AMERICAN THEATRE:
A Chronicle of Comedy and Drama, 1914–1930

AMERICAN THEATRE:

A Chronicle of Comedy and Drama, 1914–1930

GERALD BORDMAN

New York   Oxford
OXFORD UNIVERSITY PRESS
1995

Oxford University Press

Oxford   New York
Athens   Aukland   Bangkok   Bombay
Calcutta   Cape Town   Dar es Salaam   Delhi
Florence   Hong Kong   Istanbul   Karachi
Kuala Lumpur   Madras   Madrid   Melbourne
Mexico City   Nairobi   Paris   Singapore
Taipei   Tokyo   Toronto

and associated companies in
Berlin   Ibadan

Published by Oxford University Press, Inc.,
198 Madison Avenue, New York, New York 10016

Oxford is a registered trademark of Oxford University Press

Library of Congress Cataloging-in-Publication Data
Bordman, Gerald Martin.
American theatre : a chronicle of comedy and drama, 1914–1930
Gerald Bordman.
p. cm. Includes index.
ISBN 0-19-509078-0
1. Theater—United States—History—19th century.
2. Theater—United States—History—20th century.
3. American drama—19th century—Plots, themes, etc.
4. American drama—20th century—Plots, themes, etc.
I. Title.
PN2256.B6   1995   792′.0973′09034—dc20   94-13842

1 3 5 7 9 8 6 4 2

Printed in the United States of America
on acid-free paper

PREFACE

This book is the second of several projected volumes in which we hope to do for America's non-musical theatre what we did for song-and-dance entertainments in our earlier *American Musical Theatre: A Chronicle,* which Oxford University Press first published in 1978 and which has gone through a number of printings and updated editions since that time. The first volume to appear, *American Theatre: A Chronicle of Comedy and Drama, 1869–1914,* was issued in 1994. A third volume covering 1930 to 1969 is currently being prepared. Eventually a volume examining Colonial and pre-Civil War stages will be published.

With a few exceptions this volume deals entirely with first-class houses in New York, since by 1914 films had put an end to cheap touring shows and to the once healthy production of original plays for regional audiences. As a rule, plays that originated away from New York were now brought there if they were perceived to have any merit. Of course, this period also saw the rise of tiny, away-from-the-mainstream playhouses which eventually came to be called "Off Broadway." We have looked at these productions, too—at least when sufficient material survived to make discussion possible. Once again, however, we have ignored special matinees and invitational mountings as well as most bills of one-act plays (except, of course, where the one-acters were deemed of sufficient interest.)

A few caveats. Programs were sometimes careless in spelling names, and, sometimes, actors changed the spelling of their names. In the latter case, we have adopted a uniform spelling throughout, although in a few cases (such as the changes that led up to Paul Muni) we have recorded them without comment. Spelling, punctuation, and capitalization in quotations have been brought in line with the accepted modern practice.

Special thanks must be extended to the excellent staff at the library of Millersville University, notably Ray Hacker and Leo Shelley; to Geraldine Duclow and Elaine Ebo at the Theatre Collection of the Free Library of Philadelphia; to Robert Taylor at Lincoln Center's Library of the Performing Arts; to Ray Wemmlinger of the Hampden-Booth Library; to the splendid crew at the British Museum manuscript collection; to Dorothy Lester Spruill for the loan of her father's manuscripts; to the distinguished theatrical historians, Ian Bevan and Kurt Gänzl; to Jacques Kelly and to Richard Norton. Of course, sincere thanks go to my friends and colleagues at Oxford University Press: India Cooper, Joellyn Ausanka, Leona Capeless, and my great editor, Sheldon Meyer.

Kirk's Mills, Pa.   Gerald Bordman
September 1994

PROLOGUE
1914–1919

1914–1915

When the theatrical season of 1913–14 ended in mid-June, Americans were looking forward to another prosperous, carefree summer, months to come of comfortable, well-bred relaxation. Advertisements in leading newspapers and magazines promised no less. Elegant couples—carefully groomed men in tuxedos, white tie and tails, or impeccably tailored three-piece suits; attractively coiffed ladies in lovely, drapey gowns or becoming tea ensembles, and with their hairdos sometimes partially concealed by small, boxy hats, often startlingly punctuated by a single large feather—were featured in advertisement after advertisement, and not merely those for clothing. The Columbia Graphophone Company and its rival the Victor Talking Machine Company both depicted parties in huge, exquisitely furnished drawing rooms, with everyone listening attentively or dancing to the music from their large, horned instruments. This was, after all, the era of "the Dancing Craze," when America and much of the Western world went wild over tangos, fox-trots, grizzly bears, turkey trots, and similar ballroom dances. More sedentary people, just as sumptuously dressed, gathered around a Chickering piano. Even smoking Egyptian Deities, if you accepted the ads, required the finest attire. Publicity for Churchill's showed a gilded, high-ceilinged main dining room and circling balconies filled to capacity with picture-perfect patrons. Its text proclaimed, "Here, in an atmosphere surcharged with the dash and spirit of Manhattan—buoyant, brilliant, scintillating—and suffused with refinement, one finds a phase of restaurant life representing the fashionable activities of New York at their zenith." Making allowances for the oncoming heat, Arrow Shirts portrayed a handsome young man with well-combed, wavy hair playing pool—but with the jacket of his tuxedo removed. For those anxious to leave the city, sprawling, low-rising, frequently clapboarded resorts were framed by perfectly manicured lawns, serene lakes, and noble old trees. Their managements quietly assured interested readers of the best in boating, saddle horses, tennis, golf, and fishing. Regal, multi-stacked ocean liners were pictured sailing by Manhattan's skyscrapers or steaming proudly along at sea. No hint was offered that some

of these magnificent ships still carried passengers in steerage class. But those at whom these ads were aimed probably cared little about such matters. They were interested primarily in pursuing the good life—a good life which would also include starchily dressed evenings at the theatre once the new season opened. Then, on June 28, the Austrian Archduke Francis Ferdinand and his wife were assassinated at Sarajevo by a Serbian fanatic. Little more than a month later, World War I had erupted.

Of course, no society is as perfect as all too many advertisements would like to suggest. Women, even well-heeled ones, were agitating for the vote, and they and others were using spare hours to help less fortunate people. Labor unions continued to grow and flex their muscles. Malcontents were seeking outlets for their bigotry, leading to ugly lynchings and equally anti-social actions. Even the seemingly innocent "Dancing Craze" may have had a blacker subtext. The suave Maurice Mouvet, half of the popular dance team of Walton and Mouvet, observed shortly after hostilities broke out, "The Indians, and, in fact, every savage tribe dances wildly, madly, before they go to war. Is it not significant, then, that the entire world was in the throes of the dance just before the present war?"

The arts, too, were in some turmoil. Young novelists such as Sinclair Lewis and Willa Cather were breathing fresh air into their genre. Harriet Monroe had founded *Poetry* magazine two years earlier and had begun introducing American readers to such fledgling writers as E. A. Robinson, T. S. Eliot, and Robert Frost. Frank Crowninshield set about revitalizing *Vanity Fair* in 1913, and shortly afterwards two youthful gadflies, H. L. Mencken and George Jean Nathan, assumed the editorship of the *Smart Set,* filling it with their iconoclastic notions. The 1913 Armory Show called America's attention to revolutionary ideas in painting. Dissatisfaction with contemporary theatre was also swelling, as revealed in numerous articles bewailing the superficiality, commercialism (a term often preceded by the adjective "crass"), and arch-conservatism of so much period play production. One small response was the burgeoning of the Little Theatre movement. Broadway, helped by events overseas, would begin to respond with vigor in the new season.

At the same time, commentators and playgoers alike acknowledged the growing independence of American theatre, and, for all its shallowness and reluctance to experiment, they remarked with pride on its growing acceptance overseas. As articles in numerous newspapers and magazines reported, American plays were being made increasingly welcome overseas, especially in London. Traffic in plays and players was evermore a two-way affair. The war, however, shortly would throw temporary roadblocks into that traffic. One fortunate result would be a still stronger self-dependence in American theatre and, as a corollary, a newfound willingness to probe more deeply and to create more imaginatively.

A more immediate effect of the war was a disastrous plunge in theatre attendence. Uncertainty or a desire to read all the war news kept patrons away from the box office, especially on the road. *Variety* reported grosses at some theatres at between $25 and $50 a night, with the latter figure "common" ($1000 a night was about capacity for most plays at the time). In desperation many theatres offered cut-price tickets.

Whereas a large number of Americans watched with alarm the developing situation in Europe, playgoers also may have noted the curious alarms on Broadway, although there the only battle threatened was a legal one. It centered on the season's first opening, the lone play to appear between news of the assassination and the start of fighting. Several playwrights and producers claimed that Lawrence Rising's **Apartment 12-K** (7-20-14, Maxine Elliott's) was stolen from their plays, all trying out or in rehearsal just then. The brouhaha was short-lived, since the farce was greeted with scathing reviews and shuttered quickly. Rising's piece began with a black bellhop (played, as was still the practice, by a white in blackface) assisting a very inebriated, very fat man (Edward Begley) into a suite. Neither the bellhop nor the fat man is aware they have entered the wrong suite. The man promptly dons the pink pajamas he finds there. Moments later the woman (May Allison) who, with her doctor husband, occupies the suite returns. She is especially outraged since her puritanical, battle-axe mother-in-law (Helen Lowell) is asleep in a second bedroom. A burglar (Alan Brooks), the mother-in-law, the doc-tor (Robert Ober), and the police—who are chasing the burglar and mistake the doctor for their quarry—arrive in short order. One novel touch was the burglar's final exit, jumping through a window in the setting's "fourth wall" and dropping out of sight into the orchestra pit which served in lieu of the hotel's ledge.

Farces, bad or good, would loom large all season, particularly diverting Americans as the distant but disquieting news encroached upon their thinking. The season's second play and second farce was **The Third Party** (8-3-14, 39th St.), Americanized by Mark Swan from an English farce which Jocelyn Brandon and Frederick Arthur had, in turn, derived from an unidentified French piece. Hilary Chester (Taylor Holmes), to cover for his friend, Christo-pher Pottinger, (Walter Jones), a member of Parlia-ment and a married man, who has brought a lady friend, Rose Gaythorne (Marjorie Wood), to a private room in a restaurant, pretends that he and Rose are Mr. and Mrs. Garibaldi Cazzazza. This leads Mrs. Pottinger (Jobyna Howland), who has appeared inconveniently, to invite them to the Pottinger home for a weekend. Naturally, the young girl and young man to whom Hilary and Rose respectively are engaged soon turn up. The first act unfolded in the restaurant, where plates and food flew and where hats and toes were trampled on. The second act, in the Pottinger library, employed a seltzer siphon to add to the fun, while a chimney fire in the last act had players groping about in a smoke-filled room. Capitally performed, especially by the handsome young Holmes and burly Jones, the pleasantry ran three months.

The season's longest-running hit—it outran even the most popular musical—was Salisbury Field and Margaret Mayo's **Twin Beds** (8-14-14, Fulton). Despite rave reviews—"a scream," "delicious fun," "good entertainment"—the farce almost went down the drain. Playgoers, preoccupied with the new war, were not lining up at ticket windows. The show's producer, William Harris, Jr., besides taking out large advertisements in newspapers and plastering the town with billboards, resorted to a wild scheme that quickly had the whole town talking. He hired dray wagons and trucks, painted their sides with eye-catching ads, then instructed the drivers to have breakdowns at busy intersections. Before long the play was selling out. Playgoers recalling the lawsuits which threatened *Apartment 12-K* quickly saw why lawyers had been kept busy. The play begins with a drunken man entering an apartment he has mistaken for his own. He puts on the pajamas he finds and gets into bed. An all too helpful servant comes along and throws his clothes in the laundry. The man is Signor Monti (Charles Judels), and he is soon discovered by Blanche Hawkins (Madge Kennedy), whose apartment he has invaded. Because the maid threw the man's clothes away, Blanche is helpless to get rid of him before her husband, Harry (John Westley), returns. The jealous type, he becomes livid, but when he warns Monti of the scandal that can ensue he is nonplussed to realize that the publicity-starved tenor will be grateful for any attention he can get. Mrs. Monti (Ray Cox) appears. She is a harridan "born in Brooklyn, and not good Brooklyn, either." The fireworks that follow end with Mrs. Monti dragging her spouse home by his ear and Harry, hanging inside a clothes basket, receiving an impassioned lecture from his wife about the absurdity of his jealousy. The comedy's settings won high praise as the "acme" of stage design: "Here was a room in the apartment of a smart couple, with just the sort of pink and blue furnishings that a gay young woman would fancy. There were two beds, all cream enamel, with wicker panelings. . . . Even the sheets on the beds, it was to be noticed, had the correct scalloped edge." The play ran a full year and sent out numerous road companies.

William Brady, who had produced the season's first failure, was also responsible for its second. Robert Housum's **Sylvia Runs Away** (8-18-14, Playhouse) was a light comedy, not a farce, and told of a girl from finishing school who runs away only to be held, along with a friend, by three young men hoping to collect the reward for finding her. It survived a week and a half.

The season's first drama was hailed as one of the most original plays in ages, bringing to the stage the then novel device of the flashback. It was a trick which films had already utilized and thus attested to the burgeoning influence of a once deprecated medium on an older, established art. **On Trial** (8-19-14, Candler) was possibly also the first play to show a trial from beginning to end. Its forcefulness and originality earned it a 365-performance run. For many weeks, early in its run, it was the most demanded ticket and biggest money-maker on Broadway, pulling in $12,000 a week. At the beginning District Attorney Gray (William Walcott) states his case simply. Robert Strickland is accused of murdering, probably with an accomplice, Gerald Trask. Trask had lent Strickland $10,000 to save him from failure. Strickland had returned the money on schedule, but that same evening he entered Trask's home, opened the safe, and withdrew the cash. He was surprised by Trask, whom he shot. As the trial continues, Mrs. Trask (Helen Lackaye) takes the stand to recount her recollections of that evening. She recalls the phone rang. The stage darkens. A phone is heard, and when the lights come up the scene is the Trask home. Mrs. Trask answers the

phone. A woman on the other end asks for Mr. Trask but refuses to identify herself and hangs up. Mrs. Trask asks Trask's secretary, Glover (Hans Robert), if he has any idea what woman might be calling—it's not the first time—but Glover pleads innocence. Trask (Frederick Truesdell) returns and angrily dismisses his wife's concerns. Later, after everyone has gone to bed, Glover sneaks into the room, opens the safe, and removes the money. But he drops the money box. The noise wakens Mrs. Trask, and when she enters he seizes her. Strickland (Frederick Perry) enters through a window, a revolver in hand. The phone rings, and Trask comes in to answer it. He does not see the others. He has no sooner told the caller that he is Trask than he asks, "Is that you, May?" At this point Strickland shoots Trask. Glover grabs a heavy object and strikes the revolver from Strickland's hand, knocking Strickland to the floor. Back in the courtroom Glover is now on the stand. He mentions that Trask had inadvertently given Strickland a card on which he had written the recently changed combination and that, when he tried to search Strickland, Strickland had tried to keep and tear the card. One problem has been the mysterious disappearance of Mrs. Strickland, but when she finally is found she (Mary Ryan) takes the stand and tells a horrible story. She is, of course, May. Years earlier Trask had prompted her to elope with him. He had promised marriage, but she had learned he was already married. Now he had tried to force her into sex with him by threatening to reveal the story to her husband. Strickland's lawyer (Gardner Crane) shows that Strickland, who did not know the numbers on Trask's card were the combination to his safe, could not have struggled with Glover over the card since his arm had been temporarily paralyzed by Glover's blow. The jury acquits Strickland.

Critic after critic hailed not only the play's power but its daring. Most would agree with one colleague who noted, "Authors writing on stage construction will have to revise subsequent editions of their works on the technic of playwriting if dramas of the new type are accepted with the acclaim that greeted 'On Trial'." The twenty-one-year-old playwright was listed in programs as Elmer L. Reizenstein, but theatrical history would know him better as Elmer Rice.

$\cdots$

Elmer [Leopold] **Rice** [né Reizenstein] (1892–1967) was born in New York and studied law before turning his hand to playwriting. This was his first play. It had initially been called *According to the Evidence* and had dealt with feuding Kentucky mountaineers. It was accepted for production by Arthur Hopkins, who guided the tyro through the many changes the play required. When Hopkins could not raise the necessary capital, he persuaded Cohan and Harris to take over.

. . .

For all its excellences, many playgoers probably looked on *On Trial* as a criminal melodrama, or a "crook play" in the parlance of the day. Certainly Paul Wilstach's **What Happened at 22** (8-21-14, Harris) was, but it wasn't a very good one. It centered on Dave Wilson (Reginald Barlow), a forger and part owner of an employment agency, who uses his agency to gain a position as valet to the lawyer who is tracking down the forgeries. He kills the lawyer (Frank Kemble Cooper), but his attempts to pin the forgeries on the lawyer's son (Malcolm Duncan), the fiancé of the very girl (Carroll McComas) Wilson would court, leads to his unmasking.

Before the next straight play appeared a musical opened, and it, like *On Trial,* proclaimed the new vigor and creativity of the American stage in this pioneering season. The musical initially had been a West End hit, *The Girl from Utah.* As was America's wont at the time with importations, American songs were interpolated into the foreign score. But these interpolations were not the commonplace rags so regularly inserted. These songs were by twenty-nine-year-old Jerome Kern. They were head over heels above not only the English score but the other interpolations of the period. One song in particular, "They Didn't Believe Me," established the pattern for all the many dance-based love ballads to come in the succeeding half century. This and his other melodies made Kern famous and really launched his career as "Father of the American Musical Theatre."

Of course not every show could break new ground, though perhaps in a very small way the next comedy to premiere did. A whiff of impropriety hovered about **The High Cost of Loving** (8-25-14, Republic), which Frank Mandel adapted from an unspecified German play. Most critics agreed that the entertainment made for an uproarious evening in the theatre, but they also alerted their readers to the fact that the comedy presented "a not very polite story" and could be perceived as "continuously coarse." This was unexpected, since the producer and star was Lew Fields, in his first non-musical outing. Fields long had stood for good, clean fun. He portrayed Ludwig Klinke, a German mustard king. In their youth he and his buddies each had enjoyed the favors of a local young lady who then left to become a dancer in *The Black Crook* in America. Shortly thereafter each of them had received a letter from the girl telling him she had become the mother of his son, and each over the years had sent her monthly hush money. Complications arise when a young man suddenly turns up and begins to court Ludwig's daughter. Each man believes the boy to be the son. In the end it turns out the girl never had given birth to any child. Fields's admirers knew what to expect from their favorite: his palms flying outward in a gesture of despair, kneading fingers looking for a neck to choke, humorous mugging. Enough theatregoers overlooked the story's departure from perceived good taste—a sign of broadening standards—to allow the production a modest run.

The entry the following night broke no new ground, but it was a thumpingly gripping crook play—one of the best in the whole history of the genre. And it was by yet another novice playwright. Roi Cooper Megrue's **Under Cover** (8-26-14, Cort) begins in a busy office at the New York Customs House. The lower echelons there complain that things are not what they used to be. One bemoans, "I'm sick of searching trunks that's got nothin' in 'em but clothes. It ain't like the good old days. In them days if you treated a tourist right he'd hand you his business card and when you showed up at his office the next day he'd come across without a squeal." In fact the drive against corrupt officials is so bad that he adds, "If times don't change, I'm goin' into the police department." But the real drive apparently is to nab rich smugglers and its central figure is a mysterious agent, "R.J." The men's boss, Taylor (De Witt C. Jennings), appears. He is determined to catch Steven Denby, who he believes is smuggling in a $200,000 necklace. The problem is that Denby has befriended Alice Harrington, whose millionaire husband, Michael, can make trouble if the job is botched. But Taylor has a plan. He has called in a young society girl, Ethel Cartwright (Lily Cahill), who has collected insurance on the theft of some of her jewels and who is to visit the Harringtons that evening. He advises her that her sister actually pawned the jewels and made a phony claim, and that he will send the sister to prison unless Ethel helps him catch Denby. She reluctantly agrees.

The scene changes to the Harringtons' sumptuous Long Island mansion—where a bell tells the family and guests that it is time to dress for dinner. The room, done in black and white, is paneled in stripes with a motif of vases of flowers high up in the panel. "The window at the back is artistically draped in flowered linen, the mantel-piece and the doors have stencilled lines of black. The furniture is of white enamel, with luxurious upholstery and pillows. At

6

one side there is a tea table, upon which is to be seen a service of black and white striped china." When Denby (William Courtenay) and Ethel meet they recognize each other. They had met a year or so before in Paris and had fallen in love, but Denby had departed abruptly, leaving Ethel to wonder if he was truly fond of her. Their second meeting rekindles the old flame. She cannot believe Denby would be a smuggler. But before long she realizes he does have the necklace hidden in his tobacco pouch. She is torn between her feelings for him on the one hand, and her awareness that Taylor's story was correct and her concerns for her sister on the other. When she attempts to steal the necklace, Denby catches her. An emotional and intellectual struggle ensues until Taylor arrives. Denby confesses privately to Taylor that he has smuggled in the necklace and offers the officer $30,000 to overlook the matter. When Taylor agrees, Denby reveals he is R.J. (his real name is Richard Jones), and he arrests Taylor. The same underling who earlier had complained of the drive to root out corruption forlornly notes, "I've been working for a crook for two years and never knew it!" A relieved Ethel embraces Denby.

Megrue cleverly mixed amusing bits with a never-slackening tension. Thus, Mr. Harrington (William Draycott) is seen to be a genteel but determined boozer constantly defying the vigilance of his wife (Lucile Watson). Courtenay, a popular matinee idol, and a superb supporting cast lent warmth and credence to the play, which ran nearly a year.

· · ·

Roi Cooper Megrue (1883–1927) was a native New Yorker. When his first plays were rejected, he took work with Elisabeth Marbury as a play reader and learned the ins-and-outs of playwriting under the tutelage of the famous agent. He remained with her eleven years before writing this, his first successful play. (A collaboration with another playwright resulted in one drama which reached Broadway in 1912 but failed.)

· · ·

George Randolph Chester and his wife, Lillian, suffered a quick failure with **Cordelia Blossom** (8-31-14, Gaiety), which they derived from their popular short stories in the *Saturday Evening Post* and which told of the machinations of a scheming young lady.

The Beautiful Adventure (9-5-14, Lyceum) was only a little less unsuccessful, despite very favorable notices. It was adapted by George Egerton from the popular Paris piece by Robert de Flers and Gaston de Caillavet. A young lady (Ann Murdock) is persuaded by the man (Charles Cherry) she really loves to jilt her bridegroom (Ernest Lawford). They

elope to the château of her grandmother (Mrs. Thomas Whiffen), where the grandmother accepts them as husband and wife. By the time the jilted groom turns up he can only accept the inevitable. Sixty-nine-year-old Mrs. Whiffen, whom many regarded as the successor to Mrs. Gilbert, received the most accolades, but the whole cast was praised. Curiously, simply because the old lady had mistaken an unwed couple for a married one, the play's producer, Charles Frohman, had joined in the suit against *Apartment 12-K*. Was this merely a publicity stunt? If so, it was unavailing.

Only one play that opened on the busy Monday night which followed had an American setting. Paul Armstrong's **The Bludgeon** (9-7-14, Maxine Elliott's) told of a vicious wife who divorces one husband after falsely charging him with cruelty and infidelity, then is shot dead by her second husband when he realizes how treacherous she is. Critics panned both the play and the performers, and the work left hurriedly.

John Drew was made far more welcome when he arrived for what many a critic pointed out was his "twenty-second annual visit" under the aegis of Charles Frohman. His vehicle was Dario Niccodemi and Michael Morton's **The Prodigal Husband** (9-7-14, Empire). Drew took the part of an aging Frenchman who has gone downhill since he separated from his wife (Grace Carlyle). He is redeemed by the love he develops for Simone, the orphaned twelve-year-old daughter of his concierge. Time passes and the girl becomes a beauty (Jessie Glendenning), but when she understands that her guardian might want to marry her she flees to his wife. He hurries there, too. However, he comes to accept that a reconciliation with his wife is the logical answer to his loneliness. Whatever problems the play had—such as an inconsistency in tone—were glossed over by Drew's polished, throwaway performing. The comedy hung on for five weeks of disappointing business; a tour that followed was cut short when grosses on the road were even less satisfactory. The tot who played Simone in the earlier scenes was listed in the program as Helen Hayes Brown, but in a few seasons she dropped the "Brown" from her stage name.

A ripsnorting, old-fashioned English melodrama, Walter Howard's **The Story of the Rosary** (9-7-14, Manhattan Opera House) ran just as long, but did so at a huge barn of an auditorium where the gallery gods, long unmentioned in reviews, were reported to have hissed and stomped and yelled with delight. The play they so vociferously reacted to was filled with spectacle, swordplay, telltale musical accompaniment, and such happily bygone clichés as "Curse you!" Its tale, set in a mythical Balkan kingdom, focused on two kinsmen, both of whom love the same princess. The treacherous kinsman does everything he can to steal away the other's girl, even claiming she has agreed to marry him and later falsely announcing that the other man died in battle. But the hero eventually runs his sword through the red-coated villain.

Less than two weeks after he scored so brilliantly with *Under Cover*, Roi Cooper Megrue had a second smash hit on Broadway. In a change of pace, **It Pays to Advertise** (9-8-14, Cohan) was a comedy and was written in collaboration with Walter Hackett. Megrue's first play had opened in a workaday office, then moved on to a luxurious mansion. His new comedy reversed the settings. The curtain rose to disclose a plush library—"a handsome room, in tapestry and dark oak"—in the home of Cyrus Martin, the soap king. His pretty, young secretary, Mary Grayson (Ruth Shepley), is interrupted at her work by the arrival of Martin's playboy son, Rodney (Grant Mitchell), who asks her to marry him. She suggests she might do just that—if Rodney ever goes to work. This idea doesn't appeal to Rodney: "Imagine going to bed every night, knowing you've got to get up in the morning and go to business." The elder Martin (John Cope) appears and is outraged at the prospect of having to support a daughter-in-law as well as a shiftless son. He calls Rodney worthless and orders him out of the house. An angry Rodney, announcing that he will go into business and show his father that the son can outdo the old man, heads upstairs to pack. He is no sooner gone than Mary and Martin senior laughingly embrace. Their ruse has worked! They have goaded Rodney into rolling up his sleeves. The second act takes place in the offices of the 13 Soap Company, on whose walls are posters proclaiming "13 Soap is unlucky for dirt." It seems Rodney has decided to beat his father at his own game. His plan, pushed on him by his P.R. buddy, Ambrose Peale (Will Deming), is to advertise and advertise and advertise. After all, people willingly pay more for brand names they know (because they've read their advertisements) than for cheaper, equally good, but unknown brands. And they eat chicken eggs, not duck eggs: ducks lay their eggs quietly, but hens advertise their laying with their noisy clucking. Unfortunately, Rodney spends what little money he can scrounge up on his publicity, so he hasn't a cent to manufacture the soap or even pay his office rent. But when his father hears of the orders the advertisements are bringing in and realizes that Rodney is serious about

working, he invests enough to ensure Rodney's success. Read today the play seems more pleasant than funny, but contemporaries found its humor rich in "genuineness and substance."

The published text also calls to mind that curtain calls were still taken after each act. In some plays, these curtain calls were simply the usual bows, but other plays, and *It Pays to Advertise* was one, employed them for mini-scenes. At the end of the first act the text calls for "*The Second curtain: Peale and Rodney on either side of Martin, are talking advertising, while Mary has her fingers in her ears. The Third curtain: Martin is protesting angrily to Mary while Rodney and Peale are talking gleefully to each other and shaking hands.*" The play was the fourth in the still very young season to run almost a year. Oddly, none of the season's subsequent hits ran nearly as long.

For example, the next entry ran just over three months. But then George Broadhurst's **Innocent** (9-9-14, Eltinge) received sharply divided notices. Broadhurst took his play from Arpád Pásztor's Hungarian piece, which, curiously enough, had the same, seemingly English title. The reason was that "Innocent" was not an adjective but the heroine's name. She was the daughter of a dissolute Anglo-Irish couple living in Manchuria. On their death they leave the young girl to their Hungarian friend Bela Nemzetti (John Miltern). The play opens with Nemzetti's suicide, then, moving to Budapest and Nice, spins back in time to show how Innocent (Pauline Frederick) proved as dissolute and destructive as her parents. In Hungary Pásztor's play had been applauded as an interesting model of advanced dramaturgy. It could be perceived as allegorical, but more certainly as impressionistic. Much went unstated. The more tradition-bound Broadhurst took it upon himself to add characters (such as Innocent's father) and scenes, and to spell out what had been implied. In the original Innocent's hints and his own jealousy are enough to turn the character whom Broadhurst renamed Nemzetti against his best friend. In the American adaptation the friend, trusting he is helping Innocent, selflessly gives her a check. Innocent shows it to Nemzetti and purposely allows him to misconstrue its importance. Most critics who liked the play found the performances excellent. Those critics who dismissed the drama as hollow generally considered the players wooden.

Three quick failures followed. Marion Fairfax and Ruth C. Mitchell's **A Modern Girl** (9-12-14, Comedy) told of the problems that arise after a man sees his niece enter the home of a financier and misinterprets her visit. It ran two weeks, which was twice as long as did Austin Strong's **The Dragon's Claw** (9-14-14, New Amsterdam). Strong's melodrama, reminiscent of *Jessie Brown* and similar old plays, recounted the siege and relief of the British embassy during the Boxer uprising. Splendidly mounted by Henry Miller, it nonetheless could not find an audience and closed to a then staggering loss of $30,000. The longest-running of the failed trio, **The Elder Son** (9-15-14, Playhouse), survived three weeks while telling its saga of a grown son who resents his mother's remarrying. It was translated by Frederick Fenn from Lucien Népoty's *Les Petits*.

Douglas Fairbanks was the main, possibly the sole, reason that **He Comes Up Smiling** (9-16-14, Liberty) enjoyed a modest run. The play was derived by Byron Ongley and Emil Nyitray from Charles Sherman's novel. Fairbanks played Jerry Martin, a carefree young vagabond who, coming out from bathing in a pond, finds that a carefully tailored man's suit and other fine clothes have been left on the banks in place of his own tattered garments. Topping that, a sleek new car has been abandoned by the road. The clothes and the car belong to a Wall Street speculator, and Jerry is soon kidnapped by the speculator's rival (William Morris), who hopes then to have a free hand on a deal. Jerry quickly falls in love with his kidnapper's daughter, Billy (Patricia Collinge). When the kidnapper realizes his mistake he orders Jerry to leave. Jerry promises Billy that one day he'll return for her. In Sherman's novel the ending is vague, implying that Jerry may find his wanderlust more compelling than Billy. But the play concludes with Jerry's coming back to marry Billy. When the play closed after two months, Fairbanks and Miss Collinge hurried into rehearsals for a better piece.

The basic situation of George Scarborough's **What Is Love?** (9-19-14, Maxine Elliott's) recalled that at the opening of *The Beautiful Adventure,* only on this occasion it was set in a small American town. Lucy Gordon (Alice Brady) is about to marry a local attorney (Jerome Patrick) when the young man (Charles Balsar) she long loved returns from studying overseas and asks her to marry him. The play unfolds entirely in the Gordons' dreary middle-American home, during one evening, and much of that time is taken up by Lucy's inquiring of family and friends what love is and what she should do. In the end she gives the attorney his walking papers.

While raking in profits from *On Trial* and *It Pays to Advertise,* Cohan and Harris had readied a third show, this one by Cohan himself. Cohan also served as director but did not appear in the play. **The Miracle Man** (9-21-14, Astor), based on Frank L.

Packard's short story "None So Blind," was as close as Cohan ever came to writing a serious drama. In a Maine village, a huge, bearded old man has grown so respected and listened to that he is called "The Patriarch" (Wm. H. Thompson). John Madison (George Nash), a New York sharper, gets wind of his reputation and sees a way of enriching himself by it, especially after discovering that the old man will only accept money for his labors to be put in trust for his long-lost niece. In the village Madison pretends that the old man has cured him of voice problems. He tricks the old man into believing that the young girl he has brought with him is the missing niece. She is actually Madison's "queen" or mistress. Madison also brings along two men. One is Michael Coogan (James C. Marlowe), a professional "flopper," or someone who pretends to be crippled in order to solicit charity; and the other is Harry Evans (Earle Browne), a young, attractive, but highly nervous "dope fiend," who claims to have an incurable cough. They both proclaim having been made whole again by the old man, so the money begins to roll in. Then the old man actually does heal a crippled youngster (Percy Helton). The miracle converts all the crooks but Madison. However, when the old man dies and Madison's girl, who had come to have genuine affection for her supposed uncle, tells Madison she will have nothing more to do with him until he reforms, he reforms. Packard's story had ended with the death of "The Patriarch" and allowed readers to fantasize on what might have happened thereafter. Cohan was sharply criticized for tacking on a fourth act to detail the reformations. Moreover, there were complaints that, while he drew the crooks with his usual acuity, the titular figure remained cardboard and uninteresting. The play ran three months to slightly forced business.

An English comedy, **Tipping the Winner** (9-23-14, Longacre), spotlighted two American girls who try to make some money while in England by claiming to be tipsters on the races. Two weeks and it was gone.

A pair of plays—a comedy and a drama—opened the next Monday evening. Both were successful, but the drama was the less successful and has long since been forgotten. The comedy became one of the era's best-loved plays and the source of several musicals and films. Jean Webster's **Daddy Long-Legs** (9-28-14, Gaiety) was the playwright's adaptation of her own novel. The curtain rises on the dining room of the John Grier Home for Orphans. It is Trustees' Day, so the youngsters, in stiffly starched blue pinafores (for the girls) or dark knickerbockers and jumpers (for the boys), are helping set up. They are cheerful but sometimes careless and even mischievous. They break china and put salt in sugar bowls. A self-serving superintendent at the orphanage has refused to allow by far the eldest of the girls, Judy Abbott (Ruth Chatterton), to be adopted, telling prospects that the girl is incorrigibly selfish. In fact the superintendent wants to retain her as a drudge and to raise the younger children. However, this day, in front of the trustees, Judy rebels, arguing, "I might have had a home, too—like other children—and you stole it away from me. . . . I can make my own way in the world. Just give me a chance." One fortyish trustee, Jervis Pendleton (Charles Waldron), is so impressed on hearing these remarks that he quietly insists the girl be sent to college at his expense. Judy is not to be told who her benefactor is, but she has seen his shadow cast when the lights of his limousine, calling for him, throw that elongated shadow on the wall of the Home. So she calls him Daddy Long-Legs. Since Judy's roommate at college is his niece, Jervis can visit without raising suspicions. He falls in love with Judy, even though he surmises she is being courted by attractive, younger men. After college she becomes a successful writer and still is courted by younger men. Eventually he proposes, but Judy, not wishing to hurt Daddy Long-Legs, rejects him, so he walks off dejectedly into the sunset. Only after he later reveals his identity does she joyously accept. Much of the play's initial success was owed to Ruth Chatterton. *Theatre* called her "its chief charm," adding, "She is all grace." Her playing confirmed her claim to stardom.

. . .

Ruth Chatterton (1893–1961) was born in New York City. After making her acting debut in Washington, D.C., in 1909, she played there, and in Milwaukee and in Worcester, Mass., in stock for several seasons. Her first Broadway appearance came in 1911 in a short-lived failure, *The Great Name*. Only when she came under the tutelage of Henry Miller and played opposite him in *The Rainbow* (1912) did she begin to win recognition. From early on the petite beauty, with "deeply blue eyes . . . set round with shady lashes" and fluffy but well-combed brown hair, was admired for her "exquisite naturalness."

. . .

Now in his late forties, William Faversham was nearing the end of his days as a matinee idol. But he did have a success when he offered himself as star of Francis de Croisset's **The Hawk** (9-28-14, Shubert), which he and Marie Zane Taylor had translated from the French. His co-star, Gabrielle Dorziat, had been the drama's leading lady when the play had delighted Parisians as *L'Epervier*. The piece was set on the Riviera, where the Hungarian Comte George de Dasetta is forced to become a gambler and a cheat to maintain the posh life his beloved wife insists on. A young man, René de Tierrache (Conway Tearle), falls in love with the countess, and when he catches her helping her husband cheat he takes her aside and pleads with her to reform. The lecture so unnerves her that her next attempts to help the count are slipshod. He leaves her. She takes up with de Tierrache until she learns how down and out the count has become, whereupon she resolves to devote herself to his redemption. Reviewers generally praised Miss Dorziat and were gratified by her clear enunciation of English, but except for a brief appearance later in the season playing a French play in French, this was her lone American performance. Critics devoted more time to the men, and several suggested that watching Faversham, with his exaggerated movements and sometimes florid speech, and Tearle, so much less mannered and so much more natural in delivery, offered a study of evolving theatrical generations.

George Broadhurst scored a bigger hit with his second offering of the season, **The Law of the Land** (9-30-14, 48th St.). Although many aisle-sitters warned their followers that the play was often unpleasantly powerful, most concurred with the *Times*'s man who reported that he, like the rest of the audience, remained in his seat, "transfixed by his desire to watch the relentless unwinding of the thread to a dramatically inevitable end." Disregarding that the outcome was hardly inevitable, especially in light of the period's code of morality, the comment reveals what gripping theatre the piece was. Mrs. Harding (Julia Dean) has put up with her savagely sadistic husband (Charles Lane) for the sake of her little son, Bennie (Master Macomber). Of course, she herself has not been an angel. Indeed, Bennie is not even Harding's child, but rather the son of Mrs. Harding's lover, Geoffrey Morton (Milton Sills). When Harding finds he has reasonable proof of this he takes a horsewhip to the child. To stop him, Mrs. Harding shoots and kills him (in yet another of the season's richly paneled libraries). Her friends are ready to tamper with the evidence in order to defend her, and Morton is prepared to claim he did the shooting. Briefly, Mrs. Harding seems willing to let Morton go to prison, but then she blurts out a confession. Inspector Cochrane (George Fawcett), observing the whip marks on the young boy, writes a report that ensures no jury would vote for a conviction. The play ran until spring and toured profitably.

Considering the generally receptive notices H. F. Rubinstein's **Consequences** (10-1-14, Comedy) garnered, it remains puzzling that there was no call to extend the run beyond its announced limited engagement. Perhaps Broadway was still not as ready to make light of mixed marriages as London had been. So this comedy about a Christian girl and a Jewish boy, who expect to encounter all manner of obstacles to their wedding and are dismayed to discover both families welcome it, stayed for only a month. Several of the players had been in the London cast.

Only a few seasons back, Charles Klein had been one of Broadway's most promising and successful playwrights. In recent years, however, his luck had turned. **The Money Makers** (10-5-14, Booth) would be the last new play of his that he would live to see in New York, and it, too, was a flop. The *Herald* could only observe that a fine mounting allowed the play "to appear much better drama than it really is." Klein's hero was James Rodman (Emmett Corrigan), who has become a multimillionaire by the most unscrupulous means. But his money has brought him no happiness. His children and his second wife are totally unloving. So when he learns that he is terminally ill he decides to restore all his wealth to those he cheated out of it. His children and his business associates are aghast. But his wife (Alexandra Carlisle) comes to respect him and love him. Whether Klein's luck would have turned or not can never be known, since he would be among the theatrical figures lost in May in the sinking of the *Lusitania*.

Another passenger on the doomed ship would be Charles Frohman, who had a one-week failure on his hands when he presented Paul Armstrong's second play of the season, **The Heart of a Thief** (10-5-14, Hudson). This latest crook play followed a woman (Martha Hedman) from her days as an inmate in the Tombs to her redemption in the arms of a man she once had robbed.

When *Innocent* had opened a month earlier, the name of its American adaptor loomed large in programs and advertisements, while theatregoers had to look hard to discover its Hungarian author. By contrast, Ferenc Molnár's name received major billing when his *A Farkas* (*The Wolf*) was offered by David Belasco under the more felicitous title of **The Phantom Lover** (10-6-14, Belasco), even though its translator was its celebrated leading man. Its heroine (Laura Hope Crews), considering herself comfortably if unhappily married to a dull, jealous man, fantasizes about what happened to the great love of her youth (Leo Ditrichstein). She visualizes him as a dashing soldier, a suave diplomat, and a brilliant artist. But after a chance encounter with him she realizes she is probably fortunate in her actual marriage. Ditrichstein accounted for his own Hungarian accent by keeping the lover a Continental but making the other characters American. Critics applauded both play and players (with the *Herald*'s man proclaiming it "distinctly the most charming play that the season so far has brought"), but their main enthusiasm was reserved for Belasco, whom they perceived as finally coming out of a dry spell. The *Tribune* rejoiced that "the 'Belasco Myth' is once more an astonishing reality." The play was the first of three successes the producer-director was to enjoy during the season.

One quick failure, **Evidence** (10-7-14, Lyric), an English piece, arrived between Molnár's dream play and a not dissimilar work. It told of a lawyer (C. Aubrey Smith) who rashly divorces his wife because some circumstantial material suggests she is unfaithful.

Was Edward Knoblauch's **My Lady's Dress** (10-10-14, Playhouse) American or English? Knoblauch was still an American citizen, but he long ago had moved permanently to Europe, and his play was first presented in London. Anne (Mary Boland), a wife determined that her husband, John (Leon Quartermaine), shall win an important government promotion, has been playing up to the man who most can help. Her husband is annoyed at this, and he is even more upset when he learns the price of a dress that his wife has purchased for a major soirée. Before preparing for the gala the wife takes a nap and dreams of all the little tragedies required to obtain materials for the new gown. Thus, in Italy a jilted suitor destroys the silkworms that were to be the bride's dowry, and in Siberia, where furs for the collar were gathered, a peasant woman comes to despise her weakling husband when he refuses to kill her on learning of her infidelity. These dreams moved not only around the globe but back and forth in time. However, in every case the two principal figures remained the same, and even their names reflected the connection. For example, Ann became Nina or Annette or Antje. In the end, Ann learns her husband has received the promotion. Yet she recognizes the cost: "pushing, fighting, hating, loving—in one endless battle." So she hopes she and John can move on to better the world. Shortly after the outbreak of the war, Knoblauch renounced his American citizenship and became a British subject, but at the same time he muddied the waters by anglicizing the spelling of his name to Knoblock.

11

Meanwhile, his new play—the first of two New York would see this season—had a disappointingly modest run.

Another play from London ran only a little longer—72 performances, in a limited, and largely sold out, engagement—but that new comedy proved to be the most enduring premiere of the season. George Bernard Shaw had written **Pygmalion** (10-12-14, Park), the saga of a guttersnipe flower vendor who is transformed into a lady by an egomaniacal professor of phonetics, for Mrs. Patrick Campbell. She had triumphed in London, and now, despite being patently too old for the role (perhaps a vestige of old-style casting), she offered Americans "a technical exposition of rare value instinct with humor, feeling and great emotional sincerity." Philip Merivale was Higgins.

Still another London play, Harry M. Vernon and Harold Owen's lurid melodrama **Mr. Wu** (10-14-14, Maxine Elliott's), found more favor on the road than it did in New York. In Hong Kong, in the beautiful lotus garden of Mr. Wu (Walker Whiteside), a cynical young Englishman (Frank Wupperman) seduces and deserts Nang Ping (Antoinette Walker). Shamed, Wu kills his daughter, then plots his revenge. Bit by bit he destroys the business of the boy's father, and next kidnaps the young man. Finally he sends for the young man's mother (Deirdre Doyle). Before she is ushered into his magnificent room, largely done in reds and blacks, and filled with ornately carved furniture and brass ornaments, he instructs his servants not to unlock the door unless he sounds his huge gong. He soon makes it clear to the stunned woman that he demands an eye for an eye—or, in this case, a ravishing for a ravishing. He has filled two small, Oriental teacups and notices the lady secretly pouring something into one cup. He assumes she is trying to poison him, so he switches the cups. In fact, she was going to commit suicide. But Wu realizes that only after drinking the poisoned tea. He grabs a sword and tries to kill his guest, but the poison works too fast. It is the lady who must strike the gong to gain freedom for herself and her son. Whiteside, who had trained as a Shakespearean of the older school, played his Wu with stiff gestures and an impassive expression. Frank Wupperman was later better known as Frank Morgan, the comedian.

More melodrama followed—native melodrama by a writer who a short while before had been king of the cheap touring circuits but who still could not win acceptance on Broadway. What was more, the producer of Owen Davis's **Big Jim Garrity** (10-16-

14, New York) was Al Woods, himself once a leading promoter of such plays. Old notions die hard, so Woods offered his new production at a top of $1. He learned sadly that his once numerous audiences had deserted permanently to films. Davis's story centered on a man (John Mason) who had served a prison sentence for a crime he did not commit (a stock motif of the old days). After escaping, he changed his name and became a wealthy, respected citizen. Then the real villain (John Flood) tracks him down, kidnaps, binds, and gags him, and prepares to kill him. But the hero (whose new name oldtimers knew had to be Jack) manages to tap out a distress call. Just as Jack has loosened his bonds, the villain flings a lamp across the the room, but Jack pulls out a revolver and shoots him. Although Alexander Woollcott informed his readers in the *Times* that the drama was filled with "the rush and roar of old-time excitement" and with "more unblushing attempts to thrill per square act . . . than you would find in a month of first nights," the play closed quickly.

Down on 39th Street the tiny Princess Theatre was given over to a season of bills of one-act plays. The opening bill on October 17 included several English pieces as well as a revival of *The Cat and the Cherub* (9-20-97). Among later attractions was Beulah Marie Dix's little anti-war drama **Across the Border** (11-24-14). In her directions, the author specifies that the uniforms and other costumes along with the settings must suggest no specific place or nationality. Her soldiers are apparently trapped behind enemy lines, and, as the Junior Lieutenant (David Powell) worries, they have "nothing to eat, nothing to drink, and cartridges running short. Somebody's got to get back to headquarters and bring help." Since he has only an unloving mother and no girl, except in "dreamland," he volunteers. Moments after he leaves, shots are heard. But he is next shown coming to a strange house. There he sees the very girl (Jean Murdock) he has dreamed of. He tells the people at the house of "my country, the greatest country in the world, and the most enlightened . . . We do not kill unless we are forced to." They lead him to "a nook in an ice-bound place," where the dead from long-bygone wars congregate. Later, at a makeshift hospital, the girl comes dressed as a Red Cross nurse. She comforts and kisses him. But after he dies the doctor and orderly insist no woman has been present, although other patients claim that they saw her, too.

If Al Woods had come a cropper a few nights earlier with his attempt to resuscitate superannuated touring melodrama, he hit the jackpot with a voguish crook play, Willard Mack's **Kick In** (10-19-14, Longacre). Chick Hewes (John Barrymore) is an ex-convict who even the police recognize is attempting to go straight, although that has not precluded their keeping a watchful and obvious eye on him. A former cellmate is shot during a robbery and seeks shelter with Chick and Chick's pregnant wife, Molly (Jane Grey). Just before he dies they discover that a valuable necklace he had on him has disappeared. They dump the body in the river, but the police arrest them. At first Molly's tearful plea to spare her having a baby in prison seems to go for nought. Only after Molly's drug-addicted brother (Forrest Winant) confesses to stealing the necklace does a fatherly police commissioner release the couple, allowing them another chance. Barrymore already had begun to assay more serious roles, but not until late in the following season would he have an opportunity to display his gifts fully. Meanwhile, his leading lady walked off with most of the better notices. Of course, Barrymore was not necessary to the play's success. *Variety* reported shortly after the opening that nine road companies were in preparation. Still, the play allowed the stock of both Barrymore and Woods to rise sharply.

. . .

John [Sidney Blythe] **Barrymore** (1882–1942) was born in Philadelphia, the younger son of Maurice and Georgiana Drew Barrymore, and the grandson of Mrs. John Drew. He made his stage debut in Chicago in 1903 and in the same year first appeared in New York, in *Glad of It*. Supporting roles followed before he replaced the leading man in *The Boys of Company B* in 1907. Two major assignments were the principal roles in the comedy *The Fortune Hunter* (1909) and the drama *The Yellow Ticket* (1914). His "slim, proud figure, the lean wolfhound aquilinity of his profile, and the princely beauty of his full face" added to his superb acting skills.

. . .

Al[bert Herman] **Woods** [né Aladore Herman] (1870-1951) was born in Budapest and brought to America while still an infant. Growing up on New York's Lower East Side, he tried work in the garment trade and as an advance agent for a traveling show before turning to the production of cheap touring melodramas. Many of these were mounted by Sullivan, Harris and Woods, the firm he founded with P. H. Sullivan and Sam Harris. When this sort of theatre disappeared he moved on to Broadway in 1909. He became something of a legend for sitting out in front of a theatre he built on 42nd Street and welcoming all comers as "sweetheart."

. . .

What might, in a way, have been perceived as a much older crook play, though the term had not been coined when it was first presented, was Victorien Sardou's *Diplomacy* (4-1-78). On the 20th Charles Frohman brought it into the Empire with an all-star cast. William Gillette was Henry; Marie Doro, Dora; Blanche Bates, Countess Zicka; and Leslie Farber, Julian. Jeffreys Lewis, once a leading lady at Wallack's and Daly's, had the small, comic role of the Marquise de Rio-Zares. Excellent reviews kept the theatre crowded for the limited engagement.

Cyril Harcourt's **A Pair of Silk Stockings** (10-20-14, Little), with its English playwright and many from his original London company repeating their roles, recounted the comic misadventures of an actor who attempts a reconciliation with his estranged wife. The setting for the Act II "art moderne" bedroom, with its latticed gray walls and gray wicker furniture embroidered with pink roses, won special praise. The play ran longer in New York than it had in London.

There was no long run for **The Salamander** (10-23-14, Harris), which Owen Johnson adapted from his own novel and which depicted the carryings-on of a frivolous, loose-moraled girl before she finds her true love.

On the other hand, what *Theatre* hailed as "an undiluted melodramatic joy" packed playgoers into a barn of a theatre for twenty weeks. Thomas Buchanan's **Life** (10-24-14, Manhattan Opera House) took its hero, a former stroke for Yale, to Death Row at Sing Sing, where he is being held for a murder he did not commit. Since he is the hero, he escapes. "And such an escape!—in a three hundred horse-power automobile past a bewildering panorama of cubist trees and farm houses." Of course, he eventually is cleared. Other spectacular settings included a view of a regatta, a magnificent ball, a great church, and a restaurant atop a skyscraper.

A play with a similar title, **The Highway of Life** (10-26-14, Wallack's), was Louis N. Parker's dramatization of *David Copperfield*. It found few takers.

But George V. Hobart's allegory **Experience** (10-27-14, Booth) was a surprise hit and ran out the season. Youth (William Elliott, who was also the producer), goaded by the insidious but faint-hearted Ambition (Willard Blackmore), and accompanied by Experience (Ben Johnson), leaves the lush, sunny garden "where dreams begin" and heads out on his own highway of life. His journey takes him to the Street of Vacillation, the Primrose Path (where he is entertained at a late-night supper club), the Corridors of Chance (a gambling house), and the Street of Disillusion. Before long he has lost his money and his fair-weather friends. He takes a job at a seedy restaurant. Later he is arrested when he tries to shield Frailty (Margot Williams). He hits bottom in the House of Lost Souls. About to take up with Crime (Frank McCormack), he hears "Lead, Kindly Light" coming from a church on the Street of Forgotten Days and elects to return home. There, with the help of Love (Miriam Collins), he finds the good life. Characters all dressed in the latest clothing. Cabaret songs and other original, obviously contemporary music were provided by Silvio Hein. It was this knowing blend of ages-old morality play and modern materials which so delighted critics. With his profits, Hobart built a fine home and christened it Xperience Court.

Rose Stahl's meteoric career began to fade when she appeared in Channing Pollock and Rennold Wolf's slangy **A Perfect Lady** (10-28-14, Hudson). Its plot recalled her earlier, more successful *The Chorus Lady*. The small, slim star, with tangled blonde hair and hazel eyes, played Lucille Higgins. When she was a burlesque queen she had been known as Lucille Le Jambon, a name she chose off a menu. But now she has decided to retire to a little town near Kansas City and bring her convent-trained sister to live with her. She sets up as a dancing teacher. Her sister (Cherrie Carlisle) is dismayed at her big-city ways, and town gossips are malicious. But Lucille eventually wins acceptance, as well as a proposal from the local minister. Curiously, although the play closed quickly, Pollock eventually named his yacht after it.

Two more flops closed out the month. J.C. Drum's **Milady's Boudoir** (10-29-14, Garrick) spotlighted a young actress who is making her theatrical debut in a new theatre built specially for her by a cynical, rich admirer. But she jilts him for a young man who has stood by her through thick and thin. **The Battle Cry** (10-31-14, Lyric) was taken from a Charles Neville Buck story by an uncredited adaptor (though scuttlebutt said it was Augustus Thomas). It featured such respected performers as William Farnum and Grace Elliston. And several of its eighteen scenes were shown not onstage but on a motion picture screen. Yet this saga of a Kentucky mountain feud which only the encroachment of civilization brings to an end was deemed so shoddily written and lifelessly acted that it quickly was withdrawn.

Hubert Henry Davies's London drama **Outcast** (11-2-14, Lyceum) featured a streetwalker (Elsie Ferguson) who befriends a newly jilted gentleman (Charles Cherry). They go off to South America to live in peace, but Davies left up in the air whether or not they marry. The play's twenty-one-week stand was longer than its West End run, and it was, oddly enough, the only hit in November's long play list.

Even the once admired Henry Arthur Jones had no luck (or perhaps more accurately in this instance, no chance). A couple of weeks before, his **The Goal** (10-17-14), recounting how a dying man lives long enough to have a sought-after reconciliation with his son, had been on the Princess Theatre's opening bill of one-acters. His latest, and virtually his last new play to reach New York, was **Mary Goes First** (11-2-14, Comedy). The story enumerated the wiles Mary employs to earn her husband a baronetcy, simply so that she might always have precedence and lead her fellow townspeople into dinner. Mary was played by the popular West End star Marie Tempest, making what she billed as a farewell tour. It wasn't. But because she had other roles to display, she kept Jones's little comedy on the boards for only a month.

Small, dark, impassioned Nazimova could do nothing with Basil Macdonald Hastings's **That Sort** (11-6-15, Harris), in which she portrayed a once famous, now dissolute dancer who is determined to see the daughter the court years before had taken away from her. But when she discovers that she herself is the mistress of the young man who is engaged to her daughter, she walks out of the girl's life.

New York's newest theatre was one of its most unusual. The Punch and Judy was tiny (only 299 seats) and was done in a quasi-Elizabethan style. Until audience complaints forced a change, many seats were simply cushioned benches. The boyish ushers were garbed in blue Elizabethan clothes, and each night, just before the performance began, an appropriately dressed trumpeter appeared on the roof to issue a brassy alert. The playhouse's initial attraction, Harold Chapin's English comedy **The Marriage of Columbine** (11-10-14), got off to a delicious start. The scene is an English country inn. An old lady, half asleep, listens to a clock strike. When it strikes eight she sits up abruptly, surprised at the hour. But the clock continues to strike—nine, ten, eleven, twelve, and thirteen! With that, the old clock falls to pieces. Unfortunately, the rest of the play went downhill. Columbine (Mrs. Charles Hopkins) has lived with the great clown Scaramouche (Charles Hopkins) and given him two children. A local, moralistic newspaper editor (Herbert Yost) comes to interview the couple. After he learns that there is apparently no marriage certificate he persuades the empty-headed Columbine to run away with him and marry him, even though he is already engaged. Scaramouche and the man's fiancée follow and bring about a sensible ending. The witless comedy struggled on for a month.

An equally dreary but potentially more interesting

comedy, A. E. Thomas and Clayton Hamilton's **The Big Idea** (11-16-14, Hudson), ran only three weeks. Critics were torn between slamming the play's dullness and lauding its originality. Woollcott hailed its potential, seeing it as "the most novel play yet shown in a theatrical season already remarkable for the number of odd, unexpected, and fantastic works it has had to offer." Before the curtain rises, an actor appears onstage and tells the audience, "I beg to announce that the play you are about to witness is unusual in this respect: it is quite true." The curtain then rises on a darkened stage. The voices of two men are heard. When one turns on an "electrolier" they are revealed as Dick Howard (Ernest Glendinning) and his father (Forrest Robinson). The elder Howard has had a nervous breakdown and has asked his son to listen in the dark to his disclosure of what brought on his illness. It seems that the old man, a banker, had in good faith lent a huge sum to his childhood buddy, not realizing the buddy had become a crook. Now he has no way of replacing the sum—he needs $20,000—before bank examiners discover the peculation. At first Dick contemplates a cleverly disguised suicide so that the old man can collect on Dick's insurance. But a smart, pretty, and determined young visitor, Elaine Foster (Desmond Kelley), persuades Dick, who is a writer, to attempt a play about the subject, using real names and simply recording everything that has gone on exactly as it has happened. She agrees to help. That gets them through two acts of the play (with Dick's family constantly coming in to open the closed drapes in his study and Dick just as constantly protesting that he can only write by artificial light). The dialogue that Dick and Elaine read to each other is the very words they and others have spoken. But they are stuck for a third act until Elaine calls a producer friend and asks him to listen to their play. The pair rush down to his New York office, where Gilmore (William Courtleigh), the man who addressed the audience earlier, likes what he hears but says there must be a third act. Dick and Elaine assure him there now is, and that he and his comments are a major part of it. They explain why. Gilmore wonders if the public will accept it.

Elaine: Oh, they must; the darlings, they must. (*she takes a step or two toward the audience and says, with a little cry*) Oh, you do, you do, don't you?

They convince Gilmore to pay them $22,000, not just for this play (which would have been an unheard-of amount in 1914), but for all Dick's future plays. When Gilmore complains there is still not sufficient love interest, Dick proposes to Elaine.

Before long Pirandello and others would be tinkering with the line between fiction and reality with more skill and success.

The next two openings chalked up a total of two and a half weeks between them. Both recounted histories of a woman's downfall. In Oliver D. Bailey and Rachael Marshall's **The Traffic** (11-16-14, New York) the central figure was a girl of the streets. In E. H. Gould and F. Whitehouse's **What It Means to a Woman** (11-19-14, Longacre) the focus was on a well-to-do but unhappily married woman, who takes to infidelity before drinking herself to death.

Tiaraed and white-tied first-nighters crowded the Liberty on the 23rd to see Ellen Terry's lovely niece, Phyllis Neilson-Terry, make her American debut as Viola in *Twelfth Night*. She was judged to be a highly competent performer but lacking in that special charisma that made her aunt so wonderful. Her cast mixed English and American players. Among the latter were Henry E. Dixey, recreating the clownish Malvolio he once had done for Daly, and Eben Plympton as a boisterous Sir Andrew Aguecheek. Some of the most delighted comments were reserved for the scenery (alas, not described in reviews) of Joseph Urban, who would soon be one of America's most brilliant set designers.

That same evening other playgoers straggled into the opening of an old-style melodrama. A decade or so earlier Charles A. Taylor's **Yosemite** (11-23-14, Daly's) had traveled about the cheap touring circuits with his wife of the time, Laurette Taylor, in a leading role. Now it reached New York with a highly respected actor, Frank Keenan, in the title role and Grace Valentine as the heroine, Mercedes. Yosemite was a bandit (in the Yosemite Valley, naturally) who rescues Mercedes from the Indians and turns her over to safekeeping in a mission. Later, he changes his mind and kidnaps her. The rest of the play detailed the escapes, with her baby, from him, her recaptures, and further escapes. He finally kills her and is himself captured. Years later, a dying man, he is released from prison and seeks out his granddaughter, who has been raised by an old squaw, her mother's nurse, and by the man Mercedes had hoped to marry. Music of the "trembly, Liza-crossing-the-ice variety" underscored the action. As Laurette Taylor had done before her, Miss Valentine played both mother and grown daughter.

The stage of what once had been the New Theatre, an auditorium built in hopes of giving New York its equivalent of the Comédie Française and other great national playhouses, was turned over to a modern miracle play written by a Massachusetts priest, Francis L. Kenzel's **Pilate's Daughter** (11-25-14, Century). It unfolded the tale of Claudia, Pontius Pilate's daughter, who, carrying a rose that Christ once had touched, follows Peter to Rome and to her martyrdom. Most notices dismissed the drama as more well-meaning than accomplished, and the play's one-week stay added another to the growing list of the house's failures.

Edward Sheldon suffered a major disappointment with the quick closing of **The Garden of Paradise** (11-28-14, Park), his dramatization of Hans Christian Andersen's "The Little Mermaid." Swanhild (Emily Stevens), daughter of the Merman Emperor, longs to marry a mortal and afterwards enjoy the fruits of Paradise. She falls in love with the King of the Blue Mountains (George Relph), and he with her. But when she comes to understand that she might be an obstacle to him, she sacrifices herself. That sacrifice ensures her a place in Paradise. Sheldon's inventiveness should have delighted both old and young. Thus, the Captain of the Guards is forever giving his command, "Forward, swim!" And the performances were generally excellent, with Blanche Walsh, who had never held on to the stardom many felt she deserved, winning special accolades for her termagant Sea Witch. But the best and worst things about the production were its settings, again by Joseph Urban, whom *Theatre* called a "genius." The *Dramatic Mirror,* labeling him "that master of stage pictures," described some of his work: "Fancy looking through a curtain of trembling waters at a palace under the sea with mermaids and huge fish swimming gracefully about and disporting themselves gleefully amid the dark carverns of the ocean. . . . From the ocean depths to the sun-kissed shores of the Island of the Covent, back to the Cave of the Sea Witch under the sea; to the royal palace of the King of the Blue Mountains; to the Queen's Bower of the airy, sunny Southland, the wonderful Queen's garden and the scene of the bridal feast." Sadly, Urban had yet to learn to design settings in such a way that they could be changed quickly. The waits between scene changes came to almost an hour on opening night. When the show closed Florenz Ziegfeld bought some of the scenery, used it in his *Midnight Frolics,* and signed Urban to design his *Follies.* The show's failure precipitated the bankruptcy of its producers, Liebler and Co., heretofore one of New York's most adventuresome firms.

November's last entry was Anthony Wharton's **At the Barn** (11-30-14, Comedy), another comedy in Marie Tempest's repertory. In this one she played an actress who falls in love with the novelist at whose country home she had knocked for help when her car had broken down.

December was considerably more successful than November. Its very first entry won high praise, even though it looked with patent prejudice on a subject which for years had been treated disdainfully in the American theatre. Harvey O'Higgins and Harriet Ford's **Polygamy** (12-1-14, Playhouse) dealt severely with Mormonism, which still was perceived as villainous and a menace to proper society. Their play, set mostly in a comfortable middle-class home, but also in the Mormons' great Temple, centered on four people. Daniel and Zina Whitman (Ramsey Wallace and Chrystal Herne) are a happily married couple who consider themselves good Mormons, even though they still love and befriend Zina's apostate brother, Brigham (William B. Mack). Annis Grey (Katherine Emmet) is a widow who loves Brigham. Their peaceful lives are thrown into disarray after the Church orders Daniel to take Annis as a second wife. When they finally accept that to remain and rebel would be futile, they are helped to leave home by Bathsheba Tanner (Mary Shaw), an aging "plural" wife who has resigned herself to her own merely intermittently happy life. Critics not only saw the play as compelling, intelligently written drama but applauded the acting as some of the season's best. They admired not just the principals but performers such as Lizzie Hudson Collier, who played Zina and Brigham's unhappy mother. Late in the run, after the play had moved to another theatre, the authors added a curtain raiser, **The Dickey Bird** (2-22-15, Park). It recounted the revolt of a wife-dominated husband, who, having been dragged to a performance of *A Doll's House,* concludes he is a male Nora and so storms out of his house.

Willard Mack, still raking in the coin from *Kick In,* was cast as the hero of his second play of the season, **So Much for So Much** (12-2-14, Longacre). He portrayed a reporter who rescues a bright little stenographer (Marjorie Rambeau) from the advances of her libertine boss (Joseph Kilgour). Neither the critics nor the public cared for the comedy.

On December 8, a second innovative musical added to the year's claim to moving along American interests. Irving Berlin's *Watch Your Step* was announced as the first song-and-dance show with an entirely ragtime score. The boast may not have been totally accurate, but the mere fact that a new American musical was supposedly composed completely in a distinctly American idiom was telling.

A London play, E. Temple Thurston's **Driven** (12-

14-14, Empire), told of a neglected wife who, believing she has only months to live, decides to find a better husband, but it told its tale for only three weeks.

A second English play, Harold Chapin's **The Dumb and the Blind** (12-18-14, Comedy), lasted a bit longer simply because it served as a curtain raiser to a better piece. It depicted the dull existence of some London tenement dwellers. The main attraction of the evening was Marie Tempest's revival of *The Marriage of Kitty* (11-30-03).

One of the season's most controversial plays was Edward Sheldon's **The Song of Songs** (12-22-14, Eltinge), taken by the playwright from Hermann Sudermann's novel. Critics were generally agreed that the play lacked the novel's depth and richness, but beyond that they were sharply and passionately divided. Walter Pritchard Eaton, critic for the *American Mercury,* dismissed it as "five acts of highfalutin," while Arthur Hornblow in *Theatre* appraised it as "strong dramatic meat." The *Herald* reported the play was "so sensationally frank, free and vulgar . . . that sophisticated first nighters gasped, and stared at one another." Lily (Irene Fenwick) works in a small shop on Atlantic City's boardwalk until she marries the cold, manipulative Senator Calkins (John Mason). She becomes the mistress of Richard Laird (Cyril Keightley), a suave New York club man. Discovering this, the senator throws her out. In time, Lily finds what she believes is true love with young Stephen Bennett (Ernest Glendinning). "All my life," she tells him, "I've been looking for the real song of songs." But Stephen's worldly-wise Uncle Phineas (Thomas A. Wise) purposely gets Lily tipsy and shows Stephen her reckless nature. She returns to Richard. The controversy helped propel the play into a six-month run, earning nice profits for Sheldon and his unlikely producer, Al Woods, who had purchased the production from Charles Frohman after Frohman became upset at tryout notices.

Jerome K. Jerome's **Poor Little Thing** (12-22-14, Bandbox), adapted from Jules Lemaître's *La Massière,* unfolded the history of a Parisian art student who first falls in love with her teacher but later settles for his son. It was not to New Yorkers' tastes.

Ethel Watts Mumford's **Just Herself** (12-24-14, Playhouse) had even less allure. Conceived as a vehicle to allow the popular Russian ballerina Lydia Lopokova to make her debut as an actress, it assigned her the role of Euphemia Kendal. Euphemia has been raised among a very radical element in Europe and returns to her wealthy Long Island home filled with revolutionary ideals. Rejecting all the sleek young men in her set as lazy and hypocritical, she woos and wins her chauffeur, only to discover he is a young millionaire in disguise. Several feeble excuses—Euphemia has the blues or wants to show her lover how much she loves him—allowed the star to jump to her feet and go into her dances.

If Lopokova's theatrical career had begun inauspiciously, Henry Arthur Jones's was winding down with some panache. The English dramatist's third play of the season was a highly contrived but gripping stage work, **The Lie** (12-24-14, Harris). Its leading lady (Margaret Illington) has lost her fiancé (Vincent Serrano) to her younger sister (Violet Heming). Too late she discovers that the sister, who secretly had a child out of wedlock, had spread the rumor that the baby belonged to her elder sibling. The jilted woman settles for an old family friend (C. Aubrey Smith).

The musical theatre also continued to move ahead in this amazingly progressive season. On Christmas night George M. Cohan brought in his revue *Hello Broadway,* the first important revue to dispense with the till-then-requisite thin plot line tying skits and songs together.

Buxom, homely Marie Dressler was probably the lone reason to see Parker A. Hord's **A Mix-Up** (12-28-14, 39th St.). By now dedicated playgoers probably had lost count of the number of recent farces that began when a stranger mistakenly enters a wrong apartment. But Gladys Lorraine, a burlesque queen dressed in an outlandish gown, does just that. She has no sooner confronted the man of the house than the man's rich, religiously fanatic aunt and uncle arrive for a visit, so he must introduce Gladys as his wife. Gladys's misfiring attempts to be subtle and elegant provided the laughs.

Similarly, for many the sole reason to sit through Jules Eckert Goodman's maudlin **The Silent Voice** (12-29-14, Liberty), a theatricalization of Gouverneur Morris's "The Man Who Played God," was Otis Skinner. He assumed the difficult role of Montgomery Starr, a sensitive musician who is embittered by the deafness which has overtaken him. He determines to share his wealth by reading, with the help of powerful binoculars, the lips of people walking in the park below his apartment and giving money to those he learns are needful. But he also despairs that his wife (Florence Fisher) has married him out of pity and really loves his nephew. Only after he reads her lips refusing to elope with the nephew does his happiness return. Audiences did not have to read lips, for as each scene was acted out the apartment grew dark, and the others were

Prologue: 1914–1919

heard and seen, through a large window, in the illuminated park. Some critics complained that Skinner, purposely rigid, staring intently, and speaking with "the closed dead vocal tones of the deaf," had all too little to do. Nonetheless, the play had a not unprofitable nine-week New York run and a modest tour.

But Lou Tellegen, the popular matinee idol, could bring nothing but his good looks (he wasn't much of an actor) to the season's latest crook play, **Secret Strings** (12-30-14, Longacre), which Kate Jordan dramatized from her own short story. He portrayed a French thief who attempts to steal jewels from a château by drugging the hosts and guests at a luxurious dinner party. The diners turn out to be detectives.

James Forbes's **The Show Shop** (12-31-14, Hudson) was hailed by Eaton as "the most pungent, amusing, and yet the most kindly satire of stage life and the shams of theatrical production, yet written by an American." However forgotten now, it reads better today than any of the season's other hit comedies. Jerome Beldon (Douglas Fairbanks) may not be the most intelligent young man-about-town, but he is smart enough to fall madly in love with Bettina Dean (Patricia Collinge). Unfortunately, Bettina has theatrical ambitions, goaded by her harridan mother (Zelda Sears), who has never forgiven the late Mr. Dean for putting an end to her own stage career. Bettina lands a part in a play to be mounted by a hopelessly shoestring but eternally optimistic producer, Max "Rosie" Rosenblum (George Sidney). Having latched on to Bettina because his leading lady and leading man have walked out on him, Rosie has signed her despite the protests of his acid-tongued director (Ned A. Sparks), who warns Rosenblum that Mrs. Dean spells trouble. To keep Bettina interested in him, Jerry agrees to underwrite the play, and he takes over from the former leading man. The play folds out of town. Rosenblum should have known what a dud he had when the only tryout bookings he could obtain from the Syndicate took him to Montreal, Wilmington, Schenectady, Hartford, Rochester, New Haven, Troy, and Punxatawney. However, Mrs. Dean adamantly insists there can be no marriage until Bettina has become a star. So Jerry pays Rosenblum $5000 to mount a second play, with two stipulations: the play must be lousy, and it must play one performance in New York with Bettina starred. To make sure it will fail, Rosenblum again casts Jerry as leading man. The play is called *A Drop of Poison*, but Mrs. Dean orders the name changed to *Dora's Dilemma*, after Bettina's role. She also

pushes everyone else out of the way and virtually takes over rewriting and directing. She even redesigns the set. Jerry messes up on opening night, but somehow the critics love it. Now Mrs. Dean and Rosie tell the kids they cannot marry, since it will hurt the show's chances. Jerry and Bettina offer to marry quietly, but Rosie responds nothing can be done quietly in New York. So the youngsters inform Mrs. Dean and Rosie that either they accompany them to the Little Church Around the Corner or they will announce their marriage plans at a news conference. The elders agree to go to the church with them—but quietly. Fairbanks's zesty playing, Miss Collinge's well-projected charm, and the excellence of their support added to the success, including twenty weeks in New York.

The new year, 1915, was almost a week old before its first play arrived at the tiny theatre where the planned season of one-acters had ended lamely a few nights earlier. Eugène Brieux's **Maternity** (1-6-15, Princess), in a translation whose authorship seems to have been disputed, was mounted by the Purpose Play Society. If the group's name failed to scare away more casual theatregoers, reviews surely did. Critics branded it "a sermon," "a preachment," and "a thesis" rather than an honest-to-goodness drama. Brieux framed his vigorous condemnation of double standards applied to motherhood in the story of a wife who has children forced on her by her unloving, ambitious husband, and who must help her unwed sister obtain an abortion. Richard Bennett, two years before the promoter of Brieux's *Damaged Goods,* was the guiding force behind the production. Brieux himself, ostensibly here to propagandize for France, attended the opening.

Looking back years later Owen Davis would assess his **Sinners** (1-7-15, Playhouse) as "a rather stilted, old-fashioned comedy drama . . . neither a very good play nor a very well-written one but it was a big step ahead of 'Nellie, the Beautiful Cloak Model.' " Although he added, "Gentlemen of the press didn't seem to think very much of it," in fact, most reviews were the sort of money notices theatre folk pray for. Even before the play opened in New York its producer, William Brady, saw to it that it received some typical Brady publicity: on the preceding Christmas afternoon it had been given its world premiere to a packed audience of convicts in the chapel at Sing Sing. Davis's story was as moralizing as Brieux's but never forgot that it was, first of all, theatre. And the story was neither new nor complex. Mary Horton (Alice Brady) comes to New York to earn money to support her invalid mother back in New Hampshire. She succeeds handsomely, if in ways that she would have difficulty explaining at home. But when she learns her mother (Emma Dunn) is dying, she rushes back home and decides to remain there. Alice Brady, the producer's daughter, was praised for her simplicity and charm; the not-yet-forty Miss Dunn, for another "of her gentle, sweet, pathetic sketches of devoted motherhood." An excellent supporting cast included Florence Nash, Charles Richman, John Cromwell, and a fading Robert Edeson. The play ran well into summer.

In March of 1913, Winthrop Ames offered a prize of $10,000 and promise of production for the best new American play submitted to him by August. He hoped to open his Booth Theatre, then under construction, with it. It was a typical example of his idealism and progressive viewpoint.

. . .

Winthrop Ames (1870–1937) was born in New Easton, Mass., scion of a wealthy and old New England family. Although initially slated for a career in art or architecture, he turned to the theatre after graduating from Harvard. For a time he ran Boston's celebrated Castle Square Theatre stock company. After a tour of Europe, he was appointed to manage the New Theatre, a grandiose failure. Its collapse prompted him to build a far more intimate playhouse, the Little. His subsequent career witnessed a string of admired productions, but by the time he retired in 1932 he was bankrupt.

. . .

The avalanche of scripts—1646 were read—precluded an immediate mounting, so it was not until early in this new year that the winning entry, Alice Brown's **Children of Earth** (1-12-15, Booth), was brought out. Miss Brown was not an unknown figure, having long since established her reputation as a writer of novels and short stories about New England. In years gone by Mary Ellen Harstow (Effie Shannon) had renounced her chance to marry so that she might look after her parents. Alone following the death of her father (Herbert Kelcey), she seeks out the man who once had been her suitor (Reginald Barlow) but recognizes that he has become narrow and mean. She falls in love with a neighboring apple farmer (A. E. Anson), even though he has a wife. They agree to elope, but at the last minute Mary Ellen realizes the problems an elopement would create, so resigns herself to a life of loneliness and petty daily chores. Critics found the play honest and not unintelligent but almost unremittingly dull. In recent years these same critics rarely spent much time on scenery, but this time several singled out an apple orchard in full bloom

and a wood at sunrise. The play lingered five weeks, then went the way of so many other prize plays.

On the same evening, Frohman brought out a revival of *Rosemary* (8-31-96) for a short stand at the Empire. John Drew, from the original American cast, played alongside such popular actresses as Alexandra Carlisle and Mrs. Whiffen.

Guy Bolton, still a relatively unknown writer (even though he would be librettist for a musical opening two nights after his new melodrama) watched as all his labors on **The Fallen Idol** 1-23-15, Comedy) went down the drain following just nine performances. His play told of a great pianist (Albert Bruning) forced to retire by a crippling disease. His wife (Janet Beecher) takes up with an attractive young sculptor (David Powell), giving him $15,000 toward a commission. When the sculptor learns that the pianist's former mistress would blackmail the sick man, he pays her the $15,000 to keep her quiet. At first the wife thinks her young lover is unfaithful, but on discovering a photograph of her husband's illegitimate son, she understands the true story. The pianist kills himself so that his wife and the sculptor can wed.

At the start of the season, Frohman had presented John Drew in a play by Dario Niccodemi and Michael Morton; now, in mid-season, he presented a second play by the pair, this time with Drew's niece, Ethel Barrymore, as star. According to pre-opening announcements **The Shadow** (1-25-15, Empire) originally had been conceived by Niccodemi for Réjane, but the war had prevented a Paris production. No doubt by coincidence, its story was a variant on that which Bolton had offered two nights earlier. Berthe Tregnier has been confined by a seemingly hopeless, crippling disease to a chair in her drawing room. She is sure her husband (Bruce MacRae), a famous artist, is loving and loyal. Only after she is unexpectedly cured does she discover that Tregnier has set up a mistress (Grace Elliston) in his studio and that she has borne him a son. Heartbroken, Berthe gives them their freedom by leaving her home forever. Critics were impressed, praising the play, its star, and her supporting players. Even though it meant sitting "motionless in a chair for thirty-five minutes," Miss Barrymore in her autobiography recalled "*The Shadow* was a gorgeous drama . . . [and] was very sad, but it had moments of great exaltation and beauty. Many people told me they liked me better in it than anything they had seen me in. I always wanted to do it again." She never did.

The poor Princess Theatre, still desperately seeking a long-run attraction, welcomed B. Iden Payne and some other English players when they revived

Richard Brinsley Sheridan's *The Critic* on the same night. And the critics welcomed both the comedy and the comedians. More than one reviewer referred to the play as an earlier-day *The Show Shop*. Whether prior commitments or lack of patronage determined the stand cannot be said for certain. However, the troupe departed after a fortnight.

Although the war undoubtedly exacerbated a certain malaise which had disquieted intellectuals, their unhappiness had been festering for some time. Now and then it erupted to the surface. Thus, in its summer issues, *Theatre* had published a series of articles by Sheldon Cheyney entitled "The Failure of the American Producer." Much of Cheney's displeasure focused on David Belasco, whom Cheney accused of being more interested in scenery than in substance: "Belasco, in a recent magazine essay, epitomized his creed in one sentence: 'I believe in little things.' There one has the key to his whole method of artistic endeavor, the secret of his success and of his failure. . . . He believes that if he puts together enough little details that are 'real' or 'natural'—that is, true to the outer, material aspects of life—he can build a whole that will be artistically or spiritually true to life." Cheney did not confine his attack to Belasco, and he concluded ruefully, "The American stage has outgrown the exaggeration of action and thought of melodrama, but still clings to the sensationalism of scenery and stage mechanism of the ripest melodrama days." The contrast between the old and the new received stunning attention on two late January evenings.

The battle was joined when Belasco raised the curtain of Knoblauch's **Marie-Odile** (1-26-15, Belasco). Patrons entering the playhouse noted the theatre's ornate proscenium arch and boxes covered with dreary sackcloth and, once the play began, a single setting of an austere old convent in Alsace. Throughout the play no footlights were employed. Subdued lighting came from above and through the windows and doors of the convent. A spotlight followed the heroine wherever she moved. Marie-Odile (Frances Starr) had been a foundling, raised by the nuns in total ignorance of men. The only men she ever had seen were an aged priest and an even older, decrepit gardener. She wondered if there were really men as beautiful as the sword-wielding St. Michael depicted in a faded fresco in the refectory. The Franco-Prussian war breaks out, and the nuns flee. But Marie-Odile, busy shielding her pet pigeon, which the stern Mother Superior (Marie Wainright) has ordered killed, is inadvertently left behind. An Uhlan corporal (Jerome Patrick) enters, and Marie-Odile first observes him standing under the fresco. She believes he is St. Michael. He becomes her quiet defender, but after the war ends he leaves her with their baby. The nuns return, and the Mother Superior is outraged when Marie-Odile shows her the infant and tells her it is a gift from God. Marie-Odile's friend, Sister Louise (Harriet Otis Dellenbaugh), pleads that the nuns are at fault for raising Marie-Odile in such innocence. But the Mother Superior orders the girl and her baby expelled. As the Angelus is rung and the nuns begin their prayers, Marie-Odile leaves, bewildered but confident: "I do not understand. All I know is that God let a miracle happen to me. He will not forsake me and my baby."

Most critics spent the bulk of their reviews extoling the play and the performances. The conservative John Rankin Towse of the *Evening Post,* after a number of laudatory paragraphs, devoted only a single sentence to Belasco's physical production: "The setting in the convent was perfect—a notable specimen of Mr. Belasco's handiwork." A surprising count of reviewers ignored the scenery entirely, though in its austerity it was surely a marked change for Belasco. This slight apparently rankled, but he took his spleen out on a critic who had condemned the play. Samuel Hoffenstein of the *Sun* found the play "lacking in cumulative force, in human appeal, in every essential of dramatic quality." Belasco personally called on the paper's editor and demanded Hoffenstein be fired. He was. (Al Woods quickly found work for him in his office.) But the incident caused a furor, and when other producers a few weeks later tried to have another critic dismissed, they found the climate had changed. Because of the mostly favorable reviews, Belasco said little further about the play, but he issued a broadside recounting how he had first discarded footlights years earlier and how everything about his productions was the best the theatre could ever hope to offer. Despite the criticism, the aging producer continued to be his own man.

. . .

David Belasco (1859–1931) was born in San Francisco into a family of Portuguese-Jewish origin, whose name originally had been Velasco. His father had performed in London pantomimes. Raised in Victoria, B.C., he ran away from home and may have made his acting debut in 1864. By 1873 he was a callboy at a San Francisco theatre. He subsequently acted with many of the great players of the time, then began to write plays both on his own or in partnership and, finally coming to New York, in collaboration with Henry C. de Mille. Belasco helped stage the plays for Daniel Frohman. Later he co-wrote *The Girl I Left Behind Me* (1893), which opened Charles Frohman's Empire Theatre. With *The Heart of Maryland* (1895) he embarked on a long career as playwright-producer-director, famous for introducing great female stars such as Mrs. Leslie Carter, Blanche Bates, and Frances Starr (along with turning David Warfield into a dramatic actor). His productions were celebrated for their sometimes obsessive realism, which with the coming of films was increasingly perceived as absurdly overdone.

· · ·

Many felt Belasco might have learned a lesson the very next night. Harley Granville Barker, the distinguished English author, actor, and producer, had been encouraged by his government to visit America with some fellow performers in order to promote goodwill. Two rich Americans, Otto Kahn and Archer Huntington, agreed to underwrite any losses for his engagement, which, somewhat oddly, was to be in an old theatre slated for demolition. Barker also announced his repertory would be performed with each bill kept on for a strictly predetermined number of performances. These changes in bills led to some playgoers staying away, believing they were the result of poor business. His opening attraction was a double bill: Anatole France's **The Man Who Married a Dumb Wife** followed by Shaw's **Androcles and the Lion** (1-27-15, Wallack's). France's short piece looked at a man who, sad that his wife is mute, pays for an operation to cure her, only to have to make himself deaf so as not to be plagued by her incessant chattering. Shaw's comic put-down of early Christianity watched as a meek little Christian tailor is thrown to the lions. But the little man once had removed a thorn from the very lion who is supposed to eat him, so the lion simply puts his front leg around the man's shoulder and befriends him. O. P. Heggie was Androcles; Phil Dwyer, the lion; and Granville Barker's wife at the time, Lillah McCarthy, Lavinia. A majority of critics enjoyed both plays. A few of the reviewers passed over the decor briefly, noting that the producer, like Belasco before him, had dispensed with footlights. He lit the stage from the sides and from the balcony. But for some the triumph of the evening was the setting for the France play. It was the work of a young, unknown American set designer, Robert Edmond Jones. Jones threw reality to the winds. His basic setting was a flat gray-and-black drop painted in squarish planes like a Mondrian painting. On its left was a door whose vertical lines continued upward to create two more door-size oblongs, the first filled in with the basic light color of the set, the second repeating the colors

of the door. Two smaller, narrower, purely decorative oblongs were just to the right. Much of the right-hand side of the set was taken up by a large, squared window (through which a good portion of the action was seen). Its vertical lines continued down to form the sides of a stark bench. There was not a single curve in the design. Color was provided by Jones's bright costumes. Almost immediately the setting was saluted as a breakthrough in American scenic art. Some took the occasion to compare Jones's scenery with Belasco's, and Belasco came out on the distinctly short end. Thus, Francis Hackett, writing in the *New Republic*, observed, "Where Belasco would put in the skin, the seeds, the indigestible and innutritious trash, under the illusion that if anything is real orange it must be palatable, Mr. Jones has given us only golden fruit, assimilable, ripe." Small wonder the thin-skinned Belasco went public with his fury. But Jones suddenly was a celebrity.

· · ·

Robert Edmond Jones (1887–1954) Born in Milton, N.H., he studied at Harvard, where he afterwards taught drawing. He also created some apparently more or less traditional costumes and settings before leaving for Europe. In Germany he worked with Reinhardt and came under the influence of the most advanced designers of the era.

· · ·

Charles Hopkins, who had no luck when he opened his tiny theatre with one English comedy, fared better with his second try, Alfred Sutro's **The Clever Ones** (1-28-15, Punch and Judy), even though most notices claimed that he himself gave a dismal performance. A snobbish lady, her daughter, and her sister live in a home decorated with art nouveau "in its most virulent form" and are determined to embrace everything new. So they welcome a young man (Hopkins) who pretends to be an anarchist until he is shown to be a fraud.

For all the progressive developments brought forth so far in the season, traditionalists also could feel at ease. This was especially true when Robert B. Mantell came to town. In the 1880s Mantell had been a dashing leading man, but a decade later he abandoned contemporary drama to devote himself to Shakespeare. To his misfortune, this change coincided with his divorce and an order to pay such a huge alimony in New York that for many years he confined his itinerary to the road. There he won enthusiastic notices and a large, loyal following, but when he finally was able to reappear in New York in 1904, the consensus of Broadway's chauvinistic critics was that he was merely a ham. Time mellowed their judgments (and perhaps Mantell's style as well). So when this "noble-browed Scot with keen, flashing eyes, a nose like the prow of a Viking galley, and close cropped steel-gray curls" began a month-long stand at the 44th Street Theatre on February 1, reviews were largely favorable. Mantell's repertory was virtually Edwin Booth's: Edward Bulwer-Lytton's *Richelieu*, Casimir Delavigne's *Louis XI*, one Shakespearean comedy, *The Merchant of Venice* (with Mantell as the no longer comic Shylock), and eight Shakespearean tragedies from the relatively rare *King John* to such standards as *Macbeth, Hamlet,* and *Romeo and Juliet* (the sixty-year-old Mantell still portraying even the youngest heroes).

Mantell's sponsor, William A. Brady, had a still bigger hit three nights later when he presented Lechmere Worrall and J. E. Harold Terry's **The White Feather** (2-4-15, Comedy). In London the thriller, which told of a man (Leslie Faber) who is suspected of trying to evade conscription but turns out to be a secret service agent who foils the efforts of German spies, was known as *The Man Who Stayed at Home.* American critics complained the piece displayed signs of all too hasty construction, but such cavils did not prevent Broadway playgoers from flocking to the theatre until the warm weather came.

Good luck for Brady did not come by threes, so his next mounting, Salisbury Field's **The Rented Earl** (2-8-15, Maxine Elliott's), lingered only a fortnight. It revolved about a guileless, impecunious English lord (Lawrance D'Orsay) who comes to America to earn money and, without his realizing it, is rented out to social climbers by a cagey young agent (Albert Brown). D'Orsay had been playing silly, haw-hawing English lords ever since he scored in *The Earl of Pawtucket* and represented the type to perfection, while Brown won kudos for his slangy agent. But neither man could save the play.

German spies out to sink the British fleet were also the subject of Earl Derr Biggers's **Inside the Lines** (2-9-15, Longacre). The scene is Gibraltar, where the manager of a hotel is a German spy who has been advised that another German spy, disguised as an English officer, is on his way. The English officer (Lewis S. Stone) appears and is somewhat disconcerted to find there a stranded American girl (Carroll McComas) whom he had courted briefly in Berlin. He also learns that the commandant's Indian servant (Macey Harlam) is in the pay of the Germans. The Indian knows the combination to the safe where the British secrets are held, so he and the supposed British officer set out to steal the plans. But the American girl enters just

as they set about their task. No matter. The Englishman turns out to be a double agent, and the fleet is spared. A group of rich Americans, left temporarily penniless when the outbreak of the war causes all banking to be suspended, provided the comedy. The play was only a modest success, perhaps because *Under Cover* and *The White Feather* had employed many of its tricks first.

On February 15, a tiny playhouse opened its doors, a charming, bijou auditorium. But the theatre was not located on or near Broadway. Rather it sat on Grand Street amid the ethnic hubbub of the Lower East Side, and although professionals helped select its repertory and stage its productions, it was given over largely to amateurs. The theatre was called the Neighborhood Playhouse. Its initial offering was a full-length pageant play, **Jephthah's Daughter,** which retold the biblical story of Jephthah's promising God to sacrifice the first thing he sees if he returns victorious from battle. Unfortunately for Jephthah, the first thing he sees is his daughter. Most of the troupe's early bills, like those of Blinn's defunct group and those of another new group to premiere a few nights later, were composed of one-acters, a high proportion of which were fantasies. One early offering, Robert Gilbert Welsh's study of feuding Kentucky mountaineers, **Tethered Sheep** (3-3-15), foreshadowed an increasingly voguish genre when it was billed in programs as an "American folk play." With time the group became more and more professional, earning a reputation not only for its straight plays but for its dance-plays and for a series of witty, intimate musical revues.

Granville Barker's staging of *A Midsummer Night's Dream* was unveiled at Wallack's on the 16th. With its simplified, stylized settings and elaborately costumed, gilded fairies, it divided both critics and playgoers.

Richard Harding Davis and Jules Eckert Goodman failed when they enlarged Davis's vaudeville sketch "Blackmail" into a full-length play, **The Trap** (2-19-15, Booth). A young, naive Jane Carson (Martha Hedman), who owns a claim in the Yukon, is tricked into a marriage, but her husband is soon murdered. She later marries a petty, jealous man (David Powell). Mistakenly, she conceals her earlier marriage from her new husband, so a vicious idler (Tully Marshall) attempts to blackmail her. She kills him. Her first husband's brother (Holbrook Blinn) has loved Jane. He attempts to take blame for the killing and also to give her her share in her claim, which has proven lucrative. Jane's second husband misreads the man's actions, but all ends happily enough. The men generally garnered excellent notices. On the other hand, some reviewers complained that Miss Hedman's Scandinavian accent at times broke through and that she lacked depth.

Two more of those well-meaning enterprises launched every now and then in the commercial theatre came before the public at month's end. The first, the Washington Square Players, survived only a few seasons but was of crucial importance in the growth of serious theatre in America. Its founders, among them Edward Goodman, Lawrence Langner, Philip Moeller, and Helen Westley, broke away from an intellectual group known as the Liberal Club after that organization disapproved of their plans for a dramatic branch. Despite their name, they rented the petite Bandbox Theatre on 57th Street and began a three-month stand there on February 19. Undaunted by the fate of Holbrook Blinn's programs of one-acters at the Princess, they dedicated themselves to evenings of three or four short plays by different authors (native and foreign) on different themes and in different styles. Among the plays on their opening bill was Goodman's **Eugenically Speaking.** It was played out in a setting almost as simple as Jones's had been for the France comedy, a singularly sparse, modern drawing room in a rich man's home. Una Braithewaite (Florence Enright) enters, bringing with her "a handsome, well-built, magnetic-looking youth." He's a trolley car conductor (Karl Karsten), and, she tells her flabbergasted father (George C. Somnes), she picked him to be her husband after reading an article on Eugenics. "Isn't he good-looking? And I'm sure he's strong. See those hands of his—a little rough, of course, but I like that, and so firm, and, for his job, wonderfully clean." Never mind that she doesn't even know his name. It's George Coxey, the young man tells her. Nor is she particularly vexed to learn that he's married and a father and absolutely unwilling to divorce a wife "as good as gold." He tells Una that his wife had more pluck than she: "Up and told her father she would marry me if he liked it or lumped it." As he leaves, he suggests that next time she have more gumption. A stage direction tells us that *her father's shock at what George has said is increased only by noticing his daughter's reception of the words.*" Most newspapers sent critics, and most critics liked what they saw. The once stodgy *Tribune* predicted, "If the American stage is ever to extend its exhibitions beyond the 'tired business man' type of music show and the farces and melodramas which have been money makers in the last couple of seasons, it will be by reason of the competition of such organizations as the Washington Square Players."

The other high-minded ensemble was called the Modern Stage and was the brainchild of a German actor, Emanuel Reicher. Its opening shot was Gerhart Hauptmann's *Elga* (2-23-15, Garrick), performed without intermission and telling of an idealistic knight who dreams disturbingly of an unfaithful woman. The troupe's history would be fitful and extremely brief.

Undiscouraged by the failure of her American debut, Phyllis Neilson-Terry tried again, this time as a young eighteenth-century belle who must disguise herself as a man, when Anthony Hope's *The Adventure of Lady Ursula* (9-1-98) was revived at Maxine Elliott's on March 1. Her reception was no better this second time, but the intrepid beauty would persist for several seasons before resigning herself to America's indifference.

Lou Tellegen's luck improved, at least for the moment. As he had in *Secret Strings*, he portrayed a suave, Continental thief in **Taking Chances** (3-17-15, 39th St.), which Benrimo and Morgan adapted from Paul Frank and Siegfried Geyer's German hit. The comedy blended crook play and bedroom farce, telling how a man robs banks but escapes scot-free by compromising the police chiefs' wives. While Tellegen was handsome and carried himself elegantly, some commentators felt his heavily accented voice was too monotone. For all the evening's faults the play ran eleven weeks. But those faults, as perceived by one critic, led to some of the season's most spectacular, best-publicized fireworks.

Alexander Woollcott had given the play a carefully considered if mixed review. He had praised Tellegen, the supporting company, and the physical mounting but saw some, not all, of the play as "vulgar" and "quite tedious." Although a majority of critics were less kind, the Shuberts took umbrage at the notice. When they sent the *Times* tickets for their next production, they advised the paper that the tickets would not be honored if Woollcott used them. The *Times* returned the tickets and had Woollcott buy a pair of seats. At the theatre (Maxine Elliott's on April 1) he was refused admission. The paper informed the Shuberts that it would not review any Shubert productions, nor would it carry any further Shubert advertising. It also went to court and obtained an injunction barring the Shuberts from barring Woollcott. Injunction in hand two nights later, Woollcott attended the opening of *Trilby*, and the *Times* gave the critic his first byline. Now it was the Shuberts' turn to go to court, and a legal battle ensued that was not ended until nearly a year later when the Court of Appeals unanimously upheld the Shuberts. For the remainder of the season and much of the following one, the Shuberts refused to advertise in the *Times,* and the newspaper in return did not review plays at Shubert houses. Eventually the brothers accepted that their victory was a Pyrrhic one. They quietly backed away from their policy.

(Earlier in the season after Alan Dale of the *Sun* had panned a musical, the Shuberts persuaded the paper to run a series of articles promoting the show. Dale noisily resigned. In Boston the Shuberts were in a feud with the *Evening Transcript,* refusing to advertise in it unless their shows received more favorable notices.)

A famous story found a dishearteningly small audience when it was theatricalized. **Alice in Wonderland** (3-23-15, Booth), adapted by Alice Gerstenberg from both Lewis Carroll's original and his *Through the Looking Glass,* featured eleven-year-old Vivian Tobin as the little girl who has such wonderful adventures. This time those adventures did not include the White Knight or Tweedledum and Tweedledee, but most of the other principal figures had their moment in the spotlight. A Chicago production, its colorful sets and costumes skillfully combined new stylized scenic practices with copies of Tenniel's clothing. When evening audiences were sparse, the producers opted to play only matinees. Yet even that could not draw profitable houses.

Three nights later Granville Barker introduced Americans to Shaw's **The Doctor's Dilemma** (3-26-15, Wallack's). The dilemma that Shaw had first presented eight years earlier forced his doctor to choose between saving the life of a great artist (Nicholas Hannen) whom the doctor (Ian Maclaren) knows to be a scoundrel or a good but mediocre man (Edgar Kent). At season's end, when George Jean Nathan came to select the year's ten best plays, he found to his dismay that he could name only seven worthwhile new offerings. *The Doctor's Dilemma* headed the list, and the second and third plays, *Pygmalion* and *The Phantom Lover,* were also foreign.

Edward Locke, who, like Owen Davis, had cut his teeth on cheap touring melodramas, had two plays ready for New Yorkers in April. His first, **The Revolt** (4-1-15, Maxine Elliott's), lingered only a month. Locke's melodrama, more sedate than those of his earlier career, watched as an unhappy wife (Alma Belwin), obtaining proof of her husband's infidelity, storms out, announcing that hereafter she will live life to its fullest. She does, although her inherent decency often causes uncomfortable moments. Her child's nearly fatal illness causes her to reconsider and brings about a reconciliation with her husband (Vincent Serrano).

The season already had greeted the opening or the refurbishing of several minuscule auditoriums. The smallest of all opened next. It was the Bramhall Playhouse, built in an old brownstone, on 27th Street near Lexington, that more recently had served as a hall for the Knights of Columbus and as a church. It sat only 225 patrons. Its guiding light was forty-four year old Butler Davenport, a failed actor and playwright, who simply could not concede his failings. For the next three decades he would persist in mounting, directing and playing in his own plays (and sometimes those by others), eventually waiving admissions to attract playgoers. His opening salvo was **The Importance of Coming and Going** (4-2-15). At bottom it was the season's second plea for Eugenics. Davenport's heroine is an American girl who notes how much attention is paid to a dying young man, all the while she is given little instruction on what to do now that she is pregnant. Her husband (Davenport), a French count, is no help. When her baby dies at birth she resolves to pay as much attention to life's future comings as to its goings.

Broadway's next coming was a compelling revival of a twenty-year-old warhorse. With Wilton Lackaye once again a mesmerizing, villainous Svengali, *Trilby* (4-15-95) was resurrected on April 3 at the Shubert. An "All Star" supporting cast included Leo Ditrichstein, George MacFarlane, Burr McIntosh, Brandon Tynan, Taylor Holmes, and Rose Coghlan. In the title role of the girl who comes under the hypnotist's baleful influence, Phyllis Neilson-Terry, an accomplished singer, was able to perform arias onstage instead of from the wings (where someone else customarily did the real singing).

That same evening one new play opened. Charles Sumner's **The Natural Law** (4-3-15, Republic) had made headlines when it was shuttered by Boston's censors. It received close scrutiny from New York's moralists even after it announced some major changes, including dropping one seemingly objectionable scene. Some critics thought the alterations were insufficient and condemned the play as tasteless if not immoral. Others wondered in print what all the fuss was about. Sumner's heroine, Ruth Stanley (Helen Holmes), is a young portrait painter, engaged to a much older man, Dr. Webster (Howard Hall). Ruth is selected to paint the portrait of a handsome athlete, Jack Bowling (Otto Kruger). The two fall in love, and Ruth becomes pregnant. She tells Webster of her condition. He calls in Jack and at first believes the boy is an opportunistic cad. Ruth also rejects Jack, interpreting his insistence that he must leave to run a marathon in England, whether or not they marry, as a sign that he merely believes he is doing his duty. However, on realizing that both youngsters in their heart of hearts love each other, the doctor urges them to marry. Most critics came down hard on the performers, except for Kruger. Hall had for many years been a leading writer and performer of cheap touring melodramas, and certain reviewers still saw in his mannerisms the flaws of the old school. For all the carping, the play ran ten weeks.

Thanks to Mantell, Shakespeare was the most-represented playwright on Broadway during the season, but Shaw proved a healthy runner-up. His first three plays had been novelties; his last three arrived as revivals in a late-season Shavian repertory produced by and starring Arnold Daly. The series began at the Garrick on April 5 with *You Never Can Tell* (1-9-05), then moved to the Park for *Arms and the Man* (9-17-94) on May 3 and *Candida* (12-9-03) on May 18. A few morning-after assessments asked how pertinent or appropriate Shaw's anti-war comedy was at such an hour. Daly was praised for his skillful, restrained comedy as Valentine, Bluntschli, and Marchbanks, but George Giddens often stole the entertainments in such juicy roles as William (the waiter) and Major Petkoff. Daly brought Dorothy Donnelly, America's first Candida, back to recreate her interpretation. The plays continued in alternating repertory into the warm weather.

Edward Locke's second play of the season ran even longer, spanning the summer and chalking up 176 performances. **The Bubble** (4-5-15, Booth) was a sturdy enough representative of *The Auctioneer* school of drama, and as such appealed strongly to theatregoers with immigrant backgrounds. Gus Muller (Louis Mann) is the warmhearted, sometimes impulsive owner of a prosperous delicatessen. Over the years he and his equally affectionate but more reserved wife (Mathilde Cottrelly) have saved $25,000. Enter a smooth-talking bunco artist (Henry Mortimer), who persuades Gus to put all his savings into a dubious mining scheme. While Gus dreams big, Mrs. Muller has no wish to give up her comfortable if old-fashioned furniture. And she is aghast when Gus suggests she never again need set foot in a kitchen. So she proves the family's strength when the bubble seems to burst. A young newspaperman (Harrison Ford), bent on winning the hand of the Mullers' daughter (Laura Walker), helps set matters aright. Many aisle-sitters considered the play as outdated as the Mullers' furniture. And many continued to complain that Mann laid on both

his accent and his emotions too thickly. Cottrelly's rock-of-Gibraltar mother picked up some of the best notices.

Belasco and Frohman, who long had been feuding, settled their differences and combined to mount an all-star, end-of-season revival of *A Celebrated Case* (1-23-78) at the Empire on the 7th. This saga of a man unjustly comdemned for uxoricide boasted a cast including Otis Skinner, Nat C. Goodwin, Frederic de Belleville, Robert Warwick, Helen Ware, Ann Murdock, Florence Reed, Minna Gale Haynes, and Elita Proctor Otis. The producers had cut out such antiquated clutter as asides and soliloquies, yet many notices still bewailed that the piece was creaky. Audiences couldn't have cared less, crowding the theatre for the limited nine-week stand.

Paul Kester's **Beverly's Balance** (4-12-15, Lyceum) played only five weeks in New York, part of a prearranged tour that would leave its star, Margaret Anglin, on the West Coast and give her enough money to mount more of her beloved Greek tragedies there. Critics pounced on the title but failed to offer a better one. They applauded both the comedy and its star. Miss Anglin played Beverly Dinwiddie, a southern belle who had come to New York to strike it big in musicals and wound up in the back row of a chorus. When she overhears that a multimillionaire (William Boyd) is seeking a corespondent so that he may divorce his wife (Ruth Holt Boucicault), who wishes to wed a European nobleman, she volunteers for the assignment. She soon recognizes that the multimillionaire and his wife still love each other, so she locks them in an apartment until they are reconciled. Her reward is the hand of a young attorney (Pedro de Cordoba). The critic for the *Review,* a Shubert-backed publication, noted, "Miss Anglin laughs into the role, she dances into it, she smiles and coos into it, and hands it to you as a delicate and joyous soufflé."

The next evening Emanuel Reicher and his Modern Stage group offered Ibsen's *John Gabriel Borkman* (11-18-97) for three performances at the 48th Street Theatre. Reicher, an old hand in the part on Continental stages, learned English for the performance and won almost universal accolades. Two other classics received similarly brief mountings a few nights later. Isadora Duncan brought out an austerely modern production of Sophocles' *Oedipus Rex* at the Century on April 17, with Augustin Duncan in the title role and Margaret Wycherly as Jocasta. At the Longacre on the 20th *Ghosts* was offered for a couple of matinees with an unexceptional cast.

April's final new offering was **The Hyphen** (4-19-15, Knickerbocker). The hyphen in question was the hyphen in "German-American." Heinrich Brandt (W. H. Thompson) has grown rich and old in America. Still, he has given a large donation to the coffers of his native country, only to regret his generosity after reading about German atrocities. German agents, refusing to accept his change of sentiment, press him to help blow up a Pennsylvania munitions plant supplying goods to the Allies. He refuses, and the Germans' threats bring about a heart attack. Heinrich's son (David Powell) consents to drop a bomb on the plant from an aeroplane, but the treachery is thwarted by a pretty guest (Gail Kane) in the Brandt home, who is actually an American agent. For some reason, the play was ineptly mounted. Thus, *Theatre* reported, "The German conspirators followed so faithfully every tradition of the stage villain, stalking in tip-toed one after the other, hiding behind curtains, listening at keyholes, etc., that it is little wonder derisive laughter came from the sophisticated Broadway audience." The play closed after two weeks. But the Germans got a further, ghastly revenge days later, sinking the *Lusitania* and drowning the playwright, Justus Miles Forman, and the play's great producer, Charles Frohman.

While Frohman and the doomed ship were in mid-Atlantic, Butler Davenport brought in the second and final offering of his own ill-fated season. In a change of pace, Davenport's **The Lost Co-respondent** (5-3-15, Bramhall) was a farce in which "hideously-gowned female co-respondents and comic paper detectives and waiters rushed about without reason or purpose." Slammed for its "intolerable stupidity and offensive vulgarity," charges that frequently would be leveled at Davenport, it folded after three performances.

The season's last hit was another farce, Fred Jackson's **A Full House** (5-10-15, Longacre). Jackson's story concerned a newlywed man, George Howell (George Parsons), who leaves his bride, Ottily (Elizabeth Nelson), after just one day, telling her that he has been called away to Cleveland on business. Actually he goes off to Boston to retrieve letters, written to a nightclub performer, which could embarrass the writer, his buddy Ned (Ralph Morgan). On the way back his train is wrecked, and in the ensuing confusion George picks up the wrong suitcase. The bag he grabs belongs to a burglar who has just robbed Ned's mother of valuable jewels. The play begins shortly before George returns to the rented apartment, with Ottily wondering why she has not heard from him. George is hard pressed to explain his long absence and silence, and life for the couple is soon thrown into disarray by the appearance of the burglar, the police, Ned's mother, the apartment's owner, and the nightclub singer. Adding to the mayhem are Parks, a Cockney butler, and Susie, a young maid bent on saving $22.50 so that she can return to Sioux City. Her defense of her beloved hometown was not without its topical barbs:

Parks. You've talked of nothing but Sioux City since you came 'ere.
Susie. It's a grand town.
Parks. I never heard of it!
Susie. Well, you have to get close to it to do that. It's a quiet town.
Parks. Must be since *you* left it. Oh, I say now. That *was* a good one. Ha, ha! wasn't it? What? I *am* picking up a lot of these American things over 'ere.
Susie. You'd better pick up your feet and go home and join the army.

The role of Susie fell to diminutive, wide-eyed, quivery May Vokes. And for all but walking off with the show she was awarded the final curtain call, dressed up in her " 'impossible' best," carrying a suitcase with a huge "Sioux City" painted on it, and waving to her fellow players and to the audience as she made her happy exit. Less than four years later, in early 1919, Broadway applauded a musical version, Victor Herbert's *The Velvet Lady*.

Applause was not very thunderous for **She's In Again** (5-17-15, Gaiety), which Thomas J. Gray "Americanized" from Sidney Blow and Douglas Hoare's London comedy *My Aunt,* which in turn had been based on a Paris hit, Paul Gavault's *Ma Tante d'Honfleur.* The farce reused some reliable old motifs, recounting how an engaged man (William Roselle) brings home a lady from a masked ball and is chagrined to discover, when she removes her mask, that she is an unattractive street tough (Ada Lewis). He would throw her out but for the untimely appearance of his rich aunt (Helen Lowell), who concludes the girl is her nephew's fiancée.

Beautifully paneled rooms, lovely ladies in gorgeous gowns, and knowing men in black or white ties, commonplaces in so many of the season's productions, were on view again in its last play. **Three of Hearts** (6-3-15, 39th St.), a *Raffles*-like affair, was Martha Morton's dramatization of Herbert McGrath's short story "Hearts and Masks." It featured George Nash as a clever young millionaire who learns that a very attractive lady (Julia Hay) is mainly interested in reforming criminally bent men and deftly gains her interest during a masked ball by staging one crime to cover up another. Nash was lauded for his "easy-going ways and dry humor," but otherwise cool reviews and warm weather combined against a run. The *Dramatic Mirror* claimed Augustus Thomas was an uncredited co-author.

Before the next new straight play opened (albeit technically in the 1915–16 season), some devoted but rebellious theatre lovers held informal meetings in their summer cottages and decided to stage short plays written by their own coterie. Sometime, possibly July 15, they put on a double bill at the home of the Hutchins Hapgoods. **Constancy,** by Neith Boyce Hapgood (Mrs. Hapgood), dealt with the stormy relationship of their friends Mabel Dodge and John Reed. **Suppressed Desires,** by Susan Glaspell and George Cram Cook, spoofed the excesses of amateur psychoanalysis. (This second play had been written with the Washington Square Players in mind but supposedly had been rejected by that group as "too experimental.") Robert Edmond Jones reputedly supplied what minimal decor was required. The vacationers were so pleased with the results that they sought out a venue to mount further productions and obtained an unused fishhouse. It was a while before the group caused a stir. Nor it is certain precisely when they decided on a name, but since the Massachusetts village in which they summered was called Provincetown, they eventually settled on the Provincetown Players. (Not all that dissimilarly, a few months earlier—April 20, to be precise—a musical called *Nobody Home,* created in good part by composer Jerome Kern and librettist Guy Bolton, had launched a series of musicals at the tiny Princess. P. G. Wodehouse would later join them. Their literate, funny, up-to-date, and sophisticated entertainments would later be looked upon as bringing American musical comedy into the modern age.)

It had been a pioneering year, indeed.

1915–1916

Public interest in the war that had erupted the preceding summer had waned sufficiently so that the ominous drop-off of trade that had occurred in New York early last season was no longer a problem. Indeed, business throughout 1915–16 was generally good. But another problem was looming, although Broadway's smart money was uncertain what to make of it, and arguments, or at least discussions, about it abounded all season long. That new concern was the rising artistry and attraction of motion pictures.

Brief, flickering films had first been introduced to Broadway audiences in the late 1890s. Almost immediately all major vaudeville houses felt it necessary to add a few short films to their bills. By the 1906–07 season so many marginal playhouses on the road had converted permanently to films that the road began a decline from which it has never recovered. By 1910 all the cheap neighborhood theatres, home to cliff-hanging melodramas and slapdash musicals, had been forced to close or convert. During the 1914–15 season, business on the road, even in first-class houses, was so bad that many theatre owners turned to films in desperation.

In early March of 1915 the first masterful, full-length American film, *Birth of a Nation,* opened at the Liberty Theatre on 42nd Street. Charging a $2 top, it played to weeks of packed houses. A few months later the Astor Theatre on Broadway was home to *The Alien.* Based on a two-a-day sketch subsequently turned into an unsuccessful 1911 melodrama, it was a curious affair that tried to have the best of two worlds. The initial part of the evening was on film. It told of a disinherited younger brother who kidnaps his niece and tries to blame the crime on the Black Hand. The ransom is supposed to be paid at a florist shop and to be signaled by the purchase of a rose. When a poor Italian whose little daughter has been run over by an automobile comes to buy a rose for her coffin, he is suspected. At that point, after nine reels of film, the screen went dark and was lifted into the flies, revealing the same florist shop onstage, with all the characters standing precisely where they had been at the end of the film. The remaining action was live. One critic noted, "The return to speech was most grateful, the advantages of speech being apparent from the first syllable." Although the hybrid was trumpeted as a major breakthrough, it found few takers and provoked no follow-ups.

A number of the major theatrical producers, including the Shuberts, David Belasco, and William Brady, moved cautiously into the film business, only to find that many of their most luminous performers, among them John Drew, Maude Adams, Otis Skinner, and David Warfield, publicly proclaimed their refusal to desert live theatre. On the other hand, Mrs. Fiske, Mrs. Leslie Carter, William Faversham, and Forbes Robertson all tried the new medium—and failed. In articles appearing in newspapers and magazines during the season, players often suggested that films were not and never would be a true art form. Producers, more earthbound businessmen, proclaimed their disagreement. A gentlemanly, calm Daniel Frohman wrote, "As long as civilization endures, the stage will form one of its chief sources of amusement, but by the same token, the screen will always be the theatre of the many." A more panicky Brady concluded, "Pictures are surely here to stay and we might as well try to check them as to hold Niagara in leash. And for the present they have swamped the spoken drama."

The new season suggested that both Frohman's serenity and Brady's jitteriness were merited. On the one hand, interesting long-run plays were plentiful enough; on the other, they arrived early, and the last half of the season was almost a washout.

On July 14, a new enterprise, somewhat on the order of the Washington Square Players or the Neighborhood Playhouse, was launched. Stuart Walker's Portmanteau Theatre was not a bricks-and-mortar auditorium but rather a company which was devoted to novel one-act plays and which carried not only its scenery but its stage with it. Thus it could perform anywhere. Its opening bill was given at the Christodora House, a settlement building on Avenue B. Part of its initial bill was Walker's **Six Who Pass While the Lentils Boil,** in which a condemned queen seeks refuge in a peasant's hut. Over the years the company would sometimes perform in regular theatres, but just as often they played quarters that neither before nor after housed drama.

July's lone entry was a mediocrity, Paul Dickey and Charles W. Goddard's **The Last Laugh** (7-29-15, 39th St.). It opened on a sizzling hot night and critics, sitting front and center, could see the players perspiring profusely. A mad, elderly scientist (Harry Harmon) attempts to create human life. His associates are contemptuous and enlist a young man (Edward Abeles) to impersonate the manufactured human. The comic complications which followed failed to induce much laughter.

But the season's longest run was chalked up by August's first entry, Winchell Smith and Victor Mapes's **The Boomerang** (8-10-15, Belasco). The curtain rose on a simple yet elegant set. Glass-encased bookshelves, three shelves high and topped with pieces of sculpture, circle all but the right side of the room. In the center are a desk and several leather chairs of an obviously high quality. Only the right side of the room, with its white, sterile-looking cabinet, its white-metaled examination chair, and its framed diploma disclose that this is a doctor's office. The doctor is young Gerald Sumner (Arthur By-

ron), newly returned from years of study in Europe and clearly more interested in his golf game than in establishing a practice. Even his adoring father, who has built the office for him, must have his doubts, for when Gerald asks where his father is, he is told the old man doesn't feel well and has gone to consult a physician. Gerald is just about to leave for some golf when his valet announces that there is a patient to see him—Gerald's first. He quickly hides his clubs. However, Virginia Xelva (Martha Hedman), the beautiful girl who enters, turns out to be no patient. Rather she is looking for a job as a nurse. Gerald has no need for one but, smitten with her beauty and charm, hires her at once. Luckily a patient does appear. He is Budd Woodbridge (Wallace Eddinger), whose mother has insisted he is not well and has dragged him to the doctor's office. Budd denies any illness, but when he tells Gerald that he has insomnia and no appetite, has lost ten pounds in one month, and can't sit still, Gerald quickly surmises what is wrong—though he doesn't tell Budd. Gerald privately diagnoses calf love. Budd is lovesick and jealous that another man seems to be winning the girl whom Budd adores. Gerald gives him a meaningless (pure distilled water) injection and orders him to see no one for a month and to begin a regimen of strenuous athletics. He also insists that Virginia stay with Budd to look after him. When Grace Tyler (Ruth Shepley), the object of Budd's affections, writes him, Gerald has him answer her curtly and discouragingly. Gerald's theory is that love is a game, and the only way to win it is not to show one's true feelings too often. The ploy works. Grace realizes how much she loves Budd. At the same time, Virginia has fallen deeply in love with Gerald, but he seems totally unware of her feelings. So she resorts to the same tactics, letting Gerald think she has fallen in love with a handsome lawyer. Just in time for a happy curtain, Gerald realizes his game has boomeranged.

Critics were delighted with the play, the production, and the performances. The actors tilted their playing until it just verged on caricature, adding the right touch of farce to the featherweight piece. Belasco's attention to detail was manifest not only in his mounting but even in small script changes. Because the foreign-born Miss Hedman still had a trace of an accent, a line was inserted suggesting she was born and raised in Switzerland, and that her father was Swiss and her mother American. With everything falling happily into place, the comedy achieved a run stated variously as between 495 and 522 performances. *Variety,* which reported the latter figure, said the production had grossed nearly

$800,000 and, but for a booking shortage, might have continued for much of the 1916–17 season, since the play was still pulling in huge grosses.

A hit and a flop opened the next night. Roi Cooper Megrue's **Under Fire** (8-11-15, Hudson) was the success, although its popularity fell far short of his last season's triumph, *Under Cover*. The play opens in London at a posh tea, where conversations are abuzz about the outbreak of the war. Central to the story are three figures: Ethel (Violet Heming), an attractive woman married to or about to marry (depending on whether you follow the text or the reviews) Henry Streetman (Fred Krembs); Streetman himself, who is actually a German spy; and Captain Redmond (William Courtenay), a member of the British Secret Service and long in love with Ethel. The war carries all three to Belgium. Now a German officer billeted at an inn, Streetman callously orders the innkeeper killed and also attempts to have a brash American reporter (Frank Craven) shot. For his pains, Streetman is stabbed by the innkeeper's vengeful daughter, just as he is about to denounce Redmond, whom he has discovered disguised as a German soldier. Streetman recovers. He and Redmond meet again in the trenches when Streetman, now in the guise of a British officer, attempts to phone false information to the English. A bomb stymies his plans but also severely wounds Redmond. Ethel finds Redmond in a makeshift hospital in a French church and promises to nurse him back to health. Critics warned that the graphic scenes of bloodshed might dissuade many playgoers, and also noted that Megrue's ignoring President Wilson's plea for neutrality would assuredly alienate many German-Americans. They were right, so their praise for the mounting and acting went largely unheeded. One bit player they singled out for that praise was a young actor listed in the programs as E. G. Robinson. The play, by no means a failure, took to the road after 129 performances.

Who stole an eccentric old lawyer's virtually priceless ruby? **Search Me** (8-11-15, Gaiety), Augustin MacHugh's comedy-mystery, hoped to provide the answer. At first it seems that the jewel may not really have been stolen and that the attorney (Fred Graham) thought his phony claim could help a young American playwright (Howard Estabrook) gain some publicity. But soon it appears that the ruby has truly vanished. All manner of visitors are suspected, until the actual criminal turns out to be the man everyone believed to be a Scotland Yard detective (Montague Love). When, in a few years, Mary Roberts Rinehart and Avery Hopwood used a similar ending for their hugely successful *The Bat*, few people recalled this earlier use, for *Search Me* lasted a mere two weeks.

The season's second oddball scientist was featured in **Some Baby!** (8-12-15, Fulton), a farce by Zellah Covington and Jules Simonson, revised for Broadway by Percival Knight. Pudgy, balding Frank Lalor, better known as a clown in musicals, was featured as Dr. Josiah Smythe, who is convinced he has found a magical elixir which can make old folk young again. When an elderly general (Ernest Stallard) calls to ask for the hand of Smythe's daughter, the professor insists the soldier first take some of the elixir. Smythe leaves the room briefly, and immediately the general does, too, but only after accidentally spilling the elixir. A neighbor fleeing a fire dashes into the empty room, deposits her baby there, then returns to the fire scene. When Smythe comes back and sees the infant, he is flabbergasted at how powerfully his concoction works. Circumstances soon place another baby in the room, and Smythe concludes that his daughter must have tried the potion. Of course, before long the truth emerges. Smythe will have to be content with the knowledge that his discovery at least has some hair-restoring properties. Lalor's skill kept the comedy in New York for two months.

Two weeks was all that **Mr. Myd's Mystery** (8-16-15, Fulton) could muster. In that short while, Lillian Trimble Bradley's comedy focused on an author (Taylor Holmes) of mysteries who finds he is a murder suspect and makes no attempt to exculpate himself, in hopes of obtaining material for a new book. For Holmes the flop was another misstep in a career that, while long-lasting, never was as bright as his earlier admirers had prophesied.

To some extent the same fate awaited Charles Ruggles, who was to have a few important roles on Broadway but who spent most of his career as a supporting player in Hollywood. Several critics mistook his assignment in Edgar Selwyn's **Rolling Stones** (8-17-15, Harris) as his New York debut, unaware he had been performing for New York audiences as far back as 1906, when at the age of twenty he played in some of Charles Blaney's cheap touring melodramas. But there was no mistaking their delight with his acting. *Theatre*'s critic noted, "Charles Ruggles . . . has just breezed in from the West, bringing his breeze with him. His first appearance on a New York stage auspices well for his future. The word 'natural' is written all over him. He makes the play a living, natural thing." The *Times* devoted a Sunday follow-up to him. An ability to make the play a natural thing was much needed, for Selwyn's "melodramatic comedy of city life" was in reality a farce, and while it was loaded with colloquial charm its turns became increasingly preposterous. At Brannigan's Chicago boardinghouse, run by the mean-minded Mrs. Brannigan and her equally mean-minded, henpecked husband, Buck Ryder (Harrison Ford) is informed that he must give up his room, not only because he is behind in his rent but because the room is required for Jericho Braden, who, according to his late uncle's will, is to inherit the uncle's lucrative candy business so long as he marries the Brannigans' niece, Norma Noggs. That is, Braden will inherit if he has survived a train wreck which the Brannigans have every reason to believe may have proved fatal to him. Another boarder, Anna Anderson (Marguerite Skirvin), offers to pay Buck's overdue rent, but he refuses. He tells everyone that he is going out and that when he comes back he will either have the rent or he will move out. On the North Clark Street Bridge Buck paces up and down trying to work up enough nerve to carry out his plan. But before he can a very jittery holdup man demands his money. Buck, who has been contemplating staging a holdup himself, has no difficulty disarming the would-be thug. He turns out to be Dave Fulton (Ruggles), a "poor mutt" even more down on his luck than Buck. They quickly make friends, and Buck proposes they "go after the coin" together. Toward this end, Buck takes Dave back to the Brannigans' and introduces him as Braden, saying he lost his baggage and all his papers in the wreck. What Buck and Dave don't know is that yet one more boarder, Jap Walter (Arthur Aylesworth), is really Braden. But he is using an assumed name while he figures out a way to gain his inheritance even though he already is married. When Norma (Marie Carroll) falls in love with Dave, Jap decides to string along with the men, since if Norma marries Dave then she, too, could be disinherited. Happily Dave reciprocates Norma's feelings. "I'm off my dip about her," he tells Buck. Buck and Dave (the latter as Braden) take over running the candy company, hiring on Walter as an assistant. But a detective sent by Braden's West Coast lawyers, a burglar who robs the company safe, and the real Braden's unduly worried wife throw monkey wrenches into the works. Of course, all ends happily with the couples paired as audiences by the end of the first act knew they would be. The farce ran fifteen weeks and toured successfully.

Mrs. De Peyster (Flolliott Paget) of **No. 13 Washington Square** (8-23-15, Park) has long relied on dividends from one railroad company, so when that organization skips a dividend she resolves to forego her annual European vacation and, boarding up her house so no one will know she is home, spend the summer in seclusion. Naturally, a variety of intruders would frustrate her plans except for the quick, clever responses of her invaluable maid, Matilda (May Irwin). Just as naturally, blonde, hefty Miss Irwin was the real attraction of Leroy Scott's comedy, wrestling hilariously with a folding bed or finding any flimsy excuse to offer a song or two. Thanks to the star the show played to acceptable business during its seven-week engagement, although for some of that stand and for its subsequent tour the address in the title was changed to No. 33, ostensibly to placate some superstitious playgoers.

August's second smash hit was Cleves Kinkead's **Common Clay** (8-26-15, Republic). Ellen Neal (Jane Cowl) is a new maid at the Fullerton mansion, and when young Hugh Fullerton (Orme Caldara), just home from college, learns from his friend that Ellen has been seduced before, he, too, seduces her. After she gives birth she demands that the Fullertons help provide for the baby. The Fullertons call in an old family counselor, Judge Filson (John Mason). He suggests that Hugh marry the girl. His suggestion is shocking, but understandable after he confesses that years before he had seduced a girl who later committed suicide rather than hurt his career. Hugh refuses Filson's suggestion, and a trial ensues, during which it becomes obvious that Ellen is the daughter of the judge's old liaison. A contrite Filson sends Ellen to Paris to study, and when she returns years later, a rising prima donna, an equally contrite Hugh proposes. Most critics felt the play—gripping melodrama at first—fell apart following the trial scene or the subsequent dialogue between father and daughter. Many were scathing about the final scenes, especially the epilogue, which, according to Walter Prichard Eaton, "for unadulterated mush and sentimental mawkishness and falsity very nearly takes the cake."

The play had an interesting history. In 1914 John Craig of Boston's Castle Square Theatre offered a $500 prize for the best drama submitted by a Harvard student. Kinkead, who after reading for a law firm and serving as a newpaperman had come from Louisville and enrolled in Professor George Pierce Baker's famous 47 Workshop, submitted the piece and won. The award and Craig's subsequent mounting (which included a lanky young actor named Alfred Lunt, heavily made up to play the elder Fullerton) drew all the major Broadway producers. Just why Kinkead chose Al Woods, still best remembered as a peddler of cheap melodrama, is uncertain. Eaton and other critics suggested the play might have been seriously improved in other hands. The public dismissed such dismissals and packed the theatre for nearly a year. Four road companies were sent out.

Probably an additional reason for the public's interest was the play's Cinderella aspect. The beautiful Cowl was dressed as a maid in the first act and austerely in subsequent acts. But in the epilogue, returning home in triumph, she wore a gown of gilt tissue, girdled in ribbons of blue, pink, and lavender, with small bunches of black, gold, and silver grapes attached. Over this, for her grand entrance, she wore an opera cloak of tangerine velvet, with a blue fox collar and cuffs. Accessories included a huge black fan, and two "audacious brushes" of black aigrettes in her hair. Cowl's grip on stardom was assured.

. . .

Jane Cowl (1884–1950) was a slender, dark-haired beauty with eyes "so black, so limpid, it was a wonder they didn't dissolve and run down her cheeks." Born in Boston, she studied at Columbia before coming under David Belasco's aegis in 1903 in *Sweet Kitty Bellairs*. After she broke with Belasco in 1910 her luck temporarily soured until she scored a huge hit as the wronged, vengeful woman in *Within the Law* in 1912.

. . .

Perhaps because he had lacked proper guidance, Kinkead's few later attempts all failed, so in time he returned to Louisville, "found a big chair at the Pendennis Club, and from that comfortable vantage point he sat back and watched the world whirl by."

Another 47 Workshop alumnus, Fred Ballard, was the author of the lavishly praised **Young America** (8-28-15, Astor). He based his play on Pearl Franklin's *The Doray Stories*. Jack (Otto Kruger) and Edith Doray (Peggy Wood) are a typical young suburban couple whose humdrum daily life is upset when a young boy is caught stealing chickens from a nearby chicken house. The youngster, Art Simpson (Percy Helton), is the nephew and ward of the Dorays' laundress, Mrs. McGuire (Adella Barker), a selfish, mean-minded, hard-drinking woman all too ready to blame Art for her problems and anxious to be rid of him. He is hauled into Juvenile Court. There the testimony of his Huckleberry Finn–like buddy, Nutty Beemer (Benny Sweeny), although it is soon shown to be a tissue of falsehoods designed to exculpate Art, coupled with the pleas of the warmhearted Mrs. Doray ("Reformatories are preparatory schools for penitentiaries") and the sympathetic nature of the judge, allow him to be released into Mrs. Doray's care. Jack Doray is anything but happy to share his home and his breakfast with a young thief. However, when Art's faithful dog, Jasper, is nearly killed by an automobile, the concerted effort to save the mixed-breed brings everyone together. Critics extolled the play. Burns Mantle of the *Evening News* is said to have left the theatre shouting, "A real play at last!" *Variety* was less enthusiastic, seeing it as "not a great play, but its kid atmosphere, with amusing lines and situations, tend to make it a play worth while." It continued, "It bristles with kids of all descriptions and there has been no attempt to draw a color line, for in the second act there are two colored persons who have an important scene effectively done, especially on the part of a barefoot, nondescript pickaninny." That scene showed young Washington White (Norman Allen) brought before the bench for riding off with a Jewish food peddler's horse and wagon. When the same liberal judge dismisses the complaint, the poor victim, in Yiddish words not much different from those that might have been heard two generations later, bewails, "A schwartzer duyvil ganeffs a horse an wagon and noddings." Although the established professionals—Miss Wood, Kruger, and Helton—won laudatory notices, many of the most affectionate appraisals were reserved for newcomer Benny Sweeney and for Jasper, whose frantic yelps and tearing at the door after his little master was led away (a scene repeated for first-act curtain calls) and tear-jerking near-death throes were obvious high points. Yet for all the critics' loud applause, *Young America* was not the smash hit so many predicted. It set out on tour after just 105 performances. And neither Sweeney not Jasper was heard from again, although the dog is said to have returned successfully to the vaudeville stages from which he was borrowed. But the show's two producers, long since famous, would continue on for years of achievement and celebrity.

. . .

George M[ichael] Cohan (1878–1942), although best remembered as a performer and writer of song-and-dance entertainments, was a theatrical jack-of-all-trades. Born in Providence, R.I., to parents who were established vaudevillians, he joined their act as a youngster but also appeared in several straight plays. By 1901 he had expanded a vaudeville sketch into a full-length musical, and three years later he won major success with his *Little Johnny Jones*. In 1906 he formed a partnership with Sam H. Harris that produced both Cohan's own works and those of others. They enjoyed an exceptional number of successes before the partnership broke up amicably in 1920.

. . .

Sam H[enry] Harris (1872–1941) was born on New York's Lower East Side and worked as a newsboy, cough drop salesman, and steam laundry operator before becoming the manager of a popular prizefighter, Terry McGovern. He soon purchased an interest in a touring burlesque show. Then he joined with P. H. Sullivan and Al Woods to form a company which produced cheap touring melo-dramas until the vogue for them began to wane. He met Cohan in 1904 and shortly thereafter formed a new producing partnership with him, this time mounting productions for first-class theatres. With Cohan or later alone, he also built playhouses. He was admired for his shrewd theatrical judgments and for his honesty and integrity.

. . .

If several of the principals in *Young America* were beginning long, successful careers, William Hodge's had peaked. For the next thirteen years, until shortly before his death, Hodge, whose acting always retained a hayseed touch, would appear regularly if briefly on Broadway, then take his vehicle of the moment out to the more welcoming road. Such was the case with **The Road to Happiness** (8-30-15, Shubert), by Lawrence Whitman, reput-edly a pen name for the star, in which Hodge portrayed Jim Whitman, who is selling horse lini-ment to pay his way through school. Jim must reconcile a cruel farmer and his sanctimonious, suspicious wife with the stepdaughter they have unjustly sent packing after a baby is left on their doorstep immediately after the girl has returned home from school. Somehow, news of the death of the farmer's son and the subsequent realization that the news was false soften the old man's heart. Atmosphere was provided by a cornpone neighbor riding up on a white horse to buy liniment, a barn with a hen perched in the rafters, and a checker party, with homemade cookies for the guests, bringing down the final curtain.

But Hodge's six-week stand was five weeks more than was accorded Jules Eckert Goodman's **Just Outside the Door** (8-30-15, Gaiety). Critics admired the intelligence of Goodman's observations and the crispness of his dialogue, but most felt he did himself in by time and again stretching coincidence. His story focused on a girl who attempts to plead with the employer of her thieving brother. When the man agrees to drop charges if she will sleep with him she stabs him, then unwittingly takes refuge in a house where the owner's son has long loved her and where the owner's daughter is engaged to the man the heroine has just stabbed. Ernest Truex as the weak, hysterical brother garnered special encomiums.

September's first entry, Max Marcin's **The House of Glass** (9-1-15, Candler), added one more name to the season's lists of long runs. Reviewers and playgoers alike compared it to *Within the Law,* and deemed it almost as good. The comparison was not hard to make, since both plays centered on young women sent to prison for crimes of which they were innocent. After Margaret Case (Mary Ryan) is paroled, a parole she violates, she marries Harvey Lake, the president of a large railroad. Lake believes one of his employees is embezzling, and when he calls in a detective (Thomas Findlay), the man recognizes Margaret as a girl whom he once had arrested and who has broken her parole. He tells Lake, who understands that he lives in a glass house. The governor (Frank Young) of Lake's state agrees to pardon Margaret if Lake will forgive the embez-zler. One especially dramatic moment was the scene in which the detective and Margaret recognize each other. Because Lake is speaking on the phone, neither can say a word. Their insistent stares tell all. Some of the best notices went to Frank Thomas as James Burke, the thief Margaret once had loved and for whose crime she had gone to prison. The repentant Burke works devotedly to help exculpate her. George M. Cohan, co-producer with Sam Harris of the melodrama, aided Marcin to make this, his first play to see the footlights, effective theatre.

Marcin did not have to wait long to see a second play of his mounted, for Al Woods produced **See My Lawyer** (9-2-15, Eltinge) the very next evening. Stock is sold in the International Artificial Rubber Company after a scientist (Gus C. Weinburg) believes he has found a way to make synthetic rubber. The invention proves a dud, and the chief salesman (T. Roy Barnes) has to pretend he is looney to escape charges of selling worthless securi-ties. To this end, the salesman's lawyer (Sidney Booth) must bribe an alienist (John Dany Murphy) to swear to his client's looniness. Later, after the rubber trust offers a small fortune to buy the invention, the lawyer must again bribe the alienist, this time to swear to the hero's return to sanity. All ends acceptably when the material manufactured is shown to be excellent for paving blocks. Only Barnes, celebrated in vaudeville for his "nut act," received money notices. The unfunny farce folded after a week and a half.

On the 6th at the Lyceum Marie Tempest returned to Broadway in a double bill. The main item was a revival of *The Duke of Killicrankie,* in which John Drew had starred eleven years before. The star's afterpiece was a novelty, James M. Barrie's **Rosalind.** Miss Tempest played a famous actress who bravely accepts the fact that she has become middle-aged.

Two quick flops followed. Louis K. Anspacher's **Our Childen** (9-10-15, Maxine Elliott's) seemed little more than an updated version of Adolf L'Arronge's *Mein Leopold,* which New York had seen in 1878 as *My Son.* Once again a newly rich shoemaker disowns his daughter and son-in-law in favor of a worthless son. **Just Boys** (9-13-15, Comedy), by Katherine Browning Miller and Allena Kanka, spent much of its time, as had *Young America,* in Juvenile Court, but with none of the appeal of the earlier show, despite the presence of Ernest Truex in the cast. Grace Livingston (Gladys Wynne) and her little son, Billy (Master Mac Macomber), are about to be evicted from their tenement for non-payment of rent. Billy steals and sells some pigeons to help out. Caught and brought to trial, he and his mom turn out to be the long-lost son and wife of the judge (Milton Sills). How long the play ran is moot. *Best Plays* says it ran sixteen performances; the *Dramatic Mirror* gives the stay as five performances; *Variety* reported that the brutal September heat wave, more than the equally brutal reviews, prompted the show to fold after its first performance. A third work, *My Lady's Garter,* listed in *Best Plays* as having opened the night before *Our Children,* actually was called off just before its first night.

Cohan and Harris enjoyed their third and biggest hit of the season (their earlier ones had been *Young America* and *The House of Glass*) when **Hit-the-Trail Holliday** (9-13-15, Astor) was presented with Cohan's brother-in-law, Fred Niblo, in the lead. Cohan purportedly based his play on a plot suggested to him by George Middleton and Guy Bolton. Many saw it as a spoof of evangelizing Billy Sunday, but Middleton insisted it was based on a man who helped shut down racetracks after racing interests forced him out of the betting business. Cohan's Billy Holliday, a renowned New York barman, arrives in a small New England town to assist in opening a hotel. However, he turns prohibitionist after he has a falling-out with a local liquor magnate. His campaign is so convincing that all the area bars and breweries soon are out of business. He also wins the hand of Edith Holden (Katherine La Salle), daughter of the town's minister (Grant Stewart). The farce ran 336 performances.

The still young season's second war play was **Moloch** (9-20-15, New Amsterdam), a full-length drama by Beulah Marie Dix, whose one-acter *Across the Border* had impressed many reviewers and theatregoers last season. Once again the playwright attempted to be neutral, not identifying the opposing armies. But the drift of public sentiment was such that producers Klaw and Erlanger dressed the enemy soldiers in German-style uniforms and encouraged the actors who played the parts to employ such perceived German mannerisms as heel-clicking. Miss Dix (she was actually Mrs. Dix-Flebbe) offered no taut plot, preferring to depict glimpses of both sides in the loving confines of their homes and in brutal battle. In one particularly memorable scene a war-crazed servant, whose family had been wantonly murdered earlier, kills an enemy soldier billeted in her employers' house. The family had treated him kindly, and he had left a note asking that the family and their home be spared. While the old grandmother and the mother, who is attempting to shield her sick young child, plead for mercy, the soldiers drag the serving girl away. The major points out to the women that the dead soldier had been stationed three hundred miles away from the earlier atrocities. After telling the family, "You have killed the one man who would have saved you," he orders the soldier's note destroyed, the house burned, and the servant shot in front of all the neighbors. In the end, a peace treaty is signed, but the victorious allies have a falling-out and prepare to go to war. A stellar cast included Holbrook Blinn, who staged the production, Mrs. Whiffen, Lillian Albertson, Edmund Breese, and Creighton Hale. Critics praised the play's honesty and intelligence, but reading between the lines many seemed to prefer the less exalted theatricality of *Under Fire.* In his review for the *Times* Alexander Woollcott noted that grim-faced playgoers, leaving the theatre, were confronted by a nattily uniformed youngster barking the attractions of Ziegfeld's *Midnight Frolics* on the New Amsterdam Roof. The odd contrast continued for the month that the play survived.

Charles Kenyon's **Husband and Wife** (9-21-15, 48th St.) ran only half as long. Richard Baker (Robert Edeson) is as generous as any husband can be to his wife, Doris (Olive Tell), but giving her money is easy for him. Otherwise he is so shamefully neglectful of the adoring attentions a wife yearns for that Doris turns to Patrick Allston (Montague Love) for affection. Just as Doris is about to run off with Patrick she learns that Richard's generosity has brought him to the verge of bankruptcy. A reconciliation follows. Some critics apparently resented Edeson's early desertion to films and his return to the stage when his film career faltered. Woollcott, always good for a vivid picture, ruefully observed Edeson's habit of giving way "from time to time to his bad old tricks of letting his face writhe while his eyebrows mount and fall, mount and fall."

A bad old practice annoyed some loftier playgoers at a less elite house when "candy butchers" huckstered nickel boxes of chocolates in the aisles during intermissions and, more startlingly, during scene changes. The practice had been common at houses once devoted to cheap touring melodramas and was still common on the burlesque wheels. Since the attraction was an English melodrama, Cecil Raleigh and Henry Hamilton's **Stolen Orders** (9-24-15, Manhattan Opera House), done in London as *Secret Orders,* the intrusion was not entirely inappropriate. But it may have soured the play's reception. A German agent (W. L. Abington) attempts to blackmail the wife (Ivy Marshall) of a British admiral (Clarence Handyside) into handing over secret orders which had been given the admiral and which she has pilfered to pay for her gambling debts. At one point the wife's brother (John Halliday), rather than be found with letters incriminating his sister, jumps from a mast into the water. The English comedienne Connie Ediss won laughs as the girlfriend of an American magician.

On the 28th Grace George began a promised season of repertory at her husband's Playhouse. Her company included Conway Tearle, Ernest Lawford, John Cromwell, Mary Nash, and a young Guthrie McClintic. For an opener she chose Langdon Mitchell's 1906 hit, *The New York Idea.* Critics felt the play had lost none of its humor, and they admired much of the acting. On November 9, she added Henry Arthur Jones's 1898 success, *The Liars.* Not until December did she bring out a major new play.

A second sort of repertory ensemble gave October a splendid start when the Washington Square Players began their new season at the Bandbox Theatre. Except for a lone mounting at season's end, all their bills consisted of one-act plays. Among those offered at the opening was Philip Moeller's delicious comedy **Helena's Husband** (10-4-15). In his recounting of the Helena-Menelaus-Paris legend, Menelaus gladly allows Paris to elope with the bitchy, self-enamored queen only to realize that his triple alliance with Ulysses and Agamemnon means that he must go to war with Paris's father. The curtain falls on the citizens singing a paean of hate. Among the other sly topical references was an allusion to President Wilson's "scrap of paper" speech: a treaty between Sparta and Troy is deprecated as a scrap of papyrus. How pertinent the writing still is can be seen in a remark of Helena's black servant, "I've been so busy having babies I never had time to get married."

That same evening saw E. H. Sothern score a modest success when he starred in Alfred Sutro's London hit **The Two Virtues** (10-4-15, Booth). Sothern played a scholar who, despite the interferences of his sister (Haidee Wright), finally marries the woman (Charlotte Walker) he so long has loved.

Herman Scheffauer's luckless **The Bargain** (10-6-15, Comedy) was withdrawn after less than two weeks, although those critics who liked it ranked it among the season's finest plays. Its central figure was a fanatically devout Jew, Simon Lusskin (Louis Calvert), who disowns his wife (Dorothy Donnelly) after she admits she would like to go on the stage, his son (Forrest Winant) after he catches him in financial peculations, and, most dramatically, his daughter (Josephine Victor) on learning that she loves a Gentile. There are reconciliations at the close.

Three-quarters of a century later, young playwrights would have difficulty getting a hearing on Broadway, but in 1915's still healthy theatrical climate it was not unheard-of for a novice to have two new plays on Broadway in short order. Max Marcin already had done so a few weeks before. Now it was Louis K. Anspacher's turn. His second play of the season, **The Unchastened Woman** (10-9-15, 39th St.), was hailed as a brilliant achievement, possibly the season's highest. Walter Prichard Eaton rejoiced, "Here, at last, is a play which says something, and something about people." Shrewdly observed, sharply written, albeit, at least by late twentieth-century standards, excessively contrived, it focused on a totally unpleasant woman. As soon as the play caught on, its publicists were broadcasting the notion that it was pioneering in this respect, but oldtimers recalled Clara Morris's heroines and Clyde Fitch's girl with green eyes. When Hubert Knollys (H. Reeves-Smith) learns his wife has been detained at customs on suspicion of smuggling, he refuses to go to her aid. He laments that she is hopelessly immoral. He's tried to correct her, her friends have tried, society has tried, so perhaps the government can succeed where others have failed. The unrepentant Caroline (Emily Stevens) appears. She is indifferent to what has happened, utterly uncaring about her daughter's unhappy marriage, and contemptuous of her own. She tells Hubert, "Our marriage stands as a temple to the Gods of Convention. The priests are hypocrites, but be careful not to make the *congregation* laugh." Later she underscores her sentiments by insisting that "the world at best is a cruel place." On her trip she has taken a young, married architect, Lawrence Sanbury (R. Hassard Short), under her wing. She invites him to redo the Knollys' mansion and suggests he move into the house while working on it. To drive another wedge between him and his wife, Hildegarde (Christine Norman), she points out that Hildegarde's left-wing activities can only alienate the very rich people Lawrence will need. She feels she can handle a lover without recrimination since she knows her husband once had a mistress named Emily Madden. What she doesn't know is that Emily was the customs matron whom she had offered a bribe and who has returned the money to Mr. Knollys in an attempt to minimize problems. Emily (Willette Kershaw) is now engaged to a youthful Russian immigrant, Michael Krellin (Louis Bennison), who is a rising newspaperman. At a dinner which Hildegarde gives in the Sanburys' tenement apartment, Caroline is gratuitously condescending. After she becomes riled, she reveals Emily and Hubert's history to Michael. The elegantly dressed Caroline also attempts to goad the simply dressed, union-labeled, flat-heel-booted Hildegarde into falling out with Lawrence. Everyone is outraged at Caroline's self-serving callousness. They demand a written retraction. Hubert tells her that unless she agrees to the apology he or Hildegarde will start divorce proceedings and the scandal will destroy her. She signs the apology, but as she is leaving she venomously discloses details that prove Emily's earlier liaison. While she has failed to destroy either the engagement or the marriage, neither will be the same again. Caroline is clearly and incorrigibly unchastened. Eaton praised all the players, noting in particular that Stevens, who was Mrs. Fiske's niece, caught "the charm of the woman, the vampire allure, the worldly ease, the ready wit, the restless, neurasthenic vacancy of life, [and] the selfish cruelty." He criticized her only for occasional "facial contortions" and for a lack of any real sexual passion. The play ran into the spring. In December *Variety* reported that this play and *Common Clay* were "reversing" an old theatrical rule, since the cheapest balcony seats were more in demand than orchestra seats.

George Broadhurst, with far more experience under his belt than Anspacher, suffered a one-week debacle with **What Money Can't Buy** (10-11-15, 48th St.). He set his fiasco in an imaginary European kingdom, where an American millionaire (George Fawcett) is attempting to begin a transcontinental railroad, but his plans are jeopardized when his son (Calvin Thomas) falls in love with the local princess (Anne Meredith). Love triumphs.

That same evening saw William Gillette return to the Empire, first presenting four weeks of *Sherlock Holmes,* then two of *Secret Service.* Curiously, Charles Frohman, dead for six months, was listed as producer.

Another London hit, Horace Annesley Vachell's **Quinneys** (10-18-15, Maxine Elliott's), found only a lukewarm welcome in New York. It centered on a good-natured but stubborn antique dealer whose obstinacy creates problems for his family and friends.

In a marked change of pace for her, Ethel Barrymore assumed the role of the warmhearted, slightly slangy traveling saleswoman in Edna Ferber and George V. Hobart's **Our Mrs. McChesney** (10-19-15, Lyceum), a dramatization of Miss Ferber's *Saturday Evening Post* stories. Her Mrs. McChesney is anxious to give up her hard life on the road and settle down again. She is about to resign from the T. A. Buck Featherloom Petticoat Company to accept a better offer when she learns that her son (Donald Gallaher) has committed forgery and has married a showgirl (Lola Fisher). She decides to stay with her old employer and even designs a new skirt which her company enthusiastically mass-produces. Unfortunately it seems to be a costly failure until the newer Mrs. McChesney wears it in a show. To put icing on the cake, none other than T. A. Buck proposes marriage. The comedy, which had been touring profitably, stayed for five months before returning to the road.

. . .

Ethel Barrymore (1879–1959) was born in Philadelphia, the daughter of Maurice and Georgiana Drew Barrymore. She made her debut at her grandmother's famed Arch Street Theatre playing opposite her in *The Rivals* in 1894. After a brief apprenticeship, which included performing alongside her uncle, John Drew, in *The Bauble Shop,* she sailed for England to appear with William Gillette in *Secret Service* and to perform with Henry Irving. After her return to America and a few more supporting roles, Charles Frohman gave her the star part in *Captain Jinks of the Horse Marines* in 1901, and from then she moved on to a series of triumphs (with the inevitable failure here and there). She became admired for her imperious beauty, her deep, throaty voice, and her fluttery eyes. For much of her career she concluded her curtain calls by advising audiences, "That's all there is. There isn't any more."

. . .

By contrast, Georgia Earle and Fanny Cannon's **The Mark of the Beast** (10-20-15, Princess) was another of the season's two-week duds. Like the equally short-lived *Husband and Wife* a month earlier, it centered on a man (George Nash), this time an important judge, who neglects his wife (Lenore Ulrich) until she falls for the blandishments of a handsome scoundrel (Reginald Mason).

October's final hit was **Abe and Mawruss** (10-21-15, Lyric), Roi Cooper Megrue and Montague Glass's successful sequel to Glass's l913 *Potash and Perlmutter.* Stubby, slightly cross-eyed Barney Bernard was back as Abe Potash, while the taller, slimmer, and more dignified-looking Julius Tannen, a popular vaudevillian, was now Mawruss Perlmutter. Mawruss's vaulting ambitions trigger the story's problems. A glib Wall Street sharper shows him how he can make his business a million-dollar proposition almost overnight. Mrs. Potash (Mathilde Cottrelly) smells a rat and persuades Abe to have nothing to do with the scheme. He sells his share of the business for $75,000. Before long the sharper absconds with the money and Mawruss is arrested for fraudulently watering stocks. Luckily, Abe has enough in the bank to satisfy Mawruss's creditors, so the men resume their partnership. Although the comedy was a hit, like most sequels it failed to equal the popularity of the work it followed. Halfway through the six-month run the title was changed to *Potash and Perlmutter in Society,* probably in hopes of reminding some playgoers who Abe and Mawruss were.

Jenö Heltai's *A tünderlaki lányok* (The Girls of Tunderlak), received in Budapest as a powerful play of social protest, was offered to Americans in Marion Fairfax's adaptation as **Mrs. Boltay's Daughters** (10-23-15, Comedy). Reset in Washington, it focused on the widow of a Hungarian diplomat and her daughters, reduced to poverty after the man's death. To help support her mother and sisters, Boriska (Rita Jolivet) becomes the mistress of a rich government official. Later, when she would run away with and marry a young poet, the mother and sisters are furious. Only one sister, Sári (Antoinette Walker), is understanding. She offers herself to the official, who is shamed by her actions. The American reception was a far cry from that in Budapest, so the play quickly closed.

With more and more war plays appearing, it was inevitable that sooner or later one would attempt a comic approach. Regrettably for Frank Mandel's **Sherman Was Right** 10-26-15, Fulton), critics found little funny in his humor. The *Dramatic Mirror* complained that the evening "trenches closely upon burlesque." Mandel's play, suggested by the *Prinz Eital Friedrich*'s actions, unfolded on a German ship, *Prinz Karl,* whose passengers have been removed from neutral liners or from the water after being torpedoed. Berlin is demanding that the captain attempt to locate a deserter named Johann Schmitt. Several of the pickups are, or for one reason or another have been, called by that name. And then there is the young lady with a wooden leg on which her fiancé has carved the name. The production folded after a single week, but Mandel went on to become a major librettist and producer of musicals.

November's first entry was a curiosity that just missed the brass ring. Its author was Robert McLaughlin, a young Ohio theatre manager. His modern morality play, **The Eternal Magdalene** 11-1-15, 48th St.), had failed to find a Broadway producer until McLaughlin produced it to great acclaim and turnaway trade in Cleveland. The Selwyns and Al Woods, the latter uncredited, finally brought it to New York. Edenburg, a dreary small city in the Midwest, is in the throes of a religious revival, fired up by James Gleason (Alphonz Ethier), a money-grubbing, slang-spouting evangelist. His visit has been underwritten by rich, sanctimonious Elijah Bradshaw (Emmett Corrigan). On this evening Bradshaw and Gleason plan to close down the town's red light district and drive its denizens away. Bradshaw has written a statement for the local papers, but Gleason feels it is too tame: "We don't want any skim-milk in this. It's gotta be red-hot, right off the griddle. . . . Why don't you say 'Before morning there'll be a can tied to every dirty door knob on West Street.' Put some shrapnel in it!" Bradshaw is more worried about a letter he has received, cursing him and warning that his daughter will shame him, his son be found a thief, and his wife die of grief. The curses are laughed away, and Bradshaw sends his family to the evangelist's service. Left alone in his dark-paneled library, with its portrait of the Magdalene above the fireplace, he is suddenly confronted by a beautiful woman (Julia Arthur) in somber biblical robes. There is something familiar about her face. She asks why he is so cruel to the women in the red light district when so many of them are not there by choice. She tells him of one woman, deserted years before by a false lover in Montreal, who died and whose daughter, for want of a father or mother, drifted into prostitution. Throwing off her robes she stands before him in a gaudy red dress and tawdry jewels. Bradshaw realizes that he is the false lover the woman is talking about and that she must be his daughter. Against all his preachings, he gives her a position as a maid in his home. She tries to warn his children that they are about to fulfill the curses in the letter. She even finds ways of deflecting some of the difficulties, but she cannot prevent Mrs. Bradshaw from dying of grief.

The woman then discloses she is really "the Eternal Madgalene, made immortal by the touch of His hand two thousand years ago." At this point Bradshaw is shaken into consciousness and understands that he has dreamed this horrible history. But the dream has taught him a lesson. He resolves to be more compassionate. One scene-stealing figure was Blanche Dumond (Lucile Watson), the town's leading madam, whose learning, decency, and general civility put to shame the smug religious hypocrites she must deal with. Some playgoers undoubtedly recalled the 1908 drama *The Servant in the House.* Indeed, besides the basic idea of a biblical figure returning to teach twentieth-century people the true meaning of religion, there were numerous echoes. Thus the Bradshaw daughter reminds the woman, "You are a servant—in my father's house." And near the end Bradshaw himself, using the very words of the vicar in the earlier play, demands, "In God's name, who are you!" The newer work, while every bit as sincere as the earlier one, nonetheless could be faulted for resorting a little too obviously to coincidences and other theatrical claptrap.

The London stage provided a pleasant surprise with Harold Brighouse's **Hobson's Choice** (11-2-15, Princess), in which the homely but determined daughter (Molly Pearson) of a cobbler (A. G. Andrews) weds her father's most skillful assistant (Whitford Kane) and forces her father to take him on as a partner.

But Avery Hopwood's homebred **Fair and Warmer** (11-6-15, Eltinge) was even more to New York's liking. Laura Bartlett (Janet Beecher) and Jack Wheeler (Ralph Morgan) both love to go out on the town. Unfortunately, their spouses, Billy (John Cumberland) and Blanche (Madge Kennedy), are stay-at-homes. So when the gadabouts go out once too often, Billy and Blanche get together and arrange to have a little party all to themselves. If their returning spouses find them in a compromising situation—well, that'll teach them. To help the party along they mix some drinks. Of course, since they mix whiskey, gin, vermouth, absinthe, sherry, apple and apricot brandies, pink champagne, and crème de menthe, they soon pass out, with Billy sprawled on the couch and Blanche at his feet. The others return home and are outraged, especially after Blanche makes a point of announcing she's been compromised: "It's something to do—with somebody else's husband!" The next morning, Billy is in bed, extremely hungover, when Blanche arrives to apologize. Before she can say much, Laura is heard coming, so Blanche hides under the bed. Laura tells Billy that she is moving out and the moving men will

be here shortly to take the bed. Jack and the movers add to the confusion until the Bartletts' maid, Tessie (Olive May), brings everyone to their senses. The critical reception was largely favorable, with Woollcott seeing the farce as "twice as well written and about four and a half times as amusing" as earlier hits. For many the cast was even better; the *Morning Telegraph* saluted it as "one of the most competent companies that ever appeared in a play of this class." Twenty-five years before, Olive May had been hailed as one of Broadway's most promising comediennes. Hamilton Revelle, who played Laura's friend, Jack, had been a dashing leading man. Ralph Morgan and Janet Beecher were rising players who would move on to long careers. But the best performers were pudgy, balding John Cumberland and pretty, demure, if saucy-faced Madge Kennedy. The farce ran 377 performances but obviously did not need its original players, for numerous road companies toured profitably into 1920.

• • •

[James] **Avery Hopwood** (1882–1928) was already well under way by 1915 to becoming America's richest playwright. He was born in Cleveland and attended the University of Michigan. Before turning his hand to the stage, he worked for a time on newspapers. His first success, which Channing Pollock revised without his knowledge, was *Clothes* (1906). Subsequent hits included *Seven Days* (1909), written with Mary Roberts Rinehart, and *Nobody's Widow* (1910).

• • •

Some once lauded then neglected players, such as Hilda Spong and Effingham Pinto, were in the cast of **The Angel in the House** (11-8-15, Fulton), a satire by Basil Macdonald Hastings and Eden Phillpotts that Arnold Daly imported from London. Daly starred as the Bunthorne-like Hyacinth Petavel, who would impose his ultra-advanced artistic views and self-serving social schemes on his friends. In a few years, George S. Kaufman would say that satire closes on Saturday night. This play's one-week run provided an example.

Although most of November and its offerings still lay ahead, the month's last hit was Cohan and Harris's production of **The Great Lover** (11-10-15, Longacre), a comedy which its star, Leo Ditrichstein, wrote with Frederic and Fanny Hatton. Jean Paurel is the great luminary of the Gotham Opera Company. He is a spoiled, conceited philanderer. In hopes of scoring with Ethel Warren (Virginia Fox Brooks), he forces the opera company to allow her to sing with him in *Don Giovanni*. His plans for Ethel go awry, first of all since Ethel really loves a young American baritone (Malcolm Fassett), and more urgently because a soprano (Beverley Sitgreaves) whom Paurel has callously discarded threatens to make a scandal. This causes Paurel to lose his voice irrevocably. Left alone with only memories, he sits gloomily in his luxurious suite until a phone call from a charming divorcée cheers him. Ditrichstein's tour de force saw him change from a middle-aged, white-haired Paurel to a youthful Don, then back again. William Riccardi, heavyset and sporting a conspicuously twirled mustache, won laughs as a volatile conductor. The play ran seven months.

Back Home (11-15-15, Cohan), which Bayard Veiller dramatized from some Irvin S. Cobb stories, reflected both the popular muckraking of the day and the era's persistent regionalism. Robert Carter (Sidney Booth) comes to Waynesville, a southern town, to expose child labor abuses at the local cotton mills. Mr. Wayne (Charles B. Wells) hires goons to kill him. Instead, Carter kills the chief goon, who has just attempted to maim a youngster. A local judge (John Cope), who is Carter's prospective father-in-law, comes to his aid at his trial by telling the jury that Carter's father had been a Confederate hero and had asked the judge to watch over his son. The jury acquits Carter, but critics and audiences said no to the play. However, they did applaud Willis P. Sweatnam, a famous old minstrel, who blacked up to assume the role of Jefferson Davis Poindexter.

As he had last season, Emanuel Reicher tried again to earn a place on American stages for himself and neglected European drama. To this end he rented a long-dark theatre, now far below the Rialto, and offered a Björnstjerne Björnson play translated by Arvid Paulson as **When the Young Vine Blooms** (11-16-15, Garden). It told of a man who must accept that a new generation brings with it its own ideas of how to live. This obscure play in a theatre so far off the beaten track still managed to hang on for three weeks.

The Washington Square Players and the Portmanteau Theatre long since having opened their seasons they were inevitably followed by the Bramhall Players, on the 17th, but this company's opening brought more sneers than smiles to the critics. The troupe's head, Butler Davenport, was coming to seem something of a preposterous, manipulating pretender, quick to substitute titillation for genuine experimentation, and noisy publicity for quiet professionalism. Not yet the celebrated drama critic of the *World* but still writing and second-stringing for the *Tribune*, Heywood Broun observed, "Someone should spank young Butler Davenport and take away his chalk." Although critics did just that,

according him less and less attention as time went on, Davenport would prove undaunted.

But a critical drubbing did daunt one debutante, Khyva St. Albans, who, accompanied by much fanfare, came into the 44th Street Theatre on the 22nd with *Romeo and Juliet*. George Relph was her Romeo. Quite possibly the actress was aware of her limitations and anxious to face her audiences before all the mountings promised for the Shakespeare Tercentenary (of his death) raised their curtains. The consensus was that the scenery outshone the players. Miss St. Albans's returns were few and brief.

The growing fashion to dismiss John Drew as an actor capable solely of playing John Drew did nothing to dissuade his loyalists, although his annual fall engagements were becoming shorter. His latest vehicle was Horace Annesley Vachell's London hit **The Chief** (11-22-15, Empire), in which he portrayed a widower who finally recruits enough nerve to propose to the widowed ward (Laura Hope Crews) he once had let another man marry. Like several other productions that had been planned months earlier, this one still listed Charles Frohman as producer.

Three plays opened the next Monday night, two novelties and one revival. None was a major success. The longest run, ten weeks, went to Avery Hopwood's second play of the month, **Sadie Love** (11-29-15, Gaiety). No sooner are the widowed Sadie (Marjorie Rambeau) and Prince Luigi Pallavicini (Pedro de Cordoba) wed than Sadie discovers that the prince married her on the rebound from his affair with the Comtesse de Maribold (Betty Callish). In a fury, Sadie demands the marriage be called off, but so that the couple will not seem absurd to their friends, she agrees to go through the motions of a honeymoon. The countess will tag along, and so will Sadie's old friend Jim Wakeley (Franklyn Underwood), who has just happened to call on Sadie. When the puzzled Jim warns he will not know how to behave in such a situation, Sadie retorts, "We *won't* behave." The pairings move in farcical flux until, on board a luxurious ship, Sadie and the count are reconciled. Jim is reunited with his wife, while the countess falls for a nonentity who had accompanied Jim's wife. Kudos abounded for the principals, but there were serious reservations about the play. Among the most dismissive reviewers was Heywood Broun, who wrote in the *Tribune*, "Hopwood has invited into his play the divorce laws of New York State, the Mann Act, and seasickness. The divorce laws of New York State and the Mann Act are stupid and ugly. Seasickness is ugly, and not one of the three has any business in a farce." At best, he waved away the play as "merely silly."

But Beulah Poynter's **The Unborn** (11-29-15, Princess) received a far harsher reception, with critics complaining that it was more a preachment for contraception than a real play. When the fiancée (Alice Lindahl) of a young man (Everett Butterfield) learns he is a drunkard, she berates his mother (Lucy Beaumont), also an alcoholic, for allowing herself to give birth, saying there are times when it is preferable to love the unborn. Pushed by her uncle (Howard Hall), a doctor who tells her there is no hope for the man, she breaks the engagement. In drunken fury, the man attempts to rape her and when that fails he shoots her and kills himself. The play had been underwritten in good measure by the *Medical Review of Reviews,* prompting the *Dramatic Mirror* to advise it to find "better business than sponsoring plays." The production abandoned its pulpit after a fortnight.

The evening's third opening brought back *Our American Cousin,* Tom Taylor's 1858 favorite, with Sothern as Dundreary. Of course, this Sothern was E. H. Sothern, son of the original Dundreary. His makeup and costumes were outlandish, but not nearly so exaggerated as his father's had been, perhaps because he was playing out an extended season at the Booth, one of Broadway's smaller auditoriums. Sothern and the play garnered a mixed reception, albeit one more favorable than not. However, Sothern had announced this mounting would run for only five weeks, and there clearly was no demand to lengthen the stay.

A London hit, George Pleydell's **The Ware Case** (11-30-15, Maxine Elliott's) chalked up a six-week run, in some measure thanks to Lou Tellegen's popularity. He played a cruel, abusive husband who finally is made to own up to the error of his ways.

Jules Eckert Goodman's dramatization of **Treasure Island** (12-1-15, Punch and Judy) gave older playgoers a chance to bring their children or grandchildren to the theatre. This, coupled with the theatre's smallness, permitted the production to run out the season. The critical reception was generally friendly, although each man seemed to find a particular flaw. One critic complained that Jim Hawkins should not have been played by a woman. But then, she was Mrs. Charles Hopkins, wife of the producer and owner of the playhouse. Another felt there were too many scene changes, although all critics praised the scenery. Settings included the Admiral Benbow Inn, the Bristol quay, "the cave with the sight of the sea at the mouth and the gleam of pieces of eight in the corner," and the *Hispanola*

adrift. The dramatization enjoyed years of popularity with amateur groups.

An even more enduring popularity was won by the third play to be added to Grace George's repertory. As far as America was concerned, it was a new play, although England had welcomed it nearly ten years earlier. George Bernard Shaw's **Major Barbara** (12-9-15, Playhouse) unfolded a battle of wits and principles between a multimillionaire arms manufacturer and his Salvation Army daughter. Grace George's "fast-building, vivacious, chin up and tongue-sparkling" style of playing was ideal for the title role. Her clear diction was looked on as something sadly too rare in contemporary theatre. Undershaft was played by Louis Calvert, a tall, commanding English actor whom Shaw reputedly had in mind while creating the character. The supporting cast was superb.

Far down at the Garden Theatre Emanuel Reicher found a small treasure of his own when he gave New York its first important English-language production of Gerhart Hauptmann's **The Weavers** 12-14-15). The play told of the rebellion of Silesian workers against the mill owners. Critics hailed the elaborate, realistic setting, the individual players and, most of all, the powerfully effective handling of the mob scenes. With a little forcing and some discreet discounting, the drama ran for eleven weeks.

A revival of J. M. Barrie's *Peter Pan,* at the Empire on the 21st, stayed around only three weeks but might have run much longer if playgoers had realized that these would be Maude Adams's last appearances in the title part. Like *Treasure Island,* its performances, especially matinees, were crowded with children.

Ruggles of Red Gap (12-25-15, Fulton), Harrison Rhodes's theatricalization of Harry Leon Wilson's stories, centered on a valet (Ralph Herz) who is made the stakes in a card game at a posh Paris hotel. His English lord loses him to some upstart Americans, who promptly take him home with them. Since home is the still rather wild West, Ruggles has his problems acclimating. These difficulties are compounded when the valet is mistaken for a lord and his owners must treat him as one. A number of Sigmund Romberg songs larded the piece, which survived for a month. Years later a popular film version starred Charles Laughton.

According to pre-opening announcements **Cock o' the Walk** (12-27-15, Cohan) was written by Henry Arthur Jones expressly for Otis Skinner. It proved to be the last new play by Jones that New York would see. Anthony Bellchamber (Skinner) is an aging, besotted, backwater actor, seemingly doomed for the rest of his life to seedy one-night stands. However, when he saves a producer from scandal he is given his chance to realize a lifelong ambition to play Othello. He also must disillusion a lovesick, stagestruck girl (Janet Dunbar). Critics suggested the writing was competent but not Jones's best. With the Shakespeare Tercentenary so near at hand, they enjoyed his digs both at clergymen, so concerned that Shakespeare not wreck the morals of the audience, and at actor-managers, seeing only the chance for self-glorification in the festivities. While most critics praised the star, a few suggested this role, with its opportunities for overflowing emoting, pandered to Skinner's excesses. Although the play lingered for nine weeks and toured briefly, Skinner apparently had no kind memories of it. He skipped over it in his autobiography.

The old year's last entry was **The Devil's Garden** (12-28-15, Harris), which Edith Ellis adapted from William B. Maxwell's novel. William Dale (Lyn Harding) almost loses his job as postmaster, but Evarard Barradine's intervention saves it for him. Nonetheless, after Dale discovers that his wife (Lillian Albertson), when she was still a young, innocent girl, had been seduced by Barradine, he kills him and makes the murder look like an accident. Over the years Dale becomes increasingly conscience-stricken, especially after he meets Norah (Geraldine O'Brien), a sultry gypsy, and recognizes how much he desires her. He would have seduced her, but he loses his life, and thus expiates his sins, rescuing children from a burning orphanage. Aisle-sitters divided sharply over the work, deeming it everything from "a powerful tragedy" to "a gloomy play." But most lauded Robert Edmond Jones's uncluttered, impressionistic settings. They were not enough to save the production. (Curiously, critics who often devoted a whole paragraph to Urban's scenery rarely went into detail about Jones's.)

The new year's first offering was Austin Strong's **Bunny** (1-4-16, Hudson). Its notices were not the sort hoped for. As a result the comedy survived a mere two weeks. During that short time it cast its spotlight on Charles Nathaniel Disney, M.A. (Lewis S. Stone), a meek, innocent secondhand book dealer, who is known to one and all as Bunny. Only when he learns that the girl he loves is about to marry another man is he roused to action: locking away the girl, subduing a baliff, and shooting at the groom—with a "pepper pot pistol." The play was set attractively in crinoline days. Stone, who had been the lover in the 1912 hit *The Bird of Paradise*, and years later would achieve his greatest fame, in films,

as Andy Hardy's dad, was best known to playgoers in stern, solemn roles. Not all critics felt he made the change successfully.

Two nights later, on the 6th, Sothern changed his bill, bringing out a second play associated with his father. The elder Sothern had first performed T. W. Robertson's *David Garrick* in London in 1864, and though others had played it in America before him, he gave Americans his interpretation in 1873. The son's reception was not especially cordial, prompting him to drop the revival after only two and a half weeks. Its failure brought his season to a premature end.

The Pride of Race (1-11-16, Maxine Elliott's), which Michael L. Landman based on Wallace Irwin's story, proved even more distasteful to many reviewers but held on for ten weeks. Its star, Robert Hilliard, played a man who just before his marriage learns he is one-sixteenth Negro. Against all advice he fathers a child, which turns out to be black. His wife leaves him to marry another man, and he takes the baby to Cuba. The final scene shows the man as a successful plantation owner. His son works in the fields, but hopes someday to go to college.

At the Empire Maude Adams changed bills on the 11th, turning for the last ten weeks of her stay to her 1897 success, Barrie's *The Little Minister*.

January's three biggest hits came in on two successive evenings. In Edward Childs Carpenter's **The Cinderella Man** (1-17-16, Hudson) Marjorie (Phoebe Foster), an unloved heiress, learns that a young poet, Anthony (Shelley Hull), lives in a nearby garret and goes to bed hungry at night. So she steals across the roof to enter his attic and supply him with food. She does this while he is out, but one day he returns unexpectedly and finds her hiding in his closet. She tells him she is merely a rich girl's companion. A friendship quickly develops. Then She-Bear (Lucille La Verne), his harridan landlady, discovers the two together and orders Anthony to find another place to live. All ends happily after Anthony wins a $10,000 prize for an opera libretto. Critics could not take the play seriously, but most of them loved it anyway. Carpenter underscored its unreal nature by having Anthony refer to Marjorie as his fairy godmother and by other similar references. What critics liked even more was Hull's impeccable performance, catching all the play's and character's delicacy without seeming flabby. Indeed, many reviewers looked on the curly-headed, handsome Hull, who combined boyishness with an incontestable manliness, and grace with a telling force, as the best young actor in his field. (Years later a writer said that had Hull lived longer, he might have become an American Leslie Howard.) The play ran six months.

That same evening critics welcomed Eugene Walter's **Just a Woman** (1-17-16, 48th St.). They may not have welcomed it as enthusiastically as many of them had his *The Easiest Way*, as a fine, progressive drama, but they did allow it was capital theatre. The Woman (Josephine Victor) runs a boardinghouse for mill hands. She falls in love with one of them, The Man (Walter Hampden), and marries him. By her resourcefulness (she invests their savings in a new, patented process) and determination, she makes them very wealthy. Unfortunately the wealth goes to The Man's head. He becomes a drunkard and a philanderer. The Woman patiently puts up with everything until The Man sues for divorce and, with clearly perjured testimony, demands custody of their child. The Woman shocks the court by revealing the child is not his. He is sent to prison for false witness. Both the writing and the playing pulled no punches; the evening's melodrama was everywhere under-scored. Nor did the program's failure to give characters specific names mean that the play was expressionistic. In the action, the characters all had names; The Man, for example, was Jim. The play ran into May.

Erstwhile Susan (1-18-16, Gaiety), which Marian de Forest was credited with adapting from Helen R. Martin's novel *Barnabetta,* ran longer, not closing until June's hot weather. Its uncredited co-author was its star, petite, redheaded Mrs. Fiske. The great actress's heyday had passed. For the rest of her long career she would be seen in indifferent vehicles or revivals of earlier triumphs. Still, Mrs. Fiske was generally considered America's finest actress and was still able to draw profitable houses. She arrives at the home of dour, Pennsylvania Dutch Barnaby Dreary (John Cope) announcing she is an Iowan, Juliet Miller, and she has come in answer to Dreary's matrimonial advertisement. Juliet is a proud, ele-gant lady who has kept herself alive by giving elocution lessons. She learns too late that the Drearys are a hard, mean family, all except the daughter, Barnabetta (Madeline Delmar). Juliet and the girl become each other's closest friends, and Juliet stops Barnaby from horsewhipping the young-ster. After Barnaby dies, his son, Jacob (Robert Stowe Gill), tries to prevent her inheriting his father's money by disclosing that Juliet's real name is Susan Miller and that she was deserted by her first husband on their wedding night. But Juliet wins her fair share and can leave knowing that Barnabetta will marry an up-and-coming young attorney.

Woollcott, who was one of the star's most ardent admirers and had recently published some adulatory articles on her, spent most of his notice and follow-up singing her praises. He alerted his readers that "you can guess with what tremendous gusto she finally discards the high-flown familiar quotations of Juliet—erstwhile Susan—Miller and in fine fury spits out the good round oath that brings down the curtain on the second act."

. . .

Mrs. [Minnie Maddern] **Fiske** [née Mary or Marie Augusta Davey] (1865–1932) was born in New Orleans, the daughter of Thomas Davey, manager of a theatre there, and Lizzie Maddern, an actress. She was just three years old when she was first carried onstage by her mother. Her New York debut under the name Minnie Maddern came in May 1870 in *A Sheep in Wolf's Clothing,* and a month later she was seen as Little Fritz in the premiere of J. K. Emmet's long-famed *Fritz, Our Cousin German.* She later created the role of Little Alice in another drama destined for years of celebrity, *Kit, the Arkansas Traveller.* She toured for many years before winning acclaim in *Fogg's Ferry* (1882), *Caprice* (1884), and other period successes. Retiring temporarily after her marriage to Harrison Grey Fiske, she soon returned to the stage for some of her greatest triumphs, including *Tess of the D'Urbervilles* (1894), *Becky Sharp* (1899), *Leah Kleschna* (1904), *The New York Idea* (1906), *Salvation Nell* (1908), and *Mrs. Bumpstead-Leigh* (1911). Small and red-haired, with movements and speech often described as nervous and jerky, she nonetheless was generally acknowledged to be the finest American actress of her generation.

. . .

A fourth success arrived a week later. **The Fear Market** (1-26-16, Booth) was written by Amélie Rives, a Virginia girl who had married the Russian Prince Pierre Troubetsky. Her play was suggested by the history of the infamous Colonel William Mann and his notorious *Town Topics.* As Colonel Mann had done, Major Stone (Edmund Breese) runs a newspaper which publishes vicious gossip about society and political headliners—unless they pay Stone not to print the material. But he nearly destroys his daughter, Sylvia (Sydney Shields), by inadvertently publishing an article dealing with her close set of friends. Sylvia had been raised in Italy under her mother's name and knew nothing of her father's work. When she discovers the truth she bids her father good-bye and goes off with a man (Harrison Hunter) who has been opposing him. The playwright's husband designed two highly praised settings—a loggia at Maggiore and a peacock blue drawing room.

Just as Mrs. Fiske's glory days were gone by, so were Rose Stahl's. But Mrs. Fiske had risen slowly, done brilliant work in important plays, and still had years of stardom ahead of her. Rose Stahl would prove a theatrical meteor. Her swift decline had begun with last season's *A Perfect Lady* and now continued with George V. Hobart's **Moonlight Mary** (1-27-16, Fulton). It had been written to order and what the star had ordered was essentially the same story she had played in both her hits: big sister saves stagestruck little sister. In this case Laura, with only some moonlight and a lantern, climbs through a window into the apartment of a man she believes has impure designs on her sister, Helen (Francine Larrimore). He does not. And once again the background was theatrical, with Laura as a playwright and Helen as an aspiring actress. As always Miss Stahl was brash and slangy, but that was not enough to draw many playgoers.

War plays often had unusually large casts, and so required larger theatres. Thus, for the second time this season the New Amsterdam played host to a drama about the ongoing hostilities. Of course, most critics would have jumped on the word drama, suggesting "melodrama" as more appropriate, and preposterous melodrama at that. Oddly, though American-written war plays had been staunchly pro-Allies, ignoring Wilson's plea for neutrality, **Margaret Schiller** (1-31-16), by Hall Caine, an Englishman, attempted to be fair to both sides. Margaret (Elsie Ferguson), whose father has died while a prisoner of the English, wangles a job at the home of the prime minister (Norman Trevor). She hopes to assassinate him. Her plan is quickly uncovered, but the P.M. forgives her and insists she be allowed to keep working for him. She soon falls in love with him, so dresses as him and takes his place when she learns her brother is coming to kill him. She dies in his arms. Despite discouraging reviews, the play held on for ten weeks, no doubt helped by Miss Ferguson's reputation as a silent-film star and by Caine's international fame.

At mid-season, which the *Dramatic Mirror* pegged as February 1, the tradesheet published its assessment of the first six months. Noting that during the previous season "the number and importance of the misfortunes recorded were without a parallel," it continued more happily, "This season can be called one of the most active and prosperous of recent times—a remarkable achievement, indeed, when one considers the ever-increasing competition of the films, the absence of any genuinely distinctive work from our leading playwrights, and the uncertain attitude of the theatergoing public toward amusements in general." It reported that so far 104 productions (counting musicals and one-act plays individually) had opened and that no fewer than thirty-two were commercially successful.

For all practical purposes the Shakespeare Tercentenary got under way with James K. Hackett's production of *Macbeth* at the Criterion on February 7. Prior to opening, Hackett had announced that he and his Lady Macbeth, Viola Allen, would offer "innovative" interpretations. Despite his medieval dress, Hackett's Macbeth turned out to be a modern man, who sensibly scoffs at apparitions. (This gave the banquet scene a curiously lunatic quality.) Lady Macbeth was motherly, if house-proud. The *Evening Mail* bemoaned that "nothing more inept than the acting of *Macbeth* has come within our range of vision these many years." But critics admired the scenery, most of it by Urban, including the towering banquet hall and "the gray corridor with the blue sky behind against which the white figure of Lady Macbeth moves beautifully in the sleep-walking scene."

One of the season's most-talked about plays had been a one-acter, Alice Gerstenberg's *Overtones,* which the Washington Square Players had presented as part of a bill in November. It was a four-character play, featuring two ladies and their alter egos (or overtones). The same device was employed in the season's second morality play, **Any House** (2-14-16, Cort), a work by Owen Davis and his brother, Robert H. Davis. Sardus Summerfield (Edwin Arden) is a rich, unloving lawyer, about to disown his daughters and son-in-law until his better self (William B. Mack) teaches him love and charity. The play's mounting was also novel. The audience entering the theatre saw no curtain. Instead, onstage was a residential street scene, with occasional passersby and a newsboy delivering papers. The housefront was withdrawn at the beginning of each act to reveal the room in which the drama would unfold.

Grace George's next offering in her repertory season was James Bernard Fagan's seven-year-old English drama, **The Earth** (2-15-16, Playhouse). The play looked at the potential for evil of an all too powerful press and told how a young woman threatened with a scandalous divorce suit faces down the press baron who is using her situation to destroy legislation he opposes. Miss George and Calvert once again had the leads, with her excellent company in support.

Brandon Tynan, a respected actor, turned playwright with **The Melody of Youth** (2-16-16, Fulton). He gave himself the juicy part of a young Irishman who leaves his Roman seminary to find a mate for his ward, a saucy colleen (Lily Cahill), and soon concludes that he is the logical mate. He eventually wins her away from his highborn rival (William J. Kennedy). One much praised setting showed a "thatched cottage 'on the top of the hill,' set in a garden with a generous apple tree in full bloom." More than one critic suggested the play would appeal primarily to Irish theatregoers, but there were enough of them to give the romance a four-month run.

In Oliver D. Bailey and Lottie Meaney's **Pay-Day** (2-26-16, Cort) the villain (Vincent Serrano) frames the heroine (Irene Fenwick) for his thefts and later frames her for a murder he has also committed. Just before the scoundrel can marry and murder his third wife the heroine comes down with leprosy, which she purposely passes on to her antagonist. Shades of the oldtime cheap touring melodrama! Broadway scuttle-butt bruited that the play had once been tried out seriously as *Her Price* and had been laughed off the stage. As a result this revised and recast version, set on a revolve to allow quick scene changes, was openly played for laughs. A new epilogue showed the story to be a script being read by a film star, who refuses to play in it until he learns of the huge salary offered. Even in its new guise the play failed to catch on.

Like *The Unborn* earlier in the season, Marion Creighton and William Elliott's **The Greatest Nation** (2-28-16, Booth) was perceived as more preachment than play. In this case the plea was for world peace, with the story showing two mythical kingdoms led into a futile war by their silly feud. The countries are Thor and Aldon. In between them lies Donau, a small buffer state, ruled by King Alan (Elliott), son of the king of Thor. When his father is assassinated Alan finds himself ruling two countries. His good-ness and sensible pleadings prompt Aldon's soldiers to lay down their arms. Down the drain with the play went some lauded Urban settings.

At a time when a run of 100 performances was a good rule of thumb for separating hits from flops, David Belasco's mounting of George Scarborough's **The Heart of Wetona** (2-29-16, Lyceum) was a very near miss, with ninety-five performances. The play had originally been tried out under the title *The Girl* the preceding June and had dealt with midwestern Caucasians. Hastily closed, and rewritten and reset in Indian territory, it was tried out again as *Oklahoma,* then brought in under its final title. When Quannah (William Courtleigh), the Chief of the Comanches, tells his daughter, Wetona (Lenore

Ulrich), she is to be a Vestal Virgin, she confesses that she has been seduced by a white man. She refuses to reveal his name. Instead, she runs for guidance to John Hardin (John Miltern), the Indian Agent on the reservation. Quannah and his Comanche warriors have followed her and, believing Hardin to have been her lover, engineer a shotgun wedding. In truth, Hardin is not adverse, since he has secretly loved the girl. A slip of the tongue later discloses that her lover was Tony Wells (Lowell Sherman), a young engineer. Tony, who cynically stood by in silence during the wedding, just as cynically tries to resume the romance. But his words and manners convince Wetona of his perfidy. Quannah also discovers the truth. John provides Tony with a gun and a horse to allow him to escape, but the Indians have surrounded the house. After he leaves all is still for a moment or two, then a volley of shots and joyous Indian war whoops are heard. While most critics acknowledged that the melo-drama was rattling good theatre, they felt it be-longed to a swiftly passing style. However, almost to a man, they welcomed Lenore Ulrich, who soon would shorten the spelling of her last name.

· · ·

Lenore Ulric [née Leonora Ulrich] (1892–1970) The small, dark actress, who was to specialize in sultry, impassioned women, was born in New Ulm, Minn. Over the opposition of her family she went onstage, learning her trade in stock troupes in Milwaukee, Grand Rapids, Chicago, and Syracuse. In late 1913 she was given the lead in a touring company of *The Bird of Paradise*. It was during this tour that Belasco discovered her. Between tryouts of the Belasco production she made her Broadway debut in *The Mark of the Beast*.

· · ·

The envelope in Frank Hatch and Robert E. Homans's **The Blue Envelope** (3-13-16, Cort) con-tained evidence allegedly embarrassing one or more of the men who have taken refuge in a sanitorium to escape pesky wives and sweethearts. It was passed from character to character as they ran in and out of no fewer than six doors. Burly, mug-faced Walter Jones walked off with many of the laughs during the farce's short stand.

Sir Herbert Beerbohm Tree, in America to make films and to propagandize for England, took over the New Amsterdam on March 14 to begin a series of offerings as his contribution to the Shakespeare Tercentenary. For his initial presentation he im-ported the costumes and scenery from his 1910 London mounting of *King Henry VIII*. Much of the text, admittedly probably very little of which was

Shakespeare's, was jettisoned, and the emphasis was on elaborate spectacle. The archly traditional J. Rankin Towse of the *Evening Post* was delighted with the essentially pictorial staging, seeing in it "a very positive realistic and historical value," but younger critics, aware of changing notions of set design, were less happy. Tree's Cardinal Wolsey, Lyn Harding's Henry, and Edith Wynne Matthison's Katharine received generally favorable comments. Perhaps surprisingly, considering the play's position in the Shakespearean canon, the public responded enthusiastically, and only Tree's commitment to subsequent productions limited the run to sixty-three performances.

Henry VIII figured importantly in the next play to premiere, although he was not the leading figure. The play's star, Lou Tellegen, seemed to move from play to play much as Henry had from wife to wife, unable to find a major success just as Henry for so long had been unable to enjoy a male heir. Tellegen's latest disappointment was J. and L. du Rocher Macpherson's **A King of Nowhere** (3-20-16, Maxine Elliott's) in which he was Godred, who has a passionate romance with Lady Margaret Silchester (Olive Tell) while he is the prisoner of King Henry. For many the heavyset young actor who played Henry stole the show, with *Theatre* noting, "A really brilliant impersonation is contributed by Sydney Greenstreet as Bluff King Hal, racked with the gout and tortured by the recollection of his bloody deeds."

Ten days before *The Merry Wives of Windsor* opened at the Criterion on March 20, its star, Hackett, became so ill that he was forced to relinquish his role of Falstaff. In desperation, Thomas Wise was called in to replace him. Wise reputedly had never performed in Shakespeare, but his hefty build and his gift for gruff, blustering characters suggested he might serve handsomely. Nervousness and uncertainty beset the opening night, though the more understanding reviewers recognized that a few additional performances would polish the rough spots. The *Sun* reported of Wise's Falstaff, "His tremendous stomach, receptacle of uncounted flagons of sack, was encased in a doublet of bright orange. Bright orange were the tights that encased his ample legs, and jackboots of faun decorated his substantial feet. He rolled from scene to scene, quivering like a mountain of jelly, as he boozed and guzzled and boasted, and entangled himself in the snares set by those zestful wives, Mrs. Ford [Viola Allen] and Mrs. Page [Henrietta Crosman]." Although most critics usually had only the highest praise for Urban, his work on this production was not universally welcomed, one reviewer complaining, "When the expression of his art becomes so dominant that a Shakespearean classic is sacrificed to conform to its demands it is time to call a halt." Favorable word of mouth had the comedy playing to packed houses when other bookings forced it to close in mid-May. But New Yorkers would see it again.

One of the Washington Square Players' more interesting offerings was Zoë Akins's free-verse one-acter **The Magical City** (3-20-16, Bandbox). The tragedy was set in modern New York, where a love-mad poet kills the rich man who is keeping a girl the poet loves. His punishment is a blissful exile on a Greek isle. The action took place in a sumptuous wine-colored apartment, with the tower of Madison Square Garden looming just outside the huge picture window.

Haddon Chambers's **The Great Pursuit** (3-22-16, Shubert), which Marie Tempest brought out with a superb supporting cast that included Phyllis Neilson-Terry, Bruce McRae, Charles Cherry and the not yet famous Jeanne Eagels, turned out to be merely a superficial reworking of the playwright's *The Idler,* which had been done at the old Lyceum in 1890.

March ended with another revival. On the 29th Grace George brought in the final offering of her season, Shaw's *Captain Brassbound's Conversion,* a piece Ellen Terry had first shown to Americans nine years before.

If it took ten years for New York to see *Major Barbara,* it took almost as long before it could applaud John Galsworthy's **Justice** (4-3-16, Candler), although Chicago had seen a few performances five years earlier. Time has questioned their judgment, but most contemporary reviewers felt this and not the Shaw work was the best and, probably, the most enduring work of the season. In it the hero, Falder, is brought to trial for a crime he committed with the most honorable of intentions (to rescue a woman from an abusive husband). His days in court and years in cruel imprisonment drive him to suicide. The powerful drama is said to have inspired major prison reforms in England. In America it is remembered chiefly as the play which gave John Barrymore his first chance in a non-frivolous role. The *Times,* noting that Barrymore "comes into his own" in the part, continued, "It is an extraordinary performance in every detail of appearance and manner, in every note of deep feeling. He is a being transformed beyond all semblance of his debonair self, and from his speech you would think he had never dwelt a day beyond the sound of Bow Bells. He looks and sounds the undernourished underclerk . . . and in the big scene within the solitary cells he displays extraordinary power." The play ran into July.

Augustus Thomas received a largely thumbs-down press when he brought out his latest regional melodrama, **Rio Grande** (4-4-16, Empire), a play in the tradition of so many of his earlier efforts. But for all his clever construction, the result was deemed ineffectual. Nan (Lola Fisher), the young wife of the older Colonel Bannard (Richard Bennett), who is commandant of a military post in Laredo, Tex., is briefly unfaithful. Actually she and Lieutenant Ellsworth (Calvin Thomas) had hoped to marry before Nan's late father had made her promise to wed Bannard. A chance meeting accords them an opportunity neither can resist. The liaison is witnessed by an unscrupulous orderly (Frank Campeau), who attempts to blackmail her. After writing a letter to her husband, telling all, Nan tries to commit suicide by jumping into the river, but she is saved. However, Ellsworth does kill himself. The colonel reads the letter, then calls in the orderly. As the orderly viciously starts to tell his story, the colonel shoots him dead. Bannard and Nan are reconciled.

Critics divided more sharply on Alice Leal Pollock and Rita Weiman's **The Co-Respondent** (4-10-16, Booth). Those who liked it felt it might have succeeded had it not arrived just before the hot weather. The managing editor of the *Daily News,* John Manning (Norman Trevor), assigns Anne Gray (Irene Fenwick), a reporter with whom he is falling in love, to find out who has been named the corespondent in a headline-grabbing divorce. Anne had once narrowly avoided marriage with the husband in the case after discovering he already was married. To her consternation she now learns she has been named the corespondent. She must keep the news secret and clear her name.

The rest of April was devoted exclusively to revivals. The 24th saw three raise their curtains. At the huge, out-of-the-way Century Theatre, not long before the luckless New Theatre, Shakespeare's still rarely done *The Tempest* was offered in a production that had more venturesome critics and playgoers jumping for joy. First of all, the text was performed faithfully and completely, something American playgoers had never seen before. Second, there was no elaborate scenery. Instead a simple, basic box set attempted to recreate the austerity of Shakespeare's Globe. There were curtained entrances on both sides of the stage while at the rear a larger curtain opened now and then to reveal an inner stage, above which was a small gallery. A few artificial shrubs and canvas rocks were the only other decorations. Louis Calvert as Prospero and Walter Hampden as Caliban were deemed the best players. The demand for tickets allowed the mounting, originally slated for a fortnight's stand, to run a full month.

Margaret Anglin was also performing in Shakespeare during the Tercentenary (*The Taming of the Shrew* and *As You Like It*), but not in New York. There she was seen at the Fulton as Mrs. Arbuthnot in Wilde's *A Woman of No Importance*. The day when Rose Coghlan had to cancel her American tour of the play because Wilde's scandalous private life had been made public was long past. Critics did not sit in judgment on the playwright, and most who assessed the play felt it held up well. But not all. Louis Sherwin in the *Telegraph* remarked, "Miss Anglin showed us last night that all that artificiality and sentimentality can be transformed into irony by an actress with a sense of humor." Several critics were displeased with the star's leading man, Holbrook Blinn, suggesting he portrayed Lord Illington as a brash American monopolist rather than as a haughty English aristocrat. Cavils or no, the public supported the revival for seven weeks, until Miss Anglin's prior commitments forced its close.

Another respected actor, Arnold Daly, also received some brickbats in his latest assignment. Always willing to try untested new plays or bring back neglected older ones, Daly elected to mount Clyde Fitch's *Beau Brummell* (5-19-90) at the Cort. Reviewers were divided on how well the play had withstood the scrutiny of time, but a majority clearly thought the usually adroit Daly failed to bring to the title role the surefire theatricality they recalled Mansfield's displaying. The revival closed after three weeks.

His wife, Julia Marlowe, having announced her retirement several years earlier, E. H. Sothern gave notice that his revival of his old success *If I Were King* (10-14-01) at the Shubert on the 29th would mark his farewell appearances. The production ran a month, after which the play would return to Broadway only in musical guise, while the Sotherns would grace New York stages for many more seasons once the war was over.

At the New Amsterdam on May 8, Tree switched to *The Merchant of Venice*. Once again, as with all Tree's mountings, spectacle dominated. The stage was cluttered not merely with massive scenery but with such gratuitously staged bits as a sumptuous parade across the Rialto bridge, a synagogue service followed by a small riot between Christians and Jews, and gondolas floating along in a canal. As was also Tree's wont, the play was drastically rearranged and shortened. *Theatre* felt Tree's "impersonation is that of a common . . . usurer of the Ghetto. There is no underlying romance." Of the star's American Portia, it noted, "Elsie Ferguson demonstrates that that pretty and talented player has much to learn in the delivery of blank verse."

The season's last new traditional play was Cyril Harcourt's **A Lady's Name** (5-15-16, Maxine Elliott's) in which Marie Tempest starred as a a writer who advertises for a husband in order to get material for her next book.

One week later, on the 22nd, the Washington Square Players, about to abandon their tiny Bandbox Theatre, also abandoned their policy of bills of one-acters to offer New York its first professional production of Anton Chekhov's **The Sea Gull.** Critics were somewhat puzzled by the playwright's adramatic approach, but not altogether unfavorably. However, the work, played "in semi-darkness," was rejected by the company's customarily tolerant patrons.

Another novelty, but one far from traditional, opened on the 24th at the Stadium of the City College for ten special performances. The author of **Caliban of the Yellow Sands** was Percy MacKaye. The previous summer, with Thomas Wood Stevens, he had offered *The Pageant and Masque of St. Louis,* a hodgepodge of history, myth, and imagination in blank verse, to the Missouri metropolis. His new "Shakespearean Masque" was presented on a stage especially designed by Joseph Urban. The stage was more than one hundred feet wide, with two large but unadorned staircases leading up to it. Huge masks of Thalia and Melpomene, themselves flanked by classic Greek columns, framed the stage. The central sixty feet was screened off by a "cloud curtain" of layers of gauze. Beneath the stage, smack in its middle, was the squarish entrance to Caliban's cave. MacKaye's story told how the wild, vicious Caliban (Horace Braham) is civilized by exposure to the edifying comments of Shakespeare (John Drew) and by watching snatches of the bard's plays. Among the numerous other celebrated players were Edith Wynne Matthison, F. F. Mackay, Emanuel Reicher, Robert Mantell, Augustin Duncan, Etienne Girardot, and Thomas A. Wise. Of course, in days before amplification, even these stellar players could not project their voices very far, though, considering the quality of the writing, some notices suggested that was a blessing. Elaborate choreography, from early Egyptian to Elizabethan morris dances, spelled the action.

Back at the New Amsterdam on the 25th, Tree rang down the curtain on the season with his version of *The Merry Wives of Windsor.* Critics, when not carping about his overelaborate mounting, mostly agreed that his Falstaff was the best of the three interpretations he had offered during his season. Constance Collier was Mistress Ford, and, for the second time this spring, Henrietta Crosman was Mistress Page.

1916–1917

As the war became standard news and thus less of an all-absorbing interest, and as prosperity bred from supplying belligerents and from the expansion of America's own tentative efforts at preparedness, ticket sales picked up. Still, as late as October 21, the *Dramatic Mirror* ran a headline noting "Many Plays but Slim Audiences." If the season brought forth virtually nothing that would later be deemed a theatrical classic, it was rich in superb entertainments. Playgoers could ask for little more.

The season's opener came in on the summer's hottest night. Patrons entering the auditorium saw a huge, illuminated clock hanging from the proscenium arch. The clock's hands moved forward or back to indicate the flow of time in a play which employed several flashbacks. That play was Edward Clark's **Coat-Tales** (7-31-16, Cort). Its tale of a coat begins when a nervous young man pawns the garment. A mysterious, smirking lawyer enters, buys the coat, leaves, and shortly thereafter returns it. Before long the pawnbroker is arrested for receiving stolen goods. The action then moves back in time to disclose that Mrs. Allen (Margaret Greene) has brought a new fur coat back from Europe but is afraid to tell her husband (George Anderson) about it. Her gambling brother (Richard Tabor) steals and pawns it. Then Allen's tightfisted law partner, William Turner (Thomas Wise), buys it on the cheap from the pawnbroker and presents it to his wife (Louise Dresser). Before long the fur is flying. Wise, last year's Falstaff, won the biggest applause as a grouch-with-a-good-heart. But heat and indifferent notices soon removed the farce.

The season's first hit was Belasco's production of Roi Cooper Megrue's **Seven Chances** (8-8-16, Cohan). It was a rather un-Belascan endeavor, being a light comedy and having nothing extraordinary in the way of settings. All the action takes place at a swank suburban country club—in its paneled, wicker-furnished rooms and on its terrace—where the men's favorite drink is a bronx and the ladies, when they are invited for a special ladies' day, take orangeade. Its hero is Jimmie Shannon (Frank Craven), whose goals are to coast through life and keep his "bully bachelorhood." He has provoked the lovely Anne Windsor (Carroll McComas) by constantly accepting, then forgetting, her invitations. His grandfather's will leaves him $12,000,000, so he can hope to coast. But one clause is a stinger. To inherit the money he must marry before he turns thirty. Jimmie will turn thirty tomorrow. His friends, led by Billy Meekin (Otto Kruger), arrange to corral a bevy of young ladies, one of whom Jimmie must marry. He agrees, hoping to settle an income on the lady and then divorce her. Billy brings the girls to Jimmie one by one, always signaling his arrival by whistling "Cuddle Up a Little Closer," and Jimmie responds by humming the "I'm a-comin' " phrase from "Ol' Black Joe." As he proposes to each girl she surprises him by her rejection—one saying he's not virile enough, another saying he's not poetic enough, and so on. Then they all reconsider and accept. In the end, the seventh girl, Anne, realizes that in his own way he does love her, so they head off to be married minutes before the deadline. The plain-faced, homey-voiced Craven carried the show and apparently was responsible for much of its nearly five-month run. For, although the *Dramatic Mirror* praised its "life and snap and continual interest," many critics were not excited by the evening (and read today the play seems tedious).

A bigger hit and much better play came in the following night. Like *Coat-Tales,* it mixed crook play with farce, but did it far more skillfully. Several critics compared Max Marcin's **Cheating Cheaters** (8-9-16, Eltinge) favorably with Cohan's *Seven Keys to Baldpate* (9-22-13). The beautiful Nan Carey (Marjorie Rambeau) enlists several suave criminals to join her in posing as the rich Brockton clan. She has wangled an invitation to the home of the equally rich Palmers and hopes to use the occasion to steal the Palmer jewels. She herself has borrowed some very expensive jewelry to wear. But the Palmers, like the Brocktons, are actually crooks in disguise. They hope to steal the Brockton jewels. Both groups worry about a detective named Ferris, who has succeeded in catching many of their friends. Of course, Ferris proves to be none other than Nan. She arrests virtually everyone in sight, sparing only the handsome young man posing as Tom Palmer (Cyril Keightley), whom she has come to love. The play ran nearly nine months, although *Variety* reported that the show, which at one point it called the

season's number-two hit, frequently failed to sell all its more expensive orchestra seats.

Otto Harbach's **The Silent Witness** (8-10-16, Longacre) was a melodrama that had a modest run after being damned by critics with such faint praise as "far from ineffective." Like several shows that followed close on its heels, it achieved its stand by resorting to cut-rate tickets. Helen Hastings (Emilie Polini) had a child by a fellow student who reportedly died in a fire the night before their wedding. Actually the man, Richard Morgan (Henry Kolker), survived and now, years later, is a major prosecuting attorney. Helen's son, Bud Morgan (Donald Gallaher), gets into a fight with another young man over Helen's reputation. Bud's adversary stumbles, striking his head on a log, and is killed. Bud is arrested for murder. The prosecutor discovers that the accused is his long-lost son, and with the help of the silent witness, bloodstains on the log that he proves do not belong to the dead man, he helps exonerate the youngster.

A young lady also needed to exculpate herself, but from less onerous charges, in H. M. Harwood's English comedy **Please Help Emily** (8-14-16, Lyceum). Outraged by the attitude of her guardian and furious that the man (Charles Cherry) she loves is engaged to another girl, Emily (Ann Murdock), who "looks like a demi," hides in the man's apartment, putting on his pajamas and cuddling up in his bed. The expected complications follow before the man concludes he really loves Emily best. As he would be in several other later mountings, the long-dead Charles Frohman was listed as producer.

Tempers also flew in Lawrence Rising and Margaret Mayo's farce **His Bridal Night** (8-16-16, Republic). Joe Demorel (John Westley) has married Vi (Rosie Dolly) but inadvertently sets off on his honeymoon with her twin sister, Tiny (Jennie Dolly). Tiny's fiancé, Lent Trevett (Pedro de Cordoba), sets off in pursuit. The mixup was easily explained since the petite, dark, almond-eyed Dolly Sisters, so popular in vaudeville and revue, looked almost alike.

August's third and longest-running hit (a little more than a year) was Winchell Smith and John E. Hazzard's **Turn to the Right** (8-17-16, Gaiety). For much of the time it played to a weekly capacity of $10,000, leading *Variety* to hail it as the season's strongest success. Hazzard had written the original version, and Smith, the era's favorite play doctor, had then helped rework it. Like *Coat-Tales,* the play begins in a pawnshop run by an old Jew. (A small bit of the dialogue was in Yiddish—an indication of changing theatre audiences, as it had been last year in *Young America*.) Joe Bascom (Forrest Winant) comes into the Ossining Loan Bureau and buys a used suit with his meager dollars. It is quickly apparent that Joe has just been released from Sing Sing. By prearrangement he meets his two former prison buddies, Muggs (William E. Meehan) and Gilly (Frank Nelson). They are planning a new job, but Joe tells them he has gone straight and will not join them. Adding that he is off to see an old friend, he bids them good-bye. The old friend Joe has gone to see is his mother (Ruth Chester). She is the sort of woman who "whenever she's worried she just reads the Bible awhile—and then all her trouble goes and she's happy again." But he discovers that she is about to lose the family peach farm to sleazy Deacon Tillinger (Samuel Reed), whom she owes $125. Joe is at a loss for a way of making good on the debt, when Muggs and Gilly appear. Joe, who has kept his prison sentence from his mother, tells her they are business associates. When they learn of his plight Muggs sneaks off and soon comes back with the money, which he has stolen from Tillinger's safe. Joe long has loved Tillinger's daughter, Elsie (Louise Rutter), but he also discovers that her father is trying to foist her on Lester Morgan (Roy Fairchild), a rich man's son who Tillinger's unhappy employee, Sam (Edgar Nelson), insists "ain't so pretty as he is swell." Sam tells Mrs. Bascom that Tillinger is cheating her on the money he offers for her wonderful peach jam. He offers to get her a fair price, so she gives him some jars to see what he can do. When Tillinger arrives Joe pays off the debt, but before the deacon can leave Gilly has picked his pocket and retrieved the money. After Tillinger realizes the money is gone he calls in the police. But the move backfires, for although Joe must reveal the truth he also is made aware that Lester is the man who framed him and who really committed the crime for which Joe was imprisoned. The last act takes place outside the farmhouse, where the peach trees are in bloom. Joe has married Elsie. Muggs and Gilly have reformed and now sport the monikers Dudley and Lucius. They have also proposed to and been accepted by Joe's sister and her friend. Sam, who had sold Mrs. Bascom's jam to a major wholesaler, has become rich. Joe, the ex-hoods, and the bumpkinish Sam, all in white tie and tails, prepare to sit down to a sumptuous dinner.

Arthur Hornblow, writing in *Theatre*, described the play to a tee: "Sounds a shade conventional. Well it is and it isn't. 'The pathetic stuff' is piled on, to my thinking, more cloying than the jam of the plot, but the humorous touches are deliciously ingenious and the humorous side of the piece provokes a constant howl of unalloyed delight." The show was the first hit for producer John Golden.

• • •

John Golden (1864–1955) was born in New York and entered the theatre as a super at Niblo's Garden. He studied law at New York University but after producing a college show decided on his life work. He served as an actor and manager for a touring company, then turned his hand to lyric writing, including the words for "Poor Butterfly." All through his producing career he was to insist on wholesome plays.

• • •

For the second time in just over a week, with the opening of Ruth Helen Davis and Charles Klein's **The Guilty Man** (8-19-16, Astor), taken from François Coppée's *La Coupable,* a prosecuting attorney discovered his long-lost child was the very person he was prosecuting. In this instance, Claude Lescuyer (Lowell Sherman) seduces and deserts Marie (Emily Ann Wellman). Marie marries Flambon (Austin Webb), a vicious dance hall owner. Years pass. Marie's baby, Claudine (Irene Fenwick), has grown to womanhood. When Flambon attacks Marie once too often, Claudine kills him. She is brought to court, where the prosecutor turns out to be none other than Lescuyer and where his confession of his early wrongs results in her acquittal.

One of Broadway's most respected producers, Arthur Hopkins, came a cropper when he offered J. and L. du Rocher Macpherson's **The Happy Ending** (8-21-16, Shubert). A beautiful princess (Margaret Mower), desolate over the death of her soldier fiancé, is carried off to heaven, where everyone is perpetually joyful and where she is taught that death is the happiest ending. The play was thrashed as lifeless, but Robert Edmond Jones's scenery was extolled. His settings led Woollcott to observe, "Mr. Jones has what Mr. Urban lacks, a capacity for making his work serve the play at every moment. . . . It is the difference between fine art and nothing at all." Yet critics continued to describe Urban's designs at length and allowed a few words of high praise to suffice for Jones. One of the few specific descriptions, and one not very specific at that, was offered by the *Dramatic Mirror,* which recorded, "His finest achievement was the scene representing the hereafter, in which pretty children romped on a green plateau, while in the background mountains stretched interminably."

Equally unsuccessful was an English farce, Walter W. Ellis's **A Little Bit of Fluff** (8-26-16, 39th St.). After her husband's boozy night on the town a woman finds a valuable necklace in his pocket.

Naturally he gives it to her. Since he then cannot return it and must pay the owner for it, he enlists a crippled friend in a scheme to defraud an insurance company by having the friend claim to be him and state he was injured in an accident.

Another farce, Mark E. Swan's **Somebody's Luggage** (8-28-16, 48th St.), taken from a book by F. J. Randall, eked out a five-week stand solely because its star was the great rubber-faced clown James T. Powers, long a favorite in musical comedy. Of the play itself, the *World* bemoaned, "It would be hard to find one more lacking in ingenuity, cleverness, real humor or any of the other qualities that honestly provoke the merriment of an audience." Alfred Hopper (Powers) becomes helplessly drunk during a channel crossing. By error he is removed from the ship along with the luggage belonging to a passenger who has fallen overboard. Hopper and the baggage are delivered to the lost passenger's address, and there he is mistaken for the man, an Australian, who had come to claim a huge inheritance. Powers elicited laughs by trying to light his pipe in the wind, by wrestling with a collapsible steamer chair, and later by trying to jump about like a kangaroo.

August's final entry, another quick flop, was **A Pair of Queens** (8-29-16, Longacre), which Otto Harbach (still spelling his name Hauerbach) had revamped from a play by A. Seymour Brown and Harry Lewis. Critics dismissed it as an attempt to capitalize on *A Full House* and, like that play, combine crooks, angry wives, comic servants, and the police in farcical disarray. Cranby (Edward Abeles) and his brother-in-law, John Shelby (Joe Santley), have been out on the town. By mistake Cranby has grabbed the coat of a crook involved in a melee at the nightclub they visited. Two not very competent detectives (Hugh Cameron and Frank McGinn) appear, but succeed primarily in flustering Cranby's maid (Maude Eburne). Miss Eburne's dithering servant grabbed the best notices.

Nor did September get off to a good start. George Broadhurst, who had won his initial fame as a writer of farces, returned to the genre with **Fast and Grow Fat** (9-1-16, Globe), which he based on Franklin P. Adams's story "Five Fridays." The guests at a party on a posh island learn that their hostess (Marion Vantine), having read a magazine article on dieting and believing all her friends are overfed, has removed every bit of food from her estate. This proves particularly painful for two men who are both courting her: a fat drama critic (Frank McIntyre) and a thin businessman (Roy Atwell). In the end, they do find an overlooked dog biscuit. Zelda Sears provided the most laughs as a guest who luckily has

had a touch of liquor, spends the whole time intoxicated, and at one point slides down a drainpipe while clad in a scarlet evening gown.

The next evening brought in the season's longest-run hit (457 performances), Jules Eckert Goodman's **The Man Who Came Back** (9-2-16, Playhouse), taken from a story by John Fleming Wilson. It was the sort of melodrama at which Broadhurst so recently had excelled. The very rich Thomas Potter (Edward Emery) is so disillusioned by his dissolute son, Henry (Henry Hull), that he orders him to leave the Potter home. Henry takes to roaming the world, ever more and more debauched. Along the way he meets Marcelle (Mary Nash), a dance hall hostess, who becomes his associate in his debaucheries. Their lives hit bottom in a Shanghai opium den, where emissaries from his dying father find him. They beg him to return to his father but insist he leave Marcelle behind. He refuses to desert her. The decision, with its moral and ethical implications, revitalizes Henry. He returns home a reformed man but with the similarly regenerated Marcelle in tow. And they are welcomed there. As critics pointed out, the gallery patrons were especially vociferous in approval. Many of those critics had recently paid increasing attention to films and their effect on live theatre, noting especially that gallery gods had been the quickest to desert to the flickers. Given the rousing reception these more fickle playgoers accorded the work, one reviewer closed his notice, "The movie fans will love it." So did regular Broadway audiences.

Despite audible snickers from first-nighters and derisory notices, Richard Walton Tully's old-fashioned melodrama **The Flame** (9-4-16, Lyric) found an audience for three months. It told of a young couple who attempt to establish a plantation in Central America in the face of rival political factions, voodoo practitioners, hurricanes, and other obstacles. They find unexpected aid from Maya (Peggy O'Neill), "a sort of female Prospero, who lived with a weird sisterhood at the bottom of a well." There was also a little bit of dancing, which provoked one critic into writing, "The 'rhumba,' described as a new dance, is not likely to win favor as a society pastime."

In his heyday Henry E. Dixey had been an even bigger musical clown than Powers, starring in *Adonis,* the first musical to run over 500 performances in New York. But thereafter he never again found a major success, while Powers moved from hit to hit. Dixey's latest vehicle was Harvey O'Higgins and Harriet Ford's **Mr. Lazarus** (9-5-16, Shubert). Because so many cheap apartments have recently been built, times are hard for Mrs. Sylvester (Florine Arnold), who runs a rooming house. Pat (Eva Le Gallienne), her daughter by her first marriage, is the serving girl. To make matters worse for Mrs. Sylvester, she is now married to a brutal, selfish man (William T. Clarke), who also has a daughter (Marie Ascaraga), an overindulged clothes-horse. A Mr. Lazarus (Dixey) has asked for a back room and offered to pay handsomely, so Mrs. Sylvester has requested that William Booth (Tom Powers), a struggling artist who is in love with Pat but who is behind in his rent, take a less desirable room. He does so grudgingly. When Lazarus appears Booth tells him the room is haunted by the ghost of Mrs. Sylvester's first husband, Mr. Molloy, a man said to have been killed in a train wreck. Lazarus seems unconcerned. Before long it becomes obvious that Lazarus is probably Molloy. He helps the romance between Booth and Pat, gets rid of Dr. Sylvester by showing him to be a wanted criminal, settles a large income on Mrs. Sylvester and Pat— then disappears. Was he or was he not Molloy?

The play had its problems, for even the better characters were unlikable. Mrs. Sylvester was a dull flibbertigibbet; Pat was humorless and sanctimonious; and Booth, who has some old garments to dispose of, probably alienated one segment of playgoers with a remark such as "The last kike that braced me wouldn't take fifty cents to carry them away." Even Lazarus, if he was Molloy, was a scoundrel, having gone on after the accident to a new life and leaving his wife to make do on the insurance she could collect. An audience largely of oldtimers gave Dixey the same run Powers had enjoyed—five weeks.

Pierrot the Prodigal (9-6-16, Booth) was a revival of Michel Carré's pantomime, which Augustin Daly had offered unsuccessfully as *The Prodigal Son* (3-3-91). This time Americans were more receptive, so the mounting ran five months.

Six weeks was all that Edward Knoblauch's **Paganini** 9-11-16, Criterion) could manage, especially after notices such as the *Globe*'s, which lambasted it as "a silly, wishy-washy thing." In his autobiography, its star, George Arliss, conceded that it was a disappointment. His gaunt, black-garbed musician is pursued by the lovelorn Charlotte Watson (Margery Maude) until she reluctantly accepts that his only passion is for his music.

But three nights later one of Broadway's most memorable hits appeared. James Montgomery's **Nothing But the Truth** (9-14-16, Longacre) was adapted from Fred Isham's novel. The *Herald* assured its readers that "thanks to William Collier

and George Washington . . . first-nighters were kept in a gay mood." Indeed, many critics felt that Collier never had enlivened a better vehicle. E. M. Ralston (Rapley Holmes) is a rich, unscrupulous stockbroker. As he tells his partner, Bob Bennett (Collier): "A lie is just as good as the truth, if the result is all right." Bob refuses to agree, even though he is engaged to Ralston's daughter, Gwen (Margaret Brainerd). Gwen comes to Bob with $10,000 she has collected for her church and asks him to double it within a week. Since her father has promised to equal any amount she collects, that would mean that the church would have $40,000. And the church can use it, since, as Gwen's mother (Maude Turner Gordon) laments, it has become a dull place what with choirboys deserting to become caddies, the organist and tenor leaving to work at a film house, and the soprano quitting to sing in a cabaret. When Bob insists to Ralston that the truth is the only method to earn money properly, Ralston, a second partner, Dick Donnelly (Morgan Coman), and a sourpusssed customer, Clarence Van Dusen (Ned A. Sparks), bet him $10,000 that he cannot tell the truth for twenty-four hours. Bob, seeing a way to double Gwen's money overnight, takes the bet. The action moves to the Ralston home, where Bob tells a guest the insulting truth about her piano playing, nearly wrecks Ralston's marriage by revealing that Ralston has met a floozie in his office, and almost loses Gwen when he admits he has loved two other girls before her. Those loves turn out to be Maude Adams, whom he has never met, and a circus cannonball tosser, whom he did kiss once. However, all ends happily moments after the twenty-four hours are up. When Gwen asks in what sort of stock he had invested her money, Bob responds, "Steel."

A much smaller bet—just ten dollars—figured in Booth Tarkington's **Mister Antonio** (9-18-16, Lyceum). But the bettors were only Tug (John McCabe), the owner of a shabby New York bar, and Antonio Camaradonio, a hurdy-gurdy man. Indeed, Tony's standard request to passersby is "tessess [ten cents] please." Tony has come to the bar of his old friend at the very moment that Tug is bouncing a besotted customer who has slept there overnight. The man is not a Bowery bum but a "jay" who has come to the big city on business, gone on a bender, and been taken for his money, his watch, and his coat. Tony gives the man a coat and a dollar. Tug tells him he is foolish to help a stranger who has been surly and hasn't even asked for Tony's name so that he could reimburse him. But Tony says that the man is no stranger. He has recognized him as the mayor of Avalonia, Pa., who " 'ad me arrested for play de 'urdy-gurd on the street on Sunday." Since his travels with his hurdy-gurdy will take Tony back to Avalonia in six weeks, the men have bet on what the mayor's response will be. The play then moves to a tree-shaded street in Avalonia, with the shade falling not only on passersby but on two ordinary Victorian clapboard homes. One belongs to Mayor Jorny (Joseph Brennan) and his family; the other to Reverend Walpole and his clan. An after-church conversation reveals both families as puckered-faced and self-righteous. In fact, the Jornys, having learned that June Ramsey (Eleanor Woodruff), a distant relative whom they have given shelter, was seen the night before at a dance hall, order her to leave immediately. They are especially outraged at her behavior after the consideration they have shown. But she retorts that all she has been allowed to do is cook, serve, clean, and take short walks Thursday and Saturday afternoons. Onto the street comes Tony, with his beloved mule, Capitano, pulling the hurdy-gurdy, accompanied by the mentally retarded Joe (Robert Harrison), who loves to shoot at Tony with an empty gun. The chief of police would arrest Tony, but he needs a warrant, and the mayor, having recognized Tony, has run into the house claiming to have a headache. Later the mayor tries to foist a loaded gun on Joe, hoping he will kill Tony. Although for all practical purposes Tony has lost his bet, he proclaims himself the winner, since June will hereafter accompany him. Critics found the play unsatisfactory but relished Tony as performed by Otis Skinner, with his darkish makeup, his slightly shoddy if colorful jacket and pants, the large red-and-black handkerchief tied about his neck, and his gray, misshapen hat, and with "his abundant vitality, his ringing, resonant voice, and his great grandeur of gesture." The public loved the whole affair, so despite a short New York stand Skinner had a meal ticket for most of three seasons.

There was a more joyously happy ending—and what else could there have been?—for **Pollyanna** (9-18-16, Hudson), which Catherine Chisholm Cushing derived from Eleanor H. Porter's famous novel. Pollyanna (Patricia Collinge), an orphan who can find a reason to be "glad" about anything—"I'm so glad to be here—and so glad to see you—and so glad you're beautiful"—comes to the home of her stern, dour aunt (Effie Shannon). The aunt puts her on a schedule not as demeaning as, yet not unlike, the one the Jornys had forced on June, permitting her "two hours every Saturday afternoon" to herself. Before long she has coaxed the reclusive Mr. Pendleton (Philip Merivale), who has always loved Pollyanna's mother but had never been allowed to

marry her, out of his luxurious cocoon. When the girl is run over by a car, Pendleton and his friend, Dr. Chilton (Herbert Kelcey), send her to Europe for treatment. Chilton was once the aunt's suitor. However, she has cut him for twenty years. By the play's end Chilton and the aunt are married, and Pollyanna becomes engaged to a waif she had persuaded Pendleton to adopt. One reviewer described the evening as "peach melba drenched in syrup," a phrase in which most other critics acquiesced. But the public clearly liked peach melbas and syrup, with the *World* acknowledging that Pollyanna's "welcome was one of multitudinous cheers," so the play, like Skinner's vehicle, enjoyed years of touring in the face of a modest Manhattan visit (112 performances).

In December Margaret Anglin, a Canadian-born actress, was to write in *Theatre,* "I believe in American plays by American authors for American people." Yet when she came to New York in September it was an English comedy she brought with her. Somerset Maugham's **Caroline** (9-20-16, Empire) told of a middle-aged man and woman, both married to others, who have an ardent if unconsummated affair before the woman's husband dies. Then the couple's ardor wanes, until the woman conceives of the idea of pretending her husband is still alive. The star's six-week stand was part of a prearranged tour.

On the other hand, Frederic and Fanny Hatton's **Upstairs and Down** (9-25-16, Cort) ran into July. And it did so in the face of sharply divided notices, which saw the play as a vulgar comedy, a delicious satire, or a pleasing or displeasing mixture of both. Among the more ardent yeasayers was the *Journal,* which suggested, "The play is as clever as the cast." Nancy Ives (Christine Norman), a popular Long Island hostess, has become disillusioned with the pettiness, selfishness, and essential dishonesty of her guests. Especially exasperating are Elizabeth Chesterton (Mary Servoss) and her "baby vampire" sister, Alice (Juliet Day), both of whom are resorting to any means to latch on to the same man, Terrence O'Keefe (Courtney Foote). Alice is even willing to claim publicly that Terrence has seduced her. In disgust, Nancy opts for life below stairs. But there she finds her servants, with the Iveses' valet, Louis (Leo Carillo), at the top of the hierarchy, just as amoral or immoral. She concludes that her guests at least have their wealth to console them. Among those needing consolation is Alice, who must settle for a not very bright polo player (Paul Harvey).

Cyril Harcourt's **The Intruder** (9-26-16, Cohan and Harris) was a melodrama, supposedly taken by its English playwright from an unidentified French work and offered to America several years before London saw it under a different title. Set in France, it told of the dilemma of the lover of an examining magistrate's wife who can only acquit himself of an accusation of theft by revealing his liaison. It found few takers.

Grant Stewart and Robert Baker's **Arms and the Girl** (9-27-16, Fulton) attempted to extract some laughs from the German invasion of Belgium, where a young American, Wilfred Ferrers (Cyril Scott), stranded at an inn, is mistaken by the invaders for a spy. To save him from a firing squad, an American girl, Ruth Sherwood (Fay Bainter), tells the commander that she and Wilfred were eloping. The officer cancels the firing squad and instead orders an immediate wedding. The rest of the evening is spent by the couple trying to get out of their predicament. The *World* reflected the consensus of a majority of newspapers when it garlanded the entertainment as "a rattling good little play." For Woollcott, who mistakenly thought he was applauding the dark-eyed, light-haired Miss Bainter's New York debut, the young beauty was the best thing about the evening—"the most piquant and pleasing ingenue to come to our town since Madge Kennedy . . . fresh, gentle, individual, intelligent."

· · ·

Fay Bainter (1891–1968) began her career in stock in her hometown of Los Angeles. She moved to New York, first appearing there in a 1912 musical. She next toured with Mrs. Fiske before returning to stock in Albany and Toledo. However, it was with this play that New York first fully appreciated her demure charm and superb technique.

· · ·

His Majesty Bunker Bean (10-2-16, Astor), which Lee Wilson Dodd dramatized from Harry Leon Wilson's best-seller, had been a major success the previous season in Chicago. Its New York run was disappointing, perhaps because its star had been playing it too long and was now playing it too broadly. Typically, the *Post* waved away the affair as "only fairly well done." Bunker (Taylor Holmes) is a meek stenographer hoodwinked into thinking he is the reincarnation of an Egyptian pharoah, of Napoleon, and of other strong, determined men. His attempts to reconcile his incorrigible meekness with his images of his past lives sparked the farce.

Even less well received was Stuart Fox's **Backfire** (10-2-16, 39th St.). Lydia Page (Mary Boland) determines to be revenged on Mathew Garth (Ogden Crane), who has destroyed her father's business and inadvertently led to her sister's death. She gets the

goods on the old man (who had plotted arson), but when she falls in love with his son (Henry Gsell), she hands the material over to her future father-in-law.

Another failure was Violet Pearn's **Hush!** (10-3-16, Little), a play within a play. Julie Laxton (Cathleen Nesbitt) writes a comedy designed to shock her prudish fiancé and his family. In that play the freethinking Lucilla (Estelle Winwood) causes consternation in the home of her in-laws, a minister and his wife. Miss Winwood's "delicious charm" was unavailing.

So were the efforts of such respected hands as Roi Cooper Megrue and Irvin S. Cobb, whose **Under Sentence** (10-3-16, Harris) began as a muckraking melodrama and finished as a preposterous utopian comedy. The heartless billionaire, John E. Blake (George Nash), frames a young associate, Copley (Felix Krembs), for a crime Blake himself is guilty of. After her husband is jailed, Katherine Copley (Janet Beecher) uncovers the evidence she needs to exculpate him and send Blake to prison. Although behind bars, Blake engineers the election of a new governor, and the governor puts him in charge of the prison. Blake's business acumen leads to reforms that make the prison a model and the prisoners happy to be inmates. The *Herald,* a paper more accepting than most of all Broadway entries, thought the show would be a hit, unless its "lack of sex interest" told against it. Apparently it did.

Lawrence Whitman's **Fixing Sister** (10-4-16, Maxine Elliott's) ran eleven weeks, but that was all that might be expected of it. For Whitman was by then known to be the pen name for the play's star, William Hodge, who long had been more popular on the road. The *World* noted that "without the dry, genial humor of the lanky actor with the nasal twang and drawling voice, it is terrible to contemplate what might have become of the play." Hodge's John Otis was the latest in a line of laconic midwesterners who quietly but forcefully hurry to the aid of distressed ladies. In this instance, the ladies are his sister (Jane Wheatley) and his fiancée (Miriam Collins), who are being bilked by a bogus English lord (Hamilton Deane) and lady (Ida Vernon). John discreetly masterminds a police raid on a crooked roulette game the lord runs, thereby exposing him.

The heroine of **Rich Man, Poor Man** (10-5-16, 48th St.), which George Broadhurst theatricalized from Maximilian Foster's *Saturday Evening Post* story, had to be content with a happy-sad ending. Bab (Regina Wallace) is a foundling raised as a drudge in a boardinghouse. Through the well-meaning ploys of a boarder she passes into society as a wealthy girl. She even snares the crippled grandson (Rudolph Cameron) of rich, rich Peter Beeston (Brandon Hurst). But right in the middle of the posh engagement party the hoax is exposed. Beeston begs the girl not to leave, but the grandson, sensing she really loves another man, releases her and helps her beloved (John Bowers) get a head start in life.

Last season David Warfield had toured in a new Belasco production, *Van der Decken,* a version of the Flying Dutchman story. But Broadway scuttlebutt reported that Warfield was unhappy in the role and refused to play it in New York. The result was that when Warfield did return, at the Knickerbocker on the 10th, he was starred in a revival of *The Music Master* (9-26-04). Whatever Manhattan's playgoers might have thought of his Van der Decken, they were happy to support his von Barwig for twenty weeks—far longer than initially planned. On some weeks it grossed a then astonishing $15,000.

A growing number of critics had begun to rail against what they saw as theatrical sentimentality. A few condemned the Belasco-Warfield revival for it; several also chastized the next new play to appear. But playgoers ignored these complaints, agreeing instead with the *World,* which appraised the evening as "one of the most delightful of the year," and gave **Come Out of the Kitchen** (10-23-16, Cohan), derived by A. E. Thomas from Alice Duer Miller's story, a seven-month run and seasons of touring. The Dangerfields are an old Virginia family who have fallen on hard times. Father and Mother Dangerfield are in Europe, seeking a cure for father's illness. When one of their sons notes gloomily that their parents have traveled "from Wiesbaden to Marienbad and from Marienbad to Carlsbad—and poor dad getting worse all the time," his younger brother can't resist commenting, "Going from bad to worse, so to speak." (One reviewer heard the response as "going from bad to wurst.") The Dangerfield children, in dire need of cash, agree to rent the Dangerfield mansion to a Yankee for six weeks during the hunting season. The $5000 he will pay in rent will solve many of their problems. But the northerner has insisted on white servants, so when the children learn that the servants they have engaged have reneged on their agreement, they decide to pose as the servants. The beautiful, authoritative Olivia (Ruth Chatterton) will become Jane Ellen, the Irish cook. Paul (Charles Trowbridge) will be the butler, Smithfield; the pugnacious young Elizabeth (Barbara Milton), the maid, Araminta; and the rambunctious Charles (Robert Ames), the houseboy, Brindlebury. The renter turns out to be handsome, rich, unwed Burton Crane (Bruce McRae). Jane Ellen, in her false Irish brogue, assures Crane everything will be just fine: "'Tis meself can

take the sole of your honor's shoe and turn it out so's it'll melt in your honor's mouth." Before Burton realizes he has fallen in love with Jane Ellen, and before she accepts his proposal, Burton finds reason for firing the other servants one by one, a colored mammy is locked in a kitchen closet with a young man who is courting the very girl that Burton had once thought of marrying, and Jane Ellen receives several other offers of marriage. Ruth Chatterton's winsome ways enhanced the play's drolleries.

Acceptable drolleries were far fewer in Montague Glass and Jules Eckert Goodman's **Object-Matrimony** (10-25-16, Cohan and Harris), which some aisle-sitters dismissed as tasteless and unfeeling, comparing it unfavorably with the Potash and Perlmutter series. Milton Sachs (Irving Cummings) has inherited a fine garment company but, with his unworldly, arty interests, threatens to run it into the ground. To borrow the money he so badly needs, he becomes engaged to the fat, wealthy daughter (Jean Temple) of a fat, wealthy fellow Jewish garment maker (Jules Jordan). But he breaks the engagement after he and the bookkeeper (Marjorie Wood) he really loves find a way of saving the firm. The usually scene-stealing Mathilde Cottrelly was lost in the role of Milton's mama.

Critics were less happy still with **Major Pendennis** (10-26-16, Criterion), taken by Langdon Mitchell from Thackeray's novel. They found it episodic and disjointed, saved, as much as a dreary evening could be saved, by the superbly nuanced playing of John Drew in the title role. More than one reviewer rejoiced that Drew's performance—"a sound, virile and affectionate rendering of the snobbish old buck"—was his best in many seasons. Drew's reputation alone kept the play on the boards for ten weeks, with *Variety* noting that its grosses were "very low for a Drew play."

By contrast, Rachel Crothers's **Old Lady 31** (10-30-16, 39th St.), based on a novel by Louise Forsslund, was greeted with enthusiasm by most critics, even those given to sneering at theatrical sentimentality. The *Tribune* advised its readers that "Miss Crothers has handled her sentiment and her sunshine with such rare discretion that she has written a charming comedy of character." Yet read today it seems possibly the most mawkish play of the season. On a summer afternoon in 1860, Angie (Emma Dunn) and Abe Rose (Reginald Barlow) take one farewell look at the garden of their old cottage, which has just been auctioned off to pay debts resulting from Abe's bad investments. Angie is going to a home for old ladies; Abe to the county poorhouse, five miles away from her. But Angie assures Abe, "You might a giv' me all the riches in the world an still we might a bin separated further'n we'll ever be now. I'd rather be saying goodbye for the poor farm an' loving you, Abe, than sittin' with you in luxury an' not caring whether you was settin' with me or not." Suprisingly, the diverse old biddies, mostly soured spinsters, at the home agree to take in Abe, referring to him as the thirty-first tenant, old lady 31. But after a while Abe finds his position unendurable, so he runs off. When, exhausted and bedraggled, he returns, Angie hands him a letter which advises him that one of his long-forgotten investments has paid off. They now have $8000 with which to repurchase their old home. Along with the play, critics extolled Emma Dunn—"melting voice, winsome personality, splendid art"—a small, still slim, not unattractive woman in her early forties who for many years had found herself confined to playing old ladies. Despite her good notices and huge success in the play, she elected to desert the stage for films, thereafter returning to Broadway very rarely.

An English play opened the same evening, Clifford Mills's **The Basker** (10-30-16, Empire). It told of a nobleman who is shamed out of his plan to "bask" irresponsibly through life. Cyril Maude was starred.

October's final entry was another success, Arthur Hopkins's mounting of Clare Kummer's **Good Gracious Annabelle** (10-31-16, Republic). Its relatively short run—111 performances—could have been attributed to its similarity to *Come Out of the Kitchen,* although it was a brighter comedy. The *Times* extolled it as "that rarest of rarities—a brilliant farce by an American author." Once again a group of supposedly rich youngsters, actually on their uppers, agree to pose as servants. The leader of the group is pretty Annabelle Leigh (Lola Fisher), who takes the name Annie Dappledown and, like the earlier play's heroine, passes herself off as a cook. As Annie explains to John Rawson (Walter Hampden), a rich miner who has rented the estate, she was once abducted by a bearded man who took her to a cave, married her after she protested his actions, and then apparently let her escape. But for many years he has sent her money. She does not know his name, since he has been referred to only as the Hermit. The owner (Edwin Nicander) of the estate returns unexpectedly and is delighted to discover the presence there of Rawson, his archrival for mining interests. Crucial stock held by Annabelle has fallen into his hands, so Annabelle borrows some money from him, steals the stocks from his pocket, and replaces them with the cash she has just

borrowed. She helps bring about a reconciliation between the men. Only then does Rawson reveal he is her long-lost husband (he shaved off his beard years before). Since she has fallen in love with him she has no objection to his taking her in his arms, but she does ask where he is carrying her. He tells her, "Back to our cave." The play's success gave a major leg up to both its producer and playwright. Kummer's career was to prove disappointing, but Hopkins became one of the leading producers of his time.

• • •

Arthur [Melancthon] **Hopkins** (1878–1950) was one of Broadway's most high-minded, artistically aware producers. He was born in Cleveland and spent a period as a newspaperman. After a stint as a press agent he turned producer in 1912 with *Steve,* a quick failure. A year later he mounted his first hit, *The Poor Little Rich Girl.* In conjunction with the Shuberts, he built the Plymouth Theatre in 1917 and housed many of his biggest hits there.

• • •

During the preceding summer the Provincetown Players had continued their intermittent performances at their Massachusetts wharf. They had also given two very private performances of Susan Glaspell and George Cram Cook's *Suppressed Desires* for selected friends at non-theatrical venues in New York. But the sporadic New England season had expanded their repertory and introduced their audiences to Eugene O'Neill, who would become their most famous find and the reason the troupe is still remembered. Just before moving to Manhattan for a prolonged season, they had offered O'Neill's **Thirst,** a saga of three shipwrecked men on a raft, on September 1. However, earlier in the summer, sometime during the week of July 24, most likely on the 28th, they had mounted a better O'Neill one-acter, the play the company subsequently elected to inaugurate its first New York bill, **Bound East for Cardiff** (11-3-16, Playwright's). His shipmates on the *S.S. Glencairn* recognize that their mate, Yank (George Cram Cook), has been injured fatally in a fall. To their attempts at solace, he replies, "This sailor life ain't much to cry about leaving." Death calls for him in the guise of "a pretty lady dressed in black." Although major critics had regularly reviewed the one-act bills of similar troupes, most ignored the Players opening, perhaps because the ensemble had called itself a "theatre club" to evade Manhattan's stringent safety laws and had refused to offer reviewers free tickets. But Stephen Rathbun of the *Evening Sun* did take notice, reporting that the O'Neill piece "was real, subtly tense and avoided a dozen pitfalls that might have made it 'the regular thing.' " Later in their season the Players offered three more O'Neill one-acters: **Before Breakfast** (12-1-16, Playwright's), in which a nagging wife provokes her husband into killing himself; **Fog** (1-1-17, Playwright's), telling of passengers adrift in a lifeboat, who are rescued by a vessel lured to the scene by the cries of the dead child aboard; and **The Sniper** (2-16-17, Playwright's), a bitter anti-war piece in which a Belgian peasant is shot by a firing squad for having avenged the brutal deaths of his son and wife. When the German officer waves away responsibility by telling the peasant's priest that the law must be served, the priest cries, "Alas, the laws of men!"

Shaw's **Getting Married** (11-6-16, Booth) ran one performance more than *Good Gracious Annabelle*, using a marriage as an excuse to air arguments against it. William Faversham produced and directed the play and assumed the relatively minor role of the Bishop of Chelsea. Charles Cherry was St. John Hotchkiss, and Henrietta Crosman the scene-swiping Mrs. George. (A few nights later, on the 14th, Shaw's short *Great Catherine* was given its American premiere at the Neighborhood Playhouse.)

Several revivals followed, and all chalked up surprising stands. *Ben-Hur* (11-29-99), with an undistinguished cast, opened at the enormous Manhattan Opera House on the 6th and played for eleven weeks. Both *Keeping Up Appearances* (10-19-10) and *The Yellow Jacket* (11-4-12) ran twenty-two weeks. Butler Davenport's comedy opened at his tiny Bramhall Playhouse on the 8th and was aided by cut-price tickets and freebees. Hazelton and Benrimo's Chinese drama came into the Cort on the 9th and was aided by laudatory reevaluations. An excellent cast included Arthur Shaw once again as the Property Man and producer Charles Coburn as Chorus.

The knowhow of another producer, George M. Cohan, seems to have been the principal reason for the four-month run of Rida Johnson Young's comedy **Captain Kidd, Jr.** (11-13-16, Cohan and Harris), of which the *Dramatic Mirror* could say no more than that it was "pleasing in a superficial way." An old New York bookstore owner (Ernest Stallard), his granddaughter (Edith Taliaferro), and a young author (Otto Kruger) believe they can locate a treasure buried centuries earlier on Cape Cod. They are mistaken for bank robbers and nearly lose the bookstore before the inevitable happy ending. That happy ending came about not because they find the buried treasure—all they find is an empty chest—but because they had bought the piece of land for a stiff $25,000 but now learn that the railroad wants it and will pay them substantially more.

Avery Hopwood, increasingly perceived as carrying farce to the limits of good taste (and sometimes "slipping beyond the borderland of the suggestive into the risqué"), had to settle for a short run for his **Our Little Wife** (11-17-16, Harris). Herbert Warren (Lowell Sherman), upset that his wife, Dodo (Margaret Illington), flirts openly with her doctor (Charles Hampden), a young poet (Effingham Pinto), and every other man in sight, asks his friend Bobo Brown (Walter Jones) to see how far the seemingly faithless Dodo will go. At first Dodo refuses Bobo's invitation to his apartment, but after overhearing him invite her niece, Angie (Gwendolyn Piers), and unaware he and Angie are engaged, she decides to vamp in during Bobo and Angie's rendezvous. So do the doctor's irate wife and all the other characters.

November's next hit was Bayard Veiller's **The Thirteenth Chair** (11-20-16, 48th St.). Its action occurs in a single evening and takes place in an Italianate room in the Crosby mansion. (In his autobiography Veiller recalled that the producer, William Harris, Sr., "paid five thousand dollars for that one set of scenery designed by Livingston Platt, an interior picked up almost bodily from some Italian palace and slammed on the stage.") The Crosbys are delighted when their son, Will (Calvin Thomas), announces that he will wed Helen O'Neill (Katherine La Salle), even if Helen has qualms about marrying a rich young man and even if she tries to discourage the Crosbys from meeting her mother. Another of the Crosbys' guests, Edward Wales (S. K. Gardner), also expresses doubts about the marriage but refuses to be specific. For after dinner entertainment the Crosbys have planned a seance, conducted by a withered little Irish woman named Rosalie La Grange (Margaret Wycherley). They hope to discover who stabbed to death a friend of Wales. Rosalie shows the guests all the tricks employed by a medium and assures them she will use none. To her consternation, Helen recognizes Rosalie as her mother, but they remain silent about the relationship. The guests are locked in the room, and Rosalie is tied to her chair. Just as her control is about to reveal the killer, Wales groans. When the lights are turned on he is found dead—stabbed, but with no knife in sight. For a number of reasons Helen is the prime suspect. To save her daughter Rosalie employs all her tricks to expose the real murderer. She is helped when the murder weapon, which he had flung up into the ceiling, falls in front of him. Rosalie reassures Helen, "There's nothing but happiness comin' to ye. The spirits tell me ye're the favorite child af fortune." Writing thirty years later, John Chapman recalled, "Who will ever forget the first spine-chilling thrill of seeing that nasty skewer stuck in the ceiling, or the chunk with which it fell downward and stuck, quivering, in the tabletop? . . . To many of us, including myself, 'The Thirteenth Chair' remains the best of all the shriek-in-the-dark dramas." New York audiences could shriek for ten months.

But New York audiences shrugged off Harold Owen's **Such Is Life** (11-23-16, Princess), which departed this world after a single week. It focused on a silly professor who cannot believe his wife's ever-growing bank account stems from her writing sexy novels. Sam Sothern, who was the brother of E. H. Sothern but who had spent most of his career in England, was starred.

On the other hand, J. Hartley Manners's more lyrically titled **The Harp of Life** (11-27-16, Globe) attracted a sizable number of playgoers, largely because his wife, Laurette Taylor, headed the cast. She played the devoted, thirty-six-year-old mother of a nineteen-year-old lad (Dion Titheradge). He has been the absorbing interest in her life, so when she learns he is courting a not very respectable girl (Gail Kane), she is heartbroken. She eventually persuades the girl to renounce her son and finds a better mate for him. Although most critics acknowledged Laurette Taylor was one of the glories of the American stage, they were divided on how right her performance was this time. Among the yeasayers was Burns Mantle of the *Evening Mail,* who reported, "Her acting is as elusively beautiful as the color of a flower . . . perfect in her sense of theatre." Fewer critics were happy with the play, but even those who professed to admire the soap-opera-ish piece reported that many in the audience snickered at it. However, there was general agreement that the youthful, thin, slightly feline actress who played the "better mate" accomplished the remarkable feat of all but stealing the show from its star. The *World* observed, "Despite the delicate shading and fine resourcefulness of Miss Taylor's acting, the performance of a fresh ingenuous young girl—the slave of her mother's tyrannical protection—by Lynn Fontanne, . . . stood out."

Owen Davis's **Mile-A-Minute Kendall** (11-28-16, Lyceum) ended November on a down note. Critics saw it as an olio of numerous earlier and better plays, although they differed on just which ones. The *Evening World* pooh-poohed it as "a simple invention that may interest people who never stop to think." Jack Kendall (Tom Powers) is a spoiled young rich boy. He hurries into a rundown New

England inn after smashing his car into a milk wagon, a fence, and a window of the hostelry. With him is a stunning bleached blonde, Rose Howard (Adele Blood), who, he announces, he will wed. Despite the accident he insists on dancing, and in doing so knocks over some statues. He takes the shards and hurls them at the paintings hanging on the wall. Before long his father (John Flood) and the businessman (Joseph Kilgour) who has been keeping Rose appear. With the help of a large check, they convince her to leave Jack. (The first act curtain call showed Jack, who has passed out, being carried up to a room by one of the villagers, with the niece of the inn's proprietor leading the way.) The niece, Joan (Edith Lyle), knew Jack as a boy and has remembered him affectionately. She nurses him back to health, pays his bills out of her own pocket, and assists him in inventing an engine that can run cheaply on crude oil. When an automobile company offers to buy the invention, Jack and Joan agree to marry. All the villagers who bought stock in his enterprise will now be very rich—all, that is, but that cantankerous, penny-pinching innkeeper (William Sampson) who had been pressed into buying some of the stock but had sold out moments before the good news became public.

If November ended on a down note, December began by frantically seesawing down and up. The down side was George Parker's **Margery Daw** (12-4-16, Princess), which recounted the problems of a convent-trained girl who is jilted by the man she loves and then has a difficulty-plagued marriage with her former guardian. One week and it was gone. The up side was another of Sarah Bernhardt's farewell engagements. Bernhardt had permanently lost a leg and, because of a cold, temporarily lost her voice, but she courageously went on. Critics could detect little diminution in her marvelous talents—or else were too gentlemanly to underscore them. But her repertory was a little odd, consisting largely of one-acters or crucial scenes from the older plays with which she had long been identified. In one playlet, **La Faux Modèle,** she bravely assayed a scene in English. Her reputation was still so great that she packed the Empire for her three-week stand.

Growing anti-German sentiments did not stop Arnold Daly from offering Hermann Bahr's **The Master** (12-5-16, Fulton), in a translation by Benjamin Glazer. Daly assumed the role of the brilliant but arrogant surgeon, Dr. Wessley, who publicly proclaims that marital fidelity is absurd, and who must therefore put the best face he can on news that his wife is having an affair. Although the play appealed to a limited audience, it might have run longer but for Daly's illness forcing it to close.

Although amateur productions were generally given short shrift by reviewers, a number of critics gave special attention to Chester Bailey Fernald's **The Married Woman** (12-16-16, Neighborhood Playhouse), in which the heroine must choose between her unloving husband and the man who promises her genuine affection. For the most part these amateur groups, like such professional ensembles as the Washington Square Players, confined themselves to one-acters. Throughout the season, in a reflection of the growing sense of theatrical revolution and excitement, critics regularly extolled the variegated offerings of these troupes. Their plays ranged from archaic works such as *Gammer Gurton's Needle* to exotica such as the Japanese tragedy *Bushido* to contemporary pieces such as Lord Dunsany's *The Gods of the Mountain* and Susan Glaspell's *Trifles*. After the group that had presented Shaw's *Great Catherine* moved to Maxine Elliott's Theatre on the 18th, they added his examination of extramarital capers, **Overlooked** (2-2-17).

The 18th also brought in William Brady's revival of *Little Women* to the Park for three weeks.

David Belasco eked out a minor success with Horace Hodges and T. Wigney Percyval's **Little Lady in Blue** (12-21-16, Belasco). It provided Frances Starr with an opportunity to show her comic abilities. Anne Churchill, finding herself impoverished after running away from an employer who made unwanted advances, decides that if she is to succeed she must become an adventuress. She learns that the dissolute Anthony Addenbrooke (Jerome Patrick) will inherit a vast fortune if he reforms, so she sets about to reform him and then marry him. By the time she has redeemed him her better nature prevails, and she tearfully confesses her ploy. Since Anthony has come to love her as much as she loves him, no problem remains. The settings and Empire costumes of the 1820s in which the play unfolded contributed a certain charm to the story.

While an aging Sarah Bernhardt was noisily making one more of her farewell tours that was in truth no farewell, a much younger performer, for years America's favorite actress, quietly began her unpublicized farewell appearances. She was, of course, Maude Adams, and her vehicle was James M. Barrie's **A Kiss for Cinderella** (12-25-16, Empire). Miss Thing is a sweet, tiny drudge who earns a little money by cleaning for an artist and then spends that money on orphans she has adopted. Falling asleep on the doorstep, she dreams she is Cinderella and is to marry Prince Charming. That prince looks remarkably like the handsome policeman (Norman Trevor) who once threatened to arrest her for harboring her orphans. By the end of the evening she has won the policeman, if not a real prince. In an unwitting eulogy, Woollcott called the star "utterly winsome, so dauntless and gently pathetic that she almost breaks your heart." The play ran into the spring and toured.

The evening's other entry, Hulbert Footner's **Shirley Kaye** (12-25-16, Hudson), won few kudos, and but for the presence of Elsie Ferguson in the starring role it could never have kept going for eleven weeks. The *Herald* extolled her "colorful detail and delicate attention to her art." Shirley must force a flint-hearted businessman, T. J. Magen [read J. P. Morgan] (William Holden), who has ousted her father as president of a railway, to restore her father's fortune (she does this by buying up proxies in the businessman's railroad). She must also gain the affection of an avowed misogynist, John Rawson (Lee Baker), whom Magen would put in as her father's replacement (by marooning him with her on an island retreat). All this was set against a battle between old society and parvenues.

Two plays ushered in 1917. Both were backward looking. William Lindsey's blank-verse tragedy **Seremonda** (1-1-17, Criterion) starred Julia Arthur, whom critics lauded as "regal" and "queenly." They were less kind to Lindsey, an elderly Bostonian who was rumored to have paid for the production. Seremonda's groom is murdered at the altar by the vicious Count Raimon (Alphonz Ethier). He abducts her and forces her to wed him. While the count, under orders from the Church, is on a penitential pilgrimage to the Holy Land, Seremonda falls in love with his troubadour, Guilhem (Robert W. Frazer). On his return, Raimon becomes aware of the affair. He slays the poet and serves his heart to Seremonda for dinner. She commits suicide. In keeping with the superannuated nature of the play, its settings— including an oak forest and a magnificent room in a castle, with a view of a rockbound coast—were by the once admired Homer Emens, an advocate of meticulous scene painting rather than modern set design. The play survived for six weeks, five weeks longer than did its competitor.

That play was **Gamblers All** (1-1-17, Maxine Elliott's), by May Martindale, the daughter of the author of *Jim, the Penman*. It depicted the problems of a gambling-addicted woman wedded to a man opposed to gambling.

Three plays appeared the following Monday. The lone novelty was Horace Annesley Vachell's **The Lodger** (1-8-17, Maxine Elliott's), taken from the novel by Mrs. Belloc Lowndes. It had been seen in London as *Who Is He?*. The adaptation emphasized the comedy that ensues when a strange lodger (Lionel Atwill), actually a lord fleeing a broken romance, is suspected of being the killer who has been stalking young women in London.

The two revivals were A. E. Thomas's comedy *Her Husband's Wife* (5-9-10), presented at the Lyceum with Marie Tempest starred, and last year's surprise success, *The Merry Wives of Windsor,* with Thomas A. Wise repeating his Falstaff at the Park.

A preacher-turned-playwright, H. Austin Adams, was the author of **'Ception Shoals** (1-10-17, Princess). Adams's heroine was Eve, a girl reared in ignorance of the facts of life by her selfish Uncle Job (Henry Harmon) in a desolate lighthouse off the California coast. When a young, unmarried couple are stranded on a nearby shoal she swims to their rescue. The girl is pregnant, and her friend was rushing her to shore to deliver her child. The man (Charles Bryant) and Eve fall in love, and he promises to return. But Uncle Job intercepts a letter from him and writes back that Eve has died. When the man never reappears Eve kills her uncle and herself. Some critics observed that no girl in 1917 could be unaware of the facts of life. What astonished many reviewers was the performance of the girl who played Eve, Nazimova, an actress usually given to sultry roles. Her youthful innocence was remarkably convincing. She won applause when she emerged from her swim, in a bathing suit and dripping wet. But her change of style could not lure playgoers.

James Savery's **In for the Night** (1-11-17, Fulton) detailed the comic misadventures of a group of travelers stranded at an inn on the Boston Post Road (the same Boston Post Road on which the inn in *Mile-A-Minute Kendall* had been located). Savery was a graduate of George Pierce Baker's famous class and the writer of some Hasty Pudding shows, but that did not stop critics from savaging his farce.

February came roaring in with three hits. The first was Maurice V. Samuels's **The Wanderer** (2-1-17, Manhattan Opera House), a redaction of Wilhelm Schmidtbonn's *Der verlorene Sohn.* This saga of the prodigal son was given a huge, lavish mounting and a superb cast. William Elliott had the title role, Nance O'Neil was his mother, and James O'Neill, his father. Florence Reed played the siren; Charles Dalton, the elder brother; and Pedro de Cordoba, a prophet. The spectacle chalked up a fourteen-week stand at the mammoth auditorium.

Clare Kummer's second hit of the season was her pleasantly droll **A Successful Calamity** (2-5-17,

Booth). The *Tribune* observed that the young playwright "shows an ability to reach up to the heights of comedy where the laugh is tempered by just the shadow of a sob." Henry Wilton (William Gillette) is enormously wealthy. The money has made his young second wife, Emmie (Estelle Winwood), his daughter Marguerite (Ruth Findlay), and his son Eddie (Richard Barbee), irrepressible gadabouts. Henry himself is often dragged from one dull society affair to the next. He longs for "a quiet evening at home—dine with my family, perhaps play a game of cribbage and—go to bed." When he asks his butler (William Devereaux) why some people can lead unhurried lives, the butler states that the poor don't have money to spend and so must stay at home. That gives Henry an idea. He announces that he is bankrupt. To his surprise his family rallies to his support. Eddie, for the first time in his life, takes a job. And when he tells his new boss that his father is broke he inadvertently earns his father's firm $8,000,000. Marguerite ditches her querulous fiancé (Richard Sterling) and accepts the proposal of the modest, self-sacrificing Clarence Rivers (Roland Young), who is happy to have her marry him for his money. At first it appears that Emmie has run off with an artist and taken her jewels with her. But it turns out she has only gone to pawn them in order to help Henry. When Henry reveals the truth, the family agrees to spend more time together at home. The play was strengthened no end by the patrician Gillette, with his staccato delivery, his studied insouciance, and his matchless timing in what the *Herald,* apparently excepting only his Sherlock Holmes, referred to as "almost the best part he ever has had."

The longest run (172 performances) of February's hits went to Jane Cowl and Jane Murfin's **Lilac Time** (2-6-17, Republic). Its rather mushy story ("a butterfly of a plot," according to the *Herald)* was simplicity itself. Jeannine (Cowl) is a modest French villager. When some English officers are billeted in her family's home she falls in love with one of them, Lt. Philip Blythe (Orme Caldara), and he with her. He goes off to battle and is killed. As the British troops march by she stands, with her baby's garment in hand, by a window and tearfully waves to them. After America entered the war, reports tell of Cowl's changing the ending. Blythe was no longer killed, merely wounded.

The following evening brought in a new play and an old one. The novelty was Mark Swan's **If** (2-7-17, Fulton). In a small southern California town a new post office is opened to much celebration. But suddenly the Japanese in the town revolt. It quickly develops that they are part of a plan by Japan to conquer America. They even get as far as seizing San Francisco. But in the end the whole thing proves to be the dream of a man worried about America's lack of preparedness. The idea of Japan attacking America was so preposterous that the play was laughed away quickly.

The old play was *The Great Divide* (10-3-06), which Henry Miller, its original producer and star, produced and starred in again. Although many critics felt it had begun to show its age, most acknowledged its fundamental merits.

Johnny, Get Your Gun (2-12-17, Criterion) was a farce by Edmund Laurence Burke, retouched by Dorothy Donnelly. The play opens at a California movie studio, where a young actor, Johnny Wiggins (Louis Bennison), throws in the towel after being required to take too many painful pratfalls and pies in the face. His friend, Bert Whitney (Everett Butterfield), asks him to use his acting skills to help regain the affection of Bert's sweetheart, Jenet (Grace Valentine), who has fallen for the fortune-hunting Duke of No Moor (Echlin Gayer). Rushing to Long Island, Johnny not only sends the duke packing and reunites the lovers, but he forces a rapacious financier to return the moneys he has stolen from Jenet's family. Critic after critic predicted a bright future for Bennison, but he elected to serve in the army, and after the war he could never recapture his brief moment of celebrity.

The farce competed for first-nighters with a double bill of English plays. John Galsworthy's one-acter **The Little Man** (2-12-17, Maxine Elliott's) told of passengers of disparate nationalities in an Austrian railroad station. When a peasant woman with a baby needs help, only the American (Walter Jones) comes to her aid. It was followed by G. K. Chesterton's **Magic,** in which a conjurer (O. P. Heggie) teaches an atheist (Donald Gallaher) to respect religion. Cathleen Nesbitt had the romantic lead.

The next night also found an American play and an English one competing for attention. Since the American play was not a fully professional mounting, the English play, **The Morris Dance** (2-13-17, Little), corralled the major reviewers. Granville Barker's dramatization of Robert Louis Stevenson and Lloyd Osbourne's "The Wrong Box," corralled the major reviewers. It dealt with a man's attempts to see that his father wins a tontine. The American play was Elmer Rice's (still writing as Elmer Reizenstein) **The Iron Cross,** which was done at the Comedy Theatre by a mixed company of professionals and Columbia University students. It was an anti-war play, in which a soldier finds that his

wife has been seduced and had a child by an invader. At first he is bitter, but eventually he resigns himself to circumstances.

Fresh from his triumph as Falstaff, bulky, avuncular Thomas A. Wise, with his unctuous humor and deft facial comedy, provided the lion's share of fun in **Pals First** (2-26-17, Fulton), which Lee Wilson Dodd derived from the novel by Francis Perry Elliott. Wise's co-star was the debonair if stagey William Courtenay. Their first appearance came as two tramps, so hungry that when Danny (Courtenay) insists Dominie (Wise) must scrounge up some food, Dominie responds, "I'll just bite the dust." They find themselves at an old, largely shuttered southern mansion. Only the colored servants (still played by whites in blackface) are there, but they insist they recognize Danny as their master, Richard Castleman, who was traveling abroad to recruit his health. The two tramps decide to take advantage of the mistake and soon discover themselves in swell clothes, enjoying cognac and cigars after a marvelous chicken dinner. A neighbor (Albert Sackett) and Richard's fiancée (Janet Travers) are called in. They, too, insist that Danny is Richard, although they agree that Danny, cigar and snifter in hand, is virile and fun-loving whereas Richard was a prohibitionist and a ninny. Richard's mean, tricky cousin, Dr. Chilton (Lyster Chambers), arrives. He has news that Richard died aboard ship en route to Australia, and he furtively burns Richard's will, which leaves everything to Jean. A third tramp (Francis X. Conlon) appears and threatens to reveal that the men are escaped convicts. Danny's kindness dissuades the tramp from causing trouble, and the burnt scraps of the will that Danny has fished out of the fireplace allow him to humble Chilton. He admits that he is Richard, saying he changed places with the real Danny and, fed up with doctors, took to the road. He purposely saw to it that Chilton heard news of his supposed death to give Chilton enough rope to hang himself. He also confesses that Dominie, whom he had introduced as a preacher, has been a convict—a Harvard graduate gone wrong. Richard and Jean prepare to wed, and so do Dominie and the nice little old lady (Auriol Lee) who is Jean's aunt. The comedy was one of the season's lesser hits.

Having dropped *Paganini*, George Arliss returned the same evening to the Knickerbocker in a revival of Barrie's *The Professor's Love Story* (12-19-92).

Maude Fulton, a popular song-and-dance woman in vaudeville, was both author and star of **The Brat** (3-5-17, Harris). She played a girl who has just lost her job in the chorus at the Hippodrome and has been hauled into court for begging. A best-selling author, the haughty, self-serving Macmillan Forrester (Lewis S. Stone), offers to take her into his home, since he is writing a book called *The Brat* and believes she would make a perfect model. The girl rescues Macmillan's younger brother, Steven (Edmund Lowe), from the snares of alcoholism. When Macmillan, having no further need for her, tells her to leave his house, she and Steven decide to wed and to try a new life in the West. The moon-faced, heavy-featured star naturally found occasion for a little song and dance. All of which no doubt helped the comedy chalk up a four-month run.

On the same evening, E. H. Sothern was author, but not star, of **Stranger than Fiction** (3-5-17, Garrick). After all, he had already announced his retirement as an actor, insisting that hereafter he would only write, direct, or produce. The play reminded many critics of *The Big Idea* (11-16-14), which they had loved and the public had rejected. This time reviewers and playgoers alike said no. Sothern's story began when an odd assortment of people are forced to take refuge from a London fog in the home of a dramatist who uses what they tell him of themselves and what he discerns between the lines to write a play about all of them—four characters who have found their author.

A beautiful mounting and Fay Bainter helped Benrimo and Harrison Rhodes's **The Willow Tree** (3-6-17, Cohan and Harris) inch across the hundred-performance mark that, in 1917, usually meant a show had recouped its investment. Playgoers entering the theatre saw the stage apron lined with Oriental flowers and, instead of the theatre's usual dark red curtain, a six-part Japanese screen filling the proscenium opening. This screen-cum-curtain slid aside to tell the sad-happy tale of Edward Hamilton (Shelley Hull), who has left London after breaking up with Mary Temple, a girl whose financial demands were beyond Edward's means. He leads a simple, lonely life in Japan until a woodcarver sells him a statue of a beautiful princess carved from a willow tree. The statue (Bainter) comes to life, and when Edward tells the princess that she can now behold the world, she replies, "I most charmingly thank you for the world." The two fall in love, even though Edward is still haunted by his visions of Mary (also Bainter). However, the war in Europe breaks out and Edward is called home to join the army. He is reluctant to leave, so the princess turns herself back into wood in order that he can fulfill his obligations. Perhaps Mary will look at him then in a different light.

Somerset Maugham's biting dissection of rich American expatriates who have bought their way into English society, **Our Betters** (3-12-17, Hudson), was another late season success. Chrystal Herne and Rose Coghlan were outstanding as two of the more grasping Americans with English titles. John Flood, Fritz Williams, and Ronald Squire were the most praised of the male contingent. Advertisements promising "The Most Shocking Comedy in New York" no doubt spurred ticket sales. But on the road, bad business quickly forced the comedy to close, with *Variety* reporting that Chicagoans perceived it as "too dirty." The play began a succession of importations, none of which matched its New York popularity.

John Galsworthy's **The Fugitive** (3-19-17, 39th St.) spotlighted the downfall of an unhappy wife (Emily Stevens), who leaves her decent but dull husband (Edward Emery) and whose subsequent search for happiness drags her ever lower until she kills herself.

In February, while playing in *The Yellow Jacket,* Charles Coburn and his fellow actors had offered a matinee performance of Molière's *The Imaginary Invalid.* It was so well received that when the other play closed it was brought into the Liberty for a week beginning on the 19th. Tradesheets disagree on whether there was sufficient demand to have extended the stay.

Another unhappy wife (Ann Andrews) who walks out on an unsatisfactory marriage and winds up a suicide was the central figure in Ossip Dymow's Russian drama, **Nju** [pronounced "new"] (3-22-17, Bandbox). Joseph Urban and the Polish director, Richard Ordynski, were co-producers, but Urban, so accustomed to adulation, found himself the target of critical barbs. Reviewers did not mind the Gordon Craig–like simplicity of the minimal screens and flats, but they strenuously protested Urban's chiaroscuro lighting, which illuminated settings but left players in darkness.

London's prolific Horace Annesley Vachell once again disappointed New York, this time with his **The Case of Lady Camber** (3-26-17, Lyceum). Lady Camber (Mary Boland), a vulgar former music hall entertainer, whom Lord Camber (H. E. Herbert) married on the rebound from his rejection by Esther Yorke (Sydney Shields), dies suddenly while in the care of Esther, who is a nurse. Esther is suspected of murder but eventually cleared. She still doesn't think much of Camber, who is seen as a rotter, so she weds the doctor (Lyn Harding) she works for.

The string of importations came to an end when J. Hartley Manners's **Out There** (3-27-17, Globe) opened. Of course, Manners had been born in England, and much of his play was set there. But it was an American play, even if its star, Manners's

American-born wife, Laurette Taylor, had to assume a cockney accent. She played 'aunted Annie, a warmhearted drudge who is determined to do her bit at the front. "If I go, will you go?" she asks all comers. Her family, especially her cynical sister, Lizzie (Lynn Fontanne), sneer at her. So she sews herself a nurse's uniform in secret. She is not the best of seamstresses; the red cross on her uniform is distinctly askew. At an English hospital in France, she scrubs floors and does other menial jobs before she is allowed to nurse. Then she returns to Trafalgar Square to help recruit more soldiers. Just how good a play it was is moot, and even those critics who admired it agreed the last act, in the square, was anticlimactic. But Manners, Taylor, and their producer, George Tyler, had a remarkable bit of good luck, since immediately after the play opened, America entered the war. Following a highly profitable ten-week run, the show was recast with a collection of major stars (Lynn Fontanne, still not well known, was reduced to an understudy) and taken on a twenty-three-stop tour, playing each time in the largest available venue. It earned nearly $700,000 for the Red Cross.

While the Red Cross was viewed as a worthwhile charity, the *Medical Review of Reviews* was chastized for the second time in recent seasons for entering waters in which, at least according to Broadway critics, it had no business. The publication on this occasion had sponsored a special mounting of Frank Wedekind's *Frühlings Erwachen* under the title **The Awakening of Spring** (3-30-17, 39th St.). The usually lenient *Herald* was outraged, as were most reviewers who sat in judgment on this explicit look at first love, noting sourly, "Adolescent sexual perversions of unmentionable nature are discussed and depicted." The discussions and depictions were hurried away after a single performance.

Between this opening and the next, America's patience ran out. The final straw came in March when German U-boats sank several American ships. On April 2, at just about the moment playgoers watched theatre lights dim and curtains rise, Woodrow Wilson went before Congress to ask for a declaration of war. The House and Senate acquiesced, and on the 6th Wilson signed the declaration of war. World War I had come home to Americans.

If Americans heard nothing wrong when American players attempted British accents in many Broadway shows, American playgoers also saw nothing wrong when whites blacked up to play blacks. On April 5, the rarely used Garden Theatre was relit to offer three plays of black life by a white poet, Ridgely Torrence: **The Rider of Dreams, Simon the Cyrenian,**

and one play that had been done before, *Granny Maumee* (3-30-14). All three were performed by blacks. In the first of the novelties a lazy, daydreaming husband is nearly bilked out of his life savings by a sharper—the very sort of plot used comically by so many black musicals. In the second, the crossbearer, whom painters had often depicted as a black man and whom Torrence portrayed as an African revolutionary, is shown confronting death. Read today, Torrence's black speech seems no different from the speech of blacks in other plays of the period. Thus the daydreamer's wife is furious that her husband has gone to a store and charged a guitar which he knows he cannot pay for. He responds, "I'm willin' fer to be treat dat way ef dey can do hit. I says to everybody, 'What's mine's youahs—ef you can git it an' what's youah's is mine ef I kin git hit an' I'm a-goin' ter try mighty ha'd to git hit.' " Although some critics suggested there should be no reason why black actors could not play blacks as well as whites could, most agreed that these performers were hardly up to the task. One exception was Louis Sherwin of the *Globe* who noted, "There is in the race a lack of self-consciousness that gives them a greater natural aptitude for acting." The negative criticism irked many who felt that black players should be judged by special, more lenient considerations (a cry still heard eighty years later). This, in turn, angered Woollcott, who devoted a whole Sunday article to the productions and their problems. He attacked "the misguided notion that an oppressed people was being mysteriously served by the bad performance. . . . There is only one true standard, and that is the standard which asks for each separate play the best possible performance, the perfect performance so far as it is humanly obtainable." The productions, directed by Robert Edmond Jones, struggled along for three weeks.

An even shorter life (about seventeen matinee performances) was in store for Padraic Colum and Mrs. F. E. Washburn-Freund's **Grasshopper** (4-7-17, Garrick), taken from a play by Eduard Keyserling and telling of an unloved foundling who is prepared to give up her life to save another woman. What small success it had was credit to a largely unknown actress, Eileen Huban, for whom the *Dramatic Mirror* predicted overnight fame on the basis of her "vividness, poignancy and sympathy."

Four plays opened on the second Monday in April. David Belasco suffered one of his shortest-lived flops with John Meehan's **The Very Minute** (4-9-17, Belasco), which described the struggles and very-last-minute redemption of a dipsomaniac (Arnold Daly) who hopes to succeed his doting, invalid father (Forrest Robinson) as president of a small college.

Frank Mandel's **Bosom Friends** (4-9-17, Liberty) fared a little better thanks to Lew Fields and a remarkable supporting cast. Fields, still clinging to his "Dutch" dialect but discarding his most expected comic routines, was a widowed schoolteacher, Sebastian Krug, cosseted by his daughter, Gretel (Irene Fenwick), and his spinster sister, Anna (Mathilde Cottrelly). His closest friend is Dr. Aaron Mather (John Mason). They lead an idyllic life until Mather's son, Henry (Richard Bennett), goes off to New York and is nearly ruined by a crooked patent attorney. Naturally, everything is resolved happily by eleven o'clock. The rest of the cast consisted of Helen Ware as an adventuress, Helen Lowell as a busybody, and Willis Sweatnam, in blackface as usual, as a loyal darky.

Critics' rapidly growing disillusionment with the pretentious, self-glorifying Butler Davenport gave his **Difference in Gods** (4-9-17, Bramhall) short shrift and unkind comments. As usual Davenport took the leading role, this time of Amzi Barton, a man who is a pious churchgoer and a brutal father and husband. He repents his ways after a faith healer, talking to Amzi's deathly sick daughter (Jane Winslow) on the telephone, cures her. To tell this essentially thin story Davenport took four acts, each set in a different decade—1887, 1897, 1907, and 1917.

At the Knickerbocker, George Arliss revived *Disraeli* (9-18-11) for a six-week stand.

The season's second dramatized Thackeray was Michael Morton's reworking of *The Newcomes* as **Colonel Newcome** (4-10-17, New Amsterdam). The change of title hinted that the adaptation was designed as a tour de force for its star, Sir Herbert Beerbohm Tree. The range and depth of his characterization, at once austere and lovable, delighted most reviewers.

Many critics were also thrilled by Eugene Walter's **The Knife** (4-12-17, Bijou), but the unpleasantness of the subject and the lateness of the season conspired to limit its public appeal. Kate Tarleton (Olive Wyndham) goes to New York to buy her trousseau and disappears. Her fiancé, Dr. Manning (Robert Edeson), heads to the big city to find her. He discovers her drugged in the den of some white slavers. With the help of friends he forces the miscreants to become guinea pigs in an experiment. He injects them with germs of an incurable disease, then injects them with a serum he believes will cure the illness. One of the victims dies, but the other survives—proving Manning is on the right track. The law decides his experiments are justified, especially in light of the low-life on whom he experimented. The tiny Bijou on 45th Street was Broadway's newest playhouse. Its opening meant that just under fifty attractions were being offered at New York's first-class houses.

Apart from the brief return of last season's merry wives, New York had seen no Shakespeare all this semester. The half year devoted to the so-called Shakespeare Tercentenary—that first half of 1916— apparently had exhausted interest. *Life* confirmed this when, in noting the return of Robert B. Mantell and his repertory to the 44th Street Theatre on the 16th, it pontificated, "Shakespeare has again become *persona non grata* in New York." Mantell offered his Shylock, Hamlet, Macbeth, Lear, Richard III, and Brutus, as well as assuming the title role in Bulwer-Lytton's *Richelieu*. Whatever critics thought of Shakespeare, they held reservations about Mantell. Most felt that he and his mountings were better suited to barnstorming in the backwaters, but the most tolerant or kinder aisle-sitters picked and chose among his interpretations—many finding something to praise in his doddering Lear.

These same critics were not deterred from appreciating **Peter Ibbetson** (4-17-17, Republic) by a disastrous opening night—a piece of scenery fell ("disclosing shirt-sleeved stage hands, guy ropes and brick walls"), a drop refused to drop, a set change meant to be silent became noisy. The late John N. Raphael had made his dramatization of George du Maurier's famous novel many years earlier, but until now the play had seen the footlights only in a single charity performance in London. Ibbetson (John Barrymore) is a man who laments, "I have no talent for making new friends, but oh, such a genius for remembering old ones!" He has need of memories, for his life in mid-nineteenth-century England is unhappy. Since his mother's death, he has been raised by a cruel uncle (Lionel Barrymore), but on learning that the uncle is his natural father, Peter kills him. He is sentenced to death until his old friends arrange to have his sentence commuted. Throughout all this Peter escapes his distressing real world by dreaming of his childhood in a long-bygone Paris. When he was young, his little girlfriend, Mimsey (Madge Evans), taught him how to "dream true," and these dreams have helped him keep his sanity. Especially comforting have been the dreams in which the grown Mimsey, the Duchess of Towers (Constance Collier), appears. It is of her and her consoling words that he dreams just before he dies after his long imprisonment. The cast enjoyed lavish praise, although inevitably the younger Barrymore stole the limelight. Hornblow wrote glowingly of a performance, "Instinct with poetical reserve, gracious humanity and deep feeling." The play remained in New York until the heat closed it after nine weeks, but Barrymore toured with it all of the following season. Perhaps surprisingly, the drama was produced by the Messrs. Shubert, who were known primarily as theatre owners and mounters of musical shows.

· · ·

Lee Shubert [probably initially Levi] (1875?-1953), **Samuel S. Shubert** (1877?-1905), and **J**[acob] **J. Shubert** (1879?-1963), whose original family name may have been Szemanski, were born in Neustadt, in East Prussia. (These new birthdates and birthplace were unearthed by the head of the Shubert Archives, Brooks McNamara.) Their father was an unsuccessful and alcoholic peddler who settled his family in Syracuse, where Lee and Sam obtained jobs in local theatres. Sam's purchase of the touring rights to Charles Hoyt's *A Texas Steer* set the brothers on course. By 1900, leasing the Herald Square Theatre, they were ready to tackle New York and the infamous Syndicate. Their booking of *Arizona* put them on a reasonably solid footing. Their first production, *The Brixton Burglary* (1901), flopped, but they met with marked success when they turned to musicals. Some of their early nonmusical offerings were *Heidelberg* (1902), *Widowers' Houses* (1907), *The Passing of the 3rd Floor Back* (1909), and *The City* (1909).

· · ·

For all practical purposes *Peter Ibbetson* closed out the current season. May saw only three entries: a revival of *Ghosts* (1-5-94), done by the Washington Square Players at the Comedy on the 7th, with José Ruben as Oswald and Mary Shaw as Mrs. Alving; another revival, *Get-Rich-Quick Wallingford* (9-19-10), at the Cohan on the same night; and a bill of James M. Barrie one-acters—**The New Word, Old Friends,** and **The Old Lady Shows Her Medals**—at the Empire on the 14th. The first of these told how a father and mother, each in his or her own way, says good-bye to a son heading off to war. In *Old Friends* a reformed alcoholic discovers his daughter has taken to drink. *The Old Lady Shows Her Medals,* the only one of the trio to have a prolonged life in front of the footlights, centered on a familyless charlady who "adopts" a soldier she has read about in order to claim a vested interest in the war. They meet briefly and happily, and after his death she has his awards to display to her acquaintances. When business proved sluggish *Old Friends* was dropped, and *The Twelve-Pound Look* (2-13-11) was substituted, with Ethel Barrymore again in the lead.

1917–1918

Although relatively few plays dealt with the war, which America had joined, the war seriously affected Broadway. A number of actors and authors enlisted and temporarily or, in a few cases, permanently disappeared from the theatrical scene. Those left behind found themselves working overtime, not merely doing their accustomed theatrical chores but heading recruitment and war bond rallies, busily knitting for the troops, or rushing to nearby army camps to entertain trainees. Of course, the extra work often resulted in extra publicity.

Shortages led to a small inflation, and these increased costs were soon reflected in ticket prices, which had long been stable and now began to inch up. Producers tried for a $2.50 or $3.00 top. Despite their own efforts to raise prices, producers howled when Congress imposed a war tax that added another 10 percent to prices. Broadway was sure it discerned a playgoer rebellion when a number of shows closed almost immediately after they opened, and by January show after show was cutting its ticket prices. William A. Brady, always an alarmist, complained: "We are on the edge of a still panic, and in these circumstances it is only natural that the theatre as a luxury should be among the first to suffer. . . . Business, if anything, will become worse as the war continues and taxes increase."

Calmer heads noted that the better shows had no trouble attracting audiences and that their advance sales were some of the largest in memory. One problem that they did acknowledge was that Broadway had built too many new theatres too quickly. To fill their stages, theatre owners and producers were hustling in mediocrities that should never have been mounted. These were the shows the public—rightly—was rejecting.

That same public, consciously or subconsciously beset with worries about the war, also found theatregoing a little gloomier when authories, claiming they wished to avoid fuel shortages but probably merely trying to suggest that stay-at-homes must make sacrifices, ordered dim-outs of marquees. Yet for all the external difficulties, Broadway had a good enough season. And a busy one. According to *Variety* Broadway welcomed a record 156 productions, of which an even hundred were new plays and eighteen were revivals (the rest were musicals). Other tradesheets and newspapers gave slightly varying figures but told essentially the same story.

August alone brought in a dozen straight plays. The first was Al Woods's production of May Tully's farce **Mary's Ankle** (8-6-17, Bijou). Young Dr. Hampton (Bert Lytell) and his buddies, none of whom has yet hit paydirt in his career, decide to swell their bank accounts by announcing that Hampton is to be married and then pawning the gifts that pour in. They also announce that the bride-to-be is Mary Jane Smith of 201 Main Street, Elizabeth, N.J., a name and address they have invented. Sure enough a Mary Jane Smith (Irene Fenwick) of 201 Main Street, Elizabeth, comes to the doctor's office to unleash an evening of complications. Many of the gifts prove unpawnable; a passel of puzzled relatives is heard from. Not until Hampton and Mary Jane are snuggled side by side on deck chairs of a Bermuda-bound liner is a happy ending achieved. Walter Jones as a rich uncle and Zelda Sears as a noisy frump added to the fun. The *Tribune* suggested the farce might suffice for August but would "never do in September." Actually it ran into October, then enjoyed a long, profitable tour.

Edward Peple's **Friend Martha** (8-7-17, Booth) had no such good fortune. Set in Philadelphia, it told of a Quaker girl (Oza Waldrop) who refuses to marry the aging widower her father (Edmund Breese) has selected for her and instead elopes with a Main Line socialite (R. Leigh Denny). Returned home and put on trial by her co-religionists, she wins her way thanks to help from her mother (Lizzie Hudson Collier) and her young man.

William Le Baron's **The Very Idea** (8-9-17, Astor) found its fun at the expense of a contemporary fad, Eugenics. Gilbert (Ernest Truex) and Edith Goodhue (Dorothy Mackaye) are a childless young couple who decide they will adopt a baby. Dorothy's brother, Alan (Richard Bennett), a firm believer in Eugenics, warns them they cannot be certain how well the baby will turn out. He suggests they select another couple to have the child for them. His own chauffeur, tall, handsome, virile Joe Garvin (William P. Carleton), and the Goodhues' well-figured, attractive maid, Nora (Florence Oakley), are chosen. Never mind that the pair tower over the tiny Goodhues. But Joe and Nora fall in love and refuse an offer of $15,000 for their child. Just when all seems lost, Edith returns from a visit to her doctor with good news for Gilbert. The mustached Truex, sometimes ridiculously meek, sometimes absurdly determined, and, surprisingly, Bennett as his know-it-all brother-in-law supplied the best performances. Of Truex, the *Dramatic Mirror* observed, "He puts a laugh into the most obvious lines and what in other mouths might seem rough, in his seems, if not musical and low, at least snappy and amusing." The same review noted that Bennett was "so convincing . . . it was difficult to remember not to take him seriously." Critics were torn between questioning the morality of the farce and confessing how funny much of it was. The *Evening World* praised it as "delightful." Even naysayers qualified their disdain, with the *Evening Sun* suggesting the play would be "thoroughly enjoyable only to such persons as have learned to laugh not wisely but too well." There were enough such persons to give the farce a twenty-week run.

If one modern phenomenon, Eugenics, provided the basis for *The Very Idea,* another, the flickers, provided the solution in Victor Mapes's **The Lassoo** (8-13-17, Lyceum). In his search for sufficient income to support his spendthrift wife, Mildred (Phoebe Foster), Harold Brown (Shelley Hull), a young writer, decides to turn his novel into a play. Before long Mildred is jealous of Harold's leading lady (Blanche Duval). She also indulges in her own flirtation. But by eleven o'clock husband and wife have come to appreciate each other, thanks in no small measure to Harold's success in writing silent screenplays. Hull and Miss Foster had won garlands for their acting in *The Cinderella Man* (1-17-16), but even their accomplished playing here could not help a dull play.

Nor could a somewhat novel prologue save Abraham Schomer's **The Inner Man** (8-13-17, Lyric). A meeting of the Society for the Reformation of Criminals is in progress. The officers are at the dais, which is far downstage, and it is obvious all the other people attending the meeting are in front of them, in the auditorium. From seats in various parts of the theatre people rise to offer comments and suggestions. The major suggestion is to take as hardened a criminal as possible and, by putting him in charge of a charity to help other criminals reform, bring about his own reformation. The notorious "Devil Dick" Bolger (Wilton Lackaye) is selected. Despite some ominous if tentative lapses, Bolger does reform and is returned to the family he long ago deserted.

Another interesting opening scene got Jane Cowl and Jane Murfin's **Daybreak** (8-14-17, Harris) off to a good start. The scene was done entirely in pantomime. At dawn a woman (Blanche Yurka) sneaks back into her home. She does not realize that her drunken, brutal husband (Frederick Truesdell) has observed her. It turns out she is returning from a furtive visit to their young child, whose birth she has kept secret from him and whom she has farmed out so that it can be raised away from its father's baleful influences. The husband, who has a reputation of killing or crippling animals and people he dislikes, determines to learn the truth—believing his wife is having an affair. He finally is shot to death by the husband of a woman he had violated. The wife is free to marry a better man. Although the *World* condemned the play's "completely preposterous, illogical plot," it acknowledged that it was "so excellently constructed . . . that the situations pass for their face value."

Matters were happier at the season's first smash hit, the third in Montague Glass's Potash and Perlmutter series, **Business Before Pleasure** (8-15-17, Eltinge), this one written in collaboration with Jules Eckert Goodman. Despite the success of their own garment business, Abe Potash (Barney Bernard) and Mawruss Perlmutter (Alexander Carr) decide to become even richer by going into "fillums." After all, William Fox had been a furrier and Jesse Lasky a tailor. They soon discover that they have leaped "out of the frying pan into the hot water." Before they can write "The End" to their film-making they have starred their own wives, Rosie (Mathilde Cottrelly) and Ruth (Lottie Kendall), in a flicker and have had to deal with a would-be siren, Rita Sismondi (Clara Joel), who is backed by a shady banker. With Alexander Woollcott gone off to war, John Corbin had become the *Times* critic. He prophesied, "When the annals of the American drama are written it will perhaps be found that these plays of Yiddish life are the historical descendants of the Hoyt farces." The comedy ran just short of a year.

Some even more ecstatic notices failed to draw an audience to **The Deluge** (8-20-17, Hudson), which Frank Allen Americanized from a Swedish drama by Henning Berger. Since Berger had spent considerable time in America, how much rewriting the play required is uncertain. Allen's version was set in a "sumptuously appointed saloon" in a large western city. A stock ticker in the mahogany-paneled room suggests the clientele the owner hopes to attract. These include a grandiloquent shyster, O'Neill (Henry E. Dixey), a bitter, snarling promoter, Frazier (Robert McWade), and another speculating businessman, Adams (Frederick Perry). They are regulars at the bar but today have come there to escape a violent storm, which threatens to burst a nearby dam and flood the city. Frazier growls, "I wish the river'd come along and drown the whole bunch—Adams and O'Neill in particular." Among the other people who have come in for shelter are a young Swede (Edward G. Robinson), a vaudevillian (William Dick), and a streetwalker, Sadie (Pauline Lord), whom Adams once had loved but whom he

had jilted in order to marry an heiress. Seemingly trapped and doomed, the patrons set aside their meanness and self-serving, but when the threat proves to have been exaggerated the old ways return. Only Sadie, long resigned to loving and losing, is unaffected. She decides to leave town. The play closed after two weeks of no business, but its producer, the high-minded Arthur Hopkins, stored away the scenery, resolving to revive it at a later date. By the time he did, Pauline Lord had become a star, playing a girl all too familiar with low bars, in the Hopkins production of a drama by another O'Neill.

Two smash hits followed hard on Hopkins's disappointment. Charles Guerin and Max Marcin's **Eyes of Youth** (8-22-17, Maxine Elliott's) focused on Gina Ashling (Marjorie Rambeau). Her father's reduced circumstances drive Gina to visit a yogi (Macey Harlam), who gazes into a crystal ball and reveals several paths she may take. In the first Gina becomes a schoolteacher only to be fired by her school board and deserted by a two-timing lover. Path two finds her a great prima donna embroiled in the mean, duplicitous world of high art. A third choice has her marry a rich man, who divorces her on trumped-up evidence and drives her to drugs. The yogi cannot tell her of one final road, but she elects to take it as her only hope. Since the play was billed as a comedy-drama, audiences could assume her choice was wise. Hailed by the *World* as "brimful of human interest," the New York production remained in town a full year. Miss Rambeau was a beautiful if "stagey" actress, but she was not necessary to the play. Thus, Alma Tell was lauded as the lead of one of the show's many road companies.

Harry James Smith's **A Tailor-Made Man** (8-27-17, Cohan and Harris) ran just two weeks less. John Paul Bart (Grant Mitchell) is a lowly assistant in a tailor's shop, but his clothes are dapper, if a bit threadbare, and he is given to airs. Indeed he looks upon himself as a silk purse who is treated like a sow's ear. He has read the manuscript written by Dr. Sonntag (Theodore Friebus), the nasty fiancé of Tanya Huber (Helen MacKellar), who is the daughter of the tailor (Gus Weinberg), and concludes that by spouting its pro-property sentiments he can make his way in the world of high society and high finance. To this end he swipes a customer's evening clothes and crashes a gala party. The guests are the sort who attend a dinner, then rush off to watch one act of an opera, then scurry to a ball. One lady who sat doggedly through two acts of an opera assures her hostess that Caruso was in fine voice—"clear as a phonograph record." John Paul's winning personal ity, his glibness, and his quickness with half-truths gain him immediate acceptance. Most important, he catches the attention of the great financier, Abraham Nathan (Frank Burbeck). At the start, Nathan dismisses John Paul's ardent speechifying as "wonderful Cockadoodalum." John Paul agrees it is but insists "the most wonderful thing about it all is, it'll *go!* It'll *work.*" The charmed Nathan offers him employment. As John Paul and Nathan head off to dinner, John Paul avoids being exposed by another tailor's assistant who moonlights as a waiter at the party, slipping him a $50 bill he has found in the pocket of the appropriated suit. Before long he is calling many of the shots for Nathan's enterprises, even bamboozling some tough union leaders into canceling a strike. But once again he is threatened with exposure, this time by Sonntag, whom he has made his secretary and who resents his attentions to Tanya. He decides his best course is to write his own exposé by sending his true story to the newspapers. He returns humbly to the tailor shop, where virtually everyone is prepared to reject him until Nathan shows up, tells him how much he admires his pluck, and offers him $75,000 to return to his employ. He is also rewarded with the hand of Tanya, who has remained his loyal admirer. The comedy was based loosely on Gábor Drégely's *A szerencse fia* (The Son of Fortune) but was, as *Current Opinion* noted, "saturated with Americanism." Indeed Louis Bliss Gillet, writing in the *Evening Post,* observed, "When you come to think of it, all John Paul's overweening self-importance, his imperturbable *savoir faire,* his monstrous cheek, grow out of certain qualities of youth, of American youth in particular—ambition, energy, confidence." Grant Mitchell, a short, balding man who bore a remarkable resemblance to another future star, James Cagney, garnered unanimous praise for a subtle, telling performance with his thoughts always "peeping out at odd corners of [his] countenance before a word was spoken."

Another new comedy was not welcomed, although its author and star was immensely popular. **This Way Out** (8-30-17, Cohan), which Frank Craven theatricalized from a magazine story by J. U. Geisy and Octavus Roy Cohen, told of the misadventures of Joe Franklin (Craven), a practical joker whose jokes regularly misfire. No way deterred, Joe answers an ad for a husband but signs the name of a friend who has just married a blazingly jealous girl. When the advertiser (Grace Goodall) appears, Joe must pretend he is his own friend.

But New Yorkers and New York critics, always faddists eager to wave away the past, were no kinder

to George Broadhurst's *What Happened to Jones* (8-30-97), deeming it sadly old hat when it opened at the 48th Street Theatre exactly twenty years to the night after its premiere. It survived less than two weeks.

September began with a flourish when Bernhardt came into the Knickerbocker on the 1st, bringing with her the same repertory that she had offered last season. This time she had no cold, and critics once more were jubilant about her acting and her silvery voice. Advertisements told half the truth. Those that said that this was her "Farewell Tour" were correct, but those claiming these were her "Farewell Appearances" were not, for later in the season New Yorkers had a final chance to see the aging luminary on the bill at the Palace.

Two nights later first-nighters enjoyed an All-American opening. Even before critics could rush to their typewriters to evaluate Booth Tarkington and Julian Street's **The Country Cousin** (9-3-17, Gaiety), former president Teddy Roosevelt rose in his box after the performance and assured his fellow playgoers they had enjoyed a "first-class American play." More professional critics confessed to reservations but also liked the comedy. The play begins in a home in a small Ohio town. The home is comfortable but unfashionable, with nondescript Eastlake furnishings—"no 'Colonial'; no wicker; no 'Missions.' " Because Mrs. Howitt (Julia Stuart) has learned the husband who divorced her when their daughter, Eleanor, was a baby is in town, she has asked Eleanor's trustworthy country cousin, Nancy Price (Alexandra Carlisle), to come to prevent trouble. To her dismay Nancy says the grown Eleanor (Marion Coakley) has every right to go east and spend some time with her father (Arthur Forrest). She promises to go east herself if trouble brews. Eleanor, using her own money, rents a summer home by the seashore where her father and snobbish, conniving stepmother (Clara Blandick) entertain their snooty friends. They hope to marry Eleanor off to George Tewsberry Reynolds III (Eugene O'Brien), an aimless, supercilious young man with a put-on English accent. Getting wind of what is happening, Eleanor's mother dispatches Nancy to rescue her. When she arrives carrying a wicker suitcase, George sneers that people who carry wicker luggage are the same people who "drive in things called surreys—with fringe round the top—and they have engravings of Washington crossing the Delaware in what they call the 'sitting-room.' " Her father and his friends have convinced Eleanor that a marriage need not be made for love. Nancy compares George with the blustery, determined young man who has been courting her back home and who is certain he will become a famous politician and sire a long line of great men: "Sam means to be an ancestor; George the Third's content to be a descendant." In time Nancy succeeds in opening Eleanor's eyes to the unprincipled, rapacious crowd she has fallen into. She even convinces George he ought to do something with his life—like enlist and help defend his country. Sam (Donald Gallaher) arrives to take Eleanor back to Ohio, and Nancy implies she is willing to wait for a reformed George to serve out his enlistment. The comedy ran four months, then toured. One interesting sidelight is that Gallaher had been playing one of Gina's suitor's two weeks earlier at the opening of *Eyes of Youth.* In this fluid Broadway, plays changed theatres with what today seems amazing frequency, and players jumped from role to role.

One player who did not jump from role to role jumped instead from Australia to New York, hoping to repeat his success in Theodore Burt Sayre's **Lucky O'Shea** (9-3-17, 39th St.). The actor was Allen Doone, and his O'Shea was an Irishman, serving in Napoleon's army. Disguised as a gypsy while on a spy mission, he is captured by the Prussians and forcibly married to another prisoner, an Irish girl (Edna Keeley), whose father is also serving with the French. At first the girl is a reluctant bride, but O'Shea wins her over with his goodness and bravery and, in the tradition of so many older plays of Irish life, by raising his tenor voice in song. Unluckily for him, O'Shea could not win over New Yorkers.

The same evening brought in a third play, which is now forgotten but which had the longest run of any of the evening's openings—twenty weeks. John Hunter Booth's **The Masquerader** (9-3-17, Lyric) was a dramatization of Katherine Cecil Thurston's novel. Guy Bates Post assumed the dual roles of John Chilicote, a member of Parliament slowly destroying his life with drugs and philandering, and John Loder, his look-alike cousin, who is a struggling writer. The men change places. Loder, now posing as Chilicote, moves on to a successful political career and saves "his" marriage, while the real Chilicote dies of an overdose of morphine.

De Luxe Annie (9-4-17, Booth), Edward Clark's adaptation of Scammon Lockwood's *Saturday Evening Post* short story, dealt with a confusion of identities—of a different sort. Using the flashback device popularized by *On Trial,* the play opens (and ends) in a Pullman car where a doctor is telling fellow travelers about an interesting case. It concerns a notorious swindler, De Luxe Annie (Jane Grey), who suddenly came to the police's attention working with a long-known crook, Jimmie Fitzpatrick (Vincent Serrano). Detectives on her trail are puzzled by the unhappiness and disgust she has been known to admit. They soon learn that she is actually the thoroughly decent wife of a respected citizen and that she developed amnesia after a head injury. Fitzpatrick has taken advantage of her condition to enlist her support. An operation restores her health and her good name. Made plausible by fine acting, the drama ran four months.

A much better play, made especially pleasurable by an up-and-coming young actress, ran more than nine months. The curtain of George Middleton and Guy Bolton's charmer of a comedy, **Polly with a Past** (9-6-17, Belasco), rises to disclose the swank bachelor digs shared by Harry Richardson (Cyril Scott) and Clay Collum (George Stuart Christie). The sitting room is "a harmony in blue" since Clay, a not at all unmanly interior decorator, redoes it every year or two. Both men are rich society figures, and they are visited by their friend, Rex Van Zile (Herbert Yost), downcast at the refusal of Myrtle Davis (Ann Meridith) to reciprocate his affections. Harry and Clay have a beautiful new maid, Polly Shannon (Ina Claire). She has come to New York from East Gilead, Ohio, where her father is a minister. She hopes to earn enough money to become a singer. Overhearing Rex's problem, she suggests the best way for him to win Myrtle is to make her jealous by falling for another, more exotic woman. The men seize on her idea. Since Polly's mother was French and Polly speaks French fluently, they decide she could pose as a world-famous French seductress. Swaddling her in some of Clay's fabric samples and plopping down a feathery lampshade on her head, they agree she could look the part. They choose the name Paulette Bady. (Reviewers, not having access to the printed text, spelled the name Baudy or Bawdy, suggesting how it was pronounced in performance). Clay uses his newspaper connections to spread stories about her. She arrives in a beautiful, shockingly low-cut dress at the Van Zile estate. The Van Zile family and their friends are nonplussed. Polly's cover is nearly blown several times. In one instance a derelict given work by the publicly charitable Myrtle recognizes the supposed Paulette as his old friend from East Gilead. A famous pianist who, newspapers reported, committed suicide after being spurned by Paulette appears on the scene demanding to see her. Myrtle's petulant reactions to all the goings on convince Rex he would prefer to marry Polly.

Although many critics enjoyed the play, with

reservations, they felt its shortcomings were cleverly glossed over by Ina Claire. Arthur Hornblow of *Theatre* observed that she "walks through the diverting scenes with a self-assurance that is as charming as her naturalness. Her affectations and sinuosity . . . are a delightful make-believe."

. . .

Ina Claire [Fagan] (1892–1985) was born in Washington, D.C., and made her debut as a singing mimic in vaudeville in 1905. She toured in two-a-day for a number of years before making her musical comedy debut in *Jumping Jupiter* (1911). Appearances in musical comedies in New York and London continued until she appeared in the *Ziegfeld Follies* in 1915, when she introduced "Hello, Frisco," and in 1916. Her new play was the first non-musical assignment for the svelte, blonde-haired, hazel-eyed beauty with the tipped-up nose and weak chin, who would one day be called "the Comic Spirit Incarnate."

. . .

Trivia buffs may be intrigued by some curious echoes of other recent hits in Middleton and Bolton's comedy. Like the country cousin's cousin, its heroine is glad to escape Ohio. She is not unsympathetic to the response of the derelict, who, reminded that a Gilead is mentioned in the Bible, replies, "The way the Gilead folks talk you'd think they was *each* mentioned in it." And like the Ohioan Sam in that earlier play, he talks about his mother's hope that he will someday be president: "But I've disappointed her—so far." In nearly giving away Polly's pretense, he mentions her father's name was Dominie, the name the tramp in *Pals First* discloses is one of the poser's real names. Last, the suicidal pianist is called Petrowski, a name suspiciously close to the Petroskowski who is spoken of as a famous pianist and teacher in *A Tailor-Made Man*.

For the second time in as many seasons, the Japanese were preparing to go to war with America, and once again Walker Whiteside donned Oriental makeup to play an exotic villain. As Baron Takada in Azelle M. Aldrich and Joseph Noel's **The Pawn** (9-8-17, Fulton) he attempts to steal plans for a new American naval base in the Pacific. When he fails, he commits hara-kiri. As they had last season, playgoers showed no interest in the idea of Japanese treachery.

Nor did theatregoers care for the two plays that followed. George Broadhurst's **Over the 'Phone** (9-12-17, 48th St.) was an adaptation of Imre Földes's *Hallo!*, whose complications arise from a man's falling in love with a girl he knows only from a telephone conversation.

Owen Davis and Arthur Somes Roche were the authors of the equally rejected **The Scrap of Paper** (9-17-17, Criterion). A group of businessmen, led by Martin Masterman (Robert Hillard), attempt to corner the natural resources of a small country. The paper on which they record their agreement is blown out the window, and Masterman nearly loses his daughter in the attempt to recover it. His daughter's plight makes him repent his actions. Reviews for the melodrama were surprisingly favorable, so perhaps the public confused the play with Sardou's old work and therefore stayed away.

But a more interesting play opened the same evening. In his autobiography, George Arliss concluded his and Mary P. Hamlin's **Hamilton** (9-17-17, Knickerbocker) was "not a spectacular triumph, but it was a gratifying success." Indeed the play is starchy and thin, yet, as contemporary reviews suggested, it still made for satisfactory theatre. The authors helped achieve this by combining two matters that historically occurred several years apart. In their play Hamilton (Arliss) is concerned to win over Jefferson (Carl Anthony) and Monroe (Hardee Kirkland) to his bill permitting the federal government's assumption of all the states' debts. He gains their consent by agreeing to support Jefferson's desire to move the capital of the United States to the banks of the Potomac. But his plans almost come to naught when the scandal of his liaison with Mrs. Reynolds (Jeanne Eagels) is made public. Jefferson and Monroe are depicted as ardent states' righters, worried that Washington has royal ambitions. At Philadelphia's Exchange Coffee House, scene of the first act, Jefferson informs a visiting Frenchman: "I assure you Citizen Talleyrand, Citizen Giles and Citizen Monroe voice the sentiments of the great body of the American people. There is a growing unrest all over the land at the aristocratic tendencies of our President. There is bitter and righteous opposition to Alexander Hamilton's efforts to centralize the government." But Hamilton understands that they are honorable men. He can see the humor in Jefferson's deft way with a pen in defending his beliefs. Thus, when he is asked how Jefferson will explain his change of vote, he comments, "He'll just take his pen in his hand and write a cantata and his constituents will lift up their voices and sing." Queried on what they will sing, he answers, "Jefferson's praises, of course." Many critics found Jeanne Eagels, with her fragile, blonde beauty and aura of vulnerability, virtually a show stealer. The play remained in New York for ten weeks, then toured for two seasons.

Slowly but ineluctably the Washington Square Players were turning to full-length plays. One of their earliest was by the man who would usurp control of their successor, the Theatre Guild. Lawrence Langner's **The Family Exit** (9-19-17, Comedy) tells of Peter Vandusen (David Higgins), who years ago ran off to Paris to escape his too embracing family. He had lived there ever since with Elise (Alethea Luce), without marrying her. When he decides to return to America, bringing Elise, he does not count on American immigration laws, which look askance at an unmarried couple traveling together. So Peter marries Elise on Ellis Island, then divorces her so that they can live together in freedom.

Loosening moral codes also provided the background for one of the season's quickest, most dismal failures, Oliver D. Bailey's **Branded** (9-24-17, Fulton), but in this case the ending was unhappy. Ruth Belmar (Christine Norman), daughter of a celebrated brothel keeper, sinks down, down until she is a hopeless drug addict and derelict. A few lines just before the final curtain let audiences leave with a flicker of hope for Ruth's redemption. The *World,* though displeased, thought all was not lost and was prompted to offer a suggestion it would make to several other plays during the season: "With a few changes the piece might become an amusing burlesque of the old-time ten-twenty-thirty melodrama or the movies."

A not so nice young lady and the world's eternal self-serving and cynicism were to be seen as well in Frederic and Fanny Hatton's **Lombardi, Ltd.** (9-24-17, Morosco). However, in this instance they were merely the unpleasant part of a more pleasant play. Tito Lombardi (Leo Carrillo) is a good-hearted, honest dressmaker. Unfortunately, he falls in love with Phyllis Manning (Sue MacManamy), a scheming, gold-digging chorus girl, who pretends to return his affections only so long as it serves her ends. She eventually deserts him when his business seems to be going bankrupt. Fortunately, Norah Blake (Janet Dunbar), his long-suffering, self-sacrificing assistant, remains to console him and help him reorganize. In a subplot a gum-chewing model, Daisy (Grace Valentine), who has read too many torrid romances and seen too many white-slave films, is resolved to vamp Lombardi but finally settles for the "Vermicelli King," Riccardo Tosello (Warner Baxter). Whatever the play's faults, critics found ample compensation in Carrillo's performance, which, the *Tribune* exclaimed, brought to life "a real human being." Fashion parades, featuring the latest in stylish bathing suits and bustle frocks (a brief-lived fad of the day), added to the comedy's allure. The play ran out the season. But it also marked the end

of a rich two months and was followed by a prolonged period of downright failures or near misses. With one exception, not until late November would another straight-play hit emerge (though several big hit musicals did open).

Still more potential unpleasantness underscored another, far less successful comedy, Max Marcin and Roy Atwell's **Here Comes the Bride** (9-25-17, Cohan). A financially beset young man, Frederick Tile (Otto Kruger), unable to afford to marry Ethel Sinclair (Francine Larrimore), agrees to marry a woman (Maude Eburne), sight unseen, for $100,000. He plans to take the money and run, but his bride—a sight not to be seen when she lifts her veil—runs after him with equal determination. Of course, the young lovers find a way to throw over the much married bride by curtain time.

Broadway smart money held higher hopes for another entry that same evening, only to have its hopes dashed. Rachel Crothers joined hands with Kate Douglas Wiggin to dramatize Mrs. Wiggin's book **Mother Carey's Chickens** (9-25-17, Cort). What the smart money failed to recognize was that a war-bred cynicism was making too many playgoers intolerant of this old-fashioned variety of sunny sentimentality. While the *Evening World* found it "simple and appealing," its morning brother, the *World,* cried it was "too infernally good to be true." The story featured the widowed Mother Carey (Edith Barker) and her brood, headed by the charming Nancy (Edith Taliaferro), who set about restoring a deteriorating colonial home. They are heartened to discover a fine colonial fresco hidden under layers of later wallpaper and are not at all disheartened—or not for long—also to discover a will which suggests they are not the rightful possessors of the house. While all this is going on Mother Carey sets about improving the lot and disposition of her neighbors. Besides the setting for the yellowish old home, a flower-garlanded barn served as the scene for a barn dance, with three nattily dressed fiddlers and dancers in comfortable but formal (men in jackets and ties) afternoon attire.

There was no appreciable sunny sentimentality in George Bernard Shaw's **Misalliance** (9-27-17, Broadhurst), which William Faversham presented to open New York's newest playhouse. Faversham himself did not appear in this comic look at absurdly juxtaposed social relationships and romantic delusions. Portly Maclyn Arbuckle won the evening's acting laurels as the underwear magnate, John Tarleton.

William Hurlbut's **Saturday to Monday** (10-1-17, Bijou), suggested by a Jessie Leach Rector story, ran only a couple of weeks, despite some encouraging reviews. Of course, the thrust of its plot had to be obvious early on to seasoned playgoers. A militant suffragist (Ruth Maycliffe), escaping an unpleasant marriage, agrees to try another husband (Norman Trevor) on the understanding that they will be man and wife only from Saturday to Monday and that they will be free to go their independent ways the remainder of the week. The plan starts to fall apart when the lady returns home unexpectedly and discovers a strange girl (Eva Le Gallienne) in the spouse's apartment. Never mind that this lass came in by way of the fire escape while fleeing someone else's unwanted advances. By evening's end, with the husband lolling on a couch and wearing a pair of worsted bedroom slippers embroidered by the missis with pansies, the couple have decided to stay married all week long. Among the less satisfied reviewers was *Variety*'s man, who saw the work as "just enough of a play to make a rattling good 25-minute vaudeville sketch." And that was precisely what it became later.

In marked contrast to the frivolities of Hurlbut's comedy, Fannie Hurst and Harriet Ford's **The Land of the Free** (10-2-17, 48th St.) was set in the often dismal world of Jewish immigrants. Florence Nash, in an offbeat bit of casting, was featured as Sonia Marinoff, who leaves her dreary Russian village and soon finds herself, by way of Ellis Island, working away in a cramped sweatshop where the paint is peeling and the floor is littered with scraps of material and trash. She discovers her sister, Riva (Alice Lindahl), has become the mistress of their employer (Giorgio Majeroni), organizes a strike, weds a young writer (Leslie Austin), and brings her sister to live with them. The play's producer, William A. Brady, combed the Lower East Side's Yiddish theatres to enlist supporting players. Settings, especially the sweatshop, were excellent examples of theatrical realism, but the play's theme had only small appeal.

Belasco, that past master of theatrical realism, having enjoyed success on one of his rarer comedy outings with *Polly with a Past,* no doubt felt more comfortable with his next hit, Willard Mack's melodramatic **Tiger Rose** (10-3-17, Lyceum). Rose Bocion (Lenore Ulric) is a French-Canadian hellcat. She has sharply rejected the advances of a villainous Mountie, Constable Devlin (Mack), and more carefully turned down the moony Pierre Le Bey (Pedro de Cordoba), for she loves a young engineer, Bruce Norton (Calvin Thomas). Bruce kills a man who had driven his sister to suicide, then seeks Rose's aid in eluding the police, led by the vengeful Devlin. Rose

hides him in a grandfather clock in her father's house and tells him to meet her later at a remote, abandoned log cabin. A storm arises. Using the distraction of "the reverberating thunder, the revelatory flashes of lightning, the downpour of rain, the agitation of the wind-driven curtains and the flickering lamp," Norton comes out from his concealment and escapes through a trapdoor. At the cabin Devlin appears, but Rose extinguishes the only light and shoots Devlin's gun out of his hand. Norton again runs off. However, he soon returns, fearing what might happen to Rose because of her helping him. Devlin arrests him, but his influential friends promise to seek leniency for him. Belasco's theatrical pyrotechnics and the tiny, dark Ulric's fiery performance pleased theatregoers for nearly a year.

Fluttery, redheaded Billie Burke was not so fortunate when she appeared as star of Clare Kummer's **The Rescuing Angel** (10-8-17, Hudson), which her husband, Florenz Ziegfeld, presented in conjunction with Arthur Hopkins. Although Kummer had quickly developed a large coterie of admiring critics, the *World* summed up their reaction to this play by conceding that a "perceptible poverty of situation [was] effectively concealed by the sparkle of well written dialog." The star was cast as a dutiful daughter who resolves to end the financial difficulties of her parents (Marie Wainwright and Claude Gillingwater) by marrying well. She settles on a rough-hewn millionaire (Frederick Perry), but after the marriage—especially after he smashes her favorite vase—she decides she prefers a more bookish rich man (Roland Young). She then has third thoughts, so returns to the vase smasher.

It was the critics who smashed away at Charles Kenyon and Frank Dare's **The Claim** (10-9-17, Fulton), handing it some of the season's most devastating notices. The claim of the title was made by a saloon singer (Florence Roberts) who years before, unable to provide for it, had abandoned her child. Now she would like to have the grown youngster back. Since she is really not a bad woman, she succeeds. The regal Florence Roberts was a San Francisco star, never made very welcome in New York.

Grace George, who usually was greeted warmly, could do nothing to save Alicia Ramsey's **Eve's Daughter** (10-11-17, Playhouse). After the death of her tyrannical father, Irene Simpson-Bates runs off with a suave young lord (Lionel Atwill), but at Dover a storm prevents their sailing to France. In their hotel room, Irene comes upon a motto hanging in an alcove. It is her stern father's motto. In an abrupt change of heart she leaves her lover and turns as straitlaced as her strong-minded parent had been.

To many reviewers, Walter Hackett's **The Barton Mystery** (10-13-17, Comedy) seemed an unimaginative, unsatisfactory rehash of last year's *The Thirteenth Chair*. Once again a medium, this time a man (A. E. Anson), must use the tricks of his trade to exculpate a wrongly suspected person and expose the real murderer. A number of critics also disapproved of the play's single setting, a room in which walls and furniture alike were painted black.

For the second time in just over two weeks, William Hurlbut was forced to read discouraging morning-after notices for a new play of his. The girl in his **Romance and Arabella** (10-17-17, Harris) is a silly young widow (Laura Hope Crews) who sets out to find another husband. She has flings with young men, old ones, slim and fat ones, staid and wild ones. One of the wildest is a Greenwich Village poet (Alfred Lunt), a bohemian advocate of free love, who demonstrates his passionate beliefs while Arabella's chaperon hides beneath the sofa. His passion spent, he calmly, purposefully combs his hair for much of Arabella's remaining visit. Critics applauded the scenery, including a rose garden in the moonlight, but most had little or nothing to say about Lunt, making his Broadway debut. He had to derive what solace he could from the anonymous critic of the *Sun,* who reported, "Mr. Lunt has given us the most amusing character of the season."

Henry Miller, an established star, suffered one of the most abrupt failures of his long, distinguished career with the seven performance fiasco of Monckton Hoffe's English comedy **Anthony in Wonderland** (10-23-17, Criterion). Unmentioned in the critical dismissals of the play was that Miller was assuredly too old for the part of a bachelor whose ideal girls are seen only on the screen. To shove him into marriage, friends recreate a motion picture studio and "cast" Anthony as a film hero.

Paris served American audiences no better with Henri Bataille's **The Torches** (10-24-17, Bijou), as translated by Charles Andrews. It spotlighted a brilliant scientist (Lester Lonergan), whose life is destroyed by his foolish infatuation for a young lady.

Two plays that both opened five nights later must have set many a playgoer recalling not-all-that-bygone touring melodramas. One of the pair was even produced by Al Woods, so long associated with the seemingly defunct genre. (By coincidence both plays ran seven weeks.) Woods's mounting was Michael Morton's **On with the Dance** (10-29-17, Republic). A hard-working, successful husband (William Morris) is constantly taken aback by the spendthrift, flamboyantly carefree ways of his dance-mad wife (Eileen Huban). He particularly resents her running off to tango teas with the suave Billy Sutherland (John Mason). So when a scarlet lady (Julia Dean), who has been unceremoniously ditched by Sutherland, tells the husband that his wife and Billy are doing more than high-stepping, he follows the couple to a dance palace, and after the pair ignores his demand that they not dance, he shoots Sutherland. The *World* waved it away naughtily as "the most hilariously funny seriously intended play of the season."

Ernest Wilkes's **Broken Threads** (10-29-17, Fulton) was even more retrograde. Its hero, Harry Wynn (Cyril Keightley), is a prosperous mine owner who has fallen in love with and reformed a San Francisco cabaret singer, Dorothy Darrell (Phoebe Hunt). When Dorothy's vengeful ex-boyfriend (William Roselle) tries to kill her, Harry kills him instead. The dead man's powerful friends see to it that Dorothy is shanghaied to Australia so that she cannot testify for Harry and that Harry is sent to prison. He escapes and becomes even richer, and when he is eventually rearrested he uses his own influential friends to secure a pardon. He is also reunited with Dorothy.

Two very short-lived failures followed. The American dud was Sydney Rosenfeld's **The Love Drive** (10-30-17, Criterion). Bruce Markham (Fred Niblo) warns Ernestien Waite (Violet Heming) that he will stop at nothing to win her, so she decides to put as many obstacles, preferably in the form of other suitors, in his way as she can. But he wins her after all.

The hero's victory in Dion Calthrop's **The Old Country** (10-30-17, 39th St.) was less satisfying to him. Before he became an American millionaire (William Faversham) he had been an illegitimate child, and he and his mother had been hounded out of their English village. Now he resolves to employ his money to destroy the village and to make the villagers beg for mercy before him and his parent. His good-hearted mother changes his mind.

The Washington Square Players opened their latest season with another bill of one-acters, but it was only one of them that truly gripped critics—Eugene O'Neill's **In the Zone** (10-31-17, Comedy). Sailors on the *S.S. Glencairn* bind and gag one of their mates, Smitty (Frederick Roland), after learning he has furtively removed a little black box from his suitcase. They fear he might be a spy. But the box's contents prove to be merely old love letters from a girl who had left him because of his drinking. John Corbin of the *Times* proclaimed it "as simple and heartfelt as it was vivid with picturesque character, tense with excitement."

Two nights later the Provincetown Players began their season. Their first two bills, each of three one-acters, included works by Susan Glaspell, Maxwell Bodenheim, the self-publicizing Greenwich Village poet, and O'Neill. O'Neill's two offerings were **The Long Voyage Home** (11-2-17, Playwright's), recounting the plight of a sailor who is shanghaied just as he had saved enough money to abandon the sea, and **Ile** (11-30-17, Playwright's), in which a whaling captain's obsessiveness and heartlessness drive his wife over the brink into madness. Although these were among O'Neill's most powerful playlets, few critics devoted any attention to the troupe, so the plays failed to cause the stir they might have had they received major notices. Ira Remsen took the lead in the first play; Hutchinson Collins and Clara Savage, in the second.

There was precious little excitement in Florence Lincoln's **Barbara** (11-5-17, Plymouth), the story of a young lady (Marie Doro) who dreams of having children of her own and finally gets them. Two weeks and the play was gone.

But Edward Childs Carpenter's **The Pipes of Pan** (11-6-17, Hudson) ran longer, missing by less than two weeks that charmed circle of plays that run over 100 performances. No fewer than three critics, none of them young, referred to it as "a romance of middle age." One of them, Hornblow, extolled it as "sheer joy." Its story was simple. An aging artist (Norman Trevor), tired of painting pouty society women, decides to create a canvas of Pan and a dryad but cannot find a suitable model until he meets his old flame (Janet Beecher), still a titian-haired beauty. He falls in love with her again. But her jealous, puritanical husband (Berton Churchill) and her thoughtful young son (Burford Hampden) compel him to face reality.

J. Hartley Manners and his wife, Laurette Taylor, had to face the reality of dismissive notices when they offered what he termed his "thoroughly artificial and sentimental comedy," **The Wooing of Eve** (11-9-17, Liberty). Burns Mantle of the *Evening Mail* lamented that the play was "90% silly and uninteresting and only 10% Taylor, which is its only charm." She played a young woman who discovers that her cousin (Lynn Fontanne) is being pushed into marrying a man (A. E. Anson) whom the cousin does not like but whom she herself loves. She uses all her wiles to derail the wedding. She succeeds, allowing her happy cousin to marry the curate (Douglas Ross) of her dreams. Not every critic acquiesced in Mantle's assessment of the star

as the play's only charm. Corbin noted, "Miss Fontanne . . . is endlessly delightful—really an extraordinary performance."

George V. Hobart's **What's Your Husband Doing?** (11-12-17, 39th St.) received notices every bit as dismissive as Manners's play had been given. It centered on two couples who seek divorces after misconstruing their spouses' actions and on the two over-zealous, under-scrupulous lawyers they rush to.

On the other hand, John Drew garnered excellent notices when he came in as the star of a revival of Arthur Wing Pinero's *The Gay Lord Quex* that same night at the 48th Street Theatre. The comedy, advertised as "lately revised by the author," had originally been presented to New York seventeen years before to the day. Despite Drew's notices, the aging actor was increasingly perceived as caviar to the general, so the engagement was a limited one.

Away from the first-class houses, another play appeared. Ralph T. Kettering's **A Daughter of the Sun** (11-12-17, Lexington) told of an American doctor, who works in Hawaii for the secret service and who marries a native girl. But a nefarious Japanese spy nearly destroys the romance in his attempt to steal American military secrets.

Having just missed the charmed circle with his entry a week earlier, Edward Childs Carpenter came a cropper with **The Three Bears** (11-13-17, Empire). His bears are three woman-haters, camping out in a rather luxurious cabin in the Maine woods. They are made to rethink their ideas when a pretty young girl (Ann Murdock) invades their hideaway.

But Henri Bernstein's **L'Elevation** (11-14-17, Playhouse), of which much was expected, fared no better. Grace George was starred as a wife who worries more about the fate of her lover (Lionel Atwill) on the battlefield than she does about her husband (Holbrook Blinn). She is taught the truth when the lover, wounded and dying, confesses (with returning soldiers singing patriotic songs outside his hospital window) that he always looked on her as just another fling.

Another unhappy wife was featured in Fred Jackson's farce **Losing Eloise** (11-17-17, Harris). Just as she (Violet Heming) is about to elope with her lover (Francis Byrne), her husband (Charles Cherry) learns of the scheme. Being a writer, he sees useful story material in the situation. He forces them at gunpoint to spend a weekend at his Long Island bungalow, with him there as chaperon. In that time he convinces his wife to change her plans. In a futile attempt to stimulate business the title was changed midway in the run to *The Naughty Wife*.

Even the respected Mrs. Fiske could not latch onto the brass ring in this arid period, as she found to her disappointment when she appeared in the title role of Philip Moeller's **Madame Sand** (11-19-17, Criterion). The *Herald* called it "just a series of meetings and conversations and separations" and concluded, "There is no story." Mrs. Fiske's sometimes feminine, sometimes cigar-smoking, pants-wearing lady abandons her affair with De Musset (José Ruben) to embrace "poor, tired" Chopin (Alfred Cross). Ferdinand Gottschalk won laughs for a droll depiction of Heinrich Heine.

The dry spell was broken by the success of G. A. de Caillavet, Robert de Flers, and Emmanuel Arène's **The King** (11-20-17, Cohan), with Leo Ditrichstein starred. He played Serge IV of Moldavia, who is amused at how readily republican Frenchmen dote on his royal trappings. Ditrichstein had earlier announced that he would star in a translation of *El Alcalde de Zalamea,* a far superior play, but wisely discarded it when it was deemed uncommercial.

Two quick failures closed November. Harold Chapin had recently been killed in the fighting so never lived to see the New York premiere of his **Art and Opportunity** (11-26-17, Knickerbocker). The play had been done in London with Marie Tempest, who once had been a major star in musicals. In New York a younger musical star, Eleanor Painter, assumed the lead. She played a widow, a beguiling young lady who admits she has a touch of the adventuress in her. She sets her sights on a duke's son, then on the duke himself, but finally settles for the duke's secretary.

Ancella Anslee's **Six Months' Option** (11-29-17, Princess) proposed that couples about to divorce and enter into new marriages must first undergo trial divorces and trial remarriages.

Passionate bohemian love affairs were center stage in **Blind Youth** (12-3-17, Republic), which its star, the matinee idol Lou Tellegen, co-authored with Willard Mack. Tellegen played a Paris-born and trained artist, whose American mother had deserted him and his father. When he comes to America he discovers he must save his half-brother from the snares of a siren who once had enticed and then cruelly ditched him. He does, but gets little gratitude for it. Tellegen's drawing power gave the shallow melodrama a three-month run. In fact, *Variety* reported that the last nine weeks of the run, at the 39th Street Theatre, were underwritten by Tellegen, who had rented the house at $3000 per week, so that he could subsequently advertise an extended New York run.

Robert Housum's comedy-drama **The Gypsy Trail** (12-4-17, Plymouth) ran a fortnight longer than *Blind Youth.* Timid, slightly foolish Edward Andrews (Roland Young) is given to understand that his fiancée, Frances Raymond (Phoebe Foster), would prefer him to be more assertive and romantic. So he arranges to abduct her, first obtaining the permission of her father (Robert Cummings), then inviting his grandmother (Effie Ellsler) along as chaperone. Unfortunately for Edward, he also brings along his new chauffeur, Michael (Ernest Glendinning). Michael is not merely assertive and romantic, he is tall, dark, and handsome. In fact, he turns out to be a very rich young man who has hidden his heritage for reasons of his own. Naturally, Frances elects to marry him instead of the sad-eyed Edward. Because the play was relatively short, in mid-run its producer, Arthur Hopkins, added an afterpiece, Percival Knight's **A Trench Fantasy** (1-24-18), in which three soldiers— an Englishman (Knight), an American (Glendinning), and a Frenchman (Young)—are visited in their trench by the figures of Father Christmas and Death. But this addition to the bill failed to please and soon was withdrawn.

Nor was Butler Davenport's **The Silent Assertion** (12-8-17, Bramhall Playhouse) a crowd-pleaser. Davenport assumed the role of a rising statesman whose wife and mistress must regularly join hands to save him from scandal. However much in outline the play seems like so many other melodramas of the period, contemporary critics often detected an ambience of deliberate salaciousness in Davenport's writings, designed to elicit patronage from more prurient playgoers.

One of the season's most abysmal failures—it ran just one week—was Constance Lindsay Skinner's **Good Morning, Rosamond** (12-10-17, 48th St.), in which a Canadian girl (Lily Cahill) takes in a tramp (Lowell Sherman) whom she mistakes for a prince rumored to be traveling incognito in the area. She is persecuted unfairly by her neighbors until the tramp proves to have very respectable credentials and the two fall in love. They are helped by the prince, who has been disguised as a wandering fiddler.

On the other hand, despite disparaging comments by many critics (Hornblow waved the play away as "absurdly childish"), Arthur Goodrich's **Yes or No** (12-21-17, 48th St.) chalked up a five-month run, helped by some not-so-novel novelties. To begin with, the play used the flashback technique popularized by *On Trial.* A pair of sadder but wiser women are telling their histories to a third lady in hopes of preventing her from making the same mistakes. The setting for the prologue disappears, and onstage, side by side with no partition separating them, are two rooms. One, bathed in an amber glow, is in a rich man's home; the other, shown in stark white light, is a tenement. Both the rich wife (Willette Kershaw) and the poor one (Emilie Polini) are unhappy, but the rich wife succumbs to the lures of a seducer and lives to regret it, while the poor girl resigns herself to her lot.

On the next evening at the Broadhurst, William Faversham was both producer and star of a revival of his hit of eighteen years before, *Lord and Lady Algy* (2-14-99). His superb supporting cast included Maxine Elliott, Irene Fenwick, Florine Arnold, Maclyn Arbuckle, Lumsden Hare, and a young Eva Le Gallienne.

Christmas Eve brought New Yorkers another present, Al Woods's production of C. W. Bell and Mark Swan's **Parlor, Bedroom and Bath** (12-24-17, Republic). Reggie Irving (John Cumberland) is a meek, largely ineffectual young husband, but this does not alter the conviction of his wife, Angelica (Sydney Shields), that he has enjoyed a lurid past. So that he won't prove a disappointment to her, he writes himself love notes, signs them "Tootles," and sees to it they fall into her hands. When this ruse is nearly exposed, a friend arranges for Reggie to be discovered in a hotel room with another woman (Florence Moore), an ex–chorus girl who now writes for a notorious scandal sheet. The scheme almost backfires when Reggie is discovered there with several women and into the room barges the very furious husband of one of them. Reggie talks his wife into forgiving him. Of course, she is not disillusioned. The *Herald,* while warning that the evening was "naughty," welcomed it as "a true farce." Curiously, the short, dumpy, and balding Cumberland, who was featured in so many of these bedroom farces, never won more than perfunctory approval by the critics. In this instance, it was hatchet-faced Florence Moore who walked off with many of the best notices.

What should have been a second Christmas Eve present was not received by everyone as such. Ethel Barrymore opened in **The Lady of the Camellias** (12-24-17, Empire). Whether or not this was a revival is arguable, for Edward Sheldon had rewritten the older stage version, modernizing the dialogue and restoring the frame device of the auction which had begun the book and now began the play. After Marguerite Gautier's effects are auctioned off a desolate Armand (Conway Tearle) stands alone in the emptied room and cries, "Marguerite, my love, come back to me!" With that the scene flashes back to 1840. Miss Barrymore played the part in a blonde wig, but many felt she was not frail or tragic enough, with some saying her courtesan seemed singularly to lack a nineteenth-century aura. Holbrook Blinn was Duval père, while old Rose Coghlan won applause for her Mme. Prudence.

The busy evening's last offering was a British play, J. E. Harold Terry's **General Post** (12-24-17, Gaiety), in which highborn, snobbish Englishmen are taught by the war to respect those they perceive as inferiors.

Many felt that Christmas night brought in the best present of all, Jesse Lynch Williams's **Why Marry?** (12-25-17, Astor). For some time John Corbin had been proclaiming a renaissance of high comedy and seeing Clare Kummer as its driving force. But she abruptly had to take a back seat. In his Sunday follow-up Corbin anointed Williams's play as "the most penetrating satire on social institutions yet written by an American." The action takes place on John's sunporch, a bright spot with floor-to-ceiling French windows between classical pillars, climbing ivy, and wicker furniture. Jean (Lotus Robb), John's sister, has just tricked Rex (Harold West), a rich young man whom she does not love, into proposing marriage to her. She accepts, although her heart belongs to a poor boy her family refuses to allow her to see. Two more family members appear. One is Cousin Theodore (Ernest Lawford), a minister beset by dire financial problems because his wife is in a sanitorium and his children are in the best schools. The other is Uncle Everett (Nat C. Goodwin), a judge whose beloved wife is currently in Reno, applying for a divorce. She sends him doting letters, saying she wishes he were with her to enjoy the city and concluding, "Write soon, with love." When John (Edmund Breese) and his studiously pleasant wife, Lucy (Beatrice Beckley), profess to be shocked by their behavior, Everett retorts, "Is the object of marriage merely to stay married? Holy matrimony merely a vulgar endurance contest?" But the family's main concern is John's second sister, Helen (Estelle Winwood), who has spent a night with Ernest (Shelley Hull), the brilliant young scientist she assists, and who is now prepared to accompany him to Paris where he will do further research. Neither Helen nor Ernest sees much reason to marry. To Lucy's objections that such behavior is unwomanly, Helen suggests that having a hand in developing an anti-toxin to save children's lives is not unwomanly work. John advises Ernest that while the family has the highest opinion of him, they are more concerned with respecting the opinion of the world. The discussion moves back and forth, with sides seemingly changing briefly and positions sometimes dangerously atilt. But Helen assures her family that she is a New Woman: "We're at the dawn of a new era, John; women are going to do what they believe is right, not what men *tell* 'em to believe is right." She insists love is more important than law. Everett informs the rest of the family that he has a plan to get the youngsters to wed, but John's tempestuous outbursts sabotage it. So the wily Everett gets both Helen and Ernest to admit that at least in the sight of God they take each other as man and wife, after which he proclaims that since they have made these declarations, "by the authority vested in me by the laws of this state, [I] do pronounce you man and wife." There is nothing left for the family to do but to head inside for dinner.

The entire cast also won kudos, particularly Goodwin and Winwood. Contemporaries probably took a special delight in the much married, much divorced Goodwin justifying both marriage and divorce. (His arguments for trial divorces may have reminded regular first-nighters of less well couched arguments a month earlier in *Six Months' Option*.) For Miss Winwood, an exceptionally slim beauty with vivid yellow hair, blue eyes, and a cupid's-bow mouth, the notices helped consolidate her quickly growing reputation. But these same contemporaries took little stock in the fact that the critics' huzzas were reinforced when *Why Marry?* became the first play to win a Pulitzer Prize, since the prize had yet to become prestigious. Too highbrow for many, the comedy ran just four months.

Billeted (12-25-17, Playhouse), a British wartime comedy by F. Tennyson Jesse and H. M. Harwood, ran only two and a half months, but its New York stand and profitable tour gave its star, Margaret Anglin, the wherewithall she required to continue mounting her revivals of Greek tragedy. She played an Englishwoman whose husband had deserted her years before and who offers to allow some officers to be billeted in her home. Naturally, one of the men turns out to be her former spouse (Edward Emery). Playgoers could surmise the ending. Though most critics applauded the play, the star was the center of attention, with the *Herald* observing that she "shines with special lustre" and "has few if any rivals" in this sort of comedy.

The old year ended with J. Hartley Manners's second vehicle of the season for his wife, Laurette Taylor. **Happiness** (12-31-17, Criterion) originally had been written as a one-acter and now was expanded as a replacement for its disappointing predecessor. Once again critics pounced on Manners, seeing his playwriting as contrived and mawkish. *Variety* predicted correctly, "Whatever success the piece enjoys will be due in great measure to the personal popularity of the star." Indeed, the public ignored the negative notices for the play, eating up the star's little dressmaker's errand girl, who delivers gowns to rich, excruciatingly blasé Park Avenue society figures. She tells them her recipe for happiness is simply "lookin' forward." Before long Mrs. Crystal-Pole (Violet Cooper) and Philip Chandos (O. P. Heggie) are so enjoying life again that they help her lead Formoy MacDonagh (J. M. Kerrigan) to the altar and set the pair up with their own Fifth Avenue dress shop. And once again some of the best notices went to Lynn Fontanne, this time as a high-strung, clothes-mad debutante. The comedy ran until May.

The new year was rung in (and wrung in) with the late Hjalmar Bergstrom's "Ibscene" drama **Karen** (1-7-18, Greenwich Village) in which the heroine and her siblings find unhappiness in marriageless loves. The tiny playhouse was far away from Times Square and would half a century or more later have been considered off-Broadway. But no such conception existed in 1918. Still, enough avant-garde playgoers overlooked generally snide reviews to keep the theatre lit for eight weeks.

Uptown, but away from first-class houses, James Kyrke McCurdy's **A Little Girl in a Big City** (1-1-18, Lexington) told of a sweet innocent who arrives in New York and is nearly sold into white slavery by a cigarette-smoking villain (but one without the old standard—a mustache). She soon meets a charlady who says, "I have a daughter somewhere and your sweet face reminds me of her." Naturally the woman turns out to be her long-lost mother. McCurdy had spent years touring in the now defunct cheap theatres, and his play displayed all the clichés of the old-style melodrama. For example, the same dulcet melody announced each of the heroine's entrances.

At a first-class house, Eugene Walter, once looked on as one of the great hopes of American drama, again showed he was written out when his **The Heritage** (1-14-18, Playhouse) premiered. Moving between Sicily and America, it cast a harsh spotlight on Antonio (Cyril Keightley), a man torn between his skill as a fine musician and the murderous proclivities of his Sicilian ancestors. A kindly detective (Lowell Sherman) suggests the police place a discreet watch on him to see if they can explain and cure his split personality. Antonio lures the detective to Italy, where Antonio's sister (Madeline Delmar), who is given to killing kittens for the fun of it, falls in love with him. But in another murderous fit, Antonio slays the detective, driving his sister and himself over the brink.

Watching the funeral from his room, Antonio hurls a chair through the window, then leans out and screams his guilt for all to hear.

If Eugene Walter's play missed its chance to become good, old-fashioned tragedy, Walter Howard's London success **Seven Days Leave** (1-17-18, Park) grabbed every opportunity to resuscitate good, old-fashioned sensation-melodrama. The story, tilted toward American interests by an uncredited Max Marcin, centered on efforts by German spies to steal a device to detect submarines. Its inventor, an American captain (William J. Kelly), must rescue both his invention and his highborn English sweetheart (Elisabeth Risdon) from the nefarious tricksters. A huge cast added color and verisimilitude to scenes showing a destroyer's guns blazing away at a periscope, the heroine (in a black bathing suit) in danger on the high seas, and a wedding procession in front of an old church. The combination of drama and spectacle appealed to audiences for twenty weeks.

Bombast gave way to charm with the entry of **Seventeen** (1-22-18, Booth), adapted by Hugh Stanislaus Stange and Stannard Mears from Booth Tarkington's novel. As he had in the book, Willie Baxter (Gregory Kelly) has reached what his mother (Judith Lowry) calls "the painful age when he's too old to be a child and too young to be a man." In short, he's seventeen, given to envisioning himself as Dickens's heroic Sidney Carton and reacting to all his parents' obviously absurd demands with a book-learned "Ye Gods!" Then he falls madly in love—calf love—with baby-talking ("put pressus Flopit [her mutt] in a nice comfy chair wif a nice soft cushion out in the pitty sunshine"), flirtatious Lola Pratt (Ruth Gordon) and "borrows" his father's tuxedo so that he may dance with her at a party. His plans go awry, since he is found out and has to pack all his clothes and take them to a black secondhand dealer to exchange for a dress suit that had belonged to a jailed *eye*-talian waiter. Arriving late at the party, he learns that Lola has switched allegiances to a boy who will drive her in his car to the station, since she is about to return home. Oh, well, at seventeen there is such a long future to look ahead to. Willie allows that he may even try college. Critics echoed each other in lauding the play: "To see it is to laugh from the heart, heartily"; "tends to the heart of the public." The slim, dark-haired, attractive Kelly, then in his late twenties, was a skilled comedian able to milk every laugh. Gordon, whom he married during the run of the play, was a slightly coarse-featured vulgarian, loud-mouthed and pushy, but nonetheless equally skilled. They helped the comedy run seven months.

The same night saw a revival of *Experience* (10-27-14) at the vast Manhattan Opera House. By coincidence an older, more famous morality play, *Everyman,* had been presented for a pair of performances at the Cort two days earlier. The players (including Edith Wynne Matthison, Charles Rann Kennedy, and Pedro de Cordoba) who offered this English work offered a second, *The Merchant of Venice,* for daytime performances on the 25th and 26th, and a third, *As You Like It,* on the 8th and 9th of February. On March 15th Tyrone Power, Walter Hampden, Cyril Keightley, Howard Kyle, and Alma Kruger took over the stage for a matinee of *Julius Caesar,* playing Brutus, Antony, Cassius, Caesar, and Portia respectively. Hampden then brought in his Macbeth on April 5 and his Hamlet a week later. The season ended after a performance of *A Midsummer Night's Dream* saluted Shakespeare's birthday.

Three new plays competed for attention on the last Monday night in January. The longest run—just eight weeks—was awarded to Adeline Leitzbach and Theodore A. Liebler, Jr.'s **Success** (1-28-18, Harris). The play accorded Brandon Tynan a chance for a tour de force as a dissolute actor, Barry Carlton. In 1897 he wins major stardom for his Lear, but he clearly has a drinking problem, possibly brought on by accusations that his wife (Helen Holmes) has been unfaithful. Twenty years pass. Carlton has deserted his wife and daughter (Marion Coakley) and has become so undependable that he is reduced to begging for small parts. He wangles an assignment as a super in another revival of *Lear.* His neglected daughter, who is playing Cordelia in the revival and does not recognize him, is in love with the young actor (Lionel Glenister) playing Lear. But on opening night the young man, having been told that the girl is as promiscuous as her mother was, appears too drunk to perform. Carlton goes on in his place, saving the night and probably allowing his daughter and her sobered fiancé to repair their own lives and careers.

While *Success* was a drama about players, **The Madonna of the Future** (1-28-18, Broadhurst) was a play by a drama critic, Alan Dale. His fellow aisle-sitters, obviously liking their colleague, just as obviously did not like his play but out of kindness let it down gently. Dale touched on matters discussed in a number of American plays recently—Eugenics and the desire of a woman to be loved but not married. His heroine is Iris Fotheringay (Emily Stevens), who announces proudly that she is about to have a child by Rex Letherick (Jerome Patrick), a man she will not marry. But after the baby arrives and she learns that Rex is considering marrying another woman, she agrees to wed him. The law was not as kind to the play as Dale's colleagues had been. Self-appointed moralists hauled the play into court, where the straitlaced magistrate sneered that "it should have been played in a stable." Changes were ordered, but rather than comply the producer, Oliver Morosco, closed the show.

Always adventuresome, Arnold Daly emerged as producer and star of the evening's least successful entry, Hermann Bahr's **Josephine** (1-28-18, Knickerbocker). The play looked at Napoleon from Josephine's point of view, suggesting that her careful proddings made him great and that once he was in power he callously discarded her. Virginia Harned was Josephine. Even given wartime sentiments, it seems amazing that the production could have elicited howls of outrage, with the debunking of Napoleon decried as German propaganda. But that is what happened. Daly quickly came to the playwright's defense only to find that his reasonable arguments were unavailing.

In Frederic and Fanny Hatton's **The Indestructible Wife** (1-30-18, Hudson) the irrepressible vitality of the woman (Minna Gombell) nearly wrecks her marriage and her friendships, but, since this is a comedy, all ends happily.

Harry James Smith was happy to have been able to attend the opening of his comedy **The Little Teacher** (2-4-18, Playhouse) and to write to his friends that the play was going to be a hit. Just over a month later, long before the comedy ended its four-month run, he was killed while doing war work with the Canadian Red Cross, so the play, far from his best, was his last. One local figure despairs of the little Vermont backwater of Goshen Hollow, calling it "a law unto itself. It's proud and it's jealous and it's touchy and it's bad." Certainly the local biddies are shocked that the school board has gone to New York to recruit a teacher for their shabby one-room school: "A body might send to New York for a hair dresser or a dancing girl—but a *school teacher!*" That young lady is Emily West (Mary Ryan), and in short order she has patched up a French-Canadian lumberman (Edw. G. Robinson) who was attacked by a fellow worker (Curtis Cooksey) for his slurring remarks about the new marm, and she rescues two abused children from their supposed parents. When the village learns that the children were actually kidnapped, the townsfolk accept Emily. At a Red Cross sewing bee, with Allied flags decking the room and with the ladies in white, the children's mother arrives to take them home. She offers Emily a position running a shelter she has established in France for war orphans. The two lumbermen appear

in uniform, announcing they have abandoned their good-paying jobs to join the fracas. Emily tells them she will see them in France. The soldiers depart singing "Over There" by George M. Cohan, who produced the show with Sam Harris and who quietly helped rewrite it for Broadway. Mary Nash won high praise for her "wealth of feeling, youthful, gracious charm and unaffected and catching enthusiasm."

The season's oldest plays were Sophocles' *Electra* and Euripides' *Medea,* which Margaret Anglin, using profits from her current play, mounted at Carnegie Hall. Both plays were slated for one or two matinee performances, the Sophocles on the 6th and 15th, the Euripides on the 20th, but the demand for seats was such that one additional performance of each was given in March. Livingston Platt designed starkly modern, stylized settings, and in the pit Walter Damrosch provided a musical accompaniment, more Wagnerian than Greek, with a full symphony orchestra. Yet though all performances were sold out, the presentation lost money.

Ethel Barrymore's ambitions were less lofty, so when she abandoned *The Lady of the Camellias* she appeared in R. C. Carton's light English comedy **The Off Chance** (2-14-18, Empire), playing a divorced, unhappily rewedded woman who must save her daughter's troubled marriage. The play ran until May, at which time she had a third vehicle ready.

Meanwhile, her brother Lionel enjoyed a more notable triumph in Augustus Thomas's last major success, **The Copperhead** (2-18-18, Shubert). The contemporary war songs that had been sung in several of the season's plays gave way to Civil War ballads, for the play's first two acts occur in the 1860s. Their setting is the Shankses' rundown farm in southern Illinois. The clapboard farmhouse, badly in need of repair, is on the left. Just behind its cluttered yard is a split-rail fence, and behind that is a view of some gently rolling hills. Mrs. Shanks (Doris Rankin) is busy sewing uniforms for Federal troops; her sixteen-year-old son, Joey (Raymond Hackett) is molding minnie balls for the soldiers, whom he'd rather be joining; and pipe-smoking Grandma Perley (Eugenie Woodward), who did the same work in Andrew Jackson's days, is helping him. All of them are dismayed at Milt Shanks (Barrymore), who brazenly sports a copperhead in his buttonhole and refuses to help in "any *unholy* cause like an army against our own countrymen." Only Reverend Andrews (Harry Hadfield) knows that Shanks is secretly aiding the North, but he is sworn to secrecy. Joey finally runs off to enlist. However, he is later killed in action. His dying words are that his father must not be allowed to attend his funeral. Mrs. Shanks dies of grief. Fifty years pass. The farm has been tidied up, the yard now has a pretty well and modern outdoor furniture, and a bright, white picket fence has replaced the split rails. All these years Milt has been ostracized by his unforgiving neighbors. But now his grand-daughter Madeline (also played by Miss Rankin), the child of his daughter who was an infant in the first two acts, has applied to become a teacher. The villagers, believing guilt is hereditary, are opposed to her selection. So Milt discloses a plaster cast of Lincoln's hand that he watched being made and quietly kept to himself. He also shows the townsfolk a handwritten letter from Lincoln, praising his great sacrifice. When asked why he had remained silent so long, he remarks, "Couldn't tell Joey or his mother, and, with them gone—tellin' anybody seemed so—so useless." Some critics derided this explanation and said it made the play's fundamental premise absurd, but most agreed that the drama's flaws were glossed over by Barrymore's "memorable force and fervor." The often snide *World* was among those who opted enthusiastically for the work itself, hailing it as "a drama of sturdy bone and sinew, with rich blood in its veins and with its feet planted firmly in the native soil." The play ran out the season.

Last season's run of *The Master* had to be cut short because of Arnold Daly's serious illness. Now recuperated, he revived the play at the Hudson on the 19th, adding his own one-acter **Democracy's King.** It was unalloyed propaganda, allowing Daly to portray Kaiser Wilhelm. He is about to be hanged from an apple tree. In his last confession he admits that he had hoped to conquer the world, but he adds that, in fighting him, his enemies have had to adopt social and economic changes that will actually make them stronger in the long run. Thus, he has fostered democracy.

The Washington Square Players continued their drift toward full-length plays with their presentation of **Youth** (2-20-18, Comedy), the work of an English actor and author, Miles Malleson. His play took up a voguish theme—trial marriages—setting his action behind the scenes of a Greenwich Village theatre, where two youngsters, worried about the imprison-ment of marriage yet bored with their single lives, agree to live together for a time. The play seems not to have been given a major mounting in Malleson's native England.

On the other hand, Rudolf Besier and Sybil Spottiswoode's *Kultur at Home* had enjoyed a long London run before being brought to America as **Her Country** (2-21-18, Punch and Judy). Like *Democracy's King* it was more propaganda than drama. An American girl (she had been an Englishwoman in the London production) marries a German, only to discover how unloving, arrogant, and militaristic he and his compatriots are. She leaves him. Despite lukewarm notices the play ran ten weeks with Rosa Lynd in the leading role.

Sydney Rosenfeld's **Under Pressure,** which opened at the tiny Norworth Theatre on the same night, proved to be a rewritten and remounted version of Sydney Rosenfeld's *The Love Drive,* a play Broad-way had rejected earlier in the season. This time the not easily daunted author was also the producer, but Broadway still would not accept the comedy. How-ever, age was finally telling on the man who had enjoyed some fame with a few hits and considerably more notoriety with his frequently gadfly behavior. When the play closed shortly after its reopening, Rosenfeld quietly wrote finis to a career of forty years.

William Hodge pleased his faithful when he (using his nom de plume, Lawrence Whitman) and Earl Derr Biggers turned a short story by Corra Harris into Hodge's latest vehicle, **A Cure for Curables** (2-25-18, 39th St.). The *Dramatic Mirror* insisted it was "never a play," calling it instead "a Hodge-podge." Whatever it was, it was set in a swank rest home patronized by hypochondriacal rich folk. Dr. James Pendergrass (Hodge) can come into a handsome inheritance himself if he can cure ten of the regulars within thirty days. He uses tricks—such as so exhausting them that they miss the train on which they hope to escape, getting them outdoors by having them raise "Hoover gardens," and appealing to their wartime patriotism—to make them under-stand that they are really quite healthy. His actions win him the love of Phyllis Blaine (Clara Moores).

Another entry that same evening was Ethel Watts Mumford's **Sick-a-Bed** (2-25-18, Gaiety), telling of a famous African explorer (Edwin Nicander) who returns home just in time to find himself subpoenaed as a witness in his uncle's divorce case. To avoid testifying and also to escape the clutches of his libidinous aunt (Mary Newcombe), he pretends to be sick. His ruse leads to the expected farcical complications and also to his falling in love with his attractive nurse (Mary Boland).

At the mammoth Manhattan Opera House *The Garden of Allah* (10-21-11) began a short stand as the evening's third opening. An elaborate touring production that had been on the road for many seasons, it offered its audiences real donkeys, real camels, real Arabs, and a violent sandstorm that sometimes blew its cereal-cum-sand into the first rows of the orchestra.

If the sensation-melodrama that, in a way, *The Garden of Allah* represented was an all but dead theatrical genre, the old ten-twent'-thirt'-style touring melodrama had been buried nearly a decade before. Yet another attempt was made to resurrect it in this busy Monday night's fourth offering. C. W. Bell's **When Rogues Fall Out** (2-25-18, Lexington) featured all the clichés of the school: an innocent heroine caught up in a false accusation of murder; a determined, agile hero. Only the villain was a bit different, being a gentlemanly "flash yegg," a well-dressed, polite crook. The players were members of a stock company which, after two earlier offerings at the house, apparently was formed to present new plays at popular prices. Most of their offerings were ignored or given short shrift by the critics. Among them was Alfred H. Brown's **The Widow's Weeds** (3-11-18), an old-style rural drama, set in Tamarac, Maine, and telling of the romance between a lumberjack and the widowed proprietress of a boardinghouse. The play receiving the most attention was Ada Patterson and Robert Edeson's **Love's Lightning** (3-25-18), which told of the coming together of a motherless son and a sonless woman. Within a few weeks the stock company faded into history, although *Love's Lightning* was moved briefly to the Fulton.

As February faded into March Broadway received a small piece of good news. The partial blackout that had been implemented as a war effort was lifted. The Great White Way could be itself again.

Apart from some matinees given over to a presentation of **The Book of Job** (3-7-18, Booth), with George Gaul, who was then spending his evenings in blackface as a servant in *Seventeen,* as Job and Walter Hampden as Elihu, nothing but musicals appeared for the next two weeks. Then a pair of foreign plays opened in competition with one another. Arthur Hopkins, among Broadway's most admired producers, announced that his production of Ibsen's **The Wild Duck** (3-11-18, Plymouth) marked its very belated New York premiere (at least in English). Its story tells of the havoc wrought by a foolish idealist (Harry Mestayer) when he reveals to a high-strung, immature teenager (Nazimova) that her father is in truth his own father (Dodson Mitchell) and not the unsuccessful photographer (Lionel Atwill) she had been raised to believe was her parent. As she often did, Nazimova divided the critics. Hornblow praised her for displaying "a fine artistic perception. Life-like in the every movement and mood of a girl of fourteen." But Corbin, who had rarely been kind to her, complained that her major action consisted of regularly shaking her head

so that her dark, bobbed hair would not cover her eyes. She had nothing, he rued, to suggest the play's human values or spiritual implications. He even growled that her skill at English had deteriorated. In his autobiography Hopkins, who had originally thought of her as playing the mother rather than the daughter, confessed that the tiny actress still had trouble with her English but added, "she was a slight person of no age . . . one actress who never had to find again the histrionic gifts of childhood. They had never left her."

A few blocks to the south, the Washington Square Players brought out their revival of Shaw's *Mrs. Warren's Profession* (10-30-05) at the Comedy. Mary Shaw had the leading role, as she had had nearly thirteen years before. Only this time several critics suggested the play seemed little more than mid-Victorian fluff, so no police raided the theatre.

The Hattons' third play (and second flop) of the season was their spoof of the movies, **The Squab Farm** (3-13-18, Bijou). The work was deemed "a series of episodes in the life of an Anatol of the studio." He is a director (Lowell Sherman) who is not above telling an incompetent actress attempting a passionate love scene, "Just imagine he has money." Even his wife walks out on him. But he is shocked and almost led to reform after a silent-screen beauty (Alma Tell), who thinks nothing of cheating on her husband or her lovers, refuses to dress in a fig leaf to play Eve. However, the entrance of another gorgeous starlet causes his vows to behave to be immediately forgotten. Unnoticed in a tiny role was Tallulah Bankhead, making her Broadway debut. As far as the Hattons were concerned, at least, *Lombardi, Ltd.* was still raking in money.

At first it appeared that **Getting Together** (3-18-18, Lyric) would not rake in much at all. Written hurriedly by Ian Hay, Percival Knight and J. Hartley Manners, it was designed as propaganda for the British-Canadian Recruiting Mission and slated to play one-week stands in major American cities, beginning in New York. Its slim story recounted how a failing marriage was saved after the husband donned khakis. Holbrook Blinn and Blanche Bates played the leading roles. But what really appealed to the pathetic handful of playgoers on opening night was the drama's spectacle—including a mobbed Madison Avenue recruiting office, a tank (purportedly the genuine article) riding over a trench out of which soldiers poured to launch an offensive, and a destroyed French village. By its third night the show was selling out, and after its scheduled tour it returned in June for a three-month stay.

Cyril Harcourt's **A Pair of Petticoats** (3-18-18, 44th

St. Roof) also had a war flavor, with all its men in uniform. But without its khaki trappings it was simply a farce in which a gossip-mongering lady nearly destroys a couple's romance and her own in the process. She repents in time for a happy ending.

There was no hint of modern warfare in the evening's third opening, a twelve-year-old play by the British novelist and poet Maurice Hewlitt, **Pan and the Young Shepherd** (3-18-18, Greenwich Village), in which the titular figures spar over a beautiful girl.

Henry Miller welcomed the public to his new playhouse—a little Georgian gem. He was not afraid of his late-season opening since the theatre was the first to include built-in air-conditioning (however absurdly primitive and unavailing by later standards). All he lacked was a worthwhile vehicle. Louis Evan Shipman's **The Fountain of Youth** (4-1-18, Henry Miller's) saw forty-seven-year-old Gerald Place return from India after amassing a fortune there in rubber. He finds his old sweetheart (Lucile Watson), now a widow, ready to reembrace him. But he longs for more youthful joys. While backing an arty play that no one else will touch, he meets the ravishing, young Elizabeth Crichton (Olive Tell) and falls unthinkingly in love. The play proves a surprise success, but his September-May romance peters out. Still, there is the sensible widow to turn to. There was little highbrow about Miller's new vehicle, and unlike the play within his play, playgoers and critics alike politely rejected it.

Years earlier Lincoln J. Carter had been among the most prolific and popular authors of cheap touring melodramas. Now, thanks to Al Woods, a onetime producer of such shows, he was given a major Broadway hearing with **An American Ace** (4-2-18, Casino). Once more, the story—this time about a former pacifist turned American flyer (James L. Crane) who falls in love with a Belgian girl (Marion Coakley) and wins her and the war despite the nefarious ploys of the alluring Rose Matern (Sue MacManamy)—was not the thing. Spectacle was. Among the attractions were a huge parade of doughboys down Fifth Avenue with flag-waving secretaries leaning out of windows, a motorcycle brigade in Belgium, a German shot while climbing a belfry, and, most spectacular of all, an aerial dogfight, viewed from above, with the ground far below on a backdrop, while the planes "looped the loop on wires." One reviewer noted, "Not since the days of Third Avenue drama . . . has so much din hit the ears of an audience." But the days for such stagey thrillers had passed, so Woods withdrew it after a month.

The season's last long run—109 performances—went to **The Man Who Stayed at Home** (4-3-18, 48th St.), which proved to be merely *The White Feather* (2-4-15) with its original English title restored but with a new American setting.

On April 5, Laurette Taylor began a series of Friday matinees at the Criterion offering a bill of scenes from Shakespeare. She appeared as Katherine to Shelley Hull's Petruchio, Juliet to José Ruben's Romeo, and Portia to O. P. Heggie's Shylock. The roustabout condensation of *The Taming of the Shrew* went brilliantly, but trouble began when Juliet's balcony began to sway precariously and provoked titters in the audience. Nor was her Portia, in a black wig and stained face so that Bassanio might not recognize her, well received. Writing in the *Evening Mail,* Burns Mantle summed up most critics' feelings when, after lauding the star's courage, he concluded, "By all the Shakespearean standards we know anything about, she failed."

The young actress who years later would end her career heading the road company of Laurette Taylor's last success won some better notices, but in a play most critics thought little of. There apparently were two distinct sets of programs for Hubert Osborne's **April** (4-6-18, Punch and Judy), since some reviews listed Pauline Lord as playing The Woman, and others listed her as portraying Nancy Bowers. In either case she enacted the part of a young wife whose husband (Mitchell Harris) cannot provide her with the basic necessities and who dreams of how much happier she might be had she married the duplicitous but very wealthy Richard Pemberton (Alphonz Ethier). A Strange Gentleman [the same in all programs] (Charles Hopkins) steps miraculously through her wall and seemingly allows her dreams to become reality. She soon realizes how little happiness wealth would bring. But once more home, she is not discouraged to learn that her husband at last is beginning to become a good provider.

That same evening at the Plymouth, Nazimova replaced her Hedvig with her singularly repellent Hedda. As usual the critics divided sharply in their assessments of the star, with those who had long disliked her continuing to do so and those who had usually praised her praising her again. Some were also displeased with Robert Edmond Jones's stripped-down set that used only "the ugly contortions of a lambrequin border" to hint at the drama's Victorian period.

Nancy Lee (4-9-18, Hudson) was a more likable lady. Having been pressed into a cynical marriage by her family, she (Charlotte Walker) discovers after her husband's death that he was a four-flusher and has left her penniless. She takes up with a fast set, borrowing money from a young man (Ralph Kellard) who is infatuated with her. She does not know he has stolen the money. A friend (Lewis Stone) of the boy's father visits her to demand she return the money. He soon comprehends her basic decency, so he sets matters aright and proposes marriage. The play, by Eugene Walter and H. Crownin Wilson, received mixed notices, which meant so late an arrival could not expect more than a modest run.

Far more discouraging notices greeted Charles Rann Kennedy's vanity mounting of his own "divine comedy of this very day," **The Army with Banners** (4-9-18, Vieux Colombier). His doddering, palsied heroine, Mary Bliss (Edith Wynne Matthison), begins to regain her old vigor when, in her luxuriously converted thirteenth-century Gothic nunnery, she senses the Second Coming. Her hopes are nearly derailed by the arrival of a fire-and-slang-belching revivalist (shades of the Rev. James Gleason in *The Eternal Magdalene*). Tommy Trail (Ernest Anderson) harangues the assembled guests: "Warm up, warm up, you bunch of soda-fountain freezers. That's not the way to handle a hymn. Geraround it! Geraway with it! Biff! Whiz it into a goal! Some of you sissified guys have no more kick in your souls than hocked fleas." But not even the excesses of the preacher and her guests can prevent Mary from rejoicing, "The Lord is at hand! Arise and meet Him! Lazarus, I say! Lazarus, come forth!" No wonder one reviewer observed, "A curious atmosphere of lunacy weighs upon the play." When the play failed, the author presented a revival of his much superior *The Servant in the House* (3-23-08) on the 24th.

Mrs. Fiske's string of bad luck persisted with Henri Lavedan's **Service** (4-15-18, Cohan). A war play written several years before the war, it told of a pacifist mother whose husband (Lee Baker) and sons are soldiers. One (Georges Flateau) of the sons is a pacifist, too, and has invented a weapon so horrible that the user could win a war instantly. He has kept his invention secret. But after the family learns that the other brother has been killed by Germans and that France and Germany are going to war, their anger and patriotism prevail. As a curtain raiser the Fiskes offered a revival of Lord Dunsany's *A Night at an Inn,* which told of the vengeance wreaked on some Englishmen by a jade idol from whose forehead they had stolen a priceless ruby, and which had originally been done in New York two years before at the Neighborhood Playhouse.

Even Rachel Crothers was caught up in the late-season blues. Actually, the three-week stand of **Once Upon a Time** (4-15-18, Fulton) had been announced from the start as a limited engagement, concluding the season-long tour of this Chauncey Olcott vehicle. The aging actor appeared as "young middled-aged" Terry O'Shaughnessy, an inventor who is heading for New York with a little girl (Bonnie Marie) in his charge. He is in for some surprises: the little girl proves to be the orphaned daughter of his brother; he makes a fortune selling one invention; and his sweet young niece brings about a reconciliation between him and a woman who, years before, had jilted him for a richer man and who is now a widow. The tenor's admirers knew he would find occasion to warble four songs, the number of melodies that traditionally were added to such shows.

The Provincetown Players' final bill of the season included one new O'Neill play, **Rope** (4-26-18, Playwright's), in which a mean, senescent man ties a noose to the rafters of his barn, hoping his son will hang himself. As usual most critics ignored the productions rather than have to fork up the price of a ticket. But the *Tribune's* Heywood Broun did attend and reported that the play told "an enthralling story in a highly proficient way." Another of the plays was Susan Glaspell's **A Woman's Honor**, in which a group of women, uncaring about their own honor, are willing to perjure themselves to save a young man who has been condemned to death and who will not save himself because it might entail soiling his sweetheart's good name. A few weeks later the Washington Square Players also offered the O'Neill work, so the public soon learned what Broun's fellow critics thought.

On the 29th at the Plymouth, Nazimova raised the curtain on the last of her Ibsen series, her Nora in *A Doll's House* provoking the headshaking and applause that she by now must have become accustomed to.

Henry Miller, to replace his failed opener, revived Sydney Grundy's *A Marriage of Convenience* (11-8-97) at his new theatre on May 1. Billie Burke was his leading lady, with Lowell Sherman and Lucile Watson in support.

Ethel Barrymore's somewhat unsteady season concluded with A. A. Milne's **Belinda** (5-6-18, Empire). Belinda Barrington is a divorced woman courted by a poet (Richard Hatteras) and a statistician (E. Lyall Swete). So as not to dishearten them, she passes off her grown daughter (Eva Le Gallienne) as her niece. But her well-laid plans gang agley when her former husband (Cyril Keightley) unexpectedly reappears. In the end Belinda and her ex are reunited, while the daughter and the poet find that they are affinities. Barrie's *The New Word*, first done on Broadway last season, was tagged on as a curtain raiser, without the star.

An all-star cast—including Laurette Taylor, George Arliss, Chauncey Olcott, James K. Hackett, George M. Cohan, and Julia Arthur—came into the huge Century Theatre on the 17th for a week with another of last season's plays, *Out There*. It was part of an extended fund-raising tour for the Red Cross.

The season ended when yet one more of those high-hoping groups, this one calling itself the Authors' and Actors' Theatre, presented a double bill. The main play, Arline Van Ness Hines's **Her Honor, the Mayor** (5-20-18, Fulton), was a feminist tract lamely disguised as a comedy. To the consternation of the town's menfolks, Julia Kennedy (Laura Nelson Hall) is elected mayor. The men do everything they can to thwart her, but she bests them at each turn. The curtain raiser was Hubert Osborne's **The Good That Men Do,** set in Shakespeare's home the day after his death. Although his family and friends are ashamed that he wasted his life as a scribbler, that does not prevent their squabbling over his estate.

1918–1919

By the beginning of the new season things were looking up for both Broadway and America. Playgoers had shrugged off the indifference to theatricals that had hurt attendance first at the outbreak of the war in Europe and then again after America's entry into the fighting. Business was booming and, with victory clearly in sight, optimism was rampant. As a result theatres were packed. Producers again attempted to increase ticket prices, this time with more success. The old $2.00 top was all but history. More and more shows were asking and getting $2.75 ($2.50 for the basic ticket plus a 10 percent war tax). Musicals were even testing a $3.00 top. And the season could not have gotten off to a better start.

That smash-hit opener was Samuel Shipman and Aaron Hoffman's **Friendly Enemies** (7-22-18, Hudson), which came to New York after a long and profitable Chicago stand. (In Chicago it had grossed a then fabulous $18,000 a week at its height, prompting *Variety* to call it "probably [the] biggest dramatic hit in the world.") It deftly tricked its audiences into learning with a laugh the need for tolerance of divergent views. Henry Block (Sam Bernard) and Karl Pfeiffer [Pfeifer in many programs] (Louis Mann) are German-born Americans. They have been friends since their childhoods in the old country. But with the outbreak of the war they find themselves on opposing sides. Henry is so pro-American that he has changed his name from the Heinrich he so long employed, but Karl, angrily dismissing claims of German atrocities, adamantly refuses to allow Henry, or anyone else, to call him Charlie. The two men constantly quarrel. Unbeknownst to his friends, Karl has been giving huge sums of money to a man who is a secret German agent (Felix Krembs), although Karl is led to believe that he is contributing primarily to presenting the true facts of the war to Americans. Nor does Karl know that his son (Richard Barbee), with the encouragement of Karl's wife (Mathilde Cottrelly), Henry, and Henry's daughter (Regina Wallace), who is his fiancée, has left college and joined the army. Initially, on discovering this, Karl is so furious that he stalks out of his house. But after he learns the secret agent's true nature and that his son appears to have been lost in the sabotage sinking of a troop transport, he changes sides. To make for an even happier ending, the son returns home, having been saved from the sinking. Bernard, Mann, and Miss Cottrelly had been stars for years as "Dutch" dialect comedians, which most playgoers saw as more Jewish than German. Their lines were essentially the same as those which had been given to the characters they had played in more farfetched comedies or musicals and which had fun with immigrants' problems mastering English: "This is my coming daughter-in-law. . . . They are feeansayed—my son is her intention"; "You make me loose my distemper. Mr. Stuart [the secret agent] is important importance—I got important importance with him"; "In this life when we least expect the unexpected then we can always expect it." Although some critics felt the play was "crude and conventional in construction," they agreed it was superlative theatre. Capitally mounted and played, the comedy ran for over a year and sent out several road companies, even though the armistice removed some of its immediacy. For much of its New York run it repeated its phenomenal Chicago success, reportedly earning $64,000 in its first three months.

There was more anti-German propaganda in Maxine Elliott and William Faversham's production of **Allegiance** (8-1-18, Maxine Elliott's), by Prince and Princess Troubetzkoy [Amélie Rives]. Neither of the producers appeared in the play, although

Faversham directed it. In some ways it seemed a rewrite of *Friendly Enemies*. Only now a pro-American son (Charles Meredith) must confront his father and grandfather, who are loyal to the Central Powers. The sinking of the *Lusitania* converts but also kills (with a heart attack) the older man, while the father is finally made to realize he is the dupe of a secret agent. Having neither originality, fine acting, nor laughs to buoy it, the play's life was short.

John Hunter Booth's **Keep Her Smiling** (8-5-18, Astor) ran longer—104 performances—thanks in good measure to Sidney Drew, John Drew's younger, possibly illegitimate, brother, who had never found much success on the stage but had recently made a name for himself in silent-film comedies. Meek, uxorious Henry Trindle (Drew), though only a clerk, has a wife with champagne tastes. She thinks nothing of frittering away $6000 on a single party. Her spending becomes even more irresponsible after Henry, to close a legal loophole, is given one share of stock in his company and made an unpaid director. But Mrs. Trindle's extravagance soon convinces everyone that Henry must be an astute businessman, so he is pushed quickly up the corporate ladder.

More propaganda, couched in terms of an old-fashioned touring melodrama, was evident in Parker Fisher's **Mother's Liberty Bond** (8-7-18, Park), whose profits, had there been any, were to have gone to the New York *Sun* Tobacco Fund to provide soldiers with cigarettes. The play's hero was a young scholar who hits upon a way to improve the efficiency of the aeroplanes used in combat. His professor is a German spy. The rest, including the hero's eventual relationship to a pretty girl who saunters into his life, was obvious to everyone but the characters onstage. Pageantry, in the form of troop drills, added to the entertainment.

Anne Crawford Flexner's **The Blue Pearl** (8-8-18, Longacre) was a more patently commercial affair, but hardly more successful. It centered on a much wed, much alimonied temptress (Julia Bruns) who, on a moonlit boardwalk in Atlantic City, seduces a married man (Orlando Daly) into giving her a valuable pendant. When the pendant is stolen during a hypnotist's exhibition in a darkened suite, the police commissioner (George Nash) must determine who among a goodly number of guests is the thief. Actors in blackface pushing rolling chairs occupied by elegantly dressed vacationers added some verisimilitude but could not add the requisite excitement.

Nor was there the requisite buildup of laughter in Mark Swan's **She Walked in Her Sleep** (8-12-18, Playhouse), whose title gave away the basis of the plot. Daphne Arnold (Alberta Burton) is a beautiful girl who sleepwalks from her apartment into neighboring apartments, at one point picking up an important secret document and at other times sauntering into the arms of other women's husbands just as the wives enter the room. One applauded scene showed Daphne moving from apartment to apartment by way of an outer ledge on the sixteenth floor of the building.

The season's second smash hit—335 performances—was Anthony Paul Kelly's **Three Faces East** (8-13-18, Cohan and Harris). It was coming to seem, as the fighting neared its end, that one out of two new plays had a war theme. Kelly's mystery-thriller begins in a plush German war office, where a young lady (Violet Heming) is enlisted to assume the identity of a murdered Englishwoman and to take a U-boat to England, there to pose as Fraulein Helene and to make contact with an arch-spy, Franz Boelke. The play's title is the expression the spies employ to acknowledge one another. Boelke plans to blow up the cabinet, so Helene wangles a place in a minister's household. It soon appears that almost everyone who crosses her path is either a double or a triple agent. She herself turns out to be a British double agent, and she finally manages to unmask the minister's mysterious butler (Emmett Corrigan) as Boelke and, in a cellar with a bomb ticking away, thwart his scheme. She even manages to find romance with a handsome officer. Because Kelly had been a film writer, the *Times* opined, "the tenseness of the action and the swift variety of the scenic development are strongly suggestive of the screen." Miss Heming, a blue-eyed blonde with a "peaches and cream complexion," modeled a number of attractive dresses, including one "of the palest flesh-colored charmeuse with the bodice a mass of pearl passementerie" and a long, slim, draped silk skirt "drawn snugly around the ankles and tucked under . . . so that the petticoat with its metallic silver bowknots and lines of silver hemstitching may frill out below."

Martin Brown's **A Very Good Young Man** (8-19-18, Plymouth) opened on a scorching hot night and garnered a mixed press. The public sided with those who dismissed the comedy, so it was quickly withdrawn. During its short stay it spotlighted Leroy Gumph (Wallace Eddinger), a man so beautifully well-behaved that his own sweetheart (Ruth Findlay) cannot believe anyone is truly that good. To show he has a more wicked side he goes off with another girl to a pier pavilion in Sheepshead Bay.

His sweetheart then rejects him because of his naughtiness, at least until just before the final curtain. Among those who won special commendation were tiny Ada Lewis, a veteran of the old Harrigan shows, as a vinegary, vulgar undertaker's widow, and Alan Dinehart, who would go on to fame in several media, as the head of a quartet of singing waiters.

Another war play; another hit. Berte Thomas's **Under Orders** (8-21-18, Eltinge) had been done in London as *Out of Hell* but had not been very successful. Because it required only two players (each playing two parts) one reviewer called the cast Hooverized, a reference to Herbert Hoover's asking in his relief work for Americans to use less. Effie Shannon played sisters: one married to an American, the other to a German. Each sister has a soldier son, played by Shelley Hull. The American is captured but escapes and takes refuge with his German aunt. His German cousin comes to America disguised as him but inadvertently gives himself away by playing the piano, something his American relation cannot do. Although he warns his aunt that if she reveals he has come to spy her son, now a hostage, will be shot, she nonetheless turns him over to authorities, then loses her mind grieving over her son. Happily, he returns home safely in the last act and helps restore her sanity. Essentially a trick play, it still provoked Dorothy Parker to write in *Vanity Fair*, "It is certainly going to be difficult to convince me that I will ever see a better war play. . . . When a trick play can be so intensely absorbing that you forget all about the trick part and think only of the play itself, I would like to suggest that that is indeed something." However, for many the evening's strength came from Hull's brilliant playing. He was, as one reviewer noted, "handsome, manly, and tender," playing both men as basically decent human beings caught in a dehumanizing struggle. Miss Parker concluded, "If the author had let Shelley Hull get killed, not a woman in the audience would ever have smiled again." But tragedy struck during the run when Hull came down in January with the influenza that was wreaking havoc across the country. Within a few days this "virile young actor" and "matinee idol de luxe" was dead, and without him the New York troupe could not go on.

Some critics looked on Montague Glass and Jules Eckert Goodman's ramshackle farce **Why Worry?** (8-23-18, Harris) as a Potash and Perlmutter variation in which the feuding friends, owners of a Second Avenue restaurant, were female. One of the girls was Dora (Fanny Brice), the other, Stella (May Boley). Although the girls present their customers with a large menu, the only dish they can usually offer is pot roast and latkas (potato pancakes). When they encounter financial problems, a loyal patron, Felix Noblestone (George Sidney), underwrites their efforts to abandon the Lower East Side and open a roadhouse. Business remains bad, so Dora gets up to sing and dance for the guests. German spies also present difficulties. As expected, smiling solutions are found just before eleven o'clock. To contemporaries Sidney was the actor who had toured for years in musical comedies about a character named Busy Izzy (or Izzie). Singled out among the supporting players were four men who posed first as a jazz band, then as waiters, and later as detectives and who were played by vaudeville favorites, the Avon Comedy Four, headed by Joe Smith and his buddy Charlie Dale. Indeed, *Variety* found the evening "an unfortunate succession of incoherent situations made endurable by Fanny Brice and the Avon Comedy Four." It also complained about the Yiddish terms employed in the play, insisting that "not one Gentile in 100,000 knows what 'kibbitzer' means," only to add, "and many Hebrews are unfamiliar with the word." So the clowns' clowning was in vain. The farce was a flop.

By contrast, Frank Bacon and Winchell Smith's **Lightnin'** (8-26-18, Gaiety) proved the decade's biggest hit. Its 1291 performances surpassed the record of *Peg o' My Heart* and were not overtaken by another show for nearly ten years. John Marvin (Ralph Morgan) has grown to like "Lightnin' " Bill Jones (Bacon), although Jones is a teller of tall tales and a chronic boozer. But Marvin has his own troubles to worry about, since a shady lawyer bamboozled his late mother into selling their woodlands, which the railroad that subsequently bought the property has claimed have been illegally timbered by Marvin. However, Marvin is also courting Millie (Beatrice Nichols), an orphan whom Jones and his wife (Jessie Pringle) have raised and who helps the Joneses run their little hotel, which straddles the Nevada-California border. While the California half is something of a failure, the Nevada half is always packed with fugitives escaping from the law in California and, more often, with women seeking Reno divorces. The same shady lawyer (Paul Stanton) who had tricked Marvin's mother now attempts to trick Mrs. Jones into selling the hotel. When Lightnin' will not co-sign, the case winds up in court, along with the cases against Marvin and Mrs. Jones's suit for divorce. But Bill, prompted by Marvin, who has studied law, convinces the judge that Marvin is innocent and that the shyster is a crook. Mrs. Jones drops her divorce case. Lightnin' even gets Millie, who had accepted the crook's slanders against Marvin, and Marvin to agree to marry. The play was replete with down-home characters and dialogue, best represented, of course, by Lightnin'.

Bill: Did you ever know Buffalo Bill?
Sheriff: Yes, I knew him well.
Bill: I learned him all he knew about killing Indians. Did he ever tell you about the duel I fought with Settin' Bull?
Sheriff: Settin' Bull?
Bill: He was standin' when I shot him. I never took advantage of nobody, not even a Indian.
Sheriff: Say, you got a bee in your bonnet, ain't you?
Bill: What do you know about bees?
Sheriff: Not much, do you?
Bill: Yes, I do—I know all about 'em. I used to be in the bee business. Why, I drove a swarm of bees across the plains in the dead of winter. And never lost a bee. Got stung twice.

Hornblow spoke for many of his fellow critics when he wrote in *Theatre* that "Lightnin' himself is so quaintly humorous and lovable that the rusty plot never for a minute interferes with its comic effectiveness." And he added, "Bacon's impersonation of the central figure is Jeffersonian in its simplicity and understanding." The play raised the silver-haired Bacon, with his pronounced drawl and marked resemblance to Joseph Jefferson, to a belated stardom. Because of his identification with the title part, no road company was sent out. Unfortunately, Bacon died shortly after the post–New York tour began. So other men were brought in to play his part in the seasons-long tour that continued through 1925.

Overshadowed by the acclaim and success of *Lightnin'* was another far slighter hit that opened the same evening, Roi Cooper Megrue's **Where Poppies Bloom** (8-26-18, Republic). Megrue adapted his play from Henri Kistemaecker's Paris hit *Un Soir au front*. It recounted the dilemma of a woman (Marjorie Rambeau) who must choose between a husband (Lewis Stone) whom she has learned is a traitor and a young soldier (Pedro de Cordoba) whom she has nursed back to health.

During its tryout, Avery Hopwood's **Double Exposure** (8-27-18, Bijou) looked to be another hit, but Broadway felt differently, so the farce lasted less than two weeks. A swami (J. Harry Irvine) hypnotizes two husbands (John Cumberland and John Westley), each of whom believes he would prefer to be wed to the other man's wife. The swami claims that the men have exchanged "astral" bodies, while retaining their own physical appearances. Thus the timid husband played by Cumberland suddenly becomes brazen in approaching his neighbor's wife (Francine Larrimore), while his neighbor's new personality appeals to the timid man's own wife (Janet Beecher). Both men conclude they really prefer their own spouses. But then the matter is academic since the whole thing was a dream. The farce reportedly was suggested by Wilhelm Von Scholz's *Vertauschte Seelen*.

George Broadhurst, collaborating with his future wife, Lillian Trimble Bradley, did not enjoy much better luck with **The Woman on the Index** (8-29-18, 48th St.). In a prologue a policeman searches for and finds the $50,000 haul of a dead gangster while the crook's wife (Julia Dean) watches in horrified silence. Years pass. The widow has remarried and is now the wife of the American ambassador (Lester Lonergan) to England. But a supposed French diplomat (George Probert), who is actually a Turk spying for the Germans, learns her secret and sees an opportunity for mischief. Luckily a Japanese secret agent (T. Tamamoto), helping the Allies, foils his machinations. Once again the *World* suggested the drama might have been better turned into farce.

Leon Gordon and Le Roy Clemens's **Watch Your Neighbor** (9-2-18, Booth) was a war play that might have succeeded had it arrived earlier. It appealed to many critics, who suggested it was preposterous but confessed it nonetheless was great fun. Still, it was lost in the crush of dramas with war themes. It told of a peace conference in Switzerland where the participants agree to lay down arms at a specific time. Of course, this really is a nefarious plot of the Germans, who would then attack in force. But a secret service officer (Gordon), posing as a "silly ass" Englishman, gets wind of the scheme and exposes it.

There was no sign of the war in **Penrod** (9-2-18, Globe), which Edward E. Rose derived from Booth Tarkington's popular stories. The often critical *World* rejoiced that "a fragrant breath of youth wafted into Broadway." Four youngsters—Penrod (Andrew Lawlor), Sam (Richard Rose), Herman (Thomas McCann), and Vermin (Charles Whitfield)—decide to expose the suitor (John Davidson) of Penrod's sister (Helen Hayes) as a crook. Penrod buys a twenty-five-cent toy detective badge to add to his clout. But after it is shown that the suitor is, indeed, a crook he gets a real medal. In what was still a rare practice (although it had been seen in *Young America*), Herman and Vermin were two little black boys actually played by blacks. At first the show seemed to be a success, but then business fell sharply (because of the flu epidemic, according to Helen Hayes). To keep the show going it was transferred from the large Globe to the bandbox Punch and Judy. But the move failed.

Be single if you would be successful!
Ought! Nought! Cipher! Zero!
The man who marries is a hero!

So shout Robert Audrey (Bruce McRae), James Crocket (John Cope), Henry Allen (George Abbott), William Rivers (S. K. Walker), and Nicholson Walters (Edward Davis)—members of the College Bachelor's Club, who have met every fifth year since their graduation in 1903. They have sworn to remain single and must fork up $5000 if they go back on their oath. But reluctantly, and only out of a sense of patriotism and charity, each man agrees to adopt a war orphan, thereby honoring his commitment to society to raise a child. Of course, the men soon recognize that each will need a woman to help him, and so are they trapped into matrimony. The most singular case is Bob's, for his orphan turns out to be not a tiny tot but a beautiful seventeen-year-old girl, Ruth Atkins (Jeanne Eagels). Without realizing it at first, he falls in love with her. Before long he has joined his buddies in preparing to walk up the aisle. All this occurred in David Belasco's production of John L. Hobble's *Daddies* (9-5-18, Belasco). Critics split sharply in their assessments of the play, which they saw as a work of "real power and artistic distinction" or of "sugar and sentimentality . . . unhooverized throughout." As was increasingly the case, praise for Belasco's mounting was perfunctory (one critic stating that Belasco had given up trying to create stage pictures that films could easily outdo). The highest praise went to Jeanne Eagels, whose fragile, vulnerable blonde beauty awed the men on the aisle. They were especially taken by her depiction of post-crossing "land-sickness," her long, touching speech about war orphans, and her subtle courtship scenes. The play ran out the season.

· · ·

Jeanne Eagels (1894–1929) was born in Kansas City, Mo. She made her debut at the age of seven as Puck in *A Midsummer Night's Dream,* then first appeared in New York in 1911 in a musical comedy. Minor roles in both musicals and straight plays followed until she came to the attention of George Arliss, who gave her important supporting roles in a number of his vehicles. She left him to take the lead in this play.

· · ·

William A. Brady's production of Owen Davis's **Forever After** (9-9-18, Central) ran nearly as long—312 performances—even though many critics gave it short shrift. On the battlefield (played on the front of the stage), a badly wounded soldier, Ted (Conrad Nagel), asks his buddy to tell Jennie that he lied, that he always had loved her. The scene fades, and when the lights come on the setting is an American town where Ted has fallen in love with a rich girl, Jennie (Alice Brady). Unhappily, he is a poor boy, albeit bright enough to get into Harvard. Jennie's snobbish mother and Ted's own false pride scuttle the affair. Now he is taken to a hospital where Jennie is a Red Cross nurse. After a tearful reunion, she promises to love him back to health. Davis later called this maudlin claptrap "one of the biggest money-makers I have ever had." He added that no one brought the poetry to the part of Jennie that Miss Brady was able to do. *Variety* noted, "The love scenes between Miss Brady and Conrad Nagel are the sweetest, most wholesome and fetching bits of acting seen in these parts in many a day." The producer's daughter also earned gasps from the ladies in the audience when she made her first appearance in a pink gingham frock and later modeled Paris creations by Collot and Lanvin. The play was one of four openings on the same night. The other three failed.

Someone in the House (9-9-18, Knickerbocker) had originally been written by Larry Evans, on whose short stories it was based, and Walter Percival. But after an earlier, unsuccessful tryout, with Shelley Hull in the lead, its producer, George C. Tyler, had closed the show and called in several play doctors, finally asking a largely untested George S. Kaufman to liven up its comedy. Essentially another Raffles yarn, it opens in that favorite location of theatrical jewel thieves, a pawnshop. There the handsome Jimmy Burke (Robert Hudson), one of the slickest of thieves, meets with his buddies The Deacon (William B. Mack) and English (Dudley Digges). He decides to steal a valuable necklace that some high society amateurs will use in a play they are mounting. The play is written by the self-impressed J. Percyval Glendinning (Hassard Short), who seems to be followed everywhere he goes by his vacuous wife (Lynn Fontanne). Burke deftly lands a part in the play and soon falls in love with his leading lady, Molly Brant (Julia Hay), who it turns out owns the necklace. Though Burke shortly has the necklace in his possession, he leaves it behind when he disappears so that Molly will not be hurt. A police inspector (Sidney Toler) can only shake his head. (For a time, the ending had Jimmy return the jewelry case with a wedding ring inside, and Molly accept the proposal of her reformed lover.) The *World* rejoiced that the play "is rich in situations and most of the situations are surrounded by humor." Even if the leading man proved a disappointment, the supporting cast won kudos, especially Lynn Fontanne. Yet the show survived only a month, its failure blamed on the rising flu epidemic, although many plays rode out the storm successfully.

Hokum of a different sort failed to thrive in **Mr. Barnum** (9-9-18, Criterion), which Harrison Rhodes and Thomas A. Wise created as a vehicle for Wise. There was precious little plot—something about a duplicitous associate trying, and failing, to cheat Barnum out of his circus. What counted were the separate bits, such as Tom Thumb (Herbert Rice) and Lavinia Warren (Queenie Mab) falling in love and Barnum's preparing a showy wedding for them, Barnum's attempt to strike terror in some tightfisted townsfolk and drum up business by claiming his Wild Man has escaped, and Barnum's stumbling on the idea for pink lemonade. "The art of Mr. Wise is as abundant as his person," one reviewer noted. But this time it was unavailing.

Nor did Jack Lait and Jo Swerling's **One of Us** (9-9-18, Bijou) have much appeal. A suave young Harvard graduate (Arthur Ashley), the evening's second one, decides to play Pygmalion by wooing, wedding, and making a lady out of a cabaret singer (Bertha Mann). He pretends he is a hood to gain her attention. Only after he has almost succeeded does she find out who he really is. One aisle-sitter asked if a Harvard graduate would spout such a redundancy as "I haven't the fundamental rudiments of an education." The opening act, set in a cabaret, allowed for a series of specialty turns.

The busy week continued. Tuesday's two premieres, like the last three of the preceding evening and like both of Thursday's entries, were destined for short runs, six of the seven plays closing on the same Saturday three weeks later. Stuart Walker, better known as mastermind of the Portmanteau Theatre, was the author of **Jonathan Makes a Wish** (9-10-18, Princess), which featured Gregory Kelly. Kelly had rocketed to celebrity last season as the star of *Seventeen* and now was assigned the role of a fourteen-year-old. His Jonathan dreams of becoming a great writer, but his Uncle John (Ainsworth Arnold), the concrete drainpipe mogul, attempts to discourage him by locking him in a room until he gives up his preposterous notions. Jumping from a window, Jonathan is seriously hurt and in his ensuing delirium sees himself as an unloved hunchback. A nicer uncle (George Gaul) and a carefree tramp (Edgar Stelhi) help him recover his health and his ambitions.

At least Walker's play was let down respectfully, but Oliver D. Bailey's **Over Here** (9-10-18, Fulton) was derided by the critics and snickered at by audiences. It told how the fathers of two unpatriotic youngsters teach them to love their country. Only the fact that its author was also its producer accounted for its surviving three weeks.

In a slight way, Laura Hinkley and Mabel Ferris's **Another Man's Shoes** (9-12-18, 39th St.) echoed Walker's play. Years before the play begins Richard Trent had suffered from a blow on the head that seemingly had destroyed his memory. Adopting the name Richard Craven (Lionel Atwill), he becomes a successful businessman and makes a happy marriage until an injury in a railroad accident causes him to totally forget his second self and remember only his earlier life as Trent. Most of the play was occupied attempting to reconcile Trent with the friends and family he had as Craven.

Another temporarily demented man, a shell-shocked soldier, provided the love interest in Theresa Helburn's **Crops and Croppers** (9-12-18, Belmont), whose heroine was a debutante (Eileen Huban) resolved to do her bit in the war by writing the soldiers overseas (a different one each day of the week) and by becoming a "farmerette." She fails miserably as a farmer but does succeed in restoring to health a handsome poilu (Georges Flateau). In her autobiography, Miss Helburn, later a major mover in the Theatre Guild, complained that casting and decor hurt the satire. She belittled Flateau as "a plump, middle-aged Frenchman," said Miss Huban, with her thick brogue, would have been better as an Irish peasant, and complained that her simple New England farmhouse was painted "pale pink and green, like a boudoir." Even a title change to *Alison Makes Hay* could not lure in customers.

But Saturday night's entry was a big hit. Hornblow welcomed Roland West and Carlyle Moore's **The Unknown Purple** (9-14-18, Lyric) as "a 'corker' . . . a gripping, moving melodrama with a picturesque touch of the supernatural." Peter Marchmont (Richard Bennett) is a sweet, naive man but a brilliant inventor. His vicious, unfaithful wife (Helen MacKellar) and her lover (Earle Browne) send him to prison on trumped-up charges and profit from one of his discoveries. On his release, Peter is a changed person—hard and vengeful. He employs another of his inventions, a device that makes him invisible and signals his presence only by an eerie purple light, to hound his betrayers and win vindication. The play used flashbacks and even juggled time by having much of the action of its second act supposedly take place at the same time as events in the third act. Bennett won special praise for his ability to convey both the early innocent and the later, crueler avenger.

A fine, much applauded player—Otis Skinner—could do little for a creaky English vehicle, Horace Annesley Vachell's **Humpty Dumpty** (9-16-18, Lyceum). Skinner later recalled it as "the only play I ever produced that had no success whatever." For all the cross-ocean hand-clasping it proved much too English for Americans. It dealt with a hairdresser (barber in American terms) who unexpectedly becomes a lord but decides he prefers the simpler life.

The parade of novelties was interrupted by a revival of Oscar Wilde's *An Ideal Husband* (3-12-95) at the Comedy on the 16th. By now Wilde's plays could be judged on their own merits, so the comedy was lauded, as were the leading players—Norman Trevor, Constance Collier, and Julian L'Estrange.

The Hattons (Frederic and Fanny) also came a cropper this season with their comedy **The Walk-offs** (9-17-18, Morosco). The walk-offs, according to a Negro servant in the play, are people whom God forgot to give souls. One such soulless woman is Kathleen Rutherford (Carroll McComas), who lives in a posh Riverside Drive apartment with a view of the Palisades. She is a worthless society parasite until a noble Kentuckian, Robert Shirley Winston (Edmund Lowe), arrives to teach her the virtues of decency and hard work.

On the other hand, Roi Cooper Megrue had a season-long success with his **Tea for Three** (9-19-18, Maxine Elliott's). The Wife (Margaret Lawrence) dearly loves her stolid Husband (Frederick Perry), even if he is given to jealousy. But her love does not prevent her having a delightful, platonic relationship with a Friend (Arthur Byron). At lunch the two conspire to teach The Husband a lesson by allowing him to catch them in a compromising if actually innocent situation. The Husband demands that he and The Friend draw lots, with the loser to commit suicide. The Friend loses. Belatedly The Husband recognizes how absurd he has been. When The Friend smilingly reappears, the much relieved Husband urges him to continue his harmless tête-à-têtes with The Wife. Many critics singled out Shavian and Wildean lines that struck their fancy, such as "Pity is akin to love, that's why so many women pity their husbands" and "No man is so bad a woman can't find an excuse for him." In the *Times* Corbin deemed the play insubstantial but added, "It has a very rare virtue of doing what it intends with neatness and a certain finality of skill which keeps the attention of the audience throughout and ensures an evening of genuine entertainment."

Far uptown, a playhouse that years before had been home to cheap touring melodrama and then gone over to films reverted briefly to live theatre. It did so with a play by two men whose heyday preceded the last years of the old melodramas. Adolph Philipp and Edward A. Paulton's **Tell That to the Marines** (9-24-18, Yorkville) detailed the family disputes between Hein Schultz (Philipp), a German-born grocer torn between his loves for his old country and his adopted one, and his son (Joseph Striker), who has joined the marines.

The next major entry, Haddon Chambers's West End comedy **The Saving Grace** (9-30-18, Empire), received even better notices but, possibly because it was too English for many Americans, fell four performances short of the charmed century mark. It described how an army officer (Cyril Maude), cashiered for eloping with his superior's wife (Laura Hope Crews), is restored to his self-esteem and his old rank through his wife's efforts.

Two celebrated dancers—Khyva St. Albans and Theodore Kosloff—tried their luck on the dramatic stage with Ruth Sawyer's **The Awakening** (10-1-18, Criterion), in which, not surprisingly, they portrayed two dancers, who fall in love but whose romance is nearly destroyed when the girl is accused of being a spy. In a throwback, the love scenes were underscored by an orchestra wailing slow music.

Another disappointment was Jane Cowl's venture into comic waters, **Information, Please** (10-2-18, Selwyn), which the star wrote for herself in collaboration with Jane Murfin. She played the wife of a neglectful M.P. (Orme Caldara). To win him back she goes so far as to run off to America with another man. The play was the opening attraction at the newest of Broadway's theatres—a playhouse that in some notices won higher praise than the play.

October's first success was Arthur Hopkins's mounting of Tolstoy's **Redemption** [*The Living Corpse*] (10-3-18, Plymouth), with John Barrymore as a man who runs off to live with gypsies after realizing his wife has taken up with another man, and who kills himself so that she will not be convicted of bigamy. Many critics confessed to not understanding the nuances of the plot and suggested that neither did Barrymore, since his performance was so uneven. In his autobiography, Barrymore agreed with them. But the same critics extolled Robert Edmond Jones's austerely simple settings. At first, the play struggled to find an audience, but since Hopkins owned the Plymouth he was able to keep the drama on the boards until it caught on. It ran six months.

Changing times were underlined with the premiere of Hector Turnbull and Willard Mack's **I.O.U.** 10-5-18, Belmont), since the play was announced as having been based on *The Cheat,* a silent film! Reviewers suggested the flicker should have been left alone. Mary Nash, the dark-eyed, pale-skinned beauty, whose hair was described variously as "reddish-black" and "brown-black," played a society figure who diverts charity contributions she has collected and uses them to pay for her own good times. A wicked East Indian (José Ruben) lends her more money, but when she refuses to sleep with him, he brands her with a hot iron. The star's gorgeous Paris gowns elicited oohs and ahs from the audience. They included a dress of sapphire blue velvet, its skirt hem embroidered in wheat sprays of hyacinth blue; a flamingo pink dinner dress with a silver lace petticoat; and a black-and-brown dress, "the brown of tobacco duvetyn with the black of soutache and chenille embroidery." But the play's ugly story told against it.

By contrast, Sacha Guitry's light-as-air, four-character boulevard comedy *Faisons un rêve* settled in for a pleasant run as **Sleeping Partners** (10-5-18, Bijou). It centered on a young man (H. B. Warner) who is determined to have an affair with a married woman (Irene Bordoni).

Leo Ditrichstein fared less happily when he starred in his own and A. E. Thomas's **The Matinee Hero** (10-7-18, Vanderbilt), playing a popular matinee idol whose family and friends do all they can to prevent his turning serious and trying to play Hamlet. The play ends with his reading Hamlet's most famous soliloquy.

The next entry began with a priggish George Washington (Grant Stewart) and a racy, slangy Ananias (Malcolm Bradley), both bathed in eerie green lights, debating the merits and demerits of veracity. The debate concluded, the stage was once again brightly lit and a more or less real world depicted in Aaron Hoffman's **Nothing But Lies** (10-8-18, Longacre). The pivotal figure in this world is George Washington Cross, a partner in an advertising agency, but if audiences mistook him for the Robert Bennett of *Nothing But the Truth* that was understandable, since both men were (or had been) impersonated by William Collier, with the same dry, deadpan, staccato humor that Collier always displayed. This time, although once again promising to tell nothing but the truth he winds up finding it more convenient to tell fib after fib. He makes the promise to his fiancée (Olive Wyndham) and breaks it to keep her brother (Clyde North), who has publicly made some scurrilous remarks about advertising, out of prison. But the results are identical,

discomfiting all his friends. Although *Variety* embraced the comedy as "a welcome relief from war and spy plays," it was at best a modest hit.

In Oliver D. Bailey and Lottie M. Meaney's **A Stitch in Time** (10-15-18, Fulton) a pretty, young charlady (Irene Fenwick) saves a stuggling artist (Ralph Kellard) from a woman (Grace Carlyle) who is only after his parents' wealth and also shows him his talent rests with his writing and not with his painting.

The Better 'Ole, which opened at the tiny Greenwich Village Theatre on the 19th, was soon moved uptown, where it ran nearly a year. But this British war play was so jammed with old and new songs that many considered it a musical, and it has been treated as such in *American Musical Theatre: A Chronicle.*

A number of critics saw Douglas Murray's **Perkins** (10-22-18, Henry Miller's) as Henry Miller's attempt to capitalize on the success of *Come Out of the Kitchen.* They perceived the plot as being quite similar. Only this time the girl who poses as a servant, again played by Ruth Chatterton, was an heiress required by a will to marry a specific man. That man, played this time by Miller himself, was again something of an outsider—a Canadian rancher. Perkins was the name the heiress assumed in service. The public would not buy it.

But that same public kept Charlotte E. Wells and Dorothy Donnelly's **The Riddle: Woman** (10-23-18, Harris) on the boards for twenty-one weeks. The piece purportedly was based on an unidentified Danish drama. A rich matron (Bertha Kalish) and a young mother (Chrystal Herne), in the play's powerful recognition scene, realize that they are both being blackmailed by a villainous count (A. E. Anson) and that he now has set his sights on the young daughter (Beatrice Allen) of a wealthy Jew. The young mother kills herself, but the matron confronts the count and strangles him. She turns over her old love letters to her husband, who simply throws them in the fire. Although the whole cast was praised, tall, slim Bertha Kalish was accorded the lion's share. Her brown hair and brown eyes offsetting her pale beauty, with its "slavic melancholy," her fiery, compelling gaze, her regal bearing, and her magnificent, gorgeously modulated voice (even with its thick accent) ensured that she claimed the audience's attention from her first entrance in a dress of gold and silver metal-cloth, featuring large gold flowers on a silver background and a scarf of dull amethyst chiffon bordered and tasseled in silver.

In Edward Clark's **Not with My Money** (10-24-18, 39th St.), one of the season's shortest-lived flops, a young socialite (Carroll McComas) hires Dickey

Foster, alias J. Robert Fulton (Lowell Sherman), a man she has been warned is a crook, to run a $7,000,000 charity. Her intention is to reform him, and she does. She has less luck with Penknife Clay (Walter Wilson), Dickey's cohort, who is posing as the Rev. Dr. Crane.

C. Lewis Hind and E. Lyall Swete's **Freedom** (10-26-18, Century) was far more a pageant than a genuine play. Its profits were to go to disabled servicemen. Perhaps for the sake of colorful costumes, many of the examples it offered—King Alfred, Robin Hood, Joan of Arc—were from the Middle Ages. But it also brought to life the battles for freedom of Patrick Henry and Florence Nightingale.

Several reviewers considered Grant Morris and Willard Mack's **The Big Chance** (10-28-18, 48th St.) as good a war play as any Americans had written. Yet arriving, as it did, virtually on the eve of the armistice, they also suggested it had missed its own chance. It focused on some raffish Tenderloin denizens more interested in good times, such as the races, than in fighting the war. The mistress (Mary Nash) of one of them finally goads them into enlisting, thereby offering "a decent death for men not fit to live." The battles in France bring out hidden virtues in a few but leave others, including the girl's lover, dead. William E. Meehan collected the best notices as a "race-track sport." The good reviews helped turn it into a modest success, surprising some and disappointing others.

An English play also touched on the war. However, Mrs. Henry de la Pasture's **Peter's Mother** (10-29-18, Playhouse) had originally been a novel set in the days of the Boer War and was brought up to date only for its theatricalization. It centered on an Englishwoman (Selene Johnson), torn between her selfish husband (Charles A. Stevenson), who dies before the play's end, and a selfish son (Philip Tonge), who eventually loses an arm in the fighting.

"Nothing is quite so refreshing on the crowded Rialto trail as a Clare Kummer night at the theatre," the *Dramatic Mirror* rejoiced. The forewarned heroine of Kummer's **Be Calm, Camilla** (10-31-18, Booth) is a seventeen-year-old Wisconsin girl, Camilla Hathaway (Lola Fisher), who comes to the Big City to begin a career as a pianist only to find she must settle for a job as an accompanist at a film house. On her way to work she is struck down by the automobile of a very rich young man, Junius Patterson (Walter Hampden). The two fall in love, but Camilla attempts suicide by throwing herself in a lake after discovering that Junius is married. Luckily for her, Junius is not happily married, so he quickly agrees to divorce his wife and marry Camilla. Fisher and Hampden had been successfully paired in Kummer's earlier hit, *Good Gracious Annabelle*. Both again were applauded, even if some reviewers quibbled that Hampden's forte was drama rather than comedy. Robert Edmond Jones's sets were, as usual, singled out for praise but not for description. Hedda Hopper, someday to be famous as a Hollywood gossip columnist, won encomiums as a nurse, but Carlotta Monterey, someday to be infamous as Eugene O'Neill's last wife, was largely ignored. The play was lauded primarily for its subtlety, a virtue not destined to attract many playgoers, so it ran only eleven weeks.

A far less subtle play, which opened the same evening, found a far larger audience. Austin Strong's **Three Wise Fools** (10-31-18, Criterion) takes place in a home shared by three aging bachelors: a grouchy financier, Theodore Findlay (Claude Gillingwater); Dr. Richard Gaunt (Harry Davenport); and Judge James Trumble (William Ingersoll). They lead such regular lives that when their cook alters the breakfast menu, they are appalled. "How many times have I got to tell you," Findlay barks at her, "that we don't like change in this house. We are three men of settled habits—we don't want innovations." To Findlay's surprise Gaunt suddenly has a real change, a change of heart. He advises his housemates that they must reinvigorate their lives or become "unburied dead." The only youthfulness about their place is Findlay's playboy nephew, Gordon (Charles Laite), who feels that a rich man's working means he is depriving a poorer man of a job. But their lives are thrown into disarray when they learn that a woman all three had once loved and who had rejected all of them has died and left them her child, Sidney, to care for. They prepare to welcome the boy. To their astonishment Sidney turns out to be a beautiful young lady (Helen Menken). She so rejuvenates the old fogies that after she has been living with them only a month they throw a big party for the "lunaversary," showering her with gifts. Gordon has even taken a job. In fact, when the old men note they once were called Athos, Porthos, and Aramis, Gordon advises them that he is D'Artagnan. Then a dangerous escapee (Stephen Colby), who has threatened the judge, enters the house but escapes before the police can catch him. It is clear that he had inside help, and suspicion falls on Sidney. She is sent packing, and only Gordon retains his faith in her. It does turn out she helped the man, but it also develops that another prisoner who escaped at the same time was her father, who has been sent to prison for a crime he did not commit. A happy ending follows quickly. Since Winchell Smith co-produced the comedy with John Golden, Broadway scuttlebutt credited him with doctoring the hit, which ran for ten months.

Revivals ushered in November. At the gargantuan Manhattan Opera House, David Belasco brought back *The Auctioneer* (9-23-01) on the 4th, with David Warfield recreating his original role. Curiously, on the same night at the more traditionally sized 44th Street Theatre, Richard B. Mantell, whom many saw as a sad but persistent representative of the all but dead school of Forrest and Booth, opened a stand with his repertory company. His schedule began with *Richelieu* and moved on to *King Lear, The Merchant of Venice, Macbeth, Othello, Hamlet, Romeo and Juliet, Richard III,* and Delavigne's *Louis XI*—all plays of an older school that once had been performed regularly in barn-like opera houses. For the most part critics greeted the sixty-four-year-old Mantell respectfully but unenthusiastically. Although he continued to perform in the hinterlands until shortly before his death a decade later, these were his final New York appearances.

A working model of a remotely controlled cannon nearly stole the show in Robert Mears Mackay and Victor Mapes's **The Long Dash** (11-5-18, 39th St.). In doing so it also nearly eclipsed the much admired performances of two fading stars. For the German ambassador (Henry E. Dixey) attempts to steal the invention, but an altruistic twin (Robert Edeson), despite the machinations of his more covetous brother (Edeson), turns the gun on the Germans. Just before the curtain the cannon is turned ominously to face the audience. Audiences first realized that Edeson was playing a double role when the meaner brother sits down in a tall chair by a fireplace, leaving only his elbow exposed, and the good brother suddenly enters through a door. Later in a darkened room the wicked brother focuses a flashlight on his twin. Edeson delivered both men's lines using "a mild sort of ventriloquism." Admitted hokum, the play found no audiences to face after the armistice.

If audiences laughed at the gimmickry in *The Long Dash,* they giggled nervously at the gaucheries of Butler Davenport's **The Comforts of Ignorance** (11-6-18, Bramhall), which ineptly mingled the stories of social climbers, philanderers, discarded mistresses, and fortune hunters. Despairing of finding a solid story in the play, which it described as "narcotic," the *Dramatic Mirror* concluded, "It seems as if Gertrude Stein furnished [Davenport] with the plot."

Nor was there much interest in Robert Mc-Laughlin's **Home Again** (11-11-18, Playhouse), a play which used the poems and characters of James Whitcomb Riley for its source. The curtain rose to the strains of "On the Banks of the Wabash." With the help of a charlatan medicine man, "Doc" Townsend (Maclyn Arbuckle), and a genuine physician, "Doc" Sifers (Scott Cooper), Orphant Annie (Madeline Delmar), who has been made the ward of mean old Jeff Thompson (Erville Anderson), finds an affectionate suitor in a would-be poet, Jim Johnson (Henry Duffy), and learns that the strange, roving bard, The Raggedy Man (Tim Murphy), is her long-lost father. Typical of the play's homey sentiments was the real doctor's telling the village curmudgeon and hypochondriac who had purchased the quack's nostrums, "Grouches generate the rankest kind of poison. A disposition like yours will breed more rheumatism in an hour than you could soak up in a week of wet weather." The play was directed by Jesse Bonstelle, who employed what was called "the French style" by having performers talk over one another. Despite its poor motivation and slapdash construction, the play found an afterlife on the road and with amateur groups as *Little Orphan Annie.*

The just-ended war, which had prompted Edward Knoblock to change the spelling of his name, also figured in the story of his **Tiger! Tiger!** (11-12-18, Belasco), but not so urgently as to make the play seem a war drama or hurt its box-office appeal in a suddenly altered atmosphere. Clive Couper (Lionel Atwill) is a rising M.P. who has been pressed by his friend Stephen Greer (Wallace Erskine) to marry his daughter, Evelyn (Dorothy Cumming). But he and Evelyn both insist they are merely good friends. Love is another matter. Evelyn asks him, "Are we free—you and I,—caged in by our loneliness? Is there a breaking of the bars in love? A sudden soaring up into a heaven?" Clive does finally find real love, with Sally (Frances Starr), a woman he has met in the street. She is not a tramp but a decent girl who has reacted as strongly and inexplicably to Clive as he has to her. But their passionate relationship turns sour after Clive learns that Sally is a domestic, a cook. He asks her to leave such menial work and become his mistress. When she refuses, he breaks off the relationship. She marries a man of her own class, and Clive goes off to war, where he is killed. Evelyn delivers some mementos which Clive had bequeathed to Sally. One of them is a poem ending, "The earth in us shall die, / The heaven—never!" Some critics felt the story was absurd or offensive; others complained that however beautiful Belasco's stage pictures were (Clive's chambers, a Red Cross office, a servants' dining room), scene changes and the frequent lowering of the curtain to indicate the passage of time made the play drag. But they did cheer the star, "never more certain in her every movement, never more captivating in personality, never more firm in intellectual grasp." Audiences cheered for five months.

On the 16th Henry Miller revived *Daddy Long Legs* at his theatre to replace the failed *Perkins*.

Enough playgoers overlooked critical reservations to give **The Betrothal** (11-18-18, Shubert), Maurice Maeterlinck's sequel to *The Blue Bird* (10-1-10), a passable run. It told how the Fairy Berylune (Mrs. Jacques Martin) helps Tyltyl (Reggie Sheffield) choose a mate by escorting him through the realms of the past and the future. One critical complaint was that an air of unworldliness was achieved by coloring sets and costumes monotonously.

Costumes and scenery were far more colorful in Dario Niccodemi and Michael Morton's **Remnant** (11-19-18, Morosco), a play set in 1840 Paris. But they could not truly enliven the story of a street gamin, Remnant (Florence Nash), who rids an idealistic engineer (George Gaul) of his selfish mistress and helps him with his dream to build a great railroad. Several reviewers saw Miss Nash's waif as more New Yorker than Parisian.

On the afternoon of the 22nd Walter Hampden gave a special matinee performance of *Hamlet* at the Plymouth. It was so well received that several additional matinees were booked (along with a matinee of *Macbeth* on December 1). The mounting was fashionably simple and preserved the text more faithfully and more fully than was commonplace. Critics felt Hampden brought great dignity and poetry to the role, failing, as they had suggested earlier, only in lighter moments. Continuing word of mouth caused the production to be brought into the 39th Street Theatre for three weeks of regular performances beginning May 20th.

Jane Cowl enjoyed a modest success that might have been bigger had not Edgar Selwyn and Channing Pollock's **The Crowded Hour** (11-22-18, Selwyn) been perceived by many potential playgoers as a past-its-time war play. One critic evaluated it as "a curious mixture of claptrap and right feeling." At a swank dance club Peggy Lawrence (Cowl), a Follies beauty, makes it obvious to Grace Laidlaw (Christine Norman) that she is the mistress of Grace's husband, Billy (Orme Caldara). But patriotic fervor at the club prompts Billy to enlist; so does Peggy. She becomes an army telephone operator. After a British retreat she is ordered to phone for American aid. She knows this means bringing up

Billy's regiment and his almost certain death. She demurs but is finally persuaded that it is her patriotic duty. The call is no sooner placed than a German shell destroys her telephone room. One oddity, seemingly ignored by critics but recalled by Pollock in his memoirs, was Georges Flateau, as a French captain, reciting "The Star-Spangled Banner" "as I have never heard it, before or since."

Because the Provincetown Players still insisted that critics pay for their tickets, critics continued to ignore the group when they opened their new season on the same night. But their triple bill of one-acters contained two pieces of more or less enduring interest. One was a bit of Edna St. Vincent Millay juvenilia, her blank-verse comedy **The Princess Marries the Page** (11-22-18, Playwright's). Its title gave away most of its slight plot, neglecting only to mention that the page turns out to have royal blood. Another piece on the bill was Eugene O'Neill's **Where the Cross Is Made,** examining a mad sea captain's obsession with buried treasure.

War plays too long in the works continued to arrive belatedly on a Broadway all too glad that the war was over. The new mood doomed Austin Page's London hit **By Pigeon Post** (11-25-18, Cohan), although it was unusual in two respects. First, it was produced by Florenz Ziegfeld in one of his rare sorties away from musicals. Second, it featured a large number of trained pigeons, even if critics noted that because of obvious limitations they were not shown flying from place to place and delivering their messages. Page's story spotlighted a seemingly shell-shocked captain (Jerome Patrick) who thwarts a gang of German spies.

A Jewish girl marrying outside her faith provided the impetus for many a drama over the years, but in Milton Goldsmith and Benedict James's **The Little Brother** (11-25-18, Belmont), the evening's other opening and second importation from London, it took a novel twist. The girl's father is a rabbi (Walker Whiteside), and the boy's father is a Russian Orthodox priest (Tyrone Power), and when the two men, who are both opposed to the wedding, confront each other, the warm, forgiving rabbi and the narrow, hate-filled priest discover they are brothers who were separated after their parents had been killed in a pogrom many years before. Some critics protested that the characters of the men were too clearly drawn in favor of the Jew, but all hailed the performances. One of the critics with reservations about even-handedness was the *Times*'s John Corbin, already displaying the virulent anti-Semitism that would appear after his dismissal from the paper. In a Sunday follow-up he tried or pretended to try to balance his feelings, noting, "In the character of the Jew there are regions as yet unexplored—regions of suicidal meanness in trade and of truly creative industry, regions of unsocial selfishness and of far-seeing, patriotic statesmanship, regions of petty parsimony and of benefactions as liberal as they are humane. Some day our playwrights will cease posing 'the Jew' as a protagonist in a racial problem and give us many Jews who are human beings." The theatre's small capacity helped the play run for fifteen weeks.

With the opening of **Roads of Destiny** (11-27-18, Republic), Channing Pollock's supposed dramatization of an O. Henry story (he had actually written the work before being advised of its similarity), Pollock found himself with two minor hits just one theatre apart on 42nd Street. Cohan and Harris originally had been slated as producers, but after attending a performance of *Eyes of Youth*, a very similar play, they backed out. It was left to Al Woods, who had produced the Marcin drama, to bring Pollock's to New York. Whereas Marcin's play centered around a heroine attempting to avoid an unhappy fate, Pollock's focused on a hero (Edmund Lowe). But whether on a Nebraska farm, in an Alaska gambling den, or at a posh Long Island estate, he still encounters the same villain (John Miltern), the same woman (Florence Reed), and the same pearl-handled pistol. Miss Reed garnered the best notices as a love-crazed farm girl, a crafty croupier, and a French femme fatale.

November drew to a close with two openings on the same evening. One was a revival by the self-promoting Butler Davenport of his year-and-a-half-old *Difference in Gods* at his Bramhall Playhouse. The other was Cyril Harcourt's **A Place in the Sun** (11-28-18, Comedy). A farmer who has become a successful novelist (Norman Trevor) and his sister (Jane Cooper) come to London to enjoy his success. But the girl is soon compromised by a cynical aristocrat (John Halliday). The aristocrat's sister (Peggy Joyce) suggests the writer compromise her to balance matters. Despite good notices, the play failed.

The first three weeks in December saw the arrival of only a single novelty at major uptown houses, and that was a British war play that left hurriedly. Jessie Porter's **Betty at Bay** (12-2-18, 39th St.) told of an English girl who must overcome her new, aristocratic father-in-law's opposition to her marriage and who must fall back on all her inner strength when she is advised, falsely as it turns out, that her husband has been killed in the war.

Downtown, the Provincetown Players, now begin-

ning to attract critics (even though they were still asked to pay for their tickets), mounted their second bill of the season. One of the three short plays was George Cram Cook and Susan Glaspell's **Tickless Time** (12-20-18, Playwright's) in which a young couple protest the mechanization of society by dispensing with their clocks and employing a sundial. Another of the plays was Eugene O'Neill's **The Moon of the Caribbees,** which depicted the friendships and squabbles of the *Glencairn* sailors. Those reviewers who attended were not impressed. The *Tribune* dismissed the adramatic play as a "pointless tale," while the *Herald* called it "just an interlude of a drama."

Four attractions (including two long-forgotten musicals, *Listen Lester* and *Somebody's Sweetheart*) opened on the 23rd to begin just over a week filled with new hits. The most memorable was James M. Barrie's **Dear Brutus** (12-23-18, Empire), which ran five and a half months with William Gillette as star (and, more than three years after his death, Charles Frohman listed as producer). Barrie's story took its characters into an enchanted, moonlit woods where they are given the opportunity to be what they have dreamed of themselves as being. Of course, Barrie's thesis, taken from Shakespeare, was that our faults are not in our stars but in ourselves. Gillette portrayed an unhappy painter who has dreamed of having a loving daughter. As that fantasy-child, who pleaded poignantly not to become a might-have-been, Helen Hayes was complimented for conveying "a wonderful blending of dream beauty and girlish actuality." The star himself apparently set aside his customary stagey mannerisms, and so was hailed for a performance of exceptional warmth and credibility. He also set aside the traditional curtain calls after each act, thus ending a centuries-long practice. (He seems to have tried to accomplish this earlier, but without the pronounced and lasting success the policy began to enjoy from now on, though numerous holdouts continued the practice for several seasons.)

One of the few flops in this hit-packed span was William Le Baron's **Back to Earth** (12-23-18, Henry Miller's). Its main story, framed as a play within a play, found an angel (Wallace Eddinger), given two weeks leave of absence from heaven, coming back for an earthly spree.

Several critics saw something Barrie-like in the first of two George M. Cohan plays to open one night apart. **A Prince There Was** (12-24-18, Cohan) had initially been derived from a Dorrough Aldrich story by Robert Hilliard, who used it as a vehicle for himself. But after it failed on the road, Hilliard had

Cohan rework it. News of its problems out of town meant the show got off to a slow start, but largely accepting notices gave it a twenty-week run. Charles Martin is a rich man whose life has turned sour and who has taken to drink. His descent into a living hell stops abruptly when his path crosses that of a sweet little girl appropriately named Comfort (Marie Vernon). She recounts her own sad story and those of her fellow boarders, including a beautiful young woman who has failed in her ambition to become a writer. Telling Martin he could be a prince, she persuades him to leave his lonely mansion and to move to the boardinghouse. He accepts a job he has been offered on a magazine and announces to his valet, "I'm going to be an assistant editor and a Prince at one and the same time. I'm going to rescue a Princess from the grimy, sordid, tawdry prison where she dwells amid the ashes of her dreams. I'm going to bring her hope and joy and a vision of beauty. Bland, the great trouble with me is that I missed the biggest thing in life—roughing it—smashing my way through the crowd." At the boarding house he falls in love with the pretty writer (Phoebe Hunt), an heiress who has taken a room to soak up atmosphere for a story she is writing. Their romance is nearly skewered by an overimaginative film actor (Ralph Sipperly) who comes to believe they are thieves. Martin also helps an old, failed lawyer, Mr. Cricket (A. G. Andrews), receive recognition. Besides winning the girl, Martin ends up half owner of the magazine.

The only other flop to open at this time was Rita Wellman's **The Gentile Wife** (12-24-18, Vanderbilt). A Christian wife (Emily Stevens), on edge because of the behavior of the family of her Jewish husband (David Powell), spends a harmless evening with a Christian friend (Frank Conroy). Infuriated, the husband kills the man. The couple at first decide to flee to South America, but after recognizing that it would be better to go their separate ways, the husband turns himself in to the police.

Christmas night brought in one of the era's biggest successes, Samuel Shipman and John B. Hymer's **East Is West** (12-25-18, Astor). The curtain rose on a magnificent Livingston Platt setting. An oval frame, with a few Chinese markings on each side and willow branches hanging down from the top, reveals a large, ornate Chinese boat berthed at a pier. The boat fills the stage, with only a brilliant blue sky behind it. It is a "Love-Boat," whose proprietor sells "Sing-Song Girls" to whomever wants them. Hop-Toy (Harry Huguenot), a man who has brought the proprietor an unusually high number of daughters, brings his latest, Ming Toy (Fay Bainter). A visiting American, Billy Benson (Forrest Winant), is taken by her command of English, which Ming Toy tells him she learned from missionaries. To stop a wicked Chinese from purchasing her, Billy has his Chinese-American friend, Lo Sang Kee (Lester Lonergan), buy her and bring her to San Francisco. For a year she lives in Lo Sang Kee's elaborately carved and embroidered Oriental rooms. She is increasingly taken with American ways—with Christianity, winking at strangers, and the shimmy. But do-gooders, who refuse to believe that the relationship is truly platonic, take umbrage, and Lo Sang Kee is advised he will be deported if he keeps Ming Toy. He asks Charlie Yong (George Nash), the flashy owner of a chain of chop suey houses, to take her. Yong insists on buying her, so Lo Sang Kee reluctantly agrees. But Ming Toy distrusts Charlie and refuses to go with him. Fortunately, Billy appears and, over Charlie's protestations, takes her to his family's home. At first the Bensons are welcoming, amused at how easily Ming Toy is adapting to American ways. But when they realize that Billy wants to marry her they order her to leave. Billy arranges for a one week's truce. When Charlie appears and demands Ming Toy come with him or he will kill Billy, the almost American Ming Toy tells the butler to "put this chink out." Then, with the week up and the family refusing to relent, Ming Toy cries, "Oh, why didn't God make all people white?" Once again Charlie appears, this time with some Tong members who are prepared to murder Billy. But Charlie has made one serious mistake; he has brought Hop Toy with him. Hop Toy discloses that Ming Toy is not really his daughter but that he had stolen her from an American missionary married to a Spanish woman. Now that she is white, Ming Toy is welcomed by the Bensons. However, Lo Sang Kee has a final lesson for everyone.

Lo Sang Kee: The color of a man's face is not the reflection of his soul. Many white people yellow, many yellow people white.
Ming Toy: You are one of them. I bet you born in West.
Lo Sang Kee: In the infinite, Ming Toy, whence all things come, there is no East, there is no West. West is East, and East is West.

Although Fay Bainter is remembered as the star, many contemporary notices, protesting that she played too assertively, handed the palm to George Nash's skillfully nuanced Charlie Yong. Several reviewers felt Livingston Platt's scenery was the real star. Only the most brahmin critics subscribed to Heywood Broun's assessment in the *Tribune*—"a velly lotten play." The *Dramatic Mirror,* hinting at its reservations, characterized the play as "Peg o' My Heart Under the Willow Tree." Despite a few such clobberings, the play ran more than a year and a half. For a time it even raised its top ticket to $3.

Cohan's second offering of the week was a written-to-order vehicle for Chauncey Olcott, **The Voice of McConnell** (12-25-18, Manhattan Opera House), which allowed the voice of the aging Irish matinee idol to be heard in a few ballads. Indeed he played a famous ballad singer who wins a lovely American colleen (Gilda Leary) after helping her brother (Richard Taber) out of a scrape.

On the next evening Rachel Crothers's compassionate, observant, if slightly talky **A Little Journey** (12-26-18, Little) began a seven-month stand. Takers of the *World* were assured that, despite a weak second act, the play "gave a good measure of satisfaction." Its first two acts are set in a sleeping car. One by one the passengers who are starting on a four-day trip westward come in, a redcap toting their luggage. They are a mixed bag: a mean, selfish man; a flashy New York matron; an old lady who tells her granddaughter that when she was the granddaughter's age nobody dreamed of traveling on a train in a tunnel under a river; a slangy Jewish clothing drummer; two young college swells; a sickly, uncertain young girl with a baby; and, most of all, a young, beautiful, but clearly uptight, young lady who is leaving friends and family who no longer want her (Estelle Winwood), and a handsome, thoughtful, slightly older man (Cyril Keightley). The train takes off and soon is heading through the tunnel. But when the conductors appear they discover that the uptight young lady, Julie, has lost her ticket. She would be removed from the train at the first stop but for Jim's offer to loan her a second fare. When the sickly girl asks Julie to watch her baby while she goes to the diner, Julie at first refuses but then, after accepting, finds herself uncomfortable with the baby in her arms. Her discomfort amuses Jim. He tells her he is heading west to a "camp" he runs for recovered alcoholics like himself. Julie admits she is going to people who don't want her any more than those whom she has left behind. She is a very unhappy girl, even though the sickly mother tells her, "I'm sorry for *you,* lady. You look like you ought to be awful happy." Suddenly everyone's life is changed when the train is wrecked. The sickly girl is killed. The others, sitting on a hill overlooking the wreck, set aside their prejudices and conceits and become more understanding of one another. But no one is changed more than Julie, who has proved she has some unsuspected nursing skills

and a very warm heart. After she decides to adopt the orphaned baby, Jim suggests they raise it together at his place. She confesses she has fallen in love with him; however, Jim responds that it is not him but life that she has at last learned to love. "Then you are life," Julie answers. Both Keightley and Miss Winwood were praised for the richness and restraint they showed. Many critics also adored Jobyna Howland, a musical comedy favorite, as the gossip-mongering, nouveau riche matron who insists, "Nothing like New York, is there? I couldn't live any place else. When you're *in* right New York's the place." However, later, after the grandmother has announced that "our church circle is the salt of the earth—the backbone of the nation," the matron confesses she is from a small town, only to add, "Main Street wasn't wide enough for me." On the other hand, her burgeoning humanity cannot entirely overcome her prejudices. At one point, seeing a porter attempt to make coffee after the wreck, she blurts out that the "coon is human"; then, bemoaning the losses she has suffered in the crash, she reassures him, "All my jewelry gone, but I know you didn't take it, Sambo, you're a *very* honest man." The play's success meant that Crothers, after a fallow period apart from one adaptation, was again writing interesting work.

. . .

Rachel Crothers (1878–1958) was born in Bloomington, Ill., and had begun to write plays before entering the State Normal School of Illinois. She subsequently studied acting at the Stanhope-Wheatcroft School. She gave up performing when her first play, *Nora* (1904), was produced, but she directed this and all her other plays. Her initial success came with *The Three of Us* (1906). Without ever being militant, she generally wrote with the idea of liberating women from society's many double standards. And almost invariably her men characters were not as interesting or as understandingly drawn as her women.

. . .

The two plays that closed out December both ran for four months. Mark Swan's **Keep It to Yourself** (12-30-18, 39th St.) was taken from Henri Kéroul and Albert Barré's *Le No. 18* and dealt with the complications that arise at a hotel in Ostend after a honeymoon couple (Alphonz Ethier and Ethel Stanard) encounter an all too easily hypnotized man (Edwin Nicander).

In Walter Hackett's **The Invisible Foe** (12-30-18, Harris), first done in London, a dead uncle returns to haunt one nephew until the younger man confesses he has signed forgeries for which he allowed his brother to take the blame.

The first entry in 1919 also was a failure. Helen R. Martin and Frank Howe, Jr.'s **Tillie** (1-6-19, Henry Miller's), like *Erstwhile Susan* (1-18-16), was based on one of Mrs. Martin's stories of Mennonite life. In this instance Tillie (Patricia Collinge) rebels against her hardhearted family and neighbors. A young writer (Robert Hudson), coming to Schneiderville for material, proves her salvation.

More stories, this time those by Peter B. Kyne first serialized in the *Saturday Evening Post* then published as a novel, served as the source for Edward E. Rose's **Cappy Ricks** (1-13-19, Morosco). Sixty-year-old Alden "Cappy" Ricks (Tom Wise) is the most powerful figure in San Francisco's shipping world. He is cantankerous and combative, unable to allow anyone to get the better of him. So when he learns that the chief mate on one of his ships has taken over after the captain's death and has refused to consider having Ricks send another captain, he does just that—with instructions to the new man to send the recalcitrant mate to the hospital. "By the Holy pink-toed Prophet," he exclaims, no one defies Cappy Ricks. But Ricks has more immediate problems. He has fired both his secretary and his bookkeeper and so far has only been able to replace the secretary. Moreover, his beloved daughter, Florrie (Marion Coakley), wangles $20,000 from him to give to the African Pygmies Uplift Society, and an old buddy from Thomaston, Maine, has sent his flighty son, Cecil Pericles Bernard (Norval Well), out to Ricks to keep the boy away from a chorus girl named Goldie Glake and to put his nose to the grindstone. Neither Ricks nor Cecil knows that Ricks's new secretary is Goldie (Helen Stewart), whose show has folded abruptly and who has taken on this new work under her real name. Unexpectedly, the first mate, Matt Peasley (William Courtenay), appears, announcing he has brought in the ship ahead of schedule and sent the replacement captain to the hospital. To Ricks, this defiance means war. But young Matt is game. A chance meeting with Florrie, who has taken over her father's bookkeeping, leads to romance. Florrie lends Matt the $20,000 her father has given her and also provides him with information to help his enterprise. Unwilling, however, to reveal that she is Ricks's daughter, she tells him her name is Goldie Glake, having picked up the name in a conversation with Cecil. Before long, Matt's new company is giving Ricks's a run for its money. Ricks only accepts defeat after discovering that Florrie loves Matt. But his ignorance of Florrie's true identity prompts Matt to believe that Florrie prefers Cecil. The confusion is cleared up in time for a happy ending. The sharp give and take between the corpulent, avuncular Wise and

the suave, dashing Courtenay, which the public had enjoyed in *Pals First* and *General Post,* was even more finely honed this time. Excellent settings included a shipping office and the patio of a home overlooking San Francisco Bay and Mt. Tamalpais. "To sum up," *Theatre* concluded, "'Cappy Ricks' is a good evening's entertainment." But the *Sun* told its readers, "Mr. Wise is in reality 'Captain Ricks' not only in the sense that he is the character, but the whole three acts as well."

Two even longer running hits followed. The same critic for *Theatre* who had welcomed *Cappy Ricks* described Samuel Shipman and Max Marcin's **The Woman in Room 13** (1-14-19, Booth) as "an engrossing example of dramatic blacksmithing as practiced by two of America's foremost exponents of the sledge-hammer school." John Bruce (Lowell Sherman), the former husband of Laura Ramsey (Janet Beecher), vows vengeance on her and her new husband (Charles Waldron). He contrives to have Mr. Ramsey hire him as a private detective to see if his wife is faithful. They take a hotel room just below one in which Laura is supposedly meeting another man. By means of a dictograph Ramsey is led to believe he has heard his wife making compromising remarks. He dashes out of the room, and moments later shots are heard overhead. The final scene takes place in the corridor of a courthouse, but a scrim allows the audience to see what goes on both in the corridor and in the courtroom. Laura attempts to take on the burden of guilt, until it is shown that it was not her voice Ramsey heard but that of a less savory woman (Gail Kane). A bit of prurient interest was attempted by having Miss Kane wear a diaphanous kimono in her scene with Bruce and her exit by way of the fire escape. An attempt was also made to raise the top ticket to $4, but that was hurriedly abandoned. Nonetheless, *Variety* at one point termed it "the biggest dramatic hit in town."

And then there was the month's biggest hit, **Up in Mabel's Room** (1-15-19, Eltinge), Wilson Collison and Otto Harbach's farce that kept playgoers laughing into the summer. Everyone winds up in Mabel's bedroom because sometime before his wedding to jealous, tears-prone Geraldine (Enid Markey), Garry Ainsworth (John Cumberland) had presented a rose-and-pink chemise embroidered "From Garry to Mabel" to a beautiful widow, Mabel Essington (Hazel Dawn). Before he can retrieve it, the chemise is "displayed above bodices, jerked from bedposts and bathroom hooks, stuffed into pockets, and dragged about floors," while Garry watches in befuddlement from beneath Mabel's bed.

Walter Jones, as a suspicious husband, shared playing honors with the balding, boxy Cumberland, who was applauded for "his usual pantomime facial expressions."

Like Hazel Dawn of the preceding evening's farce, Eleanor Painter had won her fame in musicals. But now she was cast in the leading role of a revival on the 16th at the Comedy of *The Climax* (4-12-09), which featured Effingham Pinto recreating his original role. Since critics had not yet succumbed to the virulent faddism that condemns any play more than a year old as dated, many reviewers found the play still made for marvelous theatre. Announced as a limited engagement, it played out its four-week booking.

Leo Ditrichstein, so often seen in the part of a sensual man, was the primary reason for attending Henri Lavedan's **The Marquis de Priola** (1-20-19, Liberty), in which he portrayed a vicious Parisian libertine whose exhaustive sexual chase eventually kills him.

On the other hand, Mrs. Fiske, who had essayed a wide variety of roles and lately had found little success, finally had a money-maker with an undisguised star vehicle that she had written (without credit) with Laurence Eyre. Their "comedy of moonshine, madness and make-believe" was **Mis' Nelly of N' Orleans** (2-4-19, Cohan and Harris), and it unfolded in the rose-filled garden of an old New Orleans mansion framed by tall, ancient trees. Adding to the atmosphere were spirituals and other nineteenth-century songs sung by a quartet offstage, snatches of voodoo rites, snippets of French, Mardi Gras revelers, and, for part of the play, lovely 1886 costumes. On learning that her niece and ward, Delphine (Irene Haisman), is being courted by Felix Durand (Georges Renavent), whose father, Georges (Hamilton Revelle), had thrown her over on their wedding day, Nelly Daventry rushes back from a long self-exile in France. She is determined to break up the relationship. But after Georges barges in and attempts to humiliate Delphine by suggesting that Felix is already married, she changes her plan. Re-creating the long-gone evening on which Georges misconstrued her actions and rejected her, she shows him what really happened. By the time dawn is breaking, Felix and Delphine are again arm in arm, and so are the widowed Georges and Nelly. Although contemporary critics enjoyed the "quaint Creole English," it seems to have been employed inconsistently, with Georges and a favored priest employing it but not Nelly. Oddly, Felix's dialogue is also correct English, although the actor who originally played him was a young Frenchman. If critics saw

the play for what it was—pleasant fluff—they also concurred with the *American*'s Alan Dale when he admitted that once again "Mrs. Fiske has charmed and fascinated us by the witchery of her unique personality." And *Variety* noted that "Mrs. Fiske has a more distinct following than probably any other of the old-time actresses. It is a clientele made up of the very best people in New York." Never mind that one wag, compiling a list of "Some Things I've Yet to See," included, "A time when Mrs. Fiske didn't leave most of her lines to the imagination."

Marie Cahill was not so fortunate, and her fading career received no boost from George V. Hobart and Herbert Hall Winslow's **Just Around the Corner** (2-5-19, Longacre). Besides singing a few songs, the star revitalized a failing country store with the help of some reformed crooks and characters traditionally found in rural comedies. Critics pointed out obvious similarities with such bygone hits as *The Fortune Hunter* and *Turn to the Right*.

At the same time, *Variety* headlined the fact that every first-class theatre in New York (it called them "two dollar theatres") was occupied. There were fifty theatres then.

If Miss Cahill's fortunes were fading, Sinclair Lewis's had yet to rise—in another field. But he had a near miss with **Hobohemia** (2-8-19, Greenwich Village), which he derived from his own *Saturday Evening Post* story. To reclaim his girl from the wilds of Greenwich Village, a young midwesterner (Frank M. Thomas) comes east and sets up a "poetry factory" that will churn out verse as efficiently as Hershey manufactures chocolate kisses. Into his life stream an assortment of village types: the Nutley, N.J., married couple who pretend to be living in sin; the free-verse writer who has no idea what his verse might mean; an "ole clothes" man posing as a Russian novelist. The comedy, despite disparaging notices ("a dull and badly written travesty," "more a famine than a feast"), ran for three months at the tiny playhouse.

At a slightly larger, uptown theatre, James Cullen and Lewis Allen Browne's **Please Get Married** (2-10-19, Little) began a somewhat longer run—twenty weeks. A burglar (Edward See) has no sooner entered a minister's home than a couple (Ernest Truex and Edith Taliaferro) arrive to be married. Hastily swiveling his collar around, he performs the ceremony, then, as the newlyweds leave, he departs by way of the same window through which he came in. At their honeymoon hotel the couple are advised of what transpired, and the rest of the play consists of everyone begging them to marry while all they want to do is enjoy a honeymoon. They can after it is learned that the crook was actually a minister suffering from amnesia. *Variety* termed the comedy "a raw rarebit with the most tantalizing sex slant uncovered in this season of boudoir plays," adding it was "extremely phew, gosh and gee whiz." The play proved so popular that it was hurried into a larger, if still intimate, playhouse to finish out its run.

John Taintor Foote's **Toby's Bow** (2-10-19, Comedy) ran almost as long—chalking up 144 performances, although its title had hurt advance sales. An old family retainer, Uncle Toby (George Marion in blackface), reserves his special bow only for members of the proud but impoverished Vardeman family. He is not at all happy when a handsome young man, James Bointon Blake (Norman Trevor), whom audiences know to be a novelist traveling incognito, arrives at the Vardemans', with his Oriental valet (T. Tamamoto), a man Toby indignantly dismisses as a "yallah niggah." Blake falls in love with pretty Eugenie Vardeman (Doris Rankin), is given to understand that she is a would-be novelist discouraged by a pile of pink slips, and helps her to write a book that becomes a best-seller. When Eugenie learns his real profession she is furious, believing he was only humoring her. But true love prevails. And Uncle Toby, seeing money and gaiety once again flowing into the homestead, gives Blake his deepest bow. To bolster the box office after a time, George Bernard Shaw's **Augustus Does His Bit** (3-12-19) was added as a curtain raiser. It took a jaundiced view of a stupid, incompetent officer reduced to a backwater recruiter.

Amnesia, which had been used to comic effect in another of the evening's openings, was treated a bit more seriously in Maravene Thompson's **The Net** (2-10-19, 48th St.), the night's only flop. When a man (Charles Millward) suffering from amnesia is suspected of a murder, the murderer's wife (Kathlene MacDonnell), who could easily exculpate him, keeps silent so that her son's reputation might not be compromised. Fortunately for the man, the truth eventually comes out.

The truth also eventually comes out in Jack Larrie and Gustav Blum's **A Sleepless Night** (2-18-19, Bijou), where, like the Nutley couple in *Hobohemia* who pretended to be single, a pair of artists (Ernest Glendinning and Carlotta Monterey) hide the fact that they are husband and wife when they visit the estate of a Long Island millionaire (William Morris) hoping to obtain commissions. To their dismay the host's ward (Peggy Hopkins) and son (Donald Gallaher) fall in love with them, precipitating three acts of complications.

In the opening scene of Leighton Graves Osmun's **The Fortune Teller** (2-27-19, Republic) a haggish crystal-ball gazer (Marjorie Rambeau), in a filthy gown with zodiac signs on it, sits in her booth at a traveling circus plying her trade when she is not drunk or on dope. A young man (Hugh Dillman) appears, distressed at how plagued with failure and misfortune his life has been, and asks Madame Renee to tell him what his future holds. As they talk the woman realizes that this man was the baby she left behind when she deserted her husband twenty years before. Her maternal instincts overwhelm her, so she abandons her peripatetic life to try, without his knowing it, to help her son. Though her mean paramour (E. L. Fernandez) attempts to lure her back and, failing that, to blackmail her, she succeeds. But rather than embarrass her son, she quietly walks out of his life without revealing who she is.

The mother (Louie Emery) in Mary Stafford Smith and Leslie Vyner's **Penny Wise** (3-10-19, Belmont) was also something of a fraud. She tries to collect on her son's life insurance, even though he is quite alive, by staging an elaborate funeral and blackmailing or bribing acquaintances into silence. Regrettably for her, her not very bright son (William Lennox) gets drunk and spoils her scheme. Critics saw to it the authors didn't collect royalties for long.

Phillip Moeller was not raking in big royalties either. A little more than a year earlier Mrs. Fiske could not make a major success of his *Madame Sand*. Now, with the names of four fine players above his title, he had no better luck with **Molière** (3-17-19, Liberty), even though the *Sun* praised it as "quite the most important contribution to the American theatre that our stage has witnessed this year," and the *World* deemed it "exceptionally fine." Molière (Henry Miller) has risen from a vagabond player to the favorite of Louis XIV (Holbrook Blinn) and his mistress, Françoise, Marquise de Montespan (Blanche Bates). The playwright and actor should be happy, but he is not, especially since he has heard rumors that his much younger wife, Armande Béjart (Estelle Winwood), is unfaithful. De Montespan has come to love Molière, so she arranges for him to witness a furtive meeting between Armande and Armande's lover in the palace garden. To the courtier's fury Molière still refuses to love her. She denounces the playwright to the king, who immediately dismisses him. A year later, seriously ill and deserted by Armande, Molière resolves to perform despite his doctor's orders. The effort proves too much. He dies, but not before Armande comes rushing in to beg forgiveness. The king also appears hoping to tell the playwright that he has been reconciled to him, but he comes too late. Several critics who failed to share their colleagues' enthusiasm for the play saw it as more literary than literate. Today it seems stodgy and predictable as in the eulogy with which Louis closes the play—lines even a king would not deliver spontaneously, but might from a prepared text: "Molière is dead but in his name will live for ever the gay spirit, the brave laughter and the unconquered heart of France." All four stars were lauded for their richly nuanced, convincing portrayals, while the lush period settings and costumes also were extolled. Like Moeller's earlier historical drama, this new one held on for eight weeks.

A revival of *The Honor of the Family* (2-17-08), which opened at the Globe on the same evening, with its original star, Otis Skinner, again in the lead, ran just seven weeks—but it was a limited engagement to begin with and did good business at the large house.

Maurice Maeterlinck's **A Burgomaster of Belgium** (3-24-19, Belmont) was another war play that came in too soon after the armistice to find an audience. It told of a burgomaster who is selected to be taken hostage and shot after a German soldier is killed and of the soul-searching that follows when his German son-in-law is put in charge of the man's execution.

An even quicker failure was Marvin Taylor's **Luck in Pawn** (3-24-19, 48th St.), in which a young but penniless lady (Mabel Taliaferro) with artistic ambitions captures the heart of a very rich, very bored young man (Roland Young). She uses funds given her by a Jewish moneylender (Robert Fischer). Obstacles are thrown in the youngsters' path, and misunderstandings arise when the source of the girl's money is exposed, but the situation is resolved at a small railroad stop as dawn comes up.

The month's only incontestable hit was Rachel Crothers's **39 East** (3-31-19, Broadhurst). Breakfast at 39 East, a boardinghouse run by Mrs. de Mailly (Alison Skipworth), brings together the usual assortment of boardinghouse figures. One of them is Penelope Penn (Constance Binney), a minister's daughter who has come to New York hoping to support her mother and siblings by earning money as a singer. She has had no luck until just a few days before when she landed a job in the chorus of a burlesque show. Naturally she cannot tell her landlady of her new position or she will be asked to leave. But then she will probably be asked to leave anyway, since she has fallen far behind in her rent. Although she refuses to see it, a handsome and quite wealthy fellow boarder, Napoleon Gibbs (Henry

Hull), has fallen in love with her. She curtly rejects his invitations. But they finally agree to meet at a wisteria-covered arbor in Central Park. There she reveals that one of the producers of the show has offered to enlarge her part and increase her salary, but he has suggested they first discuss the matter over dinner at his apartment, and she has agreed. Gibbs is shocked at her naivety, and she, in turn, is livid at his response. She runs off. That evening at the boardinghouse, Gibbs has a long talk with Mrs. de Mailly; he convinces her that Penelope is hopelessly innocent and gets her to agree to help him. It turns out that Penelope's pouring out her problems to her producer resulted in the embarrassed man's quietly sending her home without taking advantage of her. Mrs. de Mailly's long talk with the girl finally begins to open her eyes, and, almost on a whim, she agrees to marry Gibbs. Although the character of Gibbs, read today, seems pesky, and that of Penelope absurdly whiny, whimpering, and stupid, critics found the figures well drawn and the play "a graceful, entertaining trifle," "without a really false touch." The curly-headed Hull, who bore a striking resemblance to his late brother and was considered by some almost as promising an actor, was applauded as heartily as the pert, winning Miss Binney. The comedy ran through August.

Shakuntala (4-8-19, Greenwich Village), a fifth-century Hindi drama, got a jump on several other plays scheduled to open that evening by premiering at a matinee. But then this saga of a bride (Beatrice Prentice) disowned by her husband-king (Joseph Macaulay) after he becomes a victim of amnesia was slated only for a series of matinee performances. Enough playgoers were intrigued by the play's notices to allow those special performances to continue right up to the summer.

Nearly three quarters of a century later, abortion would become a major political issue. But in 1919 it served only briefly as the theme of a star-filled but dreary play, William Anthony McGuire's **A Good Bad Woman** (4-8-19, Harris). A wife (Margaret Illington), fearful of the dangers of giving birth, is persuaded by a friend (Katherine Kaelred) to abort the child. The husband (Robert Edeson) learns of the situation, casts out the wife, and prepares to kill the doctor who performed the abortion. But the doctor (Wilton Lackaye) reveals he has talked the wife into going through with the pregnancy. Richard Bennett, who helped rewrite the play after it failed in Chicago under the title *Everywoman's Castle*, directed.

George V. Hobart's **Come-on Charley** (4-8-19,

48th St.) lasted only a little longer, during which time it disclosed how Charley (Lynne Overman) takes $10,000 and runs it up to half a million.

The season's last two long runs went to a pair of importations. One of the plays, **The Jest** (4-9-19, Plymouth), was Edward Sheldon's adaptation of Sem Benelli's *La Cena delle Beffe*. The version was florid and, some insisted, in free verse, although the published text was not. In Europe the leading role had been played by Bernhardt and Duse among others, but for New York the part of the seventeen-year-old Giannetto was taken by John Barrymore, while his antagonist, Neri, was assumed by John's brother, Lionel. The play was set in the heyday of the Medicis. For several years Giannetto, an almost effeminate artist, has been put upon savagely by Neri and his gang. Finally exasperated, he devises a plan for revenge. He invites Neri to a dinner and wagers that Neri cannot tweak the nose of a popular tavern owner with impunity. Neri sets out to win the bet, but his actions lead to his arrest. While Neri is in prison, Giannetto makes love to a girl whom Neri had stolen from him. Neri learns of this. On his escape, he heads home and, finding a man wrapped in Giannetto's white mantle stabs him to death. Then he notices a smiling Giannetto staring down at him. Picking up the mantle Neri discovers that he has killed his own beloved brother, whom Giannetto had tricked into wearing his clothes and visiting the girl. Neri goes mad. Giannetto, whose years of terror had kept him from praying, at last can kneel down to say his orisons. John Barrymore, dressed in a blond wig and tight green satin, displayed "a feeling knowledge of shades and moods and a personality that is poetry itself." Lionel, in a scarlet costume, made his malicious bully "comprehensibly, deliciously human." This "new milestone in American producing" also sported brilliant Robert Edmond Jones settings. The set for Acts II and IV was the woman's boudoir: "a huge room which itself suggests the castle-like luxury of of the days of Lorenzo, the Magnificent. At the left wall is a plain dressing table set with articles of toilet, but from one corner negligently but gracefully drops a soft fold of purple cloth, unconsciously giving the spectator a sense of wanton luxury. At right is a chest of gorgeous costumes in disarray. The walls are bare except for a panel of gold tapestry cloth flung across the door to the secret passage." Writing in *Vanity Fair*, Dorothy Parker paid the production the ultimate compliment, noting: "They say—they've been saying it for years—that it is impossible to hold an audience after eleven o'clock. The final curtain falls on *The Jest* at a quarter to twelve; until that

time not a coat is struggled into, not a hat is groped for, not a suburbanite wedges himself out of his mid-row seat and rushes into the night. . . . There can be no greater tribute." The play, with a three-month summer hiatus, ran until the end of February.

An American playwright, who had earned some celebrity for her one-act plays and who eventually would win a Pulitzer Prize, received a thumbs-down reception—"a boarding-house soufflé, concocted of eggs that are tired"—for her first full-length play. In Zoë Akins's **Papa** (4-10-19, Little), a father (John L. Shine), in order to recruit his failing financial situation, resolves to marry off his two daughters (Violette Wilson and Ann Andrews), even though one of them has had a child out of wedlock. He succeeds, but not before the wrong daughter claims to be the mother. Papa and his family left after a week and a half.

John Garrett Underhill's translation of Jacinto Benavente's **The Bonds of Interest** (4-19-18, Garrick) was also a failure. The story, played out against a beautiful commedia dell'arte background, told of a pair of traveling rogues who band together have-nots to achieve a rich marriage. Critics were kind, but their most telling superlatives were reserved for the costumes and scenery. They were not especially thrilled by a cast that included Augustin Duncan, Dudley Digges, Edna St. Vincent Millay, Rollo Peters (who co-designed the settings with Lee Simonson and also did the costumes), Amelia Summerville (a huge oldtimer from long-gone musicals), and Helen Westley. Nor were they in awe of Phillip Moeller's direction. Certainly no critic refered to the mounting as a new milestone in American producing, but it was just that. For this was the first production of a new organization—the Theatre Guild. Formed by many members of the now defunct Washington Square Players, it was dedicated to the staging of plays of genuine merit. Its plan, allowing for the paucity of playgoers devoted to high-minded drama, was to give each play a limited run. To ensure even that short stand, the group launched something rare in American theatre—a subscription campaign. Although audiences for this production were drawn largely from men in uniform admitted free, and although the pre-scheduled four-week run lost money, the company would soon turn the tide and become the most famous and important of all American producing organizations for several ensuing decades.

The next two plays also ran four weeks, because that was all the traffic would bear after the critical drubbings they received. There are only four characters in Thomas Broadhurst's **Our Pleasant Sins** (4-

21-19, Belmont). A wife (Pauline Lord), despairing over the love of her husband (Forrest Winant) for his mistress, takes on a lover (Vincent Serrano). A sister-in-law (Henrietta Crosman) enters to bring matters to a head, and husband and wife are reconciled.

In **Three for Diana** (4-21-19, Bijou), which Chester Bailey Fernald adapted from Sabatino Lopez's *Il Terzo Marito,* a twice-widowed lady (Martha Hedman) finds that her third husband (John Halliday) has trouble accepting her marital history.

According to some Broadway rumor-mongers David Belasco mounted W. D. Hepenstall and Whitford Kane's **Dark Rosaleen** (4-22-19, Belasco) to win back Irish audiences whom he had offended with *Marie-Odile.* Given the success of several of his productions that followed the Knoblock drama, the story is suspect. Nonetheless flags of the Irish republic were being hawked in front of the theatre on opening night, and larger versions flanked the stage. Theatregoers saw what one reviewer characterized as "a stirring entertainment of Boucicaultian order," while another saw it as belonging to the *In Old Kentucky* school. The play used a Capulet-Montague theme, transferred to Ireland. There Joe Donagh (Walter Edwin) operates a prospering store and pub. His main competition comes from Sandy McKillop, an Ulsterman whose pub is directly across the road. The men have no use for each other. At one point Joe employs a crooked lawyer in an attempt to bankrupt Sandy. Their lives are thrown into turmoil after Sandy's daughter, Moya (Eileen Huban), falls in love with Joe's son, Corny (Henry Duffey). A bitter battle looms until Corny rides Moya's horse, Dark Rosaleen, a 20 to 1 shot, to victory. If Belasco hoped New York's large contingent of Irish playgoers would give the piece a long run, he was no doubt disappointed. It closed with the coming of hot weather in July.

William Le Baron's **I Love You** (4-28-19, Booth) did not even last that long. At his Long Island estate Jimmie Farnsworth (John Westley) bets his guests $5000 that he can make any two people fall in love by giving them the right, moonlit environment. Taken up, he attempts to pair a debutante, Betty (Diantha Pattison), with an unlettered, union-agitating electrician (Richard Dix). He loses his bet when Betty falls in love with Jimmie's Harvard- and Oxford-educated butler (Gilbert Douglas) and the electrician prefers Jimmie's maid (Ruth Terry).

A boardinghouse filled with seeming misfits, much like that in *39 East,* provided the setting for H. S. Sheldon's **It Happens to Everybody** (5-9-19, Park). One of the lesser figures tries throughout the evening to commit suicide but is regularly thwarted. A more central figure was Donald Brown (James Gleason), an $18-a-week nothing, who turns out to have the gumption to expose a crooked millionaire (William P. Carelton), marry the crook's decent daughter (Josephine Stevens), and wind up with a $50,000 salary. The show reputedly had been designed merely for backwaters but after a season's touring took advantage of the availability of theatres in warmer weather to brave Broadway. It survived a single week.

The ingredients of the next play to arrive—a mean man holding a mortgage and threatening foreclosure, a girl's purity in danger, a murder, a false accusation—had been staples of the extinct touring melodrama. The play's late appearance and the fact that its producers supposedly had only $19 left in the till with which to mount it argued strongly against its success. But St. John Ervine's Irish tragedy **John Ferguson** (5-13-19, Garrick) was the season's last hit, and a resounding one at that. Ferguson (Augustin Duncan), a pious invalid, lives on his family's old farm with his wife (Helen Westley), his daughter, Hannah (Helen Freeman), and his son, Andrew (Rollo Peters), a poetically inclined young man who wanted to become a minister but has been forced by hard times to help with the farming for which he is ill-suited. When the man (S. Roger Lytton) who has threatened to foreclose attacks Hannah, Hannah's weak-willed suitor, James Caesar (Dudley Digges), goes gunning for him but cannot bring himself to kill him. Andrew takes his father's gun and shoots the man. At first Andrew allows Caesar to be arrested, but after learning that the farm is now safe, he heads off to confess. Because funds were so limited, the Theatre Guild had reneged on its promised schedule of four weeks and slated only a one-week run. But rave notices and long lines at the box office led to an immediate extension. The show ran well into the following season and saved the Guild from a premature disappearance.

Paul Potter's **Pretty Soft** (5-15-19, Morosco) was an adaptation of Anthony Mars and Leon Xanrof's French bedroom farce. It starred Edward Nicander, a dapper farceur with a quizzical face and a pencil-thin mustache, currently mired in a run of bad luck. He played Captain John, who just before his wedding, having been drugged by one of his ex-sweethearts, arrives at a supper club run by the notorious Mrs. Rapley (Rose Coghlan). There, in the midst of a zeppelin raid, mistaken identities and misunderstandings abound. Dismissed as "unusually stupid," it had a short run.

In George D. Parker's **Love Laughs** (5-20-19, Bijou) a lovesick young man (Harold Hendee) presses a misogynistic nerve specialist (Lionel Adams) to make him sick, so that a nurse (Jessie Glendinning) he loves and will hire to attend him will fall in love with him. By the final curtain the man has fallen in love instead with the doctor's fad-chasing ward (Katharine Alexander), while the doctor and the nurse are pairing.

The season's last play asked **Who Did It?** (6-9-19, Harris). Stephen Gardner Champlin's comedy cast its spotlight on Mildred Greyson (Mary Moore), a stagestruck wife who suddenly confesses to her husband (George L. Spaulding) that she has had a lurid history. Of course, the history is total fabrication, merely the misguided girl's attempt to see how convincing an actress she is. And just as naturally it leads to all manner of complications.

In its review of this last play *Theatre* observed that the 1918–19 season "had been one of the best seasons in the history of the theatre." It might have added that all five seasons from the outbreak of World War I to its end were momentous for the American stage. Although innumerable foreign plays, performers, and ideas would still be given hearings, never again would they truly dominate. Hereafter, if Americans saw value in something European they would not simply translate it (in both senses of the word) but rather would freely adapt it to American requirements. The imprisoning shackles were finally thrown off. In retrospect, if not in June of 1919, it could be clearly seen how crucial these seasons were.

These years witnessed the emergence of many of the great playwrights who would give the American stage decades of glory. True, Rachel Crothers had come to playgoers' attention some years earlier, but 1914 through 1919 saw recognition begin to alight on Elmer Rice, Susan Glaspell, Zoë Akins, Clare Kummer, and, most of all, Eugene O'Neill. Others were waiting in the wings. To offer their fledgling, shorter works groups such as the Washington Square Players and the Provincetown Players arrived on the scene, and, subsequently, to present their longer plays a new breed of producer emerged simultaneously—men such as Winthrop Ames, Arthur Hopkins, John D. Williams, and that unique group of men and women, the Theatre Guild. Robert Edmond Jones and Livingston Platt were in the vanguard of designers uncluttering our stages by using lighting and simplified settings to poetic effect. A new generation of stars was also becoming known. The competition of films had lured away many less educated playgoers, but even those more knowledgeable and demanding theatre lovers who remained loyal could not have been retained had not the level of quality—in writing, acting, and staging—been markedly raised.

All this augured well for the future. And most theatregoers were not to be disappointed.

THE GREAT ACT
1919–1928

1919–1920

The armistice was less than a year old when the next season began. The nation as a whole was looking forward to a period of peace and prosperity. But not everything was rosy. President Wilson, strenuously fighting for a League of Nations to maintain world stability, suffered a stroke—details of which were withheld from the public. But his partisan opponents in Congress, more aware of the seriousness of his illness, seized on it to scuttle America's interest in and cooperation with the new body. High-minded or simply snobbish conservative groups and uglier reactionary ones on the order of the Ku Klux Klan were recruiting and becoming vocal. American clergymen, smug in the reflected glory of victory, urged a new sort of "preparedness"—this time preaching a crusade to destroy the forces of immorality. And no small number of those forces, they insisted, were controlling influences in the theatre. John Roach Straton, pastor of New York's Calvary Baptist Church, typifying the sanctimonious meddlers, took pen in hand to write in *Theatre* that the stage must be placed under "proper control" because "the three greatest foundation stones of our Anglo-Saxon civilization . . . the home, the purity of women, and the sanctity of the Sabbath" were gravely imperiled by modern plays. He instructed readers: "You will let the editors of your newspapers know what you think of their 'dramatic critics,' when they give a clean bill of health . . . to performances that dig up unspeakable moral filth," and he exhorted those who continued to read to "never cease" their efforts until they have "rescued" the drama from "the unholy hands that today are strangling it to death." Theatre lovers and theatre folk naturally demurred, although some oldtimers, such as Daniel Frohman, did lament that "romance and sentiment" had been supplanted by "sex and sensation." The political left was also increasingly active, as Broadway would learn all too soon, with labor unions flexing their muscles and more extreme idealists extolling the promises of a new Russia in place of the genuine achievements of an older America. Of course, the economy was not all that it should be. The withdrawal of wartime farm subsidies began a precipitous slide in farm incomes, and by 1920 a post-war recession, which hit bottom in

1921, was apparent even at some box offices (although most straight plays were able to ask for and get a $3.30 top). Soon after, the economy seemed to rebound, albeit its underlying problems were ignored. So in the short run self-righteous troublemakers were more of a nuisance to the theatre than were cash flow problems. Indeed, though the 1920s technically would not begin until January of 1921, the "Roaring Twenties"—that "Era of Wonderful Nonsense," those "Années folles" as the French would eventually call them—were under way.

Business was thriving as the new season began, and all theatrical quarters were optimistic. The lone late June entry was the first of just short of 100 new plays (*Variety* counted 99) to open during the theatrical year and one of no fewer than 27 that chalked up runs of more than 100 performances (at the time a rule-of-thumb indication of success). The play was **At 9:45** (6-28-19, Playhouse). Its author was Owen Davis, who a decade or so earlier had churned out five, six, or seven touring melodramas each season. Age and changing conditions had slowed him down. He would have only two on Broadway this season. But unlike his cheap-priced thrillers, which never played longer than a week anywhere, one of his new works—this thriller of a more modern type—would enjoy a sizable New York run. Howard Clayton, the young, unprincipled son of Judge Clayton (George Backus), is found shot in his father's library. If he dies, someone will undoubtedly go to the electric chair. But who? For as the judge's chauffeur (John Harrington) tells Captain Dixon (John Cromwell), "If you was to set out to electrocute everybody—man and woman—that hates Howard Clayton, you'd run out of wire." Ruth Jordan (Marie Goff), a girl Howard jilted, confesses to the shooting. So does her current fiancé, Jim Everett (Edward Langford). Each thinks the other did it, and each self-sacrificingly hopes to be charged instead. Doane (Frank Hatch), the Claytons' longtime butler, also confesses. He has a better reason, for it turns out he has seen his daughter, Mary (Madeleine King), fire the gun. Up in Howard's bedroom Howard (Noel Tearle) admits he loves Mary, and Mary acknowledges she shot him in a moment of pique. Howard begs his father to look after her. The judge tells the captain, "If my son dies, I am going to make it my business to take care of this girl; if he lives he'll do it himself." Many critics condemned the play as crude or negligible, while granting it proved a crowd-pleaser.

Three plays arrived for inspection in July—two more murder mysteries and the first in what promised to be a parade of sagas about returning war heroes. None was a hit, although the bemedalled aviator, who came on the scene first, almost made the grade. In Guy Bolton and Frank Mandel's **The Five Million** (7-8-19, Lyric) Douglas Adams (Ralph Morgan) returns jubilantly to Clinton Falls, N.Y. His jubilation is short-lived, for he quickly learns that his law practice has been taken over by the scoundrelly Otis Weaver (Robert McWade), that his sweetheart, Ruth Hunter (Sue MacManamy), believing him dead, has become engaged to Weaver's worthless son, Albert (Purnell Pratt), and that his own weakling brother, Grant (Percy Helton), has embezzled funds and managed to make it look like Douglas's dirty work. It takes the remaining two acts for Douglas to set matters aright and find a more loyal woman (Beatrice Noyes). Comedy was supplied primarily by James Gleason and William E. Meehan as the hero's wartime buddies, while McWade, for years a respected road star, won commendation as the villain.

The Crimson Alibi (7-17-19, Broadhurst) was derived by George Broadhurst from a novel by Octavus Roy Cohen. After the detestable Joshua Quincy is stabbed to death suspicion falls on the ex-convict husband of Quincy's maid. David Carroll (Harrison Hunter), a serious composer and amateur detective, doubts the suspect's guilt and before long finds reason to point a finger at any number of regulars at the Quincy home. He finally points an accusing finger at the real killer. One exciting moment had the ex-convict's former jailmates coming to his rescue with a shootout in a darkened hotel room just as he is about to be led off.

Ralph E. Dyar's **A Voice in the Dark** (7-28-19, Republic) dealt with finding the killer of Hugh Sainsbury (Richard Gordon), a young man even more despicable than Howard Clayton. Harlan Day (William Boyd), a rising attorney, is particularly concerned, since his fiancée, Blanche Warren (Olive Wyndham), is the leading suspect. In his law office he questions the witnesses. As each person tells his or her version the action flashes back to the afternoon of the murder. A crippled, deaf old lady (Florine Arnold) tells a story that seems clearly to implicate Blanche, but a blind newsvendor (William

B. Mack) recognizes the voice of another woman whom he overheard confessing to the shooting. Blanche is released, and a young girl whom the dead philanderer had married but soon deserted is taken into custody, although there appears little chance the sweet thing will ever be brought to trial.

August promised to be busy, and it was—but not in the way Broadway had expected. As in July's first entry, August's opener, Eugene Walter's **The Challenge** (8-5-19, Selwyn), centered attention on a bemedalled aviator. Richard Putnam (Alan Dinehart) had been temporarily blinded but now, cured, returns home full of liberal ideals. He takes a job with a conservative newspaper run by Harry Winthrop (Holbrook Blinn). Putnam quickly falls in love with Mary Winthrop (Jessie Glendinning). But that does not stop him from successfully campaigning to elect a Socialist governor. After the governor sells out with dismaying swiftness to vested interests, Putnam's cohorts violently turn on their former buddy. Deserted and down-and-out, Putnam finds that only Mary retains her faith in him. When the play had opened in tryout Blinn, who remained its sole star, had been the central figure. But the slim, pale Dinehart, with his "long features and pensive expression," so stole the show that audiences would not allow an ending in which he is shot to death. The ending was altered, as was Mary's relationship to Harry, from daughter to young sister. One excellent set showed a busy newspaper room at a government office, its floor strewn with discarded papers and every desk occupied by a reporter plugging away at a typewriter or phoning in information. Yet the more elegant setting showing Winthrop's posh home won the most applause.

Thomas Dixon, whose novels *The Clansman* and *The Leopard's Spots* were the source of the famous film *Birth of a Nation,* was the author of **The Red Dawn** (8-6-19, 39th St.), a play so ineptly written, so filled with pompous dialogue and preposterous ideas, that it was hooted and laughed off the stage in less than a week. A young, misguided dreamer attempts to establish a socialist colony on an island off California. A villainous agent of the "Central Soviet of Russia" plans to usurp power. With five billion dollars in counterfeit money he believes he can enlist in his cause a million former convicts, three million workers who object to that capitalistic scheme Prohibition (Woollcott in the *Times* suggested that was a ridiculous underestimate), and ten million blacks, who, the Communist claims, were trained in bayonet practice using white dummies. The young idealist, with the help of the U.S. Navy, thwarts the plan.

Both these plays touched on the growing left-wing sentiments arising in the wake of the war. But both, at heart, were anti-liberal in their sentiments. The day after *The Red Dawn* opened, some more immediate leftish feelings engulfed Broadway. Players fed up with years of injustice—no rehearsal pay, low wages in general, frequent strandings far from home—walked out of twelve shows. The Actors' Equity strike had begun. By the 21st, virtually every Broadway theatre was dark. Although many of the more established players formed a second organization and sided with the producers, a majority of the public, many playwrights, and even a few producers such as Sam Harris supported the strikers. Harris's partner, George M. Cohan, as both an actor and a producer, offered to mediate but was met with appalling vilification, which turned him bitterly against the union. Other producers also felt betrayed. Broadhurst, who had extended generous terms to his players in *The Crimson Alibi* and believed he had a special contract, was outraged. But numbers told, so on the 28th the strike was settled on terms largely favorable to the actors' then reasonable demands. It would be a few years before theatrical unions became unreasonable.

Only one play was able to premiere during the strike. Owen Davis's **Those Who Walk in Darkness** (8-14-19, 48th St.), "a gaudily colored melodrama of the old school and an extraordinarily good sample of its kind," was based on a novel by Perley Poore Sheenan. It begins in a cheap lunch wagon where Viola Swan (Laura Walker) comes for coffee and a bun. Viola was a small-town girl who arrived in New York bursting with ambition and hope, yet was unable to find any but the most sordid work in the streets. In pops Rufus Underwood (Donald Gallaher), a small-town boy still hopeful of obtaining a good job in the city. He is clearly ill, so Viola takes him back to a seedy boardinghouse and nurses him through a bout with typhoid. They marry and move back to Underwood's small town. Viola's attempts to prevent her husband's cousin (Consuelo Bailey) from following in her footsteps and the machinations of a blackmailing former associate (Arthur Shaw) force her to reveal her past. Eventually love and inherent goodness triumph. Helen Tracy as a sharp-tongued old New Yorker provided comic relief. But the play closed abruptly when stagehands walked out.

Not until the second week in September—ten days after the strike was settled—did the awaited onrush of openings begin in force. It began with a distinct disappointment, Booth Tarkington and Harry Leon Wilson's **Up from Nowhere** (9-8-19, Comedy). George Washington Silver (Norman Trevor) is a self-made man who has risen far above his obscure early days in an East Side tenement. He wants only the best marriages for his children, but when George junior (Frederick Howard) brings home a genteelly impoverished socialite, Edith Valentine (Ann Andrews), he jumps to the conclusion that she is merely a polished fortune hunter. As a lesson to his son, he decides to woo her away from the boy. However, before long he has fallen in love with her himself, and she with him. Cecil Yapp, playing Hercules Penny, a crusty old sea captain and former cohort of Silver's, walked away with acting honors. By now critics were saying that Tarkington really had little skill in writing for the stage. They would have to eat their words less than two weeks later.

Three plays came in the next night, but only one was successful. Martha M. Stanley and Adelaide Matthews's **Nightie Night** (9-9-19, Princess) was a good, old-fashioned bedroom farce that begins in a New York–bound Pullman car. Trixie Lorraine (Suzanne Willa), fleeing a jealous husband, sublets an apartment, not aware it belongs to an old flame, Billy Moffat (Francis Byrne). Once ensconced, she sends her dress out to the cleaners, takes a bath, gets into a negligee, and then learns the cleaner will not be able to return her dress for at least a day. Naturally Mrs. Moffat (Dorothy Mortimer) appears and misconstrues everything. So does the jealous husband (Malcolm Duncan). Explanations and smiles follow at eleven o'clock.

Much of the action of Mark Swan's **A Regular Feller** (9-9-19, Cort) took place on Long Island, in and around one of the new garages springing up to take care of the swelling ranks of motorists. Two recent-model cars and an "old" jalopy were brought onstage, and, at one point, a film depicted the automobiles driving along a road. Dan Brackett (Ernest Glendinning) has been chased from home by a father (Edwin Holt) exasperated by the young man's obsession with these automobiles. Dan's friend, Charlie Winter (Everett Butterfield), has invented a puncture-proof tire, and the two set out to make their fortune with it. They succeed, and Dan wins not merely his father's respect but also the hand of Bessie Winter (Miriam Sears). Once again a secondary character stole most of the laughs. James Bradbury portrayed the burly, sarcastic, yet ultimately warm Cyrus Pond, an old horse-and-buggy devotee who finally comes around to accepting horseless carriages. Unfortunately, playgoers would not accept the play.

Nor did they want any part of Rita Olcott [Mrs.

Chauncey Olcott] and Grace Heyer's pseudo-poetic fantasy, **Lusmore** (9-9-19, Henry Miller's). Miss Heyer took the role of the hunchbacked poet of the title, forced to flee his village because the villagers fear he is a changeling. Good fairies turn him into a handsome soldier who wins not just great battles but the love of a blind girl, Eithne (Eva Le Gallienne). The fairies also restore Eithne's sight.

Even a brilliant performance by Grace George could not save Mark Reed's slight **She Would and She Did** (9-11-19, Vanderbilt). Frances Nesmith becomes so furious when she misses an easy stroke that she digs a hole in the turf with her mashie. This earns her a suspension from her club. And the suspension means she won't be able to attend the big dance or exhibit her Pekinese at the club's dog show. She uses means fair and a little foul to win reinstatement.

Cosmo Hamilton's **Scandal** (9-12-19, 39th St.) had been a huge success in Chicago the preceding season. As so often happened, Chicago success made New York critics suspicious, and many reviewers, but not all, wondered what the excitement was about. The New York public soon told them, for the "sex and society play" ran out the theatrical year. Beatrix Vanderdyke (Francine Larrimore), a teasing little devil who loves to defy convention, drops in on Sutherland York (Malcolm Fassett), an artist with a somewhat unsavory reputation. When he points out they are as alone as Paul and Virginia, she retorts she hoped he would say Adam and Eve. York replies he will if she makes his studio a Garden of Eden. When Beatrix's shocked parents enter she tells them that she wandered into the wrong apartment and meant to go across the hall to the rooms of her husband, the suave millionaire Pelham Franklin (Charles Cherry). This news further shocks them, but not as much as it shocks the proper Franklin, a bachelor. To teach her a lesson he goes along with her fib, but when they are by themselves in the bedroom he says, "If you and I were alone on an island and there was no chance of ever returning to civilization, I would build a hut for you at the furthest end of the island and treat you as if you were a man." Of course, with time Franklin falls in love with Beatrix and she sees the absurdity of her ways.

A second hit, a comedy, opened the same night. Like several earlier plays (and others to come) Thompson Buchanan's **Civilian Clothes** (9-12-19, Morosco) spotlighted a decorated ex-soldier. He is Sam McGinnis (Thurston Hall). In France during the war, as a captain in the A.E.F., he had a brief, torrid romance with a Red Cross nurse, Florence Lanham (Olive Tell), which led to an impetuous wedding and a brief, torrid honeymoon. Subsequently he was reported killed. The very social Florence returned to Louisville to resume her life as a gilded snob. Now, as she is being courted by local beaux, Sam reappears, very much alive, but "dressed in a way to make a sensitive woman scream." His store-bought suit hardly fits him; he sports a loud tie, the wrong kind of collar, a brightly colored handkerchief, and yellow shoes—"a swell dresser at the Gas House Ball." (Once again, photographs of the production belie this description.) Florence cannot conceal her horror. Sensing all this, he piles on a lowly history, including the fact that his father is a cobbler. She, of course, immediately wants out. However, Sam makes her a deal: since the family is looking for a butler, he will take the job, and if, after a certain time, he has not learned proper dress and manners, he will quietly go away. Reluctantly, Florence agrees. As everyone in the audience expected, Sam succeeds handsomely. It even turns out that while his father began life as a cobbler, he is now a successful shoe manufacturer.

The next evening brought in another superior comedy, Guy Bolton and George Middleton's **Adam and Eva** (9-13-19, Longacre). James King (Berton Churchill) has made a fortune in rubber. He ought to be happy but he is not, for his family refuses to live within his very ample means. Enter handsome, young Adam Smith (Otto Kruger), manager of King's Brazilian plantations. He tells his boss how unhappy he is, and how he longs for the noise of civilization, crowds of people, and outstretched arms. King hits upon the idea of the men's exchanging places, but when Adam quickly accepts, King warns him to expect not outstretched arms but outstretched hands. Adam takes over and puts his foot down, only to discover his new "family," furious at his refusal to let them live beyond their incomes, threaten to pawn their jewels. So Adam quietly "steals" the jewels. He also tells everyone that King has lost his entire fortune. This gets rid of the fortune hunters courting King's pretty daughter, Eva (Ruth Shepley), and forces the clan to move to a farm in New Jersey where they will raise chickens and bottle honey. In just three months (theatrical license, no doubt) the businesses are flourishing. King returns to a family changed for the better. And Adam recognizes he has fallen in love with Eva—unmindful of the apple she has given him. Welcomed by Burns Mantle as "a characteristic comedy of American home life," the comedy ran out the season.

A lame collegiate comedy, Samuel Shipman and Percival Wilde's **First Is Last** (9-17-19, Maxine

Elliott's), was all that separated *Adam and Eva* from the next wonderful laugh-provoker. Its cast of ten represented five boys from Columbia (including Hassard Short, Richard Dix, and Edward G. Robinson) and five girls from Barnard who agree, success or no, to put all their earnings in a common pot and split them. Naturally the big winners are soon unhappy with the deal.

By now critics and playgoers probably had lost count of plays whose heroes were decorated war veterans. That count climbed by one with the next opening. Not only was the leading figure a veteran, but, like non-veteran Adam Smith, he found himself embroiled in the problems of what a later generation would call a dysfunctional family, albeit a comically dysfunctional one again. Till the end of the play the characters were not even certain what his last name was. The father of the house, Mr. Wheeler (John Flood), insists it is Smun; the governess, Violet, argues for Moon. No matter, since he always answers to the name of **Clarence** (9-20-19, Hudson). However, this Clarence (Alfred Lunt) does not present the picture of a typical returning warrior. He still wears his shabby, misfitting uniform, he stoops "not only from the shoulders, but from the waist," his hair is disheveled, and beyond his large spectacles his blinking eyes disclose a touch of wildness in them. Having waited patiently for several days, he finally is brought to the anteroom of Mr. Wheeler's office. Initially the boss asks his secretary to get rid of Clarence as courteously as possible. Then Clarence overhears Mr. Wheeler's family vent their anger and exasperation on the old man. Mrs. Wheeler (Mary Boland) is his second wife, a pretty, vain, jealous woman who believes that Mr. Wheeler has fallen in love with Violet (Elsie Mackay), governess to her giddily romantic, assertive, teenaged stepdaughter, Cora (Helen Hayes). Cora's slang-spouting, playboy-in-the-making brother, Bobby (Glenn Hunter), has just been expelled from his third prep school for dicing. Embarrassed at Clarence's overhearing all his problems and impressed by the misinformation that Clarence herded army mules without ever cursing at them, Mr. Wheeler agrees to take him on as a handyman at home. The Wheelers are surprised to learn that Clarence was injured in the war, but unflummoxed when they discover it was a wound received not in battle but in target practice. In short order Clarence has mended more than a broken furnace. He has got mother, son, and possibly daughter to understand what sort of behavior is expected of them, and he has won Violet's hand. By the time he leaves the Wheelers, they have learned that he can dress and carry himself attractively, that

he can play the saxophone (which he does in one scene), and that, however young he may be, he is already a world-renowned coleopterist—a specialist in beetles. He had only taken on the job while waiting for a research post to become available. The household is happy for him, except for the love-struck Cora, who sees herself as having tragically just lost her latest true love. Oh, yes—Clarence's last name, like Adam's, proves to be Smith. Critics tripped over themselves lauding the play and apologizing to its author, Booth Tarkington, for all the slighting remarks they had been writing about him recently. Dorothy Parker, writing in *Vanity Fair*, saw it as a "faithful portrayal of all the absurdities and exaggerations of adolescence," while in the *Tribune* Heywood Broun went a step further, hailing it as "the best light comedy which has been written by an American." The brilliantly selected cast was similarly welcomed as close to perfection. Naturally the young Lunt walked off with the lion's share of the encomiums, the *Sun*'s Alan Dale calling his humane, believable, yet hilarious characterization "perfectly flawless."

• • •

Alfred [David] **Lunt** (1892–1980) was born in Milwaukee and educated at Carroll College. After abandoning his ambitions to become an architect, he made his debut with Boston's Castle Square Theatre stock company. Tours with Lillie Langtry and Margaret Anglin were followed by his Broadway debut in 1917 in *Romance and Arabella*. He was a handsome man with an elegant voice and large brown eyes that always seemed startled.

• • •

John Golden, accustomed to mounting long-run hits, found himself with an apparently short-lived dud on his hands when he presented **Thunder** (9-22-19, Criterion), which Peg (or Pearl) Franklin took from stories by Elia Peattie. It centered on "Old Thunder" (Burr McIntosh), a mountain preacher given to toting a gun, bending the law, and otherwise setting things right by his own methods. He takes under his wing an orphaned circus performer, Azalea (Sylvia Field), and, by falsely claiming she is the heir to a miserly hermit's unexpected fortune, sets her on the road to success and romance. He also performs a shotgun wedding, himself holding the gun to discourage feuding mountaineers from misbehaving while he marries a boy and a girl from enemy clans. One critic observed, " 'Thunder' is a little like 'Lightnin' '" without Frank Bacon," while *Variety*, also comparing the plays, remarked, " 'Lightnin' ' struck, but 'Thunder' crashed." The play left New York hurriedly. Yet Golden refused to admit defeat. He immediately took the play on the road, all the while rewriting (eventually with some unsolicited but crucial help from Tarkington), and by the time the play reached Chicago, where it was retitled *Howdy, Folks,* he could claim he had a minor hit.

No such good fortune befell the next two entries. Neil Twomey, who not many years earlier had churned out potboilers for cheap touring circuits, tried his hand at farce with **Katy's Kisses** (9-24-19, Greenwich Village). He himself took the lead role of Matthew Davis, a self-proclaimed "Apostle of Bluff." Coming to a New England village, he bluffs his way into a $3 room and into friendship and partnership with Ned Summers, a lawyer (Carl Jackson) who turns out to be as broke a bluffer as Davis. But a candy called Katy's Kisses starts them off on the way to wealth and wedded bliss—with Summers landing the daughter (Mary Ann Dentier) of his laundress and Davis snaring a rich widow (Geraldine Beckwith). Critics claimed the acting and staging at the tiny house was of the noisy, old fist-on-the-forehead school, adding insult to injury.

Cosmo Hamilton's second play of the season, **An Exchange of Wives** (9-26-19, Bijou), received a critical drubbing. Its title gave away much of its plot. Two friendly couples share a summer cottage on Long Island. But when the sweet little wife (Margaret Dale) of one couple and the highly conventional husband (Lee Baker) of the other suspect their spouses (Forrest Winant and Chrystal Herne) are becoming too cozy they decide to win them back by letting themselves be caught spooning together out on the sleeping porch.

George Scarborough's **Moonlight and Honeysuckle** (9-29-19, Henry Miller's) just missed entering the charmed circle of plays that ran 100 performances or more and thus could be perceived as hits. The play was produced and directed by Miller and starred the popular actress who was openly bruited to be his mistress, Ruth Chatterton. She played Judith Baldwin, a senator's daughter who is courted by three men: Washington's social butterfly, the exquisite Courtney Blue (Charles Trowbridge); the proper, up-and-coming Congressman Hamill (Sydney Booth); and a young, bemedalled aviator, Tod Musgrave (James Rennie). To help her make up her mind, Judith decides to tell all three men about her past—a scandalous, totally fictitious past. She is dismayed to discover all the men accept her fibs as truth but relieved when Tod, unlike his rivals, doesn't try to back away from his proposal. Despite intermissions the play's action was continuous.

September's last entry was not only its biggest hit but the biggest hit of the season. The play was David Belasco's production of Avery Hopwood's **The Gold Diggers** (9-30-19, Lyceum), whose title invested the language with a new phrase. (*Variety,* echoing the fears of Belasco's staff, began its notice by alerting readers that the play did not deal with forty-niners.) A group of chorus girls have gathered at the attractive apartment of their fellow chorister, Jerry Lamar (Ina Claire). Among them are the amazonian Mabel Munroe (Jobyna Howland), who makes a second career of collecting alimony, and the apparently innocent Violet Dayne (Beverly West, Mae's sister). As they join in some very late morning calisthenics, Jerry warns them, "Men will do a great deal for us now—but, oh, girls—lose your figures or your complexions—get a few lines in your face—get tired out and faded looking, and a little passé—and the fellows that are ready to give you pearls and sables now—well—they'd turn the other way when they saw you coming!" Mabel reinforces Jerry's sentiments, telling the others, "The moral of this story is—'Dig, sisters, while the digging's good!' " Jerry has promised Violet to help win over her fiancé's bluestocking uncle, Stephen Lee. Stephen (Bruce McRae) arrives and, as Jerry had hoped he would, mistakes her for Violet. She promptly "vamps" Stephen, with the idea that the real Violet will then seem virtue personified to him. Before long, he is wholly enamored of Jerry. Distressed, Jerry, like Judith the night before, concocts a story of a wicked past. To her further dismay, Stephen forgives her everything. When she confesses the truth, however, he walks out in a huff. But he soon returns to woo Jerry for herself, finding her irresistible. "What are you doing to me?" he cries. Her response: "I'm gold digging." The play was capitally performed by an excellent cast, led by the polished McRae and, most of all, the deliciously droll Ina Claire. Critics saluted them, although the same aisle-sitters disagreed on the merits of the play. Hornblow in *Theatre* dismissed most of it as "poor entertainment," but Broun, once again reaching for superlatives, welcomed it as "quite the most accurate portrayal of the type." Belasco's production was also top-notch. The girls in beautiful Bendel clothes lolled and frisked in a single sumptuous setting depicting an apartment in the "Eighties, between Broadway and Riverside," a setting, thanks to Belasco's new $80,000 lighting system, bathed in "the most breathtaking sunlight yet seen on the American stage." The comedy's run of 720 performances (broken by a summer vacation and therefore denied by some quibbling counters) made it the second-longest run in Broadway history up to its time.

By September's end *Variety* was reporting that

Broadway was breaking records and that a serious theatre shortage was looming. A few weeks later the tradesheet noted that twenty-three of the forty-six shows on Broadway were at or near capacity business. However, it also recorded the increasing disappearance of one-night stands, although it blamed the ongoing shrinkage not so much on films themselves but on the quality of mountings sent out to these backwaters. A sudden, sharp slump in November proved a passing aberration.

October's first two entries were by playwrights who, like Owen Davis and Neil Twomey, had cut their teeth creating thrillers for the old, by now defunct, cheap touring circuits. Edward Locke had moved up to triumph on Broadway with his 1909 hit, *The Climax,* which told of a young singer lured away from a promising career. His newest work, **The Dancer** (10-1-19, Harris), told of a young Russian ballerina (Isabelle Lowe), who marries a puritanical New Englander (John Halliday), is at first forced to abandon her art, then runs away to resume her dancing. Only after serving in the war and learning of his uncle and aunt's attempts to humiliate the girl is her husband made to see the light. Effingham Pinto oiled the pathos playing the ballerina's blind brother.

Langdon McCormick had much better luck with **The Storm** (10-2-19, 48th St.), a patently old-fashioned melodrama that lured in audiences for the entire season. Burr Winston (Edward Arnold), a rugged prospector, offers refuge from a storm to David Stewart (Robert Rendel), a dashing, well-educated Englishman, and later to Manchette Fachard (Helen MacKellar), whose father (Max Mitzel) has died almost immediately on reaching Burr's cabin. It soon becomes obvious not only that the trio will be marooned for some time but that both men quickly are falling in love with the girl. Manchette is unable to decide between them. When a thaw sets in, one of the men must attempt to obtain provisions. Through trickery David makes it appear that Manchette prefers Burr to go. However, before he can leave a forest fire threatens them. Burr's coolness and bravery save them and allow Manchette to choose between the men. Critics saw the play for the obsolescent hokum that it was but conceded it made for good theatre. They especially praised the stocky Arnold's performance, discovering in him a new Farnum. However, most agreed the scenery stole the show, first with an effective snowstorm and at the end with "a forest fire, which glows in the offing for a while and then sweeps right up to the footlights with choking effect. Glowing branches fall . . . [and whole trees] catch fire and burn to red-hot embers."

Cut-price tickets helped Thomas Grant Springer, Fleta Campbell Springer, and Joseph Noel's **Where's Your Wife?** (10-4-19, Punch and Judy) survive eight weeks at one of New York's tiniest auditoriums in the face of dismissive notices. The New York police begin a murder investigation, and newspapermen think they may have a hot story, all because of bloodstains, an ugly knife, and a missing woman. It turns out the blood came from a duck, the rusty knife was meant for a trash basket, and the lady had gone to Grand Central to meet her husband. One sign of the theatre's still healthy economics was that a play with sixteen principals and several walk-ons would consider booking so small a playhouse.

All of the next Monday night's openings were hits in some degree or another. One was a musical, one a drama, one a sex farce, and the last a Shakespearean revival. Of the three straight attractions, the drama ran the longest. Zoë Akins's **Déclassée** 10-6-19, Empire) prospered largely on the performance of Ethel Barrymore (especially in what reviewers extolled as the best death scene in ages) and on the brilliant dialogue and sharp observation of the author during her first two acts (the final act, even with, and to some extent because of, the death scene, had serious problems of credibility). Of the star, *Vanity Fair*'s Dorothy Parker confessed, "If, during my theatre-going life-time, there has been any other performance so perfect as the one she gives in the role . . . if there has been any other acting like that, I can only say I had the hideous ill luck to miss it." Along with the play's third-act problems critics assailed the shamefully shabby mounting (which Miss Barrymore in her memoirs attributed to Alf Hayman's determination to get back at her for her support of the striking actors). The play opens with a stunning, tone-setting scene, a once obviously gay London party in disarray and the guests desperately attempting (offstage) to calm the host and hostess. The host, Sir Bruce Haden (Harry Plimmer), is not a nice man; he is an upstart who began life as a butcher and who married the last of "the mad Varicks," a once socially important family. As one of the guests bemoans, "Here we are—all of us trying to keep them together when we ought to beg her, if she has either any pride or any courage left, to leave him, at once, forever!" Sir Bruce has accused Edward Thayer (Vernon Steel), who can most politely be termed his wife's protégé, of cheating at cards. Lady Helen finally forces Sir Bruce to apologize, but later in the evening she herself catches Thayer cheating and denounces him. To get back at her he hands Sir Bruce old letters embarrassing to his wife. The contents of the letters are never revealed, but by the beginning of the next act they have provoked Sir Bruce to divorce her. Alone in America she is snubbed by many but still loved by a small coterie of old friends. And her life, more than ever, is, as she once told Thayer, "like water that has gone over the dam and turned no mill wheels." She is courted by a rich, understanding Jew, Rudolph Solomon (Claude King), who warns her, "You're very wonderful now, Lady Helen, but there's 'tomorrow and tomorrow and tomorrow.' " Lady Helen, who has been keeping herself alive by selling off her jewels, responds, "I know. And old age around the curve, and just one more pearl, . . . [*She looks at the ring on her finger, and laughs a little*]." When Solomon proposes she gently rejects him, but he gathers her rejection comes really from the fact that she still loves someone else. After Solomon leaves she calls for her bill and hands the captain her ring in lieu of the money she no longer has. Between the acts Helen has had second thoughts and seems to have decided to reconsider her refusal of Solomon. She attends a large party that Solomon is throwing. Thayer appears, and Solomon is led to conclude that he is the man Lady Helen loves. Meaning to set her free, Solomon tells her he can no longer marry her. Lady Helen learns that Thayer is at the party and rushes away. Outside she is struck by a taxi. When she is brought back into the house, she reminisces about the good times that were and speaks of good times that might have been before she dies in the arms of the repentant Thayer.

Despite money reviews, Wilson Collison and Avery Hopwood's **The Girl in the Limousine** (10-6-19, Eltinge) ran less than half as long, 137 performances. Collison had written the farce under the more honest title *Betty's Bed,* and given it to Al Woods, who handed it over to Hopwood for revisions. Betty Neville (Doris Kenyon), fearing she is coming down with a cold, leaves her own party and returns to her streamlined, modern bedroom and takes to her modernly squarish, wicker bed. Tony Hamilton (John Cumberland), who had wooed Betty before she married another man, is on the way to the party when he stops to help a girl stranded by a seemingly broken-down limousine. She is really a lure for crooks who conk him over the head, strip him down to his underwear, and attempt to place him in a bed. Since the bed is Betty's and she's already asleep in it, they roll him underneath. Enter Aunt Cicely (Zelda Sears), who mistakes Tony for Betty's husband and forces him into the bed. She is followed by Dr. Jimmie Galen (Charles Ruggles), a friend of the family who concludes he is imagining everything, by Mr. Neville (Frank Thomas), and a partyload of

others, all programmed to misconstrue what they see. Typical of the favorable notices was Dorothy Parker's in *Vanity Fair* hailing this saga of "The most densely populated bed in town" as "undeniably very funny." Remembering that Collison was said to be a pharmacist, she asked, "What do you suppose is above that drug-store?"

At the Shubert on the 6th, Julia Marlowe and E. H. Sothern came out of a six-year retirement to offer a three-week stand in some of their best-loved Shakespearean roles. Starting with *Twelfth Night,* they followed with *Hamlet* and *The Taming of the Shrew.* Critics applauded their jettisoning their old, heavy scenery in favor of settings consisting primarily of neutral-colored drapes, which allowed for swifter and more flowing action. They also approved of the stars' decision to dispense with the insistent musical underscoring that until recently had been so commonplace. Sothern and Marlowe were both accorded kind words. Yet noting the relative slightness of many of the morning-after reviews and reading between the lines of what was written, there must have been a sense of disappointment. In a season or two, the pair would be openly accused of being retrograde in outlook and increasingly disparaging notices would help prompt a second, permanent withdrawal.

Somerset Maugham's **Too Many Husbands** (10-8-19, Booth) barely made it into the hit column with its 102 performances, despite its acclaim in England (where it had been called *Home and Beauty*), its fine mounting (surprisingly by Al Woods, who apparently was responsible for the change of title), and its laudatory notices. The surplus husbands (Kenneth Douglas and Lawrence Grossmith) belong to a slightly vacuous, demanding young lady (Estelle Winwood), who has married the second after believing the first was killed in the war. Imagine her consternation when the first returns home and each man begs the other to take her off his hands. She divorces them both and marries a nouveau riche businessman.

Frank Bacon and Freeman Tilden did themselves anything but proud with their oddball, off-putting blend of comedy and melodrama, **Five O'Clock** (10-13-19, Fulton), in which a young man (Leslie Austen), having been unjustly committed thirteen years before to a mental institution by his callous relations and kept there by an equally callous doctor (Paul Everton), finally wins freedom with the help of the doctor's compassionate daughter (Alberta Burton). The two agree to marry and to establish a place where backward youngsters can be looked after humanely and go home each night at five.

At one point the sanity of the hero of **Boys Will Be Boys** (10-13-19, Belmont), which Charles O'Brien Kennedy theatricalized from Irving Cobb's story, is also called into question. Peep O'Day (Harry Beresford) remarks, "When I hear anybody say, 'Get out o' there, white trash,' I know they means me." Unexpectedly, he inherits $40,000. He uses the money to buy his old Kentucky village's schoolhouse—so he can have the fun of breaking all its windows. Moreover, he pays to have a circus come to town, purchases the best melon field in the area—so youngsters can steal all the melons they want with impunity—and breaks into a safe to retrieve papers a pair of lovers needs. When a villager says Peep is in his second childhood, he retorts, "A man can't hardly have a second childhood when he's been cheated out of the first." Once again a large-cast play (twenty-four players) was housed in one of New York's tiniest theatres. Yet for all the good notices it received, it failed to draw. Virtually unnoticed in the casts of *Boys Will Be Boys* and *Five O'Clock* was the presence in small roles of figures once important in cheap touring melodramas—Frank I. Frayne in the former, David Higgins in the latter.

The Theatre Guild, in its first presentation of the season, met with what its leading light, Lawrence Langner, called "an honorable failure" when it offered John Masefield's poetic "Japanese drama" **The Faithful** (10-13-19, Garrick), which told of a vicious usurper (Henry Herbert) who slays the decent, popular Lord Asano (Rollo Peters), and who is then slain by Asano's followers even though it means their own deaths. While initially the Guild would rely on foreign plays to the virtual exclusion of native works, it did support American performers and creative artists. Thus, this production gave playgoers an early glimpse of Lee Simonson's work, including an austerely beautiful Japanese interior, and a view of a snow gorge painted in Oriental style on a huge Japanese-like folding screen that ran from one side of the proscenium to the other and whose top side was cut to resemble a mountain range peaking in the middle. It was backed by a curtain depicting a starry night sky. When the dead lord's avengers marched by, carrying banners, spears, and curving swords, Simonson lit the set from behind to show the progression in silhouette.

There was not a mention of Mawruss Perlmutter in Montague Glass and Jules Eckert Goodman's **His Honor, Abe Potash** (10-14-19, Bijou), yet Abe (Barney Bernard) and his wife (Mathilde Cottrelly) were able to regale Broadway for more than six months without Abe's longtime partner. It seems Abe has left the garment district and moved to Damascus, N.Y., where he has become so popular that he is asked to run for mayor. He wins the election, but, to the dismay of the politicians who promoted him, he refuses to condone a land grab. They try to throw Abe into bankruptcy and to frame his son (Ted W. Gibson). Abe toughs it through. At one point, when his son is accused, he insists the boy spend the night in jail, provoking Mrs. Potash to ask if he thinks he is playing King Lear. With Mawruss gone, was the character of Henry Block (a name out of *Friendly Enemies*) inserted as a compensatory in-joke? Hailed by *Variety* as "one of the best native comedies . . . offered the public in this generation," the play was Al Woods's fourth hit of the young season.

Mrs. Clifford Mills's **The Luck of the Navy** (10-14-19, Manhattan Opera House) was a British wartime spy melodrama with a largely British cast played out in one of Manhattan's largest auditoriums, but not for long. The British do not know (or do they?) that Sublieutenant Louis Peel, an officer in the navy, is actually Ludwig Poel, a German spy raised in England. With his mother and another spy who is posing as a Belgian officer, he plots to kidnap Lieutenant Clive Stanton, fly him back to Germany, and force him to reveal naval secrets. But when Stanton is invited to the Peel house, he turns the tables and arrests the whole rotten lot. Ignoring that Britain, like America, once had a school of cheap touring melodrama, one critic characterized the play as "written for those who like their thrills a la Theodore Kremer."

Nor did Philadelphian John T. McIntyre's **A Young Man's Fancy** (10-15-19, Playhouse) fare any better in its intimate berth. The young man is Pickering (Philip Merivale), a reclusive rich man, who falls in love with a mannequin in a department store window, breaks the window and otherwise makes a fool of himself in his infatuation, and finally finds a realistic romance when he meets Mary Darling Furlong (Jeanne Eagels), the beauty who served as the model for the mannequin. Although programs listed only one set in each act, critics reported there were numerous settings (Pickering's home, the store window, inside the store, the street, etc.) and that while they were beautiful (they were done by Joseph Urban) they created unconscionable scene-change delays and were not set solidly in place. Woollcott reported, "The 'fumed oak' panels did the shimmy, the chandelier waved like an aspen, and the old mirror shook with supressed excitement."

Woollcott's sharp memory allowed him to catch the little in-joke in Harvey O'Higgins and Harriet

Ford's **On the Hiring Line** (10-20-19, Criterion). Furious that his wife (Laura Hope Crews), a former actress who longs to be back in the big city, cannot or will not keep servants in their country home, Mr. Fessenden (Cyril Scott) resorts to hiring detectives to staff his house. (What Woollcott spotted was that the detective agency had the same name as the one in the authors' more successful *The Dummy*.) Not fully understanding their assignment, the detectives (Sidney Toler and Josephine Hall) pose as butler and cook, and snoop around. They report that Fessendens' chauffeur, Steve Mack (Donald Gallaher), is a crook, wanted in Washington. A startled Fessenden asks, "Good Lord, what do they want with another crook in Washington?" But it soon develops that Steve is a senator's son who has taken his job to be near the Fessenden's daughter (Vivian Tobin). They also cast suspicion on an actor friend (John Blair) who is visiting Mrs. Fessenden and has some old love letters he wrote to her years ago. Critics praised bits and pieces of the play and the acting of the whole cast, but the reviews could not turn the somewhat spotty comedy into a hit.

Nor did Augustus Thomas's **Palmy Days** (10-27-19, Playhouse) appeal to New Yorkers. Some critics adored it, seeing it as a capital piece of period hokum; others felt it couldn't make up its mind whether it wanted to be a comedy or a melodrama. Virtually all agreed it was superbly played. Cassius M. McBrayer once had been Edwin Forrest's dresser. But discovering Forrest having an affair with his wife, he sued for divorce and headed west, where he became a highly successful prospector and miner. He is known as Kaintuck (Wilton Lackaye), and when he is not working with his young partner, Davy Woodford (George Le Guere), at the ironically named Metamora lode, he spends time at Mrs. Curley's bar in Lone Tree. The saloon is an austere place, built of wide boards, with little or no decoration. Old crates serve as chairs. But the place is enlivened by the visit of some traveling actors. Davy instantly falls head over heels for the Lotta-like Cricket (Genevieve Tobin), who gives a performance alongside her haughty mother (Mattie Keene) and her banjo-strumming, blackfaced minstrel stepfather (Edward J. Guhl). A concerned Kaintuck moves to cool Davy's ardor, but in doing so recognizes Cricket as the daughter he has never seen (she is the image of the picture of his mother he carries about). Kaintuck's ex-wife attempts to prevent a rapprochement, while a hard-eyed gambler, Bud Farrell (Harry D. Southard), vies with Davy for Cricket's affections. Threatened shootouts do not explode, and all ends happily. At one point, when

Farrell is prevented from shooting Kaintuck, he stalks out coldly snarling, "I bid you good evening." Kaintuck drawls in return, "I sees your 'Good evening' and I raises you 'Au revoir.' "

On the 31st the Provincetown Players opened their new season with a bill of four one-acters that included Eugene O'Neill's **The Dreamy Kid,** a story of a young black fleeing from the law and determined to visit his dying grandmother even if it means he will be killed. In a bold departure, the company cast all the parts with black players.

Marjorie Blaine and Willard Mack's **The Unknown Woman** (11-10-19, Maxine Elliott's) purportedly was adapted from an unidentified Yiddish drama by one Stanley Lewis, said to have been popular recently in the Lower East Side. *Variety* added to this list by claiming that Lewis had derived his work from one by Zalmen Libin. All this led Mack to tell first-nighters that the play "was taken by the Irish from the Jews." It focused on Margaret Emerson (Marjorie Rambeau), who turns to her former lover, Gerald Hastings (Lumsden Hare), to escape her selfishly ambitious, philandering husband (Felix Krembs), a district attorney running as a candidate for governor of New York. Gerald's wife, a drug addict committed to a cure center, escapes and fatally overdoses herself. Since Gerald refuses to hurt Margaret by admitting he was with her at the time of his wife's death, circumstances allow Emerson to accuse Hastings of murder. Hastings is tried and sentenced to death. Emerson locks Margaret in a room to prevent her stopping the execution. Margaret discovers her husband has overlooked a telephone in the room and, after arguing with Central (as operators were then known), gets through to the prison in the nick of time. She and Gerald will wed after her divorce. While critics regularly praised Miss Rambeau for her beauty and diverse acting skills, they also apparently felt a little uncomfortable with her, albeit they expressed their disquiet diplomatically. Thus, they spoke of her "sometimes inexplicable mannerisms" or her "collection of old stock company tricks of histrionism." Playgoers may have shared these reservations. In any case, she could not turn the play into a success.

Similarly, Lennox Robinson's Irish drama **The Lost Leader** (11-11-19, Greenwich Village) could not lure theatregoers to its small venue downtown. Beginning in a backwater Irish inn and moving to a crossroads where two ancient monoliths rise out of the ground, it told how hypnotism goads the elderly innkeeper (Frank Conroy) into stating he is really Charles Stewart Parnell, who never died as was publicly claimed. He offers to lead Ireland to freedom but is accidentally slain by a blow a blind man was aiming at his detractor.

By contrast, Salisbury Field's **Wedding Bells** (11-12-19, Harris) was welcomed as good, clean, if slightly lamebrained fun by critics and playgoers alike, so chalked up a five-month run. On the eve of his marriage to Marcia Hunter (Jessie Glendinning), Reggie Carter (Wallace Eddinger) admits to a friend that he was married once before. He met wife number one when he was staying at a Santa Barbara hotel before sailing to the Orient. He had placed his shoes outside of his door to be shined, and Rosalie's dog had made a dinner of one of them. In two days they romanced, wed, quarreled, and separated. Reggie could not find what happened to her since "I was so busy talking about myself" that he never even learned her maiden name or home address. But he had received a notice that Rosalie had divorced him. Marcia, having also learned of Reggie's past, appears. She is irate and sorry she has not preferred Reggie's rival, Douglas Ordway (Clarke Silvernail), a poet. At her mother's insistence she will go through with the wedding but, recalling Douglas's profession of eternal love, concludes, "It's very comforting to a girl to know that someone is going to love her after she's married." The next to arrive is Rosalie (Margaret Lawrence), obviously set on winning back Reggie. She almost fails, until Reggie and Marcia return from church where the bishop, having been secretly advised that Reggie was a divorced man, refused to perform the service. Guess who sent the note to the bishop! Marcia's mother (Mrs. Jacques Martin) demands there be a wedding, what with all the guests still waiting at the church, so Marcia "in order not to disappoint mother" agrees to marry Douglas. When Douglas confesses that he, too, has been married, Rosalie quickly removes that obstacle by announcing that Douglas had wed her maid, a girl already married, and thus nullifying his marriage. The curtain falls with Reggie and Rosalie embracing.

Embraces were deadly in George Scarborough and David Belasco's **The Son-Daughter** (11-19-19, Belasco), where Dong Tong (Thomas Findlay), a leading businessman in New York's Chinatown, is prodded into selling his daughter, Lien Wha (Lenore Ulric), to raise $80,000 for the cause of the Chinese revolution. But carrying the money home Dong Tong is murdered, and Tom Lee (Edmund Lowe), who is Lien Wha's lover and the son of the slain leader of the revolution, is stabbed and dragged away. (Tom Lee was depicted as a student at Columbia and was one of the few characters in the play to dress in Occidental clothes.) A frightened but determined Lien Wha, sitting behind the rose-pink curtains of her bed, awaits the arrival of the man who has bought her, Fen-sha (Harry Mestayer), a notorious businessman and gambler, known as the Sea Crab and now revealed as a treacherous imperial agent. When he comes she invites him to join her. "You see her fondle his silken queue and then suddenly with a little gasp of fear, you see her whip the black rope around his neck and start to strangle him. There is a struggle. The towering white lamp is struck and totters. It falls and everything behind the curtains is black. You hear his death rattle and then, sobbing with fear and exultation, you see her drag him through the curtains, drag him across the floor and deliver him like an offering at the steps of the marriage altar." She prays to the gods that Fen-sha be dragged down to the seven hells. Rumors suggest Lien Wha and the wounded Tom Lee escape to the West Coast and from there to China. Most critics extolled Belasco's meticulously wrought, richly colored mounting, with its beautiful costumes and recreations of Oriental rooms in a Chinatown home and gambling den. Many, however, were not happy with the play, calling it "trite," "shoddy," "not moving," and less kind things. Dorothy Parker, dipping her pen in venom for *Vanity Fair,* wrote, "If Mr. Samuel Shipman is in the house, I should be glad to have him observe me get down and crawl abjectly along the ground for anything I may have said about his brain-child, *East Is West.* Last season, in the exuberance of youth, I used to think no play along the same lines could possibly be worse; that was before the dying year brought *The Son-Daughter.*" Critics also split, but were largely favorable, about Lenore Ulric, "garbed in brocade robes stiff with gold embroidery, plucking with tapered fingers at a two-stringed Chinese mandolin." Hot-cold reviews could not deter Belasco loyalists, who packed his playhouse for months on end.

A more literate, witty play, Somerset Maugham's **Caesar's Wife** (11-24-19, Liberty), ran only two months. It starred Billie Burke as the young wife of a much older man (Norman Trevor), a British diplomat in Egypt. When she confesses she has fallen in love with a man (Ernest Glendinning) her own age, her husband insists she put duty before personal feelings. A brilliant supporting cast (including oldtimers Hilda Spong and Frederic de Belleville) and magnificent Urban settings of a British mansion in Egypt graced the superb mounting by Miss Burke's husband, Florenz Ziegfeld.

In time Maugham would be better remembered as a novelist than as a playwright. Years earlier another novelist, William Dean Howells, had regularly tried his hand at playwriting and had been poorly rewarded. His plays are totally forgotten. In late 1919 he was an old man and in retirement (he would die in May of 1920), so it fell to Lillian Sabine to attempt a theatricalization of one of his best works. **The Rise of Silas Lapham** (11-25-19, Garrick) told of an ambitious upstart who attempts to buy his way into society but fails. He retires to Vermont, where he can spend his last years secure in the knowledge that, for all his gaucheries, he had never done a dishonest deed. In a bit of egregious miscasting, the leading role was awarded to James K. Hackett, who played the part not as a middle-aged climber but as an elderly hayseed. (Years earlier Hackett's father had won stardom with his impersonation of stage Yankees.) His performance, coupled with a pedestrian adaptation, assured the show a quick closure. For the Theatre Guild, it marked its second failure of the season in as many tries, although the group could at least claim it had mounted an American work with this theatricalized novel.

December was a busy month, and most interesting in that it redressed the balance of a season so far top-heavy with comedies by offering a number of superior dramas.

Laurette Taylor, dressed in a black wig and long, clinging garments, and setting aside her "sudden smile, the infectious twinkle of her speaking eyes and the devil-may-care humor," was the reason J. Hartley Manners's **One Night in Rome** (12-2-19, Criterion) was able to stay on New York boards for fourteen weeks. She played "L'Enigme," an Italian fortune teller popular in English high society. After disclosing to another of the season's decorated veterans, Richard Oak (Philip Merivale), that his palm suggests he is at heart a weakling, she and Richard find themselves alone together at a swank house party. He cravenly attempts to desert her, so she smashes open a jewel case to make it seem she was about to steal some valuables. The gentleman in Oak prods him into taking responsibility. His action costs him his fiancée but wins him L'Enigme, who proves to be a well-bred English girl forced to assume her disguise after her Italian husband accused her of infidelity then killed himself at a ball. The *American*'s Alan Dale warned his readers of the evening, "All the merit it contains is that it is a good vehicle for Miss Taylor."

December's lone comedy hit was Emil Nyitray and Frank Mandel's **My Lady Friends** (12-3-19, Comedy). *Theatre* rejoiced, "Of the many plays seen on Broadway this season, none has been more cordially welcomed or evoked so many spontaneous laughs as this delightful farce." It centered on Jimmy Smith (Clifton Crawford), a Bible publisher whose wife (Mona Kingsley) is so close with their fortune that she decides to spread a little sunshine by providing pretty, lonely young beauties with jewels, nice clothes, and comfortable apartments in both New York and Atlantic City. After his wife catches on she runs out and buys a $100,000 home. A shocked Jimmy suggests that's a mite expensive, only to be assured by his wife that it is not expensive for Long Island. Jimmy can merely mumble, "I didn't know you were buying Long Island." The hit ran until the warm weather. On tour, at least part of the time, and subsequently in London it was known as *His Lady Friends*. Because Crawford was as well known as a song-and-dance man as he was as a farceur, a few songs were included. But the story attained a wider vogue several years later when it was turned into the era's biggest musical comedy success, *No, No, Nanette*.

Two quick flops followed. The first was Earl Derr Biggers and Christopher Morley's adaptation of Morley's short story "Kathleen," as **Three's a Crowd** (12-4-19, Cort). Not one but four former soldiers (two Englishmen, one Canadian, and one American) all descend on the Stratford-on-Avon home of a sweet lass (Phoebe Foster) who wrote letters to them during the war. She selects the American (Alan Dinehart).

Like its first, the Provincetown Players' second bill, which premiered on the 5th, also presented one superior work, Edna St. Vincent Millay's **Aria da Capo.** It recounted how the gaily frisking Pierrot and Columbine are ordered off the stage so that two reluctantly recruited shepherds can act out a deadly war game. After the shepherds have killed each other, Pierrot and Columbine are allowed to resume their frolic. Stylized screens and props of confetti and crepe paper underscored the fantastic elements of the play.

The soldier heroes in Anthony Paul Kelly's **The Phantom Legion** (12-10-19, Playhouse) were all truly dead. But their spirits haunt both the battlefield to encourage still living fighters and places where stay-at-homes must be taught patriotic fervor. Absurd "posturing and . . . old-fashioned sepulchral rhetoric" such as "Ah, how shall we open the gate to her sorrowing heart?" were no help.

The next play was something of an oddity. It was a drama, by an Englishman, centering on a notable American. London had welcomed it, but Americans who saw it there reported that much of it was laughable. And when Woollcott sat down to review the quietly rewritten American version, he could still write that John Drinkwater's **Abraham Lincoln** (12-15-19, Cort) seemed "like a dramatized Child's History of Lincoln done by someone who did not know much about Lincoln for those who knew less." The play begins at Lincoln's Springfield home, where he accepts the Republican nomination on the condition that he not have to compromise his principles. It moves on to the White House, where the president consoles the mother of a dead soldier, upbraids the wife of a war profiteer, and forces the resignation of a cabinet member opposed to the Emancipation Proclamation, to Grant's headquarters near Appomattox, where Lincoln urges mercy on the defeated troops, and to the box at Ford's Theatre, where the president delivers snatches of the Gettysburg Address to the audience before John Wilkes Booth shoots him and runs hastily out the door (no jump from the box) and where moments later Stanton tells the stunned assemblage, "Now he belongs to the ages." Livingston Platt's superb scenery and a first-rate cast, headed by Frank McGlynn, an actor whose career was otherwise largely undistinguished, allowed playgoers to ignore the infelicities. In his makeup, McGlynn seemed Lincoln reincarnated. And his performance was "quite wonderful in its externals, while the humanity, sweetness and breadth of view of the original are depicted with graphic verisimilitude." The play ran out the season.

However, playgoers were unwilling to trek downtown to see H. Austin Adams's **Curiosity** (12-18-19, Greenwich Village). When a wife (Irene Fenwick) becomes upset by the infidelity of her husband (Ramsey Wallace), she attempts a fling with an former suitor (Cyril Keightley). But he argues so cogently in favor of a double standard that the wife returns contritely to her spouse.

Channing Pollock had a season-long success with **The Sign on the Door** (12-19-19, Republic). It employed a decades-old cliché with a vengeance. Ann Regan (Mary Ryan) goes to the apartment of Frank Devereaux (Lowell Sherman), a former lover when she was Ann Hunniwell, to plead with him not to play free and loose with her stepdaughter. Her husband, "Lafe" Regan (Lee Baker), has also learned of Devereaux's dishonorable intentions. He comes to the apartment and, not seeing Ann who is hiding in another room, kills Devereaux, places the gun in the corpse's hand, and leaves, locking the door behind him. Ann is arrested. She is eventually acquitted, as is Regan, on the grounds of justifiable homicide. The play was viewed as gripping theatre and the cast praised. Baker was hailed for making the villain reasonably sympathetic. However, be-

cause Al Woods, the producer, had Marjorie Rambeau under contract and no play immediately available for her, she was called in to replace Miss Ryan shortly after the opening.

In **For the Defense** (12-19-19, Playhouse) Elmer Rice returned to the flashback device that had made him famous with *On Trial*. This time Anne Woodstock (Winifred Lenihan) is accused of murdering a notorious "Hindoo psycho-hypnotist." The evidence is so strong against her that her fiancé, Christopher Armstrong (Richard Bennett), a district attorney, is forced to prosecute her. But flashbacks as she recounts her story in a judge's office disclose the actual killer. With some forcing, the play ran for ten weeks.

Actress, playwright, and librettist Dorothy Donnelly had far less luck with her short-lived **Forbidden** (12-20-19, Manhattan Opera House). Part of its problem may have been that it was a relatively intimate drama, lost in the vastness of its cavernous auditorium, where a theatre shortage forced it to lodge. Its simple story told of an American lieutenant (Richard Barbee) of the Army of Occupation who is billeted in the schloss belonging to a countess (Martha Hedman). They fall in love and plan to marry until it is revealed that the lieutenant was the man who shot to death the countess's twin brother. They resign themselves to going their separate ways. The pastimes of the soldiers, such as a lively crap game, and the slapdash entertainments provided the troops filled the spaces between the episodes of the doomed romance.

Critics, many of them second-stringers, who attended Arthur Hopkins's mounting of Maxim Gorky's **Night Lodging** (12-22-19, Plymouth) at a matinee could find little to cheer about. One critic predicted audiences would be "bored to extinction" by this work examining derelicts in a fetid Russian basement tenement. What little good they could say they said about a cast that included Gilda Varesi, Alan Dinehart, Cecil Yapp, Pauline Lord, Edward G. Robinson, and Edwin Nicander. The play gave only a few matinee performances, then closed, but necessity saw it revived later in the season for a short run. Subsequently, it has had a fitful if respectable afterlife on American stages as *The Lower Depths*.

James Forbes, in a departure from his slangy comedies, provided the season with one of its most brilliant successes, **The Famous Mrs. Fair** (12-22-19, Henry Miller's). Like so many of the season's plays it revolved about a decorated war hero, only this time that hero was a heroine, the wealthy Nancy Fair (Blanche Bates), who had left home and family to work with the soldiers in France and had earned herself a Croix de Guerre. Her demobilized son, Alan (Jack Devereaux), worries how well she will be able to readapt to her old life: "Take it from me. I've been through it. You're going to miss the something—I don't know what it is—but life over there gets you. You know that, mother. You'll find yourself thinking more about the people you left over there than your old friends here." His worries prove justified, for, as one of her friends agrees, she has "time to burn and no matches." So when a slick young man, Dudley Gillette (Robert Strange), offers her $30,000 for a long, cross-country speaking tour, Nancy agrees to do it. At first her husband (Henry Miller) and her daughter, Sylvia (Margalo Gillmore), are accepting, and when Alan suggests all her runnning about will lead to a nervous breakdown, Mr. Fair retorts that the only thing to give a modern woman a nervous breakdown is having to stay at home. His interest is not entirely selfless since he has been having a little fling with a seductive neighbor, Angelica Brice (Virginia Hammond). But after husband and wife quarrel, after Mrs. Fair snubs Alan's lowborn fiancée, and after Sylvia runs off with Dudley, who proves to be a scoundrel and an embezzler, a chastened Nancy recognizes her duty to her family. For the most part, critics hailed the polished playing, although one critic complained of Miss Bates's tendency to "pose and strike attitudes." Similarly, they garlanded the play, although here again not universally. In *Vanity Fair* the abrasive Dorothy Parker found it "almost impossible to discern just what all the raving is about." Playgoers disagreed with her, so the work ran for ten months.

Two failures followed. In the first an Italian actress who had won some acclaim on European stages and in Italian-language theatres in America was starred as a fiery Mexican; in the second a fine young English actor took the leading role of a temperamental Italian player. The Italian actress was Mimi Aguglia, and she portrayed Chiquita, a Mexican girl in love with dashing Captain Forest (Orrin Johnson) in George C. Hazelton and Ritter Brown's adaptation of Brown's novel **The Whirlwind** (12-23-19, Standard). But the officer's snooty mother (Rose Coghlan) throws so many obstacles in the lovers' way that Chiquita finally decides to marry a not very nice Mexican suitor. Only at the very last minute does she return to the American. *Variety* praised the star's "clear diction" but lamented, "Nowhere is an opportunity given the little Sicilian to unloose her savage command of emotional invective." She had no further career on mainstream stages.

In H. C. M. Harding and Matheson Lang's **Carnival** (12-24-19, 44th St.), taken from a German drama by Pordes-Milo, a production of *Othello* is about to be given during Carnival season in modern Venice. Unfortunately, its star, Silvio Steno (Godfrey Tearle), has reason to believe his wife and leading lady, Simonetta (Margot Kelly), is unfaithful. So he plans to really strangle her in the last act. The lady is able to prove her innocence in time to save herself and, presumably, her marriage.

The year ended on a sumptuously romantic note with Allan Langdon Martin's **Smilin' Through** (12-30-19, Broadway). Knowing critics and playgoers were aware that Allan Langdon Martin was a pen name for the show's star, Jane Cowl, and a collaborator. In the blossoming garden of an old Queen Anne house, two ghostly figures rue that their children are prevented from marrying by one man's implacable hatred. They disappear, and the garden now shows two old men playing dominoes. One is John Carteret (Henry Stephenson); the other is his lifelong friend, Dr. Owen Harding (Ethelbert D. Hales). Harding is upset because Carteret will never leave his home on moonlit nights. He accuses Carteret of "playing with the supernatural." He further argues with Carteret, trying to get him to understand that a son must not be condemned for the sins of his father. But Carteret is adamant and orders Harding off his property. The young man whom Harding is defending is Kenneth Wayne (Orme Caldara), and when Kenneth comes to say good-bye to Carteret's niece, Kathleen (Jane Cowl), before he goes off to war, Carteret orders him away, too. Kathleen demands to know why Carteret harbors such hatred. Reluctantly he agrees to tell her. The scene moves back fifty years to the same garden as a young Carteret prepares to marry Moonyeen (Cowl). He tells her that at their first meeting, "when you turned around to me under those vines—with the silver light bathing you—you looked like a little white ghost—coming down on a moonbeam to greet me." But Moonyeen's rejected suitor, Jeremiah Wayne (Caldara), appears. He attempts to shoot Carteret, but his bullet strikes Moonyeen. Dying, she recites the lyric of a song, "There's a little green gate—at whose trellis I'll wait—while two eyes so true—come Smilin' Through," and she adds, "I'll be there—waiting—just at the end of the road." The older Carteret confesses that, ever since, Moonyeen has come to him on moonlit nights to console him. After the war Kenneth returns home so badly wounded that he insists he has no right to ask for Kathleen's hand any more. But Carteret, who has been troubled that Moonyeen no longer appears to him, is touched by Kenneth's manliness. He agrees to forgive. The lovers walk off, followed by a reconciled Harding. Standing alone in his garden Carteret sees Moonyeen once again, radiant in her wedding gown. She tells John he looks as youthful as he did on their wedding day, and she points to the old John who has quietly died in his chair. They concur in how foolish it is to be afraid of death. As Moonyeen tells him, "Some poor dears are—but they'd go smilin' through the years if they knew what they'd find at the end of the road." The curtain falls to the strains of "Smilin' Through." Many critics were hard on the play (several complained about the obvious device of sometimes having one player, facing away from the audience, pose as another who was playing a double part), but most hailed the beautiful star's warm, compelling performance. Dorothy Parker, sneering that it was a work which "treats of what a perfectly corking institution death is," nonetheless granted that "if all ghosts could only look like Miss Cowl, not a woman in the audience but would gladly pass on immediately." Audiences, especially at matinees packed with handkerchief-in-hand ladies, relished the work. It ran more than six months. It was also the second show of the month to provide material for a later Vincent Youmans musical, this time the failed *Through the Years.*

Even though Broadway was prospering, too many worthwhile shows may have been hurried in, for, despite receiving enthusiastic notices, several plays to arrive in January of 1920 were only modest hits. None was a smash. The month's first two arrivals exemplified the problem.

The Purple Mask (1-5-20, Booth), taken by Matheson Lang from Paul Armont and Jean Manoussi's *Le Chevalier au masque,* was a ripsnorting romantic melodrama of the old, old school. Set in Napoleon's First Consulate, it described all the ruses of the masked Armand, Count of Trevieres (Leo Ditrichstein), to free the Duc de Chateaubriand (Burr Caruth) from his lower-class captors. It soon becomes not only a battle of swords but a battle of wits between the count and Brisquet (Brandon Tynan), a Parisian police official. In the end the rescued duke and the count flee to England, along with the duke's attractive daughter, Laurette (Lily Cahill). The acting was in keeping with the swashbuckling writing. Ditrichstein was particularly praised for his "delicacy of touch and poetry of grace." The play ran four months.

So did Rita Weiman's **The Acquittal** (1-5-20, Cohan and Harris), a murder mystery performed as quietly as its competitor was played in the grand fashion. Its novel opening had Kenneth Winthrop (Edward H. Robins) and his wife, Madeline (Chrystal Herne), returning home from a trial in which Winthrop had been acquitted of murder. Joe Conway (William Harrigan), a newspaperman, suspects a miscarriage of justice, so he plants himself and his sister in the Winthrop house to ferret out the facts. Listening behind a door, he hears an unhappy, unloved Madeline wrest a virtual confession from her husband. Conway then pretends to blackmail Winthrop, who asks only that he be allowed to drink some of the poison he had employed in the murder. After he does, Joe and Madeline look at each other with something more than admiration.

The Light of the World (1-6-20, Lyric) was a quick flop, although it had been greeted with enthusiasm on its pre-Broadway tour. Suggested by rumors concerning behind-the-scenes troubles at the Oberammergau *Passion Play,* it was set in a small Swiss village and told how the humble, pious carpenter and carver Anton Rendel (Pedro de Cordoba) is selected to play Christ in the local Passion Play. Anton had once loved Marna Lynd (Clara Joel), but she had suddenly disappeared. Now she returns with a baby, whose father is really Anton's best friend, Simon (Ralph Kellerd). When the newlywed Simon refuses to acknowledge his paternity and Marna refuses to betray him, the villagers, led by the vicious Jonas (B. Wallis Clark), who longs to assume the Christ role in the play, turn against Marna and Anton, threatening to stone her and burn Anton's cottage. Anton, arms outstretched before the prop cross he has made, beseeches Heaven, "Forgive them! For they know not what they do!" Simon's last-minute confession absolves Anton and shames the townsfolk. Perhaps rather obviously, the character names hinted at similar biblical figures. Comedy relief was provided by Nathan (Fuller Mellish), the town's lone Jew, hated by all except Anton and his mother (Percy Haswell), and by Bert Adams (Wright Kramer), an American sports reporter sent by the *Herald* to cover the play. Offered wine, he replies, "I supposed a burg that was so darn strong for all this religious dope would be dry," and he later tries to convert the village children to his religion—baseball. The play listed Pierre Saisson as author, but it was an open secret that Guy Bolton and George C. Middleton had written it. In his autobiography Middleton blamed this sham, and the fact that the play's producers were also producers of a salacious musical spectacle, for the drama's poor New York reception.

Otto Harbach also came a cropper with his **No More Blondes** (1-7-20, Maxine Elliott's), even though its star, Ernest Truex, was widely applauded for his brilliant, featherweight comedy. More than one critic saw a resemblance in the story to Truex's big hit, *Very Good Eddie*. Once again he played a honeymooner. His Jimmy Howells decides to mix business with pleasure, even if this entails his taking a beautiful blonde to lunch. Naturally the Mrs. (Nancy Fair) is furious. Matters get worse when a friend (Edward Douglas) tries to calm the bride and, in the meanwhile, puts Jimmy up in his apartment. Unknown to Jimmy, the friend's lovely blonde wife (Eileen Wilson) is in the apartment, too. So when Mrs. Howells appears the next morning to apologize for her rashness, she finds Jimmy and the blonde have spent the night (however innocently) together. Pudgy, pasty-faced Dallas Welford, in his umpteenth successive flop, again earned critical praise, this time as a blackmailing butler.

More old-school emoting was the order of the night at **The Passion Flower** (1-13-20, Greenwich Village), taken by John Garret Underhill from Jacinto Benavente's *La Malquerida*. And it was old-school emoting made all the more apparent by being performed in so small a playhouse. But then the evening's star was Nance O'Neil, a longtime proponent of a passing tradition. She expressed her feelings "with an artistic power positively terrifying in its vivid force and with such a sweep of horrible rage and frenzy as to fairly stir the blood of the most hardened old theatre-goer." As Raimunda, she learns that her second husband, Estaban (Charles Waldron), is suspected of murdering the lover of Acacia (Edna Walton), Raimunda's daughter by her first marriage. She soon comes to realize that his love of his stepdaughter may have been Estaban's motive. But when she tries to break up the relationship she is killed for her pains.

The nearest thing to a hit in the next rash of openings was Rachel Barton Butler's **Mamma's Affair** (1-19-20, Little). It arrived in town having won the annual prize for a play written by Professor George P. Baker's students in his English 47 at Harvard and Radcliffe. The hypochondriacal, maternally possessive Mrs. Orrin (Effie Shannon) and her lifelong friend, Mrs. Marchant (Katherine Kaelred), have come to a mountain hotel where they hope their children, Eve (Ida St. Leon) and Henry (George Le Guere), will marry shortly. When Mrs. Marchant has a premonition that Mrs. Orrin will soon be ill again, Henry assures her, "Mrs. Orrin will be delighted to be ill if you'll just speak to her about it." The premonition comes true, and a doctor is summoned. Dr. Jansen (Robert Edeson) realizes that there is nothing really wrong with his patient, but he also observes that Eve is not well. Sure enough, she soon breaks down. He orders rest and seclusion for her. Before long he comprehends her

problem: she has sacrificed all her young life (she's eighteen) tending her selfish mother's imaginary illnesses and now will marry a man she doesn't love, merely to please her mother again. When the doctor's compassionate old housekeeper, Mrs. Bundy (Amelia Bingham), comes to understand that he himself is falling in love with Eve and tells him so, he retorts, "Why the devil should I take an infant to rear! She's about as interesting, emotionally, as a frilled baby pillow with a blue satin bow stuck somewhere about it." But he is in love, though he won't confess it. It remains for Eve to fake another attack of hysterics to make him see that she loves him and for him to acknowledge his own sentiments. Some "old-time Broadway favorites" gilded what critics saw as a genuinely superior comedy. None seems to have found it ridiculous for Edeson, well into his fifties, to play a thirty-six year old, although some suggested that Bingham, Shannon, and Kaelred subscribed to an older style of performing that was not quite right for the comedy. Once again, this sort of playing in so small a theatre may have accentuated the contrast.

All of Grace George's finely honed comic skills could not make a success out of Frances Nordstrom's gossamer **The "Ruined" Lady** (1-19-20, Playhouse). She was cast as Ann Mortimer, who for years and years has been engaged to her neighbor, Bill Bruce (John Miltern). Her sly hints, her attempts to make him jealous, and her myriad other ploys have been unavailing—he will not pop the question. On one rainy night she decides the only answer is to compromise herself and him, so she stalks off to his house. To her dismay she learns that he is spending the night at his club in the city. But Bill's conscientious butler will not let her go back out in the storm. When Bill returns home the next day he recognizes the lengths Ann will go to, so the question is finally popped.

Another major star, Otis Skinner, had no better luck when he added one more thickly accented Italian to his catalogue of characters with Maud Skinner and Jules Eckert Goodman's **Pietro** (1-19-20, Criterion). In a Pennsylvania court in 1896, Pietro Barbano, an immigrant with almost no English, is acquitted of murdering a mean wife who killed his dog and abused their baby. Pietro himself has no real recollection of the killing, and the body of his wife has never been found. Eighteen years later, as Peter Barban, he is a rich horticulturist in California and has hidden his past. He has brought up his daughter, Angela (Ruth Rose), to think her mother was a good woman. When the wife (Mary Shaw) suddenly reappears, bent on making trouble,

Peter must find a way to send her packing. Additional complications arise from the fact that son (Robert Ames) of the very man (Thurlow Bergen) who had prosecuted him falls in love with Angela. Critics ridiculed the play, and many felt that Skinner's performance was hand-me-down. When it came to writing his autobiography, he made no mention of the work.

The failure of its mounting of Leo Tolstoy's **The Power of Darkness** (1-19-20, Garrick) nearly bankrupted the Theatre Guild. The central figure is Nikita (Arthur Hohl), who marries a woman whose husband he helped murder, deserts her for a younger girl, then strangles their baby. He repents only as the police arrive to take him to prison.

January's last entry was Willard Robertson and Kilbourn Gordon's **Big Game** (1-20-20, Fulton). Larry (Alan Dinehart) and Marie Smith (Pauline Lord) married after he stood by her when she was falsely accused of theft in the department store where they both worked. But Marie still holds some doubts about Larry's manliness. Now they find themselves stranded by a snowstorm in the Canadian woods and take refuge with John St. John (George Gaul). St. John is a scoundrel who attempts to seduce Marie. She hands Larry a gun and demands that he shoot St. John. Larry is reluctant to kill another man, so Marie tells him that the law of the woods requires her to go off with her would-be seducer. This goads Larry, who finally gets up enough nerve to kill St. John. The show failed despite some surprisingly strong notices.

February began with an ending—the ending of Maxine Elliott's acting career. Unlike many other famous actresses she said nothing about "farewell appearances." Nonetheless, after the short stand of William Hurlbut's **Trimmed in Scarlet** (2-2-20, Maxine Elliott's) she left the stage forever. Her last vehicle was sadly weak, telling of a woman who returns to New York twenty years after she deserted her family to run away with her lover. She bests a blackmailing editor who threatens to ruin the promising career of her son (Sidney Blackmer) by revealing his mother's history, then accepts the proposal of a bygone suitor (Lumsden Hare).

The next afternoon critics and enterprising playgoers attended a special matinee performance of a play that was to change drastically the perception and tenor of American drama, for the play being offered was Eugene O'Neill's **Beyond the Horizon** (2-3-20, Morosco). The bookish Robert Mayo (Richard Bennett) has come to manhood on his family's New England farm dreaming of far-off places. Now he is about to take to the sea, not just to visit these exotic lands but to escape from the pain of watching his "husky, sun-bronzed, handsome" brother, Andrew (Edward Arnold), a natural-born farmer, marry their neighbor, Ruth Atkins (Helen MacKellar), a girl whom Robert also loves. At the last moment Ruth confesses she really prefers Robert, so he changes his plans and Andrew decides to sail in his stead. Andrew's leaving so infuriates his father (Erville Alderson) that he orders him never to return. Three years pass. The still unworldly Robert has all but ruined the farm. His sole passions are his books and his sickly little daughter. His now widowed mother (Mary Jeffery) and his wife have come to despise him, holding up Andrew as an exemplar to him. Robert insists that Andrew's letters have shown he has learned nothing from his travels, a charge confirmed when a hard, unloving Andrew returns for a visit. He cruelly tells Ruth, who belatedly realized her love for him, that he had forgotten her long ago. When he returns again five years later, he discovers that the baby and his mother have died, Ruth has grown slovenly and apathetic, the farm is a wreck, and Robert is dying of consumption. Robert asks Andrew to wheel him to a window so that "I can watch the rim of the hills and dream of what is waiting beyond." He begs Andrew to marry Ruth after he dies and to save the farm. Confessing that he always loved his brother "better'n anybody in the world," Andrew berates Ruth for her behavior and demands that she tell Robert that she loves him and will do what he wants. At first Ruth refuses, but when she finally consents, she discovers Robert has died. "God damn you!" Andrew yells at her. "You never told him!"

A few of the more retrograde aisle-sitters scoffed at the play, with the *Evening Post*'s J. Rankin Towse dismissing it as "juvenile," though even he had the perception to see it as "exceedingly promising." Some, such as Arthur Hornblow, were noncommittal. But most of the younger critics, with Alexander Woollcott in the vanguard, hailed the work as a major achievement. (He and others nevertheless decried the shabby scenery and the long waits for scene changes.) These reviews lured enough customers to encourage additional matinees, first at the Morosco, then at the Criterion. When playgoers continued to press at the box office the play was moved to the Little for a run that continued into the hot weather. "By that time," Burns Mantle wrote a few months later, "there were many who were willing to accept this first long play from Eugene O'Neill's pen as representing the closest approach any native author has yet made to *the* great American play." Kenneth Macgowan, who just

121

before the play had opened suggested, "These months the American theatre is passing through the most interesting and significant period in its history," now coupled the failure of many of the season's bedroom farces with the reception accorded O'Neill's play to conclude that a "growing audience of intelligent and sensitive folk have begun to find the theatre a place worth their attention." By the spring, when the play was awarded a Pulitzer Prize, O'Neill was solidly launched on his career.

. . .

Eugene [Gladstone] **O'Neill** (1888–1953), the son of the celebrated actor James O'Neill, was born in New York but spent most of his childhood accompanying his father and the rest of his family on his father's tours. Years at Catholic schools and a year at Princeton followed before he took a job at a mail order house, then spent time prospecting in Central America. An attack of malaria forced him to return, so he accepted work as assistant manager of a touring troupe. To escape an unhappy marriage he went to sea for several years. An attempted suicide followed his next return. Subsequently hospitalized with tuberculosis, he began writing plays.

. . .

The afternoon's tragedy soon gave way to the evening's farce, **Breakfast in Bed** (2-3-20, Eltinge), which Willard Mack and Howard Booth adapted from Georges Feydeau's *Occupe-toi d'Amélie*. Feydeau would hardly have recognized his piece. Its leading lady, Emily Duval Bates (Florence Moore), is a silent-film star. Her fiancé (Will Demming) has asked a friend (Leon Gordon) to watch over her while he is away. After a masked ball, to which she came as Cleopatra and the friend as Marc Anthony, they go back to his apartment for some late-night coffee. But when the friend's girl, her own fiancé, and others appear unexpectedly she hides under a bed. The hatchet-faced, loose-jointed Miss Moore brought all her vaudeville slapstick tricks to the evening and added to the mayhem with a long, long string of sausages and a pitcher of cold water. Most critics threw their own cold water on the mounting, but a determined Al Woods kept it going for ten weeks.

Rachel Crothers's **He and She** (2-12-20, Little) had originally been tried out years earlier as *The Herfords* and failed. Apparently harboring a special fondness for the work, she rewrote it, helped underwrite the Shuberts' mounting, and assumed the leading role in the resurrection. All to no avail, for the play proved repetitive, discursive, and mechanical. Tom Herford (Cyril Keightley), a distinguished sculptor who has submitted a frieze to a competition with a $100,000 prize, sees nothing wrong in a wife's working. After all, his wife, Ann (Crothers), is also a professional sculptor, though of course she works at home. His young assistant, Keith McKenzie (Fleming Ward), holds different views. He is engaged to Ruth Creel (Ethel Cozzens), a girl whose consuming interest is her work as an editor and who has no intention of wasting time at home. As she tells Keith, "Women who are really doing things nowadays are an absolutely different breed from the one-sided domestic animals they used to be." She announces she will refuse to have children. But Tom moves over to Keith's side after Ann quietly submits her own frieze to the competition and wins. He huffily refuses to accept any of the money she has won. Matters are made worse when their daughter (Faire Binney), feeling unwanted after her mother forced her to remain at school while the other students came home for vacation, becomes engaged to a chauffeur and runs away from school. Her family's reactions to her preoccupation make Ann understand that a woman's place is at home with them. Keith throws over Ruth for a more traditional homebody. Not only did the play have its own problems, but coming so soon after the more accessible *The Famous Mrs. Fair* it could not find an audience.

Shavings (2-16-20, Knickerbocker), which Pauline Phelps and Marion Short took from a novel by Joseph C. Lincoln, garnered divided notices but ran profitably for sixteen weeks. "Shavings" is the nickname his Cape Cod townsfolk have given to J. Edward Winslow (Harry Beresford), an absent-minded, kindly bachelor, who whittles toys for children. He rents a cottage to a pretty widow, Ruth Armstrong (Clara Moores), defends her brother, Charles (Saxon Kling), who has spent time in prison, when he is falsely accused of embezzlement, but resigns himself to perpetual bachelorhood after Ruth agrees to wed a decorated veteran.

An aging John Drew found his drawing power was not what it once had been when he appeared in Rupert Hughes's **The Cat-Bird** (2-16-20, Maxine Elliott's). For the second time in the season a leading figure was a specialist in bugs and insects. Only years before his absorption in his work had cost Martin Gloade the hand of a beguiling girl. Now a widow (Janet Beecher), she again comes into his life. However, she comes with a wildly independent niece (Ruth Findlay), fleeing the advances of an importunate suitor (William Raymond). Gloade must first tame the girl and teach her suitor the art of subtlety before he can reclaim his old flame. The laid-back Drew, Lee Simonson's beautiful settings of a vivarium and a hotel, and Arthur Hopkins's otherwise meticulous mounting held small interest for New Yorkers.

Another trial matinee of another interesting play failed to stir the excitement *Beyond the Horizon* had created. The play was John Masefield's **The Tragedy of Nan** (2-17-20, 39th St.). After her father is hanged unjustly for supposedly stealing sheep, Nan (Alexandra Carlisle) comes to live with her cruel uncle and aunt. Her lover (Philip Merivale) deserts her on learning her history from her aunt, announces he will marry her cousin, but changes his mind after hearing that the government will pay Nan a large sum for the unjust execution. Nan kills her cousin and her lover and throws herself into the sea. Three additional matinees sufficed to satisfy the demand for seats.

Only Jeanne Eagels's performance kept **The Wonderful Thing** (2-17-20, Playhouse), dramatized by Lillian Trimble Bradley from a Forrest Halsey story, on the boards for fifteen weeks. She played a well-to-do French girl, Jacqueline Laurentie, who comes to live with the impoverished but snobbish Mannerbys in their home near Brighton. Upset by their rudeness, she brazenly proposes to the lone Mannerby who has shown her any kindness, Donald (Gordon Ash). She is soon led to believe he married her for her money but with time learns he truly loves her. Her goodness and resolve eventually win over the rest of the clan. The beautiful, slightly frail-seeming Eagels played her part "not only with great finesse and feeling, but with a certain witchery that is altogether enchanting." Another reviewer reported that every one of her entrances was greeted with such prolonged applause that she was forced "to wait several minutes before she could even begin her lines."

Three foreign plays opened the next Monday night. The success of St. John Ervine's **Jane Clegg** (2-23-20, Garrick) saved the Theatre Guild from a premature dissolution that might have done inconceivable harm to the American stage. It told of a bedraggled woman (Margaret Wycherly) married to a worthless man (Dudley Digges). After learning he will be jailed for stealing from his employer, she gives up a small inheritance to spare him imprisonment. But when she then discovers he is squandering money on a cheap mistress, she leaves him. Once again critics saw a contemporary production of "near perfection," with excellent actors, excellently directed, playing out their parts in a tellingly decaying sitting room designed by Lee Simonson. The drama ran out the season.

The other two plays each ran eleven weeks, to some extent on the strength of their stars' appeal. Based on his early novel *The Book of Carlotta,* Arnold Bennett's **Sacred and Profane Love** (2-23-20, Morosco) was brought out as a showcase for Elsie Ferguson, more widely known for her screen roles. As an impressionable young girl, Carlotta had had a one-night fling with the famed pianist Emilio Diaz (José Ruben). Years later, after she has become a rich and celebrated novelist, she learns that Emilio has sunk into a derelict and a drug addict. She rushes to Paris, helps restore his well-being, and brings him back to England to wed him. Critics attacked Miss Ferguson for her stagey acting, which they blamed on her screen career. Ruben's touching performance won the most applause.

Mustachioed and handsome in his French legal robes, Lionel Barrymore was starred in **The Letter of the Law** (2-23-20, Criterion), taken by an uncredited adaptor from Eugène Brieux's *La Robe rouge.* He played a prosecutor who is determined to climb to the top of the legal ladder even if he must browbeat defendants into confessions and convictions. For his pains he is stabbed to death by the wife (Doris Rankin) of one of his victims.

If an English dramatist could write a successful play about Abraham Lincoln, shouldn't an American be able to write one about **George Washington** (3-1-20, Lyric)? The answer, setting aside the obvious fact that Lincoln's life was far more dramatic, seemed to be: not if the author was Percy MacKaye. Indeed, a number of reviewers, having had their fill of MacKaye's pretensions, spent a significant share of their notices recounting his history of failures at the same time they expressed their amazement at his continuing ability to find productions. In this instance, MacKaye's producer was to have been Arthur Hopkins, but when he dropped out the rising young actor Walter Hampden, who played the title role, took on the task. To help he enlisted Robert Edmond Jones. Jones created both poetically beautiful tableaux, which were artfully posed and dramatically lighted living friezes, and simplified stylized settings that allowed for fluid scene changes. The prologue, in blank verse, saw a fiddler (George Marion), accompanied by two children, come seeking a play about Washington. He tells masked characters representing theatre, tragedy, and comedy:

> I'm Quilloquon:
> My mother hatched me—with a wild goose honkin'
> West, and a bell-wether tinkle-tonkin'
> East. Some they calls me Dellum-a-down-derry.

The rest of the "ballad play," in prose, moved on to recount Washington's agreeing to farm Mount Vernon in his dying brother's stead, his return from the French and Indian Wars and his engagement to the widowed Martha Custis, Hamilton's defending the Tory president of King's College from a mob who insist the school be called Columbia, Washington's resolving sectional differences among his soldiers, and similar incidents, ending with his refusal to be crowned king and his return to farming. After each scene the fiddler reappeared to offer another ballad. Typical of Washington's speeches was one to Martha telling of the revolutionary fervor sweeping the land: "A smoke of darkness, and our country burning: a forest of men on fire!—Wild beasts broke from their lairs.—A mad bully with a crown, driving his yoke of swine and mules, to fight the flame with fish-oil." *Variety* brushed aside the play, calling it "a flop and a thorough one. Artistically as bad as it is commercially." Critics saw the characters as puppets mouthing textbook platitudes and pompous sentiments. They felt that Hampden did all he could with a hopelessly written part in a hopelessly written drama. Two weeks and MacKaye's last play to receive a major Broadway mounting was gone. In its place Hampden brought back his Hamlet. MacKaye's work was published as *Washington: The Man Who Made Us*.

To some aisle-sitters and playgoers Victor Mapes and William Collier's **The Hottentot** (3-1-20, Cohan) was an earthbound but still uproariously funny variant of *The Aviator*. Its rather nervous, craven hero, Sam Harrington (Collier), has long loved Peggy Fairfax (Frances Carson) in silence. So when Peggy, mistaking him for a famous jockey named Harrington, asks if he will ride her fearsome horse "The Hottentot" in a steeplechase, he blurts out that he will. He spends the rest of Acts I and II unsuccessfully trying to wangle out of his promise. In the end he rides the horse, winning both the race and Peggy. The race was not shown. Instead, Peggy and her friends, standing in her open touring car, watch and describe it from a nearby hillside. Although Collier walked away with most of the acting laurels, Donald Meek gave him a run for his money as a jittery, minimally competent butler. The play ran out the season.

Phillip Moeller's **Sophie** (3-2-20, Greenwich Village) played out its story for ten weeks at its small, far-from-Broadway berth. Embellished with lovely eighteenth-century costumes and settings, it told how the Austrian ambassador (Adolf Link) to France, having wangled the leading role in *Iphegenia*, a new opera by Cristoph Ritter Von Gluck (Hubert Wilke), for Sophie Arnould (Emily Stevens), now expects a return of favors. But Sophie is awaiting the release of her lover, a poet imprisoned for writing scurrilous verses about the king, so she forges orders for the ambassador's arrest, then prepares to greet her beloved. The beautiful, blonde Miss Stevens, long praised as an actress of great promise, especially in emotionally charged roles, this time around was slated for her exaggerated mannerisms and indistinct diction.

On the 6th Arthur Hopkins brought out *Richard III* at the Plymouth with settings by Robert Edmond Jones and with John Barrymore as star. The version was not the original Shakespearean one, for Hopkins not only retained some of Colley Cibber's revisions but added a few brief scenes from *Henry VI, Part III*. Not all critics were happy with this rewriting, but none dwelt on it, preferring to devote more attention to Barrymore. Many of the more influential ones, such as Broun, Hornblow, and Woollcott, took the occasion to hail Barrymore as the greatest young player on the American stage. But there were dissenting voices. The critic for the *Literary Digest* noted: "Sardonic humor, cynical hypocrisy, inhesitant will, and malignant craft are just as strongly marked characteristics of the part as its prompt ferocity, and it was upon these that Mr. Barrymore elected to lay his chief, and perhaps too much, stress. . . . Mr. Barrymore was much too deliberate in movement. His stealthy manner, indeed, was suggestive of cunning and treachery, but was inconsistent with energy." Jones designed "a single, towering massive background, as of gray stone" for a basic set, "with such shifting disguises of lights, tapestries and iron work as each [scene] demands." One scene elicited special applause, with "Gloster, seated on a white palfrey, gorgeously comparisoned himself, a scarlet cloak thrown about him," persuading the young princes to enter the tower. Hopkins had announced that the production was to be the first in a series with Barrymore as star that would result in an ongoing repertory. But Barrymore was getting no sleep, hurrying to Atlantic City after each evening performance to be with his wife. He soon felt he was about to have a nervous breakdown, so the production was taken off after twenty-seven showings. Hopkins, who rarely compromised with his high ideals, bravely restored *Night Lodging* to his theatre's stage, this time for evening as well as matinee performances.

Leonie de Souny's **Musk** (3-13-20, Punch and Judy), supposedly taken from an unidentified Hungarian play that had enjoyed some European success, was savaged by the critics. A cast speaking a number of foreign accents played out the tale of a woman (Blanche Yurka) who learns that her husband is unfaithful. She plans to kill him but shoots herself instead.

The curious who packed the theatre and the sidewalks outside were not there to see **The Blue Flame** (3-15-20, Shubert), a play by Leta Vance Nicholson, rewritten by George V. Hobart and John Willard, but rather to watch Hollywood's notorious vamp, Theda Bara, make her debut as a Broadway star. She played Ruth Gordon (note the number of heroines named Ruth this season), a pious girl who is killed by a bolt of lightning. Her godless lover, a scientist (Alan Dinehart), brings her body back to life, but her soul has fled. She becomes a notorious seductress, until her lover wakes up and realizes he was dreaming. He resolves to reform. The play was given no serious consideration, and the critical consensus was that with years of hard work Bara might develop into a competent actress. Donald Gallaher won kudos as a drug fiend. Only Bara's reputation kept the play profitably on the boards both in New York and on tour.

Josephine Preston Peabody's *The Piper* was revived at the Fulton on the 19th for a series of matinees.

A much older play, Euripides' *Medea* was offered for a series of matinees at the Garrick, beginning on March 22. It was produced by Maurice Browne, a major figure in the Little Theatre movement, and starred his wife, Ellen Van Volkenburg. Admiring reviews allowed it to remain for fourteen representations.

The ghost of Mary Turner of *Within the Law* stalked Fred Jackson's **The Hole in the Wall** (3-26-20, Punch and Judy). Jean Oliver (Martha Hedman) has been sent to prison on charges trumped up by Mrs. Ramsay (Cordelia MacDonald), for whom she worked, after Mrs. Ramsay became concerned with her son's infatuation for Jean. On her release, vowing vengeance, she recruits a band of crooks. Sitting on a high throne, in a varicolored gown, she poses as Madame Mystera and with her group holds rigged seances, which include the newly voguish ouija board, to rob rich ladies. She also kidnaps Mrs. Ramsay's grandchild. Gordon Grant (John Halliday), a reporter with a gift for detecting, exposes her but sees to it that she is not charged and, falling in love with her, proposes. The beautiful, Swedish-born Hedman never quite gained the top rung of stardom that so many critics had foreseen for her. Even at this relatively late date, one reviewer complained she was "still not at ease with the language."

That same night at their small theatre on Macdougal Street, the Provincetown Players premiered a new bill of one-acters. Among these new offerings was O'Neill's **Exorcism,** telling of a would-be suicide who finds new hope after being saved in the nick of time by two derelicts.

Mystera's toy was also used in Crane Wilbur's **The Ouija Board** (3-29-20, Bijou). It was employed by Gabriel Mogador (Howard Lang), a fraudulent medium, to convince a rich businessman, Henry Annixter (William Ingersoll), to leave his money to his adopted son, Richard (Stewart E. Wilson), a "dope fiend," with whom Mogador is secretly in league. What is more, years earlier, under another name, Mogador had run off with Annixter's late wife. At a seance in Mogador's tricked-out quarters—where doors and curtains seemingly open and close on their own and where eerie lights create odd effects—Mogador suddenly finds he has no control over his messages. A real spirit from the beyond—Annixter's dead wife—is speaking and tells Annixter that Mogador is a charlatan. Annixter stabs Mogador to death and flees. A detective coming to investigate receives a message from the beyond that Annixter will be killed before anyone can come to his aid. He finds that Annixter has been shot by a gun which Richard had planted in a console housing a phonograph, the gun's trigger rigged to be pulled as the record concludes. Annixter's daughter, Winifred (Regina Wallace), whom Annixter had demanded marry Richard, is free to marry the man she loves, Norman Kemp (George Gaul).

In Norman S. Rose and Edith Ellis's **Mrs. Jimmie Thompson** (3-29-20, Century) Eleanor Warren (Gladys Hurlbut), having been told that the way to get the man she wants is to pretend that she is married or divorced, invents a mythical husband, Jimmie Thompson, who is supposedly somewhere in South America, only to have a real James Thompson (Thomas A. Rolfe) show up and spark the evening's complications.

April brought in only two straight plays, and both failed. Frederic Arnold Kummer's **The Bonehead** (4-12-20, Fulton) found Mrs. Campbell (Myrtle Tannehill) newly installed in a Greenwich Village apartment in order to be near all the Village types she so adores. These bohemians and other poseurs talk glibly of free love, batiks, the new Russia, affinities, and other faddist delights of the moment. Mr. Campbell (Edwin Nicander) is virtually forgotten, so he decides to behave in even more preposterous ways than his wife's friends. His outlandish search for a new soulmate brings his wife to her senses, and they are soon packing for a return to a safe and sane life in Brooklyn. New Yorkers were amused that pre-opening publicity dealt less with the play than with the fact that its producer was a son of Herbert Beerbohm Tree.

Laurence Eyre's **Martinique** (4-26-20, Eltinge) transported its audiences to the West Indies island in 1842, when the illegitimate, convent-schooled Zabette de Chauvalons (Josephine Victor) returns to seek her father. She finds he is dead and his aristocratic family will have nothing to do with her. Then she learns that the dashing Stephane Sequineau (Vincent Coleman) is being pushed into marrying her snobbish half-sister, Marie-Clemence (Helen Blair), so she seduces him. Thus she provides the heir the sonless de Chauvalons have been seeking. But for Zabette, who has fallen in love with Stephane, there is no completely happy ending. Stephane dies of wounds received in a fight, and Zabette resigns herself to living out her life in a convent. Critics admired the performances, which had just enough old-style emoting in them to complement that play's slightly *retardaire* melodrama. They also had high praise for Lee Simonson's romantic settings, showing the entrance to the de Chauvalons' mansion, Zabette's much shabbier home in a rundown area of St. Pierre, and the balconied courtyard of Seguineau's house.

The next play allowed New Yorkers to remain in their city and took them back only fifty years. The heroine of Arthur Richman's **Not So Long Ago** (5-4-20, Booth) is Elsie Dover (Eva Le Gallienne), who lives in a world of her own make-believe. She has reason to. Her father (George H. Trader) is an impractical inventor. (For example, he has just designed a fishing rod that releases a knife at the last minute, so any fish foolish enough to snap its hook is impaled.) And her father encourages her obnoxious, know-it-all suitor, Sam Robinson (Thomas Mitchell), who assures anyone who'll listen that Horace Greeley will be the next president, that George Eliot is a "he," and that he, Sam, is loved by everyone. "When I want a thing I get it," he boasts time and again. So on hearing that supposedly rich young Billy Ballard (Sidney Blackmer) is secretly courting Elsie, he snitches to Mr. Dover. Dover immediately calls on Billy, who is surprised to hear his story. To him Elsie is merely the family's seamstress. Of course, Elsie had made the whole thing up, but Billy nonetheless looks at her more attentively and likes what he sees. And Elsie confesses, "When I was a little girl and mother read me the story of Cinderella and the Prince, I used to see a figure kneeling before Cinderella and placing the slipper on her dainty foot, but the figure never had a face. Now, since I've

been coming here—Oh, but I mustn't tell you *that*!" Before long Billy has fallen in love with Elsie, and even Sam's snitching on him to Bill's snobbish mother (Esther Lyon) cannot stop him. Mrs. Ballard had been concerned that her daughter's rich suitor (Gilbert Douglas) would look askance at Billy's courting a lowly seamstress, but when the suitor proudly expresses his democratic sentiments, all can end happily. He will even take Billy, whose family is actually not rich at all, in as a business partner. The play spanned the summer heat, running into the following season. One curious feature in the printed text is the listing of curtain calls after each act, a practice by 1920 largely discarded. Were they inserted to give a period flavor to the production?

Pudgy-faced, puckered-lipped Dallas Welford, still seeking a part as fulfilling as the one he had reveled in fourteen years earlier in *Mr. Hopkinson*, failed to find it in Bide Dudley's **Oh, Henry!** (5-5-20, Fulton). He played a drunken stranger who comes to the Carsons' summer home at Long Beach and refuses to leave. The Carsons desperately try to hide him from their wealthy, prohibitionist Aunt Annabelle (Eva Condon), until it develops that he is Annabelle's new husband, out for a final fling. Prohibition, about to begin, would be an irresistible topic for playwrights. One critic noted that both this comedy and *The Bonehead* had a joke about "dear, departed spirits."

Foot-Loose (5-10-20, Greenwich Village) was Zoë Akins's adaptation of a nineteenth-century favorite, *Forget-Me-Not*. Most critics felt that relentlessly hounded Stephanie was a more congenial role for Emily Stevens than Sophie had been, and they approved of Norman Trevor's Welby. But several aisle-sitters suggested the most memorable acting of the evening was that of Tallulah Bankhead in the small role of a young widow.

Respect for Riches (5-11-20, Harris) was a vanity production, written and produced by William Devereaux, who also took the leading male role. His play spotlighted the difficulties encountered by Mrs. Kenyon (Alexandra Carlisle), who is all but broke but must keep up appearances if she is to retain her social friends. An old flame (Devereaux) discovers her plight, inadvertently broadcasts it, but atones by marrying her. The play was filled with would-be epigrams such as "She is quite uncivilized; she says what she thinks." Devereaux was a small man, and he unintentionally evoked laughter when he threatened to "thrash" tall, burly, deep-voiced Fred Tilden, who played Louis Hirsch, the cynical, sensual stockbroker who lusts after the heroine.

Shortly after Alison Heath (Lola Fisher) takes an

Irish immigrant, Norah (also Fisher), into her home as a nurse for her baby, she is killed in an automobile accident. The child soon becomes ill, but Norah tells Mr. Heath (Cyril Keightley) not to worry, since on **All Soul's Eve** (5-12-20, Maxine Elliott's) the souls of dead mothers return to save their children. And sure enough, that is what happens. Since Alison's soul has now entered Norah's body, Heath, who had resorted to drink after his wife's death but had been rehabilitated by the nurse, sees no reason not to marry her. Anne Crawford Flexner's play found little favor.

Nor did Forrest Halsey and Clara Beranger's **His Chinese Wife** (5-17-20, Belmont) win much approval. Sent on a world trip to cure him of his degenerate behavior, Rodney Sturgis (Forrest Winant) returns with a Chinese bride, Tea Flower (Madeline Delmar), by his side. His haughty, backwater New Jersey family will have nothing to do with a foreigner, and a non-white one to boot. Tea Flower is nearly driven to suicide, until the family grandmother (Mabel Burt) comes to the youngsters' defense. They decide they will be better off living in China.

Reviewers weren't certain whether Martin Brown's **An Innocent Idea** (5-25-20, Fulton) was meant to be a bedroom farce or a spoof of one. Either way, they felt it didn't work. Henry Bird (Robert Emmett Keane) is a bed manufacturer, hoping to be elected president of the bed manufacturers' trust at their annual convention. Standing in his path is his reputation as "the wickedest, wildest man in Michigan." One of his lady friends' best defense of him was "I'm just as sure that Henry never wronged a good woman as I am he never disappointed a bad one." So he decides to reform (for a night or two, anyway) and take a room with a staid friend, Ernest Geer (Russell Fillmore), a playwright who has refused to write bedroom farces. The men are no sooner in pajamas and in their respective beds, with the lights turned out, than the door opens and a bed with a beautiful blonde in it is wheeled into their room. In no time at all, a chambermaid, a lady house detective, several female delegates, a notorious vamp, and other women in various states of dress and undress have crowded into the room. After things calm down, Henry resolves to marry and reform.

The season's last show was **The Fall and Rise of Susan Lenox** (6-9-20, 44th St.), George V. Hobart's dramatization of David Graham Phillips's novel. Susan (Alma Tell) is an illegitimate child, brought up by unloving relations. After she is seduced and abandoned by Sam Wright (Harry Southard), her family forces her to marry a drunken farmer, Robert Burlingham (Robert T. Haines). She runs away, works for a time on a showboat, then leads a hard life in Cincinnati, until she becomes a department store model. The owner of the store, Roderick Spencer (Perce Benton), takes a liking to her and, after watching her deftly rebuke a nasty buyer, proposes marriage. Miss Tell was praised for her beauty and competent acting, but the heartiest kudos went to players of smaller roles, most noticeably to Haines, who two decades earlier had been one of Broadway's most sought-after leading men.

At season's end *Variety* ran an article headed "Broadway's Fifteen Biggest Hits Gross $7,000,000 During Greatest Show Year." It disclosed that two holdovers from the prior season, *Lightnin'* and *East Is West,* were still packing their theatres and had grossed about $1,170,000 and $900,000 respectively. Of four shows which had run thirty or more weeks, both *Clarence* and *Déclassée* had taken in $400,000 apiece, while *Scandal* and *Adam and Eva* had banked over $200,000 each. (The former "came to New York on velvet," having recouped its costs in a pre-Broadway Chicago run). Even a show such as *The Storm,* which rarely played to capacity and early on went to cut-rate tickets, was said to have earned a profit of $100,000 during its nine-month run.

Summing up for the first in what became his long-enduring series of *Best Plays,* Burns Mantle called 1919–20 "a fine season" with the quality of writing "much higher" than before. A heady decade was underway.

1920–1921

Worriers who fretted that the new season could not possibly match the excellences of 1919–20 were early on made aware of how unnecessary their fretting had been. The new season was very good indeed. Of course, nothing is totally right, so those who insisted on something to cry over found reason enough. A sharp, if fortunately brief, post-war recession hurt playgoers and box offices. And the road continued its dismaying decline. This drop in attendance and loss of playhouses was attributed not merely to the growing popularity of films but, with surprising candor for many theatrical pundits, to the knowingly low, shameful quality of many road companies, which discouraged would-be theatre devotees. Yet there was substantial cause for optimism. Tradesheets, theatrical magazines, and articles in newspapers all perceived and welcomed "a growing demand for better fare." The demand was by no means universal, and archly conservative middlebrows, such as George M. Cohan, pontificated on the virtues of good old-fashioned melodrama, noting, "The American play is never gloomy; we haven't reached that decadent age when we can believe in tragedy."

But tragedy and better fare would have to wait until after the hot weather. The summer's openers were given over to farce and melodrama. Margaret Mayo and Aubrey Kennedy's **Seeing Things** (6-17-20, Playhouse) featured a suspicious wife (Dorothy Mackaye), who convinces herself that her husband (John Westley) has come to prefer an attractive widow (Marion Vantine). She persuades a family friend (Frank McIntyre) to help her fake a suicide, then, with the further aid of a not entirely legitimate yogi (William Wadsworth), "returns" as a "ghost" to spy on her ex and the widow. She soon comes to understand that her husband has always loved only her, so she reveals her scheme and begs forgiveness. McIntyre milked his own rotundity for a disproportionate share of the evening's laughs. The farce spanned the summer.

Octavus Roy Cohen's **Come Seven** (7-19-20, Broadhurst) was an oddity, or at least half an oddity. What was different was that all its characters were blacks; what remained the same was that they were played by whites in blackface. When Elzevir Nesbit (Lucille LaVerne) spots her "genawine" diamond ring on the finger of the beautiful, high-living high yaller Vistar Goins (Gail Kane), she rightly suspects that her tiny "no-'count nigger" husband, Urias (Arthur Aylsworth), has once again fallen under the baleful influence of the local Beau Brummel and promoter, Florian Slappey (Earle Foxe). Sure enough, Urias lent Florian the ring, Florian pawned it, and Vistar obtained it from the pawnbroker. When the men, goaded by Elzevir, attempt to redeem their ticket, the pawnbroker is not in a position to give them the ring, so pays them $300. They use the money to buy Elzevir a new ring. What the sly Elzevir is telling no one is that she deftly substituted a paste imitation for the real one when Vistar handed it to her to examine. She now has two "genawine" diamond rings. The comedy ran nine weeks.

Owen Davis's **Opportunity** (7-30-20, 48th St.) ran almost twice as long, aided by its resemblance to the Ponzi pyramid scandal just then receiving front-page attention. At the Wall Street offices of Ladd and Werner, where ticker tapes tick noisily away, an office boy, Larry Bradford (James L. Crane), invests so wisely that he soon is a millionaire. He also helps a stenographer (Lily Cahill), who lives in the same boardinghouse, to get out of a jam and marries her. But success goes to his head. He begins playing the stock market very recklessly and comes under the spell of a voluptuous siren (Nita Naldi). Then at the same time that his house of cards tumbles down, he discovers the siren is unfaithful. He goes to her apartment and smashes eveything in sight, thereafter resolving to live quietly and simply with his loyal wife. Several critics pointed out that with its numerous scene changes the melodrama seemed more like a motion picture than a modern stage play.

But the next play to open had even more and quicker scene changes. However, its setting and subject matter were much the same. In Samuel Shipman and Percival Wilde's **Crooked Gamblers** (7-31-20, Hudson), John Stetson (Taylor Holmes) and Bob Dryden (Purnell Pratt) have developed a successful tire business, which a slick promoter, Turner (Felix Krembs), persuades them to take public. Stetson is a little reluctant, yet accedes to his partner's wishes. But when he finds that Turner and Dryden plan to manipulate the stock, drive it down until stockholders are ruined, and then buy the shares cheaply, he sets out to battle them. The big third-act scene showed "two tiers of offices overlooking the Curb Market—in the one, the hero, fighting for his life, buying frantically to stem a falling market; in the other, the scheming broker selling equally vigorously in an effort to break the stock, the lower and upper offices lighted alternately as the action shifts from one to the other until finally the scene changes to the street outside, where the mob of brokers are in delirium." Inevitably, at least in this sort of melodrama, the hero wins. Critics noted with some amusement that when Krembs took his curtain calls he was hissed, responding with a good-natured smile. But the play could not develop legs, departing after ten weeks.

That was just one week less than the run of **The Charm School** (8-2-20, Bijou), which Alice Duer Miller and Robert Milton derived from Mrs. Miller's *Saturday Evening Post* stories and their subsequent novelization. A group of pleasant bachelors suddenly find themselves on their uppers in New York. George (James Gleason) has just been fired; the twins, Jim (Neil Martin) and Tim (Morgan Farley), have had their allowances cut off for failing to get work and have been ordered home to Poughkeepsie ("seventy-five miles from a decent cabaret"), and Austin (Sam Hardy) has been told by his girl's mother that he is not good enough for her daughter. The problem, as

Austin sees it, is that "the world is run by old people. . . . I sometimes wish there wasn't anyone alive over sixty." These oldsters have conspired "to keep young people learning the wrong things." The men are visited by an attorney, Homer Johns (Rapley Holmes), who advises Austin that he is the heir to his late aunt's estate—a heavily mortgaged girls' school. Johns holds the mortgage and has his reasons for taking over the school, but Austin insists he will try to run it, teaching not all the standard "wrong things" but simply charm. Johns agrees on two conditions—that the current headmistress, Miss Hays (Margaret Dale), be retained and that no student fall in love with Austin. If one does, the school becomes Johns's property. At the school the men take over many of the teaching duties with mixed success. Since Austin is particularly good-looking all the students do sigh for him. Miss Hays tells him, "Every girl in school is taking snapshots of you—and . . . a good photograph of you commands any price." One girl, Elise (Marie Carroll), who is class president and Johns's ward, decides to woo and win Austin and, much to his amazement, does. Austin loses the school, but Johns promises to maintain most of his policies and sees to it he finds a fine job. Miss Hays, it turns out, had once been married to Johns and, who knows, may be again. Acting honors went to Gleason, who is forever being rejected by Elise, and to an oldtimer, Minnie Dupree, as the headmistress's sweet if somewhat forlorn assistant. Perhaps because there was something old-fashioned about much of the play, each act was followed by a series of special curtain calls—a practice in 1920 all but extinct.

Eugène Brieux's *Les Américains chez nous* was offered to stay-at-homes as **The Americans in France** (8-3-20, Comedy) but failed to enlist any interest and left after a single week. During that time it told how an A.E.F. captain (Wayne Arey) purchases some land from a conservative Burgundian, M. Charvet (Frank Kingdon), but immediately antagonizes him by tearing up the property to install a modern irrigation system. The battle is led by Charvet's aristocratic daughter, Henrietta (Blanche Yurka). She is thrown for a loss when her brother Henri (Franklin George), a doctor who has served with the French troops, returns and announces he will marry an American nurse who worked at his side. The furious, bitter Henrietta drives the young couple into leaving for America, but Captain Smith, admiring her spunk, proposes marriage to her.

Money notices could not turn Adelaide Matthews and Martha M. Stanley's **Scrambled Wives** (8-5-20, Fulton) into a hit. At a gay house party John Chiverick (Roland Young) and his ex-wife, Lucille

(Juliette Day), are alarmed when they spot each other. John does not want his new wife (Elise Bartlett) to know of his former marriage, and Lucille cannot allow her new beau, Larry McLeod (Glenn Anders), who professes to dislike divorcées, to learn of it. So Lucille feigns a headache and takes to her hostess's bed. Before long John, Larry, the new Mrs. Chiverick, the host and hostess, and a reporter from a local scandal sheet are all visiting, hiding, or snooping in the bedroom. The suave, sad-miened Young and the sprightly, handsome Anders won the best notices.

One reason *Scrambled Wives* failed may have been that an even funnier sex farce hurried into town four nights later. True, Avery Hopwood and Charlton Andrews's **Ladies' Night** (8-9-20, Eltinge) was bashed by most of the more brahmin critics. Woollcott slated it as "laborious" and suggested it brought to mind the dirty pictures seedy Frenchmen offered to tourists in Paris. Playgoers laughed away the criticisms and howled with delight at the farce. The cast was headed by the man many considered the era's most adept farceur, square-faced, square-bodied John Cumberland. (No one could foresee this would be his last major hit.) Cumberland played Jimmy Walters, a man so upset by the skimpy and revealing clothes which modern women wear that he refuses to go out socially, much to his wife's annoyance. To tease him, his friends take him to a somewhat louche costume ball, which in short order is raided by the police. The men, dressed as women, escape and jump through the nearest open window. They find themselves in a turkish bath on ladies' night. (The ball is not shown; Act II begins with the men's arrival at the bath.) Jimmy's growing embarrassment and befuddlement, and his consternation on finding his wife (Claiborne Foster) there, provided the fun. Charles Ruggles, as one of the friends, abetted the laughter in his absurdly curly getup. The farce ran almost a full year and later was often called *Ladies' Night in a Turkish Bath*.

A few commentators expressed dismay that Hopwood's collaborator was a well-known professor of drama. They were equally nonplussed when one of Hopwood's former collaborators, Wilson Collison, a Kansas City druggist, produced his own "dismal" sex farce, **The Girl with the Carmine Lips** (8-9-20, Punch and Judy). The young lady of the title was Mrs. Lorrington, a lawyer who arranges divorces. Her latest attempt goes awry when the girl sent in to be corespondent gets drunk ("What's one to do when they haven't tasted the real stuff since last July?"), has her clothes mistakenly taken away by a dry cleaner, and otherwise creates mayhem. Programs listed the actress who played Mrs. Lorrington as "The Girl with the Carmine Lips." *Variety* reported she was rumored to be Mrs. Collison. Poor, ill-starred Dallas Welford grabbed the best notices as yet another comic butler.

High comedy was the order of the night a week later with the premiere of Gilda Varesi and Dolly Byrne's **Enter Madame** (8-16-20, Garrick). Miss Varesi conceived the play as a vehicle for herself and based her story loosely on legends about her own mother, who had been a famous European prima donna. Gerald Fitzgerald (Norman Trevor), after twenty years of marriage to the great prima donna Lisa Della Robbia (Varesi), has tired of trailing after her in the wake of her sycophantic entourage. When a London paper refers to him as Gerald Della Robbia and a New York one as "President of the Only Her Husband's Club" he concludes enough is enough. He has met a sedate widow, Flora Preston (Jane Meredith), and fallen in love. Lisa laughs at the idea, so an angry Gerald tells her, "You're a conceited, middle-aged woman, whose career is on the wane. You never were a beauty at any time in your life. You've been spoiled and petted; self has been your god and you've served him well." A suddenly confused Lisa bemoans, "They say there are great pitch-black spaces between the stars. I think they are between the people, too, oh, quite pitch." In time she gathers herself together and invites both Gerald and Mrs. Preston to dinner. Before the evening is out she has persuaded Gerald to return to her, even if it still means carrying her puppy and tailing along with her entourage. Luminous performances by Miss Varesi and Trevor helped the comedy run until late spring. And the play's success launched the long career of its producer, Brock Pemberton.

. . .

Brock Pemberton (1885–1950) was born in Leavenworth and educated at the University of Kansas. He served on various newspapers, eventually becoming the drama editor for the *New York Mail* and the *New York World*. In 1917 he became Arthur Hopkins's assistant until he embarked on his own producing career.

. . .

Avery Hopwood's second play of the month, this one written in collaboration with Mary Roberts Rinehart, was taken from a Paris success, *Aux Jardins de Merci*. As **Spanish Love** (8-17-20, Maxine Elliott's) it was sumptuously mounted with beautiful settings, colorful Spanish costumes, superb lighting showing a sunrise, a sunset and a starry night, and even a castanet-clicking troupe of Spanish dancers.

Pencho (James Rennie) is forced to flee after wounding Javier (William H. Powell) in a fight over Maria del Carmen (Maria Ascarra). To spare Pencho imprisonment, Maria accepts that she must marry Javier. But Pencho vows the wedding will not take place. Javier agrees to meet and fight Pencho to the death, but just before the fight occurs the men overhear a doctor stating that Javier is terminally ill and has only a short while to live. Javier agrees to let bygones be bygones, gives Maria to Pencho, and slumps down dead. Besides its eye-filling mounting, the play was imaginatively staged. The orchestra pit was covered over and became an additional performing area. And when Pencho rode in to issue his threats, alarmed friends and neighbors jumped from the stage and fled up the theatre's aisles. Critics singled out Powell, whose major career would be in films, for his skillful acting. The play ran nine months, but its authors had an even better one trying out on the road and ready to brave Broadway.

Earl Carroll, who would soon be famous for his girlie shows, was the author and co-producer (with Al Woods) of **The Lady of Lamp** (8-17-20, Republic). Arthur White (George Gaul), an artist, is invited to a dinner at a private home in Chinatown. He smokes a bit of opium and is transported to ancient China where he becomes emperor, fights the treacherous Manchus, introduces gunpowder, and falls in love with a beautiful princess, who is assassinated. Waking from his dream he realizes that all the figures in it had been guests at the dinner and that the princess is really a pretty American girl well worth courting. Many of the reviews were highly favorable, praising the acting, the beautiful Chinese settings, and the basic play. What critics assailed was what they perceived as the intrusive, unnecessary injection of cheap humor. The play ran three months, but whether it was the financial failure Carroll later claimed is moot.

Guy Bolton and George Middleton's **The Cave Girl** (8-18-20, Longacre) certainly was. Dismissed as "hopelessly 'stock company,' " it told of a rich, purposeful father (John Cope) who takes his son, Divvy (Saxon Kling), into the Maine wilds so that the boy will fall in love with a girl whom the father has invited along. But Divvy quickly falls in love with a guide's daughter, Margot (Grace Valentine), sets fire to the group's canoes so that he can have more time with her, and, when the fire spreads and the band is forced to live like cavemen, is happy to let Margot take control.

Critics were no happier with Frederic and Fanny Hatton's **The Checkerboard** (8-19-20, 39th St.), which told how a stranded Russian ballet troupe latches on to some newly rich Americans by pretending that they are exiled Russian nobles. They convince the richest of the Americans to help underwrite them, but when the leading dancer (José Ruben) realizes that discovering the truth will hurt the man's daughter (Miriam Sears), whom he has come to love and who, he knows, loves him, he walks out of her life.

The next opening more than made up for a few duds or mediocrities, for that opening was Avery Hopwood and Mary Roberts Rinehart's **The Bat** (8-23-20, Morosco). An elderly spinster, Cornelia Van Gorder (Effie Ellsler) rents the summer home of a banker who reputedly has been killed. Instead, it develops he may have merely absconded after hiding stolen bank funds in the house. Miss Van Gorder is told that a number of desperate people are after the money, so she hires a detective, Anderson (Harrison Hunter), to solve the mystery. Nevertheless a series of frightening occurrences, even murder, beset the lady and her guests. Then a strange man (Robert Vaughn) appears and reveals that he is the real detective and that the other man is a dangerous impostor. Although handcuffed, the false Anderson manages to get hold of a gun. He orders everyone to put up their hands. Only Miss Van Gorder disobeys, telling him, "Why, I took the bullets out of that revolver two hours ago." In disgust, he throws the gun on the floor. The real Anderson remarks, "You see, you never know what a woman will do!" Sweet little Miss Van Gorder replies, "As it happened, I didn't. The first lie of an otherwise stainless life." Writing in *Life*, Robert Benchley observed, "From eight-thirty to eleven you are leaping about in your seat in a state bordering on epilepsy, pressing moist palms on the sleeves of the people on either side of you, reassuring yourself with little nervous laughs that this is only the theatre, and then collapsing into the aisle at the end of each act. Fortunately, you are not at all conspicuous, as the aisle is full of similar casualties." For many the evening's best performance was fragile May Vokes, as an all too easily terrified maid, quivering, shrieking, and dropping her china-laden trays. But the play also gave Effie Ellsler her first really long run since *Hazel Kirke*, more than forty years before. And a long run it was. Its 867 performances made it the second-longest-running show in Broadway history up to its time. Six road companies were sent out. By the time of his death eight years later, Hopwood and Mrs. Rinehart each had pocketed nearly a half million 1920s dollars as their shares of royalties (and their quarter shares as two of the mystery's four producers). The play's success meant that, with last season's *The Gold*

Diggers still packing in playgoers, Hopwood had four shows running simultaneously on Broadway, the only author ever to have done that except Clyde Fitch. At season's end *Variety* estimated his royalties for the one season topped $500,000.

Four failures followed. In David Carb's **Immodest Violet** (8-24-20, 48th St.) a wild Texan flapper, Violet Rose (Marie Goff), shocks her family by refusing to marry the man who has made her pregnant. Annoyed at their response, she accepts a position as delegate to the state's woman's rights meeting. Since she has no money to get there, she makes a middle-of-the-night visit to a pleasant young man, Arthur Bodkin (Kenneth MacKenna), who lives with her aunt. Instead of just borrowing the funds she needs, she persuades him to run off with her, thereby inadvertently causing him to violate the Mann Act. By the time the case is dismissed, Violet has decided Albert would make a nice husband. The play's producer, William A. Brady, unable to obtain a regular booking, ran out its short stand in a series of matinees at one of his own theatres.

Americans did not take to Ian Hay's London hit *Tilly of Bloomsbury*, which was done here using the title of Hay's original novel, **Happy-Go-Lucky** (8-24-20, Booth). It told a Cinderella tale about the daughter of boardinghouse keepers who wins the hand of an aristocrat, despite his snobbish family's objections. The cynosure was neither Tilly nor her beloved but a bailiff who comes to the boardinghouse to remove some furniture and remains to pretend to be a butler. O. P. Heggie's portrayal of the part earned him the lion's share of applause.

A second London hit, **Paddy the Next Best Thing** (8-27-20, Shubert), which Gayer Mackay and Robert Ord took from a novel by Gertrude Page, spotlighted a lovable tomboy (Eileen Huban) who vows never to marry but is finally tamed.

The fourth failure was puzzling, given the delighted reviews both the play and the cast, especially the star, received. George Scarborough's **Blue Bonnet** (8-28-20, Princess) was set on the Mexican border. Billy Burleson (Ernest Truex) is an eighteen-year-old cowboy, who has never roped a cow, has never carried a gun, and doesn't swear or drink. When his boss dies, he decides he must serve as guardian to the man's sixteen-year-old daughter, Hope (Mona Thomas). That will entail warding off sharpies who would seize the ranch by any means, discouraging Terry Mack (Richard Taber), a dashing member of the National Guard at the moment patroling the border to keep Mexican bandits away, from courting Hope, and dealing with the malicious gossip fomented by a vicious, vindictive spinster (Helen Lowell).

By coincidence the very next play to arrive was also set on the Mexican border (in fact the play had been tried out as *Borderlands*). But this time the public responded in droves to welcoming notices. The curtain rose on Porter Emerson Browne's **The Bad Man** (8-30-20, Comedy) to reveal the spartan, rundown main room of an adobe and wood ranch house. The house belongs to Gilbert Jones (Frank Conroy) but was allowed to fall into disrepair and debt by his crippled uncle (James A. Devine) while Jones served with the A.E.F. Jasper Hardy (Wilson Reynolds), who holds the mortgage, will claim the property if Jones cannot come up with moneys by evening. Visiting Jones are his old flame, Lucia Pell (Frances Carson), and her mean husband, Morgan (Fred L. Tiden). Morgan, believing there is oil under the land but keeping that belief to himself, is prepared to buy the place. The Pells fall into an argument, and Morgan, who has pinioned Lucia against a table, is about to slash her face with a spur when shots are heard. The other Americans come backing through the door, their hands held high. They are followed by a fierce-looking Mexican with a gun in his hand. The Americans recognize him as Pancho Lopez (Holbrook Blinn), and he tells them they are his prisoners. He would rob and kill them, or at least hold them for ransom once he discovers Hardy and Pell are rich. He also tells them he has spent time in America, which to him is not a land of freedom: "Every man, every woman, is slave—slave to law, slave to custom, slave to everysing. You get up such time, eat such time, every day you go to work such time; every night you go to bed such time; every week, Madre di Dios, you take a bath such a time!" Nor is he concerned how the American government will react to his behavior, assuring the onlookers that (recalling President Wilson's old phrase) all it will do is "watchfully wait." But then Jones, who has been out in the barn, comes in, and Lopez recognizes him as a man who once saved his life. His attitude changes. Discovering that Jones still loves and would marry Lucia, and will share her wealth if she is Pell's widow, he has one of his men shoot Pell. The first shot is not fatal, so he must eventually do the job himself. But Lopez is taken aback to realize that Jones is horrified at his action. He changes his attitude again, accusing Jones of having "ze liver what are white and ze soul what are yellow." Lopez announces he himself will take Lucia away. That goads Jones into pulling a gun and threatening the Mexican. But a smiling, satisfied Lopez, concluding he has made a man of Jones, bids

the Americans farewell, wishing, "May you always be so 'appy like what I 'ave make you." Browne's deliciously comic send-up of the infamous Pancho Villa and Holbrook's bravura performance in the role pleased theatregoers for the rest of the season.

Only David Belasco's fine production and brilliantly coached players made a modest, four-month success of Jean Archibald's **Call the Doctor** (8-30-20, Empire), which several critics dismissed as a dreary variation of his earlier hit, *The Boomerang*. Now it was a wife (Charlotte Walker) who is upset because she seemingly has lost the affections of her husband (William Morris), and a "doctor of domestic difficulties" (Janet Beecher) who shows her how to win him back by going out and having a spree. While supervising all this the "doctor" falls in love with the family's attractive lawyer (Philip Merivale).

George M. Cohan had dissolved his partnership with Sam Harris, and his solo production of John T. McIntyre and Francis Hill's **Genius and the Crowd** (9-6-20, Cohan) left some Broadwayites wondering out loud if he could really go it alone. Philippe Trava (Georges Renavent) is a young, brilliant violinist, so fed up with doting women and fawning sycophants that he vows to give up his career. An old cello and violin repairman, Gasparo Tagliani (Fuller Mellish), appreciating Trava's rare talents, conspires to change his mind. He knows that Trava's beautiful secretary, Mira Van Ness (Marion Coakley), loves her boss, and he suspects Trava loves her, although the violinist may not realize it. He arranges to have Trava's friend, Robert Burr (Frank Otto), a brash automobile salesman, openly court Mira. Trava's jealousy drives him back into playing and into Mira's arms. Critics particularly liked the second act, set in Tagliani's quaint, instrument-filled basement workshop, a shop also filled with passé artists dreaming of past glories and playing romantically on the instruments (or singing in accompaniment to them). But some critics were displeased with Cohan's staging, noting, for example, "Whenever two players are given over to earnest and heated dialogue, they invariably stand nose to nose, squarely in the middle of the stage, and roar their discourse down each other's throats after the fashion of Weber and Fields." Three weeks and the play was gone.

At the huge Manhattan Opera House a revival of *An Enemy of the People* with an undistinguished cast had trouble luring playgoers for its planned two-week engagement.

The stately Margaret Anglin enjoyed one of the biggest successes and longest runs (seven months) of her career with **The Woman of Bronze** (9-7-20, Frazee), Paul Kester's freely Americanized version of Henri Kistemaecker and Eugène Delard's *La Rivale*. The star played the wife of a sculptor (John Halliday) who nearly succumbs to the wiles of a guest in their home, the wife's vampish cousin (Mary Fowler). At one point the wife brandishes a dagger and threatens to kill the girl. But the husband comes to his senses, and the wife will clearly be the model for his statue of Courage. Aisle-sitters noted that Miss Anglin, famous for her portrayal of such classic Greek figures as Medea and Antigone, imbued her part with a special tragic grandeur.

Courage was the theme of Thomas Dixon's **A Man of the People** (9-7-20, Bijou), which told how Lincoln (Howard Hall) bravely fought off attempts by his party to dump him as a candidate for a second term. News of Sherman's victory at Atlanta comes just in time to make the waverers fall in line. An epilogue had the president offering his second inaugural address. Hall, who had spent much of his career writing and acting in cheap touring melodramas, surprised many reviewers by the strength and dignity of his playing. But the show could not attract attendance, and this man of the people gave up the fight at the same time as Ibsen's enemy of the people threw in the towel.

While Cohan had bad luck, his former partner, Sam Harris, scored a hit with Rida Johnson Young's **Little Old New York** (9-8-20, Plymouth). The little old town of the play was 1810 New York, and elegantly costumed actors impersonating Washington Irving, Fitz Green Halleck, Cornelius Vanderbilt, and John Jacob Astor all walked its streets. It is a town breathless at the news that a coach has made it all the way from Boston in six days and where Peter Delmonico sells sandwiches from a basket all the while dreaming of opening a fine restaurant. But the main interest lies with Larry Delavan (Ernest Glendinning) who will inherit a fortune today if one possible rival heir does not appear. To his chagrin that rival appears in Pat O'Day, who lands with his father (Alf T. Helton) on the latest boat from Ireland. The father soon dies, and Larry, who has reluctantly agreed to be the lad's guardian, taunts the boy with his girl-like mannerisms. The lad, ashamed at the fraud perpetrated, discloses that he is really a girl. That means Larry is the legitimate heir. But he and Patricia (Genevieve Tobin) find themselves falling in love, so it actually doesn't matter. Among supporting players hailed for their smaller bits was Donald Meek as Bunny, a timid night watchman.

Problems in modern New York proved far less attractive. The titular hero (George Arliss) of Booth Tarkington's **Poldekin** (9-9-20, Park) is a Bolshevist sent to America by the party to propagandize. But conversations with ordinary Americans and a visit to a baseball game (not shown) convince him that democracy is superior to communism. His old buddies try to silence him, but he wins out. Arliss, who in his autobiography wrote that the play was sadly underrated (but couldn't trouble himself to spell it correctly), gave an atypically sunny performance. It could not save the production, but he, at least, would soon have a more typical and infinitely more memorable role.

Although it was only mid-September, Sam Harris's production of Aaron Hoffman's **Welcome Stranger** (9-13-20, Cohan and Harris) was the season's seventh arrival to run through the theatrical year. In fact, it had already chalked up a hugely profitable thirty-week run in Chicago. Anti-Semitism is so virulent in Valley Falls, a backwater New England village, that when Isidor Solomon (George Sidney) comes to town hoping to set up a clothing business he is coldly informed there is no room at the local inn. He is not downhearted, and after he encourages the village's oddball inventor, Clem Beemis (David Higgins), a meek man who has been sneered at by his own townsfolk, Clem invites him to put up at his simple home. Before long Izzy's kindliness, his thoughtful actions, his success in helping the town to bring in cheaper electricity by employing Clem's electrical apparatus, and his alertness in aiding an unjustly maligned girl (Margaret Mower) win over the villagers. Only the aggressively Christian mayor, Ichabod Whitson (Edmund Breese), remains firmly against Izzy and all Jews, until Izzy receives some papers relating to the mayor's birth. They had been written in Yiddish, the language of the mayor's parents, and, indeed, one of them is a letter from his mother, who tells Izzy that her son, then known as Isaac Wolfson, ran away from home years ago because he felt inferior to some of his fellow youngsters. *Variety* reported that Izzy's reading the letter in Yiddish left many in the audience baffled, although other reviewers, most of them Christian, seemed to have no difficulty grasping its import. Critics in both Chicago and New York had found the comedy entertaining if often crude. Perhaps they recalled that Hoffman, like Higgins and Sidney, had apprenticed in the bygone cheap touring theatres. The short, stocky Sidney had spent years touring in plays dealing with a character called Busy Izzy, and he brought that Izzy's Jewish shrugs and crinkly smiles to his Izzy Solomon.

David Belasco's success with Edward Knoblock's **One** (9-14-20, Belasco) was no greater than that he had had with *Call the Doctor*. Quiet, drab Pearl Delgado (Frances Starr) for many years has em-

133

ployed telepathic communication from her London home to inspire her vivacious twin sister, Ruby, a pianist. Indeed the girls discovered they could speak to each other this way wherever they were so long as one held a rose against her breast. While Ruby is in New York preparing for a concert, Pearl receives a proposal of marriage from a man who, she had thought, preferred Ruby. She accepts, holds the rose to her breast, and tells Ruby of what has happened. She soon learns that Ruby's concert was a disastrous failure. Realizing that she will destroy her sister's career, Pearl commits suicide. "Eerie music" filled the time between the scene changes that also allowed Miss Starr to change from one character to the other.

William Hodge paid his virtually annual visit to New York with his latest, self-written vehicle, **The Guest of Honor** (9-20-20, Broadhurst). He played John Weatherbee, a failed writer living on scraps in an attic. He shares those scraps and attic with a tot he adopted after its mother, shunned by her puritanical family, had died. But later the child is recognized by his socialite aunt, who has come to invite Weatherbee to be guest of honor at a literary club which has awarded some of his poems a prize. A struggle for guardianship ensues until Weatherbee receives a big advance for a novel he has written and the aunt agrees to marry him. The play, which had been touring successfully for many months, stayed only nine weeks before returning to a more appreciative road.

Neither New York nor the hinterlands wanted anything to do with Harry Chapman Ford's **Anna Ascends** (9-22-20, Playhouse), which also had a central figure who becomes a successful novelist and which one commentator wrote off as "a ten-twent-thirt pudding and a poor one at that." Anna Ayyobb (Alice Brady) is an immigrant from Syria who starts to work her way up, meets Howard "Gents" Fisk (John Werner), a rich young man who offers to help her, but then lands in hot water after stabbing a villainous young man, "Bunch" Berry (Rod LaRoque), who tries to force her into prostitution. Believing she has killed him, she flees. She changes her name to Anna Adams, writes a thinly disguised autobiographical novel (whose title was the same as the play's), and wins fame, wealth, and Gents. When Bunch tries to make more trouble she has him sent to prison.

Another quick flop was Owen Davis's second offering of the season, his comedy **Marry the Poor Girl** (9-25-20, Little). A very drunk Jack Tanner (William Roselle), a house guest at the Paddingtons, is inadvertently put to bed by his friends in the room

of his hosts' daughter, Julia (Isabel Lowe). Come morning, the outraged Paddingtons insist that Jack make Julia an honest woman. But the wedding is no sooner performed than Jack's well-meaning friends, hoping to exculpate him and unaware of the ceremony, bring girls who are introduced as his wife or wives. The few, scanty audiences that attended the play could easily guess that by eleven o'clock misunderstandings would be resolved and Jack and Julia have fallen in love.

Although most morning-after reviews and even some later publications listed the author of **The Tavern** 9-27-20, Cohan) as Cora Dick Gantt, most showwise people knew the real author was the play's producer and director, George M. Cohan. What Cohan had done was taken a preposterously straight-faced, old-style melodrama and all but totally rewritten it as a spoof of the genre. All the action took place in the main room of a late eighteenth- or early nineteenth-century tavern. Outside the wind is howling, the thunder crashing, and a pistol shot is heard. A striking man enters, dressed in a white shirt open at the throat, a dark vest, corduroy trousers, high boots, a patched jacket, a long dark green cape, a large brown hat and a staff. The Vagabond (Arnold Daly) hails the innkeeper, Freeman (Dodson Mitchell):

Vagabond: Greetings, my friends. 'Tis a glorious storm, is it not? By God, gentlemen, it was worth being born to have lived on a night like this.
Freeman: Throw up your hands.
Vagabond: What?
Freeman: Throw up your hands.
Vagabond: What a childish idea.
Freeman: Throw up your hands, or I'll shoot.
Vagabond: Shoot and be hanged.

When Freeman insists that the Vagabond must be crazy, the stranger agrees that he is as crazy as Freeman thinks he is but also as sane as Freeman thinks himself to be. He advises the innkeeper that the shot the innkeeper heard came from an out-shed where he wrested a gun from a distraught lady, who then had fainted. The lady (Elsie Rizer) is brought into the tavern and when she is revived tells them that she is on a long trek to see the governor to ask a hearing about an injustice. By chance the governor, his wife, his daughter, and the daughter's arrogant fiancé enter, complaining that they have been attacked by robbers only moments before. Freeman sends for the sheriff. The lady reappears and, seeing the governor's son-in-law-to-be, Tom (William Jeffrey), accuses him of having despoiled and abandoned her. When the sheriff arrives Tom attempts to flee into the stormy night but is shot. At the same time, the governor's party recognize the sheriff as the leader of the gang of robbers who set upon them. Then the lady spots the inn's hired man and accuses him much as she had accused Tom. The hired man rushes out into the storm and is shot. Another man appears and is immediately accused by the lady of having despoiled and abandoned her. But he discloses that he is the head of an insane asylum and that the lady is an escaped lunatic. He prepares to take her back. But first he reveals that some years ago another inmate escaped, a man who had odd notions about life being a drama. Behind him the Vagabond picks up his things and heads for the door. "I thank you all for a few hours of delicious, delightful nonsense." He apologizes to Tom, who has recovered from the gunshot, " 'Twas my mistake to cast you for a villain." Thunder crashes as he opens the door. "Ah, what a night! What a blessing to be free on a night like this!" His exit leaves the others wondering who he was.

Throughout much of the play the Vagabond remarked on the action in comic asides. Thus, when the lady is about to tell the governor her problem but faints before she can, the Vagabond tells the audience, "Damn the luck! 'Twould have been a great scene but for that."

Immediate critical reaction was negative, with the trade sheet the *Clipper* summing up the more favorable response: "Without question it is amusing and clever, but it takes far too much time to get going." At the start the play appeared headed for failure. But then the weeklies and monthlies began to appear, their critics having had time to chew over their reactions. In *Theatre* Hornblow commented, "There's lots of fun in it, and I recommend it heartily to the legion who go to the theatre to be 'amused.' " Benchley in *Life* resorted to some tongue-in-cheek hyperbole when he called the evening "the biggest night in [my] theatregoing career, for it marked the birth of something *new* on the stage, a gorgeous insanity from which it is hoped the drama as an institution will never recover." The often acerbic Dorothy Parker, writing in *Ainslee's Magazine,* was perhaps equally hyperbolic when she spoke of "an evening to look back on for the remainder of a lifetime."

In short order the travesty was packing in audiences, although an increasingly difficult Daly (he had a drinking problem) had to be replaced by Brandon Tynan and eventually by Cohan himself. It ran nine months. The play remained one of Cohan's biggest money-makers, a favorite for nearly half a century on collegiate stages, in stock, and even off-Broadway. Cohan's biographer has pointed out one sad irony: Cora Dick Gantt died in a mental institution where she had been committed many years earlier.

The next play to arrive had begun life as a vaudeville playlet, *Dollars and Sense,* was tried out as *Easy Money,* opened as **Merchants of Venus** (9-27-20, Punch and Judy), and before its short stay was finished changed its name to *Because of Helen.* Its author and star was vaudevillian Alan Brooks, who played a wealthy man-about-town, Jack Bainbridge. He is pursued by Helen Davenport (Vivian Rushmore), who has married his best friend, Billy Hasbrouck (Robert Kelly), but who, on realizing that Jack is even richer and that Billy is about to lose his money, is willing callously to throw over her husband. At the same time, Jack must prevent Verna Cromwell (Carroll McComas), a two-a-day dancer who truly loves him but whom he does not love, from marrying a cheap roué on the rebound. Jack sees to it he loses enough money in a business transaction to Billy to prompt Helen to stay with her husband and finally decides he does love Verna. Despite the tiny theatre's tiny stage, the action of the last act took place simultaneously in several settings—rooms in two separate apartments and in an office—all shown side by side.

The author of **Don't Tell** (9-27-20, Nora Bayes), Graham Moffat, like Brooks, also took a major role in his play. He took the part of a rich, self-made former plumber who must set matters to right after his son steals to pay for gambling debts and implicates his innocent cousin in the crime. The Scottish importation had one of the season's shortest runs—six performances.

On the other hand, Max Marcin and Frederic S. Isham's **Three Live Ghosts** (9-29-20, Greenwich Village), taken from Isham's novel of the same name, ran into spring. In a grubby London lodging house, the equally grubby, boozy Mrs. Gubbins (Beryl Mercer) is in the midst of a seance, trying to speak to her stepson, Jimmie, who was reported killed in action and whose insurance she has collected, when who should walk in but Jimmie (Charles McNaughton) himself. He brings two friends with him, the American William Foster (Percy Helton) and a shell-shocked Englishman known only as Spoofy (Cyril Chadwick). They had been held prisoners in Germany, and when Jimmie tried to report his return to his old army company, he was told he was dead and had better stay dead. But Mrs. Gubbins has had a visit from an American detective who has told her that there is a thousand-pound reward out for Foster, who fled America to avoid arrest for theft. He left his name on a newspaper, but when she hurries to retrieve the paper she discovers another lodger has used it for wrapping. The girl has gone out and not returned. An alarmed Mrs. Gubbins cries out, "Maybe she fell off the embankment—and the *newspyper's drowned*." Making matters worse, Spoofy has disappeared. When he returns he returns with a baby he has kidnapped and jewels he has stolen from a safe. But he has been trailed by Scotland Yard, who suspect all the lodgers of being a gang. However, Lady Leicester (Mercedes Desmore) appears to identify the child and jewels; she also identifies Spoofy as her husband, who has been listed as missing in action. Then the American detective (Emmett Shackleford) appears. From him Foster learns that his father has died and left him enough money to repay his theft and still have lots left over. Mrs. Gubbins barks out that she still "clymes" the reward. The man (Charles Dalton) from the Yard says, "We'll divide that thousand pounds—'alf and 'alf." To which Mrs. Gubbins retorts, "Send *my* six hundred in the morning."

Although more than one critic pointed out that Edgar Selwyn's **The Mirage** (9-30-20, Times Square), which opened the Selwyns' newest playhouse, was hardly more than a tawdry rewrite of *The Easiest Way,* the public apparently enjoyed it and gave it a six-month run. Attention centers around Irene Moreland (Florence Reed), who lives "in a smart apartment with the usual coffee-colored maid." Some years before Irene had come from Erie, Pa., to New York filled with the customary noble dreams and ambitions, but by the time the play begins her dreams and ambitions are long gone, and she is the mistress of Henry M. Galt (Malcolm Williams). Suddenly her former Erie beau, Al Manning (Alan Dinehart), who has had no small success himself and has become a pillar of his local church, appears on the scene (by theatrical coincidence invited to a party at Galt's home). Thinking she is a widow, he asks her to marry him. Irene tells Galt she would like to accept Manning's proposal. He laughs at her, saying she could never go back to any place as dreary as Erie. To compound her shock, Manning learns of her past and stalks out. He returns after changing his mind, but Irene sends him away, with only the suggestion that they see what the future brings.

Hugh Stanislaus Stange's **Dawn of Ireland** (9-30-20, Lexington) told of a sturdy, good-looking Irish lad, Dan (Larry Reilly), who bests the British and their half-Irish, half-British informer and finally wins the hand of a lovely colleen. Even at $1.50 top

the poorly mounted material was too old hat for most playgoers, so ran less than a week at its much too big berth.

The Theatre Guild opened its new season with David Pinski's **The Treasure** (10-4-20, Garrick), which had first been performed a decade earlier in a Lower East Side Yiddish theatre and had subsequently been produced by Max Reinhardt in Berlin. Judke (Fred Eric), the retarded, epileptic son of Chone (Dudley Digges), the gravedigger in a Russian-Jewish shtetl, stumbles across some gold Imperial coins while digging a grave for his dog. His sister, Tille (Celia Adler), grabs them and runs to buy new clothes. She tells her neighbors of the pieces, so before long the villagers are tearing up the cemetery in hopes of finding buried treasure. When Chone tries to stop the sacrilege he is threatened with the loss of his job and house. But all ends happily, with Tille's new clothes helping her to land a husband. Although critics were respectful, they concluded the evening fell short of success. The Guild removed it after it played out its pre-subscribed performances.

Down in Greenwich Village the Neighborhood Players was a group not unlike the Guild. It would become better known than it was in 1920 but never be as preeminent as its uptown rival. Its first offering of the new season was John Galsworthy's **The Mob** (10-9-20, Neighborhood Playhouse), which told how an enraged mob kills a high-principled statesman who insists on preaching pacifist sentiments during a war. It ran eight weeks.

Reviewers were far less happy with Samuel Shipman and Victor Victor's **The Unwritten Chapter** (10-11-20, Astor), though they disagreed on why. Some saw it as blatant Jewish propaganda, some as well-intentioned but poorly written, others as a crass and inept attempt to draw in a certain clientele. *Variety*'s review, written by its founder, Sime Silverman, covered all these bases but emphasized the first. Panning the play as "sermony, preachy, and at other times a lecture," it continued, "Why dramatize the Jew at $3 a seat before the Christians will believe he is worth this much? And the Jews may not either." A socially prominent man is appalled when his son invites a Jewish war buddy to dinner, but that buddy turns out to be a descendant of Haym Salomon, and his recounting the story of how Salomon, with other Jewish friends, helped burn General Howe's stores of munitions and eventually bankrupted himself to underwrite the American Revolution changes the father's attitude. The main part of the drama took place in 1776, allowing for settings and costumes that most critics found attractive. But they were again divided on how well Louis Mann played the principal role. The majority seemed to suggest that while the actor, heretofore known as a dialect comedian, did his best in the serious, almost tragic part, his best was often not enough to save a leaden play.

George M. Cohan's second hit of the season was Augustin MacHugh's **The Meanest Man in the World** (10-12-20, Hudson), a comedy which like several earlier ones had begun life as a vaudeville sketch and which Cohan heavily altered himself. In fact, during the tryout Cohan took over the central role of Richard Clarke, an attorney so unsuccessful that would-be clients can reach him only by mail, since his phone has been disconnected. A friend says his problem is that he is too nice, advises him to be as mean as possible, and, to give him the chance to test himself, asks him to collect an overdue $850 from J. Hudson and Co. in backwater Hudsonville. But Clarke's resolve to be tough and heartless comes to naught when he discovers that J. Hudson is a beautiful young girl, Jane Hudson (Marion Coakley). He not only borrows money to help her pay off her debt but involves her in real estate deals, one of which deals with real estate that may have oil under it. In short order, in the comedy's most trumpeted, Cohanesque line, he has turned "a bum town into a boom town." The comedy ran six months and with the musical, *Mary,* which opened six nights later, gave Cohan three box-office hits at once.

Curiously, most first-stringers elected not to attend the Cohan opening but rather another that night which witnessed a popular Boston actress's grab for New York celebrity. The actress was the attractive but somewhat mature (or at least mature-looking) Mary Young, and in Harry Wagstaff Gribble's **The Outrageous Mrs. Palmer** (10-12-20, 39th St.) she played a famous, tempestuous star whose amours regularly fill the scandal sheets. Her son (Raymond Hackett), whom she sometimes coddles and sometimes neglects, runs off to war after her revelation to his fiancée that he is illegitimate destroys his engagement. When he returns badly mutilated, the actress resolves to sacrifice her career in order to tend him.

Bab (10-18-20, Park) was Edward Childs Carpenter's dramatization of a Mary Roberts Rinehart novel. Poor little Barbara "Bab" Archibald (Helen Hayes) must survive as a "sub deb" in the shadow of her beautiful older sister (Edith King), who has been introduced to society and gets to wear gorgeous clothes. She returns ahead of time from school after her story, "The Trial Marriage," is suppressed by school authorities, comes down with the measles,

nearly wrecks her sister's planned marriage when a letter Bab has written to an imaginary lover falls into the wrong hands and is misinterpreted, and causes havoc by insisting that imaginary lover is real. Almost all is forgiven by Bab's wangling, in pure storybook fashion, an important contract for her businessman father. Although critics admired Miss Hayes's handling of a role not much different from the one she had played in *Clarence,* they cared little for the character or the play. Woollcott suggested that after each of the sugary remarks figures in the play make about the girl, "there is really nothing for the little imp to do but simper and gush and bury her head roguishly in the nearest bosom, secretly wishing the while, no doubt, that she had thought to slay the author during rehearsals." The play ran eleven weeks.

But critics themselves gushed over the next entry, Frank Craven's **The First Year** (10-20-20, Little). Reviewing all the year's offerings at season's end, Burns Mantle observed, "The outstanding comedy success of this particular season was this fine comedy," and he reported, "A week after its production . . . it was practically impossible to buy seats for the succeeding three months, and by the end of two weeks the theater had been sold out for the season. Only the speculators held places in reserve, and their prices were, naturally, exorbitant." Having arrived at a very marriageable age, Grace Livingston (Roberta Arnold) is trying to choose between two suitors. Dick Loring (Lyster Chambers) is handsome and brash and about to leave little Reading, Ill., to make a big splash in the world (as he himself tells everyone). He has proposed several times. Tommy Tucker (Craven) is perhaps a little homely and so shy that he can't get up enough nerve to ask Grace's parents' permission to ask Grace. In a way, that's lucky, since if the oh-so-modern Grace believed he was that outdated she "wouldn't have him under any circumstances." But after Grace's wise old uncle (Tim Murphy) goads Tommy a bit, he proposes and is accepted. Grace's only stipulation is that they leave Reading. The second act finds the Tuckers in a tiny apartment in Joplin, Mo. They've had problems, which Tommy dismisses as merely the dark before the dawn. But Grace responds that they're stuck in "a long arctic night." They are preparing to entertain a man who Tommy hopes will buy some land Tommy has speculated on. Grace's nervousness is made worse when a young black girl (played as usual by a white in dark makeup) appears. She is Hattie (Leila Bennett), and she tells the Tuckers that her mother, their maid, "got misery" so won't be coming to help.

137

Tommy talks Hattie into helping, but in some ways she is no help at all. When Grace asks, "Did you seed the melons?" she replies, "Yes'm, I seed them." Grace has to explain she means scooping out the seeds. But Hattie proves a big help when the Tuckers discover they have no whiskey, since she has a bottle of gin in her coat: "I gets it for Mammie—she likes it for her misery." She even teaches the youngsters how to make Orange Blossoms. The guests, the Barstows (Hale Norcross and Merceita Esmonde), show up, and Mr. Barstow is about to consummate the deal when Loring arrives. He tells them he is working on the same project and that Tommy has bought the wrong land. Mr. Barstow reneges on the deal. In the argument that flares up after the Barstows and Loring have left, Grace becomes so angry she packs her bags and runs home to mother. When Tommy shows up at the Livingstons' home he is a rich man, for he has been proven right about what land the railroad wanted and Mr. Barstow has had to buy it from him at a higher price than originally agreed upon. Then Loring once more appears, the two men get to fighting, and Grace, attempting to stop Loring from hurting Tommy, accidentally knocks out her husband with a vase meant for Loring's noggin. Tommy misconstrues her actions. It takes all of Grace's uncle's diplomacy to smooth matters—plus Grace's announcement that she is pregnant. "I hope he's going to like us," Tommy remarks. When the play closed after 725 performances it was Broadway's third-longest-running show, just behind *The Bat*.

John Galsworthy's second play of the season, **The Skin Game** (10-20-20, Bijou), was also a hit, but its somber theme of the battle between landed gentry and upstart manufacturers (won by the gentry in a costly victory achieved at the price of high principles) held its run to 176 performances. The largely English cast was deemed unexceptional.

Another importation closed the month at the Greenwich Village on the 26th. *Youth,* telling of a young girl killed by her brother, who actually was aiming to shoot the man who had violated her, was a revival of the same translation of Max Halbe's *Jugend* which New York had rejected in 1911 and which it quickly spurned again.

Several critics lambasted portions of the writing and playing in A. E. Thomas's **Just Suppose** (11-1-20, Henry Miller's) as annoyingly saccharine. Some of the same men also saw it as a modern retelling of the *Old Heidelberg* story. To others the play was simply sweet, beguilingly written, charming—and modern. In fact, to many reviewers and playgoers the central figure of the comedy was a thinly disguised stand-in for the real Prince of Wales. The Staffords are southern aristocrats. They are served by a loyal old "darky" who is always saying "Yas sah" and "Yessum." The family's grande dame, Mrs. Carter Stafford (Mrs. Whiffen), is a feisty old gal, even if she retains cherished recollections of bygone days—not so much standing on the porch as a child and watching Union troops ride over her family's property as dancing with Edward VII when she was a young lady and he was visiting America as the Prince of Wales. Her granddaughter, Linda Lee Stafford (Patricia Collinge), has grown to be a beauty, though grandmother worries that the girl has not yet fully recovered from her mother's death. Still, Mrs. Stafford advises a good-looking, very eligible suitor (William J. Keighley) enough time has elapsed so that he can ask for her hand. But Linda Lee turns him down, saying she is not madly in love: "I wonder if I'm only a foolish, romantic girl crying for the moon. I wonder if it's silly of me to want to be thrilled by the voice of the man I love—to be enchanted by his touch—to be intoxicated by the thought of him—to be haunted by the memory of his smile." She thinks she is right. After the suitor leaves, the Staffords have another visitor. He is Sir Calverton Shipley (Leslie Howard), known to his friends as "Bubbles" and a diplomat assigned to the British embassy in Washington. He has come merely to say hello to the old lady, his mother's dear friend. But when the Staffords discover he has left a second young man waiting in his car, they insist the other man come in. He introduces himself as George Chester (Geoffrey Kerr), and the men's visit would be brief indeed until George spots Linda Lee. To prolong the stay he feigns illness and the Staffords press him to remain the night. In fact, he doesn't leave until the next afternoon. By that time George and Linda Lee have spent hours together admiring the treasured ring Linda Lee's mother bequeathed her, reciting poems about gathering rosebuds and about how "old echoes, wailing, die," making lots of small talk, and falling deeply in love. He is vague about who he is, calling himself merely "the loneliest beggar in all the world." (One critic heard the word as "bugger.") But when a high and angry official comes from the embassy to demand the young man return and honor his obligations, Linda Lee confesses she has known all along he is the Prince of Wales and that nothing can come of their brief fling. She recognizes that the prince had simply been seeking some desperate relief from the unending burdens of his position. They agree to write occasionally. After he has supposedly left for good he suddenly returns, having demanded his ship stop at

Hampton Roads long enough for him to say one more good-bye. Sitting with him in her garden, Linda Lee removes her mother's ring from her finger.

Linda: I want you to take it please, and keep it in remembrance of me.
George: (*She puts it on his finger—he kisses it*) Until I die!

She tells him he must leave before the storm breaks. He "*bows his head, then with a little gasp goes out hastily, not looking back.*" Linda Lee waves until the rain begins to come down. The players were also welcomed by most critics. *Variety,* commenting on Leslie Howard in his American debut, called his somewhat silly Englishman a "perfect foil" to Kerr's suave prince. In 1927 the play was musicalized as *Just Fancy.*

Amélie Rives's dramatization of Mark Twain's **The Prince and the Pauper** (11-1-20, Booth) had to settle for second-stringers, but their basically favorable notices encouraged enough playgoers to keep the play on the boards for twenty weeks. Their major complaint was that Ruth Findlay, the young actress who played both titular roles, was no more than competent. (Curiously almost none mentioned Elsie Leslie, whose performance had captivated New Yorkers in another version thirty years before. Perhaps many of the second-stringers were too young to remember her.) Best notices went to a still remarkably youthful-looking William Faversham for his somewhat old-fashioned performance as the valiant swordsman, Miles Hendon, and to the rising young Clare Eames as Princess Elizabeth. Settings seemed to have been drawn from odd corners of the Shubert warehouse and hastily repainted.

Only a handful of critics bothered to attend the evening's third opening, but their notices and some feverishly excited word of mouth sent the others scurrying hurriedly to see what all the excitement was about. That third opening was Eugene O'Neill's **The Emperor Jones** (11-1-20, Provincetown Playhouse), offered as the major part of a double bill along with the now forgotten **Matinata** by the Theatre Guild's Lawrence Langner. O'Neill's emperor, loosely suggested by Toussaint L'Ouverture and Henri Christophe, two figures in Haitian history, was Brutus Jones (Charles Gilpin). Jones had been a Pullman porter until he was sentenced to prison for a fight over a crap game. Having escaped, he fled to a West Indian island "as yet not self-determined by White Marines." He established himself as dictator, heading an abusive, corrupt regime. A white cockney trader, Smithers (Jasper Deeter), alerts him that the incessant drum beating signifies an imminent revolt. But the cocky Jones assures Smithers that only a silver bullet can kill him. However, the revolt soon forces him to flee to the forest. As his terror grows, exacerbated by the darkness, by the strange jungle sounds and ominous silences, and by the relentlessly accelerating drumming, he expends his own supply of bullets shooting at phantoms. Finally, troops led by Lem (Charles Ellis), a native chief, find him and kill him with a silver bullet that Lem has had specially fabricated. Staring down at the bloody corpse, Smithers asks, "Where's yer 'igh an' mighty airs now, yer bloomin' majesty? Silver bullets! Gawd blimey, but yer died in the 'eight of style, any'ow."

Heywood Broun, one of the few major reviewers to attend the opening, wrote in the *Tribune* that the work was "the most interesting play which has yet come from the most promising playwright in America." He called Gilpin's emoting "a performance of heroic stature." He also admired Cleon Throckmorton's simple settings and the beautiful lighting, lamenting only that the wait between scenes was "a vulture which preys upon the attention." In the *Globe,* Kenneth Macgowan, who shortly would work closely with O'Neill, hailed the drama as "an odd and extraordinary play, written with imaginative genius." He had equal praise for Gilpin: "The moment when he raises his naked body against the moonlit sky and prays is such a dark lyric of the flesh, such a cry of the primitive being, as I have never seen in the theater."

Some attention (though not as much as might have been accorded in later decades) was given to the fact that this was the first play by a white playwright produced by a white company to feature a black in a leading role. The plays of Ridgeley Torrence went unmentioned, although in their case they might have been perceived as being unquestionably about black life, while O'Neill's drama could be said to have more universal application. Only much later did students of the drama realize that for all its venturesomeness, in one respect the play represented no advance. Thus, a typical speech of Jones's—"Who dare whistle dat way in my palace? Who dare wake up de Emperor? I'll git de hide frayled off some o' you niggers sho'!"—hardly represented any change in purported black speech as heard in the "Yas sah" or "Yes'm. I seed them" of earlier entries. After running out its first weeks in the Village, the play was moved up to Broadway, first to the Selwyn and then to the Princess, chalking up 204 showings.

For O'Neill the play, with its thrilling use of

expressionism and other modern and experimental techniques (such as the constant drumming), was another major landmark. For Gilpin, it marked the beginning and the end of his heyday. Although many concurred that he was the finest black actor of his time, his arrogance (he regularly changed lines in the play if he chose to) and his growing alcoholism destroyed his chances for greatness. The drama also furthered the career of Cleon Throckmorton, whose austere, poetically stylized settings belied the restrictive nature of the tiny stage.

· · ·

Cleon Throckmorton (1897–1965) was born in Atlantic City and studied at both the Carnegie Institute of Technology and George Washington University. He had embarked on a career as a landscape and figure painter before switching callings. Although he would create many fine settings for Broadway, he remained loyal to the small playhouses in the Village throughout the decade. Later he also drew up architectural plans for many eventually famous summer theatres.

· · ·

The Charles Coburns, looking for a successor to *The Better 'Ole*, took a gamble on Reginald Berkeley's London comedy, **French Leave** (11-8-20, Belmont) and lost. The public had tired of war yarns, and this one was perceived as sadly thin. Mrs. Coburn received mixed notices, one critic saying he made her heroine commonplace. Coburn himself was seen as fitting "to a nicety" the part of the blustering English brigadier-general, while unlucky Dallas Welford was applauded for his cockney mess corporal. Mrs. Coburn played the wife of a British officer (Alexander Onslow) who attempts to visit him at a rest retreat not far from the trenches in France by disguising herself as a Parisian chanteuse, Mlle. Juliette. She is caught by the general, mistaken for a spy the British are seeking, and brought up before a military tribunal. But when the general learns the truth he is forgiving.

The new attraction at another tiny house was even less acceptable. **The Mandarin** (11-9-20, Princess), taken by Herman Bernstein from an unidentified German play by Paul Frank, was handed some of the most derisive notices of the year. A stranger (Mario Majeroni) hands a love-starved baron (Brandon Tynan) a Chinese doll which has the power of wish fulfillment. After a time the baron becomes sated with romance, finds the doll will not stop the parade of women coming to him, so attempts to strangle the stranger. He then wakes up and realizes he is an inmate in a mental institution, as are all the figures in his dream.

Many of the same critics who bashed *The Mandarin* confessed to being baffled by Shaw's **Heartbreak House** (11-10-20, Garrick), which dealt with the seeming inevitabilty of war and Englishmen's ineffectual attempts at handling it. Robert Benchley was among the confessedly puzzled, yet he urged his readers not to worry about precise meanings but simply to go and have fun. "I always feel very clever after a Shaw play," he told them, adding, "I think that I look clever, too." Critics extolled Lee Simonson's setting of Captain Shotover's home, designed, as Shaw specified, to resemble the inside of an old ship. But the aisle-sitters were not completely happy with the cast, particularly Albert Perry as Shotover. Their plaudits went to Helen Westley as the nurse, Lucile Watson as Lady Utterword, Effie Shannon as Hesione, and Dudley Digges as Mangan. For all the critical reservations the play was a major hit for the Theatre Guild, running sixteen weeks and initiating the group's long relationship with Shaw.

The fourth importation in a row was **Thy Name Is Woman** (11-15-20, Playhouse), Benjamin F. Glazer's adaptation of Karl Schönherr's *Der Weibsteufel*. Pedro (José Ruben), a cagey old smuggler in the Pyrenees, learning of a plan to get to him through his wife (Mary Nash) by sending a handsome young soldier (Curtis Cooksey) to woo her, tells her to divert the soldier long enough for him to move some contraband. But when the wife and the soldier fall in love, Pedro kills the woman and is arrested.

A fifth importation was **Samson and Delilah** (11-17-20, Greenwich Village), a translation of Sven Lange's Danish drama by Samuel S. Grossman. Peter Krumback, an idealistic poet and playwright, has written an allegorical stage piece in which Samson represents high art while Delilah stands for cheap, money-grubbing theatre happy to sell out to a low-class public. At a rehearsal Peter's wife, Dagmar (Pauline Lord), plays the siren with great fervor until Peter comprehends that she is actually playing to her lover, Sophus Meyers (Robert T. Haines), a rich furniture dealer who is sitting in the audience. He goes to shoot the lovers but instead shoots himself. The reason most critics jumped in celebration of Arthur Hopkins's production was that it marked the English-speaking debut of small, dark [Jacob] Ben Ami, a young actor who had already made his mark in Russia and in Yiddish theatre. Hornblow called him "an actor of temperament and poetic feeling with a thorough command of the continental methods of stage expression. . . . He has a fine dramatic sense and a keen disposition to the more advanced phases of naturalism." The critic did note that his accent sometimes made him unintelligible and bewailed that "his astonishing somersault after he shoots himself smacks more of acrobatics than of histrionism." Ignoring the somersault, Woollcott proclaimed him "an actor endowed with a bodily eloquence and a tragic mask unequalled in our theatre . . . mobile, beautiful, exquisitely expressive. . . . There is in his acting, when he wishes, that curious glowing quality that always defies description." Many reviewers were upset by Pauline Lord, who even at this juncture seemed to be developing the jerky mannerisms and oddly broken speech that increased with the years. But they singled out the excellent performance of Edward G. Robinson as the director of the play within the play. Such notices helped the production compile 143 performances.

The first two American plays to follow this parade of foreign entries were little credit to native dramaturgy. Kate L. McLaurin's **When We Are Young** (11-22-20, Broadhurst) reminded several critics of *The Cinderella Man*, not merely because of a similarity in story but because Henry Hull was playing a role so similar to that his late brother had assumed in the earlier comedy. Only instead of being an impoverished poet living in a garret, Carey Harper (Hull) is a once very rich young man who has squandered his fortune and has taken rooms in a boardinghouse. And instead of having his Princess Charming, food-laden basket in hand, come to him across neighboring roofs, he meets pretty Annie Laurie Brown (Alma Tell), a fellow boarder, when she knocks on his door hoping to borrow some sugar. She arrives just in time to prevent him from committing suicide and promptly gets to work injecting him with the spunk and determination to make something of himself.

Daddy Dumplins (11-22-20, Republic) was put into theatrical form by George Barr McCutcheon and Earl Carroll from "Mr. Bingle," a short story by McCutcheon. It begins and ends on succeeding Christmas Eves, which gives a clue to its nature. The first Christmas Eve finds paunchy but jolly Henry Dumplins (Maclyn Arbuckle), an almost Dickensian albeit American bookkeeper who has inherited a fortune and a magnificent country home from his late employer, entertaining seven youngsters whom he has adopted. But when the late employer's will is contested, the courts side against Dumplins. He loses not only his home and bank account but the children as well. Happily, the heart of the villain (Percy Moore), who is the late employer's son and is secretly the father of one of the children (Florence Flinn) Dumplins had taken in, eventually is softened by the child he so long denied. She reconciles the

two men. The second Christmas Eve finds everyone gathered in Dumplins's small apartment, knowing they will soon have more money and comfort again.

The first American hit in three weeks was Clare Kummer's **Rollo's Wild Oat** (11-23-20, Punch and Judy), although opening-night jitters or inadequate rehearsals played havoc with the initial performance. Rollo Webster (Roland Young), an oddball if amiable heir to an air brake fortune, has little interest in business. His burning ambition is to act Hamlet. Using his own funds, he sets up a mounting, hiring an attractive, if not very bright young lady, Goldie MacDuff (Lotus Robb), for his Ophelia. Goldie has taken to the stage to support herself, but she has lost out on a chance for a part in *The Midnight Frolics* because she cannot remain awake so late. She accepts the role of Ophelia despite her doubts about whether *Hamlet* is really a good, clean play. On opening night Goldie interrupts one of Hamlet's big scenes to tell Rollo that his grandfather is dying. After Rollo has dashed offstage to be with the old man, a flustered stage manager comes before the curtain to ask if there is another Hamlet in the house. Finally, Rollo's stagestruck, slightly effeminate butler and dresser (Ivan Simson) is hurried into a costume, which, it quickly develops, has not been sewn together properly. At home Rollo discovers his grandfather alive and well. The old man's ruse was simply to keep Rollo from making a fool of himself. Having nothing better to do, a defeated Rollo asks Goldie to marry him, and she accepts. Although the multi-scened, large-cast comedy was somewhat cramped on its tiny stage, performances quickly improved, and the comedy ran out the season profitably.

Paul Dickey and Charles W. Goddard's **The Broken Wing** (11-29-20, 48th St.) ran almost as long—22 weeks. One spectacular scene no doubt lured in some of the trade. In the beautiful Mexican home of Luther Farley (Henry Duggan), an American, his foster daughter, Inez Villera (Inez Plummer), waits in hope that a "gringo" lover will appear and sweep her off her feet. He almost literally does. For at the end of the first of four acts, "an aeroplane crashes into the setting, tears away part of a [rear] wall, and the startled audience hears a great whirring of wings, the moans from the injured men, and views the wreckage . . . through a cloud of smoke." One of the men dragged from the wreckage is handsome, blond Philip Marvin (Charles Trowbridge), and it seems the crash has destroyed his memory. But then a lot of things are not what they seem, for a number of the Americans turn out to be secret agents in disguise. While attending to government business they see to it that a Mexican bandit, Captain Innocencio Dos Santos (Alphonz Ethier), does not run off with Inez. They know how desperately he loves Inez when he agrees to bathe just to please her. She eventually flies away with Philip. The play employed lots of slang, and if Americans were always referred to by Mexicans as "gringos," they in turn called the Mexicans "greasers." One outstanding comic performance was that of George Abbott as a "breezy, uncouth pseudo oil man."

Some time earlier a youngster, Daisy Ashford, supposedly nine years old, caused a sensation by writing a novel which gave her child's-eye view of high society. As eventually dramatized by Margaret MacKenzie and Mrs. George Norman, it had a fleeting vogue in London. Now brought to America, **The Young Visitors** (11-29-20, 39th St.) garnered some encouraging reviews but so little patronage that it was hastily withdrawn. The piece, which began and ended with an actress (Grace Dougherty) impersonating the young author writing her story, was acted out with a slightly haughty seriousness against delightfully cartoonish settings while recounting how Ethel Monticue (Marie Goff) goes to London with Salteena (Herbert Yost), a butcher's ambitious but gauche son, and there meets and falls in love with Bernard Clark (Harold Anstruther), a gentleman.

More than half of December's novelties were to be importations, beginning with F. H. Rose's English fantasy **The Whispering Well** (12-5-20, Neighborhood Playhouse). The play was set in the eighteenth century and told how a greedy weaver (Whitford Kane) gives a devil who lives at the bottom of a well all his possessions in return for gold. His reward is to be pulled into the well and, presumably, all the way down to hell.

The month's first American entry was by an actor. Dodson Mitchell's **Cornered** (12-8-20, Astor), like *One* a few weeks earlier, dealt with twins—the sort of stage piece, as one critic noted, in which a player "must needs spend a large part of the performance sprinting to and fro behind the backdrop and breathlessly shifting . . . costumes." The same critic noted that a good measure of the applause usually was for these costume changes rather than for the play or players. But for many theatregoers the salient interest of the night was the return from films of Madge Kennedy, a young, much admired farceur. Naturally she played the twins, and she helped turn what might have originally been planned as just another crook play into a moderately successful comedy-drama. Some crooks, who hang out in a

New York chop suey joint, note the startling resemblance of their cohort Mary Brennan to the rich socialite Margaret Waring, so when they learn Miss Waring will be out of town for a few days they have Mary impersonate her and gain entry into her East Side home. But in the midst of the robbery Margaret returns and is shot. Mary, unable to escape, must hide and impersonate Margaret whenever someone appears. However, an amulet reveals that Mary is Margaret's long-lost sister—lost in a ship's sinking, rescued by a tramp steamer, and taken to Hong Kong, where she was raised by criminals. Mary, it also turns out, is a mind reader, further suggesting the similarity with the sisters in *One*. As Margaret, Miss Kennedy got to wear several beautiful dresses, including a dinner gown "of shell pink panne velvet girdled and sashed with satin and tulle, which balances the one-sided drapery." The consensus was that her time in films had neither hurt nor improved the star's art. Several critics reported the rumor that Zelda Sears was Mitchell's uncredited collaborator, and, curiously, one even praised her performance as the manager of the chop suey joint, although she is not listed on any program.

Several important players heretofore associated with the Theatre Guild broke away from that group after artistic differences and mounted St. John Ervine's **Mixed Marriage** (12-14-20, Bramhall Playhouse). Technically the mounting was a revival, since it had been included in the repertory of the Irish players some seasons before. It described how a unionist (Augustin Duncan), hoping to fight his employers' attempt to set workers against each other on religious grounds, discovers that he himself is hopelessly prejudiced. The play ran four months in the tiny auditorium.

James M. Barrie's **Mary Rose** (12-22-20, Empire) for a time announced as bringing Maude Adams out of her retirement, came to town with Ruth Chatterton instead. Aisle-sitters felt she was no Maude Adams, not even a Fay Compton, who had originated the role in London. Still, they recommended that their readers see this play about a strange young woman who disappears and returns decades later, still young as before, while all her family have aged or died. Enough readers complied to give the play, like *Mixed Marriage,* a four-month run.

On the other hand, aided by a splendid David Belasco production and a solid though not great performance by Lionel Atwill, Granville Barker's translation of Sacha Guitry's **Deburau** (12-23-20, Belasco) ran out the season. The wheel of fortune turns swiftly and brutally for the famed pantomimist who had put the Théâtre des Funambules on the Parisian theatrical map. Deserted by his mistress, Marie Duplessis (Elsie Mackay), he also discovers that he has lost the knack of delighting audiences. He is hissed off the stage. He grudgingly gives his costumes and makeup to his son (Morgan Farley), hoping thus to achieve a modicum of immortality. Belasco's magnificent stage pictures included a view of the outside of the theatre with the public pressing for seats, the inside of the playhouse packed with celebrities and more ordinary playgoers, and the view from backstage.

Brock Pemberton, who had scored handsomely with his first production, *Enter Madame,* earned an unexpected Pulitzer Prize with his second, Zona Gale's dramatization of her own best-seller **Miss Lulu Bett** (12-27-20, Belmont). Lulu Bett (Carroll McComas) drudges through her dismal existence at the home of her sister, Ina (Catherine Calhoun Doucet), and her brother-in-law, Dwight Deacon (William E. Holden). During a visit of Dwight's brother, Ninian (Brigham Royce), Ninian jokingly flirts with Lulu, so Dwight, keeping up the jest, reads the civil marriage ceremony to them, and Lulu and Ninian respond in a playful spirit. Then Dwight realizes he has actually married them. The pair goes off on their honeymoon, only to have Lulu return disconsolately, announcing she has found out that Ninian is already married. News that Ninian's first wife has died leads to a happy ending. The play gave Carroll McComas, until now a leading lady in musical comedy and straight plays, a chance to appear as a bedraggled slavey before metamorphosing into a beautiful woman. She carried off both aspects well. While some reviewers were pleased with the dramatization, many others felt it was inferior to the novel or even essentially undramatic. But playgoers kept the work running into the summer. Even so, especially considering some of the more original works to premiere during the season, a consensus suggested the Pulitzer Prize was as undeserved as it was unexpected.

O'Neill's growing fame still could not lure most first-string critics to his opening nights, particularly, as in the case of **Diff'rent** (12-27-20, Provincetown Playhouse), if they conflicted with an opening at an uptown playhouse. But most critics came on the second night, albeit some waited until this new play followed the route *The Emperor Jones* had taken in moving up from the village. The tragedy centered on Emma Crosby (Mary Blair), who is engaged to Caleb Williams (James Light), a sea captain. But she breaks off the engagement after learning he has slept with girls he came across in the South Sea islands. Thirty

years later she remains a spinster, plying on hair dye and makeup to give an image of perpetual youthfulness. Finally the lonely woman succumbs to the entreaties of a dashing, self-serving, good-for-nothing soldier, Benny (Charles Ellis). Williams learns of this and confronts Emma. She begs him not to hurt the soldier. He assures her he won't but adds sneeringly, "Thirty o' the best years of my life flung for a yeller dog like him to feed on. God! You used to say you was diff'rent from the rest o' folks. By God, if you are, it's just you're a mite madder'n they be!." He hangs himself, and, after Emma learns of his suicide, it is obvious that she will kill herself, too. The play was seen as not up to *Beyond the Horizon* or *The Emperor Jones* but worthwhile nonetheless. The *World* lauded O'Neill's "boldly drawn and closely scrutinzied" characters, while the *Sun* hailed "the strongest, truest, finest and most inherently honest dramatic dialogue" on the American stage. As a result, partly "on the waves of renown" newly achieved by O'Neill, the drama ran for 100 performances.

At the Lexington Opera House, a barn of a theatre that served various functions, Fritz Leiber, an attractive young Shakespearean player, came in on the same night offering a repertory that allowed him to play Hamlet, Romeo, Othello, Marc Antony (in *Julius Caesar*), Shylock, and Macbeth. His settings were designed to be interchangeable from play to play, and he charged less than standard Broadway prices. So with critics welcoming him as an intelligent, theatrically effective if not brilliant player, he did acceptable business.

The new year began with a hit. In Thomas Louden and A. E. Thomas's **The Champion** (1-3-21, Longacre) William Burroughs (Grant Mitchell) returns after fifteen years to the snobbish English home he ran away from as a teenager. He ran all the way to America. His old home is the sort of place where "attorney" is considered vulgar American slang for "barrister." And where, when William tells his father he has served for a spell as an ordinary seaman, his shocked father asks, "Have you *ever* had any sort of decent, gentlemanly occupation?" William discovers that one of his pliable brothers has dutifully become a minister, the other a politician— conservative, of course. To their horror William is for the common man: "The tide of democracy is rising and the man who tries to dam it will *be* damned." However, their horror knows no bounds when they learn that William has become Gunboat Williams, a prizefighter.

Burroughs: My son—a common prize-fighter!
William: No, Father.

Burroughs: You deny it?
Williams: Not common, Father. I was the champion.

It soon develops that was several years ago, and since then William has been elected a congressman ("a man who goes to Washington to misrepresent the people"). In short order, William uses his fists to put a snooty nobleman in his place, his father comes to realize how admired and wealthy his son is, and William wins the hand of a gracious English lady who had been intended for one of his wimpy brothers and who had been cheated by the snooty nobleman. The play was slight and the English accents of most of the cast heard as ridiculous. But Mitchell's charm, crisp delivery, and comic flair lured in patrons.

Hallem Thompson's **Transplanting Jean** (1-3-21, Cort), which he took from de Flers and de Caillavet's *Papa,* proved less alluring. Produced by Arthur Byron as a vehicle for himself it described how an old boulevardier of a count decides to legitimatize a son (Richard Barbee) he has allowed to languish far away in the Pyrenees. He soon falls in love with his son's fiancée (Margaret Lawrence) and decides to marry her himself and take her back to Paris. The young man is perfectly happy remaining in the backwaters.

The popular composer Sigmund Romberg, having broken with the Shuberts, had set up his own production company with an associate. The men produced a pair of musicals (by Romberg) and a straight play whose failures sent Romberg back to allowing other men to mount his works. The straight-play flop was Charles Anthony's **Pagans** (1-4-21, Princess). Its leading figure was a crippled artist who has married a nice but uncomprehending girl (Regina Wallace) on the rebound, after being rejected by the woman he loved. That woman (Helen Ware) is now a great opera singer, yet when she learns that the artist is dying she throws up her schedule to be near him and help him. While the two women quibble over who can best aid the man, he dies. The evening was memorable only for the Broadway debut (as the artist) of Joseph Schildkraut, who had already won attention for his Shylock at the Jewish Art Theatre.

The Jonathan of Hatcher Hughes and Elmer Rice's **Wake Up, Jonathan!** (1-17-21, Henry Miller's) was Jonathan Blake, a man (Charles Dalton) so obsessed with running a business and making money that his wife (Mrs. Fiske) has declined to continue living with him and his children hardly know him. Small wonder, then, that when he tries for a reconciliation everything seems against him, especially since his family has become fond of Adam West (Howard Lang), a failed writer who once had courted Mrs. Blake. But with persistence Blake wins a second chance. The play won only lukewarm notices, and the sole reason for its modest run (105 performances) was the lure of its star, who was not Dalton but Mrs. Fiske. The *American*'s Alan Dale, an admirer of hers from way back, told his readers, "Not in the halcyon period labeled heyday did Mrs. Fiske give as deliciously and artistically perfect a performance."

Luther Reed and Hale Hamilton's **Dear Me** (1-17-21, Republic) ran a mite longer. It begins in the Amos Prentice Home for Artistic and Literary Failures, where April Blair (Grace La Rue) is a beloved slavey who writes herself encouraging "Dear Me" letters. Enter a new resident, seedy but young and handsome Edgar Craig (Hamilton), who overhears April singing, turns her into a musical comedy star, and by eleven o'clock has started all the other residents on their own roads to success. Edgar's real name, it seems, is Edgar Craig Prentice, and he is the son of the home's founder. He is also Prince Charming, who wins the hand of April, née, no doubt, Cinderella.

In 1921, William Archer was known as a respected English drama critic, the first important English translator of Ibsen, and a friend of Shaw. Strangely, his one and only original play of any importance was a claptrap melodrama and was given its first production not in England but in America. Yet the claptrap was so astute and literate, and the production so splendid, that **The Green Goddess** (1-18-21, Booth) not only became one of the era's most successful and memorable plays but also gave its name to a salad, a salad dressing, a distinct type of jewelry, and possibly other more ephemeral fads. For the second time in recent weeks a crashed plane figured importantly in a play, only this time the curtain rose to show the plane already down. Little more than a wing is visible atop some rocks, for the plane has landed in a gorge in the Himalayas. On the right, a cave in the hills has been converted into a temple dominated by a huge green idol. The victims of the wreck are three English citizens: Traherne (Cyril Keightley), a distinguished scientist and amateur flyer; Lieutenant Cardew (Herbert Ransome), a querulous, alcoholic soldier; and Lucilla (Olive Wyndham), his long-suffering wife. The crash brings to the site a procession of savage warriors, elaborately bedecked court figures, and their raja (George Arliss). The raja is a suave, Western-educated man, who politely welcomes his guests. But there is something menacing in his smiling suavity. The newcomers hope that he is unaware that three of his countrymen have been sentenced to death by the British in India. Unfortunately for them, he is aware, and it soon becomes obvious that the three English arrivals will be killed if the raja's half-brothers are executed. The English eventually attempt to send a wireless for aid but are caught, and Cardew is shot to death. Fortunately the message got through. The British fly in soldiers to rescue their stranded compatriots. The raja had promised to spare Lucilla if she would become part of his harem. With the soldiers and his hostages gone, he can only rationalize, "Well, well—she'd probably have been a damned nuisance." For all its theatrical excellences, the chief virtue of the evening was Arliss's performance. Woollcott celebrated it by noting, "With countenance at once gentle and diabolic, with his cat-like tread, and with his uneasy but sinister hands, he seems to have been roaming our stage all his days in wistful quest of a play about a raja with richly encrusted garments, a sardonic humor and an evil heart."

The few critics who attended Butler Davenport's revival of *The Importance of Being Earnest* at the Bramhall Playhouse on the 20th (with Davenport naturally assuming the role of Jack Worthing) waved it away much as they did Davenport's novelties.

A critical drubbing was also the lot of the Theatre Guild's latest mounting, David Liebovits's **John Hawthorne** (1-24-21, Garrick). It survived its evening opening only long enough to play for a few special matinees. Its hero (Warren Kreck) is an atheist in love with the wife (Muriel Starr) of his fanatically religious employer (Eugene Ordway). He kills the man and runs off with the wife, who, failing to convert him, turns him over to the police.

Ruth Draper, who had played only briefly in regular stage works, had taken to presenting monologues, all of which she wrote herself. She had been acclaimed in London and now, after repeating her best pieces at the Princess on the 27th, had New York at her feet. For the next several decades she would return at intervals with these and new monologues. She never again was seen in a standard play.

Good acting gave **In the Night Watch** (1-29-21, Century), which Michael Morton took from Claude Farrère and Lucien Népoty's *La Veille d'armes,* its modest success. Captain de Corlaix (Robert Warwick) of the crusier *Alma,* having a birthday party for his wife, Eugénie (Jeanne Eagels), aboard ship, suddenly must get all his guests ashore without their knowing war has been declared. His wife, hurt at his apparently abrupt behavior, takes refuge in the cabin of Lieutenant Brambourg (Cyril Scott), her lover. The ship sails with her on board and is sunk by the Germans. The captain and his wife are rescued, but when the captain is brought up for court-martial only Eugénie's testimony saves him. He forgives her peccadillo.

Although Harold Chapin's comedy **The New Morality** (1-30-21, Playhouse) was written some years before he was killed in the war, this was its first Broadway hearing. It received far better notices than *John Hawthorne* but, like that drama, lasted only for a few matinees following its evening premiere. During that time it told of how Betty Jones's verbal attacks on a woman who lives in a neighboring houseboat for entertaining a strange man nearly lead to a lawsuit. The appearances of Jones's lawyer brother (Warburton Gamble) and the neighboring woman's drunken husband (Lawrence Grossmith) complicate matters. Betty Jones was played by Grace George; the other woman never comes onstage. All the action took place in a few hours of a single evening.

A number of actors already had shown up this season in plays of their own writing. Willard Mack was the latest. His **Near Santa Barbara** (1-31-21, Greenwich Village) unfolded the adventures of a gambler (Mack) after the man to whom he owes $14,000 is found shot to death. It turns out that a good number of people wanted the man out of the way, and the hero is finally exonerated when the sheriff reveals he himself killed the man. Easterners got a fascinating glimpse of California weather during an evening thundershower when they were offered "a view of total blackness out of one window, brilliant moonlight out of another, and a warm, glowing sunset out of a third." But they had to hurry to see the phenomenon, for the play lasted only two weeks.

A second opening in the Village drew less attention. Actually, George Cram Cook's **The Spring** (1-31-21, Provincetown Playhouse) had given a single preview performance a week earlier. The play begins in 1813 at a spring near the Mississippi frequented by Sauk Indians. Looking in the waters, an Indian princess sees her father, the chief, shot at by a white sniper. As it happens, the shot misses, and the chief, admiring the sniper's courage in finally confronting him, adopts him into the tribe. A hundred years pass, and the site, with the spring still there, is the home of the sniper's grandson and great-grandson, Elijah (William Rainey). Elijah is a young professor working on psychic manifestations. He is visited by his superior, Dr. Chantland (Howard Smith), and Chantland's daughter, Esther (Lark Bronlee). When Elijah discovers that Esther sees visions in the spring he tells her, "I want a new sensitive—yourself—to approach the whole thing from a new angle. I want a new body of experiments in which the profound dramatic imagination of the unconscious shall not be enlisted in advance in the service of spiritualist doctrine. I want the subconscious to reveal its own sources of knowledge. Instead of suggesting to *your* unconscious: 'Reveal the spirits of the dead,' I want your writing to be born of the suggestion: 'Reveal yourself!' " But the experiments lead to tragedy, for the cold, unbelieving Chantland, feeling his daughter is being driven over the brink into insanity, vents his anger by striking Elijah, and Elijah, hitting back, accidentally kills the older man. Those critics who wrote about it found the play humorless and speechy. But Cook, who had been the prime mover in founding the Provincetown Players and who had grown jealous of O'Neill's success, insisted the play be moved uptown. It was, but soon succumbed to a lack of business. The financial setback eventually drove Cook away from the company and led to a reorganization. The troupe was never again the same.

Twenty-four performances, mostly matinees, was the fate of Johann Sigurjonsson's Icelandic tragedy **Eyvind of the Hills** (2-1-21, Greenwich Village), which was admired by many commentators but correctly deemed too strong and unyielding for most theatregoers. It told of a cruel widow (Margaret Wycherly) who murders her own children and runs off with an outlawed thief (Arthur Hohl). Their hard life in a hard land destroys their love for each other, so they commit suicide by heading out together into a blizzard. Once again winning special commendation was Edward G. Robinson, this time as a young man who loves the widow and tries vainly to help her.

A theatre shortage and divided notices confined to a series of matinees the run of **The White Villa** (2-14-21, Eltinge), which Edith Ellis took from Karen Michaelis's Danish novel *The Dangerous Age*. After a legacy makes her independent, Elsie Lindtner (Lucile Watson) leaves her husband and builds herself a villa on an isolated island. When she grows lonely, she summons a young architect (Frank Morgan) who once had said he loved her. She learns he is engaged and no longer interested, so she tries to rekindle the ardor of her husband (Edward Ellis), but he, too, is about to marry a younger, more sympathetic woman. Elsie is left to accept that her life will probably remain empty.

Hours after the curtain rang down at the Eltinge it rose at the Cort on a return of *Peg o' My Heart*, which had first played there nine years earlier. What counted most was that Laurette Taylor once again was Peg, and, as an added bonus, Michael was still her shabby little mutt, albeit by now he seemed a bit better fed. The play did eleven weeks of good business.

Three nights later, on the 17th, Arthur Hopkins brought in his production of *Macbeth,* with Lionel Barrymore as star. The reaction was one of outrage, typified by Benchley, who wailed, "The Hopkins theory, as nearly as can be ascertained, was to eliminate all nonessential things from the stage and the acting, leaving Shakespeare in the essence. Unfortunately they left the eliminator on too long, and not even Shakespeare was left." Reviewers agreed that Barrymore's king was dissuadingly flat, but what really stoked their annoyance were Robert Edmond Jones's scenery and costumes, which Hornblow condemned as "abnormal and artistically perverted . . . aberrations." Woollcott, equally disturbed, described some in detail. He was not unhappy with occasionally stunning moments, such as the king and queen (Julia Arthur), in blood-red robes, standing in a pool of light surrounded by blackness. On the other hand, there was the opening: "The curtain rises on a black-curtained stage of infinite depth and height. Glaring down on the centre are three five foot masks of dull silver. The eyes of these masks focus on a ring around which stand three indeterminate figures in crimson crepe. These red and midnight hags wear masks of bronze through which their girlish voices drone something inaudible." The production was withdrawn quickly.

Down at the Neighborhood Playhouse, the company restored Arnold Bennett's *The Great Adventure,* a failure in its initial American production, to the stage on the 25th.

For the second time within a month Willard Mack took on the leading role in a play he himself wrote, **Smooth as Silk** (2-22-21, Lexington). In fact, he announced that he had written and staged the whole affair in a mere ten days. "Silk" Malone (Mack) is allowed to escape from prison so that he can get the goods on Freeman Holding (Joseph Sweeney), an internationally sought crook posing as an investigator of civic corruption. He does, but when he also wins the heart of a sweet young thing, he tears himself away lest his own shady life spoil hers.

The last Monday in February brought in a bill of four one-acters by Clare Kummer (to mixed notices), an importation, a revival, and a new offering downtown. There was also a special matinee performance of **The Cradle Song,** a play which would not be given a major mounting on Broadway for several years. The importation was A. A. Milne's **Mr. Pim Passes By** (2-28-21, Garrick). It depicted the consternation Mr. Pim (Erskine Sanford) creates when he happens to mention to Mr. Marden (Dudley Digges) that he has just seen the first husband of the widow (Laura Hope Crews) Marden recently has wed. Affairs are set right after the dim-witted Pim realizes it was not the late Mr. Tellworthy he saw but one Mr. Polwittle. The comedy gave the Theatre Guild a solid hit.

The revival at the Playhouse was the 1913 success *Romance,* with Doris Keane, fresh from her London triumph in the play, repeating her original role.

In the Village, Evelyn Scott's **Love** (2-28-21, Provincetown Playhouse) received its premiere. A virago of a mother-in-law (Virginia Chauvenet) drives her new daughter-in-law (Ida Rauh) into the arms of the son (William Rainey) of the husband's first marriage, and this drives the husband (Marlyn Brown) to suicide.

The Tyranny of Love (3-1-21, Bijou), which Henry Baron Americanized from Georges de Porto-Riche's *Amoureuse,* was another work forced by the theatre crunch to premiere at a matinee. Its notices were sufficiently encouraging to allow, after a string of additional afternoon performances at several theatres, for it to move into another playhouse for a brief run in May. Estelle Winwood earned the loudest kudos for her performance in a role Réjane had played in French for Americans on her visit thirteen years before. That was the part of a young, love-starved, clinging-vine wife who so exhausts her aging, preoccupied scientist-husband (Charles Cherry) that he tells her to find a lover. For a time she does, but the couple eventually reach a workaday understanding.

March's biggest hit was Rachel Crothers's **Nice People** (3-2-21, Klaw), which opened yet another new playhouse. When his sister-in-law, Margaret Rainsford (Merle Maddern), tells the widowed Herbert Gloucester (Frederick Perry) that his twenty-year-old daughter, Teddy (Francine Larrimore), is too young to go around unchaperoned and criticizes her smoking, drinking, and kissing in public, Gloucester insists, "It's the way things *are.* The manners of yesterday have nothing to do with the case. This is to-day." But when Teddy pops in very late to change coats and go out again until the wee hours, Gloucester changes his tune and orders her to stay in. She waits until after the old folks have gone to bed to sneak out again. And she stays out the whole night with friends, then drives around all day before actually spending a quite innocent second night with one of the young men (Hugh Huntley) at a country cottage her mother had bequeathed her.

Gloucester and Aunt Margaret find her there and insist she marry the boy. She refuses, and her father for all practical purposes disowns her. But Aunt Margaret stays with her and comes to understand that Teddy is a fundamentally decent girl. Moreover, that night she supposedly spent alone with the young man, another young man, Billy Wade (Robert Ames), storm-driven, took refuge with them. He is a bright fellow, unseduced by the ways of the modern smart set. He not only teaches Teddy how to turn the place into a working farm but, when Teddy comprehends that he loves her for herself and most definitely not for her father's money, gets her to accept his marriage proposal. Critics applauded the play, although some chafed at the well-off Miss Crothers's sometimes heavy-handed attacks on money. They had mixed feelings about the leading lady, decrying her voice as "cacophonous," "husky, unpleasant at times, and seemingly not under full control," and displaying "all the dissonance of a jazz band." They also berated other "numerous faults" such as her careless posture and curiously brash walk. Yet most conceded that for all her flaws her performance was effective. So were those by Ames, Perry, and Miss Maddern. Unmentioned for the most part was the playing of young Katharine Cornell as one of Teddy's friends. Another young actress, Tallulah Bankhead, as the booziest, cattiest of Teddy's friends did win several commendations. Interestingly, her very first speech foreshadowed the sort of talk she later would become ridiculed for. Wearing a pale purple-and-green dress, she is told she looks like an orchid. "That's what I'm supposed to look like—darling" is her reply.

On the afternoon of the 14th, Gilbert Emery's **The Hero** launched a series of trial matinees at the Longacre. The acclaim was such that the play was put away until it could be readied for a regular run the following season. (It will be dealt with at that time.)

George Atkinson's **The Survival of the Fittest** (3-14 21, Greenwich Village) was laughed off the stage after two weeks. It recounted how a big, strong man (Montague Love) wins a beautiful society woman (Laura Nelson Hall) away from an effete rival (George Le Guere). If one review is to be believed, one of the weakling's speeches, addressed to his more virile brother, ran, "Nay, Will, women have always fondled you and licked your boots because of your robust health and rosy cheeks."

John Drinkwater's **Mary Stuart** and a companion pantomime, Austin Strong's **A Man About Town** (3-21-21, Ritz), were the initial attractions at yet another new auditorium. Naturally Drinkwater's history was favorable to Mary (Clare Eames) and far less so to the craven, perfumed Riccio (Frank Reicher), the besotted, vicious Darnley (Charles Waldron), or the unprincipled Bothwell (Thurston Hall). But neither his approach nor his subject was of interest to New Yorkers.

They were perhaps a bit happier with Achmed Abdullah's **Toto** (3-21-21, Bijou), which was so freely Americanized from Maurice Hennequin and Félix Duquesnil's *Patachon* that Parisians might no longer recognize it. Antoine "Toto" de Tillois (Leo Ditrichstein) long ago left his dull, pious wife (Frances Underwood) to live the life of a boulevardier in Paris. But when his daughter Louise, (Phoebe Foster), insists she will not wed until her parents are reconciled, Toto agrees to try. Comic complications and a reconciliation follow.

Those critics who betook themselves to the Village were not deeply impressed by Susan Glaspell's **The Inheritors** (3-21-21, Provincetown Playhouse), but they were bowled over by the performance of a beautiful young blonde, Ann Harding. In no time, Broadway producers were beckoning to her. The play begins in the late 1870s when an idealistic midwestern pioneer, Silas Morton (George Cram Cook), founds a college dedicated to raising the level of each succeeding generation's knowledge and ethics. Forty years later Morton College needs to go to the state legislature for subsidies. Unfortunately, the problem of a radical professor (James Light) arises. Most of Morton's heirs are willing to sacrifice both Morton's principles and the professor to gain the funds, but Morton's granddaughter, Madeline (Harding), risks her reputation and even her personal well-being to save them.

According to several aisle-sitters, Vincent Lawrence's **The Ghost Between** (3-22-21, 39th St.) was good escapist entertainment even if it could not make up its mind whether it wanted to be comedy or drama. The reviews were enough to keep the play running comfortably into the summer. After the groom of less than a year of Ethel Brookes (Laura Walker) dies, the family physician (Arthur Byron) proposes to her. She demurs, but he offers a marriage in name only, if that will please her. She finally accepts, although she is not certain she can love Dr. Dillard. But when the husband's friend and protégé, the unconscionable, scampish Richard Hunt (Glenn Anders), suggests he and she elope, she realizes that she does love Dillard.

Considering the harvest of money notices that Augustus Thomas's **Nemesis** (4-4-21, Hudson) collected, its short run was unexpected. When aging, paunchy John Kallan (Emmett Corrigan) discovers his wife, Marcia (Olive Tell), is having a torrid affair with a youthful, strikingly handsome sculptor, Jovaine (Pedro de Cordoba), he plans a diabolic revenge. He takes some of Jovaine's fingerprints off a clay model Jovaine had been working on and has rubber stamps made of them. Following an impassioned quarrel with his wife, he stabs and kills her with a tiny nail file. Then, using the rubber stamps, he strews Jovaine's fingerprints on the file and elsewhere in the room and calls the police. The prosecuting attorney (John Blair) employs the prints to convict the protesting sculptor. At the gates to Sing Sing, once Jovaine has been executed, Kallan shows the prosecutor the stamps. The mortified man can only suggest forgetting the whole matter. Superior settings included a paneled courtroom filled with spectators as well as lawyers, jurors, and a judge. Whatever the reason for the play's failure (possibly the oncoming heat), Thomas passed over the work in his autobiography.

While many critics had ignored the premieres of several new American plays, which went on to runs and lasting fame, they all gathered at the Manhattan Opera House on the 7th for the single announced performance of Euripides' *Iphigenia in Aulis,* with Margaret Anglin starred as Clytemnestra. Walter Damrosch conducted a full symphony orchestra in his own background music. Apart from some disagreement on the formalized staging, reviewers rejoiced. Even the hardly intellectual *Telegram* proclaimed, "This splendid production is by far the supreme dramatic achievement of the season," and, calling Anglin "America's greatest tragic actress," added that the star's "lines were beautifully read, so clearly they could be heard even in the last rows, and yet none of their finer shadings were lost in the huge auditorium."

Recently Miss Anglin had given another special performance, a benefit for the Herbert Hoover Relief Fund, at the Century Theatre on Easter Sunday, March 27, of Astrid Argyll's translation of Émile Moreau's *The Trial of Joan of Arc.* The play was accompanied by music from Tchaikovsky's opera about the maid. (Bernhardt had played the original text for New Yorkers in 1910.) So lauded was the offering that it was remounted at the Shubert on the 12th for a month's stand. Although the forty-five-year-old star was growing buxom, Alan Dale reported, "The Joan of Arc that I saw in the person of Margaret Anglin was the visionary girl, the dreamer, the hearer of voices, the unforgettably pathetic figure."

Four nights later, on the 16th, a group of youthful players, led by Thomas Mitchell, revived *The*

Playboy of the Western World at the Bramhall without causing a stir.

But there was a stir a little further uptown. Ticket prices for what was touted as the most eagerly awaited premiere of the season were raised to a then shocking $5 per seat—and not only was the opening sold out, but speculators had a field day. The play was a family affair, for **Clair de Lune** (4-18-21, Empire) was by Michael Strange, whose husband and sister-in-law, John and Ethel Barrymore, were starred. The play did everyone in. John played Gwynplane, an aristocrat who became a mountebank clown after his face was savagely scarred by conniving courtiers. He travels with a blind dancer, Dea (Jane Cooper), who loves him although, of course, she cannot see him. The pair are soon romantically involved with a degenerate duchess (Violet Kemble Cooper) and a cynical prince (Henry Daniell), even though the duchess and the prince are supposed to wed. The Queen (Ethel Barrymore) intrigues to stop the wedding. The machinations end in tragedy. Dea, thinking she has lost Gwynplane, dies of a broken heart; Gwynplane commits suicide. Barrymore made his first entrance doing somersaults, then did a small bit in pantomime. But afterwards he was stuck with such awkward, pretentious speeches as "But my heart is here, underneath your slender foot. O, my heart has no will of its own but is only a reckless fever leaping, shivering after crumbs of your favour." Ethel Barrymore, slim after a recent illness, looked gorgeous in a series of beautiful period gowns, but she, too, was burdened with lines on the order of "There are many things you might not understand: for instance, there is a love that is half hatred. It is sprinkled into life in a rather strange manner—by wounds. However, I am becoming sentimental and I hate sentimentality. It reminds me of people with colds in their heads who have lost their pocket handkerchiefs." A strong advance sale, and Barrymore's angry letters assailing critics and published in the newspapers, allowed the drama to run out its ten-week engagement.

The Barrymores' bad luck was called to mind again the next night as Walter Hampden began a stand in a Shakespearean repertory at the Broadhurst. He opened with the same *Macbeth* that had so thrown Lionel and followed this with *The Taming of the Shrew* and *The Merchant of Venice*. His Shylock surprised some commentators, for it was a throwback, much like Mansfield's, to the pre-Macklin days, a filthy, venal old Jew. Critics welcomed all the player's presentations as solid and acceptable but unexciting. Woollcott suggested that for all his

virtues, Hampden was an actor "whose mechanics are ever as visible as those of a machine making breakfast food in a shop window, one who is merely lugubrious where a fine actor would be tragic." At the end of his engagement he gave a few performances of his 1908 success *The Servant in the House.*

The season's last major success was an importation, but it was also one of the most memorable productions of the era, Benjamin F. Glazer's translation of Ferenc Molnár's **Liliom** (4-20-21, Garrick). In Hungarian the word, although it also means a lily, connotes a roughneck, and Molnar's subtitle can be translated as "The Life and Death of a Chickensnatcher." But in the play Liliom (Joseph Schildkraut) is the name of the central figure, a carnival barker. Julie (Eva Le Gallienne), a serving girl, falls in love with him, despite her friends' admonitions, and marries him. He is an abusive, unfaithful spouse, until he learns his wife is pregnant. Then it is not hard for a vicious hood known as "The Sparrow" (Dudley Digges) to talk Liliom into helping in a robbery, so that Liliom can obtain funds. But Liliom stabs himself to death when the robbery goes awry and he foresees capture. In heaven he pleads for a chance to return to earth, and the plea is granted. Regrettably, an unregenerate Liliom steals a star to bring to his daughter (Evelyn Chard), who is now sixteen years old, and he slaps her when she rebuffs him. He is led back to heaven. Lee Simonson's settings, including a carnival, a lonely spot in a park, a railroad embankment, a celestial court, and a modest home, were poetically atmospheric. All but the park, whose silhouetted trees rose almost to the flies, were simple and low-lying with a large expanse of sky in the rear, the lighting altered from scene to scene to imply different times of day or night. Reviewers understood and accepted Molnár's dichotomy of reality and fantasy and, for the most part, praised all the principals. A few dissenting words were heard, with, for example, Le Gallienne being slapped as "too refined" and for her off-putting mannish bob. While some of the most glowing comments went to Helen Westley for her overpainted, sharp-tongued carousel owner, the plaudits accorded them confirmed Le Gallienne as a star and rocketed Schildkraut to stardom as well. Glowing comments also smoothed the road for the play's designer.

· · ·

Eva Le Gallienne (1899–1992), the daughter of the English novelist and poet Richard Le Gallienne, was born in London and trained at the Royal Academy of Dramatic Arts. She performed for a short time in England before making her New York debut in *Mrs. Boltay's Daughters* (1915) and won celebrity with her performance in *Not So Long Ago* (1920). She was a tiny woman, with a small, tight-featured face. Even in later years her acting would be criticized for being too studiously mannered, but her intelligence and dedication were never questioned.

· · ·

Joseph Schildkraut (1896–1964), the Viennese-born son of the famous German and Yiddish actor Rudolf Schildkraut, prepared for his stage career both in Germany and at New York's American Academy of Dramatic Arts. He made his American debut opposite his father in German-language productions at the Irving Place Theatre in 1910, then spent time in Germany working with Max Reinhardt and others before returning to America to make his English-speaking debut earlier in this same season in a quick failure. He was a swarthy, dashingly handsome man, whose performances onstage were said to vary greatly from evening to evening. At his best, especially in his early years, he conveyed a sex-laden charm.

· · ·

Lee Simonson (1888–1967) was born in New York. He studied at Harvard, including courses with Professor George Pierce Baker. His earliest commercial work was with the Washington Square Players. After serving in World War I, he became one of the founders of the Theatre Guild and did much of his subsequent work for them, creating not only settings and lighting but sometimes even costumes. In later years he wrote several books on set design.

· · ·

Rave notices gave the Theatre Guild its biggest hit to date, with a run listed variously from 285 to 311 performances. In 1945 it was turned into *Carousel* by Rodgers and Hammerstein.

In Adelaide Matthews and Anne Nichols's **Just Married** (4-26-21, Comedy) a very drunk Robert Adams (Lynne Overman) staggers into a stateroom, peers out into the night at the sea, and indignantly phones the purser to ask, "What is the idea of all this water?" He then passes out on a bed. By mistake Adams has been given the key to the cabin of another passenger, Roberta Adams (Vivian Martin), and when she awakes in the morning a very startled young lady in pink pajamas confronts a slightly headachy, puzzled man in creased evening wear in the next bed. The usual complications ensue, until Roberta decides that while she will not change her name, she will marry Robert. Critics did handstands saluting Overman's brilliant, throwaway farcical underplaying and hailing him as a future star. That was not to be, but the farce, which had excellent settings showing the ship at its pier and

various public places on the vessel, ran until the cool weather returned.

Morris Wittman's **The Sacrifice** (5-2-21, Greenwich Village) apparently was a vanity production since the leading role was played by a woman listed, depending on whom you read, as his wife or his daughter. Yolan Wittman played Camilla Tauber, a Philadelphia Jewess courted by Benedict Arnold (George McManus). She comes to realize how perfidious he is, berates him, and goes on to fight and die for her country in stolen regimentals. The dud lasted one week.

The season's last play was Eugene O'Neill's **Gold** (6-1-21, Frazee). It spotlighted a sea captain (Willard Mack), who stumbles on what he believes is buried treasure, kills to keep it, reburies it, and becomes obsessed with the idea of returning to dig it up. He begins to lose his mind. His son, Nat (E. J. Ballantine), for a time comes to accept his father's word, but after the old captain shows him a small piece of the hoard he has cached away all these years, the boy realizes it is merely brass and tells him so. The shock is too much for the man. To his daughter (Geraldine O'Brien) went the last words of the season: "Oh, Nat—he's dead—I think—he's dead!" Even critics who liked the play conceded that it was not up to O'Neill's best, while the naysayers frequently pointed to its unrelieved gloom. The play's run was short. Interestingly, although O'Neill had enjoyed a good season, he later told friends that he earned only about $15,000 in 1921. The more commercially minded Avery Hopwood had grossed more than thirty times as much.

1921–1922

Variety counted 142 new straight plays during the season, plus a handful of non-musical revivals; *Best Play*'s figure was 130. No matter which total is accepted it represented a huge jump over prior figures and, as such, a new record. That could be seen as good news, but wasn't by everyone. Although the quality of the top entries remained satisfyingly high, the deluge brought with it a distressingly large amount of flotsam and jetsam. And playgoers found ticket prices beginning to creep up again. However, the dismaying number of flops soon took a toll on costs of admission. At the beginning of the season *Variety* noted that last year *Clair de Lune* had ventured a $5.00 top, which had failed largely because the mounting itself was not fully satisfactory, and the tradesheet reported several major producers planned price increases in the new term. By mid-September those optimistic plans had evaporated. In its issue of the 16th, the publication gloomily headlined "Broadway Bad—Worst Legit Season in Years," and when a late summer and early fall heat wave hit, business plummeted further. On October 5, the paper predicted lower, not higher, prices, and a little over one month later it carried an item announcing one producer's plan to bring in a new show at a $1.50 top. That particular show never came in, and during the season $2.00 and $3.00 remained the basic top ticket prices. Whether playgoers decided on the basis of quality or prices, they remained unhappy. Business continued limp throughout the theatrical year.

The new actors' union, increasingly coming under the control of left-wing troublemakers, raised an outcry against foreign performers playing on Broadway. In the very issue in which it assailed the proposal to restrict them, *Theatre* ran a full page of portraits entitled "Foreign Actors Dominate Broadway," offering photographs of Leo Ditrichstein (Austria), George Arliss (England), Joseph Schildkraut (listed inaccurately as coming from Hungary), Jacob Ben Ami (Russia), Pedro de Cordoba (Spain), and José Ruben (France). Miles away from Broadway in Washington religious extremists badgered Congress to pass a theatrical censorship law. Congress considered a bill, but cooler heads prevailed. William McAdoo, a politically cynical politician with his eye on the 1924 Democratic nomination, opened fire on Broadway at the same time, writing an article for the *Saturday Evening Post* proclaiming the need for censorship. In January a large rally was held at the Belasco Theatre. *Variety*'s banner for the item covering the meeting noted, "Warning Sounded Against Half-Way Measures to Fight Play Censorship," but the paper in the same issue reported that the actor Harry Davenport was taking his Sundays off from performing to appear at churches where he supported ministers inveighing against the theatre. The growingly reactionary *Theatre*, while denouncing the move in the legislature, nonetheless published a series of editorials which proffered such excited, exaggerated conclusions as "Our stage is in a parlous state" and "The grand, divine eternal Drama, freed from indecency and sordid commercialism, must again reign."

Eternal drama did not reign in the season's opener. Ernest Howard Culbertson's **Goat Alley** (6-20-21, Bijou) was produced with the backing of the

Medical Review of Reviews, which in earlier seasons had helped bring controversial works to the New York stage. The play was seen as the latest rewriting of *The Easiest Way*. Lucy Belle Dorsey (Lillian McKee) wants to work hard and lead the good life with Sam Reed (Barrington Carter), but after Sam is sent to prison she discovers it simpler to allow another man to keep her. On his release, Sam finds out and leaves Lucy Belle to fend for herself and her child. What little controversy the play ignited came from its employing an all-black cast. A few seasons before, Woollcott had bewailed in the *Times* the use of and overpraising of incompetent black actors. Now one of the paper's second stringers said much the same thing, remarking, "The play suffers considerably . . . by reason of an inadequate performance of the leading role. As a matter of fact, the piece would probably have been just as realistic throughout had it been played by professional actors in blackface." The work ran less than a week.

Thomas P. Robinson's **The Skylark** (7-25-21, Belmont) ran only a couple of weeks longer. It recounted how Daisy (Charlotte Walker), three years married to John (Fred Eric), doesn't know what she wants but at least knows that she does not have it. So the couple agree to a trial divorce. That seems just as unprofitable until a beautiful, clever widow (Marguerite Sylva) sets out to reunite the pair by vamping John and thus making Daisy jealous. Sylva, from the lyric stage, won applause for her glamorous gowns and one song she was able to work in. Good notices were also accorded Eugene Lockhart as a parson who cannot talk and sit at the same time.

The knowledgeable William Brady fared no better, despite encouraging notices, when he offered Martha M. Stanley and Adelaide Matthews's **The Teaser** (7-27-21, Playhouse). Teddy Wyndham (Jane Grey) invites her orphaned niece, Annie Barton (Faire Binney), to live with her, unaware that Annie is an incorrigible flirt and tease. Men fall over themselves entertaining her, until Annie nearly blows it all by allowing a married philanderer (John Cromwell) to invite her to supper. Matters end happily when Annie decides to wed a traveling salesman (Bruce Elmore) she met on the train coming to her aunt.

The season's first hit was not as big a success as legend has suggested, but the truth is the play's fame rests largely on its name—**Getting Gertie's Garter** (8-1-21, Republic). The farce had been written by Wilson Collison and then largely reworked by Avery Hopwood at the behest of its producer, Al Woods. Now that she has married Teddy Darling (Louis

Kimball), Gertie (Hazel Dawn) decides she ought to return the diamond-encrusted garter that Ken Walrick (Donald MacDonald) had given her when she and Ken were dating last year. After all, the garter does have Ken's picture sewn into it. Imagine what Teddy or Ken's new wife, Pattie (Dorothy Mackaye), might think! But Gertie's best-laid schemes gang agley, especially when Pattie, trying to make Ken jealous, winds up in a hayloft with her clothes off. Critic after critic pointed out that the play was not truly risqué. In the *Herald* Percy Hammond insisted, "There is no more interest in a garter as a naughty thing than there is in a virgin's wimple," while the *Tribune*'s Heywood Broun observed, "Mr. Hopwood made his reputation as a farce writer back in the days when the favorite sport was skating on thin ice. Since then audiences have learned how to swim." The farce chalked up a profitable if disappointing run of 120 performances.

Roi Cooper Megrue's **Honors Are Even** (8-10-21, Times) had a novel beginning—motion pictures of silhouettes show an apparently attractive girl rejecting a proposal made in a rolling chair on the boardwalk, a proposal made in a modern touring car, and a proposal made on a beach. That attractive girl turns out to be Belinde (Lola Fisher), who finally finds the man of her dreams in a worldly dramatist, John Leighton (William Courtenay). But being the knowing man he is, he decides to play it cool. So Belinde pretends to elope with another man to force John to propose. He does. Honors are even.

While some aisle-sitters professed to be delighted with Harry Wagstaff Gribble's **March Hares** (8-11-21, Bijou), more found it "a bit of bore," "effeminate," or "unfocused." Geoffrey Wareham (Alexander Onslow) and Janet Rodney (Adrienne Morrison) share an elocution studio. They have been engaged for several years and live with Janet's mother (Lucile Watson). But when Janet invites Claudia Kitts (Norma Mitchell) to stay with her, an annoyed Geoffrey retaliates by asking a relative stranger, Edgar Fuller (Brandon Peters), to stay with him. Complications follow, before Geoffrey and Janet are happily embracing. Those complications consisted of such things as Claudia's being thought to have stolen the maid's boyfriend, since he has the same name as the maid's suitor and calls Claudia by her middle name, which is the same as the maid's first name. Pseudo-epigrammatic, grammatically awkward dialogue included such speeches as "I regret to say that I have never been in the tropics. That's one of the things that are wrong with me. A man is never fully awake until he has crossed the equator."

The two mediocrities were succeeded by a smash hit, George S. Kaufman and Marc Connelly's **Dulcy** (8-13-21, Frazee). Ambitious, feather-brained, bromide-spouting Dulcinea Smith (Lynn Fontanne) is forever landing in the soup when she tries to help her husband Gordon (John Westley). Gordon is planning to merge his business with one belonging to C. Rogers Forbes (Wallis Clark), so Dulcy invites the Forbeses and their daughter, Angela (Norma Lee), for a weekend. She also invites Vincent Leach (Howard Lindsay), a film writer in love with Angela, her brother, Bill (Gregory Kelly), and Schuyler Van Dyck (Gilbert Douglas), a rich young man she has met. She infuriates the Forbeses by encouraging Angela and Vincent to elope and by having Schuyler offer to support Gordon in a venture to rival Forbes. Only after Schuyler is shown to be a harmless madman who merely thinks he is rich, and Angela elopes not with Vincent but with Bill, are affairs finally settled. Dulcy, promising never again to meddle, observes, "A burnt child dreads the fire. Once bitten—." Hornblow, in *Theatre*, predicted the comedy could win a Pulitzer Prize, applauding it as "clean, wholesome and jolly, knit together with a nice sense of cumulative interest, peppered with dialogue, salient with native, naive wit." The comedy ran until spring, making Lynn Fontanne, with her brilliantly pointed yet gentle comedy, a star and establishing Kaufman and Connelly as writers of the first rank.

· · ·

Lynn Fontanne [née Lillie Louise Fontanne] (1887–1983) was born in England and studied there with Ellen Terry before making her debut in 1905. She came to America in *Mr. Preedy and the Countess* (1910), returned to England, then came back to America in 1916 and appeared with Laurette Taylor in several plays. The willowy, dark-haired, sharp-eyed actress had a feline grace, a regal bearing, and a throaty voice.

· · ·

George S[imon] Kaufman (1889–1961) was born in Pittsburgh and served on the staffs of newspapers in Washington, D.C., and New York City before collaborating with Connelly on this comedy. A master of the barbed riposte, he soon became famous for his impeccable sense of theatrical timing and for his skills as a play doctor, as well as director and writer.

· · ·

Marc[us Cook] Connelly (1890–1981) was born in McKeesport, Pa., a steel town near Pittsburgh, and began writing plays while working as a newsman in the larger city. His first works to be mounted there were musicals, and his first major Broadway assignment was to update the old musical *Erminie* for a 1921 revival.

. . .

Although Alexander Woollcott snarled that Max Marcin and Guy Bolton's "mystery comedy" **The Nightcap** (8-15-21, 39th St.) was "mongrel entertainment," it ran twelve weeks and remains fun to read. Since Robert Andrews (Jerome Patrick) has played free and loose with $600,000 of his bank's money and cannot replace it before federal examiners come to check the books, he has two problems. First, how can he leave his money to his ward, Anne Maynard (Flora Sheffield), without making it seem she was his mistress, since she has been living in his magnificently paneled, high-ceilinged mansion? That problem is solved early on—he marries her. The second problem is how to commit suicide yet have it seem like a murder, so that his estate can collect on his insurance and thus save the bank (as well as provide for Anne). He tells his board of directors what he has done and tries to provoke one of them to shoot him—any one of them, but none obliges. Then one of the directors is murdered. The murderer turns out to be Anne's brother, disguised as a policeman (John Wray), who was aiming for Andrews in the belief he had despoiled his sister. When it is discovered that the dead man had entered the bank vaults and stolen papers, Andrews realizes he is off the hook. The authors created suitable tensions but had fun as well. Thus, one especially crotchety director (John Daly Murphy) is confronted by the coroner (Halbert Brown):

Coroner: Now tell me what's been going on here.
Jerry: Well, it started with a party. It was rotten when it began, and it's been getting worse every minute. The music was rotten—the supper was rotten—
Coroner: I don't want to hear about the music or the supper. What about this murder?
Jerry: The murder? Yes—well, the wrong man was killed—(*Catches himself.*)
Coroner: What's that?
Jerry: Did I say that? I didn't mean to—I—
Coroner: The wrong man, eh? Who ought to have been killed?
Jerry: Why—the saxophone player.

Sonya (8-15-21, 48th St.), which Eugene Thomas Wyckoff translated from a Polish play by Gabryela Zapolska, ran just a half week longer than *The Nightcap*. The play was a Graustarkian operetta without music. To embarrass Prince Alexander (Otto Kruger), who is the heir apparent, his shifty cousin, Prince Paul (Edward Emery), dresses Sonya (Violet Heming), a famous circus trapeze artist, as a boy and brings "him" to Alexander's room ostensibly as a gymnastics teacher. Alexander sees through the scheme soon enough but then quickly falls in love with the girl. When, just one month later, his father dies, he insists he will not be crowned without Sonya as his queen, and the reluctant courtiers are brought around by Sonya's sweet, prayerful entreaties. Kruger, so accustomed to laudatory notices, must have been shocked to be called "fustian" and "unconvincing."

A series of flops was led off by William Le Baron's **Nobody's Money** (8-17-21, Longacre), which had a funny idea but could not develop it properly. John W. Hamilton (Wallace Eddinger) is a tired businessman, so tired, in fact, that he hires a burglar (Will Deming) to teach him the art of being a crook. He then poses as a book salesman, going door to door in a swank area to case potential victims' homes. In the process he meets two successful authors (Frederick Raymond, Jr., and Robert Strange) who are themselves a little larcenous. They have written some of their books under a fictitious name, so that their publisher cannot hold them to older, low-figured contracts and in order to sidestep the tax man. Those books have become runaway best-sellers, and while their publisher may still be blissfully ignorant, Uncle Sam cannot look the other way. Hamilton agrees to pose as the author, and all the characters are in and out of hot water before the evening ends. Deming walked away with acting honors as the burglar who had spent time in stock and lards his speech with quotations from old melodramas.

Le Baron had a second, even shorter-lived failure five nights later with **The Scarlet Man** (8-22-21, Henry Miller's). It was seen as another good idea gone wrong. Diffident Wilbur Lawrence (John Cumberland) is taken aback when his fiancée, Mary Talbot (Frances Carson), appears at his apartment demanding to spend the night. It seems that in Act I Mary had been outraged when her parents (William Morris and Olive May) demanded that her brother (Don Burroughs) break his engagement to his sweetheart after a whiff of scandal had arisen about her. The next morning Wilbur loses his job and is snubbed by his acquaintances as a scarlet man until matters are resolved happily just before the final curtain. The farce was short, the final curtain falling less than two hours after the first curtain rose. Although critics cheered for Cumberland, some saying his was the only truly comic performance of the evening, the play's failure marked the beginning of the end of his career as a leading farceur.

Some dispute arose as to whether Ario Flamma's **The Mask of Hamlet** (8-22-21, Princess) had been written in stilted English or in Italian and then was badly translated. There was no dispute about its utter lack of merit and its short run—one week (although the producer had booked the house for a full month). The play professed to answer the still unsolved mystery of who had set off the murderous bomb on Wall Street a year earlier. According to Flamma a disguised Bolshevik mastermind (Cecil Owen) induces the beautiful Katia (Laura Walker) to set up Marx Martin (Harmon MacGregor) to do the deed. On learning that his father may have been one of the victims Marx has second thoughts so is murdered by Katia, who then disappears in the company of the mastermind.

The next failure was a most honorable one, with Burns Mantle assessing Owen Davis's **The Detour** (8-23-21, Astor) as "a splendid character study" and Davis himself subsequently calling it "the best play I have ever written." For many years Helen Hardy (Effie Shannon) and her daughter, Kate (Angela McCahill), have been saving so that Kate, who Helen is convinced has the ability to become a great painter, can leave their isolated farm and go study in New York. They cannot tell Stephen Hardy (Augustin Duncan), since he would take the money to buy more land. Stephen works hard but never has made good as a farmer, always insisting that he needs more and more land to turn a profit. He would like to buy the property of Tom Lane (Willard Robertson), his neighbor who has been courting Kate and who has just opened a garage to service the burgeoning automobile traffic. But the highway department closes the road for repairs, leaving Tom badly short of money. He offers to sell Stephen the land.. When Stephen discovers the women's cache he tries to appropriate it, but Helen balks, so he orders both of the women out of the house. Then a famous artist (Harry Andrews) who is passing through looks at Kate's work and tells her she has no talent. She hands the money over to her father, thereby allowing him to buy more land and allowing Tom to save his garage, and she resignedly accepts that she will become Tom's wife. An undefeated Helen starts saving for her first grand-daughter. The gist and tragedy of the story were recorded in a few lines which disclose how the changes automobiles were bringing about were also enlarging our vocabulary.

Helen: The road's pretty bad; it's a good thing they're fixing it. Detour, that's a new word; seems we're borrowing lots of things from France. It ain't a bad word—Detour—only I don't know as I get the meaning of it exactly.
Kate: It means a turning.
Dora [a visitor]: Another way round, to get to the same place.
Helen: Oh, well, so long as a person gets where they want to go, I guess a detour don't matter much.

The Samuel French acting edition is interesting in that unlike most such editions it contains a long preface—by the then famous theatrical historian Montrose J. Moses—pleading that Davis's reputation as a writer of old melodramatic clinkers not prevent his new works from being judged fairly.

. . .

Owen Davis (1874–1956) was born in Portland, Maine, and studied at Harvard. After graduation he attempted to write some blank-verse tragedies but abandoned them and turned to cheap touring melodramas to support his family. In short order he became one of the most prolific creators of the genre—under his own name and aliases—pouring out such popular potboilers as *Driven from Home*, *Convict 999*, and *Nellie, the Beautiful Cloak Model*. When the market for these plays disappeared after 1909 he wrote for the Hippodrome and suffered several short-lived Broadway failures. But he also enjoyed some success with *The Family Cupboard* (1913), *Sinners* (1915), *Forever After* (1918), and *Opportunity* (1920).

. . .

Carlos Wupperman had written **The Triumph of X** (8-24-21, Comedy) several years before his death at the front during the war. His loyal elder brother, Frank Morgan, and Jessie Bonstelle worked for a number of seasons to achieve this mounting. Phillis (Helen Menken) becomes drunk at her engagement party, provoking her fiancé, Ralph Armstrong (Robert Keith), to walk out on her, but not before revealing that her father had been a notorious dipsomaniac, her mother an infamous scarlet lady, and that she clearly cannot override her genes. She responds that she will join all the other "denizens of the gutter" and "laugh her way to hell." Phillis's guardian, Robert Knowles (Morgan), attempts to save her. He is almost dragged down himself before Phillis finds the inner strength to rescue the pair of them. She points out that both heredity and upbringing can be conquered by the vigor of the soul she calls "X." Morgan was attacked for his "elocutionary over-emphasis," but Menken's "exquisitely beautiful and gripping performance" marked her as an actress to be watched.

The parade of failures was put to an end by one of

the decade's most joyful comedies, William Anthony McGuire's **Six-Cylinder Love** (8-25-21, Sam H. Harris). It also gave Ernest Truex his first smash hit in several seasons. Richard and Geraldine Burton (Donald Meek and Eleanor Gordon) are faced with eviction, having gone broke living beyond their means. As far as Richard is concerned the villain, as he tells Donroy (Ralph Sipperly), a car salesman who is attempting to dispose of the Burtons' car, is the expense of maintaining an automobile.

Donroy: Why that isn't an expensive boat to run, is it?
Burton: No, I can go about forty miles on five gallons of gas, a quart of oil, three quarts of Scotch, chicken dinners for five or six, theatre tickets, cigars and cigarettes for the bunch.
Donroy: And do you pay for it all?
Burton: When a man buys an automobile he purchases that permanent position of host, and none of his friends ever question his right to it.

But Donroy, looking across the fence that separates the Burtons' home from that of Gilbert and Marilyn Sterling (Truex and June Walker), spots two perfect suckers—newlyweds who "dear" and "sweetheart" each other ad nauseam. He soon bamboozles the Sterlings into buying the car. Before long the Sterlings are living beyond their means, and the hangers-on have deserted the Burtons and taken up with the Sterlings, whom they once had sneered at. A sudden visit by Gilbert's staid boss, Mr. Stapleton (Berton Churchill), costs Gilbert his job when Stapleton is offended at what he sees. Like the Burtons, the Sterlings are forced to move to simpler quarters. Gilbert sells the car and gains back his job just in time to learn he will be saddled with a new expense—a baby. The comedy ran for more than a year.

Meanwhile, the parade of flops resumed. In the prologue of Philip Bartholomae and Jasper Ewing Brady's **Personality** (8-27-21, Playhouse) Ruth Kent (Dorothy Bernard), waking up to find a burglar in her bedroom, hurls a slipper at him. He flees. The next morning, at the office of her businessman father (Dodson Mitchell), who is looking for an assistant, she encourages him to hire a handsome but somewhat bedraggled man (Louis Bennison) she has spotted in the waiting room and who tells her he is Robert Wainwright. Within two years he is so successful that Ruth determines to cut him down to size. Instead he moves from success to success. Only after Ruth confesses she loves him rich as well as poor does he hand her the slipper she once threw at

him. Bennison, who had been praised to the skies as a most promising comedian in 1917's *Johnny Get Your Gun*, won no more than polite approval. He would never reclaim that early excitement.

Winchell Smith's **The Wheel** (8-29-21, Gaiety) told of a pretty, street-smart owner of a Fifth Avenue millinery shop, Kate O'Hara (Ida St. Leon), who marries a socialite, Teddy Morton, Jr. (Charles Laite), only to discover he is hopelessly addicted to gambling. To cure him she approaches an old friend, Ed Baker (Thomas W. Ross), a professional gambler, and the two of them set up a fake casino, where Teddy soon comes to play. After he loses all his money, he demands to see the boss. His shock on having the boss turn out to be Kate cures him of his addiction. Several critics pointed out an apparent bit of contemporary typecasting when Leila Bennett, who had played the black maid in *The First Year*, played a white maid in this piece. (Later in the season *Theatre* would publish a full page of photographs of actresses playing maids in Broadway shows. Although half of the maids were supposed to be black, all were played by whites.)

Ralph Morgan had no better luck this month than his brother had. At the beginning of Leon Gordon, LeRoy Clemens, and Thomas Grant Springer's **The Poppy God** (8-29-21, Hudson) he was seen as Stanley Bennett, who is occupying a stateroom on a ship sailing from Hong Kong to San Francisco. Bennett has lived for some time in China to escape accusations back home in England of cowardice. But with the outbreak of the war he has resolved to enlist and disprove the charges. He never gets beyond Frisco, where he seduces the wife (Edna Hibbard) of his Chinese host (George MacQuarrie). To be avenged the betrayed husband does not kill Bennett but rather slowly and deliberately destroys him by making him an opium addict. The curtain comes down on all the smiling Chinese gloating around Bennett's prostrate figure.

So much ballyhoo preceded the opening of Fannie Hurst's **Back Pay** (8-30-21, Eltinge) that even downbeat notices could not deprive it of at least a modest ten-week run. It centered on Hester Bevins (Helen MacKellar), who, having been raised by a brothel-keeping aunt (Mary Shaw), believes fine things more important and more permanent than true love. So she rejects her decent small-town suitor (Leo Donnelly), runs off to New York, and soon finds many rich men willing to keep her in silk, sables, and jewelry. But in the middle of a lavish party she is holding, she learns that her hometown suitor, wounded in the war, lies blinded and dying at a nearby hospital. She rushes off to his bedside, where she is so moved (much like last season's outrageous Mrs. Palmer) that she has him brought to her apartment and nurses him until he dies. Even then the memory of his empty eyes haunts her until she abandons her glittering highlife and accepts work as as ordinary shopgirl. One interesting performance was that of Lucille LaVerne. At last season's start she had blacked up to play in a work about blacks performed by whites. Now she blacked up again, this time as the traditional black maid in a white society.

If Miss LaVerne seemingly could not break away from blackface roles, Barney Bernard did break away from Abe Potash. But not by much. For in Aaron Hoffman's **Two Blocks Away** (8-30-21, George M. Cohan) he was now Nathaniel Pommerantz, a poor but kind and generous East Side shoemaker who inherits a fortune, moves those short two blocks to a Fifth Avenue mansion overlooking the park, and there becomes reclusive, mean, and miserly. Since this was a comedy, Nathaniel sees the light by eleven o'clock (five o'clock at matinees). Typical of Hoffman's lines was one in which Nathaniel tells visitors that his adopted daughter (Marie Carroll) will be seeing "Westminster Abey" when she goes to London. Although the comedy received warmer reviews than had Miss Hurst's play, it ran only a little more than half as long. Later in the season, Abe would rejoin his old associate Mawruss, and Miss Carroll would confront a different Abie.

The month ended with a modest success—although a subsequent road tour was a disaster—Zoë Akins's **Daddy's Gone A-Hunting** (8-31-21, Plymouth). While her husband, Julien (Frank Conroy), was spending time overseas supposedly learning his art, Edith Fields (Marjorie Rambeau) had become friendly with the rich Walter Greenough (Lee Baker) and allowed him to shower her and her young daughter, Janet (Frances Victory), with gifts. But Edith is stunned when Julien returns to find him a changed man. He has become a bit of a poser, seemingly more interested in his bohemian friends than in his family. "Love's not everything," he tells his wife, "as you women think. Love is damned little—when a man's got work to do." He claims what he wants most is freedom, and stalks out. Edith sings Janet an old song about daddy's gone a-hunting, and when Janet asks what he is hunting, Edith sobs, "God knows." The marriage goes from bad to worse, especially after newspapers headline the sensational accusations against a society woman, with Julien named as corespondent. A fight about this with Julien provokes Edith into running outside. Janet asks Julien where mother is going, and Julien

answers, "God knows." Three years later, Edith has been set up in style by Greenough, but Janet's dangerous illness brings her and Julien to the child's bedside. Still, when Greenough asks Edith to promise that once the child recovers, Edith will not see Julien again, she agrees. Janet does not recover; she dies. Sensing that Edith needs Julien more than she needs him, Greenough seems to walk out of her life. But Julien comes in and makes it clear that he does not want to resume any matrimonial fetters. Greenough's cousin asks Edith what she will do now, and her reply is "God knows." For all that the play seems reiterative, leisurely, and contrived today (with each act ending with the same phrase), contemporaries felt it was "a triumph" that "immeasurably enriched" the season. Some critics chided producer-director Arthur Hopkins for his languid staging (were they confusing the staging with a problem inherent in the text?). But there were paeans aplenty for Marjorie Rambeau, who finally could sink her teeth into a meaty role and who gave a deeply felt, finely modulated performance. The rest of the cast was also applauded. And Robert Edmond Jones's settings of a small flat in Harlem (Act I), shabby bohemian digs near Washington Square (Act II)—the pair referred to by *Theatre* as "speaking likenesses"—and "a small exquisite room" in a luxurious apartment overlooking Central Park (Act III) were also singled out for commendation.

More Jones settings stole the show from Sidney Howard's maiden effort, **Swords** (9-1-21, National). Howard's story was set in the late Middle Ages, when Guelphs and Ghibelines were at each other's throats. The savage Ugolino (Charles Waldron) has captured and imprisoned Donna Fiamma (Clare Eames), a beautiful jewel of the Popish party. Papal emissaries and knights disguised as friars try unavailingly to rescue her. Ugolino plans to bend the woman to his will, but he is clumsy and slow, so his more wily, depraved jester, Cannetto (José Ruben), takes his place. In the dawning light, with the sounds of matins being chanted in the distance, the lustful Cannetto stealthily enters her room. Suddenly, he pitches forward—dead. Fiamma, torch in hand, runs to freedom. Critics felt that neither Ruben nor the attractive if sharp-nosed Eames had the depth of tragic fervor that might have glossed over Howard's infelicities. However, even many of those who dismissed the play—and they were in the majority—saw the young author as a writer of distinct promise.

Gilbert Emery's **The Hero** (9-5-21, Belmont) had critics clapping their hands when it was given a few trial matinees last season and again when it began what was hoped would be a long run now. But when its run proved disappointingly short (ten weeks at the tiny house), Broadway pundits suggested this was not the time to produce a play touching on the recent war, especially one that exposed some unpleasant truths. Mixed emotions in the Lane household greet the news that their long-missing Oswald has been spotted in a French army hospital with numerous decorations to show for his soldiering. Old Mrs. Lane (Blanche Friderici) is nervously anxious to see her younger son again, but his brother, Andrew (Richard Bennett), recalling that Oswald ran away after deflowering a neighborhood girl and stealing money, is not so certain. Andrew, who with his late father paid back the money to avoid scandal, is a struggling insurance salesman, who lives with his wife, Hester (Alma Belwin), their young son, and Marthe (Fania Marinoff), a Belgian refugee they have taken in. Andrew hopes that Oswald's wartime experiences may have changed him, but when Oswald (Robert Ames) does return it quickly becomes evident they have not. He makes brazen advances toward Marthe, more subtle ones toward Hester, then runs off again, pocketing $500 with which Andrew, as church treasurer, had been entrusted. However, as he is heading for the station, Oswald runs into a burning school to save some children and dies in the fire. Not wanting Andrew to know the truth, Hester tells him she gave Oswald the money to take to the bank. Though he doesn't realize it, Andrew once again will have to pay for his brother's crimes. A sympathetic Hester tells Andrew he is a good man. "Me? I'm just old Andy, I am," he responds. "But Os—Os was a hero." Emery was better known under the name Emery Pottle as a short-story writer; his real name was Gilbert Emery Bensley Pottle.

An importation fared better, chalking up 112 showings. Cosmo Hamilton's **The Silver Fox** (9-5-21, Maxine Elliott's), a reasonably faithful reworking of Ferenc Herczeg's *A kék róka* [The Blue Fox], was reset in England and told how a woman (Violet Kemble Cooper) blatantly compromises herself so that her charming novelist husband (Lawrence Grossmith), who has come to view her as little more than an amusing spendthrift ("A beautiful woman is a more expensive hobby than old furniture") can divorce her and she can marry his best friend (William Faversham), a poet who has lived with them. For a time, the poet brutally rejects her, believing her a loose woman having an affair with a notorious roué (Ian Keith), and he threatens to turn the matter into "a tragedy by refusing to put you back on your pedestal and going out with no more faith in womanhood." In response, she demon-

strates that his reaction is a mask for his jealousy and cowardice. "A woman must follow the ways of a fox to break the poet and find the man," she tells him, and she eventually brings about a satisfactory ending when her husband admits to a new love.

The attitudinizing matinee idol Lou Tellegen was cast in the lead of **Don Juan** (9-5-21, Garrick), Henri Bataille's *L'Homme à la rose* as adapted by Lawrence Langner. When an infuriated husband kills an innocent man, thinking he has slain his wife's infamous seducer, the Don allows the man to be buried under his name and even attends the funeral. But thereafter he discovers he must buy his favors, since it was his reputation that allowed him to enjoy such easy conquests. Lee Simonson had quickly become Robert Edmond Jones's major competitor. He needed only "two great pillars, some iron grillwork, and some shadows" to beautifully convey the impression of the Cathedral at Seville.

The only work to come before first-nighters the following evening, the 6th, was a revival at the Lyceum of Eugene Walter's 1909 hit *The Easiest Way*, with Frances Starr and Joseph Kilgour in their original roles as a kept woman who futilely tries to break away and as the man who has kept her. Most reviewers felt the work was as powerful as ever, but it remained on the boards just for the eight weeks initially slated for it.

However, Broadway wanted nothing to do with its next importation. Its credits were listed as "A melodrama in four acts and ten episodes by Major Herbert Woodgate and Arthur Gibbons, based on the novel of the same name by Edgar Rice Burroughs. American version by George Broadhurst." Of course, **Tarzan of the Apes** (9-7-21, Broadhurst) would not have been hurt by having been a 1914 best-seller, but since 1918 a number of film versions and fresh sequels, many with Elmo Lincoln and Enid Markey, had won wide popularity and could offer a breadth of action and scenery no stage mounting could hope to rival. Clinging closely to the original story, this version of a young aristocrat raised by apes featured Ronald Adair in the title role.

The days when Ristori or Duse could perform their Italian plays in their native language at first-class New York theatres had passed, so when Giovanni Grasso, a fine Sicilian player, brought a company to Manhattan, he was assigned a shabby theatre in the Bowery for his twelve-week visit and was ignored by most critics.

Just as Ario Flamma had professed to solve the Wall Street bombing mystery in *The Mask of Hamlet*, William Devereux offered a possible solution to another recent real-life mystery, the once sensational, now forgotten Elwell case. Joseph Browne Elwell was a prominent horse breeder and whist expert. He was also suspected of being a philanderer and a bootleg kingpin. All through July of 1920 newspapers were filled with columns on his murder and on the women and suspected bootleggers who were questioned by the police. The killing went unsolved. In **The Elton Case** (9-10-21, Playhouse) Robert Elton (Byron Beasley) is a famous bridge player and almost equally notorious philanderer. To win the money that will keep her brother out of prison for misappropriating funds, Marjorie Ramsey (Chrystal Herne) offers to play Elton for extremely high stakes. She loses. At this juncture, Elton, understanding her plight, offers to give her the money if she will become his mistress. Marjorie shoots him dead but learns that the district attorney, to avoid a weak case and further scandal, will not prosecute her. The public showed no more interest in Devereux's theories than they had shown in Flamma's.

For much of that public, interest in the next opening centered on the long-absent Mrs. Leslie Carter, who returned to New York to head a superb cast that also included John Drew, Ernest Lawford, Estelle Winwood, and John Halliday in Somerset Maugham's **The Circle** (9-12-21, Selwyn). They played out a deliciously witty story of some aristocrats who years before broke up their own marriages by eloping. But when the now somewhat remorseful Lady Catherine tries to prevent her daughter-in-law from repeating her own behavior, she fails. The play ran five months and has been revived regularly ever since.

Two other plays, presented that same evening at smaller venues away from Times Square, found little popularity. Augustin MacHugh's **True to Form** (9-12-21, Bramhall Playhouse) followed the prickly but ultimately successful rebellion of a newlywed (John Warner) whose in-laws, goaded by a self-impressed philosopher (Edwin Nicander), try to force him and his more pliable wife (Verna Wilkens) into their own narrow, conservative ways. The philosopher writes a novel which he hopes will resolve the situation. Instead it drives the husband into the arms of another woman (Sue MacManamy), but the novelist himself eventually proposes to the new woman and all ends happily.

Edwin Milton Royle's dramatization of a Tennyson poem as **Launcelot and Elaine** (9-12-21, Greenwich Village) was a family affair, with his wife, Selena Fetter Royle as Guinevere and their daughter, Josephine, as the tragic Elaine. Pedro de Cordoba was Launcelot. Livingston Platt's impressionistic scenery, including a trackless waste, the courtyard of Arthur's palace, and, most especially, a sunken garden, walked off with the best notices.

Notices for A. E. Thomas's **Only 38** (9-13-21, Cort) were lukewarm, so the play could do no more than muster a slightly forced eleven-week run. Depending on one's viewpoint, the not-so-young or not-so-old heroine was Mrs. Stanley (Mary Ryan), the widow of a strict, killjoy minister who was twice her age. Now she must find a home for herself and her two priggish children (Neil Martin and Ruth Mero), both of whom reflect their late father's sour thinking. Mrs. Stanley receives a visit from her own aging father (Percy Pollock), a farmer determined to enjoy the big city and the good life before he dies. His attitude sets his daughter thinking, especially after he reveals that he has sold a large woods he owns so that she can send her children to college and have a suitable place of her own. Though the children insist she decorate their new place with a Rogers group of a prayer session, portraits of clergymen, and drab horsehair furniture, she slowly introduces Japanese art, colorful slipcovers, and other cheery amenities. When her children, especially her daughter, continue to want her to be joyless, she purposely smokes a cigarette. Before long the children have started to come around to her thinking, and in time an attractive young professor (Harry C. Browne), at forty only two years her senior, proposes. She accepts, but he is puzzled when she breaks out in tears. However, she assures him she now even understands how to enjoy a good cry.

There was something a bit Tarzan-like in Norman MacOwan and Charlton Mann's **The Blue Lagoon** (9-14-21, Astor), a dramatization of H. De Vere Stacpoole's novel, which concerned two children who are shipwrecked and raised on a lonely tropical island by the lone sailor (Cecil Yapp) to survive the sinking. He dies, and the grown Dick (Harold French) and Emmeline (Frances Carson) fall in love and create so idyllic a world for themselves that when rescuers finally appear they evince no interest in returning to a more brutal world. The play had been a success in London, but New Yorkers received it with "yawns, titters and occasional murmurs of mutiny," so the work was hastily ushered out.

By contrast, the Irish Players from the Abbey Theatre were greeted enthusiastically when they offered Lennox Robinson's **The White-Headed Boy** (9-15-21, Henry Miller's). The badly spoiled pet (Arthur Shields) of the Geoghegan family flunks out of school and gets a lowly job as a street cleaner after a threat of breach of promise forces him to marry the girl (Gertrude Murphy) his family had selected for him. But despite every setback, he always seems to land on his feet and smile.

So did the heroine of **Bluebeard's Eighth Wife** (9-19-21, Ritz), which Charlton Andrews—of *Ladies' Night* fame—worked over from Alfred Savoir's Paris hit. The girl is Monna de Briac (Ina Claire), a moneyless French aristocrat's daughter, who demands that John Brandon (Edmund Breese), a much divorced, hotheaded American billionaire, help restore her father's fortune and guarantee her financial well-being before she will become his eighth bride. The marriage soon seems to take a turn for the worse until Monna invites a former beau (Barry Baxter) to her home, gets him drunk, and, when they hear Brandon enter, tells him to strip and hide in her bed. Of course, Brandon explodes with rage and jealousy, but then comes to understand how much he loves Monna. While Ina Claire again walked away with excellent notices, Baxter, a young English actor who died suddenly later in the season, walked away with better ones. They kept audiences laughing for twenty weeks.

Yet a third central figure to land on his feet after a series of vicissitudes was James W. Elliott's **The Man in the Making** (9-20-21, Hudson). Elliott was known as a man who created advertisements promising pots of gold to those who worked hard and followed his how-to-succeed manuals. His hero was Jimmy Carswell (Donald Gallaher), who returns home from college having learned how to drink and party, but not much else. His father (Paul Everton), a rich, self-made manufacturer, cuts off his allowance and tells him, "Make good or make room." Jimmy drifts to San Francisco, where he falls in with a louche crowd, gets hold of himself, returns home to take a job at his father's factory (unbeknownst to the old man), berates his father for mistreating employees, then heads off to found a community in which boys work to earn money to gain an education. On the gate of the community is the slogan "Work Is Life and Good Work Is Good Life." Playgoers felt any life was too short to waste on such drivel.

But they had hardly any more time for Tom Cushing's dramatization of Vicente Blasco Ibañez's **Blood and Sand** (9-20-21, Empire), with Otis Skinner in the leading role of the bullfighter betrayed by both his vixenish paramour and his insatiably bloodthirsty followers. In his autobiography, Skinner gave an interesting glimpse of the play and his own perhaps more queasy admirers: "In the third act, the hero *Juan Gallardo* is brought in on a stretcher, his leg, broken a month before in the bull-

ring, is still in a splint. At a juncture in the scene, *Juan* disobeys the doctor's orders and cuts the bandages from the wounded leg. Mistrusting his superstitious faith in the cards that have told him his wound has healed, and doubting whether he should have gone against the doctor's command, he gingerly lifts his leg from the cot, holds it out while he bends his knee—his brow in a cold sweat of terror lest the leg should prove to be permanently stiff. The foot finally resting on the floor, he rises slowly until his entire weight is on the broken leg. Every night somebody in the audience fainted. . . . In the last act when *Juan* is carried in covered with blood, not a soul minded." Most critics admired Skinner's bravura performance, all the while agreeing that he was too old for the part. The following year a much younger if less practiced performer, Rudolph Valentino, scored a major success in a silent-film version.

While the drift toward films may have been inexorable, Broadway still cherished old plays and players, so when Belasco brought back David Warfield in *The Return of Peter Grimm* at the Belasco on the 21st, aisle-sitters and playgoers reacted joyously, giving this saga of a man who comes back from the dead a healthy stay.

Three maiden aunts who live determinedly in the past stole the show in Hutcheson Boyd and Rudolph Bunner's **Wait Till We're Married** (9-26-21, Playhouse), especially when they got tipsy one by one, by mistake. Most comical among the aunties was Auntie Meridian (was that meant as a laugh?) as played by Edna May Oliver. But the old gals were not the main figures of this failed comedy. They were Marion Livermore (Marion Coakley), a very wealthy socialite who rescues William Plumb (Henry Duffy), a down-and-out war hero, from drowning, tries to get him to accept her set's frivolous ways, dumps him when he seemingly will not, then agrees to wed him after he shows her how nonsensical and artificial her society's manners are by carrying them to extremes.

A rather dreary September faded out with an appropriately dreary comedy, Edward Childs Carpenter's **Pot Luck** (9-29-21, Comedy). Amy Jewell (Clara Moores), worrying that she will become an old maid, advertises for a husband. She lands Stephen McCauley (James Rennie), who is really a crook on the run. Luckily, McCauley has some writing ability, and an article he sells to the *Saturday Evening Post* proves so popular that it looks like he may be asked to run for mayor. But his old partner in crime, Jim Patterson (Rockliffe Fellowes), appears and attempts to blackmail the couple. His hackles up, McCauley writes an autobiographical novel, leaving only the ending blank. When Patterson arrives to collect his hush money he finds a meeting of the Hebron Wednesday Evening Literary Circle in progress and McCauley reading them the novel. McCauley then asks for ideas on how to end the book. The townsfolk say the hero should not pay the blackmail since he is a good man at heart and has reformed. Patterson, accepting that he is licked, leaves.

John Golden had a season-long hit on his hands when he presented Winchell Smith and Tom Cushing's **Thank You** (10-3-21, Longacre). It offered a different perspective than *Only 38* had on the clergy. The very underpaid Rev. David Lee (Harry Davenport) cannot get by on his meager salary of $800, so relies on "donations" from his Connecticut parishoners until his orphaned, Paris-befrocked niece, Diane (Edith King), returns from Europe to stay with him. Offended that her uncle is little more than a beggar, she wages a campaign to get him a decent stipend and to restore his self-respect. Annoyed vestrymen try to remove Lee by threatening to lower his salary further. Fortunately, a rich businessman (Frank Malone), who is a member of the congregation and in love with Diane, comes to his defense, seeing that he is properly provided for. Diane is grateful but elects to wed the man's black-sheep son (Donald Foster), whom she is sure she can reform. The comedy was welcomed as the sort of good, clean entertainment John Golden stood for, and Davenport's minister was eulogized as the kind that "makes you feel like going to church again." (Remember Davenport himself was going to churches to endorse theatrical censorship.) After leaving New York, the piece played four years on the road, where, according to Golden, it was "hailed by ministers and teachers as a powerful argument for underpaid educators and as the best friend the clergy ever had." Much of the time on the road it was billed as *Thank-U*.

Connecticut was also the setting for another of the evening's entries. The same critics who regularly panned William Hodge for bringing his "jay plays" to the big time did so again when he came to town in **Beware of Dogs** (10-3-21, Broadhurst). *Variety*, sneering at the play and the acting, especially that of an actress who played a vamp "hysterically," concluded, "If this seems valueless on Broadway, it is not in the sticks." For this go-round the once respected star took on the role of George Oliver, who rents a country place just off the Boston Post Road near Greenwich. His plan is to care for an invalid sister there, but because the lease requires that he maintain a boarding kennel that comes with

the property he soon finds himself dealing with unsavory characters such as a businessman and his chorus-girl mistress who use the place for a rendezvous, and his cook, who employs her kitchen as a "blind tiger"—a place to sell liquor illegally. Oliver chastens and chases the scalawags and wins the affection of a pretty girl (Ann Davis). Transplanted rubes and some forcing earned the piece an eleven-week stand.

For the second time in just short of a month, a decorated war hero was shown as being not all he was reputed to be. Only this time, in John Hunter Booth's **Like a King** (10-3-21, 39th St.), the situation was played for laughs and had a happy ending. Like Oswald Lane before him, Nathaniel Alden (James Gleason) was a mischievous boy who ran away from home. However, in the army in France he won medals for bravery. Since the war he has tried several ventures; all have failed, leaving him broke. This has not stopped him from writing home that he is not merely successful but a millionaire. Home is Lower Falls, Mass. And when he returns he returns in a new $15,000 Rolls-Royce, escorted by the town's band, both its fire engines, and all the hoopla the town's biggest hero and richest man deserves. The town needs something to celebrate, since the new census shows how rapidly it is losing population to nearby burgs with more to offer youngsters. Pressed to save the town, Nat proposes bringing in industry. Stuck-in-the-muds are horrified: "We wun't have no fact'ries. Lower Falls is a stric'ly residential kermun'ty." Most villagers support Nat until problems arise. First, one old codger demands Nat pay off the elder Mr. Alden's $10,000 debt, unaware Nat has only $10 to his name, and the Rolls proves to be stolen, although Nat had thought a friend had legitimately borrowed it. Nat bamboozles its real owner into letting him buy it and pay him in a few days. Then he accepts a $100,000 check from a manufacturer who has heard of his schemes and wants to locate in Lower Falls. That money allows Nat to buy the car, pay off the debt, continue to be thought of as a rich promoter, and get a yes from the girl he loves, Phyllis Weston (Ann Harding). Handclapping was reserved for the leading players; the comedy was snubbed. *Variety*, again interested primarily in a play's money-making chances, correctly predicted, "In these troublesome days in the theatrical business, 'Like a King' doesn't seem to have sufficient 'kick' to go over." Two weeks and it was gone. The play was published as *Rolling Home*.

The evening's only importation, **The Fan** (10-3-21, Punch and Judy), derived by Pitts Duffield from de Flers and de Caillavet's Paris hit, found Hilda Spong starred as a Parisian widow of a certain age, who visits friends in her Normandy hometown, sets right their romantic problems, rediscovers her first and only real love (Ian Maclaren), and marries him.

Mildred Harker (Marie Doro), divorced by her philandering husband on trumped-up evidence and denied custody of her child, is consoled by her old friend, Maisie Lee (Josephine Drake), in William Hurlbut's **Lilies of the Field** (10-4-21, Klaw). At first Mildred keeps herself at arm's length, since she recognizes that the bejeweled and befurred Maisie and her glittering friends are merely modern-day courtesans. But after she is informed that her child has died she allows herself to be kept by Lewis Willing (Norman Trevor). She is fortunate that Willing is a kind, understanding lover, for when she subsequently learns that her child is not dead, and that her mean ex-husband purposely spread the rumor, she plans to kidnap the child and run off with it, until Willing not only insists she marry him but goes to her ex and wrests custody of the child from him. Although Hornblow spoke for a majority of his colleagues when he assailed the piece's "tawdriness" and scoffed at "perhaps the most preposterous *deus ex machina* final solution . . . that local footlights have blazed on in many a season," enough playgoers were lured by its salaciousness to give the melodrama a five-month run. It might have run longer but for complicated legal battles that led to its closing.

One major disappointment was Harvey O'Higgins and Harriet Ford's dramatization of Sinclair Lewis's **Main Street** (10-5-21, National). Critics felt Higgins and Ford had done their job rather well but asked if it was worth it. They concluded that the year-old best-seller was better read between its covers. Alma Tell was cast as Carol Kennicott, who vainly strives to bring a little excitement and sophistication to backwater Gopher Prairie, Minn.

Unlike Lewis, Booth Tarkington moved easily between writing novels and writing plays. His latest stage work, **The Wren** (10-10-21, Gaiety), did his reputation no good. (Though today, for all its simplicity and obviousness, and with the reader envisioning and hearing its leading players in his or her imagination, it seems quite charming.) Its brevity (it was only two hours long) prompted Woollcott to protest that audiences came away from the theatre "undernourished." Tarkington's story cast its gaze on Seeby—short for Eusebia—Olds (Helen Hayes), a young lady who manages Cap'n Olds's New England boardinghouse. She effectively manages to keep her father, the captain (George Fawcett), and his caretaker (Sam Reed) in line, too.

She manages them so efficiently that she soon finds herself managing all the off-season guests' lives, especially that of Roddy (Leslie Howard), an attractive, insouciant Canadian artist, who has been showering a bit of attention on her. When he turns his attentions to another guest, Mrs. Frazee (Pauline Armitage), Seeby is momentarily bested and dejected. A suspicious Mr. Frazee (John Flood) appears on the scene unannounced, and in no time (the action of the play transpires over less than a full day) Seeby manages to have Mr. Frazee cart his wife off. Seeby explains to Roddy that Mrs. Frazee's presence distracted him from his work and he must go off to the beach and paint by himself. But a few moments after he has gone out, Seeby disappears. Then the captain spots her running toward the young man. "Seeby's caught up with him. Mr. Roddy, he looks like he don't know which way to go. . . . Yes, suh, she's a leadin' of him—she's a leadin' of him—by the hand." During all of the play's twenty-four performances, audiences could surmise the ending well in advance. Notices did little more for Miss Hayes than they had for Tarkington, with Franklin P. Adams in his famous column complaining her performance "suffered from fallen archness."

But the Theatre Guild won some fine, if damagingly qualified, reviews when it brought out Arthur Richman's **Ambush** (10-10-21, Garrick). "The finest American play of its sort . . . but stays rather overly on the surface," "vivid, if sordid," and "powerful . . . [but] perhaps too unrelentingly painful" were among the critical assessments. Walter Nichols (Frank Reicher) has not been much of a breadwinner, so his high-mindedness has become particularly galling to his mercenary wife (Jane Wheatley) and his even more grasping, immoral daughter, Margaret (Florence Eldridge). She lives off money she receives from the men she sleeps with, although her father does not know this. But the women's pressures finally drive him to gamble in the stock market. He loses his investment and also loses his job. A friend (George Stillwell) of Margaret's offers to give him employment as well as money to pay the rent that has come due. Only after Walter accepts does he discover that the man is married and that Margaret is his mistress. What is more, he learns that the man is merely the latest of his daughter's keepers. Yet he cannot refuse the job or the money. He bewails to a family friend (Katherine Proctor):

Walter: Everything I stood for—everything I lived
  for—everything God put me on this earth for—
  turns out wrong. What can I do now?

Mrs. Jennison: Whatever has happened—you must go on just the same.
Walter: Why? (*His voice louder*) Why? Why?

Helped by the Guild's subscription, the play ran three months.

Two foreign plays opened the same night as the two native works. Clemence Dane's **A Bill of Divorcement** (10-10-21, George M. Cohan) had been a hit in London but opened to almost no advance sale. Reviewed with "guarded enthusiasm" by second- and third-stringers, it enjoyed no box-office rush. Not until rave Sunday follow-ups by major critics did a crush develop at the box office. A closing notice had been posted, so the show's producer, Charles Dillingham, hurriedly booked the Times Square, where "for the next several months it was the biggest kind of success." The story unfolded in the future, when England was to have more liberal divorce laws. Considering her husband, Hillary (Allan Pollock), hopelessly deranged after he was shell-shocked in the war, Margaret Fairfield (Janet Beecher) divorces him and prepares to marry Gray Meredith (Charles Waldron). Shortly after the divorce is granted, Hillary appears, somewhat better, but he reveals that his problems were actually a manifestation of the insanity that runs in his family. His daughter, Sydney (Katharine Cornell), learns this history, abandons her own plans for marriage, and resolves to dedicate her life to taking care of her father. One of the few first-stringers to attend the opening was the *American*'s Alan Dale, who rued that Miss Cornell "performed flippantly as a flapper." Not until the follow-ups appeared did reviews truly start the young player on her way to stardom.

· · ·

Katharine Cornell (1893–1974) was born in Berlin, the daughter of a former stage manager who had gone to Germany to study medicine. After growing up in Buffalo, she made her stage debut with the Washington Square Players in 1916, then performed in stock—first in Buffalo and subsequently with Jessie Bonstelle's company in Detroit. She spent a brief period acting in London before calling attention to her skills in New York in *Nice People* (1921). Although she seemed tall and regal onstage, she was not quite five feet seven inches, with dark hair, a dark complexion, and broad features that were called Oriental or even negroid.

· · ·

There were no critics to rescue Benjamin F. Glazer's translation of Karl Schönherr's **The Children's Tragedy** (10-10-21, Greenwich Village). The children—the play's only characters—were apparently not meant to be tots but the teenaged offspring of an immoral peasant mother, the wife of a Tyrolean forester. Their reactions to seeing their mother take on a lover lead to the death of one, a second's insanity, and the driving of the third into exile. The play was accompanied by a one-act comedy, Cosmo Gordon Lennox's **The Van Dyck**, taken from a French piece attributed variously to Eugène Fourrier or to André Savoir and Pierre Ducrox. In it Arnold Daly played a supposed art lover who goes mad after seeing a collector's paintings and telling the man (William Norris) that all are magnificent except the Van Dyck. The man helps attendants from a mental institution take the visitor away, but when the man returns he finds all his paintings have been stolen except the Van Dyck. The double bill was taken away at the end of its first week.

Many commentators remarked that Arthur Hopkins's production of Henri Bernstein's **The Claw** (10-17-21, Broadhurst)—in a translation by Edward Delaney Dunn and Louis Wolheim—was put on the boards as an effort to supply Lionel Barrymore with a tour de force that would erase unpleasant memories of Barrymore's *Macbeth* debacle. If they were right, then Hopkins succeeded only partially, for the play and its star received good but not unqualified endorsements, and the production ran a modest 115 performances. Barrymore was cast as Achille Cortelon, a distinguished French newspaper editor and Socialist politician, so besotted with his vicious wife (Irene Fenwick) that, under her baleful influence, he prostitutes his high ideals and ruins both his careers. When his wife learns he is about to be tried for his behavior, she deserts him for a young lover, and Cortelon dies.

Last season, farces by those erstwhile collaborators Wilson Collison and Avery Hopwood had opened on the same evening. This year they came in one night apart. Collison's work was called **A Bachelor's Night** (10-17-21, Park) and told of the comic complications that pile one atop the other after Dicky Jarvis (William Roselle) cuts short a vacation and returns home unaware that his maid, Cleetie (Amy Ongley), has rented his apartment to a pretty flapper, Frederica Dill (Leila Frost). The women's attempts to hide while Dicky throws a party for some not very sedate young ladies was supposed to provide the laughs. Apparently they didn't. The party was over after just eight performances.

But Hopwood's **The Demi-Virgin** (10-18-21, Times Square) ran all season, thanks in good measure to some unsought publicity. Hopwood took his play—

very freely—from a French farce by Marcel Prévost, whose similar title spoke of more than one virgin. It spotlights two film stars who separated on their wedding night after Wally Dean (Glenn Anders) received a phone call at one in the morning from an old girlfriend, prompting Gloria Graham (Hazel Dawn) to jump out of bed, rush to Reno, and obtain a divorce. The farce begins with the pair back in Hollywood to finish the film their marriage had interrrupted. They are at each other's throats, and each flaunts a new partner, but that doesn't prevent Gloria from inviting Wally to spend an evening with her. While he is there, but out of the room, Gloria's lady friends appear and indulge in a version of strip poker called "stripping cupid." The visitors rush off when they realize Wally is watching. By the time Wally tells Gloria her Reno divorce has no legal standing in California, the two are on the road to reconciling. Critical consensus was that playgoers who relished earlier Hopwood hits would enjoy this one—regardless of what the critics thought—and that was enough to send many to line up at the box office. The additional help provided by the probably unexpected publicity began during a Pittsburgh tryout ended abruptly by the police. In New York the politically ambitious magistrate William McAdoo went to court to close so "lustful and licentious" a piece. The play was still running profitably in May when the court decided in favor of its producer, Al Woods.

One short-lived failure in an irregular theatre was Charles Mackaye's **As Ye Mould** (10-19-21, People's). It centered on a woman reluctant to tell her husband that she once had a child out of wedlock. When the father of that child, for his own self-serving reasons, demands she adopt the boy, she is forced to reveal her secret. Her husband is compassionate, but the father's would-be bride, disgusted at his behavior, walks out on him.

The lonely farm and the farmer's wife in Kate McLaurin's **The Six-Fifty** (10-24-21, Hudson) reminded some aisle-sitters of the farm and farmer's wife in *The Detour*. Hester Taylor (Lillian Albertson) is unhappy with her isolated existence on a farm where she and her husband (Leonard Willey) have come to take care of his aging parents and grandfather. Each night the sound of the six-fifty express train passing in the distance sets her dreaming of better things she enjoyed in the city. Then one evening the six-fifty is derailed just as it passes the farm. The passengers bring some brief excitement into Hester's life, especially the attractive young, former lover (John Merkyl) of a famous prima donna (Lolita Robertson). The lover, recognizing

that his affair with the singer cannot be rekindled, quietly woos Hester, and Hester almost falls for him, until the prima donna comes between them. After the travelers leave, Hester is prepared to sink back into her old, dreary ways. But news that the railroad wants to buy the farm gives her a little hope of better days to come. Most of the play took place in the drab farmhouse, but one scene, no doubt for variety and effect, occurred in the train's dining car immediately before the accident. Many of the best notices went to Reginald Barlow, who just before the war had been hailed as one of Broadway's most promising young actors. His eighty-nine-year-old grandfather was applauded as a superb bit of character acting, even if one critic described the role as "one of those obvious old-man parts with every angle heavily shadowed, the sort of role that always makes the uninitiated pop-eyed with wonder." But Barlow, like Bennison, was never to recapture his early glory. The play folded after three weeks.

Railroads figured in a second play the same evening, a ferociously left-wing bit of English union propaganda whose inflammatory rhetoric and retrograde fist-on-the-forehead acting caused it to be hissed off the stage by the end of its first week. Ernest Hutchinson's **The Right to Strike** (10-24-21, Comedy) told of brutal railroad strikers who kill a protesting young doctor, and this murder prompts local doctors to refuse to treat strikers or their families until the pleadings of the dead man's widow break the impasse.

Two more English plays followed, both achieving middling runs. The principal attractions of E. Temple Thurston's **The Wandering Jew** (10-26-21, Knickerbocker) were its lavish scenery and Tyrone Power—"a sonorous and majestic player . . . of the old school"—in the title part. Large, colorful settings and costumes moved with the action from the day of the Crucifixion to a Crusader camp in Syria to thirteenth-century Sicily and finally to the Spain of the Inquisition, where the Jew is condemmed to burn at the stake. The curtain falls as flames lick at his feet.

Critics with advanced points of view were more delighted with Harley Granville Barker's eleven-year-old **The Madras House** (10-29-21, Neighborhood Playhouse), an amorphously plotted piece which examined the relationships between the men and women of the Madras and Huxtable families, families partnered in a drapery concern about to be sold. There are the spinster daughters, the young, unmarried, but pregnant employee, the flirtatious wife, the nagging wife, the straitlaced wife, and others, most of whom are thrown off balance when one of the Madras men, who had run off after deserting his family, returns to announce that he lives in Arabia and has converted to Mohammedanism because he prefers its way of dealing with women.

On the 31st, Sothern and Marlowe unpacked their bags at the huge Century Theatre—which years before they had helped open as the New—with a repertory that offered *Twelfth Night*, *The Taming of the Shrew*, *Hamlet* and *The Merchant of Venice*. Critics clearly wanted to see more Shakespeare on the stage, and their notices were respectful, especially to Marlowe. But it was also becoming very obvious that there was something hopelessly pedestrian about the pair and that, while their mountings might be satisfactory, they would never be fully satisfying, certainly never compellingly thrilling. Yet business was astonishing. With only seven performances a week the pair grossed $14,000, $17,000, $19,000, and $24,000 in the first four weeks, pulling in more than $5000 for a Saturday matinee. Such attendance was sufficient to induce the stars to remain an extra two weeks.

Helen Hayes suffered her second failure of the season when she was cast in the lead of Sidney Toler and Marion Short's **Golden Days** (11-1-21, Gaiety). She played Mary Anne, a country girl whose sweetheart breaks off their friendship when he comes under the spell of a city sophisticate. To help her win back the unfaithful young man by making him jealous an attractive neighbor, Dick (Donald Gallaher), agrees to pose as her beau. The ploy works, but by that time Dick and Mary Anne are in love. The comedy was directed by Toler, who had begun his career in cheap touring melodramas and would become one of filmland's Charlie Chans.

Golden Days's failure meant that November's first hit—albeit not a big one—was Sacha Guitry's **The Grand Duke** (11-1-21, Lyceum), in a translation by Achmed Abdullah. It unfolded the story of the exiled, penniless Russian Grand Duke Feodor (Lionel Atwill) who takes a job teaching languages to the daughter (Vivian Tobin) of a rich Parisian plumber (John L. Shine). He discovers that the girl's singing teacher (Lina Abarbanell) is his old flame and that the teacher's pleasant son (Morgan Farley) is also his son. He deftly arranges for his son and the plumber's daughter to marry. Then he convinces the singing teacher and the plumber to wed, implicitly trusting he can be his old flame's lover once more.

A slightly bigger (177 performances) but more memorable success came in the next evening, Eugene O'Neill's **Anna Christie** (11-2-21, Vanderbilt). Chris Christopherson (George Marion), loung-

ing at Johnny-the-Priest's seedy waterfront saloon between trips on his coal barge, receives a letter from a daughter he has not seen since she was a child, when she and her mother went to live with relatives on a Minnesota farm. "Ay tank it's better Anna live on farm," Chris explains, "den she don't know dat ole davil sea, she don't know fader like me." Anna (Pauline Lord) soon shows up, and it is obvious to everyone except Chris that Anna has been beset by her own devils. At sixteen she had been seduced by a cousin and soon after ran off to St. Paul, where she became a prostitute. Since Chris is about to go to sea again, Anna hesitatingly agrees to join him. The sea seems to regenerate her, "like I'd found something I'd missed and been looking for." Her father rescues some sailors whose ship has sunk. One of the men, burly, boastful Mat Burke (Frank Shannon), falls in love with Anna and proposes to her. Before she can accept, Anna feels she must tell her history to Mat and her father. As a result, the men get drunk and sign on with a ship heading for Africa. Before the men leave, the threesome are reconciled, with Anna promising to wait and "make a regular place for you to come back to." Chris cannot be sure what that means, telling everyone, "Only dat ole davil sea, she know." Critics praised a cast that was "as nearly perfect as could be hoped for" and Robert Edmond Jones's settings of the bar and the barge, "remarkably successful in creating the desired Joseph Conrad sea atmosphere." Of the play, Kenneth Macgowan wrote in the *Globe*, "For sheer realism, stripped to its ugly vitals, *Anna Christie* is the finest piece of writing O'Neill has done," while the *Daily Mail*'s Burns Mantle proclaimed it "towers above most of the plays in town." Yet many of the same critics blasted what they perceived to be the drama's tacked-on happy ending, which Mantle branded "the happy ending all true artists of the higher drama so generously despise" and Woollcott dismissed more succinctly as "dross." Thirty-six years later the happy ending was repeated in a musical version, *New Girl in Town*.

At the beginning of Booth Tarkington's **The Intimate Strangers** (11-7-21, Henry Miller's), which the author had written in the ultimately unrealized hope of luring Maude Adams out of retirement, the curtain rises on a darkened stage. Only a faint oblong of luminous blue hints at a large window. Then a door is pushed opened; a man with a lantern enters and switches on a light, which discloses the main room of a drab, rural railroad station. A man "somewhere in the early forties" is seen sleeping on a bench. He is Ames (Alfred Lunt), and he has been stranded by a devastating storm. So has one lovely lady, Isabel Stuart (Billie Burke), who is huddled outside in the cold, since she and Ames have quarreled after misunderstanding each other's willingness to share a sandwich and hardboiled egg that the lady brought with her. In time she comes back in, Ames lights a fire in the stove, and the two soon are reconciled. In fact, it becomes clear that Ames is falling in love. He tells Isabel, "I'm going to talk as sentimentally as I *feel*, just for once in my life—when I looked at you I caught a—a perfume of sweeter days—yes, *better* days than this!" Yet he is taken aback to realize that his mustache, his conservative dress, and his earlier statement that no "brazen little hussy in breeches with a flask of homemade gin in her pocket" could possess any charm have caused Isabel to take him for an older man. However, both are too tired to prolong their discussion and soon fall asleep. They are awakened at dawn by the arrival of Isabel's niece, Florence (Frances Howard), and Florence's suitor, Johnnie White (Glenn Hunter), who have come to rescue Miss Stuart. The foursome return to Isabel's country estate, where Florence proceeds to vamp Ames, much to Johnnie's ire and Isabel's amusement. Intrigued by Ames's persistent attempts to discover her age, and also uncertain if Ames really dislikes flappers as much as he claims, Isabel pretends to be older than she is. She talks knowingly of Tilden and Hayes, and the 1876 Centennial Exposition, dons a granny cap, and claims to be a bit arthritic. It turns out that Isabel is the daughter of her father's second marriage when he was a very old man and that Florence is actually her great-niece. So Ames and Isabel are embracing as the last curtain falls. Although Percy Hammond, who had recently replaced Broun on the *Tribune*, was, like many of his colleagues, ambivalent about the play, he called the long opening scene "one of the most sweetly sophisticated interludes of Mr. Tarkington's achievements as a playwright." Again in line with other critics, he gave long and flattering attention to the show's star, suggesting she was unfortunately underrated as a comedienne and lauding her characterization with "its twinkling pathos, its sagacities, its mockery and banter." Praise was also poured on Glenn Hunter for his latest embodiment of a mercurially pleased, mercurially angered adolescent. Since reviewers could not look into the future, most passed over Lunt's performance with perfunctory, though not unfavorable, comments. The play ran just short of three months, then toured.

Two other plays that opened the same night both closed the following Saturday. Bessie Barriscale, a blonde beauty who had left the stage to win celebrity in films, returned briefly in Howard Hickman's **The Skirt** (11-7-21, Bijou). She played Betty Price, who disguises herself as a boy named Bob and heads for the Arizona ranch of Jack Warren (Paul Harvey), the sweetheart with whom she has had a falling-out. Her disguise fools no one, and the ranch hands give her a rough time. So in Act III she puts on her most elegant dress and wins an apology from Jack.

The Great Way (11-7-21, Park) apparently was a vanity production. At least its leading lady, Helen Freeman, was also its producer, co-director, and, with Horace Fish, its co-author. She played Dulce, a Spanish prostitute, who nurses back to health a young man, José Luis (Moroni Olsen), after he has been wounded in a duel with her jealous lover. She falls in love with him and is heartbroken when he tells her he must return to his fiancée. But his goodness inspires her to leave her trade, learn to sing, and become a renowned prima donna. She must go on singing even after she discovers José Luis again many years later—happily married to a lady who has befriended her. Miss Freeman went on to a long but undistinguished acting career.

Things were looking up, for George Scarborough's **The Mad Dog** (11-8-21, Comedy) ran twice as long as its two predecessors, fifteen performances. At twilight, a befouled, unshaven figure is seen creeping about a quiet mission near the Mexican border. The figure proves to be Rab Mobley (Conway Tearle), escaped from a Colorado prison where he was serving a life sentence for murdering a faithless sweetheart. He spots the pious Maria (Helen Menken) praying at an altar, seizes her, drags her into another room to rape her, then flees across the border. But he soon comes back, repentant, and begs Maria to shoot him. Fearing he might attack her again, she does. However, the wound is not fatal, and by the time Padre Francolon (Forrest Robinson) has restored him to health, Rab and Maria are in love. The priest assists the pair in fleeing again to Mexico.

Then Frederic and Fannie Hatton's **We Girls** (11-9-21, 48th St.) came along and doubled *The Mad Dog*'s stay. It reemployed a motif that Pinero's *The Magistrate* and several earlier plays had used with more comic skill. Mrs. Carter Durand (Mary Young), in reality forty-six, has a facelift and determines to pass herself off as thirty. But she also has a nineteen-year-old daughter, Harriet (Juliette Day), who leaves her convent school (in a stolen automobile) and comes to New York to prevent her mother's making a foolish move. She does not relish being "on the brink of an infant stepfather." She also seeks an eligible bachelor for herself. The one she eventually lands is the very one her baby-talking mother had her own eyes on.

Eugene O'Neill's second play of the season, **The Straw** (11-10-21, Greenwich Village), extended the procession of failures. The drama focused on two inmates at a sanitorium for tubercular patients. Eileen Carmody (Margalo Gillmore) is the more seriously ill of the two, her glimmer of hope shattered when she realizes her fiancé will not remain loyal. Stephen Murray (Otto Kruger) is a newspaperman whom, prior to his release, Eileen encourages to try loftier writings. They are success-ful. Before he leaves, Eileen confesses her love for him, a love he does not return. But he is grateful for her friendship and comes back later to visit her, only to find her dying. Desperate to give her hope, he feigns affection and proposes marriage. Although Eileen sees through him, she accepts, clinging to the only straw she can grasp. When Stephen berates a nurse who has told him that Eileen's case is hopeless, the nurse can only retort emptily, "God bless you both!" Otto Kruger, brought in as a very last-minute replacement (opening-night programs still listed his predecessor's name) won the best notices; Gillmore was seen as perhaps too inexperi-enced to bring out all the nuances in her part. While several critics liked the play, none thought it among the author's best; and his growing reputation for gloom and doom kept playgoers away. Producer George Tyler withdrew the piece after twenty showings.

Playgoers looking for escapist entertainment might have thought that at least one of the three plays to open the next Monday evening would have broken the succession of failures. None did. The longest run—seventy-four performances—went to William A. Brady's mounting of **Nature's Noble-man** (11-14-21, Apollo), Samuel Shipman and Clara Lipman's vehicle for Lipman's husband, Louis Mann. Following last season's fiasco with a serious, propagandizing drama, Mann reverted to the comparative safety of dialect comedy. That safety really was not much, since *Variety* echoed most critical sentiment when it put down the play as "the most hopeless failure of the legitimate sea-son." Mann played Carl Schnitzler, the proprietor of a Catskills boardinghouse, who must rein in a kittenish wife (Louise Beaudet), a son (John Roche) in love with a married woman, and a flapper daughter (Sue MacManamy). Since the daughter is pursued by the very man (Morgan Wallace) whose wife (Allyn Gillyn) her brother desires, she convinces the husband to allow his wife

to divorce him. But then the young girl marries an ad man instead.

The precise message in Susan Glaspell's **The Verge** (11-14-21, Provincetown Playhouse) eluded critics. They agreed only that the play revolved about Claire Archer (Margaret Wycherly), a women displeased by her two marriages, her unresponsive daughter, her puritan ancestors, and everybody else she encounters. Her determination to put her past behind her and enter a more enlightened world drives her to the verge and finally over the brink into insanity. She strangles a kindly lover (Henry O'Neill) and keens "Nearer My God to Thee" to the empty air as the curtain falls. All that reviewers could readily praise was Wycherly's intense and moving performance and Cleon Throckmorton's imaginative settings. Audiences viewed his first- and third-act greenhouse through a greenhouse-like framework, while his second-act tower suggested fantastically twisted masonry. The settings were strikingly lit by a large suspended lamp covered with intricately patterned grillwork.

Arnold Bennett's **The Title** (11-14-21, Belmont) told of an English politician who would reject a baronetcy because he believes his government's selection of honorees is dictated by mercenary considerations. But his socially ambitious wife forces him to accept it. The play proved too English for Broadway.

From the moment the curtain rose to disclose the Marvins' cabin in Colorado, with guns scattered about the room and talk of how Hal Marvin (Lowell Sherman) has become a crack shot, in Marjorie Chase and Eugene Walter's **The Man's Name** (11-15-21, Republic) playgoers could expect lots of loud, smoky gunfire in short order. Their disappointment may explain the play's quick failure. Marvin's wife (Dorothy Shoemaker) has brought her husband, a mostly unpublished author, out west in hopes of curing his tuberculosis. However, Marvin learns she obtained the money for the trip from her wealthy former boss, Marshall Dunn (Felix Krembs), a known womanizer. Dunn appears, hoping for more favors from Mrs. Marvin. Hal shoots him, but only once and in the hand, and, after Dunn leaves, forgives his wife.

A. A. Milne's **The Great Broxopp** (11-15-21, Punch and Judy) could not lure playgoers for all that it delighted many reviewers. That English jack-of-many-theatrical-trades Iden Payne was producer and director and assumed the leading role of James Broxopp, who has made a fortune with baby foods but who is forced into very comfortable but unsatisfy-ing retirement until his wife (Pamela Gaythorne), sensing his problem, sees to it he loses his money and must start a new business.

What was becoming a dismaying string of flops continued with Rachel Crothers's **Everyday** (11-16-21, Bijou). Its heroine was Phyllis Nolan (Tallulah Bankhead), who returns to her stodgy Midwest home after two eye-opening years in Europe. She rebels against her hectoring, corrupt father (Frank Sheridan), her milquetoast mother (Minnie Dupree), and all her other narrow-minded townsfolk. Ignoring her father's commands, she decides to wed the son (Henry Hull) of the town butcher, a much decorated, idealistic veteran. In her autobiography Bankhead noted that the critics considered the play "something south of Shakespeare or Sheridan," neglecting to add that their primary complaint was that the playwright missed a golden opportunity for social satire and a comedy of manners by opting to write instead another obvious piece about the postwar generation gap.

Apparently no critic could resist an allusion to Sherlock Holmes in reviewing **The Dream Maker** (11-21-21, Empire), which William Gillette took from a story by Howard E. Morton. Gillette assumed the principal part of Dr. Paul Clement, a physician who has served time in prison and who discovers that Marion Bruce (Miriam Sears), the daughter of a woman with whom he was once in love, and her seemingly feebleminded husband (Charles Laite), are being held by a gang of blackmailers (called "badger-crooks" in the parlance of the time), who hope to compromise her and then demand a sizable ransom. But Clement is not a doctor for nothing. He drugs the crooks' food, making them so sick that they are happy to confess, tell Marion she dreamt the whole horrible affair, and be on their way. Some Broadway smart money attributed the play's disappointing ten-week run to a title that failed to suggest it was a rather good thriller, with Gillette performing in his best, insouciant Holmes style.

No producer publicly took the blame for **Marie Antoinette** (11-22-21, Playhouse), but since its star was William A. Brady's wife and since Brady owned the Playhouse, he was generally held responsible. Insiders did know that Edymar, which was given as the playwright's sole monicker, was actually a pen name for Aubrey M. Kennedy and Margaret Mayo. Grace George, herself mired in a succession of more or less unprofitable plays, found herself in the latest Broadway dud, cast in the title role of the frivolous queen whose amorous hints are politely rejected by a high-minded Count Axel Fersen (Pedro de Cordoba) but who nobly tries to save her unloved husband (Fred Eric) and children from the guillotine as she is led to her own execution. De Cordoba, another last-minute replacement, annoyed some writers by constantly snapping his fingers in an effort to recall his lines.

The players in Forrest Rutherford's **Her Salary Man** (11-28-21, Cort) may have learned their lines well but had little time to repeat them. A will provides that, until she marries, Emily Sladen (Ruth Shepley) must remain under the supervision of her prim, prissy, and haughty spinster aunt, "Mrs." Sophie Perkins (Edna May Oliver). This leads Emily to tell a friend she plans to "rent" a husband at a handsome fee, provided he agrees to always keep his distance. A newspaperman overhears her and prints the story. Emily is swamped by applicants. The man she chooses is actually not an applicant, but Emily mistakes him for one. He is John "Bunny" Brown (A. H. Van Buren), a wealthy bachelor. On a lark, he accepts, only to find himself falling in love with her. He returns the rent money and demands his matrimonial rights. Luckily, Emily has fallen in love with him.

Even the Theatre Guild could not override the doldrums. Its double bill of Denys Amiel and André Obey's *La Souriante Mme Baudet*, done in Ruth Livingstone's translation as **The Wife with the Smile,** and her translation of Georges Courteline's **Boubouroche** (11-28-21, Garrick) lasted only as long as the Guild's regulars could be counted on. In the former a wife (Blanche Yurka), driven to distraction by her fault-finding, nagging husband (Arnold Daly), a man who likes to put an empty gun to his head and pull the trigger to frighten guests, secretly loads the pistol. In an argument the next day, the husband takes the gun, points it at her, and shoots. The bullet misses. But the husband now comprehends his wife's feelings. The shorter piece, a farce, tells of a hopelessly dupable old man (Daly), who believes the lies of his mistress, Adèle (Olive May), even after he finds her hiding a lover in her closet.

November's lone smash hit came in at the end. The entry was David Belasco's somewhat bowdlerized production of André Picard's **Kiki** (11-29-21, Belasco). Kiki (Lenore Ulric) is little more than an overgrown Parisian street urchin who sometimes has held odd jobs at the Folies Monplaisir Music Hall. She is convinced she merits more attention, especially from the music hall's distant, matter-of-fact manager, Victor Renal (Sam B. Hardy). A doorman who attempts to eject her is stabbed with her hatpin for his efforts, and she subsequently wrestles Renal's valet to the ground. Attracted by her tenacity, Renal takes her to dinner and then to his apartment. His attempt to kiss her earns him a kick, but she refuses to leave the apartment. The appearance of his prima donna ex-wife [mistress in the Parisian version] (Arline Frederick) rouses Kiki to further frenzy. At one point she even feigns a cataleptic trance. But she ultimately succeeds in driving the woman away and winning a proposal from Renal. Most critics found the play competently written and entertaining. Many were amused by Kiki's insistence that she was a good girl, which they saw as a concession to American prudery. What made the evening for virtually all the men on the aisle was Ulric's Kiki. "You simply must go to see 'Kiki' if for no other reason than to witness Lenore Ulric's astonishing performance," Hornblow urged his readers. Woollcott concurred, noting Ulric "is Kiki, and the relish and the fire and the comic spirit with which she undertakes the embodiment of this naive, ignorant, aspiring, ardent little Parisian chorus girl is a joy to behold . . . and in her one little collapse of discouragement and freshet of tears you recognize a touching and authentic actress." Thanks in no small measure to its star, *Kiki* stayed around for 600 performances.

The sedate but fun-loving Madame Leland was no Kiki, but to friends whom she had often helped and who gather at her Monte Carlo hotel after her funeral, the little and very old lady had been the "sinners' saint." When most of the mourners depart, leaving her last lover (Charles Francis) to his thoughts, the dead lady's ghost (Elsie Ferguson) appears and tells him her true history. So begins Zoë Akins's **The Varying Shore** (12-5-21, Hudson). But Madame Leland herself does not begin at the beginning. Instead she recounts her tale in a reverse chronology, telling how in 1870 in Paris, when she was forty, she sacrificed her own feelings and refused to tell her son (Rollo Peters), who was unaware of her true identity, that she was his mother, lest his social standing be destroyed; moving back to 1859 New York, she leaves her wastrel lover (James Crane), on learning he prefers another woman; and finally she reveals that as a teenager in 1847 Richmond, she was seduced by a dashing, cocky neighbor (Rollo Peters) and ran away just before their wedding rather than enter what she recognized would be a loveless marriage. Critics split on their assessment of the play, with even those who admired it admitting the reverse chronology made for certain difficulties. The cast, except for Peters, was judged inferior. To save the show, the play was restaged to allow the scenes to be offered in their normal chronological order. Yet playgoers remained uninter-

ested, so the piece called it a day after sixty-six performances.

At least Akins was an experienced dramatist with a feeling for theatre. The famous novelist Theodore Dreiser had neither theatrical experience nor a genuine theatrical instinct. His shortcomings were made obvious with the opening of his **The Hand of the Potter** (12-5-21, Provincetown Playhouse). The Berchanskys, Jewish immigrants, live in a tenement whose tin roof makes life almost unbearable in the summer. The younger children are concerned that their father, a poor tailor, and their mother refuse to have their son Isadore institutionalized. He has just been released from prison, having served time for molesting a young girl. When Isadore next rapes and kills a young Irish girl who lives in the same tenement, his siblings and mother lie to defend him, but his emotional father breaks down and confesses to a grand jury. Isadore has fled but, finding his situation hopeless, inhales enough gas from a gas jet to kill himself. The landlord whom Isadore owes money berates Berchansky for not bringing up his son properly. The old man snarls back, "Vy pull at de walls of my house! Dey are already down!" Not only was Dreiser's ear for Jewish speech defective, but his use of extended soliloquies added to his problems. And his curious stage directions further demonstrated a lack of contemporary restraint. Thus, when Isadore approaches the young girl whom he assaults, Dreiser's directions read: "*His shoulder jerks. As she looks, he stands and stares at her in a greedy, savage, half-insane way, his face coloring. . . . His expression flares to one of fierce, demonic hunger. He snatches the glasses away, puts them behind his back, laughs a playful, semi-idiotic laugh.*" Those reviewers who wrote about the play attacked both the writing and the production. It struggled on for only two weeks, with the foul-tempered Dreiser reportedly railing about the ineptitude of his actors, director, designer, and his critics.

What Gladys Unger thought about the one-week failure of her **The Fair Circassian** (12-6-21, Republic) is unrecorded. It was set in early nineteenth-century England, where the new Persian ambassador (Claude King) arrives carrying numerous gifts for the gouty, leering Prince Regent (Louis Wolheim), including a beautiful young slave girl, Zora (Margaret Mower). The court accepts the jewels but rejects the girl, whom the ambassador then claims as his own. Zora, given to understand that in England she is a free woman, in turn spurns the envoy until she concludes he is preferable to any of the stuffy, cold Englishmen she has met.

The next two evenings brought in a pair of

revivals. On the 7th at the Playhouse, George Broadhurst's 1911 hit, *Bought and Paid For*, came to life again with Charles Richman recreating his original role as a wealthy businessman who treats a wife as just some more property. Helen MacKellar was the wife, and William Harrigan played the comic role that had made Frank Craven famous. The 8th saw the Gaiety house the return of Paul Armstrong's 1910 thriller, *Alias Jimmy Valentine*, with Otto Kruger starred as the reformed safe-cracker. Both plays had only modest runs.

Somewhat inexplicably, since several of the most influential reviewers panned the comedy, Clare Kummer's **The Mountain Man** (12-12-21, Maxine Elliott's) enjoyed a profitable twenty-one-week run. A young, largely untutored mountain boy, Aaron Winterfield (Sidney Blackmer), is brought to town by his relatives to claim an inheritance. To wheedle as much of that inheritance from him as they can, his relatives have Paris-schooled Delaney McCloud (Catherine Dale Owen) vamp and marry him. But after Aaron discovers that Del has a lover still waiting for her in France, he angrily enlists, hoping to be sent to France where he can shoot at both Germans and the lover. After the war he returns, a decorated hero who has killed lots of Huns but not the lover. However, Del has come to love him, so all ends happily.

If Dreiser's saga of Jewish life had been swept away swiftly, so was a more authentic view, Peretz Hirschbein's *Di Puste Kretshme*, translated as **The Idle Inn** (12-20-21, Plymouth) by Isaac Goldberg and Louis Wolheim. Its simple story depicted how Maite (Eva MacDonald) comes to love wild but attractive Eisik (Ben Ami), a self-assured horse thief, who kidnaps her at what was to be her wedding to the unworldly Mendel (Edward G. Robinson). Were, as some of Maite's villagers believe, the kidnappers not really Eisik and his buddies but evil spirits in league with Eisik? The cast also included Mary Shaw, an actress never raised to the heights many thought she deserved, and two future celebrities, the co-translator, Wolheim, and Sam Jaffe. Despite its short run, the play would be given a second hearing years later by the Federal Theatre Project.

The four productions brought in immediately before Christmas found varying fates. Cosmo Hamilton's **Danger** (12-22-21, 39th St.) was a ten-week near miss. It told how ambitious, passionless Mrs. Scorrier (Marie Goff) locks her husband (H. B. Warner) out of her bedroom on their wedding night, telling him she has no intention of being a dutiful wife. Her continuing aloofness drives him to

think of suicide until he encounters Mary Hubbard (Kathlene MacDonell) and falls in love with her. Because his cruel wife will not consider a divorce, Scorrier knowingly sacrifices his own promising legal career for happiness with Mary. Critics were not happy with the actress who played Mary, one calling her more monotonous than passionless, and they gave the other principals short shrift. Nor did they like the stilted, emotionally charged dialogue. In a supporting role, young Leslie Howard gave "a delightful performance" as "a blissfully happy English husband."

But almost everyone approved of A. A. Milne's **The Dover Road** (12-23-21, Bijou), which had yet to be done in Milne's native England, but which ran out the New York season. His fey, Barrie-like story featured an eccentric Englishman, Latimer (Charles Cherry), whose home on the Dover Road is used by elopers heading for the Continent. Whenever possible Latimer detains the young couples for a day or two, giving them the opportunity to observe each other in domestic circumstances, and thus often changing their minds. One couple he has just detained sees no reason to alter their plans, but the would-be husband (Reginald Mason) of the second pair opts to return home, while his fiancée (Winifred Lenihan) decides to remain with Latimer.

That same evening saw a another revival of the 1895 success *Trilby*, with Wilton Lackaye still as the evil mesmerist Svengali, at the National.

Chester Bailey Fernald, who had been an American when he wrote his 1897 failure, *The Cat and the Cherub*, had long since moved to England, where Londoners reportedly had enjoyed his **The Married Woman** (12-24-21, Princess). Not enough New Yorkers agreed to give it an extended run. It told of a lady (Beatrice Maude) who resolves to keep her first marriage undyingly romantic. When she fails, she turns for comfort to the philosophizing bachelor (Norman Trevor) who had warned her of the impossibility of her dreams.

After a one-night respite—after all, it was Christmas—four plays came in to stand trial. Olga Petrova—a film and vaudeville favorite—was both author and star of **The White Peacock** (12-26-21, Comedy). She played Revette di Ribera y Santallos, who has left her wicked husband (Leon Gordon), the Spanish premier, and set up as an artist. The ever vivid Woollcott sets the scene in her sleeping room: "It looks rather like the corner of a museum and is fairly giddy with atmosphere. Outside the blue moonlight of old Spain streams across the fragrant crescendo, and out of the romance-laden night floats the strumming of a guitar. . . . Dona

Revette casts off her burdensome frock of blue-green brocade, puts on a simple nightgown of silver (with a train eight feet long) and, turning down the candles, goes to bed." But her room is invaded by the swashbuckling Don Caesar (Malcolm Fassett), who hopes to avenge wrongs the premier has done to him by getting at Revette. Though at one point he shoots her, the pair soon are in each other's embrace, and the premier's death promises to keep them there.

The other American entry of the evening, a revival of Edwin Milton Royle's 1905 success, *The Squaw Man*, relit the Astor with William Faversham once again in his original role of an expatriate Englishman who makes a tragic liaison with an Indian girl.

The evening's most successful importation was "Sapper" [Cyril McNeill] and Gerald du Maurier's London favorite **Bulldog Drummond** (12-26-21, Knickerbocker). Drummond (A. E. Matthews) advertises for adventure and finds it when he is visited by Phyllis Benton (Dorothy Tetley), his dead buddy's sister. She gets him to rescue a rich American who has been kidnapped by a gang of international criminals, drugged, and held until he turns over much of his fortune. He refuses. Phyllis's concerns are exacerbated because her uncle, whom she does not know is a forger, is in league with the crooks. Although the uncle kills himself, Drummond nabs the gang (except for the mastermind, who uses a ruse to make a clever escape), frees the American, and kisses Phyllis. The play kept audiences on edge for twenty weeks.

Even with Leo Ditrichstein as star, Solita Solano's Americanization of Sabatino Lopez's Italian comedy as **Face Value** (12-26-21, 49th St.) could not find an audience. In a grotesque brick-red pompadoured wig and thick horn-rimmed glasses, Ditrichstein impersonated a Cuban-American stockbroker so homely that men refuse to believe he can charm any woman. But he does more than that, and always walks away scot-free when an irate husband or suspicious lover takes a good look at him.

Students might insist that there was a fifth opening that night, when Fritz Leiber came into the Lexington with a Shakespearean repertory that included his Macbeth, Hamlet, and Romeo. But he returned later in the season to a genuinely first-class house, and his productions will be examined then.

The year ended on a high note, with the nearly year-long success of Walter Hackett's **Captain Applejack** (12-30-21, Cort). Hackett, like Chester Bailey Fernald, was an American who had found better luck in England. His comedy already was a success

there. Bored with his dull English country existence, Ambrose Applejohn (Wallace Eddinger) plans to sells his Cornwall estate and travel. He places an advertisement in a magazine. Shortly afterwards, a woman (Mary Nash) claiming to be a dancer fleeing from communism, a psychic and his wife (Ferdinand Gottschalk and Helen Lackaye) claiming their car has broken down, and a Russian (Hamilton Revelle) saying he is seeking the runaway dancer all come to Applejohn's home. Applejohn refuses to believe they are not house hunters. When the frightened dancer faints in his arms he remarks, "It's awful. She may die before she has a chance to make an offer for the place." But after they go, he falls asleep and dreams he is a pirate and his visitors are all mutineers. Only his ward, Poppy Faire (Phoebe Foster), figures as a goodie in his dream, which proves to be more or less prophetic. The visitors turn out to be crooks attempting to steal a map which is hidden in the house and which shows the whereabouts of buried treasure. Applejohn bests the villains (by using an alarm clock to simulate the ringing of a phone they believe they have disabled) and decides life with Poppy would not be boring anywhere. Although only Eddinger and Nash were starred, a splendid cast that included a number of old favorites added to the play's attraction.

The new year also opened with another season-long hit, Samuel Shipman's **Lawful Larceny** (1-2-22, Republic). Marion Dorsey (Margaret Lawrence) learns that her husband (Alan Dinehart) has been having an affair with Vivian Hepburn (Gail Kane), the notorious proprietress of gambling rooms, and that Hepburn has stolen her husband's securities. She assumes her maiden name and takes employment as Vivian's personal secretary. Before long she has recovered the securities, plus all the money in the lady's safe. She then discovers that she can be sent to prison for stealing the money but that Vivian cannot be jailed for borrowing a husband. Her repentant husband helps bring about a happy ending. Played more as a comedy than as a melodrama, the play pleased both critics and the public.

Not many critics or playgoers cared for John Colton and Daisy H. Andrews's **Drifting** (1-2-22, Playhouse), which some saw as *The Man Who Came Back* with the sexes reversed. Having been kicked out of her home by her fanatically religious father, Cassie Cook (Alice Brady) sails to China, becomes a cabaret singer there, then begins to hit the skids. Just as she is about to touch bottom, she meets Badlands McKinney (Robert Warwick), an unjustly cashiered soldier who is also heading for perdition.

But the two fall in love and help each other to do a bootstrap recovery.

Nor was there much enthusiasm for **The S.S. Tenacity** (1-2-22, Belmont), which Sidney Howard adapted from Charles Vildrac's French original, *Le Paquebot "Tenacity."* In it, two unemployed printers, the shy Ségard (Tom Powers) and the more forceful Bastien (George Gaul), are about to take a ship to Canada when they spot a sweet little waitress (Marguerite Forrest). All night Ségard dreams of the lovely life he and the girl could have together, but in the morning, when he calls for Bastien, he discovers that his friend has run off with the girl, and he must sail to Canada alone. Augustin Duncan, the play's producer, took the part of a boozy old tar who served as a sort of Greek chorus.

The next week brought in an American failure and a foreign hit. The American play was Edward E. Rose's **Rosa Machree** (1-9-22, Lexington), which featured one of Jacob Adler's daughters, Julia, as the offspring of an interfaith marriage. Her aristocratic English grandparents will accept her only if she agrees never to see her Jewish mother again. Her mother (Sonia Marcelle) contrives to obtain a position as a servant in the aristocrats' home, and by curtain time all the principals are reconciled.

The foreign play was a Russian piece, the work of Leonid Andreyev, which the Theatre Guild mounted in Gregory Zilbourg's translation as **He Who Gets Slapped** (1-9-22, Garrick). To escape an unhappy marriage, false friends, and money problems, a Frenchman (Richard Bennett) joins a circus as a clown called merely He and earns laughs by letting fellow clowns batter him much as the world has. But he cannot escape reality, for he falls in love with Consuelo (Margalo Gillmore), a young bareback rider, then learns her unscrupulous father (Frank Reicher) is about to sell her to a lecherous old nobleman. To bring an end to both their agonies, he poisons the girl and himself. Simonson's brightly colored setting of a circus "greenroom," with caged animals, gaudily dressed trainers, acrobats, and clowns passing through, set the light comic tone with which the work was played. Bennett gave a Mercutio-like performance, which proved satisfactory but left many longing to see a more probing actor in the role.

Fritz Leiber, who earlier had offered some of his Shakespearean repertory at cheap prices in the huge Lexington Opera House, now began a brief stand on the 16th at the far more intimate 48th Street Theatre asking more traditional prices. Critics saw in him a young, attractive-looking player, given to much that was accepted practice in his interpretations but not nearly as fustian as his mentor, Robert Mantell. His youthfulness allowed for more spirited productions than Marlowe and Sothern presented, but his settings and costumes often lacked their richness. For this visit he brought out *Macbeth, Julius Caesar,* and *Romeo and Juliet.*

J. Hartley Manners's **The National Anthem** (1-23-22, Henry Miller's) suggested that playgoers didn't have to run off to China to set foot on the road to hell. New York and Paris would serve as well. Teetotaling Marian Hale (Laurette Taylor) finds that out when, against everyone's warnings, she marries an incorrigible playboy, Arthur Carlton (Ralph Morgan). At first it appears that she can keep him under control, but in due course his hard-drinking, high-living ways take command of both of them. They are surely headed for self-destruction when a drunken Marian inadvertently takes some bichloride of mercury to relieve a headache. Carlton, even more drunk, is killed in a dash for a doctor. A much sobered Marian seeks solace with a quiet homebody, Tom Carroll (Frank M. Thomas). Throughout the play a small, concealed jazz band played "The Sheik of Araby" over and over again, providing the play with a sustained background not unlike the drums in *The Emperor Jones.* Whatever critics thought of the play—and many found it too stridently opposed to modern ways, too ready to point to jazz and gin as the fount of all of America's current ills—they adored the star. In one of his last reviews before his unexpected death, Louis V. Defoe wrote in the *World* that hers was "a human, moving, deep and persuasive performance." *Variety*'s man, thrilled with her acting, called her "America's most brilliant, most able and most worth-while artiste of the stage." The production's disappointing fifteen-week run was blamed on its off-putting title, which few theatregoers realized referred ironically to contemporary jazz.

The Deluge, which Arthur Hopkins brought into his Plymouth Theatre on the 27th, was a revival of the same play he had offered Broadway in 1917. It failed once again.

It was Grace George, producer, and not Grace George, actress, who met with success when she presented her adaptation of Paul Géraldy's *Les Noces d'argent* as **The Nest** (1-28-22, 48th St.), even though some critics slammed the show for reemploying scenery and costumes that had been used in some of the season's failures and had not been so much as retouched. It centered on a mother (Lucile Watson) who is dismayed when her coddled children (Juliette Crosby and Kenneth MacKenna) leave to make lives of their own—her son going so far as to have a liaison with her dearest friend (Christine Norman).

The popular London star Marie Löhr, grown matronly though only in her early thirties, began a visit by offering Robert Hichens's **The Voice from the Minaret** (1-30-22, Hudson). She played an unhappily wed English lady who has a brief romance with a dashing young man (Herbert Marshall) until the man chooses a life in the Church. Edmund Gwenn, as the lady's unkind husband, won the most glowing notices.

Down in the Village a minor American poet, Arthur Davison Ficke, came badly a cropper with his retelling of an old legend in modern terms as **Mr. Faust** (1-30-22, Provincetown Playhouse). This latter-day Faust was a wealthy New York business-man and socialite who sells his soul to Nicholas Satan (Moroni Olsen) and travels to India and Europe searching for happiness before the customary ending. Maurice Browne, founder of the Chicago Little Theatre and one of the guiding lights in the whole Little Theatre movement, assumed the title role, while his actress-wife, Ellen Van Volkenburg, served as producer.

Edward Sheldon and Doris Keane, no doubt praying to repeat their fabulous success of *Romance*, found instead that they had only a squeak-by hit with a play which Sheldon derived from Menyhért Lengyel and Lajos Biró's *A cárno*, and translated literally as **The Czarina** (1-31-22, Empire). The romantic comedy-melodrama recounted how a roughneck officer, Count Alexei Czerny (Basil Rathbone), becomes the lover of Catherine II after alerting her to an impending coup. No matter that Alexei is supposedly betrothed to Catherine's lady-in-waiting, Annie (Lois Meredith). But he eventually begins to resent Catherine's subtly condescending treatment of him, so plots his own coup. He nearly carries it off, but at the last minute the tables are turned and he is condemned to death. Catherine forgives him after she finds a new lover. Reviewers accepted the play as a passable vehicle but disagreed on whether the star was "brilliant," "triumphant," and "radiant" or "stiff" "unregal, harsh of voice and theatrical," and "unconvincing."

A revival of John Galsworthy's 1912 entry, *The Pigeon*, at the Greenwich Village on the 2nd got February off to a quiet start. His story of a man who shelters street people ran for twelve weeks at the tiny house.

Uptown, Jules Eckert Goodman's **The Law-breaker** (2-6-22, Booth) ran just as long. Its central figure was a handsome, suave crook, Jim Thorne (William Courtenay), who has stolen $60,000 from a bank and would be heading for prison but for Joan Fowler (Blanche Yurka), the banker's daughter. She subscribes to a new school of thought that says criminals are more swiftly reformed by being al-lowed to develop their own sense of moral responsi-bility than by jail terms. To back her ideas, she pledges her $75,000 pearl necklace if she is allowed to try her theory on Thorne. After laughing off the whole idea, Thorne's next reaction is to return the $60,000 and swipe the more valuable jewels. But in time Joan brings about his reformation. Her own reward must be personal vindication, since the new Thorne heads to the altar with Kit Grey (Marguerite Maxwell), a feisty street gamin who professes her own willingness to go the straight route. If critics could not see eye to eye on the play's merits, performers could not agree on acting styles. At nearly fifty, Courtenay was his usual charming, superficial self, while Yurka played with Ibsenite intensity.

The same evening saw Mary Shaw and a small supporting company open at the tiny Punch and Judy Theatre with a repertory of two plays—Ibsen's *Ghosts* and Shaw's *Mrs. Warren's Profession*. Nei-ther provoked the hubbub they once had, and the engagement lasted an uneventful nine weeks.

The next night brought in John Willard's **The Cat and the Canary** (2-7-22, National). Critics in their following-day notices were virtually unanimous, with the *Sun*'s Acton Davis's "Not even *The Bat* has more suspense" being echoed in the *Globe* by Kenneth Macgowan's "more exciting than *The Bat* . . . the creepiest mystery play I ever saw." When lawyer Crosby (Percy Moore) comes to Glencliff Manor, which has lain deserted but for its voodoo-obsessed caretaker, Mammy (Blanche Fri-derici), since its owner died two decades earlier, he scoffs at the black woman's claim to have seen spirits. She retorts, "Yes sir—I see 'em! And they done warn me there's an evil spirit working around this house." The lawyer has come to read the eccentric owner's will, a will he demanded be revealed at midnight in these long-silent rooms twenty years after his death. Seven expectant heirs gather to hear that he has left all his money to Annabelle West (Florence Eldridge), unless she proves to be of unsound mind. If she turns out to be unstable, another will is to be read, which will declare a substitute heir. That second heir may know who he or she is, for the safe has been opened somehow and the seals on the wills broken. Crosby also discloses that the dead man secreted a priceless sapphire and ruby necklace somewhere in the house. A man claiming to be from a nearby mental institution warns everyone that a homicidal maniac has escaped and may be hiding in the house. Later, while Annabelle and the lawyer are talking and Annabelle has her back to him, an arm reaches out from a panel and grabs the attorney, pulling him into some hidden passage. Annabelle's concern about his strange disappearance sets the others to wondering if she is sane. Gathering up her courage, Annabelle turns out the lights and heads for bed. In the empty room she has just left, now lit only by the moon outside, a monstrous head rises from behind an armchair. Thereafter doorknobs turn although no one is near to turn them, screams and other frightening sounds rend the evening quiet, and, in Annabelle's bedroom, a claw reaches out to seize her throat. In the end, another possible heir, "a tall, handsome leading-man type" (Ryder Keane), who had broken into the safe, read the wills, and discovered he was the replacement heir, is shown to be Crosby's killer. He had rented a monster costume and persuaded a friend to pose as the asylum director. Annabelle finds a future husband in another of the would-be heirs, a seemingly timid soul (Henry Hull) who shows his bravery during the crisis. The play terrified delighted audiences for ten months in New York and subsequently for seasons on the road.

Following her disappointment with her first offering, Marie Löhr switched her bill to a revival of Victorien Sardou's forty-year-old *Fedora* on the 10th at the Hudson. Her playing (perhaps dictated by her choice of plays) had a whiff of the old grand manner which many younger critics sniffed at contemptuously. Enjoying no better luck as the aristocrat who realizes she has come to love the man she has betrayed, the star soon packed her bags and returned to a more welcoming West End.

There were only four characters in Wilson Collison's equally unwelcomed **Desert Sands** (2-13-22, Princess). All the action took place at a lonely desert encampment in the few hours between moonrise and dawn. Hugh Berndon (Norman Trevor) has fled to the Sahara after spending time imprisoned for a murder he did not commit, and though he still loves the wife of the man he was accused of killing he has taken up with an Arab girl (Anzonetta Lloyd). Into the camp wander the real killer (Edmund Lowe) and, not much later, the widow (Virginia Hammond). The killer is himself slain by the Arab girl for making a pass at her, and Berndon and the widow decide to return to England and be married. Although *Variety* called the play "three or four times as good as 'A Bill of Divorcement,' " most critics, perhaps unwilling to accept

Collison even as a farceur, slammed it, so it folded quickly.

A French drama, played at a similarly bandbox house, fared much better. **Montmartre** (2-13-22, Belmont), which Benjamin Glazer translated from Pierre Frondaie's original, traced the decline and fall of Marie-Claire (Galina Kopernak), a girl of easy virtue, who is taken away from her free-and-loose world by an idealistic young composer, Pierre (Arthur Hohl). The first time she runs off and becomes a rich man's mistress, Pierre forgives and takes her back. But the second time that boredom with the good life becomes too unbearable, she runs away and he does not follow her. Several years later, he spots her, down and out, at the Moulin Rouge, but accepts that he cannot help her.

A second French play might have been considered a revival since it had been given a few trial performances as *The Incubus* thirteen years earlier. Now in a fresh translation by Arthur Hornblow, Jr., Eugène Brieux's *Les Hannetons* was called **Madame Pierre** (2-15-22, Ritz). It raked in enthusiastic notices, including a highly laudatory one from Arthur Hornblow, Sr., in *Theatre*, yet failed. The playing could not have been at fault, since the two principals garned notices every bit as friendly as the play's. Pierre (Roland Young) and Charlotte (Estelle Winwood) have lived together, out of wedlock, for several years. When Pierre accuses her—quite justly as it happens—of having affairs with his friends, she storms out, expecting the heartbroken Pierre to come begging her to return. He does nothing of the sort, so she concocts all manner of sad rumors about herself and even stages a ludicrously inept attempt at suicide by drowning. Pierre remains unmoved, but his friends finally persuade him to take her back.

Not all the players hailed as promising would find roles to rocket them to stardom or keep them there. Helen Hayes was one of the more fortunate ones. George S. Kaufman and Marc Connelly's **To the Ladies** (2-20-22, Liberty) saw to that. *Variety* commented, "Helen Hayes has not had very much luck in the allotment of roles that came her way. But all that is gone, and with the opening of *To the Ladies* there is no further cause to worry on her part." Leonard Beebe (Otto Kruger), a salesman for the Kincaid Piano Company, is a dreamy visionary. Not so his wife, Elsie (Hayes). The Kincaids visit the Beebes and are most impressed with Elsie, who arranges with Mrs. Kincaid to wangle a promotion for Leonard. Their plan is for him to speak at a banquet. Embarrassingly, when the time arrives he becomes tongue-tied. Elsie makes the speech for him and wins him the promotion. Although *Variety* went on to hail the comedy's "knockout opening night," it enjoyed only a modest run of 128 performances and proved too arcane for the road. Still, Miss Hayes's credentials were fully established.

. . .

Helen Hayes [Brown] (1900–1993) The tiny, small-featured actress was the daughter of a minor actress and a traveling salesman. She made her debut in her native Washington at the age of five. New York first saw her when Lew Fields cast her in the musical *Old Dutch* (1909). She appeared in several other musicals before touring in 1917 as Pollyanna in the show of the same name. Important teenager roles followed in *Penrod, Dear Brutus,* and *Clarence.*

. . .

Only the Kaufman and Connelly comedy interrupted the short procession of French plays, which concluded with Henry Baron's adaptation of Edouard Bourdet's **The Rubicon** (2-21-22, Hudson). It became one of the season's surprise hits, running until the hot weather closed it. Germaine (Violet Heming) has married on the rebound and determined to be a wife in name only. To the chagrin of the man (Kenneth Hill) she really loves and who had hoped to become her lover, she boasts she has made her husband (Warburton Gamble) sleep on the drawing-room sofa. A bottle of champagne given to her and her husband by a wise old family friend (Edna May Oliver) sets the marriage on the right road. The would-be lover will have to look elsewhere (at least in the American version).

Earl Carroll, not yet preoccupied with his girlie revues, opened his new playhouse with a drama he reputedly wrote himself, **Bavu** (2-25-22, Earl Carroll). Critics devoted most of their precious paragraphs to describing and remarking on the new theatre and gave the play the shortest shrift. It recounted how a half-caste Turk (Henry Herbert) pretends to string along with the Russian Revolution, all the while looting his province. His plans to hide his loot are nearly thwarted by an aristocrat-turned-revolutionist, Michka (William H. Powell), who is attempting to aid a princess (Helen Freeman) escape. Bavu endeavors to seal up Michka in a secret room, but the young man escapes in a laundry basket. Stolen signet rings, interchanged passports, sliding doors hidden behind an altar, another door which pivots so that one figure may exit unseen while another enters, and swords all are featured in the action. By the time Bavu makes his hurried escape, he realizes that he has accidentally walled up his own sweetheart (Carlotta Monterey) in the same secret room in which he has hidden his loot and

where he planned to immure Michka. Unable to help her, he kisses her limp hand, which somehow protrudes through the wall.

Cleves Kinkead, never to repeat the success of his *Common Clay,* found few takers for his **Your Woman and Mine** (2-27-22, Klaw). Certainly the critics slammed it. Kinkead's story told how a self-righteous, sanctimonious Governor Moreland (Byron Beasley) refuses to pardon Joe Harney (Henry Mortimer), who is about to be sent to prison for stealing funds, even though he only stole the money so that Mrs. Prewitt (Minnie Dupree) could get Mr. Prewitt (Reginald Barlow), a lawmaker, to the hospital. A furious Prewitt succeeds in dredging up some history that the governor doesn't want brought to light.

That same evening marked the first of three opening nights for the Theatre Guild's mounting of George Bernard Shaw's history of the world from Adam and Eve (which was sometime before the year one) to the year 31,290. **Back to Methuselah** (2-27-22, 3-6-22, and 3-13-22, Garrick) was a collection of five almost full-length plays, so the Guild presented two each on the first pair of openings and the remaining one at the final opening. Critics extolled Simonson's settings and most of the cast, which included Margaret Wycherly, Mary Lawton, Albert Bruning, Dennis King, Claude King, and George Gaul, but questioned whether the five plays were truly worth sitting through. Robert Benchley, writing in *Life*, suggested someone should advise the Guild "that there is no law compelling it to produce Shaw's longest and dullest play," but he did add that since the second play had some good moments, playgoers might find it "worthwhile leaving a call at the box office to be awakened at 10:15, in time to see it." Woollcott concluded the last of his three reviews, "Better fifty minutes of 'Candida,' than a Cycle of Methuselah." The Guild was happy to lose only $20,000 on the venture. It had expected to drop $30,000.

Minor O'Neill ushered in February. **The First Man** (3-4-22, Neighborhood Playhouse) caused several critics to despair that the playwright could only depict the harshest, ugliest side of life, unrelieved by hope or humor. Later students would see the play as O'Neill's earliest use (however loose) of classic legend. Years before the story begins Curtis Jayson (Augustin Duncan), an anthropologist, and his wife, Martha (Margaret Mower), have lost their two young daughters. Now Jayson is about to embark on a major expedition and assumes his wife will join him. He is furious when his wife tells him she is pregnant. After she dies in childbirth, he would reject the baby as its mother's killer but finally agrees to help raise his son. A third act whose dialogue was underscored by Martha's incessant cries while giving birth had critics howling, too. The play ran twenty-seven performances.

Several of the same critics thought Owen Davis must be in league with J. Hartley Manners when his **Up the Ladder** (3-6-22, Playhouse) echoed Manners's sentiments in *The National Anthem*, once again seeing jazz and bootleg gin and high living (plus, according to Davis, the relentless quest for success) hurling the country to its destruction. Davis's hero and heroine were Jane (Doris Kenyon) and John Allen (Paul Kelly). At the time of their marriage, Jane had been the more financially secure of the pair, and moving into the cheap apartment that John had selected was something of a comedown. But John, a bond salesman, is a driven man. His ruthless pushiness by day and wild socializing by night, though it helps them move to a fine home in Westchester, nearly wrecks their health and their good name. They pull themselves together in time for a happy ending.

Applause was perhaps a bit perfunctory for George M. Cohan's **Madeleine and the Movies** (3-6-22, Gaiety), which Cohan had written as a vehicle for his daughter, Georgette, who had scored a hit some months before in London as Peter Pan. The celebrated film star Garrison Paige (James Rennie) is startled to find a pretty young lady in his apartment. She reveals she is Madeleine Madigan, and she warns Paige that her father and brother are gunning for him, since they have found her cache of Paige photographs and believe that he is attempting to seduce her. Farcical complications pile up until the whole affair is shown to have been the dream of Paige's butler (Frank Hollins), who fell asleep reading a movie script. Cohan had fun with contemporary filmdom, especially that centered in Fort Lee, N.J., and with the voguish Irish-Jewish relationships. Thus, Paige phones his studio: "Is Goldberg there?—No? Then give me Finkelstein.—No? Oh, well, give me Lesinsky.—No? (*Resignedly*) Oh, all right, give me O'Hollaran." When business lagged, Cohan took over the role of Paige, but even Cohan could not push the play's run past ten weeks.

The big flop of the evening was Emil Nyitray and Herbert Hall Winslow's **Broken Branches** (3-6-22, 39th St.). It, too, told a story that proved to be merely a bad dream. A vicious old man, John McCann (H. R. Irving), plants enough suspicions in the mind of Karl Martens (Hyman Adler) to allow Martens to believe his children care only about his money. He puts his foot down, forcing his son

(Raymond Hackett) to abandon his married mistress and provoking his daughter (Beatrice Allen) to elope. At a seedy bar, the boy becomes a dope fiend and the girl commits suicide before Martens awakes and resolves to trust his children.

O'Neill's second play of the month more than compensated for the failure of the first. In **The Hairy Ape** (3-9-22, Provincetown Playhouse) Richard "Yank" Smith (Louis Wolheim), an apish coal stoker on a luxury liner, encounters Mildred Douglas (Mary Blair), the do-gooder daughter of the shipping company's president, when she visits the boiler room. His brutish appearance upsets her and causes her to faint. The incident leads Yank to question his worth and his place in society. Leaving the ship, he strolls up Fifth Avenue until his boorish behavior lands him in jail. Lowlife cellmates urge him to join the left-wing "Wobblies," but the union will have nothing to do with him. Confused and disturbed, he heads for the zoo. There he asks a gorilla, "Where do I fit in?" Taking pity on the caged animal, he attempts to free it. But the beast, misunderstanding him like everyone else, kills him. Critics divided sharply on the drama, with Woollcott calling it "a turbulent and tremendous play . . . so vital and interesting and teeming with life," while the *Evening Post*'s old, reactionary J. Ranken Towse dismissed it, as he had some earlier O'Neill, as "juvenile." Writing of the hulky, broken-nosed Wolheim, Burns Mantle commented, "No actor we know could roar more effectively, swear with more freedom and give less offense, or suggest the pathetic groping of a primitive human being better than he did last night." Robert Edmond Jones's expressionistic settings also received accolades, with Robert Gilbert Welsh of the *Telegram* reporting, "The stage pictures are remarkable, especially the scenes in the firemen's forecastle, with half naked stokers at their drunken orgy, and the scene where the stokers feed the fire." O'Neill, for all the praise he received and controversy he engendered, still was caviar to the majority of playgoers, so, while Arthur Hopkins moved the production briefly uptown, it compiled only 120 performances. A subsequent road tour was limited.

Henry Myers's **The First Fifty Years** (3-13-22, Princess) was an oddity for its time—a two-character play. It looked at Martin and Anne Wells (Tom Powers and Clare Eames) in 1872 as they arrive at their new Harlem home from their honeymoon, with Martin asserting, "I suppose every husband thinks he's married the finest girl in the world, but in my case it just happens to be true." A year later, on their paper anniversary, disillusionment has begun to set in for both of them, with Anne accusing Martin of being a poor provider and Martin dissatisfied with Anne's housekeeping. By their wooden anniversary their marriage is a public sham; by tin they no longer speak to each other (the play's shortest scene). An accommodation is reached by the time Martin becomes ill shortly before their crystal anniversary. They pass their twenty-fifth landmark resignedly and eventually reach their golden anniversary. Playing cards, they wonder how different their marriage might have been had they had children, and they discuss what color flowers to place on Martin's grave when he dies. Martin suggests they start anew:

Anne: Why? We haven't many years to live.
Martin: Can't we—at least—forgive each other.
Anne: When life is wasted, what good is forgiveness?

Suddenly Martin begins to talk happily, as if they had just returned from their honeymoon. Anne reminds him it is his turn to deal. Although the play received some encouraging reviews, many critics were not yet prepared for so intimate, quiet a play. The producers, who included a young Lorenz Hart, removed it after six weeks.

But England's A. A. Milne found success with a play that amateur groups would delight in for decades to come, **The Truth About Blayds** (3-14-22, Booth), which featured O. P. Heggie as an aging, much admired poet who confronts his family with a dilemma when he confesses that all his published poetry, except for the single book that was slated by critics, was actually the work of his long-dead roommate. His only writings were the book that failed.

One reason Hopkins could move *The Hairy Ape* to his theatre was the abrupt closing of his production of a work by two recent Columbia College graduates, Leila Taylor and Gertrude Purcell's **Voltaire** (3-20-22, Plymouth). Their play allowed Arnold Daly to paint wrinkles on his face, don a white wig, and speak in the squeaky voice of an old man, long retired but still interested in French affairs. At the behest of the beautiful Mlle. Clairon (Carlotta Monterey) he helps a young atheist (George Le Guere) escape the French police. He also probably saves France from war with Prussia by having the boy return to the Prussian king scurrilous verses the king has written about his French counterpart. When the comedy closed, Hopkins moved Monterey into the leading female role in the O'Neill play, thus introducing the playwright to his future wife.

The Green Goddess and *The Cat and the Canary* were mingled unhappily in Gordon Kean and Carl Mason's **The Hindu** (3-20-22, Comedy). The inscrutable Indian Prince Tamar (Walker Whiteside), fearing rebellion in his province, asks for aid from Scotland Yard. He hides his shock when the Yard sends Clarice Cartright (Sydney Shields) to assist him. Doors and chest lids open and close unaided, odd chanting seems to come from nowhere, and there always looms the threat of death in the local quicklime deposits. And why does the prince himself make advances at Clarice? Whiteside was a good actor, who many thought might have been much better had he not sold out early on to such roles, but he totally lacked Arliss's genuine artistry and finesse. *Variety* thought the piece was written "not so much for the tired businessman . . . as for the pop-eyed shoe-clerk and the agitated stenographer." The play, with some forcing, ran nine weeks.

Woollcott, who days earlier had expressed his preference for *Candida* over *Back to Methuselah,* was, like many of his colleagues, not altogether satisfied when the play was revived on the 22nd at the Greenwich Village. He admired Moroni Olsen's Morell, was not displeased with Maurice Browne's Marchbanks, but balked at Ellen Van Volkenburg's "arch, even roguish" heroine. And he used his notice to reiterate that the play would still be enjoyed when dusty copies of *Back to Methuselah* sat unread on library shelves.

The reception accorded the socially prominent Mary Hoyt Wiborg's **Taboo** (4-4-22, Sam H. Harris) put the kibosh on any extended run and confined its stay to three matinee performances. During those few representations its racially mixed cast recounted how Grandmother Gaylord (Margaret Wycherly), frustrated in her attempts to make her eight-year-old grandson talk, allows her family's black servants to set up a voodoo ceremony in hopes of curing the boy. Dream sequences propel them across to Africa and back in time to the origins of the voodoo cult. When the excitement of the wild rituals proves too much for the old lady and she dies, the blacks attempt to kill the man who encouraged the affair. But the child's suddenly talking silences their fury. One of the players was Paul Robeson.

Zinaida Hippius's **The Green Ring** (4-4-22, Neighborhood Playhouse) reputedly had been a prerevolutionary Moscow success. It told of an organization—the title's Green Ring—made up of intellectual Russian youngsters who strive to better the miserable world their elders have created. They have not succeeded by the play's end, but one attractive girl (Joanna Roos), whose self-involved parents have largely ignored her, has agreed to marry the middle-aged man (Ian Maclaren) whom the youngsters have allowed to observe their meetings. The material was not to New Yorkers' tastes.

They were even less happy with Frances Nordstrom's **The Lady Bug** (4-17-22, Apollo), which could have been deemed the farcical side of the same material offered six weeks before in *The Lawbreaker*. Tutwiller Thorton (John Cumberland) is dismayed by his faddist, do-gooder wife (Marie Nordstrom). Her latest thing is coddling notorious ex-convicts with the idea of permanently reforming them. Thus the Thortons' current house guest is Daniel Dill (Edward Poland), a killer newly released from Sing Sing. (Act I begins with the welcoming party that Mrs. T. is holding in Dill's honor.) At his wit's end and fearful for both himself and his wife, Tutwiller gets the family butler, Viddlars (Denman Maley), to hide in the attic, so that Tutwiller can lead the missus to believe Dill has murdered the servant and disposed of the body. However, Tutwiller neglects to remember the cache of liquor he has hidden in the attic and which Viddlars finds. A boozy butler lets the cat out of the bag.

But, despite a number of critical turndowns, Paul Armont and Marcel Gerbidon's *L'École des cocottes*, translated by Gladys Unger as **The Goldfish** (4-17-22, Maxine Elliott's), was embraced by playgoers. The electricity which Marjorie Rambeau generated for so many of these ticket buyers also helped. She played Jenny Jones, who has married Jim Wetherby (Wilfred Lytell), a minor songwriter, on a whim that she comes to regret. Guided by a baleful, penniless Polish count (Wilton Lackaye), she ditches Jim—"giving him the goldfish," their prearranged signal should either believe the marriage has run its course—and embarks on a series of ever richer marriages. At the same time, she changes her name first to Genevieve, then to Guinevere. But after two divorces and the death of her latest husband, she begins to recognize how hollow her life is. When her maid speaks joyously of an evening with a date at the automat, the movies, and Roseland, her despair seems boundless. Happily, Jim, still no big deal, comes knocking at her door. The play ran into the autumn months.

Leonard Praskins and Ernest Pascal's **The Charlatan** (4-24-22, Times Square) took place in the drawing room of Mason Talbot's Florida home. There a famed magician from India, Cagliostro (Frederick Tiden), is offering an exhibition of his art. He has placed his wife in a cabinet and made her disappear—until a secret chamber in the box is opened and she tumbles out with a poisoned needle in her back. As they had in several earlier plays this season, doors and boxes open and shut of their own

accord, terrifying noises come from empty rooms, and, for a touch of novelty, a large portrait drops inexplicably from the wall. Cagliostro is shown to be an American who had gone to India to find his father's murderer and had traced the killer back to the Talbot home. That killer was none other than Talbot (William Ingersoll). He is fingered by the "spirit" of Cagliostro's supposedly dead wife.

Eden Phillpotts's English drama **The Shadow** (4-24-22, Klaw) was rejected by most critics as implausible and unconvincing. It told how a gentle, loving man (Noel Leslie) confesses to murdering his cruel uncle, even though he is innocent and knows that the real killer is the man (Percy Waram) who has married a girl (Helen MacKellar) who spurned him. Since he feels he has little to live for, this is his way of ensuring her happiness. The play's short stay marked another disappointment in the disappointment-studded career of Dallas Welford, who nonetheless received garlands for his portrayal of a comic butcher.

Critics also slammed Ossip Dymow's Yiddish fantasy **The Bronx Express** (4-26-22, Astor), which had been a popular attraction on the Lower East Side and which Samuel Golding translated into English and Owen Davis then adapted. Actually, the critics were ambivalent about the play itself. What they disliked was Davis's adaptation and the largely Anglo-Saxon cast's inability to accurately capture Jewish speech and mannerisms. David Hungerstolz (Charles Coburn), a no more than moderately successful Canal Street button-maker, fights with his daughter (Hope Sutherland) about her marrying a poor boy. She storms out of the house, and he boards the subway to chase after her. (A storm of applause greeted the disclosure of the subway setting, showing a car packed with carefully dressed and business-suited riders, including at least one honest-to-goodness Negro.) On the train he meets a now successful old friend who bewails that success is as flat as the advertisements lining the subway car. Hungerstolz falls asleep and dreams he is at a party where the other guests are figures out of the ads, such as the Smith Brothers and the Arrow Collar Man. They confirm his friend's sentiments. So when he awakes and learns that his daughter has married, he is content.

So ill rehearsed was Adeline Hendricks's **The Night Call** (4-26-22, Frazee) that all through the evening playgoers could hear a prompter feeding the cast not only lines but stage directions, too. The mystery found Alice Dodge (Elsie Rizer) stranded in a deserted mansion on the Jersey shore during a violent storm. She cannot call for help, since the phone lines have been cut. The appearance of several nice but secretive young men, and the discovery of a hidden tunnel and of a corpse, lead to the disclosure that the house is a base for rumrunning bootleggers.

April's last offering was Susan Glaspell's **Chains of Dew** (4-27-22, Provincetown Playhouse). Seymour Standish (Edgar Reese) comes to New York, where he hopes his career as a poet will flourish now that he has left his dreary midwestern town, his uncomprehending wife, and his dominating mother. His New York friends, sympathetic to his problem, head for River Bluff to aid him in more completely breaking his ties there. They discover that his wife, Diantha (Louise Treadwell), is a sharp, progressive gal whom Standish condescendingly calls Dotty, and that his mother is just as warm and understanding. Indeed, at one point she has perceptively asked Diantha, "Do you love him enough to be his cross?" The friends return to New York alone, certain Standish will be better off seeing himself as a martyr. The play closed after three weeks, and with its closing the old order at the Provincetown Players came to an end.

Casting its eye on Broadway just as these last plays were opening, *Theatre* counted slightly fewer than fifty first-class attractions on Broadway, a fine count remembering that it was relatively late in the season. But the magazine's division of these plays would give modern theatre lovers cause to ponder and sigh, for while sixteen were musicals, the rest were straight plays—fifteen dramas and sixteen comedies. Small matter that several of the dramas were mysteries or melodramas.

After much of a season going separate ways, Potash and Perlmutter were reunited in Montague Glass and Jules Eckert Goodman's **Partners Again** (5-1-22, Selwyn). Abe (Barney Bernard) and Mawruss (Alexander Carr) have said good-bye to the garment trade and now are trying to sell automobiles. As usual they are forever questioning each other's judgment. Having had no luck pushing the Schenkmann Six, they switch to the Climax Four. They sell not only cars but a fortune in the company's stock only to find themselves the victims of some clever crooks and the subject of a U.S. government investigation. For a time, it looks as if they may have to go to prison, so Abe prepares a list of things he will need there, like "warm underwear, aspirin, nujol, and mathematic spirits of ammonia." But in the richly paneled, high-ceilinged office of the U.S. Commissioner, with a portrait of Lincoln staring down sagely at them, the partners resolve the difficulties in time for a happy ending. Well, perhaps

not totally happy, because Mawruss has agreed with Abe on an important matter, and that leaves Abe to worry if he could be wrong. Alan Dale of the *American* summed up critical reaction when he wrote that the comedy was "the least funny of the Potash and Perlmutter combinations, but it will nevertheless make plenty of friends." Although the play was a hit, running into the following season, it was not quite the money-maker earlier ones in the series had been. Glass would attempt only one more Potash and Perlmutter play, four years later, after Barney Bernard had died, and six years further on would offer another similar play that would not call the partners Potash and Perlmutter.

The Theatre Guild closed its main season with Arnold Bennett's **What the Public Wants** (5-1-22, Garrick). Giving the public what it wants has allowed Sir Charles Worgan (Charles Waldron) to create a huge publishing empire. Into his life comes high-minded Emily Vernon (Margaret Wycherly), who persuades him to print better stories and support an art theatre. But when she comprehends that he will do this only out of love for her and not simply because it is the right thing to do, she walks out of his life.

Both plays to open the next Monday evening were quick failures. Annie Nathan Meyer's **The Advertising of Kate** (5-8-22, Ritz) examined the plight of Kate Blackwell (Mary Boland), who has inherited her father's share of an advertising agency. To everyone's amazement, not the least her own, she proves a first-class businesswoman. But her handsome young partner, Robert Kent (Leslie Austin), won't give her a second look until she decides to advertise her femininity. That lands her proposals from Robert and a slew of other men. Disgusted, she announces, "I'm going back to the business world, where a woman is what she is, and not what a dressmaker makes her." But over breakfast at Aunt Maisie's, the dear old lady (Mrs. Whiffen) persuades Kate to accept the often topsy-turvy ways of the world.

If the still lovely, skillful Mary Boland could not save a mediocre play, a cast of relatively inexperienced and unknown performers could not hope to save a drama characterized by Hornblow as "one of the most puerile plays of the season." Ruth M. Woodward's **The Red Geranium** (5-8-22, Princess) was set in wicked Greenwich Village, where a naive Massachusetts country schoolmarm, Mary (Florence Rittenhouse), comes to live for a time and taste the bohemian life she long has dreamed of. In short order, she bobs her hair, witnesses the agonizing death of a dope fiend during a wild party, is seduced and deserted by an advocate of free love, and, after realizing that her behavior has alienated her home-town sweetheart, jumps to her death from a hospital window.

The play might have had a somewhat different reception had it been offered down at the Greenwich Village Theatre, but that little playhouse was host to *Billeted*, a comedy which had starred Margaret Anglin in 1917 and now was given a brief, unprofitable revival beginning on the 9th.

Fanny Hawthorn (5-11-22, Vanderbilt) also proved to be a revival, for it was merely the 1912 *Hindle Wakes* dressed in a new name. Once again this English drama of a young girl's rebellion against the stifling conventions of her time and her willingness to lose her virginity without losing her freedom failed to interest Americans.

The title of J. C. and Elliott Nugent's **Kempy** (5-15-22, Belmont) might also be seen as misleading, but that didn't prevent its becoming a hit and delighting New Yorkers for more than six months. Kempy (Elliott Nugent) is the nickname of a young man who hopes to be an architect but, until he can establish himself, works as a plumber. He comes to the Bence household to fix a leak. There he meets the Bences' aggressive, wishfully multi-talented middle daughter, Kate (Lotus Robb), who has just quarreled with her fiancé, "Duke" Merrill (Grant Mitchell). She no sooner learns that Kempy has read a book she has written (which she does not know Duke has paid to have printed) and has been inspired to design a church based on ideas in the book than she rushes him off to a justice of the peace. "Don't just stand there staring at me—*come on!*" she barks. All Kempy can say as he is being led away is "Gee whiz!" The leak is left unfixed. Within hours of the marriage, Kempy realizes he has made an unfortunate mistake, for not only is there no love bewteen the couple but Kempy, in the few minutes he had been in the Bence home, had fallen in love with the youngest daughter, Ruth (Ruth Nugent). More complications follow before it is discovered that Kempy is too young to be married without his parents' consent. When Kate also learns that Duke has bought the Bence home so that they can continue to live there, she recognizes where her future lies. The play's major problem was that Kempy was its least interesting figure. The Bences, deliciously varied in nature, constantly hogged the spotlight. There was the cantankerous father (J. C. Nugent), the worrying, not very bright mother (Jessie Crommette), the brash married daughter, Jane (Helen Carew), and the quietly sensible if love-besotted Ruth. Thus when the family discovers Kate

and Kempy are not to be found, the following scene unfolds:

Ma: I don't s'pose the boy will ever be back to turn the water on—it's so late now.
Dad: If he does, I'd like to see them try to charge me for the time we've been waiting. Young smart aleck!
Ruth: I think you'll find it isn't his fault!
Dad: What have you been stickin' up for him? If it ain't his fault, it's Harger's [Kempy's boss]— they're all the same—plumbers!
Jane: Why don't you 'phone Harger's house?
Dad: He ain't in the 'phone book—I told you!
Jane: It might be an intelligent idea to ask Information.
Dad: (Going to 'phone) Oh, shut up, Jane! If it was an intelligent idea, where would you get it?

Curiously, although J. C. was a popular vaudevillian and Elliott, his son, would go on to fame as an actor, director, and playwright, young Ruth Nugent walked off with many of the best notices. For its young producer, Richard Herndon, the play marked a high point in a short but fascinating career.

· · ·

Richard [Gilbert] **Herndon** (1873–1958) was born in Paris and educated at private schools. After his first mounting closed on the road in 1914, he began importing celebrated foreign stars and ensembles. With his profits from these ventures he took over two of Broadway's most intimate playhouses, the Belmont and the Klaw. Besides *Kempy* his noteworthy offerings included Philip Barry's *You and I* and Maxwell Anderson's *Gypsy*.

· · ·

The Theatre Guild, having ended its "official" season, brought out another novelty for some special performances and received sufficient encouragement to continue it for a summer-spanning run. The play was **From Morn till Midnight** (5-21-22, Garrick), which Ashley Dukes translated from Georg Kaiser's expressionistic German work. Its main figure was a cashier (Frank Reicher), who comes under a woman's malevolent influence, embezzles money, and by day's end has grown mad with guilt, so shoots himself in a Salvation Army shelter. The play had an exceptionally large cast—which may have prevented a still longer run—but its initial mounting cost only $2000, Simonson having simply used projections on a screen to allow numerous scene changes. Even then suggestion had to suffice. A bicycle race was represented merely by a man in a box watching the proceedings through binoculars.

A second foreign piece was H. F. Maltby's **The**

Rotters (5-22-22, 39th St.), in which a British politician (Harry Corson Clarke) who has constantly boasted of his own and his family's respectability must fend off damaging revelations about his children, his wife, and even himself. Clarke had been touring English-speaking theatrical centers around the world with the piece but was coldly received in New York.

His premiere competed with Oscar Wilde's *Salome,* which arrived at the Klaw in an expanded, evening-long version that had Salome (Thelma Harvey) doing her dance to Strauss's music. Perhaps not coincidentally, protesting religious extremists earlier in the season had frightened the Metropolitan Opera into dropping the Strauss opus from its schedule.

Abie's Irish Rose (5-23-22, Fulton) opened the next night. With few exceptions (one of whom was the *Times*'s second-stringer) critics savaged the comedy. Robert Benchley began his review in *Life*, "On the night following the presentation of *The Rotters*, residents of Broadway, New York City, were startled by the sound of horse's hoofs clattering up the famous thoroughfare. Rushing to their windows they saw a man in Colonial costume riding a bay mare whose eyes flashed fire. The man was shouting as he rode, and his message was '*The Rotters* is no longer the worst play in town! *Abie's Irish Rose* has just opened.' " The comedy appeared almost certainly doomed until its author, Anne Nichols, obtained money from the notorious gangster Arnold Rothstein to keep the play alive and launch a huge promotional campaign. Her success paid off beyond anyone's wildest dream. Mrs. Isaac Cohen (Mathilde Cottrelly) is boring the patient Rabbi Samuels (Howard Lang) with her ongoing recounting of her recent surgery. They and Mr. Cohen (Bernard Gorcey) are trying to soothe Solomon Levy (Alfred Wiseman), who is anxiously awaiting word from his son, Abie. The boy had not shown up at work that day. Abie finally phones to tell his father that he is bringing a girl home. Solomon will be delighted to welcome any future daughter-in-law—so long as she is Jewish. It seems Abie has not been dating many Jewish girls. But a happy, hoping Solomon is already looking forward to a dozen grandchildren. "Right away you talk wholesale," Cohen reprimands him. When Abie (Robert B. Williams) arrives, he feels compelled to introduce his girl as Rosie Murpheski (Marie Carroll), even though she was really Rose Mary Murphy before they were married by a Methodist minister. Naturally they cannot tell Solomon that a Christian cleric has wed them. Eager to see his son married, Solomon insists on planning a wedding for them the

following week, with the rabbi officiating. Since orange blossoms are out of season Solomon decorates the room with oranges, observing, "Ven the wedding is over, we can *eat* the fruit." The wedding has just ended when Rose Mary's father, Patrick Murphy (John Cope), arrives from Chicago, bringing with him his old friend, Father Whalen (Harry Bradley). Murphy believes his daughter has found a fine Irish lad. But his appearance blows all covers. The fathers are more than aghast, they are instantly at each other's throats. Solomon says he'd sell his new daughter-in-law for a nickel, and Patrick retorts he will take her away for nothing. While the fathers squabble, the priest and the rabbi chat amicably, discovering they both ministered to the troops in the last war. "Shure," recalls Father Whalen, "I have comforted a great many boys of your faith in their last hours when there wasn't a good rabbi around." And Samuels assures the priest that he did the same for dying Catholics. He agrees with the father when Whalen adds, "Shure, we're all trying to get to the same place when we pass on. We're just going by different routes." So the rabbi suggests that, since "the young folks have made a business of getting married," the priest wed them according to Roman rites. While the old men continue assailing one another, the priest calls home and obtains permission for the marriage. During a lull in the name-calling, the fathers hear the priest say from the next room that he pronounces the couple man and wife. "My God! They've done it again!" a staggered Murphy exclaims. The last act takes place at Christmas, in Abie and Rose Mary's small apartment, where Abie is putting finishing touches on a Christmas tree. They are surprised first of all by a visit from the Cohens. Abie and Rose Mary confirm that they have heard from neither of the fathers (both mothers were long dead) since the weddings. But the fathers have learned that Rose Mary has given birth. Patrick sneaks in, bearing gifts for a granddaughter—it had better not be a boy. He is followed minutes later by Solomon—who has presents for a baby he is sure will be a boy. He wants nothing to do with a granddaughter. Happily, Abie and Rose Mary have accommodated both men, since she has given birth to what Solomon terms "Twinses." But after Patrick learns the boy is named for him and Solomon is told the girl is named for his late wife, they accept both babies. Bells ring.

Solomon: Vod iss it? A fire?
Patrick: A fire! 'Tis Christmas! Merry Christmas, Sol!
Solomon: Good Yonteff, Patrick!

The play's comedy was superficial and based largely on one or two notes—the characters' ethnicity and the ethnic disagreements. Nor was Miss Nichols's ear for Yiddish speech all that accurate. Note the inconsistencies and errors of sound in one of Solomon's short speeches: "And dot schimiel he's known her since de var! They should have been married with the childrens py this time." Oddly, read today, it is the comedy's underlying sentimentalities which hold up best—such as Mrs. Cohen's inherent warmth and the friendly understanding of the clergymen. (As with *Kempy,* the title figures are the play's least interesting.) But for contemporaries that seems not to have mattered. By the time the comedy closed it had left far behind all other Broadway plays with its run of 2532 performances, its numerous road companies enjoyed record stands in city after city (it ran three weeks in Erie, normally a one-night stand), and it made Miss Nichols a millionaire. How many patrons truly enjoyed the play and how many afterward felt sucked in by its notoriety is uncertain. Benchley never forgot or forgave the play's overriding his dismissal of it. He had to prepare brief comments for his magazine's weekly rundown of current shows. Deciding that thumbnail appraisals such as "something awful" served little purpose, he took to comments such as "People laugh at this every night, which explains why democracy can never be a success" or "Where do the people come from who keep this going? You don't see them out in the daytime." When he once wrote, "What the public wants—God forbid!" advertisements for the comedy soon read " 'What the public wants'—Benchley, *Life.*" One of his most succinct put-downs read merely "Hebrews 13:8." Readers looking up the reference found it said, "Jesus Christ the same yesterday and today and for ever."

Some critics felt Frederick Lansing Day's interesting **Makers of Light** (5-23-22, Neighborhood Playhouse) might have been better served had it been opened earlier in the season. For this drama by one of Professor George Pierce Baker's playwriting students closed as soon as the heat approached and the company's subscription list was exhausted. Millville is a typical, unimaginative New England town. Its school board votes money for a bronze plaque with members' names inscribed but will not consider giving teachers even the smallest pay increase. But then the teachers are their own worst enemies. One frustrated schoolmarm, Sally Morton (Adrienne Morrison), takes up with a shy student twelve years her junior, Jimmy Grupton (Albert Carroll), whose schoolmates have rejected him and call him "fish-eye." When she realizes she is pregnant she decides to move away, but she refuses Jimmy's pleas to allow him to go with her. The terrified, brokenhearted youngster kills himself, leaving Sally more alone and frustrated than ever. Carroll, a member of the company virtually since its founding, won long-lasting fame in the next few seasons not as an actor but as a pantomimist and mimic in the troupe's musical revues.

The Drums of Jeopardy (5-29-22, Gaiety) was Howard Herrick and Harold McGrath's theatricalization of McGrath's *Saturday Evening Post* short story. Critics felt it should have been left between the magazine's covers. A Russian prince has fled the Communists, taking with him two priceless emeralds knowns as "the Drums of Jeopardy." The jewels are reputed to be cursed, dooming their owner. The prince has come to New York and assumed the name John Hawksley (C. Henry Gordon). He has also befriended Kitty Conover (Marion Coakley), a charming newspaper reporter, and her godfather, Cutty (William Courtleigh), a secret service agent. The agent's help will be useful, since Hawksley is pursued by a nefarious Russian spy, Boris Karlov (Paul Everton). The men thwart his plans, leaving John and Kitty time to think about a wedding.

The season's last novelty was an unappealing British comedy, H. M. Harwood's **A Pinch Hitter** (6-1-22, Henry Miller's), in which a financially strapped young man (Allan Pollock) agrees to be a corespondent in a divorce. But on realizing what an unprincipled fellow (Charles Waldron) the unhappy wife (Pamela Gaythorne) is planning to marry after her divorce, he finds ways to show her her error. He also finds love with the woman's niece (Helen Stewart).

The season ended at the Empire on the 5th with an all-star revival of Richard Brinsley Sheridan's *The Rivals,* mounted for a limited one-week stand by members of the famous actors' club, the Players. Tyrone Power was Sir Anthony; Robert Warwick, Captain Absolute; Pedro de Cordoba, Faulkland; Francis Wilson, Bob Acres; John Craig, Sir Lucius; Henry E. Dixey, Fag; James T. Powers, David; Mary Shaw, Mrs. Malaprop; Violet Heming, Lydia Languish; and Patricia Collinge, Lucy. Truly all-star, even if some of the stars were a bit long in the tooth and had seen their glory days slip away. Norman Bel Geddes's stripped-down settings employed simple screens and flats, augmented only by an occasional prop—a divan, a window, a tree—to suggest where the action was occuring. The Players promised to make the event an annual affair, and they kept their promise until rising costs and the absurd rules of their own profession's union put an end to the series.

1922–1923

Writing in mid-summer of 1923 in the preface to his latest *Best Plays*, Burns Mantle made a startling statement. "If the particular season of which this volume is a record, does not recommend itself to future historians of the theatre as the most notable of a generation," he remarked, "it should at least be given credit for being the first theatrical season in a generation that has not been described as 'the worst in years.' " That last clause is the eye-catcher. After all, in his first volume Mantle had called the 1919–20 season "the best we have enjoyed in years in the general quality of the productions made," and he had more or less echoed those sentiments in subsequent years. (And we have quoted the excited commentary those same seasons evoked elsewhere.) The rash of failures and poor turnout at the box office last year was a minor matter when put in perspective. Indeed, producers began raising ticket prices again this season, with many straight plays now asking a $3.50 top ($3.85 with tax). In the fall these increases met with some resistance, especially the still higher admissions for musicals. And a few plays that relied heavily on cut-rate tickets, such as *Abie's Irish Rose*, saw a goodly portion of the increase go into the pockets of Leblang's and other cut-raters. Yet by early December, *Variety* noted that half the shows on Broadway were pulling in "exceptional profits," and at year's end its front-page banner read "Wealth of Broadway Hits."

With time, Mantle would reveal himself as a happy pessimist, forever enjoying a theatrical decline. Nor would he be alone. But, despite ongoing cries by self-serving religious figures for censorship, most commentators and playgoers were mightily pleased. True, a relatively healthy theatrical economy and a growing supply of available playhouses led to the mounting of too many plays that should never have seen the footlights. But the season's better offerings, whether hit or failure, more than compensated.

Unlike recent seasons, no new straight plays premiered in June or July. And while August was not exceptionally busy, it was hit-packed. The parade of successes was led by Kate McLaurin's **Whispering Wires** (8-7-22, 49th St.), taken from a *Saturday Evening Post* story by Henry Leverage. Montgomery Stockbridge (Ben Johnson), a rich but hated businessman, hurriedly hires a detective (George Howell) to protect him after he receives a

warning that he will be murdered within two hours. The detective's best is not enough, and in "a scene in the first act which is just a little more filled with suspense than any other scene . . . ever witnessed" Stockbridge sits silently if nervously alone in his library hoping he is safe, yet fearful he is not. The phone rings, he answers it and drops dead. Before long his daughter, Doris (Olive Tell), receives a similar threat. Fortunately, the detective unmasks the telephone repairman (Malcolm Duncan) who is in reality the inventive, vengeful brother of a man Stockbridge helped send to prison. The killer has hidden "a single-shot pistol actuated by the human voice" in the receiver and is killed by his own mechanism. A relieved Doris embraces her fiancé, Barry McGill (Paul Kelly). The thriller ran into June.

Hubert Osborne's **Shore Leave** (8-8-22, Belasco) ran a little less than half as long and might have been completely forgotten had it not a few years afterwards served as the source for Vincent Youmans's *Hit the Deck!* Connie Martin (Francis Starr) is a shy dressmaker in a small New England seaport. Perhaps more important, she is a pretty but aging spinster, reluctant to see what remains of her life slip away wasted. So she invites a handsome "gob," "Bilge" Smith (James Rennie), whom she has met in the park, home for dinner. As he departs, he kisses her, and she realizes she is actually in love. Since he has promised to return, Connie waits and waits. And while she waits, she gathers together all her savings to purchase a small freighter so that he can be a captain. When Bilge finally does return two years later he has no recollection of their short time together, but he starts to fall in love with her until he learns of her purchase and runs away, dreading to be tied to a wife richer than he. Not until she finally agrees to turn everything over to any child they may have can the pair head for the altar. One critic summed up his colleagues' consensus by branding the evening "a second rate comedy made first class by Belasco care and a performance of unusual appeal by Frances Starr." Besides Connie's homey cottage in the first and last acts, the settings included a flag-bedecked, handsomely crewed deck of the S.S. *Zonoma*, which Connie (and Belasco) had dolled up for Bilge.

August's third successive hit was a play by actor Crane Wilbur, **The Monster** (8-9-22, 39th St.). The reclusive Dr. Gustave Ziska (Wilton Lackaye) lives with his hulking, mute, and sinister-eyed black servant, Caliban (Walter James, a white playing in blackface), in a secluded, reputedly haunted house not far from a major city. The home overlooks a bridge off which a number of cars have plunged mysteriously, after which the cars' occupants have disappeared. A newspaperman, Alvin Bruce (McKay Morris), decides to investigate. Just before he arrives, another automobile crashes on a stormy night. He comes with its driver, Julie Cartier (Marguerite Risser), and a tramp (Frank McCormack) to the house where the distinguished-looking, white-haired Ziska, dressed elegantly in slightly bohemian clothes, welcomes them. Soon, chairs and doors move of their own accord, candles go out, an arm bursts through a wall, and apparitions appear in a mirror. Before long, in the cavernous depths of the house, Alvin is tied to an electric chair and Julie is strapped to an operating table where the now entirely white-garbed, clearly mad doctor plans to dismember her. Luckily the tramp is not a tramp, and the goodies are rescued. The piece was praised in *Theatre* as "highly sophisticated entertainment," "in a class by itself as a purveyor of gruesome chills."

Another actor, Henry Hull, was co-author with Leighton Osmun of **Manhattan** (8-15-22, Playhouse), a comedy which received mostly disparaging notices yet almost managed to become a hit. In the *Times* Woollcott insisted that "this study of an exceptionally poor and almost obtrusively pure girl . . . who goes right, rings about as true as a lead quarter." The girl was Lory (Marguerite Maxwell), a typist (reviews referred to her as a typewritist) whose spelling and grammar ain't as strong as her moral fiber. She lives down below Fifth Avenue on Fletcher Street, "where Greenwich Village stops kidding itself," and is courted by wealthy Duncan Van Norman (Norman Trevor), whose mother (Hilda Spong) has pressured him into finding a wife. His courtship flourishes until Lory learns she is an heiress. That sends Duncan scurrying away, but Lory rushes after him and all but blackmails him into a proposal.

The economical Edward Locke, a pioneer in small-cast plays, had only three characters in his **The Woman Who Laughed** (8-16-22, Longacre). When Freida Neilson (Martha Hedman) realizes that her husband, John (William H. Powell), and her half-sister, Minna (Gilda Leary), are lovers, she drugs them, ties them up, threatens them with death, and leaves them to chew over their fate. Minna decides enough is enough, and a repentant John is accepted back by his wife. For New Yorkers enough was enough after two weeks.

A week and a half was all New Yorkers granted to Paul Dickey and Mann Page's **Lights Out** (8-17-22, Vanderbilt). It had a clever idea which its authors

could not capitalize on. In the observation car of the Pennsylvania Limited crooks hear Egbert Winslow (Robert Ames) boast that he has papers worth $1,000,000 in his briefcase, so they steal the briefcase. Unable to see the value of the papers, they demand that Egbert tell them why they are so pricey. He discloses they are film scripts he believes will make him rich. That gives the head crook, Walt Sebastian (Felix Krembs), an idea. He agrees to back a film dealing with a bank robbery, and he provides Egbert with all the details. Those details are the real facts behind a robbery Sebastian committed with High Shine Joe (C. Henry Gordon), who subsequently double-crossed the gang. When the film, a serial called *The Red Trail,* is released, police suspect Egbert, and High Shine turns up at a showing, gun in hand, to silence his erstwhile buddies. High Shine is nabbed, Sebastian escapes, and Egbert finds romance.

Romances happy and unhappy were the subject of Louis Evan Shipman's **Fools Errant** (8-21-22, Maxine Elliott's). Eric Brierly (Cyril Keightley), returning from a rejuvenating stint in some Minnesota mines, learns that his old sweetheart, Fanny (Lucile Watson), is unhappily married to a man (Vincent Serrano) who is having an affair with an art student (Alexandra Carlisle), so Eric nobly woos and weds the student, hoping that Fanny's problems are over. The newlyweds move west. A year later, Fanny, now a widow, appears, but when she discovers the Brierlys are living in married bliss, she heads home, more unhappy than ever. Nor was Broadway happy with the play.

But there was lots of rejoicing at the appearance of humorist Don Marquis's **The Old Soak** (8-22-22, Plymouth), a character the playwright had written about in his newspaper columns. Clem Hawley (Harry Beresford), whom his neighbors refer to as "the Old Soak," never was much for work, but with the coming of Prohibition he must spend so much time hunting for liquor that any thought of work is out. When his wife, Matilda (Minnie Dupree), berates him for not being a good provider he responds, "Ain't I pervided you with a couple of children to work for you?" And when she suggests he has no will power, his answer is, "What do you think kept me drinkin' if twasn't my will power?" After stocks Matilda has put away for a rainy day disappear, she accuses him of stealing them and Clem prepares to leave home. Then Clem learns that his playboy son, Clem junior (George Le Guere), actually stole them and sold them at a discount to the Hawleys' cousin, Webster Parsons (Robert McWade). Parsons is the town's banker, a prissy, self-righteous teetotaler—and the money behind the local bootleggers. When Clem learns this he blackmails Parsons into returning the stocks. "Web," he tells him, "your soul is so small that if there were a million souls the size of yourn in a flea's belly they'd be so fur apart they couldn't hear each other holler." Assisted by "richly humorous" performances from Beresford (which *Variety* compared favorably with Joseph Jefferson's in *Rip Van Winkle*), Miss Dupree, and an excellent supporting cast, the comedy ran for more than a year.

A second worthless son figured importantly in Arthur Richman's **A Serpent's Tooth** (8-24-22, Little). Indeed, Alice Middleton (Marie Tempest) is upset because many people refuse to believe the lies she tells in defense of her son, Jerry (Leslie Howard). However, she is happy to learn that Jerry is engaged to Janet Trendell (Ann Merrick), the daughter of an old suitor, Morgan Trendell (W. Graham Browne), whom she has long looked upon favorably. And she is especially pleased when Janet informs her that her father calls the widowed Mrs. Middleton "the most attractive girl he ever knew" and when Trendell, a widower, adds, "I'll need company now. It'll mean a great change in my life to have Janet leave me. . . . You're still very good looking, Alice. It'll be a pleasure to take you where we'll be seen." Alice has come to consider herself "a middle-aged Cinderella who sits at home dreaming of other people's parties." But after she discovers that Jerry is not only a philanderer but a forger, she tells Janet the whole story. Janet agrees to wait for Jerry, while the boy goes away "long enough to prove I can be different." When he returns he will have both a bride-to-be and a new stepfather to greet him. Coming after Richman's admired *Ambush*, critics felt the play was a letdown, and they divided sharply over Miss Tempest's performance. The main salutes were offered to Howard, one critic calling his work "a notable performance, and quite the best thus far this season. . . . There is truth in his playing, sincerity, intelligence, no exhibitionism, no trick technique."

The growing amateur Little Theatre movement was brilliantly satirized in George Kelly's **The Torch-Bearers** (8-29-22, 48th St.). There were sufficient allusions in the play for Philadelphians to gather that the comedy was set in their city, albeit that was not specified. When the husband of the woman who was to play an important part dies of a heart attack after watching his wife try to act, Paula Ritter (Mary Boland) is drafted into the role. It's not a big play, she assures her skeptical husband, Fred (Arthur Shaw)—"just a one-act play—in one act, you

know." The players invade the Ritter household for a rehearsal, led by the autocratic, pompous director, Mrs. J. Duro Pampinelli (Alison Skipworth), who has recently spoken on "Technique in Acting as Distinguished from Method." She informs the disbelieving Ritter, who has questioned whether all this is worth a man's life, that "whenever the torch of essential culture has been raised—(*She raises the lead-pencil as though it was a torch*)—there has unfailingly been the concomitant exactment of a human life. (*She stands holding the torch aloft until the little cuckoo clock over the door at left cuckoos the half-hour.*)" The rehearsal is a disaster, possibly causing Mr. Ritter to fall down the stairs in a faint. But such problems are nothing compared with the performance: players stumble over a door sill; a telephone bell will not ring when it is supposed to but rings wildly later; half of an actor's mustache falls off; lines are forgotten, and the prompter (Helen Lowell), busy with important gossip backstage, cannot find her place in the prompt book. After the show, though everyone praises Paula to the skies, Fred convinces her to give up theatricals by suggesting she "vanish, as the poet says, right in the heyday of your glow." He assures her that her performance will never be forgotten by those who saw it. "You're awfully sweet, Fred," the silly woman says.

For the most part critics threw imaginary hats in the air to celebrate both the play and the acting. Stark Young, writing in the *New Republic*, welcomed a work of "real wit" and predicted, "The chances are that Mr. Kelly, if he remembers what is joyous, will be our best writer of comedy." Although the play's Broadway run was a somewhat disappointing 135 performances, it remained for many years a favorite with the very amateur troupes it spoofed.

· · ·

George [Edward] **Kelly** (1890–1974) was the Philadelphia-born brother of vaudevillian Walter C. Kelly and the uncle of actress Grace Kelly. He began his career as an actor, by 1916 performing in his own sketches in two-a-day. His first full-length play was *Mrs. Ritter Appears* in 1917. It failed to reach Broadway but contained the seeds for his initial Broadway success.

· · ·

Crane Wilbur's second play of the month was **I Will If You Will** (8-29-22, Comedy). The curtain rose on this bedroom farce to disclose three connecting hotel rooms with a total of seven doors. The four male and three female principals were shortly running from room to room slamming doors, hiding in closets, and offering unhelpful explanations to an irate hotel staff. The main reason for the comings and goings was one man's attempt to keep an unhappy wife from trying to sell a stolen $30,000 necklace. He (Edmund Lowe) pretends to be a crook, but in the end a detective he cavorts with turns out to be the real crook. Louis D'Arclay sought laughs—and got them—as a hotel manager suffering from St. Vitus's Dance. Given some of the sharpest pans in a long time, the piece departed after a single week.

Ostensibly, Arthur Goodrich was the author of **So This Is London** (8-30-22, Hudson), but insiders knew that its producer, George M. Cohan, had a large hand in revamping it. The comedy might well have been called *A Yankee's English Rose*, all the more so since the heroine was played by the same actress who first had played Rose Mary Murphy on Broadway. American Hiram Draper (Donald Gallaher) and British Eleanor Beauchamp (Marie Carroll) have fallen in love and announced their engagement. Their parents, most of all their respective fathers (Edmund Breese and Lawrance D'Orsay), are appalled. Old man Draper pictures the English as la-de-dahing snobs, while Sir Percy Beauchamp envisions Americans as gum-chewing, spittoon-prone barbarians. (Both men's imaginings were depicted in special scenes that followed quick blackouts.) But in the end the parents are not only reconciled, they agree to merge their rival shoe factories. Played to the hilt in the best Cohan style ("Cohan snaps his stuff over"), the comedy ran out the season.

Edward A. Paulton's **Her Temporary Husband** (8-31-22, Frazee) just missed the charmed circle of 100 performances by a single week. Its plot had served handsomely for a number of bygone musicals. Blanche Ingram (Ann Andrews) will lose her inheritance if she marries Clarence Topping, a man her late father detested. So Blanche arranges with a friendly doctor at a home for incurables to wed a doddering old man on his last legs. After he dies, she can marry Clarence without forfeiting her estate. But when the marriage ceremony is over, the groom pulls off his long, gray beard and dark glasses and reveals himself as a handsome young buck, Tom Burton (William Courtenay). It takes the remaining two acts for Blanche to accept that Tom is preferable to Clarence or the old geezer.

September was very busy, yet only one entry managed to run more than six months, and that was an importation. A number of reliable old hands found just modest success or no success at all with their latest offerings. James Forbes was among the latter. Unable to move with the times, his handful of

pre-war and immediate postwar triumphs were behind him; his remaining career would be marked by one disappointment after another. **The Endless Chain** (9-4-22, Cohan) could be seen as treating the more serious, uglier side of the story told in Kaufman and Connelly's *To the Ladies*. Believing her husband, Kenneth (Kenneth MacKenna), will never rise to the top on his own, Ann Reeves (Margaret Lawrence) determines to push him there herself. Her method is to have an affair with an influential businessman, Andrew Hale (Harry Minturn). The affair nearly destroys her marriage and Kenneth's career, until Ann is brought to her senses. Critics garlanded Miss Lawrence, seeing in her an actress of continuing promise who could turn a cardboard figure into a believable person. But her career was to be undistinguished.

MacDonald Watson's **Hunky Dory** (9-4-22, Klaw) was an English play set in a small Scottish bootmaking shop. It was not to New York's taste. The boozy, conniving Hunky Dory (Walter Roy) is trying to blackmail the bootmaker (Robert Drysdale) into selling his old building to a developer. But his schemes are thwarted by the local plumber, Peter Maguffie (Watson), who hopes to become a painter and who eventually wins the affection of Dory's sweet daughter (Nell Barker).

The luckless Edwin Nicander and Dallas Welford won their usual quota of fine notices when they appeared in **The Plot Thickens** (9-5-22, Booth), which Thomas Beer took from an Italian play by Luigi Barzini and Arnaldo Fraccaroli. But the comedians could not save the comedy from a quick demise. Adonis Duckworth (Nicander) hires a film director to inject some excitement into his life but requires the director not to reveal his plans to him. So he treats as part of the joke his sweetheart's genuine infatuation with the director's leading man and the real burglars (led by Welford) who break into his home and steal his valuables.

Nor could the hefty Maclyn Arbuckle, his career slowly creeping to its end, do anything for **Wild Oats Lane** (9-6-22, Broadhurst), which George Broadhurst dramatized from Gerald Beaumont's *Red Book Magazine* short story "The Gambling Chaplain." Father Joe (Arbuckle) presides over a slum parish popularly known as Wild Oats Lane and is in charge of a "get-away fund" a gambler left to help criminals escape prosecution and turn over a new leaf. Into his life come The Up-and-Down Kid (Richard Barbee), a hardened hood, and Sweet Marie (Marion Coakley), a prostitute. Years earlier the Kid had seduced the innocent girl back in her hometown, forcing her to flee. When they confront each other, the good priest asks the hood what he will do about the story. The Kid hands Marie his gun, bares his breast, and tells her to shoot. Father Joe comes between the pair, reconciles them, and sends them off to start a fresh life on a western ranch. Audiences reportedly snickered at the scene.

The series of failures was shoved aside with the arrival of Avery Hopwood's comedy **Why Men Leave Home** (9-12-22, Morosco). At the Long Island country house of Tom (John McFarlane) and Fifi Morgan (Florence Shirley), Tom and Grandma (Jessie Villars) sit waiting for Fifi to return from her latest European trip. When she comes back she is accompanied by her two fellow travelers, Nina (Theresa Maxwell Conover) and Betty (Audrey Hart), and their spouses, Artie (Herbert Yost) and Sam (Paul Everton), who had met their ship. The girls rush off to plan their next excursion, leaving the morose men to admire Grandma's old-fashioned ideas and to complain that their plight would make an excellent play. They even have the title for it: "Why Men Leave Home! And the answer would be 'Because their wives leave home first—and the man hasn't any HOME to leave!' " The men talk about flings of their own, scaring the wives into realizing they must be homebodies more often, with Fifi donning her sexiest negligee to underscore her decision. Critics were tiring of Hopwood and were baffled by his attempts to mix farce with preachment. They were also annoyed at Hopwood's public boasting that he was the richest playwright in America. In *Life* Robert Benchley, with his tongue in his cheek as usual, noted, "Stung to the quick by the taunts of this department at his lewd farces and chagrined that his royalties cannot possibly reach the two-million mark until several weeks after Christmas, Mr. Hopwood has taken the ingredients of what would ordinarily have been another bedroom farce and has made them into a bedroom problem play by having the hero get out of bed in his pajamas to deliver a short talk on the shortcomings of the modern American wife." Less able to turn his annoyance into humor, Hornblow concluded his review succinctly, "Mr. Hopwood recently made a self-conscious announcement to the press that he has made a million and a quarter out of his plays. In the name of Eugene O'Neill, he is welcome to it!" Playgoers reacted with mixed emotions to the critics, giving the farce a run of 135 performances. As so often happened, Broadway smart money blamed the title for the comparatively short run.

Many of the same critics could not decide whether Owen Davis's **Dreams for Sale** (9-13-22, Playhouse) was meant to be a comedy, a farce, an old-style melodrama, or a mixture of all three. For many years the Nashes and the Baldwins have been feuding fiercely over business and personal grudges. But the feud promises to end when Anne Baldwin (Helen Gahagan) shows interest in Arthur Nash (John Bohn) and old Peter Nash (William Holden) agrees to let bygones be bygones if Anne marries Arthur. Then Anne realizes she prefers her childhood beau, Jim Griswold (Donald Cameron), reigniting the feud. She cleverly delays a Nash truck from bringing machinery that will start up an old pulp mill and will allow the Nashes to win a legal claim. The delay permits the Baldwin men to blow up the truck, thereby defeating the Nashes for good and permitting her to wed Jim. Two weeks and the play was gone.

The slight but charming comedy that came in next delighted audiences for eighteen weeks, thanks in no small measure to the skillful playing of Ina Claire, Bruce McRae, and their associates and to Gilbert Miller's deft staging. In Arthur Richman's second play of the season, **The Awful Truth** (9-18-22, Henry Miller's), the hard-up-for-cash divorcée Lucy Warriner (Claire) decides she must marry again. She selects a nice but somewhat uncouth westerner, Daniel Leeson (Paul Harvey). His snooty aunt (Louise Mackintosh) objects strongly, citing rumors of indiscretions that led to the divorce. So Lucy invites her ex, Norman Satterly (Bruce McRae), to meet the aunt and acknowledge Lucy's innocence. Being a gentleman, he does just that. When the others leave, Lucy and Norman sit together reminiscing. In short order, they appreciate that they are still in love. So Lucy sends Daniel away. Of course, Norman admits he still has doubts about what really happened. This time Lucy invites that man who was mentioned in the divorce, Rufus Kempster (Raymond Walburn), to visit her, and she arranges for Norman to overhear their conversation. The dialogue clears Lucy, and Norman agrees to a second marriage. But was that conversation prearranged? The audience can only guess. As the wayward, vexatious, but frequently adorable Lucy, Claire was at her sparkling best. And she was surrounded not only by excellent players but by some of the season's loveliest settings, including a darkly paneled and richly furnished library (in her friends' home) and her own brightly elegant, flower-filled drawing room. The play served as the basis for three films, most successfully one with Irene Dunne and Cary Grant.

William Anthony McGuire's **It's a Boy!** (9-19-22, Sam H. Harris) was the latest play to preach to New Yorkers about the virtues of small-town life over the snares of the big city. Naturally, not many New

Yorkers bought it. The baby proclaimed in the title arrived in the prologue and was rarely spoken about again. Instead the plot recounts how Charles Blake (Robert Ames) runs a small store successfully in Carbondale, Pa. He would remain there even after he receives a lucrative offer of $10,000 a year to come to New York. His ambitious wife, Dorothy Mackaye) pushes him into accepting. In no time they are beset by freeloaders and growing debts. The loss of his position drives him into bankruptcy, so the couple head home to Carbondale's suppposedly simpler, more honest ways.

Banco (9-20-22, Ritz) was Clare Kummer's adaptation of Alfred Savoir's Paris hit. Count Alexandre de Lussac (Alfred Lunt), known to his intimates as "Banco" because of his passion for gambling, is furious when his wife, Charlotte (Lola Fisher), appears at the Casino to beg him to return home. He informs her that he will continue to gamble so long as she remains in the waiting room. She stays for eighty-four hours, consoled only by a kindly baron (Francis Byrne). She finally leaves, having decided to divorce her husband. A year later she is about to marry the baron. Banco shows up at the wedding to talk her out of her plans, but fails. That evening a suspicious fire breaks out on the baron's estate, forcing him to run to obtain aid. He is no sooner gone than Banco enters Charlotte's bedroom and sweet-talks her into agreeing to an annulment and returning to him. Critics applauded Kummer's delicate touch and the players' flair, especially Lunt's. Many welcomed his abandonment of cute comic mannerisms that they perceived were starting to mar his performances. The *Telegram* hailed his "sure lightness of touch and never failing variety." A few, such as Kenneth Macgowan and Heywood Broun, still held reservations about his "chasing gestures." A major critical complaint was that Livingston Platt's settings offered almost no suggestion of France. Yet for all the money notices, *Banco* could not find an audience.

Somerset Maugham's **East of Suez** (9-21-22, Eltinge) did, at least until its star had a violent, public disagreement with the producer, Al Woods, and walked out in a huff. That star was Florence Reed. She played a half-caste vamp who drives the man (John Halliday) who genuinely loves her to suicide after he weds his best friend (Leonard Mudie), a somewhat innocent young fellow. Exotic settings enhanced the sultry atmosphere.

In Martin Brown's **The Exciters** (9-22-22, Times Square) a fast-living flapper, "Rufus" Rand (Tallulah Bankhead), part of a high-flying coterie that calls itself "The Exciters," is seriously injured after driving her car into a ditch. She may die. If she dies unwed her family stands to lose a $2,000,000 fortune. By disturbing coincidence, the only single man around the Rand house is "Five Minute" Dan MacGee (Alan Dinehart), who happens to be burglarizing the Long Island home just as Rufus is brought back from the hospital. He agrees to become the groom if no charges are brought against him. The wedding takes place at once at Rufus's insistence. To her family's happy surprise, Rufus recovers; to the family's horror, she refuses to divorce the handsome, personable Dan. But then he turns out not to be a real burglar. Rather, he is the scion of the Philadelphia Stafford MacGees and is a detective posing as a crook to get the goods on other burglars. The *Tribune*'s Percy Hammond, among the minority who approved the play, called it "a delirious charade." He may have been damning with faint praise when he added, "Few actresses can portray more convincingly than Miss Bankhead the difficult part of a pretty girl." But Hornblow, this time seeing the humor of a situation and allowing that she was "radiantly beautiful," reported prophetically, "Miss Bankhead has literally too vast a sense of humor to be able to act with any conviction or sincerity."

Frank Craven's **Spite Corner** (9-25-22, Little) was looked on as a marked comedown from his earlier *The First Year*, although producer John Golden kept it going with some profit for four months. The comedy took place in an archaic, low-ceilinged, beamed and wooden-pegged room that had been built a century or more ago. When it was constructed it had been the street floor of the first building in what became the town of Dean. The little burg never really flourished, and certainly the Dean family has fallen on hard times. Its last member, Elizabeth Dean (Madge Kennedy), runs a dressmaking establishment in the room. Old biddies sit there sewing or come to make small purchases and small talk. Over the years, the Lattimers have become the town's richest family. But there has been bad blood between them and the Deans. However, Elizabeth had fallen in love with John Lattimer, who left town when the family patriarch, Nathan Lattimer, opposed his seeing Elizabeth. John promised Elizabeth to make good on his own in the big city and then marry her. That was five years ago. For much of that time, she has not heard from him. Nonetheless, the townsfolk are certain she is still in love. After all, "there ain't nobody in town between the high school and the soldiers' home to make her forget him." Now Elizabeth discovers that Nathan wants to buy her property so he can erect a modern business block on the street. John (Jason Robards) returns unexpectedly, though he is forced to admit he has not been a success. But he seems strangely indifferent to Elizabeth and urges her to sell. She declines. Most of the townsfolk, feeling that she is holding back progress, refuse to sell her groceries, boycott her store, and patronize a competitive shop which Nathan spitefully underwrites. A furious Elizabeth will not even see John, despite his unceasing entreaties. Finally she is told that the town has employed eminent domain to seize her property. She must leave. Just then a fire seriously damages the building. At the same time, Nathan dies, leaving John his heir. His behavior in her distress convinces Elizabeth he loves her. The first act, with the old biddies exchanging malicious gossip, was charming, but the play's development was mechanical. (The play was also very short.) One effective bit had the curtain drop after smoke begins to pour into the room; when it rose again a third of the room was a fire-gutted skeleton.

Exotic, mad villains and haunted houses continued to appeal to playwrights. The exotic, mad villain in William Hurlbut's **On the Stairs** (9-25-22, Playhouse) was the Swami Abhukevanda (Arnold Daly), who attempts to woo Elsa Carroll (Maragret Dale), an heiress whose father he had murdered. The house is reputedly haunted by the dead man's ghost. Elsa is rescued by the stalwart Merritt Lane (James Crane). Frustrated, the swami climbs the stairs of the old house, then falls backward down the long flight, dead.

Two other established favorites, Henry Miller and Ruth Chatterton, also met with disappointment when they were starred in Henri Bataille's **La Tendresse** (9-25-22, Empire). A great dramatist (Miller), suspecting his mistress (Chatterton) is unfaithful, hides stenographers in a room where she entertains her friends. At first they cannot obtain material, but finally she entertains her lover, and her conversations are reported to the dramatist. He writes a play in which he includes her own remarks and reads it to her, then orders her to leave. Eventually, loneliness goads him to call her back, and since she does love him in her fashion, a compromise is reached.

Ethel Barrymore encountered similar resistance from both the press and the public when she starred in Ludwig Lewisohn's translation of Gerhart Hauptmann's **Rose Bernd** (9-26-22, Longacre). Rose is a peasant girl who has a child out of wedlock and is driven both to killing it and contemplating suicide.

The month's biggest hit was also an importation, John Galsworthy's **Loyalties** (9-27-22, Gaiety). It was enthusiastically greeted and ran for seven months. Ferdinand De Levis (James Dale) is a rich Jew who has been more or less accepted into English society. While a house guest, he finds his money has been stolen. When he accuses another guest, a war hero named Dancy (Charles Quartermaine), his host and all the others present defend Dancy. Dancy would take the matter to court, but when proof of his thievery is forthcoming he drops his charges and commits suicide. The Jew, however, remains ostracized for having publicly accused him.

Another English play, Percival Knight's **Thin Ice** (9-30-22, Comedy), concluded September's entries and found some small success. The author himself took the leading role of an impoverished English aristocrat who comes to America and takes work as a butler with a man (Felix Krembs) who had served under him during the war. He solves the man's marital problems, weds the man's rich sister (Olive Wyndham), and returns home.

October's first novelty continued the parade of importations. Actors' Equity, announcing it would turn producer and mount plays commercial interests ignored (as if the Theatre Guild, Arthur Hopkins, and Winthrop Ames did not exist), formed the Equity Players to offer **Malvaloca** (10-2-22, 48th St.), which Jacob S. Fassett, Jr., took from the Spanish of Serafín and Joaquín Álvarez Quintero. It told how the loose-moraled Malvaloca (Jane Cowl) meets and falls in love with the upright Leonardo (Rollo Peters). He has doubts about her dependability but concludes that his love has reformed her. Rejected by most aisle-sitters, it ran six weeks largely on the strength of Jane Cowl's appeal.

There was even less interest in Louis Anspacher's **That Day** (10-3-22, Bijou). Elinor Wyndham (Helen Holmes) was the mistress of a man she did not know was married. When she discovered the fact, she threw over the man. At the same time, she learned that she had kept her part in the affair so quiet that another woman was suspected. Elinor marries, only to find that her new brother-in-law is about to marry the suspected woman until he hears of her supposed behavior. The truth comes out, but Elinor's husband is forgiving.

Its five performances made B. Iden Payne's **Dolly Jordan** (10-3-22, Daly's) one of the season's most ignominious failures. In its short stay it recounted the history of Dorothy Bland (Josephine Victor), who, as Dorothy Jordan, became a famous London actress in the late eighteenth century, had aristocratic lovers, and died all but forgotten in France. Daly's was not the celebrated old playhouse but an out-of-the-way theatre on 63rd Street that had won attention by housing the black musical *Shuffle Along*.

188

One of the era's most memorable plays was Karel Capek's **R.U.R.** (10-9-22, Garrick), which the Theatre Guild produced in Paul Selver and Nigel Playfair's translation. R.U.R. stood for Rossum's Universal Robots and gave the term "robot," taken from a Slavic word root meaning "work," to the English language. Rossum's factory turns out soulless robots who have no human emotions but work unquestioningly. They are supplanting humans everywhere. As time passes, however, the robots begin to display human traits and finally rise up against their human masters. Only one human remains, but when he goes to dissect a pretty robot girl, a male robot objects. The man realizes these robots have learned to love. Since they have found a cottage with two puppies, he tells them they must become the new Adam and Eve. The robots all wore closely cropped black wigs and had white-washed faces; they were dressed in dark pants and long-sleeved, turtlenecked shirts with sewn-on triangular patches showing their numbers. Many critics saw the play as biting satire, others as what a later generation would call science fiction. Either way, despite reservations about uneven staging and performances, they liked it. The public sustained it for just short of six months.

Neither playgoers nor reviewers cared much for Monckton Hoffe's **The Faithful Heart** (10-10-22, Broadhurst), a "sentimental melodrama" from England, which some saw as a watered-down, sugared retelling of the Anna Christie story. Just as Lieutenant-Colonel Waverly Ango (Tom Nesbitt), a much decorated war hero, is about to make a splendid marriage for himself, a young lady (Flora Sheffield) appears and tells him she is the child born of a fling he had when he was in the merchant marine twenty years before. Ango backs out of the marriage and becomes captain of a tramp steamer, taking his daughter with him.

A pleasant if not wholly original idea got nowhere in Abby Merchant's **The Ever Green Lady** (10-11-22, Punch and Judy). When the newly rich O'Hallorans leave their swank Riverside Drive apartment for a holiday in Palm Beach, they also leave behind—at her own insistence—Grandma O'Halloran (Beryl Mercer), whom they pretentiously call Madame O'Halloran. As a young woman, the old gal had taken in laundry, and she has never felt at ease in her posh surroundings. So her family is no sooner gone than she heads for Greenwich Village and takes a job as a laundress. Part of the laundry had been converted into a still. Since she has no qualms about mixing washing and whiskey she soon finds herself in trouble with the district attorney (Jack Murtagh).

Her snobbish son (Robert T. Haines) and daughter-in-law (Jane Meredith) are mortified. But after the D.A. comes down with a cold and she shows him the curative powers of booze, a happy accommodation is reached. Granny also helps the romance of her granddaughter (Beatrice Miles).

The **Swifty** (10-16-22, Playhouse) of John Peter Toohey and W. C. Percival's comedy was Swifty Morgan (Hale Hamilton), a former boxing champion who has been hired as a bodybuilder for Tom Proctor (Humphrey Bogart), the playboy son of Jefferson Proctor (William Holden). As they become friendly, Tom starts confiding in Swifty, including the proud fact that he has seduced a young girl and has no intention of making an honest woman of her. When Swifty discovers the girl is his own sister, he determines to be revenged by eloping with Tom's sister, Miriam (Frances Howard). But his better nature prevails, so after spending the night walking with her along Fifth Avenue and breakfasting at the Plaza, he brings her home. The elder Proctor tells Tom he must marry Swifty's sister. Swifty and Miriam shake hands and go their separate paths. Most critics silently passed over young Bogart's performance. He probably wished *Variety* had, too. The tradesheet saw him as "deplorably lost" in his part.

The season's second three-character play was Grace George's adaptation of Paul Géraldy's **To Love** (10-17-22, Bijou). Just as Helene (George) is about to run off with the fun-loving Challange (Robert Warwick), memories of her years with her devoted if somewhat dull husband (Norman Trevor) flood back and overwhelm her. She sends Challange on his way. Superbly polished acting by all three principals could not enlist support for an unexciting play.

There was little support at first for Channing Pollock's **The Fool** (10-23-22, Times Square), but sermons by numerous important religious figures extolling the piece soon sent members of their congregations rushing to the box office. (In a publicity booklet released by the Selwyns, who produced the play, no fewer than forty clerics were mentioned, beginning, inexplicably, with six rabbis. The booklet also listed prominent public figures who lauded the work.) The congregation of the Church of the Nativity in New York is rich and selfish. They believe donating things they have worn out or have no use for makes them charitable, and they are aghast at the notion of foreigners worshiping alongside them. They are also disgusted with their minister, Daniel Gilchrist (James Kirkwood), even if he is the son of a man who had been one of their wealthiest, most loyal members. As one outraged churchgoer bemoans, "He said we couldn't take credit to ourselves for returning a small portion of our *ill-gotten gains*!" And they are further appalled when he gives his only overcoat to a man shivering in the cold—a Jew, at that. His father's friend, George Goodkind (Henry Stephenson), tries vainly to reason with him, pointing out that Gilchrist already has given away all the moneys he has received so far from his father's trust. Gilchrist responds, "What would happen if anybody really tried to live like Christ?" He sets out to learn. But his behavior costs him his job and the girl he loves. Goodkind gives Gilchrist work attempting to mollify the miners whom Goodkind employs, only to discover that Gilchrist is totally committed to their cause. Fired again, Gilchrist establishes a shelter for the homeless. He takes in a miner's wife who has become a prostitute, but when he fails to convert her, he is beaten by the miner and the miner's buddies. However, he does find work for Grubby (Arthur Elliott), a cabman who no longer can find trade for his horse and carriage, by getting him a taxi. And somehow his goodness allows a crippled girl (Sara Sothern) to walk again. That miracle brings him standing in the community. When Goodkind visits him, the older man confesses, "I wonder if *you're* the failure, after all." Within a few weeks demand for seats was so great the play was giving twelve performances a week and seven road companies were sent out. In his autobiography Pollock recounts the play's fascinating history, including the meteoric career of Miss Sothern, whom he discovered when the play was first tried out in stock on the West Coast, and who walked off with the best notices.

Another surprise hit was Thomas F. Fallon's **The Last Warning** (10-24-22, Klaw), taken from Wadsworth Camp's novel *The House of Fear*. Since both Fallon and his producers were fledglings, the play opened with no ballyhoo and no appreciable advance sale. Rave notices changed that. *Variety* spoke of its being "as spooky as 'The Bat'—only battier." A famous old actor-manager, Thomas Woodward, had disappeared mysteriously during the performance of a play called *The Snare* and has never been seen again. Since that time his playhouse, which one character notes "would give anybody the creeps," has remained dark, until Arthur McHugh (William Courtleigh) decides to relight the theatre with a revival of the play, employing most of the original cast. But the old actor's "ghost," plodding around in an eerie green spotlight, besets rehearsals. Even close-range gunshots cannot affect him. The words "The Last Warning" appear on the backstage wall,

the dead man's perfume wafts through the auditorium, a heavy sandbag falls from the flies, an actor cast as the new leading man is electrocuted picking up a supposedly harmless candle, another goes mad, and tarantulas the old actor had collected are inadvertently let loose. The police arrive, fanning out over the whole of the real theatre and blocking exits, and remain until the mystery is solved during a performance of *The Snare* (the last act of the real play being the first act of the fictitious one). McHugh is actually a detective and, telling the other players she is a former burlesque queen, has cast his statuesque wife, Evelynda Hendon (Marion Lord), in a minor role to allow her to snoop about. Pretending she is a modern-day Mrs. Malaprop, she is forever calling him Mr. McHuge. Together they point the finger at Robert Bruce (Clarence Derwent), co-owner of the playhouse, who killed Woodford because the actor refused to help in Bruce's criminal sidelines. Bruce, who earlier had sneered, "Good detectives never solve mysteries. . . . They follow clues—it's more lucrative," plunges offstage through a canvas setting and kills himself. McHugh steps before the footlights, apologizes to the audience for not being able to complete the play, and urges them to return tomorrow for a full performance. The play ran out the season.

A second mystery, Robert Housum's **Persons Unknown** (10-25-22, Punch and Judy), failed to provide many thrills and was consigned to oblivion after just five performances. Peter Sheridan (Hugh Huntley), a reformed wastrel, is suspected of stealing his widowed father's Rembrandt. The father (John Miltern) and the father's new love (Martha Hedman) cannot believe it, for they are convinced that Peter's reformation is genuine. However, when the father's friend, Nicholas Gregory (Philip Lord), threatens Peter with seemingly conclusive evidence of the boy's guilt, Peter kills him. It soon develops that Gregory was the thief, so everyone conspires to provide Peter with an unbreakable alibi.

The month's and the season's longest-run hit was Austin Strong's **Seventh Heaven** (10-30-22, Booth). Old Boul' (Hubert Druce)—like Grubby in *The Fool*—is a cabman who has become a taxi driver, even if his jalopy, "Eloise," does not want to work. He parks it in a sinister-looking cul-de-sac, just in time to rescue the lovely but bedraggled, blonde Diane (Helen Menken) from her vicious, crooked sister. However, he needs help in fighting off the sharp-nailed Nana (Marion Kerby). Up from below the streets pops a smiling sewer cleaner, Chico (George Gaul), who assures all listeners that he is "a very remarkable fellow." The men chase away Nana and console Diane. That done, Boul' is dismayed to learn that Chico does not believe in le Bon Dieu. Chico says all that he wants in life are three things: a promotion to street cleaner, a lovely blonde wife, and a grand tour in a taxi. Chico then prevents the despairing girl from killing herself. A priest comes from the church in front of which all this has occurred. He has overheard much of the discussion and recognizes Chico as a man who once saved his life, so he gives Chico a card which will allow him to become a street cleaner. Just then Nana returns with a policeman, demanding that Diane be arrested. But Chico lies that he and Diane are married, offering to present proof the next day. The skeptical policeman leaves. Chico and his "wife" jump into the old taxi, which unexpectedly starts up without difficulty, and the three drive off for a grand tour of Paris, or at least a short ride to where Chico lives. In her shabby but neat attic home with Chico, Diane is visited by a rich aunt (Isabel West), who leads her to believe that a rich admirer, Brissac (Frank Morgan), will look after the girl and has paid Chico to abandon her. Diane is happy to discover that she has misunderstood and that Chico wants her. The war breaks out, but before he leaves to join the fight Chico marries Diane in his own way, asking le Bon Dieu, "If there is any truth in the Idea of You, please make this a true marriage." After several years, a nattily uniformed Boul' returns telling of Eloise's brave end at the front and offering Diane a bar of soap. Sadly he has no news of Chico. Nonetheless Diane is happy to reminisce about "that glorious ride when you brought us here—to heaven!" A somber Brissac appears and hands Diane a package containing the keepsakes that Chico had taken to the front with him. He tells her as gently as possible that Chico is dead. A celebration breaks out down in the street. The war is ended. Diane falls into Brissac's embrace, and Brissac tells her he loves her. Suddenly a hatless, disheveled Chico comes into the room. A hospital attendant hurries in after him, yelling that he should not have run away from the hospital. Diane breaks loose from Brissac and, sensing something is wrong, slowly passes her hand over Chico's face. When she realizes he is blind, she falls to her knees. Chico raises her up. He assures her he cannot stay blind since he understands now that le Bon Dieu is watching over them and, what is more, he himself is "a very remarkable fellow."

Critics deemed the play flawed but eminently workable. The physical production with the reproduced taxi of the first act won applause. The best notices went to Helen Menken, with more than one critic comparing her to Duse and lauding her "exquisite pathetic quality," her "sense of simple actuality, shot through always with divinations of the spirit." When John Golden's production closed after 704 performances, it was the fifth longest running show in Broadway history. Golden himself had produced two of the others, *Lightnin'* and *The First Year*. In 1927 the play became a successful silent film, and in 1955 it was turned unsuccessfully into a musical.

Less popular with the public was **Six Characters in Search of an Author** (10-30-22, Princess), Luigi Pirandello's play as translated by Edward Storer. For all the difficulties it presented to the tired businessman, it was no flop, chalking up 136 performances and moving on to numerous revivals. The work purported to deal with six figures whom the author had dropped from a play and who, obtaining lives of their own, come to the rehearsal of another play, demanding they be allowed to act out their stories. Among the players were Margaret Wycherly as "the Mother" and Florence Eldridge as "the Daughter."

Karel Capek, this time with his brother Josef, gave Broadway yet another interesting play with *Ze zivota hmyzu*, adapted by Owen Davis as **The World We Live In** (10-31-22, Jolson). A vagrant (Robert Edeson) falls asleep and dreams of insect worlds not unlike that of humans. There are carefree, amorous butterflies (who dance the bunnyhug), murderous, self-serving, greedy beetles, and land-mad, warring ants. Waking from his dream the despondent vagrant dies, but a woodcutter comes along to proclaim that life will go on. Lee Simonson's stylized settings and imaginative costumes won high praise. The decor consisted largely of "oddly colored drapes . . . of sombre tones of blue, misted greens, and subdued browns." The drapes carried batik-like motifs. Earthly items were grotesquely enlarged; pebbles, for example, became huge rounded rocks. Scenes faded away as transparent, patterned curtains were lowered. The ants wore headdresses suggesting Prussian helmets; the moths cavorted in diaphanous drapey gowns; the beetles had derby hats and dark, menacing businesslike jackets, shirts, and ties, but equally dark drapery instead of pants. A grub was garbed in a ringed outfit not unlike the figure in the modern Michelin logo. All the insects wore colored sashes or eccentric masks. Between the acts a special "shining curtain of silver cloth" hid the stage. Even some reviewers preferred to call the play *The Insect Comedy*, and that is the title it became known by. Its original run was three months.

November began with a big splash, for **Rain** (11-7-22, Maxine Elliott's), which John Colton and Cle-

191

mence Randolph took from Somerset Maugham's short story "Miss Thompson," was the season's "most talked of play" and "most consistently popular dramatic success." Some newly arrived travelers are detained temporarily at a ramshackle hotel in Pago Pago [pronounced "pango pango"] when a cholera outbreak prevents their heading for their ultimate destination. One is a heavily painted, gaudily dressed, and somewhat faded beauty, Sadie Thompson (Jeanne Eagels), a woman who has clearly worked the streets. Among the others are the belligerently sanctimonious Reverend Davidson (Robert Kelly), his grim wife (Catharine Brooke), and their more humane companions, Dr. and Mrs. McPhail (Fritz Williams and Shirley King). Mrs. Davidson finds nothing to like in the loose-living port, a place "far below the moral standard," while the minister boasts of the trouble he has made for those who refused to adopt properly Christian ways. The hotel owner, Joe Horn (Rapley Holmes), has other ideas, suggesting that "these reform folks fighting depravity are only fighting their own hankering for the very indulgences they suspect in others." In no time the Reverend has turned on the fun-loving Sadie, who openly entertains marines and sailors in her room and dances to jazz records she plays on the phonograph. Their arguments grow increasingly heated, with Sadie opining that Davidson as a child must have stuck pins in frogs for the joy of it and calling him a "dirty two-faced mutt" and a "psalm-singing son of a . . ." (she is hustled out of the room before she can finish the latter epithet). In revenge, Davidson convinces the governor to order Sadie onto the next ship returning to America even though the minister knows she faces jail if she returns. While they await the ship, Davidson continues to work on Sadie, and for a time it even seems that she may be converted. Davidson himself is troubled by strange dreams of mountains back in Nebraska. But McPhail points out that there are no real mountains in Nebraska and wonders if the so-called mountains were not "curiously like a woman's breast." Torrential rains confine everyone to the hotel, and one evening, the Reverend's deepest yearnings finally overwhelming him, he goes to Sadie's room and closes the door behind him. The next morning it is learned that he has drowned himself. Surprisingly, Mrs. Davidson, who earlier had boasted that the minister had never touched her sexually, comes face to face with Sadie and tells her she understands and is sorry for both her late husband and for Sadie herself. Sadie replies, "I guess I'm sorry for everybody in the world." And she prepares to sail for Sydney.

Most critics agreed with Burns Mantle, who called the play a "supreme dramatic triumph." The production's suggestion of languorous tropical heat and, even more, the brilliant re-creation of tropical downpours were also singled out. But it was Eagels who garnered many of the most passionate endorsements for playing Sadie "with an emotional power as fiery and unbridled in effect as it is artistically restrained." For a brief time she became one of Broadway's brightest stars, and her reputation has lived on after many other players' have faded away.

The play ran 648 performances, just a little short of *Seventh Heaven*'s stand. A 1944 musical version, called *Sadie Thompson*, failed.

Down in the Village, matters were not so happy. After a lapse of thirteen years John Luther Long was heard from again with his blank-verse drama **Crowns** (11-9-22, Provincetown Playhouse). His story told of a prince (Benjamin Kauser) and a princess (Margaret Mower), each of a different country, who were once imprisoned in an olive garden and there came to love one another and to embrace Christ's teachings. Years later, called to their respective countries' thrones, each is assured by war-like ministers and generals that the other is preparing for war. When the prince fights his way through the opposing army, he discovers the princess has poisoned herself, grieved to think he has become an aggressor.

Uptown, Broadway's fifth successive hit was George S. Kaufman and Marc Connelly's **Merton of the Movies** (11-13-22, Cort), theatricalized from Harry Leon Wilson's *Saturday Evening Post* novelette. Merton Gill (Glenn Hunter) is so film-struck that he is a laughingstock in his small hometown, Simsbury. He has used some of his meager savings to buy the various outfits—a cowboy suit, swank vestments—he believes a star requires, and he has had photographs taken to resemble those of one of his idols, Harold Parmalee. At Amos Gashwiler's general store, where he works, he spends his time acting out fantasies. He uses a mustachioed window dummy that is clothed in a raincoat carrying a sign saying "Rainproof or Get Your Money Back" as his villain, tussles with him, and tosses him over a cliff, which happens to be the store's counter. Caught in the act, he loses his job, so he heads for California. Before he leaves he prays that God make him a good movie star: "Make me one of the best! For Jesus' sake, Amen!" In Hollywood he assumes the name Clifford Armytage. While waiting in casting offices he meets Miss Montague (Florence Nash), who has played some bit parts and who tries to help him. Disillusionment sets in quickly. Parmalee (Alexander Clark, Jr.) ignores him. And another of his idols, Beulah Baxter (Gladys Feldman), who has starred in the truly dramatic serial *Hazards of Hortense* and who has publicly sworn she never uses a double, uses a double. His first assignment is a fiasco, since he plays everything too seriously. Then his helper has a marvelous idea. She tells a director that Merton is so serious he is funny. Without letting on to Merton, they cast him in a comedy which he plays with such innocent, deadpan earnestness that it makes him a star. He sadly accepts his success. Hailed as "corking entertainment," the comedy ran nearly a year.

Inevitably the string of hits had to end. Leon Cunningham's **Hospitality** (11-13-22, 48th St.) saw to that. This second mounting by the Equity Players was billed as a "tragi-comedy." It centered on Jennie Wells (Louise Closser Hale), who takes in boarders to make ends meet. When her son, Peter (Tom Powers), marries Muriel Humphrey (Phyllis Povah), a girl Jennie rightly suspects of few morals, Jennie pretends to lose her life savings and comes to live with the young couple. She makes life so miserable for Muriel that the girl runs off with a man with whom she has been flirting. Peter is free to marry Ruthie (Margaret Borough), a better girl whom Jennie had wanted Peter to marry in the first place. But Jennie's victory is short-lived. For the strain kills her. Though the performers and, in many instances, the play were well-received, theatregoers had too many superior offerings to choose from.

Nor did players from the Comédie Française, led by Cecile Sorel, attract large audiences when they arrived the same evening at the 39th Street Theatre to present a repertory that included *L'Aventurière*, *Le Demi-monde*, *Le Duel*, *La Dame aux camélias*, *Le Misanthrope*, *Tartuffe*, and one oddity, *La Mégère apprivoisée*, a free French redaction of *The Taming of the Shrew*.

But an adaptation from the French did find favor. In **The Love Child** (11-14-22, Cohan), which Martin Brown drew from Henri Bataille's eleven-year-old Paris hit, Eugene Thorne (Sidney Blackmer) learns that his mother's longtime lover (Lee Baker) refuses to keep his promise to marry Laura Thorne (Janet Beecher) after his wife has died. So Eugene threatens to make a mistress of the man's daughter (Juliette Crosby) unless the lover honors his pledge. The man sourly agrees, but Laura now will not have him.

The public would not have A. A. Milne's **The Romantic Age** (11-14-22, Comedy) in which Melisande Knowles (Margalo Gillmore) dreams of finding a romantic knight in armor. She thinks she has spotted one when she see Gervase Mallory (Leslie Howard) garbed exactly like her dream man. But she changes her mind when she discovers he is merely a stockbroker heading for a costume ball. By the final act Gervase has convinced Melisande that contemporary dress is no bar to love.

The season's shortest run—three performances— went to William Everett's **Virtue(?)** (11-16-22, Nora Bayes). It was based on the Nashville killing several years before of Senator Carmack by Duncan B. Cooper, a local political boss. Now the senator became McCormack and the villain, who himself is killed at the end of the play, Robert Duncan. A love interest told the story of a district attorney forced to patronize a seedy roadhouse after the car he and his lady friend were driving in breaks down. Second-stringers who covered it gave it very short shrift. *Variety*, suggesting it was "unlikely there have been many" worse plays, bemoaned the drama "talks itself unconscious."

First-stringers had something far more exciting to cover—John Barrymore's Hamlet, which Arthur Hopkins brought into the Sam H. Harris Theatre the same evening. Heywood Broun began his review in the *World*: "John Barrymore is far and away the finest Hamlet we have ever seen. He excels all others in grace, fire, wit and clarity. This final quality should be stressed. Back in high school we remember being asked whether Hamlet was really mad. If we had seen Barrymore it would have been possible for us to tell the teacher, 'Don't be silly.' " He especially admired how clear the star made Hamlet's "unconscious motives" and faulted him only for some of his diction. Similarly thrilled, Woollcott opened his *Herald* notice: "It lacked but twenty minutes of midnight last evening when the four tawny clad captains of Fortinbras lifted the slim, young body of the dead Prince of Denmark to their mailed shoulders, bore it slowly up the great stone steps of Elsinore and out of the brilliant, gory, earthy castle into the cool of the moonlight. They stood there for an instant, they had their burden silhouetted for us as a final memory. There was a wail of trumpets in the distance, the lights faded out and the curtain fell. Thus ended an evening that will be memorable in the history of the American theatre." Extolling the added credibility Barrymore's relative youth gave, Woollcott went on to the performance's intelligence and lack of outmoded stage tricks. To him Hamlet's soliloquies "seemed for once just a lonely, unhappy man's thoughts walking in the silent darkness." (Heard today on record, the reading of the great soliloquy sounds excessively stagey.) In one bold departure, the dead king's ghost (Reginald Pole) was never seen. When he was heard to speak a flickering, spectral light appeared on the curtain behind the arch high up at the back of the stage. About the supporting players critics were lukewarm, with Blanche Yurka's Queen coming out best and Rosalinde Fuller's Ophelia often the least approved. Robert Edmond Jones's single basic setting was hailed as poetically beautiful but was also said by many to have cramped the action. It consisted of one huge room whose two high walls on both sides were broken only by a lone, tall window in each. Almost from the footlights a wide, long staircase ascended to a magnificent, towering arch, sometimes closed off by curtains, sometimes, as in the final scene, opened to reveal the sky beyond. (For a few scenes, such as Gertrude's bedroom, curtains were lowered to achieve a sense of intimacy.) Virtually every critic admired Jones's sensitive lighting. Costumes, apparently, were unexceptional. The run of 101 performances surpassed Edwin Booth's longest stay by a single performance and probably exceeded John Kellard's suspect claim to a longer stand.

Playgoers were brought back to earth with Zoë Akins's **The Texas Nightingale** (11-20-22, Empire), one of a number of plays still being produced under the aegis of "Charles Frohman." The casting of the leading role was one of the strangest in years, one the long- dead producer probably would not have stood for. Steven Tillerton (Cyril Keightley) and a friend return from hearing Brasa Canava sing Brünnhilde at the Met. By his own admission Tillerton was "the second and most obscure of Madame Canava's four husbands." And that is now confronting him with a problem. To help Hollyhock Jones, as Canava was then known, study for a career, he borrowed $8000 from a rich acquaintance, who subsequently promised to tear up Tillerton's note. Twenty years have passed, and the rich man has just died, without, it seems, having kept his promise. Tillerton is a not very successful writer and will be hard put to honor the estate's demand for the money. But Tillerton assures his friend it was worth it to promote "greatness." After the friend leaves, Canava (Jobyna Howland), accompanied by four German shepherds, appears unannounced. She has become, perhaps always was, a not very pleasant woman, self-assured and demanding. She, too, is having problems. She reveals that six months after Tillerton left her she gave birth to a son. Tillerton has never known that. But now she finds the youngster "the damnedest poor excuse for a nineteen-year-old boy I've ever seen in my whole life." To make matters worse, the son, Raymond (Percy Helton), is in love with a superficial flapper, Inez (Beth Varden). The moody, slightly irresponsi-

ble Raymond is furious when Canava tries to break up the relationship. He tells his much married mother that her affair with the flamboyant violinist Sascha Bloch (Georges Renavent) is far more scandalous. Can Tillerton help? The best he can do with Raymond is extract a not very firm agreement to postpone any wedding. But it seems more likely that, having visited with Tillerton again, Canava may give up Bloch and return to her number two. She tells him, "There's always been something in me that's belonged to you, Stevie. Those three years were the best of all." The casting of the Junoesque, beautiful Jobyna Howland, far better known for her work in musicals and straight comedies, threw some critics off balance. Still, she was deemed unexpectedly competent. Percy Helton's touching performance as the son grabbed the best adjectives. The play, which had tried out and was afterwards published as *Greatness*, managed only a one-month run.

A. A. Milne's second failure of the season, **The Lucky One** (11-20-22, Garrick), ran just a week longer. It told how Pamela Carey (Violet Heming) leaves her charming, charmed husband, Gerald (Dennis King), to live with his luckless brother, Bob (Percy Waram). Since nothing flusters Gerald, he goes blithely on his way.

A third short-lived production was William A. Page's **The Bootleggers** (11-27-22, 39th St.) It contrasted the fate of two bootleg "Kings," who for several years have fought murderous territorial wars. The low-born Vicarelli (Barry Towsley) dominates the East Side until he steals Rosa (Lenore Masso) from Tony (Antonio Salerno). Tony attempts to poison Vicarelli, but Rosa drinks the poison by mistake. Vicarelli then stabs Tony to death. He is arrested and is certain to receive the electric chair. By contrast, the Waspish lawyer, William T. Rossmore (Robert Conness) controls the West Side until his high-minded daughter, Nina (Catherine Dale Owen), who loves both noble principles and a treasury agent, threatens to turn him in. Rossmore agrees to reform and walks away scot-free.

Elmer Rice, who had introduced the flashback device to Broadway in *On Trial*, employed it again in **It Is the Law** (11-29-22, Ritz), which he based on an unpublished novel by Hayden Talbot. The play begins in the card room of the Gotham Club, where members, including a district attorney, are playing bridge. They have no sooner commented that their old friend Justin Victor has received a pardon and is out of prison than Victor (Ralph Kellard) appears. Moments later a goateed Englishman enters only to be shot to death on the spot by Victor. The D.A.

tells the stunned men that there is no chance Victor will have to return to prison, and, with a story that turns the calendar back several years, he tells them why. Albert Woodruff (Arthur Hohl), believing Victor has deceived him, finds "Snifer" Evans, a "snowbird" [cocaine addict] second-story man, who is a double for himself, kills him, then phones Victor to come to his place. Victor arrives moments before the police, who arrest him for Woodruff's murder. He is sent to prison. Later a goateed Woodruff returns, poses as an Englishman, and gloats over what happened. But Woodruff's wife (Alma Tell), who had once almost married Victor, finally sees through his disguise and turns him over to the police. The play scored a modest success, tallying 125 performances.

December's first play, Carlyle Moore's **Listening In** (12-4-22, Bijou), was a failure, but it contained one moment that had critics saluting it rapturously. On a totally darkened stage a bit of glowing "ectoplasm" appears, slowly takes on human form, moves to a chair, and ends by becoming the seated ghost of the late owner of Bleeker Hall. The ghost befriends John Coomber (Ernest Glendinning), who has accepted a wager to prove or disprove the ability of humans to communicate with the dead. The ghost gives excellent tips on the stock market and warns, rightly as it turns out, that someone attempting to leave the house before a specified time will be murdered. In the end, a mesmerist (Giorgio Majeroni) offers a scientific explanation for the goings-on. Unfortunately, beyond the goose-pimply ectoplasm scene, the play wavered unacceptably between thriller and farce.

From ghosts to saints. At least Peter Jubasz (O. P. Heggie), the central figure in **Fashions for Men** (12-5-22, National), translated by Benjamin Glazer from Ferenc Molnár's *Uri divat*, seems too saintly to survive in a dog-eat-dog world. His wife (Beth Merrill) and best salesman (Clarke Silvernail) run off together, taking so much money from the safe in his haberdashery that he is forced into bankruptcy. He takes work with an old friend, a count (Edwin Nicander), where he encounters his former secretary, a greedy girl (Helen Gahagan) hoping to marry the count. His inability to run the count's farm and his attempts to preach generosity to the girl are only half successful. He must leave the count's estate, but the girl helps him restart his old store. Indifferently received, the play could not catch on even when it moved to a smaller theatre and changed its name to *Passions for Men*.

Another put-upon—or in this instance stepped-upon—figure was the principal interest of H. S.

Sheldon's **The Doormat** (12-7-22, Punch and Judy). But Lucy Cavender (Lois Bolton) rebels at the end of Act I, takes work with a popular novelist (Harry Benham), and finally marries him. The comedy left after four showings.

Sophie Treadwell's **Gringo** (12-12-22, Comedy) was written off by several aisle-sitters as a hand-me-down rehash of *The Bad Man*, albeit most admitted that Guthrie McClintic's production and staging were superb. Years before the action begins, a young Mexican sold his wife to an enterprising American miner. The Mexican is now Tito, el Tuerto (José Ruben)—*tuerto* means one-eyed or unfair—a politically powerful bandit; the American, Chivers (Frederick Perry), has become a rich mine owner, so rich, in fact, that Tito decides he sold his wife (Olin Field) too cheaply. He invades the Chivers household to demand more cash, but recognizing that Chivers's new wealth is far greater than he was led to believe, he kidnaps Chivers, his wife, his half-breed daughter (Edna Hibbard), and a couple who live with the Chivers. He holds them for ransom. The ransom is finally paid, but the not unlikable Tito gets more than he bargained for when the half-breed elects to remain with him.

A number of people got far more than they bargained for shortly after the next mounting arrived. The Provincetown Players had temporarily disbanded, leaving their playhouse in the village dark until Alice Kauser booked it for a production of Sholom Ash's **The God of Vengeance** (12-20-22, Provincetown Playhouse), with Rudolph Schildkraut re-creating the role he had enacted in various European capitals for more than a decade. The star played Yekel, the owner of a brothel in the Jewish section of a Polish city. He has brazenly taken it upon himself to purchase a Holy Scroll, even though anyone as defiled as he has no right under Jewish law to possess one. However, Yekel is determined that his daughter, Rifkele (Virginia MacFayden), shall remain pure, and he proposes to give the Scroll to the man who marries her. To his horror he discovers that Rifkele has been seduced into a lesbian relationship by one of his whores (Dorothee Nolan). He, his wife (Esther Stockton), and Rifkele are prepared to lie when Reb Ali (Sam Jaffe), asking all the ritual questions, demands to know if the daughter is pure. But on discovering that the bridegroom is a rabbinical student, Yekel's deepest religious instincts well up and, like the father in *The Hand of the Potter*, he cannot lie. He goes mad. The *Tribune*'s Percy Hammond was one of the favorable reviewers, reporting that "they were still cheering and hat-waving when we left for the subway, all excited ourselves at the things we had witnessed." But he warned that if playgoers were "abashed" at the thought of a brothel, they had best stay away. " 'The God of Vengeance,' " he concluded, "was only for post-graduates. Or, as Kin Hubbard used to say, it is 'artistic, but ornery.' " On the other hand, the *American*'s Alan Dale spoke for a majority when he suggested that "there are some themes that have no place upon the stage." Ignoring the naysayers, the play did so well in the Village that in February it was moved to the Apollo Theatre on 42nd Street, and all hell broke loose. Cries of indecency and blasphemy—supported by a notoriously self-promoting rabbi, Joseph Silverman—saw to it the play was hauled into court. There a multitude of distinguished rabbis spoke in its defense, but an Irish judge ruled against the play, fining Schildkraut and the owner of the English rights each $200. The initial outcries had aided business. At first the move uptown had been disappointing, but attendance improved markedly, if briefly, after the indictment. All in all, the drama compiled 133 performances, not a bad stand for a somber drama.

One interesting point was the judge's statement that the play's translation did not reflect the dignity of the original. Actually the Isaac Goldberg translation that was employed had been published four years earlier, with a preface by Abraham Cahan, the well-known editor of the *Jewish Daily Forward*. Naturally fluent in the original Yiddish, he had commented, "Dr. Isaac Goldberg's translation is not only a thoroughly correct and felicitous equivalent of the original, but a piece of art in itself." And, considering the subsequent to-do, Goldberg's own introduction is noteworthy for underlining his belief that the drama "is not a sex play." Curiously, Woollcott was the only major morning-after reviewer to remark—unfavorably—on the translation. But his displeasure came from a "lumpy, clubfooted translation" and not from a salacious one. However, he did use the occasion to suggest that probably "no play can ever really be lifted from one language to another" and to note further on, "Most translations for the American stage seem to be done by men who can read the French or German or Russian original, but who just do not happen to be able to write English."

André Picard and Francis Carco's Parisian hit *Mon Homme* was a quick New York failure in an uncredited translation as **The Red Poppy** (12-20-22, Greenwich Village). A Russian princess (Estelle Winwood), who years before had been a member of the French underworld, revisits Paris, goes slumming, and in an Apache haunt falls for a handsome Spanish thug (Bela Lugosi). She invites him to come to her place later. He agrees, believing her to be a servant and hoping to rob the place. But when he comes there he is shot and killed, dying in the saddened princess's arms. The two principals, Lugosi newly arrived from the Hungarian National Theatre, received excellent notices, but they could not sustain the play.

Few productions had been so long promised or so eagerly awaited as David Belasco's mounting of *The Merchant of Venice* with David Warfield as Shylock. The play opened at the Lyceum on the 21st. Belasco, conceding nothing to modern ideas of scenic design as exemplified by the highly lauded works of Robert Edmond Jones, Lee Simonson, or Livingston Platt, called on his longtime associate, Ernest Gros, to provide an opulent, archaically detailed collection of settings that required long waits for changes: "The scenes in Venetian residential streets, one of them showing the front of a synagogue, are admirable architecturally as pictorially. The scene at Portia's villa is richly beautiful in the internal decorations and gives outward upon a landscape of vibrant aerial spaces. The scene of the trial is a riot of rich color and sober ornament, truly Venetian. The final outdoor scene at Belmont is an enchantment of moonlight and stars." Several critics evoked memories of Irving and Daly's elaborately Victorian settings. The production was said to have cost $250,000, as much as a *Ziegfeld Follies* and many times more than virtually any other Broadway show of the period. The jewel-encrusted caskets used in one scene supposedly set Belasco back $16,000. Moreover, as was the wont of older producers, Belasco tampered cavalierly with the text, writing in a whole scene, merely described in the original, in which Shylock comes home to find his daughter gone and, after frantically searching the house, runs back out into the street wailing, "My daughter, my ducats!" But the primary attention naturally focused on Warfield. Hornblow typified the majority reaction: "His interpretation is quiet, scholarly, sincere. . . . But he lacks the terror, the fierceness and the tragedy of Shylock." The production played for twelve weeks, then toured, without ever returning Belasco's full investment. For reasons now not completely understood, Warfield and Belasco quarreled during the time and, when the production closed, ended their long-standing relationship. Warfield announced his retirement and, though he lived for more than another quarter of a century, never returned to acting.

Charles Méré's **The Masked Woman** (12-22-22, Eltinge), in Kate Jordan's translation, was a squeak-by hit, thanks in good measure to playgoers who knew what to expect and generally liked whatever Al Woods produced. The vicious, lascivious Baron Tolento (Lowell Sherman), having been spurned by Diane Delatour (Helen MacKeller), plots revenge. Aware he is about to die, he leaves everything to the lady, surmising rightly that her husband (John Halliday) will conclude she has been his mistress. But an old courtesan (Ethel Jackson), having overheard everything, reassures M. Delatour.

Scenery stole the show in the next arrival but couldn't make a hit out of it. **Johannes Kreisler** (12-23-22, Apollo) was Louis N. Parker's adaptation of Carl Meinhard and Rudolph Bernauer's *Die Wunderlichen Geschichten des Kapellmeisters Kreisler*, which in turn had been taken from a story by E. T. A. Hoffmann. It told of a probably mad musician (Jacob Ben Ami) who relives the histories of the loves he has lost. The play contained forty-two scenes, some played on a part of the stage, some on a raised stage, some on the full stage—all flowing quickly into one another thanks to devices recently patented and employed in Germany. At one point a room appeared upstage, and as it moved downstage it grew ever larger. Patented lighting effects also speeded up scene changes.

Effects were not as advanced in Lady Gregory's **The Dragon** (12-25-22, Earl Carroll), but the audience for which it was designed probably could not have cared less. The play was given for a short series of matinees as a children's entertainment. It told how a fierce, damsel-distressing dragon (John Waller) is turned into a lovable, nut-munching pet after a brave prince (Albert Carroll) tears out its heart and substitutes a squirrel's heart.

Eight shows competed for attention on Christmas night. Six of them were straight plays. The best of the American entries almost certainly was Jesse Lynch Williams's **Why Not?** (12-25-22, 48th St.). Just as Williams's *Why Marry?* had examined the difficulties of wedded life, so his new comedy treated the problems of divorce—problems imposed on divorced people by society's absurd and arbitrary rules. Because Leonard Chadwick (Tom Powers) has failed to make money with his poetry, he and his wife, Mary (Margaret Mower), have taken work as butler and maid at the Thompson home. They were hired while the Thompsons were away and are surprised, when the couple returns home, to discover they know them. Indeed, Leonard had loved Evadne Thompson (Jane Grey) but had run away from her because "you were so enormously rich, and I was too romantically poor." And Mary had almost married Bill Thompson (Warburton Gamble), but

for her stand on woman's suffrage and the fact that she insisted on remaining an Episcopalian while he was a dedicated Presbyterian. Both the Chadwicks and the Thompsons allow that their marriages are dutiful but loveless and that they still love their old partners. They confess that they are not truly happy. So, ignoring the Thompsons' lawyer uncle (Cecil Yapp), who tells them that, being married, they have no business being happy, they decide to divorce and switch partners. But after the divorces and second marriages take place, problems arise. For example, Bill is forced to resign from his law firm, even though one of his partners had also thought of suing for divorce. But that partner and his wife have agreed that he can set his love up as a mistress in a swank apartment while the wife, a devout churchwoman, looks the other way. That is socially acceptable. And the judge has ordered that the Thompsons' son and the Chadwicks' daughter must live with their mothers for ten months of the year. The couples have also fallen on hard times financially. Why, Leonard and Evadne have even had to close down a wing of the Chadwick mansion. But that provides the solution. It is decided that one pair will occupy the east wing, the other pair the west wing, thereby saving money and permitting the fathers to see the children all the time. "But nice people won't understand," the uncle protests. "Nice people never do," Leonard retorts; "let 'em rave." Some critics must have been among the nice people, since the comedy received sharply divided notices, forcing this third Equity Players production to depart after a modest 120 performances.

Florence Ziegfeld gave Booth Tarkington's **Rose Briar** (12-25-22, Empire) a typically opulent Ziegfeld production. Luckily for the producer, the play began at a cabaret, the Pompadour, with a small revue in progress. Elaborately dressed showgirls paraded across the stage, backed by a lovely Joseph Urban setting colored primarily in his famous blue. The girls then posed in a Ben Ali Haggan tableau, "the equal of any that the producer has shown us in his revues." Jerome Kern even wrote a special song for the scene. To the cabaret comes the clever, vicious Mrs. Valentine (Julia Hoyt) to enroll a performer who she hopes will serve as a corespondent for her husband (Frank Conroy), so that she may divorce him and remarry. She selects Rose Briar (Billie Burke), a well-bred but poor young lady who has become a nightclub singer to support herself. At first Rose will not even consider the suggestion, but when she learns that the man Mrs. Valentine hopes to marry is the very man (Alan Dinehart) she herself has had an eye on, she consents. At Mrs. Valentine's country home (another sumptuous Urban setting, with blossoming trees seen through the windows), Rose employs all her wiles to win the man. The Valentines will go on with their own marriage, at least for the time being. Despite fine acting and a beautiful-to-look-at mounting, the play was dismissed as dull and was withdrawn after eleven weeks.

Leo Ditrichstein's career was fast drawing to a close. He long since had won a reputation in "Great Lover" roles, and his new vehicle, Ben Hecht's **The Egotist** (12-25-22, 39th St.), gave him another such part—with a twist. For the famous matinee idol Felix Tarbell is a man who dreams of sexual conquests but usually cannot turn his fantasies into reality. His leading lady, Norma Ramon (Mary Duncan), finds that out to her regret when she invites him to her apartment and attempts to seduce him. But his wife (Maude Hanaford), tired of his boasting and believing much of it, runs off with a lover, leaving Tarbell desolate and alone at the final curtain. Playgoers were apparently tiring of Ditrichstein in such roles, and since the play was viewed as no great shakes, it soon departed.

The evening's other openings were importations. The most successful was Rudolf Besier and May Edginton's **Secrets** (12-25-22, Fulton). A wife (Margaret Lawrence), at the bedside of her dying husband (Tom Nesbitt), looks back on the highlights of their half-century romance, from their elopement to America, their pioneering struggles there, their return to England, and the husband's rise to political power. So what if he had become unfaithful; the wife always knew all his secrets and never stopped loving him. The play's five-month run silenced pundits who sneered that Broadway would never accept so gentle, undramatic an evening.

Only the Theatre Guild's regulars kept Paul Claudel's **The Tidings Brought to Mary** (12-25-22, Garrick), in L. M. Sill's translation, before the footlights for a lone month. It told how the strong religious faith of a leper (Jeanne de Casalis) restores the life of her sister's dead baby—a baby fathered by a man the leper once had loved and hoped to wed.

There were also religious aspects to the evening's third importation, Monckton Hoffe's **The Lady Cristilinda** (12-25-22, Broadhurst). A young painter, Martini (Leslie Howard), in love with a circus bareback rider, Cristilinda (Fay Bainter), paints her in the manner of a medieval saint. They sell the painting to a crooked dealer, Iky-Mo (Ferdinand Gottschalk), for twelve pounds. Circumstances separate the youngsters, and years pass. Martini has become a famous painter, and Cristilinda has been crippled in a fall. Word comes that the painting,

represented as a centuries-old masterwork, has been sold for a huge sum to a church. When the hoax is about to be exposed, Cristilinda pleads with officials not to reveal the truth for her sake and for the sake of her old love. She pleads so touchingly that they acquiesce. Once again, despite colorful settings—of a circus, a music hall, and an old church—and highly praised performances, the play found no favor, folding after three weeks.

The year ended on a distinctly down note, with Arthur Hopkins mounting another Shakespearean tragedy in Robert Edmond Jones settings and offering a Barrymore as star. Only this time the star was Ethel Barrymore and the play was *Romeo and Juliet*. One critic, his feelings mirroring those of most of his colleagues, wrote, "The Hopkins *Romeo and Juliet* was all doom. Its settings and lighting were doom. Its acting was doom." Another reviewer said the star appeared to be acting in a trance. A third dismissed the whole affair as "dull beyond belief." McKay Morris was Romeo; Basil Sydney, Mercutio. (In her autobiography the star insisted she had wanted to do *As You Like It,* and indeed that play had been announced earlier in the season as her vehicle. But she claimed that for some reason Hopkins had Jones design *Romeo and Juliet* settings and then insisted that since he had the scenery she would have to do the tragedy.) The play was taken off after twenty-nine performances, immediately before a vigorously applauded competitor could open.

But the play also turned up in the importation that launched the new year, Clemence Dane's **Will Shakespeare** (1-1-23, National). Shakespeare (Otto Kruger), fed up with the lack of understanding shown by Anne Hathaway (Winifred Lenihan), leaves Stratford for London. There his writings call themselves to the attention of Queen Elizabeth (Haidee Wright), who orders her lady-in-waiting, Mary Fitton (Katharine Cornell), to do whatever necessary to inspire the poet. Never mind that Mary prefers Kit Marlowe (Alan Birmingham). But the dutiful, lively Mary does her work so well that she prompts Shakespeare to make her the dark lady of the sonnets and serve as a model for Juliet. In fact, when the boy playing Juliet is hurt, she goes on in his stead. However, Shakespeare soon comes to realize that she really prefers his rival. Although Kruger, Lenihan, and Cornell all were admired, most critics felt that Wright's strong, observant queen stole the show during its ten-week run.

Edward Locke's **Mike Angelo** (1-8-23, Morosco) ran just about half as long. Its hero (Leo Carrillo) was supposed to be a descendant of the great artist and a young man who hopes to win fame as a modern painter. He is a surprisingly generous artist, going so far as to let a Russian (Robert Strange), who he mistakenly believes is loved by the girl (Dorothy Mackaye) he himself adores, claim credit for his painting at a judging. But the Russian proves perfidious, damages the painting, and loses any chance to win the girl, who preferred Mike from the start. More than one critic bewailed that Carrillo was an exceptionally fine actor who had no luck finding suitable roles. His luck would never change.

Huzzas of a kind probably rarely if ever heard before on Broadway rang out when the Moscow Art Theatre came into Jolson's on the 10th with a repertory, all naturally played in Russian, that offered Tolstoy's *Tsar Fyodor Ivanovitch*, Gorky's *The Lower Depths*, Chekhov's *The Cherry Orchard* and *The Three Sisters*, and Turgenyev's *The Lady from the Provinces* coupled with dramatized excerpts from Dostoyevsky's *The Brothers Karamazoff*. True, a few critics, such as the *Times*'s dour John Corbin, carefully reined in their enthusiasm. Yet the often stodgy Hornblow welcomed "the finest acting unit I have ever seen in this country or abroad" and time and again in his notices called the troupe "incredible." At the *Herald*, Woollcott, reviewing the Gorky play, insisted, "Never before had we seen scenes on the stage so actual, so alive. 'The Lower Depths' as it was acted last evening . . . was the finest performance of a play within this reviewer's experience as a playgoer." In short order, Konstantin Stanislavsky and his notions of theatrical realism, ensemble acting, and psychological probing became Broadway buzzwords. A few of the players—such as Maria Ouspenskaya and Akim Tamiroff—later made careers for themselves in America.

The new year's first successful novelty was Guy Bolton's **Polly Preferred** (1-11-23, Little). Polly Brown (Genevieve Tobin) sits morosely at a table at the automat. She has just lost her job as a chorus girl to a young lady more willing to respond to the producer's advances. Along comes Bob Cooley (William Harrigan), himself an out-of-work salesman. The two get to chatting over cups of coffee, and before long the enterprising Bob has an idea. He borrows some elegant, eye-catching clothes and parades Polly around the Biltmore in them. This leads to a Hollywood contract for Polly, but also to problems, especially since she has fallen in love with Bob but her contract prohibits her from marrying. Of course, by the end of the last act all difficulties have been swept away. The critical consensus was that the final two acts, while good, could not approach the brilliant first act (set at the automat

and in the Biltmore). Playgoers were not so picky, keeping the show on the boards into the summer.

As she had been several years earlier, vaudevillian Maude Fulton was both the author and star of her latest vehicle, **The Humming Bird** (1-15-23, Ritz). She played a Parisian Apache dancer who has fled to America to escape her abusive partner. She is terrified when he (Walter Wills) suddenly appears in New York, but it develops he has only come over to bring her back to France so that she may be decorated for her valor during the war. A once celebrated oldtimer, Frederic de Belleville, played the general who pins on the medal. But soon he was unemployed again and Miss Fulton back in two-a-day.

Bertha Kalish had no better luck when she appeared in Siegfried Trebitsch's **Jitta's Atonement** (1-17-23, Comedy). She played a writer's wife who has an affair with his collaborator, is then spurned by her husband, and is reunited with him only through the efforts of the now dead collaborator's compassionate daughter.

But audiences did delight in Aaron Hoffman's **Give and Take** (1-18-23, 49th St.), even if many critics gave it thumbs-down notices. Just as he encounters financial problems at his California cannery, John Bauer (Louis Mann) is persuaded by his college-miseducated son (Robert W. Craig) and his old foreman (George Sidney) to turn the company over to its employees. Perhaps not completely, but at least in the form of an "industrial democracy," with the elder Bauer still as president, but with the workers as a sort of Congress. The employees' interference makes matters worse. The old man can only shrug, "This isn't the first time Congress put the president on the bum." A millionaire (Douglas Wood) enters the scene with a scheme to refinance the company. The scheme succeeds even though the millionaire is exposed as an escaped inmate of an insane asylum. Once again Bauer can only shrug, "The only man who believes in industrial democracy and he has to turn out to be cuckoo." But Bauer really is not brokenhearted. The tired businessmen who constituted a large quota of Mann's loyalists kept the play running until the season's end.

Yet even the multitudes who flocked to see Nazimova on the silent screen would not support her for long when she starred in **Dagmar** (1-22-23, Selwyn), which Louis K. Anspacher took from Ferenc Herczeg's *Tilla*. Critics were dismayed that an actress who had made her name in high-minded drama could sink into this sort of play. Dagmar is a sex-obsessed but faithless woman who carelessly tells one lover (Charles Bryant) to kill her if she is ever disloyal to him. When he finds her vamping a former love (Gilbert Emery), he does just that, slitting her throat. Before the bloody denouement the star paraded in a show of diaphanous negligees, slinky gowns, and glamorous furs. Plush settings included Dagmar's bedroom, a terrace overlooking a tennis court, and an ornate corner in an opera house.

In Jack Alicoate's **Extra** (1-23-23, Longacre) John King (Howard Truesdell), a tricky politician and newspaper publisher, decides to buy the outstanding shares of his paper; to drive down those share prices, he turns the paper over to his playboy son, Wallace (Chester Morris), assuming the youngster's indifference and incompetence will wreck circulation. At first it almost does, but after Wallace learns of the plot, he turns the paper into a smashingly successful crusading journal. He even uses his influence with a reform mayor he has helped elect to keep his father out of prison.

The next evening brought in the season's second *Romeo and Juliet*, at Henry Miller's Theatre. This time Juliet was dark-haired, dark- and limpid-eyed Jane Cowl. Although she was only five years younger than Barrymore—she had just turned thirty-eight—she seemed infinitely more youthful and vital than her matronly rival. A few reviewers were unhappy, a few unthinkingly rapturous. But Stark Young, writing in the *New Republic*, spoke for a thoughtful, perceptive majority. Noting that the performance "could not be called great, if one itches for that threadbare word," he continued on that it was nonetheless "a performance full of fresh and persuasive life." Of the star he observed, "Miss Cowl's Juliet is beautiful, first of all, to see. She is a child, a tragic girl, a woman convincing to the eye as few Juliets ever have had the good fortune to be. She has quiet too and naturalness and a right simplicity of method." Rollo Peters's Romeo and Dennis King's Mercutio also came in for praise. So did the "vivid and beautiful" scenery (by Peters), far simpler and less cluttering than Jones's had been. Playgoers responded by packing the small playhouse for twenty weeks.

But a large number of laudatory notices could not make a success of January's last entry, Lewis Beach's **A Square Peg** (1-27-23, Punch and Judy). It presented a harsh picture which audiences seeking escapism had no wish to confront. Rena Huckins (Beverly Sitgreaves) is a mother and wife, but not a very good one. She is more than domineering, she wants to control every facet of her family's life without providing a measure of love in return. At heart, she is a businesswoman unable, because of the mores of her time, to run a huge corporation.

Her son (Walter Abel) takes to drink, her daughter (Leona Hogarth) elopes in an especially noisy and scandalous way, and her husband (William B. Mack), caught embezzling funds with which he hoped to buy a farm in Canada, far away from Rena, kills himself.

February brought in a goodly share of rewards, beginning with a fine new play and a notable revival. The novelty was Rachel Crothers's **Mary the Third** (2-5-23, 39th St.). In 1870 the first Mary (Louise Huff) uses all her coquetry to ensnare William (Ben Lyon). Twenty-seven years later her daughter, the second Mary (also Huff), induces Robert (again Lyon) to propose. Now, in 1923, the latest Mary (Huff) is debating whether to marry Lynn (Lyon) or Hal (William Hanley). She announces that, with another girl, she is going to spend some time with the men in the wilds. Her argument is that most marriages do not really work because the lovers know so little about each other and that they should have experimented before marrying. Her stuffy grandmother (now played by May Galyer) is outraged, while her mother (Beatrice Terry) warns the youngster that marital problems will still occur. Paying no heed, Mary and her friends drive off. (The first scene of the second act begins with the youngsters enjoying their ride in the automobile.) But Mary soon is back home, having had second thoughts. However, she returns in time to overhear a heated argument between her parents in which her mother admits her marriage has been a failure. Once again she changes her mind, telling Lynn, "I'll live with you till we're *sure* what we really mean to each other, and when we *know* we'll either be married or quit." Then the second Mary decides to leave her husband, who insists he will do everything he can to win her back. The youngest Mary realizes that nobody can ever know how love or marriage will turn out. In a lame, possibly ironic fashion, she asks Lynn about their love: "It *is* one of those great eternal passions that will last through the ages—isn't it, dear?" Several critics hailed the play as Crothers's best, ignoring that the men in the play were uninteresting, cardboard figures and that only the women, as was Crothers's wont, were superbly drawn. The play ran into the summer.

Although Ibsen had long since been accepted as a great playwright, not all his works were considered theatrically effective. The result was that when the Theatre Guild mounted William and Charles Archer's translation of *Peer Gynt* at the Garrick on the same night, many critics still expressed doubts about its stageworthiness. Most, however, applauded the beautifully set and finely acted evening. While a few balked, a majority saw Joseph Schildkraut, with his good looks, his charm, his verve, and his passionate, sometimes reckless intensity, as an almost ideal Peer. An excellent supporting cast included Louise Closser Hale as Ase, Dudley Digges as the Troll King, Helen Westley as the Troll King's Daughter, and Edward G. Robinson in several parts, among them the Button-Moulder. The celebrated Russian director Theodore Komisarjevsky staged the production. Edvard Grieg's well-known musical accompaniment was utilized. Despite reservations, the ayes had it, so the revival scored an impressive 120 performances.

A third successive hit was Owen Davis's **Icebound** (2-10-23, Sam H. Harris). The loveless, self-serving Jordans are sitting in their mother's austere parlor in northern Maine, waiting for her to die and worrying how she will divide her limited moneys. They all assume she will leave nothing to her favorite son, Ben, who has been running from the law. As Henry (John Westley), Ben's older brother, says, "Don't talk Ben to me after the way he broke his mother's heart and hurt my credit." To their consternation, Ben (Robert Ames) shows up. But before he can go upstairs to see his mother, the old lady dies. Judge Bradford (Willard Robertson) tells the horrified family that Mrs. Jordan left everything to Jane (Phyllis Povah), a distant cousin who has been looking after her. It was Jane who sent for Ben, and when the sheriff comes to arrest him, she pays his bail on the understanding that he will stay and help restore the Jordan farm. He reluctantly accepts the deal. But their relationship is often stormy, especially after Ben learns that the villagers are calling him Jane's "white slave." He refuses to see Jane's goodness and describes the Jordans as "icebound, that's what we are—all of us—inside and out." But Ben eventually learns that Jane has arranged to have the charges against him dropped, and when he reads a letter his mother left for Jane, in which she stated he can only be redeemed "through a woman who will hold out her heart to him and let him trample on it as he has on mine," he recognizes Jane's goodness and that they both love each other. Reviewers hailed the play and said it forever laid to rest the complaint that Davis had not overridden his apprenticeship in a tawdrier school. Coming after *Rain* and *Secrets*, it gave Sam Harris his third hit of the season. In the spring it was awarded the Pulitzer Prize. The award stirred a bit of controversy, with even some critics who liked the play insisting there were better choices. Woollcott, for example, opted for *The Texas Nightingale*, Mantle for *You and I* (a later February opening).

Arthur Hopkins's production of Alfred Sutro's **The Laughing Lady** (2-12-23, Longacre) enjoyed good business during its limited stand—limited because Ethel Barrymore was unhappy in her part and refused to play when hot weather threatened. She portrayed a Mayfair lady who is courted by the attorney (Cyril Keightley) who had represented her husband (McKay Morris) in their divorce trial. She sends him back to his own wife and reluctantly decides to give her ex a second chance.

Feast gave way to meager pickings. In Charles Rann Kennedy's **The Chastening** (2-12-23, 48th St.), the author and his wife, Edith Wynne Matthison, played a carpenter named Joseph and the carpenter's wife, Mary, who return to a stable where the woman's son had been born twelve years before. They rest there for the night before the boy (Margaret Gage, in a trouser role) is to go to meet wise men at the temple. Both have plans for the boy, but he convinces them to allow him to go his own way. The talky, boring play was mounted by the Equity Players but was quickly withdrawn.

Four plays opened the next Monday evening. The lone success was Philip Barry's **You and I** (2-19-23, Belmont). It arrived at its tiny house having already received the accolade of being one of the prize plays written by students of George Pierce Baker. Veronica "Ronny" Duane (Frieda Inescort) persuades Roderick "Ricky" White (Geofrey Kerr) to abandon his plan to study architecture in Paris and marry her now, even though both are aware that Ricky's father sacrificed his dream of being an artist to marry Ricky's mother. His mother (Lucile Watson) warns him, "When you're forty or so, you may look on love as a kind of captivating robber—who chatted so sweetly, as he plucked your destiny out of your pocket." And his father, Maitland (H. B. Warner), better known as "Matey," tells him a true artist must think of "I—I—I—I and my work" while a married man can only deal with "you and I." Ricky's insistence brings out long-repressed urgings in Matey, who takes a sabbatical from his work to spend a year painting. To his dismay, his best painting, a portrait, is purchased by his boss, who hopes to use the face in advertisements. Ronny, understanding what Ricky's sacrifice will mean, agrees to delay the marriage so that Ricky can go to Paris, and Matey, unwilling to join "the ranks of the agreeably mediocre," returns to his job. The play garnered almost universal raves and, for the second time in the season, launched the career of a major writer of comedy.

. . .

Philip [Jerome Quinn] **Barry** (1896–1949) was born in Rochester, N.Y. His father, who died while the youngster was an infant, was an Irish immigrant who became a successful businessman; his mother came from an older Philadelphia Irish-Catholic family. Despite defective eyesight, he entered Yale, but left to serve with the State Department in London during the war. Returning to Yale, he wrote his first play, then enrolled in Baker's famous 47 Workshop at Harvard.

. . .

The evening's other openings were failures. Thompson Buchanan's **The Sporting Thing to Do** (2-19-23, Ritz) was "a poor play, poorly acted." It centered on Jean Thornton (Emily Stevens), who divorces her philandering husband, knowing full well that some day he will come back to her.

William Hurlbut's **Hail and Fairwell** (2-19-23, Morosco) was set in France in the 1870s, where a notorious Spanish courtesan, Isabella Echevaria (Florence Reed), sets out to capture an American millionaire (Harold Salter). But her quest is derailed when she meets Philippe, Comte de Villenueve (Paul Gordon). For the first time in her life she is overwhelmed. The affair progresses passionately until Isabella learns that she stands in the way of Philippe's advancement. She drinks poison and dies in her lover's arms, assuring him, "This love was real."

The season's second faithless prima donna was the focus in **Rita Coventry** (2-19-23, Bijou), which Hubert Osborne took from Julian Street's novel. Rita (Dorothy Francis) marries a rich Virginian (Charles Francis) but, while on a visit to the Ritz in Atlantic City, falls in love with a cute piano tuner (Dwight Frye) and runs off to Europe with him. Even the settings were lambasted, with a midnight sky depicted in a bright Maxfield Parrish blue evoking giggles.

Several superior comedians could do nothing with Edgar Selwyn's **Anything Might Happen** (2-20-23, Comedy). Richard Keating (Roland Young) and Hal Turner (Leslie Howard) have both been jilted by their sweethearts. On the rebound—and in a rainstorm—Richard bumps into and falls in love with Helen Springer (Estelle Winwood), Turner's ex. They go to Richard's apartment and get tipsy on a bottle of champagne. Then Hal appears with a new flame (Ruth Findlay), Richard's ex. By evening's end matters and lovers are repaired.

William Ricciardi's **Mister Malatesta** (2-26-23, Princess) had a somewhat forced run of twelve weeks at its small berth. Its author served as its leading figure, a father who forces his son (Burdette Kappes) to marry his foster daughter (Rhy Derby) after learning the boy had violated her. It turns out

that is what the boy wanted to do anyway, even though the girl has already killed the baby born of the affair. Humor ran on the order of one man saying he wanted to press his suit for a lady's hand, and Malatesta retorting the suit he was in was nicely pressed. The play was subsequently retitled *Papa Joe*.

Laurette Taylor met with disaster when she starred in **Humoresque** (2-27-23), Fanny Hurst's dramatization of her own novel. In a marked departure from earlier roles she played a young, heavily accented Jewish immigrant who, by the last act, has lost her youth but not her accent. She is Sarah Kantor, the long-struggling mother of a large family and a woman obsessed with the notion that her little boy, Leon, will grow up to be a great violinist. He does, but his insistence that he must go off to fight in the war breaks her heart. Leon was played by Alfred Little in the first act and later by Luther Adler, billed at the time as Lutha J. Adler. Most critics slated the play but had high praise for the star. Broun wrote in the *World* that "the fidelity of the portrait was much deeper than eyes or ears could convey to the spectator." Her old admirer Woollcott noted in the *Herald* that her performance was "astounding in its rich resourcefulness and now again austere in its tragic beauty." However, he went on to lament that she continued to act in plays by mediocre dramatists, when her talents demanded she try greater works, especially the classics. Playgoers refused to buy tickets, and the show was taken off after a month. Calling the role the most difficult she had ever attempted, she blamed her heretofore loyal Irish and Jewish supporters for the play's failure, saying neither group wanted to see her as a Jew.

March offered few successes, but several failures were interesting and memorable. Nonetheless some commentators abruptly bewailed that the season had suddenly fallen apart. The month's opener was **Roger Bloomer** (3-1-23, 48th St.). An Equity Players production, it was the work of John Howard Lawson, who eventually would win notoriety for his extreme left-wing leanings. It was written in the modern expressionistic style and played out in appropriately expressionistic settings by Woodman Thompson, with sharply colored facades, rooms, and even an elevated station tilting at various aggressive angles. Roger (Henry Hull) is a rebellious young man who comes to New York, a place described in the play's most quoted phrase as "the city of women, death and garbage." He meets up with the equally dissatisfied Louise (Mary Fowler). Their unavailing search for truth and happiness leads them to take poison. Louise dies. Roger survives and is carted off to jail, where nightmares confirm the absurd and cruel ways of the world. His father (Walter Walker) comes to take him home.

Another ugly aspect of life was represented in a more traditional play, **Morphia** (3-2-23, Eltinge), which Duncan McNab took from the German of Ludwig Herzer. Julian Wade (Lowell Sherman) had become a drug addict after accidentally killing a girl he loved. But a woman (Olive Tell) who long has loved him in silence takes a position as his nurse, restores his health, and gains a proposal of marriage.

A vanity mounting of *King Lear* at the Earl Carroll on the 9th, produced by, directed by, and starring Reginald Pole, who had played the Ghost to Barrymore's Hamlet, was hooted off the stage after just two showings, although it had Genevieve Tobin as its Cordelia. Edgar was played by a young Lawrence Tibbett.

Philip Bartholomae and John Meehan's **Barnum Was Right** (3-12-23, Frazee) was a near miss, chalking up an eleven-week run. Several aisle-sitters, perhaps influenced by the star and some of his supporting cast, saw it as a musical comedy without music. The star was song-and-dance favorite Donald Brian (America's original Danilo), and his associates included Ziegfeld beauty Lilyan Tashman. Brian was seen as Fred Farrell, who loves Miriam Locke (Marion Coakley) but cannot gain her father's consent to marrying her until he proves his worth as a businessman. So Farrell takes a deserted Long Island estate, turns it into a swank inn, and, to lure trade, spreads rumors (by loudly denying them) that the grounds contain buried treasure. Guests are provided with whatever tools they might want for digging. In true song-and-dance fashion, everything ends happily.

Two Sacha Guitry plays followed back to back. The first was unusual in several ways, for **Pasteur** (3-12-23, Empire), in a translation by Arthur Hornblow, Jr., was a literate, episodic piece with a large, all-male cast, yet often seemed little more than a monologue for its central figure. It recounted the highlights of the great scientist's life. The star was Henry Miller. Writing in the *Times*, John Corbin informed his readers that Miller "cast upon his audience a spell of warm humanity." Theatregoers were not intrigued, so the play closed after just two weeks.

Belasco's adaptation of **The Comedian** (3-13-23, Lyceum) survived nine weeks longer. The Comedian (Lionel Atwill) is a consummately vain actor, who refuses to acknowledge the passing years. Imagine his chagrin when he is asked to disillusion a lovesick girl (Elsie Mackay) by allowing her to see him at close range, without his toupee or makeup. He grudgingly consents, then discovers to his delight that the very beautiful youngster is still completely enamored of him. He, too, falls in love, and the pair marry. One night, when his leading lady is ill, he presses his wife to go on in her stead. She does and acts atrociously. But now she is stagestruck, insisting she must have more roles. Feeling she could destroy his career, he abandons her. Critics praised Belasco for his superb staging and for eschewing the overelaborate settings that he customarily employed. But they were annoyed by his translation, in which, unlike the original, the actor and the girl wed. They suggested it was more immoral to desert a wife than a mistress.

Decades later the problem of stalkers would become a menacing one, but in **The Love Habit** (3-14-23, Bijou), which Gladys Unger took from Louis Verneuil's *Pour avoir Adrienne*, it was treated humorously. Nadine (Florence Eldridge) is disturbed by the unwanted attentions of a handsome young man (James Rennie), so she orders her husband (Ernest Cossart) to chase him away. Unfortunately for the husband, the young man knows he is seeing a cabaret dancer on the sly and threatens to tell his wife. The husband is helpless to do anything. In time, the wife discovers his secret, and that allows her to send the young man packing—but not before she obtains his address. Generally delighted notices somehow could not prevail on playgoers to attend, and the show closed after two months.

Although the next play to open, Elmer Rice's **The Adding Machine** (3-19-23, Garrick), ran no longer, it has become a classic of American dramaturgy. Its small initial reception was no fault of the critics. Corbin, speaking for a majority of his colleagues, called it "the best and fairest example of the newer expressionistic theatre . . . yet experienced." The cast, too, was showered with praise. On his twenty-fifth anniversary with The Firm, Mr. Zero (Dudley Digges) is told by The Boss (Irving Dillon) that he is to be replaced by a modern adding machine. In his fury, Mr. Zero kills his employer, a fact which his nagging, indifferent wife (Helen Westley) learns only when the police interrupt dinner to arrest Mr. Zero. He is tried and executed. In life, Mr. Zero had been a bigot and a hypocritical moralist, denouncing, at his wife's instigation, a girl for indecent exposure. Now the girl (Elise Bartlett) dances on his grave, but a corpse (Edward G. Robinson) arises to console Mr. Zero by telling him that he, too, had been a murderer. Then Daisy Diana Dorothea Devore (Margaret Wycherly), who had befriended

Mr. Zero at the office, appears. In despair over his death, she has committed suicide. But the puritanical Mr. Zero pushes her away, leaving her to lament, "Without him I might as well be alive." In the hereafter Mr. Zero finds brief satisfaction operating a gigantic adding machine, until he is ordered back to earth. He refuses to go but is told he will do so until he is a totally crushed soul doomed to "sit in the gallery of a coal mine and operate the super-hyper-adding machine with the great toe of his right foot." Along with the play and the cast, Lee Simonson was lauded for his imaginative settings. Besides the stage-engulfing adding machine, these included a modernistic courtroom whose pillars and railings were distorted, and numbers and blood-red banners flying across the stage to suggest Mr. Zero's fury.

Thomas Loudon's **The Love Set** (3-19-23, Punch and Judy) was a one-week flop. To prevent his daughter, Gertrude (Catherine Dale Owen), from marrying a bounder (Kenneth Daigneau), John Lamont (George Alison) attempts to bribe a likable tennis star (Gavin Muir) to woo her. The athlete refuses the bribe but falls in love with Gertrude anyway, and she with him, once she realizes what a fortune hunter his rival is.

Pauline Frederick, so long popular in films, had met with great success on the road all season with Michael Morton and Peter Traill's **The Guilty One** (3-20-23, Selwyn), but Broadway would not buy it. She played a woman who assumes blame for the murder of her lover (Noel Leslie) after she learns that her husband (Charles Waldron) has killed him. She gives Scotland Yard a detailed confession, only to be informed that no killing took place. It was merely a ruse to get her to understand how much she loved her husband.

Mercedes de Acosta's **Sandro Botticelli** (3-26-23, Provincetown Playhouse) was a dismal failure, as even its star, Eva Le Gallienne, admitted in her autobiography. She played Simonetta Vespucci, a young Italian beauty who flourished at the time Botticelli (Basil Sydney) was painting. Smitten by him, she offers to come to his studio and pose in the nude. But when she realizes that he cares more for his art than for her, she rushes off, gets caught in the rain, sickens, and dies. Botticelli must finish his *Birth of Venus* from memory.

Thomas F. Fallon, who scored such an unexpected smash with *The Last Warning*, just missed having a second hit with **The Wasp** (3-27-23. Morosco). He did so in the face of damning notices. The play told how a woman (Emily Ann Wellman), about to be tried a third time for a murder after two hung juries,

discovers evidence that will clear her, thanks to a lightning strike which exposes material hidden in an old chimney. The best thing about the play seems to have been the deafening thunder that accompanied the storm, even if the rain poured down outside one window, but not another. Otto Kruger was cast as two brothers—one of whom was evil while the second was good.

Another March entry that failed to find support but thereafter enjoyed a long career in stock was Arthur Wing Pinero's **The Enchanted Cottage** (3-31-23, Ritz). To escape a nagging family, a crippled war veteran (Noel Tearle) marries a homely girl (Katharine Cornell). They honeymoon in an enchanted cottage which lets them see each other as beautiful. Even when reality is forced upon them, they understand that genuine beauty is in a loving beholder's eye. Reviewers thought it was the sort of tale James M. Barrie might have recounted more deftly.

Cries of a theatrical downturn grew a bit more shrill in April. The month's first offering was **If Winter Comes** (4-2-23, Gaiety), taken from A. S. M. Hutchinson's best-selling novel by the novelist himself and B. Macdonald Hastings. It featured Cyril Maude as a not all that young war veteran who loses his unsympathetic wife and nearly loses his reputation after the suicide of a young unwed mother he selflessly befriended. Despite the novel's wide popularity, the stage version engendered little interest. Fortunately for Maude, he had a much better piece waiting in the wings.

A surprise if modest success was **Uptown West** (4-3-23, Earl Carroll), the work of Lincoln Osborn, an actor who for years had been seen in minor roles, mostly with touring companies. Carroll mounted it for a few trial matinees at his own theatre, but after it was hailed as "a play with a punch" and "an excellent play," he moved it late in the month to the smaller Bijou for a regular run. Sakamoto (Henry Herbert), although Japanese-born, is now an American citizen and a successful businessman. He has married Mildred (Florence Mason), and they have had a baby, whom he adoringly calls Kuma San. But Mildred is not happy. Except for a kindly Jewish neighbor, she is ostracized by her fellow whites. She is also beset by having to look after her drug-addicted sister, Florence (Grace Heyer). When the baby dies after an accident Sakamoto puts up a brave front, telling a friend, "I am still of a family of soldiers! But my heart is weeping!" The baby's death, coupled with the return of Mildred's old sweetheart (Carlton Birckert), dooms the marriage. His realization of this is too much for Sakamoto.

Going into his darkened bedroom he strangles the woman on the bed, then returns to the living room, removes his sword from the wall, and crying, "We will *both* be with you, Kuma San!" commits suicide. He dies not knowing the woman in the bed was actually his bedrugged sister-in-law.

Like the younger Laurette Taylor, the much admired Mrs. Fiske met with a resounding rejection when she returned to town, this time in Lillian Barrett's **The Dice of the Gods** (4-5-23, National). The consensus, as it had been with Taylor, was that, while she gave a marvelous performance, she had selected an uncongenial role in yet another undeserving play. But whereas Taylor had portrayed a Jewish immigrant, Mrs. Fiske took the role of a Virginia aristocrat, albeit a drug-addicted one—"a part that exhibits her impish malice, subversive wit and iridescent charm more delightfully than ever before." Her Patricia "Paddy" Baird has lived loosely but has come to want the best for her daughter (Ernita Lascalles) by one of her numerous liaisons. When she cannot convince the girl to marry a rich, older man, and when her daughter discovers her sordid history, she purposely takes an overdose of morphine.

Another star, Alice Brady, chose her vehicle more wisely and enjoyed a hit with Salisbury Field's **Zander the Great** (4-9-23, Empire). After his mother dies, five-year-old Alexander (Edwin Mills) finds himself left in the care of his family's devoted housemaid, Mamie (Brady). They decide to seek his long-lost father who is reported to be somewhere in Arizona, so they pile the family car with all their belongings, including Zander's pet rabbits, and head west. (Although the prologue was set in Weeweedin, N.J., the automobile conspicuously sported a Pennsylvania license plate.) Once in Arizona they seek shelter at a ranch occupied by three men: the forlornly pessimistic Good News (Joseph Allen), the sentimental, tobacco-chewing Texas (George Abbott), and the stalwart Dan Murchison (Jerome Patrick). But when it dawns on Mamie that the men are bootleggers, she draws a pistol to allow her and Zander to escape. The men stop her, but in time (in time, as well, for a third-act curtain) they agree to reform and she agrees to marry Dan. Thanks in good measure to the star's "vivacious, tender, defiant, saucy" performance, the comedy spanned the summer.

By contrast, Sidney Toler's **The Exile** (4-9-23, George M. Cohan) barely spanned the month. Jacques Cortot (José Ruben) returns from exile in England to take part in the Revolution. He falls in love with an aristocratic actress, Bernice Millet (Eleanor Painter), from the Comédie Française.

When the mobs begin to lust for blood he tears off her elegant gown and forces her to dress like a peasant, with a red bandana on her head. As the rioters break into the room she is singing the "Marseillaise," accompanied by none other than its author, Roget de L'Isle (Sidney Riggs). What better passport to safety could there be? Because of her celebrity as a singer (she was not much of an actress) Painter was given several additional songs to warble, but neither her vocalizing nor Ruben's fine, swashbuckling performance could save the show.

One of the season's great successes downtown at the Yiddish Art Theatre had been Leonid Andreyev's **Anathema** with Maurice Schwartz (at the time transliterating his name as Swartz) in the title role of the devil, angry for being refused readmittance to heaven. He plots revenge in a shtetl through the medium of a pious, innocent Jew, by making the man wealthy then stripping him of his wealth. When he once again applies for entry he is again refused, at the same time that he is informed his faithful victim has been given a seat at God's right hand. (In the Yiddish production the Jew had been played by Muni Weisenfreund, whom Broadway audiences one day would know as Paul Muni.) For Broadway, where the show opened at the 48th Street Theatre on the 10th in Herman Bernstein's translation, Schwartz assumed the role of the Jew and Ernest Glendinning was cast as Anathema. But Broadway was not in a religious mood.

Nor did it seem to want the sort of fictional reminiscences offered in Glen MacDonough's **Within Four Walls** (4-17-23, Selwyn). The decaying, rat-infested Minuit mansion down in the Village is about to be razed. The last of the Minuits, Gerrit (Leonard Doyle), comes for a final look at the old place. There he meets Agnes Meade (Anne Morrison), a newspaperwoman assigned to write an article on the house. The pair uncover a manuscript retailing the building's history, and in flashbacks the loves, murderous hatreds, ambitions and failures of the Minuit family are relived again. By the time Gerrit and Agnes are sitting outside on the steps, they muse over whether the two of them might contrive to keep the Minuit clan ongoing.

Two revivals followed, both opening on the 23rd. At the 44th Street Theatre Augustus Thomas, hoping to start a national repertory company, and the Producing Managers' Association, possibly hoping to show up the Equity Players, combined to offer *As You Like It*. The cast included Marjorie Rambeau as Rosalind, Margalo Gillmore as Celia, Ian Keith as Orlando, A. E. Anson as Jacques, and Ernest Lawford as Touchstone, with the veteran

John Craig and the young Walter Abel in lesser roles. For the most part the players were awarded encouraging but hardly excited notices. The most enthusiastic comments were saved for Lee Simonson's settings—"gorgeous settings with richness and warmth of color, great open spaces and wonderful blue skies"—among them the terrace of Duke Frederick's palace "with its hangings of autumnal tints and its gorgeous marquee beyond" seen against one of those spacious blue backgrounds. Sadly, the public proved so indifferent that the production closed at the end of its first week.

Because of its many loyalists, the Theatre Guild did much better with George Bernard Shaw's *The Devil's Disciple* at the Garrick. The cast included Basil Sydney in the central role of Dick Dudgeon and Roland Young in the scene-stealing assignment as General Burgoyne.

Leighton Osmun's **Sylvia** (4-25-23, Provincetown Playhouse), a play possibly inspired by the recollection that "all our swains commend her," was thumbed off as too silly for words. Sylvia (Catherine Cozzens) could lose the inheritance her grandfather has promised her if he discovers she has married a man he despises. Then Sylvia is advised that her husband has died while on a trip overseas, so she weds her grandfather's choice. When her first husband turns up very much alive, she ditches both men and runs off with a rich old bachelor.

With the failure of the English version of *Anathema*, many of the same players switched to Nikolai Gogol's **The Inspector General** (4-30-23, 48th St.), with Schwartz as the clerk who lives it up when he is mistaken for a government inspector. The translation was by Thomas Seltzer and Samuel S. Grossman. Once more, the public stayed away, so the play closed after a single week.

Broadway's doldrums continued well into May before the season concluded in a brief display of theatrical pyrotechnics. Paul Gavault's *Ma Tante d'Honfleur* became **My Aunt from Ypsilanti** (5-1-23, Earl Carroll) in Henry Baron's adaptation. Few remembered or cared that another adaptation had failed in 1915 as *She's In Again*. This adaptation also failed, although its emphasis on two gay blades and their lady friends followed the original more closely. And this time the men run from Greenwich Village to one man's home in Virginia.

After years away from Broadway, Thompson Buchanan had had one play mounted in February. Now he had a second one, **Pride** (5-2-23, Morosco), but this was an even quicker dud, closing after less than two weeks. It featured Hilda Spong as an American heiress who became a French duchesse,

eventually returning home with her young daughter on tiring of her husband's blatant philanderings. When the play begins, many years have elapsed. The Duc (Fred L. Tiden) has been impoverished and has come to America to take work as a waiter in a chain of hotels run by his former valet (Robert Fisher). He meets his now grown daughter (Juliette Day) and, without disclosing his true identity, takes her under his wing. This leads to a meeting with his long-separated wife and to their reconciliation.

The first Monday in May brought in five openings. The four that arrived hoping for long runs were failures. W. J. Locke and Ernest Denny's **The Mountebank** (5-7-23, Lyceum) was a theatricalization of Locke's novel. Petit Patou is a beloved circus clown in France, where he cavorts in the ring with a comic, beribboned French poodle. He is also Andrew Lackaday (Norman Trevor), a self-exiled Englishman. After the dog is killed in an accident he teams up successfully with a sweet young girl, Elodie (Gabrielle Ravine). When the war breaks out, Lackaday returns home, rises to the position of brigadier general, and falls in love with the aristocratic Lady Auriol Dayne (Lillian Kemble Cooper). The war over, he would return to Elodie, but learning that she has eloped with another circus performer, he proposes to Auriol.

In Ethel Clifton's **For Value Received** (5-7-23, Longacre) an aging, blind, and egomaniacal author, Almeric Thomson (Augustin Duncan), has lived for some years with the pretty and much younger Beverly Mason (Maude Hanaford). She has willingly sacrificed her best years so that she can support her giddy sister. She finally decides to leave Thomson, only to be accused of misappropriating his funds. She retorts by showing that she actually wrote many of his best works. She then hopes to find happiness with a man (Louis Kimball) her own age, but after learning how fickle he is, she is reconciled with Thomson.

The most sourly received of the evening's entries was Josephine Turck Baker's **The Apache** (5-7-23, Punch and Judy). Monsieur Le Von (Juan de la Cruz) is married to the celebrated pianist Madame Viennese (Thais Magrane), but he is suspicious and jealous, so he decides to become an Apache and plots to kill his wife and strangle her lover. The whole affair turns out to be an unpleasant dream. Eerie green lighting effects and lots of exits and entrances through windows accentuated the play's absurdity.

A group of black players, calling themselves the Ethiopian Art Theatre, offered a double bill consisting of Oscar Wilde's *Salome* and Willis Richardson's one-act comedy **The Chip Woman's Fortune** (5-7-23, Frazee). In the novelty, Aunt Nancy digs up her cache of money so that Jim can pay to celebrate his release from jail. She discovers she has hidden so many old bills and coins that there is some left over to help her neighbors buy items they long have hoped to own. One neighbor has wanted a victrola, so the curtain falls on everyone dancing to a jazz record. There was more jazz the following week, when the company replaced Wilde's drama with *The Comedy of Errors*. In some respects the production was trailblazing, set as it was not against a traditional Elizabethan background but in a modern-day circus, with characters shimmying and fox-troting. The Duke of Ephesus was performed by a falsetto-voiced midget. In his *Times* review, sour John Corbin referred to the player as a "pigmy" and added insult to injury by continuing that Shakespeare did not need "complexions of the various shades of café au lait and dissonances suggestive of the African jungle." Evenings of black music and dancing had become voguish on Broadway, but not blacks in serious drama or even in comedies. Moreover, the consensus was these black actors were not first-rank.

To help the Equity Players, by now wallowing in red ink, the Players (the theatrical club) remounted at the 48th Street Theatre their highly praised *The Rivals* from last season. But both the Equity Players and the Players had more interesting productions in the offing.

Besides all these professional attractions the evening witnessed the first Little Theatre Tournament. The Little Theatre movement had been flourishing in America for about a decade. Almost any town with pretensions to culture had its group of dedicated amateurs. For the most part they put on plays that had won Broadway's stamp of approval, but they occasionally staged original works and, more rarely, classics. For the rest of the week, each night saw three or four such ensembles offer one-act plays at the Nora Bayes.

Professionalism returned on the 18th, when the Equity Players brought out Paul Kester's *Sweet Nell of Old Drury* at the 48th Street Theatre. No matter that most critics agreed with Woollcott, who characterized the play as "a gaudy piece of rubbish which tottered rheumatically through this town three and twenty years ago." The play could still be captivating theatre, especially when Laurette Taylor was its Nell Gwynne. Even Woollcott would have agreed with *Variety*'s man, who wrote, "Our Laurette makes the unreal seem actual and the maudlin seem gospel truth." Among the supporting cast were newlyweds Alfred Lunt and Lynn Fontanne, playing together for

the first time. Both were embraced. Woollcott observed that "in a generally sumptuous cast, one performance stood out as something of fine mettle, something true and shining. That was the performance of Lynn Fontanne as the frustrated and embittered Lady Castlemaine." Writing in the *Globe*, Kenneth Macgowan proclaimed, "The real news about *Sweet Nell* is of course the fact that Alfred Lunt is having a fine time of it playing Charles II of England." In her curtain speech Taylor announced, "We hope to please the tired businessman—and to make some money." The two goals were happily achieved, with profits from the limited stand putting the Equity Players back into the black.

Three nights later one of the season's most brilliant comedies opened. Frederick Lonsdale's **Aren't We All?** (5-21-23, Gaiety) was a London hit. It told how the marriage of Margot and Willie Tatham (Alma Tell and Leslie Howard) is nearly wrecked when Margot stumbles upon Willie kissing Kitty Lake (Roberta Beatty). The return of Willie's father, the long-absent, womanizing Lord Gresham (Cyril Maude), helps resolve matters, particularly after it is discovered that Margot has done some away-from-home kissing herself.

Fred Jackson and Pierre Gendron came a cropper with **Cold Feet** (5-21-23, Fulton). At her wedding Coralie Prentice (Annette Bade) becomes so nervous that Dr. Harry Nolles (Glenn Anders), the man she jilted to marry a French count (Louis D'Arclay), consents to give her something to calm her. By mistake he gives her chloral, knocking her out. For the rest of the evening he carries the limp bride about, pursued by irate members of the wedding party and their guests. He tries hiding the unconscious girl and even must administer the drug to his more vociferous accusers. To exculpate himself, he claims he dreamt that the train the couple were to take would be wrecked. Humor ran to the order of one person accusing the doctor of being a quack, and his responding by telling the accuser not to sound like a duck. Some of the best laughs were grabbed by May Vokes as a silly serving girl who has tippled too much of the wedding champagne on the side.

Apparently riding on the crest of Taylor Holmes's popularity in films, Conrad Westerfelt's **Not So Fast** (5-22-23, Morosco) managed to run through the summer. Holmes's Henry Watterson Blake is a thoughtful but slow-moving Kentuckian who finds himself appointed co-guardian of two New York heiresses. His fellow guardian is a young hotshot Wall Streeter, James Acton (Leon Gordon), who has fallen under the spell of some financial sharpers and is prepared to risk the girls' fortune in dubious stocks. The girls, in turn, fall under Acton's spell and resent Blake's interference. But Blake not only proves right, he wins the hand of the older girl, Mary (Ann Davis).

Lula Vollmer's **Sun-Up** (5-25-23, Provincetown Playhouse) is set in the backreaches of the North Carolina mountains. It is 1917, and rumors of some sort of war have reached the mountain folk. The pipe-smoking Widow Cagle (Lucille LaVerne) assumes the South has had to do battle with the Yankees again "for the way they air bleedin' us to death." At the same time, she worries about her son, Rufe (Alan Birmingham), and the young man's refusal to make moonshine, the way his father did before he was shot by federal agents. So she is taken aback when Rufe informs her that he has registered for military service. Advised the war is in France, a place she never heard of and which she is told is about forty miles from Asheville, she complains that is "going a mighty long way to fight." Rufe assures her that he is a good shot and that they must not allow themselves to become enslaved. Before he goes, Rufe marries his sweetheart, Emmy (Anne Elstner). Months pass. A letter comes for the widow, but she is unable to read. Emmy reads it and tells her it is from the government, advising her that Rufe is dead. At the same time a stranger (Eliot Cabot) appears. He is a deserter and is being sought by the authorities. Widow Cagle hides him, saying, "I've been a-breakin' the law fer nigh on to sixty years, and I ain't afeered to break it agin." Then she learns that he is the son of the man who killed her husband. She rushes for her gun but is stopped from pulling the trigger by the voice of the dead Rufe. Repeating the words which she alone can hear, she acknowledges the boy's plea for more love and less hatred. She lets the stranger escape, then, imagining Rufe is with her again, she says to him, "I never knowed nothin' about lovin' anybody but you till you showed me hit was lovin' them all that counts. It was sundown when yer left me but hit's sun-up now and I know God Almighty is a-takin' care of you, son." Greeted by "as thunderous an ovation as the tiny Provincetown Theatre could hold," the drama played to packed houses, was moved to a small auditorium far uptown, where it continued to draw, and then was taken over by the Shuberts, who moved it to the Princess. To everyone's surprise, it ran there for much of the 1923–24 season.

The season closed with the Players' second revival, Richard Brinsley Sheridan's *The School for Scandal* at the Lyceum on June 4. What was virtually an ideal cast for the time included John Drew as Sir Peter, Tom Wise as Sir Oliver, McKay Morris as Joseph, Charles Richman as Charles, Henry Dixey as Backbite, Etienne Giradot as Crabtree, Robert Mantell as Snake, John Craig as Careless, Albert Bruning as Rowley, Ernest Lawford as Trip, Grant Mitchell, Walter Hampden, and Francis Wilson as servants, Ethel Barrymore as Lady Teazle, Violet Kemble Cooper as Lady Sneerwell, Charlotte Walker as Mrs. Candour, and Carroll McComas as Maria.

1923–1924

One fine season followed another. Late in the new theatrical year, *Variety,* surveying the crop of attractions available to theatregoers at the moment, characterized it as "of the first order." In his annual *Best Plays,* Burns Mantle commented, "The general quality of the drama was higher than it ever has been before. There were fewer trivial plays and . . . of cheap farces there were practically none at all." The number of productions inched up, while ticket prices held steady or, in a few instances, tried some inching up of their own. However, while the season was busy from beginning to end, its early months brought in few major successes. Bucking historical patterns, most of them came in later. And for all the season's excellences, there was no standout hit, no runaway smash.

Two comedies by a playwright with only one other produced work to his credit inaugurated the festivities. The thirty-three-year-old, Massachusetts-born Vincent Lawrence would continue to offer Broadway plays for twenty more years, but this pair of novelties would remain his most successful. The first to arrive was **Two Fellows and a Girl** (7-19-23, Vanderbilt). Lee Ellery (Ruth Shepley) flips a coin to decide whether she will marry Jack Moorland (John Halliday) or Jim Dale (Alan Dinehart). She fudges a bit, since she really prefers Jack. When Jack is pronounced the winner, a dejected Jim says his good-byes and leaves town. Several years later he returns. He is still single but now he is very rich. For a time it seems that Lee may desert Jack and run off with Jim. Then a pretty flapper, Doris Wadsworth (Claiborne Foster), catches Jim's eye and leaves Lee no choice but to remain with her husband. George M. Cohan's staging did wonders for the slim piece, giving it "snap" and filling it with such surefire Cohan stage tricks as having performers play brazenly to the audience. The comedy chalked up 132 playings.

In Love with Love (8-6-23, Ritz) ran four performances less, although many deemed it the better comedy. It could easily have been called *Three Fellows and a Girl*. Like Lee Ellery, Ann Jordan [Jordon in the acting edition] (Lynn Fontanne) cannot make up her mind whom she would marry. She has promised several young men that she will wed them some day. When Bob Metcalf (Henry Hull) whines, "All you want to do is to play a little while," she assures him, "We can be married any time. It's much nicer being sweethearts." Yet before long she has announced her engagement to the more demanding Frank Oakes (Robert Strange). Then, after arguments with him, she breaks it off and agrees to become engaged to Bob. Meanwhile, Bob has brought his friend, Jack Gardner (Ralph Morgan), a young engineer with a novel idea on how to construct bridges, to meet Ann's father (Berton Churchill), who is in a position to help Jack find builders. While Frank and Bob squabble and glower at each other, Jack pays little heed to Ann, only stopping now and then to point out how childish she is, then turning back to his business and ignoring her. His behavior opens Ann's eyes. She finally drops Bob and tells Jack that with Bob and Frank she had always been happy—the shallow happiness of being in love with love. "Then you came," she goes on, "and I never was so happy in my life—ever since I've known you I've been sick because I was afraid I'd lose you. Oh, please marry me and put me out of my misery." A startled Jack accepts. Most critics approved of the play, agreeing with Arthur Hornblow when he advised readers in *Theatre,* "It's only a trifle, but you'll enjoy every minute of it." In his *Herald* review, Alexander Woollcott took a slightly different tack by casting his spotlight on Lynn Fontanne and insisting this "ingrained American comedy" was too inconsequential for her great talents, though he did acknowledge that "her uncommon skill and resourcefulness as a player had carried her triumphantly through," despite "the English color to her voice." He suggested several Ibsen characters she might more profitably be performing.

The season's first flop was Myron C. Fagan's Thumbs Down (8-6-23, 49th St.). Having been disowned by his family when he was revealed as a bootlegger and sent to prison, Emmett Sheridan (Howard Lang) vows revenge on them. But he goes too far when he tries to blackmail his daughter (Sue MacManamy), who is engaged to the son (John Marston) of a prominent judge. She shoots her father. Her fiancé attempts to take the blame, but the district attorney (Purnell Pratt) will not allow it. At her trial, the district attorney is revealed as a bootleg king on the side and is shown to have been the real killer. Simultaneously, the girl learns that she is not Sheridan's child but the long-lost daughter (shades of oldtime melodrama), by an early marriage, of the judge.

The season's second dud was Barry Conners's comic melodrama The Mad Honeymoon (8-7-23, Playhouse). By pretending to oppose their marriage, Rufus Colgate (George Pauncefort) hopes to provoke his daughter, Peggy (Boots Wooster), and her milquetoast beau, Wally Spencer (Kenneth MacKenna), into eloping. What he does not count on is a slew of theatrical coincidences that almost wreck his plan. His ex-convict butler (Edward Arnold) is suddenly confronted by one (George Probert) of his old cronies, who has come to blackmail Peggy. It seems he is the twin brother of a man she secretly married but who was killed on the way to their honeymoon. When the butler refuses to cooperate the crook leaves a coonskin coat (with stolen bonds hidden in a pocket) where it will be found and suspicion will fall on the butler. But Peggy's maid, not understanding Mr. Colgate's plans, hides all of Peggy's clothes, so Peggy is forced to run off in little more than the coonskin coat she sees thrown over a chair. The youngsters elope to the same dingy, small-town hotel where the crooks are hiding and where one of them is posing as a minister. All sorts of misunderstandings ensue until the butler bravely tricks the crooks into confessions. Typical of the play's humor was Wally's, on learning that old man Colgate has a shotgun, asking Peggy: "What good is a dead husband? He's of practically no use to anyone but an undertaker, is he?" Moments later his manliness returns and he asserts, "As soon as we're safely married and it's too late to stop us—I'm going to call your father on the long distance and tell him about it—right to his face."

Booth Tarkington and Harry Leon Wilson's Tweedles (8-13-23, Frazee) was a near miss, despite largely delighted notices. Winsora Tweedles (Ruth Gordon), a waitress at her aunt's antique shop and tea room in Maine, and Julian Castlebury (Gregory Kelly), a young summer resident who has been buying Bristol glass at the shop so as to be near Winora and who is a scion of the Philadelphia Castleburys, discover to their chagrin that their snooty families oppose their romance. After all, a Castlebury signed the Declaration of Independence, so they can look down at the Tweedles clan, while Tweedleses came over to America two or three years before the Castleburys, whom they therefore look on as recent immigrants. The families are reconciled and the sweethearts allowed to announce wedding plans only after the youngsters go looking into family closets and find skeletons in them. Kelly and Gordon (husband and wife offstage) had performed together in Tarkington's earlier *Seventeen*. This time Woollcott observed, "In addition to the gentle, blinking, immensely engaging Kelly, one must certainly mention Miss Gordon who has a genuine and forthright actuality which is immensely nourishing to a play like this, and who, at times, can fill the brief love scenes with the shining light that is all one needs by which to see what goes on under Juliet's balcony." Donald Meek also won applause, playing with unctuous humor a government Prohibition agent who has a way of drinking the evidence.

Prohibition was the subject of Aaron Hoffman's **The Good Old Days** (8-14-23, Broadhurst). Like *Tweedles* it raked in mostly money notices, yet it would probably have to be called a near near miss, since, while it did well out of town, it survived only a little more than two months in New York. The play opens in 1916 in Nick and Rudolph's bar, a comfortable and traditionally elegant place of muslin-covered mirrors, ornate mahogany fittings, a brass rail, a mouth-watering free lunch counter, and waiters serving huge schooners of foaming beer. Nick Schloss (George Bickel) and Rudolph Zimmer (Charles Winninger), both thickly accented German-Americans, have been friendly partners. But with the coming of Prohibition, Nick gets religion and becomes a Prohibition agent, while Rudolph turns bootlegger and runs the old place as a speakeasy. Rudolph prospers while Nick becomes increasingly disillusioned with the corruption Prohibition has bred. Just in time to help unite the children of both families, Rudolph sees the light, announcing, "I feel that Prohibition is right, but I know it's wrong." Oldtimer Mathilde Cottrelly won laughs and handclaps as a tippling social climber.

Living together experimentally before marriage, which had been touched on by earlier plays such as last season's *Mary the Third* and others, was dealt with crucially in Bernard K. Burns's **The Woman on the Jury** (8-15-23, Eltinge). So was a more ongoing problem—men's attitudes toward women. Betty Brown (Mary Newcomb) has been living in a Vermont summer cottage with George Wayne (Fleming Ward) and without benefit of clergy. But when George callously walks out on her, Betty shoots at him and gets away with it. Years later she is chosen for a jury trying another woman who this time shot and did kill the cynical George, by whom she had had a baby. The eleven men on the panel demand the defendant get the chair as an example to all women. They have no understanding of her posi-

tion. So, risking her reputation and the marriage she has subsequently made, Betty tells the men her own story and sufficiently humbles her fellow jurors that they vote for acquittal. Al Woods's production, like *The Good Old Days,* ran for a little more than nine weeks.

But even Mary Roberts Rinehart's name could not push her **The Breaking Point** (8-16-23, Klaw) beyond an eight-and-a-half-week stay. The play was taken from her own novel and also dealt with a past that is dredged up again. In this case out in Wyoming Judd Clarke killed the husband of an actress he loved, then ran away to New York. Years later Dick Livingstone (McKay Morris) is a successful physician and about to make a socially advantageous marriage. But he knows that he has suffered for some time from amnesia and that there is something ugly in his background that he must first uncover. On a trip to Wyoming the horrible truth comes out, and he flees once again. But now he finds he cannot recall anything about his later New York days. Confronted at the New York home of a friend by authorities from Wyoming and by the actress, who claims she was the real killer, he suffers yet another shock, which now completely cures all his amnesia. Since the actress was the only witness to the killing, he is a free man. *Variety* was amused that the veiled, deep-voiced, and sultry woman who played the actress "made Theda Bara look like Bebe Daniels."

Considering some of the notices it received, Martin Flavin's **Children of the Moon** (8-17-23, Comedy) should have been the season's first major hit. "Not in the past ten years has the American stage received so valuable a contribution, from either foreign or native sources," *Theatre* exclaimed, while Broun, writing in the *World,* suggested that it contained some of the best playwriting of the last two decades. But the play's theme and treatment apparently dissuaded many playgoers, so it ran only fifteen weeks. Taken in after his plane crashed on the Atherton property, Major John Bannister (Paul Gordon) has had time to recover and to fall in love with attractive, young Jane Atherton (Florence Johns). But he also has had time to recognize that there is something odd about the family. They are not called the "Moon-Mad Athertons" for nothing. As old Judge Atherton (Albert Perry), who spends much of his time on the terrace peering up at the sky through the family's telescope, tells the flyer, "The Moon is our mother, and gave us birth. And you, sir, do you know that from the Moon we came, and to the Moon we must return? Do you realize that we are all Children of the Moon?" The idyll of Major Bannister and Jane is almost destroyed when Jane's mean, self-serving mother (Beatrice Terry) returns and, over the protestations of grandmother Atherton (Henrietta Crosman) and a thoughtful family physician (Grant Stewart), does all in her power to prevent a marriage. The youngsters defy both her and heredity and fly off in the repaired "air machine." The family watches from the terrace until an incoming fog blocks their view, so they cannot be certain whether the couple has reached the moon or has crashed.

None of the entries arriving the next Monday was a hit. The longest run—seven weeks—went to Edward Laska's **We've Got to Have Money** (8-20-23, Playhouse). Laska was better known as a lyricist and a sometime composer. His comedy was seen as a hand-me-down rehashing of the *It Pays to Advertise* school. Instead of studying for his degree at Columbia Dave Farnum (Robert Ames) has changed places with the bookish Thomas Campbell (Stewart Kemp), paying for Tom to earn a degree while he himself cavorts in the best New York night spots. The truth does not emerge until his fiancée, Olga Walcott (Vivian Tobin), and his prospective father-in-law (Robert McWade) realize a stranger has accepted his degree at his commencement. The old man has the power to cut off Dave's income and does just that, telling him he will not support a wastrel or allow him to marry his daughter. That leaves Dave "as broke as the Ten Commandments" but does not stop him from forming the American Promoting Company and taking offices in the Woolworth Building. There, using all manner of bluff, he induces inventors to let him try to market their often absurd inventions. He eventually lands some profitable deals, and all ends happily after he prevents a tricky rival from getting an edge on a new idea that could enrich Mr. Walcott's firm.

There were even fewer takers for Owen Davis's **Home Fires** (8-20-23, 39th St.) The Bedfords do well enough on the $10,000 a year Mr. Bedford (Charles Richman) brings home, but they are restless and not truly contented. Troubles come when father goes driving with a neighbor's wife, and both daughters date boys they are not supposed to be seeing. In fact, when the older daughter (Juliette Crosby) spots her father with the neighbor at a seedy roadhouse, she breaks a leg jumping out a window in an effort to avoid his seeing her. Before long Mr. Bedford loses his job and the family's dreams of owning a Ford go down the drain. But Mrs. Bedford (Frances Underwood) is a happy stay-at-home, ready to welcome everyone back when they realize how silly their behavior has been and to encourage them to face the future bravely.

Least of the evening's three openings was Thomas P. Robinson's **Brook** (8-20-23, Greenwich Village). Brook Blackburn (Mary Carroll) is a naive Allegheny mountain girl who falls in love with and has a child by a summer visitor, Bryce Hammond (Donald Cameron). Bryce would forget Brook and marry his city sweetheart (Ellis Baker), until the depth and fervor of Brook's love makes him understand his place is with the mountain girl. Some critics complained that the mountain folk were given names reflecting plants and other natural phenomena and that Robinson too aggressively punched home his point that the closer to nature we are, the better we are.

The week's two other premieres both chalked up eleven-week runs. Probably only Al Woods among Broadway's major producers would mount a play called **Red Light Annie** (8-21-23, Morosco), though curiously his co-producer was the respected Sam Harris. The drama was the work of Norman Houston and Sam Forrest. Like Brook Blackburn, Fanny and Tom Campbell (Mary Ryan and Frank M. Thomas) are naive. But they reverse Brook's situation, leaving their small hometown and coming to the big city, where they fall under the evil influence of the only people they know, Fanny's stepsister and brother-in-law (Warda Howard and Edward Ellis). Before Fanny and Tom realize what the Martins are truly like, Tom is framed and imprisoned for the theft of bonds from a bank and Fanny becomes a snowbird (drug addict) and prostitute. After Tom's release and Fanny's reformation, they attempt to go straight, but the brother-in-law tries to blackmail them. Fanny kills him. However, a compassionate detective sees to it that she walks away scot-free. The first act contained "Ten Thumbnail Sketches," beginning at an upstate New York railroad station as the Campbells leave home and continuing through all the scenes of the couple's degradation. Reviewers praised the excellence of the numerous settings and the quickness with which they were changed.

Many of the same aisle-sitters also lauded the eerie effects employed in Joseph F. Rinn's **Zeno** (8-25-23, 48th St.) No one knows who the criminal mastermind called Zeno really is. His orders to his cohorts are always given by wireless. A psychic named Dr. Moore (William B. Mack) persuades Inspector Parker to attend a seance in which Moore will call upon a recently murdered young man to identify Zeno. In the room's strange green light, ghostly hands and black hooded figures are seen before the inspector discloses that the house had been wired by the police, and that from listening to earlier conversations he now knows who Zeno is and that Moore is Zeno's confederate.

Reviewers also lauded Leo Carrillo's performance but had few kind words for Booth Tarkington's **Magnolia** (8-27-23, Liberty), a misfiring spoof of old southern traditions. Tom Rumford (Carrillo), having been reared by Philadelphia Quakers, opposes the use of firearms and fisticuffs. When he returns to his Mississippi home, his notions so infuriate his belli-cose father (J. K. Hutchinson) that he is chased away. At a Natchez gambling den, he comes under the tutelage of warmhearted General Jackson (Malcolm Williams), who teaches him various methods of self-defense and shows him there is nothing morally wrong with them. So when Tom returns home, advertising himself as the "notorious Cunnel Blake," he is a changed man.

The busy Al Woods enjoyed the season's longest run to date —twenty-two weeks—when he pre-sented playgoers with John Emerson and Anita Loos's **The Whole Town's Talking** (8-29-23, Bijou). Since Mr. Simmons (James Bradbury) has selected his timid, disheveled partner, Chester Binney (Grant Mitchell), as husband for his daughter, Ethel (June Bradbury), he is taken aback when she returns from Chicago with a brash, French-spouting man of the world, Roger Shields (Gerald Oliver Smith). But Simmons is undaunted. He tells Chester:

Simmons: We are going to sow some wild oats.
Chester: What are you talking about?
Simmons: We are going to make you a man of the world, a man who has lived his whole life in an oat field.
Chester: Well, I was brought up on the farm.

Simmons sends Chester out to buy a photograph of a great beauty, with whom, the men will then claim, Chester has had an affair. Chester's selections dismay Simmons, for he returns with photographs of the Queen of Roumania (too far away), the Mona Lisa (dead too long), and Julian Eltinge (a man in drag). Fortunately Chester has also bought a fourth photograph, one of the famous film star Letty Lythe. Simmons forges a sexy comment and auto-graph on it and lets Mrs. Simmons (Lucia Moore) accidentally find the picture. Before long the whole town—Sandusky, Ohio—is talking about Chester and Letty. All the girls are after Chester, and Ethel has dumped Roger in his favor. Simmons is de-lighted with himself until Letty Lythe (Catherine Owen) comes to town for a personal appearance. Learning of what has been going on she barges into the Simmons house, followed by her jealous fiancé (Harold Salter), and vamps Chester. All hell breaks loose, leaving Simmons to wail, "Oh, ye Gods! Why didn't we pick the Mona Lisa!" A battle in the darkened Simmons parlor (darkened to copy a scene in Letty's latest flicker) wrecks the place but leads to a happy ending. John Corbin of the *Times* spoke for a majority when he concluded his review, "There is small scope for critical appraisal; the only question is how infectious its humor will prove to be."

The month ended with Walter Hampden, prior to launching his announced Shakespearean season, producing A. E. Thomas's **The Jolly Roger** (8-30-23, National) for a limited run. He did not appear in the play, which featured Pedro de Cordoba as Adam Trent, who somehow manages to board a pirate ship on which the pirate king lies dead and the crew is in mutiny. He takes over, and his bravado wins him the respect of the sailors, including a charming cabin boy in pirate shorts and woolen hose, who turns out to be an even more charming girl (Carroll McComas) in disguise. Though they eventually are marooned on a deserted island, love triumphs. The cast was panned, with de Cordoba being assailed as "too mincing in manner" to be believable, but the color-splashed settings (the deck of a ship, the captain's cabin, the lonely tropical island) and costumes were deemed worthy of the best operetta.

September began on a down note with Edward Childs Carpenter's **Connie Goes Home** (9-6-23, 49th St.), taken from a story by Fannie Kilburn. Having failed in her attempt to find "kid" roles on Broad-way, Connie (Sylvia Field) rejects the notion of becoming a rich man's mistress and opts to return to the orphanage in which she had been reared. Since she lacks sufficient train fare, she dons her kiddy togs and goes out to buy a half-fare ticket. When we next see her, she is at the Chicago home of peppery old George Barclay (Berton Churchill). It seems that she was almost kicked off the train by an unsympathetic conductor until she was rescued by Jim (Donald Foster), who is Barclay's nephew and has brought her to his uncle's home. There Connie not only helps Barclay out of little domestic difficul-ties but routs a vamp who had her clutches on Jim. Naturally the grateful Jim proposes.

Four in Hand (9-6-23, Greenwich Village), trans-lated by Roy Briant and E. L. Gerstein from a play by Paul Frank and Siegfried Geyer, was even less cordially received. It told of a wife (Galina Kopernak) who walks out on her husband (Robert Rendel) when he refuses to show signs of jealousy and returns to him when he does.

Another young girl come to New York to make good was the central figure of Samuel Shipman and Alfred C. Kennedy's **The Crooked Square** (9-10-23,

Hudson). Like Connie, sweet, southern Barbara Kirkwood (Edna Hibbard) has no luck. Worse, when she approaches a man for help she is arrested and imprisoned for soliciting sexual favors. She is bailed out by crooks who pose as legitimate detectives and who set her up to uncover a scandal which they can use in their blackmailing schemes. But she falls in love with the suave socialite (Kenneth MacKenna) she was to victimize and turns the tables on the crooks. Generally bullish business on Broadway kept the play going for eleven weeks.

Eleven weeks was also how long Mrs. Fiske and David Belasco allowed St. John Ervine's **Mary, Mary, Quite Contrary** (9-11-23, Belasco) to remain on Broadway before heading out to tour. Mrs. Fiske portrayed a famous actress who, on a lark, visits a country vicarage and flirts there both with the vicar's son, an aspiring young playwright (Francis Lister), and with a not so young diplomat (C. Aubrey Smith), before she returns to the West End to do her latest play. One comic scene found the actress and diplomat, both drenched, returning home having spent a rainy night on a nearby lake after losing their oars. Of the star's playing, Woollcott cooed, "It was such a performance as her devotees have in mind when they say there is no comedienne like her anywhere in the world." One footnote: Belasco took the occasion to announce he had installed a new lighting system inspired by his study of the rainbow. This led Robert Benchley to muse in *Life* that it "only goes to show what great strides Nature is making."

Henry Miller found himself with a modest but highly praised hit on his hands when he brought out Lee Wilson Dodd's **The Changelings** (9-17-23, Henry Miller's). Hornblow greeted it as "perhaps our first genuine American comedy of manners, of a distinct literary quality." Wallace Aldcroft (Miller) is a rather tradition-minded publisher married to the more progressive Karen (Blanche Bates). They have long been friends with a liberal writer, Fenwick Faber (Reginald Mason), and Faber's less imaginative wife, Dora (Laura Hope Crews). Bonds of friendship have been tightened since the Fabers' son, "Wicky" (Geoffrey Kerr), married the Aldcrofts' daughter, Kay (Ruth Chatterton). Their reactions to a book that a young Jew has written calling the family the last bulwark of tyranny against freedom can be imagined. Aldcroft is outraged, but not nearly as upset as when Wicky suddenly appears and discloses that Kay has left him. In no time, the more freethinking Fenwick and Karen are aligned against Wallace and Dora, who demand immediate action. Karen explodes, "For years we've been discussing these things in a vacuum—all of us. We've made a sort of word-game out of it! And now, it isn't a game any more." Kay soon appears, having run out on the man (Felix Krembs) she had run away with. He appears, too, and his nastiness puts an end to the constantly altering side-taking and unites the others against him. After he leaves, they realize their relationships will never be the same again, but they understand that they must make the best of imperfect marriages.

Edward Knoblock's **The Lullaby** (9-17-23, Knickerbocker) was also a modest success, running eighteen weeks. In present-day Paris a bedraggled old hag (Florence Reed) attempts to stop a young girl from destroying her own life by telling her history to the girl. She had fled her Normandy home after the boy who seduced her refused to marry her. In Paris she becomes the mistress of a rich American initially but with time sinks lower and lower. As a painted street walker in Tunis, she offers herself to anyone but sailors. She refuses to sleep with sailors because she has been told that her son, whom she has not seen since he was a child, has become one. But when a sailor, who proves to be her son, appears and demands her favors, he is so infuriated by her refusal that he pulls a gun. They tussle for it and the gun goes off, killing the boy. The police come, arrest her, and send her to prison.

Frank Keenan, a character actor who many felt never received the recognition he deserved, won good notices in Frank Dazey and Leighton Osmun's **Peter Weston** (9-18-23, Sam H. Harris). He played an ironwilled man who drove his wife to an early grave and cruelly attempts to dominate his three children. He has forced his sons into his pumping business, even though one wanted a career as a writer and the other as an artist. The artist (Clyde North) accidentally kills the firm's bookkeeper (Wilfred Lytell), who had discovered irregularities in the books. But the police accuse him of first-degree murder. Weston's daughter was pregnant by the dead man and had hoped to marry him, but her father forces her to perjure herself at her brother's trial. Her lies fall on deaf ears, and her brother is sentenced to death. The old man's attempts to bribe the governor are unavailing. All this drives the younger brother (Jay Hanna) to drink himself to death. On the morning of his son's execution the old man goes mad, attempting to talk over the telephone to the birds outside his window. Most critics extolled Keenan's acting, although a few seemed to resent his having spent so much time recently in films. The best reviews went to Judith Anderson as the daughter. One reviewer, saying that she "puts up some thrilling fights," concluded she "rises to rather important heights." Another said her big scene with Keenan reached "genuinely tragic heights." *Variety* predicted major stardom for her.

Another of the early season's modest successes—this time fifteen weeks—was William A. Brady's production of Jules Eckert Goodman's **Chains** (9-19-23, Playhouse), which Corbin saw as "an intimately true and finely realized comedy of family life." Harry Maury (Paul Kelly) tells his parents (William Morris and Maude Turner Gordon) that he wants to go with his Uncle Richard (Gilbert Emery) to South America to try his luck there. It soon comes out that Harry's real reason for going is to run away from a romance that has turned sour. Uncle Dick has known about all this, but he feels that the Maurys, including Harry, look at matters jaundicedly—their interests lie in maintaining their respectability by avoiding scandal and in doing their duty. Dick scoffs, "We have taken the commonest and most powerful instinct in human nature and have deliberately set to work to shroud it in mystery and false values." To clear the air he has brought the girl, Jean Trowbridge (Helen Gahagan), to them. The Maurys cannot believe that she refuses to accept the money they offer her to go away nor that she really does not want to marry Harry. When Uncle Dick blurts out that there is a baby involved, Harry offers to wed Jean. But Jean points out that she is not talking about money, love, revenge, or duty. What has happened has happened, and that is that. Harry and his parents, all uncomprehending, can only shrug their shoulders. An amused Jean tells Dick, "They are going to shudder deliciously at what might have happened and so heave a great sigh and, piously or otherwise, thank God that they have saved their son." The admiring Dick offers to marry Jean, but, having cleared the air the best she can, she insists she prefers to go her own way.

In Rudolf Besier and May Edginton's **A Lesson in Love** (9-24-23, 39th St.) the very French Captain André Briquette (William Faversham), disgusted by the haughty, sanctimonious behavior of Beatrice Audley (Emily Stevens), who has slammed the door on an old friend because the friend left a loveless marriage, decides to teach her a lesson. He so deftly woos Beatrice that she deserts her own fiancé (Hugh Buckler). But when it comes time to publicly discard and disgrace her, the captain finds he has fallen in love. Miss Stevens was praised for controlling her nervous mannerisms; Faversham, gently chided for his inconsistent French accent. But the stars pleased Broadway for nine weeks.

Guy Bolton's **Chicken Feed** (9-24-23, Little) was another less than runaway hit—staying profitably for eighteen weeks. Nell Bailey (Roberta Arnold) is about to marry Danny Kester (Stuart Fox), a young man attempting to interest his small town in prefabricated homes—"made out West, sent on in sections and stuck together in a week." But hours before the wedding she discovers her father (Frank Mc-Cormack) has appropriated family funds and invested them unwisely. She tells her father that even at servant's wages he owes his wife (Marie Day) thousands of dollars. When he retorts that his wife is not a servant, Nell angrily replies, "No, if she had been she would have been paid for all her hard work—that's the difference." Nell finds that Danny agrees with the men, so she, her mother, and some other local women decide to take rooms in a nearby hotel and not return until they receive their fair share of their family incomes. Before that happens, some other matters intervene. Nell must both save Danny from losing his enterprise to a dishonest judge (Sam Reed) and save her father's investments. She does. Small lines in these plays offer interesting period pictures. Thus, in *Chains* Mrs. Maury is shocked to see her daughter wearing rouge, while in *Chicken Feed* one character complains that bobbed hair does not require hair pins and thereby deprives women of a weapon.

Sidney Howard's translation of Lorenzo de Azertis's **Casanova** (9-26-23, Empire) lasted ten weeks, or long enough to deprive its leading lady of the title role in a Shaw play which many felt she would have been ideal for. Following a pantomime featuring Columbine and Pulcinella, and choreographed by Fokine to Deems Taylor's music, it told how Casanova (Lowell Sherman) wins Henriette (Katharine Cornell), the lone great and true love of his life, how he gives her up when he fears she will have to live with him in poverty, and how he later seeks in vain to find her. Years afterwards, he encounters their daughter (again Cornell) but cannot reveal his identity to her, so he dies kissing the carpet on which she has just passed. Critics had few kind words for the play or for Sherman but rejoiced that Cornell, who so short a time ago had played an ugly, deformed girl in *The Enchanted Cottage,* could be "the same vision of beauty and grace who smiled and curtsied in the fantastic hoop skirts of the early eighteenth century."

Luigi Pirandello's **Floriani's Wife** (9-30-23, Greenwich Village), in a translation by Ann Sprague MacDonald, received divided notices and folded after two weeks. It centered on a woman (Margaret Wycherly) whose husband (George Bergen George) had left her because of her seemingly loose ways. Years later he takes her back with the understanding that she not acknowledge that she is the mother of their child, who was a baby when they separated. Since the daughter (Mary Hone) has beatified her mother's memory, she will not accept the interloper. Battles wax so fierce that the wife, after blurting out the truth, leaves home.

Not until October did non-musical plays arrive which would enjoy runs of six months or more. One of three novelties opening on the first Monday of the month, Gilbert Emery's **Tarnish** (10-1-23, Belmont), stayed around for seven months. Adolph Tevis (Albert Gran) has squandered his life on liquor and women, much to the fury of his wife (Mrs. Russ Whytal), a southern belle who is forever lamenting that she married beneath her station. Their daughter, Letitia or Tishy (Ann Harding), is in love with Emmett Carr (Tom Powers), who works in the same office that she does and whom her mother openly looks down upon. When Tishy learns that her father, who was supposed to deposit a check to cover rent money, has cashed the check and given the money to a prostitute, she decides to go after the girl and retrieve the money. The girl (Fania Marinoff) refuses to return it, insisting that her work is as mean and hard as any. While the two are arguing Emmett appears, and the girl, who had known him long ago and who has tricked him into coming to her, makes it seem that he is still a voluntary and regular visitor. Tishy storms out. Back at her home, Tishy will not listen to Emmett's tearful pleadings and chases him away. But the Tevises' understanding Irish cleaning woman tells Tishy, "They're a poor lot, the men, all of 'em, and dirty, too—but the thing is, darlin', to get one that cleans easy." So when a still contrite Emmett returns again to beg Tishy to take him back, she does. Critics saw the play as inferior to Emery's *The Hero* but nonetheless gripping theatre even if it sometimes sacrificed honesty for theatrical effect. Harding, however, won almost universal praise for coupling "unforced sincerity and poignantly emotional power" with "golden beauty and girlish charm."

In Herbert Hall Winslow and Emil Nyitray's **What's Your Wife Doing?** (10-1-23, 49th St.) Christopher and Beatrice Skinner (Louis Simon and Dorothy Mackaye) learn that Chris's uncle (Shep Camp) may disinherit him for marrying over the uncle's opposition and so decide to go through the motions of a very public divorce, then remarry after Chris gets his inheritance. They enlist their friend Jerry Warner (Glenn Anders) as corespondent. Chris invites his uncle to join him in "discovering" the lovers' tryst at Jerry's apartment. Of course, everything goes awry, including the appearance of Jerry's

fiancée (Isabelle Leighton). The uncle, who turns out to be a good soul, engineers a happy ending. The play served as the source of the 1925 musical *Mercenary Mary,* which despite Broadway's relative indifference to it, became an international hit.

A good uncle and aunt-to-be engineered a happy ending in the long-unheard-from Sydney Rosenfeld's **Forbidden** (10-1-23, Daly's). An automobile accident in front of his mansion prompts Roger Carlyle (Cyril Keightley) to offer shelter to Alice Carson (Mary Young). The middle-aged pair are taken with one another, but their brief acquaintance is threatened when Roger's niece, Virginia (Josephine Stevens), bursts in, having run away from her convent school. The kindly Alice agrees to take in Virginia and straighten her out. She soon discovers Virginia's boasts of wild behavior have no truth to them. At the same time, the doctor (Harry Minturn) whom Roger had called in to examine Alice has taken a liking to Virginia and successfully courts her. Roger and Alice, both of whom have claimed fictitious spouses, send themselves telegrams announcing the deaths of those spouses. Burns Mantle lists the play as *Virginia Runs Away.*

On the 2nd Sothern and Marlowe offered New Yorkers their version of *Cymbeline* at the Jolson. Critics such as Broun, Corbin, and Woollcott, who once had adored Marlowe, pounced on her absurdly exaggerated and stagey reading. They gave Sothern slighting attention. The almost ancient John Ranken Towse, writing in the *Post,* blamed his displeasure largely on "the dead weight of the plot." The *American*'s Alan Dale was one of the few admirers of the elaborate mounting, which set the stars back $60,000. Later in their visit they brought out *The Taming of the Shrew, Twelfth Night, Hamlet, The Merchant of Venice,* and *Romeo and Juliet.* But at sixty-five and fifty-eight, and rooted in Victorian theatrical traditions, Sothern and Marlowe had seen their sun set. When they finished their engagement and short post-Broadway tour, they said their final farewells to the stage as a pair, albeit Sothern returned alone for a few later modern plays.

The Theatre Guild's production of John Galsworthy's **Windows** (10-8-23, Garrick) was a major disappointment. It told of an idealistic family's attempt to help reclaim a serving girl (Phyllis Povah), just out of prison for killing her illegitimate baby. The attempt fails, since the girl, like Jane in *Chains,* has strong ideas of her own.

October's second long run—thirty-five weeks— went to **The Nervous Wreck** (10-9-23, Sam H. Harris), which Owen Davis dramatized from "The Wreck," an *Argosy* story by E. J. Rath and G.

Howard Watt. The old Ford flivver in which Henry Williams (Otto Kruger) and Sally Morgan (June Walker) have been riding has broken down on a lonely, narrow canyon road. When Sally presses him to hurry with repairs, he begs her not to get him more nervous than he is. "It isn't safe for a man in my state of health." He has a bag full of medications, and he must be careful not to take the wrong ones: "That's the worst of these complications of diseases. One's got to be fair to all of them." But Sally makes Henry rush for his pills and powders when she confesses that she has lied to him. He is not, as he has believed, driving her to the train station. Rather, to escape an unwanted marriage to hotheaded Sheriff Bob Wells, she has left a note at her father's ranch saying she has eloped with Henry. On the other hand, Sally can be helpful. She discovers their problem is that they have run out of gas. When another car pulls up behind them and threatens to shove their jalopy into the ravine, Henry grabs a gun that Sally has shown him and forces the others to share their gas. Sally and Henry wind up at a ranch where the tables are turned and they, at gunpoint, are forced to become the ranch's cook and waiter to replace the "Chinks" who have run off. The other car soon pulls in, and its owner, Mr. Underwood (William Holden), who is also the ranch's owner, phones for Sheriff Bob to hurry over and find the bandits who held him up. With each retelling the number of bandits grows. For the rest of the evening, Sally and Henry first try to avoid being identified and, after they are, being carted off to jail or shot by the trigger-happy sheriff (Edward Arnold). In the end Henry's often inadvertent bravery impresses Sally and she convinces him that he is in the pink of health, so they are married and head back home. The play's humor was often slapdash and reliant on puns. Thus, when Henry, as the waiter, finds Sally being courted by a tough ranch hand, he asks her how to make a salad dressing. The annoyed ranch hand chimes in with an order to "beat it!" Henry vigorously beats the dressing with a spoon, tosses the salad and dressing together, then tosses the melange over the ranch hand and runs out. In 1928, the comedy was made into the successful Ziegfeld musical *Whoopee*, for Eddie Cantor.

Edna St. Vincent Millay's adaptation of Ferenc Molnár's **Launzi** (10-10-23, Plymouth) found few takers. Its Hungarian title, *Egi és földi szerelem*, could have been translated more accurately as "Heavenly and Earthly Love." It recounted the tragedy of Launzi (Pauline Lord), who, frustrated that the man she loves prefers her mother, unsuccess-

fully attempts suicide. Rescued, she insists on being considered dead, and doctors tell the family to humor her. To further the illusion, she dons a pair of angel-like wings and attempts to fly by jumping off a tower.

On his more or less annual visit, William Hodge introduced his latest play, **For All of Us** (10-15-23, 49th St.). And he received his more or less annual drubbing from critics who were starting to wonder if even rubes could still accept his vehicles with a straight face. For the occasion he assumed the role of a wholesome ditch digger, Tom Griswald, who found religion while serving a jail sentence for drunkenness. Attracted by the way Tom whistles while he digs, a crippled banker (Frank Losee) invites him into his home. In no time at all, Tom has cured the man's paralysis by teaching him good, honest thinking. He also discovers—shades of bygone melodrama—his long-lost daughter. To the surprise of Broadway's smart money, this "Christian Science drama" chugged along profitably for six months.

Hodge had to compete for first-nighters with the Grand Guignol of Paris, which began a ten-week engagement at the Frolic. As was the case with Hodge, Broadway smart money guessed wrong. The company, especially in light of its huge advance sale, had been expected to cause a sensation, but it left most playgoers cold. In a turnover of bills of one-acters, the group offered not only horror plays but short farces and didactic pieces as well.

With the arrival of Lula Vollmer's **The Shame Woman** (10-16-23, Greenwich Village) the young playwright had two successes running at once in New York. That surprised a number of critics who questioned whether playgoers would support two such stark folk dramas. As in *Sun-Up*, the action unfolds largely in a cabin somewhere in the North Carolina mountains. Lize Burns (Florence Rittenhouse), an unmarried woman ostracized by her neighbors for letting herself be seduced, has raised an orphan girl, Lily (Thelma Paige), so that she might have companionship. Lily commits suicide after she, too, is seduced. When Lize learns that the same man has been responsible for both incidents, she stabs him to death. Her refusal to name the dead girl—and thus brand her "a shame woman"—in the trial that follows leads to Lize's being sentenced to hang.

A second opening in the Village that evening saw the Neighborhood Players inaugurate their new season with William Butler Yeats's **The Player Queen** (10-16-23, Neighborhood Playhouse), coupled with a revival of Shaw's *The Shewing-up of*

Blanco Posnet. In Yeats's strange work a loud, vulgar actress (Aline MacMahon) takes the place of an unpopular, religiously obsessed queen. The Shaw play details the comic contretemps that arise after a cowboy steals a horse in a town where everyone delights in doing bad.

Richard Bennett was increasingly perceived as an ambitious, high-minded actor of unfortunately limited scope. The perception was furthered by his performance in Gerald du Maurier's London hit **The Dancers** (10-17-23, Broadhurst). Tony (Bennett), a successful Canadian immigrant, learns he has inherited a fortune back in England, so he leaves his Canadian sweetheart (Jean Oliver), a dancer, returns home, and resumes a long-dormant affair with another dancer (Flora Sheffield). But the English girl proves a self-destructive hedonist, leaving Tony to patch it up with his Canadian friend. While not a failure, the play fell far short of its West End popularity.

Brock Pemberton, the producer, often took gambles that paid off handsomely, but when he presented a blank-verse drama by a fledgling playwright he met with disaster. Pemberton would move on to better things, and so would the writer, Maxwell Anderson. In **White Desert** (10-18-23, Princess) Anderson depicts the tense marriage of Mary and Michael Kane (Beth Merrill and Frank Shannon), whose home is an isolated cabin on the bleak, often snow-covered North Dakota prairie. Michael is a sexually repressed, puritanical man, disturbed by his wife's obvious pleasure in their lovemaking. She, in turn, is shocked by the names he calls her for confessing her pleasure. A storm sets in shortly after Michael heads off on a two-day trip for supplies. Sverre Peterson (George Abbott), a friendly, manly neighbor, takes shelter with Mary, and she, embittered by her husband's behavior, seduces him. Michael, on his return, is apologetic; he has come to understand that different humans have different needs and desires. But when Mary tells him what she has done and goes out to walk for a bit in the snow with Sverre, Michael rushes for a gun and kills her. He can understand, but he cannot forgive. Although a few reviewers, among them, surprisingly, Corbin, detected great promise in the work, a majority condemned it as dull or salacious. A week and a half, and it was gone, with *Variety* recording that it grossed only about $100 a performance.

Two hard-working, more experienced craftsmen, Frank Mandel and Guy Bolton, were not that much more successful with their comedy **Nobody's Business** (10-22-23, Klaw). The mercurial Francine Larrimore was featured as Marjorie Benton, an upstate New Yorker who heads for the big city to seek the proverbial fame and fortune. On the train she meets Jerry Moore (Louis Bennison), who offers to underwrite her if she will become his mistress. She refuses. Some time later, Moore and his attorney are writing Moore's will, and the attorney tells his client that he can understand his healthy bequests to *Follies* girls, since those beauties need more to live on, but he asks why Moore is leaving so large a bequest to Marjorie. The scene flashes back to the digs Marjorie sometimes shares with Vera Smith (Josephine Drake), a sharp-tongued, man-hungry, out-of-work vaudevillian. Vera has warned Marjorie that nice girls have a way of falling for rotten men (the line reportedly got the biggest audience reaction of the evening). Sure enough, she has bad luck with a lecherous pianist (Frank Conroy). When Moore learns of this, he attempts to profit by her despair. He is turned away again. His visit is misunderstood by a decent young banker who is courting Marjorie and nearly costs her his love. But all ends satisfactorily, with a colored maid (Elaine Davies) echoing the sentiments of the Irish maid in *Tarnish:* "Just when you's made up yo' mind that all men are bad, you up an' discover that they's one real gemman lives close roun' de cohner." The two scenes in Vera's apartment offered a view from a window showing a "moving" electric sign in which a white-bulbed kitten plays with a white-bulbed ball of yarn.

One of the season's most memorable hits was Melville Baker's translation of Ferenc Molnár's **The Swan** (10-23-23, Cort). Eva Le Gallienne had the leading role of a princess whose mother (Hilda Spong) orders her tutor (Basil Rathbone) to escort the girl to a ball in hopes of making a neighboring prince (Philip Merivale) jealous. The love interest awakened between the princess and the tutor nearly wrecks plans for royal nuptials until moments before the final curtain. (Programs still listed Charles Frohman as producer, eight and a half years after his death.)

In the face of Ramon Novarro's hugely popular film version, Rafael Sabatini went ahead and dramatized his own best-selling **Scaramouche** (10-24-23, Morosco), the saga of a French revolutionist (Sidney Blackmer) sworn to revenge the killing of his best friend, until he learns the killer was his own father. The play could not compete with the silent, black-and-white film.

Nor did anyone expect Sophocles' *Oedipus Rex* (in Gilbert Murray and W. L. Courtney's translation) to compete with Broadway's more commercial fare when it was offered at the huge, out-of-the-way

Century Theatre on the 25th, and it did not. Still, with Sir John Martin-Harvey as a dignified if not especially impassioned king, it did respectable trade for its two-and-a-half-week stand. After it was taken off, the English star offered some performances of Sybil Amherst and C. E. Wheeler's translation of Hugo von Hofmannsthal's **Via Crucis** (beginning on November 12), a modern-day retelling of the Every-man story; Alexander Teixera de Mattos' translation of Maurice Maeterlinck's *The Burgomaster of Stilemonde* (on the 15th), which Broadway had seen before as *The Burgomaster of Belgium* and which told of a burgomaster who sacrifices his life to spare his Belgian city during the war; and *Hamlet* (on the 19th).

Eleonora Duse began what was announced as a farewell visit with a matinee performance of Ibsen's *The Lady from the Sea* at the Metropolitan Opera House on the 29th. Her subsequent performances, again mostly matinees, were given at the same Century Theatre where Martin-Harvey was holding forth in the evenings. Besides a second Ibsen drama, *Ghosts,* and d'Annunzio's *La Città Morta,* she offered Tommaso Gallarati-Scotti's **Così Sia** (on November 13), in which she played a devout, self-sacrificing mother left to die alone by her ungrateful son, and Marco Praga's **La Porta Chuisa** (on the 19th), assuming the role of a mother who must confront her son's distress on learning he is illegitimate. Some reviewers complained about the star's choice of plays, particularly the Praga drama, but concurred that her artistry was as luminous as ever. These were, indeed, her last New York performances, for the great Italian actress died in Pittsburgh in April during her post-Broadway tour.

A cast consisting in good measure of Irish-Americans made a hash of Albert Koblitz and S. J. Warshawsky's **Steadfast** (10-29-23, Ambassador), recounting how an orthodox Jewish rabbi (Frank McGlynn) must face up to the seduction of his daughter (Leona Hogarth) and the announcement that his son (Rexford Kendrick) wants to marry a Christian. Noting that McGlynn conveyed none of the intense emotion or depth of Semitic feeling to be expected from an orthodox rabbi, more than one aisle-sitter chortled that he still seemed to be playing Abe Lincoln.

Probably no other success of the season was as unlooked for as Walter Hampden's revival of Edmond Rostand's *Cyrano de Bergerac,* which the actor offered to playgoers at the National on November 1, employing Brian Hooker's translation. The *American*'s often clownish Alan Dale, whose theatregoing career stretched far enough back, grew serious as he insisted that Hampden's performance surpassed Mansfield's and Coquelin's, asserting, "It was so full of poetry and mystic qualities that it made me think I had never seen the play before." The starchier, hidebound John Rankin Towse virtually concurred in the *Evening Post,* rejoicing, "His Cyrano puts those of all other English performers completely into the shade and is no whit inferior to that of the great Coquelin himself." Many reviewers were unhappy with Carroll McComas's Roxane and Charles Francis's Christian but remarked that the magnificent settings and costumes as well as Hampden's staging glossed over their failings. Music from Walter Damrosch's 1913 opera on the story was used for background. With everything, including a general boom at the box office, falling into place, the revival achieved 250 performances.

The success of the next drama to premiere was probably also unexpected and left a number of critics shaking their heads. The play was Leon Gordon's **White Cargo** (11-5-23, Greenwich Village). The river steamboat that chugs its way up to a small West African clearing every three months will take home an employee of the nearby rubber plantation who can no longer stand the heat and loneliness and filth, and it will bring with it his replacement. Witzel (A. E. Anson), the boss, is contemptuous of quitters. He will stay for his contracted ten years if it means he must finally be carried out on "a nigger stretcher." His sole white companions are a besotted physician (Conway Wingfield) and a platitudinous missionary (J. Malcolm Dunn). The men discuss the newcomer, wondering how long he can hold out and whether he will succumb to the native women—especially the notorious mixed-race Tondeleyo. She has proven a thorn in Witzel's side: "Tondeleyo is the only really good looking nigger I've ever seen. Of course she is more than half white, but her blood and her instincts are all nigger." The newcomer is Langford (Richard Stevenson), and while he is full of confidence and optimism, there is instant animosity between him and Witzel. Witzel warns him that if he is not careful he will soon go native, first giving up shaving, then letting his clothes become filthy. On his very first night a figure (Annette Margules) appears in his doorway, announcing, "I am Tondeleyo." Six months later, Langford no longer shaves. The doctor warns him that he is showing dangerous signs and ought to go home, but Langford defiantly ripostes that he is all white, that he will remain white, and that in time he will become fully acclimatized. His use of the word "acclimatize" drives Witzel to fury. It soon is general knowledge that Langford is living with Tondeleyo—what the whites contemptuously call "mammy palavering"—but he truly astounds his associates by demanding that the missionary marry him and the girl. Telling the others that it is better than living in sin, the missionary agrees. However, Tondeleyo proves a poor wife, constantly begging Langford for more and more trinkets and sulking when she is not instantly gratified. The doctor attempts to teach her the obligations entailed in marriage, but she cannot or will not understand. Meanwhile, Langford grows slovenly and begins to drink too much. When Witzel catches the unhappy Tondeleyo attempting to poison Langford, he forces her to drink the poison and arranges for Langford to be returned home as useless white cargo. His replacement arrives on the same boat that will carry Langford away, and the new young man unwittingly gets off on a wrong foot by repeating much of what Langford had said on his arrival and assuring the others that he will soon be acclimatized. Although the play received some raves and some pans, Hornblow spoke for many when he wrote that it "leaves a bad taste, but it makes a strong impression." The play ran two years in New York and shortly sent out companies to span the nation. Its strong reception by the distinguished H. T. Parker of the *Boston Evening Transcript* went a long way to silencing that city's notorious censor.

Uptown, George S. Kaufman and Marc Connelly ran into a critical crossfire with **The Deep Tangled Wildwood** (11-5-23, Frazee). Their tale of a Broadway playwright (James Gleason) who satisfies his longing to return to his small-town roots only to discover that small towns have adopted big-city vices was pulled after just sixteen performances.

Carlos de Navarro and Sydney Stone's **A Love Scandal** (11-6-23, Ambassador) eked out eight performances more while detailing the story of a stylish American woman (Edith Taliaferro), who wins the Scotsman (Percy Waram) she has her eye on, despite her married rival's claiming that he is her lover. With the help of the husband (Norman Trevor) of the rival (Mona Kingsley), the American makes the other woman see the error of her ways.

On the other hand, Frederick Lonsdale had a season-long hit with **Spring Cleaning** (11-9-23, Eltinge). The London success describes how a husband (Arthur Byron) cures his wife (Violet Heming) of her predilection for a too raffish set by inviting a lady of the evening (Estelle Winwood) to a dinner party.

The next week brought in nothing but failures. Zoë Akins's **A Royal Fandango** (11-12-23, Plymouth) starred Ethel Barrymore as a princess who

seeks out an affair with a celebrated matador (Jose Alessandro) only to have him swoon at her feet. Later she runs off to the man's castle in Spain, but when she hears that there is a plot to kill the prince (Cyril Keightley), she grabs the first plane back home.

There were more lowly doings in William Hurlbut's **The Cup** (11-12-23, Fulton). Although Mary (Josephine Victor) is a pious Catholic she thinks nothing of living in sin with a common thief, Eddie (Tom Moore). But then her priest (O. P. Heggie) tells her that a cup believed to have been used in the Last Supper has reportedly come into the possession of a New York hood. Mary discovers Eddie has the cup and risks her life, defying her infuriated lover, to deliver it to the forgiving priest.

The least of the evening's openings was Fay Pulsifer and Cara Carelli's **Go West, Young Man** (11-12-23, Punch and Judy). It depicted the dilemma of Claude Merrill (Percy Helton), who must chose between his doting mother's wish to make him an artistic dancer or a young lady's determination to see him become a real man. The title gave away the answer, as if audiences couldn't tell anyway.

Even Somerset Maugham had no luck this week. His **The Camel's Back** (11-13-23, Vanderbilt) ran just a fortnight. During that time it recounted how an English politician (Charles Cherry) bumblingly attempts to rule his own roost but is thwarted by his clever wife (Violet Kemble Cooper).

David Carb and Walter Prichard Eaton's **Queen Victoria** (11-15-23, 48th St.) chronicled seven episodes in the monarch's life, beginning with her crowning and concluding with the celebration of her diamond jubilee. Beryl Mercer was Victoria. A dozen years would have to pass before a better play and a better player (though Miss Mercer was unsurpassed as a boozy sloven) would do justice to the story.

In Kilbourn Gordon and Arthur Caesar's **Out of the Seven Seas** (11-19-23, Frazee) Phyllis Stanton (Audrey Hart) is a drug addict who pays for her drugs by helping opium smugglers. She also turns her prospective brother-in-law, Ted Mason (Norval Keedwell), into an addict. Ashamed of himself, he flees to Hong Kong, followed by his loyal fiancée, Ann (Lotus Robb). There at a seedy den called the Café de Petit Paris, run by the louche Papa Dubois (George Marion), they encounter all manner of degradation until Ted springs the news that he is not really an addict but a Secret Service agent.

The Theatre Guild's second failure of the season was Winifred Katzin's translation of Henri-René Lenormand's **The Failures** (11-19-23, Garrick).

Against a background of Lee Simonson's purposely dingy settings, He (Jacob Ben Ami), a failed playwright, and She (Winifred Lenihan), an unsuccessful actress, struggle to make ends meet. But when He learns that She has been selling herself for pin money he kills her. In a dreary train station, the other members of their pathetic company, including their penniless producer (Dudley Digges), comment languidly on the incident, then doze off while waiting for their train.

The same evening, the Moscow Art Theatre began a return engagement at the Jolson, offering not only most of the plays they had offered last year but such additional pieces as Carlo Goldoni's *The Mistress of the Inn,* Ibsen's *An Enemy of the People,* Knut Hamsun's **In the Claws of Life,** Chekhov's **Uncle Vanya** and **Ivanoff,** and several other Russian works.

With Americans offering a stage biography of an English queen, England's John Drinkwater returned the compliment by presenting a study of an American general, **Robert E. Lee** (11-20-23, Ritz). The play begins with Virginia's secession and continues through the end of the war. Berton Churchill made a somber, dignified Lee, but neither his performance nor the play caught fire the way Drinkwater's earlier *Abraham Lincoln* had. In the minor role of the pessimistic Private David Peel, Alfred Lunt was praised (by Woollcott) for giving "a performance of distinguished beauty."

A booking crunch forced J. C. and Elliott Nugent's **Dumb-Bell** (11-26-23, Belmont) to premiere at a matinee. Critical reaction was so negative that the comedy was withdrawn after its second afternoon performance. Romeo (J. C. Nugent) is dismissed as hopelessly stupid by his village neighbors. His inventions are absurd, reflecting the fairy-tale world in which he lives. But he does help the romance of a neglected girl (Ruth Nugent) and her charming beau (Kenneth MacKenna). The grateful suitor turns Romeo's unsaleable mousetrap into a best-selling Christmas toy, letting all three live happily ever after.

Comedy and cast came together delightfully in Lynn Starling's **Meet the Wife** (11-26-23, Klaw). Mrs. Lennox (Mary Boland) is a bossy but less than brilliant matron, not so preoccupied with preparations to welcome a famous English writer who is to speak to her ladies' club to be unable to find time to accept a marriage proposal from the prissy, peevish esthete Victor Staunton (Clifton Webb). Of course, it's no real problem since she is accepting the proposal on behalf of her daughter, Doris (Eleanor Bellamy). Never mind that her daughter knows

nothing about it or that she adores a young newspaperman, Gregory Brown (Humphrey Bogart). After all, Gregory kept the girl out overnight, and thus got her into trouble at school. As for Mrs. Lennox, she is married to her second husband, the pliable, resigned Harvey Lennox (Charles Dalton), whom she wed just weeks after her first husband disappeared in the San Francisco quake. However, when the English author arrives he turns out to be husband number one. It seems that he used the excuse of his office's burning to escape his hectoring wife and to head overseas for a new life. Of course, there is consternation since Mrs. Lennox is now a bigamist. Number one, who calls himself Philip Lord (Ernest Lawford), takes it upon himself to see that Doris and Gregory are quietly wed, leaving the huffy Victor out in the cold. He is also sympathetic to Mr. Lennox's failed attempt to emulate him by setting fire to his own office (the place had been fireproofed). In the end, he heads back for England promising never to make public what the other characters and the audience have learned. Hornblow, who called the play "an original, witty, expert farce," went on, "Mary Boland has created a comedy character . . . the lovable fool, which deserves immortality. She is far funnier than the bromidic Dulcy, of whom she might have been mother." Thus, when Gregory, offering to fasten her dress, tells her that he often does it for his own mother, she accepts, saying, "Oh, well, of course if you have a mother of your own, I suppose there's no harm." And when it dawns on her that she is a bigamist, she muses, "I may as well take the veil for the rest of my life." Most of the supporting players also received glowing notices, although poor Bogart again was ignored by many of the critics. (*Variety,* which called Boland "the whole show," but then went on to praise most of the cast, passed over Bogart by noting that he was "a clean-looking juvenile and made a pleasant lover.") The play ran until hot weather and an actors' strike discouraged playgoers.

The evening's other comedy, Arthur Henry's **Time** (11-26-23, 39th St.), went out with the old year, five weeks later. Jim Prescott (A. H. Van Buren) has tired of his wife (Dorothy Francis) and wants to divorce her in order to marry their widowed neighbor (Margaret Mower). But Prescott's mother (Marie Curtis) concocts a story about his father's relationship to a scarlet lady that scares him out of his plan. After the Prescotts' daughter (Lucile Nikolas) and the widow's son (William Kirkland) elope—with Grandma's help—and have a child of their own, all the parties are reconciled. One small novelty was the play's setting—a camp in the Maine woods.

The run of **Sancho Panza** (11-26-23, Hudson), which Sidney Howard adapted from Menyhért Lengyel's Hungarian play, paralleled that of *Time*. It told of Sancho Panza's being made governor of Barataria on orders from the Duke (Russ Whytal). The Duke means it to be a joke, humoring the delusions of Sancho (Otis Skinner) and the demented knight (Robert Robson) with whom the peasant travels. He governs so wisely and so fairly that the people demand he remain after courtiers, tiring of the joke, depose him. But Sancho has found his responsibilities too worrying, so he mounts his donkey (Robert Rosaire) and heads home. Imagine Skinner's dismay when he was mentioned only briefly or even totally passed over in some notices, especially when the actor who played the ass was regularly singled out for praise. Richard Boleslawski's staging was also lauded, but the main kudos went to the colorful, stylized costumes and settings by Emilie Hapgood and James Reynolds. Besides the lavish rooms of the castle, the sets depicted an empty roadside in Andalusia and a cathedral square. Broun, treating the evening largely as spectacle, called it "constantly enthralling." For most of his remaining career, Skinner stuck with revivals of plays from his heyday or of classics, only twice, some years on, chancing new vehicles (one of which failed to make it to New York).

The same busy Monday also saw John Barrymore come into the mammoth Manhattan Opera House for three more weeks as Hamlet.

Eleanor Robson (long since Mrs. Augustus Belmont and retired from the stage) and Harriet Ford combined their talents to write **In the Next Room** (11-27-23, Vanderbilt). Playgoers who might have expected the actress-turned-society-lady-and-philanthropist to write something arty (especially after noticing that Winthrop Ames and Guthrie McClintic were co-producers) misjudged the situation. The new play was a spine-chilling mystery. Philip Vantine (Wright Kramer) has ordered a copy of a famous buhlwork cabinet made and shipped to him. But when the cabinet arrives it proves to be the original, which is believed to have secret compartments housing embarrassing love notes and some fabulous diamonds. Its arrival is followed promptly by the appearance of a man who identifies himself as Felix Armand (Claude King), the son of the Frenchman who sold the piece to Vantine. He has hurried to America to correct the mistake. But his visit is interrupted, first by the murder of an unidentified foreigner in Vantine's waiting room, then by the murder of Vantine himself. James Godfrey (Arthur Albertson), a reporter for the *New York Record* and in love with Vantine's niece (Mary Kennedy), gets word that a famous French jewel thief, Crochard, is in the country for reasons unknown and that Scotland Yard's equally famous Colonel Piggott has come to America in pursuit of him. Act II ends with Godfrey surprising a burglar at the Vantine home and the supposed intruder coolly identifying himself as Piggott. The New York police are baffled, but Godfrey is eventually able to wrestle the killer to the floor. He tells the policeman, "I've got your man inspector! Allow me to introduce Monsieur Crochard, alias Felix Armand, alias Colonel Piggott." The killer had murdered the real Armand and had stuffed the compartments with a chemical that released poisonous vapors when exposed to the air.

David Belasco and Tom Cushing's **Laugh, Clown, Laugh!** (11-28-23, Belasco), taken from Fausto Martini's Italian drama, starred the third Barrymore to come before the critics in just over two weeks, Lionel. A famous Italian clown, Tito Beppi (Barrymore), consults a psychologist (Henry Herbert) to learn why he is always unhappy and prone to crying jags. He is told his malaise stems from his repressed love for his ward, Simonetta (Irene Fenwick), who has accompanied him to the doctor's office. Unfortunately, an attractive young nobleman, Luigi Ravelli (Ian Keith), given to uncontrollable laughter, is in the waiting room at the same time. The doctor tells the nobleman to give up drinking and try living with the traveling players for a while. He does, and Luigi and Simonetta fall in love. When Tito tearfully confronts Luigi with his suspicions, Luigi again breaks out in laughter. Tito recognizes that for all her decent intentions Simonetta can never love him, only pity him. Going to his room and surrounding himself with mirrors and candles, he goes through his best routines, finds them more pathetic than funny, and so stabs himself to death. Critics viewed Barrymore variously as "uneven," "without tragic feeling," or "without flaw," yet even those who admired his work conscientiously reported a lack of audience response. The drama ran for 133 performances, the last run of any size Barrymore would enjoy before leaving live theatre for films.

Hutcheson Boyd's **The Talking Parrot** (12-3-23, Frazee) was one of those plays that critics pounce on and gleefully label the "worst of the season," long before the season is finished. During its one-week stand it described the antics of a dead husband (Jack Cherry) who returns to haunt his widow's suitors.

Flashbacks helped Martin Brown tell his story of

The Lady (12-4-23, Empire). At a bar she runs in Le Havre for sailors and travelers, Polly Pearl (Mary Nash) recounts her history to a sympathetic customer. The cockney Polly had married a well-born Englishman who ultimately deserted her for more elegant ladies. She fell on hard, occasionally sordid times and had her young son taken away from her by court order. She has no sooner told her story than two young customers get into an argument and one kills the other in self-defense. The shooter turns out to be her son, so she self-sacrificingly claims she fired the gun. A kindly police officer knows better and lets both mother and son go. This hodgepodge of unoriginal motifs and techniques gave some promise of appealing to the public but ultimately was withdrawn after eleven weeks.

Less than two weeks had to suffice for Jane Cowl's mounting of Maurice Maeterlinck's *Pelleas and Melisande,* which Mrs. Patrick Campbell had offered to Broadway twenty-one years before and which the younger actress brought into the Times Square on the 4th. Cowl assumed the role of the beautiful princess who dies after her lover, Pelleas (Rollo Peters), is slain by his jealous older brother (Louis Hector). Jazz-age reviewers found the acting and production beautiful but the play deadly static.

By contrast, they found much to enjoy in **The Potters** (12-10-23, Plymouth), dramatized by J. P. McEvoy from his *Chicago Tribune* stories. The Potters, led by the amiable but not very adroit Pa Potter (Donald Meek), have to struggle to make ends meet. Then the daughter, Mamie (Mary Carroll), crosses paths with a bunko fortune teller (Josephine Deffry), who advises her to invest in oil stocks. The credulous Mamie convinces her equally gullible father to do just that, and she also dumps her adoring beau, the dashing carrot-topped lifeguard Red Miller (Douglas Hunter). Matters take a turn for the worse until the loyal Red and the worthless stocks prove more valuable than the fortune teller could have imagined. The action moved swiftly from the Potter house to a trolley car, a train, and a street with the family in a rundown old auto. Typical of the play's humor was a line by one of the strap-hangers in the packed trolley: "A sardine has this on us, he doesn't have to stand on end." The comedy ran into the summer.

The fading Leo Ditrichstein closed his career after the disappointing run of Gladys Unger's **The Business Widow** (12-10-23, Ritz). He played a rich, middle-aged businessman whose inconsiderate young wife (Lola Fisher) uses his associates as errand boys and has furriers deliver her chinchillas and ermines to her husband's office so that she can try them on there. He

lets her run off with a skirt-chasing Greek (John Davidson), but when she comes humbly back he tells her she can return only if she agrees to be more thoughtful and less of a spendthrift.

A revival of *The Shadow,* Ethel Barrymore's 1915 success, this time without a star of her caliber, came into the 39th Street on the 18th and left a fortnight later.

Belasco's career still had a number of years to run, but the once all but infallible producer was increasingly identified with too many failures, such as **The Other Rose** (12-20-23, Morosco), George Middleton's Americanization of Edouard Bourdet's *L'Heure du berger.* When Rose Coe (Fay Bainter) rents a summer cottage in Maine, she discovers that the owner's son (Henry Hull) is furious, since he had wooed another woman named Rose in that very cottage. The two glower at each other but in time fall in love, so when the first Rose (Carlotta Monterey) reappears she is politely sent on her way.

Christmas Eve brought in two quick failures. Anne Morrison's **The Wild Westcotts** (12-24-23, Frazee) spotlighted a zany family, which is never more so than on the day Agatha (Vivian Martin), having been ditched by an older man she doted on, plans to wed Eddie Hudson (Elliott Nugent). Her elder sister (Isabel Withers) arrives bearing her newborn babe and the news that she has left her husband. Problems are ironed out and the wedding finally allowed to proceed.

In **The Alarm Clock** (12-24-23, 39th St.), Avery Hopwood's adaptation of Maurice Hennequin and Romain Coolus's Paris hit, comic complications set in after the polished Bobby Brandon (Bruce McRae) invites his country cousin (Harold Vermilyea), the cousin's fiancée (Marion Coakley), and the fiancée's mother (Blanche Ring) to visit him in New York. Bobby and the fiancée quickly fall in love, as do the cousin and a *Follies* beauty (Helen Flint).

The lone non-musical novelty to open on Christmas night was Olga Petrova's **Hurricane** (12-25-23, Frolic), with the playwright starred as Ilka, a Russian immigrant abused by her cruel Texas stepfather. She kills hims, runs off to Kansas City, and there makes so much money as a prostitute that she comes east and sets up as a fashionable interior decorator. She is courted by two men who are aware of her past but nonetheless love her. However, her own feelings of guilt drive her to take an overdose of morphine.

A revival of Materlinck's *The Blue Bird* also opened on Christmas night. But the highly praised mounting at the Jolson found only enough takers to keep it going for a month.

The curtain rose on Leon Cunningham's **Neighbors** (12-26-23, 48th St.) to reveal the interiors of two modest midwestern suburban homes, side by side. One home belongs to the Hicks family. The father (Frederick Burton) of the house is a horticulturist experimenting with odorless onions in his garden. The other house is owned by the Stones. Mrs. Stone (Helen Strickland) has a pet rooster. After the rooster, set free by a malicious neighbor, plays havoc with the onions, all hell breaks loose, and even the love of young Phoebe Hicks (Ruth Nugent) for Crawford Stone (Warren Lyons) is no help. Thanks to an odd arrangement, supposedly not uncommon in the area, the Stones turn off the Hickses' gas just as the Hickses are about to prepare dinner. In revenge the Hickses shut off the Stones' water supply when Mr. Stone, having swept his chimney, is about to take a bath. A quiet, sensible Mrs. Hicks finally brings reason and peace to the households. The actress who played her won the most favorable reviews. She had begun her career as Josephine Sherwood, retired after marrying, and, now a widow, returned using her married name, Josephine Hull. Yet many seasons would have to pass by before she achieved full recognition and late stardom.

Percy MacKaye's **This Fine-Pretty World** (12-26-23, Neighborhood Playhouse) received no recognition and so fell permanently from view. His story was set in the Kentucky mountains and focused on the effort of Gilly Maggot (Perry Ivans) to "get shet of" his wife (Aline MacMahon) so that he can wed the voluptuous Goldy Shoop (Joanna Roos). He hires Beem Spaulding (E. J. Ballantine), a notorious "defamin' attorney," to handle the case. But for all the "lie-swearin'" Gilly loses. His consternation is doubled when he then learns that Goldy has eloped with another man.

The theatre crunch continued, forcing yet another play, Wilson Collison's **The Vagabond** (12-27-23, Apollo), to grab for attention at matinees. A duel of guns and wits ensues when Sheriff Buck Jepson (Robert T. Haines) goes seeking a suspected murderess and finds her in the arms of a mean-faced, gun-laden bandit, Señor Santchez (Louis Bennison). In the end, Santchez is shown to be a gentlemanly California landowner, and he is allowed to head home with his new bride, who has proved to be innocent. By way of compensation, the sheriff arrests the real killer.

In George Bernard Shaw's **Saint Joan** (12-28-23, Garrick), Joan of Arc (Winifred Lenihan) helps to save France only to be betrayed in the end by jealous courtiers and the church. Even her ghost cannot change the narrow vision of her former friends, and she falls on her knees asking God how long it will be before the world can understand its saints. The Theatre Guild gave the Shaw play a magnificent mounting. Lenihan was praised for her admirable if not truly impassioned performance. The play ran out the season.

That oddity of the era, a play about Negroes enacted by whites in blackface, surfaced again with Nan Bagby Stephens's **Roseanne** (12-29-23, Greenwich Village). In her backwater Georgia community, the pious laundrywoman Roseanne (Chrystal Herne) has such blind faith in the Reverend Cicero Brown (John Harrington) that she hands over her adopted daughter, Leola (Kathleen Comegys), to him for spiritual guidance. Instead the corrupt, hypocritical minster leads the girl into thievery, drugs and death. Roseanne, her eyes opened at last and blazing with fury, harangues the congregation to lynch the cleric, but when her fury is spent she agrees to let God decide the man's punishment. Having been exposed to Charles Gilpin's emperor and to other adroit black performances, critics were coming to see the absurdity of casting whites in blackface, and the practice would soon disappear on more serious stages.

At another theatre "off Broadway"—although the expression had yet to be coined—this one uptown on East 78th Street, Nance O'Neil appeared briefly in Rafael Marti Orbera's Spanish drama, **Madre** (12-29-29, Lenox Hill), portraying a mother whose son is killed by her stepson in a fight over a girl.

George M. Cohan rang down the curtain on the old year as **The Song and Dance Man** (12-31-23, Hudson). Hap Farrell (Cohan) a small-time vaudevillian, falls on hard times after the death of his partner, the Carroll of Farrell and Carroll. Yet the good-hearted Hap empties his pockets to help a struggling actress, Leona Lane (Mayo Methot). Now totally penniless, Hap attempts to hold up a man. The man, after foiling Hap's scheme, turns out to be a rich illustrator (Frederick Perry), who, with a producer friend (Louis Calhern), agrees to underwrite Hap and Leola for a time. Leola proves a big success; Hap, a talentless failure. He heads west, where he eventually makes a pile in mining. But the call of the footlights is irresistible, and he returns to take his chance again in New York. He learns that Leola had become a big star and then retired. He convinces her "there's no happiness for people of the theatre outside of the theatre," and the two agree to face the uncertain future together. Critics found the play creaky and contrived but were awed by Cohan's performance, especially his ability and willingness to do a turn as a patently mediocre trouper. Without any irony Broun observed that Cohan "is cast as a bad actor and he does it so beautifully that you believe him." Nonetheless *The Song and Dance Man* fell four performances short of the charmed century mark.

The new year was launched down in the Village, where Kenneth Macgowan, Eugene O'Neill, and Robert Edmond Jones had taken over the quiescent Provincetown Players. (The three men changed the group's name to The Experimental Theater, Incorporated, but the public ignored the change.) Their first offering was August Strindberg's **The Spook Sonata** (1-3-24, Provincetown Playhouse), a "half-fantasy" featuring a cripple (Stanley Howlett), his wife (Clare Eames), who lives in a cupboard, thinks she is a parrot, and is called "The Mummy," his crippled daughter (Helen Freeman), and a young student (Walter Abel) who admires the girl. The cripple is eventually shown to be a murderer and hangs himself in his wife's cupboard. The play baffled critics and audiences, and the actors' employment of masks further confused matters. The production closed after three weeks.

The same theatre shortage that forced *Dumb-Bell* and *The Vagabond* to try for a normal run by first presenting matinee performances forced Hatcher Hughes's **Hell-Bent fer Heaven** (1-4-24, Klaw) to do the same thing. But unlike the earlier failures, the play received rave notices and was hurriedly moved into a regular run. Its setting was the increasingly voguish Appalachian Mountains. Here the Lowrys and the Hunts have been feuding violently for generations, but all that may be set aside now that Sid Hunt (George Abbott) has been courting Jude Lowry (Margaret Borough). Only Rufe Prior (John F. Hamilton) is opposed. He was a draft dodger, and his guilt about that has made him a warped religious fanatic. He craves Jude for himself, so he hopes to rekindle the feud by having Jude's brother Andy (Glenn Anders) kill Sid. He almost succeeds before his treachery is exposed. Then Andy would shoot him, but grampa Hunt (Augustin Duncan) contrives to allow the craven Rufe to escape. "You darned old Christian! You'll save me from hell yit!" Andy tells the old man. Shortly after it closed, the play was awarded the Pulitzer Prize, immediately sparking a controversy, since the judges had voted for another work and were overruled by higher-ups.

Critics felt that Cosmo Hamilton's **The New Poor** (1-7-24, Playhouse) was a good idea mishandled. In a desperate search for servants the Welbys hire some exiled Russian nobles, led by Princess Irina (Lillian Kemble Cooper) and the Grand Duke Boris (Lyn Harding). The younger Welbys fall in love with the younger immigrants even though the Russians are mistaken for art thieves for a time. Finally the new servants are seen to be neither thieves nor Russians, but all ends happily.

Endings were the subject of Sutton Vane's **Outward Bound** (1-7-24, Ritz), set on a ship carrying the newly dead to the hereafter. Most applauded among the cast were Alfred Lunt as the hard-drinking young Mr. Prior, Beryl Mercer as the cockney who is shown to be his mother, Dudley Digges as the Reverend Thompson, the Examiner who determines where each character will spend Eternity, and Leslie Howard and Margalo Gillmore as a pair of suicidal lovers who are given another chance. The play ran into the spring.

Oscar Hammerstein II and Milton Herbert Gropper were the authors of **Gypsy Jim** (1-14-24, 49th St.). The colorfully garbed gypsy (Leo Carrillo) appears suddenly at the unhappy Blake household. He seems omniscient, telling them what they had for dinner and how much money Mr. Blake (George Farren) has in his pocket. He finds the suicidal son (Wallace Ford) an outlet for his inventiveness, prevents the daughter (Martha-Bryan Allen) from eloping with a scoundrel, then helps her get her writing published, sets Mr. Blake's failing law practice on the road to recovery, and finds a long-lost daughter of Mrs. Blake's (Elizabeth Patterson) late, beloved brother. Then Jim disappears. It later turns out that he is an eccentric, half-gypsy millionaire, who, with the aid of associates and using his influence with companies he owns, has played the same game elsewhere. In this instance, he wins the hand of the daughter. All through the evening Jim breaks out in lyrical couplets (Hammerstein's?) such as "A gypsy in an automobile, I fear, / Is much like putting roller skates on a deer." Woollcott summed up the critical reaction with a couplet of his own: "Oscar Hammerstein 2nd and Milton Gropper / Wrote a comedy that came an awful cropper."

Henry Miller also came a cropper with Laurence Eyre's **Fanshastics** (1-16-24, Henry Miller's), in which the paths of two sisters (Grace George and Laura Hope Crews), separated at birth, later cross without their recognizing one another. One has become a society grande dame, the other is married to an Irish squatter who lives in a shack across from Central Park. Their husbands squabble over who owns the land the shack sits on; their children fall in love. The action was set in 1873. Even an immediate change of title to *Merry Wives of Gotham* could not save the play.

Probably the most talked about production of the season was Max Reinhardt's mounting of Karl Vollmoeller's **The Miracle** (1-16-24, Century). For this story of a nun (Rosamund Pinchot) who runs away from her nunnery to try the pleasures of the world and years later returns to discover that the Virgin Mary (Lady Diana Manners) has taken her place while she was away, Norman Bel Geddes turned the huge auditorium into a breathtaking medieval cathedral, and, at times, several hundred performers crowded the stage. Because of the vastness of the house, much of the play came across as pantomime, but there was no misunderstanding the basic story.

. . .

Norman Bel Geddes [né Norman Melancton Geddes] (1893-1958) was born in Adrian, Mich., and studied at art schools in Cleveland and Chicago. His first designs were for *Nju* in 1916 in Los Angeles. Otto Kahn brought him to New York to create sets for the Metropolitan Opera. He then moved to the legitimate stage. Although a dedicated modernist who would draw beautiful art deco settings for many shows, especially musicals, some of his finest and best-remembered achievements were to be in more traditional designs, such as those for *The Miracle*.

. . .

In George Middleton's **The Road Together** (1-17-24, Frazee) an argument between a devoted, high-principled wife (Marjorie Rambeau) and her husband (A. E. Anson), a district attorney who wants to sell out to vested interests, leads first to the realization that both have taken on lovers and then to the acknowledgment that they still love and need each other. Critics complained that Rambeau stumbled over her lines, but that they were not all that interesting anyway, and dismissed the whole affair as "uneven, faltering and turgid."

Nor did reviewers welcome the Theatre Guild's production of Wilhelm von Scholz's **The Race with the Shadow** (1-20-24, Garrick), as translated by Graham and Tristan Rawson. It told how a novelist (Arnold Daly) brings troubles on himself by writing a fictionalized account of a love affair his wife (Helen Westley) once had with a younger man (Jacob Ben Ami).

Brock Pemberton, having garnered prestige and enjoyed a certain success with Pirandello's *Six Characters in Search of an Author*, tried again with the playwright's *Enrico IV*, in an Arthur Livingston translation pretentiously entitled **The Living Mask** (1-21-24, 44th St.) It told of a reveler (Arnold Korff), disguised as Henry IV, who comes to believe

he truly is the king. The play's failure prompted Pemberton to rush back in *Six Characters*.

Pemberton had a second failure when he offered **Mr. Pitt** (1-22-24, 39th St.), Zona Gale's dramatization of her novel *Birth*. Marshall Pitt (Walter Huston) is an openhearted, charming oaf—"a masculine Pollyanna," whose wife (Minna Gombell), craving more excitement and sophistication, runs off with a trombone player from a tent show, taking her baby son with her. Twenty years later the grown boy (Borden Harriman) meets his now prosperous father but also rejects him as too uncouth. Corbin, reporting that "the lobby was buzzing with the excited query as to just who this Walter Huston may be," hailed him as an actor "of the first order."

A far more dismal failure was Julia Chandler and Alethea Luce's **The Gift** (1-22-24, Greenwich Village), which unfolded the teary tale of Yvonne Dubois (Doris Kenyon), who sets about to reform Richard Bain (Pedro de Cordoba), an irresponsible American expatriate studying art in the Latin Quarter, and who dies in his arms as soon as she has accomplished her goal.

For a third time, Katharine Cornell attempted a role in a Clemence Dane play. In **The Way Things Happen** (1-28-24, Lyceum) she portrayed Shirley Pride, who long had loved her foster brother, Martin Farren (Tom Nesbitt), in silence. He is about marry the vulgar Muriel Hanbury (Helen Robbins) when it is learned he has stolen bonds to pay for his fiancée's jewels. Bennett Lomax (Ivan Simpson) holds the incriminating evidence and agrees to give it to Shirley if she will sleep with him. She does. Martin, horrified at her sacrifice, which he holds against her, confesses and is sent to jail. Two years later his mother's death brings Martin home. He is still cold to Shirley, until her fury makes him realize his true feelings for her. While condemning the play's absurdity, Hornblow asked about Cornell, "With a singularly expressive face, one which reflects physical as well as spiritual beauty, a strangely pliable mask, now of surpassing loveliness, now repellently ugly, a keen intelligence, a cultivated, appealing voice . . . what role is there this actress might not attempt?"

Lewis Beach's **The Goose Hangs High** (1-29-24, Bijou) broke the run of flops and near misses. It was produced by the Dramatists' Theatre, a soon-to-disappear group of playwrights determined to chart their own course, much like the later, more enduring Playwrights' Company. When Granny (Mrs. Whiffen) learns that her daughter and son-in-law (Katherine Gray and Norman Trevor) have sacrificed to buy one of their sons an expensive book he wants, she moans, " 'Wanting' and 'getting' mean the same thing in this house. Oh, their goose hangs high!" Indeed, the children are thoughtless and selfish, until they learn that their father has had to resign from his government post and cannot afford to help with expenses for the wedding of the older brother (John Marston) or continue the college education of his young son (Eric Dressler) and daughter (Miriam Doyle). Then they willingly give up their ambitions and pitch in. A plan to allow Mr. Ingals to open a nursery, a dream he has long held, offers a glimmer of promise at the final curtain. Although a number of reviewers complained about the unconvincing happy ending, they otherwise enjoyed what Burns Mantle welcomed as a "true and observantly written" comedy. It played until the hot weather.

Despite largely unfavorable notices, Robert Presnell's **Rust** (1-31-24, Greenwich Village) held out for more than ten weeks. Believing he killed the villainous, hulking Miguel (Leslie King) with a rusty nail, José (Clarke Silvernail) has fled to Valencia, where his work with smugglers and his songwriting sideline make him rich. He returns to his old home to discover that Miguel has survived and has married the girl (Selena Royle) José loves. But when Miguel again looms threateningly over the scene, José's father (Ralf Belmont), a junk dealer, grabs another rusty nail and finishes him off.

Although it was not a novelty, February's first entry might well have been considered one, for it was Anna Cora Mowatt's 1845 success, *Fashion,* revived by the new order at the Provincetown Playhouse on the 3rd. The story of how Mrs. Tiffany (Clare Eames) is taught the virtues of a simple life, thanks in good measure to a sensible Yankee, Adam Trueman (Perry Ivins), was rearranged, played as a spoof, and larded with period songs touched up by Deems Taylor. Joyously welcomed, it ran for 235 performances—more than ten times the run of the original.

Oliver Morosco, his career sliding fast, was the producer of Willis Maxwell Goodhue's **Myrtie** (2-4-24, 52nd St.), which was openly scoffed at by critics and playgoers alike. Its heroine (Selma Haley) defies both her father (Pete Raymond) and her priest (Harry Minturn) to run off, without benefit of clergy, with a rich old man.

The next entry was even more rapturously received than *Fashion* had been and became the season's biggest success, with 571 performances to its total when it closed. Expanded from a vaudeville sketch the author had written, **The Show-Off** (2-5-24, Playhouse) indisputably consolidated George Kelly's reputation. The Fishers are lower-middle-class Phila-delphians, and they are chagrined that their younger daughter, Amy (Regina Wallace), is in love with Aubrey Piper (Louis John Bartels). When he parades around their parlor in his patent leather shoes and his slick toupee, with a carnation in his buttonhole, calling himself "the pride of old West Philly," the Fishers conclude he is not only a nut but crazy as well. Yet Amy agrees to marry him despite the barbed warnings of her mother (Helen Lowell). He proves a poor provider, constantly borrowing from his brother-in-law (Guy d'Ennery), who must also go bail for him after, driving a borrowed car, he hits both a trolley and a policeman. Of course, Aubrey is not worried about losing his license, since he hasn't any. Just after Mr. Fisher (C. W. Goodrich) dies and the future looks darkest, the family learns that brother Joe (Lee Tracy) has been awarded $100,000 for a rustproofing invention, inadvertently suggested to Joe by Aubrey. In fact, Aubrey has barged into the office of the people dickering with Joe and bulldozed them into doubling their initial offer. He tells the family that a little bluff goes a long way. The deflated Mrs. Fisher can merely sigh, "God help me, from now on." Broun, in his preface to the published play, called it "the best comedy which has yet been written by an American" (a hyperbolic statement he had earlier made about *Clarence* and several other plays), and the Pulitzer jury more or less agreed, only to be overridden by Columbia University officials.

The New Englander (2-7-24, 48th St.) of Abby Merchant's drama was stern, moralizing Mrs. Ellery (Katherine Emmet), who urges her prospective daughter-in-law (Louise Huff) to sue her son, Seth (Alan Birmingham), when she discovers he has misappropriated the girl's moneys. Seth runs away, prompting his mother to kill herself to teach him what high principles mean.

A much younger girl attempted suicide in Robert Presnell's second play in as many weeks, **Saturday Night** (2-9-24, Cherry Lane). She is a shopgirl prone to dance by her Greenwich Village apartment's open window. A not very nice producer, seeing her, offers her fame. But his price so repels her that she jumps from the window. An attractive jazz drummer is there to comfort her and offer her a happier life. Those critics who bothered to review the play gave it a sharp thumbs down.

The month's second hit was George S. Kaufman and Marc Connelly's **Beggar on Horseback** (2-12-24, Broadhurst), a reworking of Paul Apel's *Hans Sonnenstössers Höllenfahrt* that many of New York's critics felt ended up singularly American in tone. Because Neil McRae (Roland Young) can barely scrape by doing hack orchestrations, his neighbors

Cynthia Mason (Kay Johnson) and Dr. Rice (Richard Barbee) quietly look after his welfare. Just before the arrival of friends from Neil's hometown, the doctor gives Neil a sleeping pill. The friends are the Cadys, whose daughter, Gladys (Ann Carpenter), wants to marry Neil. Mr. Cady offers to take Neil into his prosperous widget business; he will even allow Neil to write songs on the side, so long as they make a million dollars. The Cadys leave and Neil takes the pill. He dreams he is marrying Gladys, whose wedding bouquet is composed of banknotes. At home, two butlers appear and Gladys orders them, "Announce somebody!" With each announcement the butlers increase, until at least twelve are announcing visitors. At work, Neil is required to fill out endless forms to requisition a simple pencil. Exasperated, he murders the family. Newsboys run up and down the aisles hawking a paper detailing the crime. "Judge" Cady presides at Neil's trial and proclaims, "This thing of using the imagination has got to stop!" Neil awakes from his nightmare and realizes it is Cynthia whom he must marry. The expressionistic settings of the dream ("interminable corridors and endless mirrors"), a dance-pantomime to more Deems Taylor music, and Roland Young's droll playing all helped the comedy, which Woollcott called "a small and facetious disturbance in the rear of the Church of the Gospel of Success," run more than six months.

Critics, if not the public, were equally delighted with another dream play, **The Wonderful Visit** (2-12-24, Lenox Hill), dramatized by St. John Ervine from an H. G. Wells story. A rather unworldly curate (Robert LeSueur) falls asleep and dreams that an angel (Margaret Mower) comes to him to help set things right in his village. The villagers' reactions embitter the angel, but she assures the minister that someday there will be a better world.

All the while playing in *The Swan,* Eva Le Gallienne and many of her supporting players combined their efforts to mount a revival of Gerhart Hauptmann's *The Assumption of Hannele,* with the young star as the visionary, abused little girl who dies and goes to heaven. The mounting was offered for a series of matinees, beginning on the 15th. Le Gallienne stirred up controversy by refusing to admit patrons who arrived late. Woollcott was one of the latecomers and subsequently wrote an article urging all managers to follow the policy, provided they kept to the announced curtain time.

Oscar Hammerstein II and Milton Herbert Gropper had even less success with **New Toys** (2-18-24, Fulton) than with *Gypsy Jim.* Despite their new baby, Will and Ruth Webb (Ernest Truex and Vivienne Osbourne) have pressing outside interests. She wants to be an actress, and he looks to an extramarital affair. Only Ruth's mother (Louise Closser Hale) keeps matters on an even keel until the failures of Ruth's play and Will's playing around bring them home again. Almost all the good notices went to Truex but could not save the "comic tragedy."

Critics let Jane Cowl's revival of *Antony and Cleopatra* at the Lyceum on the 19th down as gently as possible, for they admired her willingness to take risks and the basic good taste she offered. But she was hardly the brash, earthy queen that Shakespeare drew, and Rollo Peters's warrior lacked the requisite snarling toughness and driven sensuality. Peters's settings were beautiful to look at but cumbersome to change, so that even with substantial cuts the evening ran long.

Critics also saw the choice of performers as wrong in **The Moon-Flower** (2-25-24, Astor), Zoë Akins's version of Lajos Biró's *Az utolsó csók* (The Last Kiss). A young lawyer, Peter (Sidney Blackmer), decides to use a small inheritance for a gorgeous fling and then commit suicide. Coming to Monte Carlo, he falls in love with a duke's mistress (Elsie Ferguson), so sets aside his desire to die. But after a brief night together, the woman sets off with the duke on his yacht, leaving Peter once again to reconsider his future. Critics felt the red-wigged Ferguson sounded too American to be taken for a worldly courtesan, and Blackmer conveyed no sense of fervent passion.

Karen Bramson's Danish play **The Strong** (2-26-24, 49th St.), translated by Henry Baron, was yet another play hoping to find a regular berth after starting out at matinees. It told of a girl who kills herself after being forced to choose between the hunchback who rescued her from a cruel father or her young, good-looking lover. Two matinees were enough.

The Theatre Guild, continuing its devotion to foreign plays, sponsored Ernö Vajda's *A délibáb* (The Mirage), in James L. A. Burrell's translation, as **Fata Morgana** (3-3-24, Garrick). Its story of a short, impassioned night of love that leads nowhere was a little like *The Moon-Flower*'s. In this instance a beautiful, married woman (Emily Stevens) finds an attractive young relative (Morgan Farley) alone in his village home after his family has gone away. She seduces him, but when her husband arrives the next day, she tells the boy to think of their affair as a pleasant mirage. In a run broken for a time by an actors' strike, it ran into the fall.

A second foreign play, Dorothy Brandon's London drama **The Outsider** (3-3-24, 49th St.), ran just half as long. What limited success it had was credited to Katharine Cornell, brought in as a last-minute replacement. She played Lalage Sturdee, a girl deemed a hopeless cripple. But Anton Ragatzy (Lionel Atwill), called a quack by all the great doctors, including Lalage's father (Lester Lonergan), believes he can cure her by stretching her on a rack. When his work is done and he tries to show the doctors his achievement, Lalage remains helpless on the floor where she has fallen. But the doctors' sneers infuriate her. She struggles to her feet, nearly falls again, then walks totteringly into Ragatzy's embrace. "Thrilling" and "covers herself with glory" were critical assessments of Cornell's restrained, moving performance.

Benjamin F. Glazer's **Tyrants** (3-4-24, Cherry Lane) was taken from something called *The Tragedy of Eumenes* by someone named Thaddeus Rittner—those critics who reviewed the play were unsure who Rittner was. It took a comic view of a timid soul (Henry Wagstaff Gribble) drafted by revolutionaries to kill a dictator and of his life as a galley slave after he bungles the job.

At the Fulton Maurice de Feraudy, advertised as a modern day Coquelin, began a short engagement offering such plays as Octave Mirbeau's *Les Affaires sont les affaires* and Molière's *L'Avare*. He was received politely but failed to generate the excitement Coquelin and some of his contemporaries had.

In Israel Zangwill's **We Moderns** (3-11-24, Gaiety) Richard Sundale (Kenneth MacKenna) and his sister, Mary (Helen Hayes), react against the stodgy Victorian attitudes of their parents (O. P. Heggie and Isabel Irving) and live in a wild, hedonistic manner until Richard finds true love (with a woman pregnant by another man) and Mary has to tend to her dangerously ill mother.

Still another flop was Alice and Frank Mandel's **The Lady Killer** (3-12-24, Morosco). To prove a point about the uselessness of circumstantial evidence, Jack Kennedy (Paul Kelly), the son of a film writer, and his lawyer friend, Henry Meecham (Harold Vermilyea), stage a fake murder, with the lawyer as the supposed victim. When Jack is accused of the crime, his sweetheart (Claiborne Foster), believing no pretty girl is ever convicted, takes the blame. Comic misunderstandings and a romantic denouement follow, aided by a not wholly cynical detective (James Gleason) and the lawyer's timely reappearance.

Critics applauded James K. Hackett's manly, introspective Macbeth, divided over the Lady Macbeth of Clare Eames, and condemned the heavy,

old-fashioned scenery. The public remained indifferent to the production, which opened at the 48th Street Theatre on the 15th.

But the public was even less receptive to Eugene O'Neill's **Welded** (3-17-24, 39th St.). Michael Cape (Jacob Ben Ami), a playwright, and his wife, Eleanor (Doris Keane), find their love is strangling and intimidating. Both attempt to seek satisfaction with others and fail. They recognize that they are welded in love for better and worse, with Cape stating, "We'll torture and tear . . . fail and hate again . . . but!— fail *with pride*—with joy!" Reviewers objected to Ben Ami's heavy emoting and Keane's curious hollowness. They respected O'Neill's integrity but wrote the play off as a failure, some gently ("can scarcely be called a highly original or distinquished play"), some more harshly ("prodigiously dull").

A virtual committee—Leonidas Westervelt, John Clements, Harvey O'Higgins, and Harriet Ford— were the authors of **Sweet Seventeen** (3-17-24, Lyceum), in which a teenager called Peeks Farnum (Marian Mears) resorts to all sorts of tricks, including dressing as a boy and attempting to run off with her sister's fiancé, to bring order into what she perceives as her disorganized family.

A second French performer, Mme. Simone, an actress described as subscribing to an older, emotional school, began a series of matinee performances at the Gaiety on the 21st. Her repertory started with Henri Bataille's *La Vierge folle*. Interestingly, along with her fellow French players, José Ruben and Eva Le Gallienne joined in the presentations.

The sad parade of failures continued for the rest of the month. Richard A. Purdy's **Across the Street** (3-24-24, Hudson) came first. Two men who have grudgingly followed in their fathers' footsteps look longingly on each other's occupation. So the newspaperman and the store owner agree to change jobs. Their new positions help them find happiness, success, and two nice girls.

There is no happiness for an English nobleman who loses all his friends after he persists in eating a vile-smelling Chinese fruit. Their rejection drives him to suicide. Another lord, who eats the fruit but encases himself like a deep-sea diver, finds his eccentric solution brings him social success. Such was the saga of W. J. Turner's English play **The Man Who Ate the Popomack** (3-24-24, Cherry Lane). After a short stand downtown, it was transferred uptown for a second, brief engagement.

As might be expected, Grace Griswold and Thomas McKean's **The Main Line** (3-25-24, Klaw) was set in the most prestigious residential area of suburban Philadelphia, in the home of rich social-ites with the old Philadelphia name Rittenhouse. But the action revolves around one of their servants, Betty (Jo Wallace), who thwarts the theft of the Rittenhouse jewels, sets the family's way-ward son on the right track, and realigns the relationships between "the help and the helpless."

Moving from Philadelphia to New York society, Dorothy Heyward's **Nancy Ann** (3-31-24, 49th St.) addressed the problems of Nancy Angeline Van Cuyler Farr (Francine Larrimore). Stifled by soci-ety's restrictions, she runs away from her coming-out party, tries her luck in the theatre, and ends up discovering romance. The play had won the Harvard Prize, given to the best yearly work by a student of Professor George Pierce Baker, but held no interest for New Yorkers. *Variety* noted with some relief that Larrimore managed to get through the entire play without lighting a single cigarette or resorting to any of her other high-strung, jazz-age mannerisms.

The new heads of the Provincetown Players had deserted their own playhouse to present O'Neill's *Welded* uptown. In early April, on the 6th, they coupled some very minor O'Neill with some lesser Molière down at their Village base. **George Dandin** unfolded the humiliation of a cuckolded upstart. **The Ancient Mariner** was O'Neill's dramatization of Coleridge's poem. Molière's comedy was given a traditional staging, but the O'Neill-Coleridge opus employed impressionistic settings and a rhythmically moving chorus of sailors in "gangrenous" masks. Neither the stagings nor the performances of unex-ceptional players impressed critics.

Better players in a lesser play also displeased reviewers. The best of the performers was Mrs. Fiske. In Ida Lublenski Erlich's **Helena's Boys** (4-7-24, Henry Miller's), taken from a short story by Mary Brecht Pulver, she played a mother who feels obligated to show her radical sons the absurdity of their politics by becoming even more wildly radical, boozing in public and threatening to live in sin with a local businessman. Six years would have to elapse before Mrs. Fiske again ventured a new play.

Fritz Leiber left the relative security of his Shakespearean repertory to try his luck with Myron C. Fagan's **Two Strangers from Nowhere** (4-7-24, Punch and Judy). He first appeared, spotlighted in green, after an ominous thunderclap. But then his Angelo Desdichado was actually the Devil, who can raise a trapdoor in the stage and drag his victims to a reddish hell glowing below. He does not live up to the standard notion of Satan, since he has been told he can return to heaven if the whole world reforms. One current problem is a man (Theodore Babcock)

who believes he can buy any woman's love. But Satan walks away relieved when he can spare a pretty girl (Frances McGrath) who sees the light in the nick of time, after beseeching his aid in providing her with the baubles her dedicated researcher-husband (Richard Gordon) cannot af-ford. Leiber, who emphasized the unreality of his role by his slow movements and precise speech, soon found himself dusting off his Shakespearean cos-tumes.

The Theatre Guild's production of Ernst Toller's expressionistic **Man and the Masses** (4-14-24, Gar-rick), in Louis H. Untermeyer's translation, contin-ued the onrush of failures. The Woman (Blanche Yurka) attempts to lead the Communists in a peaceful revolution, but more bloody-minded party members see to it that she is executed for treason.

Except for the late-season actors' strike Samuel Shipman's **Cheaper to Marry** (4-15-24, 49th St.) might have caught on. Evelyn Gardner (Florence Eldridge) is a bright, self-supporting girl who loves Jim Knight (Robert Warwick) and, since he has vowed never to marry, agrees to become his mistress. She stashes away the money and expensive jewels he gives her for a rainy day. But when it is disclosed that he stole money from his business to provide for her she leaves him and refuses his plea to marry, stating she would have happily taken that cheaper course long before. She points to the quiet, rock-sure marriage of his partner (Alan Dinehart) and his partner's wife (Claiborne Foster).

Rachel Crothers's **Expressing Willie** (4-16-24, 48th St.) was the first long-running hit in two months—running, in fact, until just before Christ-mas. Willie Smith (Richard Sterling), having built a toothpaste company into a multimillion dollar enterprise, has also built himself a mansion on Long Island. He lives there with his mother (Louise Closser Hale), who boasts that she has "always been able to steer him without letting him know it." Now, aghast at the pseudo-fashionables he has chosen to associate with and especially concerned about his attraction to svelte, conniving Frances Sylvester (Merle Maddern), who has advised Willie "that absolute freedom—the expression of oneself, is the most important and developing thing in the world," Mrs. Smith has invited his long-ignored, hometown sweetheart, Minnie Whitcomb (Chrystal Herne), to spend a weekend. Minnie has remained a backwater music teacher, but her innate artistry and her warm reasonableness soon rout Willie's pretentious friends. When Willie finally under-stands this, he hugs Minnie and proposes to her, assuring her, "I'm expressing myself all right—and

I'm going to keep right on—to the end." Corbin exemplified the cheering when he wrote, "The sallies of [Miss Crothers's] wit took the audience by storm. . . . The varied group of her characters was so subtly and saliently limned that half a dozen actors, long loved and honored, seemed lifted above themselves as by the touch of genius."

Maurice V. Samuels and Malcolm La Prade's **Flame of Love** (4-21-24, Morosco) was billed as "a romantic drama of ancient China." Wu-chen (Brandon Peters) hopes to win a weaving contest by replicating the flaming pattern associated with the goddess Si-Ling. To do that he must be pure. But he finds he cannot resist the beautiful Circassian girl, Zara (Lenita Lane). So when he does win the contest he realizes that the goddess has forgiven his lapse.

C. M. S. McLellan's *Leah Kleschna*, Mrs. Fiske's old vehicle, was revived on the same night at the Lyric with Helen Gahagan as Leah, Arnold Daly as her father, José Ruben as Schram, Lowell Sherman as Raoul, and William Faversham as Paul Sylvaine. The story of a girl who is rescued from a life of crime by an understanding gentleman was coolly received; its four-week booking was not extended.

Having so dramatically called attention to herself earlier in the season, Judith Anderson was awarded the title role in Martin Brown's **Cobra** (4-22-24, Hudson). Jack Race (Louis Calhern), once the star of Yale's crew, has always been a woman-chaser, but his rich buddy, Tony Dorning (Ralph Morgan), time and again has paid to get him out of scrapes. Tony tells Jack of a trip to India in which he watched a huge white bull so fascinated by a cobra that it was unable to stamp on and kill the snake. That allowed the cobra to attack. Tony warns Jack that some women are like that cobra. Elsie Van Zile is a money-clutching vamp from Jack's hometown, who comes to New York hoping to snare Jack. But on learning of his much richer friend, she switches her efforts to Tony. Four years later, as Mrs. Dorning, she is bored with Tony and so agrees to an assignation with Jack at the disreputable Van Cleve Hotel. After Jack leaves, the hotel catches fire and Elsie is killed in the blaze. Jack debates whether or not to tell Tony the truth. He decides not to, but Tony learns what sort of girl he married anyway after coming across a cache of her letters to and from other men. Athough Tony realizes that Jack was one of those men, he forgives him and congratulates him on finding a prospective spouse in an understanding secretary (Clara Moores), who had argued that Jack should tell Tony the story. Most critics thought the play claptrap and were not overwhelmed with

Anderson's seductress. Hornblow, seeing her as too youthful for the role, nonetheless suggested she conveyed sufficient venom or artistry to make her performance "one of the most virile and satisfying characterizations of the season." The public, deciding for itself, kept the play on the boards for seven months.

. . .

Judith Anderson (1898–1992) was born in Australia, where she was christened Frances Margaret Anderson-Anderson. After acting for some time in her homeland, she came to America, played in stock in New York, then toured with William Gillette. She was a small, dark, hard-faced woman, best in roles of smothered or explosive passion.

. . .

Henri-René Lenormand's **Time Is a Dream** (4-22-24, Neighborhood Playhouse), in Winifred Katzin's translation, was a five-performance flop. Romée (Esther Mitchell) dreams that her fiancé, Nico (Albert Carroll), will die plunging helplessly from a green boat into a lake, and all her efforts to prevent the accident are futile.

Uptown, the fate of John Goldsworthy and Charles McNaughton's **Whitewashed** (4-23-24, 52nd St.) was not much better. It told of a man who is wrongly suspected of being a burglar in his own home and is thrown into a coalbin. Emerging in blackface, he vows revenge by literally whitewashing those responsible. One critic said the unusually wide aisles of the tiny new playhouse allowed audiences to escape quickly.

Out of the coalbin and into Bernard J. McOwen and Paul Dickey's **The Dust Heap** (4-24-24, Vanderbilt)! A half-breed (Inez Plummer) is kidnapped from the cabin of a Catholic priest (Albert Tavernier) who raised her by the God-cursing villain, Jules Toussaint (Louis Bennison), and his cohorts. They auction her off, and Jules is the highest bidder. He is about to drag her to his room when he is struck by lightning. He is not killed and revives in time to confront Pat O'Day (George W. Barnum), a Mountie who makes a belated appearance. They fight on the stairs and up on the roof, then tumble down the chimney together. The half-breed attempts to interfere and her clothes are torn, revealing a birthmark on her shoulder. That mark proves she is no half-breed at all but is the long-lost daughter of Abraham Levy (George Farren), who has been wandering around for three acts seeking her. Critics agreed that if by some stretch of charity the play did not belong on a dust heap, it did belong on a dust-laden shelf devoted to long-gone cheap melodramas.

Abandoning his religious plays, Charles Rann

Kennedy offered his three-character **The Admiral** (4-24-24, 48th St.). It was mainly a dialogue between Columbus (Kennedy) and Isabella (Edith Wynne Matthison), with Columbus insisting that he would not find a new route to India but rather a new world where the demon rum would be banned. The absurdity played just four matinees.

Leon Gordon's obsession with degenerates was shown again in his **Garden of Weeds** (4-28-24, Gaiety). In the Asbury Park mansion he owns, Phillip Flagg (Lee Baker) likes to entertain parties of chorus girls, who confirm for him his theory that the most beautiful flowers and humans are weeds at heart. When Dorothy Deldridge (Phoebe Foster) has had enough of his orgies, she makes a sane and sober marriage with Douglas Crawford (Warburton Gamble) but fails to tell him of her youthful flings. Flagg sees an opportunity to play the spoiler. He promises not to squeal about her past if she will spend twenty-four hours with him. Dorothy reveals her history to her husband, who invites Flagg into the corridor outside the Crawfords' apartment, then moments later returns alone to phone the building superintendent and advise him that a visitor has broken his neck in a fall down the stairs. Several former Ziegfeld beauties appeared in the party scenes, most notably Lilyan Tashman as a flashy, slangy chorus girl. *Variety* suggested, "Only an Equity strike can spare this one from disgrace and disaster." But by the time the strike erupted a month later, the play was long gone.

Peggy Wood moved from the lyric to non-musical stage in Stuart Olivier's **The Bride** (5-5-24, 39th St.). Marie Duquesne appears one stormy night at the Travers home on Washington Square. She is in her bridal gown and claims to have fled an unwanted marriage. The two bachelors, Mortimer and Wilson (Ferdinand Gottschalk and Donald Cameron), take her in. Mortimer is much older than the handsomer Wilson. The one man is a student of discomedusae (jellyfish), the other of pigeon-blood rubies. When the rubies are stolen the men recall seeing Marie, in Mortimer's slate blue dressing robe and old gold pajamas, signaling an organ grinder outside with a flashlight and suspect her. But she and the men's aunt (Isabel Irving) soon demonstrate that the thief was actually the Traverses' amiable family doctor (Robert Harrison). By that time, Marie has also discovered whom she ought to marry.

One scene in Roscoe W. Brink's **Catskill Dutch** (5-6-24, Belmont) sent several critics reaching for their most glowing encomiums. But it was not enough to save the play, which opened on a Tuesday night and failed to finish out the week, closing after Friday's performance. A leader (Frederic Burt) of the most orthodox Dutch community in the Catskills in the 1870s has seduced and then denounced Neelia-Anne (Ann Davis), a serving girl in his home. Blame for fathering the child is placed on Peetcha (Kenneth MacKenna), who is forced to marry Neelia-Anne. But some while later, at an emotional revival meeting, Neelia-Anne blurts out the whole story, ruining the elder's standing and nearly wrecking her marriage. Whether they were moved by the scene or not, critics compared it to a similar one in the earlier *Roseanne*.

At the Provincetown Playhouse a revival of *The Emperor Jones* was offered on the same night with Paul Robeson in the lead. The reason for the revival was to call positive attention to Robeson and thus deflect less desirable attention from the next play the group was to mount, already the subject of much controversy. Most critics took the bait, calling him, among other things, "a giant in stature and possessed of a magnificent voice."

A coterie of knowing Broadwayites was aware that the Herbert Richard Lorenz who wrote **The Melody Man** (5-13-24, Ritz) was actually three young men struggling for recognition in the musical theatre—Herbert Fields, Richard Rodgers, and Lorenz Hart. They even included a couple of purposely mediocre songs in their story. Franz Henkel (Lew Fields), an immigrant composer devoted to the finest in music, is reduced to making arrangements for a writer of popular songs, Al Tyler (Donald Gallaher). He is shocked when Tyler appropriates one of his themes to use in "Moonlight Mama." But he accepts the ways of his adopted country after Al proposes to Elsa Henkel (Betty Weston). Woollcott, having moved to the *Sun* following the merger of the *Herald* and the *Tribune,* thought the play had some "enormously comic interludes," but Percy Hammond, now the critic for the merged papers, spoke for a majority in dismissing the entertainment as "feeble, immature and meandering."

A revival of Jacob Gordin's *The Kreutzer Sonata* at the Frazee on the 14th, with Bertha Kalish recreating her role of the Jewish woman unhappy in the choice of both Christian lover and Jewish husband, found some favor. But a series of *Hedda Gabler* matinees at the 48th Street, beginning on the 16th, was less well supported although the cast included Clare Eames as Hedda, Fritz Leiber as Lovborg, Dudley Digges as Tesman, Margalo Gillmore as Mrs. Elvsted, and Roland Young as Judge Brack.

Between these two openings the season's most

controversial drama appeared. Even before it premiered, Eugene O'Neill's **All God's Chillun Got Wings** (5-15-24, Provincetown Playhouse) was beset by howls of outrage in the more conservative press over the prospect of a Negro kissing a white girl and by the city's refusal, in an effort to cripple the production, to permit children to perform in the play. The blaring headlines probably whetted playgoers' interest, and the cast got around the injunction by cutting some scenes and reading others. Ella Downey (Mary Blair) and Jim Harris (Paul Robeson) have known each other since childhood, but as they matured they drifted apart because of their different races. However, after she is seduced and deserted by a white lover, Ella marries Jim. Racial prejudices shortly drive her over the brink of sanity. The problems cause Jim to fail his bar exams. Ella retains enough basic sense to see that she has hurt Jim, and when she begs his forgiveness and asks him to play marbles with her, the loving Jim reassures her, "I'll play right up to the gates of Heaven with you!" Robert Welsh of the *Telegram-Mail* predicted the drama "was likely to take a permanent place in the American theatre." But the more negative Hammond, again speaking for a majority, wrote, "It is a vehement exposition of a marriage between a stupid negro and a stupid white woman. If it is possible for you to get an emotion out of that situation, here is your opportunity." Despite its difficulties, and possibly because of some of them, the play made money during its short stand.

Jessy Trimble and Eugenie Woodward's **The Leap** (5-22-24, Cherry Lane) told how the drab daughter (Minette Buddecke) of a beautiful mother (Anna Cleveland) finds self-confidence and happiness thanks to a thoughtful English nobleman (Herbert Standing, Jr.) and an American beau (John Goldsworthy).

There was no happiness in Irving Kaye Davis's **The Right to Dream** (5-26-24, Punch and Judy) for David Dean (Ralph Shirley), an unsuccessful writer pushed by his ambitious in-laws into a mundane job he hates. He kills himself.

At the end of the month Equity struck. This time it did not close every show but chose selectively until the strike was settled.

Off and on, all season long, critics had been seeing hints of bygone cheap melodramas in many of the newer plays. Now they were confronted with the genuine article when Theodore Kremer's 1901 tourer, *The Fatal Wedding,* was revived at the Ritz on June 2. At the time this tale of a malicious couple's endeavoring to destroy a decent marriage first played the Grand Opera House twenty-three

years earlier, the *Dramatic Mirror* had reported, "It suits the popular taste." Now the *Times* assured its readers it was "excellent fun" (except where it tried to be funny). Its 1924 run was the same as its 1901 stand—one week.

Jo Swerling's **One Helluva Night** (6-2-24, Sam H. Harris) was a borderline curiosity, mounted by members of the Cheese Club, a group which included a number of professionals. This spoof of the mystery play genre employed some of the insanities Olsen and Johnson would use years later in their zany revues. Thus, the man who was supposedly the author and producer fired his leading man in mid-scene and took over himself, other figures replaced other actors in mid-act and decided to change the names of the characters they were impersonating, and the stagehands, supposedly bored and anxious to go home, removed the settings while players were performing the second act. One performance sufficed.

As they had in the last two seasons, the Players enjoyed the last word. Their admired revival of Oliver Goldsmith's *She Stoops to Conquer* was brought into the Empire for a single week, beginning on the 9th. Frazer Coulter was Sir Charles; Basil Sydney, young Marlow; Dudley Digges, Hardcastle; Ernest Glendinning, Tony Lumpkin; Henry E. Dixey, Diggory; Francis Wilson, Jeremy; Maclyn Arbuckle, Stingo; Effie Shannon, Mrs. Hardcastle; Elsie Ferguson, Kate; Helen Hayes, Constance Neville; and Pauline Lord was a maid.

1924–1925

The roaring twenties roared on. And the theatre flourished and prospered along with so much else in American society. According to *Variety,* first-class houses introduced a record 228 attractions, 162 of which were new dramas or comedies. Other surveys offered slightly different figures, but all attested to the indisputable vigor of the American stage, especially in New York. Moreover, in his latest *Best Plays* Burns Mantle pointed with pride to the fact that he did not have to consider importations to fill out his list of ten top entries—for the first time in the series all ten were native works.

Of course, some problems did arise. A new form of competition was emerging—radio. William Brady, a professional alarmist, who a decade earlier had bewailed the growing menace of films, now cried out that the new medium "threatens the very existence of the drama in this country." In fact, since October of 1922 WGY had been broadcasting more or less uncut versions of recent Broadway hits. A few astute producers, Arthur Hammerstein among them, had begun to advertise their offerings on radio and reported good results. Out-of-work players found a fresh source of income. So clearly, radio was not all bad. It would be a different matter if someone could combine radio's sightless sounds and film's soundless scenes. Any number of people were attempting just that and a few years down the road would accomplish the task.

In the meanwhile a more pressing problem was the growing pressure from religious extremists and self-promoting politicians to "cleanse" the theatre—or close it. Several of the season's finest plays would come under attack from these sanctimonious do-gooders, and a few bowed to the pressure. Shockingly, the increasingly hidebound, puritanical *Theatre* supported the troublemakers, suggesting producers should agree to blue-penciling rather than padlocking and even proposing a "red light theatre" district where bawdy or foul-languaged plays would have to be confined.

Late June was busier than ever, albeit only its initial entry scored a hit. Just days before the Democrats gathered at Madison Square Garden to begin what proved to be America's longest convention (103 ballots) in a futile effort to unseat taciturn Cal Coolidge, Barry Conners's **So This Is Politics** (6-16-24, Henry Miller's) opened the season. Its politics were local, centering on the attempt of Nina Buckmaster (Marjorie Gateson) to become mayor of her hometown in the heartlands. Her husband (Glenn Anders), more interested in his country club than in city hall, is contemptuous, and so is most of the political establishment. But Butch McKenna (William Courtleigh), a "blarneying" ex-saloon keeper and notorious ward boss, takes her side and helps her win. The comedy ran more than four months, but when business started to slip (perhaps because playgoers had become surfeited with politics), the title was changed to the more alluring *Strange Bedfellows*.

Martin Lawton's **The Locked Door** (6-19-24, Cort) spotlighted a pair of honeymooners. The husband, Richard (Charles Trowbridge), tells his naive, baby-talking wife, Muriel (Florence Shirley), that they ought to throw away their wedding rings and license in order to keep their romance as passionate as it was before their marriage. They play a game of chess to see if they will spend the night together, and after Richard loses Muriel locks him out of her bedroom. Although Richard tries unavailingly to pick the lock, the newlyweds soon come to their senses.

Sex and politics mingled in Edwin Milton Royle's **Her Way Out** (6-23-24, Gaiety). When the idealistic, crusading young Senator Daniel Norcross (Edward Arnold) comes to Washington, older politicos set Mrs. Hamilton (Beatrice Terry), the city's most glittering hostess, on to him, to rein him into line. The two fall in love, forcing Mrs. Hamilton to confess to him that she rose to wealth by running a bordello in New Orleans. (The third of the play's four acts was a flashback to the earlier days.) Norcross is forgiving, and they agree to marry. On opening night, Royle made a curtain speech complaining that commercial pressures compelled him to insert a happy ending instead of allowing Mrs. Hamilton to commit suicide, as he originally intended and as his title suggested. But the change could not save the play.

Hubert Osborne fared no better with **The Blue Bandanna** (6-23-24, Vanderbilt). Sidney Blackmer was starred in the dual roles of Richard Haskell, a rich, benevolent clubman, and his look-alike, the thieving "Gentleman Jim" Delano. For a time Delano makes it seem that Haskell has committed Delano's crimes, and he also almost wins over "the Girl" (Vivienne Osborne), a lady whom Haskell has caught burglarizing his home but who turns out to be a real lady after all.

The evening's third opening, Allen Leiber's **Try It with Alice** (6-23-24, 52nd St.), had the shortest run, one week. Set in a future when a twenty-fourth amendment requires all bachelors over twenty-five to marry (and when not only liquor but tobacco also is proscribed), it followed the efforts of two old college buddies to evade the law by having one of them, who had played in drag in school theatricals, pose as a girl.

Henry Fisk Carlton and William Ford Manley's **Shooting Shadows** (6-26-24, Ritz) ran half a week longer. It told of the comic misadventures encountered by summer vacationers, including a pretty girl (Ann Reader) who is attempting to blackmail a handsome millionaire (Howard Miller), when they visit a supposedly haunted old farmhouse in the Berkshires.

In the Village, Katherine Browning Miller's **Mud** (7-3-24, Cherry Lane) told of "a perpetual college student" who tries to make a killing with a new formula for mud packs at beauty salons. Deemed this early on as "the dark horse entrant for the nomination of the worst play of the season," it survived less than one full week.

July's lone uptown entry, which opened at the Frazee on the 16th, was a double bill of rare oldies—George Dibdin Pitt's *Sweeney Todd* and W. Barnes Rhodes's *Bombastes Furioso*. The former told of a mad barber (Robert Vivian) who slits his customers' throats and has the corpses baked into pies. It later became a source for Stephen Sondheim's controversial 1979 musical. The afterpiece spoofed early eighteenth-century opera. Critics found the first piece, apparently played reasonably straight, entertaining but felt the burlesque hopelessly dated. Notwithstanding reviewers' reservations, the bill survived two months.

The first hit to run out the season was Edgar Selwyn and Edmund Goulding's **Dancing Mothers** (8-11-24, Booth). Ethel "Buddy" Westcourt (Mary Young) gave up a promising stage career to settle down contentedly as a wife and mother. But her philandering, uncomprehending husband (Henry Stevenson) and her wild, flapper daughter, "Kittens" (Helen Hayes), treat her with indifference, even contempt. Declaring enough is enough, Buddy takes up with Gerald Naughton (John Halliday), the very man Kittens has been seeing. She also encounters Irma Raymond (Elsie Lawson), who has been courted by both Gerald and Mr. Westcourt. Westcourt's reaction, when he discovers his wife's change of ways, is one of intolerant male outrage. Ethel responds, "I have become a woman of today. I have become a dancing mother. I have begun to step out with my foot on the gas and I like it, Hughie." She packs her bags and heads off, leaving a baffled husband and tearful daughter to fend for themselves. The play succeeded despite largely lukewarm notices, but fine performances, the public's fascination with the new flapper morality, a lively jazz-filled act at a chic cabaret, and the startling ending were seen as overriding the reviews.

Nothing could override the pans received by **Dr. David's Dad** (8-13-24, Vanderbilt), which Carrington North and Joseph J. Garren derived from Armin Friedmann and Louis Nertz's German hit *Dr. Stieglitz*. It recounted the rebellion of a young physician (Bruce Elmore) against the authoritarian ways of his aging father (Egon Brecher). Because part of the conflict concerned lovers' religious differences, some saw the comedy as a middle-European *Abie's Irish Rose*.

Nor was Ralph Thomas Kettering's **Easy Street** (8-14-24, 39th St.) made welcome. In its brief sojourn it related how a stingy, surly husband (Ralph Kellerd), suspicious of his wife's frequent trips to town, orders her (Mary Newcomb) to leave and to go live with whomever she is seeing there. Having packed and

unaware her husband is hidden by a huge chair, she confesses to a friend that she has been going to town to work as a secretary in order to have household money and put away something for the baby she is expecting. The husband jumps up and grabs her bag, which opens to disclose some baby garments. "Darling, can this be true?" he asks. It is, and they are reconciled.

By contrast much had been looked for in David Gray and Avery Hopwood's **The Best People** (8-19-24, Lyceum), which was based on Gray's *Saturday Evening Post* story "The Self-Determination of the Lenoxes" and which had enjoyed a long run the previous season in Chicago. Like *Dancing Mothers* it examined the jazz-age generation. In this case the staid, snooty Lenoxes (Charles Richman and Margaret Dale) have a pair of all too modern children. Marion (Frances Howard) rebuffs her parents' attempt to marry her off to a titled Englishman (William Valentine), preferring instead the family's attractive chauffeur (James Rennie). Bertie (Gavin Muir) is chasing a seemingly gold-digging chorus girl (Hope Drown). When the parents are unable to change their children's minds, Mr. Lenox can only rationalize that the family needs new blood. Writing in the *American Mercury,* the brahmin George Jean Nathan devastated the play, assigning a numerical statistic to each of its clichés by noting, "It is the one hundred and eighty-first play about the unruly generation, the 269th play in which the irate father starts out to bribe and unmask the girl his son is engaged to and learns that she is really a very decent sort," and, injecting ever higher figures, concluding it was "the 1995th play in which the daughter, called to accounts by her parents, retorts that she didn't ask to be born." The play's New York run was a disappointing 143 performances, but it again met with enormous success when it returned to the road and when it played London.

The month's second German importation was **The Werewolf** (8-25-24, 49th St.), which Gladys Unger adapted from Rudolph Lothar's play. A lustful duchess (Laura Hope Crews), living in a castle once owned by Don Juan and aware that someone is making advances to her serving girls, is told that the dead roué's spirit now inhabits a local professor. She invites the shy man (Leslie Howard) to the castle and attempts to seduce him, only to discover that her own butler is the prowler. Despite sharply divided notices the play ran three months.

So did an American comedy, Jack Larrie's **The Easy Mark** (8-26-24, 39th St.). Sam Crane's sister, Hattie (Lulu Mae Hubbard), tells her mother (Kate Morgan), "Sam's an X, Mom. . . . An X—an easy mark. He's so honest himself, it never occurs to him the world's full of bunk." Sam (Walter Huston) is also a dreamer and something of a loafer, always eyeing the chance to make millions and always refusing real work. Inevitably, Sam is bamboozled into spending his family's $6000 savings on land that he is told has oil under it. He soon finds there is nothing beneath the soil but brackish water. His family is about to be evicted when a friend stages a fake gusher on the land, sending the bamboozlers rushing back to Sam and agreeing to repurchase the property for a small fortune. Has Sam learned his lesson? You bet he has! Instead of squandering his wealth on worthless oil lands he will put it in a pie-in-the-sky asbestos mine. For all the play's cheerful naiveties, it was replete with good comic lines. Thus Hattie's busy suitor, Joe (G. Pat Collins), tells Hattie that "when a feller likes a girl, he ought to marry her and get her off his mind." And Sam's girl, Mary (Pauline Armitage), suggesting to Hattie that Sam needed to lose $6000 to wake him up to his real nature, is told, "Six thousand dollars for an alarm clock! They come high."

Three new plays, plus a three-month return of *Rain*, began September's onslaught of offerings. (In fact *Variety* had announced that the week's seventeen entries would make it the busiest in Broadway history. Actually, because of one last-minute folding and two postponements, only fourteen opened.) The sole hit among Monday's trio was its only comedy, Anne Morrison and Patterson McNutt's **Pigs** (9-1-24, Little). It was the sort of good, clean show—"the home-made pie type of play"—that John Golden specialized in, and he was rewarded with a season-long run. Its simple story told how Tommy Atkins, Jr. (Wallace Ford), with the help of his long-loyal, flapper sweetheart, Mildred Cushing (Nydia Westman), finds the money to set up a farm to cure sick pigs and then sell them profitably. Actually the $250 he needs to purchase the pigs is gotten by Mildred's gently blackmailing the local vamp. Among the minor characters was a brother who writes poetry in which "Lenore" rhymes with "saw." Maude Granger, a star and beauty of yesteryear, said her farewells to the stage as Tommy's gossipy, bossy grandmother.

The two dramas had not dissimilar war themes. In John Farrar and Stephen Vincent Benet's **Nerves** (9-1-24, Comedy), three socialites, Jack (Kenneth MacKenna), Ted (Paul Kelly), and Bob (Humphrey Bogart), have all enlisted in the same flying unit, the Tiger Squadron. But in battle Jack loses his nerve and refuses to fly his mission. Bob, though he already has flown his own mission, takes his place

and then is reported missing. Ted's patent contempt finally steels Jack and he flies off. He shoots down a Hun, but his own legs are shattered. Back home Peggy Thatch (Winifred Lenihan), who has been courted by both Ted and Jack, berates Ted for goading Jack. She is supported in her feelings by Bob, who has come back after all. She proposes that Jack marry her. But Jack wants to be loved, not pitied, so a compromise is reached. Critics praised the play and the men's performances, but more than one reviewer complained that Miss Lenihan seemed to believe she was still playing an overwrought Saint Joan. The play might have succeeded had not a much better war play followed a little later.

The second war drama that evening came from England—Harry Wall's **Havoc** (9-1-24, Maxine Elliott's). It, too, featured a girl caught between two suitors. Although Violet (Joyce Barbour) is engaged to Roddy (Leo G. Carroll), she decides she prefers his comrade in arms, Dick (Ralph Forbes). Dick brings the news to Roddy at the front, and the hurt, furious man falsifies orders that will probably send his rival to his death. Dick is not killed but blinded, and the guilt-ridden Roddy commits suicide. However, when Dick returns to Violet, the fickle girl tells him she has found another love. Happily for Dick, Roddy's sister Tessie (Mollie Johnson) is there to care for and love him. The drama was received politely but, like *Nerves*, quickly faded away.

Owen Davis's first play of the month was **The Haunted House** (9-2-24, George M. Cohan). Like a number of plays in recent years, particularly those touted as expressionistic, its program listed its characters as the Tramp, the Bride, etc., instead of by name. But the play was not expressionistic. Rather it was a send-up of voguish whodunits, and its characters did have names. Despite the warnings of Edward Evans (Frank Monroe), the bride's father, Emily and Jack Driscoll (Flora Sheffield and Saxon Kling) decide to spend their honeymoon at Evans's "haunted" country lodge. Gunshots, blood, and apparent murder follow as does a host of figures, including a know-it-all writer, Desmond Duncan (Wallace Eddinger), his wife (Isabel Withers), a tramp (John Irwin), a cowardly, incompetent sheriff (Denman Maley), a bucolic milkman named Ed (Arthur Aylsworth), and a publicity-mad detective (Dudley Clements). Just as Duncan is about to proclaim his own wife to be the killer of the as yet undiscovered victim, Ed rushes in announcing he has found the body. It's the body of Nellie, he tells his listeners. "Not your wife?" a horrified Duncan asks. "No," Ed replies, "the best cow I ever had." The play was a squeak-by success, running fourteen weeks. In his autobiography Davis suggested a cabal of mystery writers, angry at being spoofed, conspired somehow to hurt business.

However, John Willard, the author of a famous mystery (*The Cat and the Canary*) found a less receptive welcome for his **The Green Beetle** (9-2-24, Klaw). His new work was not so much a whodunit as a willhesucceedindoinit. Years before the action starts a drunken Robert Chandos had entered a sacred garden and there had despoiled and deserted the girl Chang Hong had loved. Now Chandos and his wife (Percy Moore and Florence Fair) are lured into the San Francisco curio shop run by Chang (Ian Maclaren), who prattles about love while planning the murder of any and all foes. Chandos, who has a weak heart, is frightened to death by Chang's sudden clanging on a huge cymbal, and his wife is drugged and turned into a servant. Years later, Chang would also seize the couple's daughter (Lee Patrick), but she takes refuge in the hotel room of a girl-shy young man (Louis Kimball), who happens to be the son of Chang's American partner and who gets up enough nerve to help her escape Chang's murderous emissaries. Chang himself dies when he is accidentally pricked by a poisoned fan intended for the daughter. *Variety* dismissed the play as "just another Chink melodrama."

The same night that saw these two plays open also applauded the premiere of Rudolf Friml's *Rose Marie,* which rekindled the popularity of operetta and became the era's biggest musical hit.

Two and a half weeks sufficed for William F. Dugan and John Meehan's **The Tantrum** (9-4-24, Cort). The play opens in a theatre where the audience is assembling. Two of the playgoers, obviously man and wife, are arguing, with most of the spleen coming from the nagging wife. Then the lights are lowered. The De Pipers (Joe King and Roberta Arnold) return home from the theatre, and the wife continues to so nag and demean her husband that he storms out, determined to live separately. She later finds him at a friend's apartment, reveling in a wild party filled with scantily clad girls and lots of bootleg hooch. The infuriated spouse shoots her husband. The scene returns to the darkened auditorium, where the playgoing wife is so upset by the story she has been watching that she promises her husband she will never again nag him.

Friday night's combat drama sent Monday's war plays into hasty retreat. In the *Sun,* Alexander Woollcott opened his review of Maxwell Anderson and Laurence Stallings's **What Price Glory?** (9-5-24, Plymouth), "No war play written in the English language since German guns boomed under the walls of Liege, ten years ago, has been so true, so salty and so richly satisfying." He continued, "Compared with these men, who have their little day in the three acts of 'What Price Glory?,' all the other stage officers and soldiers that have charged upon us from the embattled dressing rooms of Broadway have seemed to step glistening from some magazine cover." He also reported that "the first audience gave the play such a welcome as we have seldom seen matched in these many years." Heywood Broun agreed, writing in the *World* that this was "far and away the most credible of all war plays" and confirming, "Almost everybody remained at the end to shout for the authors. This reviewer did. That is why his review must be curtailed." With more time to consider even the crotchety Nathan fell in line, noting in the *American Mercury* that the piece was "the finest thing of its kind I have ever seen . . . infinitely superior to every other play born of the late war." Among the few quibblers was Arthur Hornblow in *Theatre,* who called the play's pacifist stance "illogical" and complained the story failed to depict the more noble side of war. Two career soldiers, Captain Flagg (Louis Wolheim) and First Sergeant Quirt (William Boyd) have long been friendly enemies. When Flagg goes on leave, Quirt is placed in charge of his company and has a fling with Charmaine (Leyla Georgie), a local belle whom Flagg has considered his personal property. Flagg returns, learns that Charmaine is pregnant, and orders Quirt to marry her. But orders come for the men to head for the front. There the battle is fierce. One officer (Clyde North), beset by a sniper and confronting a wounded buddy, exclaims, "What price glory now? Why in God's name can't we all go home? Who gives a damn for this lousy, stinking little town but the poor French devils who live here?" Quirt is also wounded and resumes his affair while convalescing. When a second call to the front arrives, Flagg heads out yelling to Charmaine to put her money in real estate, while Quirt, equally unconcerned about her, hurries after, shouting, "Hey, Flagg, wait for baby!" The play ran for more than a year, abetted no doubt by publicity when bluestockings in the church, the armed services, and city hall took loud umbrage at the play's damn this, damn that, and "tout goddamn suites." Along with his playing in *The Hairy Ape,* his acting in this play marked the pinnacle of burly, battered-faced Wolheim's career. The play's success also truly launched the career of at least one of its authors, Maxwell Anderson.

· · ·

[James] **Maxwell Anderson** (1888–1959) was born in Atlantic, Penn. He was educated at the University of North Dakota and at Stanford. Subsequently he tried his hand at teaching and at journalism. His first produced drama, *The White Desert* (1923), was a quick failure. With the success of his new play, he abandoned newspaper work, to devote himself full time to the theatre.

* * *

Ann Harding's still uncertain hold on stardom suffered a setback when she appeared in Lewis B. Ely and Sam Forrest's short-lived **Thoroughbreds** (9-8-24, Vanderbilt). She played pretty Sue Wynn, a young lawyer who has set up a practice in Tuckytown, Ky., after leaving her native village, which long has held something in her hush-hush past against her. She has had no cases until the local judge (William Corbett) assigns her to defend "Doc" Pusey (George Marion), an accused horse thief. She soon realizes that Pusey is her long-lost father, chased from his home by her late mother's snooty relations. A happy ending ensues.

In Willard Mack's **High Stakes** (9-9-24, Hudson) Richard Lennon (Wilton Lackaye), a lonely, aging widower, marries a beautiful young blonde, Dolly (Phoebe Foster), unaware the girl is a crook. Dolly wangles a confederate, Louis de Salde (Fleming Ward), a position in the house. But Richard's wily brother, Joe (Lowell Sherman), pretending to be a silly ass, gets the goods on the pair and sends them fleeing. Richard decides to adopt an orphan. Al Woods's mounting chalked up a four-month stand.

Chester Bailey Fernald's **The Mask and the Face** (9-10-24, Bijou) was taken from Luigi Chiarelli's Italian original. Count Mario Grazia (William Faversham) has become a local hero after keeping a vow to kill his wife (Catherine Willard) if he ever found her with another man. Only he hasn't kept his vow. Rather, he has quietly exiled her. She returns in black weeds to attend her own funeral, prove her innocence, and effect a reconciliation. Faversham's old-style acting could not sustain the light comic touch required, so Brock Pemberton's production was soon withdrawn.

Al Woods had another modest hit on his hands with Don Mullally's **Conscience** (9-11-24, Belmont). It too dealt with a man and his unfaithful wife. Jeff Stewart (Ray B. Collins) comes out of the storm into the dubious comfort of his smoky, dirty Yukon cabin, where the snow creeps in between cracks in the logs and where his only real company is a cackling, caged jackdaw. For a time he sits gazing dreamily but restlessly into the fire. Then he turns to the bird: "Do you know what, Gompers, you're watchin', without knowin'. Do you know what you're watchin', Gompers? You're watchin' a great

race. Spring and insanity are racin', with me for the stake. Right now it looks as if Spring is goin' to lose." And sure enough, he soon is visited by ghosts from his past. His thoughts go back to the home he and his wife (Lillian Foster) shared; his leaving her, after being fired for union activity (thus the bird's name), to find work in another state; his return months later, after being jailed for vagrancy, to discover his wife supporting herself by prostitution; and his killing her. The memories drive him to dash out into the storm and certain death.

The **Schemers** (9-15-24, Nora Bayes) in Dr. William Irving Strovich's comedy were James Darlington (William Harrigan), a Broadway producer, and Marty Evans (Ralph Sipperly), his press agent. The pair lure in four famous drama critics—A. Wood Brown, Perry Almond, Alan Olcott, and Alexander Dale (read Alan Dale and Alexander Woollcott for the last two)—to discuss a play before it opens. The play deals with a sweet Wichita girl's attempt to star in a Darlington play and the obstacles her jealous Kansas boyfriend throws in her path. Stark Young, now the critic for the *Times,* concurred with the fictitious reviewers on the other side of the footlights, who suggested the play-within-a-play (and, according to Stark, the whole affair) had "neither wit, point, entertainment, [or] humor."

One night Broadway, the next, Hollywood. Lillian Trimble Bradley and George Broadhurst's **Izzy** (9-16-24, Broadhurst) was based on the "Izzy Iskovitch" stories by Lillian George Randolph Chester that had appeared in the *Saturday Evening Post*. It told how ambitious Izzy Iskovitch (Jimmy Hussey), still in his teens, gets his five adoring uncles (one of whom was played by Sam Jaffe) to come up with the $10,000 he needs to start a film at the Magnificent Pictures Corporation's studio. Two and a half hours later he is the head of the corporation. On the way to the top he is vamped by a famous writer (Helene Lackaye) and comes to the aid of and wins the heart of Prudence Joy (Isabelle Lowe), a starlet who is being held back supposedly because she is a "schicksa," but who turns out to be really Rosie Rosenberg. Hussey, a small, slim, youthful-looking Irish vaudevillian, walked off with the best notices but couldn't turn the comedy into a hit.

One totally unexpected, season-long success was Martha Stanley's **My Son** (9-17-24, Princess). Set in the home and store of Ana Silva (Joan Gordon), a Portuguese immigrant in Cape Cod, it described how she discovers that her son, Brauglio (Herbert Clark), is so smitten by a conniving little flapper (Martha Madison) that he has no qualms about stealing an emerald necklace belonging to the girl's mother (Sarah Truax) in order to pay for their good times. Unable to deal with the boy, Ana arranges with some friendly Portuguese-American fishermen to shanghai him, hoping that a year or two on a whaler will set him straight.

A fisherman of sorts also figured importantly in Owen Davis's second play of the month, **Lazybones** (9-22-24, Vanderbilt). Steve Tuttle (George Abbott) of Milo, Maine, is the village ne'er-do-well. Returning from a fishing trip he discovers an abandoned baby and announces that he and his mother will adopt it. His suspicious fiancée abandons him and the townsfolk snub him, but he does not care. Years pass and the baby grows into an attractive young lady (Martha Bryan-Allen). She and Steve fall in love. Nor is their romance shattered after it is learned that her mother was the sister of Steve's former sweetheart. Many critics compared the play favorably to *Lightnin'*, and praised the players. But the public supported the play for only ten weeks.

On the other hand, an elaborate, expensive, and highly publicized importation was a two-week failure. **Hassan** (9-22-24, Knickerbocker) was an Arabian Nights tale, written by James Elroy Flecker, who had been killed in the recent war. It recounted the unhappy experiences of the confectioner-poet (Randal Ayrton) both in love and at the sumptuous court of Haroun Al Raschid (James Dale). Disillusioned, he embarks on a pilgrimage.

The Hungarian playwright Ernö Vajda would be represented by no fewer than three works during the season, two in the waning days of September alone. (Counting last season's *Fata Morgana*, that gave him four Broadway productions in the calendar year.) First to arrive in the new season was **Grounds for Divorce** (9-23-24, Empire), Guy Bolton's reworking of his *A válóperes hölgy* (The Divorce Court Lady). With Ina Claire, Philip Merivale, and H. Reeves-Smith heading a capital cast, the story centered on a beautiful woman, neglected by her husband, the busiest and handsomest of divorce lawyers. She uses the divorce court to free herself of him, then wins him back. The comedy received a split verdict from the critics and only enough backing from the public to linger four months.

An American comedy that opened the next night fared only slightly better but enjoyed a long afterlife in Little Theatres and in stock. George S. Kaufman and Edna Ferber's **Minick** (9-24-24, Booth) was based of a Ferber short story, "Old Man Minick." It recounts how the seventyish Minick (O. P. Heggie) leaves his Bloomington home to live in Chicago with his son and daughter-in-law (Frederic Burt and Phyllis Povah), how for all his good intentions—

such as fixing the lamps in the house—he merely throws things into disarray, and how, recognizing the problems, he waits until the others have gone out for a night, then packs his bags and moves to a nearby home for the elderly. Determined to lead his "own life, same as anybody," he tells the family maid, "I ain't going to waste it teaching pinochle to anybody!" The critical consensus was that the plot was exceptionally thin and the acting, especially of the admired Heggie, disappointing (the English-bred Heggie could not master a midwestern twang), yet that for all its faults the play provided a pleasant evening.

Vajda's *Rozmarin Néni* (Aunt Rosemary) was offered to New Yorkers as **The Little Angel** (9-27-24, Frazee) in a translation by J. Jacobus. A young count (Edward Crandall) takes advantage of a pretty girl (Mildred Macleod) who has fainted to render her pregnant. At first, he refuses the demands of her outraged aunt (Clare Eames) to marry the youngster, but eventually he falls in love with her and agrees to a wedding. The play gave Vajda his first American failure of the year.

Three plays opened on the next Monday. William A. Brady, who had produced John Farrar and Stephen Vincent Benet's failed war drama four weeks earlier, tried again with their **That Awful Mrs. Eaton** (9-29-24, Morosco). As historically minded playgoers realized, the work dealt with the attempts of Andrew Jackson (Frank McGlynn) to force Peggy O'Neal Eaton (Katharine Alexander), a tavern keeper's daughter, on Washington's snobbish society. Like the men's earlier effort, it was a quick flop.

So was John Clements and Leonidas Westervelt's **Made for Each Other** (9-29-24, 52nd St.). A vanity production, whose producer was also its leading man, it attempted to tell in farcical terms what happens when a bridegroom (Upson Rose) is kidnapped on the eve of his wedding. He makes matters worse for himself after he is tricked into lying about what happened. In a novel departure foreshadowing the Japanese *Rashomon*, one incident is repeated three times—each time from the self-serving viewpoint of a different character. *Variety* concluded its short, dismissive review by alerting the company which took away unwanted scenery, "Cain's, keep the front door open."

Dorrance Davis's **The Busybody** (9-29-24, Bijou) ran a bit longer than its opening-night competitors but was still a flop. It followed the comic mishaps created by a well-to-do do-gooder from Riverside Drive, who must interfere in everyone's lives. Its sole attraction was the brash clowning in the title role of small, pugnacious Ada Lewis, once a favorite in the later Edward Harrigan shows and afterwards a character comedienne in musicals. This proved to be her last outing, for she died suddenly, just fifty years old, at the beginning of the next season.

Arthur Richman was having difficulty clinging to the promise of his early plays (and indeed would never again have a major success). His latest effort was **The Far Cry** (9-30-24, Cort). It spotlighted the self-willed Claire Marsh (Margalo Gillmore), taken by her divorced mother (Winifred Harris) to live in Paris. There mama lands a French lover, while the unsettled Claire marries and divorces a worthless local (José Alessandro), has a fling with an American art student (Kenneth MacKenna), then attempts a liaison with an Italian count (Frederick Worlock). Finally the long-absent father (Claude King) reappears, to set his daughter on the right road. While critics trounced the play, they had glowing words for Margalo Gillmore ("astonishingly brilliant," "drew out the whole sum of drama that lay within the situations") and Livingston Platt's settings of a Paris hotel and a villa in Florence ("gorgeous," "enhance and dilate the quality of the dramatic elements").

October's first six or seven entries were failures. An ailing Edward Sheldon and a young Sidney Howard combined their talents to write **Bewitched** (10-1-24, National). The play was a fantasy, but the cast listing in the program suggested it might have a touch of expressionism, too, since among its characters were A Native of the Enchanted Forest, Another, Still Another, and One More. But a principal figure was the Aviator (Glenn Anders), whose plane crashes near a magnificent château. The building's owner, the Marquis (José Ruben), welcomes the man and tells him that the castle is haunted. The Aviator falls asleep and dreams that he encounters a beautiful sorceress (Florence Eldridge) who attempts to seduce him. When his goodness makes her desist, her grandfather (Ruben), a most evil sorcerer, attempts unavailingly to coerce her. The next morning, the Aviator recognizes that the sorceress of his dream is simply the marquis's lovely granddaughter (Eldridge). Critics viewed the play as a good but faulty, sometimes tedious, work, made all the less acceptable by Anders's uneven, unfeeling performance. Eldridge and Ruben were praised, but the highest accolades were accorded Lee Simonson for his richly but subtly colored château, magical forest, sorcerer's gloomy, ominous study, and final sundrenched mountain top.

Programs for Martin Brown's **Great Music** (10-4-24, Earl Carroll) announced the play's subtitle as "A Dramatization of Eric Fane's Symphony in D Minor" and gave titles to each of the play's four acts—Theme, Scherzo, Largo, and Rhapsodie and Finale. Appropriately a large orchestra—billed as a "full symphony orchestra"—performed excerpts (actually by one C. Linn Seiler) from the fictitious piece before sinking out of view as the curtain rose. The story recounted how Fane (Tom Powers) spends a year in Rome trying to prove himself a composer, runs off to Paris with a girlfriend (Christine Norman) to seek inspiration there, falls out with her and flees to Port Said where "hoochee-coochee dancing and screeching harlots," including a notorious wanton called San Francisco Sal (Helen Ware), provide no afflatus, and finally hears the music of the spheres in the Marquesas Islands after discovering he has become a leper.

In Mark Swan's **Judy Drops In** (10-4-24, Punch and Judy) Judy Drummond (Marion Mears), rather than sneak home in the wee hours, takes refuge in a Greenwich Village garret shared by three disorganized young artists—Tom, Dick, and Harry. She not only brings order to their haphazard world but meets and falls in love with their friend Jack Letheridge (Donald Gallaher)

Frederick Lonsdale's London melodrama, **The Fake** (10-6-24, Hudson) found few takers on this side of the Atlantic. To rescue the girl (Frieda Inescort) he loves from her unhappy marriage to the vicious, dishonest, drug-addicted earl's son (Frank Conroy) her opportunistic, politician father (Orlando Daly) has foisted on her, Gerrard Pillick (Godfrey Tearle) kills his rival with a drug overdose after making it seem like suicide and creating an ironclad alibi for himself in case the police were unconvinced.

George Broadhurst and Lillian Trimble Bradley (soon to be the next Mrs. Broadhurst) tried for a second time this season, only to fail again. Their **The Red Falcon** (10-7-24, Broadhurst) was set in the fifteenth century. In a prologue, a marauding warrior (McKay Morris), busy burning the Sicilian town of Badia, comes to the local convent, realizes that the Mother Superior (Thais Lawton) is the woman he once loved and was prevented from marrying, so agrees to spare the nunnery if she will sleep with him. Many years later the son (Morris) of that liaison has become a priest, but his father's genes eventually goad him to don his parent's red garments and to try a little marauding of his own, until his guilt feelings, inherited no doubt from his mother, lead him to abandon his warring and enter a monastery.

Neither critics nor playgoers were impressed with Edmund Wilson's **The Crime in the Whistler Room**

(10-9-24, Provincetown Playhouse), even though Stark Young suggested that "Wilson's fantastic comedy or tragedy, or whatever it is, proved to be engaging." Its focus was "Bill" McKee (Mary Blair), the daughter of a ne'er-do-well dreamer (Perry Ivins). Bill has been taken from the Y.W.C.A. by the socially prominent Miss Streetfield (Mary Morris), who hopes to elevate her. But Bill believes she is more confined then elevated, and she prefers to party with the rebellious, fist-swinging radical writer, Simon Delacy (E. J. Ballantine). In a nightmare she dreams that she has killed Miss Streetfield's brother (Edgar Stehli) and that Simon has become a wolf. Awake again, she runs off with Simon after confessing that she is pregnant. Besides filling his play with unlikable characters, Wilson also filled it with long speeches and with strange dialogue (obviously meant to capture Bill's lack of a proper education): "Why, I've knownum to come into Cincinnati with only forty-five cents inuz pocket, and inside of two weeks' time raise seven thousand dawllars." Among Cleon Throckmorton's settings was a dream sequence which showed a man on an exceptionally high stool, writing on an equally high desk. He was flanked by two oversized blackboards (suggesting Bill's tutoring) covered with unintelligible algebraic formulas. Some implied that the acting shifted from realistic to stylized in the dream sections.

A modest little hit from England broke the run of flops. Eden Phillpotts's **The Farmer's Wife** (10-9-24, Comedy) told of the attempts of Samuel Sweetland (Charles Coburn), a Devonshire farmer and widower, to find a new wife. To help him he enlists his housekeeper, Araminta Dench, and since Araminta was played by Mrs. Coburn knowing playgoers had a good idea early on whom Samuel would marry.

As a critic, Stark Young would later come to be perceived as a precursor of a new order. More so than most earlier reviewers he was a faddist, with little tolerance for older traditions. He was often a petty quibbler. He injected what a later generation would call political correctness into many of his notices. And, perhaps worst of all, he was an uninteresting writer. His stint on the *Times* would be brief, though he would move on to other publications. Similarly, he would persist in his attempts at playwrighting despite the cold shoulder given him by his fellow critics and the public. Even as accomplished and admired, if ill-lucked, an actor as Leo Carrillo could do nothing for Young's **The Saint** (10-11-24, Greenwich Village). Carrillo played Valdez, a cowboy-turned-seminarian, lured away from his studies and devotions by the voluptuous Marietta (Helen Freeman). After he learns that she has run off with a knife thrower from a touring vaudeville band, he attempts to return to the seminary but in time recognizes that he is better suited for a cowboy's life. The play was given a fine production, with religious processions passing by the portico of the Texas seminary and with lively slices of backstage life at the vaudeville tent. Young's paper, in an unsigned review, lauded the play for its "lofty aim," "great delicacy," and "many moments of beauty," and blamed its obvious failure on the cast, making an exception only of Maria Ouspenskaya, so recently of the Moscow Art. She played the knife thrower's discarded mistress. *Variety,* concurring with the *Times* as far as Ouspenskaya was concerned, noted that she won "bravos" although she was "shrivelled, intentionally ugly and handicapped by an obviously limited control of English and a marked accent" in her brief second-act appearance.

Three comedies arrived the next Monday night. Two were American, and neither of these was well received. Lynn Starling's **In His Arms** (10-13-24, Fulton) detailed the adventures of Elise Clarendon (Margaret Lawrence), who is engaged to the priggish painter Ernest Fairleigh (Geoffrey Kerr) but is not above flirting with the more fun-loving Dutchman, Tom van Ruysen (Vernon Steele), whom she has only just met. Ernest's worldly-wise mother (Effie Shannon) is good-natured and perspicacious enough to try to warn Elise off her son. She tells the younger woman that she must be prepared "from now on to take second place, put yourself out of your thoughts, submerge your individuality." And Ernest, though he is more preoccupied with the exhibition of his latest painting, *The Evolution of a Soul,* than he is with wedding plans, is condescendingly prepared to forgive Elise if such an affair does not happen again. But it does. When an angry Ernest brings up this flirtation on their wedding day, Elise decides to elope with Tom, who is sailing home the next morning and has reserved a cabin big enough for two. Asked by Mrs. Fairleigh where she will spend her wedding night, Elise replies, "In his arms." Several reviewers remarked that Miss Lawrence was growing too old for such roles. Kerr was praised, but some older players were even more applauded in secondary roles: Effie Shannon as Ernest's understanding mother, Edna May Oliver as Elise's outspoken mother, and Grant Stewart as her peppery father. The cast also included such rising performers as Eliot Cabot and Cornelia Otis Skinner. The Sam Harris production lingered for just five weeks.

Rida Johnson Young's **Cock o' the Roost** (10-13-

24, Liberty) was produced by the same group of playwrights, operating as the Dramatists' Theatre, who last year had offered *The Goose Hangs High.* It seems the luxury-loving Mrs. Dawn (Elisabeth Risdon), discontent that Mr. Dawn (Harry Davenport), a writer of dime novels, is so poor a provider, is determined that her daughter Phyllis (Katherine Wilson), shall marry the rich if otherwise worthless Henry Barron (Purnell Pratt), even though Phyllis prefers the brash, show-offy Jerry Heyward (Donald Foster). All ends happily after Jerry, while the women are away visiting Barron, convinces Mr. Dawn to give up his fancy Park Avenue apartment and take a cheaper one at the Sheridan Model Tenements. Freed from money worries Dawn writes a worthwhile novel that could become a best-seller. His wife sees the light.

The evening's third comedy was Ferenc Molnár's *A testör,* which Broadway had seen and rejected more than a decade earlier as *Where Ignorance Is Bliss* and which was now bravely resurrected by the Theatre Guild at the Garrick. Although reset in Vienna, the new version retained the saga of the Actor, so suspicious of the Actress, his wife, that he claims a nonexistent engagement out of town and reappears disguised as a Russian officer to woo and seemingly win her. The dejected Actor returns to their elegant apartment as himself. He decides to confront his wife with the truth. In her foreword to the printed play Theresa Helburn described what followed: "At the moment when the Actor rises from behind the trunk in the partial make-up of the Guardsman and reassumes his Russian accent, the Actress is lying prone on the couch, reading a book. There is no sudden gesture. Very slowly the book is lowered, the actress looks back and up at the figure towering above her and her lips gradually curve into a smile. It may be the moment of recognition for her, it may be she has recognized him a few minutes before, it may be she has known him all along. Every member of the audience is free to answer the question." Although an excellent new adaptation largely by Philip Moeller, a fine supporting cast which included Dudley Digges and Helen Westley, some excellent settings by Jo Mielziner, among them a red-and-black marbled opera house lobby, and a new and more succinct title, **The Guardsman,** all helped turn an old flop into a fresh success, there was little disagreement that the evening's most magnetic attraction was the playing together of Alfred Lunt and Lynn Fontanne, their first major acting as a couple. Writing in the *Herald Tribune,* Percy Hammond called their playing "perfect" and saw it as "superior to the play itself." Broun

characterized them as "brilliant." But it remained for Woollcott to pen the most prophetic, often quoted lines: "They have youth and great gifts and the unmistakable attitude of ascent and those who saw them last night bowing hand in hand for the first time may well have been witnessing a moment in theatrical history. It is among the possibilities that we were seeing the first chapter in a partnership destined to be as distinguished as that of Henry Irving and Ellen Terry. Our respective grandchildren will be able to tell." The play, in its season-long run, gave the Guild its biggest money-maker to date. Besides securing the Lunts a lasting celebrity, it immeasurably aided Mielziner's rise.

. . .

Jo Mielziner (1901–76), a descendant of a long line of rabbis and cantors, was born in Paris and studied at both the Pennsylvania Academy of Fine Arts and the National Academy of Design. He entered the theatre by working as an actor, then a designer, for Jessie Bonstelle in Detroit. Subsequently he served as an actor and stage manager for the Theatre Guild, before that group enlisted him to create the settings for this production. His brother was Kenneth MacKenna, the actor.

. . .

Leslie Hickson and W. Lee Dickson's **Clubs Are Trumps** (10-14-24, Bijou) lost its entire investment and folded after just six performances. In that short time it unveiled the tale of William Augustus Jones (Harry Green), who decides that learning golf is the easiest road to success. Apparently he is right, because his experiences at the Tutley Country Club bring him a nice job with a soup company and a nice girl to cook his soup for him.

According to Edwin Justus Mayer's **The Firebrand** (10-15-24, Morosco) Benvenuto Cellini (Joseph Schildkraut) led a more dangerous existence. As he returns home, he slams the door behind him and locks it, for although he is under orders of the Duke of Florence to maintain the peace, he has just killed another man in a brawl. He hopes a friendly Cardinal, for whom he is making a golden cup, will intercede. He tells his servants that "genius is in itself a charm" and that his cups and vases and statues are better protection that any law or dagger. The Duke (Frank Morgan) himself, a lascivious scatterbrain, arrives, prepared to have Cellini hanged. But the artist's smooth words and the sight of Cellini's beautiful mistress, Angela (Eden Grey), whom he instantly appropriates, mollify him. After the Duke departs, his cousin Ottaviano (Edward G. Robinson) tries vainly to get Cellini to kill the Duke. Then the Duchess (Nana Bryant) appears and pours out her love for Cellini. A liaison is arranged. But it never takes place, for in the comic comings and goings at the Duke's moonlit palace, Cellini manages to steal away with Angela, leaving the puzzled Duke and Duchess, standing together on their balcony, to explain matters to each other. Back at Cellini's workshop, the artist has had his fill of Angela, so when an angry Duke and an angrier Duchess come on the scene again, Cellini must use all his glibness and subtlety to hand Angela back to the Duke, blame Ottaviano for all the mischief, and arrange another liaison with the Duchess. The play's dialogue was fast-moving and impassioned, with just enough formality to suggest long-gone days.

Duchess: You are not only a villain, Cellini, but a clever villain. You try to put me on the defensive. You will not succeed.
Cellini: Madam, whatever you speak from, I speak from the heart.
Duchess: You have no heart!
Cellini: No, for your ladyship has torn it out of my breast and flung it in my face!

Schildkraut was applauded for his "dash and verve," Morgan for his "deliciously" comic playing, and Miss Bryant for her "authority," while Robinson was seen as "a more than satisfying villain." And all this was acted out in Woodman Thompson's superb costumes and settings, particularly the Duke's moonlit, shadowed garden and balcony. Hornblow, so often repelled by even a hint of raciness, put aside his strictures and called the evening "a buoyant, boisterous and genuinely amusing comedy-farce." And Woollcott embraced this "jovial entertainment." It ran out the season and in 1945 was turned into an unsuccessful musical, *The Firebrand of Florence,* by Kurt Weill and Ira Gershwin.

A less inspired piece, Reginald Goode's melodramatic **Ashes** (10-20-24, National), disappeared quickly, despite some fine performing by its star, Florence Reed. She played an actress, Marjorie Lane, married to a self-serving scoundrel (Warburton Gamble). He persuades her to hand their baby over to a relation so that raising it will not interfere with her career. But on the night of her greatest triumph she learns that the child has died (at which point she tearfully holds up to the audience the baby clothes she was about to send to it), and as if that agony is not enough, she discovers her husband is unfaithful to her with her own sister (Gladys Hurlbut). She decides to go out into the big, lonely world to seek happiness somewhere else.

Anne Nichols, using some of her huge profits from *Abie's Irish Rose,* turned producer to bring a French company headed by Mme. Simone to Henry Miller's Theatre on the same night. Opening with *L'Aiglon,* the troupe moved on to *Madame Sans-Gêne, La Parisienne, Un Caprice, Amoureuse,* and one Italian play, Pirandello's recent *Vestire gli Ignudi,* performed in French but advertised as **Naked** (10-27-24), which told of how a prevaricating minx cons a gullible author into writing a totally fictitious biography of her. The Frenchmen were received politely but no more, and Miss Nichols was reported to have lost a bundle on the venture.

David Belasco also lost money on his latest venture. **Tiger Cats** (10-21-24, Belasco) was Michael Orme's version of the Danish Karen Bramson's Paris hit *Les Félines.* It unfolded the tempestuous relationship of André Chaumont, a dedicated psychologist, and his demanding wife. She had been one of his many former admirers but after their wedding had come to resent what she perceived as his neglect. Her nagging and patent disdain drive him to attempt to kill her, but his shot misses. Totally cowed, he gives up his career to devote himself to pleasing his wife. The play had been a major London success with Robert Loraine and Edith Evans. But Miss Evans, who had brought some striking pyrotechnics to her interpretation, refused to come to America with the play. Belasco cast Katharine Cornell in her role, only to discover that Miss Cornell pleasantly but firmly refused to mimic the English actress. Hers was a subdued performance, smoldering but never exploding. Perhaps amazingly, Belasco capitulated. But he must have regretted his capitulation after reading the reviews, many of which blamed Cornell for the evening's failure. (The often carping Stark Young was one of the few critics to admire her playing.)

A second French play was also dismissed the same night. Henry Baron served as his own producer when he brought out his adaptation of **Comedienne** 10-21-24, Bijou), taken from Paul Armont and Jacques Bousquet's Paris hit. Facing up to the news that her lover has become engaged to a younger woman, the fiftyish Helen Blakemore (Charlotte Walker) decides to abandon her long career as an ingenue. She goes to live with her son (Alexander Clark, Jr.) and his family in Virginia but soon finds their petty squabbling unbearable. Luckily the offer of a fine new role and the discovery that her lover (Cyril Keightley) has not wed after all, bring about a happy ending.

After several disappointing seasons, Ethel Barrymore alighted on a congenial role when Arthur Hopkins revived Arthur Wing Pinero's *The Second Mrs. Tanqueray* for her at the Cort on the 27th. In this story of a woman with a past, driven to suicide by a society that will neither forget nor forgive, Henry Daniell, Lionel Pape, G. P. Huntley, and Margot Kelly were among her supporting players. The revival did good business during its nine-week engagement, which was part of a pre-booked national tour.

A pair of novelties that opened the same night were soon gone. By coincidence, mill town life figured in both, but more directly in Robert Ritz's **Alloy** (10-27-24, Princess). Pansy and Bill Jorgan (Minna Gombell and Byron Beasley) are an unhappily married working-class couple. He is a drunkard and frequently abusive when in his cups. The miserable Pansy throws herself into the arms of John Walton (Ivan Miller), a boarder Bill has insisted be taken in to add to their income. At first John demurs, but after he witnesses Bill's attacking Pansy, he agrees to go off with her.

J. C. and Elliott Nugent, still seeking another *Kempy,* didn't find one in **The Rising Son** (10-27-24, Klaw). J. C. cast himself as Jim Alamayne, who years earlier left another steel town where his father was employed because the old man wanted him to become a priest and he wanted to write. Now a successful humorist, he tries to force his own son (Elliott), who would rather marry and become an innkeeper, to follow in his footsteps. Only after Jim realizes his prospective daughter-in-law (Ruth Nugent) is a skillful writer does he bow to the theatrically inevitable. Interestingly, as with *Kempy,* it was neither J. C. nor his son, Elliott, who walked off with the best notices, but Elliott's sister, Ruth. But she alone could not turn a mediocre comedy into a hit.

At the Provincetown Playhouse on November 3rd, four of Eugene O'Neill's early one-act sea plays—*The Moon of the Caribees, The Long Voyage Home, In the Zone,* and *Bound East for Cardiff*—were staged together in an evening named for the ship about which all four plays revolve, **S.S. Glencairn.** Well received, the combination ran for three months.

A far more lavish mounting ran as long but wound up in the loss column when the release of a silent film curtailed its post-Broadway tour. This, too, was a revival—James M. Barrie's *Peter Pan*—which Charles Dillingham brought out at the Knickerbocker on the 6th with musical comedy queen Marilyn Miller in the role heretofore played only by Maude Adams in America. Critics admired the star's beauty and charm but felt she left much to be desired as an actress. To gloss over her inadequacies, she sang some minor new Jerome Kern material.

Jules Eckert Goodman and Edward Knoblock could take small comfort from their dramatization of Robert Keable's novel **Simon Called Peter** (11-10-24, Klaw), which told of a priest (Leonard Willey), serving at the front, who falls in love with a nurse (Catherine Willard). He leaves the priesthood in order to marry her, after she dashes down the aisle of a church to embrace him during a sermon.

There was still less interest in Laurence Eyre's **The Steam Roller** (11-10-24, Princess). William Trimble (Bruce McRae), a writer of popular fiction, has long loved Dorcas Dill (Olive Wyndham), but her steam-rolling sister, Amelia (Janet Beecher), covets Trimble for herself. For a time Trimble runs off, but later, steeling himself, he comes back and offers to marry Amelia on such threatening and humiliating terms that she consents to his wedding Dorcas.

For the second time in less than a month a French troupe made itself at home on Broadway. This one was headed by Firmin Gémier, supported by players from the Paris Odéon, and came into the Jolson on the same night. Besides Molière's *Le Bourgeois Gentilhomme,* the company performed such lesser-known works as Pierre Frondaie's **L'Homme qui assassina** (in which a lover kills his mistress's brutal husband), Henri de Gorsse and Louis Forest's **Le Procureur Hallers** (centering on a Jekyll-and-Hyde lawyer), and Henri-René Lenormand's **L'Homme et ses fantômes** (dealing with the repentance of a Don Juan), and French versions of *The Taming of the Shrew* and *The Merchant of Venice.*

Just over a week after some of his old plays were revived, O'Neill had a new one ready for inspection, **Desire Under the Elms** (11-11-24, Greenwich Village). With the help of his three sons, the unsparing, miserly, seventy-five-year-old Ephraim Cabot (Walter Huston) works the New England farm he inherited from his second wife. His youngest son, Eben (Charles Ellis), blames his father for his mother's death from overwork. Simeon (Allen Nagle) and Peter (Perry Ivins), Eben's older half-brothers, hope for a better life in California—"at t'other side of the world." After Ephraim takes Abbie Putnam (Mary Morris), an ambitious young widow, for his third wife, the older boys sell out to Eben and head for the gold fields. Abbie seduces Eben, and when she has a child she lets Ephraim believe he is the father and make the baby his heir. A furious Eben denounces Abbie. To prove that she has come to love him she kills the baby. Eben calls in the authorities, but since he, in turn, has come to love Abbie, he claims that he is her accomplice. As Abbie and Eben are taken away, Ephraim muses that he will be lonelier than ever. But then, "God's lonesome, hain't He? God's hard an' lonesome!" Considering the play's later prestige, its initial reception is surprising. In the *American* Alan Dale cried out against "hideous characters" caught up in "cantankerous, cancerous proceedings." As if bridging the yeas and nays, Broun saw the playwright as a would-be pioneer still enmeshed in the superannuated traditions of his father's day. And Robert Benchley, who thought O'Neill had "tortured" his theme "into a terrific catastrophe," noted the play "has moments of unconscious comedy, a terrible thing for a tragedy," and that it became overheated and repetitive in the last half. Highly approving, Stark Young hailed the work as "mature" and "imaginative." Huston's performance was also praised. (In later years O'Neill would claim that Huston was one of only three players over the years to fully capture the playwright's intent.) Surprisingly, Robert Edmond Jones's setting caused serious controversy. It showed the old farmhouse (with one or more of its rooms exposed at different times in keeping with the characters' movements) coming right down to the footlights and ancient elms overhanging it. Young called it "profoundly dramatic," but Woollcott complained that it was little more than "a mechanical toy, not unsuited to farce, but disastrous when used as the background for so dour and grave a play." For all the critical quibbles, the drama ran more than six months, some of the time at a larger house uptown.

Max Marcin's **Silence** (11-12-24, National) ran just a week less, helped by notices that called it "one of the best melodramas of recent seasons" and "one of the best [crook plays] New York has seen since *Within the Law*." In five hours Jim Warren (H. B. Warner), a man with a criminal past, will be executed, unless he tells who really did kill the blackmailing Harry Silvers (John Wray). Long ago Jim had had an affair with Norma Drake (Flora Sheffield), but finding him unfaithful she had left him and married Phil Powers (Frederick Perry), who had accepted Norma and Jim's baby as his own. Jim had wandered about the country as a carnival gamester. Just before Norma and Jim's daughter, also called Norma (and also played by Sheffield), is about to make a brilliant marriage, Silvers appears and threatens to disclose letters revealing the girl's illegitimate birth. Jim had tried to alert Powers but was accused of being Silvers's crony and chased out. However, he lingered long enough to see the girl kill the blackmailer. He remains silent until prison officials plant a phony priest (H. Cooper Cliffe) to trick him into a

confession. The girl, learning who her father really is and how far he will go to protect her, admits her guilt. But a timely pardon lets the curtain fall on a smiling father and daughter.

No long run awaited Langdon McCormick's **Shipwrecked** (11-12-24, Frazee). Probably only the most dedicated playgoers recognized that McCormick was a voice out of the past, a prolific creator of cheap touring melodramas of an earlier day. Those were the days when heroines regularly jumped into huge stage tanks representing a river or lake or ocean to be rescued in the nick of time by the hero. And when, quite frequently, the same hero later had to rescue the heroine from a burning building. Now, in 1924, a despairing Loie Austin (Gilda Leary) jumps from a wharf into the East River and is rescued by dashing, life-loving Steve Calvin (Clay Clement), the son of a wealthy shipowner. (The act took only eleven minutes and was set on a dimly lit wharf, with a "rippling water effect" in the background.) He takes her aboard the S.S. *Corsican,* one of his father's vessels, sailing for warmer climates. But the vicious, lustful captain (Edmund Elton) has his own ideas about Loie. During a storm at sea, the ship catches fire, but just as the captain is about to have his way with the defenseless girl, who has grabbed an elephant tusk to ward off the villain, Steve suddenly appears and again saves her. Back on dry land, the pair decide to wed. One critic singled out "the burning of a ship in a manner so realistic as to cause visible signs of discomfiture in . . . the beholders." The outside of the ship had been shown at the start of Act II, but moments later the inside of the bridge and captain's quarters was revealed to allow the action to proceed.

Frank Craven vainly continued to seek a successor to *The First Year*. His **New Brooms** (11-17-24, Fulton) certainly did not fill the bill. Thomas Bates (Robert McWade), a successful broom manufacturer, resents the playboy ways and attitudes of his son, Thomas junior. (Robert Keith): "You'd think I was a relic from Noah's Ark, the way he talks." The old man is admittedly a grouch, as any hardworking, down-to-earth fellow should be, while the son has a foolishly sunny disposition. The men decide to change places. Before long the elder Bates is relaxed and smiling, while Junior has not only become snappish but is something of a failure at work. In the end, the two agree they need each other, and young Thomas decides to marry a pretty housekeeper he had hired and later fired, when he questioned her interest in his father. The play had homey lines such as "Men don't take so much pride in their sons as they do in the fact that they are the boy's father," but it was "absolutely devoid of dramatic situations" and too "slow moving."

The second unhappy priest in just over a week was the central figure in Alice Sidman and Victoria Montgomery's **Blind Alleys** (11-17-24, Punch and Judy), a play mounted for the benefit of the Disabled American War Veterans. The priest comes home from the war recognizing that he no longer loves his wife. Instead he has fallen for an attractive ambulance driver he met in France, and she for him. So he breaks up the old marriage for the sake of a newer one. The play survived for merely one week.

The same night also saw a revival of Congreve's *The Way of the World* at the Cherry Lane with a cast of unknowns who would remain unknown. But unexpectedly good notices kept the play going at the tiny, out-of-the-way house for fifteen weeks.

The Desert Flower (11-18-24, Longacre), Don Mullally's second melodrama of the season, received a fair share of enthusiastic reviews yet failed to find its public. The play was set in the construction camps and crude mining communities of 1903 Nevada. After Maggie Fortune (Helen MacKellar) is beaten by her demoniacally abusive stepfather, Mike Dyer (Robert Cummings), for consorting with a young, college-educated tramp, Rance Conway (Roberts Ames), she and Rance run off together. Rance seems to be an alcoholic wastrel until Maggie finally goads him into prospecting. Having found gold, he returns. But he also finds that Maggie has shot and killed Mike, who came looking for her and attacked her. Rance attempts to take the blame for the murder, but both he and Maggie are exonerated when the true story is revealed. Even critics who disliked the play admired MacKellar's impassioned, stirring performance.

Cosmo Hamilton's **Parasites** (11-19-24, 39th St.) was also unable to develop legs. Joan Millett (Francine Larrimore) has squandered her inheritance and so attempts to support herself by her winnings at bridge. She is apparently not the best of players, for she is badly in debt when Langdon Pomeroy (Cecil Humphreys) slips her the money to cover her losses. Since she loves Langdon she is overjoyed until Langdon proposes she show her gratitude by becoming his mistress. The shocked girl is clever enough to agree but to stall, and, in the ensuing time, Langdon falls in love with her, so proposes marriage instead. Critics admired Larrimore's playing, even with her "everpresent cigarettes," her "sharp, restless mannerisms," and her "baby-blue diction." However, the best notices went to Clifton Webb as Eliot Phelps, an effete society pet who is forever kissing ladies' fingertips

and murmuring "Tell Elie" to grandes dames seeking consolation.

Sidney Howard, who had been working primarily as a translator and collaborator, hit the jackpot when he struck out on his own with **They Knew What They Wanted** (11-24-24, Garrick). Tony (Richard Bennett) is an aging, not particularly attractive wine-maker in the Napa Valley who proposes by mail to a San Francisco waitress named Amy. But afraid that the youngster would reject him as too old and too ugly, he sends her the photograph of his handsome hired hand, Joe (Glenn Anders). When Amy (Pauline Lord) arrives she quickly discovers the truth, and the shock drives her into Joe's arms. Tony soon learns what has happened and that Amy is pregnant, but his need for love and his innate decency allow him to forgive: "What you done was mistake in da head, not in da heart. . . . Mistake in da head is no matter." Deeply moved by his compassion, Amy consents to remain with him. Most critics admired the play, even though many held reservations. Thus, the sniffy Hornblow characterized it as "an unusually well-constructed play, smudged up with repellent situations." But Benchley, feeling it did a better job with the same theme than had *Desire Under the Elms,* observed that the "comedy has moments of great pathos, a necessary thing for comedy." There were virtually no reservations about the players, and nearly twenty years later Brooks Atkinson could write, "Those of us who saw the Theatre Guild's production . . . will never be able to read the racy dialogue without hearing the voices of Pauline Lord, Richard Bennett and Glenn Anders rising and falling over the crises of the story. Those voices, all distinct and individual with remarkable contrast in tone and inflection, still haunt the text of the play." Most haunting for many were Lord's husky, jerkily delivered utterances. The play ran nearly a year (the Guild's second smash-hit money-maker in a row), won the Pulitzer Prize, and in 1956 was made into a successful musical, *The Most Happy Fella,* by Frank Loesser. The play's success made Howard a name to be reckoned with.

• • •

Sidney [Coe] Howard (1891–1939) was born to pioneer stock in Oakland, Calif. After studying at the University of California, he moved east to take courses under Professor George Pierce Baker in his 47 Workshop at Harvard. Employment on magazines and newspapers followed before his first play, *Swords,* was produced in 1921.

• • •

That same evening saw the opening of yet another drama about the flapper problem and the generation gap, Tom Barry's **Dawn** (11-24-24, Sam H. Harris). When Matthew Slayton (Howard Lang) learns that his daughter, Judith (Zita Johann), a cigarette-smoking, booze-guzzling, shimmying eighteen-year-old, is no longer a virgin, he demands she marry the boy who deflowered her. Judith claims she is not certain which boy it was. (She does know but, since she no longer cares for him, doesn't want to be involved with him anymore.) Her more understanding mother (Emma Dunn) comes to her rescue by confessing that she was no virgin when she married Matthew. Judith is free to head for the altar with the boy she would choose. The play failed.

So did December's first entry, Dorothy Parker and Elmer Rice's **Close Harmony** (12-1-24, Gaiety). In suburban Homecrest, which is just forty-five minutes from Grand Central and where the homes all seem look-alikes, Ed Graham (James Spottswood) is married to a garrulous, pushy wife (Georgie Drew Mendum), while his next-door neighbor, Belle Sheridan (Wanda Lyon), is wed to an unloving, preoccupied spouse (Robert Hudson). But since Belle gives piano lessons to the Grahams' daughter, she is in their home a lot. Soon Ed has dusted off his mandolin, which his wife has prohibited him from playing, and is performing duets with Belle in Belle's living room. Before long Ed and Belle decide to run off together. Then Ed's little daughter becomes ill and other problems crop up, prompting Ed to back away from the scheme. Belle runs off alone. Reviewers praised the often witty dialogue but regretted the cleverness did not add up to a genuine comedy.

A handful of matinees was all that a revival of Stephen Phillips's *Paolo and Francesca* could muster, beginning on the 2nd at the Booth. Morgan Farley was Paolo; Phyllis Povah, Francesca da Rimini; and Claude King, Giovanni Malatesta.

But that evening did usher in a hit, **The Harem** (12-2-24, Belasco), David Belasco's mounting of Avery Hopwood's adaptation of Ernö Vajda's comedy. In a sense the play was the counterpart of *The Guardsman*, with a wife testing a husband and finding him less than perfect. In Budapest, Carla (Lenore Ulric), having learned that her husband (William Courtenay) of just three years has kissed another woman and enjoyed himself in doing it, arranges for him to supposedly meet that woman on the sly. The husband invents an excuse for leaving the house. As soon as he is gone, the blonde Carla puts on a black wig and a Turkish odalisque's costume and veil and runs off to meet him. They have a flaming night in a hotel room, where Carla has conveniently smashed the lamps. The next day the wife confronts the husband, but he claims that he

knew who she was all along. While critics disagreed about the play's merits, though even many of those who questioned its worth conceded it was entertaining, they united in praising Ulric's fetching performance.

A capital comic, Gregory Kelly, breathed enough life into Max Marcin and Edward Hammond's **Badges** (12-3-24, 49th St.) to give it a three-month run. A naive Brooklyn hotel clerk, Franklyn Green, has earned his tin detective's badge from a correspondence school. Although he has served no apprenticeship he is convinced that pretty Miriam Holt (Lotus Robb) is being trailed by a bevy of suspicious-looking figures. That bevy turns out to be a motley but interrelated gang of bond thieves, false impersonators, and a murderer. Led by Miriam's father, who wanted to get enough money to send his daughter to college, they had stolen $2,000,000 worth of bonds. His cronies had then murdered Holt, but only after he had given each one of them a partial clue to where he had hidden the loot. Since the survivors have had a falling out, they are hard put to combine the clues and find the money. Green's pursuit, after he stumbles on one of the clues, takes him from New York to somewhere out west before he nails the criminals in a "haunted" house and wins Miriam. That Kelly was not yet a top drawer was suggested by *Variety*'s remarking that the "$3.30 top . . . seems a high scale for an attraction without a star."

The Man in Evening Clothes (12-5-24, Henry Miller's), which Ruth Chatterton adapted from André Picard and Yves Mirande's French comedy, earned neither laurels nor profits. Believing his wife no longer loves him, the Count de Lussange (Henry Miller) dissipates his entire fortune and in the end is left with only the evening clothes that French bankruptcy laws allow a man to retain. The French version ended with the count reduced to taking tickets at a theatre, but Miss Chatterton tacked on a happier curtain, with the wife (Carlotta Monterey), proving she loves her husband, promising to help restore his fortune.

On the other hand, the Neighborhood Players won applause and some small success with their unusual offering, **The Little Clay Cart** (12-5-24, Neighborhood Playhouse). This ancient Hindu work, translated from the Sanskrit by Arthur William Ryder, told how a courtesan (Kyra Alanova) saves the merchant (Ian Maclaren) she loves from being unjustly hanged.

No kudos and a Saturday night closing awaited Thomas P. Robinson's **Artistic Temperament** (12-9-24, Wallack's). Its action occurred in an elegant, purple-draped room whose windows overlook fruit orchards in bloom. The room is where Archie Stanwood (Donald Foster) receives his inspirations and writes his novels. Alice Huntington (Gail Kane), a thirtyish friend of his wife (Elisabeth Risdon), comes visiting with her professorial fiancé (Austin Freeman), with whom she is at the moment having an argument. Stanwood takes advantage of their rupture and his wife's temporary absence to seduce Alice. It will provide material for a new book.

Katharine Cornell set a long string of disappointments behind her when she assumed the title role in a revival of Shaw's *Candida* at a matinee at the 48th Street Theatre on the 12th. In this story of a woman who must choose between her dreary minister husband and a lovesick poet, Pedro de Cordoba was the Reverend Morell and Richard Bird, Marchbanks. Clare Eames was Prossy, the secretary, and Ernest Cossart was Candida's rascally father. Young hailed Cornell's playing as "a deep revelation," continuing, "Her frail presence had something in it of the light of another world. She was strong, not with womanly aplomb and maternal astuteness, but with an exquisite power to feel and understand." Demand for seats to the slated matinees far exceeded expectations, so the play soon moved on to a regular run, not closing until it had chalked up 143 performances.

Raymond Hitchcock, whom Stanley Green described as "a lanky, raspy-voiced comic with sharp features and straw colored hair that he brushed across his forehead," for years had been a musical comedy favorite but recently had spent time touring in *The Old Soak*. Now he tried another bit of homespun comedy with William A. Grew's **The Sap** (12-15-24, Apollo). His wife, Betty (Miriam Sears), his younger sister-in-law, Jane (Doris Eaton) and her husband, Ed (Norval Keedwell), and his sharp-tongued, older, spinster sister-in-law, Kate (Peggy Allenby), have all resigned themselves to considering Bill Small as a hopelessly cheerful idiot. He cannot or will not hold a job. Kate suggests he "take a tin cup and get a dog and go from house to house," but Ed warns that Bill's "a yokel that never earned a dime and never will." Then a frightened Ed confesses he has stolen $10,000 from the bank where he works and looks to be exposed. He stole it to invest in wheat futures, which promptly went south. Bill gets Ed to invite his manager over, and Bill coyly tricks the man, James Belden (A. H. Van Buren), into confessing that he had stolen even more—for the same reason and with the same disastrous outcome. So Bill blackmails the pair into letting him

steal $50,000. Before they realize what has happened, they read in the paper that Bill has bought the bank. Seems he made the same investment they had, but at the right time. By using the $250,000 he netted in the deal, he purchased the bank and thus precluded anyone from learning about the theft before the men can make good. Suddenly his family all love Bill. And Jane announces that she will wed Mr. Belden.

While his son Joseph was basking in the success of *The Firebrand*, Rudolph Schildkraut garnered little acclaim as star of **The Mongrel** (12-15-24, Longacre), which Elmer Rice took from Hermann Bahr's *Der Querulant*. Schildkraut played an old man whose beloved dog is shot by a forester. Feeling that the court's order to the forester to pay him a token sum for the mutt is grossly inadequate, he plans to strangle the forester's daughter. But her patent humanity—she had loved the old man's now dead son—brings the mourner to his senses.

Producer Edgar Selwyn, having pulled Helen Hayes from a leading role in his production of *Dancing Mothers*, gave her the leading part in F. Tennyson Jesse's **Quarantine** (12-16-24, Henry Miller's). Once again she portrayed a flapper with a mind and will of her own. Dinah Partlett loves Tony Blunt (Sidney Blackmer), the very man her married cousin hopes to run off with. She craftily takes the girl's place on board ship. Blunt discovers the ruse and, to embarrass Dinah, introduces her as his wife. But an epidemic breaks out, quarantining the passengers on Pigeon Island. At a bungalow the supposed honeymooners have been assigned Tony ineluctably succumbs to Dinah's charms. Both the play and its star received appreciative notices. The comedy ran five months, but long before it closed Miss Hayes had deserted it for a more newsworthy mounting.

Henry Hull played Richard Winslow, the title role of Philip Barry's **The Youngest** (12-22-24, Gaiety). Poor Richard, having been almost an afterthought and born following his father's death, is used shamefully by his haughty siblings. An attractive, socially prominent visitor, Nancy Blake (Genevieve Tobin), takes pity on him and bets his somewhat supportive sister (Katharine Alexander) that she can make the would-be writer assert himself in his business-minded family. She states that she will treat him as the most important family member, until he comes to believe it. She tells Richard he would be better off in a world of "less do-as-you're-told, more do-as-you-please." Nancy's remarks and clever ruses are coupled with his sympathetic brother-in-law's revealing to him that a quirk in the law, concerning offspring born after a parent's death and therefore unmentioned in the will, means that the family is deeply in debt to him. This provokes Richard into taking over. But his glee is destroyed when he learns of the bet. He concludes it was all a game on Nancy's part, a heartless way of demonstrating her social position. Of course, since she has come to love Richard, she patiently and thoughtfully explains her side of the situation. Then she asks him to marry her, assuring him he is her equal. Richard can tell her "something better than that." To Nancy's "What?" he responds, "You're mine." Critics, while deeming the comedy "one of those pleasant little entertainments" and "always entertaining," felt it failed to fulfill the brilliant promise of *You and I,* but the public supported it for three modestly profitable months.

If Barry had greater successes ahead, Louis Mann was approaching the end of a long, successful, albeit largely undistinguished career, primarily as a dialect comedian. His latest vehicle was B. Harrison Orkow's **Milgrim's Progress** (12-22-24, Wallack's). The action see-sawed between suburban Connecticut and Central Park West. David Milgrim, a wealthy Jewish businessman, is goaded by his children into moving to New York. There his children and his life all seem to go astray, prompting him to move the family back to their old Connecticut home. But he himself now finds the tug of the city irresistible, so, when the children promise to behave, the final curtain finds him preparing to head for Manhattan again. Only Mann's dwindling crowd of loyalists kept the show alive for eight weeks.

That was five weeks more than Thompson Buchanan and John Meehan's **Bluffing Bluffers** (12-22-24, Ambassador) could muster. Josephine Dawson (Enid Markey) spearheads a women's reform movement that has enlisted Dr. Barnes (Edward H. Robins) as its reluctant candidate. That should surprise some, since Josephine is the daughter of one of the state's crooked senators. Although they are innocent, the candidate's late-night meetings with the ladies could lead to some scandalous headlines. So the girls buy up the town paper (much as Bill Small had bought the bank) to preclude problems.

Another play with a crucial motif echoing a recent work was Milton Herbert Gropper's **Ladies of the Evening** (12-23-24, Lyceum). Sitting with friends at his posh club (seen at first through the balcony windows) Jerry Strong (James Kirkwood), a sculptor, bets that he can turn a streetwalker into a lady by treating her with consideration. He selects Kay Beatty (Beth Merrill). Returning with her to her cheap hotel room, he astonishes her by offering her a job as his model. She soon falls in love with him and abandons all ideas of her former life until she learns of the wager (shades of *The Youngest*). Sorely hurt, she runs off to Atlantic City, where she tries to resume her old ways but realizes that she cannot. Returning to New York, she accepts a job at a restaurant in the downtown business district. Jerry finds her there and convinces her of his love. The play ran until the hot weather scared off playgoers. But midway in its run it was attacked by the local moralists. To please them, Belasco cleaned the piece, leading *Variety,* which reviewed it again, to bewail that it had been "sterilized."

George Arliss was another aging player nearing the end of his career, a far more noteworthy one than Mann's. Although John Galsworthy had described the hero of his **Old English** (12-23-24, Ritz)—based on his short story "The Stoic"—as a big, fat man, Arliss was small and slim. Nevertheless he turned Sylvanus Heythorp into a memorable tour de force. Sylvanus, well into his eighties, still rules the Island Navigation Company with an iron fist. So he is not above arranging a shady ship sale in order to provide for the children of his late, illegitimate son. The threat of exposure and an epicurean feast prove too much, but Sylvanus dies satisfied that he has accomplished his goals and enjoyed life to the full. The play ran out the season and had so profitable a tour that Arliss later claimed it was his biggest money-maker. However, apart from one stab at Shakespeare, it marked his last appearances before the footlights, although he subsequently had a distinguished film career.

Critics felt that so high-minded a group as the Actors' Theatre should have offered something more high-minded—and well written—than Dana Burnet's **The Habitual Husband** (12-24-24, 48th St.). Anne Kingsley (Margalo Gillmore) is a spoiled, demanding wife, in for a shock. When her husband Rodney (Grant Mitchell) returns from showing Anne's friend Hilda (Diantha Pattison) the sights—including the top of the Woolworth Building, where the pair recited poetry to each other—they tell Anne that they have fallen in love and want to run off. Anne reminds Rodney of a compact they signed on their wedding night, three years ago, agreeing to an amicable separation if the marriage bogs down. She tells the pair they are welcome to go, but that she will go with them. At a roadside inn, presided over by a highly allergic ex-butler (Ernest Stallard), Anne slowly wears down Rodney, until he consents to become her habitual husband again.

Broadway did not view the lone Christmas night entry as a present. Taking a page out of *Cheating*

Cheaters, Julie Helene Percival and Calvin Clark's **The Bully** (12-25-24, Hudson) recounted how George Moare (Emmett Corrigan) and his supposed wife, Grace (Margaret Cusack), answer an advertisement looking for servants. George is a crook who worms his way into rich folks' homes, steals what he wants, then disappears. The trusting Grace does not understand what sort of work he does. The ad was placed by Stanley Winton (Barry Jones) a writer whose eyesight is failing, and who is looked after by his doting mother (Olive Oliver), owner of a fine pearl collection. In the end, it turns out that the Wintons placed the ad to trick Moare into coming. He is exposed as a thief and a killer. Furthermore, it seems he never actually married Grace, so Winton, who actually can see a pretty girl a mile away, is free to propose to her.

Nor was there much celebration when the year ended with **Carnival** (12-29-24, Cort), taken by Melville Baker from Molnár's drama. Each year the lovely Camilla (Elsie Ferguson) and her conventional, much older husband come to Budapest for the carnival season. Inevitably handsome young men flirt with her. At a ball Camilla picks up a valuable diamond that has fallen from a princess's crown. She shows the gem to the dashing Nicholas (Tom Nesbitt) and proposes they use it to elope. But Nicholas proves as conventional as Camilla's husband, suggesting she either obtain a divorce or simply become his mistress. So she reluctantly resumes her dull life.

At mid-season *Variety* reported that Broadway was booming as never before. The grosses for Christmas week, inflated in some cases by one or two additional performances to handle the holiday press, were astonishing. Of course, with their higher ticket prices, musicals led the field. *Rose-Marie* topped the list with $52,500, followed by *The Student Prince* with $45,000. Among straight plays *What Price Glory?* led the way with $27,500. *Old English* was not far behind with $27,000, while *The Firebrand* took in $23,000. Many another hit reported between $12,000 and $18,000, very healthy figures at the time.

The first Monday of the new year brought in two hits. In fact, James Gleason and Richard Taber's **Is Zat So?** (1-5-25, 39th St.) tallied the season's longest run—618 performances. With its gate exceeding $26,000 a week, the play became a top straight grosser for some while. Sitting dejectedly on a Central Park bench, Hap Hurley (Gleason), a small time boxing manager, tells Chick Cowan (Robert Armstrong), "You ain't worth the half a pint o' river water it'd take to drown you." Hap is referring to

Chick's going down for the count when a trainer's white towel distracted him long enough for his opponent to land a solid punch and to Chick's forfeiting his previous fight when he failed to show up in Newark because he had to escort a girl to her Brooklyn home. But a drunk in evening clothes staggers by, gets into conversation with the men, and, when they agree to teach him how to slug, invites them to his mansion, directly across the street. He is C. Clinton Blackburn (Sydney Riggs), who lives there with his sister, Sue (Marie Chambers), and her mean, conniving husband, Robert Parker (John C. King). Clint is convinced Parker has libeled Clint's dead brother and cheated the Blackburns out of their estate, and he is anxious to get revenge. More immediately, he arranges for Chick to fight a championship match. But before that time a friendly bout is arranged at the Blackburn home. In the middle of it Chick remembers where he long ago met Parker—during the war, when the latter attempted to bribe soldiers sparring in amateur matches just behind the front. The brainwave distracts him long enough for his latest opponent, a friendly chauffeur, to knock him out. Thinking he did it intentionally, Clint orders Chick to leave. However, after Chick wins the championship the whole story comes out, solid proof of Parker's chicanery is offered, and the curtain falls with Chick and Hap listening as the now properly trained Clint gives an unwanted boxing lesson to his brother-in-law in the next room. Hap and Chick were given subsidiary love stories, with Hap attempting to learn proper English in order to win his lady but eventually confessing, "The gang I trail wit' don't get me when I talk it, so I went back to the old way. S'easier anyway." The title came from Chick's constant, indignant question, to which Hap usually retorts, "Yes, *zat's* so!" and Chick comes back even more vociferously, "*Is zat so?*" A large segment of Broadway playgoers undoubtedly concurred with Bide Dudley, who wrote in the *Evening World,* "Wish we had a season ticket good for the run of the show. . . . We'd wear it out showing it to the doorman."

The second comedy hit was of a more sophisticated order and accordingly ran only 144 performances. Mary Kennedy (Mrs. Deems Taylor) and Ruth Hawthorne's **Mrs. Partridge Presents** (1-5-25, Belmont) was the latest comedy to explore the seemingly increasingly wide generation gap, and one of the best. Burns Mantle characterized it as "a sane and humorous preachment on the determination of parents to rule." Speaking of her children, the long widowed Maisie Partridge (Blanche Bates) informs a family friend, "They let me live my life over again, only now I can do all the things I ever wanted to do. They are correcting all my mistakes. Do you suppose all children turn out so perfectly?" Her friend (Charles Waldron) hints that she may be in for a rude awakening, but she ignores him. After all, daughter Delight (Sylvia Field) is going to be the actress that Maisie had wanted to be before her early marriage, and Philip (Edward Emery, Jr.) will become the family's Whistler. The intrusion of Sydney Armstead (Eliot Cabot), a rich young man whom Delight is obviously falling for, presents an obstacle, so Maisie takes all her savings and buys Delight a part in a forthcoming Broadway play. Then she learns that Philip has left art school and will join a friend building a bridge in Spain. Even worse, Delight leaves a rehearsal and runs off to marry Sydney. Wailing "I have no life to lead outside my children," Maisie is left to salvage what she can, alone. Critics agreed that Miss Bates was disconcertingly nervous on opening night. But she had already told producer Tyrone Guthrie that this would be her last play. It almost was. She subsequently played some short engagements on the road and, goaded by financial considerations in the depths of the Depression, returned briefly to Broadway a decade later. But an apparently very unnervous, relative newcomer stole the show and took a huge step forward. As Katie, Delight's closest buddy, Ruth Gordon "made the little feather-brain an appealing and wistful creature, living a vicarious love affair because her own dominating parents suppressed her. . . . Every line she spoke caused laughter, but it was the kind of laughter which is tempered with understanding of the pathos of the stupid little flapper's plight."

A good idea went sour in Gordon Morris's **Jack in the Pulpit** (1-6-25, Princess), where Jack Faber (Robert Ames), sharing rooms with some of his equally crooked buddies, learns that he has been left half a million dollars by his late aunt on the condition that he become a minister. The men urge him to go through the motions, then abscond with the money. Jack brings such zest and novelty to his preaching at St. John's in Rosedale Junction that the congregation grows by leaps and bounds. This leads to articles about him and photographs in newspapers, and the photographs bring a New York detective on the scene. But Jack has come under the spell not only of his own sermons but of lovely Doris Granger (Marion Coakley), so his past is forgiven. Even his buddies settle into small-town stalwarts.

Nor did New Yorkers want much of Flora Le Breton, who had been called England's Mary Pickford but who also had won applause in the West End. Her vehicle, Edith Carter and Nan Marriott Watson's **Lass o' Laughter** (1-8-25, Comedy), was set in Scotland and recounted the rise of a cruelly snubbed slavey into the ranks of the peerage, where, it developed, she should have been from the start.

Walter Hampden's revival of *Othello*, which restored many traditionally cut scenes, such as all the Cassio-Bianca dialogues, was brought forth at the Shubert on the 10th. Baliol Holloway was the Iago, Jeanette Sherwin the Desdemona. Oldtimers, savoring roseate memories of Booth and Salvini, were disappointed. Younger men found much to praise, albeit their praise was clearly muted. The lavish mounting chalked up fifty-seven performances, a far cry from the long, hugely profitable run of Hampden's *Cyrano*.

An ominous hint of the leftish, propaganda-laden stage pieces of later years could be seen in John Howard Lawson's **Processional** (1-12-25, Garrick), described in programs as "a jazz symphony of American life." Critics felt it was not so formally orchestrated but rather was a sometimes moving, sometimes dismal melange of vaudeville, burlesque, melodrama, and tragedy. As Hornblow reported, "The dominant note is noise and confusion. There is shooting and flag waving, murder, violence, rape." Burns Mantle, clearly not in the play's corner, summed it up, "In a West Virginia mining town there is a strike of miners, offering a background of industrial slavery for the play and silhouetting against it scenes in which the blatant agitator, the purse-proud and psalm-singing capitalist, the howling one hundred percent Ku Kluxer, the whining and protesting Jew and the ignorant, befuddled common citizen struggle to express themselves and their common protests against life in America." Most moving among the scenes were those concerning Dynamite Jim (George Abbott), a blind man who is arrested for killing a soldier and who has a harrowing meeting with his mother (Blanche Friderici) in prison and later is allowed, in a jazz wedding, to marry the Jewish shopkeeper's daughter (June Walker), who is pregnant by him. Playgoers, not yet surfeited with slanted political plays, kept the drama on the boards for three months.

None of the plays that opened the next night succeeded. Blanche Upright's **The Valley of Content** (1-13-25, Apollo) told how Marjorie Benton (Marjorie Rambeau) dreams of the lush life she and her husband will lead in New York, far away from their dreary hometown, after Mr. Benton sells the invention he has patented. However, the dream soon becomes a nightmare of disrespectful children, seductive courtesans, and other big-city horrors, so, when she awakes from her dream, Marjorie is glad to learn that the sale fell through.

Vincent Lawrence's **Two Married Men** (1-13-25, Longacre) actually focused more on the men's discontented wives and the suave bachelor in their midst. James Hunter (George Gaul), recognizing that both Eve Devant (Ann Andrews) and Cora Stevens (Frances Carson) are his for the taking, makes public passes at Cora to hide his more serious pursuit of Eve. Both husbands assault their wives rather than James. Eve, afraid of her forceful John (Minor Watson), capitulates, but the frustrated Cora locks out her fundamentally timid Frank (James Dale).

A light-as-air double bill of importations lured theatregoers for only a month, despite pleasant notices. In **Isabel** (1-13-25, Empire), adapted by Arthur Richman from Kurt Goetz's German original, a handsome, lovesick young man (Leslie Howard) visits a professor (Lyonel Watts) so absorbed in his biological dissections that he has little time for his beautiful, bored wife (Margaret Lawrence), to whom the young man was attracted when he saw the mole on her knee while she was swimming in a stream. Aunt Olivia (Edna May Oliver), wise in the ways of love although she herself is a spinster, counsels the girl to have the best of both worlds. The curtain falls with the professor having gone to bed and the wife staring out into the moonlit garden, where the babbling stream and the lovesick young man await her. The afterpiece was J. M. Barrie's "unfinished" **Shall We Join the Ladies?,** in which a host tells the guests at his dinner table that the murderer of his brother is in the house. Is it one of the guests, one of the servants, or the host himself— since all had motive and occasion for the killing? The play cuts short without pinning the blame on the criminal.

Leon Gordon's **The Piker** (1-15-25, Eltinge), taken from a short story by Oliver Eastwood, was the first of three failures that Lionel Barrymore would appear in during the season. Their cumulative effect convinced the actor to abandon the footlights permanently. Barrymore played Bernie Kaplan, a bank messenger. Noticing an envelope left carelessly on a cashier's desk, he pockets it, hoping it might contain enough money to allow him to buy a decent suit with two pair of pants, so that he can court June Knight (Irene Fenwick). Unwisely, he opens it in front of his shady roommate (Alan Brooks), who realizes that the envelope contains $50,000 and thereupon blackmails him. June proves no better than the roommate and his crooked buddies. Al-

though Bernie loses $20,000 of his cash in bad investments the men advise him to make, he still has enough left to buy the girl a comfortable apartment. But when he goes to visit her he finds her in the arms of her lover (Frank Conroy), who chases him away. Bernie goes to the police to confess his crime, but since the theft has already been solved, with an innocent man sent to jail, the police pack Bernie off to Bellevue for observation. Barrymore, acting in a black wig and with marked Jewish intonations and gestures, received scathing notices—"decidedly monotonous," "never convincing . . . monotonous and distressingly in the same shambling, sobbing key and hoarse voice," "dreary." Woollcott suggested that Barrymore was giving bad performances because he was "slovenly and negligent in his choice of plays," adding, "Vide 'The Piker.' Or rather, don't."

The three openings on the last Monday of January divided first-stringers on which was the right play to attend, but first-stringers and their backups largely agreed that none of the three was very good. The loftiest of the critics deserted Broadway to attend the opening of Rita Matthias's translation of Walter Hasenclever's expressionistic **Beyond** (1-26-25, Provincetown Playhouse), in which a man (Walter Abel), coming to visit an old friend, learns of his death and takes his place in the life of his widow (Helen Gahagan) until events outside the couple's grasp drive him to kill the woman.

A second foreign play was **The Stork** (1-26-25, Cort), which Ben Hecht adapted from László Fodor's *Navarrai Margit* (Margaret of Navarre) and which told how a young man (Geoffrey Kerr) called away on his wedding night by urgent political problems is forced by his dismayed bride (Katharine Alexander) to choose between her and a premiership.

In Barry Conners's **Hell's Bells** (1-26-25, Wallack's) two seemingly successful prospectors return to the hometown of one of the men. The hometown boy's selfish sisters are all honey until they learn that their brother really has no money. They try to have him committed to a mental institution, but he runs off with his buddy, who brings along an attractive widow. Although the comedy received anything but money notices it somehow managed a four-month stand—and not because playgoers with a sense of history wanted to see Olive May or those prescient enough to know the future wanted an early glimpse of Shirley Booth (making her debut) or Humphrey Bogart, all of whom had small roles. Perhaps the presence in the cast of the ever popular "George Spelvin" was an attraction.

Even Jane Cowl's luminous persona could not

nudge Hans Mueller's tawdry **The Depths** (1-27-25, Broadhurst) past a four-week stay. She played Anna, a Viennese prostitute, who falls so in love with a young composer (Rollo Peters) that she is happy to abandon her old trade. The couple go to live in the man's attic, but on the night his symphony is to be played he refuses to take her with him to the concert hall, fearing the snobbish society gathered there would condemn him as well as her. After being refused admission on her own, she walks the streets, briefly and despairingly sells herself, then returns to the attic and jumps from its window.

Knowles Entrikin's **The Small Timers** (1-27-25, Punch and Judy) spotlighted Tommy Devlin (Leslie John Cooley), a young man rebuffed in love and determined to make the girl who rejected him sorry by becoming a famous vaudevillian. His curious selection for a partner is Abigail Mallory (Julie Bernard), his spurner's sister. But the pair prove distressingly untalented, even for the bottom-rung vaudeville house where they present their act. They return home sadder and probably a bit wiser.

Theatrical dreams also figured in another quick failure, A. A. Kline's **Out of Step** (1-29-25, Hudson). Young Henry Harrison (Eric Dressler) has won celebrity as a jazz dancer at Atlantic City's famed Paradise Pier, so he naturally looks forward to a brilliant theatrical career. But then he falls in love with a summer visitor, Edith Rayder (Marcia Byron), and agrees to give up dancing to run the Rayders' Zaneville, Ohio, department store. After a few years, especially after he has tried to form a little jazz ensemble on the side, the Rayders let Henry know that he is grossly unfit to manage a store. Angered at their stance, Henry decides to return to Atlantic City and pick up there where he left off. Following a struggle between her love of comfort and family, and her feelings for Henry, Edith decides to join him.

"Dull" was the descriptive adjective of choice of several critics in their notices for **She Had to Know** (2-2-25, Times Square), which Grace George adapted from Paul Géraldy and Robert Spitzer's *Si je voulais*. Although she has been happily married for ten years, Gerry (George) one night unexpectedly asks her sleepy husband (Bruce McRae) if he still finds her seductive. When she receives only a yawn in answer, she decides to make him jealous and so lures her house guests, including her impetuous cousin (H. Tyrrell Davis), into public embraces, which poke her husband into a more positive, wide-awake response.

Harry Beresford was a first-rate character comedian who rarely found congenial roles in equally first-rate plays. William H. McMasters's **The Undercurrent** (2-3-25, Cort) certainly was not one. Beresford was seen as Jason Mills, one of the world's richest and meanest men. He cares nothing about his miners' poverty and dangers, is a pain to his wife and daughter, and will not tolerate the opposing political views of his daughter's fiancé. Then he is struck down by a Fifth Avenue bus in front of his home. The nightmares he suffers before he regains consciousness change his outlook and behavior.

The ignominy of the season's shortest run—two performances—went to E. B. Dewing and Courtenay Savage's **Don't Bother Mother** (2-3-25, Little). The play had been brought in not for a run but for a series of test matinees. Still, the cancellation of the third and final performance must have been humiliating. During its short life the comedy told of the fortyish Millicent Ray (Mary Hall), who has been keeping her career as an ingenue alive by carefully concealing her husband and grown children and by having publicized romances with her young leading men. She knows the jig is up when her latest co-star (Joseph Macaulay) lets everyone see he prefers the actress's charming young seamstress (Margaret Mower).

Gilbert Emery was also caught in this theatrical dry spell. His **Episode** (2-4-25, Bijou) recounts how the discovery of an emerald ring in his wife's jewel box leads Arnold Ryesdale (William Courtleigh), a neglectful husband, to realize his wife (Kathlene MacDonnell) is having an affair with his best friend (Emery). Mrs. Ryesdale will probably seek a divorce.

William A. Brady long had railed against the production of so many of what he deemed obscene plays. Aware of a growing movement decrying them, he decided to do something about it. He got more than he bargained for, including the public ire of many of his colleagues. In league with Al Woods, who had profited so often and so handsomely from suggestive comedies and dramas, he produced William J. McNally's **A Good Bad Woman** (2-9-25, Comedy). Eileen Donovan (Helen MacKellar) returns to her hometown after years as a New York streetwalker and a chorus girl in questionable shows. No sooner is she back than she seduces Archie Cooper (Donald Cameron), the son of the rich woman who has offered her work. She becomes pregnant, only to have the baby die. But when she discovers that Archie truly loves June Lawler (Edith King), the unhappy wife of a mean, uncaring local doctor (Robert Strange), she compromises the physician, provokes her father (Walter Law) into killing him, then goes out to see what other happiness she can find and good she can do. *Variety* called the show "dirty," complaining it edged "close to the limit in language." The tradesheet concluded, "Its chief value appears to be in its luridness." The outcry that followed from the self-appointed moral crusaders roused ever compliant politicians, with District Attorney Joab H. Banton and Commissioner of Licenses William F. Quigley in the fore, to establish "juries" to sit in judgment on plays. These groups could demand any changes deemed necessary for the welfare of a public unable to look after itself and could proceed to close productions. Banton and his cronies made the mistake of going after the season's most respected plays—*What Price Glory?*, *The Firebrand*, and *Desire Under the Elms*—along with some more patently cheap offerings. In the case of the O'Neill play, business, which had been dwindling, perked in the face of all the publicity, while the larger hits picked up even greater advance sales. A few of the plays made token alterations (albeit O'Neill refused to make any), and for a short while the brouhaha died down. By the time all this happened, *A Good Bad Woman*, which survived for only two weeks, was long gone. But it would return in the next season.

Down in the Village an uncontroversial Irish drama found small audiences for nine weeks. Ralph Cullinan's **Loggerheads** (2-9-25, Cherry Lane) told how Norah Halpin (Joanna Roos), whose father had been killed by the vengeful Barretts for having married the girl—Norah's mother—whom a Barrett wanted, brings about an end to the feud when she takes the veil.

The next afternoon James Faller's **A Play** (2-10-25, Cort) was presented by the adventuresome Richard G. Herndon. But it required only one additional matinee to satisfy the demand for this saga of Ku Klux Klansmen hunting down a suspected but actually innocent black, while other blacks cringe with terror in a hut near a swamp.

Two English dramas met varying fates—one becoming a modest hit, the other a respectable failure. Although David L'Estrange was listed as author of **The Rat** (2-10-25, Colonial), theatre folk were aware L'Estrange was a pen name for Ivor Novello and Constance Collier. When an Apache known as "The Rat" (Horace Braham) realizes he has been lured away from his beloved, chaste Odile (Katherine Revner) through the trickery of Baron Stetz (C. H. Croker-King), who hopes to seduce her, he returns and kills the baron. Odile attempts to take the blame, but she is acquitted. Earl Carroll's production featured the former West End musical comedy favorite Teddy Gerard as the baron's accomplice.

In H. B. Trevelyan's **The Dark Angel** (2-10-25, Longacre) a woman (Patricia Collinge) who believes that the man she was engaged to has been killed in the war falls in love with and agrees to marry another man (John Williams). Just as the pair are to be wed, the supposedly dead man (Reginald Mason) appears. However, since he is blind, he refuses to stand in the way of the woman's happiness by holding her to her prior vow.

That night also saw an opening in the Village, where Sherwood Anderson and Raymond O'Neil's **The Triumph of the Egg** (2-10-25, Provincetown Playhouse) served as a curtain raiser to a revival of Eugene O'Neill's *Diff'rent*. Set in a failing Pickleville's eatery, it watched as the restaurant's incompetent owner (John Huston) tries to entertain his only customer by showing him egg tricks—making an egg stand on end and squeezing one into a bottle without breaking the egg. He fails miserably, prompting the customer to dash away.

Critics echoed one another to salute David Belasco's newest offering, **The Dove** (2-11-25, Empire), which Willard Mack drew from an unidentified story by Gerald Beaumont: "Good, old-style, rattling, romantic melodrama"; "a rattling, bright-colored, old-styled melodrama." They also sang paeans to his superb cast and production. Yet the play ran only 101 performances and apparently ended up in the red. At the Purple Pigeon Café, a Mexican cabaret run by the bespangled Mike Morowich (Sidney Toler), the strutting, swaggering Don José Maria Lopez y Tostado (Holbrook Blinn) is throwing a champagne dinner for his many lady friends. But he loses all interest in them when he sees and hears the beautiful singing guitarist, Dolores Romero (Judith Anderson). However, she rebuffs him, having eyes only for Johnny Powell (William Harrigan), an American who works in the gambling house across the street. Furious, Don José arranges to have Johnny framed for shooting a drunken gambler. The Mexican tells Dolores Johnny will rot in jail unless she comes to live with him. To gain Johnny's freedom, she consents. But the released man goes after Don José and is arrested. He is facing a firing squad when Dolores's tearful pleadings move Don José to stop the execution and allow the lovers to go off.

At the 52nd Street Theatre on the same evening a double bill of O'Neill revivals coupled *The Emperor Jones*, with Paul Robeson in the lead, with *The Dreamy Kid*.

Like they had *The Dove*, many critics saw Walter Archer Frost's **Cape Smoke** (2-16-25, Martin Beck) as a good, old-fashioned melodrama. More than one compared it with *White Cargo*. And like the Belasco entry, it ran only three months. A group of Englishmen, who have come to South Africa to strike it rich in the diamond mines, have failed miserably and are anxious to return home. With the help of a corrupt witch doctor (Frank Corbie) and of Catherine Bradbroke (Ruth Shepley), a lovely, indentured girl who is unaware of their chicanery, they trick John Ormsby (James Rennie), a rich Texas oil man, into buying the mine. The witch doctor convinces the suprisingly gullible Texan that he has put a curse on the four Englishmen and on the Texan, who will die last. It is only after three of the Britishers have apparently succumbed and Ormsby has paid the surviving Englishman half a million dollars to get out of the country and away from the witch doctor's reach that the hoax is exposed. Happily, Ormsby, who has fallen in love with the girl, discovers Catherine's innocence. The witch doctor's bone-and-feathers costumes and his spectacular dance against a background of lightning and thunder were high points of the production.

Nocturne (2-16-25, Punch and Judy), Henry Stillman's dramatization of Frank Swinnerton's novel, was one of the season's duds—lasting a mere three performances. The story told of two lower-middle-class sisters, taking care of their worthless father and sharing an indifferent lover. One of the girls at least enjoys a brief fling with a rich man on his yacht.

Two American novelties vied unsuccessfully for attention the next evening. G. Marion Burton's **Houses of Sand** (2-17-25, Hudson) told of Arthur Demarest (Paul Kelly), who wonders how he can possibly marry the beautiful Japanese-American known both as Miss Kane and Golden Fragrance (Vivienne Osborne). The answer turns out to be that he has Japanese blood in him.

Gertrude Purcell's **Tangletoes** (2-17-25, 39th St.) had Arthur Griswold (Morgan Farley), a high-minded writer, marry Francie (Mildred MacLeod), a pretty chorus girl, and take her to suburbia, where he will show her the good, dull life. When Francie concludes she prefers the bad, fun-filled world of her New York buddies and hurries back to Manhattan, Arthur first throws up his hands, then resumes his writing.

Exiles (2-19-25, Neighborhood Playhouse), James Joyce's only play, was received coolly by both the press and the public. It relates how a writer (Ian Maclaren) is driven to despair and garrulousness after refusing to take action against his unfaithful wife or her lover.

Four plays premiered the next Monday night. One of the two American plays in the group was the evening's only hit. Edith Ellis's **White Collars** (2-23-25, Cort), taken from a story by Edgar Franklin, was already in the midst of a long Los Angeles run when a second company was created for New York. Joan Thayer (Mona Kingsley), the only college-educated Thayer, startles her family by bringing home a husband, her millionaire employer, William Van Luyn (John Marston). To the family's surprise, he agrees to move in with them; to their consternation, after listening to their left-leaning Cousin Henry (Clarke Silvernail), he proposes to gave away his wealth to establish a hospital catering to the indigent. At the same time, Thayer senior and Joan's brother lose their jobs, but they are embarrassed to take money from Van Luyn, which the obnoxious Henry had told them would make them charity cases. A happy compromise is worked out, with the Thayer men given jobs at the hospital. The comedy ran three months (backed by Anne Nichols's money), far short of its L.A. stand.

In John Turner and Eugenie Woodward's **Two by Two** (2-23-25, Selwyn), middle-aged Mrs. Cleves (Charlotte Walker), about to marry the much younger Richard Graham (Howard Lindsay), decides to teach her terribly shy daughter, Elinor (Minette Buddecke) the art of nabbing a husband. She teaches Elinor so well that Elinor snatches Richard from her, leaving her to settle for an Englishman she once had been fond of, Lord Leighton (Lawrance D'Orsay). The play had been done in May in Greenwich Village as *The Leap*, at which time the authors had been listed as Miss Woodward and Jessy Trimble. Broadway scuttlebutt was that the two J.T.'s were the same person.

Support for A. A. Milne's **Ariadne** (2-23-25, Garrick) came largely from the Theatre Guild's faithful. When their numbers were exhausted the play closed. Milne's tale tells how an inconsiderate businessman (Lee Baker) insists his wife (Laura Hope Crews) entertain a client (Harry Mestayer) who, she has warned her husband, is a notorious libertine. To teach her husband a lesson, the wife pursues the affair with gusto.

Henri Bernstein's *Judith* came to Broadway in Gladys Unger's translation as **The Virgin of Bethulia** (2-23-25, Ambassador). Those critics who did not find this retelling of the Judith (Julia Hoyt) and Holophernes (McKay Morris) story sexually offensive found it boring.

Some reviewers also balked at the theme of Roland Oliver's **Night Hawk** (2-24-25, Bijou), in which a surgeon (Byron Beasley) rejuvenates Masie Buck, an aging prostitute (Mary Newcomb), who has agreed to lead a virtuous life if her youthful appearance is restored. After the operation succeeds, the surgeon advises her to write off her past and find a good man. However, the doctor is stunned when his younger brother (Leonard Doyle) falls in love with Masie. Still grateful to the surgeon, Masie breaks off the affair and heads out alone to Kansas, to help her own brother on his farm.

But critics did handsprings to celebrate the revival of Ibsen's *The Wild Duck* at the 48th Street Theatre on the next night. Hornblow unequivocally called this Actors' Theatre mounting "the most satisfying production of the season." Warburton Gamble was Hjalmar; Blanche Yurka, Gina; Tom Powers, Gregers; Helen Chandler, Hedvig; and Cecil Yapp, old Ekdal. As a result of the rave notices, the play ran 103 performances.

With the rage for psychoanalysis growing, a psychoanalyst, Louis E. Bisch, offered Broadway a play centering on a single fictitious case. **The Complex** (3-3-25, Booth), was initially presented for a few matinee performances, but playgoers evinced sufficient interest for a short regular run to follow. Bisch's case focused on Felicia Windle (Dorothy Hall), whose image of her late, ideal father prevents her consummating her marriage. Dr. Dale (Robert Harrison) must show her that her father was a scoundrel and is still alive but kept from seeing her by her protective aunt (Percy Haswell). The truth sends Felicia into the arms of her husband (William A. Williams).

Gladys Unger's second play in as many weeks was **Starlight** (3-3-25, Broadhurst), which she dramatized from Abel Hermant's *Dialogues* and which was bruited to be based on the life of Sarah Bernhardt. With Doris Keane as star, the play had been touring the country for many months. Its action moved from 1865, when Aurelie is discovered performing in her father's dingy Montmartre cabaret to a gala evening at Aurelie's Theatre in 1924. In between, and played out against lovely period settings and costumes, the story followed the actress's rise to fame, her romances and the social ambitions that nearly destroy her career, and her final triumph when in her eighties. Unfortunately for Miss Keane—apart from, to a small extent, with *The Czarina*—she was never able to recapture the glory of her own real triumph in *Romance*.

There was no triumph of any sort in Charles Vildrac's weepy **Michel Auclair** (3-4-25, Provincetown Playhouse), recouting how Michel (Edgar Stehli), jilted by his faithless sweetheart (Helen Freeman), who marries a worthless soldier (Walter Abel), self-sacrificingly sees to it that they obtain comfortable positions and a nice country cottage.

Nor were there many kudos for a revival of Michel Carré's pantomime *L'Enfant prodigue* which the Actors' Theatre presented as *Pierrot, the Prodigal* in a series of matinees at the 49th Street Theatre, beginning March 6. Returning to the stage after nearly two years' absence, Laurette Taylor had no better luck with the mute figure than Ada Rehan had had many decades earlier.

In a sense it was only a small step from pantomime to **Puppets** (3-9-25, Selwyn), but there was no more cordial welcome for Frances Lightner's stage piece about a puppeteer (C. Henry Gordon) in New York's Little Italy, who, at the outbreak of the war, marries a charming orphan (Miriam Hopkins), goes off to battle, is reported dead, but returns in the nick of time to rescue her from white slavers. Young Fredric March played the part of the puppeteer's cousin, who dreams of marrying the orphan after his cousin is rumored to be dead. All the action was set in a room behind the stage of the puppet theatre.

A short life was also in order for Fred Wall and Ralph Murphy's sermonizing comedy, **The Handy Man** (3-9-25, 39th St.) Its central figure was a blandly preachy carpenter named Chris! He is given to the sort of "trite and true sayings" that one reviewer compared to those found in grammar school texts of the period. Into the small upstate New York village where Chris (Tim Murphy) works and lives comes Nellie Nelson (Margaret Cusack), a sweet, attractive "dip"—a professional pickpocket. She soon spots sweet, attractive Willie Weller (Glenn Burdette) and resolves to convert him into an accomplice and a lover. She does not count on Chris's somewhat mysterious ways. Chris gently opens Willie's eyes and, with the help of a timely flash of lightning and a loud thunderclap, and of a badge recovered from a Prohibition agent who lost it while he was drunk, leads Nellie to the straight and narrow. In a day when large casts were commonplace, *Variety* remarked on the play's "short cast . . . only eight characters," but its low budget was no help.

Abraham Goldknopf, a doctor by profession, was the author of **In the Near Future** (3-10-25), which was presented at a matinee and managed to eke out two more matinees before being hustled away in the face of some of the season's most dismissive reviews. Goldknopf's saga drew attention to an unhappily married woman who has a brief affair with a doctor in order to see if he would be a good match for a friend of hers, whom she hopes to spare her own disappointments. Under ether in surgery, she babbles about the affair, leaving her surgeon, who is also her husband, to debate whether to save her or to let her die.

Matters improved no end that evening. James Gleason, this time working with George Abbott, had a second smash hit (although not as big as *Is Zat So?*) in **The Fall Guy** (3-10-25, Eltinge). Percy Hammond of the *Herald Tribune* placed it "among the top notchers of American shows." Gullible little Johnnie Quinlan (Ernest Truex) suddenly loses his job. Since he has a wife and a sponging brother-in-law and sister to support, he agrees to deliver a suitcase filled with "valuables" for "Nifty" Herman (Hartley Power), even though he suspects the valuables are merely bootleg hootch. "How can you be sure," he muses, "about this here Eighteenth Amendment, huh? Some guy says there must be something wrong with a law that so many people want to break." Complications follow when Johnnie attempts to hide the valise. For example, his sister's suitor, Charles Newton (Henry Mortimer), who may be a member of a rival gang, appears and concludes the suitcase is loaded with drugs. Herman arrives and Johnnie tricks him into admitting he is a gang leader, whereupon Newton discloses that he is a federal agent. He arrests Herman and offers Johnnie a job. Anchoring the comedy was Truex's performance—"easy, never out of key, cleverly and truly varied." As a result the piece ran well into the summer.

Charles Horan's whodunit **The Devil Within** (3-16-25, Hudson) asked audiences to guess the killer of rich, mean John Blackwood (Henry W. Pemberton), who has whipped his Indian servant, told his niece he is cutting her out of his will, chased away his mistress and illegitimate son, and quarreled with his attorney after revealing that he will remarry. Yet he was alone in his library when he fell to the floor, with blood oozing from his neck. The consensus was that the play was so boring no one cared who really did it or how. In fact, one aisle-sitter said he could not figure what the ending was meant to suggest.

The 23rd saw a return engagement of *Beggar on Horseback* at the Shubert, with many of the original principals still in the cast, and, more interestingly, Charles Dillingham's revival of Barrie's *The Little Minister* at the Globe, with Ruth Chatterton in the role created by Maude Adams. Both mountings, limited enagements to begin with, lingered only a fortnight.

E. Temple Thurston's **The Blue Peter** (3-24-25, 52nd St.) had enjoyed some modest success in London but failed to find a large American audience. It told of a former African adventurer (Warren Williams), who is almost seduced away from a sedate life with his wife and child by the lure of excitement and the sea but in the end resists the temptation. The play, despite some very favorable notices, marked an inauspicious debut for the Stagers, a high-minded group hoping to rival the Theatre Guild.

Harry Chapman Ford's **Eve's Leaves** (3-26-25, Wallack's) centered on Eve Corbin (Elwyn Harvey), a woman whose husband (Ray Collins) cannot afford to buy her expensive clothes, so she devises the trick of buying them herself, wearing them once, then returning them for some trumped-up reason. Her couturier catches on but agrees to lend her clothes if she will become his agent. In time he adds a more sinister condition, but since Eve has discovered that she and her husband are about to become parents, she spurns the offer.

Wealthy, young, and socially prominent Dwight Deere Wiman, working in conjunction with William A. Brady, launched his career as producer on a sour note when Edward Wilbraham's **Ostriches** (3-30-25, Comedy) proved a one-week bomb. Its story was an unfunny variant of that in *Two by Two*. In this case, Margaret Charlton (Janet Beecher) is aghast to learn that her daughter, Kit (Katharine Alexander), is enamored of her lover, George Lorrimer (Orrin Johnson). All ends happily when Kit recognizes the foolishness of a May-September romance.

Although critics were saddened to see its text cut (but not bowdlerized) and its playing a somewhat dismaying mixture of American and British acting styles, virtually to a man they joyfully embraced the mounting of Congreve's *Love for Love* at the Greenwich Village the next evening. Once again the crafty Valentine (Stanley Howlett) prevents his father, Sir Sampson Legend (Walter Abel), from disowning him in favor of his uncouth seaman brother, Ben (Perry Ivins), and wins the hand of the lovely Angelica (Helen Freeman). The comedy played only forty-seven performances but was brought back in the fall to a larger house prior to embarking on a brief tour.

Sadly, critics could not embrace April's initial novelty, Lula Vollmer's **The Dunce Boy** (4-1-25, Daly's). Nor could they agree on why they did not like it. Some found the basic story too unpleasant, others saw its execution as faulty. Whatever their reasoning most felt it marked a comedown from *Sun-Up* and *The Shame Woman*. Ma Huckle (Antoinette Perry) does all she can to keep her mentally defective son, Tude (Gareth Hughes), away from their boarder, the pretty schoolteacher Rosy Pierce (Mary Carroll). She tells him that if he were to touch her, Rosy would die like a crushed flower. However, when he sees another man embrace the girl, he shoves his mother to the floor and rushes after them. His mother is horrified to spot Tude coming home with a limp Rosy in his arms. It turns out Rosy was molested by the mill boss (John Clarendon) whose advances she has rejected. Distraught and disoriented by the events, Tude kills the mill boss, then rushes to the mill and throws himself on a buzz saw. Whatever reservations reviewers held, a majority lauded Miss Perry, seeing her "fine restraint and convincing expression" making for "a performance of unusual merit." The play was the first of several folk plays to arrive in quick succession, none of which lived up to advance expectations.

The second was Hatcher Hughes's **Ruint** (4-7-25, Provincetown Playhouse). Unlike most folk plays which New Yorkers had seen, this was not a tragedy—although its story could easily have led to a tragic denouement—but a "folk comedy." Rich, spoiled Reginald Vanderpeet (William Leonard) has come to the Carolina backwoods to build, with his mother's money, a mission school. But while he understands the ways of Palm Beach and Long Island he has no idea of backwater mores. So when he gives pretty Mary Jane Horton (Jeannie Begg) a seemingly harmless kiss in a laurel brake he thinks nothing more of it. Mary Jane takes the kiss as an indication that Reginald will marry her, but he informs her that the law would not allow a man to marry every girl he kissed, since he'd have too many wives. Mary Jane's family and friends howl that she has been "ruint" and attempt to lynch Reginald. At the last minute, just as his mother (Anne Sutherland) arrives in her limousine, they relent. Instead Reginald is ridden out of town on a rail. Speech patterns provided much of the laughter. Thus, the backwater women are baffled by Reginald's expressions such as "Charmed, I'm sure" on being introduced to them, while Reginald is thrown for a loss when Mary Jane's mother (Jane Burby) asks him what sort of pie he prefers. He replies, " 'Kivered' er open? I'm afraid I'm not competent to settle that question off-hand." The play's principal problem was that it was much too long for the simple story it had to tell and employed too much talk and too little incident to stretch out the evening.

Earlier that afternoon, the Actors' Theatre initiated a series of matinees featuring a revival of Charles Rann Kennedy's *The Servant in the House* at the 48th Street Theatre. Pedro de Cordoba assumed the role of Manson, the Christ-like figure who poses as a servant in his brother's home—a role generally associated with Walter Hampden.

Byron's closet drama **Cain** (4-8-25, Lenox Little Theatre) came out of the closet briefly. Billed as the work's first theatrical performance anywhere, it won some applause for its unusual staging—with all of the play performed behind a transparent scrim to suggest a distance from modern realities. The poet's tale reveals how Lucifer (Albert Howson) influences Cain (William P. Carleton) after the expulsion from Eden, how they visit Hades together, and how Cain kills Abel (David Leonard) in an argument over worship practices. Slated for only a two-week stand, it closed on schedule when there was no call for an extension.

April's third folk drama, Dan Totheroh's **Wild Birds** (4-8-25, Cherry Lane), arrived in the East after having won a play contest at the University of California. The judges had been Susan Glaspell, Eugene O'Neill, and George Jean Nathan. But when he later reviewed the drama Nathan condemned it (justly) for a lack of dramatic discipline and confessed he had originally voted for it because the rest of the submissions were so patently inferior. As he is about to leave rather than continue to work for the vicious John Slag (Dodson Mitchell), George Marshall (Thomas MacLarnis) says a fond farewell to Mazie (Mildred McLeod), the orphan whom the Slags have adopted and treat callously as a drudge. He calls her a trapped little wild bird and says someday he may return and release her from the trap. To replace Marshall, Slag takes on Adam Larsen (Donald Duff), a runaway from a reform school (where he had been sent for beating his father when the man abused his mother). Slag threatens to report the boy to the authorities if Adam refuses to do his bidding. Before long Adam and Mazie fall in love, although Slag refuses to allow them to wed. Disgusted with Slag's brutalities, the pair run off. They meet various people, including a fiery preacher and a philosophic tramp, on their trek, but eventually they are caught and returned to the Slag farm. Slag is so outraged when he learns that Mazie is pregnant, he whips Adam to death, driving Mazie to commit suicide by jumping down a well. Just then Marshall returns. He tells Slag he has found Mazie's long-lost father, who has promised to take in the girl, but now all he can do is report Slag to the police. For all its flawed construction, the play did have intriguing characters and some stabs at poetry. Thus, when the eloping youngsters reach "the top of a billow where star-fires are very thick," they embrace and Adam exclaims, "How strong the star-fires air. They make my head swim." Mazie responds dreamily, "Everything air white an' silver, an' now the wind air warm an' singin.' " Like its predecessors, the play failed. One interesting point is that none of the plays, despite their authors' reputations or awards, was assigned a major house.

The Great Act: 1919–1928

Two played in what would later be considered off-Broadway venues, the third in one of Broadway's least desirable and most out-of-the-way theatres.

A less imaginative, more traditional drama, booked into one of New York's prime houses, fared no better. In Paul Dickey and Mann Page's **The Backslapper** (4-11-25, Hudson), the title figure is a rising young midwestern politician (Harry C. Browne) who gladhands anyone who can be of help to him but coolly ignores his own wife (Mary Fowler) now that he has won her away from his former buddy. At a dinner party at their home, where he hopes to promote his candidacy for senator, his disgruntled wife exposes his hypocrisy and decides to go off with her old flame (Charles Trowbridge).

The busy night of Monday, April 13, saw the opening of two new musicals (*Tell Me More, Mercenary Mary*), a revival of one old musical (*Princess Ida*), the return of *Aren't We All,* two novelties and a Shavian restoration. Normally the two novelties would have usurped the limelight, but since *Caesar and Cleopatra* was the initial attraction at the Theatre Guild's spanking new playhouse, it drew the first-string critics and the swank first-nighters. Only half a dozen years had elapsed since the Guild had been formed, yet here it was welcoming its friends to its spacious new home on 52nd Street. For their part, its friends welcomed the return of what Stark Young called "the greatest" of Shaw's works. The players received a less enthusiastic greeting. As the worldly, humane, and aging Caesar, Lionel Atwill was assailed for his flat interpretation, his poor enunciation, and even his posture. As the childish, kittenish queen, Helen Hayes split the aisle-sitters, with a pleased Woollcott seeing her casting as "inevitable" and a soured Nathan waving her off as sexless. Helen Westley's Ftatateeta garnered some of the best notices. A number of complaints about slow pacing didn't help matters at the box office. However, almost all the reviewers took space to hail the new playhouse, called simply the Guild, albeit a prophetic Woollcott, eyeing expensive tapestries on the walls of the small seater, warned, "The Gobelins will get you if you don't watch out!"

Another Caesar, one Caesar Dunn, known as a comic gangster in vaudeville, was author of **The Fourflusher** (4-13-25, Apollo), which was listed in its program as "a comedy radiating the hustling spirit of American youth" and which had enjoyed some success earlier in Chicago. A dreamily ambitious shoe clerk, Andy Whittaker (Russell Mack), is passed over for promotion at the store where he works and generally ignored by his fellow townsfolk. Then the rumor gets noised about that Andy is heir to his fabulously rich uncle (Spencer Charters)—the uncle with the weak heart. Suddenly he is showered with attention and credit—on which he buys an automobile, jewels, and fancy clothes. Why, even snooty Mrs. Allen (Margaret Dumont) sees him as the logical mate for her daughter (Sue Mac-Manamy). But when news comes that he is not his uncle's heir, he is snubbed again, until he invents a shoe arch that makes a fortune for him. He buys the shoe store and weds the pretty young thing (Louise Allen) who worked with him there. Broadway displayed little interest in Andy's history.

But then it displayed even less interest in Myron C. Fagan's **Mismates** (4-13-25, Times Square). *Variety*'s critic branded it "one of those countless in-betweens, almost beaten before they start." The curtain rose to disclose a baby sitting in a highchair and playing happily with a rattle. (The opening won a huge hand but also the ire of the Gerry Society, which successfully went to court to have the baby removed.) The infant belongs to wealthy Jim Blake (C. Henry Gordon), who has been disowned by his family for marrying beneath his place, and the poor manicurist he wed, Judy (Clara Joel). Unfortunately, their life is increasingly quarrel-filled, so Judy walks out. Then Judy is sent to prison for a murder her brother committed. Jim takes charge of the baby and afterwards, believing Judy dead, remarries. Judy escapes from prison, comes to Jim's home hoping to kill him, but is talked out of it by a man (Minor Watson) who has loved her for many years and who, having become a detective, will work to prove her innocence.

The next evening the Shuberts revived *Taps,* which Sam Shubert had first presented in 1904. The new mounting at the Broadhurst starred Lionel Barrymore as the Prussian soldier who attempts to kill the officer (McKay Morris) who has had an affair with his daughter (Irene Fenwick) but kills the girl by mistake. In 1904 the drama had run for three weeks; this time it ran four.

Sophie Treadwell's **O Nightingale** (4-15-25, 49th St.) ran just as long. It recounted the story of Appolonia Lee (Martha-Bryan Allen), an innocent small-town beauty, who comes to New York hoping for stardom on the stage. Advised the best way is to employ the aegis of a rich man, she persuades the Marquis de Severac (Ernest Lawford) to help her. Since he is unhappily married, he buys her jewels and introduces her to important people. While she realizes that the marquis is not at all a wicked man, Appolonia finds the whole matter sordid, so settles for a young sculptor (Lyonel Watts). Constance Eliot, who played a mean, embittered Russian dancer, was said to be a stage name for the playwright.

The Sapphire Ring (4-15-25, Selwyn) was Isabel Leighton's translation of László Lakatos's Hungarian play. The title was an exact translation of the original, and the play's text also followed the Hungarian closely. It told of a wife (Helen Gahagan) who has been given a magic ring by her husband (Frank Conroy). The ring will expose her any time she lies about an infidelity. Fortunately for her she does not have the ring when she visits a handsome young doctor (Kenneth MacKenna). Actually the arrival of the doctor's old mistress and the mistress's new lover prevent the wife and the doctor from carrying out their plans. So, when the wife tells the husband the story and when he sees her wearing the ring, he feels he must believe her. Or must he? A magic ring in modern Budapest could not grip modern New Yorkers.

"Platitude and twaddle" filled William Francis Dugan's unexciting **Thrills** (4-16-25, Comedy), which Dugan, unable to find a producer, produced himself. After quarreling with her husband, Horace (W. L. Thorne), Mozella Benson (Elisabeth Risdon) sets up a tryst with the celebrated author and ladies' man Armand Valry (Ramsey Wallace). When she appears she discovers that Armand has had his Japanese serving boy lock the doors from the outside and has also alerted his neighbors not to be concerned by any untoward noises. He carries Mozella into the bedroom as the curtain falls. In the next act Horace comes seeking his wife, and Armand blandly tells him that she has resisted all his efforts and that nothing came of their evening. But one scene and four years later Horace has left Mozella, who has wed Armand and proven a genuine inspiration to him.

Platitudes and twaddle of a somewhat different sort also abounded in John B. Hymer and LeRoy Clemens's **Aloma of the South Seas** (4-20-25, Lyric), which hoped to recreate the success of such older works as *The Bird of Paradise, White Cargo,* and *Rain.* Bob Holden's sweetheart, thinking him killed during the war, married another man. That man had been Bob's best friend and knew that he had been gassed and was a prisoner of war, but said nothing in order to steal the girl. Returning home and discovering this, Holden (Frank Thomas) sailed away to a lush tropical island to manage a business there for his uncle. But he soon was managing mostly to get drunk. The beautiful native girl, Aloma (Vivienne Osborne), takes pity on him and sets about to rescue

him, even though Nuitane (George Gaul), her native lover (who makes his entrances and exits playing on his "sweet potato"), has killed several white men she looked longingly at before and now warns her he will kill Holden. He tells her, "Sharks no like dark meat; they like white meat." However, Aloma has fallen so deeply in love that she not only ignores the warnings but perfumes a pink nightie she has bought and places it alongside the white pajamas she finds on Holden's bed. At this juncture, Holden's old flame (Anne Morrison), along with her hopelessly alcoholic husband (Richard Gordon), appears on the island. Nuitane, meaning to kill Holden, mistakenly feeds the drunken husband to the sharks, leaving Holden and the new widow to head back for America, and leaving Aloma to resign herself to wedding her native suitor. Livingston Platt's scenery was praised, and an electric storm won applause but was deemed inferior to the great storm in *Rain.* An offstage Hawaiian ukulele band supplied background music.

Even worse followed. Edward E. Rose, a name from a fast-receding past, and Frank S. Merlin were the authors of a strange hodgepodge called **The Three Doors** (4-23-25, Lenox Little Theatre). It apparently began as a send-up of the recent rash of play juries, then disintegrated into a murder mystery with a Hindu villain, who sported the typical Hindu moniker Raymond (John O. Hewitt). Critics threw up their hands in disbelief.

All these duds were followed by two hits which brought April to a happy end. J. C. and Elliott Nugent's **The Poor Nut** (4-27-25, Henry Miller's) came first. John Miller (Elliott Nugent) is a shy, bumbling botany major who works in the bookstore at Ohio State. He has just been given a charming young assistant, Margerie Blake (Norma Lee). Margerie is visited by an old friend, the luscious Julia Winters (Florence Shirley), who has been selected Miss Wisconsin and who has come not only to see her fiancé run a race against Ohio State but also to meet somebody named Jack Miller, who has been writing her mash notes after seeing her picture in the paper. Jack has told her he is a big fraternity man and a star athlete. When she learns that John and Jack are one and the same she is not angry. Rather she sets about to help him, stating that he is "an emotional introvert" and must turn his libido outward. Then John is informed that he is to substitute in the race for an athlete taken ill. Hearing of this, Julia tells him that if he wins the race they will become engaged (her boyfriend has broken their engagement after being teased about Julia's interest in Miller). However, just before the race John's nerves get the best of him and he faints. Luckily, Margerie is there, and she revives and encourages him. After he wins the race, the fraternity that once had rejected him for spilling his noodle soup and then fainting at the dinner table now pledges him. And Julia is there to announce that they will be wed immediately and that she will then help start him in the business world. All this comes as a shock to John, who wants only to be a botany professor. He says good-bye to a stunned Julia, telling her that his libido is now turned outward, and walks off with Margerie. Fine and offbeat settings included the bookstore, the athletes' tent, a corner of the stadium (where parts of the race could be seen), and a fraternity dance. Welcomed for its "refreshing humor" and "delicate satire," the comedy ran for nine months.

Ralph Spence's **The Gorilla** (4-28-25, Selwyn) was a surprise hit. When Alice Stevens (Betty Weston) learns that her sweetheart, Arthur Marsden (Robert Strange), has written a mystery play, she gets her father (Frederick Truesdell) to listen to Arthur read it. It concerns a criminal who is called "the Gorilla" because he always leaves a gorilla's imprint at the scene of his crimes. Stevens laughs that the story is unbelievable. But fact and fiction become totally mixed up when a real gorilla escapes from a sailor who kept it as a pet. Is it a crook just like the one in Marsden's play or the wild animal that carries off Alice? Before the adventures are over two inept, easily terrified detectives (Frank McCormack and Clifford Dempsey) make fools of themselves—"putting you on the detective force is like putting a ukulele in Sousa's band," one of them is told—and an even more easily terrified black servant, Jefferson Lee (Stephen Maley, the usual white in blackface,) gets more than his share of occasions to quiver and an "Uncle Tom death" turn. Much of the humor was wild and slapdash, with the gorilla at times jumping over the footlights and running through the audience. Hailed by Hornblow as "about the funniest thing on Broadway," and by *Variety* as the "shootingest, shoutingest melange of chills and thrills and yells ever concocted," the merry lunacy chalked up 257 performances. Spence was best known as a writer for the screen comedian Harold Lloyd.

In late April *Variety* reported that Broadway was still booming. Fifty-seven shows were competing for trade. But then, a week later, an early heat wave struck, and the tradesheet noted that business at many playhouses plunged 50 percent. It concluded the "season has definitely shot [its] bolt." One small bit of encouragement was the note that a prominent legal expert had concluded play juries could have no legal standing. (He was subsequently overruled.)

The Stagers launched May with a revival of Ibsen's *Rosmersholm* at the 52nd Street Theatre on the 5th. Only a few critics were displeased with the mounting, which featured Margaret Wycherly as Rebecca West.

Disaster, albeit comic in many ways, followed. The A. J. Lamb who wrote **Flesh** (5-7-25, Princess) was reputedly the same Arthur Lamb who had served as lyricist for "Asleep in the Deep" and "A Bird in a Gilded Cage." His story, told with numerous changes of setting, watched as Dell Morland (Madeline Davidson), a respectable but sex-deprived young lady, learning that her fiancé patronizes a prostitute, goes to the woman's rooms and arranges to switch places with her. However, the prostitute's lover arrives just before Dell's own sweetheart, and the men fall to fighting. Dell leaves and elects to wed a squeaky-clean physician. The audience laughed so heartily at all the wrong times that even the actors joined in, and after the first night it was announced that the piece would be performed as a satire on sex dramas. The ploy failed, and the work went the way of all flesh after four performances.

May's second revival was brought forth by the Neighborhood Players on the 8th at their little auditorium on Grand Street. Their staging of Sheridan's *The Critic* featured Ian Maclaren as Mr. Puff, Charles Warburton as Mr. Sneer, and Whitford Kane and Dorothy Sands as Mr. and Mrs. Dangle. Although the revival was fundamentally faithful, a handful of characters were purposely dressed in anachronistic costumes (including a Santa Claus outfit) and a few topical references were inserted.

All three plays to premiere the next Monday were quick flops. John Hastings Turner's **His Queen** (5-11-25, Hudson) begins just after Maria Avilon (Francine Larrimore), a model at a Yonkers dress shop, has married the store's floorwalker (Charles Brown). An unexpected wedding gift is news that she has inherited the throne of far-off Pyrrichos. By the second act she is the queen, disillusioned with her spouse and in love with Thales (Robert Warwick), leader of the country's malcontents. In the final act she dies, protecting Thales from the bullets of her own palace guard.

There was much less plot, all of it predictable, in DeWitt Newing's **The Big Mogul** (5-11-25, Daly's). Peter Quinn Quilt (Fiske O'Hara), a Troy, N.Y., plumber turned Wall Street multimillionaire, falls in love with his stenographer, Marie Lamb (Pat Clary), unaware her father, Van Cortland Lamb (Cameron

Mathews), is conspiring to bankrupt him. However, aided by a song in each act, Peter frustrates all Lamb's machinations and weds Marie. O'Hara was always more popular on the road than in New York, and this play had long since earned back its costs traversing the hinterlands.

Most first-string critics elected to sit through the evening's lone importation, Frank Wedekind's *Erdgeist,* which was offered in Samuel A. Eliot, Jr.'s translation as **The Loves of Lulu** (5-11-25, 49th St.). They came out into the night extremely dissatisfied. Those reviewers not offended by this tale of a temptress (Margot Kelly) who destroys her lovers, whether male or female, condemned the uncomfortable translation and almost amateurish acting.

Even the respected John Galsworthy could come a cropper, as he did when the Actors' Theatre presented his **A Bit of Love** (5-12-25, 48th St.). It examined the plight of a minister (O. P. Heggie), assailed by his own parishoners for allowing his wife (Chrystal Herne) to pursue an affair with another man. Despite fine performances and staging, there was no call to extend the run beyond the handful of matinees initially slated.

A French comedy did only a mite better. In **The Bride Retires** (5-16-25, National), taken by Henry Baron from Félix Gandéra's seven-year-old *Le Couché de la mariée,* a young couple (Lila Lee and Stanley Ridges) marry to please their parents, although both prefer other mates. At first the bride demands the groom sleep on the floor, instead of in bed with her. But by eleven o'clock the pair have fallen in love with each other.

The promise Martin Flavin had displayed in his *Children of the Moon* went unfulfilled in **Lady of the Rose** (5-19-25, 49th St.). Years ago John Meredith (Henry Herbert) had written a play about the woman of his dreams. Later he married Lorraine (Margaret Mower), who he believed personified that ideal. However, he was soon disillusioned. When the old manuscript is discovered, Lorraine has it produced with herself as star. The furious husband dies cursing his wife for exposing his vision. However, on his deathbed that very vision—the Lady of the Rose (Margaret Mosier)—comforts him. Young dismissed the work as "wandering and sentimental and unconvincing as a whole."

Jerome K. Jerome's **Man or Devil** (5-21-25, Broadhust) was set in a gloomy house in seventeenth-century Holland and starred Lionel Barrymore as the miserly old Dutchman, Nicholas Snyder, who employs a magic wine purchased from a strange peddler (Thurlow Bergen) to exchange personalities with a pleasant younger man (McKay Morris). But as a good man, his guilt feelings get the better of him, so he once again drinks the wine, thereby allowing the young man to be sweet again and to marry the girl both men have loved. By way of reward, his behavior and the experience are powerful enough to turn Nicholas permanently into a good person as well. Barrymore received fine notices, but not the play. Mindful of the failures Barrymore had suffered during the year, Woollcott warned, "Such stature as he has enjoyed in the American theater cannot long stand the whittling process of such a season as he has just passed through." In a manner Woollcott could not have expected, Barrymore took his words to heart. He packed his bags and entrained to California, never again to play on Broadway.

May's last two productions were no more successful. Those who liked "sophisticated" and "epigrammatic" dialogue found something to enjoy in Paul Fox and George Tilton's **Odd Man Out** (5-25-25, Booth). Others found little to approve of. Sitting in the lovely "farmhouse" she and her husband have restored so elegantly, the selfish, immoral Julie Bancroft (Alma Tell) is advised that Dickon Bancroft (Lee Baker) has been killed in a hunting accident in Morocco. She thereupon debates which of her two lovers she will live with. Should it be the cynical, old, but very rich Karl Spalla (A. E. Anson) or the love of her younger days, Jerry Ames (James Crane), who left for China when she jilted him for the richer Dickon but has now returned? When her husband unexpectedly reappears, in perfect condition, she inadvertently blurts out her thoughts. Amused, he advises her to choose Spalla, and she does. That pleases Dickon since he knows the affair will not last and that Julie will in time return to him.

Charles Horace Malcolm's **Bachelor's Brides** (5-28-25, Cort) found Perry Ashfield (Charles Davis), a young Englishman, on the eve of his wedding to a wealthy, pushy young American, Mary Bowing (Lee Patrick). When one of the wedding gifts proves to be a baby he desperately attempts to hide it. His exertions and befuddlement so exhaust him that he falls asleep and has a nightmare in which all his friends appear in strange guises. The dream convinces him he has been about to marry the wrong girl. Many an aisle-sitter pointed out the similarity to *Beggar on Horseback,* noting all the while how inferior the new offering was.

If *Bachelor's Brides* reminded some of *Beggar on Horseback,* Robert J. Sherman's **Spooks** (6-1-25, 48th St.) could have recalled *The Cat and the Canary.* During most of his life Simon Blackwell had been shunned by his own family and, in turn, had refused to receive any visitors. His will leaves the bulk of his estate to any of four designated heirs who can stay in his house for three successive nights and the rest to be divided between his deaf and dumb black servant (Dixie Lofton) and his secretary, Silas Willoughby (Arthur Olmi). The four would-be inheritors are Elliot Butterfield (Roy Gordon), Marion Blackwell (Ethel Wilson), Douglas Blackwell (Grant Mitchell), and Laurette Payne (Marcia Byron). When Douglas arrives he brings with him his own servant, an easily terrified black named Sam (Cy Plunkett). Before long, having gotten all the figures to sign an agreement and having placed it in an envelope to be taken to the attorneys by a messenger, Willoughby chokes to death. In short order white spirits are seen in the hallways and a hand comes out of the paneling to grab a gun. When an inspector (Cecil Owen) attempts to re-create the murder he, too, chokes to death. It takes a supposed nurse (Emmy Bartin), who is really a policewoman, to show that the poison was in the envelopes' seals, that the servant can hear and speak, and that the killers are the two blacks, angry that Blackwell had not done more for Sam, his son by the woman. The play's humor was rather pathetic: "What's the fun in being a sheik—without a sheikess?" However, some of the staging was relatively novel. Audiences entering the theatre saw not the playhouse's regular curtain but a show curtain depicting the front of a dilapidating colonial mansion. The first character to enter, Elliot, made his entrance down one of the theatre's aisles, climbed up steps leading to the curtain, knocked on the front door, and, when no one answered, opened the door and walked in. The curtain then rose. But all other characters who came from the outside made similar entrances, employing an imaginary knocker before coming onstage. Given the use of the terms "nigger" and "coon" by the whites at some points to describe the blacks (both of whom were played by whites in blackface), could the title have hidden a clue in a nasty pun?

A pair of revivals enhanced the same night. In what was becoming an annual affair, the Players restored an old theatre piece to the stage. This time they brought out Pinero's *Trelawny of the Wells* at the Knickerbocker. Rose Trelawny, a young actress who finds that marrying above her station has its problems, was played by Laurette Taylor. Her remarkable supporting cast included Mrs. Thomas Whiffen, Amelia Bingham, Violet Heming, John Drew, Charles Coburn, William Courtleigh, Claude King, John Cumberland, and O. P. Heggie.

Far less warmly embraced was a mediocre revival of Brandon Thomas's beloved *Charley's Aunt* at Daly's, filled with a cast of second-raters. However,

there was one curiosity, with Harry Lillford, who had been the first American Brassett, recreating his old part.

The season's second French pantomime about Pierrot was Fernand Beissier's **The Bird Cage** (6-2-25, 52nd St.). It described in actions louder than words how Pierrot wins Louisette away from the villainous Julot, then almost loses her after he flirts for a time with Fifine.

Sheldon White's **The Right to Love** (6-8-25, Wallack's) brought the season to a dreary end. A rich capitalist is murdered while supposedly in the Maryland countryside to buy real estate. The stir that the killing arouses brings out that a young man was not really Mary Barton's adopted child but rather her illegitimate son by the dead man. The boy, convinced his mother is guilty, attempts to take the blame. But a shrewd lady detective, Belinda Perkins (Edith King), posing as a domestic, unearths the real killer.

1925–1926

Looking back, decades later, the 1925–1926 season seems very good indeed. Like the rest of the nation, Broadway was raking in the money. *Variety* counted a record 178 new plays. And the quality of these new plays was often high. Yet contemporaries were not entirely pleased. They perceived a discernible drop from the preceding season. There was no smash hit on the order of *What Price Glory?* or *Is Zat So?*. Proportionately fewer novelties were seen as truly exciting. To many commentators the swelling list of revivals suggested a shortage of good new works rather than, as it probably should have, a healthy attempt to balance the new with the old, to keep alive bygone traditions.

Possibly the season's dreadfully bad and slow start set the stage for subsequent judgments. Only one squeak-by hit overcame the exceptionally hot weather in the first two and a half months. The lone late June entry was a return of last season's controversial *A Good Bad Woman*, which Brady, forgetting his arguments that he had produced it to provoke an outcry from right-thinking folk, restored to his Playhouse on the 22nd. Its return was short-lived. (Hereafter, the season's numerous return engagements will be ignored unless they hold some special interest.)

July brought in only three novelties. Willis Maxwell Goodhue's **All Wet** (7-6-25, Wallack's) was set in the Yonkers mansion of the Thomas Fitch Ingrams. When personal matters take the couple away, the butler, Higgins (Edward Emery), takes over. He is a bolshevist and attempts to follow the Russian scheme for "nationalizing" women. But one determined maid (Elizabeth Dunne) resents his leftist ideas and turns the tables on him. He is finally deemed to be off his rocker.

The personal affairs that had sent the Ingrams away from home centered on Mrs. Ingram's resolve to have a career and her consequent neglect of her husband. The situation was reversed in Lila Longson's **What Woman Do** (7-20-25, Bijou). Resentful of her physician-husband's neglect, Mrs. Steadman (Irene Purcell) decides to make him jealous and attentive by having a very public affair. Her plan backfires when the doctor (Ben Taggart) orders her out of the house. But the illness of their little boy reunites them. Opening night was awkward, since, at the last minute, the Children's Society had gone to court, much as they had last season with *Mismates,* and forced the removal of the child actor.

In Len D. Hollister and Leona Stephens's **The Morning After** (7-27-25, Hudson) Will Sumner (A. H. Van Buren) discovers that the formula for his patent is missing, so he maroons his oddly assorted guests on his Maine island until the thief is unmasked.

Many of the critics liked Vincent Lawrence's **Spring Fever** (8-3-25, Maxine Elliott's), but the public wouldn't buy it. As a reward for teaching him how to play golf, David Waters (Joseph Kilgour) gives his shipping clerk, Jack Kelly (James Rennie), a visitor's pass to a swank golf club. There Jack's fine playing, not to mention his good looks, draws the attention of a pretty little snob, Allie Monte (Marion Coakley). Jack and his boss are nearly expelled after Jack defends himself in a fistfight, but the boss prevails by telling the committee that Jack is the son of a shipping magnate worth $80,000,000 and his expulsion could embarrass the club. The news that Jack is heir to a fortune only further whets Allie's interest. Not until after they are on their honeymoon does she learn that Jack is a mere shipping clerk. However, by that time she has come to love him. The play's first act was set on the links, at the eighteenth hole.

Harry Lee's blank-verse drama **The Little Poor Man** (8-5-25, Princess) recounted the life of St. Francis (Jerome Lawler) from his early, roistering days to his later years of self-sacrifice and good deeds. Nearly forty players (on the stage of one of New York's tiniest theatres) and beautiful scenery and costumes could not enliven a dull, pretentious work.

Nor could some encouraging notices and fine playing save Kate McLaurin's **It All Depends** (8-10-25, Vanderbilt), in which a young flapper (Katharine Alexander) sees nothing wrong in her liaison with a middle-aged, married man (Felix Krembs) until she discovers her father (Norman Trevor) embracing her best friend (Lee Patrick).

Even "a clean, simple entertainment to which one need not hesitate to take one's grandmother" could not defy the summer heat. But then perhaps most playgoers did not consider taking grandma to the theatre with them. So Zelda Sears's **A Lucky Break** (8-11-25, Cort) quickly went down the drain. In its brief life it looked at what happened when very rich John Bruce (George Macfarlane) came back to the village where he was raised. To test his old friends, he pretends to be poor. But they love him anyway. Miss Sears, best known as a comedienne and a librettist, afterwards helped turn the comedy into a musical, only to watch it, too, fail.

Edgar Selwyn and William LeBaron's **Something to Brag About** (8-13-25, Booth) wasn't. It was hurried away after just four performances. Meek Willie Harrington (Richard Sterling) gets no respect from his wife (Sylvia Field), who seriously thinks of running off with a neighbor (Charles Bickford). But after a trip to town Willie finds he is missing $1500. Believing the man who sat next to him on the train stole it, he buys a gun and forces the man to give him the money. Then he finds that he had actually left the cash at home. His victim has him arrested, but the night he spends in jail makes him a local hero and gives his wife something to brag about.

Harry Delf, a vaudevillian, surprised some Broadway critics by writing a small and honest comedy of lower-middle-class life, **The Family Upstairs** (8-17-25, Gaiety). The Hellers are a family of five, living in a modest walk-up in an unfashionable part of town. Mrs. Heller (Clare Woodbury) is a pushy, socially ambitious woman who prods her younger daughter (Lillian Garrick) to play the piano, is disgusted that her sixteen-year-old son (Theodore Westman) will not get a job—a cake-eater, in the slang of the day—and worries most that her older daughter, Louise (Ruth Nugent), is not yet married. Her son tells her not to worry, someone will like Louise—"there's a lot of guys who ain't so particular." To the family's surprise Louise brings home a pleasant young man, Charles Grant (Harold Elliott), a bank teller. However, mama paints such a loftily impossible picture of Louise and the family that Charles is frightened and tells Louise he cannot go through with their engagement. But shrewd Mr. Heller (Walter Wilson) finds a way of luring Charles back and resolving the problem. This leaves Mrs. Heller unhappy that she is about to lose a daughter. Mr. Heller consoles her by offering to take her to the movies.

Alice Brady was the star of **Oh, Mama!** (8-19-25, Playhouse), which Wilton Lackaye and Henry Wagstaff Gribble derived from Louis Verneuil's *Mademoiselle ma mère*. She played the young wife of a philandering old man (Edwin Nicander), so unhappy that she finally arranges a tryst with her friend Julien (John Cromwell). However, that tryst is interrupted in the hotel dining room by her stepson Georges (Kenneth MacKenna), and when the two realize that they are in love, she agrees to divorce his papa and marry him. The piece was a tour de force for Miss Brady, who managed to play the piano and even sing a couple of songs on the way. But like every other show in the young season, it failed to catch on. The play later became the musical *Boom Boom,* which featured Jeanette MacDonald.

Elliott Lester's **The Mud Turtle** (8-20-25, Bijou) examined the problems faced by Kate Tustine (Helen MacKellar), a city lass who comes to live in northern Minnesota on the isolated farm belonging to the family of her husband, Lem (Buford Armitage). She admits, "This place ain't exactly the kind of love nest I'd a picked out for myself. . . . I always figured on a cozy little flat on the avenue with a dollar-a-week old-rose parlour." Her treatment at the hands of Len's father (David Landau) is so brutal that she agrees to sleep with a farmhand if he will sabotage the farm machinery. He does, but then she reneges on her promise. Her retaining her virtue allows even the old man to accept her. The critical consensus was that Lester had a good idea and interesting characters but failed to write a credible drama. Lester, who was to have several other failures on Broadway, spent much of his life teaching at a high school for selected, superior boys in Philadelphia and was the father of Richard Lester, the film director.

Two new straight plays opened the next Monday night. Most first-stringers elected to review Willard Robertson's **The Sea Woman** (8-24-25, Little), which the *Times*'s man (was it a young Brooks Atkinson?) dismissed as "ten-twenty-thirt" and Hornblow assailed as "rank melodrama." True to the promise she made on her deathbed to a lighthouse keeper who had saved her life, Molla Hansen (Blanche Yurka) looks after his daughter, Pearl (Rea Martin), even though it means she must refuse her long-lost sweetheart (Clyde Fillmore) when he reappears

after many years. But Pearl proves to be a vixen. After she becomes pregnant she claims her seducer was a young engineer (Paul Kelly) who had actually rebuffed her advances. Molla shoots the man, then learns of his innocence. However, Pearl accidentally sets fire to the lighthouse. She and her lover are killed in the blaze, but Molla is rescued from the flames by her old sweetheart. The lighthouse setting won praise as did the last-act fire—"flames were heard roaring in the wings and a black, sinister smoke crept across the stage."

The other opening was Kane Campbell's **The Enchanted April** (8-24-25, Morosco). Lotty Wilkins (Elizabeth Risdon) and Rose Arbuthnot (Merle Maddern), both unhappily married, decide to rent an Italian villa for a month's vacation. To minimize the expense they agree to take two other women into the party. One is the reticent, unsatisfied Lady Caroline Dester (Helen Gahagan); the other a haughty grande dame, Mrs. Fisher (Alison Skipworth), a woman boastful of all the great Victorian figures she knew personally and obstinately Victorian in her outlook. Their stay is dull and not very pleasant, although Lotty tells Rose, "The great thing is to have lots of love about. Since I've been here I've been seeing that it doesn't matter who loves as long as somebody does." The women's husbands arrive. Mr. Wilkins (Herbert Yost) is gently made to see that his absorption in his law practice has been unfair to Lotty. Rose, too, has a reconciliation with her husband (Gilbert Douglas), a writer, never learning that under his pen name he has enjoyed a prolonged affair with Lady Caroline. And Caroline falls in love with Thomas W. Briggs (Hugh Huntley), the painter who owns the villa. Much of the rapprochement has come about through the quiet maneuvering of Mrs. Fisher, who is not nearly as forbidding as her austere facade might suggest. One interesting feature of the printed text was the inclusion of tableaux for curtain calls at the end of the first act, a practice by this time virtually extinct.

The only play of the month to inch across the 100-performance barrier was Al Woods's mounting of **A Kiss in a Taxi** (8-25-25, Ritz), taken by Clifford Grey from Maurice Hennequin and Pierre Veber's *Le Monsieur de cinq heures*. Ginette (Claudette Colbert) has been set up in a Montmartre café by her sugar daddy, Leon Lambert (Arthur Byron), who visits her every day at five o'clock. When she falls in love with the yokelish but attractive Lucien (John Williams), she tells the boy that she is Lambert's illegitimate daughter. This leads Lucien to run to Lambert and urge him to legitimize his "blossom of inadvertence." Mrs. Lambert (Janet Beecher) hears of Ginette but does not know of her relationship to her husband. Meeting the girl, she decides to adopt her as a daughter. From that point both the complications and the ending become evident. In 1928 it was musicalized as *Sunny Days*.

August's last entry was John Emerson and Anita Loos's **The Fall of Eve** (8-31-25, Booth). Just because her husband (Albert Albertson) spent a night at the home of a beautiful, divorced actress (he was, in fact, doing nothing but help her with her income tax returns), Eva Hutton (Ruth Gordon) is led to believe he is unfaithful. At the home of some bachelor friends, she gets drunk, makes futile advances at one of the men, and passes out. When she soon is pregnant she thinks one of the bachelors was involved. No, they were perfect gentlemen. The father of her child is her husband, so all ends merrily. Few reviewers had kind words for the play, but most adored Gordon's performance as a raucous, absurdly gauche, wide-eyed "child bride."

September's first two offerings were no more promising. In Helen Broun's **Clouds** (9-2-25, Cort) Richard Adams (Ramsey Wallace) has returned from the war blinded as a result of shell shock. His mother (Louise Carter), worried that the girl Richard loves, June Phelps (Marian Swayne), seems ready to jilt him for a rich young man, feigns sudden insanity in hopes that a second shock will restore her son's sight. It does, and Richard goes off to retrieve June.

Another ruse of sorts played a prominent part in John Kirkpatrick's **The Book of Charm** (9-3-25, Comedy). Joe Pond (Kenneth Dana), fearful his sweetheart, Ida May Harper (Mildred MacLeod), is about to run off to the big city, buys a book telling how to put on supposedly sophisticated airs and, in cahoots with Ida May's parents, puts on enough airs to keep the girl home. Rachel Crothers was the play's producer and director.

The season's first smash hit was one of the decade's funniest comedies, Russell Medcraft and Norma Mitchell's **Cradle Snatchers** (9-7-25, Music Box). Three women, Kitty Ladd (Margaret Dale), Ethel Drake (Edna May Oliver), and Susan Martin (Mary Boland), see their husbands off on the men's annual hunting trip, which, according to Kitty, occurs at least every three months. But Kitty is not fooled. She has discovered her husband is having an affair with a flapper, so she has bought herself a cute little cake-eater, Henry (Raymond Hackett). It doesn't take much to see the other gals also have become disappointed with their husbands and are in a "dangerous mood." As Susan suggests, "A man is a pill in any case, but if you need one, get one just covered with sugar!" Little prodding is required to

convince Ethel and Susan to allow Henry to phone his fraternity house and enlist two of his friends for a swell party the gals will throw at Kitty's luxurious summer cottage on Long Island. One of the boys, Oscar Nordholm (Raymond Guion), proves to be somewhat reserved and shy, but the other boy, Jose Vallejo (Humphrey Bogart), who is introduced as a Spaniard although he is really an Italian kid from Brooklyn, has quite a flair. Luring the awed Susan into the darkened garden, he tells her, "Am I not Don Jose Vallejo, the matador, whose two strong arms have choked the breath out of the bulls in the rings of Barcelona? Am I not Don Jose Vallejo, who, with one grip, tore the bars from the Palace windows at Madrid, that I might better see the black eyes of a lady-in-waiting to the Queen?" The party has grown hot and heavy when the husbands appear suddenly and profess to be outraged. But then the three flappers they have left in their car barge in, and the cats are out of the bag. Susan warns her husband that if he creates a stir she will soon be a widow. Leaving the men to fend temporarily for themselves, the gals resume the party. The settings were lovely: the Drakes' apartment, its walls covered with satiny drapes, giving way to the Ladds' wainscoted estate. Even the often nitpicking George Jean Nathan succumbed and called it "the funniest show in town," a superlative echoed in many other reviews. Among the players Oliver and Boland received the best notices, with poor Bogart again being ignored by many critics, albeit others praised him highly. The play established itself as the biggest comedy hit of the season, sometimes grossing as much as $25,000 in a single week, and ran for more than a year. It later became the 1941 musical, *Let's Face It*.

Maxwell Anderson's **Outside Looking In** (9-7-25, Greenwich Village), based on Jim Tully's *Beggars of Life,* ran only fifteen weeks at its small, out-of-the-way venue. It looked uncompromisingly on the world of hoboes and filled its dialogue with tough talk and drifters' jargon ("darbs," "frails," "yeggs," "stiffs"). In settings that moved from a riverside hobo camp by a railroad bridge in North Dakota, to the inside of a boxcar, and finally to a deserted shack in Montana, its story described some hours in the life of a hobo pack. Among them are a fiery young Irishman, Little Red (James Cagney), and the "boy" with whom he is traveling. The boy is actually a girl, Edna (Blythe Daly), fleeing the police after murdering the stepfather who had assaulted her. Although they all agree they would not like to go back to jail— "I'd rather be outside lookin' in"—at the promptings of the seemingly brutish Oklahoma (Charles

Bickford), they sacrifice their freedom so that Little Red and Edna can escape capture and possible hanging.

David Belasco came a cropper when he produced Willard Mack's **Canary Dutch** (9-8-25, Lyceum), based on an unidentified story by John A. Moroso. The playwright assumed the central role of a newly released convict, a Swiss jailed for counterfeiting, who has gotten his nickname for keeping a canary in his cell. He moves into the Try Again Home, an establishment run by his long-lost daughter (Catherine Dale Owen), whom he does not recognize. His old cronies appear, demand he resume his former trade, and, revealing the truth about his daughter, threaten to tell her all about him. He kills the leader. His daughter, learning the facts, comes to his defense.

Raymond Stevens (Norman Trevor), the central figure in Arthur Richman's **All Dressed Up** (9-9-25, Eltinge), has invented a truth-telling drug and decides to test it on some dinner guests. Personalities are turned inside out. Most startling is the change in Donald West (James Crane), the seemingly restrained fiancé of Stevens's daughter, Emily (Kay Johnson). He turns out to be violently passionate. While Emily is not all that upset, her father concludes that hypocrisy is not so bad after all.

More old-fashioned melodrama could be savored in Marian Wightman's **The Dagger** (9-9-25, Longacre). Deprived of his rightful inheritance, Pierre (Ralph Morgan) has become a Parisian Apache known as "The Dagger." His behavior lands him in jail, but he bribes his way into a pardon and marries Colette (Sara Sothern), a slum girl, but a decent one.

From France to Mexico, where Joe Byron Totten's **Love's Call** (9-10-25, 39th St.) was set. There the "tall, cold, handsome" Clyde Wilson Harrison (Mitchell Harris) tells the streetwalking Piquita (Galina Kopernak), "Although you are a wanton, you fire my senses." She falls in love with him even if she is kept by the villainous Don Pedro de Scarillo (Robert Glecker). When Don Pedro kidnaps Clyde and goes to shoot him, Piquita dashes into the bullet's path. Woollcott reported that an "audience of old meanies . . . tittered helplessly through its three steaming acts." He noted that at one point, after Don Pedro has announced his intention of torturing Clyde Wilson Harrison (Joe Byron Totten was apparently given to always using all three names), and Clyde Wilson Harrison has replied, "The thrill of the passion I have just experienced was worth it," "two dramatic critics and four laymen had to be picked up out of the aisles and put back in their seats before the play could resume."

A London comedy also flopped. A. Kenward Matthews's **Courting** (9-12-25, 49th St.) was a sort of Cinderella-ish tale in which Jeannie Grant (Jean Clyde), kept from the pleasures of life by a stern father (J. Nelson Ramsey), runs off to a ball and wins the man (Vernon Sylvaine) of her dreams.

Samson Raphaelson's **The Jazz Singer** (9-14-25, Fulton) ran out the season. It described the dilemma confronting the fast-rising singing star Jack Robin (George Jessel), born Jakie Rabinowitz, the son of a cantor. Torn between his celebrity and new wealth on the one hand and his religious upbringing on the other, and branding himself "half a cantor and half a bum," he finally heeds the call of his dying father (Howard Lang) on the eve of Yom Kippur, abandons show business and the cute actress (Phoebe Foster) he has come to admire, and plans to return to the synagogue. Sam Jaffe won laughs for his comic relief as a diamond merchant who sits on the synagogue's board. Some critics felt Jessel was weak in the more emotional scenes, but by and large his performance was applauded. However, when the play was made into the first "talkie," Al Jolson was starred.

A more Waspish America was displayed briefly in Larry E. Johnson's **Brother Elks** (9-14-25, Princess). Since Walter Woodward (Richard Mayfield), for all his obvious abilities, has never been a success, he decides to turn himself into a corporation and sell shares. Everything goes smoothly until one stockholder tries some chicanery. But Walter is able to thwart him. He also has a problem when several young ladies, wanting to own shares of him, buy stock. That problem fades after he proposes to the prettiest of them.

The Theatre Guild won kudos for its revival of Shaw's *Arms and the Man* at the Guild on the same night, with Lunt and Fontanne in the leads and with a fine supporting cast, headed by Pedro de Cordoba as Sergius. Fontanne was so nervous on opening night that she went up on her lines and had to be prompted audibly, but she soon got hold of herself and went on to give what Woollcott saw as a performance "glowing with vitality, immensely skillful and at times richly comic." He found Lunt's acting "flawless," and especially marveled at the actor's depiction of fatigue in the first act. (Lunt had hidden lead plates at the bottom of his boots to enhance his own sense of weariness.)

Two newer English plays also became hits, even though George Jean Nathan, remounting his high horse, dismissed them both as "flapdoodle." Michael Arlen's dramatization of his own novel, **The Green Hat** (9-15-25, Broadhurst) centered on the self-destructive Iris March (Katharine Cornell), who takes the blame for her husband's suicide (although he killed himself on his honeymoon after disclosing he had a venereal disease), watches the man (Leslie Howard) she truly loves marry another girl (Margalo Gillmore), then kills herself by driving her Hispano Suiza into a tree. Setting aside his own disdain for the play, Nathan acknowledged in the *Morning Telegraph* that it was "superbly acted in its leading role by that one young woman who stands head and shoulders above all the other young women of the American theatre." But Robert Benchley, who could rarely take anything seriously, while also admiring the players, suggested in *Life,* "May we not please some afternoon have a special matinee . . . in which this sensible cast are allowed to broaden their performances one-eighth of an inch, making the whole thing the most delightful burlesque of the season?"

Noel Coward's **The Vortex** (9-16-25, Henry Miller's) unfolded the sad saga of an amoral mother (Lillian Braithwaite), desperately clinging to her fading youth, and a son (Coward) driven to drugs by his own need to be admired and by the "vortex of beastliness" around him. Its English premiere at a playhouse in Hampstead had caused a furor, shocking many with its theme and delighting others with its excellence. New Yorkers seem to have taken something of a middle ground.

Although critics found redeeming features in Maxwell Anderson and Laurence Stallings's **First Flight** (9-17-25, Plymouth), with Nathan suggesting it had "a fine ring of brave beauty and the soft melody of an understanding tenderness," this somewhat artificial, pompous, and exceedingly talky drama had a short life. The "free and sovereign State of Franklin" will never become a part of North Carolina if the vicious, grasping George Dozier (Blaine Cordiner) and his foolishly aristocratic crony Major Singlefoot (J. Merrill Holmes) can help it. They are especially concerned about the man the government is sending to force unification. He turns out to be Captain Andrew Jackson (Rudolf Cameron). In no time, both men force Jackson into duels. He kills Dozier but purposely spares Singlefoot. Dozier had been about to marry Charity Clarkson (Helen Chandler), backed by her intimidated father's insistence, even though she would prefer Lonny Tucker (John Tucker Battle). But she has quickly fallen in love with Jackson. After the duels, she tells him, "If I let ye leave, there won't never be anything like ye again. And I'll live to be old, and ye'll be the one thing I've wanted, and I won't have never had you." But while Jackson is

adamant about his going, he confesses, "You'll belong to me always . . . above me white and shinin' forever." Jo Mielziner's settings of an eighteenth-century tavern and of the clearing alongside a log barn, where a barn dance was held, earned plaudits.

Kate Horton's **Harvest** (9-19-25, Belmont) also looked at unfulfilled love, and also failed. Old Man Sonrel (Augustin Duncan) and his daughter, Rose (Ethel Taylor), love their hardscrabble Michigan farm, but his wife (Louise Closser Hale) and her embittered, socialist son (Elmer Cornell) despise it. During the summer a rich Chicagoan (Wallace Erskine), his spinster sister (Hilda Spong), and his spoiled son, Richard (Fredric March), visit the area. Rose and Richard fall in love, even ignoring the drought-breaking rain that drenches them at the end of Act II. But Rose soon realizes that Richard is irresponsible and, to her father's dismay, sends him on his way.

Modern New York suburbia was the setting for Crane Wilbur's **Easy Terms** (9-21-25, National). Persuaded by the blandishments of her chiropractor (Wilbur), who has his eye on her daughter, Pet (Susanne Caubet), Lou (Mabel Montgomery) goads her husband, Ed (Donald Meek), a lowly paper-shuffler, into buying a suburban nest on "easy terms." However, when she hands the family savings over to the ambitious doctor he nearly squanders it all before sanity is restored. The program referred to the play's acts as installments.

F. Tennyson Jesse and H. M. Harwood's English drama **The Pelican** (9-21-25, Times Square) spanned a number of years, during which the family of an Englishman (Fred Kerr) press him to divorce his difficult wife (Margaret Lawrence) and declare the child about to be born illegitimate. When that baby grows to manhood (Herbert Marshall) and attempts to enlist in the army his illegitimacy prevents him until his father consents to rewed his mother, who must abandon a happy liaison to do so. Pelican mothers were said to pluck their breasts in order to feed their own blood to their offspring.

George S. Kaufman's **The Butter and Egg Man** (9-23-25, Longacre) brought playgoers back to New York and hurried them behind the scenes on Broadway. Joe Lehman (Robert Middleman) a crass, cigar-chomping former agent turned producer, and his partner, Jack McClure (John A. Butler), are vainly attempting to raise money to bring in their latest clinker. Joe had hoped to use his wife's savings, but she (Lucille Webster) has put her foot down. The result is some acrimonious give and take, with Joe reminding the woman she was once a vaudeville juggler and snarling, "There ain't a stage between here and California ain't got dents in it from them clubs of yours," and his wife, when he later moans that he can't throw the whole show away, retorting, "Why not?" But luck seems to come Joe's way in the person of Peter Jones (Gregory Kelly), a gullible young yokel from Chillicothe, with $20,000 to burn. Peter hopes to use the profit from any investment to buy a hotel back home. On opening night in Syracuse the play is a dud, so Joe and his partner jump when the obviously hopeless Peter offers to buy up the whole affair. To almost everyone's surprise the show becomes a smash hit. The only fly in the ointment is the arrival of a lawyer (George Alison), who informs Peter that he has a client and an ironclad case of plagiarism. Peter will have to surrender two-thirds of the take. Just then Joe and Jack return and offer to buy back in. Peter, who has assumed all the proper Broadway manner-isms and airs, agrees to sell it back to them for $100,000. Peter and Joe's attractive secretary, Jane (Sylvia Field), who have fallen in love, head back to Ohio together. Gilbert Gabriel of the *Sun* hailed the comedy as "the wittiest and liveliest jamboree ever distilled from the atmosphere of Broadway," while Walter Winchell reported in the *Graphic* that "first-nighters roared." As a result, the play prospered until the warm weather arrived.

Alice Conway (Carroll McComas), the leading figure in F. S. Merlin and Brian Marlow's **The New Gallantry** (9-24-25, Cort), has languished since returning home from a stint as an ambulance driver in wartime France. Her family doctor (Cyril Scott) tells her that her problem is "sex starvation." "Do you advise a love affair for a cure now?" she asks. "Why not?" the doctor answers. So when an engaging, philosophy-spouting hobo (G. Pat Collins) appears at her door, she invites him in, and before long, despite his claims of indifference to women, the two become lovers. Neighbors are shocked, but a happy ending ensues after Alice shows everyone a French wedding certificate and falsely claims that the hobo was the man she had wed during the war. Max Montesole won fine notices as Alice's "nearly male" friend, who tells people that they can talk to him as if he were their mother. (Remember Clifton Webb in *Parasites* last season?)

J. C. and Elliott Nugent suffered a humiliating failure when their **Human Nature** (9-24-25, Liberty) folded after just four performances. Learning that Jim Trayne (John Marston), the man she loves, is marrying another woman (Sue MacManamy), Bess Flanders (Mary Duncan) agrees to wed the aging novelist (Brandon Tynan) for whom she has served as secretary. Time passes and Bess hears that Jim's wife is now a useless invalid. She rushes back to Jim's arms. Before long she is pregnant, but Jim, of course, will not divorce his wife. So Bess confesses everything to her husband, who agrees to accept the baby as his own. Fine acting and some beautiful Joseph Urban settings could not save the play.

Of the three plays to open the following Monday only Barry Conners's **Applesauce** (9-28-25, Ambassador) came anywhere near the charmed 100-performance circle, playing eleven weeks. (It had run for twenty-nine weeks in Chicago.) Billed as "An American Comedy," it opens in the simple but comfortable home of the Robinsons. Ma (Jessie Crommette) is something of a scatterbrain, and Pa (William Holden) a peevish old soul. They are discussing the engagement of their daughter, Hazel (Gladys Lloyd), who has selected Rollo Jenkins (Walter Connolly), a man who counts every penny, over Bill McAllister (Alan Dinehart), a ne'er-do-well given to getting what little he wants by flattery. Pa dismisses Bill as mere applesauce and a man who is "twenty-five dollars short of having twenty-five cents." And though he believes that Rollo has opted for a long engagement so that he won't have to buy Hazel's new winter dresses, he is not opposed to the idea since a long engagement means they won't have to be married so long. But after Bill points out to Rollo the cost of wedded life, Rollo is happy to use the excuse of Hazel's seeing Bill without his permission to end the engagement. In their shabby little flat above a drugstore, Hazel and Bill scrimp by happily, hoping something good will eventually come their way. The play was filled with little touches of contemporary Americana, such as Pa's complaining that the women use his razor as a scissor for cutting patterns, as a blade to cut their corns, and as a can opener. And there's Ma's touching, homey observation, "It seems to me the curse of growing old is that every new generation is so much better looking than the last one was." Hornblow concluded that Conners gave his conventional characters "real life."

A less cozy look at American life was presented in Winchell Smith and George Abbott's **A Holy Terror** (9-28-25, George M. Cohan), with Abbott himself in the leading role of Dirk Yancey. (Abbott also directed John Golden's production although Smith was credited in the program.) Raised among feuding West Virginia mountaineers, Yancey knows how to shoot, even if he prefers not to. He is made police chief just as a bloody mine strike erupts. When the mayor of the town is killed, Yancey is arrested, despite his position, since it was general knowledge that he coveted the mayor's wife (Leona Hogarth). But Yancey makes mincemeat of the arguments against him and fingers the actual killer.

It was a huge hop from modern America to modern and bygone China and not spanned satisfactorily by John and Ella Scrymsour's **The Bridge of Distances** (9-28-25, Morosco), as revised by Irma Kraft. When Lady Susan Herryot (Mary Newcomb) and Li Wenk Lok (Ulrich Haupt) meet in China, they realize that they were lovers in an earlier, tragic reincarnation. Back then the Princess Tzu-Tsan was abducted from her wedding by an English buccaneer. Although he had been caught and killed, the young couple were forced to commit suicide because the girl's kidnapper had left her with child. Beautiful settings—"patterned columns, golden thrones, pagodas, shrines; and . . . human figures in silhouette against the shimmering waters of a moonlit lake"—could not gloss over the play's inadequacies.

Eugène Brieux's *L'Avocat,* translated by George Middleton as **Accused** (9-29-25, Belasco), was another near miss—ninety-five performances— although David Belasco mounted it with his usual skill and brought E. H. Sothern out of retirement to star. Actually, the play had been booked for only eight weeks, but Sothern's draw prompted an extension, after which it was taken out on the road where Sothern's name led to more profitable grosses. Sothern played a distinguished attorney who must defend a woman (Ann Davis) he once loved for killing her husband. He knows she is guilty, but he wins her freedom, after which she confesses that she killed because her husband was jealous of her old affair and considered murdering the attorney.

Having failed with Maxwell Anderson and Laurence Stallings's earlier drama, Arthur Hopkins tried again with their **The Buccaneer** (10-2-25). Her servants describe the haughty Donna Lisa (Estelle Winwood) as "cold like the slopes of a volcano in winter" but with "a smoldering hell under the snowcap forehead." Donna Lisa is actually Lady Elizabeth Neville, an English widow living under the roof of Don Jacinto de Esmeraldo (J. Colvil Dunn) in Panama City. The piratical Henry Morgan (William Farnum) lands and begins to ransack the town, but when he comes to her house, she demands he respect her and spare her mansion and servants. Her courage awes Morgan and he obeys. In short order the pair seem to have fallen in love, notwithstanding the lady's distant demeanor. When British sailors arrive to seize Morgan, she begins by hiding him, but after she discovers he has spent the night with

one of her serving girls, she turns against him. He is taken to England for trial. There King Charles (Ferdinand Gottschalk) is reluctant to hang him and employs Morgan's own clever arguments to acquit him, knight him, and make him Governor of Jamaica. Impressed by his bravery and reasoning, Lady Elizabeth changes her feelings. So when Morgan throws down his glove and challenges the snobbish courtiers to come with him, the glove is picked up only by the woman who will now call herself Lady Elizabeth Morgan. The play reads well today but failed to please its contemporaries.

If George M. Cohan's **American Born** (10-5-25, Hudson) chalked up a money-making eleven-week stay, it did so largely on the draw of Cohan's name as author and star. Indeed, Woollcott suggested it would not have run a single week without Cohan's presence. *Variety,* calling Cohan "America's most popular actor" and noting that he was "just the same old Georgie," nonetheless continued by noting that he "doesn't hog downstage center, tells no witty after-dinner stories, and gives himself no long speeches at all. . . . Yet one who had never seen him would 'fall' for him instanter. He has that magnificent simplicity which only genius can and only genius does assume." Joe Gilson was born and raised in America after his mother was disowned by her snooty English family for marrying their gardener. Now he finds he is heir to Malbridge Hall. Unmoved by England and its aristocracy, he prevents the closing of the family's factories, which would have thrown hundreds out of work, makes provisions for the main estate, and returns home with one nice thing he did find, sweet Jocelyn Pettering (Joan Maclean).

In Kate McLaurin's **Caught** (10-5-25, 39th St.) a luxury-loving young man (Lester Vail) throws over a sweet young girl (Gladys Hurlbut) to marry a rich, much older woman (Antoinette Perry). Later he learns the girl is about to give herself to a cynical, aging roué (Boyd Clarke). Realizing that he is unhappy and has probably doomed the girl, he kills his wife (accidentally when she attempts to prevent his leaving), runs to the girl's home, and, when the police come there for him, kills himself.

Catherine Chisholm Cushing's chronicle play **Edgar Allan Poe** (10-5-25, Liberty) was a one-week dud. It followed the poet (James Kirkwood) from his early manhood, through marriage, his time as a magazine's poetry editor, and his wife's death, and ended with his reciting "The Raven" in a cheap Baltimore bar in exchange for a drink.

Time would show that Broadway was wrong to dismiss the evening's lone importation, Noel Coward's second play of the season, **Hay Fever** (10-5-25, Maxine Elliott's). This delightful comedy, describing how a self-absorbed family, with the actress Judith Bliss (Laura Hope Crews) as its best-known member, invites friends to their home for a weekend, and then totally ignores the visitors, survived a mere six weeks. Part of the show's problem may have been that, because of so many openings, the producers invited critics to a dress rehearsal, where one thing after another went wrong.

Another importation, arriving the next night, ran fourteen weeks, albeit that meant **These Charming People** (10-6-25, Gaiety) was far less successful than Michael Arlen's earlier entry. It unfolded the saga of a press mogul (Alfred Drayton) who threatens to call in the debts of his father-in-law (Cyril Maude) if the man cannot prevent the mogul's wife (Edna Best) from running off with another man (Herbert Marshall).

Still two more importations opened the following evening. The more successful of the pair was **Stolen Fruit** (10-7-25, Eltinge), which Gladys Unger took from Dario Niccodemi's *La Maestrina*. The tearjerker ran twelve weeks, telling the story of a young French girl (Ann Harding) who is hurried off to South America after being seduced by a rich farmer (Felix Krembs). She returns eight years later, believing the child taken from her at birth to have died, and becomes a schoolteacher. After the mayor (Rollo Peters) reveals that the child remains alive and is one of her pupils, the girl looks with new interest not only at the youngster but at the mayor. While critics thought little of the play, Harding received some of the season's best notices. Hornblow, praising not only her "gentle voice—with its rich, well-modulated, cultured tones," lauded "a depth of sincere emotion, such perfect poise and naturalness, such unforgettable appeal, allied to a ravishing golden beauty."

Molnár's *A Farkas,* which Leo Ditrchstein had offered New Yorkers successfully in 1914 as *The Phantom Lover,* was presented again, in a Melville Baker translation, as **A Tale of the Wolf** (10-7-25, Empire). This time Roland Young was the dull husband; Phyllis Povah, the fantasizing wife; and Wallace Eddinger, the man of her dreams. But this time there were few takers.

Mary Borden's **Jane, Our Stranger** (10-8-25, Cort) premiered on Thursday night and closed shop on Saturday. In that flicker of time it watched as naive Jane Carpenter (Selena Royle) weds a money-chasing French nobleman (Clarke Silvernail) but wisely refuses to take him back after he runs off for a fling with a vixenish princess (Kay Strozzi).

Yet one more of the month's numerous importations, Monckton Hoffe's **The Crooked Friday** (10-8-25, Bijou), ran only a little longer. It told of a youngster who finds a baby in a sack and turns it over to a foundling home. Years later he (Dennis Neilson-Terry) seeks out the girl, finds she is a thief named Friday (Mary Glynne), arranges to give her $2000 a month to go straight and sees to it that she uses some of the money supposedly to support him, believing women love men who are dependent on them.

The Call of Life (10-9-25, Comedy), Dorothy Donnelly's translation of Arthur Schnitzler's play, starred Eva Le Gallienne as a girl who kills her dying, tyrannical father (Egon Brecher) so that she may run off and have an affair with a young officer (Derek Glynne). The officer subsequently is killed, and the girl faces a bleak life alone.

Hamlet was brought out on the 10th at Hampden's Theatre (the former Colonial at 62nd and Broadway), with Walter Hampden's "carefully studied interpretation" of the Dane and with Ethel Barrymore as a "kittenish . . . lovelier than ever and slender" Ophelia. Settings were a mix of traditional and less cluttered modern pictures. The revival's good but not truly excited notices allowed the tragedy to survive for sixty-eight performances, not a bad showing all told.

"You want your house, Harriet, and that's all you do want," Miss Austen (Anne Sutherland) tells her nephew's spouse, in George Kelly's **Craig's Wife** (10-12-25, Morosco). But then Harriet Craig (Chrystal Herne) has no qualms about stating that "if a woman is the right kind of a woman, it's better that the destiny of her home should be in *her* hands than in any man's." And that destiny means that no scratch can appear on the furniture, no cigarette ashes anywhere, and none of her husband's friends or the Craigs' neighbors are welcome to spoil the hard-won perfection. When she brings home the daughter (Eleanor Mish) of her ailing sister, she tells the girl's fiancé that the girl cannot be disturbed and rudely hangs up the phone. And when she discovers that her husband had visited the home of a man who subsequently killed his wife and committed suicide, she lies to the police to ensure that the Craig name will not be mentioned. His eyes finally opened, Mr. Craig (Charles Trowbridge) smashes his wife's favorite knickknack, then purposely smokes several cigarettes and drops the ashes on the rug. He then walks out, accompanied by his aunt and the niece. Mrs. Craig receives a telegram informing her of her sister's death, forcing her to realize that she is now alone not merely in her precious home but in the world.

Reviewers had mixed feelings about the play, with Brooks Atkinson noting that Kelly "has written an earnest study of character which he seems to confuse with a problem play." But like most of his colleagues, Atkinson admired Herne's performance: "One feels in her acting a strong, malignant force sweeping through every scene . . . a solid substance of smiling, overbearing, relentless duplicity." Business was slow at first but soon picked up. Aided by its winning of the Pulitzer Prize, which some suggested was given to compensate for *The Show Off*'s not having been awarded it, it ran into and through the summer.

Several critics gave Patrick Kearney's **A Man's Man** (10-13-25, 52nd St.) more enthusiastic notices than they had accorded Kelly's play, yet this unflinching look at middle-class life ran only fifteen weeks and long has been forgotten. It was set in a modest apartment in the shadow of the El and examined the gullibility of a bookkeeper named Melville Tuttle (Dwight Frye) and his wife, Edie (Josephine Hutchinson). Edie wants to be a film star, and Melville wants to join the Elks. They easily succumb to the wiles of a brash, swaggering con man, Charlie Groff (Robert Gleckler), who promises, for a proper recompense, to let them realize their ambitions. Of course, once he has the cash from Mel and the night in bed with Edie, Charlie disappears, leaving the disillusioned couple to get on with their lives.

In Lynn Starling's **Weak Sisters** (10-13-25, Booth) a sanctimonious reformer (Osgood Perkins) receives his comeuppance when the madam of a brothel he would close reminds him publicly that he has been a good customer. Jed Harris's production included some "daring" dialogue and scenes, especially when several of the prostitutes discussed their trade over tea.

Much was made of the fact that Garland Anderson, the author of **Appearances** (10-13-25, Frolic), was a black bellhop in San Francisco. Al Jolson and Governor Al Smith were both said to have helped get the play produced, even if Nedda Harrigan is reputed to have walked out of rehearsals when she learned she would have to appear with black actors instead of the usual whites in blackface. Anderson's story told of another black bellhop (Lionel Monagas) and his buddy, Rufus (Doe Doe Green), both accused by a white woman (Mildred Wall) of raping her. At their trial everything seems to prove them guilty until the woman is shown to be really a light-skinned, blackmailing Negress. The play survived for three weeks.

The month's seventh importation (not counting *Hamlet*) was **The Grand Duchess and the Waiter** (10-13-25, Lyceum), which Arthur Richman took from Alfred Savoir's Paris success. It did not succeed here with its tale of an exiled Russian noblewoman (Elsie Ferguson), who falls in love with a waiter (Basil Rathbone) at a Swiss hotel but runs away when she learns he is the son of the country's president, since she despises republicans. He follows her and wins her.

If a black could write about black experiences, two immigrants, Mr. and Mrs. M. H. Gulesian (the husband was said to be a prosperous Boston merchant), could do the same for the immigrant experience. Their play was **Made in America** (10-14-25, Cort), and it followed the history of Hagop Turian (Horace Braham) from the time he lands at Ellis Island, through his meeting Mildred (Jane Chapin), the daughter of the immigration commissioner, his borrowing $50 from her, his rise in the world until he has an art shop on Park Avenue and his marriage to Mildred. Uninteresting as all this sounds, it managed to run for nine weeks.

A modern vampire (Elisabeth Risdon) sets out to get either Mr. Linton (Bruce McRae), a successful attorney, or his handsome, nineteen-year-old son (William Hanley), in Jesse Lynch Williams's **Lovely Lady** (10-14-25, Belmont), but their love for Mrs. Linton (Lily Cahill) prompts both men to send the vamp on her way. The son settles for a pretty flapper (Miriam Hopkins), at least temporarily. Burns Mantle found the figures "impossibly exaggerated and quite unbelievable," and since many agreed, the play itself soon was sent on its way, too.

The next evening witnessed the opening of the American Laboratory Theatre, a small, high-minded organization founded by actor-director Richard Boleslawski and Maria Ouspenskaya, both of whom had been with the Moscow Art Theatre. Their policy demanded extended rehearsals and plays performed in repertory fashion. The group's first public offering was *Twelfth Night,* followed by Amélie Rives's **The Sea-Woman's Cloak** (11-4-25), in which a fisherman plunges to his death in an effort to live with an Ondine-like sea creature, and a new version of **The Scarlet Letter** (1-7-26). The productions and players were frequently greeted with kind notices but never moved on to major Broadway success.

Richard Barry's **Barefoot** (10-19-25, Princess) found few takers. Jessal Tabor (Evelyn Martin) lives in the Virginia mountains, but that has not stopped her from wanting to become an artist, so when slick Kemp Owen (Byron Beasley) invites her to come study in France and stay at his home in Barbazon, she accepts. Only after she learns Owen is a married man and lecherous does she run back home. There her father (John M. Kline) would shoot Owen when he comes after her, but Grey Langham (Eugene Weber) dissuades him and offers to marry Jessal, whom he has loved since way back. The play had been a hit when it was mounted on Long Island, but Manhattan was a different sort of island.

The Theatre Guild's regulars allowed Molnár's *Az üvegcipö,* presented in an uncredited translation literally as **The Glass Slipper** (10-19-25, Guild), to have a modest run. Its heroine (June Walker) works as a maid in a boardinghouse and loves one of the tenants (Lee Baker). When she learns that he has married the scruffy landlady (Helen Westley) she is so distraught that she applies for work in a brothel. The to-do that follows makes the boarder recognize that he prefers the girl.

In his *Best Plays,* Burns Mantle noted that Channing Pollock's **The Enemy** (10-20-25, Times Square) received such laudatory reviews during its tryout, "followed by such editorial endorsement as not half a dozen plays receive in a generation," that its Broadway premiere almost inevitably was a letdown. Still, New York notices were largely favorable, so the drama did good business for six months. At the home of Professor Arndt (Russ Whytal), his daughter, Pauli (Fay Bainter), and her sweetheart, Carl (Walter Abel), discuss the pacifist drama that Carl has written. Carl's stern, militaristic father (Charles Dalton) disapproves of such nonsense. The Germans and Austrians are superior and deserve to rule the world, he says. And he is contemptuous of Bruce Gordon (Lyonel Watts), a British student who boards with the Arndts. Then the archduke is killed by a Serb in Bosnia and war declared. Carl, forgetting his play, joins up although Pauli pleads, "More than ever you must remind people that the enemy is hate—the real enemy." Things go from bad to worse at the home of the idealistic Arndts, while Carl's father becomes rich as a war profiteer. Carl is killed, and Carl and Pauli's baby dies from lack of proper food. Pauli can only thank God that her baby is now safe from the scourge of war. After the armistice, Bruce comes back to Vienna and urges Pauli to marry him and live in England. Looking out of the window, Pauli watches the children playing. They are playing solider. Bainter, a last-minute replacement, won applause for her "sweet, patient and brave" heroine.

Norman Bel Geddes, who designed, staged, and co-produced Cloyd Head and Eunice Tietjens's **Arabesque** (10-20-25, National), was the hero of the night. His employment of huge colored blocks on three different levels to suggest various settings (with action often taking place on all three levels at once) and his use of dimmed or distracting lights, rather than a curtain, to cover scene changes garnered tremendous praise. Not so the play, an Arabian Nights affair, set in Tunisia, where the Sheik of Hamman (Bela Lugosi) is diverted from his pursuit of the Pearl in a Bed of Oysters, M'na (Sara Sothern) by the voluptuous Bedouin, Laila (Hortense Alden) and later finds that in the interim he has lost the girl to an ordinary young man (Curtis Cooksey). One scene caused a minor furor: Laila "dressed down to the utmost finesse of nakedness (she would be far less conspicuous were she utterly naked) straddles [the] sheik, who lies full-length on a cloak on the floor of a savage tent at midnight, alone with her. Only the blackout saves what might have gone much further." A short time later the girl reveals she is pregnant. Etienne Giradot was lauded for his performance as comic Caid. Some also were amused by the players pronouncing "sheik" as "sheck."

Antonia (10-20-25, Empire) was yet another importation, taken by Arthur Richman from Menyhért Lengyel's play of the same name. The title figure (Majorie Rambeau) had been a famous prima donna before her marriage and retirement. Now, after ten years on her husband's farm, she craves the excitement of the great town. Returning there, she meets the dashing Capt. Pierre Marceau (Georges Renavent) and nearly runs off with him. But common sense prevails, so she heads wistfully back to the farm. A nightclub setting and her character gave Rambeau a chance to sing several songs and to perform a wild dance to some fiery gypsy fiddles. Joseph Urban assisted by designing a lovely garden and atmospheric boîte. But plusses could not override the languors of a less than thrilling play.

Although many critics found much to praise in Sidney Howard's **Lucky Sam McCarver** (10-21-25, Playhouse), it lasted slightly short of a month. Sam (John Cromwell) runs a successful speakeasy and has not done badly on Wall Street. He is a rough-hewn Irishman, in love with Carlotta Ashe (Clare Eames), a much divorced, somewhat dissolute member of an old society family. After Sam deftly covers up a shooting in which her friends had been involved, Carlotta agrees to marry him. She feels she can give him polish; he is sure her name is his stepping-stone to greater fortune. But only a few months later, staying at the Venetian palazzo of an aunt (Hilda Spong) who is wed to a homosexual Italian count, Carlotta has despaired of changing her husband, while Sam is infuriated by his wife's hangers on. They separate, and Carlotta, increasingly ill with heart trouble, moves into an apartment provided for her by a rich Jew (Austin Fairman). Sam goes to visit her, to offer her a handsome yearly allowance, but they argue and the strain proves fatal to Carlotta. Howard gave his raffish characters raffish dialogue. For example, the nightclub's doorman warns its orchestra leader, "It 'ud be a fine thing for me to go off an' leave Sam at the mercy of a jazz-crazy Broadway highbinder like yourself." And his characters were sometimes singularly frank for the time, with Sam rejecting the chits of one of Carlotta's leeches as "fifty thousand liras worth of a fairy's calling-cards." Unfortunately, interesting characters, good dialogue, and fine acting did not prevail.

Mrs. Gladys Insull, in her earlier years an actress known as Gladys Wallis, had mounted a revival of *The School for Scandal* in Chicago to raise money for charity. She had employed Daly's old redaction, cast herself as Lady Teazle, and hired a mediocre supporting cast. She brought the production into the Little Theatre on the 22nd and kept it going for eighty-five performances in the face of mostly discouraging notices. On December 6th George Tyler and Basil Dean brought in a company they had assembled for the road to give a single performance at the Knickerbocker. That troupe included O. P. Heggie as Sir Peter, Henrietta Crosman as Lady Sneerwell, and the old musical clown Jefferson DeAngelis as Moses. Some more important roles were assigned to less known performers.

Owen Davis enjoyed a five-month success with **Easy Come, Easy Go** (10-26-25, George M. Cohan). Several of the performers, including its co-star Otto Kruger, had played in Davis's earlier hit, *The Nervous Wreck*. Now Kruger became Dick Tain, who, in cahoots with Jim Bailey (Victor Moore), robs a bank. The pair make their escape in a Pullman car. On the train they pull some more subtle heists, including robbing Mortimer Quale (Edward Arnold), an eccentric millionaire, of his wallet and cigars. He nonetheless takes a liking to Tain and unwittingly suggests a perfect hideaway, Dr. Jasper's Health Farm. Overhearing a detective say that the robbers are known to be on the train and that all the exits at Detroit are now guarded, Tain and Bailey get off with the patients at a special stop for the farm's clients. There Quale, who preaches the virtues of bluff, passes Tain off as a rich man. Tain promptly sells the patients nonexistent Florida lots, telling them, "Look at Wall St. Think of it— land down there is worth millions an acre and you can't even grow an orange, while here we are offering . . .". Tain also manages to steal Quale's daughter, Barbara (Mary Holliday), from the stuffy fellow her father had planned for her to wed. Love makes Tain promise to go straight, so he turns over

the stolen money to the police and claims the $5000 reward. Poor Bailey has no choice but to reform, too. The farce later became the musical *Lady Fingers*.

All seemed to end happily, too, in Ashley Dukes's English comedy **The Man with a Load of Mischief** (10-26-25, Ritz). A lovely lady (Ruth Chatterton), ignored by her gambling husband, takes off. Her carriage breaks down on the road, and she finds herself accosted at a country inn by an imperious, boastful nobleman (Robert Loraine). Finding him detestable, she takes off again—this time with the nobleman's good-looking, surprisingly suave servant (Ralph Forbes). The title came from the name of the inn.

Don Mullally's **Laff That Off** (11-2-25, Wallack's) was one of two plays that opened on the first Monday in November to run out the season, and the only American one. A broke and homeless young lady, Peggy Bryant (Shirley Booth), thinking of jumping in the river, is stopped by a nice but rather dense Leo Mitchell (Alan Bunce), who brings her back to the apartment he shares with two other men and sets her up as their housekeeper. The other men fall in love with her, but Leo appears indifferent. Then one day Peggy slips away, taking the men's $600 savings with her. She comes back on Christmas Eve, bejeweled and befurred, having landed a film contract. At that somewhat late juncture Leo realizes he loves her. Miss Booth won plaudits for her "natural manner" and "was tense enough at times to indicate good dramatic possibilities."

Sidney Blackmer was a young actor who regularly received flattering notices (although some reviewers claimed he whined too much) but was almost never to find a sturdy vehicle (one would come decades later when he co-starred with Miss Booth). His latest disappointment was Rafael Sabatini and J. E. Harold Terry's **The Carolinian** (11-2-25, Sam H. Harris), in which he played Harry Latimer, one of the most vociferous rebels in 1774 Charles Town. After the Revolution breaks out, his marriage to Myrtle Carey (Martha-Bryan Allen), daughter of a Colonial governor, brings problems when she is accused of being a spy and he is given reason to suspect the accusations are justified. However, a happy ending follows her acquittal.

J. Palmer Parsons's **White Gold** (11-2-25, Lenox Little Theatre) took place on an isolated Australian sheep ranch, where a prolonged drought has killed off many of the sheep and has driven the rancher to drink and his English wife to thoughts of eloping with another man. But the rains finally come, saving both the ranch and the marriage.

The other play to open that same evening was an importation, but in a few years its playwright would settle in America and become an American citizen. John Van Druten's **Young Woodley** (11-2-25, Belmont) focused on a student at an English "public school"—a shy, gauche, poetry-penning boy (Glenn Hunter) of seventeen. His rites of manhood come through a brief romance with the bored wife (Helen Gahagan) of the overbearing headmaster (Herbert Bunston), who discovers the couple at an awkward moment and forces Woodley to leave school. Hunter's "sensitive and finely grained" acting provided "a splendid portrait of a boy overwhelmed with the perplexities of ordinary living." The play, with what for the time was some candid talk of teenage sexuality, had been banned in London, but after its season-long success in New York, Basil Dean, who had directed the play here, launched a campaign that finally allowed its production in the West End.

Em Jo Basshe's **Adam Solitaire** (11-6-25, Provincetown Playhouse) begins at the wedding of John Stafford (Robert Lynn), where his Aunt Minnie (Eda Heinemann), reading from her ten-cent fortune-telling book, sees a gloomy life ahead. As the dire prophecies begin to come true, Stafford attempts suicide but fails. He must suffer through all the catastrophes foreseen by his aunt. Cleon Throckmorton's expressionistic settings underscored the nature of the writing. One scene was played in a vaudeville style, while white-coated hucksters walked up and down the theatre's aisle peddling soft drinks, much as they might in cheaper vaudeville houses.

November's third season-spanning hit, Frederick Lonsdale's **The Last of Mrs. Cheyney** (11-9-25, Fulton), was aided immeasurably by the brilliant clowning of Ina Claire and Roland Young. An English aristocrat discovers the elegant Australian widow he is courting is, in fact, merely a sophisticated jewel thief. He presents her the choice of sleeping with him or being exposed. After she chooses exposure, he looks at her with renewed respect and offers to marry her. Miss Claire, "radiantly lovely and in supreme command of the impishness and slyness and cuteness that were in her role," and Young, "smooth . . . and most engaging," were abetted by A. E. Matthews as the butler who secretly heads the widow's crime clique.

The Last Night of Don Juan (11-9-25, Greenwich Village) enjoyed no similar acclaim or success. In Sidney Howard's redaction of Edmond Rostand's play, Don Juan (Stanley Logan), having won his plea for some extra years on earth and lived them to the fullest, returns haughtily to hell, where the Devil (Augustin Duncan) shows him that most of the women he thought he had conquered actually laughed at him behind his back. Coupled with this piece was Sigourney Thayer's adaptation of Charles Vildrac's **The Pilgrimage,** in which a black sheep (Augustin Duncan) returns to the scenes of his dissipated youth only to find he is still unwelcome.

One novelty that straddled the fence between straight plays and song-and-dance entertainments was **Naughty Cinderella** (11-9-25, Lyceum), derived by Avery Hopwood from René Peter and Henri Falk's *Pouche.* A woman used as a decoy by a man to conceal his affair with another lady wins the man for herself just before the final curtain. Irene Bordoni starred.

Two revivals, both of English shows, opened the same evening. A modern-dress *Hamlet,* having caused a stir in London, came into the Booth with Basil Sydney in the lead, Charles Waldron as Claudius, Ernest Lawford as a monocled Polonius, and Helen Chandler as Ophelia. A new-model touring car was onstage for a time, Polonius was shot with an automatic, and the First Grave Digger (Walter Kingsford) sported a bowler. The novelty, plus some basically excellent acting, allowed the production to outrun Hampden's, piling up eighty-eight performances.

Lovely Peggy Wood and the skilled Morgan Farley (who walked away with the best notices) could not push the Actors' Theatre revival of *Candida* beyond its originally announced three-week engagement at the Comedy.

Eva Le Gallienne did so much better with her restoration of *The Master Builder* at Maxine Elliott's on the 10th that she began to muse seriously about founding a repertory company. Many critics still confessed to being baffled by the play, but Miss Le Gallienne's Hilda Wangel, dressed the entire evening in mannish work clothes, was seen by Woollcott as "alive with a finely communicated exaltation." Her reward was a ten-week stand.

Although second-stringers who reviewed William Anthony McGuire's **Twelve Miles Out** (11-16-25, Playhouse) gave it short shrift, it enjoyed the longest run of any of the evening's many openings—188 performances. No sooner have bootleggers, led by Gerald Fay (Warren William), commandeered the Long Island home of John (John Westley) and Jane Burton (Mildred Florence) in order to cache their liquor than Mike McCue (Frank Shannon) and his hijackers seize the booty and take everyone aboard their yacht. There John's sniveling behavior infuriates Jane, whom both Gerald and Mike have come to covet. However, Mike is stabbed to death, so the chances are good that Jane will ditch John and link up with the attractive rumrunner.

The night's second-longest run—seventy-three performances—went to a more high-minded work, Philip Barry's **In a Garden** (11-16-25, Plymouth). A playwright, Adrian Terry (Frank Conroy), has decided to abandon writing and live an ideal life with his ideal wife, Lissa (Laurette Taylor). He scoffs when his more realistic friend, Roger Crompton (Ferdinand Gottschalk), warns him that "every wife is at heart another man's mistress—the man who just happened to be on hand when first romance came to flower in her." In his wife's case that man would be Norrie Bliss (Louis Calhern), who made love to her years ago in a moonlit garden. Since Bliss, a diplomat who has spent many years out of the country, will be visiting the Terrys, Adrian has an idea. Using old stage settings and theatrical lighting, he recreates that garden in his library and leaves the pair alone there. The old love is momentarily rekindled, but Lissa then learns not only of her husband's curious scheme but that Bliss had contrived the first meeting. She walks out on both men at least until she can discover her true self. Critics divided on the merits of the play, but Woollcott admired it and Miss Taylor as well. He described her Lissa as "an earth woman, the composition of whose music is full of half notes and accidentals . . . and who is so fashioned for just living that she could have made an Arcady in a flat under the El," and he saw the play as "brushed with a kind of gentle graciousness of its own."

Sports were coming to have a larger and larger place in the lives of all Americans, so it was not too surprising that Theodore Westman, Jr.'s **Solid Ivory** (11-16-25, Central) should have baseball-wise, baseball-mad "Babe" Ruth Holden (Lillian Ross) as its principal figure. She is the daughter of the manager of the bush league Hyenas and in love with the team's best pitcher, Jimmy Buck (James Burtis). Trouble is, the self-awed Jimmy has eyes only for the redheaded vampire, Shirley Griffen (Marie Adels), whose daddy owns the team. Then one day Babe's father misses a train connection and cannot get to a game. Babe takes over and refuses to send Jimmy to the showers when he starts to lose. She lets him lose but good, his failure costing the team the pennant and his fellow players a $500 bonus for each of them. That brings Jimmy down to earth. There is a reasonable probability that Babe will soon be Mrs. Buck, watching as Jimmy pitches for McGraw's Giants. The dialogue was said to have a Lardneresque ring to it (no pun intended), and much of the action occurred at the clubhouse entrance, in the dugout, and in the press box—refreshingly different stage settings. But for all its success during its tryouts, the play failed in New York.

Arthur Goodrich and W. F. Payson's **The Joker** (11-16-25, Maxine Elliott's) found the high-living, seemingly irresponsible Dick Hamill (Ralph Morgan) accused of stealing bonds from the office where he works. He sets out to unearth the real thief and does—his best friend, Grant Nugent (Walter Gilbert).

The English acting team of Dennis Neilson-Terry and Mary Glynne, having failed with *The Crooked Friday,* tried to recoup with an evening premiere and some subsequent matinee performances of Mordaunt Shairp's **The Offense** (11-16-25, Ritz). It studied a man terrorized by the memory of a beating his father gave him for breaking a valuable vase. It requires his breaking another vase to exorcise the obsession. The performers sailed back home shortly after the opening.

Rachel Crothers had a moderately bankable property in **A Lady's Virtue** (11-23-25, Bijou). When the charming diva Madame Sisson (Mary Nash) visits the Halsteads, a small-town couple bored with each other after eight years of marriage, Mrs. Halstead (Florence Nash) sees little wrong after her husband (Robert Warwick) starts to fall in love with the singer. She herself heads for New York where she attempts to rekindle the ardor of a former suitor (Joseph King). She succeeds more than she meant to. Before long, the Halsteads accept the fact that their somewhat dull marriage is preferable to the dangerous excitements their flirtations might offer. The play was referred to in the trade as a "lower floor show," which meant it relied on dowagers and matrons, and any men they could induce to join them, to keep it going by buying the more expensive orchestra seats.

Unfortunately, Henry Myers could not make the most of the Pirandellish undercurrents in his **Me** (11-23-25, Princess). Kate Sims (Norma Millay) has lost her mind fretting over her fiancé Donald Hood (Gerald Cornell), who has spent seven years in a cabin in the Rocky Mountains, attempting to recover from tuberculosis. Kate finally visits him. That visit and his embrace restore her sanity. What she is unaware of is that the man in the cabin is not Donald but a tramp (Jerome Lawler) who has killed Donald and taken his place. He even convinces Kate's doctor-father (Fred Tiden) that he is really Donald.

The Theatre Guild had become Shaw's chief American exponent. For mid-season it offered revivals of two more of his older plays, *Androcles and the Lion* and *The Man of Destiny.* The double bill opened at the Klaw on the 23rd with Henry Travers and Romney Brent in the title roles of the first piece and Tom Powers playing the title part in the second. Their reception was unexpectedly cool, even if Edward G. Robinson, who assumed the parts of Caesar and Giuseppe, could delight in some highly clippable comments.

John B. Hymer and Le Roy Clemens's **Alias the Deacon** (11-24-25, Sam H. Harris), an obvious, naive comedy that some critics saw as a poor man's *Lightnin',* came in with good advance notices and ran until late summer. For the second time in recent weeks, a supposedly empty freight car served as a setting. In this instance, several hoboes who occupy the car are astonished when a young boy who enters turns out, like the boy in *Outside Looking In,* to be a girl. She is Phyllis Halliday (Mayo Methot). The youngest and best-looking of the hoboes, John Adams (Donald Foster), saves her from a lecherous and murderous Italian (Clyde Veaux). When the train stops in Herrington, the youngsters jump off. Phyllis takes work as a waitress and helper at the local hotel, while John gets employment cleaning cars. They have obviously fallen in love and plan to marry. Another of their trainmates was a distinguished-looking cardsharp known as "the Deacon" (Berton Churchill). He appears at the hotel and is accepted as a clergyman. In short order, he saves the widow who runs the hotel from a man who would trick her out of her property, fingers the Italian when he attempts another seduction, and sees to it that John and Phyllis get enough money to set up house. While he is talking with the Deacon, the sheriff (John F. Morrisey) is handed a telegram listing the Deacon as a wanted man and describing him in unmistakable detail. The Deacon assures the sheriff that he is at his disposal, but the sheriff, aware of the good deeds the man has done, tells him he first must attend to seeing the Italian sent off to Denver. He asks the Deacon if he will be there when he returns. When the Deacon replies "Extremely unlikely," the sheriff smiles, wishes him good luck, and leaves. The Deacon also departs, after stating he hopes he can return some day. Churchill's "engagingly unctuous" performance aided no end in carrying the play.

James Forbes's slang-laden melodrama **Young Blood** (11-24-25, Ritz) overcame largely scathing notices to run nine weeks, primarily on the strength of its performers' reputations. Although Alan Dana (Norman Trevor), a prosperous widower, has been a neglectful father, he explodes with fury when his son, Alan junior (Eric Dressler), flunks out of college. The dejected boy seeks solace in booze and while drunk is seduced by Dana's attractive but loose-moraled maid (Florence Eldridge), who then claims she is pregnant and demands young Alan marry her. Luckily for Alan, his pretty, wily neighbor, Georgia Bissell (Helen Hayes), exposes the maid's deception and wins Alan for herself. For once, Helen Hayes, in a relatively subdued part, did not collect the best notices, which went to Florence Eldridge, applauded for playing with "real skill and power."

Maurice V. Samuels and Hymen Adler's **Drift** (11-24-25, Cherry Lane) spotlighted a gypsy fiddler (Adler) who assists in proving that two sweethearts are not blood relations and therefore can wed.

Sam Forrest, better known as a director, was author of **Paid** (11-25-25, Booth). A penniless inventor, John Ramsey (Carl Anthony), finds $5000 dropped in haste by a thief. He decides to keep it and not report it. However, once his inventions begin to bring in money he quietly assigns a share of the profits to the man he knows was robbed. Yet when the truth comes out the man is not at all grateful. Only the fact that the inventor's son loves the victim's daughter prevents further problems.

Charles Recht and Sidney Howard were responsible for **Morals** (11-30-25, Comedy), taken from Ludwig Thoma's German play. It echoed *Weak Sisters* in recounting how a police official (John Craig), attempting to stifle accusations that the police are in league with the city's madams, discovers that the noisy head (Edwin Nicander) of the Society for the Suppression of Vice is one of the main clients of the best local brothel. The noise-maker is embarrassed into helping the owner set up shop elsewhere.

December got off to an uncertain start. In Owen Davis's **Beware of Widows** (12-1-25, Maxine Elliott's) Joyce Bragdon (Madge Kennedy), determined that her next husband should be her old flame, Jack Waller (Alan Edwards), manages to set a houseboat adrift with only the pair of them aboard. The plot was flimsy, and it necessitated Miss Kennedy's skilled and varied antics, "smearing her lines with the proper insinuations," to keep the play alive for seven weeks.

Some aisle-sitters deemed Reginald Goode's **Just Beyond** (12-1-25, National) a variation on the story of *White Gold,* since it was set on an Australian sheep farm during a drought and it took the rain to bring about a reconciliation between the farmer and his American wife, whom he suspected of planning to elope with his younger brother. The play's title came from the name of the ranch, Gundramundra, which meant "just beyond" in the aboriginal tongue.

Herman Heijermans's Dutch drama *Eva Bonheur*

276

was brought to New York in Caroline Heijermans-Houwink and Lillian Saunders's translation as **The Devil to Pay** (12-3-25, 52nd St.). Learning that the parents of Marie (Mary Ricard) are poor and no longer even own their home, Nanning Storm (Alexander Kirkland) deserts her after seducing her. When he has second thoughts and returns to do the right thing, Marie's father (Whitford Kane) orders him out. All this is watched with malicious interest by Eva (Margaret Wycherly), a poisonous lodger who has managed to become the home's owner. A much praised double-decked setting showed both the family's and Eva's apartments.

Gypsies were not confined to Graustarkian operettas, as *Drift* had demonstrated. Allan Davis's **Gypsy Fires** (12-7-25, George M. Cohan) was set in a Romany encampment not in Graustark but in New England. Morella Oneil (Lillian Foster), a half-breed, loves Carroll Lankford (Arthur Albertson), an American artist from old New England stock. Her gypsy grandmother (Alice Fischer), queen of the band, is adamantly opposed to the relationship, as is her Irish father (J. M. Kerrigan). But after he is killed by the villainous full-blooded gypsy who wants to marry Morella, and the villain himself is killed by his own bear, Morella is free to wed Carroll.

The evening's lone hit was Noel Coward's third play of the season, **Easy Virtue** (12-7-25, Empire). It is soon obvious to Larita (Jane Cowl), a woman with a past, that the stuffy English family she has just married into will never accept her. So she puts on quite a display at a family soirée, even smashing a favorite statue (shades of *Craig's Wife*). Having mortified them all, she stalks out. Woollcott, ruing that the star had stepped down from the high world of Shakespeare and Maeterlinck, surmised that she had an easy time of it, nonetheless playing with "humor and resourcefulness and immense, contagious spirit."

A second importation, **Cousin Sonia** (12-7-25, Central Park), which Herbert Williams adapted from Louis Verneuil's *Ma cousine de Varsovie,* received a chillier greeting. Marguerita Sylva was starred as the "cousin" who discovers her friends' marriage is in jeopardy because the wife (Katherine Hayden) is falling for a persuasive bachelor (Douglas MacPherson), whom she promptly vamps.

The producing team of Robert Edmond Jones, Kenneth Macgowan and Eugene O'Neill brought in O'Neill's own **The Fountain** (12-10-25, Greenwich Village), in which Juan Ponce de Leon (Walter Huston), hearing an Arab sing of a fountain of eternal youth, sails with Columbus on his second voyage and spends the rest of his life seeking the waters. Eventually he is shot full of arrows by treacherous Florida Indians. Brought back to Cuba, he comes to understand that youth can only belong to each new generation for a brief time, and he dies praying, "Youth of this earth—love—hail—and farewell! May you be forever blessed!" In his Sunday follow-up Brooks Atkinson complained that the drama "rarely stirs the emotions or gives spur to the imagination" and regretted that the playwright "filled [the play] with a profusion of irrelevant ornaments that clog the action and imprison the meaning." Even Jones's eight elaborate settings, which moved from a Moorish courtyard to Columbus's ship to various places in the New World, seemed less than helpful. The drama closed quickly, losing the men their entire $18,000 investment—no small amount at the time (when *Desire Under the Elms* had cost $4000).

At a theatre which Jones, Macgowan, and O'Neill had recently relinquished, Charles Webster's **The Man Who Never Died** (12-12-25, Provincetown Playhouse) had a slightly shorter run but at least cost a mere fraction of what the O'Neill play had. John Gerald Holt (Harold Vosburgh) kills his wife's lover to save his own honor and is acquitted in court; Albert Edward Uwyng (Bennett Southard) kills his wife's lover at the man's behest to save the man's honor and is sentenced to a long prison term. Yet Uwyng insists it is his sort of killing that makes him above the law. The point of the play baffled reviewers, with Burns Mantle stating it was performed "to the complete understanding of everybody except the audience" and Robert Benchley in *Life* concluding, "Unfortunately for a coherent review we lost track of what it was all about."

The plots of the four plays which opened the following Monday were not hard to understand. Samuel R. Golding was both the author and producer of **Open House** (12-14-25, Daly's), in which Eugenie Bellamy (Helen MacKellar), pressed by her ambitious husband (Ramsey Wallace) to accommodate his potential clients in anything they might demand, demonstrates the insulting nature of his request by having an affair with a Russian customer (Bela Lugosi).

Marcel Pagnol and Paul Nivoix's **Merchants of Glory** (12-14-25, Guild), in an English version by Ralph Roeder, examined a French family who lost a son during the war. The mother and sister (Helen Westley and Armina Marshall) have mourned for ten years, but the father (Augustin Duncan) has profited by his son's reflected glory and is about to be elected to the Chamber of Deputies. So imagine his consternation when his son (José Ruben), an amnesia victim and still not quite right in mind, turns up. The father demands the young man take another name and not acknowledge his relationship.

Audiences tittered at Joe Byron Totten's **So That's That** (12-14-25, Cherry Lane) much as they had at his earlier *Love's Call,* only this time they were meant to laugh, since the play was "a comedy of youth, romance and adventure." Regrettably it was a very bad one, so was gone after just two performances. In those it told how a failed author wins a bet that he can marry the daughter of the publisher who has rejected his books.

A number of first-stringers elected to attend the fourth opening, even though it was given in Russian and limited to a week's stand. This was the Moscow Art Theatre's mounting at the Jolson of Aristophanes' 2336-year-old anti-war comedy, *Lysistrata,* recounting how the women of Athens deny their husbands their beds until peace is restored. Staged in a simple, Greek-like setting, the production made especially effective use of the lively mob that served as anything but a staid chorus.

Similarly, the next night the new American play was once again not the center of interest. The native work was William Hurlbut's **Chivalry** (12-15-25, Wallack's). In its concern with killers who seem to be above the law, it bore a resemblance to *The Man Who Never Died,* but while it was less ambiguous it was also too preachy to enlist much support. Having won an acquittal for Lucy Meredith (Violet Heming), a cold-blooded golddigger who shot her rich lover when he attempted to end their affair, the great criminal lawyer, Emerson Jarvis (Edmund Breese), then berates the jury—and the whole modern American system of justice—for being so lenient on pretty women.

The drama that received much more attention was S. Ansky's **The Dybbuk** (12-15-25, Neighborhood Playhouse), even though it was a foreign work and presented by a small but respected group some distance from mainstream Broadway. The play, initially written in Russian but translated into Yiddish after being banned in its original language, had been presented on several earlier occasions in America by Yiddish theatres. Its English version was by Henry G. Alsberg. The spirit of a dead boy (Albert Carroll) haunts the girl (Mary Ellis) he was prevented from marrying by her ambitious father (Marc Loebell). An attempted exorcism kills the girl, allowing her to join her lover in the afterworld. Greeted by enthusiastic notices, the mystical piece ran for 120 performances.

Respected critics do not always make the best playwrights, as Gilbert Seldes found out when his **The Wisecrackers** (12-16-25, Fifth Ave. Playhouse)

premiered at a small, out-of-the-way venue. The play was reputedly a send-up of the Algonquin roundtable crowd. Its hero was Tony Cooper (Russell Hicks), a notoriously barb-witted editor, who eventually comes to see that a quiet, happy marriage is worth more than afternoons of smart repartee. Atkinson typified his colleagues' reactions when he branded this "assault upon the citadel of waggery" as "lugubrious entertainment."

The Taming of the Shrew was brought out at the Klaw for a series of matinees beginning on the 18th. Richard Boleslawski directed a cast that included Estelle Winwood as Kate, Rollo Peters as Petruchio (he also designed the scenery), and Ann Harding as Bianca. Although a number of reviewers praised the revival, the players' other commitments prevented a regular run.

Snobberies of a different sort than Seldes had depicted were highlighted in Kenneth Webb's **One of the Family** (12-21-25, 49th St.), a sleeper which delighted playgoers into the summer. Henry Adams (Grant Mitchell), oppressed by his family's heavy-handed worship of their ancient lineage, marries a lovely, lively girl (Kay Johnson) with the common surname Smith and no pedigree whatsoever. His family, lorded over by the spinsterish Priscilla Adams (Louise Closser Hale), is outraged. A good, stiff cocktail of bootleg hootch provokes Henry into telling the snobs where to get off.

But Broadway turned thumbs down on Catherine Chisholm Cushing's theatricalization of Robert Herrick's novel **The Master of the Inn** (12-21-25, Little). The "inn" of the story is a hospital run by Geoffrey Thorne (Robert Loraine), who tells some of his patients that he established it after his sweetheart (Virginia Pemberton) ran off with a young surgeon (Ian Keith). His story is barely concluded when the surgeon, now a shameless alcoholic, and his brutally abused wife appear. Thorne rehabilitates both and sends them on their way. Playing a small part in the drama was a young man who would some day take over running the little eatery his father operated just a few doors away, Vincent Sardi, Jr.

Barry Conners's **The Patsy** (12-22-25, Booth) ran out the season. Pop Harrington (Joseph Allen) is a moderately successful salesman, much put upon by his harridan wife (Lucia Moore). Her latest demand is that he buy an automobile so his older daughter's rich fiancé will not think the Harringtons are paupers. Harrington responds, "You've got just as much chance of me buying another automobile as you have of seeing a Swiss battleship sinking off the coast of Nebraska." That older daughter, Grace (Mary Stills), is a mean-tongued version of her mother. She has just thrown over the pleasant Tony Anderson (Herbert Clark) for the wealthy Billy Caldwell (John Diggs). Moreover, she thinks nothing of stealing money belonging to her younger sister, Pat (Claiborne Foster), even if that means that Pat, unable to bank the money to cover a check she has written, might go to jail as a result. Pat has long suffered such treatment in silence and has long loved Tony. She finally stops being a patsy and gets her revenge after Grace antagonizes and loses Billy and then decides to pursue Tony again. Grace has asked Tony to meet her at the country club, but, before Grace can arrive there, Pat calls the club and asks Tony to come talk to her about an important matter. Tony, no dumbbell, tells Pat he has caught on to Grace's vicious ways, and, besides, he has come to love Pat. He proposes and Pat accepts. Pop has also had enough. He alerts Pat, "Wait till you see what happens from now on!"

In the prologue to A. E. Thomas's **Fool's Bells** (12-22-25, Criterion), dramatized from a story by Leona Dalrymple, a hunchbacked young man (Donald Gallaher) is urged by his uncle not to consider serving in the war, so the man begins to read a play he has written to his uncle. The main part of the play brings to life that drama. In it the hunchback becomes Mr. Pan, and he is encouraged by a Pollyannaish Lucy Grey (Sara Sothern) to perform all manner of good deeds. These good deeds and his noble thoughts straighten his back. In the epilogue, the uncle agrees the boy should do his duty. Beryl Mercer once again won applause as a bedraggled if good-hearted sot (as well as for her spoof of Queen Victoria), and Donald Meek was admired for his fey performance as a corn-salve salesman. But, as was so often the case, the good acting was not sufficient to keep the play going.

Walter Hampden and Ethel Barrymore, having combined their talents in their earlier *Hamlet,* now brought out *The Merchant of Venice* at Hampden's Theatre on the 26th. Hampden's lonely, embittered Shylock drew little sympathy, nor did many critics feel that Barrymore put much fire into her straightfoward Portia. In her autobiography Miss Barrymore states that she purposely delivered the "quality of mercy" speech so softly and unobtrusively that audiences did not realize it was the famous speech till after she had finished, and then there was a silence rather than applause.

Two importations closed out 1925. **The Monkey Talks** (12-28-25, Sam H. Harris), which Gladys Unger took from René Fauchois's Paris hit, ran twelve weeks, missing by just two performances the charmed 100-playings mark. Having been ostracized by his family for his flirtation with a circus performer, Sam Wick (Philip Merivale) joins a circus, performing with Faho (Jacques Lerner), a tiny man in a realistic monkey outfit. They become a tremendous success until Faho is kidnapped by a rival. His having to disclose that he is not actually a monkey ruins the act. But Faho helps Sam find romance by way of consolation. Circus settings and a glimpse of a performance at the Folies-Bergère added gaiety and color.

Stronger Than Love (12-28-25, Belasco) was adapted by an uncredited writer from Dario Niccodemi's *La Nemica.* Marius (Ralph Forbes) asks his mother (Nance O'Neil) why she has always preferred his younger brother (Borden Harriman) and learns that he is not really her son but rather is his late father's illegitimate offspring. She also admits that she is resentful that he, rather than her own son, is to inherit his father's wealth. But the war comes, the younger man is killed, and the old lady accepts the bastard as her own.

The new year, 1926, opened with an oddity. **Dope** (1-3-26, 48th St.) began life as a short vaudeville drama written by and featuring Hermann Lieb and was expanded into a full-length play by Joseph Medill Patterson. It was scheduled for an evening premiere and subsequent matinees but lasted only for two performances. The play told how a district attorney (Robert T. Haines) discovers that a rich society lady (Jennie A. Eustace) is the landlord of properties employed by a drug ring.

Willis Maxwell Goodhue's **Head First** (1-6-26, Greenwich Village) ran only six performances. It followed the career of Anne Beckwith (Selma Paley), who, discovering that her husband (Louis Kimball) has been fired for ineptitude, takes his place at work and does so well she is soon made assistant manager and then the firm's Paris representative. Coming home, she finds her husband has prospered in the garbage-collecting trade, but, recognizing their fundamental incompatibility, she divorces him.

Alexander C. Herman and Leslie P. Eichel's **Down Stream** (1-11-26, 48th St.) did nothing to break the new year's doldrums. Set mainly on an Ohio River towboat, it unfolded the sad story of Mazie (Roberta Arnold), the cynical, hard-fisted wife of the boat's cook, who is bored by her husband and who falls in love with Pig-Iron (Rex Cherryman), a soft, young, moonstruck lad who takes employment on the boat, though he is patently unfit for it. However, when he tells her he wants to introduce her to his family, she is shocked into facing facts. By a campfire at the base of some cliffs, with a railroad bridge looming in the distance, she gently sends him back to his "Kaintucky" home, realizing that any further liaison can only end in tragedy.

The same issue of *Variety* that reviewed *Down Stream* attested to the growing discomfort even many professionals felt with what they perceived as "dirt shows" (today we might say "dirty"). A semi-professional group had mounted an English drama and, in reviewing it, the tradesheet dropped its customary practice of heading its notice with the play's title. Instead, the review was headed "England's Dirtiest Play," and the critic began, "These modern dirt show writers don't know the meaning of filth." The drama in question was not new. It was John Ford's Caroline tragedy, *'Tis Pity She's a Whore.*

H. V. Esmond's **The House of Ussher** (1-13-26, Fifth Ave. Playhouse) was not a misspelled redaction of Poe's tale. Rather it focused on a family of English Jews and purportedly had been written for George Arliss, who rejected it. The daughter, Constance (Rosalinde Fuller), is disowned by her father (Clarence Derwent) after she insists on marrying a Christian (Fairfax Burgher). She forges her father's name to a large check and threatens to reveal some of his shady business practices if she denounces her. With grudging admiration for her toughness, her father accepts her decision to wed. Burned out of its home shortly after its opening, the play moved from theatre to theatre before throwing in the towel after seven weeks.

Charles Bamfield Hoyt's **Move On** (1-18-26, Daly's) was a one-week flop relating the adventures of a tramp printer, Muscogee (Claude Cooper), who is something of a boozer and a "$2 touch boy" (a beggar). Given temporary work at a Topeka newspaper, he uses his small advance salary to go on a bender. At one speakeasy he stumbles upon the governor's daughter, who has been kidnapped and is being held for ransom. He rushes back to the paper, writes up the story, refuses to publish his real name, John Andrian Gookins, in a byline, gives the byline to a cub reporter in love with the girl, and heads back out on the road.

Even Lew Fields's somewhat tarnished popularity couldn't win a run for Oscar M. Carter's hackneyed **Money Business** (1-20-26, National). Fields, resorting to all his old tricks of dialect and Jewish gestures, played Jacob Berman, who has saved $3000 from the profits of his East Side delicatessen. He is thinking about investing it in the laundry operation of young Sam Madorsky (Luther Adler). Knowing her husband disapproves, Mrs. Berman (Pola Carter) quietly hands the money over to their boarder, George Braun (A. J. Herbert). His investments make them rich, and the Bermans move to Park Avenue, where they find the often arbitrary formalities of high life leave them uncomfortable, but not nearly as uncomfortable as learning that Braun is a crook and their investments have become worthless. Without too much regret, the Bermans return to the delicatessen business. Typical of Fields's (or Carter's) humor was Berman's response to his wife's assuring him she would trust Braun with her life: "But would you trust him with anything valuable?"

August Strindberg's **The Dream Play** (1-20-26, Provincetown Playhouse), in which Indra's daughter (Mary Fowler) comes to earth in various guises to study humans, whom she comes to look on with pity, was hailed by many of the loftier critics but met with public indifference. The translation was by Edwin Bjorkman.

On the other hand, **The Makropoulos Secret** (1-21-26, Charles Hopkins), Randal C. Burrell's adaptation of Karel Capek's *Komedie*, eked out eleven weeks at its tiny venue. It spotlighted a three-hundred-year-old opera singer (Helen Menken) who finally sacrifices the papers that hold the secret to eternal life.

There was more unreality in the year's first play to achieve something of a run, albeit initially at another minuscule house—Eugene O'Neill's **The Great God Brown** (1-23-26, Greenwich Village). Margaret Anthony (Leona Hogarth) married her husband, Dion (Robert Keith), unaware that his mocking, cynical ways were merely a front, a mask. (All the characters wore masks for their public selves and dropped them to reveal their true selves.) Beneath Anthony's mask is a tortured, sensitive, artistic soul. Margaret is revolted when she sees him without his mask. He leaves the business to his partner, William A. Brown (William Harrigan), attempts to become a painter, but soon withers and dies. Assuming Anthony's mask, Brown takes his place as Margaret's husband. But the inner Brown languishes, and after he is accused of slaying his true self, he can find solace only with a prostitute, Cybel (Anne Shoemaker), who wears no mask. Years later, when both men have died, Margaret vows eternal love to Anthony—or at least to Anthony's mask. She takes it from under her cloak, *"as if from her heart,"* and exclaims, "You can never die till my heart dies!" Many critics were baffled by the play, with its characters putting on and removing their masks, but on the whole welcomed it. In one of the earliest reviews actually carrying his byline, Brooks Atkinson observed that O'Neill had not always made himself clear, "but he has placed within the reach of the stage finer shades of beauty, more delicate nuances of truth and more passionate qualities of emotion than we can discover in any other single modern play." Following five weeks in the Village, the play ventured uptown and ran for a total of 278 performances. It was reputed to have remained the playwright's favorite among his works.

Although several American plays premiered on January's active last Monday night, most first-stringers opted for the Theatre Guild's importation, Ruth Langner's translation of Franz Werfel's **Goat Song** (1-25-26, Guild), yet another excursion into unreality. (The word "tragedy" comes from Greek roots meaning "goat song.") In the late eighteenth century, Serbian revolutionaries, led by Juvan (Alfred Lunt), have seized a strange creature, half man and half beast, who has escaped from the hiding place where his aristocratic parents have confined him. The rebels see him as a symbol of their rotten superiors. Juvan only agrees to release the man-beast to the intended bride of the monster's brother. The girl, Stanja (Lynn Fontanne), bravely accepts. After the goat-man is burned to death and Juvan is captured and executed, Stanja announces that she is pregnant and carries within her the seeds of further horrors for Serbia. Critics again were baffled and often annoyed. Even the Lunts were on the receiving end of less than enthusiastic notices. The best comments were reserved for the fine supporting cast, particularly Helen Westley as a superstitious peasant and Edward G. Robinson as a Jewish peddler who provided some comic relief.

Another importation was Hans Bachwitz's *Yoshiwara,* offered in an uncredited translation as **The Love City** (1-25-26, Little). Its main attraction was the appearance of Sessue Hayakawa, a popular silent-screen actor. Although he was Japanese, he portrayed a Chinese brothel keeper, Chang Lo, dispensing exotic wine, opium pipes, and girls from his flowerboat to Caucasian clients. The play's story, like several before it with similar settings, centered on a dream. The dream is that of an English patron, Richard Cavendish (Earle Larimore), who fantasizes that the prostitute he meets, Tse-shi (Catherine Dale Owen), is his wife and the proprietor her lover. After Cavendish wakes, a disillusioned Tse-shi comes to understand that he does not love her, so she hands him a gun. In the shootout in the dark that follows, the two men kill each other. Hayakawa was hailed as being "as clever as when before the camera," but his cleverness did not save the show. Nor did some applauded Oriental dances staged by Michio Itow, a celebrated dancer and choreographer of the day.

Harry Chapman Ford's **Shelter** (1-25-26, Cherry Lane) was perceived as *The Lower Depths* "done into Manhattanese." It unfolded in a secret den under a North River wharf and depicted some hours in the lives of its ragtag denizens, including an anarchist girl, a man who specializes in robbing sailors, a shell-shocked ex-soldier, a hopeless drunkard, and a refuse collector.

The title role in Ada Sterling's **Nica** (1-25-26, Central Park) was that of a girl whose father, prone to using a whip, sets a trap to kill the boy his daughter loves. Instead it kills the young man whom he was attempting to foist on the girl.

Tuesday was just as busy as Monday. Its only new "American" play was Howard Irving Young's **Not Herbert** (1-26-26, 52nd St.). Herbert Alden (Clarke Silvernail) is a sort of Raffles—"a sappy Westchester poet" during the day and a jewel thief at night. He outwits the police and more professional jewel thieves, running off in the end with nice, young Ruth Webster (Karen Peterson) to a Mediterranean island where there is no extradition. The group that produced the play had proclaimed their allegiance to new American works, leaving some critics to point out that Young was English-born and still lived there much of the time. For all that, the show was a modest success.

Delightful performances by its three principals were the lone underpinning for **A Weak Woman** (1-26-26, Ritz), which Ernest Boyd took from Jacques Deval's original. Arlette (Estelle Winwood) cannot make up her mind whether to marry Henri (Frank Morgan) or Serge (Ralph Morgan), but after a passionate night with Henri she selects Serge.

The evening's two other entries were revivals. *Hedda Gabler,* at the Comedy and in William Archer's translation, featured Dudley Digges as Tesman, Patricia Collinge as Mrs. Elvsted, Frank Conroy as Brack, Louis Calhern as Lovborg, and, in her last appearance before her suicide, Emily Stevens as Hedda. The dimissive notices Stevens received may have played a part in her killing herself several years later, although the production ran for nearly eight weeks.

Nor were many critics pleased with Bertha Kalish's slightly old-school emoting in Hermann Sudermann's *Magda* at Maxine Elliott's Theatre. The production employed Charles Edward Amory Winslow's translation of this story of a famous prima donna whose defiance of conventional morality causes her father to die of shock. Advertised as a limited three-week booking, its run was not extended.

Anne Nichols, again turning producer, had a small hit with Adelaide Mathews and Martha Stanley's **Puppy Love** (1-27-26, 48th St.), a slam-bang, no-holds-barred farce. Byron Lockhart (William Hanley) would love to marry Jean Brent (Vivian Martin), but he is considered ineligible until he takes a job as chauffeur to the girl's uncle (Charles Abbe) and helps Jean and her mother (Spring Byington) out of all sorts of scrapes, some of which he inadvertently got them into. Critics complained that Jean, who was supposed to be sixteen, and Byron, who was supposed to be twenty, were played by performers "too mature to depict adolescence." The best notices went to Maude Eburne as a comedy cook who "slapsticks all over the place even unto a Keystone bit with a pie." Among the lines singled out were "I'm pure as snow, but not drifting" and "Puppy love usually leads to a dog's life."

The presence in its cast of tennis star Bill Tilden did nothing to help Bernard S. Schubert's **Don Q., Jr.** (1-27-26, 49th St.). The Kid (Billy Quinn), a mere twelve-year-old, gets $150 in a holdup and gives the money to a friend who suffers from tuberculosis and can use the cash to head west for a cure. When the boy is caught he is sent to a reform school, where a bashful young social worker (Tilden) befriends him and aids in his rehabilitation. The play was subsequently retitled *That Smith Boy.*

Eva Le Gallienne closed out the month with a revival of Ibsen's *John Gabriel Borkman* at the Booth at a matinee on the 29th. Egon Brecher assumed the title role, to Miss Le Gallienne's Ella Rentheim. Only six further performances were given, but the praise the mounting received for its fine ensemble playing was one more incentive to Miss Le Gallienne to found a repertory company, which she did later in the year.

February got off to a sensational start with John Colton's **The Shanghai Gesture** (2-1-26, Martin Beck). Conceived initially for Mrs. Leslie Carter, it came to Broadway with Florence Reed in the lead after tryouts proved the older actress unable to give full value to the role of Mother Goddam. Goddam once had been a Chinese princess who had married a dashing young Englishman. Later, tiring of her and wanting to marry an English girl, he had sold her "down the river" to junkmen. Twenty years afterwards, having risen to duenna of the largest brothel in China, she invites a group of Englishmen to an elegant dinner. One of them is Sir Guy Charteris (McKay Morris), who, though he does not realize it, is the man who sold her into slavery. In the play's most famous scene, with its "I survived" speech, Goddam tells her history, including the tortures she received at the junkmen's hands, such as having pebbles sewn into the soles of her feet. In the stunned silence that follows, she brings in a beautiful

Caucasian girl and sells her to similar junkmen. Then she reveals to Charteris that the girl was his daughter by his marriage to his English wife. Goddam had switched babies, and Charteris had unknowingly raised his own bastard (Mary Duncan). But she has grown into a degenerate drug addict, so Goddam strangles her. Settings, by Frederick S. Jones III, were "bewilderingly beautiful." One critic predicted they would become the talk of the town. Moving from "The Gallery of Laughing Dolls" to "The Grand Red Hall of Lily and Lotus Roots," "The Little Room of the Great Cat," and finally to "The Green Stairway of the Angry Dragon," all at the "Far-famed House of Mother Goddam," they were "lavish in their traditional gold ornaments, their regal panelings, their mosaics and Chinese reds." The latticed stairs and platforms of the final scene climbed "to dizzy heights above the stage." Spangled and brocaded costumes added to the pictures. A number of stuffier critics, such as Hornblow, condemned the play for its immorality; more liberal writers found other flaws. But a majority admitted it was a spellbinder. For all his reservations, Woollcott characterized the play as "a gaudy, bawdy melodrama," and he acknowledged the power of the "I survived" speech, reporting, "When Florence Reed spat it out last night the thunder and applause shook the surprised and inexperienced Martin Beck to its shiny foundations." As soon as the notices appeared, ticket prices were raised from a $3.30 top to $3.85. With excited word of mouth boosting sales, the play ran for ten months, not counting a short summer vacation.

What proved to be Henry Miller's last appearance was all but lost in the hue and cry raised by the opening at the Beck. His vehicle also dealt with baby-switching. **Embers** (2-1-26, Henry Miller's) was A. E. Thomas's adaptation of Pierre Wolff and Henri Duvernois's *Après l'amour.* A man's wife (Laura Hope Crews) and his mistress (Florence Shirley) have babies at the same time. The mistress dies in childbirth, and since the man wants to raise the son she bore him, he secretly exchanges the infants. Later, he arranges to adopt the other child, supposedly that of the dead woman. Miller's final notices included one extolling his deft mixing of "simplicity and sincerity with outward urbanity." The play ran a month, and another month later, while rehearsing a new show, he died.

The next afternoon saw another of the season's many Ibsen revivals, with William A. Brady and Dwight Deere Wiman renting the Guild for eight performances of *Little Eyolf.* The title role went to William Pierce, but he was outshone by Reginald

Owen as Allmers, Clare Eames as Mrs. Allmers, Margalo Gillmore as Asta, John Cromwell as Borgheim, and Helen Menken as the Rat Wife.

Owen Davis's third play of the season was his dramatization of F. Scott Fitzgerald's best-selling novel **The Great Gatsby** (2-2-26, Ambassador), depicting the rise and fall of one of the era's many high-livers. James Rennie played Gatsby. Apart from some minor changes, such as Gatsby's death now coming at the hands of his chauffeur, Davis's redaction was faithful and delighted many critics. Atkinson assessed it as "able and moving," retaining "the novel's peculiar glamour." But the public apparently concurred with the *Herald Tribune's* Percy Hammond, who, while admiring it, felt it was only "half as satisfactory as entertainment as it is in the book," so the play had to be content with a fourteen-week stand.

George Abbott and John V. A. Weaver, the latter better known for his slangy verses, had a little more luck with their harem-scarem comedy **Love 'Em and Leave 'Em** (2-3-26, Sam H. Harris). Two sisters, Janie (Katherine Wilson) and Mame Walsh (Florence Johns), work at Ginsberg's Department Store and share a room at Ma Woodruff's boardinghouse. The unscrupulous Janie nearly steals Mame's beau, Billingsley (Donald MacDonald), a fellow clerk, and does steal the money she had been entrusted with as treasurer of the store's Welfare Service Association and which had been set aside for the group's charity pageant. During a dress rehearsal for the pageant, where almost everything else goes comically wrong, Mame wins the money back in a crap game with a crooked bookie and reclaims Billingsley, too. Donald Meek garnered special commendation as the boardinghouse's "slippery, shiftless, easy-going" co-manager.

For some inexplicable reason Arthur Hopkins chose to revive *The Jest* at the Plymouth on the 4th—but to do it without the Barrymores. Basil Sydney and Alphonz Ethier assumed the parts once played by John and Lionel. Ethier, who had replaced Lionel during the original run, was hailed, but most reviewers felt Sydney was no match for John Barrymore. Still, Hopkins kept the play going for nearly ten weeks.

The two plays that opened a few nights later both closed on the same night two weeks down the road. Considering the scathing notices accorded screenwriter Olga Printzlau's **The Jay Walker** (2-8-26, Klaw), a run even that long is amazing. Mary (Mary Daniel) is not a nice girl. In fact, looking at herself in her mirror, she concludes that she is "a little tart." She lives with her hard-working mother and brother in a dreary apartment on 112th Street. Although she is engaged to a policeman, she runs off with a wealthy man, returns home after he beats her, steals her mother's savings, heads for California, is indicted for manslaughter, jumps bail, and returns home en route to the Mediterranean. But mama calls the police, and the cop she once deserted puts handcuffs on her and takes her away.

J. O. Francis, an English dramatist admired in some circles, was the author of **The Beaten Path** (2-8-26, Frolic). His title referred to the road between birth and death, and a leading figure in the play, an old gravedigger (St. Clair Bayfield), was seen as the personification of Death. The story focused on the attempt of a grandmother to live to see the birth of a great-grandchild. But the gravedigger will not let her wait.

Only two non-musicals among the season's entries ran for more than a year, and the one that opened the next night marked the last time David Belasco would have a hit of such magnitude. **Lulu Belle** (2-9-26, Belasco) was a collaboration between young, vital Charles MacArthur and an aging, hopelessly crippled Edward Sheldon. For the title role, Lenore Ulric donned blackface to portray a flamboyant prostitute who pounds the pavements of San Juan Hill and Harlem. She lures George Randall (Henry Hull), a black barber from White Plains, away from his family, then deserts him for a rugged prizefighter, Butch Cooper (John Harrington). Cooper winds up with a knife in his ribs, for which Randall is sent to prison. Lulu Belle deserts Cooper, too. Then, after a fist-swinging, hair-pulling battle in a nightclub with a rival (Evelyn Preer, one of some eighty-five genuine blacks in the cast), she wins over the lascivious Vicompte de Villars (Jean Del Val), who takes her to Paris and sets her up in a luxurious apartment. Cooper reappears, warning her that Randall is lurking across the street, but she sends him away. The probably demented Randall enters, and, after Lulu Belle yells at him, "You dirty rat, five years ago I gave you the best bum's rush in the history of Harlem, and you don't know it yet," he strangles her. The usually tolerant Atkinson joined his colleagues in dismissing the play, but he, like many of them, admitted to being awed by Belasco's production. The first act took place on the sidewalks of San Juan Hill (in a setting reputed to have cost $24,000) "with tenement houses represented exactly from door to fire-escape, and the square is set with lampposts, fire signal boxes, electric signs . . . to the last detail. Every episode of street life is likewise represented by a huge mob of colored actors—crap shooting, Salvation Army serenaders, hair-pulling, a wedding party reproduced from the taunts of the jealous neighbors on the fire-escape to the Ford automobile rolling the principals and relatives down the street toward the church." A glimpse of a Harlem boardinghouse was followed by the scene in the Harlem nightclub, where white slummers watch blacks do the Charleston. The last act took place in a sumptuous apartment on the Avenue Marigny, with the perfume from Lulu Belle's atomizer wafting out into the audience.

As with *The Shanghai Gesture,* Belasco's premiere so monopolized attention that the evening's other opening fell by the wayside. George W. Oliver's English play **Port o' London** (2-9-26, Daly's) looked on as a hunchbacked artist (Basil Rathbone) marries a demented half-caste (Joan Lowell) to save her from her abusive father (James Carroll). But when her senses are restored, she does not recognize her savior and instead runs off with a sailor.

The only success among the four openings on the next Monday was Marc Connelly's first major solo effort since breaking up with George S. Kaufman, **The Wisdom Tooth** (2-15-26, Little). Bemis (Thomas Mitchell) is a meek and docile man, willing to change his opinion on any subject if someone suggests he is wrong. One of his fellow boarders notes snidely, "He looks like a clerk, he talks and thinks like a clerk." Only another fellow boarder, Sally Field (Mary Philips), sees something of value beneath his drab exterior. But even she finally comes to wonder. Left alone, Bemis falls asleep and dreams that he is visited by his long-dead grandparents, by the little girl he adored as a child, and even by his own youthful self, when he was known as Skeeter. The apparitions transport him to an old circus, where no less than Barnum and Bailey are there to sing his praises, and they recall for him what a brash and promising youngster he had been. When he wakes from his dream, he phones his boss and berates the man for unjustly firing a stenographer. The call costs him his job but wins him Sally. Among the play's admirers was Woollcott, who paeaned "this gentle and glowing and gallant play which seemed so good and true," adding, "I have not had a better time at a play since the season began." At first business was slow, but word of mouth in time turned it into a modest money-maker.

The other American play to premiere that evening was Daniel Rubin and Edgar MacGregor's **The Night Duel** (2-15-26, Mansfield). It starred Marjorie Rambeau as a devoted wife whose husband (John Marston) has taken $50,000 from a bank so that a friend may cover a shortage until after the bank examiner has audited his books. A detective (Felix Krembs) attempts to blackmail her into sleeping with him by threatening to disclose the story. But she goes to his room and holds him at gunpoint until her husband can replace the money. *Variety's* review suggested a different ending, noting, "In the final scene the audience is given to understand that 'the worst' happened, but that the husband is never going to know and the detective if he tells has the promise of the wife that she will kill him."

H. F. Maltby's English comedy **The Right Age to Marry** (2-15-26, 49th St.) followed a successful Lancashire mill owner (Charles Coburn) into a happy retirement, until the mill's burning impoverishes him. He decides to start all over, helped by his loyal housekeeper (Mrs. Coburn).

The Right to Kill (2-15-26, Garrick) was Herman Bernstein's Americanization of an unspecified Russian play by Leo Urvantzov. When a woman (Anna Zasock) discovers her lover (Robert Rendel) threatens to reveal their affair to her husband (Clyde Fillmore), she shoots him and blithely returns home.

Ralph Cullinan's **You Can't Win** (2-16-26, Klaw) lost out after two matinee performances during which it recounted the tale of a woman (Carroll McComas) who keeps her past from her new husband (Jack Roseleigh) and finds her marriage is nearly destroyed when the truth comes out.

Critics bewailed that a revival of Louis K. Anspacher's *The Unchastened Woman* at the Princess on the same evening sadly showed the drama's age. Violet Kemble Cooper assumed the role originally played by Emily Stevens. But another revival that night, *The Emperor Jones* at the Provincetown Playhouse, with Charles Gilpin recreating the title role, fared much better and drew packed houses for several weeks.

Still another revival was Hampden's mounting of *Cyrano de Bergerac* at his theatre on the 18th. Ethel Barrymore had left the company, and Marie Adels became his Roxane. The restoration of his most popular offering allowed Hampden to add another ninety-six performances of it to his record.

February's last three entries arrived in tandem on its last Monday night. All three failed. In Jack McGowan and Mann Page's **Mama Loves Papa** (2-22-26, Forrest) newlywed Nan Turner (Sara Sothern) is led by her much married, gossipy friend, Margie (Helen Broderick), to believe her insurance-selling husband, Joe (Lorin Baker), is having a fling with a beautiful dancer (Zola Talma) whose legs he has insured. Nan goes out to find some male companionship and winds up at the bachelor digs of Sonny Whitmore (Robert Emmett Keane). Sonny is throwing a party, and who should pop in but Joe and the dancer. Vinegar turns to sugar at eleven o'clock. The comedy's best reviews were stolen by John E. Hazzard as an irredeemable lover of bootleg hootch and by Miss Broderick, in the sort of role she would become known for, a wisecracker, with lines such as "This cheating business in no longer a gentleman's game." Later in the year, the comedy was musicalized as *Sweet Lady*.

More serious matters were the subject of Arthur Corning White and Louis Bennison's **The Virgin** (2-22-26, Maxine Elliott's). The Reverend Elias Whipple (Lee Baker) has come to the woods in northern New Hampshire to spread his gospel of "Holy Thinking" and abstention from sex. A naive, deeply religious lumberjack, Louis Le Bombard (Bennison), mistakes Whipple's wife (Phyllis Povah) for the Virgin Mary and worships her until he sees her in the arms of another local (Arthur Albertson). After knocking out the man, Louis takes the woman to his shack and attempts to make love to her. But his rival rushes to her rescue. The minister is then exposed as a fugitive from a mental institution. He kills himself, leaving his wife free to marry Louis, if she will have him. She won't, so Louis returns to Mag (Bertha Mann), a girl he had jilted for the other woman.

A play that had enjoyed some London success, Allene Tupper Wilkes and Roland Pertwee's **The Creaking Chair** (2-22-26, Lyceum), came the closest to succeeding of the night's offerings—surviving for ten weeks. Filled with the usual doors which open unaided, hands coming out of the paneling, and shrieks in the dark, it unfolded the saga of a crippled archeologist (Reginald Mason), possessor of a priceless ancient Egyptian headpiece, and the murderous attempts to steal it from him. After the expected false turns, the villain proves to be a pleasant young Egyptian with the un-Egyptian name of Philip Speed (Brandon Peters), who wants to take the piece back to its homeland.

Unlike Henry Miller, who died almost immediately after his last appearance, Augustus Thomas would live for nearly another decade. Wittingly or no, he offered Broadway his final play in **Still Waters** (3-1-26, Henry Miller's), ironically at Miller's playhouse. Critics viewed it as a far-fetched, preachy anti-Prohibition tract. His state's political power—the "dry-as-dusts"—oppose the liberal views of Senator Cassius Clayborn (Thurston Hall), so they attempt to have the more unyielding Congressman Ponder (William Norton) replace him. To this end they try to smear the widowed Clayborn's lady friend (Mona Kingsley) by involving her in a scandal with the fiancé (David Tearle) of the senator's daughter. But

Clayborn is aware of a black bag containing $100,000 in his opponents' possession and—snarling, "Cash in Washington?"—sends them headlong into retreat.

That same night saw another of the season's surprise hits arrive, James P. Judge's **Square Crooks** (3-1-26, Daly's). Eddie Ellison (Russell Mack) and Larry Scott (Norval Keedwell) have both served time. Now they have gone straight. But the stolen Carsen pearls, famous jewels belonging to the wife of Ellison's old boss, suddenly fall into their laps, and a detective (Harold Salter), out to get back at Ellison for once refusing to help railroad another thief, attempts to nab the men with the goods. After three acts of trying to elude the detective, they decide honesty is the best policy. So they take the pearls to Carsen, tell how they came to have them, and walk away with clean hands.

George Dunning Gribble's **The Masque of Venice** (3-2-26, Mansfield) faintly echoed *In a Garden*. Its central figure is a novelist, Jonathan Mumford (Arnold Daly), who likes to bring people together and employ their unusual reactions in his plots. In his rented Venetian palazzo, where he is vacationing with "a latter-day nymph," Egeria (Selena Royle), he observes the meeting between Jack Cazeneuve (Kenneth MacKenna), a descendant of the famous lover, and Sophia Weir (Antoinette Perry), a literary lion. But when the pair run off and Sophia falls into the canal, it is Mumford who must dive in to rescue her. Egeria, who proves as manipulative as Mumford and a nymph who is also a good fairy, having achieved her purpose of getting the author to become a man of real action, packs her bags and moves on.

Characters in John Howard Lawson's pretentious **Nirvana** (3-3-26, Greenwich Village) included "A Hungry Girl," "A Giggling Girl," "A Nice Young Man," and "An Even Nicer Young Man," all of whom cross the paths of Dr. Alonzo Weed (Crane Wilbur), a scientist, and his novelist brother, Bill (Earle Larimore), as the two men attempt to skirt the "gaiety of despair" everywhere around them and seek out a proper new religion for modern times, perhaps one inspired by an "electro-magnetic Christ."

But even the more down-to-earth J. C. and Elliott Nugent could not find success with tried and true material in **The Trouper** (3-8-26, 52nd St.). J. C. played a seedy actor in a broken-down touring company, who for many years has been writing the daughter (Ruth Nugent) his puritanical in-laws have raised and prevented him from meeting. The actor has written about himself in glowing terms, so Tilly believes her father is a great tragedian and star. The truth emerges when his troupe is stranded in Shanesville, the daughter's hometown. But the actor stages an impressive benefit to raise money to get the actors back to New York, and Tilly, involving herself in the affair, decides she, too, will become a player.

Tadema Bussiere's **Find Daddy** (3-8-26, Ritz) continued the parade of duds. Ruth Todd (Dorothy Peterson) returns to the Todds' Hollywood bungalow after giving birth to a baby in Texas. Wanting to surprise her husband (Horace Braham), whose birthday is the next day, she asks her friend Jane Potter (Enid Markey) to pretend the infant is hers until she can spring the news on Jerry Todd. Naturally, several hours of complications ensue.

A revival of the old warhorse, Mrs. Henry Wood's *East Lynne,* which told of a disgraced mother who returns in disguise to help raise her children, was unveiled at the Greenwich Village on the 10th. Unfortunately, the producers did not have the courage of their convictions. The mounting, with Mary Blair in the lead, was played for laughs, and played unskillfully at that.

Nor did John Dos Passos's **The Moon Is a Gong** (3-12-26, Cherry Lane) create any excitement. Jane (Helen Chandler) and Tom (Allyn Joslyn), wandering home together after a dress ball, pass by a group of soiled, exhausted workers returning from their jobs. The couple wonder about their own futures. Jane becomes hard as nails, even a bit corrupt, in her climb up the social ladder, while Tom turns into a vagabond and thief, before the pair meet again for a more or less happy ending in which they sing the praises of the moon. The Garbage Man (Edward Reese), a personification of Death much like the gravedigger in *The Beaten Path,* wandered in and out of the action.

The three plays that opened the next Monday night—two American and one Irish—were also failures. Alfred G. Jackson and Mann Page's **Hush Money** (3-15-26, 49th St.) starred the former *Follies* beauty Justine Johnstone. Like *Square Crooks* it featured a reformed thief, this time called Harry Bentley (Kenneth Thomson), some stolen jewels, this time a diamond necklace, and a venal detective (Richard Gordon). Harry hopes to wed gorgeous, rich Kathleen Forrest and does, after lifting the veil of suspicion and discovering that the diamonds were merely paste. The story was supposedly based on true incidents, made public after F. W. Woolworth's daughter was robbed at the Hotel Plaza and the private detective who collected the reward for recovering the jewels was indicted for masterminding the theft.

Francis De Witt's **90 Horse Power** (3-15-26, Ritz) told of a war ace (Ramsey Wallace) who takes work as a chauffeur to earn enough money to manufacture a new type of carburator he has invented. He not only earns the money but also earns the love of his employer's comely daughter (Allyn King).

Although Sean O'Casey's **Juno and the Paycock** (3-15-26, Mayfair) would become a twentieth-century classic, it made no waves at its Broadway premiere. A highly uneven mounting was no help. Louise Randolph was Juno and Augustin Duncan the hard-drinking, boastful, lazy peacock, Jack Boyle, whose lives are thrown in turmoil by the false news that Jack has inherited a fortune. The production ran for seventy-four performances at its tiny house.

Early in December a Danish actress, Hilda Englund, had given some matinee performances of Ibsen's *Ghosts* at the Princess. The Actors' Theatre brought out their own version at the Comedy on the 16th with Lucile Watson as Mrs. Alving and José Ruben as Oswald. Greeted by divided notices, the drama struggled along for one month before folding.

Daniel N. Rubin, now working without a collaborator, was the author of **Devils** (3-17-26, Maxine Elliott's). An innocent girl, Jennie (Ruth Mero) is sent to live with her vicious Uncle Joel (David Landau) in a home in the backwoods of Mississippi. She falls in love with her cousin, Amos (Reed Brown), who runs away from home but promises to return and rescue her. That night her uncle seduces her. When crop failures and other disasters plague the area, the Rev. Matthew Dibble (John Cromwell) ascribes them to local sinfulness and alights on Jennie as a scapegoat. Joel claims publicly that Jennie was the seducer. Led by Dibble, the neighbors drive Jennie to suicide.

Strindberg's **Easter** and Joseph Conrad's **One Day More** (3-18-26, Princess) formed a double bill offered by the Stagers. In the Conrad piece, which served as a curtain raiser, a demented father (Whitford Kane) and a lonely neighboring girl (Josephine Hutchinson) await the return of the long-absent Harry Hagberd (Warren Williams), but when the young man appears his father does not recognize him, and the girl is disappointed that he does not live up to her exaggerated expectations. The Strindberg opus was set over the Easter weekend during which a family whose father has been imprisoned for embezzlement awaits with trepidation and bitterness the coming of a creditor. But when he appears he is friendly and encouraging.

The two plays that premiered the next Monday were both importations and did nothing to break the chain of flops. **The Chief Thing** (3-22-26, Guild) was Herman Bernstein and Leo Randole's translation of Nicholas Evreinoff's Russian comedy-drama. A fortune teller (McKay Morris), supposedly a reincarnation of John the Baptist's Comforter, listens to the complaints of tenants at a cheap boardinghouse, then hurries to a nearby theatre, where he hires the actors to pose as modern-day comforters and lighten the people's woes. Even Lawrence Langner in his autobiography dismissed the Theatre Guild's production as "a resounding failure."

But for all the brouhaha surrounding it the Countess of Cathcart's **Ashes of Love** (3-22-26, National) was a worse bomb. American authorities had tried to prevent her entering the country on the grounds of moral turpitude for eloping to South Africa with an earl, though she was still married. Her play, which she produced and with her in the leading role, recounted the events of her elopement, albeit she used fictitious names. When the play closed after a single week, the lady was also shown the door.

Martha Hedman, having closed out her acting career, and her husband, Henry Arthur House, were the authors of **What's the Big Idea?** (3-23-26, Bijou), the tale of a woman (Lillian Ross) who proves that wishing things to end happily allows them to. She makes some woman-haters enjoy feminine charms, reunites her quarreling relations, prompts her wall-flower gray-haired maiden aunt (Ethel Strickland) to dye her hair before going out on the town, and starts her fiancé (Pierre Gendron) on the road to riches. *Variety* reported that there was so little interest on opening night that the Shuberts attempted to pack the house with free tickets and that "a stack of passes a foot high" could be seen in the box-office window.

Franz Werfel's second failure of the season was **Schweiger** (3-23-26, Fifth Ave. Playhouse), offered in a translation by Jack Charash and William A. Drake. Its hero (Jacob Ben Ami) had been a child murderer until a doctor had cured him and erased any memory of the deeds. In his new life he has married the beautiful Anna (Ann Harding). When his memory is restored he confesses his history to his wife, who aborts their unborn child. Schweiger then rescues children from a burning ship, but the pain of his own burns drives him to kill himself.

Jack McClennan's **The Half-Caste** (3-29-26, National) was billed as "a story of love and sacrifice in a Land of Forgotten Men." Dick Chester (Fredric March), a rich, bored, and hard-drinking San Franciscan, decides to sail on his yacht and throw a wreath into the ocean at the spot where his father

was thought to have disappeared many years before. He is accompanied by his icy fiancée, Marjorie Farnham (Helenka Adamowska), and her scheming, pushy aunt (Isabel O'Madigan). They land on the island of Savaii, where Dick falls in love with the voluptuous Tuana (Veronica). But then he discovers that his father (Frederick Perry) is still alive, living as a beachcomber, and that Tuana is his father's daughter. After Tuana kills herself, Dick and his group sail on. Muscular native dances and a ukulele band spelled the action. The single-named Veronica had been a vaudevillian and was whispered to be the show's producer along with her husband, a Prohibition enforcement official.

Not until month's end did two hits arrive. And they arrived on the same night. William Hurlbut's **The Bride of the Lamb** (3-30-26, Greenwich Village) examined the latest religious revival to sweep small towns in the Middle West. Ina Bowman (Alice Brady) is fed up with her alcoholic husband (Edmund Elton) and her dreary life, so she welcomes the coming of the Reverend Albaugh (Crane Wilbur), a vaudevillian turned evangelist. He no sooner arrives for a week of revival meetings and is lodged in the Bowman home than Ina takes it upon herself to shine his shoes. By the end of the week Ina's daughter (Arline Blackburn) is speaking in tongues and Ina herself is walking on clouds. She steals the family's money to buy the preacher a gold watch, then seduces him. The next day, when he must move on, she begs him to take her with him. While he is upstairs packing, a lady (Julia Ralph) appears and announces the preacher is her husband, although he long ago ran out on her. The minister's refusal to let Ina accompany him and this new shock prove too much for Ina. When she reappears she is carrying paper flowers, wearing mosquito netting like a bridal veil, and humming a wedding march. Pointing to an imaginary figure, she tells the startled crowd in her living room, "Let me introduce the bridegroom—Mr. Christ. Oh, I am such a proud and happy girl!" The preacher falls to his knees, begging God to forgive him. Although a number of critics rued the contrivances of the final act, the notices were good enough to send playgoers scurrying to the Village. After a month the play was brought uptown, where it ran through June.

A lesser play enjoyed a slightly longer run. Chester De Vonde and Kilbourn Gordon's **Kongo** (3-30-26, Biltmore) was set in a primitive store surrounded by African jungle. The store is run by a tall, bearded cripple, Deadleg Flint (Walter Huston), who is confined to a wheelchair but can drag himself across the floor when circumstances require it. His main aim in life is to be avenged on a man called Kregg (Frederic Burt), who had run off with Flint's wife and crippled him by breaking his spine. Flint drives Kregg's daughter (Florence Mason) into prostitution, only to learn the girl is actually his own child. Later he helps her to escape howling natives who would use her for a sacrifice. She takes with her a young doctor (Richard Stevenson) whose drug addiction she has cured. Kregg loses his mind, and the natives spear him to death, leaving Flint to realize that he is the only civilized person left in the area—he is alone in a savage world. Sharing plaudits with Huston was a black—"one of the cleverest actors of his race"—Clarence Redd in the small role of Fuzzy.

Stuart Olivier's **Beau Gallant** (4-5-26, Ritz) is more formally known as Caton Beale Carrington (Lionel Atwell), the last of the Carringtons and, by his own lights, a consummate gentleman, even if he must scrounge off his butler's daughter (Marguerite Burrough) for spending money and to prevent the sheriff removing his furniture. However, when his vulgar uncle (Dodson Mitchell), an Argentine cattle baron, dies and leaves him $5,000,000 with the stipulation that he marry the girl, he waves the will aside, lets the girl inherit the money, and looks to marry someone of his own set.

Most first-string critics skipped the Olivier opening to attend the premiere at the Cosmopolitan of an all-star revival of one of the 1870s' great successes, Adolphe d'Ennery and Eugène Cormon's *The Two Orphans*. The two girls who undergo so many tribulations after coming to eighteenth-century Paris were played by Fay Bainter and Mary Nash. May Robson was La Frochard; Henrietta Crosman, Countess de Linières; and Mrs. Whiffen, Sister Genevieve. Among the men, Robert Loraine was Chevalier de Vaudrey; Wilton Lackaye, Count de Linières; Henry E. Dixey, Picard; Robert Warwick, Jacques; and José Ruben, Pierre. Despite the carpings of some faddist critics, the production did land-office business for its four-week stand.

On a lazy summer day, a motley group of roomers in the lobby of a cheap Bowery hotel that is the setting for Thomas Mitchell and Bertram Bloch's fantastic **Glory Hallelujah** (4-6-26, Broadhurst) learns that a comet is about to come between the sun and Earth, casting the world into darkness and freezing millions of people to death. The tenants—tramps, crooks, and other lowlife—each react differently. The hotel's young charlady, Lilly (June Walker), so comes to welcome the hopes for a better life in the hereafter which she listens to on radio broadcasts that, when the comet moves on and the

sun returns, she kills herself rather than resume her everyday drudgery. Mitchell quickly found he had more luck playing in a fantasy than writing one.

A happier fate than Lilly's awaited the heroine of Amélie Rives and Gilbert Emery's **Love in a Mist** (4-12-26, Gaiety). Diana Wynne (Madge Kennedy) has "always thought white lies better than black truths." That's why she has to explain to Gregory Farnham (Sidney Blackmer), who had stormed out after discovering that Diana was engaged not only to him but to another man, that she only told the other fellow she would marry him because he still had not fully recovered from being shell-shocked in the war and she wanted to make him feel good. Just as Gregory and Diana are ready to kiss and make up, Count Scipione Varelli (Tom Powers) arrives from Italy, rejoicing in the knowledge that Diana has written to say she will be delighted to marry him. This is almost too much for Gregory, until Diana explains that Scippi's mother, a family friend, wrote her that Scippi was dying and asked her to write him an encouraging note. Her rejection makes Scippi rush off and attempt suicide. For a time both men are disgusted with Diana, but Scippi finally falls for Diana's cousin (Frieda Inescort), and Gregory agrees to marry Diana, only stopping to warn her, "If you ever lie to me again . . .". The comedy ran through most of the summer. A 1928 musical version, *Say When,* failed.

One most unexpected hit was William Brady's revival of James M. Barrie's *What Every Woman Knows* at the Bijou on the 13th. Brady had foreseen a month's run, thereby keeping the playhouse lit until the end of his lease. But his choice of Helen Hayes to play Maggie Shane, who quietly employs her charms to help her husband (Kenneth Mac-Kenna) rise in the world, not only delighted critics but further consolidated the star's fast-growing reputation. She reputedly took lessons from a Scottish fortune teller to perfect her accent. John Mason Brown, writing in the *Evening Post,* rejoiced that she "lights up the whole play and brings out of it the enchantments of pure magic." Some critics implied she consciously imitated Maude Adams's well-remembered performance, but they saw nothing wrong in that. Instead of one month, the production ran eight, and Miss Hayes would return to the work at intervals throughout much of her career.

Another revival that same evening languished briefly. Leopold Lewis's *The Bells* had never been popular in America unless Henry Irving was performing in it. Rollo Lloyd was no Irving, so the production at the Nora Bayes lasted only two weeks.

Clare Kummer's **Pomeroy's Past** (4-19-26, Long-acre) had been tried out unsuccessfully with the author's son-in-law, Roland Young, in the lead and had been announced with other comedians before Ernest Truex brought the play to Broadway, with himself as co-producer, director, and star. He probably wished he had not, since the play ended up a near miss. Dejected because he believes his sweetheart (Helen Chandler) is going to marry his best friend, Edward Marsh (Richard Barbee), Pomeroy Chilton decides to adopt a little girl (Eleanor Frances Shaw). At the same time, Edward adopts a boy of identical age. Pomeroy's older sister (Laura Hope Crews) insists the child must be his own, so he lies that it is but that the mother refused to marry him because she found the Episcopal service boring. Complications pile on after a maid (Marjorie Kummer) claims the girl is hers. By curtain time the two children prove to be twins and are restored to their real mother, and Pomeroy finds that his sweetheart does prefer him after all.

April's biggest hit was Jane Mast's **Sex** (4-26-26, Daly's), which ran for nearly a year before the sanctimonious D.A., Joab Banton, raided it and hauled its star, Mae West, into court. By that time her show (for she was also the playwright, Jane Mast being merely her nom de plume) had made her so much money that she scoffed at the $500 fine and ten-day jail term. Meanwhile Mae had become Margie, Margie Lamont—a streetwalker in Montreal who specializes in entertaining naval officers. When she selflessly attempts to help a socialite who has been drugged, the socialite accuses her of robbery. To be revenged Margie seduces the lady's son, before heading back to her sailor boys. In its review, *Variety* gave a foretaste of what would happen, slamming the play as "a nasty red-light district show—which would be tolerated in but few of the stock burlesque houses in America." It also derided West's performance, suggesting she could not differentiate between the openly wicked woman of the early and later scenes and the "good" woman of the the middle part: "She doesn't change when the play calls for it, and . . . she's still slouching and showing the figure just as if she were drumming up business."

Bernard Voight and Clayton Hamilton's **A Friend Indeed** (4-26-26, Central Park), needed one, found none, so quickly gave up the ghost. The friend (Roland Hogue) of an Indiana newspaper publisher, whose paper is jeopardized by corrupt politicians, takes over the paper for him, boosts circulation by articles involving the politicians in the theft of John Hancock's snuffbox, and weds an heiress (Ruth Easton), who may or may not be one of Hancock's descendants.

The two English plays that opened the same evening were both by C. K. Munro. The more successful (seven weeks on the Theatre Guild subscription) was **At Mrs. Beam's** (4-26-26, Guild). A snoopy boarder (Jean Cadell) tells her fellow tenants that she is certain the new tenants, Mr. Dermott (Alfred Lunt) and Laura Pasquale (Lynn Fontanne), are actually a notorious French lady killer (with thirty-nine murders to his credit) and his next intended victim. The guests seem to believe her. But the couple turns out to be a pair of international thieves in hiding, who loot the establishment before they disappear. A knock-down-drag-out battle between the pair in Dermott's bedroom, with Fontanne at one point hurling Lunt over a sofa, was a highlight of the comedy.

Beau-Strings (4-26-26, Mansfield) took place in a similar setting—a backwater hotel—and followed the misadventures of a promiscuous hussy (Estelle Winwood), who could not care less whether her prey is single or married.

Revivals accounted for much of the remaining season. Two ushered in May. Walter Hampden concluded his season by resurrecting Charles Rann Kennedy's *The Servant in the House* at his theatre on the 3rd, with Hampden again as the Christ-like central figure. The same evening saw the Actors' Theatre's version of *The Importance of Being Earnest* with Vernon Steele and Reginald Owen as John and Algernon, Haroldine Humphreys and Patricia Collinge as Gwendolen and Cecily, and Lucile Watson as Lady Bracknell. Dudley Digges, who directed, also assumed the role of Canon Chasuble. Kennedy's play was given only a handful of performances, but the Wilde comedy ran for a surprising eight weeks.

Neither of the imported novelties that came in the next evening found favor. Major Ian Hay Beith's **The Sport of Kings** (5-4-26, Lyceum) centered on a straitlaced magistrate (O. P. Heggie), who for years has railed against all manner of sin, especially gambling. But when his taxes threaten to cripple him financially he secretly begins to bet on the horses. He is exposed, to the glee of his track-loving menage, but at least he wins enough to stop worrying.

The Romantic Young Lady (5-4-26, Neighborhood Playhouse) was Helen and Harley Granville Barker's adaptation of Gregorio Martínez Sierra's comedy. Rosario (Mary Ellis) is startled when a man's hat flies in through a window while she is reading a novel. The stranger (Ian Maclaren) who knocks on the door to reclaim his hat falls into a discussion with the lady and tells her he will introduce her to the novel's author if she will come to his house. She discovers the stranger and the author are one and the same.

More Spanish plays were offered New Yorkers on the week of the 17th, but they were all done in Spanish and at the Metropolitan Opera House. With Maria Guerrero, touted as the Spanish Bernhardt, heading the company from Madrid's Princess Theatre, the troupe presented a different play, some old, some new, each evening. Neither the plays nor the players caused the stir or influenced American stages the way the Irish and Russian players had a few years before.

Competing with the Spaniard's opening night was a revival of Edward Locke's *The Climax* at the 48th Street Theatre. Effingham Pinto was back in the role of the forlorn composer he had played in the original production seventeen years earlier, as was Albert Bruning in a smaller part. Dorothy Francis was the young singer whose career is nearly destroyed by a treacherous doctor. Walter Marshall took the role of the doctor. As they had several months earlier with *The Unchastened Woman,* New York's faddist critics waved the work away as a hackneyed period piece. It left after a single week.

Michael Kallesser's **One Man's Woman** (5-25-26, 48th St.), which came into the the the theatre just abandoned by *The Climax,* was the month's last novelty. It was also a vanity production, with the playwright serving as his own producer. Kenneth Regan (Curtis Cooksey), a woman-hating sugar-mill manager in Hawaii, finally falls in love with Betty Davis (Margaret Barnstead), who he believes to be a lady. When he discovers she is a prostitute, he takes to drink. But he cannot stop thinking of her, so he decides to marry and reform her. As with dramas having similar backgrounds, a Hawaiian string orchestra supplied incidental music and the action was stopped at one point for a chorus of hula dancers. *Variety* closed its notice predicting, "Cain [the warehouse for old scenery] will have this one this week unless the Leblangers [cut-rate ticket offices] or a house arrangement forces it a few more days." The tradesheet proved wrong. Helped by the producer-author's willingness to underwrite losing weeks, the play defied the critics and ran for five months.

May closed with the Players' fifth annual revival— *Henry IV (Part I)*—at the Knickerbocker on the 31st. John Drew greeted the audience as the Prologue. William Courtleigh was the king; Basil Sydney, the Prince of Wales; Philip Merivale, Hotspur; and Otis Skinner, Falstaff. Blanche Ring

was Mistress Quickly; Peggy Wood, Lady Percy. In the very minor role of Francis, the thick-witted tapster, musical comedy clown James T. Powers walked off with some of the best notices. And serving merely as soldiers and other supernumeraries were such club members as Don Marquis and Irvin S. Cobb.

Two disastrous first nights brought the season to a close. N. Brewster Morse's **The Half-Naked Truth** (6-7-26, Mayfair) might have known trouble was brewing when its leading man came down with the mumps on the morning of the opening. Ray Collins was rushed in to play Charlie Smith. Charlie's sweetie, Mamie (Marguerite Mosier), is ready to put an end to their romance after she learns Charlie has been spending time with a notorious vamp, Clarice Van Doren (Eva Balfour). However, Clarice is gifted in more arts than vamping. She is also an accomplished sculptor, and her interest in Charlie turns out to be purely professional. He has served as the model for her latest statue. Charlie and Mamie head off into the sunset, or at least to Hollywood, where Charlie's good looks have won him a film contract. On opening night, late in the second act, during a tense scene between the lovers in Charlie's drab tenement, a gray cat wandered onstage and sat down to watch the audience. He (or she) refused to leave, sending playgoers into howls of laughter. "What drama could vie with the reality of a cat?" Brooks Atkinson asked. Yet for all the mishaps the new play was able to struggle along for more than a month.

By contrast, only one performance marked the life of David Thorne's **Beyond Evil** (6-7-26, Cort). The unhappy wife (Mary Blair) of a New Jersey druggist runs away from her small town and comes to Harlem, where she is soon having an affair with a mulatto (Edouardo Sanchez). Their affair finished, she returns to New Jersey but finds the thought of living again with her dreary husband so repulsive that she drinks poison. First-nighters were clearly unhappy. They whistled and booed and hooted so loudly that the actors could not be heard.

1926–1927

Burns Mantle, waxing increasingly Cassandraic with the passing years, bemoaned that the 1926–27 season "was one of comparatively few successes and several rather conspicuous failures." Admittedly, some of those failures, at least by his lights, were the failure of the play jury system, the failure in the battle against ticket speculators, and the failure of producers of a few so-called dirt shows to avoid fines and jail terms. Still, he also listed "the expected failure" of 70 percent of the shows produced, including the 163 new straight plays plus a handful of "revivals and what not." The more businesslike *Variety* reported a higher toll of paybacks, since a number of plays that flopped on Broadway enjoyed subsequent success on the road. Moreover, the trade sheet counted 188 new plays and 26 revivals and return engagements, albeit it failed to note how many of the revivals were not straight plays.

Only one play opened in late June, Douglas Murray's **The Man from Toronto** (6-17-26, Selwyn). It was not a new play, since Henry Miller and Ruth Chatterton had starred in it when it was done as *Perkins* in October of 1918 and had failed after twenty-three performances. A London revival prompted this New York rehearing with a far less distinguished cast. Once more Broadway said no, even if the revival ran five performances more than the original.

A month went by before the appearance of the next play, Robert Weenolsen and Sherill Webb's **Honest Liars** (7-19-26, Sam H. Harris). The wife (Kathleen Lowry) of a doctor (Alfred Kappeler) and a young man (Robert Woolsey) engaged to another girl go out together for an evening at a lively but somewhat disreputable roadhouse. When the place is raided, the pair escape, only to discover two babies in the backseat of the taxi they have stolen. All this could be expected to irk the husband, who runs a sanitarium outside Philadelphia. However, the gadabouts employ an anesthetic machine the doctor has invented to knock him out. They place him in the bed of a sleeping nurse. So when he awakes he finds he cannot complain about their escapade. In the face of cool notices, the comedy ran twelve weeks.

That same night saw the opening of Samuel Ruskin Golding's **Pyramids** (7-19-26, George M. Cohan). It had its highly theatrical moments but didn't add up to a good play. By pyramiding stocks he has bought with embezzled money, Robert Amory (Roy Gordon), a young lawyer, hopes to please his luxury-loving wife (Carroll McComas). But his broker ignores his orders, bankrupting him. The scandal sends Amory to prison. Martin Van Cott (Charles Waldron), his boss, sets up Mrs. Amory in a swank apartment and promises to get Amory pardoned, a promise he has no intention of keeping. When Mrs. Amory learns that her husband

has escaped, she has a heated argument with Van Cott. The lights go out, and when they are turned on again, she and Van Cott's Japanese butler (Harry D. Southard) find him shot to death. Believing Amory did it, Mrs. Amory tells the police she is the killer. Amory, thinking his wife is the murderer, says he fired the shot. It turns out the butler did it. The drama lingered for one month.

Samuel Shipman and Neil Twomey's **No More Women** (8-3-26, Ambassador) didn't last a full week. When the vamping Lorna Morton (Nana Bryant) jilts Mel Hardy (John Marston), that's the final straw. Mel heads off and establishes a ranch for misogynists outside Cody. He tacks a sign saying "Damn the Women" above his door. However, Nancy (Mildred McLeod) turns up, fleeing an abusive father and the man her father has sold her to, Roarin' Bill Slade (Charles Bickford). She enlists Mel's sympathies, so when Lorna, who has changed her mind about Mel, reappears, Mel cleverly foists her on Bill. The play opened on a sweltering evening, and that led to applause when one character remarked, "On a night like this I feel like Hell."

William J. Perlman's **My Country** (8-9-26, 46th St.) was an *Abie's Irish Rose* with a vengeance. When snooty, bigoted Robert Van Dorn (Frederick Burton) learns that his son (Earl House) intends to marry an Italian (Erin O'Brien Moore), and his daughter (Marguerite Mosier) a Jew (Roy R. Bucklee), he storms out, threatening to disown his family. But Mrs. Van Dorn (Louise Randolph) reveals that while Van Dorn was ill, the Jewish boy's father (Lee Kohlmar), their neighbor, lent her money to keep the family going. After all, Mr. Blumberg makes $20,000 a year in the pants business and Mr. Palmieri earns a handsome sum in his wholesale fruit business, while Van Dorn, when he is well enough to work, is a clerk getting only $3000 a year. All is made well at the Van Dorns' silver anniversary party. Broadway thought one *Abie's Irish Rose* (still playing to big houses) was enough.

The two plays that opened the following Monday were the season's first non-musical hits. Myron C. Fagan's **The Little Spitfire** (8-16-26, Cort) examined the sometimes rocky marriage of newlyweds James Ralston (Raymond Van Sickle), the vice-president of the United Cigar Company, and his wife, Gypsy (Sylvia Field), whom he had culled from the chorus of *Rose-Marie*. Her gadfly brother, Marty (Russell Mack), works as a clerk in one of Ralston's stores and is goaded into stealing some cash from the firm. Gypsy's attempts to correct matters lead to complications, especially after she is found in the rooms of another man. The comedy ran six months.

Sam Janney's **Loose Ankles** (8-16-26, Biltmore) ran almost as long. A man-hating young lady, Ann Harper (Kathleen Comegys), is left a fortune by her grandmother on the condition she marry. Ann's response is to advertise for a husband. The ad is answered by Gil Barry (Harold Vermilyea), an amiable cake-eater who shares his apartment with two money-mad "dancing sheiks" (Charles D. Brown and Osgood Perkins). His buddies goad Gil on, while Ann's relations give her a push. Ann learns that Gil had to be prodded and that her aunts have known the sheiks, paying them to take them out for good times. Of course, by the final curtain Ann and Gil have fallen in love.

Even O. P. Heggie was unable to draw an audience for Henry C. White's **Sunshine** (8-17-26, Lyric). He played David Whitaker, a small-town Connecticut attorney, known affectionately as "Sunshine." He discovers that his daughter, Emily (Eleanor Griffith), is really not his but the child of an affair his late wife had with a perfume salesman (Byron Beasley). The man has come to Sunshine's office, asking him to find the girl, whom he has never seen, and his story leaves no doubt of the situation. Sunshine is loath to take action, since a scandal would hurt Emily. He tells her the story in the guise of a fable. She understands and refuses to meet her real father, dismissing him as a moral coward. She will stay with Sunshine.

George M. Cohan missed paydirt with **The Home Towners** (8-23-26, Hudson). *Variety* cheered, "If this isn't a clean home run knockout, New York is crazy." New York may have been, for it also ignored a slew of favorable notices in the dailies. Vic Arnold (William Elliott), an Indiana boy who has made good in New York, invites his old buddy, P. H. Bancroft (Robert McWade), to be best man at Vic's wedding to Beth Calhoon (Peg Entwistle), daughter of Park Avenue socialites. Bancroft warns that the Calhoons are probably just gold diggers and sets out to prove it. In the end, after almost wrecking the wedding plans, he sheepishly admits that he was wrong. A second-act setting, which moved quickly and cleverly to offer different views of a suite at the Waldorf-Astoria, won favorable mention from the press.

Lawrence Langner of the highbrow Theatre Guild offered Broadway a slick, commercial farce-comedy with his **Henry—Behave!** (8-23-26, Bayes) and was rewarded with a twelve-week run. The sober, proper Henry Wilton (John Cumberland), head of a major Long Island realty company, suffers amnesia after a blow on the head in a taxi accident. Some instinct leads him back home, but he does not recognize his wife (Justina Wayne) or son (Elisha Cook, Jr.) or battle-axe mother-in-law (Carrie Weller). In his mind he is once again the gay blade he was a quarter of a century earlier, so with his son he goes out to relive the evenings when he and Mazie Gay of the Casino painted the town. Guzzling illicit liquor at his Yacht Club he philosophizes, "Here's to the love that lies in women's eyes, and lies and lies and lies." His antics shock his family and nearly cost him an important sale, but another blow on the head brings him back to earth. He will have to be content with his son's marrying Evelyn Hollis (Gladys Lloyd), who turns out to be Mazie's daughter. The career of Cumberland, a brilliant farceur, had long since begun to fade. Even so, he received good notices, but not as good as those won by Edward G. Robinson as Wilton's "smug, oleaginous" partner.

Arnold Ridley's **The Ghost Train** (8-25-26, Eltinge) was a long-running London hit that failed to delight Americans, even though it was extensively rewritten for New York and won numerous approving notices. An unhappily wed couple (Robert Rendel and Gypsy O'Brien), honeymooners (John Williams and Claudette Colbert), and a prim old maid (Gladys Ffolliott) are stranded at a small, unused railroad station near Rockland, Maine. They are especially annoyed with a sixth passenger, a silly-ass Englishman (Eric Blore), dressed absurdly in plus fours and other golfing togs, who caused the problem by pulling the emergency cord while the train's wheezing engine negotiated an incline. He wanted to rescue his hat, which had blown out the window. The spinster growls at him, "Things like you are found in cheese. Only better looking!" A night watchman (Walter Wilson) appears and warns them they must leave, since the station is haunted. A mysterious train passes by every evening. No one knows where it comes from or where it goes, but anyone who sees it soon dies. The night watchman obviously has seen it, for he slumps over dead. Some neighbors in evening clothes also appear. It finally develops that they and the night watchman have been in league to smuggle booze and drugs, using the station as a hideaway. They are unmasked by the Englishman, who tells the others that he is actually Detective Inspector Morrison of Scotland Yard. A number of reviewers thought they heard perfect English accents from the whole cast, even the Americans who played Americans.

Owen Davis enjoyed a minor success with another mystery, **The Donovan Affair** (8-30-26, Fulton). The excitement begins in the library of Peter

Rankin (Robert T. Haines), with gruff Inspector John Killian (Paul Harvey) warning assembled guests to remain where they are, since Jack Donovan has been stabbed to death at the dinner table when the lights were out briefly. Donovan had asked that the lights be turned off so that he could demonstrate his ring, which glows in the dark and has an irresistible appeal to women. Now the ring is missing. It soon is found, but when the inspector goes to test it in the dark a second man is killed. The investigation shows that the ring was a fake, smeared with a radiating chemical, that all the guests had some reason to kill Donovan but that, as in *Pyramids,* the butler (Ray Collins) done it, because Donovan had secretly married the maid (Georgie Lee Hall) whom the butler loved and because the second man had figured it out. When Donovan's father (Edwin Maxwell) says it could not have been the butler, whose courtesies and humor he had admired, Killian replies, "Why not, it had to be somebody, didn't it?"

Two other plays competed with Davis's for first-nighters. Both failed. The title of Roy Briant and Harry Durant's **The Adorable Liar** (8-30-26, 49th St.) gave away much of the plot. Karith Barry (Dorothy Burgess) is a seventeen-year-old who dreams of medieval knights on white chargers and is given to telling lots of little falsehoods. When a young realtor, Alan Davis (Eric Dressler), drives into her small Florida town in a white automobile, she concludes this is her modern Galahad. So after he is accused of breach of promise, and possibly more, by the local vamp, Tansy Roque (Nelly Neil), and Tansy's irate father (William B. Mack), Karith hides him in her room. There coffee and sandwiches soon lead to kisses. Although he runs off for a time, on his return some more of Karith's little lies rid him of the Roques and win him for her. Advance ballyhoo suggested Miss Burgess was another Helen Hayes or Katharine Cornell. Her failure to live up to expectations no doubt hurt the show and led to her own very short career.

Most first-string critics, aware of the great promise Martin Flavin had shown, attended his **Service for Two** (8-30-26, Gaiety). They came away disappointed, for Flavin had written a farce and not a good one. In his simple tale, Sam (Hugh Wakefield), the Earl of Bagshote, brings his bride, Edith (Florence Fair), to New York's Hotel Alabaster for a stopover on their way west. His old flame, Peggy (Marion Coakley), now a film queen, discovers he has the adjoining suite and proceeds to vamp him. In fact she is snuggling on his lap when his wife returns from shopping. Wakefield, hailed as an English

Ernest Truex, and Miss Coakley were applauded for their skilled clowning; the play was dismissed.

Even more disappointing was Montague Glass and Jules Eckert Goodman's **Potash and Perlmutter, Detectives** (8-31-26, Ritz). In a rare move for modern days, the authors gave their play a subtitle, **Poisoned by Pictures.** The subtitle had little, if anything, to do with the play. The quarreling partners ("You agree with me? Then I must be wrong," one repeats from an earlier episode) find themselves heirs to a detective agency. They are asked to locate the missing McAdams jewels, which just happen to be sitting in their safe. The discovery of the jewels almost sends them to prison, but all ends happily. Typical of the sight gags was a police inspector praising Abe for having so many facts at his fingertips. As soon as the man leaves, Abe carefully examines his fingertips in wonderment. Critics praised the new Mawruss (Robert Leonard) and, even more so, the new Abe (Ludwig Satz), but though Satz made himself up to resemble the late Barney Bernard, he somehow lacked his predecessor's appeal. Held over from previous editions was Mathilde Cottrelly as Abe's practical wife.

B. M. Kaye's **She Couldn't Say No** (8-31-26, Booth) centered on a lovelorn stenographer, Alice Hinsdale (Florence Moore). Aching for the love of her attorney-boss (Ralph Kellard), she takes on, in his absence, a breach-of-promise suit and heads upstate to try the case. There she discovers her boss is the opposing attorney. She wins the case and, apparently, the boss. Only the broad clowning of the hatchet-faced comedienne gave this "rickety" farce a modest run. Some of her touches were pure Groucho Marx: "As attorney for the defendant . . . she proceeds to examine the plaintiff, she first walks up and down the court room imposingly before she says a word. [Then] she bellows her first question, 'How old are you, you liar?' " At another point she looks at the jury through the back of a chair to suggest how unjust it would be to put her client behind bars.

September began with a near miss, William Anthony McGuire's **If I Was Rich** (9-2-26, Mansfield). Jimmy Sterling (Joe Laurie, Jr.) is a $40-a-week shipping clerk who would be happy going his own simple ways. His ambitious wife (Mildred McLeod), on the other hand, grumbles about their probably being evicted for late rent payments and prods him into bluffing his way into society as the supposed son of a rubber magnate. Things progress swimmingly until a jewel robbery discloses that Mrs. Sterling has been accepting very expensive baubles from a rich admirer. After that the couple return resignedly to their walk-up apartment. The diminutive Laurie, a vaudevillian, garnered high praise. So did Raymond Walburn as a smooth-talking radio announcer, who "slips the folks a few snappy gags." Indeed, new radio jargon—"static," "sign off"—peppered the comedy's dialogue.

An unsatisfactory ending damaged the chances of Vincent Lawrence's **Sour Grapes** (9-6-26, Longacre). The Overtons (John Halliday and Alice Brady) understand that romance eventually dies; at least Mrs. Overton does. Therefore, when a family friend, James Milburn (Frank Conroy), presses her to elope with him she seriously considers accepting, even though she knows he is engaged to Marjorie Lawson (Flora Sheffield). That does not sit well with Marjorie. She tells Frank that she is pregnant, and he agrees to marry her. Mr. Overton suggests that he and his wife pretend to be still deeply in love, and in short order the idea seems to work wonders. For all its flaws, the comedy was beautifully acted, especially by the radiant Miss Brady and the suave Halliday.

There were no compensations in Pauline Fain's look at Jewish life, **What's the Use?** (9-6-26, Princess). This vanity production recorded the unhappy times of William Salen (Harry R. Irving) and Rita Ginsberg (Yvonne Manon). After their marriage Salen proves abusive until he becomes a successful nightclub owner. Then he turns loving and considerate again.

Matters were not much better in the Christian world of John Hunter Booth's **No Trespassing** (9-7-26, Sam H. Harris). At a swank Long Island party, Zoe Galt (Kay Johnson), the only single woman there and a notorious vamp, casts her eyes on David Druce (Russell Hicks). He may be handsome, but he is also a missionary, about to sail away to proselytize South Sea natives. Zoe is undaunted. She climbs through his bedroom window at three in the morning and goes to work on him. Initially she is rebuffed, but after a while the two fall in love, with Zoe promising to abandon her vamping and accompany him to the South Seas as Mrs. Druce. A Ben Bernie orchestra supplied music during intermissions.

The season's second London mystery, Joseph Jefferson Farjeon's **Number 7** (9-8-26, Times Square), found few takers for its tale of eerie doings in an untenanted London house during a fog.

Gladys B. Unger's **Two Girls Wanted** (9-9-26, Little) was the first hit of the season to run until the warm weather returned the following July. It was a typical John Golden production. As one critic observed, "His stuff is always clean, his plots hackneyed, and his belief in the ultimate victory of Right over Might unfaltering." The reviewer added that Broadway wags termed Golden's plays "comiclean." In this instance, the title was a bit inaccurate, for while the play began in the drab apartment shared by the Miller girls, Marianna (Nydia Westman), a stenographer, and Sarah (Charlotte Denniston), a clerk, attention focused primarily on Marianna. She falls in love with Dexter Wright (William Hanley), only to faint when she overhears that he is engaged to another young lady. The girls decide to leave New York City and take work as servants at a posh Westchester home, which, they soon discover, is the home of Dexter's fiancée and her parents. But after Marianna unearths a plot there to drug and defraud Dexter and tips him off to it, Dexter realizes where his heart truly lies.

Fred Ballard, another young playwright failing to live up to his early promise, and Arthur Stern were the authors of **Henry's Harem** (9-13-26, Greenwich Village). As with *Two Girls Wanted* its title was inaccurate, here probably intentionally so. Henry (Al Roberts) promised his dying father that he would not marry until his large flock of sisters all were wed. Now, after several years, his sweetheart gives him only six months more to accomplish the task or she will start looking around for another man. This prompts Henry to throw a wild party, during which all his siblings win engagement rings.

Once again Marjorie Rambeau found herself stuck in a hopeless vehicle, John Bowie's **Just Life** (9-14-26, Henry Miller's). She played Madame Bernice Chase, a once famous prima donna whose voice has lost its bloom. She struggles along, singing in second-rate opera houses and even in nightclubs, to support her worthless, philandering husband (Clyde Fillmore) and her daughter (Vivian Tobin). But when she finds her husband, who had sworn he would behave, in another woman's arms, and recognizes that her daughter is growing irresponsible, she walks out on Mr. Chase, sees to it her daughter makes a sober marriage, and heads back to Rome.

The season's first sensational smash hit was Phillip Dunning and George Abbott's **Broadway** (9-16-26, Broadhurst). In fact it was deemed so sensational that *Variety*, deviating from its normal policy, gave it three reviews—one by a theatre critic, one by its nightclub critic, and one by an out-of-town critic to assess its appeal for the hicks from the sticks. At the Paradise Night Club, a young hoofer, Roy Lane (Lee Tracy), is putting the chorus girls through their routine in a private party room just before the midnight show. But he is concerned because his own favorite, Billie Moore (Sylvia Field), has not shown up and he fears Nick (Paul Porcasi), the proprietor, will fire her. When she belatedly enters, she is on the arm of Steve Crandall (Robert Glecker), the notorious bootlegger who provides Nick with his all his illegal booze, so there is no chance of her losing her job. Crandall has a problem of his own when "Scar" Edwards (John Wray) shows up. Crandall is attempting to seize Edwards's territory north of 125th Street and has hijacked some of Edwards's liquor. Edwards warns Crandall to lay off or he will tell the police what he knows about some unsolved murders, so Crandall shoots him. They are carrying him off when Roy and Billie return. Crandall says they are just removing a drunk. Roy, anxious to keep Billie away from the sordidness, tells her, "I guess you know pretty well that I'm very strong on you, but I ain't said nothing about matrimony on account of my old man has just recently died. But since this big four-flusher is talking about a wedding ring, I'll play my own ace. Listen, honey, how about getting hitched up?" In no time, the police start to close in on Crandall. Roy tells them of seeing Crandall taking out the supposed drunk, but Billie, still somewhat under Crandall's spell, denies it happened. Then one of the other chorus girls, who was Edwards's mistress and whom he had planted as a spy in the club, hears of Edwards's murder. She shoots and kills Crandall, but a sympathetic detective insists it was suicide. Roy and Billie go on with their performance, with the probability that they will have two engagements, their own and one together in vaudeville. Throughout the evening an offstage jazz band, supposedly in the main room of the nightclub, provided a rhythmic, saxophony accompaniment. Praise for the show was almost unanimous, with the *New Yorker*'s Charles Brackett calling it "faultless" and Walter Winchell telling his readers that "in the language of the stem, *Broadway* is the pay-off!" Tracy's "magnetic gusto" also earned loud applause. Jed Harris's production, which Abbott directed, paid off for 603 performances. Curiously, though the play still makes fascinating reading, a revival in the 1970s folded out of town, while a second one ran only a single performance in New York in 1987. Nonetheless, the play was probably the first of many peaks in Abbott's long career and the first of a series of triumphs for the controversial Harris.

. . .

George [Francis] **Abbott** (1887–1995) was born in Forestville, N.Y., and studied with Professor George Pierce Baker at his famous 47 Workshop at Harvard. His earliest plays were failures, so he turned to acting, making his New York debut in *The Misleading Lady* (1913). Apart from some rewriting for *Lightnin'* (1918), he did not resume work as an author until 1925, when he collaborated with James Gleason on *The Fall Guy*. He remained associated with melodrama through the twenties, switching to comedy in the thirties and then to musicals for the rest of his career.

. . .

Jed Harris [né Jacob Horowitz] (1900–1979) was born in Vienna and brought to America while still a boy. He was educated at Yale, then did a brief stint as a journalist. His first mounting, *Weak Sisters* (1925), was a flop, but he enjoyed some small success with *Love 'Em and Leave 'Em* (1926). He quickly earned a reputation as a "wonder boy," although he was despised for his gratuitous abrasiveness and rudeness.

. . .

Broadway saw no reason to keep Pierre Gendron's **Kept** (9-17-26, Comedy). Oldtimer Minnie Dupree was featured as Netty Estel, who lives in an old folks' home called the Autumn Lodge and rescues a drunken, injured Norman Henderson (Robert Williams), a prominent architect, after an automobile accident. In gratitude he adopts her as a sort of live-in mother and takes her to his comfortable New York apartment. His mistress (Zola Talma) howls and demands he throw her out. He does, but then has second thoughts. So he gives the mistress the boot.

Nor did New Yorkers care for Patrick Hastings's London comedy **Scotch Mist** (9-20-16, Klaw), in which a lady (Rosalinde Fuller) decides she prefers her importuning lover (Philip Merivale) to her dull husband (Fred Tiden). In London, Tallulah Bankhead had played the lady.

Margaret Vernon's **Yellow** (9-21-26, National) came in under George M. Cohan's aegis and scored a small success. Self-serving Val Parker (Chester Morris) ditches his pregnant girlfriend, Daisy Lingard (Shirley Warde), to marry a fellow socialite, Polly Sayre (Selena Royle), but at least he gives his buddy, Jack Crompton (Hale Hamilton), $5000 to look after Daisy. The embittered Daisy refuses the money and takes to prostitution to support herself. When Val returns from a disastrous honeymoon, he attempts to take up with Daisy again. Daisy shoots but does not kill him. Later they meet at a nightclub where Daisy is accompanied by an old roué (Frank Burbeck). Daisy creates a scene. The police enter, tell Daisy to ply her trade "below the line," and suggest Val find another town. Several critics singled out the performance of Spencer Tracy as a crude but pleasant bank clerk.

Fanny Brice, venturing into straight theatre, came a cropper in Willard Mack and David Belasco's

Fanny (9-21-26, Lyceum). She was seen as Fanny Fiebaum, who accompanies the philanthropic Leah Mendoza (Jane Ellison) to a rest cure at the ranch of Mendoza's late brother. She foils would-be robbers and becomes a Yiddish vamp, with slightly crossed eyes, a broad grin, and pronounced gawkiness, to trick the villainous foreman "Gyp" Gradyear (John Cromwell) out of the $60,000 the dead brother had cached away and Gradyear had found. At one point, sporting an oversized sombrero, she sat down with the cowpunchers to play poker, dealing from the bottom of the deck and stopping to perform card tricks. Both the play and the acting were dismissed by *Variety* as "unreal and unfunny."

Owen Davis dramatized Fulton Oursler's novel **Sandalwood** (9-22-26, Gaiety). It takes Faith Waring (Gilda Leary), an old flame, to cure Eddie Carpenter (William Harrigan) of his mysterious, languishing illness and his death wish, even though it means Mrs. Carpenter (Pauline Lord) is ordered out of their home. But when he is well again, Eddie turns the tables by ordering Faith out, and the Carpenters decide to move to another town. In Oursler's novel Faith had committed suicide after Eddie refused to run off with her, but Davis had opted for a less dramatic ending—one of many changes that critics felt diminished the play. Although her part was the least significant of the three principals, Miss Lord transmuted its "common substance . . . into precious metal" with her "vivid and profound" performance.

William Hodge, long more popular on the road than in New York, nonetheless chalked up a fifteen-week run with the latest vehicle he had written for himself, **The Judge's Husband** (9-27-26, 49th St.). Joe Kirby has become the housekeeper-husband for his wife (Gladys Hanson), a judge. But when he disappears for two nights, she decides to sue for divorce. She elects to sit in judgment herself, and he opts to be his own attorney. The trial brings out that his two nights away from home were spent extricating their daughter (Ruth Lyons) from a mess she had gotten herself into. Several critics wondered aloud why Joe couldn't have told his wife that in the first place, but then there would not have been any play.

Dorrance Davis's **The Shelf** (9-27-26, Morosco) had a more tenable idea but failed to capitalize on it. Overhearing the town harpies say she is ready for the shelf where older women are relegated after they have lost their youth, Stella Amaranth (Frances Starr) elects to show them a thing or two. She goes out and sells iced tea and kisses at a church fair, then vamps her niece's fiancé (Louis Kimball), a minister (Donald Meek), a governor (Lawrence Leslie), and finally a senator (Arthur Byron). Among the menfolk Meek and Byron earned extra bows—Byron for his smooth but slightly depraved politician, and Meek for his milquetoast clergyman henpecked by his juggernaut wife (Leah Wilson).

Anita Loos and her husband, John Emerson, enjoyed a six-month success with their adaptation of her best-seller **Gentlemen Prefer Blondes** (9-28-26, Times Square). June Walker, in a blonde wig, played the baby-talking, gold-digging Lorelei Lee, who insists diamonds are a girl's best friend. Pug-nosed Edna Hibbard was her lively companion, Dorothy Shaw. Having said their farewells to Gus Eisman (Arthur S. Ross), a rich Chicago button manufacturer, and Lorelei having promised to remain faithful, the girls sail for Europe. On the ship they meet an inarticulate, "bone-spectacled," but very wealthy Philadelphian, Henry Spofford (Frank Morgan), and by the time they return from a stay at the Ritz in Paris to Lorelei's New York apartment, Lorelei has nailed the poor galoot. Never mind that she has also wheedled Sir Francis Beekman (G. P. Huntley) into buying her a diamond tiara. George Jean Nathan commented that the play's "characters are completely alive, reported with an ear of absolute pitch and caught brilliantly in detail." In 1949 the story was successfully musicalized.

Some good acting was the main claim to patronage of Denison Clift's **A Woman Disputed** (9-28-26, Forrest). Bitter at having been jailed for an offense she did not commit, Marie-Ange (Ann Harding) takes to prostitution. A client shoots himself in her room, and his brother, Captain Von Hartmann (Lowell Sherman), calling to investigate, is smitten by the girl. His friend, Yank Trinkard (Louis Calhern), also falls in love with her. When the war breaks out she elects to stick by Yank. The furious Von Hartmann attempts to seduce her after she is captured, but the girl tricks him into releasing some prisoners, one of whom alerts Yank. He returns to claim Marie-Ange and give the German his comeuppance.

The season's most controversial play was **The Captive** (9-29-26, Empire), taken by Arthur Hornblow, Jr., from Edouard Bourdet's *La Prisonnière*. Irène de Montcel (Helen Menken) refuses the demand of her diplomat father (Norman Trevor) that she accompany him to his new post in Brussels. De Montcel is worried about Irène's unhealthy relationship with another woman. To avoid leaving her lover, she agrees to marry Jacques Virieu (Basil Rathbone), a friend from childhood days. Jacques is warned against the marriage by the other woman's husband (Arthur Wontner) but goes through with it. A year later the marriage is patently a failure, even though Irène has genuinely tried to escape the feelings that keep her in bondage to her illicit passion. Irène returns to her lover, while Jacques seeks solace with a heterosexual lady (Ann Andrews). (Irène's lover never appears in the play.) In his introduction to the published text, Brooks Atkinson called the work "a restrained though uncompromising tragedy." Earlier, *Variety* had hailed it as "The most daring play of the season . . . and one of the best written and acted in years." It then went on to devote a whole paragraph to discussing the theme, observing that such relationships were common in Greenwich Village and adding, "There are millions of women, sedate in nature, who never heard of a Lesbian, much less believing that such people exist. And many men, too." It ended its review, "What a play to promote censorship! And what a play!" When the D.A., Joab Banton, decided to pounce late in the season, *The Captive* was high on his list of obscenities. Other producers gave battle to save their mountings, but the Charles Frohman Corporation (Frohman himself had been dead eleven years), owned by Jesse Lasky's movie interests, wanted no trouble. They threw in the towel, forcing the play to close after just twenty weeks, although it was still drawing packed houses.

Lord Lathom's **Red Blinds** (9-30-26, Maxine Elliott's) had been shuttered in London by the English authorities, so he himself brought it over to New York with its London cast intact. It told of a woman (Iris Hoey) discarded by her husband and lover when she confesses she is a prostitute. Undiscouraged, she sets off to find a new man. Banton had no opportunity to close this play. New York's playgoers did it by showing their complete indifference.

These same playgoers, on a Broadway reveling in prostitutes, uncertain wives, and lesbians, displayed a similar indifference when Walter Hampden returned to the religious theme which had proved so popular for him in *The Servant in the House* and inaugurated his new season with a not unrelated tale. The earlier play had dealt with a Christ-like figure; Tom Barry's blank-verse drama, **The Immortal Thief** (10-2-26, Hampden's), looked at one of the men crucified alongside Christ. Marius Rufinus (Hampden) is a vicious malefactor, callously willing, from his secret hideout in an abandoned catacomb, to betray his own comrades if necessary. Yet he is not ignorant of higher ideals, for his mother (Mabel Moore) is a follower of Jesus and has attempted to teach him some of Christ's lessons. So after he is captured, he takes on himself the blame for the murder of a brothel keeper, actually killed by a girl the proprietor had abused but whom Marius had loved. The last act was set first in the bare country-side near the Jerusalem city gate and showed the women watching as far off in the distance Marius, Christ, and the third man carry their crosses to Golgotha, and then moved to Calvary, with only Marius's cross visible. In the darkness and crackling lightning, Marius's mother urges him to turn toward Jesus and be saved. He obeys her.

Frederic and Fanny Hatton's **Treat 'Em Rough** (10-4-26, Klaw) depicted a more mundane, modern redemption, but with no more success. Tony Barudi (Alan Dinehart), the adopted, spoiled son of Tomasso Salvatore (William Ricciardi), owner of the Café Salvatore, not only treats the club's chorus girls roughly, he looks on them as little better than tramps, which some of them are. Then in walks Nora O'Hare (Genevieve Tobin), fresh off the boat. He would give her the same treatment, until the fiery lass teaches him what respect and love mean.

George S. Kaufman suffered the worst failure of his career when he collaborated with Herman J. Mankiewicz on **The Good Fellow** (10-5-26, Playhouse). Wilkes-Barre's Jim Helton (John E. Hazzard) has a single ambition in life, to merit his election as Grand Napoleon of the Ancient Order of Corsicans. He is not above hocking his life insurance policy or borrowing from his prospective son-in-law (Lester Vail) to raise the $10,000 necessary to bring the group's national convention to Wilkes-Barre instead of Little Rock. (His attempts to get the community to contribute had raised merely a pathetic $254.) His actions alienate his family, especially his mother-in-law (Clara Blandick), who tells him she hopes someone starts a new lodge and refuses to admit him. When his lodge members also turn against him, he resigns and takes work in the Welfare Department of the mine owned by his future son-in-law's family. The satire was perceived as unevenly written and poorly acted, so Kaufman was probably not too surprised when it closed after its first Saturday night.

Paul Robeson was responsible for what little run (thirty-seven performances) Jim Tully and Frank Dazey's **Black Boy** (10-6-26, Comedy) achieved. (Tully, a professional hobo "whose unconventional existence does not bar him from dining in the Algonquin on occasion," had been the author of the book used as the source of last season's *Outside Looking In*.) Black Boy, a shambling, ignorant Negro, saunters into the training camp of "The Mauler" (Charles Henderson), offers to spar with him, and promptly knocks him out. The trainers seize on him, and in two years' time he is world champion. But he soon takes to the high life, begins losing fights, and is deserted by former rooters.

Most painfully, the white girl he has loved, Irene (Edith Warren), is revealed as a half-caste. His illusions shattered, he wanders off. In one indication of growing technological change, the big fight was not seen but was "graphically word-pictured via a radio receiving set." The voice was that of the celebrated sports announcer Major J. Andrew White. (All through the season, *Variety* reported on still another technological advance, noting that Warner Bros. was leasing playhouses to exhibit its new Vitaphone process for sound films.) Atkinson characterized Robeson's performance as "a fine-grained, resilient bit," adding, "His full, deep voice has a sustaining beauty."

An oddity called **The Jeweled Tree** (10-7-26, 48th St.) ran exactly as long as did *Black Boy*. Its author, Garrett Chatfield Pier, was an Egyptologist working at the Metropolitan Museum. In dialogue filled with "thous," "thees," "dosts," and "dursts," the widow of Tutankhamen, Queen Ankhesen (Olive Valerie), sends Rames (Walter Petrie) in search of a jeweled tree whose fruit keeps its eaters eternally young and beautiful. He finds the tree and its lovely guardian, Ata (Reva Greenwood). They conspire to give Ankhesen fruit that will make her old and ugly, after which the young lovers will live on forever. The play's scenery was gorgeous, particularly a glittering throne room and part of the Sea of Forgetfulness (with its illusion of tremendous depth). Scenery aside, the evening was dismissed as "Tut tosh."

Two other plays that opened the same night had even shorter runs. Credits for **Buy, Buy, Baby** (10-7-26, Princess) read "by Russell Medcraft and Norma Mitchell based on a play by Francis Bellamy and Lawton Mackall." Esmeralda Pottle (Alison Skipworth), "52, white, virgin but reconciled," fearing race suicide if other whites remain as childless as she, offers $1,000,000 to the first niece or nephew to have a baby. The niece, Janice (Laura Hope Crews), has been married, without offspring, for ten years, and her husband is away in South America. Ronald (Edwin Nicander) is a society bachelor and woman-hater. Together they agree to keep news of the offer from another nephew, Hal (Maurice Burke). Janice wires her husband to hurry home; Ronald latches on to a dumb flapper. But their efforts go for naught when Hal learns of the challenge, discloses that he has been secretly wed for several years, and produces his wife (Shirley Booth) and their three-month-old infant.

Alfred Savoir's *Le Dompteur* was offered in Wilfred Katzin's translation as **The Lion Tamer** (10-7-26, Neighborhood Playhouse). Lord Lonsdale (Ian Maclaren), disturbed by any sort of oppression, follows a circus in hopes of watching the lions turn on their whip-prone tamer (Otto Hulicius) and kill him. When nothing happens, he attempts to unnerve the man by having an affair with the tamer's wife (Dorothy Sands). Still, nothing occurs, so the frustrated lord feeds himself to the lions.

In Maurice Clark's **Tragic 18** (10-9-26, Charles Hopkins) Teddy Bowman (Neil Martin) comes from Red Oak, Iowa, to New York to begin his college studies and moves in with his older brother (Frank Roberts). Neil steals his brother's girl, Dot Dixon (Maude Hanaford), a struggling dancer, so the brother writes home to mother (Jennie Eustace), who rushes east. She uncovers the fact that Dot is a divorcée with a five-month-old baby. But Dot is not a bad girl, and she agrees to send Neil away as gently as possible. She suggests he come back to her when he is twenty-five, knowing by that time he will have forgotten her.

Patrick Kearney's theatricalization of Theodore Dreiser's **An American Tragedy** (10-11-26, Longacre) ran just over six months at stiff musical comedy prices in the face of divided notices. (That was two weeks longer than the more light-hearted and more welcomed *Gentlemen Prefer Blondes* did, for whatever that might mean.) *Variety*'s glowing notice hailed it as a "mighty offering." The perennially snide Robert Benchley, writing in *Life*, began his disparaging review with a disclaimer that could have come back to haunt him: "We are usually quite prepared to be proven wrong in our opinions, because we usually *are* wrong, but in the matter of the dramatization of Dreiser's 'An American Tragedy' all the expert testimony in the world cannot shake us from our belief that it is a heavy-handed, obvious, badly done play. Just the kind of play, in fact, that the novel deserved." As he had been in the book, Clyde Griffiths (Morgan Farley) is sentenced to death for killing Roberta Alden (Katherine Wilson) so that he could be free to wed a rich girl.

The Theatre Guild attempted to establish something approaching a repertory system (its idea was to change plays weekly) when it presented Ruth Langner's translation of Franz Werfel's **Juarez and Maximilian** (10-11-26, Guild). The drama recounted the history of the Austrian nobleman (Alfred Lunt) from his assuming the Mexican throne until his execution by a republican firing squad. The consensus was that Lee Simonson's magnificent settings and costumes—"the Indians in their blankets, the brilliant royal assemblies, the native and foreign uniforms, the lace robes of the archbishop"—were too cumbersome and made the drama sluggish. Even Lunt's performance split the critics, with

Alexander Woollcott calling it "magnificent" in the *World,* Atkinson complaining the actor "seldom penetrates the obvious surfaces," and Benchley fence-straddling in his comment, "It may have been the 1865 frock coat, but we were conscious throughout, in the sensitive performance of Mr. Lunt, of the presence of a futile and inexperienced Lincoln." The large, brilliant cast included Morris Carnovsky, Arnold Daly, Dudley Digges, Clare Eames, Earle Larimore, Philip Loeb, and Edward G. Robinson as well as several figures who would later make their mark behind the scenes—Harold Clurman, Cheryl Crawford, and Sanford Meisner.

Yet another novel—E. J. Rath's *The Dark Chapter*—was brought to the stage in Courtenay Savage's **They All Want Something** (10-12-26, Wallack's). The play was the second attempt of Bill Tilden, the tennis star now billed as William T. Tilden II, to gain equal prominence onstage. He was seen as William Rawlins, the son of a wealthy automobile manufacture. He has loved Hilda Kilbourne (Katherine Revner) from afar but has never been able to meet her. Learning that her mother is given to taking in hoboes, he appears at her door in tattered clothes and is invited in. Made chauffeur, he soon clears up some family difficulties and wins the girl. Performing with more vitality than artistry, Tilden kept the play on the boards for eight weeks, double its initial booking.

Milton Herbert Gropper and Max Siegel's **We Americans** (10-12-26, Sam H. Harris) was a minor success. The Levines (Clara Langsner and Muni Wisenfrend) are largely unacclimated immigrants. Their foreign ways prompt their American-born daughter (Ailsa Lawson) to run away from home. To become more American, they enroll in Sam Korn's night school, where, along with others like themselves, they learn to speak better English and adopt American customs. Before long their daughter, who was not able to make her way as readily as she had assumed, is back home and everyone is happy. Critics complained that the second act, in the night school, was little more than a series of vaudeville turns dear to old dialect comedians. But this could have pleased playgoers, since, according to *Variety,* patronage came largely from cut-rate tickets offered in East Side outlets. Muni Wisenfrend later changed his name to Paul Muni.

A pair of revivals followed, though both sported new names. **The Humble** (10-13-26, Greenwich Village) was Laurence Irving's adaptation of Dostoyevsky's *Crime and Punishment,* the same play E. H. Sothern had starred in when it was called *Rodion, the Student.* It failed once again.

The American Laboratory Theatre opened its season with **The Straw Hat** (10-14-26, American Laboratory), a new translation by Paul Tulane and Agnes Hamilton Jones of Eugène Labiche and Marc-Michel's *Un Chapeau de paille d'Italie,* telling of a bridegroom who cannot get to his wedding until he replaces a straw hat his horse has eaten.

Having bravely mounted a play he had informed its author had no chance of success, Winthrop Ames was forced to close Philip Barry's **White Wings** (10-15-26, Booth) after twenty-seven performances, just as it appeared to be catching on. Certainly the critics were little help, providing anything but money notices. Atkinson waved it away as "completely mad," although he was gentleman enough to acknowledge that the audience had a good time. The curtain rose on a somewhat stylized 1895 street scene to disclose a horse and carriage standing in front of a seafood restaurant. The horse was not a real horse but an actor in costume, and the actor was George Ali, celebrated for playing all sorts of animals in musical comedies and in vaudeville. Throughout the evening Ali's horse sat down and rose up, cocked his head to listen to conversation, struck postures of defiance, and rolled his eyes. A young couple emerge from the restaurant. The boy is Archie Inch (Tom Powers), the latest in a long line of Inches, white wings who have proudly swept up after horses. The girl is Mary Todd (Winifred Lenihan), whose father has perfected a marvelous invention, a horseless carriage. Since there is no cabby in sight she suggests they wait ten minutes; then, realizing how happy she is, she changes that to eleven minutes. But Archie is reluctant to sit in the presence of a standing horse. That would be disrespectful. As the years progress, the horseless carriage replaces the horse. The Inches are aghast, with father Inch (William Norris) even puncturing tires to discourage people from buying the vehicles. But by 1915 Mary has shot the horse—"the last goddamn suffering horse in the city," Archie gets behind the wheel of a new flivver, and old man Inch takes to peddling strawberries in the street.

J. P. McEvoy's **God Loves Us** (10-18-26, Maxine Elliott's) spotlighted another replaceable man, Hector Midge (J. C. Nugent), who has worked loyally for twenty-five years at Dawson and Co., a greeting cards firm, and has risen to assistant sales manager. But just as he comes in line for promotion to sales manager, the boss's son (Cebra Graves) appears and is given the post. To add injury to insult, when the boss (Malcolm Williams) goes on vacation, the son fires Hector. The best that Hector can wangle on the boss's return is restoration of his old job at his old salary. During the short run, the show's title was changed to *The Go-Getters* and the ending was altered to have Hector take work elsewhere as a book salesman.

An importation, Frederick Lonsdale's **On Approval** (10-18-26, Gaiety), fared better, surviving for twelve weeks and enjoying numerous subsequent revivals. It told of two pair of lovers—a young man (Wallace Eddinger) and a divorcée (Violet Kemble Cooper), and a youthful pickle heiress (Kathlene MacDonell) and a duke (Hugh Wakefield)—who go off to an isolated Scottish estate to see how they like living together. Before long, the youngsters have run away arm in arm, leaving the duke and the divorcée to fend for themselves.

Willard Mack, rebounding quickly from the failure of his Fanny Brice vehicle, smiled all the way to the bank during the six-month run of **The Noose** (10-20-26, Hudson), which he took from a short story by H. H. Van Loan. Some critics suggested he might have had an even bigger hit had his play opened before *Broadway*. Ignoring even his wife's pleadings, the governor (Lester Lonergan) has refused to spare the life of a young murderer, Nickie Elkins (Rex Cherryman). The action then flashes back to the time of the killing. Nickie has been raised in a rough environment and has joined a gang of bootleggers. But when the leader of the gang, Buck Gordon (George Nash), threatens to blackmail the governor by revealing that Nickie is his wife's illegitimate son, Nickie kills him in the office of a nightclub the gang supplies with liquor. Back at the governor's mansion, a tearful chorus girl (Barbara Stanwyck) finally moves the executive to spare Nickie, without revealing the true story. The cast was superb, with Cherryman promising to become a sought-after leading man, and Stanwyck stopping the show with her big scene. Stanwyck also participated, with the four other nightclub chorus girls, in a second show-stopping moment, a frenzied "Black Bottom."

Rolph ("formerly Ralph") Murphy's **Sure Fire** (10-20-26, Waldorf) opens in the office of John Kenderton (William Jeffrey), a Broadway producer. He is described as "a manager filthy with money from clean plays." (Broadway read John Golden into that description.) He is explaining to Robert Ford (Robert Armstrong) why he has rejected his play about sordid Greenwich Village and suggests that he "screw out" to a small town to see how most Americans live. So Ford heads for Clayville, Ind. There he saves the postmistress (Mina C. Gleason) from losing her home after she has paid her erring son's gambling debts and wins the hand of the lady's

daughter (Nancy Sheridan). They are enjoying a clinch in the good lady's workplace when a startled villager enters and asks what they think they are doing. "Playing post office" is their reply. Robert then decides to write the whole story as a comedy. The play failed in New York but did well on its post-Broadway tour.

An opening two nights later, J. Frank Davis's **The Ladder** (10-22-26, Mansfield), made Broadway history. Margaret Newell (Antoinette Perry), weary of this "rag bag" and "tiresome puzzle" called life, is proposed to by the charming but soft Roger Crane (Vernon Steele) and by the ruthless Stephen Pennock (Hugh Buckler), who has ruined Roger's business. Sitting at the piano in her luxurious 1926 apartment, she feels she has had to make a similar choice before. She falls asleep and dreams of her earlier lives. When she was Lady Margaret Percy in fourteenth-century England, Stephen, then the Earl of Orleton, slew Robert in order to win her. Much the same thing occurred when she was Mistress Margaret Sanderson in seventeenth-century London and simple Margaret Wright in nineteenth-century New York. After she wakes, Margaret accepts Roger's proposal. Reviews were damning, yet its nearly 800 performances made *The Ladder* the fourth-longest-running Broadway show on record at the time. Why? Because a wealthy oil man, Edgar B. Davis, believed so strongly in reincarnation that he underwrote the drama for its entire stand, reputedly casting away between half a million and a million dollars. Some nights audiences were allowed in at no charge, and at other times tickets were reduced to a fraction of the stated cost. Moreover, Davis persisted although there were evenings when only two or three people were in the audience.

A much better play, George Kelly's **Daisy Mayme** (10-25-26, Playhouse), had a much shorter life. For years Cliff Mettinger (Carlton Brickert), a bachelor, was looked after by his mother and, following her death, by a widowed sister. Now the sister has died, and Cliff has taken her daughter, May (Madge Evans), to Atlantic City for a short vacation. On the day he is expected to return, his surviving sisters, Olly Kipax (Josephine Hull) and Laura Fenner (Alma Kruger), along with Laura's daughter, Ruth (Nadea Hall), all of whom he has helped to support, come to put the place in order. They are taken aback when he arrives not only with May but with Daisy Mayme Plunkett (Jessie Busley), an outgoing but slightly vulgar woman whom he met at the shore. Laura is certain she knows Daisy Mayme's type, the sort of woman who "has no more home than a tomcat" and who will "hang around fashionable hotels, with their ear to the ground." There has never been much love among the siblings, but the sisters set aside their animosities in an attempt to chase Daisy Mayme away. She fights back, even as the sisters strive to convince her that Cliff wants her only as a companion for May. It remains for May to tell Cliff that at forty-two he is not too old to marry and that Daisy Mayme would make an excellent wife. When he proposes, she accepts and purrs, "I'll sit here in the lady's chair. I've always wanted to be a lady." Critics felt that the play was inferior to Kelly's earlier offerings. It ran only fourteen weeks and failed on a subsequent tour.

That same evening saw the start of the Civic Repertory Theatre, which Eva Le Gallienne founded. Because no Broadway theatre owner would give her a reasonable lease, especially after learning that she insisted on a ticket scale ranging from thirty-five cents in the balcony to a $1.50 top, she took over and renamed the old, out-of-the-way 14th Street Theatre. At least at the start, her company included numerous fine players, but none who would go on to lasting fame. Among her early rosters were Josephine Hutchinson, Rose Hobart, Beatrice Terry, Egon Brecher, and Alan Birmingham. Her first offering was Jacinto Benavente's **Saturday Night** (10-25-26, Civic Repertory), in a translation by John G. Underhill. Benavente's tale told of the rise, near fall, and ultimate grasping for salvation of a sculptor's model, Imperia (Le Gallienne), in medieval Italy. Critics were kind, despite a problem-beset first night. The next evening she brought out Chekhov's **The Three Sisters** (10-26-26, Civic Repertory), in a translation supposedly by herself and recounting the unfulfilled dreams of sisters longing to visit Moscow. The excellent notices received by this production secured Miss Le Gallienne's longed-for success. In short order she added both of the Ibsen dramas that she had mounted last season to offer New York for the first time in decades a true repertory ensemble.

Medieval Italy was also the setting for **Caponsacchi** (10-26-26, Hampden's), which Arthur Goodrich and Rose A. Palmer took from Robert Browning's "The Ring and the Book." It described, with flashbacks to the incidents brought up, the trial of a high-minded monk (Walter Hampden) who has been falsely accused by a brutal nobleman (Ernest Rowan), who is the real killer, of murdering the nobleman's wife (Edith Barrett), a woman the monk admired. He is acquitted by the Pope (Stanley Howlett). At the end he kneels gratefully to God and assures Him, "I mean to do my duty and live long, / Meet straight the fate Thou hast prepared for me, / To try to mold the golden ring of truth." The play was a resounding success, running until summer and brought back by Hampden several times in later years.

T. C. Murray's **Autumn Fire** (10-26-26, Klaw) was an Irish play, presented with an Irish cast. Its central figure, a middle-aged man, marries a young girl who really prefers his son. After the old man is injured and tended back to health by his wife, he finds her in his son's arms and comprehends that he should not have wed her. The only player whom most Americans soon would come to recognize was Una O'Connor, and she won the best notices as the old man's sharp-tongued spinster daughter.

Owen Davis's **Gentle Grafters** (10-27-26, Music Box) was touted as the author's 107th play. Sally (Katharine Alexander), a $35-a-week secretary, and her older friend, Cora (Charlotte Granville), whom she passes off as her mother, are gold diggers who agree "there is nothing so annoying in this world as to live with a virtuous woman." They live in a spiffy apartment on Central Park East and wear all the latest fashions. So when Cora finds Sally falling genuinely in love with Dick (Robert Keith), she tells her that Dick is actually engaged to another woman and pushes her into the embrace of Jim (Morgan Wallace). Dick hears of Sally and Jim, and leaves her. Only too late does she discover she has been tricked. She heads out for a ride to Westchester with a couple of rich young men. When the play closed after two weeks, no press agent counted how many flops Davis had suffered.

November was heavy with importations, although only one of the three openings on its first night was foreign. *Variety* characterized Knowles Entrikin's **Seed of the Brute** (11-1-26, Little) as "a play that for bald and shocking profanity, salaciousness, and obscenity, outranks any of the rank ones in town." Why, it even went so far as to call a whorehouse a whorehouse. In a prologue, a young farm boy uses his family's barn to rape women, then sends them away telling them they are sluts. Years pass, and that boy, Calvin Roberts (Robert Ames), has married a rich girl and become a power in his state. He is cruel and corrupt. But he broods because his only son (Donn Cook) is a weakling. The sole figure willing to stand up to and defy Roberts is a young newspaperman, David Carr (Harold Elliott). Roberts discovers Carr is his illegitimate son and attempts to use the fact for a rapprochement. But Carr has his father's blood in him and prefers to continue the fight. One irony of the production was that William Brady, who had spoken loudly against dirt shows on many occasions, was co-producer.

Robert McLaughlin, a Cleveland theatre owner,

had been offering his morality play to Broadway producers for several years. Curiously, only the most unlikely were interested. Al Woods had taken an option, then dropped it, and it remained for the Shuberts to finally stage **The Pearl of Great Price** (11-1-26, Century). Their reasoning may have been that they needed something to fill the huge Century. The play opens at "The Little House Among the Hollyhocks," where Pilgrim (Claudette Colbert) is left alone by the death of her mother (Effie Shannon), with only a rare pearl—her chastity—to sustain her. Moving on to such places as "The Abode of Luxury," "The Street of Indecision," and finally to "The Trysting Place of Happiness," she encounters among others, for better or worse, Adventure, Beauty, Despair, Indolence, and Shame, this last portrayed by the all but forgotten Amelia Bingham in what Alison Smith of the *World* called "her most stately and Shakespearian manner." The Shuberts mounted the piece lavishly but, taking another tack as well, included a scene in an artist's studio with a model posing totally in the nude (legal so long as she didn't move). But the public would have nothing of it, concurring with the critic who snarled, "It's the bunk."

The evening's importation was Dion Titheradge's **Loose Ends** (11-1-26, Ritz). A fast-living actress (Violet Heming) falls in love with a man (Titheradge) she accidentally knocked down with her car. He is contemptuous of her boozy set, until she learns he is a former convict. They would part in a huff, but love keeps them together.

The month's first smash hit was **The Play's The Thing** (11-3-26, Henry Miller's), which P. G. Wodehouse drew from Ferenc Molnár's *Játék a kastélyban* (A Play in the Castle). Interestingly, its tryout at Great Neck had been its world premiere, and Budapest would not see the original play until the end of the month. The story was simple but deliciously presented. A young composer (Edward Crandall) overhears his sweetheart (Catherine Dale Owen) and a man who is obviously her lover (Reginald Owen) talking in her room. He is ready to break up with the girl until his crafty librettist (Holbrook Blinn) writes a skit employing the very words the couple used. Led to believe he listened in on a rehearsal, the composer can pursue his courtship. The play ran more than nine months and has had several successful revivals. Sadly, it also marked the versatile Blinn's last role before his rather premature death.

First Love (11-8-26, Booth) was Zoë Akins's version of Louis Verneuil's *Pile ou face*. Jean (Geoffrey Kerr) and Maica (Fay Bainter) are lovers.

Their idyll is endangered when Jean's father, the Count de Varigny (Bruce McRae), insists Jean marry a rich girl. This leads Maica to write to a rich man who has been offering her money. When the man is shown to be the count, the lovers convince him to let them alone. Several critics rejoiced that Bainter was giving her best performance since *East Is West*, but fine acting failed to prop up a featherweight comedy.

Only New Yorkers who understood French or Italian could have seen Luigi Pirandello's *Vestire gli Ignudi* before it was presented in Arthur Livingston's translation as **Naked** (11-8-26, Princess). A lady (Marguerite Risser) is stopped by several men from committing suicide. After debating for a time which of the men to marry, she decides she would rather be dead and appears to kill herself. But then one of the men, a writer (Augustin Duncan), comes onstage and muses to the audience whether he would not be better off with a happy ending that allows the lady to live.

The same night saw the Neigborhood Players bring back their 1924 production of *The Little Clay Cart*.

November's second Hungarian play, László Lakatos's *Fej vagy irás*, was brought out in Garrick Truman's closely translated **Head or Tail** (11-9-26, Waldorf) and ran a single week. It offered the not unfamiliar saga of an irrationally jealous husband (Philip Merivale) put in his place by an adroit wife (Estelle Winwood).

Old Bill, M.P. (11-10-26, Biltmore) was Bruce Bairnsfather's sequel to his wartime hit *The Better 'Ole*, and, like that show, wavered between straight play and musical. This time Old Bill (Charles Coburn) runs for Parliament, supports striking miners, and is caught in a mine blast but escapes. Lacking the universal appeal of the earlier show, it was withdrawn after three weeks.

Competing with the British comedy for attention was another revival of *The Emperor Jones*, this one at the Mayfair. Moss Hart was Smithers, and he recalled in his autobiography that while Gilpin was fine on opening night, later he was often too drunk to perform well, or to perform at all. Still, the tacky production survived for two months at the tiny house.

One of the season's longest runs (444 performances) was chalked up by Jean Bart's **The Squall** (11-11-26, 48th St.), a run prolonged in good measure by cut-rate tickets and because the producers owned the theatre. The critics lent no helping hand, condemning the play as "tawdry," "meretricious," and "cheap," albeit their comparing it to

White Cargo may have sent some theatregoers to the box office. The play, whose author was a doctor's wife, was set in Spain, near Granada. Nubi (Suzanne Caubet), fleeing her gypsy chief (Ali Yousuff), seeks refuge in the home of the Mendez family: "Me Nubi. Nubi good girl. Nubi stay." The family acquiesces. Then, while señora Mendez (Blanche Yurka) watches and bides her time, Nubi seduces both the husband (Lee Baker) and the son (Horace Braham) before the gypsy chief, alerted by the Señora, comes to claim her. The show's press agent gained paragraphs of publicity reporting that Robert Benchley stalked out of the theatre on opening night, audibly muttering, "Me Benchley. Benchley bad boy. Benchley go." The less show-offy Atkinson, who reported that Nubi was pronounced to rhyme with "heebie-jeebie," at least could praise the play's devastating thunderstorm effects.

Carlo Gozzi's dramatization of an old folk tale was worked into English by Henry G. Alsberg and Isaac Don Levine and presented as **Princess Turandot** (11-12-26, Provincetown Playhouse). The Russian director, Leo Bulgakov, staged this story of an icy princess (Barbara Bulgakov) who kills all suitors unable to answer her riddles and who is finally bested by a handsome Kalaf (Kirby Hawkes). But his staging was so capriciously slapstick that many playgoers and reviewers were put off. Puccini's opera on the same subject was presented at the Metropolitan Opera House the following week.

Tadema Bussiere's **Gertie** (11-15-26, Bayes), like *The Squall*, resorted to cut-rate tickets to thumb its nose at the critics and win a lengthy run—248 performances. Gertie (Constance McKay) is "a dese, dem and dos girl, good looking, but just a hick from the west side." Because she is absurdly ambitious she spurns Steve (Pat O'Brien), the garage mechanic who likes her, and convinces herself that a rich Long Island socialite is in love with her. But when the rich boy, drunk on illicit Scotch, appears and attempts to go too far too fast, she chases him away and returns to Steve. At this point she learns that Steve is no mere mechanic but the owner of the garage and several other garages, too.

Cut-rate tickets could not save Arthur Richman's **A Proud Woman** (11-15-26, Maxine Elliott's). Marion Taylor (Florence Eldridge) stands by helplessly as her dominating older sister, Mrs. Cates (Elizabeth Risdon), pushes Marion's prospective in-laws to delay Marion's wedding and replan it on a grander scale. Mrs. Cates also drums into Marion's ears her belief that the in-laws and their rich friends look down condescendingly on a poor girl from way out west. Too disturbed to reason with herself, Marion runs off to get back some order and control into her life.

Most first-string critics passed up the two new American plays to attend the Theatre Guild's revival of Shaw's *Pygmalion* at the Guild. The evening's star was clearly Lynn Fontanne as Eliza. Woollcott cooed that she was "richly satisfying." *Variety* went further, saying she was "never truer," then continued, "Her Whitechapel dialect is delicious and her animated moments are glorious. If there is a finer young actress in America than Miss Fontanne where is she?" There was not much praise for Reginald Mason's Higgins, but Henry Travers beguiled playgoers as Eliza's philosophizing cockney father. With the production's success the Guild began its so-called repertory policy, a policy that was not true repertory and that the failure of the Werfel drama had forced the company to hold in abeyance.

The busy Willard Mack, David Belasco again serving as his producer, bombed with **Lily Sue** (11-16-26, Lyceum). Flaxen-haired Lily Sue (Beth Merrill), the nicest "bit of calico" in Montana, is wooed by three men: Sheriff Joe Holly (Mack), Duke Adams (Curtis Cooksey), a cowpuncher, and Louis Lingard (Joseph Sweeney). Discovering Lingard peeping into the tent where Lily Sue is undressing, Adams drags his boss away, and a fistfight ensues. A short while later Lingard is found shot to death. Adams is arrested, although no one supposedly saw the shooting. On a moonlit night, Lingard's twin brother and his cohorts break into the log jailhouse, seize Adams, and take him outside to lynch him. Just then Lily Sue rides up on a horse and tells all. Seems the killer was her brother, who murdered Lingard for violating his girl. Like Amelia Bingham some weeks before, another star of earlier nights was relegated to a minor role, with William Courtleigh portaying Charlie Highhorse, a pleasant Blackfoot Indian.

Even less interest was evinced in **The Witch** (11-18-26, Greenwich Village), A. H. Wiers-Jenssen's *Anna Pedersdotter* in a version by the English poet John Masefield. It told of the daughter (Alice Brady) of a witch who had been burned at the stake in sixteenth-century Norway. Now she is married to a cold, elderly minister (David Landau). Sensing that she has her mother's powers, she seduces her husband's son (Hugh Huntley) by a former marriage and wills the minister to die, which he does. At her trial for witchery, she goes mad. The best notices went to Brady, and to Maria Ouspenskaya as a witch who is hounded out of hiding and burned at the stake early in the drama.

Another Harvard Prize play, Henry Fisk Carlton's **Up the Line** (11-22-26, Morosco) won no awards in New York. Ellie (Florence Johns), a hired girl on a North Dakota ranch, falls in love with Slug (Louis Calhern), a member of a group of militantly unionist drifters called Wobblies. He consents to marry her and settle down, but after a while the wanderlust gets him and he disappears. He is gone so long that the courts declare him dead, allowing Ellie to rewed. When Slug, who had been in prison, reappears, Ellie can do nothing but send him on his way. Calhern's picturesque and engaging performance was "the chief distinction of the play."

The same evening Eva Le Gallienne added Carlo Goldoni's *La Locandiera* to the Civic Repertory programs, using Helen Lehmann's translation as **The Mistress of The Inn.** In a role last played in New York (and in Italian) by Duse, Miss Le Gallienne enacted the attractive innkeeper who makes a woman-hater love her, then jilts him for a pleasant young man.

For the second time this season, New York was given an oportunity to see a London show banned by the Lord Chamberlain. Noel Coward's **This Was a Man** (11-23-26, Klaw) apparently offended some English sensibilities by reversing the position of the sexes in a story of infidelity. Edward Churt (A. E. Matthews) refuses to divorce his openly unfaithful wife (Francine Larrimore) until her seduction of his best friend (Nigel Bruce) proves too much. He swallows his pride and institutes action. The little interest the play held for New York was in Miss Larrimore's performance. She finally combed her usually rumpled hair to ape the slicked-down English society fashions, but she could not rein in her intense, slightly jittery, tempestuous, if rather un-English, mannerisms.

Two of the season's best plays came in on the same night, virtually at month's end. The American work was Sidney Howard's **Ned McCobb's Daughter** (11-29-26, John Golden). At Carrie's Spa, which his wife (Clare Eames) runs, across from the Mayberry terminus of the Kennebec Ferry, George Callahan (Earle Larimore) confesses that he has stolen $2000 while collecting ferry fares and that the company has given him until noon tomorrow to repay it or face prison. Having already served time, he is not anxious to do it again. But a visit from George's bootlegging brother, Babe (Alfred Lunt), seems to solve matters. He will give Carrie the money if she, in turn, will allow him to hide his liquor on her premises. She grudgingly consents, only to find that Babe quickly ups the ante. She just as quickly cows him by threatening to call in the federal authorities.

Before long the couple work out a way to deal with each other on more friendly, equal terms. Miss Eames, Howard's wife, gave a convincing performance as a woman with a tough, cold exterior but with a genuine warmth deep down. Lunt's hood, with his conspicuous gold-capped front tooth and his raucous voice, surprised and captured the critics. Playgoers who knew only the suave Lunt of later years might wonder how he put over a speech that ran in part: "Dat's what counts in dis world. Character. By God, if it don't! Beauty fades, but character goes on forever. You know, huh?" Or, more succinctly, "What's your name, hot lips?" Unfortunately critics held innumerable reservations about the play, which nonetheless ran up 132 performances.

Somerset Maugham's **The Constant Wife** (11-29-26, Maxine Elliott's) ran more than twice as long and gave Ethel Barrymore, who "looked her loveliest and played superbly," her biggest hit in years. Reversing the situation in Coward's play, and therefore obviously not offending male feelings, Maugham's heroine is aware that her husband (C. Aubrey Smith) is a philanderer. She even enjoys watching her friends struggle with keeping from her the truth that she already knows. And in her own good time, she announces that she is going out and perhaps have a fling of her own.

The month ended with the arrival of Cécile Sorel at the Cosmopolitan on the 30th in a repertory of French plays that began with Adolphe Aderer and Armand Ephraim's chronicle of Du Barry's last years, **Maîtresse de roi,** and included older plays once performed for New Yorkers by Bernhardt and Coquelin. She stayed for six weeks.

A revival of O'Neill's *Beyond the Horizon,* with Thomas Chalmers as Andrew, Robert Keith as Robert, and Aline MacMahon as Ruth, began a ten-week sojourn the same night at the Mansfield.

Employing players who were acting in regularly scheduled offerings, Brock Pemberton planned to run Pirandello's *L'Uomo, la Bestia e la Virtu* at a series of midnight performances, in Alice Rohe's translation as **Say It with Flowers** (12-3-26, Garrick). A professor (Osgood Perkins) has been having an affair with a woman (Carlotta Irwin), whose husband (Hugh Buckler), a sea captain, refuses to sleep with her on his rare visits home. The professor, eager to end the liaison, has a special cake baked and tells the wife to feed it to her husband and to place flowers on her balcony if all goes well. The next morning there are flowers on the balcony. Two late night performances satisfied the demand for seats.

A single week sufficed for the first of three English plays to come in, one right after the other. Edward Percy's **Slaves All** (12-6-26, Bijou) led the short procession. A writer (Lionel Atwill), driven to drink by his cold, sanctimonious sister (Marion Abbott), contemplates killing her. She dies before he can carry out his plan. He then learns that the sister's maid (Marguerite Mosier) is actually her illegitimate daughter.

Benn W. Levy's comedies almost never repeated their West End success in New York. Witness **This Woman Business** (12-7-26, Ritz), in which a band of misogynists discover a comely young girl (Genevieve Tobin) burglarizing their weekend retreat. In no time at all, the leader (George Thorpe) of the band falls in love with her.

But enough New Yorkers did embrace **The Constant Nymph** (12-9-26, Selwyn), which Basil Dean and Margaret Kennedy adapted from Miss Kennedy's best-seller, to give it a four-month run. It centered on a dead man's daughters, his cousins, and his protégé. The protégé (Glenn Anders) marries one of the cousins (Louise Huntington), regrets his actions, then marries one of the daughters (Beatrix Thompson), only to have her die.

Several years would pass before Thornton Wilder achieved fame as a playwright. His first professional mounting, **The Trumpet Shall Sound** (12-10-26, American Laboratory), was given rather short shrift by the critics, mostly second-stringers. The play, which some saw as a morality play whose central figure was really God, pictures what happens in 1871 when Peter Magnus returns to his Washington Square mansion to find his servants have turned the place into a boardinghouse. Rather than chase away the riffraff he attempts to inculcate spiritual values. One serving girl, Flora, who had suggested the rooms be rented and hoped to use her share of the money to help a sailor she loved, finds he is unfaithful, so she commits suicide. The others plead their cases before Magnus, and he, in turn, suggests means for redemption.

Anne Nichols frittered away more of her profits from *Abie's Irish Rose* when she produced Mark Swan's **Howdy, King** (12-13-26, Morosco). Johnny North (Minor Watson), a cowboy from Arizona, is visiting Europe, where he falls in love with Helen Bond (Harriet MacGibbon) to the consternation of her haughty aunt (Lorna Elliott). He impresses the girl by winning in a touring rodeo, after its bronco busting star is taken ill. Learning that Helen is traveling next to Eldorado, he follows her. There he is told that he is the long-sought heir to Eldorado's throne. As king, he quells a revolution, turns the country into a republic, then marries Helen. Nichols spared no expense, so the settings, including a view of Nice, a Saracen tower, a throne room, and a lavish royal apartment, were as eye-filling as the gold-braided, ermine-lined outfits of Eldorado's courtiers.

The same evening ushered in the Habima Players from Moscow. Performing in Hebrew, they began their visit at the Mansfield with *The Dybbuk.* Atkinson exclaimed, "No other performance in this city has been so bold in its stylization, so daring in its treatment of details, and so skillful in evoking the latent moods of a production." The company also offered *The Eternal Jew* and *The Deluge,* which had been seen before in English-language mountings, as well as Richard Beer-Hoffman's **Jacob's Dream,** relating the biblical tale of Jacob, Esau and Rebecca, and H. Levick's **The Golem,** in which a rabbi in medieval Prague creates a monster who destroys persecuting Christians before it turns on the Jews and so must be killed. The company was slated to remain for five weeks, but attendance caused them to extend their stay to fourteen weeks (some of it at the out-of-the-way, less desirable Irving Place Theatre) and to raise their top ticket from an initially hefty $4.40 to an even heftier $5.50 on some nights. Perhaps not coincidentally, the Neighborhood Players brought back their own version of *The Dybbuk* three nights later.

Hangman's House (12-16-26, Forrest) was based on a Donn Byrne novel and was Willard Mack's fourth play of the season. It also was a one-week dud. The "hangman" was Ireland's harsh Lord Chief Justice O'Brien (Joseph Kilgour), who forces his daughter, Connaught (Katharine Alexander), to marry the mean, toping John D'Arcy (Frank Shannon), even though she loves Dermot McDermot (Walter Abel). Shortly afterward, Connaught is horrified to learn that her husband is not only betting against the horse she has entered in the derby but doing his nefarious best to see it does not win. She tells all this to McDermot, who, casting aside his promise to his mother to keep away from horses, shouts, "I'll ride the bairn!" The race was then shown with two horses on treadmills, one of them clearing "an obstacle as high as a croquet wicket." After the race D'Arcy commits suicide, and McDermot is able to plan his wedding to Connaught.

Atkinson's review of Sidney Howard's **The Silver Cord** (12-20-26, John Golden) was headlined "Craig's Mother," a marvelous dig, since instead of a house-proud woman it dealt with a child-proud one. When her architect son, David (Eliot Cabot), returns from Europe with a bride, Christina (Elisabeth Risdon), who is a smart, attractive biologist, Mrs. Phelps (Laura Hope Crews) first ignores the girl then sweetly and quietly attempts to destroy the marriage. Christina is finally provoked into calling her mother-in-law a civilized cannibal, to which Mrs. Phelps retorts, "I would cut off my hands and burn out my eyes to rid my son of you." She has better luck with her weaker son, Robert (Earle Larimore), and his fiancée, Hester (Margalo Gillmore), who is a guest in their house. She keeps at Hester until the girl, in disgust, attempts to call a cab to take her to a hotel, at which point Mrs. Phelps, worried about appearances, pulls out the phone plug. Hester then attempts to leave, but in crossing the pond just outside the home, she falls through the ice. When the men rush to rescue her, Mrs. Phelps's sole worry is that they might catch cold. Hester is saved but walks out. So do David and his wife. Left alone with Robert, Mrs. Phelps assures him there is nothing to compare with mother love. The weakling can do nothing but respond, "Yes, mother." Hailed by Burns Mantle as "a weightier and more significant study of American character [than *Ned McCobb's Daughter*]," the drama came to be perceived as the best American stage portrait of a domineering mother. It played alternate weeks with Howard's other drama, running for 130 performances.

That same evening saw a revival of *Twelfth Night* at the Civic Repertory Theatre. Eva Le Gallienne's supporting players were never quite of the first order, although they were very good. In this instance the production was enlivened by some almost surrealistic settings and costumes.

Arnold Bennett's *The Great Adventure,* which told of an artist who feigns death to escape his fawning admirers, was rejected by New Yorkers in 1913 and rejected by them again after it was brought out at the Princess on the 22nd.

Nor did Otis Skinner create any special excitement when he resurrected his 1908 vehicle, *The Honor of the Family,* at the Booth on Christmas night. His one-month stand was part of a cross-country tour, with him once more giving a bravura performance as a man who must rid his relations of parasites.

But a revival that evening at the Frolic of a more recent play, *Night Hawk,* outran the 1925 original by three weeks for a run of 144 performances.

The customary screams in the dark, strange disappearances, and a comic-relief detective helped John Floyd's **Wooden Kimono** (12-27-26, Martin Beck) play for six months. No sooner have Richard Halstead (Alden Chase), a famous mystery writer, and his detective friend, Sandock (Bennett Southard), arrived at the spooky Red Owl Tavern to investigate three recent murders there than Sandock is killed. That brings the bumbling John Dryden (Dudley Clements) on the scene to conduct his own investigation. Other characters include the innkeeper whose hobby is building coffins, which he refers to euphemistically as wooden kimonos, and a girl who turns out to be yet another detective. By curtain time the tavern is shown to be a hangout for dope smugglers, and the killer is caught.

The Padre (12-27-26, Ritz) was Stanley Logan's adaptation of André de Lorde and Pierre Chaine's *Mon curé chez les riches* and served as a vehicle for the usually unlucky Leo Carrillo. He was unlucky this time, too. Father Pellegrin's attempts to help his wartime buddies land him in hot water with both church and public officials as well as his rich parishioners until a sympathetic Cardinal takes his side.

David Belasco and his star, E. H. Sothern, were also unlucky, in their case with **What Never Dies** (12-28-26, Lyceum), which Ernest Boyd translated from an unidentified comedy by Alexander Engel. When the sixtyish Tiburtius leaves Vienna and runs off to Rome with a young Italian beauty (Rosalinde Fuller), his children and grandchildren are shocked. But his eightyish mother (Haidee Wright) squares everything once she is assured that her son is properly married.

For several months before it opened, Tom Cushing's **The Devil in the Cheese** (12-29-26, Charles Hopkins) had been boldly advertised in bright lights atop the tiny theatre. The interest built up by this sign possibly aided the play to run well into the spring. Certainly it was an oddball affair. Summoned by Father Petros (Bela Lugosi), Quigley (Robert McWade), the noted archaeologist, and his family are lifted in crane-held baskets to a monastery perched high in the Greek mountains. Quigley has brought along his daughter, Goldina (Linda Watkins), hoping her time there will make her forget her love for Jimmie Chard (Fredric March). After Quigley eats a piece of cheese which he has removed from an ancient vase he has dug up, he finds himself transported into his daughter's brain. (The whole, long second act took place in the brain.) Her fantasies include a visit with Jimmie to a South Sea island where he saves her from cannibals and a gorilla, and a presidential campaign in which she deftly bests Jimmie's rival. "Imagine a handsome man like that as President," Quigley growls, only to be assured, "It might be an agreeable change." Back in the real world Jimmie proves his worth by chasing away some Greek bandits. Quigley has no choice but to acquiesce in Goldina's marrying Jimmie. Even on the theatre's small stage Norman Bel Geddes performed wonders. For the monastery, he caught the illusion of vast heights, and, after covering the forestage with small steps, "by some dark sorcery of perspective he has indicated fabulous elevations on one side of the stage and a dizzy drop on the other." His inner head contained a revolve which allowed Goldina's fantasies to move from one place to another quickly.

Four plays opened the next evening, including two of the season's best. Paul Green's "biography of a negro," **In Abraham's Bosom** (12-30-26, Provincetown Playhouse), was set near the Turpentine Woods of eastern North Carolina. Abraham McCranie (Jules Bledsoe) has had a hard life as the son of white Colonel McCranie (L. Rufus Hill) and a black woman. His ambition is to "rise him up wid eddication" so that he might become the black man's savior and "lead 'em up out'n ignorance." Unfortunately, his all-white half-brother, the colonel's vicious son, Lonnie (H. Ben Smith), is equally determined to keep him in his place. Lonnie would close the school that Abraham wants to open, where he could teach all black youngsters to read. Abraham encounters further rebuffs on every side. Only Goldie McAllister (Rose McClendon) offers him the encouragement and affection he seeks. After losing employment for beating one of his students, he and Rosie move to the city but return after his young son (R. J. Huey) gets in trouble there. When Lonnie's tormentings become too much for him, Abraham kills him. He, in turn, is lynched by other local white men. Beautifully acted, especially by Miss McClendon, whom many considered the best black actress of her day, it was greeted with enthusiastic notices. The *Herald Tribune* hailed it as "so well-written and so well-played that even near-Southerners who applaud *Dixie* the loudest may be urged to sympathy." It had already closed when the announcement that it had won the Pulitzer Prize prompted additional performances. In all it ran for more than 200 playings, although the exact number is disputed.

· · ·

Paul Green (1894–1981) was born in Lillington, N.C., and later attended both the University of North Carolina and Cornell. His earliest efforts at playwriting appear to have been one-acters, with *The No 'Count Boy* bringing him his first real attention.

· · ·

Maurine Watkins's **Chicago** (12-30-26, Music Box) begins when Roxie Hart (Francine Larrimore), in a bedroom she should be sharing with her husband, whips out a pearl-handled revolver and shoots a lover who has just told her their affair is over. After a quick blackout, the same scene is shown with the room filled with police and newspaper reporters. One of the reporters, Jake (Charles Bickford), takes Roxie under his wing, promising to get none other than Billy Flynn to represent her and assuring her that if she plays her cards right she will not only get off but will be as famous as a movie queen. Roxie protests that she has killed a man, but Jake tells her, "What if yuh did? Ain't this Chicago? And gallant old Cook County never hung a woman yet!" Jake even consents to pose as the dead man, since the body has been taken out, and the photographers snap Roxy, leaning over the supposed body, half in tears and half trying to smile for the camera. In jail she befriends other murderers, especially the now celebrated Velma (Juliette Crosby), who killed her husband for not offering a large enough divorce settlement. Amos Hart (Charles Halton) arrives, tries to claim he is the killer, and is berated by Roxy for not paying enough to have better meals brought in to her. Flynn (Edward Ellis) enters and warns Roxy and Amos that if they cannot scrounge up $5000 he will not take the case. Roxy raises the money by selling her furniture and clothes to curious collectors. Flynn also contrives a phony history for her, so as the photographers come in again and bulbs start flashing, she tells them she is a refined girl, born in a convent. At her trial, having profited from Flynn's coaching, she is acquitted. But when Amos comes to take her home she chases him away, saying he will ruin a vaudeville career she plans. The police bring in the latest murderess, Machine-Gun-Rosie. Fearing the newcomer will grab the limelight, Roxie cajoles Rosie to pose for the photographers with her alongside. Miss Larrimore, her hair once more rumpled, was a last-minute replacement for Jeanne Eagels. Her "intense yet brittle" performance illuminated the show, which ran until spring. It later was musicalized successfully by John Kander and Fred Ebb.

Peter Glenny's **New York Exchange** (12-30-26, Klaw) opened in a nightclub run by Dallas Dinon (Lelya LeNoir), whom knowing New Yorkers took as the play's answer to Texas Guinan. She is pushing a young tenor, Ernest (Donn Cook), and begging her patrons to give "this little boy a great big hand." Having gained attention, Ernest ditches Dallas for a rising musical comedy favorite, Sally Parks (Sydney Shields), who for a time foots his bills. But along comes Mrs. Ella May Morton (Alison Skipworth), who carries him off to Paris. To his dismay, Ernest soon realizes that Mrs. Morton is not very generous. Luckily for him, Sally has come to Paris and made a name for herself. He tells Sally that the old girl has proved a "philanthropic louse" and asks her to take him back. For some reason, she does. The play managed to survive for ten and a half weeks, or ten weeks longer than the evening's fourth opening.

That calamity was Samuel Ruskin Golding's **The Black Cockatoo** (12-30-26, Comedy). While *New York Exchange* began in a nightclub, the new play ended in one. In fact, the play's title came from the name of the nightclub, where a George Olsen orchestra held forth. Its proprietress is a half-caste, Lily Chang (Anne Forrest), known unaffectionately among her employees and rivals as "the tiger girl of Singapore." When her club is padlocked, she gets an assistant D.A., Roy Beekman (James Crane), drunk and tricks him into thinking they have been married. Even though she is involved in drug smuggling along with her other activities, she and Beekman fall truly in love in time for a happy ending.

With Sidney Howard's two plays in alternate-week repertory at the John Golden, the Theatre Guild initiated the same policy—and the new year— at its home base with its mounting of **The Brothers Karamazov** (1-3-27, Guild). This version of Dostoyevsky's novel came by way of France, since the group employed Jacques Copeau and Jean Croué's adaptation in Rosalind Ivan's translation. Copeau came over to stage the work. A brilliant cast included Dudley Digges as the besotted and eventually murdered father, Alfred Lunt as Dmitri, the son wrongly accused of the crime, Lynn Fontanne as Grouchenka, Dmitri's fiancée, George Gaul as Ivan, the brother who incited the killing, Edward G. Robinson as Smerdiakov, the dim-witted, illegitimate brother who actually committed the crime, and Morris Carnovsky as the religious brother. However, the play's theme was not meat for many playgoers, so its life was relatively short.

That same night at the tiny Edith Totten Theatre a group of young players revived Henry Irving's version of Goethe's *Faust,* with Parker Fennelly (later a comedian on Fred Allen's radio programs) in the title role, Eleanor Laning as Marguerite, and Gene Lockhart as Mephisto.

Kate Horton's **Ballyhoo** (1-4-27, 49th St.) was the first of two January offerings to depict carnival life. After Starlight Lil (Minna Gombell), a carnival bronco rider, falls in love with a charming socialite, Cameron MacDonald (Eric Dressler), she decides she is not good enough for him, so attempts to alienate him by being publicly promiscuous. In response, he takes up with loose women until an accident in which both he and Lil are hurt by her rampaging horse brings them together again.

Like Horton's drama, Edwin B. Self's **Junk** (1-5-27, Garrick) lingered only a week. Ernest John (Sydney Greenstreet) is a corpulent hobo given to conversing with God, whom he calls "the old man." Coming across a sweet young girl, Nancy (Marguerite Mosier), and her seriously ill grandmother (Alice May Tuck), he connives with Nancy's sweetheart, Chick (Calvin Thomas), and a former convict (Jay Fassett) to rob a bank to get the money needed for the lady's surgery. Twenty years pass. Both women have died, and Chick has become governor. A sinister doctor (Herbert Ranson) who has stumbled on the ex-con's dying confession attempts to blackmail the governor. John, now a junkman, moving in and out of his shack, where he lives in the company of a ragged crone (Emma Dunn) and where he stores the cart he uses to collect his junk, determines to thwart the blackmailer. A shootout ensues. The doctor falls dead and John is mortally wounded. As the crone shrieks in despair, John dies while holding his hand out to the vision of Nancy he sees standing in the doorway. Dunn won applause for a convincing departure from her usually saccharine old ladies, but some critics felt Greenstreet spoke with too many Shakespearean flourishes for the tramp.

The year's first substantial hit was Howard Lindsay and Bertrand Robinson's **Tommy** (1-10-27, Gaiety). The comedy focused on the Thurber family of Peoria, Ill., who have their hearts set on seeing their daughter, Marie (Peg Entwistle), marry their nice neighbor, Tommy (William Janney). But their entreaties have rubbed the girl the wrong way, and she defiantly announces she prefers another young man, Bernard (Alan Bunce). Fortunately, Mrs. Thurber's brother, David Tuttle (Sidney Toler), lives with them. He is not a cagey politician for nothing. Like his idol, Lincoln, he often resorts to roundabout methods to get what he wants. In this instance, he seems to make Tommy appear greedy enough to prevent Mr. Thurber's selling his failing livery stable, all the while seeing to it that a fine deal is arranged. Thus he turns the family against the boy. Now that her family no longer prefers him, Marie has second thoughts. With a marriage license that Bernard has purchased, she and Tommy run off to be wed. The comedy pleased audiences for seven months.

Another young lady bored with the boy she really ought to marry was the principal figure in David Tearle and Dominick Colaizzi's **The Arabian Nightmare** (1-10-27, Cort). Mamie Marshall (Marion

Coakley) lives in Amesbury, Mass., with her spinster aunt, Caroline Twiggam (Helen Lowell). Having come under the spell of too many Valentino movies, she is tired of her Babbitt-like beau, Bobbie Mudge (Lorin Raker). So when she inherits some money, she and her aunt pack their bags and head for Arabia, where she is promptly kidnapped and thrown into a harem. Luckily for her, Bobbie is hot on her trail and rescues her by posing as an odalisque. Since the producer was a set designer, the scenery, including an Arabian palace and a harem room, was outstanding. But even with changing its title to *The Galloping Sheik,* the play mustered only a three-week stand.

Some critics were disturbed by the modern-dress version of *Ghosts* which brought Mrs. Fiske into the Mansfield the same night. Her husband had gone so far as to rework William Archer's translation by introducing contemporary slang. In a moment reminiscent of several of her bygone triumphs, the star sat with her back to the audience throughout a scene between Pastor Manders (Walter Ringham) and Engstrand (William C. Masson), only her mop of reddish hair hinting at her reactions. Theodore St. John was the highly praised Oswald.

Sacha Guitry and Yvonne Printemps, who were appearing in their Paris musical *Mozart,* also offered a few performances of Guitry's **L'Illusioniste** (1-10-27, 46th St.), in which the battle of the sexes is fought out by two people both handy with bags of tricks.

On the 12th a group headed by Georges Renavent began a series of one-act Grand Guignol–type plays at the intimate Grove Street Theatre in the Village. Good notices kept the repertory alive for sixty performances.

Another attraction in the Village received devastating notices. In Ben S. Gross's **Where's Your Husband?** (1-14-27, Greenwich Village), an uncle (Henry Lewellyn) has promised Elsie (Alice Fischer) $50,000 if he likes her husband. But on the day the uncle is supposed to arrive, the husband stalks out after a fight. Elsie calls on her friends to find a substitute, and by the time Uncle Daniel appears, two are on the scene. Then the real husband returns, making three.

Since *Ballyhoo* had usurped its title and come in first, the month's second carnival play was now called **The Barker** (1-18-27, Biltmore). Superbly written and beautifully played, Kenyon Nicholson's drama chalked up a seven-month run. Nifty Miller (Walter Huston) is a pitchman with Colonel Gowdy's Big City Show, a carnival which, despite its name, plays only backwater towns where hicks are often shortchanged unless they prove to be on the local council. Nifty has refused to wed Carrie (Eleanor Williams), a hootchie-cootchie dancer, since he wants to use his little spare cash to put his son through law school. Carrie is bitter. Then Chris (Norman Foster), the son, shows up asking his father to allow him to work with the carnival for the summer. Nifty is reluctant but finally consents. However, when he catches Carrie allowing Chris to drink her bootleg liquor, he explodes, even though Carrie reminds him that he himself is a lush. To be revenged, Carrie offers Lou (Claudette Colbert) $100 to vamp the boy. Lou is also bitter, having been cast off by none other than Colonel Gowdy (George Barbier). Although she tells Carrie, "I got *my* belly full of this kind of life," she agrees, since she is broke. Within a week Chris and Lou have fallen genuinely in love, and when Nifty learns that Chris has been smitten by the "crummiest broad in the outfit," he punches his son, knocking him unconscious. Chris and Lou run off to be married, then head out. Nifty fires Carrie and quits the show, blaming it for all his problems. But then he watches his replacement haltingly attempt Nifty's old spiel and learns that Lou has taken work while Chris is spending the rest of the summer in a law office, so he reconsiders. Some reviewers questioned how the supposedly educated Chris could say things such as "Well, shucks, I don't know's I could be a lawyer, even if I did go to all them colleges." But for the most part they fell in line with Woollcott, who deemed the show "endlessly entertaining" and confessed that he "enjoyed every moment of it." Huston was hailed as "a really great actor . . . living the ballyhooer and show manager."

William Francis Dugan's **The Virgin Man** (1-18-27, Princess) was an Americanization of H. F. Maltby's London comedy *Three Birds.* A young man (Don Dillaway) from Yale comes to New York, where his guardian's wife, her friend, and his host's maid all try, unavailing, to seduce him. The next afternoon, another London play, Isabel Kemp's **Courage** (1-19-27, Princess), began a series of matinee performances at the same house. It told of a tragic triangle between an African explorer, the ghost of his dead mistress, and his deserted wife. Critics noted that stagehands were kept busy since a version of *Snow White and the Seven Dwarfs* was being presented for children in the mornings.

Anne Nichols added to her string of failed productions with **Sam Abramovitch** (1-19-27, National), derived by Charlton Andrews from François Porché's *La Race errante.* It told of a Russian immigrant (Pedro de Cordoba) who becomes rich, loses his money through the treachery of a partner

(Arthur Hohl), but determines to start all over again.

Another superb performance by Alice Brady failed to inject much life into Laetitia McDonald's talky **Lady Alone** (1-20-27, Forrest). Nina Hopkins, hard up for cash, considers a proposal from a kind, much older widower (Joseph Kilgour) but rejects it, since she clings to the hope that another man (Austin Fairman) will divorce his wife and marry her. When he backs away from his promise, she swallows an overdose of sleep medicine.

A doomed young man was the subject of William Gaston's **Damn the Tears** (1-21-27, Garrick), which told of the fall of a baseball player (Ralph Morgan) from stardom to vagrancy. Film clips, radio broadcasts, puppets as cheerleaders, and a Norman Bel Geddes panorama of a grandstand filled with mannequins whose arms waved excitedly were the drama's most interesting features.

By contrast, two real rotters find a happy ending in Martin Brown's **Praying Curve** (1-24-27, Eltinge). Daisy Bell (Florence Rittenhouse) is a shoplifter and a gin-joint souse, who has been corresponding with a reformed dope fiend. To escape the advances of a brutish rumrunner (Walter Connolly), she and her streetwalking friend (Grace Huff) head for Praying Curve, where her correspondent lives. There she discovers that the man she was writing to has long died, and his place has been taken by a recovering alcoholic, Angel (Frank M. Thomas). She hurries off, but her train is wrecked, and Angel's bravery in helping the injured travelers prompts Daisy Bell to reconsider. Like *The Arabian Nightmare*, the play quickly changed its title—to *The Love Thief*. The change did not save the show.

Eva Le Gallienne's Civic Repertory won kudos when it revived Gregorio and Maria Martínez Sierra's largely adramatic story of nuns and the foundling they adopt, *The Cradle Song,* on the same night. John Garrett Underhill's translation was employed.

Maxwell Anderson's still uncertain reputation received a marked boost with **Saturday's Children** (1-26-27, Booth). Mantle deemed this look at "home life among the native middle class, an amusing exposure of human and familiar weaknesses touched with an individuality in characterization that sets it apart from the common run of plays of its type." Percy Hammond of the *Herald Tribune* lauded the "hushed little comedy" and "the quiet speed with which it tells its story." Although feisty Bobby Halevy (Ruth Gordon) insists she will not employ any of the tricks her manipulative sister (Ruth Hammond) suggests she use to snare Rims O'Neil

(Roger Pryor), she resorts to several of them to wangle a proposal from him. But married life proves difficult for them, with money troubles arising from Rims's insistence that she quit her job and allow him to be the sole breadwinner, and from his playing cards with his buddies. She tells him, "I think all day how marvellous it's going to be when you come home—and then you get here—and I don't know—it isn't marvellous at all." Fights and making up follow one after the other until Rims, in a fury, storms out. Bobby takes a room at a boardinghouse run by a suspicious landlady (Beulah Bondi). Rims comes there, only to discover that Bobby's boss, whom she has been dating, has sent her not merely flowers but a bolt to place on her door so that the landlady cannot snoop. The youngsters' conversation suggests that they still love each other, but the landlady chases Rims off when the hour turns late. A forlorn Bobby starts to get ready for bed. She has no sooner doused the lights than Rims climbs in through the window by the fire escape. In a happy, whispered exchange, the two start to fit the bolt against the door. With Gordon doing "her best acting in years," the comedy ran for more than nine months. Humphrey Bogart replaced Pryor during the run.

Willard Mack's fifth play of the season, **Honor Be Damned!** (1-26-27, Morosco), had to be content with a little more than one month. John Connell (Mack) has risen from the slums to become a famous lawyer, but he remains loyal to his old cronies, who are, for the most part, slum politicians, gamblers, and crooks. He regularly defends them successfully in court, even when he knows they are guilty. He only asks that they stay away from his mother and his sister, Mary (Lizzie McCall). So he is prepared to defend Lou Buckley (Carl Gerard), until he learns that Lou has seduced his sister. He reads his buddies the riot act. They turn against Lou. At the same time, John is informed that Mary will marry, with her seduction not standing in her way. Only then does John proceed to manufacture the evidence that can acquit Lou.

For the third time in recent weeks, a play attempted to save itself from failure by changing its name following its opening. Once again, the ploy did not work. In this case, David Arnold Balch's **The Scarlet Lily** (1-29-27, Comedy) became *The Red Lily*. Soon after Elmer Strong (Malcolm Fassett) returns to his Vermont home from fighting in France and introduces his French bride, Marcelle (Marguerite Risser), he and his family are told by a neighbor (Edwin Redding) that Marcelle had been a common prostitute. Marcelle confesses, but her contrition leads to a happy ending.

The month ended with two notable successes. One was **The Road to Rome** (1-31-27, Playhouse). Although her pompous, impotent husband, Fabius Maxius (Richie Ling), has just been made Dictator of Rome, Amytis (Jane Cowl) is more interested in the peacock green silk gown she has just bought from an Antioch merchant. She sighs that her husband cares little about lovely, fun-filled things in life. He concedes that respectability, modesty, economy, devotion to duty, and the like are what really count. To which Amytis adds, mediocrity. Nor is she concerned about Hannibal's alarming victories over the Romans. In fact, to her husband's astonishment, she has never heard of Hannibal. Just then a soldier hurries in to announce a Roman rout and the news that Hannibal is at Rome's gates. While the others make plans for a last-ditch, possibly suicidal stand, Amytis tells her husband that she is going to visit her mother, who lives a safe distance from the city. Only her mother-in-law (Jessie Ralph) notices something odd about her departure—she is wearing her peacock green gown. Shortly thereafter, Amytis, claiming she has lost her way, is brought before Hannibal (Philip Merivale), who orders her executed as a spy. But she begs a few moments to speak with him alone. She questions him on his purpose in life, which seems only to win bloody wars, a medal or two, and possibly a statue of himself after he is dead. Has he not ever thought of the human equation? She finally gets him to admit, "For ten years I've followed the road that leads to Rome—and it's a hard road to travel, Amytis. It's littered with the bones of dead men. Perhaps they know why they died. I don't." Her soft words and her beauty finally compel the warrior to seize her and kiss her. The next morning he tells a delegation from Rome and his own troops that he has had a portent from a goddess and been warned to turn back. He hands Amytis over to Fabius, a member of the delegation, telling him that he hopes the son Fabius may someday have will be as much a man as "his father." Of course, Fabius misconstrues the words, and the Romans leave smug in the knowledge that Roman superiority has prevailed again. Not only was Miss Cowl applauded for her "shining artistry," but the play was effusively welcomed, with Charles Brackett of the *New Yorker* calling it "A hymn of hate against militarism—disguised, ever so gaily, as a love song." Its year-long run was an auspicious debut for Robert Sherwood.

. . .

Robert E[mmet] Sherwood (1896–1955) was born in New Rochelle, N.Y. He studied at Harvard, where he was active on the *Lampoon,* which his father had helped found, and with the Hasty Pudding Club. He took Professor George Pierce Baker's course in theatre history but did not enroll in his playwriting course. After fighting in World War I with the Canadian Black Watch, a group where his 6'6" height gave no difficulties, he grew disillusioned with the governments that had allowed the carnage. Subsequently, he served in various capacities at *Vanity Fair, Life,* and *Scribner's,* and also as one of the earliest serious critics of films, before this play was produced.

. . .

Three other novelties, all failures, opened in competition with Sherwood's comedy. They ran three weeks, two weeks, and one week, respectively. Michael Kalleser's **Trial Marriage** (1-31-27, Wallack's) was conceived as a sequel of sorts to the author's *One Man's Woman* and had tried out as *Any Man's Woman.* After Peggy Hall (Grace Valentine) and Dick Saunders (Howard St. John) call a halt to their trial marriage, Jack Wales (G. Pat Collins) attempts to lure her into prostitution. She shoots him for his pains but does not kill him. Still, when Dick returns and learns about Jack, he decides not to resume the relationship. Years later, Dick, a married man, visits Peggy, but during the visit, Jack, now a hophead, enters through a window, shoots and kills the woman, and runs off, leaving Dick to explain matters to the police when they come.

The two-weeker was Allen de Lano's **For Better or Worse** (1-31-27, Mansfield). A spoiled, college-educated young man (Tom Powers) is forced to wed a pregnant serving girl (Gladys Hurlbut), but the disparities in their backgrounds—with his spouting high-minded, socialistic platitudes and her thinking mostly about films and film stars—drive them apart. Somehow, her claim that he is not the child's father brings about a reconciliation.

John Tucker Battle and William J. Perlman's **The Bottom of the Cup** (1-31-27, Mayfair) echoed *In Abraham's Bosom* in some ways. A Negro (Daniel L. Haynes), sent north by the colonel whose family his own family had worked for, returns home hoping to set up a college for blacks. His plans go awry after his brother (George W. Nixon) is involved in a bank robbery and then killed by an accomplice. Pretending to be his brother, he is lynched by a white mob.

The evening's fifth premiere was George C. Tyler's revival of *Trelawny of the Wells* at the New Amsterdam. Inspired by the success two seasons earlier of the Players' mounting of the piece, its all-star cast retained several performers from that production, including John Drew as Sir William

Gower, Mrs. Whiffen as Mrs. Mossop, and O. P. Heggie as Mr. Albett. Newcomers included Wilton Lackaye and Henrietta Crosman as the Telfers, Otto Kruger as Colpoys, John E. Kellerd as Gadd, Rollo Peters as Tom Wrench, Eric Dressler as Arthur, Estelle Winwood as Avonia Bunn, Pauline Lord as Imogen Parrott, Effie Shannon as Mrs. Gower, and Helen Gahagan in the title role. Showered with encomiums, the revival did fine business for seven weeks, after which it went on tour. Drew was singled out for some of the best notices, which mentioned the extended applause he received when he made his first appearance from behind a newspaper covering his face during an after-dinner nap. For all his brilliant company, he "came as near to running away with the honors as was possible," speaking condescendingly to his grandson, flinging his cards up in annoyance, or barking at Rose, who has sat on the floor, "Have we no cheers? Trafalgy, have we no cheers?" But during the tour (which saw some major replacements) Drew took ill, left the cast, and died shortly thereafter.

February was as busy as the preceding months but was virtually devoid of artistic interest. Its first novelty, Martin Brown's **The Dark** (2-1-27, Lyceum), prefigured the lackluster weeks ahead. An inventor, Chris Landers (Louis Calhern), is blinded and scarred after a new electric tube he is working on explodes. His wife (Ann Andrews) has never been completely faithful, and she has a phobia about ugliness, so, with the heightened sense of hearing that follows his loss of sight, he comprehends that he is losing her. He forces her to confess, then pulls off the mask that has covered his face. But instead of sickening her, the sight of his empty eye sockets moves her to compassion.

The Wandering Jew was revived that night at the Cosmopolitan, with Matheson Lang in the role Tyrone Power had performed five seasons before.

Few people thought much of Francis Edwards Faragoh's expressionistic view of lower-middle-class seediness, **Pinwheel** (2-3-27, Neighborhood Playhouse). The Jane (Dorothy Sands), a loose-moraled stenographer, tricks the Bookkeeper (Albert Carroll) into marrying her, lets herself be seduced by the Guy (Marc Loebell), and "in general she misbehaves shamefully." Sands, who was onstage the entire time, won praise for her admirable performance. However, Donald Oenslager's scenery and costumes usurped paragraphs of attention. His "constructivist" setting, a "steel-like construction with two stage levels and flights of steps," served for all sixteen scenes. Clever lighting, slightly grotesque costumes, and superbly recreated city noises—horns

honking, a creaky carousel in operation, distant jazz music—furthered the play's illusions.

Thompson Buchanan, now spending most of his time writing for Hollywood, returned east with **Sinner** (2-7-27, Klaw) and scored a modest hit. After living with Tom Page (Alan Dinehart) before his divorce, Cynthia Pemberton (Claiborne Foster) at first refuses to marry him once he is free. Then, in an ugly incident at a roadhouse where she has come with Tom, she discovers her sister-in-law (Vera Allen) with another man. The elder Pembertons show up, and the woman claims that she and the man are there to attend Cynthia and Tom's wedding. To avoid troubles Cynthia marries Tom. But she soon is having an affair with the artist (Hugh Huntley) who once painted her in a picture he called *The Sinner*. She tells Tom she wants out, so he slugs her into submission.

John Willard, the author of *The Cat and the Canary,* had a near miss with **Fog** (2-7-27, National) at the same theatre where his earlier success had played. An odd assortment of men, and one woman, are invited to a decrepit yacht moored to a deserted dock on Long Island. Their host is nowhere in sight, and the ship is lorded over by a huge, glowering black man, who sports one large earring and is able only to grunt and point. Before they realize it, the ship is out at sea, and one by one the men fall overboard, screaming. One of the guests is finally unmasked as the demented host.

After a fourteen-year absence, Mrs. Patrick Campbell made an ill-judged return to the New York stage in Frederick Witney's **The Adventurous Age** (2-7-27, Mansfield). Some ungentlemanly critics observed that the star had lost her looks and figure, but many felt she had not lost all of her old fire. Still, there was little she could do to save this story of a middle-aged couple who attempt romances with their children's prospective spouses.

Martin Brown's third play and third Broadway flop of the season (a fourth play folded out of town) was **The Strawberry Blonde** (2-7-27, Bijou). Herbie Salute (George Anderson) is the redheaded Sheik of Steinway Avenue in Astoria, a happily married man dutifully stashing away his racetrack winnings to save for a nice little home in Flatbush. But the Salutes' more or less peaceful world is shattered after three redheaded babies are born to women in neighboring apartments and all fingers point to Herbie. However, it eventually is shown that the culprit is meek Adolf Linkworthy (Frank Howson), whose wife (Frances Victory) complains that months have passed since "Adolf looked cockeyed at me." First-nighters could have known that Herbie was innocent when the actor's red wig came off accidentally.

The basic plot of Arthur Caesar's quick flop, **Off Key** (2-8-27, Belmont), paralleled that of *Sinner*. A wife (Florence Eldridge) fails to tells her husband (McKay Morris) about an old affair, takes up again with her former beau (Kenneth Hunter), and is cured of her wandering by some rough treatment.

The title figure (Claude Rains) of Henry Stillman's **Lally** (2-8-27, Greenwich Village) is a widower and a genius, a fine conductor and composer who lives with his illegitimate son, Stravinski, and his three daughters, Elsa, Isolde, and Brunhilde. Having reached the end of his affair with his mistress (Zola Talma), he finds he lacks the inspiration to finish his new opera. Just then a delegation from Boston call on him, asking him to become the conductor of their symphony orchestra. Among the group is Judith Montifiori (Anne Morrison), and she provides the needed inspiration. However, once the opera is finished, she leaves him.

The story of Dorothy Manley and Donald Duff's **Stigma** (2-10-27, Cherry Lane) raised some hackles among New York's critics. An unhappily married professor's wife (Joanna Roos) in a southern college lusts for the bright and attractive young student (Duff) who boards with them. But he is a dangerously outspoken advocate of miscegenation. She goes mad on learning her black maid (Doralyne Spence) is carrying his baby.

Sybil Thorndike and Lewis Casson had starred in Clemence Dane's **Granite** (2-11-27, American Laboratory) in London, but the American Laboratory Theatre's less noted players failed to inject the requisite tragic nobility into this story of a woman who lives a lonely existence on a rocky, isolated island and who, after her first two, cruel husbands are killed by a Nameless Man, recognizes that her life with him will be no better. Like the Civic Repertory Theatre, albeit at a much smaller house, the group asked only a $1.50 top, so its shows could run a little while thanks to price-conscious playgoers.

Three performances were all that Walter Elwood's **Spellbound** (2-15-27, Klaw) was able to muster. A mother, obsessed with temperance ideals, drugs her sons' coffee, believing the drug will keep them from becoming alcoholics. Instead one becomes mute, the other paralyzed. She runs off, ostensibly to do missionary work, but returns eighteen years later, patently demented.

Larry E. Johnson's **What Ann Brought Home** (2-21-27, Wallack's) ran twelve weeks largely because it proved, as *Variety* had predicted, "a great Leblang and 2-4-1 entry." What Ann (Mayo Methot) brought to her Bennet's Mills, Ind., home after a shopping trip in the city was a husband, Dudley Purdy (William Hanley). Her family turns up its nose at such an obvious nonentity until he carries out the biggest real estate coup in the village's history.

With *The Captive* forcibly closed, the theatre where it had prospered was given over to Edward E. Paramore's **Set a Thief** (2-21-27, Empire). Because he is being blackmailed by a notorious gang of ex-convicts who sign their notes S.Q.V., a young banker, Walter Martson (Calvin Thomas), plans to steal bonds from his own bank. His querulous but shrewd aunt, Mrs. Dowling (Margaret Wycherly), has other ideas, and she uncovers the man (James Spottswood) behind the blackmailing. However, before she can do that, mysterious green hands are seen at the French windows of Marston's elegant library, bookcases move to disclose secret vaults, and two men are found murdered, with S.Q.V. tattooed on their foreheads.

Olga Printzlau's **Window Panes** (2-21-27, Mansfield) was set in a primitive Russian village where most of the townspeople have gone to church after hearing that the second coming of Christ is imminent. Marya (Eileen Huban) is left behind with her mute little son (Cathryn Randolph). A tattered beggar (Henry Herbert) appears, and after Marya gives him something to eat he washes her windows so that the light will come through. He says the boy needs only to have light in his mind and that the child can will himself to speak. The boy does just that. Marya is grateful, but her husband, Artem (Charles Dalton), spotting a mark on the beggar, recognizes him as a wanted man and kills him for the thirty-ruble reward offered. Then he is informed that the man was placed on the wanted list by mistake and is ostracized by his neighbors, so he commits suicide.

Many of the best critics elected to attend what proved to be the shortest-lived of all the evening's openings, Dorrance Davis's stab at writing a modern-day Restoration comedy, **A Lady in Love** (2-21-27, Lyceum). Clarissa (Peggy Wood) married the crabbed, much older Sir Barnaby (Rollo Lloyd) because he saved her father from debtors' prison. Her gallant lover, Bragdon (Gavin Gordon), was off at the wars. Now he has returned, and their former passions remain undiminished. She invites him to her house, and, after the jealous Barnaby has had the younger man set upon, she tricks her husband into thinking Bragdon has been slain. She also suggests that if left alone with the corpse she may been able to bring it back to life, so that Barnaby will not be prosecuted. The lovers are thus able to spend the night together and to plan for Clarissa's divorce. Views of Sir Barnaby's living room and gardens, and the Stag's Head Inn (clearly in this season the play's answer to the modern nightclub), attractive 1680 costumes, and dialogue sprinkled with the likes of "Zounds, girl!" and "Odd's life" were unable to spark a leaden comedy. However, Miss Wood garnered praise for her charm, and hefty Sydney Greenstreet earned applause as a Restoration fop who turns aside to the audience at a particularly malicious moment to observe, "Here's fun!"

The month's longest run—if 186 performances can be considered long—went to Samuel Shipman and John B. Hymer's **Crime** (2-22-27, Eltinge). That was a far cry from the success they had enjoyed with *East Is West.* Annabelle (Sylvia Sidney) and Tommy (Douglass Montgomery), out for a stroll in Central Park, are held up and robbed of the $130 they had saved toward a wedding. An angry Tommy vows to get the money back from the robbers. At a gang member's Riverside Drive apartment where they have ventured to retrieve their savings, the youngsters are held at gunpoint and forced to join in a robbery. The leader of the gang is polished Gene Fenmore (James Rennie), who operates by his own code of ethics, and their next objective is Goldberg's Jewelry Store. A more mercurial, gum-chewing hood, Rocky Morse (Chester Morris), shoots the fat jeweler during the holdup. Back at his apartment, Fenmore kills Morse for violating his code. This angers the rest of the gang, and at a meeting at the Hellsden Club (nightclubs were truly in vogue this season) they put Fenmore on trial. He shows them that Morse was pilfering the gang's funds and underscores how successful they have been under his leadership, so, as one of the hoods tell him, he is acquitted by a "synonomous" vote. However, Fenmore's mistress (Kay Johnson), who was having an affair on the side with Morse, squeals to the police. Not only Fenmore but Annabelle and Tommy face the electric chair. Self-sacrificingly, Fenmore exculpates the youngsters and puts all the blame on himself. Rennie's suavity and the youngsters' charm served as excellent foils for the snarling gang members.

In Pirandello's **Right You Are If You Think You Are** [*Cosí é (se vi pare)*] (2-23-27, Guild) Ponza (Edward G. Robinson) keeps his mother-in-law (Beryl Mercer) and his wife (Armina Marshall) in separate apartments. He tells snooping neighbors that his mother-in-law is a bit crazy, that her daughter died and his current wife is his second. The mother-in-law insists that Ponza is mad, that he believes his wife has died and that he has remarried

but reallly has been wed only once. The neighbors approach the veiled wife, who suggests that certain things must be left unsaid. She admits only that the mother-in-law is her mother and that she is Ponza's second wife. Who's crazy? The superior cast and Jo Mielziner's austerely simple setting added to the play's appeal. Its low cost—$1500—allowed the Guild to make a handsome profit. No translator was given credit.

A second Italian play, Pier Maria Rosso di San Secondo's expressionistic **Puppets of Passion** (2-24-27, Masque), in a translation by Ernest Boyd and Eduardo Ciannelli, found no favor, though it remains a classic in its homeland. The Gentleman in Gray (Frank Morgan), The Gentleman in Mourning (Manart Kippen), and The Lady in the Blue Fox Fur (Rose Hobart) meet in a telegraph office, where they intend to send messages to lovers they believe have betrayed them. Then the man in gray drinks poison, the woman learns her husband still wants her, and the other man remains to wonder what life and love are all about. The play was the first attraction at the Masque (for many years now the Golden), which the Chanins built to house experimental works.

Another dud was E. D. Thomas's **Babbling Brookes** (2-25-27, Edyth Totten), which scuttlebutt said was actually by its director and star, Edyth Totten. It told of the Brooke family which, in the early nineteenth-century, owned much of Long Island. After one member betrays an Indian princess she places a curse on the clan. The family struggles unsuccessfully to maintain its estates through the years (1847, 1867, 1890, 1923, and 1927) until one member, a lady lawyer, settles matters.

The star and director of **Money from Home** (2-28-27, Fulton) was also its author, Frank Craven. He played Doc Durham, a physician turned con artist. When Jennie Patrick (Shirley Warde), a small-town waitress and the niece and ward of the cranky village scold, inherits a few thousand dollars on her twenty-first birthday she heads for New York and a good time. Durham, thinking she is a millionaire, sets out to relieve her of her riches. Before long the pair have fallen in love, but Jennie, convinced she has deceived Durham, tells him the truth about herself. He blithely assumes that she is now conning him. They return to Falls Creek, Pa., where he is dismayed to discover not everyone is a con artist. He would run off, but a mill explosion brings out the best in him. He decides to reform and settle down. His brazen character was a change of pace for Craven, who had usually portrayed hangdog, picked-on figures. *Variety,* which regularly took a cold, hard look at all new plays, suggested it hadn't much chance and that it was "a little prototype of the clean play—the sort that used to run a season some ten seasons ago" and that it would not be able to hold its own against "the high-power and high-voltage sex, crime, intrigue, spectacle and nudity banquets" of the day. It proved right. But all during the season, the tradesheet had also suggested that several plays, some wittingly, some not, would make money on the sale of film rights. Film rights were becoming a major consideration for producers, who, according to the paper, had started to mount certain obvious bombs simply for their potential movie money. Whether *Money from Home* was saved by a film sale is unknown.

A number of critics saw Knud Wiberg and Marcel Strauss's **We All Do** (2-28-27, Bijou) as an inept rehashing of the basic theme of *The Constant Wife*. Aware that her own husband (Charles Richman) is having an affair with a countess (Kathryn Givney), Pauline Chester (Ann Shoemaker) is startled to learn that the lovers oppose the marriage of the Chesters' daughter (Virginia Williams) to the countess's son (Herbert Clark). She helps the youngsters by threatening a scandal, then runs off to divorce her husband and marry an old flame. Critics were baffled by Richman's stuttering and frequently repeating his lines. They asked if he was egregiously misdirected. Or perhaps he was too concerned about his having to file for bankruptcy immediately after the opening.

Another constructivist set—"Stairways run up and down with goodnatured abandon; chutes lead on and off on either side; doors, windows, desks, divans, a fireplace, a safe, a trusty musket and a screen complete the whirligig stage fittings"—was a principal attraction in John Howard Lawson's **Loud Speaker** (3-2-27, 52nd St.). And as with *Pinwheel,* sounds from a jazz band underscored the story. That story, the critics complained, wasn't much. Despite the desertion of his wife (Margaret Douglass), the public rebellion of his daughter (Agnes Lumbard), and the revelation that he has been making whoopee with Miss New Lots (Reba Garden), a beauty contest winner, Harry U. Collins (Seth Kendall) persists in running for governor. Finally fed up with the whole affair, he takes to the radio, telling his listeners not only that newspapers and the government are "blah" (a foreshadowing of Stuart Chase's best-seller, *The Tyranny of Words*) but that they themselves can go to hell. The public finds his candor so refreshing that Collins is elected. Several songs larded the action, with one new face, Leonard Sillman, doing a mean black bottom to accompany

the most lilting number. The play was produced by a group of young writers (Em Jo Basshe, John Dos Passos, Francis Edwards Faragoh, Michael Gold, and John Howard Lawson) calling themselves the New Playwrights Theatre. They promised more novelties shortly.

An array of critical pans helped to close Zoë Akins's dissuadingly titled **Thou Desperate Pilot** (3-7-27, Morosco) after a single week. Woollcott, in one of the kinder notices, warned his followers it was "a strange mixture of beautiful letters, fine theatre and red plush pomposity." It is set on the Riviera, where its heroine, Zelda (Miriam Hopkins), loves two men. The wealthy man (Charles Henderson) she agrees to marry quickly drinks himself to death. The English lord (David Hawthorne) she had spurned then spurns her, so she plunges into the sea and drowns.

Many of the same critics who found little to like in Lawson's and Miss Akins's plays also wondered aloud why Eva Le Gallienne elected to revive Susan Glaspell's 1921 drama, *The Inheritors,* at the Civic Repertory on the 7th. But Miss Le Gallienne kept the play on her programs virtually as long as the organization survived.

Backcountry religion took over Broadway for the next two nights. Devil Ace Gibson (Louis Bennison), one of the three pivotal figures in George Scarborough and Annette Westbay's **The Heaven Tappers** (3-8-27, Forrest), runs a lucrative moonshining operation in the Blue Ridge Mountains. He is a ruthless man. A detective who wanders into his territory is given a draft of wood alcohol, goes blind within minutes, and after being set on a trail can be heard shrieking as he falls off a cliff. David "Parson" Calvin (Charles Waldron), newly out of the penitentiary, decides to horn in on Gibson's work. He and his girl, Red Belwyn (Margaret Lawrence), appear at Gibson's shack, dressed in long white biblical robes and posing as prophets. Before long, Gibson has fallen for Red's blandishments and she herself has come to accept her own preachments. Calvin is left dry, but not high. Aisle-sitters suggested that the performers, especially Lawrence, were ill at ease with their backwoods twangs. When the play soon closed, Bennison ("of the expansive teeth and French-Canadian accent"), who a little over a decade earlier had made such a sensational New York debut, took the lead in the West Coast company of *The Barker* and never again performed in New York before his early death.

The New Playwrights Theatre added a second play to its promised repertory with Em Jo Basshe's **Earth** (3-9-27, 52nd St.). Deborah (Inez Clough), a backwoods Negro in the 1880s, turns against both her Christian god and her voodoo spirits after she loses all her babies and the gods she worships refuse to at least bring one of them, her favorite boy, back to life. To make matters worse, a huge fire devastates much of the countryside. Deborah comes to a mountain revival meeting where a blind preacher, Brother Elijah (Daniel L. Haynes), is holding forth. He seizes on her as the sinner who has brought such catastrophe on herself and her neighbors, and she is lynched. For many the most moving moments were the singing of tradional black hymns, such as "The Time Has Come" and "Count Your Sins, Sinnin' Sister," under the direction of Hall Johnson.

Gustav Blum, a producer who, by resorting to cut-rate tickets, had defied critical shellackings to earn profitable runs for such cheap-to-mount, cheap-to-run shows as *Gertie* and *My Son,* did the same with Edgar M. Schoenberg and Milton Silver's **The Mystery Ship** (3-14-27, Garrick). The detective who sets out to uncover the murder of a man aboard a liner heading for Europe finds that no murder has been committed. The whole thing was an insurance fraud. As usual, most critics enjoyed listing the clichés sprinkled throughout the show, one itemizing "the gun shot in the dark, the hands from nowhere, the grisly laugh, the ghastly groan."

Arthur M. Brilant's **Menace** (3-14-27, 49th St.) was perceived as a modern-day *Madame Butterfly.* Setsu (Eva Casanova), a graduate of Smith College, lives on an isolated Japanese island and offers shelter there to Lattimer (Jack Roseleigh), who has escaped from an American prison where he had been confined for killing a man who had violated his sister. He is a gifted painter and, like Setsu, well educated. Their idyll ends when the prison warden (Alan Ramsay) and by his daughter (Pauline MacLean) appear on the island in their search for Lattimer. It is clear that the daughter and Lattimer are in love. Setsu's samurai relations would kill the Americans, but she prevails on them to permit the whites to escape. She then commits suicide. No Puccini emerged to give this dud immortality.

Louis Mann and Clara Lipman offered what proved to be their last Broadway performances in Samuel Shipman and Neil Twomey's **That French Lady** (3-15-27, Ritz). Karl Kraft, still staunchly pro-German, has never quite forgiven his son, Fred (Robert Williams), for fighting in the A.E.F. Now he is appalled when Fred brings home an older French lady, whom Kraft assumes to be the boy's mistress. It turns out she is merely his mother-in-law, come for an advance view of the family her daughter will be joining. Ethnic differences explode, such as

when Kraft proclaims, "Frenchmen do things to ladies that I would not even think about," but the disputes finally are settled amicably. Mann's followers expected to see his "dialectic tantrums." They did, but his followers no longer were numerous enough to give the show a run.

Hatcher Hughes received scathing notices for his farce **Honeymooning** (3-17-27, Bijou). A young couple (Lorin Raker and Marie Louise Dana), about to set out on their honeymoon, learn that they are not legally married. In the contretemps that ensue a spiritualist (LeRoi Operti) attempts to intervene, and at one point the husband, pretending to be dead, sits up in his coffin to hurl flowerpots and spray soda water.

Her fiery temperament having lost her the lead in *Chicago,* Jeanne Eagels at least enjoyed one small hit before her early death. **Her Cardboard Lover** (3-21-27, Empire) was Valerie Wyngate and P. G. Wodehouse's adaptation of Jacques Deval's *Dans sa candeur naïve.* Its story was simplicity itself. Simone, fearing she still loves the husband she has divorced, hires André (Leslie Howard), a broke young gambler, to keep her away from him. André is so charming and forceful that she soon cares only for him. Abandoning the raspy voice she had employed as Sadie Thompson, Miss Eagels spoke with "a melodious, almost baby-talk vocal ingenuousity," and her blonde beauty was more elegantly ravishing than ever. An extended monologue on the phone, while sitting on the edge of her bed, brought down the house, and, as one first-nighter reported, the ovation she later received "was such as rarely has been adventured in a modern playhouse. For 10 minutes the salvos, the cheers and the bravos rang against the respectable rafters of the staid Empire." Howard also won kudos. But the play, plagued by Miss Eagels's drinking and drug problems, ran for only nineteen weeks. A subsequent road trip had to be shortened when her problems worsened.

At the Tivoli, a vaudeville house, the overture is followed by some film clips and then by a slick roller-skating act and by two black-faced dancers ("The Chocolate Cake-Eaters"). The next act is that of Chatrand the Great (John Halliday), a magician. After performing feats of legerdemain, he begins his mind-reading turn by introducing Alexander (Roy Hargrave), a masked young man whom he had found wandering dazedly in the streets of Washington and took on to prevent the boy's being institutionalized. He adds, "I keep him masked because I am afraid that some evening my performance will be interrupted by someone in the audience recognizing this lost boy—perhaps his mother, his father, or his sweetheart." But he also promises to remove the mask after the performance. He then proceeds to have the boy identify objects members of the audience offer but which the boy, of course, cannot see. One young lady (Eleanor Griffith) hands the magician a necklace. The man with her tries to stop her, the lights go out, a shot is heard, and when they go on again the man is seen to be mortally wounded. Thus began Fulton Oursler and Lowell Brentano's **The Spider** (3-22-27, 46th St.). A doctor (Arthur Stuart Hull) in the audience offers to tend to the dying man, and two men offer to rush him to the hospital. But the man dies, shot, the doctor states, from the stage. It develops that Alexander is the brother of the girl with the necklace and that the dead man was his guardian, from whom he fled after the guardian attempted to kill him. The two men who offered to ride to the hospital turn out to be hoods, and they reveal that the necklace was to be used that evening as a signal for a major dope deal. The dead man was a higher-up in the gang, but no one knows who the leader is. Chatrand suggests that he knows and that the man is still in the theatre, since no one has been allowed to leave. (Actors dressed as police pretended to restrain the audience from leaving during intermissions.) Chatrand convinces the police to allow him to restage the mind-reading turn in order to catch the head man and killer. He does, and the man is shown to be the doctor. He then tells the audience that it can leave. But he suggests that the girl, whose picture he had found on Alexander and with whom he has fallen in love, remain. George Jean Nathan spoke for many of his colleagues when he commented that as a play *The Spider* was worthless, "but as a show it is excellent." It ran for more than nine months.

Zoë Akins's second play of the month was **The Crown Prince** (3-23-27, Forrest), which she adapted faithfully from Ernö Vajda's drama. It was the latest attempt to explain the incidents at Mayerling, when the heir apparent to the Austrian throne and his mistress were found dead under never truly explained circumstances. In this version the emperor (Henry Stephenson) promises the mistress (Mary Ellis) that she could be his queen if she poisons the prince (Basil Sydney). She does poison him, then drinks more of the poison herself.

Like many other players, Louis Calhern jumped from flop to flop during the season. In Harry L. Foster and Wynn Proctor's **Savages Under the Skin** (3-24-27, Greenwich Village) he played Francis Xavier O'Rourke, the vengeful son of a missionary slain by the natives, who seizes Saba Saba and establishes himself as dictator. Aided by the Reverend Brown (William B. Mack), a native prince, Hadi (Clay Clement), returns from college and initiates a successful rebellion. But O'Rourke regathers his forces, invades the island, and winds up once again the boss. As usual in such plays, hula dancing and ukulele music were interspersed.

Another ill-starred player this year was Pauline Lord. She was cast as the low-bred, suspicious wife of a high-minded clergyman (Arthur Wontner) in Clemence Dane's **Mariners** (3-28-27, Plymouth). He catches influenza and dies after she locks him out on a rainy night. The neighbors then find her dead on his grave. For all her bad luck, Miss Lord was voted actress of the year by New York drama critics for her performances in her two failures.

A. E. Thomas and George Agnew Chamberlain's **Lost** (3-28-27, Mansfield), taken from Chamberlain's novel, was an even more dismal failure. Gerald and Alice Lansing (Ramsey Wallace and Mona Kingsley) are so unhappy that Alice decides to run off to Brazil with Alan Wayne (James Crane). Not aware that Alice has reconsidered and is returning, Gerald rushes to Brazil and challenges Alan to a duel. Since Alan is suffering from a debilitating fever, the duel is delayed, and Gerald falls in love with Margarita (Rosalinde Fuller). But when Alice arrives on the scene, Margarita jumps off a cliff.

David Higgins and Bennet Musson's **The Scalawag** (3-29-27, 49th St.) was set in a teetotaling Clear Water Springs, Vt. Most of the villagers ignore the fact that eighty-year-old "Uncle Sam" Appleby (Higgins) is often a bit soused. He's a nice man. And when Jim (Robert Toms), the stunt-piloting fiancé of his granddaughter, Myra (Isabel Dawn), gets into trouble for stashing some liquor in the garage that Appleby runs with the boy's stern grandfather (Carleton Macy), Appleby sells the rights to an invention of his—a cheap substitute for gasoline—to pay the fine. He would be hard strapped thereafter, but a kindly judge (Duncan Penwarden) remits the fine.

That same night saw a short-lived revival of James M. Barrie's *The Legend of Leonora* at the Ritz, with Grace George as the woman acquitted for pushing a man out of a train window after he refused to close it.

April's first entry was Hugh Stanislaus Stange's **Fog-Bound** (4-1-27, Belmont), a vehicle for an old timer, gaunt, deep-voiced Nance O'Neil. Hester Penny's mother (Clara Blandick) has forced her to marry Capt. Ezra Tuttle (Alfred Hickman), a cruel fisherman and a sometime parson, who has terrorized his neighbors into submitting to his every wish.

Hester would have preferred Lem Ross (Curtis Cooksey). Eighteen years pass. Lem returns from his sailing trips and offers to take Hester away, but Hester, having seen what happened when she tried to assist a young lady who found herself pushed into an unwanted marriage, demurs, fearing her daughter (Betty Linley) might be made to suffer by a vindictive Tuttle.

A majority of critics thought that Jed Harris was about to profit from a hit as big as his earlier *Broadway* when he produced George S. Brooks and Walter B. Lister's **Spread Eagle** (4-4-27, Martin Beck). Atkinson hailed it as a "thumping" and "searing" melodrama. A few days later *Variety* proclaimed, "If this newcomer isn't dirty with money, then all the standard values have switched and all the established equations have warped." Yet the play, which still makes compelling reading, closed after ten weeks. The multimillionaire magnate Martin Henderson (Fritz Williams), determined to have the U.S. Army seize Mexico and protect his interests, promises General De Castro (Felix Krembs) hundreds of thousands of dollars if he will start a revolution. He also hires Charles Parkman (Allen Vincent), his daughter's fiancé and the son of a former American president, to work at his Mexican enterprise, even though the manager (Donald Meek) of his Mexican operation thinks it is too dangerous a place for so callow a young man. De Castro's troops seize the operation, shoot the boy, and then take the widow (Aline MacMahon) of the operation's treasurer, who had been killed some time before by bandits, in front of a firing squad. Reaction is swift. At a Broadway theatre the manager steps before the curtain to inform the audience that all military men and reservists are being called up. A radio broadcast tells its listeners that it has only been two weeks since Parkman was murdered but that Congress and the country have been galvanized into action. A motion picture theatre uses animated cartoons recalling the blowing up of the *Maine* and a flag-draped photograph of Parkman in its "News of the Week." From his private railroad car, Henderson watches events with satisfaction. But to his dismay, Parkman, who had only been wounded and had escaped, arrives. He is no longer innocent. He yells at Henderson, "You tried to murder me and failed. . . . You don't care how many soldiers are killed to make Mexico safe for the Spread Eagle Mining Company," and he vows to expose Henderson. But Henderson's right-hand man, Joe Cobb (Osgood Perkins), warns Parkman they will claim that Parkman ran away like a girl. However, Cobb, who has helped Henderson

engineer everything, has grown disgusted. He tells Henderson he is going to enlist. Henderson scoffs. Then, as the band outside the train starts "The Star-Spangled Banner," Henderson slumps down in an easy chair. "You son-of-a-bitch," Cobb barks angrily, "stand up." Perkins won special praise as Cobb, who supplied much of the evening's comic relief, and one aisle-sitter noted that the director, George Abbott, fresh from his success with *Broadway*, "has quickly, but surely, come to mean convincing realism."

Hearts Are Trumps (4-7-27, Morosco) was derived by Henry Baron from Félix Gandéra's *Atout . . . coeur*. A young lady (Vivian Martin) comes to the country estate of a French duke (Frank Morgan), telling him her mother (Alice Fischer) forced her to wed an impostor pretending to be the duke. The sympathetic duke sets the girl up in a Paris apartment with the cousin (William Phelps) she says she loves, but in short order the girl and the duke are paired.

According to its program **Rapid Transit** (4-7-27, Provincetown Playhouse) was "translated by Gustav Davidson and Francis Edwards Faragoh and adapted by Charles Recht" from Lajos N. Egri's *Hakuba és Hekuba* (Hakuba and Hekuba). According to Broadway scuttlebutt Egri was not a Budapest playwright but an East Side pants presser. Acted out in Cleon Throckmorton's "impressionistic machine-mechanism" setting, the play told of existence in an imaginary land where all lives last a mere twenty-four hours; it wove into its tale diatribes against the rich, big business, and taxation.

The last durable new play of the season was S. N. Behrman's **The Second Man** (4-11-27, Guild). Clark Storey (Alfred Lunt) is barely successful young writer, happy to live more than comfortably off the largess of a rich widow, Mrs. Kendall Frayne (Lynn Fontanne), whom he hopes to wed. In his heart of hearts, however, he loves a relatively poor girl, Monica Grey (Margalo Gillmore), to whom he confesses, "There's someone else inside me—a second man—a cynical, odious person, who keeps watching me. . . . He never lets me be." Storey attempts to foist Monica on a brilliant if socially inept scientist, Austin Lowe (Earle Larimore), and he almost succeeds. But after Monica discovers a $500 check made out to Storey by Mrs. Frayne, she claims that she is pregnant with Storey's child. Mrs. Frayne walks out on Storey, and Monica, also dismayed by his behavior, leaves him, too. As the curtain falls Storey is phoning Mrs. Frayne, trying to make up with her. The entire small cast was garlanded with praise although Lunt, whom the critics subsequently chose actor of the year, was patently the show-stealer. Brackett said his Storey was "the best high comedy performance I have ever seen given by a man," while Hammond thought his performance established him beyond doubt as America's leading actor. (Lynn Fontanne's role was the smallest of the four and she is said to have insisted thereafter that her roles and Lunt's must be balanced.) Equally exciting was Broadway's discovery of a new playwright in Behrman. Nathan rejoiced in his "talent for whipping the English language into a sparkle," and John Mason Brown hailed the play's "shimmering dialogue." Several critics pointed to the same bit—Storey's response to Lowe's complaint that he cannot follow Monica's small talk: "Her talk is not small. It is infinitesimal. Your microscope training should help you." The comedy remained in the Theatre Guild's repertory for 178 performances.

· · ·

S[amuel] N[athaniel] **Behrman** (1893–1973) was born in Worcester, Mass. He studied at Clark University before enrolling in George Pierce Baker's playwriting course at Harvard, then did graduate work at Columbia under Brander Matthews and St. John Ervine. He worked as a book reviewer, play reader, and press agent and collaborated on several unproduced plays before this solo effort reached New York.

· · ·

All the remaining novelties to open in April were failures. Lynn Riggs's main claim to fame would be that one of his plays was the source of the musical *Oklahoma!* But those plays themselves were always to meet the same rejection accorded his maiden effort, **Big Lake** (4-11-27, American Laboratory). In 1906, when Oklahoma was still Indian Territory, a murderer persuades a sheriff that the real killer he seeks is a young man who is out on the lake with a girl. The sheriff kills the boy, and the girl dives into the lake and drowns.

In years gone by, spring's coming had often been the cue for a spate of revivals. This year the pattern reemerged with a vengeance, led off by Githa Sowerby's English drama of a daughter's rebellion against her iron-fisted father, *Rutherford and Son,* at the Grove Street Theatre on the 12th.

One Glorious Hour (4-14-27, Selwyn) was Ella Barnett's translation of an unspecified German play by Gerhardt Falkenberg. It centered on a baroness (Vivienne Osborne), a believer in women's sexual freedom before marriage, who has a fling with three male vacationers at a resort near home before her father and fiancé come to reclaim her. It left quickly.

Nor was Robert Keith, an actor, lucky when he turned playwright with **The Tightwad** (4-16-27, 49th St.). Tommy (King Calder) is so extravagant that his sweetheart (Lucile Nikolas) insists she will not marry him. So he becomes a real cheapskate, wearing rubber collars, buying his girl the smallest boxes of inexpensive candy, and crediting his personal account with seventy-five cents whenever he eats at his prospective in-laws'. The girl and the would-be in-laws are ready to chase him away until Tommy makes a killing in a business deal.

S. N. Behrman and Kenyon Nicholson, both with hits running, struck out when they collaborated on **Love Is Like That** (4-18-27, Cort). Cassandra Hopper (Ann Davis) and Graham Delano (Edward Wever) had been childhood sweethearts back in Oklahoma. Now, in New York, Graham is a writer under the spell of a wealthy divorcee, Kay Gurlitz (Catharine Willard), so Cassandra has headed for Europe. On her way back she stops an exiled Russian prince (Basil Rathbone) from jumping overboard. Cassandra's wily aunt (Lucile Watson) puts the prince up and sets him on Kay. More complications follow, including a hint of romance between Cassandra and the prince, before Graham and Cassandra are brought together and the prince walks off to meet an old Russian flame, now singing at a New York bistro.

One revival that same evening was *Mr. Pim Passes By* at the Garrick.

Since Lawrence Grattan's **The Gossipy Sex** (4-19-27, Mansfield) was a farce, its title referred to men. One particularly gossipy man, Danny Grundy (Lynne Overman), causes all manner of mischief in three marriages by spreading rumors of infidelity, miscegenation, and financial chicanery. Is he at all abashed? No way! After some stocks he had sold his friends rebound handsomely from a sickening plunge, he is last heard of still trafficking unconcernedly in tantalizing rumors.

James L. A. Burell and Lawrence R. Brown's **The Comic** (4-19-27, Masque) was supposedly derived from an unidentified Hungarian play by one Lajos Luria, who also remained unidentified. When the Comedian (J. C. Nugent) suspects the Actress (Patricia Collinge) is having an affair with the Author (Cyril Keightley), he adds some dialogue to the play in rehearsal to test them. They are alerted by the Pupil (Rex O'Malley), after which the Actress runs off with the Manager (Malcolm Williams).

James N. Rosenberg's **Wall Street** (4-20-27, Hudson) spanned twenty years and was played out in Cleon Throckmorton's skeletonized sets on a revolving stage that allowed numerous quick scene changes, during which players rushed on and off in full view of the audience. Although John H. Perry (Arthur Hohl) describes himself as a "Massachusetts hick," he is ambitious and ruthless. He deserts his wife (Margaret Douglass) and later allows her to die in poverty, blackmails his way to the top of a New York brokerage house, is deserted by his second wife, finds that his son (John Warner) is a vicious chip off the old block, and is confined to a wheelchair after a stroke following the suicide of the son, who jumps out of a window after costing the firm $14,000,000.

Goat Alley, a 1921 failure, was revived at the Princess on the same night and failed again.

Fritz Leiber, once a promising Shakespearean and long absent from Broadway, played the leading role in Paul Green's **The Field God** (4-21-27, Greenwich Village). Hardy Gilchrist is a hard-working but godless North Carolina farmer who ignores the insistent pieties of his wife (Adelaide Fitz-Allen). When his wife catches him in the arms of her niece, Rhoda (Ruth Mason), she curses them and dies. Later Hardy and Rhoda's baby also dies, leaving Hardy to suggest that if there is a God in heaven, he is murderous and destructive. He offers the awed Rhoda an alternative: "We are God—Man is God. That's the light, that's the truth. . . . And love shall abide among us to the end."

Leigh Hutty's **The House of Shadows** (4-21-27, Longacre) described the adventures of a Harvard psychologist and ghost-story writer (Tom Powers) who decides to examine a supposedly haunted house. While he is there a frightened girl (Marguerite Churchill) rushes in, pursued by an abusive crook (James S. Barrett). There are mysterious rappings and shrieks, and the three find themselves in a hidden subterranean passage. The crook dies of shock on spotting a live monster through a lighted cubbyhole, leaving the young couple to discover that the house is actually occupied by a deranged old miser (Frank Peters), who wears the monster costume to scare away intruders.

Another revival, and a successful one, was William Brady's resurrection of *The Thief* for his daughter Alice at the Ritz on the 22nd. The story of a pretty woman who steals so that she may have clothes and jewels to please her husband (Lionel Atwill) gripped oldtimers and younger playgoers for ten weeks.

Two British plays closed out the month. Frank Stayton's **Mixed Doubles** (4-26-27, Bijou) found Betty (Margaret Lawrence) telling her new husband, Lord John Dorle (Thurston Hall), that she

was once married to a Howell Jamess. Then Reggie (Eric Blore), who turns out to be her real ex, appears with his new wife (Marion Coakley), who has told him that she was once married to Jamess. Jamess (John Williams) arrives and proves merely to be the maid's swain.

Joseph Jefferson Farjeon's **Enchantment** (4-27-27, Edyth Totten) unfolded in a snowbound English cottage. Two ordinary people come there and pretend to be nobility. Two others appear and claim they are a great detective and a crook. Another pair profess to be nobodies. When the snow melts and the first four leave, the nobodies, really a duke and a duchess, can reclaim their own cottage retreat for themselves.

For all practical purposes, the season had collapsed. Only one of May's novelties ran longer than a week (although two others attempted to extend their stays in odd ways). Everett Chantler's **The Lady Screams** (5-2-27, Selwyn) began the dismal procession. Tough, swaggering Lucy West (Betty Weston), given a suspended sentence for shooting the crooked Walter Henson (Anthony Hughes), is sent to live with a rich woman, Ruth Harrison (Dana Desboro). When Henson burglarizes Mrs. Harrison's home after Lucy refuses to help him steal the woman's $50,000 pearls, he blackjacks Mrs. Harrison's son (Allan Tower), who has fallen in love with Lucy, and attempts to carry off the girl. Lucy screams, and keeps screaming till the police come.

Sarah Ellis Hyman's **The Seventh Heart** (5-2-27, Mayfair) was bruited to have been produced by the eightyish authoress's sons as a gift to her. It dealt with the amours and hypocrisies of the idle rich in Palm Beach and in turn was dealt the most scathing notices of the season. Although a second week was announced by the devoted sons, there remains some doubt of how many, if any, performances were given that week.

Gregorio Martínez Sierra offered dedicated playgoers some better evenings when he brought his Spanish Art Theatre into the Forrest that same night with a repertory (all in Spanish) of plays that included Shaw's *Pygmalion* and his own *The Romantic Young Lady* and *The Cradle Song.*

On the evenings of the 3rd and 4th, Margaret Anglin added a little luster to the dying season by offering *Electra* at the Metropolitan Opera House. Both evenings were sold out, and many disappointed playgoers were turned away. Her cast included William Courtleigh as the Guardian, Ralph Roeder as Orestes, Ruth Holt Boucicault as Clytemnestra, and Charles Dalton as Aegisthus. Livingston Platt's austere, somber settings were employed.

Frank Vreeland, reviewing the tragedy in the *Telegram and Evening Mail,* noted of the star, "In spite of her soon-forgotten matronly appearance, she managed to convey magically, hypnotically, the sense of a young, passion-driven creature caught up in a storm of grief and hate and vengeance." The Shuberts urged Miss Anglin to move the production to a regular house for a brief run, but she declined.

Echoes of *The Spider* were so loud and clear in F. S. Merlin's **Triple Crossed** (5-5-27, Morosco) that a defensive notice was printed in the program stating that the play had been copyrighted in 1922. In response Fulton Oursler said his story had been originally serialized in 1921. But that became a matter for the courts. At the theatre, the curtain rose on an ordinary triangle play. But then one (Robert Toms) of the characters shoots and kills another (Frederick Smith). Witnesses later claim that they saw a hand thrust through a doorway on the set and switch guns. Since the stage could have been entered from the auditorium, everyone is suspect. Once again the police come in, the audience is told it cannot leave, an investigation ensues, including a reenactment of the shooting, and the killer is revealed. Among the comic relief was a lawyer who rises from a box and alerts the audience to its rights. For all the head-shaking the piece survived for 52 performances.

Two more one-weekers appeared the next Monday. Willis Maxwell Goodhue's **Katy Did** (5-9-27, Daly's) allowed Katie (Juliette Day), a waitress at Childs', to fall in love with a dishwasher and part-time bootlegger (Romney Brent), who turns out to be the exiled king of Suavia. When he is offered his throne back and the hand of beautiful if haughty Princess Amalia (Carolyne McLean) of Moronia, Carlo opts to remain where and what he is, and to marry Katie. Although one scene occurred in a Childs' restaurant and another just outside, nobody compared the sets to Belasco's famous one in *The Governor's Lady.*

Arthur Corning White, a Dartmouth professor who had collaborated a year earlier with Louis Bennison on *The Virgin,* a play about French-Canadian life, had another one ready in **Julie** (5-9-27, Lyceum). Her booze-addicted mother (Alison Skipworth) is prepared to sell Julie (Betty Pierce) to a mean bootlegger (Edward Arnold) for two dozen bottles of whiskey. Julie loves Lee Stone (Alexander Clark, Jr.), but her mother lets Stone's puritanical mother (Blanche Friderici) believe Julie has had an illegitimate child. However, the child proves to be that of the very girl (Mildred Southwick) Stone's mother had favored. So all ends happily for Julie.

When the will of Hamilton Wayne, the founder of Waynesburg, is read in Herbert Hall Winslow's **He Loved the Ladies** (5-10-27, Frolic) the shocked townsfolk learn he has left everything to an illegitimate daughter (Lillian Ross). The town ladies snub her until she uncovers some letters which reveal that Wayne had had affairs with many of them. The girl settles down and weds Wayne's charming nephew (Lyons Wickland). One critic said the best thing about the comedy at the roof theatre was the songs wafted up now and then from the musical playing in the New Amsterdam Theatre below.

The Nugents were reunited for a revival the next evening of *Kempy* at the Hudson. It enjoyed a month-and-a-half stay.

Ernest and Louise Cortis, two vaudevillians, were the authors of **One for All** (5-13-27, Greenwich Village). Knowing that her husband (Allyn Joslyn), who is dying from tuberculosis, is on the verge of discovering a cure for the disease but requires additional money to finish his work, Mrs. Brent (Madeline Delmar) sleeps with a man willing to provide the funds in exchange for bedding her. The work ended, and his own life saved, Brent learns that his wife is pregnant even though he was in no condition to have sex with her. She tells him the truth, and he is forgiving. The production was awash in controversy and puzzlements. Jasper Deeter, the cantankerous eccentric who ran the Hedgerow Theatre outside of Philadelphia, was listed as the director, but just before the opening he sent the critics telegrams disclaiming the credit. And while the show was abruptly closed, it was reopened a few weeks later at the Princess Theatre, apparently by a different management (possibly the authors themselves), and given a brief, forced run.

The season's final novelty was Sam Janney's **A Very Wise Virgin** (6-2-27, Bijou). "It's a wise virgin who knows her own boiling point," exclaims Betty Brent (Joan Bourdelle), an eighteen-year-old flapper who thinks she knows it all. She steals the boyfriend (John Buckler) of her best friend (Gail DeHart) only to have an international courtesan (Joan Gordon) vamp him away from her. A little wiser now, she accepts a proposal from the young doctor (Dennis Clough) who has watched with amusement from the sidelines. Her best friend forgives Betty when her own boyfriend returns to her. The show ran two and a half weeks.

Four revivals brought the season to a close. On the 6th at the New Amsterdam the Players offered their annual presentation—this year, *Julius Caesar,* with William Courtleigh in the title role, James Rennie as Marc Antony, Tyrone Power as Brutus,

Basil Rathbone as Cassius, and such names as Joseph Kilgour, Pedro de Cordoba, Frazer Coulter, James T. Powers, Mary Eaton, Marion Coakley, and Mary Young in lesser roles. Possibly New York critics were beginning to take these annual affairs for granted, for the reviews were filled with carpings about the individual performances and the direction as a whole, particularly of the less adept members (often playwrights, not actors) who came on in crowd scenes. On the other hand, Norman Bel Geddes was applauded for his settings, which consisted primarily of "huge and impressive draperies, punctuated here and there with a column, a throne, or a set of massive steps."

With a series of recent failures on his scorecard, Leo Carrillo took refuge in his hit of ten years earlier, *Lombardi, Ltd.,* at the George M. Cohan on the same night. His reward was a meager three weeks of employment.

An even shorter stay was accorded the 1910 hit *Baby Mine,* in which a wife sets out to borrow a baby in order to win back her husband but finds that a friend supplies her with too many tots. The revival at the 46th Street Theatre on the 9th had Lee Patrick as the wife, Humphrey Bogart as the husband, and Roscoe "Fatty" Arbuckle as the friend.

But at reduced prices for its limited engagement beginning on the 15th at the Lyric, Margaret Anglin's revival of *The Woman of Bronze* did excellent business, despite a thrashing for the play itself.

1927–1928

Broadway peaked in 1927–28. Whether one accepts *Variety*'s figure of 264 entertainments or Burns Mantle's of 270, no season before or since has brought forth so many productions. True, a jump in the number of musicals and revivals helped push up the figure, while the count of new straight plays slipped a notch or two. Still, the tradesheet recorded 183 new comedies and dramas. Even more so than in the preceding season, they were packed in tightly. The early summer months were a washout, and in the spring the season collapsed more strikingly than the year before. For all that, it was a great season, probably the greatest. Among its musical delights were *Good News, My Maryland, Manhattan Mary, The 5 O'Clock Girl, Funny Face, A Connecticut Yankee, The Three Musketeers, Blackbirds of 1928,*

Rosalie, and, best of all, *Show Boat.* The high percentage of straight plays still revived now and then, or remembered glowingly, will become evident as the season progresses.

No non-musical novelties came in during late June, and July saw only two straight plays open. One was a revival of a French drama long associated with Bernhardt, *Madame X.* Presented at the large Earl Carroll Theatre at a $2 top, it offered Carroll McComas as the fallen woman and Rex Cherryman as her legal defense counselor, who also discovers he is the woman's long-lost son. The mounting lingered for just three weeks.

That was all William A. Grew's **The Mating Season** (7-18-27, Selwyn) managed, too. Grew, a sometime revue-sketch writer, was also the star, leaving critics to ponder if he was more embarrassingly inept as a playwright or a player. He wrote himself a hefty part that kept him onstage all but "2$\frac{3}{4}$ minutes by a stopwatch." Jack Stratford is a playwright on vacation in Atlantic City. He is irresistible to women, especially his brother's bride (Lillian Walker), his uncle's gray-haired but red-wigged wife (Ethel Martin), and an actress (Gladys Feldman) for whom he is writing a play. The husband, the uncle, and the actress's tough-boy lover all show up in the playwright's bedroom to add to the confusion.

Some much better acting prodded John McGowan and Lloyd Griscom's "melodrama of New York's underworld," **Tenth Avenue** (8-15-27, Eltinge), into an eleven-week run. (Griscom had been American ambassador to Italy.) Lyla Mason (Edna Hibbard) is a charitable woman who tries to reform the crooks who room at her 38th Street boardinghouse. She is especially fond of a slick gambler, Guy Peters (Frank Morgan). When he and another lodger, Elzy Everetts (William Boyd), learn Lyla is short $400 of rent money, Guy wins some of what she needs in a questionable card game, while Elzy gets the rest by shooting a treacherous bootlegger. Though they try, the others can't save Elzy from the police.

There were clear echoes of last season's *Buy, Buy, Baby* in **Babies a la Carte** (8-15-27, Wallack's). The play was a vanity production since Seaman Lewis, the playwright, and S. L. Simpson, the producer, were one and the same. Their uncle's will leaves a small fortune to the first child born to either of his nieces. One niece (Harriet Rempell) is nice and married. The not so nice niece (Mildred Southwick) rushes out to wed, then employs every trick she knows to win. The babies are born within minutes of each other, but what with one having been delivered in New York and the second in Chicago, lawyers start to haggle over precedence. The discovery of a later will settles matters by insisting the baby must be a boy. Naturally the not so nice niece had a girl. The comedy was the young season's third three-week dud, but that would not deter its author and producer from offering a rewritten version a year down the road.

Caesar Dunn's **What the Doctor Ordered** (8-18-27, Ritz) could not even survive three full weeks. In its simple tale, a quack doctor (Hale Hamilton), given a $25,000 stipend by a wife (Ruth Abbott) in hopes that he can stimulate her bookish, amorously tepid husband (Herbert Yost), sends him to a hotel in Florida where he can find lots of beautiful gals parading around in one-piece bathing suits. The husband's sexual interests are finally reawakened by the lovely woman in the adjoining room—his wife. The humor was rather pathetic, with one exchange going: "Did he ever go out with the boys?" "No, he was practically grown in a hot-house." "That may be why's he's so cold." And a colored bellhop asks a resident if he was the man who left a six o'clock wake-up call. On being told he was, the bellhop remarks, "Well, it's five o'clock now. You've got another hour to sleep."

As he had last season, Gustav Blum used a low-budget play and cut-rate tickets to win a modest but profitable run at his roof theatre, this time for Merrill Rogers's **Her First Affaire** (8-22-27, Bayes). Ann Hood (Grace Voss), an impressionable flapper, is determined to have a pre-marital affair and elects Carey Maxon (Stanley Logan), who writes free-thinking, convention-defying novels. Being a good girl, Ann first insists on getting the permission of Mrs. Maxon (Aline MacMahon), and, being an innocent girl, she fails to catch the amused glint in the wife's eye. To her dismay, Ann soon finds that Maxon, unlike his writings, is hopelessly conventional and proper. In no time she has run off with a young man (Anderson Lawler) who had been courting her.

George Middleton based **Blood Money** (8-22-27, Hudson) on a short story by H. H. Van Loan. Immediately following the funeral of his father, who was a distinguished senator, James Bolton (Thomas Mitchell) gives out that he is heading for New York. But the senator's pretty secretary, Julia Jones (Phyllis Povah), discovers that he is actually sneaking off elsewhere. After he has gone an unsavory couple, Tom and Mary Jefferson (Beatrice Nichols and Malcolm Duncan), appear and claim that there is a brown envelope containing $100,000 in the senator's desk and that it was money the senator accepted from them as a bribe to vote against an important bill. Julia suspects the couple, particularly after the

man makes a call to the senator's lawyer (whom Julia knows to be away) and supposedly speaks to him. She points out the man never took his finger off the hook. The senator's chauffeur (Robert Brister) enters, proves to be in league with the couple, and points a gun at Julia. Julia switches off the lights in the library, and, when they come on again, she is gone and the chauffeur has been stabbed to death. Julia heads for the senator's yacht, a boat whose beautiful, paneled lounge has a huge skylight. There she finds Bolton. It soon develops that the money was not a bribe for the senator but had been stolen by the senator's drug-addicted young son, whom James has hidden on the yacht, in order to have Mary run off with him. The senator had hoped to return the money to the bank. Certain they can straighten everything out, James and Julia acknowledge that they love each other. The play, which had a gripping first act but became repetitious and patently padded later, struggled along for eight weeks.

Peter Glenny and Marie Armstrong Hecht's **Such Is Life** (8-31-27, Morosco) was the month's fourth two-and-a-half or three-weeker. It, too, looked at young people who would defy convention. Noel Gignon (Ralph Sprague) first married one sister secretly, then a second. The girls have sons at about the same time, and, after Noel deserts them, they and two other sisters raise the boys together, claiming they are twins belonging to one of them. Twenty years later Noel turns up, needing a wife and child for public appearance. But the girls, threatening him with charges of bigamy, send him on his way. One bit of casting elicited some surprise—the lovely Marie Carroll playing a third sister, a petulant, troublesome spinster with a humped shoulder.

The season's first smash hit was George Manker Watters and Arthur Hopkins's **Burlesque** (9-1-27, Plymouth). Skid (Hal Skelly) is an excellent but booze-addicted comic in a cheap burlesque troupe. His wife, Bonny (Barbara Stanwyck), knows that he is good enough for Broadway, and, sitting in their shabby dressing room, she tells him that his excuses for not trying to move up are "applesauce." She also knows he is unfaithful, while she herself has rejected an attractive proposal to leave him and wed a wealthy, amiable rancher (Ralph Theadore). An offer finally comes from the great producer Charles Dillingham to appear in a New York revue. Bonny arranges for Skid to be fired from the burlesque company, thus forcing him to accept the offer. In New York, without Bonny, Skid is a big hit. However, his drinking has been made all the worse by Bonny's starting divorce proceedings. Still, she has come east to see him and is shocked that he appeared onstage patently drunk. "Your two weeks' notice is printed on every bottle of scotch," she warns. Sure enough, Dillingham fires him. And Skid returns to Bonny's hotel suite and creates a scene with her husband-to-be. The friendly manager (Charles D. Brown) who had helped Bonny nudge Skid onto Broadway has now found a "sugar daddy" to back a new burlesque outfit. He has tried to hire Skid but found him on a days-long bender. Bonny, realizing she still loves Skid, decides to rejoin him. Although he is still a bit woozy, she and he head onstage to do a routine together. Critic after critic welcomed the show, all the while insisting it was no *Broadway*. What made it was its scintillating performances. *Variety* reported, "Hal Skelly as the hick comic is an inspiration. . . . He doesn't exaggerate; he doesn't play for sympathy. It is a sublimated characterization and a superfine performance." Calling Stanwyck "a fine ingenue," the tradesheet observed, "Her chief virtue is poise and her salvation is restraint. She is winsome, withal." The play immediately began to play to capacity weeks of $28,000 and ran eleven months.

Cosmo Hamilton and Frank C. Reilly were the latest to attempt to adapt Charles Dickens for the stage. Reilly, a rich inventor and manufacturer, produced **Pickwick** (9-5-27, Empire), lavishing $100,000 on it—more than most musicals of the time cost. The settings and costumes were brilliant, and the performances, particularly that of John Cumberland in the title role, admired. But the play itself was rather dull, so languished for a somewhat forced run of nine weeks.

More burlesque performers were pivotal characters in Harry Wagstaff Gribble and Wallace A. Manheimer's **Mister Romeo** (9-5-27, Wallack's). Henry Trundle (J. C. Nugent) is a fifty-year-old printer and a middle-aged Lothario. Taking on the name Carleton Hazelton and pretending to be an author looking for material, he latches on to two burlesque chorus girls, Maisie (Jane Meredith) and Babe (Isabelle Lowe). They are good kids, so as soon as they understand his real intentions, they get in touch with his wife (Thais Lawton). The three agree to teach him a lesson. Maisie rents a flat and plays the gold digger; Babe allows herself to be caught in Hazelton's embrace by her gorilla of a boyfriend (G. Pat Collins).

Seeking a change of pace from the comedies in which she had been performing, Mary Boland took the lead in Daniel L. Rubin's **Woman Go On Forever** (9-7-27, Forrest), and kept it going for 117 performances. Daisy runs a boardinghouse where she gives

her lover, Jake (Morgan Wallace), the room next to hers, rent free. But when Jake starts to flirt with other roomers, Daisy's blind son (Douglass Montgomery), whom she dotes on, kills him. The boy then runs off and marries a much older, ugly woman (Elizabeth Taylor) who he believes is young and beautiful. The police conclude that Jake was killed by another boarder, Pete (Osgood Perkins), who in turn is killed by Jake's brother, who is struck down and killed fleeing the cops. Daisy claims to be fed up with men, until a handsome, hunky, blond Swede (Hans Sandquist) knocks on her door. She offers him the room next to hers, at a reduced rent.

Another quick flop was an English play, Eden and Adelaide Phillpotts's **Yellow Sands** (9-9-27, Fulton), in which a wise old aunt (Madge Burbage) bequeaths her moneys to the quiet, leftish nephew (Lester Matthews) who least expected anything.

The next Monday night saw two non-musicals open. The lone success was George M. Cohan's **Baby Cyclone** (9-12-27, Henry Miller's). Baby Cyclone is a Pekinese, whose owner, Mrs. Hurley (Nan Sunderland), smothered it with kisses and baby talk. After Mr. Hurley (Spencer Tracy) had enough, he sold it for $5 to the first lady who was willing to take it off his hands. Mrs. Hurley, on hearing the news, started screaming, and a passing stockbroker, Mr. Meadows (Grant Mitchell), ran to her aid and was punched by Mr. Hurley. The play begins as Meadows has brought the distraught woman to his home. Just then Meadows's fiancée (Natalie Moorehead) arrives and is revealed as the lady who bought the dog. She claims proprietary rights. Hurley sides with her; Meadows, jeopardizing his own engagement, tries to argue from Mrs. Hurley's viewpoint. "Cohan, the old wizard, made something out of nothing," noted Richard Watts, then a second-stringer on the *Herald Tribune*. But the wizard's skill at theatrical magic kept audiences coming for nearly six months and called further attention to Tracy.

In **Revelry** (9-12-27, Masque), which Maurine Watkins took from Samuel Hopkins Adams's controversial novel suggested by the scandals surrounding Harding and his administration, Willis Markham (Berton Churchill), the President of the United States, likes to sneak away from the White House and play cards with the boys at a house on K Street known as "The Crow's Nest." He subsequently learns from a lady (Eleanor Woodruff) he admires that the men he so trusted have played free and loose with oil deals which will engulf his administration in scandal. He feels he has no choice but to kill himself. With Churchill made up to resemble the late Warren Harding, the production left little doubt that it was a drama à clef. It also left some reviewers shocked at its frequent resort to foul language, especially the "four-worded oath." Brooks Atkinson of the *Times* regretted that what might have been a powerful play, had it been more bravely written, suffered "the stigmas of cheapness and meretriciousness."

Some Broadway know-it-alls were amused that Eugene Davis's **Ten Per Cent** (9-13-27, George M. Cohan) was produced by two casting agents, since its story centered on two men in a similar partnership. Rumor also had it that one of the producers, H. S. Kraft, was the real author. In any case, two casting agents (Albert Hackett and Walter Plimmer, Jr.) are trying to produce what everyone else knows is a lousy drama, *Love's Torrent*. They find a rich Jewish real estate man, Rudolf Schwartz (Robert Leonard), who is willing to back the play if his daughter (Patricia Calvert) is star. The play proves a smash hit, since the writing and acting were so bad the critics mistook it for a farce. Its obvious debt to *The Show Shop* and *The Butter and Egg Man* underscored its inadequacies.

An even shorter life awaited another play about the theatre world, Marc Connelly and Herman J. Mankiewicz's **The Wild Man of Borneo** (9-13-27, Bijou). Their comedy was set in the late 1890s. At a theatrical boardinghouse run by the fluttery Mrs. Marshall (Josephine Hull), J. Daniel Thompson (George Hassell), who looks a lot like William Jennings Bryan, has apparently bamboozled his fellow boarders into believing he is Richard Mansfield's understudy. He is particularly anxious to maintain the fiction after he meets the daughter (Marguerite Churchill) he has not seen in many years. But the girl visits the Hall of Living Wonders on 14th Street and finds her father in a cage impersonating the wild man. Since the play was a comedy, a happy ending was contrived for the last act.

Owen Davis's **The Triumphant Bachelor** (9-15-27, Biltmore) survived a mere week and a half. To win a bet proving women do not trust their husbands, Jack Sylvester (Robert Ames), a confirmed bachelor, slips love notes into three of his buddies' pockets, knowing their wives will find them. All hell breaks loose, but in the end Jack himself is snared by an aggressive secretary (Elsie Lawson), who may or may not be trusting later on.

Two hits came in the next Monday night. By far the bigger was Bayard Veiller's **The Trial of Mary Dugan** (9-19-27, National). The audience entering the theatre saw no curtain. Onstage was a courtroom, with the judge's raised bench on the right, and the witness box immediately downstage of it. No jury box was in evidence, since when the play started the audience learned it was to be the jury. Court officials, reporters, onlookers all saunter in much in the same slow fashion as the audience. Before the new trial can begin, old business must be taken care of. An Italian woman who speaks little or no English is sentenced to death for murder and dragged screaming from the courtroom. District Attorney Galway (Arthur Hohl) then states his case against Mary Dugan (Ann Harding), who is accused of stabbing her lover to death after he tried to end their affair. Witnesses are called, and Mary's attorney, Edward West (Cyril Keightley), cross-examines them in a somewhat desultory though not ineffective fashion. For example, he elicits the fact that a loud argument had occurred just before the murder, but that the police made no attempt to interview neighbors. And he surprises the court by telling it that he lives in the very next apartment. The most damaging testimony comes from the dead man's wife (Merle Maddern), who states that the dead man had gone to the apartment to break the news of the end of the affair to Mary. At this point a young man speaks out. He says he is Mary's brother, Jimmy (Rex Cherryman), an attorney from California, and begs Mary to dismiss West, who he states is not conducting a proper defense. Mary agrees to the new arrangement, but when Jimmy goes to cross-examine the widow, she claims she has become ill. The court adjourns. Jimmy puts Mary on the stand. She reveals that she and Jimmy were orphans, and she confesses that she has been a kept woman since she was sixteen and that she earned the money so that she could put Jimmy through the best schools and get him started. She also claims that the dead man had learned his wife was unfaithful and that he was about to divorce her and cut her out of his will. Jimmy finally demonstrates that the knifing was committed by a left-hander. Having subpoenaed West, he throws the murder weapon at him. West instinctively catches it with his left hand. "I offer in evidence the left handed lover of Gertrude Rice, and the knife with which he committed the murder," Jimmy exclaims. Mary is acquitted. *Time* reported that the play "moves more swiftly than the law with all its ruthless direction. Its plot has the fascinating features of a front-page murder story." The public agreed, keeping court in session for more than a year.

Dana Burnet and George Abbott's **Four Walls** (9-19-27, John Golden) had a less universal appeal, so ran only a little over four months. Having served five years in prison, Benny Horowitz (Muni Wisenfrend [Paul Muni]) vows to remain a free man, with ties to neither criminals nor women. But after he accidentally kills his old gang leader by throwing him off a roof in a fight to protect a girl, he gives himself up although the girl would have lied to exculpate him. The action moved from the Horowitzes' cheap apartment on the East Side, to a bar, and finally to the roof. Wisenfrend was clearly the strength of the evening, with one critic calling him not only "the possessor of all the trade's tricks and a master of expression" but also "one of the best actors in town."

Slated for at least four matinee performances, Michael Artzibashev's **Lovers and Enemies** (9-20-27, Little) closed after just two. In a translation by one Mme. Strindberg, it told of a scientist's attempt to demonstrate that love and hate were much the same, and marriage was futile.

But an unidentified German play by Rudolph Lothar and Fritz Gottwald, translated by Herman Bernstein and Brian Marlow as **The Command to Love** (9-20-27, Longacre), delighted playgoers for seven months. Its story told of a French attaché (Basil Rathbone) in Spain ordered by the ambassador (Henry Stephenson) to flirt with important Spanish ladies. His brief affair with one (Mary Nash) helps promote a treaty. Police threats to close the play for indecency no doubt prompted some playgoers to buy tickets.

Some equally licentious doings failed to save Samuel Shipman and Kenneth Perkins's **Creoles** (9-22-27, Klaw) from a quick shuttering. The action of the play occurred in 1850s New Orleans, in a sumptuous mansion setting designed by Norman Bel Geddes. Madame Hyacinthe (Princess Matchabelli) tries to force her daughter, Jacinta (Helen Chandler), newly returned from convent school, to marry the sinister Monsieur Merluche (George Nash), who holds the mortgage on the family's home. But Jacinta has a better idea, vamping the pirate El Gato (Alan Dinehart), who marries her and buys off Merluche. The cost of a huge cast of supporting players, all in beautiful costumes, sped the closure.

With six openings (including two musicals) to choose from, none of the first-stringers opted for James Gleason's **The Shannons of Broadway** (9-26-27, Martin Beck). But this engaging bit of claptrap won the longest run of the evening, entertaining Broadway for almost nine months. Two vaudevillians, Mickey and Emma Shannon (Gleason and his wife, Lucile Webster), are stranded in a small New England town because they are refused rooms for their poodle, sit in the lobby wondering where to go, and overhear a conversation that reveals the town skinflint is about to foreclose on the hotel's mortgage. They use their savings to buy the place, which becomes a haven for theatrical folk, who often do their acts in the lobby. But some other of Mrs. Shannon's investments seem to go sour, and deadbeat actors could bankrupt the hotel. At that point a Mr. Albee (Bertram Millar) appears and offers to buy the hotel. He tells them he represents a big hotel chain, but they think he might be *the* Mr. Albee. At the same time, Mrs. Shannon's investments turn very sweet. Assisted by a saxophone band, the Shannons and their guests perform a routine they hope they will do in the big time. *Variety*, which enjoyed the show, wondered aloud how so many actors found their way to "a tank burg" and how professionals could not know that Mr. Albee was not the vaudeville king.

Another unexpected hit of the busy night was Myron C. Fagan's **Jimmie's Women** (9-26-27, Biltmore). By the terms of his father's will, Jimmie Turner (Robert Williams) could lose his inheritance if he does not allow a trustee of his father's estate to select a bride for him. The self-serving, hypocritical trustee (Charles Abbe) and his termagant wife (Beatrice Terry) select their own giddy, flapper daughter, Teddie (Lucia Laska). To ensure that Jimmie weds Teddie, who prefers another young man, Teddie's family brings in a girl (Minna Gombell) to make Teddie jealous by vamping Jimmie. The girl tells Teddie, "The best way to get a man is to go into his room and spend the night there." To the girl's delight, Teddie backs off, so she enters the bedroom. How does Jimmie react? Well, the girl brought in to vamp him is, after all, the very girl he has secretly wed. In the face of many disparaging notices, the comedy ran more than six months.

The shortest run of the night among the native offerings (albeit one of its authors had long since become a British subject) was seven weeks. In Edward Knoblock and George Rosener's **Speakeasy** (9-26-27, Mansfield), Alice White (Dorothy Hall), an innocent country girl, walks into the notorious club in Hell's Kitchen run by "Min" Denton (Anne Shoemaker). "Cannon" Costello (Arthur R. Vinton), a tough habitué of the joint, would have his way with her, but Alice's Princeton beau (Edward Woods) rushes to her rescue.

Fresh off her triumph in *The Green Hat*, Katharine Cornell scored a lesser but nonetheless memorable success in Somerset Maugham's **The Letter** (9-26-27, Morosco). (This was the play most first-stringers attended.) A resident of colonial Singapore, Leslie Crosby, would claim she killed Geoffrey Hammond (Burton McEvilly) in self-defense, but she is blackmailed into buying a letter that proves her lover deserted her for a Chinese girl. In the *World*, Woollcott, who admired the play, felt that it would help the star "hold and increase her following," not quite the highest of praise. Similarly, Atkinson suggested Miss Cornell's acting was "not great, but extraordinarily telling." She took the show on the road after three months in New York.

Three more plays competed for attention the next evening. All three folded quickly. Avery Hopwood's **The Garden of Eden** (9-27-27, Selwyn), taken from an unspecified play by Rudolph Bernauer and Rudolf Oesterreicher, had been a hugely successful comedy-drama, with lesbian overtones, in London, where Tallulah Bankhead had starred in it. The watered-down version which New York saw was played as broad comedy. A young lady (Miriam Hopkins) who has danced in cheap cabarets finds her aristocratic suitor (Douglass Montgomery) has a change of heart after learning her history, so she doffs her wedding dress, walks out in her undies, and lands a Spanish prince (Russ Whytal). The play was a downbeat ending to Hopwood's so frequently upbeat career. He was drowned some months later while swimming on the Riviera. But Hopwood's three-week run was the longest any of the evening's openings achieved.

Willard Robertson's **Black Velvet** (9-27-27, Liberty) ran just two weeks. General John William Darr (Arthur Byron) is an eighty-four-year-old, unreconstructed southerner, with the typical drooping white mustache all good southern colonels sport. He applauds the killing of a northerner come to recruit black workers and the lynching of an arrogant black. And then, learning that his grandson (Nelan Jaap) is having an affair with a high yellow, he sets off to kill the boy himself but drops dead before he can.

Bernard J. Owen's **The Uninvited Guest** (9-27-27, Belmont) ran a single week. Johanna (Peg Entwistle), the child bride in a December-May marriage, has a baby by the local minister (Robert Conness). After the infant dies, the minister wants to carry on their affair, but Johanna kills him.

September's last play was also a failure. Leslie Howard's **Murray Hill** (9-29-27, Bijou) was set in an old Victorian brownstone sitting doggedly between two modern skyscrapers. One of the Tweedle sisters has died and left her estate to a surviving niece, Amelia (Genevieve Tobin), and a worthless, playboy nephew, Worthington Smythe (Glenn Anders), whom the remaining sisters have not seen since he was a toddler. He turns up in such a disreputable condition that the family lawyer (John Brewer) asks a deputy assistant mortician named Wrigley (Howard) to take his place, so the aunts will not be offended. Amelia faints on seeing Wrigley, and it soon develops that she had fallen in love with him when their eyes met while she was caught in a traffic jam. Smythe reappears, and the quick-thinking Wrigley introduces him as his friend Vandenbock, son of the famous multimillionaire. It also turns out that Wrigley is not a mortician. He, too, fell in love on seeing Amelia, and so bribed his way into the funeral cortege. Smythe takes the livelier of the aunts (Gaby Fay), who earlier had said, "I would rather endow a home for misguided gunmen than I would endow dear little Worthington," for a wild night on the town. Amelia and Wrigley elope but come back having been unable to secure a license. All is forgiven after Smythe admits who he is and Wrigley confesses to being the real Vandenbock heir.

Louis Bromfield adapted his own novel *The Green Bay Tree* for the stage as **The House of Women** (10-3-27, Maxine Elliott's), but it proved unexciting in the transfer. Julia Shane (Nance O'Neil), grande dame of the wealthy Shane clan, watches as over the years one of her daughters, Lily (Elsie Ferguson), takes man after man away from her sister (Helen Freeman). The acting nearly redeemed a tedious evening. O'Neil, "almost a Bernhardt in her . . . characterizations, her vocal modulations and her unctuous deportment," had two big scenes. Her first-act history of her life was touted as one of the longest monologues ever heard onstage; at the end she had a moving death scene. Ferguson ran her a close second with "her God-given voice and her well-known delsarte of poise and feminine eloquence." Robert Edmond Jones's setting of the Shane's drawing room "caught the heavy, grandiose dignity of that broad room in a splendidly suggestive background."

In Conrad Westervelt's short-lived **Romancin' Round** (10-3-27, Little) a sailor (Ralph Morgan) is nearly convicted of murder after the man whom Neena Dobson's rich, racketeering father has selected for her dies in an argument with him. But she testifies at his court-martial, and the man is shown to have died from a heart attack. Neena (Helen MacKellar), who had run away from home and taken work in a coffee shop near the Brooklyn navy yard, can then resume slinging the hash until her new husband returns from his final tour of duty at sea.

The evening's longest run went to Walter Hampden's revival of *An Enemy of the People* at Hampden's Theatre. The actor-producer's Stockmann was "benign, thoughtful, at times almost quaint" and helped the production to its run of 127 performances, an American record for the play.

Only Belasco's name seems to have allowed William Hurlbut's **Hidden** (10-4-27, Lyceum) to remain on the boards for ten weeks. As had *The House of Women*, it dealt with the rivalry of two sisters, and the leading figure's second-act monologue vied in length with that in the earlier play. Violet (Beth Merrill) is a neurotic spinster who lives with her sister, Ellen (Mary Morris), and Ellen's husband, Nick (Philip Merivale). She grows faint and suffers headaches whenever she is left alone with Nick, whom she believes to be a lady-chaser. And she drives Ellen from the house with her tales of advances Nick has made to her. Left together, Nick and Violet spend one night together before she kills herself and Ellen can return to salvage her marriage.

Mercedes de Acosta's **Jacob Slovak** (10-5-27, Greenwich Village) takes place in a New England village where Jews, such as Slovak (José Ruben), a Polish immigrant, are made unwelcome. For all that, he is vamped by Myra Flint (Miriam Doyle). But she refuses to marry him although she becomes pregnant. She answers his pleadings by stating she will claim he raped her, so he leaves town after pointing out that her child's Jewish blood will probably help it become an important local figure. Myra gets a local boy to make her respectable.

Uptown, that same evening, an importation became one of the season's big hits. **Dracula** (10-5-27, Fulton) was theatricalized from Bram Stoker's famous novel by Hamilton Deane and John Balderston. A vampire, one of the "undead dead," is stalking female patients at an English sanitarium, dooming them by sucking blood from their necks. When Lucy Harker (Dorothy Peterson) displays the same markings and symptoms as a girl who recently has died, Dr. van Helsing (Edward Van Sloan) is summoned. He soon realizes the vampire is none other than Count Dracula (Bela Lugosi) and, after trying vainly to capture him, finds his daytime grave and drives a spike through the sleeping vampire's heart. Lugosi, in the evening dress and cape he would later wear in picture versions, used his foreign accent to underscore his sinister portrayal, amid the eerie howlings and mysteriously billowing curtains.

If Belasco's name could increase a play's run, Shirley Booth's could not—at least not yet. But some critics felt her "corking," "fluttery" performance was the only good thing about Larry E. Johnson's **High Gear** (10-6-27, Wallack's). She played a young wife who has been writing to her rich old Uncle Elmer about the elegant life she has been leading. Actually, she's just another struggling newlywed, so when Uncle Elmer (Erman Seavey) announces he will visit her she has to scurry to find some suitable furniture, china, and silverware. The staff she hires includes a felonious butler, whom she immediately replaces with her husband (William Shelley), even if, in true farce fashion, that means she must now latch on to someone to play the husband. A sharp-tongued maid (Edith Gordon)—the very sort of figure Booth often would impersonate in later years—added to the complications.

A more significant opening occurred the same evening. The first major sound film, *The Jazz Singer*, premiered. It was one of two devastating October bombs that would bring about a swift end to the heyday of live theatre. (The second bomb would explode two years later.) In short order, many of Broadway's best talents were heading for Hollywood. Many would never return. Whether it was the excitement the new talkie created or the unseasonably warm weather, *Variety* reported in the next few weeks an "unprecedented ebb" in business all along Broadway.

But the next Monday night did bring in something by way of immediate compensation—the Theatre Guild's brilliant mounting of Dorothy and DuBose Heyward's adaptation of the latter's novel, **Porgy** (10-10-27, Guild). As the house lights dimmed, the bells of St. Michael's church could be heard tolling the time. The curtain rose to disclose the dilapidating court of Catfish Row, a once elegant colonial building in Charleston that had become a Negro tenement. The windows and doors of its numerous apartments are seen on three sides, but at the rear the lower floor is pierced at its center by a magnificently carved wrought-iron gate. The walls are mottled in pastel shades. A crap game is in progress, with an argument bursting out when one of the players, Sporting Life (Percy Verwayne), a nattily dressed high-yellow bootlegger, who also supplies tenants with their happy dust, is shown to have loaded dice. One of the women, Clara (Mary Young), is singing a lullaby to her newborn, telling it, "Hush, li'l baby, don' yo' cry." A worse fight soon breaks out over the game, with strapping Crown (Jack Carter) killing Robbins (Lloyd Gray). Crown flees, and the tenants all run for cover. Crown's girl, Bess (Evelyn Ellis), seeks refuge in the room belonging to Porgy (Frank Wilson), a crippled beggar who rides about in a cart made from a soap box and pulled by a dirty goat. In the room belonging to Robbins's widow, Serena (Rose McClendon), the neighbors all come to contribute to the funeral expenses and sing hymns. The women would shun Bess, but seeing that she has made Porgy so happy and that "Porgy t'ink right now he gots a she-gawd," they grudgingly accept her. She joins them on an island picnic, but just as the group is about to leave, Crown emerges from his hiding place and makes Bess stay with him. She finally escapes and returns in a delirious state to Catfish Row. Porgy realizes what has happened and is forgiving. Later, when Crown comes back to claim Bess, Porgy finds the strength to kill him. He is arrested. Sporting Life feeds Bess happy dust, tells her Porgy will not return for many months, and lures Bess into sailing to New York with him. Porgy returns much sooner and finds Bess gone. The women attempt to convince him it is futile trying to find her. But he demands they tell him where New York is and, learning it is "Up Nort'—past de Custom House," heads out in his cart to seek her. As he rides off, the gates are closed and the bells of St. Michael's chime the quarter hour. Cleon Throckmorton's evocative setting received "a roar of honest applause on first rise," but the play and the actors were the main thing. Woollcott, never very sympathetic to shows about blacks or, more particularly, to black players, changed his mind, observing, " 'Porgy' is the first good job the American theatre has done with the Negro, and certainly it is the first fine performance of a play I have ever seen given by a Negro troupe." Since most other critics were firmly in its corner, the mounting, with one hiatus, ran nearly 400 performances. In 1935, Heyward, along with George and Ira Gershwin, turned the play into one of the best of all American musicals, *Porgy and Bess*.

No jubilation greeted Frederic and Fanny Hatton's **Synthetic Sin** (10-10-27, 49th St.). With her flop closing in Easton, Pa., Betty Fairfax (Dorothy Burgess), a young southern girl trying for a stage career, is told by the playwright (Geoffrey Harwood) that she will not be a great actress unless she experiences life. She rejects the experience he has in mind but takes a shabby apartment on the West Side. The people she meets are largely unsavory, and she is just about to throw in the towel when a handsome gangster (Alan Birmingham) comes on the scene. Any doubts she may have had about cavorting with a hood are swept aside when she discovers he is merely another playwright, posing as a criminal to soak in atmosphere.

Frank Craven enjoyed a small hit with his **The 19th Hole** (10-11-27, George M. Cohan). Vernon Chase (Craven) is a henpecked, weak-kneed bookworm who moves for the summer to suburbia. There he is pressed into trying his luck at golf. At first his attempts are pathetic, but he soon catches on and finds himself vying with the bullying Colonel Ham-

mer (Robert Wayne). It takes a nineteenth hole to break the tie, and, while Vernon loses, he finally wins the respect of his wife (Mary Kennedy), to whom he sets out to teach the game. During intermission, slow motion films showed leading golfers of the day demonstrating their strokes. Many critics predicted the still somewhat restricted interest in golf would limit the comedy's appeal, and apparently they were right.

Several flops followed. Sidney Blackmer and Madge Kennedy, who had played together in *Love in a Mist* two seasons before, were reunited for Alice Duer Miller's **The Springboard** (10-12-27, Mansfield). Victor is a notorious philanderer. He gets Mary to abandon her trip to Paris and a promising career as a painter, and marry him, but his philanderings continue until Mary walks out. After a time, he shows up at her studio, wearing his pajamas under his overcoat and telling her he is seriously ill. She agrees to nurse him and take him back, since she knows that while he will never be faithful he genuinely loves her.

The Matrimonial Bed (10-12-27, Ambassador), which Seymour Hicks had taken from Yves Mirande and André Mouëzy-Éon's *Au premier de ces messieurs* and which reportedly Hicks had made into a London hit under a third title, was a variation on an old theme. Adolph Noblet (John T. Murray), suffering from amnesia after a railroad accident, has embarked on a new life, remarrying and becoming a hairdresser. He is called to the home of his former wife (Lee Patrick), also rewed, and the two husbands must decide who is really her legal spouse.

Harold Hutchinson and Margery Williams's **Out of the Night** (10-17-27, Lyric) was a cliché-riddled mystery comedy, set in a Maine summer home during a howling winter snowstorm. The murdered owner is found by his nephew (James Spottswood), and all manner of relations and neighbors are suspected. Characters included the usual "boob detective," a servant whom reviewers called a Hindu despite his references to Allah, and a pair of bootleggers. The detective, Ichabod Blivens (Spencer Charters), is so startled on hearing a radio blurt out, "This is Station KDAK," that he drops his revolver, raises his arms, and pleads, "Don't shoot! I surrender!" The killer proves to be the dead man's wife (Diantha Pattison). She is unmasked because the dead man had furtively installed a microphone and radio sending unit in the house and had hired a stenographer at the other end to transcribe his last argument over money with his wife. She dies after being accidentally locked up by one of the bootleggers in a secret room.

Lynn Starling's **Skin Deep** (10-17-27, Liberty) was a one-week flop. Long after he has married another woman (Chrystal Herne), Mr. Weston (Reginald Owen), a fashionable composer, comes across an old flame (Marian Warring-Mauley) and finds his bygone ardor rekindled. The woman, perhaps a bit buxom, is his wife's cousin and is now a celebrated singer. Although she herself is no bargain, being a slightly venomous cat, Mrs. Weston wisely allows the affair to run its course. She knows that for the long haul her husband will prefer her and her pampering ways to the mercurial, self-involved diva. A four-piece orchestra (two violins, a cello, and a piano) provided incidental music and accompanied the singer in an aria.

For a change, it was a Tuesday night that brought in the next spate of plays. Both American plays to premiere that evening were failures. Audiences entering the theatre to see the prolific Willard Mack's **Weather Clear—Track Fast** (10-18-27, Hudson) were greeted by ushers dressed as jockeys, and a bugle call, then common at tracks, announced the rise of the curtain. The first scene depicted stables at Havre de Grace, Md., with real horses being walked about. Joe McGinn (Joe Laurie, Jr.) and his sweetie, Mary Marlo (Janet McLeay), hope to marry and buy a small store in Baltimore with the money Joe will win betting on Dr. Patrick, a horse owned by his old buddy Silent Johnson (William Courtleigh). But a vengeful Alex Cerinac (Joseph Sweeney), whom Johnson had once fingered for drugging a horse, attempts to bribe the jockey to throw the race. He is exposed, and another jockey rides the horse. Although Dr. Patrick fails to win, Johnson forces Cerinac to buy the store for Joe. The race was not shown, as it almost assuredly would have been a few decades earlier, but was described by Joe, standing on the roof of a stable shed. Two blacks, Joe Buck and Jim Bubbles, subsequently famous as just Buck and Bubbles, played Chicken Man and Baltimore Sleeper, a pair of racetrack hangers-on, and stopped the show with a hot song-and-dance routine that culminated in "the darkest kind of Black Bottom."

Arthur Corning White's **Love in the Tropics** (10-18-27, Daly's) was set on a Philippine plantation. Middle-aged Hugh Blanton (E. J. Bunkall) fires his foreman, Dick Gray (Walter N. Greaza), when the man confesses his affection for Blanton's young wife (Isabel Baring). After an embittered native (Effingham Pinto) stabs, but does not kill, Blanton, Mendoza (Benedict MacQuarrie), a Spaniard who also lusts after Mrs. Blanton, finishes the job. Dick is accused but is ultimately cleared.

The evening's two new importations both enjoyed good runs. Roland Pertwee and Harold Dearden's **Interference** (10-18-27, Empire) told of a prominent Englishman (Arthur Wortner) led to suspect his wife (Elsie Landford) of killing a woman (Kathlene MacDonnell) who was blackmailing her with the news that the wife's first husband, supposedly dead, was still alive. The dissolute first husband (A. E. Matthews) is shown to be the real murderer.

In A. A. Milne's fantasy **The Ivory Door** (10-18-27, Charles Hopkins), a king (Henry Hull) is believed to be a devil after reemerging from a mysterious room hidden behind an ivory door. To prove she loves him, the princess (Linda Watkins) he is set to wed also visits the room. Seeing that their people now reject both of them, the couple walk through the door again, never to return.

A third foreign entry that evening was the Civic Repertory Theatre's revival of Heijermans's *The Good Hope*, which Ellen Terry had offered years earlier and in which a mother's two sons drown after sailing in an unseaworthy ship.

The New Playwrights organization took over the tiny Cherry Lane Theatre, renamed it for the group, and offered Paul Sifton's **The Belt** (10-19-27, New Playwrights). The play was a harbinger of the left-wing diatribes that would pester Broadway during the Depression. Jim Thompson (Ross Matthews) has worked for ten years on the assembly line of an automobile plant. He is exhausted. On his anniversary the company's owner, The Old Man (George N. Price), visits Jim's home and, though he can't remember Jim's name, dances a lively Black Bottom to show he is one of the boys. Jim's daughter, Nance (Gail de Hart), is courted by a young radical, Bill Vance (Lawrence Bolton), who is determined to stir up trouble by telling employees that the Belt (the assembly line) is pulling the life out of them and dehumanizing them. Jim and his buddies would lynch Bill after the youngster spends the night with Nance, but news that all of them are going to be laid off for nine months changes their minds. Bill yells, "Don't forget! Nine months, no pay. Remember all the extra time they sweated out of you for nothing. . . . Get up and walk on your two hind legs and we'll spit in The Old Man's eye!" The workers rebel, but the police rush in to quash the trouble. Critics took The Old Man to be a slap at Henry Ford, whose hectic assembly line was shown in darkish colors while an ominous Mob, armed with saxophones, banjos, and trombones, played and jazz-danced in the background. The piece was dismissed as "one-sided" vitriol.

The small and few audiences that saw Adelaide Matthews and Martha Stanley's **The Wasp's Nest**

(10-25-27, Wallack's) knew what to expect after the curtain rose on a deserted, reputedly haunted house at Halloween. The ghost bathed in a green light turned out to be a realtor looking over the property. Other characters included a crooked lawyer, several train robbers in hiding, and a courting pair.

Lord Dunsany's **If** (10-25-27, Little) was the month's second imported fantasy. It recounted the story of a man (Walter Kingsford) given a magic crystal and thus allowed to see what might have happened had he not missed a train ten years before. Although he would have married a beautiful girl and become ruler of much of Persia, he concludes he is happy in his English home.

Basil Sydney and Mary Ellis starred in the evening's most successful mounting, their modern-dress version of *The Taming of the Shrew* at the Garrick. The characters wore brightly striped, sporty clothing, used a radio and an Eastman Kodak camera, and finally drove off in a Ford flivver. For all the up-to-date shenanigans, the revival also faithfully restored much of the text that was so often omitted, including the Christopher Sly induction.

England further supplied both the hit and the flop that opened the next night. The hit was John Galsworthy's **Escape** (10-26-27, Booth), which depicted the failed attempt by a gentleman (Leslie Howard) to flee from the prison where he is serving a sentence for manslaughter. Howard portrayed Denant as "an extraordinarily engaging young man of excellent sensibilities."

The flop was Edward Knoblock's **The Mulberry Bush** (10-26-27, Republic). When Anne Lancaster (Isobel Elsom) realizes that Harry Bainbridge (James Rennie), who is in the process of being divorced by his wife, Sylvia (Claudette Colbert), will never marry her, she locks the couple in a bedroom. That, according to English law, puts an end to the divorce proceedings. Besides disliking the play, critics complained that Colbert and Rennie were miscast.

Lawton Campbell's **Immoral Isabella?** (10-27-27, Bijou) attempted to play with history much as *The Road to Rome* had done. According to Campbell, the queen (Frances Starr) pawned her jewels so that her lover (Julius McVicker) could make his voyages, and the king (Reginald Mason) acquiesced in order to get Columbus out of his way. Jokes included a reference to the Knights of Columbus and a ring known as the Columbus Circle.

Beset with a snappish wife (Patricia O'Hearn) forever wishing God would strike him dead, and working at the Strictly Strickler Brush factory run by his bourgeois father-in-law (Dodson Mitchell), Char-ley Turner (Glenn Hunter), the hero of Fulton Oursler and Aubrey Kennedy's **Behold This Dreamer** (10-31-27, Cort), which the writers took from Oursler's novel, escapes from reality by sitting in his room, playing his ocarina and daydreaming about becoming a famous painter. In desperation, Mr. Strickler has the boy committed to a mental institution. There he tells a committee of inmates who wish to have him join their group of intelligentsia that he thinks the worst thing in the world is common sense; the best, imagination. After all, common sense said man could not survive under water or fly; imagination invented the submarine and aeroplane. And he tells them of the pictures he would paint: "streaks, globs, blocks of color—orange, violet and quivering greens—a tangled profusion of color, shape and movement." A member (Thomas A. Wise) of the committee calls him a "post-pillar-expressionist." After one of his paintings wins an award and is declared a masterpiece by art critics, Strickler forces him to return home and launches a publicity campaign. This would be bad enough, but when Charley catches his wife in the arms of another man, he packs his bags, leaves the crazy world, and returns to the quiet sanity of the insane asylum. The *Telegram* saw the play as "Pirandello, with a touch of John Golden," but most reviewers felt that for all its patent charms, it failed to add up to a full evening's entertainment.

Gordon Kean's **The Arabian** (10-31-27, Eltinge) was designed for the road, where its star, Walker Whiteside, was far more popular than he was in New York. Indeed, it had been playing to good business in the hinterlands for more than a season. It seemed to some *The Desert Song*, without music. The mysterious Sontra is plaguing the British from his desert hideaway. The polished Abd el Rey (Whiteside) gives the British a safe-conduct through the desert, but the suspicious British take a different route and are set upon by Sontra, who guessed the Englishmen would react the way they did. Sontra and Abd el Rey turn out to be one and the same. He is prepared to kill the soldiers until Diane (Ellis Baker), an English girl who pleads for him to spare the men, is shown to be his long-lost daughter. In return for sparing the soldiers, Sontra's clan receive land and he is allowed to go to England to seek the lady he once loved.

Elliott Lester's **Take My Advice** (11-1-27, Belmont) focused on a schoolteacher, Bradley Clement (Ralph Morgan), and his visit to the Weaver family. He is one of their son's teachers, although the son, Bud (Raymond Guion), describes him as "more like a human being than a teacher." Learning that Bud plans to leave school without graduating, he hopes to change the boy's mind. He finds the Weaver home in turmoil, with Mrs. Weaver (Lucia Moore) giving her savings to a go-getter oil stock salesman (Ray Walburn), Bud in the snares of a seductive, gold-digging actress (Mary Stills), and Bud's pretty sister, Ann (Vivian Tobin), under the influence of an effeminate, lorgnetted phony (Herbert Yost) who runs a drama school. By pretending to want to buy oil stocks and enroll in the school, and by offering to make whoopee with the actress, Clement exposes them. He even uncovers the fact that the stock peddler and the supposed actress are husband and wife, and professional swindlers. Clement's reward is Ann.

The author of **Ink** (11-1-27, Biltmore) was a Minneapolis newspaperman writing under a pseudonym made up from the last names of three famous editors, Dana Watterson Greeley. Franklin Jerome (Charles Richman), the crusading publisher of the *Morning Chronicle*, a paper owned by his rich wife (Sue MacManamy), is having an affair with Jeanne Keenan (Kay Strozzi), unaware she is also going the rounds with the paper's drama critic (Robert Hyman) and a bootlegging politician (Brandon Evans). One evening, after he passes out drunk in her room, she and the men go driving. Their car kills a woman and child. The paper's high-principled managing editor, Robert Buchanan (William Harrigan), publishes the story, which immediately threatens to involve Jerome. The bootlegger's death helps relieve the pressure, but Mrs. Jerome seriously considers divorcing her husband and marrying Buchanan.

Waved away by Gilbert Gabriel in the *Sun* as "a richly decorated disaster," Philip Barry's **John** (11-2-27, Klaw) closed ignominiously after eleven performances. Not only was the play damned, but the players' poor enunciation, Guthrie McClintic's uninspired direction, and even the "bronchial tubed spectators" were assailed. Only Norman Bel Geddes's settings, particularly the gold-surfaced living-hall at Machaerus, received general praise. Barry's story followed John the Baptist (Jacob Ben Ami) from his condemnation of Herodias (Constance Collier) and Antipas (George Graham), and his refusal to accept their bribes ("He may not be able to move mountains," Antipas remarks, "but mountains cannot move him"), to the moment before his beheading when he first fully comprehends the mission of Christ.

Even Mae West could come a cropper, as she did in her own play, **The Wicked Age** (11-4-27, Daly's). The plot was minor. When an uncle (Hal Clarendon), who has ordered his flapper ward, Babe Carson, not to go to questionable roadhouses, returns home and finds Babe has brought the roadhouse gang to his living room, he kicks her out. So Babe enters a beauty contest, wins, and sets herself up in a posh New York apartment. A small Negro jazz orchestra accompanied the star as she sang some slightly suggestive songs between offering such fly lines as "He was a quarterback at Notre Dame; he's now a fullback for this dame" or, in response to a French count's saying, "I kiss your hand, Mademoiselle, and later I will kiss you some more," commenting, "Fifty million Frenchmen can't be wrong." One critic noted that the men West surrounded herself with were all bruisers over six feet tall.

All three plays to open the next Monday were also bombs. The lone American entry was a totally amateur botch, Stephen G. Champlin and Fredric S. Isham's **One Shot Fired** (11-7-27, Mayfair). It apparently dealt with the search for the body of a philanderer an outraged flapper had killed in a Greenwich Village apartment. In fact the drunken man was not dead but had regained consciousness and scampered out a window.

Whatever London thought of Miles Malleson's **The Fanatics** (11-7-27, 49th St.), New York had no time for it. Malleson's tale looked at youngsters who have come of age during the war and their more modern notions of love and marriage.

But Broadway was even less receptive to Rosso di San Secondo's **The Stairs** (11-7-27, Bijou), which recounted the vengeance of a lawyer (Lester Lonergan) who forces his unfaithful wife (Dorothy Sands) to live alone in a shabby tenement he owns. She is left with no reason to live after hearing that her daughter has died.

The month's first hit was George Abbott and Ann Preston Bridgers's **Coquette** (11-8-27, Maxine Elliott's). Dr. Besant (Charles Waldron), a conservative southern widower, is unhappy that his daughter, Norma (Helen Hayes), is seeing Michael Jeffery (Eliot Cabot), whom he considers an ungentlemanly ruffian. She pleads that Michael is still suffering from having been shell shocked in the war. The youngsters ignore Dr. Besant's orders not to see one another, and spend the night together. After an angry Michael blurts out the truth, the doctor shoots and kills him. Norma is told that the only way for her to save her father is to appear on the witness stand, claim she is still a virgin, and insist Michael attempted to attack her. Since she is pregnant with his child, she refuses. When her father is brought home briefly, she pleads, "Just for one minute I want you to be as you used to. Let's just pretend we're like we used to be before any of this happened."

Then, with her father's gun in her handbag, she walks off and shoots herself. John Anderson of the *Evening Post* welcomed "a fragile and exquisite tragedy, a truly rare and touching evening," while Atkinson noted of Miss Hayes, "From the coquettish dissembling, the bright irresponsibility of the first scenes, she passes to the anguish of the conclusion without changing key—from girlhood to sudden, cruel womanhood. What a range of emotion!" The play ran for more than ten months. On its subsequent tour Miss Hayes became pregnant and left the cast to have her "Act of God" baby, prompting the play's notorious producer, Jed Harris, to win headlines by suing her in order to keep her in the cast or win compensation for her leaving. She won when the court agreed a baby was an "Act of God."

James B. Fagan's "sequel to the diary of Samuel Pepys," **And So to Bed** (11-9-27, Shubert), delighted New York much as it had London with its saga of Pepys (Wallace Eddinger) calling to receive the thanks of a lady (Mary Grey) whom he rescued from a cutpurse and having to hide when Charles II (Charles Bryant) arrives to make love to her. Later he also has some explaining to do to Mrs. Pepys (Yvonne Arnaud).

A seeming committee wrote **Nightstick** (11-10-27, Selwyn). The program gave credit to John Wray, Elaine Sterne Carrington, and J. C. and Elliott Nugent, while insiders knew that Max Marcin had done a major, uncredited rewrite. Officer Glennon (Thomas Mitchell) has two grievances against Chick Williams (Wray), since Williams has killed another cop and married the girl, Joan Manning (Lee Patrick), that Glennon himself loved. Joan is prepared to provide Chick with an alibi, since both of them were at *The Trial of Mary Dugan* at the time of the slaying, until Glennon uncovers the fact that the intermission was long enough for Chick to dash off to the warehouse, kill the cop, and return before the next act began. He corners and captures Chick in a cabin in the Catskills.

The lone American entry the next Monday, Samuel Ruskin Golding's **New York** (11-14-27, Mansfield), was slammed by most critics, one of whom suggested, "If they closed shows on Wednesday, this one should qualify." And he continued by blasting the playwright as "the barrister with a Shipman complex, [who] still bats a 1,000 as the prolific author of theatrical sewage." A girl (Ruth Shepley) imprisoned for stealing a woman's purse to pay medical expenses after her father's employer (George MacQuarrie) refused to help the man when he was injured in a workplace accident eventually becomes the employer's mistress, has an affair with the man's son, then is put on trial for shooting a detective. Gershwin's "Rhapsody in Blue" was used as background music.

Of the two importations to premiere that evening, Noel Coward's **The Marquise** (11-14-27, Biltmore) had the longer stay—ten weeks—thanks in good measure to Billie Burke. "Loveliness itself in the powdered wig and the frills and the ruffles" of the eighteenth century, she played a French aristocrat who must prevent her daughter (Madge Evans) by one marriage from wedding her son (Rex O'Malley) by another. She succeeds in finding them new mates, landing a proposal of marriage for herself as well. A second critic, noting that Miss Burke played a woman in her early forties, suggested she could still pass for a girl in her twenties.

Although Pauline Lord was more admired as a great actress than the beautiful but shallow Billie Burke, years would pass before she enjoyed another hit. Her latest vehicle, Frank Vosper's **Spellbound** (11-14-27, Earl Carroll), had been banned in London because it touched too closely on a recent English murder. Bitterly disappointed in her marriage, Ethel Carter encourages the advances of her lodger (Donn Cook) and eventually provokes him into killing her husband (Campbell Gullen). Both are sentenced to death. Miss Lord's most poignant scenes were with her father (O. P. Heggie), whom she cannot reach in the prison visiting room after her conviction: "Her constricted, pleading gestures, her twitching body, bending forward in a kind of mute supplication . . . make the playgoer's heart stand still."

The central figure in Chester De Vonde and Kilbourn Gordon's **Tia Juana** (11-15-27, Bijou) is Sprutt (Frederic Burt), an ex-convict who now smuggles Chinese into California from his Mexican base. Sprutt is determined to get back at the judge who sent him to prison. He lures the man's son (Harold Elliott) to his place and contrives to have it seem the boy killed a man in defense of his girl (Carolyn Ferriday). But his plans go for nought, and Sprutt is killed by a man (Paul Wright) whose bride he attempted to seduce. The play ran less than a week.

The next play to appear lasted twice as long. F. S. Merlin's **The King Can Do No Wrong** (11-16-27, Masque) unfolded in a Graustarkian South American kingdom. Baron Reus (Lionel Atwill) sets out to catch the man who assassinated the crown prince. He can do little after he realizes the womanizing prince was killed by an American diplomat (Larry Fletcher) for raping his fiancée, but he does quell a rebellion led by Baron Almeria (Felix Krembs) and, following Almeria's death, weds his wife (Leona Hogarth).

Max Reinhardt brought over his celebrated Berlin company and began a stand at the huge Century Theatre on the 17th with *A Midsummer Night's Dream*. A circular, staircased platform served as the grotto and for most subsequent settings. "There are cavern entrances, sloping pathways down which fairies and characters come, and the whole extends down over the footlights, for various people of the play come from under the orchestra pit and descend upon occasion." Reinhardt's leading actor, Alexander Moissi, was Oberon, and Lili Darvas was Titania. Among the other productions the troupe offered were Hugo von Hofmannsthal's version of *Everyman*, with Moissi triumphing in the title role, *Danton's Death*, and *The Servant of Two Masters*.

On a much smaller scale the next evening the American Laboratory Theatre revived *Much Ado About Nothing*. Lively, slightly stylized performances were given in front of a gold checkerboard background, with red, white, blue, and black panels to hint at scenes.

Although the Theatre Guild's revival of Shaw's *The Doctor's Dilemma* at their playhouse on the 21st included Helen Westley, Morris Carnovsky, Dudley Digges, Earle Larimore, and Henry Travers in its cast, Lunt and Fontanne were given the most glowing notices. Woollcott, almost always passionately in their corner, told his readers, "It may be doubted if ever anywhere the crucial roles of the dying blackguard of an artist and his exalted, exalting wife have ever been so illuminatingly acted as they were last night by Alfred Lunt and Lynn Fontanne." More specifically, *Variety* reported that "their range, power, charm and 'class' are captivating." The play chalked up 115 performances.

A gripping new American melodrama, Barlett Cormack's **The Racket** (11-22-27, Ambassador) managed to compile just four more performances than the Shaw play. Burns Mantle hailed it as a work that "bears unmistakeably the stamp of authenticity in character, scene and speech and reflects vividly a phase of civic life in America." The outlying station house to which Captain McQuigg (John Cromwell) has been exiled for defying Chicago's political bosses and going after the notorious gangster Nick Scarsi is a dilapidating, high-ceilinged Victorian mansion with besmoked wainscoting and soiled walls. For all that, McQuigg remains determined to get Scarsi. He even refuses an offer of his old post from a state's attorney (Romaine Callender) if he will lay off. McQuigg sees a chance when Scarsi's kid brother

(Edward Eliscu) is brought in for stealing a car. He ignores an order to release the boy. A man in a brown form-fitted overcoat and soft hat appears at the station, and when a policeman refuses to allow him to see Joe Scarsi he shoots the cop and runs off. He is soon captured and brought back. McQuigg realizes the man is Nick (Edward G. Robinson), and though Scarsi warns, "I'll take anythin' you four-thousand-dollar-a-year harps can think up for me," McQuigg tricks the hood into a confession. The cornered mobster threatens to squeal on the big politicians whose darkest secrets he knows. This upsets the state's attorney, who has long been in his pay, so Scarsi is prodded into attempting an escape and is shot dead. McQuigg hopes he can be done with the coroner and the press in time for an early mass.

Lyon Mearson and Edgar M. Schoenberg's **People Don't Do Such Things** (11-23-27, 48th St.) looked with a wink at a philandering cad (Lynne Overman) who is perfectly content to allow his wife (Isobel Elsom) and mistress (Millicent Hanley) to swap places. But when he decides to spend his evenings with another gal (Elsie Lawson), all three women rebel, leaving him to run for his little black book and start phoning bygone flings.

Two foreign plays that arrived on the next Monday both found only small audiences, albeit one has since come to be considered a classic—Sean O'Casey's **The Plough and the Stars** (11-28-27, Hudson). Acted by the Irish Players, it spotlighted an impressionable man (Michael Scott) goaded into leading a band of rebels in the 1916 uprising. He is killed, and his wife (Shelah Richards) goes mad. The best notices went to performers in subsidiary roles, especially to Arthur Sinclair as the excitable, hard-drinking Fluther and to Sara Allgood as an equally bibulous, blaspheming fruit-vender.

The Civic Repertory Theatre added a Danish play to its schedule. **2 × 2 = 5** was Ernest Boyd and Holger Koppel's version of Gustav Wied's *Ranke Viljer*. It recounted the history of an unhappily married writer, who is jailed for publishing an obscene book, comes out of prison to find his wife changed for the better, and so settles down to a respectable existence.

The most striking thing about Em Jo Basshe's **The Centuries** (11-29-27, New Playwrights) seems to have been the setting disclosed on the small stage—a triple-decked view of four tenements and the stairs leading from one to another. In these shabby quarters, Jewish immigrants arrive, thrilled to finally be in a free land. Slowly life in sweatshops, strikes, corrupt city officials, and ubiquitous indifference or even cruelty whittle away their early optimism. In the end, the more acclimated head for better homes in other boroughs.

Moving to another home was also the subject of Jessie Hein Ernst and Max Simon's **Storm Center** (11-30-27, Klaw). Tricked by a devious, skinflint uncle (John Daly Murphy) into buying his Long Island house, with a large swamp attached, the Todds (Betty Lawrence and Russell Mack) encounter so many problems with drunken moving men, a fang-tongued servant (Maude Eburne), striking repairmen, falling plaster, and no running water that they arrange to sell the house for a handsome profit to a developer (who plans to drain the swamp and build a canal to the bay) and never leave their Manhattan apartment.

There was almost no story to Noel Coward's **Fallen Angels** (12-1-27, 49th St.). Two married women (Fay Bainter and Estelle Winwood) get soused and catty while awaiting the appearance of a Frenchman they once both adored. Panned as hopelessly thin and dull, the comedy had to wait nearly thirty years before Nancy Walker demonstrated how to make an uproarious evening out of it.

On the same night, Margaret Anglin began a twelve-performance visit at the Gallo in the *Electra* she had offered so briefly late last season.

Don Marquis was the unlikely author of **Out of the Sea** (12-5-27, Eltinge), a tragedy set on the Cornish coast. Raised by people who found her as a baby adrift in a boat, Isobel (Beatrix Thomson) has wed the malevolent Mark Tregesal (Lyn Harding). However, true love comes to her in the guise of an American poet, John Marstin (Rollo Peters). A fight between the two men solves nothing, so Isobel and John attempt to sail in a small boat to France. Mark tries to stop them and is stabbed to death by Isobel, who then commits suicide by leaping off a crag, thus returning to the sea from which she came.

Another suicidal foundling, Rosie (Muriel Kirkland), is prevented from killing herself by a policeman, Dan Flynn (Frank Shannon), in John Hunter Booth's **Brass Buttons** (12-5-27, Bijou). He learns that she is pregnant by a prizefighter, Kid Dickson (Gerald Kent), but when Dickson refuses to accept responsibility, Flynn marries the girl.

W. D. Hepenstall and Ralph Cullinan's **The Banshee** (12-5-27, Daly's) begins with the killing in his home of a wealthy Irish immigrant shortly after the ominous cry of a banshee has been heard. The dead man had been about to change his will. At first an evil-looking doctor (Herbert Ranson) with a knowledge of exotic poisons is suspected. But the killer is finally shown to be a Brazilian Indian

servant boy (Richard Whorf), who keeps a shrunken head in his room and who used a blowgun to commit the crime.

The title of Lula Vollmer's **Trigger** (12-6-27, Little) came from its leading figure, a North Carolina mountain girl (Claiborne Foster), who is half hoyden, half religious fanatic. She has stolen prayer cards from Sunday school to give away and kidnapped a sick baby so that she might heal it. Some neighbors believe the girl, whose wardrobe seemingly consists of torn gingham dresses, is a witch. Two engineers helping construct a nearby dam fall in love with her. One is a scoundrelly married man (Walter Connolly), but he backs off when he sees that his young associate (Minor Watson) has deeper, more honest feelings toward her.

The Norwegian Nobel Prize winner Knut Hamsun received a brief hearing with the presentation of **At the Gate of the Kingdom** (12-8-27, American Laboratory) in which a man's marriage is destroyed because of his preoccupation with his philosophic interests.

A group of Argentine players came into the Manhattan Opera House on the 8th and for the next two weeks offered a collection of native plays. The players and the plays were greeted with distinctly divided notices.

The ladies' room at the Club Pierrot in New York is the opening scene of Max Marcin and Donald Ogden Stewart's **Los Angeles** (12-19-27, Hudson). Mrs. Jones (Alison Skipworth), the maid there, has mixed feelings when her friend, Ethel (Frances Dale), reveals her cynical plans to dig for gold among the Hollywood rich. The pair head west posing as an aunt and her convent-trained niece. Once on the coast, a film magnate (G. Davison Clark) selects Ethel to keep his troublesome comedian, Eddie Trafford (Alan Brooks), in line. Of course, Eddie and Ethel really do fall in love. Eddie's last gal (Mary Robinson) attempts to shoot Eddie but hits the film magnate's son (Harold Vermilyea) instead. To prevent the very sort of scandal she initially had sought to capitalize on, Ethel marries the boy and leaves Eddie. But back in New York at the Club Pierrot, Ethel and Eddie meet again and set matters to right. The play struggled for two weeks, one week longer than another novelty which opened the same night managed.

That dud was Bruce Reynolds's **Playing the Game** (12-19-27, Ritz). The swank wedding of Gerald and Rose has to be delayed following the discovery that Gerald is already married. Gerald himself has little recollection of the ceremony since he was too far in his cups. However, all ends happily. Among the examples of the play's humor quoted by reviewers was "The lips of those Park Avenue Lotharios were so hot they couldn't eat ice cream."

On the same evening, the Irish Players, having moved to the Gallo, replaced one O'Casey play with another—in this instance a revival of *Juno and the Paycock*, with Sara Allgood and Arthur Sinclair in the title parts. To Atkinson, the performance seemed "vexatiously slow."

Gustav Blum, who had successfully strung out the runs of several plays on his roof theatre thanks to Leblang's cut-rate tickets, found he could not do the same with Virginia Farmer's **Spring Song** (12-20-27, Bayes). Believing his marriage to have been a mistake, a young sculptor reconsiders the offer of a famous prima donna to keep him. However, after a while he longs for his wife again, and the prima donna lets him go. According to one reviewer, the best thing about the play was the "genuine New York skylight art studio" of the final act.

The Love Nest (12-22-27, Comedy), Robert Sherwood's dramatization of a Ring Lardner short story, was the latest in December's growing parade of disappointments. Her husband's total absorption in his motion picture work drives Celia Gregg (June Walker) to drink. After creating a furor with a tell-all interview, she packs her bags and heads east with her ex-actor butler (G. G. Thorpe). Her husband (Clyde Fillmore) is so busy spreading the news that Sid Grauman wants his next film that he hardly notices.

Two more failures came in a night later. Cosmo Hamilton drew **Caste** (12-23-27, Mansfield) from his own novel. His story of two wealthy families—one Christian, one Jewish—who are at first opposed but eventually acquiesce to the religiously mixed marriage of their children had been told too many times to evoke much interest.

Olga Petrova was the author of **What Do We Know?** (12-23-27, Wallack's), the play that brought her back to the stage after some years in films. Kasha is still a virgin four years after her marriage to a dedicated member (Bradley Page) of the Purity League, so she runs off to live with a bohemian (Carlton Brickert) in Greenwich Village. Both men are killed by a lightning bolt. Kasha tries to reach them in a seance but succeeds only in talking with the lover before she, too, dies.

John Willard's **Sisters** (12-24-27, Klaw) presented three siblings in seemingly no-win situations. Ann (Irene Purcell) is courted by a rich married man who wants her for a mistress and by a poor but caddish one willing to marry her. The sister (Millicent Hanley) who is kept in luxury on Park Avenue tells her to choose marriage at any price; her other sister (Roberta Arnold), wed to a poor man, tells her to look for money and comfort. The sudden death of the rich man's wife allows Ann to have the best of both worlds.

Monday, December 26, 1927, was the busiest night in Broadway history. Eleven shows opened—one musical and ten straight plays. True, only one of the plays was a hit, but a second, much superior work came close. Reviewers suggested that John McGowan's **Excess Baggage** (12-26-27, Ritz) did for vaudeville what *Broadway* had done for nightclubs and *Burlesque* for its field. Its main story centered on a small-time two-a-day juggling act consisting of Eddie Kane (Eric Dressler) and Elsa McCoy (Miriam Hopkins). Because she simply stands around while Eddie does the real juggling, Elsie feels she is excess baggage. Spotted by a movie sheik who rushes her to Hollywood, she becomes a star at $500 per week and soon is supporting Eddie. Shame drives him back to the stage, but his new wire-walking act, heading foot before foot up to the gallery then sliding back to the stage, seems headed for disaster after he slips and falls, until Elsie runs up to rejoin him. There were several delicious subsidiary stories and characters. The best told of Jimmy Dunn (Frank McHugh), another vaudevillian. He attempts to court the younger of the Ford Sisters, a singing-dancing team that actually consists of mother (Suzanne Willa) and daughter (Doris Eaton). Jimmy's fast talk is countered by mama's slashing retorts, since mama wants all the nice young men on the bill for herself. One of the men she goes after is George McCarthy (Mort Downey), a song plugger whose bellowing Irish tenor voice helps put over the songs. The play ran till July.

Although some critics professed to be baffled by George Kelly's **Behold the Bridegroom** (12-26-27, Cort), especially its ending, the *Herald Tribune*'s Percy Hammond spoke for many when he saluted the work as "a good, sane, theatrical study." Bored and lonely, the hopelessly pampered Antoinette Lyle (Judith Anderson) returns home abruptly from Europe. She not only rejects her friends' suggestion that she marry Gehring Fitler (Lester Vail), an alcoholic ne'er-do-well who long has courted her, but she spurns all her wealthy suitors. Then she meets Spencer Train (John Marston), a handsome, reserved businessman—"the first man that ever held me cheap." She recognizes that she is in love and that her life heretofore has been a waste. She admits that she has been "the notorious Tony Lyle—that ridiculed every sincerity and thought it smart to say and do the meanest and most embarrassing thing to everybody on every occasion." Beset by an affliction as much spiritual as physical, she languishes. Her father (Thurston Hall) asks Train to speak with her, but she understands that she is not yet prepared to receive her "bridegroom" or the redemption he might offer. The play ran eleven weeks.

Conrad Westervelt's **Mongolia** (12-26-27, Greenwich Village) ran half as long as at its bandbox playhouse. General Oronoff (Frederic Burt), commander of White Russian forces in northern China in 1919, is also the uncle of the last of the Romanoffs (Warren McCollum), whom he is bent on getting safely to Paris. He gets an American couple (Thomas Carrigan and Mildred Florence) to escort the boy, after first testing their loyalty by having a subordinate attempt to seduce the woman and by subjecting the husband to indignities.

The consensus was that pug-nosed, Waspy Edna Hibbard was egregiously miscast in Fanny Hurst's latest look at American Jews, **It Is to Laugh** (12-26-27, Eltinge). Morris Goldfish (John Davidson), newly rich, moves his parents and sister Birdie to an expensive uptown apartment. But Birdie, seeking a life of her own, marries a crook (Frank Beaston) and takes work as a waitress in Atlanta after he is sent to the federal prison there. Although she subsequently reforms the man, her brother slams the door on her. He will not even allow her to come when her dying father (Irving Honigman) begs to see her. But her mother sneaks her in, and effects a reconciliation after the father dies.

Of the remaining six plays to open that evening, three ran three weeks; the other three ran a single week. Alice Brady was the lone reason to see John Meehan and Robert Riskin's **Bless You, Sister** (12-26-27, Forrest). Some audiences saw more than a touch of Aimee MacPherson in Mary MacDonald, the daughter of a small-town preacher. Prodded by a go-getting, totally irreligious Bible salesman (Charles Bickford), she dons white robes and, basking in a spotlight, evangelizes the susceptible. Since she herself understands her preaching is merely a business racket, she is aghast when her small-town sweetie (Robert Ames) falls for it. Although the salesman would happily bed her, Mary abandons her work, confesses all to the boyfriend, and prepares to settle down to a very ordinary life.

If playgoers could read a headline-seeking evangelist into one play, they had even less difficulty seeing a heavyweight champion and his world in another, Willard Keefe's **Celebrity** (12-26-27, Lyceum). A shrewd prizefight promoter, Circus Snyder (Crane Wilbur), latches on to a good but low-life boxer,

Barry Regan (Gavin Gordon). Snyder's superb training and his clever publicizing of Regan as bookworm and intellectual on the side bring both fame and knockouts. A brief rebellion occurs when a sleazy racketeer, Solly Gold (Maurice Freeman), attempts to push too far, too fast. But all ends happily. The play closed before Gene Tunney, Tex Rickard, or Arnold Rothstein apparently could comment.

In Sydney Stone's **Restless Women** (12-26-27, Morosco) several wives lament their disillusionment with marriage. One (Mary Young) decides to flee to Greenwich Village and take up with a good-looking young artist (Robert Crozier), only to have her flapper daughter (Leila Frost) steal him from her.

Brooks Atkinson began his review of **Venus** (12-26-27, Masque) with the sort of puckerishly balanced sentence that would become one of his trademarks: "Writing on an uncommonly imaginative theme, Rachel Crothers has put together an unimaginative play." (Atkinson had caught the show at a Sunday runthrough and attended George Kelly's opening the next night, so that two of the eleven notices in Tuesday's paper were his.) The curtain rose to the sounds of airplanes taking off and radio broadcasts crackling away. Since this is the world of some undated future, the planes are heading for Venus. Much of the action unfolds on an apartment house roof used by planes for take-offs and landings. In order to equalize the sexes, a doctor (Arnold Lucy) has concocted a pill which makes assertively masculine men feminine and simperingly coy women agressively macho. Thus, Herbert Beveridge (Tyrone Power) is reduced to weeping into his handkerchief and donning drag to dance a fandango, while Agnes Beveridge (Patricia Collinge), his meek wife, and Virgie Gibbs (Cecilia Loftus) take to guzzling booze and cussing like troopers. Only those whose intellectual interests make them relatively indifferent to sex are left unaffected.

William Hurlbut's **Paradise** (12-26-27, 48th St.) was the second of the evening's one-weekers. Having left her hometown of Paradise, Ohio, to escape the taunts of her married sisters and neighbors, Winnie Elder (Lillian Foster) moves to New York. From there she writes home that she has married and includes a picture of her handsome husband with her letter. The truth is that Winnie is still a spinster, so when one sister announces she will come to New York for a visit, Winnie writes that her husband has died suddenly. She wangles a corpse from the morgue and takes it back home for burial. Her ruse is discovered when her aunt (Minnie Dupree) has the coffin opened to disclose the body of an old derelict. But not to worry, for Winnie finds real love with a local doctor (Warren William).

John Barrymore's wife, Michael Strange, found she was no attraction—and no Bernhardt or Maude Adams—when she was starred in a revival of *L'Aiglon* at the Cosmopolitan.

Only two plays premiered the next evening. One was *Show Boat,* the first truly all-American operetta, which, with its great Jerome Kern score, remains one of the towering masterpieces of our lyric stage. The other was Philip Barry's **Paris Bound** (12-27-27, Music Box). At the wedding of Jim and Mary Hutton (Donn Cook and Madge Kennedy), Jim's father (Gilbert Emery) berates Jim's mother (Martha Mayo), who years ago had divorced him for an infidelity: "For following a physical impulse which I share with the rest of the animal kingdom, you destroyed a spiritual relationship which belonged only to us." Jim and Mary swear they will avoid such problems. But five years later Mary discovers that Jim, whose business takes him regularly to Europe, is having an affair there with an old flame. She prepares to divorce him, but then realizes that Jim has ignored her own flirtation with an attractive young composer (Donald MacDonald), so decides to live and let live. Hailed by Atkinson as "a comedy of manners, rich in quality, true in temper and buoyant in its social criticism," it ran for seven months.

The living room of the Cavendishes' duplex apartment in George S. Kaufman and Edna Ferber's **The Royal Family** (12-28-27, Selwyn) is a magnificent, high-ceilinged affair. At the rear, in the center, a winding staircase leads to a balcony containing the bedrooms. A large portrait of Aubrey Cavendish, the great actor who founded the line, looms above the stairway. His wife, Fanny (Haidee Wright), is the duenna of the clan and still looks forward to one more tour. Their daughter, Julie (Ann Andrews), is a leading actress, while Julie's daughter, Gwen (Sylvia Field), is a promising ingenue. Gwen's socialite beau, Perry (Roger Pryor), attempts to show her the futility of a theatrical life: "Get your name up in electric lights, and a fuse blows out—and where are you?" Gwen retorts by suggesting she can name dozens of players from bygone centuries and challenges Perry to name just two seventeenth-century stockbrokers. The apartment is thrown into an uproar by the unexpected arrival of Julie's mercurial brother, Tony (Otto Kruger), who has slugged his director, broken his film contract, and apparently is in line as well for a breach of promise suit. With the help of a businessman (Joseph King) who is trying to persuade Julie to give up the theatre

and marry him, Tony gets a passport and, after changing clothes with a callboy to avoid the mob of reporters outside, sneaks off to Europe. He returns a year later, having started a small war with his amours. For a time both Julie and Gwen seem ready to quit the stage, but their excitement at Tony's return and the new play he describes convinces the men in their lives that they must go along with them or else leave them completely. Indifferent to the men's decisions, the family, and their ever loyal producer, Oscar Wolfe (Jefferson De Angelis), prattle on until they realize that Fanny has died quietly in her chair. Critics praised the comedy, with *Variety* placing it "among the blue-blooded shows of the season." Although the authors strenuously denied it, the play was perceived as a send-up of the Barrymores and the Drews. It delighted Broadway for ten months.

Alexander Berkman, a professed anarchist who had been involved in numerous brushes with the law, was the translator of Emil Bernhard's *Das reizende Lamm* as **The Prisoner** (12-28-27, Provincetown Playhouse). The play described the brutal torture by a sadistic jailer of a man imprisoned for preaching pacifist ideals to czarist troops. This "peasant-saint" has refused both the authorities' bribes and the revolutionists' entreaties to launch a bloody reign of terror. But the man's dying word—"Brothers"— moves the jailer to free his other inmates.

Wilson Collison, who had enjoyed some success as a writer of farce, had no luck with his melodramatic **Red Dust** (1-2-28, Daly's), which launched the new year. Van Tene (Sydney Shields), an Indo-Chinese wanton, creates problems on the plantation of Lucien Fourville (Curtis Cooksey), even killing a man who attempts to whip her. But then she saves Fourville from a crazed neighbor, earning herself a proposal of marriage. This last scene elicited snickers from the audience with its improbable turn of events, exaggerated, no doubt, by Miss Shields's performance, which one critic suggested resembled "a feeble imitation of Mae West."

Interest moved from Indo-China to China itself (when it was known as Cathay) in Eugene O'Neill's **Marco Millions** (1-9-28, Guild). Young Marco Polo (Alfred Lunt) is sent to Cathay on business in the company of his father and uncle. His drive to succeed is matched by his insensitivity to more delicate matters. Thus, he has no idea of the deep love Kukachin (Margalo Gillmore), granddaughter of the Great Kaan (Baliol Holloway), feels for him. So he unconcernedly piles one commercial success upon another before returning home. The Kaan, who had enjoyed Marco's strange mixture of adeptness, vulgarity, and naivety, and had favored the boy, now must watch Kukachin waste away. He broods, "My hideous suspicion is that God is only an infinite, insane energy which creates and destroys with no other purpose than to pass eternity in avoiding thought." In Italy Marco joins his bride-to-be for a lavish orgy while, back in Cathay, Kukachin dies. Critics were uncertain whether to emphasize the play's serious undertones or its more superficial satire of Babbittry. Hammond warned some playgoers would find the evening too long and possibly boring but continued, "To the knowing postgraduate of the Guild audience it will afford pleasure as a splendid and thoughtful burlesque." The scenery and costumes were universally lauded. Lee Simonson's basic, stepped triptych allowed for quick changes from the solid buildings of Venice to the beauties of Persia and India and the filagreed grace of Cathay. To these were added "costumes of refulgent splendor and bizarre variety, brilliantly composed groupings of Oriental figures, gongs, bells, chants, dirges, voices in chorus and mysterious declamation." The same critics ran a wide gamut in assessing Alfred Lunt's performance, albeit most were captivated by Margalo Gillmore's Kukachin. The play remained in repertory, alternating weekly with *The Doctor's Dilemma*, for the rest of the season.

When Wyn Hayward (Richard Bird), the young lawyer who is the central figure in John Van Druten's **Diversion** (1-11-28, 49th St.), learns that the lovely actress Rayetta Muir (Cathleen Nesbitt) wants to end their affair, he strangles her. He then cajoles his physician father (Guy Standing) into giving him poison.

There was more murder in Philip Barry and Elmer Rice's **Cock Robin** (1-12-28, 48th St.). The curtain rose to disclose an eighteenth-century English grog shop where a man is shot and falls dead. The problem is the man should not have been dead, since the grog shop was a setting for a play and the figures involved were actually members of the Cole Valley Community Players in a dress rehearsal. Someone had substituted real bullets for the blanks. It also develops that the murdered man, the most detested member of the troupe, was not merely shot; he was stabbed in the back as well. One eagle-eyed member (Beulah Bondi) spots the clue that leads to the apprehension of the group's director (Edward Ellis). A high point was the simpering curtain speech given by a muddle-headed dowager (Beatrice Herford) to thank the audience and explain the errors in the program and any other matter that came into her head. The comedy ran an even 100 performances.

Another opening that evening ran exactly as long. Willard Mack's **A Free Soul** (1-12-28, Playhouse) was taken from Adela Roger St. John's novel. Jan Ashe (Kay Johnson) was raised by her father (Lester Lonergan), a famous trial lawyer, to think for herself, so he cannot protest too strenuously when she marries a suave, blond-haired gambler, Ace Wilfong (Melvyn Douglas). And she sticks by Ace after he kills a young man she has kept on seeing. Her father dutifully defends her husband and wins an acquittal. But after the verdict is announced, it is discovered that the lawyer has died quietly in his chair (shades of *The Royal Family*). As someone in the court remarks, "The defense rests."

Finally abandoning its reliance on foreign works, although admittedly it had revived one native play, the Civic Repertory Theatre produced a new American drama, Walter Ferris's examination of the marital double standard, **The First Stone** (1-13-28, Civic Repertory), which was based on a story by Mary Heaton Vorse. John Peri (Egon Brecher), a New England fisherman-turned-trucker, is not always faithful to his wife (Eva Le Gallienne) on his trips away from home. But when he learns that she, too, is having an affair, he explodes. His wife leaves him, but then returns to have it out, and he realizes he must accept what has happened. Tepid notices for the play and Miss Le Gallienne resulted in the work's being withdrawn from the repertory after only about twenty performances.

Critics gave short shrift to John Howard Lawson's "excruciatingly uninteresting," "hectic and cacophonous" piece of left-wing balderdash, **The International** (1-14-28, New Playwrights), in which a pair of vicious American capitalists were shown prepared to bring chaos to Tibet and to start a second world war in their greedy quest for oil. As was customary with the New Playwrights, the work was performed on a constructivist setting to a background of jazz music. The "limited group of radicals" who supported this sort of material was so limited that the play closed after less than a month.

Two disappointing revivals followed. The more disappointing of the pair was Winthrop Ames's mounting of *The Merchant of Venice* for George Arliss at the Broadhurst on the 16th. Reviewers found it polite and bloodless, with Peggy Wood's Portia faring no better than Arliss's curiously gentleman-like Shylock. But Arliss, extremely popular on the road as well as in New York, took the production out for an extended cross-country tour after its eight-week stand. Then, without any flourishes, he retired from the stage and confined the remainder of his career to films.

John Galsworthy's study of unequal justice, *The Silver Box*, with Isobel Elsom in the part Ethel Barrymore had played twenty-one years before, elicited scant approval when it opened at the Morosco on the 17th.

Nor were five novelties that came in next made welcome. Milton Herbert Gropper's **Mirrors** (1-16-28, Forrest) showed what happened when the children of some high-living suburbanites attempted to emulate their parents. Luckily, one sensible daughter (Sylvia Sidney) is present to call a halt to the orgiastic smoking, drinking, and necking, and thus shame her parents.

The Patriot (1-19-28, Majestic), Ashley Dukes's translation of Alfred Neumann's drama, recounted the attempt of a Russian count (Leslie Faber) to assassinate an insane czar (Lyn Harding) and replace him with the young Grand Duke (John Gielgud). After the killing the count commands his orderly to shoot him, then kill himself. The curtain falls, and two slightly spaced shots are heard.

Although George Jean Nathan blasted his fellow critics for not appreciating Vincent Lawrence's **A Distant Drum** (1-20-28, Hudson), most of those colleagues agreed that for all its superb acting, the play failed to live up to its early scenes. John Milburn (Louis Calhern) is a totally unprincipled gigolo. But just as he is about to throw over Lynn Wilson (Mary Newcomb) for her much richer friend, Edith Reed (Katherine Wilson), Mr. Wilson (Felix Krembs) learns of his wife's liaison and shoots John dead.

Owen Davis, "the most prolific of American stage writers" in the eyes of one contemporary critic, had to settle for a single week's run after reviewers finished with **Carry On** (1-23-28, Masque). Horace Marston (Berton Churchill), determined to pay off every debt after his family's hundred-year-old woolen mills are thrown into bankruptcy, all but bankrupts himself and in the process drives his daughter into an affair with a cigarette-puffing, married cad, and his son and wife into thievery.

A playwriting novice, Daisy Wolf, had only slightly better luck with **We Never Learn** (1-23-28, Eltinge). James Bruce (Charles Trowbridge) is a prominent attorney and likely to be governor of his state. At first he is reluctant to defend a boy (Richard Romero) accused of murder. But his wife's pleadings finally persuade him. The boy is acquitted, since he really was innocent. In fact, the killer was the lawyer, who committed the murder when the dead man had made advances to the lawyer's mistress (Estelle Winwood). The lawyer's wife (Elisabeth Risdon), having discovered the truth, prepares to leave him. But he is more interested in phoning his mistress to make a date to meet out of town.

The string of flops was broken by Robert E. Sherwood's **The Queen's Husband** (1-25-28, Playhouse). Since King Eric VIII (Roland Young), titular head of "an anonymous kingdom, situated on an island in the North Sea, somewhere between Denmark and Scotland," is more interested in watching penguins at the zoo, playing checkers with a courtier, or riding his bicycle than in carrying out his duties, his kingdom is ruled by his harridan wife (Gladys Hanson) and his ambitious premier, General Northrup (Reginald Barlow). To gain sorely needed funds for the kingdom the queen heads for America, determined to raise the money even if it means going straight to the President of the United States. All Eric can say is, "God help the President of the United States." While she is abroad, the populace rises up, and Eric, finally asserting himself, sides with the rebels. Having read the constitution the night before, he learns he can abolish Parliament, which he promptly does to the consternation of Northrup, who long has had it under his thumb. However, on the queen's return she demands that they proceed with the wedding she arranged for her daughter, Princess Anne (Katharine Alexander), without the girl's knowledge or consent. The sympathetic Eric quietly contrives to have Anne elope with the man she truly loves, then he sets out to enjoy what will assuredly be an unusual, brideless state wedding. Aisle-sitters held reservations about the play's mixing comedy with serious social problems, and as a result the play ran only four months. But it subsequently was a bigger hit in England and remained popular for years with amateur groups.

The latest of Gustav Blum's cheapies for his roof theatre was Morris Ankrum and Vincent Duffey's **The Mystery Man** (1-26-28, Bayes). It had an interesting first act. Robert Wheeler, quite in his cups, returns to his apartment to find a dead man on his sofa. He calls in his buddy, who seems to know something about the man but will not speak out. Wheeler's fiancée also arrives and also seems to know something but won't say what. Then, with all the other characters offstage, Wheeler's Japanese valet enters and signals somebody on the outside by turning lights off and on. Finally, a stranger (Allyn Joslyn) from Chicago comes on the scene and confesses to the killing. Of course, since that was only the first act, the confession cannot hold water. A paternalistic detective takes two more acts to show that the killer was Wheeler's maid and that she killed the man because he threatened to reveal that he was the father of Wheeler's fiancée and that the maid was her mother. Like two other plays this month, *The Mystery Man* ran an even 100 performances.

Several critics expressed their surprise that Edward Locke could write anything as inept as **57 Bowery** (1-26-28, Wallack's), although they were willing to concede that its outdated dialogue might well have come from his pen. In Locke's story, Manny Schiller (John D. Seymour), ashamed that his father (Herbert Adler) is a Jew and a Bowery pawnbroker, falls in with a suave socialite, Edward Van Cleve (Robert Brister). Besides being a socialite, Van Cleve is also a thief, and the jewels he leaves in hock with old David Schiller are all stolen. A friendly Irish detective (Harold Healy) nabs Van Cleve, who employs a poisoned cigarette to escape justice, and exculpates Schiller. A secondary story recounted the dealings the older Schiller's radical daughter (Joan Blair) had with fellow left-wingers.

C. M. Selling's **So Am I** (1-27-28, Comedy), taken from an unspecified Italian comedy by Camillo Scolari, told of a convent-trained wife (Betty Linley), her sex-starved husband (Walter Kingsford), and the architect (Vernon Steele) hired by him to make the wife's room less like a nunnery. The architect gives the wife a copy of a Boccaccio story about a woman, her unhappy husband, and her lover. The wife dreams that she and the two men in her life are playing out the story. But when she wakes, she realizes she must send the architect away and be more of a true wife to her spouse.

No play of the season created more advance excitement than Eugene O'Neill's **Strange Interlude** (1-30-28, John Golden). To most critics and playgoers the advance ballyhoo was merited. Nina Leeds (Lynn Fontanne) is bitter that her father, Professor Leeds (Philip Leigh), refused to allow her to marry the man she loved and who was killed in the war. Now, she is admired by three men. Charles Marsden (Tom Powers) is a shy writer, too attached to his mother's apron strings to admit to his feelings openly. Dr. Edmund Darrell (Glenn Anders), for all his affection, prefers the distant safety of his career. So Nina marries the third man, Sam Evans (Earle Larimore), a weak if all-American type, and becomes pregnant, only to learn from her mother-in-law (Helen Westley) that insanity runs in the family. She has an abortion, then secretly allows Edmund to father a child by her. Eleven years pass. Her son, Gordon (Charles Walters in early scenes, then John J. Burns), grows up preferring Sam to his real father or his increasingly possessive mother. Recognizing that she has lost both Edmund and Gordon, she is stunned by Sam's death. Only Charles remains

loyal, so she marries him. He urges her to regard the past as an interlude, and she agrees, concluding, "Our lives are merely strange dark interludes in the electrical display of God the father!" (Compare that with the Kaan's remark in *Marco Millions*.) She can only congratulate Charles, "who, passed beyond desire, has all the luck at last." The action was stopped frequently to allow the characters lengthy Freudian asides, expressing their inner thoughts. The play ran from 5:15 until after eleven, with a long intermission at 7:40 for dinner.

A few critics disliked the play. Woollcott had jumped the gun by offering a slashing review in *Vanity Fair* before the opening. (As a result, he was not allowed to review the opening in the *World*, and his arguments with his editor about this led in a few months' time to the end of his career as a drama critic.) Another dissenter was Robert Benchley in *Life*. Conceding that the work was "probably" a great play, he nonetheless went on to report that he himself was "irritated to the bursting point by the pretentious banality of the lines," and added facetiously, "If Samuel Shipman had written the first act of 'Strange Interlude' (and he could have), the play would have been laughed off the stage. If Mae West had written the boat race scene in Act 8 (and she wouldn't have), every reviewer in town would have taken the day off to kid it." Without resorting to the more formal, slightly pompous phrasing of other critics, *Variety*'s man best caught the excitement and approval of most of his colleagues and fellow playgoers when he reported, "There were some 20 curtain calls at the conclusion of the show—cheers and calls for the author, director and about everybody else. In other words, this long, long play with a small cast held its audience tight and didn't lose a customer." He then added, "Nor will it. It is one of the season's cinches and certainly the best thing by far that O'Neill has ever written." The cast was also praised, even if the praise usually seemed lost in the extensive paragraphs devoted to the play itself. The large number of glowing notices and the ongoing, excited word of mouth, coupled a few months later with the Pulitzer Prize and the drama's highly publicized banning by the Boston censor, kept the show running for 426 performances at a then steep top of $4.40. The drama also helped the spreading vogue for psychoanalysis and sometimes showy public self-analysis.

Aimee MacPherson and her ilk were depicted onstage for the second time in just over a month in Sidney Howard and Charles MacArthur's **Salvation** (1-31-28, Empire). But audiences that would not buy Alice Brady would not buy Pauline Lord either, even though Atkinson extolled her performance as "moving and enthralling, magnetic in its stream of impulses across the footlights." Bethany Jones is a decent girl turned by her grasping, pushing mother (Helen Ware) and the mother's cynical friend, a former circus man named Brady (George MacFarlane), into a money-making evangelist. The handsome tenor, Victor (Donald Gallaher), who travels with the group gets Bethany to marry him. She believes he truly cares for her until she overhears a battle between him, her mother, and her mother's lover over how to split her earnings. She walks out on all of them, vowing to continue her religious life in an unmercenary manner. Only the company's facile-tongued but disillusioned publicity agent (Osgood Perkins) cheers her on. To his "Hallelujah!" she walks away with a "Hallelujah!" of her own.

A fiery performance by Claudette Colbert could not save Tom Cushing's **La Gringa** (2-1-28, Little). Believing her to be an heiress, Captain Bowditch (George Nash) takes Carlota from her Mexican convent school, pretends to marry her, and brings her to his New Bedford home. While he heads out to claim her money, he leaves her with his cold, bigoted relations. Thus alone and lonely, she falls in love with a sympathetic schoolteacher (Paul Wright). Bowditch, having learned there is no fortune and suspecting her feelings, casts out the girl. Since she has come to realize that her love of the teacher can wreck his career, she reluctantly breaks off the relationship. Donning a flaming red dress, she does a stomping dance for the drunken Bowditch, poisons his drink, then grabs a ship sailing back to Mexico. For additional color, the play was set in the mid-1880s.

The Atlas of Harry Delf's **Atlas and Eva** (2-6-28, Mansfield) was Elmer Nebblepredder (Delf), a $40-a-week floorwalker who has taken the burdens of all his family on himself. His grouchy father (George Marion) has lost his job as a stage doorman for insulting the actors, his mother (Helen Lowell) is a hypochondriac, his little brother (Tom Brown) is forever running away, and his sister (Dorothea Chard) wants to marry a man (Donald Dillaway) who may be a thief. Even when he merely mentions his own name on the phone Nebblepredder must inevitably go to the trouble of spelling it. He finally has a nervous breakdown. But things look up after the sister elopes with her man—now cleared of the charges against him—and the family agrees to move into her new home. Elmer can at last be alone with his Eva (Leona Hogarth). Although it survived in New York for only three weeks, it subsequently toured as *Too Much Family*.

Frank Wilson's **Meek Mose** (2-6-28, Princess) also survived a mere three weeks, even though Wilson was the black postman who played Porgy eight times a week after completing his route, and even though on opening night the meager audience included Mayor Jimmy Walker, Otto Kahn, the financier, and Max Reinhardt. Mose (Charles H. Moore) is the spiritual leader of the poor blacks in Mexia, Tex. The town authorities order the blacks to move their shacks from land sought by a developer and rebuild them next to the town dump, on a piece of land known as "The Gut." One baby dies in the process, and the blacks are about to turn against Mose, when oil is discovered on the property. The curtain falls as the blacks joyfully sing a Negro spiritual, "Who'll Be a Witness?" With all their goodwill, the critics dismissed the play and the acting as childish.

To keep some of his actors busy, Chamberlain Brown, an agent, mounted a revival of *Mrs. Dane's Defense* at the Cosmopolitan on the same night. Violet Heming was the woman whose past comes back to wreck her hopes for a happy marriage.

February's first hit was an importation, John G. Brandon and George Pickett's **The Silent House** (2-7-28, Morosco), in which a will leaves a man (Alan Dinehart) $4,000,000 worth of bonds provided he can find where they are hidden in his late uncle's spooky house. A sinister Chinese doctor (Howard Lang) does everything he can to prevent their discovery, but a loyal Chinese houseboy (Clarke Silvernail) helps to uncover them.

Lawrence Langner's **These Modern Women** (2-13-28, Eltinge) was the month's third three-week flop. Mrs. Haynes is better known as Roberta Coakley (Chrystal Herne), since among her absurdly modern notions is one that says a wife should retain her maiden name. To justify her own infidelity with a blasé English author (Alan Mowbray), she encourages her soft-spoken, unflappable husband (Minor Watson) to have an affair with his secretary (Helen Flint). But when the two take her up on it and lock their bedroom door on her, she pounds futilely at the door for admission. Imagine her consternation when hubby says he has enjoyed himself so much that he is taking their son and his secretary and moving out.

Vincent Lawrence's brother, Warren F. Lawrence, was the author of **Quicksand** (2-13-28, Masque), which sank out of sight after a mere fortnight. Having postponed a long-contemplated vacation at the behest of blonde, statuesque Mrs. Spencer (Anne Forrest) in order to win an acquittal for Roger Spencer (C. W. Van Voorhis) on a murder charge, Robert Clayton (Robert Ames) discovers the Spencers are criminals who were instrumental in sending his brother to the chair. However, just before the pair are sent to prison for another crime, Clayton learns that Mrs. Spencer was a reluctant accomplice, so he promises to work for her release and marry her after she divorces her husband. If the play was dull, it was mercifully short—running less than two hours.

The month's fourth three-weeker was Ralph Thomas Kettering's **The Clutching Claw** (2-14-28, Forrest). The play opens with a monstrous hand reaching out and choking a man to death as he sits by his fireside on a stormy night. A policeman (Charles Slattery) would arrest a neurotic lad (Duncan Penwarden) who is the obvious killer until a smart aleck reporter (Ralph Morgan) starts snooping around. He discovers the house is used by dope smugglers and haunted by ghosts (one of which, with the help of some radiumized cloth and a crane, flies out over the footlights and above the audience). He finally photographs the killer attempting another murder. Who is the killer? The very man the policeman wanted to arrest in the first place.

Argyll Campbell, Joseph H. Graham, and Willard Mack's **Spring 3100** (2-15-28, Little) lasted a mite longer—three and a half weeks. Mike Callahan (Owen Martin) is shocked to hear that Larry O'Day (Jack McKee), the prizefighter he manages, may be engaged to Josephine Douglas (Mariposa Haynes), a society girl. He warns Larry that the girl's need for expensive baubles will drive him to become a criminal and that to reach him people will have to phone Spring 3100—the number for police headquarters. During a fight Larry is knocked to the canvas. The next thing he knows he is at Josephine's apartment, where all of Mike's predictions seem to come true. Larry finally is forced to shoot it out, a gun in each hand blazing away. Then Larry realizes he is still on the canvas and has been dreaming. He gets up and finishes the fight. Aisle-sitters reported that the transition from fight to dream was so clumsily handled that many playgoers were baffled and lost interest.

Michael Swift's **Hot Pan** (2-15-28, Provincetown Playhouse) gave up its struggle after two and a half weeks, although another producer later reopened it at a similar theatre far uptown with even more disastrous results. Hot Pan is a mining settlement during the California gold rush. A Mexican-American and his mistress are thrown out of their home by gamblers who want it for a casino and saloon. They in turn are evicted by greedy miners when gold is discovered beneath the house. "If anyone voices anything that meets with momentary

displeasure he is casually but convincingly rewarded with a dose of lead," one reviewer noted of this "three-act exposition in hysteria" designed to ridicule American avarice.

Matters at the New Playwrights Theatre were worse. Even the staid, tolerant Atkinson observed, "They are the only avowedly die-hard radical theatre in the city. Yet in their second season they seem to have made no progress toward any discernible goal." The play that prompted this assessment was Michael Gold's **Hoboken Blues** (2-17-28, New Playwrights). Other critics agreed, one noting that "some 45 amateur players, all in blackface and revealing in their total not a single smack of talent," acted out this hodgepodge in which a black man returns to Harlem after a long absence and finds it preoccupied with typically American money-grubbing. In one scene, two barkers try to lure customers into neighboring cabarets by supposedly offering

—Charles Lindbergh, Champeen.
—Napoleon, Super-Champeen.
—Cleopatra, the Oriental Dancer.
—Helen of Troy.
—Adam and Eve.
—The Devil Himself.

A gaudily painted, constructivist setting featured two doors, between which placards were unrolled to suggest various locations. *Variety* ended its devastating notice, "If it weren't that Otto Kahn supports the group one would suspect they were pulling a Cherry Sisters." The Cherry Sisters were a bygone vaudeville act so hilariously bad that a transparent mesh curtain was placed in front of them to catch the rotten fruit and vegetables hurled at them.

Two hits brought some welcomed relief the next Monday night. Like his earlier *The Home Towners*, George M. Cohan's **Whispering Friends** (2-20-28, Hudson) dealt with the consequences of bad advice from untrusting buddies. In this instance, a struggling insurance salesman (William Harrigan) weds a rich widow (Anne Shoemaker). Her best friend (Elsie Lawson) thinks Joe married Emily for her money; his best friend (Chester Morris) is convinced that Emily married Joe for convenience's sake. Their attempts to test their ideas lead to arguments and misunderstandings before the happy ending audiences knew would come. Benchley assailed "the dullest dialogue that we have heard in many a day," and, while admitting that the audience laughed its head off, he warned Cohan that audience laughter could not ensure a success: "That was what they tried to tell us about that play—what was the name?—the one about a Jewish boy who wanted to an Irish girl, or maybe it was an Irish boy who ...anted to marry a Jewish girl—anyway, there was a rabbi and a priest in it, and you know what happened to *that* play." Actually, the new comedy had paid off during its profitable tryout, so its modest run of 112 performances simply added a bit more to the till.

Ina Claire, "with the spirit and the sort of refulgent comic intelligence that makes her a positive figure in any play," headed a brilliant revival of Somerset Maugham's 1917 look at expatriated Americans in England, *Our Betters*, which began a four-month stand at Henry Miller's.

Two other revivals the same night were far less successful. *Sherlock Holmes*, with Robert Warwick in the role playgoers still identified with William Gillette, at the Cosmopolitan was another attempt by Chamberlain Brown to keep his clients employed. And Butler Davenport, who had struggled along for years, largely ignored, in his tiny theatre on 27th Street, brought his revival of *The Passing of the Third Floor Back* to Wallack's, he himself assuming the role of the Christ-like boarder.

Mr. Dempsey and Mr. Kelly, two comic detectives played by Clifford Dempsey and Harry Kelly, find the cab taking them back to New York from a job on Long Island breaks down and, hearing a scream in the night, they rush to a lighthouse to investigate. Thus begins Ralph Murphy and Donald Gallaher's **Sh! The Octopus** (2-21-28, Royale). They soon confront a motley assortment of characters including a man with a hook for a hand and a villainous figure called "the Octopus." It seems everyone is after the plans to a submarine so terrible it could end all wars. The man known as the Octopus is finally killed by a "real" octopus that thrusts its tentacles through a trap door. Several other figures prove to be international detectives. But then, for the second time this month, the whole affair proves to be a dream.

In his review of Ernest Boyd's translation of Simon Gantillon's **Maya** (2-21-28, Comedy), Woollcott observed, "It is so beautiful a play, and at the Comedy they play it so well, that it cannot fail. But, brought face to face with such a testing play, there is always the chance that New York will fail. There is always the chance, for instance, that New York will snigger or simper or utter shrill, embarrassed calls for the Black Maria." And, sure enough, in two weeks' time Assistant District Attorney James G. Wallace resorted to the Wales Padlock Law to close this "symbolical" play about a Marseilles prostitute (Aline MacMahon) and the varying reactions of her rivals and her customers to her.

The murderous behavior of American rednecks and their often colorful language did not bother the authorities. **Rope** (2-22-28, Biltmore) was taken by David Wallace and T. S. Stribling from Stribling's novel *Teeftallow*. A northern railroad engineer, Henry Ditmas (Crane Wilbur) comes to work in the village of Irontown, Tenn. He falls in love with a local girl, Nessie (Mary Carroll), unaware that she is also courted by the brutish Abner Teeftallow (Ben Smith). One of Abner's gang is killed, and his buddies, in KKK outfits, lynch the killer, as well as an innocent colored boy, at night behind the local hotel with automobile headlights illuminating the murder and a huge billboard promoting the anti-evolutionist views of a local evangelist (Leslie Hunt) and his vicious-mouthed supporter (Elizabeth Patterson). Nessie had kept Abner from joining the mob by sleeping with him, and as a result the evangelists want to stone her as a loose woman. Henry prevents the stoning and, realizing that it is best for everyone if Nessie and Abner marry, gets drunk and prepares to leave for home.

Jules Romains's *Knock* was offered to subscribers of the American Laboratory Theatre in Harley Granville Barker's translation as **Doctor Knock** (2-23-28, American Laboratory). Using the power of suggestion, a charlatan physician soon has a whole French village coming to him for imaginary ailments. In no time he is a rich man, being sought out by sick people from all over.

A second foreign play was **Improvisations in June** (2-26-28, Civic Repertory), adapted by Susan Behn and Cecil Lewis from Max Mohr's German original. It was an anti-American work, showing how a young American man is saved by high-principled Germans from following in his father's money-mad footsteps.

Arnold Ridley and Bernard Merivale's London hit **The Wrecker** (2-27-28, Cort) was too English for American tastes. A maniac is wrecking England's best trains and seemingly cannot be stopped even though he announces his plans in advance. He is eventually shown to be an old railroad man gone mad. One striking scene had the hero run into the tower to pull a crucial switch. He is not sure which of two switches is the right one, so he flips a coin. His action saves the train, which speeds by the tower, filling the room with engine smoke.

The month closed out with what proved to be the last long-running hit, but one, David Belasco was to enjoy. In Edward Childs Carpenter's **The Bachelor Father** (2-28-28, Belasco) Sir Basil Winterton, V.C., K.C.B., K.C.G.M., K.W. (C. Aubrey Smith), is taunted by his doctor (David Glassford) into acknowledging and meeting his illegitimate children. He sends his young attorney, John Ashley (Geoffrey

Kerr), to bring them to him. In Manchester, John gets the mother of a young composer, Geoffrey Trent (Rex O'Malley), to prod her son into agreeing to visit his father. In Italy, calling up from a trapdoor opening below stage, he persuades Maria (Adriana Dori) to leave her balcony and come to England, and on a New York slum stoop he cajoles Tony Flagg (June Walker), the tough-talking orphan of a vaudeville belter, to sail back with him. At Sir Basil's Surrey estate the children decide to put their astonished father "on probation." Within a few weeks he comes to love them, and they him. He provides Geoffrey with piano lessons, Maria with singing lessons, and the tomboyish Tony with flying lessons. But in time he must lose the children. Maria accepts a contract to sing in opera in Italy, and Geoffrey, who has fallen in love with her, is relieved to discover his mother was merely milking Sir Basil and he is not Sir Basil's son. This allows him to hurry off to rejoin Maria. Tony will leave, too—to wed John. She consoles Sir Basil, who is angry at what he deems John's duplicity, "But you've got to hand it to him, Chief—it'll be the first wedding in *this* family!" Critic after critic complained about the excessive use of slang in Tony's speeches. Thus, she tells a New York beau, "You act as if I'd plugged you the wrong number." And when he responds, "Ain't you the cute biscuit," she retorts, "Oh, fade—comic strip!" These reservations aside, reviewers concurred with Burns Mantle, who in his *Daily News* review called the play "a happy, wholesome, trivial, brightly spiced, honestly theatrical comedy, full of healthy laughs and topped by a pleasant finish." The comedy ran for eight months.

Last season Michael Kallesser produced his own *Trial Marriage* and watched it quickly fail. On March 1 at Wallack's he offered a revised version, **Marriage on Approval**, and once again watched it flop.

New York's first English-language mounting of Anton Chekhov's **The Cherry Orchard** (3-5-28, Bijou), in a translation by George Calderon, was offered for a series of matinee performances. The more discerning critics hailed the play but had only small, if any, praise for the players, led by Mary Grey as Madame Ranevskaya. Five representations sufficed.

For about a decade, Howard McKent Barnes and Grace Hayward's **Her Unborn Child** (3-5-28, Eltinge) had been raking in substantial grosses in backwaters across the country. Now, in a somewhat revised version by Melville Burke, New Yorkers were allowed to assess it. Doris Kennedy (Ivy Mertons) is refused an abortion and rejects the half-hearted offer of marriage from Jack Conover (Theo-

dore Hecht), the young socialite who fathered her child. Doris tells all to her grief-stricken mother (Effie Shannon) and is given moral support by her brother (Elisha Cook, Jr.). In time, however, Doris and Jack do wed. Critics noted that many girls and older women in the audience wept unrestrainedly. They also noted that birth control literature was being distributed in the lobby. At matinees a doctor gave an intermission lecture on the topic. While New Yorkers were not as accepting as playgoers on the road, the drama nonetheless ran for ten weeks in two separate engagements.

That evening also saw the day's second revival, this time Chamberlain Brown's performers, headed again by Violet Heming, at the Cosmopolitan in *Within the Law*.

Taylor Holmes, long busy in films, was starred in another Brown production, a novelty that Holmes had first played in Los Angeles, Elmer Harris's **The Great Necker** (3-6-28, Ambassador). The title was a play on words. Arthur Pomroy (Holmes) is forty-five, very rich, and given to backing films. He is also given to pretty young ladies. He is certain he will have no difficulty getting around Pansy Hawthorne (Irene Purcell), the sixteen-year-old daughter of a rigidly straitlaced film censor (Blanche Ring). To his horror, he finds Pansy more knowledgeable and almost as experienced as he is. He finally settles for a young lady (Marjorie Gateson) from Great Neck, although the elder Hawthorne abruptly had bobbed her hair and turned kittenish in hopes of attracting him. One interesting feature was clippings from a torrid film the censor had to view—*Aching Lips*.

Laurette Taylor met with a major disappointment when she appeared in Zoë Akins's **The Furies** (3-7-28, Shubert). Fifi Sands arrives at a dinner party with the joyful news that her mean husband has at last consented to a divorce. But then more news arrives—the husband has been found murdered. Fifi thinks her lover (Frederic Worlock) did it. He suggests Fifi is the killer, thereby losing her affection. Her son (Alan Campbell), who has been reading Shakespeare, suggests the two conspired in the killing and brings down the second-act curtain by parroting Hamlet: "Mother, you have my father much offended." The killer proves to be the demented family lawyer (A. E. Anson), who also has loved Fifi. He ends the play by jumping out of the window of his forty-second-floor apartment. Critics lauded James Reynolds's three "conspicuously well-composed and well-imagined" interiors, without describing them except to note that one gave a remarkable illusion of depth. They thought much less of the play, although they applauded the star. She achieved, according to Gilbert Gabriel in the *Telegram*, "the subtlest and most glowing piece of playing many of us have seen her do in many years." But for Miss Taylor's admirers this would be their last opportunity to see her for some years, since her growing drinking problem soon led to her being institutionalized. Among her superb supporting cast, John Cumberland walked away with honors as an unwittingly funny social climber.

Critics were not nearly so happy with Lionel Atwill's strutting about in the title role of B. Harrison Orkow's **Napoleon** (3-8-28, Empire). One even complained that the actor had grown unbecomingly paunchy and that his sumptuous costumes were ill-fitting. The drama recounted the emperor's history from his escape from Elba to his death in a vermin-filled room on St. Helena. It also represented the Polish Countess Walewska (Selena Royle) as the only true love of his life.

More fictionalized history was served up in William A. Drake's adaptation of Bruno Frank's **12,000** (3-12-28, Garrick), in which Frederick the Great thwarts a Hessian prince's attempt to send thousands of drafted soldiers to fight for the British against American rebels. The principal roles of the Hessian's enlightened secretary and his favorite were taken by Basil Sydney and Mary Ellis.

Louis E. Bisch and Howard Merling's **Killers** (3-13-28, 49th St.) begins with a shooting in a speakeasy and ends with the green door to Sing Sing's Death Row being opened to admit another prisoner. In between several stories were loosely woven together. One told of the killing of a woman out with a married man for an evening of fun. Suspicion falls first on the woman's husband, then on two supposed hired killers, but the murderer turns out to be the philanderer's unhappy wife (Cynthia Blake). A related tale told of an innocent-faced kid (Harold Vermilyea), newly released from prison after serving time as a lookout in a holdup. Although a killing occurred during the robbery, he was the only one convicted. Now sent to jail again after circumstantial evidence makes it seem he was one of the hired hoods in the nightclub, he is sentenced to death when he is caught picking up a gun his cellmate has just used to shoot a warden. Its huge cast of thirty-four meant the show virtually had to sell out at its small house to break even. It did not, so it soon closed.

Two worse disasters came hard on *Killers'* heels. Irving Kaye Davis's **Veils** (3-13-28, Forrest) told of twin sisters (Elsa Shelley). One becomes a nun who eventually decides to leave the nunnery and marry the artist who had painted a chapel mural. The other

is a streetwalker who decides to take the veil. One reviewer dismissed it as "nunsense." It survived half a week.

Another aisle-sitter branded Courtenay Savage's **The Buzzard** (3-14-28, Broadhurst) "the most inept, dull and impossible production within memory." It lasted a week and a half. To the public John Collier was an upright district attorney; to those who knew him well he was a scoundrel. So when he is shot, everyone who knew him well is suspected. A wronged woman finally confesses, but no one seems ready to arrest her—especially after her confession brings about the reunion of a long-separated mother and daughter.

A brace of Shakespearean revivals briefly illuminated Broadway. Walter Hampden had followed his successful production of *An Enemy of the People* with short remountings of *Hamlet* and *Caponsacchi*. Now he offered his loyalists *Henry V* at Hampden's on the 15th. The production was relatively simple, relying on drapes, a few sticks of furniture, and lighting to suggest settings. But the performance, more stately than vibrant, was not to many's liking. Still, it ran longer than the multi-starred Shakespearean comedy that came next.

Mrs. Fiske, Henrietta Crosman, and Otis Skinner had toured the country for a number of months in *The Merry Wives of Windsor* before bringing it into the Knickerbocker on the 19th for a three-week stand. A good number of critics confessed to their readers that the play was not truly all that funny, nor were the stars inspired, even though the ever loyal Woollcott called Mrs. Fiske "the foremost artist of our stage" and continued, "I know no actress in the English-speaking world who is half so good a comedian." Atkinson missed a hint of "Tudor vulgarity" in Skinner's Falstaff.

In Harry Segal's **The Behavior of Mrs. Crane** (3-20-28, Erlanger) Mrs. Crane (Margaret Lawrence) is understanding when her husband (Charles Trowbridge) announces he wants a divorce in order to wed Myra Spaulding (Isobel Elsom). All Mrs. Crane asks is that, since the couple are depriving her of a husband, they find her a suitable replacement. They offer her a chuckleheaded English lord (George Thorpe), a fiery Cuban (Walter Connolly), a Wall Street genius (L'Estrange Millman), and a charming, handsome multimillionaire (John Marston). In fact, Bruce King is so charming, handsome, and rich that Myra decides she wants him instead of Mr. Crane. But Mrs. Crane holds everyone to their agreement.

Down in the Village, Nicholas P. Heisdorf served as both playwright and producer for **The Schoolmas-**

ter (3-20-28, Provincetown Playhouse). According to Samuel L. Leiter, in his study of the decade, the play dealt with New York–born siblings of ancient Dutch heritage fighting over a $200 piece of property in the early nineteenth century. A schoolteacher helps settle the dispute and wins the sister. It was gone almost immediately after its arrival.

When *Variety* reached the newsstands that week, it told a sad tale. With a headline reading "Future Glum," it reported that, although more than fifty shows were playing on Broadway, "an unusual number of dark theatres is still a Broadway problem." Even desirable playhouses on Broadway and on 42nd Street were said to be going begging. Two weeks later, reviewing a new melodrama, it stated the work "gets a break by coming in at a time when the new show crop is the most meager in years."

Before that play arrived, Samuel Ruskin Golding added to his string of failures with **Divorce a la Carte** (3-26-28, Biltmore). Because Mr. Maitland (Hale Hamilton) spends too much time playing golf, Mrs. Maitland (Regina Wallace) has taken to drinking too much. They agree on a Mexican quickie divorce, but since Mr. Maitland cannot spare the time to go south, their mincing friend Chapman Pell (Geoffrey Harwood) goes, posing as Maitland. Divorce obtained, Pell weds Mrs. Maitland, and Mr. Maitland marries a simpering flapper (Kathleen Lowry). Then, at about the same time the Maitlands decide they should have stayed together, word comes that the divorce has no legal standing in New York. Like several other supposedly full-length plays of the season, this comedy ran less than two hours.

That same night the Civic Repertory Theatre revived *Hedda Gabler*. The mounting was done in modern dress against simple gray drapes and, for the most part, was panned as lifeless. Curiously, considering the negative notices several of her recent productions received, Eva Le Gallienne makes a strange, suspicious leap in her autobiography, jumping from *2 × 2 = 5* to one of the group's 1928–29 productions.

The play that *Variety* said was given a better chance because of the paucity of competition was Willard Mack's **The Scarlet Fox** (3-27-28, Masque). In a small sense it was a sequel, since eleven years earlier Mack had played Mike Devlin of the Royal Canadian Mounted Police in *Tiger Rose*, and he portrayed him again in his "flamboyant Irish style" in the new play. Although Devlin gives out that he suspects strikers killed a hated strike-breaker in the mining town of Drumheller, Alberta, he knows there is more to the matter. He finds Swede Cora (Marie Chambers), the local madam, is in cahoots as

a dope runner with Harry Spatz (Joseph Sweeney), who owns the haberdashery on the brothel's ground floor, and Ling Foo Loo (Sam Lee), who operates the basement laundry. Just as it seems that Devlin is about to be shot for his pains, his buddies spring out of the clothes hampers and nab the malefactors. A program note told playgoers, "The story is borrowed intact from the Royal Mounted records of Drumheller's last coal strike." For all the histrionic flamboyance, there were no gunshots, and at least one critic suggested a good shootout might have enlivened the evening. Still, in the face of tepid notices, the play ran ten weeks. Whether that fulfilled the tradesheet's prophecy is moot.

A less likely candidate for popularity ran somewhat longer—fourteen weeks—after opening at Wallack's on the same night. Once a touring warhorse, the seventy-year-old *Ten Nights in a Barroom* told how the boozy barfly Joe Morgan at first ignores the pleas of his little daughter— "Father, dear father, come home [with me now]"— but eventually reforms. Prohibition audiences undoubtedly found a perverse relish in the drama, played straight by a cast of minor professionals, before rushing off to their favorite speakeasies.

A successful London production of Harry Wagstaff Gribble's 1921 comedy *March Hares* prompted a third attempt, at the Little on April 2, to get Broadway to accept the play. Broadway would not, though critics showered the cast with garlands. Richard Bird was Geoffrey; Vivian Tobin, Janet; and Dorothy Stickney, Claudia. But the show stealer was Josephine Hull, "who can cling breathlessly to the edge of a raging tornado more comically than anyone else in our theatre," in the lesser role of Mrs. Rodney.

Jean-Jacques Bernard's **Martine** (4-4-28, American Laboratory), in Helen Grayson's translation, told of a little farm girl who settles for a life of drudgery after the newspaperman of her dreams marries someone else.

But another lady did find true love, and her name was **Diamond Lil** (4-9-28, Royale). Actually her name was Mae West, who wrote and starred in the play and provided her admirers with a fun evening. Lil is a dance hall mistress and, no doubt, a madam on the side. She runs Suicide Hall, a far more respectable joint than the neighboring Paresis Hall, for her lover, the local political bigwig, Gus Jordan (J. Merrill Holmes). With Gus in hot water and looking to be sent to the pen, she falls in love with Captain Cummings (Curtis Cooksey) of the Salvation Army. Learning that the Army is about to be evicted from its current digs, Lil manages to scrounge up the money to purchase the building and present it to the captain. At the same time that he admits he has fallen in love with her, he also reveals he is actually a detective assigned to find out what is going on in her place. Nothing surprises Lil. As she tells Cummings, "I knew you could be had." Among the evening's divertissements were Lil's show-stopping rendition of "Frankie and Johnnie," although that had to be cleaned up a bit on orders from the district attorney. The fun went on for twenty-two weeks.

Ben Jonson's comic look at greed and hypocrisy, **Volpone** (4-9-28, Guild), took a roundabout way of reaching New York, since what the Guild's first-nighters heard was Ruth Langner's translation of Stefan Zweig's German adaptation. Although the whole cast, headed by Dudley Digges in the title role, won kudos, Alfred Lunt once again garnered the lion's share of critical attention. In a real change of pace he made Mosca into a low clown. Surmising that Lunt was having "the time of his life," Woollcott noted how "swift, sure, gleaming—he darts and buzzes and stings his way through the play." He added that only John Barrymore, now playing truant in Hollywood, could have equaled Lunt, since no others brought such high imagination to the stage. Oddly enough, the district attorney made noises about shutting down both this play and *Strange Interlude*, but he was shortly brought to his senses, so settled merely for having closed the defenseless *Maya*.

Lionel Atwill attempted to revive the four-year-old *The Outsider* at the Ambassador the same evening but found, like the producer of *March Hares*, that it is all but impossible to get New York to reconsider a negative judgment.

Across the country in California the only major early play by Eugene O'Neill never to be given a Broadway mounting was offered that night. In **Lazaurus Laughed** (4-9-28, Pasadena Playhouse) O'Neill returned to the use of masks, and only Lazarus (Irving Pichel) remained unmasked. And he alone does not fear life, since he does not fear death. A jealous wanton, Pompeia (Dore Wilson), kills his wife (Lenore Shanewise), but Lazaurus can still find love for the murderess. When he is sent by the swinish Caligula (Victor Jory) to burn at the stake, Pompeia throws herself into the fire. Yet the flames make Lazarus laugh, and he shouts to the groveling Caligula, "Fear not, Caligula! There is no death." Beating himself, Caligula begs forgiveness. A few New York newspapers published reviews by West Coast critics, who devoted most of their paragraphs to praising the costly, lavish mounting and avoiding harshly critical comments on the play

itself. Those less approving comments were reserved for the published text a few months later. Thus, Conrad Aiken, writing in the *Post*, decried it as "too romantic, too purple, too humorlessly serious; there is a kind of grandiosity about it which if not intellectually hollow is very close to it."

Back in New York, some pleasant notices failed to turn Anne Collins and Alice Timoney's **Bottled** (4-10-28, Booth) into a hit. Although her grandfather died fifteen years ago, a special clause in his will had to remain unread until Mary Lou (Mildred McCoy) came of age. That clause reveals that she and her cousins inherit the family's distillery. However, their harridan grandmother (Maud Durand) has no intention of giving up the reins. So the kids, like grandmother, become bootleggers, and a comic battle for territory explodes, with booze being shipped in golf bags, hat boxes, and anything else that comes in handy. A compromise is finally reached with grandmother paying the kids $75,000.

Bottled was the work of two sisters. **The Breaks** (4-16-28, Klaw) was by a better-known father-and-son team, J. C. and Elliott Nugent. Rather than have his property fall into the hands of his despised cousin, Jim Dolf (Elliott), the narrow-minded Jed Willis (J. C.) tries to force his serving girl, Amy (Sylvia Sidney), to have his child, thus giving him an apparent heir. After a fight between the men, Jim and Amy run off, and Jed, told by his doctor he can never have children, shoots himself. The play ran for just one week, as did another novelty which opened the same evening.

Hutcheson Boyd's **A Lady for a Night** (4-16-28, 49th St.) recounted the problems faced by the Dexters of Staten Island after Mr. Dexter (Warren Ashe), to solve the servant problem, brought home a serving girl enticed away from a department store ribbon counter. The girl (Esther Howard) involves the Dexters in mayhem, murder, problems of a broken family, and more before Mrs. Dexter (Dorothy Hall) awakes from her dream. (The third such dream in recent weeks.)

One foreign play also premiered that evening. **Forbidden Roads** (4-16-28, Liberty) was Roland Oliver's version of José Lopez Pinillos' *El Caudal de los Hijos*. A father cannot kill his unfaithful wife for fear the killing will bring shame upon their son. Years later the son cannot kill his own wife for the same reason.

Few critics could make heads or tails of e. e. cummings's **him** (4-18-28, Provincetown Playhouse). But then in a program note cummings had warned playgoers, "Don't try to understand it." The central figures were Me (Erin O'Brien-Moore) and Him

(William S. Johnstone). As three weird sisters sit in their rocking chairs and knit, Me is etherized for an operation. The rest of the play may be her dream. At one point Me and Him discuss their love, then she asks him to read from a play he has written. Scenes follow in which, among other things, a Negro's singing of "Frankie and Johnnie" is interrupted by a member of a society dedicated to the suppression of vice, and Mussolini (who looks amazingly like Me's doctor) tells admiring homosexuals (bluntly called fairies) that he will destroy communism. Finally, Him says, "I wish I could believe this," only to state he cannot, "because this is true." For all the head-shaking, the play survived nearly a month.

The heroine of Edward Massey's **Box Seats** (4-19-28, Little) was Hazel Lawrence (Joan Storm), a woman with a past and a tab show singer with a sordid present. But when her young daughter (Patricia Barclay) is sent to her after the death of the girl's father, she decides the girl cannot be like her. A falling out occurs after the girl becomes enamored of the spoiled son (Paul Guilfoyle) of the woman who runs the show, only to discover he has had an affair with her mother. But all ends happily after Hazel becomes a Ziegfeld star.

Diamond Lil and *Volpone* aside, the nearest thing to a hit in April—and it just missed—was Bernard J. McOwen and Harry E. Humphrey's **The Skull** (4-23-28, Forrest). The play was set in a long-abandoned church on a deserted Connecticut road. Since this was a mystery, the building was the sort where doors open unaided and slam shut suddenly with a frightening bang. The church is sometimes used by a self-proclaimed professor of psychic phenomenan (C. W. Van Voorhis) to hold seances, so an international jewel thief (Allan Davis), known as "the Skull," must pose as a detective and let himself be drafted into one of the rap sessions while seeking to reclaim jewels he has hidden there.

Kidding Kidders (4-23-28, Bijou) turned out to be another ragged old play tatted up in new garb. In this case it was a rewrite of November's one-week disaster *One Shot Fired*, and once again it ran just a single week. Things were growing desperate on the Great White Way.

They grew worse the next evening. Although Lester Lonergan and Charles Andrews were respected professionals, their oddball play **The Golden Age** (4-24-28, Longacre) collected some of the meanest notices in quite a while. The *Journal*'s John Anderson characterized it as "the season's most stupefying bore," while Robert Littell in the *Evening Post* found it "so incredible it's almost worth

seeing." The Barneses, living in primitive contentment in a log cabin in Enchanted Land, Utah, have only native Indians for friends until they take in a bearded stranger (Warren William). He soon is betrothed to the pretty young daughter of the family, Peggy (Leila Frost). Then a mail plane crashes nearby. The two aviators recognize the stranger as a man who has been sought for killing his colonel during the war. To prevent word from leaking out, Peggy shoots the plane's mechanician (Donald Gallaher) with her bow and arrow. He is not killed, and after the stranger wanders off to seek his freedom elsewhere, Chief Silver Cloud (George Marion) persuades Peggy and the mechanician to tie the knot.

Down in the Village, **The Waltz of the Dogs** (4-25-28, Cherry Lane), taken by Herman Bernstein from Leonid Andreyev's Russian original, followed the saga of a bank clerk from disillusionment to disillusionment until his suicide. Because the clerk exited waving a revolver yet no gunshot followed, the first-night audience, uncertain the drama was finished, sat on its hands until the embarrassed cast appeared for curtain calls.

Billie Burke's loyalists kept Harrison Owen's English comedy **The Happy Husband** (5-7-28, Empire) on the boards for nine weeks. She played a wife who grows furious when her complacent husband (Lawrence Grossmith) refuses to believe she has enjoyed a fling with another man (A. E. Matthews). The play's top price of $4.40 was matched among non-musicals only by *Strange Interlude*.

There were echoes of *Easy Come, Easy Go* in Louis Sobol's **The High Hatters** (5-10-28, Klaw), which came and went in less than a fortnight's time. Sitting in their dilapidated dressing room, two down-and-out, crooked vaudevillians, Bim (Gilbert Douglas) and Cookie (Thomas H. Manning), conspire to have themselves committed to a mental institution. From this new base they pull robberies at swank nearby Tarrytown homes until several other inmates turn out to be detectives.

Robert Whittier was producer and star of a poorly received revival of Strindberg's *The Father* at the Belmont on the 11th, with Florence Johns as the wife determined to drive him insane.

Two more revivals came in on the 14th. One, at the Cosmopolitan, was Vincent Lawrence's 1923 comedy *In Love with Love*. Regarded with indifference, it crept away after a single week. The other was the first of several "all-star" mountings brought in for strictly limited engagements. The stars in Oliver Goldsmith's *She Stoops to Conquer* at the Erlanger included Fay Bainter as Kate, Wilfred

Seagram as young Marlow, Glenn Hunter as Tony Lumpkin, Lawrance D'Orsay as Charles Marlow, Lyn Harding and Mrs. Leslie Carter as the elder Hardcastles, and Marie Carroll, Patricia Collinge, Horace Braham, and O. P. Heggie in lesser roles. Pauline Lord appeared briefly to recite the prologue. The actors were cheered, even if some critics, as they had with *The Merry Wives of Windsor*, insisted the comedy itself was not particularly funny. But the production drew good audiences for its two-week stand.

The actors were the only reason to see **Anna** (5-16-28, Lyceum), which Herman Bernstein derived from an unidentified Rudolph Lothar work. Aware that the brilliant sculptor Peter Torrelli (Lou Telegen) has not only insisted that marriage is foolish but specifically has sworn not to touch her since she is the daughter of his patron, Anna Plumer (Judith Anderson) adopts a phony name, bets the man that he will marry a rich girl in three months, then lures him into wooing her. Tellegen, his accent still thick, his good looks fading, gave a stormy performance, while Miss Anderson was afforded some small opportunity to show subtle comic skills as well play out more impassioned moments.

In the Sunday edition of the *World* for May 20, Alexander Woollcott said farewell to his readers. His battles with his editor, culminating in the feud over *Strange Interlude*, prompted him to call a halt to his career as a theatre critic. Referring to himself, as he had when he left the *Times*, as the First Grave Digger, he wrote, "With an uneasy glance over his shoulder, he exits hurriedly, almost unnoticed, save for a faint murmur in one corner of the scene where Alfred Lunt, Harpo Marx, Mrs. Fiske and Ruth Gordon sob quietly in chorus, as the curtain falls. Then, to a great blare from the orchestra pit, it rises again in a street scene. Enter Lee Shubert, Walter Hampden, Ruth Chatterton, Lowell Sherman, Billie Burke and a great happy throng tossing roses in the air. They dance. Curtain." No one could have claimed that Woollcott was a deep critic, and, like all reviewers, he had his prejudices and blind spots. But his record of calling early attention to superior young players probably was unequaled. And his ability to gauge both a show's merits and its likely public appeal was as good as any. What always came through in the warmth of his writing was his love for good theatre, and none of his colleagues could hold a candle to him for penning deliciously extractable quotes. Reading (or culling) theatre reviews was never to be quite as enjoyable again.

Poor casting merely underscored the inadequacies of Charlton Andrews and Philip Dunning's **Get Me in the Movies** (5-21-28, Earl Carroll). Johnny Loring (Sterling Holloway), a yokel from Sheboygan, Mich., is brought to Hollywood after winning a contest run by Decent Pictures for a clean movie scenario. The studio's boss (Paul Ker) awards him some silvery bed linens and a contract which requires him to stay away from women and provide a new, full-blown scenario every Monday morning. The studio's female star and lots of would-be starlets all try to muss the bed linens, which could be put on the revolving folding bed that Johnny finds in the apartment he has been given, but Johnny remains true to his hometown girl. The tall, blond, gawky Holloway, with his "humming bird's voice," had delighted Broadway in revue skits but seemed unable to carry a whole evening's script. His support was small help.

Most first-string critics attended the Andrews-Dunning opus, leaving second-stringers to sit in judgment on the evening's other openings. It was one of these other openings that, despite being waved away in the *Times* as "just passable," enjoyed the season's last long run—448 performances—and went on to a singular fame. There would come a time in the 1930s and the 1940s when the characters from Aurania Rouverol's **Skidding** (5-21-28, Bijou) would be better known to most Americans than those from any other of the season's plays. Marion (Marguerite Churchill) returns to Idaho after studying political science back east. She discovers that one of her sisters is leaving her husband because he neglects her and that the other sister is walking out on her spouse because he cares only for good times. She also realizes that her father (Carleton Macy) has little chance to be reelected judge if he keeps fighting the corrupt powers that rule the roost. Her fiery speech turns the tide in his favor and leads to her being offered a chance to run for the legislature, and that in turn alienates her old-fashioned fiancé, Wayne Trenton III (Walter Abel), who insists a woman's place is in the kitchen. But all ends happily after Wayne sees the light. The play was filled with down-home touches. The judge's wife (Clara Blandick) complains the only jewelry he ever has bought her is a pair of opera glasses that he himself wanted to use, while the judge observes that his wife's latest birthday gift to him is new curtains for the living room. The comedy's odd title comes from a line early in the first act, when Marion's spinster aunt (Louise Carter) suggests that marriages "start skidding" after five or seven years. Although Marion would soon be forgotten, her father, Judge Hardy, and her scrappy kid brother, Andy (Charles Eaton), would win fans in a long series of MGM films.

No afterlife awaited **Dorian Gray** (5-21-28, Biltmore), David Thorne's theatricalization of Oscar Wilde's famous tale. Critics found the version clumsy and the acting mediocre.

Two more "all-star" revivals followed. Victorien Sardou's *Diplomacy*, one of the best-loved of nineteenth-century melodramas, had been touring the country in this mounting for several months, generally playing to turn-away business before George C. Tyler brought it in for five weeks at the Erlanger on the 28th. Once again, Henry Beauclerc (William Faversham) saves his brother, Julien (Rollo Peters), from ruin by exposing the treachery of the Countess Zicka (Helen Gahagan). Other major players included Tyrone Power, Cecilia Loftus, Jacob Ben Ami, Margaret Anglin (in the small comic part of Lady Fairfax), Frances Starr (Dora), and Charles Coburn. At a time when old plays were increasingly waved away with condescension, the *Times* critic observed, " 'Diplomacy' is so well-made that it stands the test of revival in the tenth year after the war that is supposed to have changed everything. It is still good theatre in New York in the year of 'Strange Interlude.' "

Although it was given just as good notices, the Players' resurrection of George Farquhar's *The Beaux Stratagem* at Hampden's on June 4 followed the group's practice of confining its annual outing to one week. Fay Bainter and Helen Menken were Mrs. Sullen and Dorinda, while Wilfred Seagram and Fred Eric were their would-be seducers, Aimwell and Archer. Raymond Hitchcock and James T. Powers romped in the low comedy parts of Boniface and Scrub. Among the other performers were Dorothy Stickney, Lyn Harding, William Courtleigh, Henrietta Crosman, O. P. Heggie, and, as one of the servants at the inn, Josephine Hull.

A pair of failed comedies brought the season to a sad close. At the start of Fred Ballard and Charles Bickford's **The Cyclone Lover** (6-5-28, Frolic), Betty Black (Emily Graham) cannot be dissuaded from eloping with a portrait painter, Tony Mariochetti (Theodore Hecht), a man her shipping magnate father (Thomas McLarnie) knows to be a crook. After Mr. Black attempts to take out an insurance policy with Bob White (Harold Elliott) against Betty's marrying, Bob tricks her on to a yacht captained by her father's friend (William Crimans) and wins her for himself. The elaborate yacht setting of the last two acts won applause when it was first revealed, reminding some playgoers of similar settings so voguish a decade or more earlier.

Ray Hodgdon's **Married—and How!** (6-14-28, Little) found the newlyweds Phil and Flo Ballinger (Robert Bentley and Dulcie Cooper) wondering if their marriage had not been a mistake, especially since Phil's rich, noisy, and pigheaded father (Walter Jones) has disowned him for marrying a chorus girl. But Phil is struck down on Eighth Avenue by his own car with his brother-in-law (George Le Guere) behind the wheel. In helping restore him to health, father and son are reunited and the marriage saved.

EPILOGUE
1928–1930

1928–1929

The seasons of 1928–29 and 1929–30 constitute an epilogue to the great years that Broadway enjoyed, or should have, from the end of World War I until the waning months of 1927–28. Broadway would never again be as lively, generous, diversified, or insistently exciting. With a few small exceptions, from 1928–29 onward each year saw a discernible drop not only in the total number of productions but in the number of new plays offered as well. The arrival of sound films unquestionably took a serious toll, and the stock market crash of October 1929 with the ensuing Depression aggravated matters. Some of Broadway's best talents and a far larger group of lesser, but heretofore dependable, figures deserted live theatre, most of them permanently. Even some of the great figures who remained did so because they were deemed unphotogenic or could not adapt to Hollywood's often different methods.

Looking back, modern theatregoers would be grateful for any season whose successes ranged from the raucous comedy of *The Front Page* to the gripping drama of *Street Scene*, yet the often Cassandraic Burns Mantle spoke for many when he rued, "The legitimate theatre came a cropper this last season. I am without record of the number of times the report has been sent out from New York that . . . the season of 1928–29 was, in very fact, the worst theatre season the Broadway stage has suffered within the memory of living playgoers." In its annual summation the *Times* concurred, observing that the theatrical session had been "lamented up and down Broadway as the worst in many years."

Mantle and producers such as Lee Shubert put most of the blame squarely on "articulate films." But Mantle listed other problems, too. He cited the public's disgust with salacious presentations, the rush of inexperienced and tasteless producers to make a quick killing, and the persistence of gouging ticket speculators. Still, films took an unmistakable toll on live playhouses. Indeed, they had been doing a little of that for some time. The old Broadway on 41st Street was demolished during the season, but its stage, which had seen the likes of Fanny Davenport, Modjeska, and Salvini, had long been surrendered to silent flickers. The desirable Astor, a few blocks up in the heart of Times Square, had been devoted to films for several years and now was joined by the Globe, the Gaiety, the Central, and several others. Most of these theatres never returned to the legitimate fold.

Three entries appeared, and quickly disappeared, in July. Don Mullally's **Wanted** (7-2-28, Wallack's) recounted how pretty, redheaded Penelope Merton (Alney Alba) comes from Baton Rouge to New York with only $7 in her pocket. She is given rooms in the swank Park Avenue apartment of family friends, where she finds her old black mammy (Teresa Brooks) is now employed. But she also finds herself under suspicion after the family's jewels are stolen. At the police station, a young admirer (Ken Cartier) helps pin the blame on the real thief and proposes marriage to Penelope. Despite favorable, if not enthusiastic, notices, the heat killed the play in two weeks.

Seaman Lewis's **The Lawyer's Dilemma** (7-9-28, Belmont) proved to be a rehashing of last season's *Babies a la Carte* and failed again.

The year's first drama was Paul Eldridge's **The Intruder** (7-25-28, Biltmore). It dealt with a problem which seventy years later still made headlines. A serving girl, Katy (Viola Frayne), is seduced by a doctor (Richard Gordon) in his office when she comes for a consultation. Six years later she confronts the doctor and demands that he divorce his wife (Anne Sutherland), marry her, and support their young son. But when she discovers how loving and forgiving the wife is, she quietly walks out of their life.

Social drama gave way to melodrama in August's first entry, and melodrama would loom large all month long. One critic branded James Hagan's **Guns** (8-6-28, Wallack's) a fine "old-fashioned thriller," noting machine guns firing away in Act I, "a really good, hair-raising murder" in the next act, and lots of pistol-play in the final act. Hagan's somewhat diffuse plot centered on bootleggers and moved from speakeasies in New York and Chicago to a lonely spot on the Mexican border, where the same criminals also smuggle illegal Chinese immigrants into the country. Its heroine, Cora Chase (Suzanne Bennett), is a decent girl who unwittingly becomes involved with the hoodlums until she is rescued by

Jimmy Plankey (Hugh Thompson), alias "the Colorado Special." Jimmy appears to be one of the gangsters until he reveals himself as a special agent. The play ran six weeks.

So did **Elmer Gantry** (8-7-28, Playhouse), a dramatization of Sinclair Lewis's novel, which had undergone a temptestuous tryout. Major cast changes occurred several times, both the director and the producer disclaimed responsibility for what emerged, and Thompson Buchanan was hurried in to provide a new third act for Patrick Kearney's theatricalization. As much as possible, however, the play remained faithful to Lewis's saga of a hypocritical, self-serving evangelist (Edward Pawley). One interesting touch had actors running up and down the theatre's aisles during the revival meeting, exhorting playgoers to be born again. On opening night they were joined by the play's disgruntled press agent, who proclaimed, "I love Jesus more than William A. Brady [the original producer]."

Irving Berlin's marriage to socialite Ellin Mackay, which had been grist for numerous revue sketches, was generally perceived to have been the inspiration for Crane Wilbur's **The Song Writer** (8-13-28, 48th St.), although both Wilbur and his producers strenously denied the rumor. David Bernard (Georgie Price), a young Jew who has made a name and a fortune for himself with his songwriting, marries a rich, Christian debutante, Patricia Thayer (Mayo Methot). But her family's disdain and the unceasing glare of publicity drive her to run off with the equally social J. Rodman Peck (Hugh Huntley), until Bernard's love songs, which she hears wherever she goes, call her back to Bernard. Several original songs were included in the piece, among them "You're Gone," designed to recall Berlin's "Remember," which was bruited to have determined Miss Mackay not to abandon Berlin. Price, a comic and singer in vaudeville, also sang another "Bernard" song, "You Are My Heaven," whose lyric proclaimed, "I'm in heaven when you're near, living in another sphere."

The season's first smash hit broke the long jinx on newspaper plays. Ben Hecht and Charles MacArthur's **The Front Page** (8-14-28, Times Square) remains one of the greatest American comedies, although, curiously, many reviewers, including Brooks Atkinson on the *Times*, deemed it essentially a melodrama. To no small extent, it was. The action unfolds in the seedy press room at Chicago's criminal court. A motley group of hard-drinking, foul-mouthed reporters are playing poker, while another reporter is phoning around for any news tidbits. There is a sudden silence when the phoner is told of a double shooting in a love triangle, but he hangs up in disgust and the reporters return to their game when the caller learns the killer and his victims were merely "niggers." Yet the very reason so many reporters are in the room is that they are awaiting the hanging of Earl Williams, a poor bird who "had the tough luck to kill a nigger policeman in a town where the nigger vote is important." As one reporter remarks, "If he'd bumped him off down South they'd have given him a banquet and a trip to Europe." One persistent caller to the press room is Walter Burns, the fiery editor of the *Examiner*, who is seeking his reporter, Hildy Johnson. The other reporters know where he is but aren't telling, for Hildy is about to get married and leave Chicago. The arrival of Molly Molloy (Dorothy Stickney), a prostitute who served as a defense witness for Williams, prompts a round of razzing by the cynical reporters. Molly berates them for their callousness. Then Hildy (Lee Tracy) enters to say his good-byes. He has barely appeared when all hell breaks loose. Williams has escaped after tricking the sheriff into giving him a gun. Sirens go off and searchlights flood the press room, casting a silhouette of the gallows on the walls. The reporters dash out, leaving Hildy alone when Williams enters through a window. Hildy hides him in a rolltop desk and, forgetting both his appointment to meet his fiancée and his disdain for Burns, phones the paper with his story. Burns (Osgood Perkins) promptly shows up, and when Hildy's distraught mother-in-law-to-be (Jessie Cromette) also appears, Burns has her kidnapped to keep her quiet. More pandemonium follows until the police discover that Burns and Hildy are hiding the fugitive. The pair are about to be arrested when a drunken employee from the governor's office discloses the governor has reprieved Williams. Burns turns the affair into an account of his paper's heroic efforts. Hildy's girl (Frances Fuller) comes, and Burns oozes sweetness. He even gives them a farewell gift—his own watch, engraved with his name. He smilingly waves the lovers off, but he has no real intention of losing his best reporter. Once Hildy is out of earshot, Burns goes to the phone and arranges for Hildy to be arrested. The charge? "The son of a bitch stole my watch!" (Although the curtain line became possibly the most celebrated of its era, it is interesting to compare it with Perkins's curtain line of *Spread Eagle*.) Alison Smith, Woollcott's successor at the *World*, rejoiced, " 'The Front Page,' with its rowdy virility, its swift percussion of incident, its streaks of Gargantuan derision, is as breath-taking an event as ever dropped . . . on Broadway." Brilliantly directed by George S. Kaufman and lustily played, the show ran out the season. (Reading the play provides an additional pleasure, since the authors' directions and comments are every bit as delicious as the rest of the piece.)

Frances Lynch and the seemingly foredoomed Michael Kallesser had little luck with **He Understood Women** (8-15-28, Belmont), which Kallesser himself produced. Set in Paris, it centered on a notorious roué, Julian Romain (Joseph Granby). He discovers that none of the women he courted ever really loved him and that even the girl (Peggy Allenby) he finally married—in order to have a son to whom he could pass on his ideas—has been unfaithful. He settles for the best of a bad deal. The play included lines such as "Women always tell the truth by lying." Oldtimer Hilda Spong stood out in an otherwise mediocre cast.

Edward Clark's look at the Jewish business world, **Relations** (8-20-28, Masque), chalked up 104 performances, making it a squeak-by hit. Uncle Wolfe Michaels (Clark) is so fed up with all the troublesome relations he has employed in his millinery store that he fires them. Just then David Lubin (Horace Braham), a distant cousin from Australia, enters and agrees to buy the whole business for $17,000. He rehires all the fired relations, whom he soon finds as troublesome as Uncle Wolfe had. To make matters worse, Uncle Wolfe opens a competing store. Learning that still another member of the Australian branch of the family has died and left him a fortune, David heads back home.

Pistol shots rang out early in Willard Mack's **Gang War** (8-20-28, Morosco), with a leading gangster shot dead on the steps in front of St. Dominic's Church. The dead man had been the leader of the Castoldi gang; the killers belong to the Kelton gang. The leader of the Keltons is then stabbed to death. There are more killings before the Castoldi boys hire an aeroplane to bomb the Kelton headquarters. Who really cares? Even a policeman tells a gang member, "The police don't give a good god damn so long as you shoot each other."

In George Middleton and A. E. Thomas's **The Big Pond** (8-21-28, Bijou), Henry Billings (Harlan Briggs), a cantankerous "rubber king" from Ohio, visiting Europe for a year, is so upset at the attentions suave Pierre De Mirande (Kenneth MacKenna) pays to his daughter, Barbara (Lucile Nikolas), in Venice that he decides on an unusual method to cure his daughter's infatuation. He invites Pierre to return to America with him and join his company. The plot seems to work, for Pierre is so successful in business that Barbara no longer views him as a romantic European. She marries a nice

hometown boy (Reed Brown, Jr.). Audiences, and some critics, objected strongly to the ending, forcing the authors to change it and allow Barbara to select Pierre. But even the change could not save the show.

Brock Pemberton, at the time one of Broadway's more adventuresome producers, took another gamble when he presented Ransom Rideout's study of miscegenation, **Goin' Home** (8-23-28, Hudson). The playwright attempted to take some of the edge off his subject by setting his story in France. Lise (Barbara Bulgakov), a rather louche café owner, believes Israel Du Bois (Richard Hale), a black American who has served in the Foreign Legion, when he tells her he is rich and socially prominent back home. Only after she marries him does she learn the truth from Major Edward Powell (Russell Hicks), who reveals that Israel was merely a servant boy to his family and that blacks are never socially important in America. Lise makes advances to Powell, and he succumbs. Learning of their relationship, Israel sets out to shoot Powell. Before he can, an irate Senegalese (Clarence Redd), who had served with Israel in the Legion, attempts to stab Powell. To prevent so quixotic a killing, Israel shoots his buddy. Powell agrees to take Israel back to America before the authorities can act. The café setting allowed for some wild Senegalese dancing and a lively crap game among the boisterous blacks. Despite its excellences, the drama was unable to lure in playgoers.

There were no compensations in Edward Elsner's vanity production, **The Lido Girl** (8-23-28, Totten), which one critic branded as "so bad as to defy description." Its Greenwich Village heroine, the voluptuous, promiscuous Claire Carson (Ethel Fisher), sleeps with poets and painters until she finds true love with a young engineer, Robert Gordon (Frank R. London). Gordon loves her even after he discovers she was the model for the infamous nude statue that gives the show its title. Recalling the hero in Clyde Fitch's *Sapho*, he carries her up the circular stairs to his bedroom.

The jinx on newspaper plays may have hurt Ward Morehouse's **Gentlemen of the Press** (8-27-28, Henry Millers), but probably not as much as its coming so soon after *The Front Page*. Its hero, Wick Snell (John Cromwell), was a polished, polite Hildy Johnson. Like Hildy, he has had it with the crudities of newspaper life. He takes a job heading the publicity department of a large real estate company, but when his boss fails to appreciate his efforts and goes over his head, he returns to newspaper work. For many the show was stolen by Hugh O'Connell as a boozy reporter, so drunk that he inadvertently phones in a story to a paper from which he has been fired. (Critics noted this was supposedly based on a true incident, ignoring the fact that it had been used in *The Stolen Story* in 1906.) Atkinson wrote of another player, "One L. Russel Crouse, who has been pilfered from the Evening Post staff to bring a touch of verisimilitude to a newspaper play, spoke his lines gently last evening. His performance was as muted as Duse." The production survived for sixteen weeks.

Roy Horniman's **The Money Lender** (8-27-28, Ambassador) was an English drama dealing with Jewish-Christian relationships. A rich Christian moneylender has left his fortune to his daughter (Katherine Standing) on the condition that she marry the son (Herbert Clark) of his Jewish partner, but when the young man insists their children be raised as Jews, she rejects him. Although the will would then give the young man all the money, he generously agrees to split it with her. The play departed after a mere fortnight.

Kenyon Nicholson and John Golden failed to find favor with a bit of clean hokum, **Eva the Fifth** (8-28-28, Little). For years the Hartley girls have been touring backwaters playing Eva in "Ed Blondell's Uncle Tom's Cabin Company." Hattie Hartley (Claiborne Foster), the fourth in her line, is approached by the company's seedy manager (Edward M. Favor) when the company looks to go broke in Hiawatha, Kans. He asks her to cozy up to a rich hick who has fallen in love with her. Hattie reluctantly consents. The hick is Newton Wampler (Philip Barrison), the local furniture store owner and also the town's undertaker. That night Blondell absconds with what is left of the funds, leaving the players stranded in their private railroad car in the middle of nowhere. Hattie's little date with Newton has infuriated the nice, eager young man who long has loved her, Mal Thorne (Buford Armitage), the group's Simon Legree. Exasperated by his jealousy and the stranding, Hattie consents to wed Newton. But the resourceful Mal organizes a benefit performance at a nearby town, with half the money going to local flood victims and half to the players. To further Hattie's annoyance he enlists her obnoxiously bratty young sister, Oriole (Lois Shore), to become the company's fifth Eva. Hattie is furious and, although she won't admit it, jealous, even if she herself actually has become too old to continue to play Eva. Unfortunately, Oriole so overindulges in chocolates that she becomes sick. "Oriole has thrown up her part," Topsy (Nila Mack) announces. So Hattie, recognizing her own need to be a trouper, abandons her undertaker and agrees to finish the

performance. "I'll show them who's the greatest Little Eva!" she barks. A subdued Oriole can only moan, "I'll bet she won't be as good as I was."

Several prizefighting dramas would open during the season, beginning with Edward E. Paramore, Jr., Hyatt Daab, and George Abbott's **Ringside** (8-29-28, Broadhurst). Abbott, who directed the play, had also directed *Gentlemen of the Press*, which had opened two nights earlier. Hoping to get Bobby Murray (Richard Taber), the lightweight champion, to throw a title bout, the notorious racketeer John Zelli (Robert Glecker) uses booze and the beautiful Paula Vornoff (Suzanne Caubaye) to undermine the boy's principles. But Bobby's father, who is also his trainer, has vowed to kill his son if he ever throws a fight. He shoots Zelli instead. The last scene showed the fight. Glecker walked off with acting honors, playing "the part for every drop of poison it contains." However, once again a stellar performance was unable to save a weak show.

Clifford Pember and Ralph Cullinan's **Caravan** (8-29-28, Klaw) had an even shorter run. It was dismissed as "an operetta libretto for which some one forgot to supply the tunes." Alza (Virginia Pemberton), who was kidnapped as a child and raised by French gypsies, is suspected of murdering unwanted suitors. But the real killer is unearthed, and Alza is free to stay with the gypsies or find a noble lover.

The Phantom Lover (9-4-28, 49th St.) was not a revival of Ferenc Molnár's 1914 success but rather Herman Bernstein and Adolph E. Meyer's adaptation of Georg Kaiser's *Oktobertag*. Broadway would have none of this story about a handsome soldier (David Newell) who marries out of pity the young girl (Edith Barrett) who has loved him from afar and even claimed he is the father of her illegitimate child by a butcher's boy.

Nor was New York all that interested in Arthur Richman's latest opus, **Heavy Traffic** (9-5-28, Empire), although its epigrammatic dialogue delighted a number of critics. Rosalie West (Mary Boland) is a discreet but promiscuous wife. Her husband, Malcolm (Reginald Mason), is indifferent until he falls in love with Isabel Mancini (Kay Strozzi), the sister of his wife's latest paramour (Edward Crandall). Then he asks Rosalie for a divorce. She hotly refuses. But after she attempts to seduce the suave detective (A. E. Matthews) her husband has set on her trail, he has her where he wants her.

Sophie Treadwell's **Machinal** (9-7-28, Plymouth) was briefly "the talk of the early season" but failed to find a sufficiently large audience and closed after only ninety-one performances. Scuttlebutt had it that the play was based on the sensational Ruth Snyder–Judd Gray murder trial, a trial Treadwell had covered as a journalist. But she and her producer, the distinguished Arthur Hopkins, denied this, much as Crane Wilbur and his producer had denied that their production had been inspired by the Irving Berlin–Ellin Mackay romance. The play was the latest catering to the fashion for expressionism, so Hopkins hired Robert Edmond Jones to design the numerous settings required. They were simple, stylized settings, doing little more than suggest the whereabouts of the action, and were changed quickly during the blackouts that followed each short scene. The dialogue was often equally brusque. For example:

Husband: You know what?
Young Woman: No.
Husband: Guess.
Young Woman: I can't.
Husband: Then I'm coming in and tell you.
Young Woman: No! Don't! Please don't.

The Young Woman (Zita Johann), whose name is later revealed to be Helen Jones, is so discouraged by having to live with her nagging Mother (Jean Adair) that she grudgingly marries the Boss (George Stillwell), even though she is repelled by his fat, sweaty hands. Despite the arrival of a baby, their marriage is difficult. At a speakeasy she meets an attractive young Man (Clark Gable) and goes back with him to his room. He tells her he escaped from captors in Mexico by filling a bottle with stones and hitting his captors over the head with it. Hoping he will marry her, she kills her husband by the same method. Brought to trial, she denies everything until a letter from the Man is read, incriminating her. After being consoled by a Priest, she goes benumbedly to her execution. On an empty stage the lights change from a dim blue through red and pink to a glowing amber, suggesting that the Young Woman has at last found peace. Atkinson hailed the play and production as "fraught with a beauty unfamiliar to the stage."

Frederick Lonsdale, abetted by the incomparable Ina Claire, had better luck with **The High Road** (9-10-28, Fulton). The star played an actress who falls in love with several noblemen but in the end recognizes she belongs on the stage.

Two quick flops opened the next night. Myron C. Fagan's **The Great Power** (9-11-28, Ritz) begins in the real world, where the arrogant, cigar-puffing John Power (John T. Doyle) exclaims, "I will cover the Wray name with such filth that even the carrion of Wyoming will shun the spot where she is buried."

She is Joan Wray (Minna Gombell), who has been fighting Power's attempt to smear her senator brother (John Anthony). Joan is more than the mogul has bargained for, and before long he collapses on the floor of his elegant library. He dreams that he is at the Judgment Seat and is denied a place in heaven. To finish his humiliation he is told that Joan is the daughter of a marriage he shamefully abandoned years earlier. Joan agrees to wed his decent stepson (Alan Birmingham).

Samuel Shipman and Max Marcin's **Trapped** (9-11-28, National) began and stayed in the real world, at least the real world as seen in Broadway melodrama. Despite the efforts of the police and her rich banker father (William Ingersoll), who have been warned of a planned kidnapping, Helen Lorrimore (Janet McLeay) is abducted by an Italian gang, along with the bank messenger, Guthrie Daniels (Edward Woods), who was escorting her. They are taken to a hideaway in Westchester, where Helen's life and honor are both threatened. But Guthrie, by playing along, tricks the gangsters into letting him collect the $500,000 ransom. And Helen is rescued in the nick of time by the police on an old wharf. By then Helen has fallen in love with Guthrie.

Philip Dunning's eagerly awaited **Night Hostess** (9-12-28, Martin Beck) was produced by, of all people, the unlikely John Golden. Although the tough-talking melodrama chalked up 117 performances, it went down as one of the season's major disappointments. The play was set in the "ultramodern" lounge of the splashily art deco Little Casino. The furniture is all painted in shiny silver, bright green, and Chinese red. Doors lead to the bar and an office, and an elevator at the rear takes customers up to the gambling rooms. At the rise of the curtain several professional hostesses have lured in "chumps," well-heeled southern yokels who are out for an evening on the town and who are made to leave their bottle of white mule in the cloakroom. Ben Fisher (Maurice Freeman), the honest co-owner, is complaining that while he was in the hospital for some surgery a lot of cash has disappeared. His crooked partner, Chris Miller (Averell Harris), contemptuously denies it. Although Chris has dropped one boozy, aging hostess, Julia (Gail De Hart), for her attractive, younger colleague, Buddy Miles (Ruth Lyons), he persuades Julia to help lure a customer who had just won $20,000 to a nearby restaurant. There Chris's men kill him. When Julia realizes that Chris is about to lure Buddy to Chicago with the promise of a job in a new musical, she threatens to reveal the truth. Chris uses a waiter's apron to strangle her and dumps her body into a trunk. But Julia's ex-husband (Charles Laite), a detective who still loves her even though she succumbed to Chris's blandishments, and Rags Conway (Norman Foster), a composer-performer who loves Buddy, discover the trunk. Chris grabs the detective's gun and starts to back away, but he backs into an open elevator shaft and falls to his death. Buddy embraces Rags and bewails what a wicked town New York is. "Well, we shouldn't complain about the town," Rags replies; "after all, we only paid the Indians a bottle of whiskey for it."

Edwin Burke's **This Thing Called Love** (9-17-28, Maxine Elliott's) was a modest hit, running seventeen weeks. E. W. Osborn of the *Evening World* welcomed it as "the happiest comedy this reviewer has seen in many a long day." When Tice Collins (Minor Watson), newly back in New York after fifteen years running mines in Peru, abruptly proposes to Ann Marvin (Violet Heming), she is reluctant to accept, even if her little tea room has just been seized for debt by the sheriff. Her reluctance stems from the vicious battle she has just witnessed between her mercurial sister (Juliette Day) and her philandering brother-in-law (Malcolm Duncan). She agrees to a compromise. She will become Tice's wife for hire and the entire arrangement will be conducted on a businesslike basis. That way, she insists, "it has all the excitement of a gamble. If we win—how glorious! If we lose—well, we lose!" A few months later they have taken over her sister's magnificent apartment. Ann knows Tice is already having some side flings, but then, so is she. Her affair is with a roué, Normie De Witt (Harry Whittemore), notorious for courting married women. But when Normie learns that both are aware of each other's affairs and don't care, his sense of propriety is outraged, and he even attempts to shoot Tice. Tice and Ann soon understand how much they have come to love each other and agree to marry, for all their faults and flings. Even Ann's sister and brother-in-law may get together again.

Jack Dempsey, following in an old tradition, was greeted with wild applause when he made his first entrance as star of Milton Herbert Gropper and Max Marcin's **The Big Fight** (9-18-28, Majestic), but all his celebrity could not make the play go, and the huge take the producers obviously hoped for at the large-capacity theatre normally given over to musicals never materialized. Yet one of the producers was the knowing Sam H. Harris, and the director was David Belasco. The story was simple and old hat. The heavyweight champion, Tiger Dillon, hopes to win both his next match and the hand of the lovely manicurist, Shirley (Estelle Taylor [Mrs. Dempsey]). His manager, Steve Logan (Jack Roseleigh), also covets the girl, so when the crooked Chuck Sloan (Arthur R. Vinton), who owns the barbershop where most of the action unfolds, makes him a generous offer, Steve is willing to trick Shirley into drugging Tiger. She doesn't, and after the action shifts to Madison Square Garden, Tiger goes into the ring and flattens his opponent in two rounds. Dempsey, who received $5000 a week, delivered such memorable lines as "I'll say so!" and "Is that so?" in a "somewhat piping voice." But he got a big hand when he snarled at Steve, who spoke leeringly of Shirley, "You cut that out or I'll break your jaw!"

The ring gave way to the baseball diamond without any more luck in Ring Lardner's **Elmer the Great** (9-24-28, Lyceum), albeit the show had been a modest hit in Chicago. Producer George M. Cohan tried unavailingly to rewrite the show before bringing it into New York. The best thing about the evening proved to be Walter Huston's vivid performance as the lunkhead pitcher, so brilliant in the minor leagues that a New York team desperately tries to sign him. But he won't go, since he loves Nellie Poole (Nan Sunderland), the gal who owns the grocery store in Gentryville, Ind., where he is a delivery boy. Sensing the problem, Nellie fires him. In New York Elmer is successful, but he takes to gambling. The gamblers try to get him to throw a big game and, shades of *The Big Fight,* attempt to con Nellie into helping them. She outwits them, so at the end Elmer is about to sign a new contract, with Nellie put down as his business manager and wife-to-be.

The same producers who had offered *The Big Fight,* a week earlier also offered **The War Song** (9-24-28, National), which listed Sam and Bella Spewack and George Jessel as its authors. Jessel was also its star. He played Eddie Rosen, who goes off to fight in the World War even though his widowed mother (Clara Langsner) is dying and his sister (Shirley Booth) is pregnant but unwed. His girl (Lola Lane) and his buddy (Raymond Guion) come to entertain the troops, so he also learns that she is leaving him for his pal. Taken prisoner by the Germans shortly after receiving news that his mother has died, he puzzles his captors with his moans until a German officer (in German) reveals that he in praying in Jewish fashion. Scenes at Camp Upton in Yaphank provided comic relief. The play ran ten weeks—more than twice as long as *Elmer the Great*— but *Variety* suggested it would do well on the road.

The evening's longest run—seventeen weeks— went to **Jarnegan** (9-24-28, Longacre), which Charles Beahan and Garret Fort took from Jim Tully's novel.

Jack Jarnegan (Richard Bennett) is a rough-mouthed, hard-drinking, womanizing Hollywood director until he falls in love with a would-be star, sixteen-year-old Daisy Carol (Joan Bennett). But when Daisy dies from an abortion after being seduced by a fellow director (Robert Cain), Jarnegan goes on a bender and tells everyone off, then reluctantly agrees to continue directing. Many critics, while admiring Bennett's "splendid shouting pipes," felt he could not capture the necessary hardness for the part. His daughter was given short shrift.

None of September's last three entries ran a full month. The hero of John Willard's **Adventure** (9-25-28, Republic), Michael O'Shane (John B. Litel), is a member of the Adventure League, a group of veterans from "the big war and who still are imbued with the over-there spirit." He meets and falls in love with Dolores Hampton (Roberta Arnold), whose father runs a cattle ranch in Bitter Creek, Wyo. Curiously, he takes work as a sharpshooter whose job is to kill Hampton's cattle so that there will be more land for a neighbor to graze his sheep. He is exposed by malicious Angel Evans (Harry D. Southard), kills Evans in a shootout, but somehow is forgiven by Dolores.

Samuel Shipman joined hands, this time with John B. Hymer, to write **Fast Life** (9-26-28, Ambassador). Patricia Mason (Claudette Colbert) has secretly wed Douglas Stratton (Donald Dillaway). Another suitor, Rodney Hall (Donald McClelland), finds them in bed together and, unaware of the true situation, berates them. Shortly afterwards Rodney is shot dead and Douglas is arrested and convicted. But just before he can be executed, a third suitor, Chester Palmer (Chester Morris), confesses.

Producer George M. Cohan and writers J. C. and Elliott Nugent wasted their efforts with **By Request** (9-27-28, Hudson). Bill Abbott (Elliott Nugent), assistant editor of a paper in Massilon, Ohio, comes east to see the paper's new owner and falls in love with pretty Claudia Wynn (Verree Teasdale), albeit he is honest enough to tell her he has a wife back home. That wife (Norma Lee) soon appears and realizes what is happening. On the advice of an old friend she encourages Bill and Claudia to go on with their plans for a trip to Bar Harbor. In the Pullman sleeper, Bill drinks too much, which annoys Claudia and prompts her to leave. Bill is unaware of this, and when he sees a woman in a dressing robe just like Claudia's, he climbs into her berth. Of course, the woman is his wife, and all ends happily.

Five attractions simultaneously ushered in October. Two were musicals. Of the three straight plays, one was a French classic, one a curious British novelty, and one American. The American play had the shortest run thanks to the police, who closed it after its second performance. Mae West's **Pleasure Man** (10-1-28, Biltmore) takes place at a drag party. "It's the queerest show you've ever seen. All of the Queens are in it," *Variety* observed. Characters, all played by men, had such names as Bird of Paradise, It (after Clara Bow), and Peaches. Rodney Terrill (Alan Brooks), either straight or a bisexual, has violated a young girl, and her brother uses the occasion to castrate him. The closing reputedly forced West and her producer to refund a record $200,000 advance sale.

Nigel Playfair's **When Crummles Played** (10-1-28, Garrick) resurrected characters from Dickens's *Nicholas Nickleby*. In 1827 they gather on the stage of the Portsmouth Theatre and offer their version of George Lillo's eighteenth-century mercantile tragedy, *George Barnwell*, then conclude with a harlequinade. Halliwell Hobbes was Vincent Crummles. Played with a light touch of satire, the production had been a success at the Lyric Hammersmith, near London, and was offered as the first in a planned repertory by the English Company of the Garrick Players. It delighted knowing theatregoers for its limited stand.

Eva Le Gallienne began the third season of her own Civic Repertory down on 14th Street—still at a bargain $1.50 top—with Molière's *The Would-Be Gentleman* in a version by F. Anstey (Thomas Anstey Guthrie). Miss Le Gallienne herself took no part, although she did direct. The company's stalwart Egon Brecher was Jourdain. Brecher's German-tinged accent annoyed some critics, and most felt all the performances left something to be desired. Comedy was never to be the Civic's strong point. However, they praised the lavish settings and costumes (by Cleon Throckmorton and Aline Bernstein).

Edgar Selwyn was the producer of his own comedy, **Possession** (10-2-28, Booth). Exasperated by twenty-five years of mothering and babying at the hands of his histrionic wife (Margaret Lawrence), Stanley Whiteman (Walter Connolly) runs off with pretty, black-haired Edythe Grange (Roberta Beatty). Mrs. Whiteman refuses to grant him a divorce and vows revenge. Then Whiteman is accidentally shot, and his wife's thoughtful nursing convinces him that being mothered and babied are not all that bad. While this is going on the couple's handsome but spoiled-rotten son (Robert Montgomery) has a fling with pert Molly Russell (Edna Hibbard). The comedy could not find its audience.

Nor could C. Stafford Dickens's **The Command Performance** (10-3-28, Klaw), which allowed Ian

Keith to enact the dual roles of the irresponsible Prince Alexis of Moldavia and Peter Kraditch, a look-alike actor. Authorities force Kraditch to woo Princess Katerina (Jessie Royce Landis) of Wallachia in Alexis's stead. The prince may have good reason for being loath to court the lady, since, like Turandot, she has had all her spurned suitors put to death. When Alexis runs off, his mother, Queen Elinor (Beatrice Terry), declares that Kraditch is the real prince and heir and allows him to marry Katerina.

William Hodge, always more popular on the road than in New York, fared poorly with his latest self-written vehicle, **Straight Thru the Door** (10-4-28, 49th St.). Eugene Thomas, an actor who is building a suburban home for himself and his wife (Ruth Gates), hears one of the builders gossip about a supposed romance between Mrs. Thomas and the architect. When the gossip is shot dead, suspicion falls on Thomas, especially since he has been seen kissing his vampish interior decorator (Jeanette Fox-Lee). But it turns out the vamp was the aggressor in that clinch and that the architect was the killer.

The Civic Repertory's second offering of the season was even less welcomed than its first. Jean-Jacques Bernard's **L'Invitation au Voyage** (10-4-28, Civic Repertory) was presented in a translation by Ernest Boyd which retained the original title. It told of a woman (Eva Le Gallienne) who long believes she loves her husband's partner. For years the man has been away, managing their interests overseas, but when he returns she realizes she has been deluding herself. The loved partner never appears in the play.

The Theatre Guild inaugurated its latest season with Graham and Tristan Rawson's translation of Goethe's *Faust* at the Guild on the 8th. A magnificent mounting "with the extraordinary beauty of Lee Simonson's sets, the perfection of detail in exorcism, the puffs of smoke and the glare of fire, the musical roulades, the starry heavens in the open"—all of this within the confines of a large arch, could not fully overcome the languors of the drama. Nonetheless, Dudley Digges as Mephistopheles and George Gaul in the title role acquitted themselves handsomely and pleased subscribers for six weeks.

Tom Barry's **Courage** (10-8-28, Ritz) pleased even more theatregoers and, as a result, ran out the season. It did so in the face of numerous critical barbs about its sentimentality. The improvident Mrs. Colebrook (Janet Beecher) has frittered away the small inheritance left her by her late, brutally cruel husband. Determined to educate her large brood, whom she adores uncritically, she has moved to Cambridge, Mass. But her children, except for the youngest, the spunky, outspoken Bill (Junior Durkin), are totally selfish and not the least grateful. So when they discover that she is bankrupt and that their mean, vengeful aunt (Helen Strickland)—Mrs. Colebrook's sister-in-law—is willing to pay for all the comforts they feel they are entitled to, they leave their mother to go live with the aunt. The aunt wants nothing to do with Mrs. Colebrook or Bill. She even buys the house Mrs. Colebrook has rented, just for the satisfaction of dispossessing her. But then Bill, who has befriended a lonely spinster, is found to be the old lady's heir after she dies. With their brother now the possessor of $500,000, the children return home. But Mrs. Colebrook, her eyes finally opened, tells them she is going back to Iowa to marry her childhood sweetheart: "I am going to marry an illiterate man. That is the only reason I have not married him sooner. I could not reconcile him in the lives of my children." And she confesses that the man is Bill's father, whom she turned to in order to escape Mr. Colebrook's "cruelty and fiendishness."

Another season-long success arrived the next evening, although once again many critics—mostly second-stringers—had reservations about its merits, particularly its "wobbly" last act. **Little Accident** (10-9-28, Morosco) was adapted by Floyd Dell and Thomas Mitchell from Dell's story *An Unmarried Father*. Hours before his wedding rehearsal, Norman Overbeck (Mitchell) receives a letter from a Chicago maternity hospital advising him he has become a father and asking him to recall an art exhibition he attended in Cambridge. He needs only nine fingers to count back to the time of the exhibition, so he rushes off to Chicago, leaving his bride-to-be (Elvia Enders) and the minister perplexed. There he discovers that the baby's mother has no intention of embarrassing him. He has been asked to come so that he may have a physical that will allow the baby to be placed for adoption. One look at his new son and he is outraged that its mother, Isabel Drury (Katharine Alexander), a young artist determined to pursue her studies in Paris, could do anything so inhuman as walk away from a baby. Told she has every right to do so, he kidnaps the child. At a small boardinghouse, he tries to raise the infant himself. But he dares not call the hospital to get the baby's formula, and since it has gained only one ounce during the week, he fears that would mean only fifty-two ounces a year and the boy would still be a midget at twenty. His fiancée arrives and learns that in his desperation he has virtually proposed to the daughter (Patricia Barcley) of the lady who runs the boardinghouse. There is a further shock when Isabel, whom he has announced has died, also appears. Although his fiancée has offered to accept the child, Isabel tells him she, however reluctantly, will marry him—"just so you can have some claim on him." They argue, but in the end Norman and Isabel acknowledge that they love each other, and they set out to change the baby's diapers together.

Walter Hampden's penchant for often pompous, high-flown religious drama was seen again when he began his season with Georgina Jones Walton's **The Light of Asia** (10-9-28, Hampden's). Hampden played Siddartha, Prince of the Sakyas, who is appalled by the death and depravity all about him and runs off to become a contemplative recluse. When he emerges years later to "cast away the world to save the world," he is known as Buddha. The huge spectacle was embellished with dances by Ruth St. Denis, but a critical drubbing prompted its quick removal.

Three plays opened the next Monday. The two new plays did little to help what *Variety* was already bewailing as "the most sluggish legit autumn season in a decade." In the first scene of Willard Mack's **The Common Sin** (10-15-28, Forrest), Jim Steele (Thurston Hall), unable to convince his faithless wife (Milicent Hanley) to help him in a financial crisis, writes a suicide note and prepares to kill himself. Before he can, his old flame, Bobo Aster (Lee Patrick), appears and offers to save him. She plans to get the $300,000 he needs from her own lover, but when she goes to him she finds Mrs. Steele there. She threatens Mrs. Steele with exposure. Later that evening, Mrs. Steele returns and picks up the note, which Jim had crumpled and discarded. She kills him and plants the note beside him. Bobo is suspected. She confronts Mrs. Steele and, with the police listening in the next room, tricks her into a confession. The play marked Mack's swan song as a dramatist.

During its tryout, Fredric March had played the lead in Walter De Leon and Alethea Luce's **The K Guy** (10-15-28, Biltmore), but he left to take a lucrative screen offer and so had no part in its ignominious one-week New York stand. The Kid (Alan Ward), a pleasant young man who claims he is suffering from amnesia and can't remember his real name, is suspected of being the sought-after forger known as "the K Guy" because he always uses the letter *k* in the phony names he signs on his checks. The suspicion hurts his chances of finding romance and a career in Hollywood. But later the real forger, a fake Egyptian prince (Francis Compton), shoots

him, grazing his head. The wound restores his memory, and all ends happily in the lunchroom of the Idol Film Company, where the action unfolds. Oh yes, the Kid had been a promising comedian before hurting his head in a fall from the stage.

Eva Le Gallienne finally struck paydirt with her mounting of Chekhov's *The Cherry Orchard*, in Constance Garnett's translation, at the Civic Repertory on the same night. She brought in Alla Nazimova to portray Madame Ranevsky, while she herself took the lesser role of Varya. The women's performances were hailed; not so the men's. Whatever its shortcomings, Miss Le Gallienne kept this story of a Russian lady's inability to accept and deal with her family's impoverishment in her repertory for several seasons.

According to Channing Pollock his **Mr. Moneypenny** (10-16-28, Liberty) "was produced at a cost of more than $100,000, with scenery by Robert Edmond Jones, two orchestras, and a company of 112, . . . with the best seats at two dollars." Critics felt this tedious, expressionistic parable was not worth the trouble. The curtain rises on a bank vault over which looms briefly a devil-like shadow. For twenty years John Jones (Donald Meek) has been employed in the vault, employment which he sees as a treadmill going nowhere. "Every night I quit my job, and go home, and get some sleep, and get up, and play golf with the lawn mower, and come back to my job." Just as bad, he is cursed with a family totally satisfied with this humdrum existence. So when Mr. Moneypenny (Hale Hamilton) offers him riches galore—"Millions—Billions"—in return for his soul, Jones quickly accepts. He soon is John Jones of Jones and Co., 60 Gold Street, New York, where employees work in unison to the beat of a giant metronome. At first his family wallows in wealth. His son even orders a new roadster, since his Hispano does not match the color of his purple blazer. At a wild, jam-packed jazz nightclub, where all that can be seen are lighted tips of cigarettes, the feet of the dancers, and a huge plaster head of his Satanic Majesty, frenzy passes for pleasure. But slowly his wife (Margaret Wycherly) and children rebel. Finally, Jones himself recognizes how unhappy he is and reneges on his bargain with Mr. Moneypenny, to return to his old ways and old job.

Sidney Howard's faithful—even to retaining the original title—adaptation of Molnár's **Olympia** (10-16-28, Empire) was perhaps too faithful, since the nuances of European royal romances were lost on Broadway's tired businessmen and their wives. Fay Compton played a princess who cruelly rejects the polite wooing of a dashing hussar (Ian Hunter) only to be even more savagely rejected in turn after her family discovers he is actually a suitable prospect and she gladly spends a night with him.

Lemist Esler, a graduate of Professor George Pierce Baker's class in playwriting, which Baker had moved to Yale, was the author of **The Grey Fox** (10-22-28, Playhouse), purportedly a history of Machiavelli (Henry Hull). At first he is an idealistic young man until he is betrayed by Caterina Sforza (Chrystal Herne). Some years later he becomes the murderous cohort of Cesare Borgia (Edward Arnold). At last, as an old man in exile, he sits down to write his famous book, *The Prince*. Lavish settings (by Jo Mielziner) and costumes and a huge cast meant that the drama had to draw virtual capacity at its small house to remain profitable. Discouraging notices saw to it that it did not.

Yet laudatory reviews peppered with adjectives such as "poignant" and "honest" and with favorable comparisons to Maxwell Anderson's *Saturday's Children* could not win Caroline Francke's **Exceeding Small** (10-22-28, Comedy) a profitable run, either. So the play went down as another succès d'estime for the Equity Players, now rechristened the Actors' Theatre. The drama opens on a Saturday evening at a Chinese restaurant and dance hall, where a stout, balding immigrant (Eddie Garvie), a man who has made a small sum of money, hopes to lure Gert (Ruth Easton) away from Ed (Eric Dressler), her freight-handler beau. That leads to the couple's latest argument, which they continue the next day at Gert's bare apartment. For all their fiery words, Ed stills begs Gert to marry him although neither of them has much of an income. She finally consents. However, just a week after their hasty wedding, Ed collapses, and Gert learns that he is dying of an incurably bad heart. A doctor (Halliam Bosworth) tells her that even with a long rest, which he cannot afford, Ed has only two or three years at most to live. In despair, they turn on the gas and commit suicide. Audiences, growing increasingly accustomed to realistic talk, may have felt that the play, with lines such as "I'd like to see any son-of-a-gun come pawing at Gert" or "I'll bust this fat sap on his beezock," was not all that honest. Or they may have been bored with the characters' irredeemably lower-class dreariness and their semi-literate speech. Whatever the reason, they stayed away. Perhaps in hope of future amateur productions, the playwright offered an alternate, happy ending in the Samuel French acting edition.

While the two new American plays to open on the 22nd had larger than normal casts, **Jealousy** (10-22-28, Maxine Elliott's), which Eugene Walter derived from Louis Verneuil's *Monsieur Lambertier*, was a rarity for the time—a two-character drama. Since the two characters were played by Fay Bainter and John Halliday, and since the reviews were largely favorable, the piece ran seventeen weeks, despite its unpleasant story. An artist discovers that his wife is having an affair with a rich man in order to help support her husband. He strangles the lover, then confesses to the police rather than see an innocent man inculpated.

Lula Vollmer's *Sun-Up* was revived the same evening with Lucille La Verne again as Widow Cagel. The Princess Theatre was briefly renamed after the star for the three months during which the revival survived.

While the authors of plays which seemingly were based on the Berlin-Mackay and Snyder-Gray headlines went to some pain to deny their works' origins, Maxwell Anderson and Harold Hickerson made no bones about their **Gods of the Lightning** (10-24-28, Little). It was provoked by the Sacco-Vanzetti case, in which two anarchists were convicted in an alleged kangaroo court and executed for a killing they probably did not commit. Macready (Charles Bickford) is a rabble-rouser who boasts, "Everywhere I go there's a strike." He hates all successful men, big business, religion, and the military, the latter two deemed tools of the former pair. Even Rosalie (Sylvia Sidney), the girl he is engaged to, tells him, "You like strikes because you like to be in a fight and you run them because you like to act like a tin Napoleon!" A paymaster has been killed and robbed of the money meant to pay replacements brought into a mill where Macready has goaded the regular employees into striking. Along with his friend Capraro (Horace Braham), a pacific anarchist, he is arrested, although the police know neither man is guilty. The district attorney (Robert Brister), for all his doubts about the men's guilt, is too interested in furthering his own career to go against the will of the authorities and has filled the jury with "a hundred and forty proof Shriners and Chamber of Commerce." Even the judge (Willard Dashiell) is happy that the panel is "not too intelligent." The trial is a mockery, and the men are sentenced to death, despite the testimony of one witness (Leo Bulgakov) that he himself and a partner were the actual killers. At the cheap lunchroom where the play begins and ends, the men's friends await the executions. A socialist tabloid across the road posts banners announcing that they have been "murdered." Seeing the banners Rosalie exhorts, "Shout it! Shout it! Cry out! Run and cry! Only—it won't do any good—now."

Anderson and Hickerson attempted a little even-handedness by making Macready unlikable, leaving *Variety* to note that "these heroes seem hardly heroic." But The *Times* hailed the play as "a strong, harrowing drama." Perhaps tired of the whole Sacco-Vanzetti affair, theatregoers would not buy the play. Anderson's biographer dimissed the piece as "certainly not a good one," adding it was "too much in the socialist vein of what Clifford Odets would soon be doing." Of course, playgoers could not foresee that.

Barry Conners's **Girl Trouble** (10-25-28, Belmont) spotlighted Jimmy Lockhart (Alan Dinehart), whose mother (Lucia Moore) had annulled a runaway marriage he contracted at seventeen with a fifteen-year-old carnival girl, Evelyn Waldron (Dorothy Hall). Finding that Jimmy cannot stay out of girl trouble, Mrs. Lockhart finally consents to his remarrying Evelyn.

All the rest of October's entries were also failures. Saxon Kling's **Crashing Through** (10-29-28, Republic) takes place in an aging Gramercy Park mansion, where young, bored Consuelo Poole (Rose Hobart) lives with her aristocratic grandmother (Henrietta Crosman), while her divorced parents (Frederick Truesdell and Eleanor Woodruff) caper their separate ways about the world. A large, new apartment house is being built on the site of several neighboring mansions, and one day Consuelo finds her boredom relieved when a handsome, blond construction worker, Chris (Gavin Gordon), comes plunging through a skylight. They are soon in love, then, almost as soon, expecting a baby. Consuelo's parents are aghast when they learn of the situation, but, surprisingly, the old grande dame is understanding and enlists a bishop (Albert Bruning) to make matters right. Matters are made even more right after the Pooles learn that Chris has invented and patented a silent riveter, which promises to bring in big bucks.

The Unknown Warrior (10-29-28, Charles Hopkins) was taken by Cecil Lewis from Paul Raynal's *Le Tombeau sous l'Arc de Triomphe*. A soldier (Lester Vail) returns from the front for a short leave, hoping to marry his sweetheart (Beatrix Thomson). She sleeps with him but also tells him she no longer loves him the way she once did. Embittered, he heads back to his outfit and probable death. The play was one of several small-cast entries during the season, having only three characters.

There were only four characters in Samson Raphaelson's **Young Love** (10-30-28, Masque). It, too, dealt with a young woman, Fay Hilary (Dorothy Gish), who doubts her feelings about the man,

David Hallowell (Tom Douglas), she is to marry. She proposes that they each have a fling with another partner and suggests a married couple with whom they are friendly, Peter and Nancy Bird (James Rennie and Catherine Willard). Fay and Peter spend a happy night together, but David cannot even muster sufficient nerve to make the proposal to Nancy. Yet Fay concludes that she does love David, after all. Despite some critical cavils about the play being "lurid," its eleven-week run was as close as any late October entry came to making the grade.

At the opening of Leonard Ide's **These Few Ashes** (10-30-28, Booth) four women in Kenneth Vail's life and his Oriental valet assemble at his swank apartment in St. Moritz, Switzerland, and gather around an urn containing his ashes to remember him. In flashbacks their relationships are relived. A French woman would ensnare him in an unhealthy ménage à quatre, a gambling lady hopes to win all his fortune, a German baroness proves to be a collector of bad debts hired by Kenneth's creditors, and a sweet little girl loves him for himself. All four refuse to claim his ashes, but after the first three have departed, Kenneth (Hugh Sinclair) appears, very much alive, and proposes to the sweet little thing.

Two other plays focused on real suicides. Down in the Village, David Pinski, heretofore known as a writer for the Yiddish theatre, though *The Treasure* had been translated into English and presented by the Theatre Guild, offered his **The Final Balance** (10-30-28, Provincetown Playhouse). A baker (E. J. Ballantine) is led by a dream to believe that new flour turns people insane and that old flour can cure them. He buys up all the old flour, then sets out to destroy his enemies, especially the husband (Berne Lenrow) of the woman (Emily Graham) he loves, by selling them bread made with fresh flour. Finding that the woman spurns him, he gives her bread made with old flour to cure her husband, then he hangs himself.

In Harry Wagstaff Gribble's **Revolt** (10-31-28, Vanderbilt), the world of a fiery, fundamentalist preacher, Barnabas Ford (Hugh Buckler), begins to fall apart when his children (his three daughters are Faith, Hope, and Charity, and his son is Paul) rebel against his ironclad, religious ways. To recruit a dwindling congregation he enlists the help of a celebrated girl evangelist (Eloise Keeler), only to have her become hysterical and faint when he attempts to submerge her in water. Further humiliation follows when his congregation suggests he take an extended vacation. Too depressed to go on, the minister shoots himself.

The doldrums persisted during November's first three weeks, with only two revivals even approaching genuine hit status.

Despite its title, Hugh Stanislaus Stange's **Tin Pan Alley** (11-1-28, Biltmore) was merely the latest of Broadway's nightclub melodramas. Believing her songsmith husband, Fred Moran (Norman Foster), indifferent to her, Jill O'Dare (Claudette Colbert) leaves her job in the chorus of the *Scandals* to take employment as secretary to the notorious gangster and nightclub owner Joe Privadi (John Wray). She resists all of Joe's efforts, pleasant or otherwise, to seduce her, and when she realizes that Fred's lack of interest stems from consumption, she throws up her work and prepares to accompany him out west for a cure. Privadi and his hoods shoot Fred before he and Jill can board the train at Grand Central, but Fred survives and Privadi, tricked into a confession by a recording device hidden in a telephone, is sent to prison. Settings included another bare apartment, another garish nightclub, and the station.

To replace the failure of his religious spectacle, Walter Hampden brought back *An Enemy of the People* for three weeks at his playhouse, beginning on the 5th.

A revival of George C. Hazelton and J. Harry Benrimo's *The Yellow Jacket* was offered two nights later by Mr. and Mrs. Charles Coburn at a theatre, far up on 63rd Street, they renamed the Coburn. The producers assumed the roles of Chorus and Chee Moo, the kind mother. Arthur Shaw, as he had been in November of 1912 and in subsequent restorations, again was the bored Property Man, and Schuyler Ladd once more was Daffodil in this Chinese fantasy recreated in the style of traditional Chinese drama.

Paul Osborn, another student of George Pierce Baker, and a dramatist soon to make his mark on Broadway, launched his writing career with **Hotbed** (11-8-28, Klaw), a play that reminded some critics of *Revolt*, since its central figure was an unbending, fundamentalist minister, this time called David Rushbrook (William Ingersoll). He has made life miserable for his weak, fluttery wife (Josephine Hull) and hopes to dominate and mold his children. Having already seen ominous signs of rebellion in his son (Richard Spencer), he demands that a nearby college purge itself of godless liberals, and he particularly goes after one young instructor (Richard Stevenson) rumored to have seduced a student. The instructor's fellow teachers—depicted, according to one critic, as "spineless, ingrown, jealous and selfish"—acquiesce in the minister's demand. The young man refuses to identify the girl, but she will not let him be persecuted. She storms into the meeting and reveals that she is Rushbrook's daughter (Alison Bradshaw). The minister disowns her and walks out of the meeting.

The English Company of the Garrick Players, now called simply the Garrick Players, since most of the performers enlisted for their latest effort were Americans, mounted **A Man with Red Hair** (11-8-28, Garrick), theatricalized by Benn W. Levy from Hugh Walpole's novel. It told of the sadistic Mr. Crispin (Edward G. Robinson), who lures victims to his isolated mansion and tortures them, with the aid of Oriental slaves whose tongues he has cut out. The slaves turn on him after his latest victims escape. Albeit some critics considered Robinson's red wig absurd, they ranked "this cruelest of his stage portraits" among the top of his career.

More loose morals were on display in Roland Oliver's **On Call** (11-9-28, Waldorf). When John Smith (Ray Collins) discovers his wife (Emily Ross) having an affair with a charming young piano player (Charles Dosch) living at the Y.M.C.A., he demands a divorce, albeit he consents to be the defendant. To this end he calls a celebrated madam and asks her to send over a girl to serve as corespondent. The girl, Margie (Dorothea Chard), turns out to be a lass whom the madam saved from committing suicide and who is an innocent on her first job. She also turns out to be the piano player's sister. Before long Smith, Margie, and her brother are all heading for honest, pure Kenyon, Ohio, leaving Mrs. Smith to fend for herself in wicked New York. *Variety*, noting that Margie thanks Smith for saving her from "a fate worse than death" but that she suggests no gratitude for the madam's having prevented her killing herself, observed, "Death apparently is not worse enough."

Irving Stone, whose fame would come from other literary forms, was the author of **The Dark Mirror** (11-9-28, Cherry Lane), which traced the history of Alvin Atkins from the time he was a ten-year-old in 1910 to his death—well in the future as far as 1928 playgoers were concerned—in 1960. He watches his father die after losing his job, his mother run a successful family business only to commit suicide when problems arise, and his daughter turn streetwalker and starve to death. Some performers, all unknown, played several roles. Those critics who reviewed the show were mostly dismissive.

For some time Broadway scuttlebutt had claimed that Mark Linder had been a silent co-author for *Diamond Lil*. True or not, he was accorded full credit—or blame—for **The Squealer** (11-12-28, Forrest), which was billed as a "melodrama of the days when the villain WAS a villain and the hero had a heart of gold." The drama was set in 1906 and played out for the most part in Charlie Wong's Oriental Palace. Like the Little Casino in *Night Hostess*, the Oriental Palace is a gambling joint as well as a nightclub, but it is also a drug den. Scantily clad girls parade across the room now and then, a fire-eater entertains, and a "kind o' hot Chinese band" offers its version of American ragtime. Charlie (Robert Harrison) is determined to keep "Slippery" Jimmy (Robert Bentley), a dope-runner with a heart of gold, and Jimmy's gal, the cabaret singer, Dora Deane (Ruth Shepley), who would reform Jimmy, from going straight. Charlie employs any number of immoral and corruptible cohorts to help him, while Jimmy's friend, the crippled "Gimpty" Kelly (Guy Harrington), who proves late in the game to be a secret service agent, does all he can to thwart the machinations of the "slinky chink." Kelly succeeds, aided at the very end by a device straight out of the long-gone touring melodramas from the era in which the play was set—the great San Francisco earthquake, which destroys the Oriental Palace.

Not all of George Pierce Baker's students were welcomed on Broadway, as Katharine Clugston learned when her **These Days** (11-12-28, Cort) folded after one dismally attended week. Coming from an unhappy home, Virginia MacRae (Mildred McCoy) cannot adapt to life at her stern boarding school. She elopes with the son (William Johnstone) of a celebrated actor, finds she is just as unsatisfied in married life, divorces her husband, then, still unhappy, sets out to get him back. Among the "fresh, attractive types" playing other students was another Katharine—Hepburn.

Owen Davis was a far more famous name at the time. But age had begun to slow him down and, apart from the book of one musical comedy, **Tonight at 12** (11-13-28, Hudson) was his only offering for the season. When Alice Keith (Anne Shoemaker) observes her husband (William Roselle) slip a note into a cloisonné box before a dinner party, she takes it out, sees that it reads "tonight at 12," and replaces it. Later in the evening the note has disappeared, so Mrs. Keith confronts all the ladies and asks which one is having an affair with Mr. Keith. The Keiths' son (Owen Davis, Jr.) runs in to say the note was meant for him and later tries to save his father at the risk of ruining his own romance by suggesting he has been dallying with a pretty housemaid (Viola Frayne). The maid herself is able to provide more real answers about skeletons in closets or lovers in

concealed embraces than anyone wants to hear, so she is silenced with a handsome bribe.

Five revivals and one imported novelty vied for attention the next Monday. The novelty was Somerset Maugham's **The Sacred Flame** (11-19-28, Henry Miller's). Knowing that Stella Tabret (Casha Pringle) is pregnant by her brother-in-law (Anthony Bushell), Nurse Wayland (Clare Eames) demands that the police investigate the death of the hopelessly crippled Maurice Tabret (Robert Harris). After several false leads and false confessions, Maurice's mother (Mary Jerrold) confesses to giving her son an overdose to put him out of his misery. Some critics felt that Eames emoted too strongly in this, her last appearance before her premature death.

Two of the revivals enjoyed excellent notices and ran ten weeks apiece. At its own playhouse the Theatre Guild restored Shaw's *Major Barbara*. Dudley Digges walked off with acting honors for his Undershaft, but Helen Westley as Lady Britomart Undershaft, Eliot Cabot as Cusins, and Percy Waram as the resourceful cockney, Bill Walker, also garnered praise. Only Winifred Lenihan in the title role of the idealistic Salvation Army lass battling with her munitions-maker father was deemed a disappointment, failing to convey the same religious devotion she had shown as Saint Joan.

Ibsen's *The Wild Duck* at the 49th Street Theatre was almost a revival of a revival, since it employed the same scenery that had been used in 1925 and Blanche Yurka, now also credited as director, was once again a highly lauded Gina. Linda Watkins was Hedvig, Dallas Andersen was Hjalmar, and Ralph Roeder, Gregers.

The principal attraction of George Tyler's mounting of *Macbeth* at the Knickerbocker was neither Lyn Harding's rather vigorous usurper nor Florence Reed's cynically coquettish Lady Macbeth but Gordon Craig's stripped down settings and modern lighting. Much of the scenery consisted of "a series of groups of large masses, probably 12 feet high, and arranged with three sides square and a fourth surface curved. The masses are manipulated with the addition of stairways to form stately backgrounds." Some aisle-sitters complained that such a mounting was a halfway measure, still cluttered and heavy enough to present problems in scenes such as the banquet.

While rehearsing a return of *Cyrano*, Hampden replaced his *Enemy of the People* with a fortnight of *Caponsacchi*.

The last revival was an oddity in that it was offered in German. *Redemption* was given two and a half weeks of New York performances at the

Ambassador before heading out on a pre-planned tour with the great Berlin favorite Alexander Moissi in the role most American theatregoers identified with John Barrymore.

The lone new American play of the week and one more revival came in the next night. Only Jane Cowl's name allowed **The Jealous Moon** (11-20-28, Majestic), which the star wrote with Theodore Charles, to eke out a nine-week stand. The play, which ran for more than three hours, was howled down as an excruciating bore. Judy plays Columbine, Peter Parrot (Philip Merivale) is Pierrot, and Desti (Guy Standing) is Harlequin in a traveling show run by Papa Louis (Harry Davenport). But Peter takes the loving Judy for granted until he nods off and dreams that he has rejected her and fallen for a redheaded minx (Joyce Carey), then, after losing interest in his new amour, suffers the agony of Judy's dying in his arms. He wakes up and resolves to do right by Judy.

The evening's revival was *The Royal Box*, which Charles Coghlan had taken from the elder Dumas's *Kean* and first presented in 1897. This romanticized dramatization of incidents from the English actor's life now starred Walker Whiteside, a player generally better received on the road than in New York. His ample, largely superannuated style of acting was just right for the play. But the piece found only a small audience during its five weeks at the tiny Belmont.

Nearly three dozen plays had opened since *Little Accident* in early October, more than six weeks earlier, and only *Jealousy* and the revival of *Sun-Up* sneaked by the 100-performance mark. Relief came when six works opened on Monday, November 26, and half of them were hits.

The biggest and best—"the smartest of the season's comedies," "delightfully witty and thoroughly humane as well"—was Philip Barry's **Holiday** (11-26-28, Plymouth). The play was written with Hope Williams in mind. A slim, pretty socialite who bobbed her hair mannishly and walked with a brazen stride, she had called attention to herself in a supporting role in the playwright's *Paris Bound*. Having set aside a comfortable nest egg while still a young man, Johnny Case (Ben Smith) decides to use his wealth to live a carefree, easy life. As he tells his prospective sister-in-law, Linda Seton, "I just want to save part of my life for myself. There's a catch, though. It's got to be the young part." He can work again later, if need be. The philosophy sits well with Linda. Like Johnny, she does not share her fabulously wealthy family's "reverence for riches." Johnny's prospective father-in-law (Walter Walker)

and his bride-to-be, Julia (Dorothy Tree), urge him to compromise by waiting a few years before acting on his plans. For a time, Johnny seems willing to comply, but after Mr. Seton offers to give him a mansion and a vacation retreat, Johnny, eschewing all such encumbrances, balks and rushes off to grab a ship for Europe. Learning of this and making certain that her sister actually does not love Johnny, Linda heads out to join him. The play's second act unfolded in an unusual setting: an attic room which had been converted into a child's playroom and still was cluttered with children's toys, even two swings suspended from the ceiling. The comedy ran seven months.

Although Alice Brady continued to search in vain for a first-class vehicle, her name was such that she sometimes could coax a run out of a play that received largely negative notices ("too talky," "it will not bear too close examination"). She did just this with Townsend Martin's **A Most Immoral Lady** (11-26-28, Cort). Laura Sargent and her husband, Humphrey (Austin Fairman), are badger artists. She lures chumps into their apartment, allows them to be caught with her by her spouse, and then blackmails them into handing over a sizable check. By this method they have relieved John Williams (Robert Strange) of $10,000. But then Laura falls genuinely in love with Williams's nephew, Tony (Guido Nadzo), only to have him learn of her trade and stalk off to marry a sweet flapper. Laura is so upset that she gets Humphrey to agree to let her have a quick Paris divorce. At a nightclub there, "between a futuristic dance by a naked man, and a violin solo by the cafe virtuoso," Laura runs into Tony. She learns that his marriage was a failure, so the chance remains for her to recapture him.

All of Peggy Wood's charm could not turn Austin Strong's **A Play Without a Name** (11-26-28, Booth) into a hit. When John Russell (Kenneth MacKenna), a young banker, fails to get an appointment that he sought to a post in Germany, he places the blame on his wife, Anne, whose loving attentions suddenly appear to him to be demeaning naggings. John finds consolation with a pretty, world-weary brunette (Katherine Wilson). However, after discovering that he was passed over so that a more important position could be offered him, he is reconciled with Anne. As it had in 1926's *The Devil in the Cheese*, some of the action takes place inside a central figure's brain, in this case the hero's. A pair of eyes look backstage, and above them a screen shows motion pictures, revealing John's thought processes. In the center a veiled figure sits before an altar, while two slaves, stripped to the waist, control switches on each side of the brain. The voices of all the play's characters come from the wings, as if entering John's ears. The play ran six weeks.

John Meehan's **The Lady Lies** (11-26-28, Little) ran half as long. A widower (William Boyd) would like to marry his mistress (Shirley Warde) but worries what his teenaged children would think. The children, appreciating the woman's warmth and consideration, urge him to go ahead with the marriage.

The evening's worst failure was Olga Printzlau's **Back Here** (11-26-28, Klaw). The action of her drama shifted from a hospital housing some of the most gruesomely injured war veterans to a dance hall and back again. Sergeant Terry O'Brien (Melvyn Douglas) lost his legs and his right hand in France, and his torso is strapped in a steel jacket to hold everything together. He is ready to throw in the towel on life, particularly when his Bible-spouting, cripple-legged buddy, Peter Linden (George Meeker), spews religious platitudes at him. If God is so wonderful, Terry asks Peter, why can't Peter walk? At the dance hall, where the men are largely sidelined, Terry grows furious after a heel (Donald McClellan) who took advantage of Terry's old flame and later tried to bilk a woman of her jewels makes a pass at Peter's flapper sweetie (Jeanne Greene). Flailing with his iron hand, he nearly kills the man. Terry's bravery and the affection of his own girl give Peter the courage to get up and walk a few steps. Even Terry is moved. Audiences were not, so the play closed after a single week.

But the evening's lone revival proved its other hit. The play was James M. Barrie's *Peter Pan,* and it became the biggest success Eva Le Gallienne and her Civic Repertory Theatre would enjoy during the group's six-year existence. (Its 129 representations would surpass by two those of the runner-up, *Alice in Wonderland.*) To the surprise of many, the grave, studious Miss Le Gallienne let herself go and made an excellent Peter. If she lacked a bit of Maude Adams's sweet wistfulness, she injected an interesting and legitimate touch of boyish aloofness. Changing mores allowed her to display her real legs instead of donning russet-colored tights, as Miss Adams had been compelled to do. Egon Brecher's Hook had no lisp but did have a hint of a German accent. In this season alone the revival was given forty-eight times.

Three plays came in the following night, and all three garnered respectable runs. Most first-stringers opted for **The Age of Innocence** (11-27-28, Empire), which Margaret Ayer Barnes and Edward Sheldon, the latter uncredited, drew from Edith Wharton's famous novel. It recounted the futile romance of an American girl (Katharine Cornell), unhappily married to a Polish count, and a dashing young society figure (Rollo Peters), engaged to his own cousin. While Percy Hammond hailed the play as "the best theatre approximation of a book" in several years, most laurels were reserved for the star. Writing in the *World*, St. John Ervine conjured verbal pictures of her "magnificent in her gray furs, magnificent again in a long white dress which caught the firelight" and reported that Miss Cornell "makes us aware again that in her America possesses a great actress. Her fine, intelligent face, as sensitive as a seismographic instrument which records the most intimate and remote tremblings of the earth, has a dark, ivory-colored beauty that is almost Amerindian in its quality. Her dusky eyes have a stillness in them that is found in deep, dark water. . . . It is the stillness of life so quick that the whole of a thought or a feeling can be expressed with a flicker of an eyelid." Aided by the star's appeal, the play ran six months.

The other American novelty had to settle for fifteen weeks. **Congai** (11-27-28, Harris), which Harry Hervey and Carleton Hildreth took from Hervey's novel, was set in the lush jungles and Europeanized cities of Indo-China. French officers there—wearing skirts instead of trousers because of the heat—appropriate beautiful half-caste girls, whom they refer to as congai, as mistresses, then forget them when they are ordered back home. One such girl is Thi-Linh (Helen Menken), who has raised the son she had by a native boy whom tribal differences prevented her from marrying. She becomes the mistress of successive French officers, but when one colonel (Felix Krembs) attempts forcibly to seduce her, her son kills him. She takes the blame, and the governor agrees to sweep the charges under the rug if she will become his woman. She has little choice but to agree, even though it means her dream of freedom in the jungles for herself and her boy must be held in abeyance. Menken, sporting both skimpy native garments and fashionable Paris gowns, blended a remarkable intensity and pathetic weariness in her playing, while one oldtimer, Felix Krembs, won special applause as the lascivious colonel. Native musicians accompanied the story on "strange, thumpy instruments," and a Senegalese dancer offered supposedly authentic choreography.

The evening's importation, A. A. Milne's **The Perfect Alibi** (11-27-28, Charles Hopkins), ran out the season in its minuscule venue. Judge Ludgrove (Ernest Stallard) is murdered in full view of the audience, but the police (Harry Beresford and Leo G. Carroll) arrive and declare his death a suicide.

Ludgrove's nephew (Alan Bunce) and ward (Vivian Tobin) refuse to accept the verdict and set out to trap the killers, who turn out to be a convict the judge had sent up and the convict's buddy (Richie Ling and Ivan Simpson).

David Pinski, the celebrated Yiddish playwright, seems to have been his own translator for **Three** (12-3-28, Edyth Totten), in which two men (Eduard Franz and William Challee) throw dice to see who will win the woman (Dorothy Ellis) they both covet. Furious at such cavalier behavior, she seduces the loser, then walks out on both. The play's fourth character, heard but not seen, proclaimed himself the Voice of Fate (Harry O'Neil).

Although Upton Sinclair's **Singing Jailbirds** (12-6-28, Provincetown Playhouse) had found a welcome on some European stages—where pictures unfavorable to America were often eagerly applauded—its New York reception was cold, critical comments ranging from "impossibly stilted" to "shrilling melodrama" to "should have a long run in Moscow." Sinclair's principal jailbird was Red Adams (Grover Burgess)—note the attempt to chain a suggestion of radical politics to an old Yankee name. Adams, an agitator for the Wobblies, is arrested and placed in solitary confinement, where he is given only bread and water. Since the bread is made of white meal, its lack of mineral content ruins his teeth and prevents his eating. He dies while his fellow unionist convicts sing left-wing anthems.

A loftier menace was featured in the Theatre Guild's mounting of Robert Nichols and Maurice Browne's talky and womanless but riveting **Wings over Europe** (12-10-28, Martin Beck). The authors were English, albeit Browne earlier had been a seminal figure in the American Little Theatre movement before returning home. Their play was not offered to London until 1932. A brilliant young scientist (Alexander Kirkland) tells the British cabinet that he has harnessed the atom, giving him life-and-death control over the whole world. He demands the cabinet take action to ensure mankind benefits or he will unleash a cosmic disaster. Fearing the young man's stability, one cabinet member shoots him dead. But the group's complacency is shattered when they received a telegram from a mysterious league of scientists, announcing that it, too, has learned how to control the atom and that aeroplanes carrying atomic bombs will drop them on any capital unwilling to cooperate in a plan for world order. Thanks in good measure to the Guild's subscription, the play ran ninety performances.

Yet another bit of terror, one that had long since become a laughable theatrical and cinematic cliché, sent hit-hungry New Yorkers scurrying over the river to Hoboken, where Christopher Morley, Cleon Throckmorton, Harry Wagstaff Gribble, and their colleagues had taken over an old theatre, the Rialto, and on the 10th had brought out Dion Boucicault's sixty-year-old *After Dark*. The play was a typical Boucicault compilation of period motifs knowingly interwoven. But when the play had opened in New York in 1868 it had landed its producers in court, since its most celebrated scene had a figure, tied to railroad tracks, rescued at the last minute from an oncoming train. Unfortunately for Boucicault's associates, Augustin Daly had used the motif a year before in *Under the Gaslight* and had copyrighted it. The court sided with Daly, who thereafter received a percentage of the show's gross. Most 1928 playgoers probably cared little for this history. They were simply out for fun. The production had been slated for a fortnight; then the run was extended an additional week. Demand continued to grow, so before the revival closed it had run through the season and through the summer at a $1.25 top (later raised slightly).

Edgar Wallace's **Sign of the Leopard** (12-11-28, National) had been done in London as *The Squeaker*. Like another recently imported English mystery, *The Perfect Alibi*, it allowed its audience to witness a killing and so identify the killer. The play was framed in a newspaper office where a reporter (Campbell Gullan) writes his story telling how he proved a very suspicious ex-captain (Warren William) did not commit the murder at the Leopard Club and how the real culprit was the suspect's boss (Murrey Kinnell), a man who had fingered any number of criminals so as to throw people off the scent of his own crimes.

The season's most expensive production—in fact, costing more than any of the year's musicals—was **Mima** (12-12-28, Belasco), which David Belasco had adapted from Ferenc Molnár's *A vörös malom* (The Red Mill). The producer was bruited to have expended between $300,000 and $325,000 (about four to six million in 1993 terms) on it. He had closed his theatre for several months, ripped out part of the proscenium to widen the stage, covered the orchestra pit with metal stairs, and even hidden the playhouse's boxes in sinister metal sheathing. Molnár's story was relatively simple and was further pruned by Belasco. Magister (A. E. Anson), the Devil's right-hand man, erects a huge (stage-filling) "psycho-corrupter," an elaborate, frightening-looking machine, with two gigantic turbines, a mammoth piston, fire-escape-like stairs, and elevators, that he boasts is capable of doing in an hour what New York requires twenty years to do: totally corrupt the soul of even the most saintly man. To prove his point he seeks out a victim and finds him in a good-hearted forester, Janos (Sidney Blackmer). He sets his chief seductress, Mima (Lenore Ulric), onto the young man. In no time, Janos is lying, thieving, and killing. (The setting was capable of opening to reveal scenes in various other places.) But when Janos realizes what has happened and forgives Mima, it proves too much for the machine, which self-destructs in an orgy of flame, smoke, and deafening noise. The performances, including a large corps of devils and imps, who ran up and down the aisles and climbed the metal stairs to the stage, were admired, but the play divided the critics. Some self-appointed highbrows, such as George Jean Nathan, sneered in showy contempt. But *Variety*, reporting the "salvos and bravos" at the final curtain, concluded, "The master had unveiled his masterpiece." Atkinson, taking a middle ground, acknowledged that the mounting was "a monument to Mr. Belasco's genius for display," but in a Sunday follow-up he used the production as cue to bewail the season's emptiness. The drama ran for 180 performances—not a bad run in so troubled a season, especially at a new record top of $5.50. However, perhaps because many potential playgoers were driven off by the high ticket prices, it closed with a reported loss of nearly a quarter of a million dollars.

The notorious, publicity-seeking beauty Peggy Hopkins Joyce was the only reason to see **The Lady of the Orchids** (12-13-28, Henry Miller's), which E. Ray Goetz adapted from Jacques Natanson's *Le Greluchon délicat*. The slim blonde was first seen under the ermine blankets of a large, silk-pillowed bed. Later she paraded in an ermine-trimmed boudoir suit and in a cloth-of-gold evening gown with an ermine wrap. All these goodies belong to Simone, who is kept by rich, aging Michel (Kenneth Hunter) and cheating on him with Emile (Hugh Sinclair), a young actor. Then Henri (Edward Crandall) walks into her life. He is too high-principled to allow Michel's money to be spent on him until Michel simply endows Simone with a sizable dowry. With that the two run off to Cannes. Critics suggested the incidents in the story had been tailored to mirror Joyce's headlined scandals. Clearly, New Yorkers had grown tired of them, so the play was withdrawn after two and a half weeks.

By contrast a saintlier play found enough patrons to run ninety-two performances. Of course, Ethel Barrymore's starring in it and opening a new theatre named in her honor helped. **The Kingdom of God** (12-20-28, Ethel Barrymore) was taken from the Spanish of G. Martínez Sierra by Helen and Harley Granville Barker. It rather adramatically followed the life of a devoted nun. At nineteen she helps at a home for the aged. Ten years later she works with unwed mothers. At seventy, lame but much revered, she runs an asylum for orphans. Miss Barrymore was hailed for her "great depth and earnestness."

Having abandoned the Bayes roof theatre, Gustav Blum was nonetheless able to use cut-rate tickets to keep Howard Chenery's **That Ferguson Family** (12-22-28, Little) alive for sixteen weeks. It told of a family, not unlike that in George Kelly's *The Show-Off*, dominated by a sharp-tongued mother (Jean Adair). The children all hurriedly head out to married life, with one daughter (Marienne Franks) landing a cocky, boastful young man (Arthur Kohl) who saves her from being indicted for stealing gowns from her workplace.

Bella and Sam Spewack's **Poppa** (12-24-28, Biltmore) was a near miss, running ninety-six performances. It focused on Pincus Schwitzky (Jachial Goldsmith), who is too intrigued by East Side politics to bother to earn a living for his family, so his wife (Anna Apple) and daughter (Mary Ricard) run his insurance business. Jake Harris (William E. Morris), the local ward leader, pushes through Pincus's election as alderman, only to discover Pincus is an idealist with a mind of his own. Harris attempts to frame him and nearly succeeds, until Pincus's wildly imaginative son, Herbie (Harold Waldridge), first stages a fake jailbreak then incriminates Harris by having him unwittingly confess into a hidden dictaphone.

There were more murderous shenanigans in Beulah Poynter's **One Way Street** (12-24-28, George M. Cohan). Goaded by the attractive Sheldon Colby (Robert Hudson), a pretty chorus girl has been helping him transport drugs from Canada and finding potential users until her body is discovered in a trunk. Lots of folk are suspected before one drug-addicted girl (Wilhelmina Morris) blurts out that her brother (John R. Hamilton) did the killing to avenge his sister's ruination. The police are certain the courts will be lenient with him. Somehow the requisite chills were missing, and the thriller gave up after a seven-week struggle.

An English play, Edgar C. Middleton's **Potiphar's Wife** (12-24-28, Craig) opened what turned out to be the last new theatre to be built in the Broadway area for many decades. In this instance, the wife (Frances Carson) is a countess, and the man (Barry O'Neill) she attempts to seduce and then accuses of attacking her when he balks is the family chauffeur. The play was a two-week flop, a harbinger of the bad luck that would hound this often renamed 54th Street playhouse during its history.

Christmas night brought in a rash of openings. The longest run—eight months—went to Herbert Ashton, Jr.'s **Brothers** (12-25-28, 48th St.). No small part of the play's success could be attributed to Bert Lytell's assuming the title roles. Lytell had spent much of the twenties in films and received a huge hand on his first appearance. In order to learn whether heredity or environment is the major determinant of character, three scientists take orphaned identical twins and place one in a rich home, the other in the slums. Years pass. The slum-bred Eddie Connelly is charged with murder. His lawyer is his natural brother, Robert Naughton. Naughton is a scoundrelly drug addict and the real murderer. However, he has a conscience. He wins his brother's acquittal and commits himself to a sanitarium while quietly allowing his brother to take his place at home. Robert dies in the hospital, so Eddie marries his brother's sweetheart (Grace Menken). Lytell's quick changes, such as walking out of one door dressed in evening clothes and moments later reentering through another in different garments, earned him further applause.

The other two regular straight-play novelties to open that evening were quick failures, one running two weeks, the second, only one. Larry E. Johnson's **Back Seat Drivers** (12-25-28, Wallack's) won the longer run, telling of two wives convinced their husbands' investments are foolish. They form a fake company, get their men to invest in it, but are nearly fleeced by some clever crooks until the husbands come to their rescue.

Walker Whiteside, so partial to Oriental characters calling for "beautiful flowing kimonos, a coppery complexion, half-closed eyes, and a voice that moves on a single key," was producer, director, and star of Atherton Brownell's **Sakura** (12-25-28, Belmont). He played Prince Hagane, who thwarts the Russians' nefarious plans to steal and expose a secret treaty and to kidnap a beautiful noblewoman (Franc Hale), then claims the woman for his bride.

One quirky entry that same evening was James Plaisted Webber's **Falstaff** (12-25-28, Coburn), which strung together the various Shakespearean episodes dealing with the preposterous Sir John (Charles Coburn) and embellished them with a handful of original songs and a chorus line of girls in Elizabethan costumes. Credits listed someone named Porter Steele as composer, Brian Hooker as lyricist, Richard Boleslawski as co-stager and co-choreographer, and Ted Shawn as Boleslawski's

collaborator with the dances. Critics dismissed the result as neither a musical nor a legitimate straight play. With both purists and tired businessmen evincing no interest, the affair was sent to Cain's warehouse after two weeks.

Walter Hampden's Christmas gift to his loyalists was a return of *Cyrano de Bergerac* at Hampden's Theatre. The loyalists acknowledged their gratitude by keeping the revival on the boards into the spring.

In Hull Gould and Saxon Kling's very short-lived **Tomorrow** (12-28-28, Lyceum) a villain attempts to steal a patent for a new electrical device and to elope with his friends' daughter. What little interest this show, set in a distant 1982, held was in the far-fetched appliances it suggested would be available more than five decades later: a telephone worn like a wristwatch, a typewriter that writes in response to a human voice and can talk back, "airflivvers" instead of automobiles, a table that opens up to offer an immediately ready dinner along with cocktails. As at least one other play dealing with the future had implied, tobacco will be outlawed and thus bootlegged.

The lone success among New Year's Eve's entries was **Caprice** (12-31-28, Guild), which Philip Moeller adapted from the Austrian comedy *Mit der Lieb spielen* by Sil-Vara (Geza Silberer). When his mother (Lily Cahill) brings sixteen-year-old Robert (Douglass Montgomery) to visit Counselor Albert Von Echardt (Alfred Lunt), the father he has never seen, Albert's sharp mistress, Ilsa (Lynn Fontanne), suspects that Albert's old flame is trying to rekindle their amour. She vamps the boy, then discloses her own relationship with his father to him. Straitlaced mama and son decamp in a huff. The play, waved away by one critic as "too fragile for the subway riders," ran until June—or just after the Lunts left the cast to take the play to London. Indeed, the Lunts walked away with the reviews, although many critics did not yet see them as equal mates. True, Atkinson hailed them as a "matchless pair of volatile comedians." But Ervine probably spoke for many more when he commented, "Mr. Lunt's performance was a delightful exhibition of accomplished comedy acting, a fine and accurately observed show of manners. Miss Fontanne startled me with her brilliant artifice. I had not expected to see anything so good." *Variety*, almost always in Lunt's corner, passed over his wife with a perfunctory compliment, then praised him for bringing to all his roles "faultless grooming, diction, and poise with a left-handed twist to his lines that makes commonplaceness seem like iridescent wit."

Margaret Anglin received some polite plaudits,

but her vehicle was slammed, when she took the customary dual roles of the title part and the redheaded, outspoken maid in **Lady Dedlock** (12-31-28, Ambassador), Paul Kester's retelling of Dickens's *Bleak House*. Thus, Wilella Waldorf, writing in the *Post*, reported, "Miss Anglin acts . . . with all her might, but the result is curiously lacking in drama." The *World*'s Alison Smith was even less pleased, complaining, "As her Ladyship with her 'insolent resolve' and her 'exhausted composure,' Miss Anglin gives a neatly designed picture, only to shatter it with her next entrance where the shrewish Hortense rips out her Gallic insults with the uneasy consciousness that she must soon dash into her other make-up and become a lady again." By the end of the five-week stand, the production was grossing less than $700 a night.

Hyman Adler and Edward Paulton's one-week dud **The Street Wolf** (12-31-28, Garrick), which Adler also produced and directed, was the latest in the era's numerous melodramas of nightclub life. It told of a white slaver who attempts to lure an elegant lady into his trade, only to discover she is his long-lost mother. A dissipated client of the rathskeller, who swings a heavy, blunt instrument at the white slaver in an attempt to kill him, turns out to be his long-lost father. All this is revealed by an old nurse, who somehow also happens to be there at a New Year's Eve party.

A week before the year ended, Atkinson used his Sunday article to decry the state of contemporary American theatre. Noting that "hollowness permeates most of the current theatre in New York," he continued, "In a world steaming with things to say and equipped with the means of saying them, the current theatre either remains silent or stammers like an awkward plowboy. Most of its diseases the medicine men can describe—overproduction, lack of first-rate talent in creative writing, pandering to audiences by managers who have no respect for their art, high prices for tickets as well as for labor, competition from screen and radio." Whatever the obvious truths of most of these complaints, it also was becoming clear that the warped, destructive notion that "art" must come before entertainment in the theatre was obtaining a dangerous foothold.

The first week of the new year, 1929, went by without ushering in anything new. Nor did the three openings on January's first Monday augur well. The longest run—nine weeks—went to Ernest Pascal's dramatization of his own novel, **The Marriage Bed** (1-7-29, Booth). Mary Boyd (Ann Davis) is told that George (Alan Dinehart), her husband of ten years, is having an affair with Christine Kennedy (Helen Flint), but she refuses to be disturbed by the news. She reacts in a similar fashion on learning that George has set up Christine in a swank apartment. But when Christine appears, falsely claims she is pregnant, and asks Mary to divorce George, Mary reads the lovers the riot act. They are chastened, and George resumes a monogamous life.

Young Preston Sturges, heretofore a minor actor, turned author with **The Guinea Pig** (1-7-29, President). His story looked at another fledgling author, a playwright named Catherine Howard (Mary Carroll), who is told by her shoestring producer, Sam Small (Alexander Carr), a Jewish furrier turned theatrical impresario, that to achieve the proper verisimilitude she must experience the lovemaking she depicts. So Mary latches on to Wilton Smith (John Ferguson) and seduces him. When he learns why he naturally is furious, but with time, and two more acts, the couple fall genuinely in love. Carr brought all his Potash and Perlmutter mannerisms with him, but they were insufficient to save a promising but unfulfilled comedy, allegedly autobiographical, even in the tiny venue that until now had been the Edyth Totten Theatre.

The show that many thought would have the longest run among the evening's premieres had the shortest—a mere two weeks. One reason for high expectations was that A. E. Thomas's **Vermont** (1-7-29, Erlanger) was produced by George M. Cohan. It dealt with some hard-pressed New Englanders, the Carter family, who live near the Canadian border and succumb to the lure of easy money from smuggling booze across the boundary. The family's upright daughter (Phyllis Povah) objects, demanding her father (John T. Doyle) return money he was given for use of his barn. Old man Carter had hoped to use it for medical expenses for a son blinded by bad liquor and toward another boy's college tuition. He is killed in a shootout between bootleggers and hi-jackers before he can do that. The daughter, for all her high-mindedness, falls in love with the handsomest (Allyn Joslyn) of the crooks, so sets out to reform him. Some of the Cohan touches reminded critics of James A. Herne's or Belasco's heyday, for the Carter hardscrabble homestead included a practical wood stove, and audiences could smell cabbage cooking on it during the evening.

The 9th saw a revival of Eugene O'Neill's four one-act sea plays as *S.S. Glencairn* at the Provincetown Playhouse. Among the principals, Lionel J. Stander was Yank; Walter Abel, Olson; and E. J. Ballantine, Smitty. The mounting ran eleven weeks.

The season's best new American drama came in

the next night. All of Elmer Rice's **Street Scene** (1-10-29, Playhouse) took place on a sidewalk in front of an aging brownstone tenement. On one side of the building, another brownstone is being demolished; on the other side, a new apartment house is under construction. Trash cans and carelessly discarded items litter the sidewalk. (The setting was an outstanding example of Jo Mielziner at his realistic best.) It is summer, and the building's windows are opened, with some tenants leaning out of their windows for a bit of fresh air and gossip. Much of that chatter deals with Anna Maurrant (Mary Servoss), a woman married to a cold, mean man and having an affair with Steve Sankey (Joseph Baird), a collector for Borden's milk company. "Someday her hoosban' is killing him," the Scandinavian janitor predicts, and one of the tenants concurs, saying Maurrant is liable to, since "he's got a wicked look in his eye, dat baby has." Another family who lives in the brownstone is the Kaplans. Its patriarch is Abraham Kaplan (Leo Bulgakov), a radical who argues with everyone when he is not reading his Yiddish newspaper. His son, Samuel (Horace Braham), loves the Maurrants' grown daughter, Rose (Erin O'Brien-Moore), but her affections are divided between him and one of her fellow employees at a real estate office. When Maurrant (Robert Kelly) comes home unexpectedly early one day, he discovers his wife and her lover together and kills them. Sam and his rival both offer to marry Rose and take her away, but she tells Sam that "loving and belonging aren't the same thing" and that she will raise her twelve-year-old brother (Russell Griffin) in hopes of sparing him the life their parents knew. Through much of this, the screams of a young woman in labor on an upper floor pierced the dialogue. Among the numerous favorable reviews—though some were qualified—was John Anderson's in the *Evening Journal*. He wrote, "It is a play which builds engrossing trivialities into a drama that is rich and compelling and catches in the wide reaches of its curbside panorama the comedy and heartbreak that lie a few steps up from the sidewalks of New York." With the help of a Pulitzer Prize, which it was awarded in the spring, the drama compiled 601 performances. In 1947, it was made into an opera by Kurt Weill.

The hero of Mark Reed's **The Skyrocket** (1-11-29, Lyceum) is Vic Ewing (Humphrey Bogart), who earns $29.75 a week collecting pennies from chewing-gum machines. In his spare time he invents gadgets. Neither his bellicose father (J. C. Nugent) nor his waspish mother (Clara Blandick) is happy with him. Even his loving wife (Mary Phillips) wishes he were different. But then one of his inventions makes him rich. He moves his wife to a plush Park Avenue apartment complete with a Japanese butler, but when she finds Vic flirting with a blonde musical comedy dolly (Dorothy Bigelow), for whom he promises to back a show, she storms out. Vic also loses all his money in foolish stock market speculation. Only then is he reconciled with "wifie." The play was produced by Gilbert Miller. A short while earlier, he had announced he was giving up Broadway as a lost cause. He didn't, but this play certainly could not explain his change of heart.

First-nighters and critics had a choice of four openings the next Monday night.

Many of the leading critics chose Maxwell Anderson's **Gypsy** (1-14-29, Klaw). Ellen Hastings (Claiborne Foster), called "Gypsy" by her adoring husband, David (Lester Vail), a failed violinist who conducts a film-house orchestra, cannot conceal her restlessness, which she blames on her hated mother, a woman she recalls having numerous lovers. She herself has had affairs, although David has been forgiving, and she also has aborted a child by David. When she falls in love with an up-and-coming novelist, Cleve (Donn Cook), she leaves David and sets up in her own apartment. But after another affair and a tiff with Cleve, she sends Cleve off, telling him, "I'm perfectly unreliable and indecent!" She locks herself in her room and turns on the gas ("a corking effect of escaping vapor," one critic noted). Although this was Anderson's original ending and reportedly was employed during much of the New York run, on opening night the play ended with Ellen turning off the gas after receiving an encouraging call from her latest lover. Burns Mantle called the work "an honestly written drama inspired by changing social standards and values." But neither ending could keep the work alive beyond eight weeks.

That was one week less than the run of McElbert Moore, Earle Crooker, and Lowell Brentano's **Zeppelin** (1-14-29, National), whose settings struck many as more interesting than its story. The setting was the German dirigible *Barbarosa*. One scene showed the ship's girders and catwalks, the other its forward gondola and observation section. The plot was reminiscent of *Wings over Europe*, only more action-packed. A scientist (Charles Abbe) has invented a leprosy gas so horrible that he hopes it will end all wars. He is flying to Berlin to meet with other scientists and world leaders to ensure his discovery will not be abused. But other passengers on the zeppelin are out to steal the formula for one reason or another. Even the ship's captain has been enlisted by certain German higher-ups to secure the information for their benefit. Moreover, one of the scientist's assistants, who contracted leprosy when an experiment went awry, is also aboard. He is insane and vengeful. (His movements were followed by a green spotlight always illuminating his face.) Several people are killed before the madman shoots a hole into the gas bag. As in *Mima*, the whole set falls to pieces. An anticlimactic final act occurred in the gondola, which was miraculously floating on the sea. Jimmie Cooper, the producer, was better known for shows he sent out on the nation's burlesque wheels.

James Forbes, whose glory years were long gone, was the author of **Precious** (1-14-29, Royale), which featured the month's second blonde gold digger. Actually Eva Mills (Dorothy Hall) is not calculating, she is merely an overgrown child who needs instant gratification and can be manipulated by her money-grubbing sister (Cora Witherspoon). But after she marries the middle-aged Andrew Hoyt (John Cumberland), her high living threatens to bankrupt him, so he adroitly foists her on a young man (Edward Leiter) her own age.

Although critics failed to wax enthusiastic about Eva Le Gallienne's new double bill, she kept it in the Civic Repertory's schedule for three seasons (if for only a handful of performances each year). **The Lady from Alfaqueque**, adapted by Helen and Harley Granville Barker from Serafín and Joaquín Álvarez Quintero's *La Consulesa*, told of a Madrid lady (Alma Kruger) so enamored of her old hometown that she happily and sometimes gullibly takes in any stranger claiming to be from there. Accompanying the Spanish comedy was Chekhov's **On the High Road**, as translated by Constance Garnett. It recounted how a rich woman (Alla Nazimova), who years before had deserted her husband on their wedding night and run off with a lover, takes shelter at a rundown inn during a storm and there discovers her former spouse (Egon Brecher), now a drunken derelict. For some reason, Nazimova played the part in a large blonde wig.

Like the Japanese film *Rashomon* decades later, Len D. Hollister and Lester Lonergan's **House Unguarded** (1-15-29, Little) looked at a murder from three points of view. Two newsmen (James Dailey and Frank Knight), sitting in a café in the Panama Canal Zone, offer their ideas of who killed Colonel Thorne (Lonergan), an American officer whose wife (Shirley Warde) is having an affair with a young naval lieutenant (John Marston). One man believes the wife accidentally killed her husband; the other suggests the naval officer did it to be rid of him.

Then the officer himself appears and gives his version, which implicates a trouble-making orderly (Raymond Bramley). Who is right?

In a season during which traditional producers were bewailing the state of the American theatre all the while they were still producing, a number of unlikely novices, as Atkinson had bewailed, tried their hands, too. The latest were vaudevillian Phil Baker and bandleader Ben Bernie. Their mounting was **Café de Danse** (1-15-29, Forrest), translated by Eugenie Leontovitch, Helen Mitchell, and Clarke Silvernail from Fernand Nozière and Charles Muller's twenty-year-old *La Maison de danses*. The producers ballyhooed the production as "a Spanish Diamond Lil." It told of a drudge, Estrellita (Trini), at a Barcelona dance hall run by the imperious Tomasa (Alison Skipworth). The drudge would like to try her skills as a dancer, but Tomasa's lascivious son (Leonard Ceeley) puts too shameful a price on giving her a chance. Then the dance hall's star (Enid Romany) disappears, and Estrellita is shoved on in her place. She wins not only the clients' applause but the hand of the handsome Luisito (Martin Burton) as well. Comic relief was provided by Gregory Ratoff, who also directed, as an older lecher. The play survived for one month.

Apart from Lucille La Verne's performance—and many critics failed to make an exception for even that—there was little reason to see Helena Dayton and Louise Bascom Barratt's **Hot Water** (1-21-29, Lucille La Verne). Duckie, years ago as Jessica Dale a famous Lady Macbeth, now runs an apartment house filled with sponging theatre folk. In her spare time she invents a disposable paper umbrella which she calls a "showersol." Her attempts to market it and to make a comeback both fail. She is snubbed by most of the spongers after she is discovered dirty and hungry on a park bench. But a decent former tenant succeeds in selling the umbrella idea and proposes marriage to her. She consents, assuring him she will keep him "in hot water" for the rest of their lives. Some reviewers suggested that the acting was far too broad for the confines of so intimate a playhouse. *Sun-Up* was hastily, if briefly, restored to the stage when the new play folded.

Lewis Beach's **Merry Andrew** (1-21-29, Henry Miller's) was received no more cordially. At sixty Andrew Aiken (Walter Connolly) is pressed by his wife (Effie Shannon) to sell his pharmacy and retire. He does, then finds having nothing to do so upsetting that he upsets everyone else. The solution is simple. He repurchases the store.

One curiosity arrived the same evening. Financed by Universal Pictures to help publicize their film version of *Show Boat*, a troupe of real showboat players, Norman F. Thom's Princess Showboat Company, normally unemployed off season, were brought in to the Belmont with a repertory of **The Parson's Bride** (the name of the play supposedly being performed in the first act of the Kern-Hammerstein operetta) and **The Shadow of the Rockies**. In the former, a pretty schoolmarm's plan to marry a parson is nearly derailed by the parson's lustful brother and by the sudden appearance of the girl's long-lost husband, now an ex-convict. The other play told a not dissimilar yarn, this time about moonshiners and revenue agents. In both instances audiences were encouraged to cheer the heroine and hiss the villains. The actors also tripled or quadrupled in brass, one playing the calliope before the show, several hawking candy at the same time and also during intermission, and most of them performing in the olio (with one of the villains revealing a fine baritone in a tender ballad). The public, apparently having attended and been sated by *After Dark*, failed to buy the enterprise, albeit one second-stringer suggested another reason: he observed these were just bad plays, "and that has ceased to be a novelty hereabouts."

But a very good play came in two nights later, and Broadway still was not all that interested. S. N. Behrman's **Serena Blandish; or, The Difficulty of Getting Married** (1-23-29, Morosco) was a dramatization of a novel of the same name. The novel was initially announced as being by "a Lady of Quality," who subsequently proved to be Enid Bagnold. A rich Jewish jeweler, Sigmund Traub (Clarence Derwent), lunching at a Soho restaurant overhears that the young lady at the next table has been left in the lurch by the seemingly pleasant young man with whom she was dining and cannot pay the two-pound bill. He pays it for her and learns she is Serena Blandish (Ruth Gordon), a pretty young thing more or less on her uppers. He suggests he can make a good marriage for her if she will let him, telling her men only give diamonds to women who already have them and that they buy jewelry "more to placate than to please." Serena consents to let herself be turned over to a fabulously rich, highly eccentric countess (Constance Collier) who sees immediately that Serena is too good and too docile, and so sets about teaching her how to snare a rich husband and passing her off as one of her own set. She is introduced to a hundred-year-old invalid (Wallace Erskine) and to a rich, bored, caddish man-about-town (Henry Daniell), then meets a poet (Alfred Shirley) on a London bus—but each time she continues to play her cards wrong. By the time she gets a proposal from Traub she has made

up her mind to run off with a rakish young man (Hugh Sinclair) who has warned her he will never marry her. She tells the countess's sardonic, protesting butler (A. E. Matthews), who Serena has discovered is the young man's secretive father, "Don't sneer, Martin. No man has taken me—only my good will, my weakness, my docility." Robert Garland in the *Telegram* characterized the play as "bitter, ironic and tender, all at the same time. Beautifully written by a dramatist who knows his nuances." The performance, directed by Jed Harris, was a joy. Serena became "a finespun study of character in Miss Gordon's orchidaceous acting." Miss Collier, always with a monkey or a cat or a bird on her shoulder or in her arms, contributed "no little portion of the enjoyable features," and Matthews was "delightfully droll." A hidden band played everything from Gershwin to Strauss throughout the evening. Robert Edmond Jones's myriad settings also won applause. The front seat atop a London bus and the interior of the countess's limousine were seen as "flecks of soft light plucked out of foggy spaces," while his countess's anteroom was "a fantasy in black patent leather curtains, oddly erotic gold statues flanking columns of lavender gold and with a background-vista of a corridor hung in green and white." Yet for all its many virtues, the production ran for only ninety-three performances—a near miss.

Behrman's light, elegant touch gave way the following evening to "pretension and bombast" with Walter Ferris and Basil Rathbone's **Judas** (1-24-29, Longacre). Rathbone himself took the title role, in a work which attempted to suggest that the disciple was no heartless, greedy villain but rather a misguided fanatic who, by setting the authorities on Jesus (never seen), hoped to incite him to the violence necessary to overthrow entrenched malefactors. Rathbone, heretofore known primarily as an impersonator of reserved sophisticates, suprised some with the chest-pounding ardor of his emoting.

Elmer Rice's second offering of the month was **The Subway** (1-25-29, Cherry Lane), a play he had written shortly after *The Adding Machine* but for which he had sought a producer unavailingly. Its story, again told in expressionistic terms although the characters were all given names from the start, followed Sadie Smith (Jane Hamilton), who is helped by Eugene Bohm, a personable young artist (Louis John Latzer), after she faints in an overcrowded subway car. A romance ensues, but when she finds that she is pregnant and Eugene will not marry her, she throws herself under the wheels of another subway train. At times characters stopped suddenly and without moving spoke their inner thoughts—a device Rice insisted was in the play before he saw *Strange Interlude*. The play was performed by a company designated variously as "amateurs" or "amateur professionals" and was actually too demanding for so restricted a stage. On opening night, the subway set collapsed and had to be dispensed with. Despite cool notices, William A. Brady, who had produced *Street Scene*, moved the play uptown, then promptly closed it when playgoers would not come.

February's first entry was the Actors' Theatre revival of *Hedda Gabler* at the 49th Street Theatre on the 2nd. Blanche Yurka's quieter Hedda was deemed inferior to the sharp, cruel woman Eva Le Gallienne had retained in the Civic Repertory's schedule.

The pair of plays that opened the next Monday both lasted a mere four weeks. Fulton Oursler's **All the King's Men** (2-4-29, Fulton) spotlighted a widower (Grant Mitchell) who weds a woman (Mayo Methot) determined to erase all vestiges of his former marriage. However, when his new wife expects the couple's first baby at any moment, the man hurriedly sails for Europe to be with his son, reportedly dangerously ill at school. The wife is furious, and a year later she decides to elope with another man (Hugh Huntley). But after her lover refuses to allow her to bring her baby daughter with her, she understands her husband's deep attachment to his son and accepts the realistic demands of a second marriage. Mitchell's brusque acting style was seen as wrong for the part and a reflection of his days in Cohan comedies. The reflection was accentuated by the fact that his widower was an advertising man, not unlike the one Mitchell had portrayed in *It Pays to Advertise*, fifteen years before.

Monkey glands and rejuvenation had made headlines for more than a decade and had provided musical comedies and revues with laughing matter. Thomas P. Robinson and Esther Willard Bates's **Be Your Age** (2-4-29, Belmont) took the subject only a tad more seriously. Mrs. Merriam (Spring Byington), a comely grandmother, shocks her unctuous bishop (Halliwell Hobbes) and her ex-diplomat admirer (John Miltern) when she returns from three weeks of treatment by the celebrated young Dr. Gage (Romney Brent). She has summoned the diplomat by cable and is disheartened to see his white hair and cane. She announces that she is actually thirty years younger than she was a month before and, misconstruing some of the doctor's remarks and movements, even concludes he is in love with her. She is annoyed when her old admirer refuses to subject himself to the same treatment she has received, but then she is made to realize that the doctor's warmth stemmed from his love for her granddaughter (Mary Stills). Mrs. Merriam, acknowledging that you cannot truly defy the passage of time, consents to wed the diplomat, cane and all.

Apart from the Theatre Guild's subscribers, Broadway demonstrated little interest in Eugene O'Neill's **Dynamo** (2-11-29, Martin Beck) in the face of sharply divided notices. "The play opens dully," Ervine lamented, continuing, "The drama slowly drips out of it as we listen to infinitely dreary dialogue." Conversely, Atkinson concluded, "Writing on the most essential theme of modern life, Mr. O'Neill has strength and breadth, and a lashing, poetic fury." O'Neill questions whether man has any true replacement for the God he has come to reject. The Reverend Light (George Gaul), a devout if rather arrogant Christian, and Ramsay Fife (Dudley Digges), an atheist, have long been unfriendly neighbors. After the minister's son, Reuben (Glenn Anders), falls in love with Fife's daughter, Ada (Claudette Colbert), Reuben and his father have a falling-out in which Reuben renounces religion and heads off in search of a more modern truth. Returning years later after having seemingly made science his god, he is seduced by Ada. He kills her, then in strange terms begs the dynamo, "I don't want to know the truth! I only want you to hide me, Mother! Never let me go from you again!" He embraces the machine and is electrocuted. The work was removed after fifty performances. Removed with it were Lee Simonson's superb settings, first a skeletonized view of the neighbors' homes side by side, then the startling interior of the hydro-electric plant.

Percy Robinson and Terence de Marney's **The Whispering Gallery** (2-11-29, Forrest), a mystery, supposedly by two Englishman, that had been so successful in Boston that a second company was hurriedly assembled for New York, outran the O'Neill play by several weeks but left not a rack behind. It was set in an artist's studio, where the painter (Hugh Miller) strangles his wife after voices tell him she is unfaithful. Years later, his son (Miller) is murdered in the same studio after bringing friends there. The killer turns out to be the father, who has escaped from a mental institution. Some of the stock characters won the most laughs and handclaps. Frank Frayne blackened up to portray a jittery, shrieky serving man, while Bertha Belmore was a comically sarcastic grande dame.

Some of the season's most scathing notices were slapped on William A. Grew's **My Girl Friday** (2-12-29, Republic). "Drivel," "smut," and "filth" were among the adjectives leveled, and the writer and producer were promptly hauled into court, all of which may have aided the comedy in running seven months. Three chorus girls—a dainty, tiny brunette (Alice Weaver), a willowy blonde (Esther Muir), and a dark, sultry one (Lucille Mendez)—are ordered by their producer to attend a boozy stag party thrown by the show's backer. In revenge, after parading about in bathing suits, they drug the men's drinks, leave ladies' underwear strewn about, and notify the men's wives. Those wives and the girls' sweethearts create complications.

With largely favorable notices, Jo Swerling and Edward G. Robinson's **Kibitzer** (2-18-29, Royale), billed as "a karakter komedy," ran less than half as long, although *Variety* reported "internal trouble," and not poor grosses, forced its closure. Robinson was featured as Lazarus, who runs a cigar store on Amsterdam Avenue and who freely gives advice to his friends and customers on how to play pinochle, what horse to bet on, or what stock to buy. Learning that his daughter (Jeanne Greene) is being courted by the son of the famous millionaire James Livingston (Eugene Powers), he calls on the man at his mansion. There the two discover that the so-called son is actually Livingston's secretary and is an embezzler as well as a fraud. When the man pulls a gun, Lazarus stops him by dumping a basket of ticker tape on him. In gratitude, Livingston gives Lazarus 10,000 shares in American Steel, worth $52 a share. Larazus returns to his shop, sets up his own ticker tape, and watches the stock first rise then drop by half in a few minutes. His friends all sneer. However, it soon develops that the broker had called Lazarus urging him to sell the stock at its peak. Lazarus's dim-witted brother had answered and to all the broker's comments had casually said, "Sure, go ahead." Lazarus is very rich. The evening was all Robinson's, giving him a superb chance to demonstrate his versatility and ability at homey comedy. A high point was his hilarious indecision in a scene in which he must select what sort of reward he wants from Livingston. His inability to choose becomes so painful that Livingston must decide for him.

Susan Meriwether and Victor Victor's **Flight** (2-18-29, Longacre) was merely another of the season's innumerable duds. Miriam Hopkins played Cynthia Larrimore, daughter of an unhappily married couple who have remained together for her sake. She is a wild young lady, confessing to her aviator suitor (Donald Dillaway) that she has been having an affair with another man (John D. Seymour) and does not know who is the father of the baby she is expecting.

The suitor runs off but later reconsiders and agrees to marry her.

William Jordan Rapp, a white man, and Wallace Thurman, a black, were the authors of **Harlem** (2-20-29, Apollo). Its program called the play "An Episode of Life in New York's Black Belt" and contained a glossary of terms with which playgoers might not be familiar. Among those terms were Monkey Chaser, "a West Indian negro"; 38-and-2 and 40, both signifying "Okay"; Numbers, "a gambling game, peculiar to Harlem"; Chippy, an "Undiscriminating young wench"; and Rent Party, a "Saturday night orgy to raise money to pay the landlord." Rent parties charged admission and, for an additional fee, set out corn whiskey and pigs' knuckles. The drama began and ended with such parties at the railroad flat of the Williamses, southern blacks who have emigrated to Harlem and found rough going there. The Williamses' daughter, Delia (Isabell Washington), has been having an affair with a West Indian law student (Richard Landers) but ditches him for Roy (Billy Andrews), one of a pair of "big boys" in the numbers game. Then she switches to Roy's partner, Kid Vamp (Ernest R. Whitman), unaware that he has killed Roy in the belief that Roy has double crossed him. When the police show up at the Williamses' rent party to arrest him, he pulls a gun and runs out, but the police shoot through the door and kill him. Delia heads off to seek a new lover. The noisy party dances offered "that amazing rhythm and style seen only in Harlem," including one particularly lewd dance known as "The Belly Rub." *Harlem* ran twelve weeks and returned in the next season for an additional fortnight.

William J. Perlman's **The Broken Chain** (2-20-29, Maxine Elliott's) dealt with another group of New Yorkers outside the city's mainstream, ultra-orthodox Jews known as Hassidim. Having already written off his playboy boxer son, Reb Velvele Slomner (Frank McGlynn) is stunned to learn his married daughter (Mary Fowler) is having an affair. He brands her an adulteress, declares her dead to himself and to the world, and recites the Hebrew prayer for the dead. ("The scene had the audience slobbering heavily," *Variety* reported.) After misfortunes pile one atop the other on the rabbi and his congregation, he understands he is guilty of false pride. He turns his pulpit over to his daughter's husband and tries to forgive her and his son. Offstage chants, a procession of robed, bearded rabbinical students, and the lighting of candles added flavor to the piece, but McGlynn was seen as miscast and the play's appeal very limited.

John Dos Passos's **Airways, Inc.** (2-20-29, Grove

Street) had even less appeal. Its "incoherent, undisciplined" plot attempted to belittle big business and glorify unions. In the latter case it was reminiscent of *Gods of the Lightning*. An ambitious aviator (Winston Lee) believes anything is allowable in his attempt to build a large airline. His sister (Edith Meiser) loves a fiery union agitator (Harry Gordon), who is framed by the authorities for a murder he did not commit and sent to the electric chair. The aviator dies after his spine is broken in a plane crash.

The next evening ushered in one of the season's best comedies and biggest hits, Rachel Crothers's **Let Us Be Gay** (2-21-29, Little). A prologue is set in the drapey, dimly lit bedroom of Kitty Brown (Francine Larrimore). She has locked out her husband, Bob (Warren William), who she believes has been unfaithful. She admits him only after he threatens to break down the door. But she still insists he go away, and he finally agrees, vowing never to return. Three years pass. Kitty has been invited to a dinner in Westchester by a tart, cigar-puffing dowager, Mrs. Boucicault (Charlotte Granville), who has asked Kitty to disillusion her granddaughter, Diedre (Rita Vita), about a divorced man that Diedre has become besotted over, even though she is engaged to marry an eligible young bachelor. Of course, the man turns out to be Kitty's ex. He instantly understands why she is there. Bob would spill the beans, but Kitty urges him not to, and he consents. Even Diedre, although she does not know that Kitty was once Bob's wife, grasps why she had been invited. Kitty and Bob have a long chat on a romantically moonlit balcony. The next morning Bob asks Kitty if he could make love to her again. "That's what I'm afraid of. That's why I'm running now." But they quickly kiss and make up. Some critics, while acknowledging that she was in many ways superb, lambasted Miss Larrimore's still slovenly diction and uncontrolled voice. Nonetheless, the comedy ran ten and a half months.

A. A. Milne's fairy-tale-ish **Meet the Prince** (2-25-29, Lyceum) centered on another quarreling couple (Mary Ellis and Basil Sydney). They separate. Going out into society, he pretends to be a prince; she pretends to be the widow of a famous warrior. They meet and fall in love again. In England the play was called *To Have the Honor*.

On the same evening the Civic Repertory Theatre added Leonid Andreyev's **Katerina** to its slate. The play was translated by Herman Bernstein, and Alla Nazimova was starred as a woman unjustly accused of infidelity by her husband (Walter Beck). The shock drives her into increasingly degraded behavior.

Arthur Schnitzler's *Liebelei*, done in 1905 as *The Reckoning*, was revived at the Cherry Lane on the 26th in a new, uncredited translation as **Playing with Love**. It again narrated a young woman's unrequited passion for a man who prefers a married lady and is killed in a duel with the lady's husband. The "draggled handful" of theatregoers attending its opening night foretold its short life.

Savage notices on a par with those handed *My Girl Friday*—"witless," "dullness and stupidity personified," "one of the world's worst"—did not prevent George Rosener's low-budget comedy **She Got What She Wanted** (3-4-29, Wallack's) from achieving a somewhat forced run of fifteen weeks, sustained in large part by Leblang's cut-rate tickets. Mahnya (Galina Kopernak) deserts her bookseller husband, Boris (Alan Brooks), for Dave (William Pike), a gambler, then runs off with Eddie (Franklyn Ardell), a wise-cracking vaudevillian, before returning to Boris.

Myron C. Fagan's **Indiscretion** (3-4-29, Mansfield) ran just five weeks. Its first-night audience reportedly hissed and booed the drama, which seems to have been played in a slightly overmelodramatic fashion. Bob's father, a Canadian railroad magnate, has refused to give his consent to Bob's marrying Margaret (Minna Gombell), so Bob (Harland Tucker) and Margaret have lived together in Venice. Falsely informed that his father is dying, Bob returns home and is railroaded into a society marriage. Years later the widowed Bob, now a senator, and Margaret, now a famous actress, meet again. Bob discovers that she has had a daughter by him, and they both realize they have been the victims of trickery and slander. They are permanently reunited just before the final curtain.

Inveterate playgoers who hustled themselves down to Greenwich Village could, briefly, attend a double bill which began with a revival of O'Neill's one-character *Before Breakfast*. Mary Blair enacted the role of the nagging wife who drives her husband to suicide. The evening's main event was Vergil Geddes's **The Earth Between** (3-5-29, Provincetown Playhouse). Nat Jennings (Carl Ashburn), a dour backwater farmer, sees his daughter, Floy (Bette Davis), as the embodiment of his late wife and lusts after her. To prevent her being courted by his farmhand, Jake (William Challee), he forces Jake to sleep on a damp pallet in the barn. Jake contracts pneumonia and dies after Nat withholds his medicine. Nat continues his unnatural relationship with Floy. The play's settings were done in the expressionistic style so common to Village mountings. Davis, in her New York debut, was hailed for her "soft, unassertive" innocence.

The succession of flops continued with Warren F. Lawrence's **Conflict** (3-6-29, Fulton). Aviators were popular again this season. The new play looked at a disgruntled clerk, Richard Banks (Spencer Tracy), who is snubbed by a beautiful socialite, Ruth Winship (Peggy Allenby). Drafted during the war, he becomes a decorated pilot and returns home to find Ruth willing to wed him. He soon is lounging away on Ruth's money. Then he overhears a phone conversation in which she tells an old beau that she made a mistake by marrying Richard. He leaves her to become a commercial pilot. Tracy was lauded for doing "an excellent job," making Richard seem more misguided than calculating.

Martin Mooney and Thomson Burtis, two newspapermen, had to produce their own drama, **The Town's Woman** (3-11-29, Craig), and close it after two weeks of atrocious business. The snobbish William Hudson (Frank Monroe) is extremely chagrined to learn that his son, Robert (Jack McKee), is fond of Nancy North (Helen Baxter) After all, Nancy had been an actress and now runs a tea room patronized by gamblers from a nearby racetrack. She even has cost Robert money by giving him a tip that failed. (The back part of the tea room setting disappeared for a time to show the race—run on a treadmill in a virtually extinct theatrical tradition.) But Nancy makes good on Robert's losses by selling the tea room and, when the elder Hudson is brought down on being shown to be not all that ethical in his business dealings, agrees to marry Robert, who has become an aviator.

Ancient history was given new life in Hardwick Nevin's **Young Alexander** (3-12-29, Biltmore). Alexander was Henry Hull—the second historical figure Hull played during the season (the first was Machiavelli)—while A. E. Anson was his mentor, Aristotle. The young warrior, believing himself a god, feels he is too good for women. Then the wife (Jessie Royce Landis) of Darius (Charles Dalton), whom he has just routed, teaches the boy how to be a man. Similar to *The Road to Rome*, but lacking that show's panache, the drama closed at the end of its first week.

Frederick Rath and Kolby Kohn's **Solitaire** (3-12-29, Waldorf) could not even finish out a single week. Its story told of a midget (Master Gabriel) who kills the man attempting to steal his normal-sized wife (Dorothy Libaire). He is acquitted by a compassionate jury.

Along with aviators, nineteenth-century plays had become a small rage during the season. The latest to be resurrected was Dion Boucicault's seventy-year-old *The Octoroon*, which saw the light of night once more on the 12th at Maxine Elliott's. It recounted the tragic fate of the beautiful octoroon Zoe (Inez Plummer), doomed by the racial prejudices of her era. But this time, the public would not buy it for all the appreciative notices it received. Like *Young Alexander*, it lasted only a week.

Still a third one-week flop, A. W. and E. L. Barker and Charles Beahan's **Buckaroo** (3-16-29, Erlanger), had an unusual and interesting setting. The action took place under the stands of Soldier's Field in Chicago, where a rodeo is being held. A stilt walker, a knife thrower, and buxom cowgirls contributed color. Stray Murfee (James Bell), a not too bright champion broncho buster, is vamped away from his loving sweetheart, Lee (Nydia Westman), by the glamorous Maxine Madison (Ruth Easton), who bilks him of $1500 by promising him a vaudeville contract. Lee retrieves the money, which Maxine has placed for safety in the depths of her bosom, in a hair-pulling slugfest. But Benny (Clyde Dilson), Maxine's jealous gangster beau, shoots Stray in the shoulder, which does not stop the cowboy from winning another rodeo prize. Of course, Lee is an even better prize.

Two revivals began the next week. The Actors' Theatre brought out Ibsen's *The Lady from the Sea* at the Bijou on the 18th, with Blanche Yurka as Ellida. A group called the Jitney Players, which had been busing and trucking through New England and the New York suburbs, settled in for a time at the Cherry Lane Playhouse. Their first offering was Richard Brinsley Sheridan's *A Trip to Scarborough*, which had not been done in the lifetime of modern playgoers. In fact, the revival was bruited as the comedy's first New York mounting in 150 years. Although ostensibly dealing with the attempts of a lovely belle to be avenged for her lover's philanderings, the center of attention fell on the comically and rather appropriately named Lord Foppington.

In recent years, critics had rarely deigned to accord any attention to Butler Davenport and his Free Theatre, but some did attend his presentation of the New York premiere of Somerset Maugham's early drama **The Tenth Man** (3-20-29, Davenport). Playing with a "Machiavellian touch and great relish," Davenport himself took the role of the blackmailing politician who even blackmails his wife when she asks for a divorce that could ruin his career. His philosophy is that nine out of ten men are scoundrels. But he fails to heed his wife's warning that sooner or later that tenth man will appear and will destroy him. Her prophecy comes true.

No drama of the 1928–29 season has been revived as often or as welcomedly—even if virtually all the revivals have been in England—as R. C. Sherriff's **Journey's End** (3-22-29, Henry Miller's). Generally acknowledged as the best play about World War I, it was set in a front-line dugout and followed the foredoomed fate of a group of young English soldiers and officers. Several of the men are sent on suicide missions, but the remainder die at the end when the dugout is blown to bits. The characters included the hard-drinking Captain Stanhope (Colin Keith Johnson), a high-minded recent arrival, 2nd Lieutenant Raleigh (Derek Williams), the schoolmarmish Lieutenant Osborne (Leon Quartermaine), and the frightened 2nd Lieutenant Hibbert (Jack Hawkins). The play ran for more than a year.

The Jitney Players' second offering of their visit was Lady Gregory's dalliance *The Dragon* at the Cherry Lane on the 25th, in which a king and queen must marry off their daughter before she can be gobbled up by a dragon (a character in the play) who dines solely on unwed maidens. The king announces she will be wed to the first man entering the palace, only to find that man is a cook. But, in true fairy tale fashion, the cook is revealed as a prince traveling incognito.

Esme Wynne-Tyson's English drama **Security** (3-28-29, Maxine Elliott's) found little favor, even with Margaret Anglin playing the wife who remains married to her unscrupulous, philandering husband (Thurston Hall) so that her children can have some security and is freed only by his suicide. The artificial, stilted dialogue was pounced upon, but Robert Littell wrote in the *Post* that its pompousness was not obvious when the star spoke "with an extraordinary skillful naturalness and variety, and an expertness in change of pace that takes your breath away."

Only one novelty competed with the revivals that launched April. In a move possibly foreshadowing its movement away from the serious, high-minded works it had been presenting for so long, the Theatre Guild continued its season with a comedy-drama that many critics felt might well have been presented by a more commercially bent management. **Man's Estate** (4-1-29, Biltmore) was an effort by two more newspaper people, Beatrice Blackmar and Bruce Gold. It followed the fate of Jerry Jordan (Earle Larimore), who has hoped to study architecture at Yale and then in Paris, instead of entering his uncle's hardware store, as his parents (Dudley Digges and Elizabeth Patterson) would prefer. Unfortunately for his lofty ambitions, Jerry falls in love with Sesaly Blaine (Margalo Gillmore), and she

soon is pregnant. She is willing to have an abortion or have the child in Europe, if that will help Jerry. He elects to accept responsibility for his behavior and, giving up his dreams of "bumping the stars," enters the hardware business. Larimore was applauded for poignantly depicting Jerry's metamorphosis into a man, while Gillmore played the heroine with "beauty and anguish."

Of the evening's three revivals, Mrs. Fiske's recreation of her role as the scheming climber in Harry James Smith's *Mrs. Bumpstead-Leigh* at the Klaw was the most successful, staying in town for nine weeks and breaking to some extent her streak of ill luck. Heywood Broun observed in the *Telegram* that she could still "mug and clown with the best," adding that even if she continued occasionally to swallow some of her dialogue, "I would rather hear twenty-five percent of Mrs. Fiske's speeches than get a full hundred percent from any other actress." "Lanky, easy-going" Sidney Toler thrived in the scene-stealing role of the blackmailing Peter Swallow.

There was also high praise for Jane Cowl and Philip Merivale in Miss Cowl's resurrection of Stephen Phillips's *Paolo and Francesca* at the Forrest. But so few playgoers lined up at the box office that the run was not extended beyond its originally announced two weeks.

A strange revival ran longer. In 1926, *Appearances*, a play by a black San Francisco bellhop, had been a quick flop. Brought back inexplicably to the Hudson, it flopped again, although forcing kept it on the boards for eight weeks.

The next night brought in yet another nineteenth-century melodrama, Augustin Daly's sixty-two-year-old *Under the Gaslight*, whose railroad-track scene had been lifted by Boucicault for *After Dark*, a revival of which was still flourishing in Hoboken. Once again, the one-armed Snorkey (John Ferguson) was tied to the rails and saved by Laura (Helene Dumas) just as a locomotive appears in view from the right side of the proscenium. The play was mounted by a Bowery saloon keeper at what he called Fay's Bowery Theatre. This was not the famous old Bowery but an auditorium which once had offered cheap touring thrillers when it was known as the People's Theatre and which since had become a Yiddish stage. *Variety* was amused by the juxtaposition of "gaping hobos and bread-line citizenry" outside with "Rolls-Royces, Hispano-Suizas and Isotta-Fraschinis" disgorging elegantly garbed first-nighters at the curb in front of the house. But playgoers apparently had become quickly surfeited, so the melodrama was removed after three weeks.

Except for *Street Scene*, British plays grabbed the season's long-run honors among straight works, with John Drinkwater's comedy **Bird in Hand** (4-4-29, Booth) tallying 500 performances to beat out *Journey's End* by a mere fifteen representations. The story followed the daughter (Jill Esmond Moore) of the owner of a humble inn that has been in their family for three centuries through her courtship by the son (Charles Hickman) of a local squire. Her father (Herbert Lomas) suspects the young man's intentions, but true love triumphs.

Two American efforts fared less well. Hugh A. Anderson and George Bamman's **Mystery Square** (4-4-29, Longacre) was derived from Robert Louis Stevenson's *Suicide Club* and *The Rajah's Diamond*. Its hero was a prince (Gavin Muir) who uncovers a plan by some criminals to help rich men to suicide and thereby gain some of their wealth.

Norman Cannon's **He Walked in Her Sleep** (4-4-29, Princess) dealt with a man who believes his wife is unfaithful. While she is sleeping he runs off to have an affair of his own, then learns his wife has not been disloyal.

Another of the season's near misses was Anne Morrison and John Peter Toohey's **Jonesy** (4-9-29, Bijou), taken from some of Toohey's short stories. Henry Jones (Donald Meek) is an unsuccessful lawyer who hopes getting work from Stanley Jackson (Percy Moore), his town's biggest businessman, will give his practice a boost. His son, Wilbur (Raymond Guion), known as Jonesy, falls in love with Diana Devereaux (Helen Brooks), the buxom beauty from the local stock company. His mother (Spring Byington) and father do everything they can to break up the romance, especially after learning that this week's attraction requires Di to parade across the stage in a sarong. To add to their concern, the play is raided by the police. They also find out that Jonesy has sold his car to pay off a gambling debt. But then they discover that Di is Jackson's pet niece. All ends happily with Jonesy taking a job driving the town's water wagon and becoming engaged to Di.

Leo Bulgakov's mounting of *The Sea Gull* at the Comedy on the 9th was slated for just a handful of matinee peformances, but glowing notices prompted it to stick around for a brief run. Among the actors in Chekhov's piece were Walter Abel as Trigorin, E. J. Ballantine as Sorin, Barbara Bulgakov as Nina, and Dorothy Sands as Irina.

Considering his celebrity, F. Scott Fitzgerald got singularly short shrift from the reviewers when his play, **The Vegetable; or, From President to Postman** (4-10-29, Cherry Lane), premiered. The comedy

had been tried out with Ernest Truex and had failed. Now it was brought in by a group of semi-professionals whose inadequacies only underscored the play's own. Fitzgerald's subtitle gave away the story of a young man who dreams of becoming president of the United States but settles for being a postman.

Two Middle European plays vied for attention the next Monday. One succeeded in winning a long run; the other did not actually fail but had a limited run because of its star's commitments. The hit was the Theatre Guild's mounting of a Czech play by František Langer, adapted by Philip Moeller as **Camel Through the Needle's Eye** (4-15-29, Martin Beck). An amiable but not bright rich boy, Alik (Eliot Cabot), runs off with Susi (Miriam Hopkins), illegitimate daughter of some down-and-out schemers (Henry Travers and Helen Westley). Alik's father (Claude Rains) tries to separate the pair, but they have a child and make something profitable out of a small dairy. The play ran six months.

Zoë Akins was the adaptor of **The Love Duel** (4-15-29, Ethel Barrymore), which was taken from the Hungarian of Lili Hatvany and which starred Ethel Barrymore. Miss Barrymore had closed *The Kingdom of God* when she became ill, but the fact that she did not reopen it suggests it was probably deemed ready to fold shortly in any case. That she had been ill was indisputable, with critics remarking on her pallor and thinness. Both Carlo (Louis Calhern) and Lydia—listed simply as He and She in programs—have had many affairs. When they meet and fall in love, they refuse to openly acknowledge their strong emotions. Instead they agree to match wits, a love duel. Of course, the duel ends with their marrying after she has his child. The following season, Miss Barrymore took both plays across the country, performing them in semi-repertory fashion. Despite its limited run, the play was the season's last success. Everything hereafter went downhill.

In some ways, Kenyon Nicholson's **Before You're 25** (4-16-29, Maxine Elliott's) resembled *Man's Estate*, telling of a young idealist made to face reality. Clement Corbin (Eric Dressler) would rather publish a radical monthly and face arrest than join an established family business. His girlfriend (Mildred McCoy) has his child out of wedlock but finally convinces him to marry her and go into his family's furniture business.

A string of flops had not discouraged Michael Kallesser, but after the failure of **Rockbound** (4-19-29, Cort), which he wrote with Amy Wales, Broadway would not hear from him for many years. Some reviewers laughed off the new work as pseudo-

O'Neill. Set in a Maine fishing village where Ellen Higgins (Emily Ann Wellman) lives with her soured-on-life family, it recounted her dilemma when her son, Amos (John F. Hamilton), falls in love with Lucy (Renita Randolph), a visitor. Ellen is forced to admit that Lucy is her illegitimate daughter. The women are turned out of the house. Ellen eventually arranges a suitable marriage for Lucy, then returns to look after her menfolk.

Herbert Ashton, Jr., played the lead in his own crook play, **The Come-On Man** (4-22-29, 49th St.). A gang who steal rich women's jewels catch Jimmie McGuire attempting to burglarize their home. Since he is handsome and suave they press him into luring victims into their clutches. The gang leader, William Strange (George MacQuarrie), has a beautiful daughter, Betty (Mary Wall). Jimmie and Betty naturally fall in love. A detective (Harold Jack) tries to expose the group, but then Jimmie reveals that he himself is a detective and that the detective is a crook. He persuades Strange to reform.

Jean Archibald's **Marry the Man** (4-22-29, Fulton) was billed as "a compassionate comedy." Its leading lady was thoroughly modern Mollie Jeffries (Vivian Martin), who wants to hold on to Gregory Martin (Lester Vail) without anything so old-fashioned as marriage. She even convinces her younger sister (Joan Peers) and the serving girl to follow her practice. But by eleven o'clock all the ladies are heading for the altar.

The fad for nineteenth-century melodrama hit bottom with a revival of Boucicault's *The Streets of New York* on the 23rd at the Spanish Theatre, a hastily converted hall on 14th Street. Originally done as *The Poor of New York* in 1857, the play told of financial finagling and contained a celebrated rescue from a burning building. Its cast mixed unknown professionals and amateurs.

"It takes brains to be a swell tart, and we ain't got 'em," says one of the cooch dancers in William R. Doyle's **Carnival** (4-24-29, Forrest). Its heroine, another carnival dancer, might have been better off had she given her actions some thought. For a brief time Helen Herbert (Anne Forrest) has a hot and heavy affair with a small-town young man, Bobbie Spencer (Norman Foster), but then realizes she will only harm his chances. She attempts to discourage him by inviting him to a specially staged "smoker," where he can see her perform lewd dances. Failing in her ploy, she substitutes for a parachute jumper and refuses to open the chute.

On the 29th at the huge Hippodrome, Morris Gest imported the Freiburg (Germany) **Passion Play**. The play was restaged for the occasion by Gest's father-in-law, David Belasco. The production was "a sublimated pageant," mounted with "vast realism to the extent of the hammer blows that drive the nails through [Christ's] hands and feet." Performed in German, the evening lasted nearly four hours. The attraction ran for six weeks, although prices had to be halved for the last several weeks to keep the house crowded.

The author of **Congratulations** (4-30-29, National) was listed as Morgan Wallace, the name of the play's central figure. Those in the know realized that Henry Hull, the actor who assumed the role, also used the moniker as his nom de plume. He set his play in Hokum City, where Wallace heads a dying stock company. A corrupt local political boss, hoping to ensure his slate's reelection, prods Wallace to run in opposition, certain he will lose. Wallace accepts, assuming the race at least will provide his troupe with publicity. He wins and sets about reforming the town. He also announces that he will write the whole story as a play.

The First Law (5-6-29, Masque) was ballyhooed as the first Soviet play to receive a Broadway hearing. But Broadway would listen to it only for a week. The drama was by Dmitry Scheglov, as translated by Herman Bernstein and Leonid Snegoff. A wealthy American woman (Francis Carson) and her equally highborn American fiancé (Reginald Goode) take refuge in a peasant's hut during the Russian revolution. A dashing Bolshevist (Snegoff) appears. For a time the woman and Bolshevist fall in love, leading to a fight in which the Russian kills the American. But when the woman is confronted with the choice of going home alone or remaining in Russia with her new man, she chooses home.

William E. Barry's **The Jade God** (5-13-29, Cort) was theatricalized from a novel by Alan Sullivan. In a short prologue, two servants are seen standing in shock over the dead body of John Millicent, a traveler murdered with an exotic Malay knife. Weeks later Jack Derrick (Richard Nicholls), who loves the dead man's daughter, Jean (Lyle Stackpole), takes over his house and determines to find the murderer. Disembodied voices are heard, and knives gleam in the dark. Several people are suspected, including an East Indian who admits he has come to recover a precious if ill-omened idol the dead man had taken away. But the killer turns out to be one of the servants, an odd woman (Margaret Wycherly) who speaks "enigmatic lines in a sepulchral tone of voice" and who has believed herself cursed by the idol. Jack smashes the jade to bits.

Some critics perceived Elmer Harris's **Stepping Out** (5-20-29, Fulton) as a feeble attempt to copy

Cradle Snatchers, with the sexes reversed. Two Hollywood moguls (Herbert Corthell and Walter Connolly) decide to have some fun while their wives are away and call on two gold-digging starlets (Lillian Bond and Martha Sleeper) to join in the partying at their posh mansion. They do not hear one of the girls tell the other, "Keep your love letters and your love letters will keep you." But the men's wives (Jobyna Howland and Grace La Rue), having forgotten some of their luggage, return unexpectedly. Seeing the situation, the woman head off to a cabin at Yosemite, intending to find some nice college boys. Not until the final curtain is everyone properly repaired.

In Captain Cushing Donnell's **Chinese O'Neill** (5-22-29, Forrest), the title figure (Donald R. Dumbrille) is a sailor of fortune who rushes to the rescue of Gerson St. George (Hugh Buckley) and his party, captured by associates of the notorious and murderous warlord Chang Kai Chang. O'Neill soon learns that St. George is as much a villain as Chang, so is not too sorry when he is killed. But O'Neill blows up Chang's gunboat and also falls in love with the Hon. Nancy Beresford (Audrey Ridgwell), whom St. George had hoped to marry against her will. Stabbings, stranglings, and machine gunnings spiced the action.

Morris Carnovsky, "in a make-up that unhappily suggests Shylock," played the lead in a mounting of Chekhov's *Uncle Vanya* at the Morosco on the 24th. It was booked for a series of matinee performances, but tepid reviews saw to it that only two matinees sufficed.

Rehearsed for just over a week before its opening and the recipient of some of the season's coldest shoulders, Carl Henkle's **Decision** (5-27-29, 49th St.) stayed on for eight weeks, aided by cut-rate tickets and forcing. Its story centered on a young woman (Margaret Barnstead) who adopts her dead sister's children when their other relatives refuse to take them in. But these same relatives try to have her declared unfit after they learn the kids have inherited scads of money. The good woman wins the case and finds true love.

But nothing could sustain Luther Yantis's **Chippies** (5-29-29, Belmont). Reviewers reported that first-nighters tittered in embarrassment at the play's ineptness. Beth Ramsey (Maud Brooks) breaks off her engagement to a decent chap in her hometown of Painesville and runs off to the allures of Cleveland. There she finds love as the mistress of an Italian hood (Cullen Landis). She finally convinces him to marry her, but when she brings him home to mother, she hears the parlor organ playing her mother's favorite song, "In the Gloaming," and finds her mother in a coffin. The poor old gal died of a broken heart. Only vaudevillian Fred Ardath earned real laughs and applause by doing his popular vaudeville turn as an inebriate.

At month's end, *Variety* gave an interesting picture of business on Broadway. For the most part it was not good. Among straight plays only *Journey's End* and *Street Scene* were packing them in and grossing over $20,000, with *Bird in Hand* a fairly strong third at $17,000. Hits such as *Holiday* and *Let Us Be Gay* had to be content with between $12,500 and $14,500. And the crushing hot weather was just around the corner.

Lyle Weaver Hall's **The Tired Business Man** (6-3-29, Waldorf) took a comic gander at the problems of Henry Gilbert (Harlan Briggs), a Topeka editor who is running for mayor even though he is estranged from his wife (Frances McGrath). His rivals foist a cute manicurist (Mary Vance) on him and, when he naively brings her back to his home, snap seemingly incriminating photos of the pair. But his wife helps him outwit the conspirators and effects a reconciliation.

With Mrs. Fiske about to close her production, the Players brought out another work with which she was associated for their annual mounting. Among the performers in Langdon Mitchell's *Becky Sharp*, which began a week's stand at the Knickerbocker on June 3, were Mary Ellis in the title role, Patricia Collinge as Amelia, Cecilia Loftus as Miss Crawley, Moffat Johnston as the Marquis of Steyne, and Basil Sydney as Rawdon. Other celebrated players assumed lesser roles. But the consensus was that this production was not on a par—either as drama or as performance—with the club's prior offerings.

Rich, aging Mark Chandler (Robert Warwick), the protagonist in William A. Grew's **Nice Women** (6-10-29), does not at first realize that her father (George Barbier), whom he employs, and her mother have pressured their daughter, Bessie (Sylvia Sidney), to break off with the boy she loves and become engaged to Chandler. The parents believe he will keep them in style for the rest of their lives. When Chandler learns of this, he backs away. But there is Bessie's kid sister, Gerry (Hope Drown), ready to take her place. Good reviews, a far cry from those the playwright received for *My Girl Friday*, could not buck Broadway's slump or the hot weather that arrived in short order.

The season concluded on a very down note with Test Dalton's **Adam's Apple** (6-10-29, Princess). A burglar (Charles Kennedy), having overheard Adam Van Alstyne (Stanley Price) confess to a friend that whenever he wants a night on the town he tells his wife he is going to visit his imaginary Uncle John, enters the Van Alstyne house and is caught by Mrs. Van Alstyne (Helen Holmes), so tells her he is Uncle John. The expected complications follow.

1929–1930

Having been dealt a shaking blow by the advent of sound films in 1927, live theatre was hit hard again in the new season—this time by the stock market crash and the onset of the Depression. After an all too brief period in which it seemed like the crash downtown would not seriously affect playhouses uptown, business tumbled. A very few hits bucked the trend for a while, but failures were more frequent and more quickly hurried off the stage. Nearly seventy, or approximately half the new plays which premiered, ran three weeks or less. Several of these three-week runs were forced, since twenty-four or more performances allowed a producer to share in screen rights and other additional royalties. Twenty-five of these duds were so feeble that a forced run was out of the question and they were closed in the same week in which they opened.

As usual, statisticians and commentators could not agree on figures or evaluations. Both *Variety* and the *Times* reported a very slight increase in the number of new plays offered (giving 169 and 156 as their respective totals), while Burns Mantle insisted, "We had fewer plays last year." Brooks Atkinson became curiously equivocal when assessing the merits of the season, noting that "thoughtful observers" found Broadway "steadily improving," but nonetheless continuing, "People who love the theatre repeatedly discover that their love is not returned." On the other hand, at year's end Mantle looked back to hail "a more interesting season than many of those that have preceded it."

Certainly the season's early weeks offered no encouragement. Bide Dudley, drama editor for the *Evening World*, launched the outing with **Borrowed Love** (6-18-29, Times Square), which its programs called "a new angle on the sex triangle." John Carter (Richard Gordon), a war veteran and onetime star Illinois football player, wangles his way into the box office of a Chicago theatre and convinces Tom Bradford (Barry O'Neill), the company's young, handsome, and unmarried manager, to come home to meet his wife. Tom soon learns that John is impotent and has hoped that Tom could make Mrs. Carter (Mary Fowler) happy. Tom hastily backs away. So John decides to head for New York, where a famous psychoanalyst may be able to help him. Several critics questioned whether bringing up such a subject as impotence was in good taste. Their notices and an unusually hot June doomed the play, even though it had only four performers, none of whom received a high salary.

The opening night of Louise Carter's **Bedfellows** (7-2-29, Waldorf) had to be delayed for one evening after a falling balustrade injured an actor during a dress rehearsal. At least one critic suggested "the balcony must have fallen directly on the play itself, producing an effect varying from complete vacuousness to a sustained yawn." When Felix Cornwall (Hal K. Dawson) falls in love with Elinor Charlot (Anne Bronaugh), who is married to Jack Charlot (John Vosberg), a man enamored of Mrs. Cornwall (Lee Smith), the couples attempt to change partners but by the end of Act III decide that the original pairing was better.

Another seemingly mismated couple initiated the fireworks in C. Stafford Dickens's **Freddy** (7-16-29, Lyceum). The strong-minded Jane Gommery (Beatrice Terry), knowing her husband (Dickens) has eyes for the voluptuous actress Queenie Mellish (Vera Neilson), sets her own sights on Freddy Hale (Raymond Walburn). To avoid her clutches, Freddy announces he has a mistress—Queenie. She agrees to go along with the gag, so when the Gommerys comes to Queenie's apartment they find her and Freddy embracing. The complications that ensue end with Freddy and Queenie heading off in her car, and the Gommerys looking for new romances.

Down in Greenwich Village a black ensemble attempted a revival of Oscar Wilde's *Salome* the next evening at the Cherry Lane and were laughed off the stage. (Another black group had mounted the same play on Broadway six years before.) Heading the newer company was a female impersonator, Hemsley Winfield, "in nothing but a symbolic brassiere and a Belmont Park girdle, lisping indecencies to John the Baptist's severed head or whirling in wild abandon before Herod."

For many the new season began with William A. Brady's mounting of Arthur F. Brash's **Now-A-Days** (8-5-29, Forrest). It was the latest drama to take an unhappy look at modern youth but marked "no happy augury for the new season." Boyd Butler (Melvyn Douglas), a star football player, is a nasty drunk. Barbara Herford (Irene Blair) loves him and would reform him, but the flashy, debauched Paula Newhall (Mayo Methot) lures him to a speakeasy where, in a fight with a bootlegger, Paula kills the rumrunner. Boyd is held for the killing until Paula confesses and kills herself by swallowing poison. Barbara is left with a repentant Boyd, while all the detective who handled the case can ask is "Good God, what is this country coming to?"

Laurence E. Johnson's **It's a Wise Child** (8-6-29, Belasco), the season's first hit—and David Belasco's last—came in the next evening. To avoid having to marry G. A. Appleby (Harlan Briggs), a stuffed-shirt, middle-aged banker, Joyce Stanton (Mildred McCoy) announces that she is going to have a baby. After all, the family maid had used the same gimmick and wound up with a lovable if mercurial iceman, Cool Kelly (Sidney Toler). Joyce's ploy works too well, for not only is Appleby alienated, but so is the boy she really loves, Roger Baldwin (Humphrey Bogart). Then the polished, attractive family lawyer, James Stevens (Minor Watson), who long has loved Joyce, offers to take the blame. He wins Joyce's affections and, of course, a confession of innocence. Belasco's direction and the fine players glossed over "lines which are not so funny in themselves" and kept audiences delighted for just short of a full year.

Fiske O'Hara, who usually sprinkled his vehicles with a handful of tenor solos, reserved the songs for the curtain calls at William A. Grew's **Jerry for Short** (8-12-29, Waldorf). The play was also a change of pace for Grew, who last season had offered the more questionable *My Girl Friday* and *Nice Women*. O'Hara played John Hartwell, who has made a fortune in Montana mines and brought his daughter, Betty (Lorna Carroll), east in hopes of wedding her into society. At first society snubs them, but then it is learned that the Hartwells have hired a father and daughter (Joseph Fay and Marie Louise Dana) as butler and maid, and that the butler has inherited a fortune. Since the money was inherited rather than earned, society is more sympathetic. However, the news is shown to be spurious. Still, Betty finds true love, and so does her father—with their pretty maid. O'Hara's aging loyalists kept the play in New York for two months.

A pair of plays that followed each ran less than a week. Alan Mowbray, later a celebrated character actor in films, was the author and featured player of **Dinner Is Served** (8-15-29, Cort). Mary Bishop (Beatrice Hendricks), desperate to rekindle the ardor of her husband, Billy (Mowbray), tries to foist him on their pretty maid (Gaby Fay). But it turns out that Mary herself still inspires Billy, so the maid goes off with Mary's father (Edward Emery). To some the best thing about the evening was its posh

country-house setting, "with period portraits, a stained glass window, and the lush night color in the sky brooding over the garden."

There were thirty-four episodes and twenty-two players in Nathaniel Wilson's **Getting Even** (8-19-29, Biltmore), and not much to compel real attention. Many a reviewer informed his readers that the play and the acting were so bad that first-nighters were sometimes doubled over in laughter at supposedly serious and moving moments. The multiple scenes traced the decline and fall, and ultimate death, of Veronica Matilda McConnell (Georgia Clarke), "a Pollyanna of the slums, too good to be true," who is slowly embittered and destroyed by life. Having found a husband after a flirtation with a garbage collector, Veronica Matilda McConnell enters a hospital for an abortion. The surgery kills her. "Then the nurse says to the husband 'I think you'd better take a walk' and the audience howled."

George M. Cohan enjoyed a modest success with his **Gambling** (8-26-29, Fulton). When the show went into tryouts the lead had been played by Clark Gable, but Cohan let him go and rewrote the central part to his own needs. Al Draper is a foursquare gambler, who learns that the body of his adopted daughter, his late partner's orphaned child, has been found in a shabby hotel. She had been seeing a rather dissolute young man named Braddock (Douglas MacPherson). However, the police cannot pin the crime on him, so Draper sets out to do so. He starts by befriending two of Braddock's louche, gold-digging ladies, Mazie and Dot (Mary Philips and Isabel Baring). Finally assembling everyone at the office of the D.A. (Jack Leslie), he unwittingly wheedles a confession from Braddock, who then commits suicide. Critics felt Cohan was the whole show, giving "the sort of performance that would chase people away from the dinner table to be there on time for the curtain."

Murder and the younger generation, two matters already touched on in plays such as *Gambling* and *Now-A-Days*, would figure importantly in many September plays, sometimes separately, sometimes interwoven. Indeed, the onrush of murder plays prompted some surveyors of the Broadway scene to suggest that the competition confused playgoers and caused one or two better examples to fail. Paul Hervey Fox and George Tilton's **Soldiers and Women** (9-2-29, Ritz) was not one of the better instances, albeit excellent acting kept the play alive for eight weeks. Brenda Ritchie (Violet Heming), the cold-blooded, selfish wife of a British colonel posted in India, is rebuffed when she proposes a liaison with Captain Branch (Derek Glynne). Meaning to kill Branch, she inadvertently kills the husband (Leonard Mudie) of Branch's mistress (Verree Teasdale). Branch is held for the killing and looks to be convicted until the clever General Sir Charles Conant (A. E. Anson), in charge of the investigation, unearths enough evidence to force Brenda to swallow a vial of cyanide.

The younger generation came to the fore in Howard E. Koch's **Great Scott** (9-2-29, 49th St.). Delancey Scott (Ray Harper), the only member of his working-class family to go to college, returns from school full of big words, high-falutin' notions, and a marked left-wing bent. He takes a job at the can factory where his father and brother work, organizes a strike, and wins the workers shorter hours, profit sharing, and a garden to look out on. He also wins the hand of Ruth Watson (Adele Ronson), his boss's daughter. However, he costs his father, his brother, and himself their jobs. Father and brother are finally taken back, but Delancey must settle for a job at the local high school.

Walter Huston, offering yet another memorable performance, was the chief attraction of **The Commodore Marries** (9-4-29, Plymouth), which Kate Parsons derived from incidents in Tobias Smollett's *Peregrine Pickle*. The play was set colorfully in the early eighteenth century. Commodore Trunnion, a retired seaman, lives in a house made over like a ship. He has, for example, removed the stairs. The only way from one floor to another is to climb a mast. To his friends' dismay, he falls in love with and marries a young spinster, Miss Pickle (Eda Heinemann). The ceremony is no sooner finished than he tells her, "Well, let's go aloft and get the business over with." His friends help the bride up the mast. But they have also loosened the ropes of the couple's hammock, which comes down with a thud. Regrettably, the new Mrs. Trunnion proves a shrew and a gold digger. Trunnion, learning she has not become, as she claimed, pregnant, rues he truly believed she was "carrying cargo." He forces her to "walk the plank," then celebrates his restored freedom with his old buddies. Huston was lauded for a performance "not merely virile, but illuminating." Yet the play survived just for five weeks.

The month's first hit was Kenneth Phillips Britton and Roy Hargrave's **Houseparty** (9-9-29, Knickerbocker), which managed to combine successfully youth and murder. The play begins and ends with parties, complete with a jazz band, at a Williams College fraternity. But the fun is spoiled for one sophomore, Alan Bradford (Hargrave), when Florence (Harriet MacGibbon), the "town bag," calls on him, tells him she is pregnant, and, while admitting

that she has no idea who the father is, adds that she has "elected" him to take the blame unless he pays her $10,000. In a scuffle, Florence falls into the fireplace, crushing her skull on an andiron. At first Alan hides the body in a cupboard, then, his nerves on edge, breaks down and confesses. Six months later he has been acquitted and returns to the fraternity in the midst of another giddy party. But he still is a nervous wreck and suicidal, especially when he sees the fireplace. A fraternity brother takes him aside, calms him, and persuades him that the past is passed. The play ran twenty-two weeks.

Samuel Shipman and John B. Hymer's **Scarlet Pages** (9-9-29, Morosco) had too many obsolete contrivances to please most critics. The play begins in the office of Mary Brancroft (Elsie Ferguson), a famous and beautiful criminal lawyer, where Nora Mason (Claire Luce), a hostess at the Hellbound nightclub, her mother (Jean Adair), and Nora's beau, Robert Lawrence (Robert Williams), a $50-a-week motion picture projectionist at the Roxy, are trying to convince the attorney to accept Nora as a client. Nora has been accused of murdering her father, who she says made advances toward her. Mary refuses until Nora hands her a slip of paper. The second act showed the trial. The orchestra pit was replaced by wide stairs and witnesses came up from seats in the theatre to offer evidence. The jury was supposedly out in the auditorium, too. The trial reveals that Nora was adopted and that Nora's father was not her real father, thus explaining his actions to a district attorney (Lee Baker) who could not believe a father would assault his child. It also discloses that Mary was Nora's true mother. On learning this, the D.A. would quash the evidence, but Mary insists it be made public. She also urges Nora to come live with her. Nora elects to remains with the only mother she has known. At the close, Mary "disappears into an aureole light-effect, symbolizing the radiance of eternity and the love of an honest woman for her child."

Murder at a suddenly darkened Chicago radio station—where all the action occurred—was the central incident in Clyde North, Albert C. Fuller, and Jack T. Nelson's **Remote Control** (9-10-29, 48th St.). Knowing playgoers read the real Norman Brokenshire into the character of Walter Brokenchild (Walter N. Greaza), whose interview with bejewelled Junior League debs is interrupted by a gang who rob the ladies of their baubles. A spiritualist (Edward Van Sloan) is suspected of engineering the robbery by having asked for the lights to be lowered, but when the lights go out again and the mind reader is found dead, suspicion turns on Brokenchild. As was often the case, a character whom few would have fingered is shown to be the leader of the gang and the killer.

There was obviously more mayhem in Frank Vosper's London play **Murder on the Second Floor** (9-11-29, Eltinge). A young playwright (Laurence Olivier) is pressed by his landlady's daughter (Phyllis Konstam) to write a mystery as good as those in the West End. He chooses his characters and his victim from among the boarders, and his story comes to life as he recounts it. When the landlady's daughter says she approves, the playwright confesses he used the plot in a mystery which opened the night before. Olivier, in his American debut, was seen by Atkinson as "offering an alarming suggestion now and then of Alfred Lunt." However, Olivier was still unknown to American playgoers, and the piece survived for a mere six weeks.

Two new plays and one revival vied for attention on a busy Friday night, an unusual night for so many openings. Leo de Valery's **A Comedy of Women** (9-13-29, Craig) was a vanity production which the author also produced and starred in. He wrote himself "some of the longest winded lines ever spieled on any man's stage," in the role of Pierre Preval, a playwright pursued by numerous ladies. He finally elopes with one of them.

Back down in the Village, the same black group which had offered *Salome* now switched to a new work, Mrs. Jeroline Hemsley's **Wade in de Water** (9-13-29, Cherry Lane). Set in Georgia in 1885, it told of a black man who vows vengeance after his wife is lynched and his son kidnapped. Its best scene was said to be a fervent revival meeting at a small church.

Blacks acquitted themselves more notably when *Porgy* was returned for a brief stand at the Martin Beck, with Frank Wilson still as the crippled hero.

The following Monday was also busy, although the only run of any duration (scattered over time in true repertory fashion) went to the Civic Repertory Theatre's mounting of Chekhov's *The Sea Gull*. Eva Le Gallienne was Masha; Josephine Hutchinson, Nina; Merle Maddern, Irina; Jacob Ben Ami, Trigorin; Egon Brecher, Shamraev; and Robert Ross, Konstantin. A majority of critics praised the group's ensemble acting. Later in the week several of the company's older productions were also restored.

The new plays were not so welcomed. The longest run—four weeks—went to S. John Park's "melodramatic satire" **Philadelphia** (9-16-29, Mansfield). Reviewers discerned the melodrama but were at a loss to discover the satire. Young, idealistic Robert

Crawford (Walter Regan) has paid the corrupt John Bradshaw (Jack Motte) $25,000 to become a partner in his firm, unaware of Bradshaw's crookedness or that he has snarled, "College boys are dumb enough to believe in justice and equity." In fact, the play begins with Bradshaw attempting successfully to bribe the D.A. (John A. Bennett) to withhold information at a killer's trial. But after the man is convicted the killer's gang attempt to retrieve the money and shoot Bradshaw when he refuses to hand it over. The police—called "bulls" in the patois of the time—rush in, and more shenanigans follow before Bradshaw pops up and laughingly admits he was only playing dead since a bulletproof vest had protected him. Crawford agrees to defend the man who shot Bradshaw. He also finds romance with a judge's daughter (Eleanor Hayden).

Another dead body was seen on the stage where Howard Irving Young's **Hawk Island** (9-16-29, Longacre) premiered. At his summer home off the New England coast, Gregory Sloane (Clark Gable) is so bored with his guests that he contrives with one of them, Anthony Bryce (Charles Halton), a mystery writer, to arrange a phony murder with the novelist as victim. The plan works swimmingly until the novelist quietly returns after the other guests have gone to sleep. Then he is really shot and killed by the husband (Joseph Ganby) of a woman (Mary Fowler) he has been flirting with. The killer nearly manages to pin the blame on Sloane, using the story that Sloane and the dead man had invented, but he is finally exposed.

No killings enlivened Lee Wilson Dodd's **A Strong Man's House** (9-16-29, Ambassador), though a principal character did die peacefully. That figure was Sam Bannerman (Howard Lang), a crusty old millionaire, who is disillusioned with his weakling son, Roy (Lester Vail), and who has persuaded his nurse, Janet Hale (Mary Nash), to marry the boy. Janet needed little persuading, since she has been out to get hold of the Bannerman money. However, after the wedding Roy proves to have a spine, battling local politicians and setting up a foundation for deprived children. Before long, Janet has come to love her husband. And she remains loyal even after his father's venal associates see to it that Roy is paralyzed in an automobile accident.

The group calling themselves the Provincetown Players abandoned their Village venue and moved uptown to present Michael Gold's **Fiesta** (9-17-27, Garrick). Gold, an editor of *Masses*, had a thesis as well as a play to offer. His thesis seemed to be that the masses must be educated before they can be elevated by social progress. Don Enrique (Carl

Benton Reid), a wealthy caudillo imbued with Tolstoy's teachings, hopes to raise the standards of living of his peons, especially a beautiful, young orphan, Guadalupe (Virginia Venable). But the peasants are more interested in the wild revels at a local fiesta, where even Guadalupe lets herself be seduced by Don Enrique's brother (Jack La Rue). The disillusioned Don Enrique renounces his holdings and heads off to further the revolution.

The season's biggest comedy hit—"a hit and no foolin'," "quick, witty and delicately risque"— Preston Sturges's **Strictly Dishonorable** (9-18-29, Avon) defied the box-office slump to chalk up 557 performances. There are no patrons at Tomaso Antiovi's small speakeasy except for Judge Dempsey (Carl Anthony), who lives in an apartment above the bar. The room's quiet is broken with the arrival of Isabelle Parry (Muriel Kirkland), a lively southern girl, and her petulant fiancé, Henry Greene (Louis Jean Heydt). She is disappointed that he has not been as romantic a beau as she envisaged and, worse, that he insists they live in West Orange, N.J., after their marriage. Another arrival is Gus, Count Di Ruvo (Tullio Carminati), whom Antiovi (William Ricciardi) looks on as a ward, since he had once been a servant of Gus's parents. Gus lives upstairs in another apartment, and he is known to the world as Tino Caraffa, the great opera singer. Before long he has swept Isabelle off her feet and the pair are dancing to a phonograph. This so infuriates Henry that he calls everyone polite names such as Wop and Dago, thereby provoking Isabelle to throw her engagement ring back at him. Henry storms out and returns with an Irish policeman (Edward J. McNamara), but the judge assures his fellow Irishman that nothing is amiss. Gus invites Isabelle to his apartment, confessing his intentions are "strictly dishonorable." There he gives her his line that a singer is no different from a bear trainer. People want to hear him sing or see the trainer's bear perform, but the singer and the trainer remain unloved. The judge, claiming it is his birthday, makes a sudden appearance, hoping to avoid problems. But he need not worry, since Gus is so impressed with Isabelle's loveliness and fundamental innocence that he leaves her in his apartment and spends the night on the judge's couch. The next morning Henry returns, demanding that Isabelle come home with him. He will wait in his car downstairs. Isabelle and Gus meet, spar verbally for a few minutes, then confess their love to each other. However, Gus warns that he must have four sons and seven daughters. Whereupon the judge remarks that under the circumstances, he'll tell Henry not to wait.

A comedy with a more original idea opened on the same evening and got nowhere. **The Crooks' Convention** (9-18-29, Forrest) was by Arthur Somers Roche, a popular novelist of the day. A cynical newspaper editor (Joseph Sweeney) and a crusading evangelist (Stuart Fox) call representatives of all the nation's leading crooks into convention and persuade them to reform. The police have no one to arrest, ministers no souls to save; playwrights lose a popular source of melodrama. To everyone's relief the crooks return to their old trades. Defying George S. Kaufman's aphorism, the satire did not close until its second Saturday night.

Far uptown, at 180th Street and the Boston Post Road, a group calling itself the Bronx Theatre Guild garnered attention when it offered its first production, Michael Artzibashev's Russian drama **War** (9-18-29, Intimate Playhouse). The play followed the disintegration of a happy Russian family under wartime stresses. Further mountings were announced, but if they saw the footlights they were ignored by major reviewers.

Just as playwrights last season had strenuously denied that their dramas were inspired by recent headlines, so Patrick Hamilton, author of the London thriller *Rope*, insisted he had never heard of the Loeb-Leopold case when he wrote his play, which was presented in New York under the slightly altered title of **Rope's End** (9-19-29, Masque). Two young Oxford students (Sebastian Shaw and Ivan Brandt) murder a friend merely for the thrill of it, hide his body in a chest, then invite the boy's relations and another friend to dinner, which they serve on the chest. That friend (Ernest Milton), a crippled youth, finds a stub the dead boy had dropped. Suspecting the horrible truth, he subtly hounds the pair into a confession. Even though one critic complained, "There certainly are a record number of shows with killings in them on Broadway," and saw the entertainment as one of the milder examples, the play found enough of an audience to run 100 performances.

John McGowan's latest play premiered on a Friday night as **Nigger Rich** (9-20-29, Royale), changed its title to *The Big Shot* on Monday, and closed on Saturday. Mike Kelly (Eric Dressler), a war hero, has been sponging off his buddies at the Dugout Club ever since. His friend Gunny (Richard Taber) lends him a few bucks. Mike wins big at the races, moves to the Ritz, and ignores his old comrades. He even steals the girl of his former colonel, a stockbroker who has given him helpful stock tips. In revenge, the group sees to it he is given a bad tip. Mike takes it and loses everything. Broke and ashamed, he makes his insurance over to

Gunny, then kills himself. When the play tried out, its ending had Mike coming into an unexpected inheritance and once again going off on his own selfish ways. But neither ending was helpful. Spencer Tracy, as Mike's tolerant old sergeant, won particular applause for his vigorous performance.

Two novelties raised their curtains the next Monday. Both were quick flops. In John Kirkpatrick's **The Love Expert** (9-23-29, Wallack's), Miss Alice (Helen Holmes), a writer of a column giving advice to the lovelorn, decides to interview Mary Jackson (Natalie Wykes), who has written her asking whether she should marry a loud-mouthed, successful insurance salesman (Owen Cunningham) or a quiet but stupid Italian (William Lovejoy). Miss Alice advises her to marry the salesman, but she has unfortunately brought her own fiancé (Earl McDonald), a theatre reporter, with her. The reporter and Mary fall in love at first sight, leaving Miss Alice to ponder the wisdom of her own behavior.

Philip Dunning, still looking for another drama about nightclub life to repeat the success of *Broadway*, came a cropper with **Sweet Land of Liberty** (9-23-29, Knickerbocker), which survived for one lone week. At the seafood restaurant and speakeasy run by Charlie Hunter (George Barbier), two bootleggers, Jack Richards (Ralph Theadore) and Joe Davis (John Sharkey), are told by a corrupt federal agent (Thomas Coffin Cooke) that payoffs will have to increase by 10 percent. Davis has the agent shot. Hunter agrees to provide Davis's men with alibis, but Richards, determined to quit the racket and go straight, refuses to perjure himself. He is killed by a shot through a skylight. Davis's crooked lawyer (Hermann Lieb), a leading light in the Better Government League, arranges to have an innocent girl framed for the killings and laughs off the whole affair.

Still another critic wailed that "the town is crawling with homicide puzzles," but that did not stop Eva Kay Flint and Martha Madison's **Subway Express** (9-24-29, Liberty) from delighting playgoers for eight months. And that in the face of a huge nut for a cast of more than forty players—all crammed into a superb re-creation of a Seventh Avenue subway car. (Part of the time the setting rocked as lights whisked by during its supposed dash from Times Square to 72nd Street.) Edward Tracy (Jack Lee) and Whitney Borden (Edward Pawley), partners in a brokerage firm, are riding with Mrs. Tracy (Dorothy Peterson) when two drunken Italians attempt to annoy her. Borden and the men fight, the lights go out briefly, and when they return Tracy is seen to have been shot. The police are called.

Learning that Mrs. Tracy and Borden have been lovers, the authorities at first suspect them. Then it is discovered that Tracy had been electrocuted moments before the shot, thus explaining why he didn't join in the fight. The police finally show that Tracy had arranged to have Borden killed, but his accomplice had botched the job, killing Tracy instead. Lee, who had to sit upright and still for most of the evening, won a big hand at the curtain call.

The most successful of the next evening's entries was an English play with another large cast (although here many players assumed several parts) and numerous scene changes. The play was Monckton Hoffe's **Many Waters** (9-25-29, Maxine Elliott's), and it brought Ernest Truex back to New York after a prolonged absence. A producer (Aubrey Dexter) and a playwright (C. Stafford Dickens) argue whether playgoers prefer true-to-life dramas or roseate romances. They ask the opinion of a modest couple (Truex and Marda Vanne), who have come hoping to rent their cottage to the producer for the summer. The playwright is contemptuous of the pair when they say they prefer romance. But then the producer bit by bit elicits the story of their lives and the tragedies of their business failure, their daughter's dying at childbirth, and other misfortunes. No wonder they want escapism. Although some critics regretted the show was "shabbily produced," they saw Truex giving "the most genuine performance of his career" and endowing "insignificance with dignity." The play ran for 110 performances.

A feud between hill folk and valley folk in the Allegheny Mountains of Pennsylvania provided the subject for David Davidson, Jr.'s **Mountain Fury** (9-25-29, President). Myra (Mary Miner) of the hills loves Paul (Herbert Ashton, Jr.), son of the valley sheriff (Carleton Macy), but her father, Ezra (Jack Roseleigh), will not hear of her marrying "a valley rat." The sheriff feels the same way, since Ezra once killed a member of the sheriff's family. Furthermore, Ezra has decided Mary must wed Bill Strunk, a mountain loafer. When Strunk is killed, Paul appears to be the murderer. But then Fenicle (Barry Macollum), an idiot who hears voices in the wind, confesses he is the guilty one and jumps off a cliff. A climactic moment came when Paul and Strunk fight in a cabin, with a forest fire seen blazing outside, followed by a violent thunderstorm which leaves the cabin in darkness. Reports said the young playwright could not attend the opening because he was near death from overwork. Whether or not the rumors were true, he was never heard from again.

Over in Hoboken, the same group that had brought back from the dead both *After Dark* and the old musical *The Black Crook* now offered a new melodrama written in a consciously superannuated style, Thompson Buchanan's **The Star of Bengal** (9-25-29, Lyric). Buchanan's wife, Joan Lowell, who had recently published a controversial book supposedly recounting her adventures at sea, was featured. As Jerry Waite she made her first entrance sliding down a rope from the yardarm of a ship captained by her crusty father (William Carleton). She runs away with Dan (Charles Starrett), a crew member, and the captain vows to find them and hang the boy. For a time Dan proves unfaithful, but Jerry discourages her rival by nearly strangling her. The captain finally locates them and holds a trial aboard ship during which Jerry discloses that she is expecting. The thought of a grandchild mollifies the captain, and Dan is allowed to head for Australia, where he promises to be waiting for Jerry when the ship returns to Sydney.

The latest offering in the Village was Roland Oliver's **Kansas City Kitty** (9-25-29, Gansevoort), "a creaky story, loosely played by an incompetent cast." That story told of Kitty (Evelyn Platt), a dance hall hostess and mistress to "a sheik buyer" (John Negley) at the Kansas City emporium. She falls in love with an executive (Will Claire) who is told he has tuberculosis and must move to Arizona. He responds to Kitty until her connection with the buyer is exposed. Then he walks away alone. Kitty shoots, but does not kill, the sheik, who is gentleman enough to cover for her. She and her new love head out to the desert air.

Although Elmer Rice had written **See Naples and Die** (9-26-29, Vanderbilt) before *Street Scene*, he had been unable to find a producer. With his Pulitzer Prize in his pocket, he persuaded a minor composer, Lewis Gensler, to mount it. Then, as so often happens, things went sour. Rice called the play "an extravagant comedy," but most critics found it merely puzzling, with Atkinson allowing only that "parts are more enjoyable than the whole." Some of the problem was the leading lady, Claudette Colbert, a last-minute miscasting who Rice felt never understood the role. Nanette Dodge has broken her engagement to Charles Carroll (Roger Pryor) and married the blackmailing Prince Ivan (Pedro de Cordoba) to regain possession of incriminating letters. Having obtained the letters, she runs off to find Charles, who is about to marry Kunegunde Wandl (Margaret Knapp Waller). He does not believe Nanette's story, but after the prince is shot dead by revolutionaries, he and Nanette are reconciled. The action was set on the terrace of a pension on the Bay of Naples, where one amusing touch was "the hoof

and patter of a donkey cart with intermittent brays by the donk." The comedy lingered for two months.

Denison Clift's **Scotland Yard** (9-27-29, Sam H. Harris) was alleged to have been banned in England. Dakin Barroles, the greatest thief ever to elude capture by Scotland Yard, has served in the war under the alias Captain John Leigh (Paul Cavanaugh). When his face was severely disfigured a plastic surgeon restored it but unwittingly used a photo of Sir John Usher, the head of the Bank of England. Sir John has been missing in action, so Barroles-Leigh takes his place, hoping to be able to rob the bank in partnership with his old crony, Charles Fox (Gerald McCarthy). But to play his part, Barroles-Leigh must deal with Sir John's wife, Lady Xandra (Phoebe Foster). She is at first a bit suspicious, but the pair are soon genuinely in love. So when the real Sir John reappears, Barroles-Leigh scuttles the robbery. Fox is killed, but an understanding detective sees to it Barroles-Leigh escapes to the Continent.

Winnie Baldwin's **Divided Honors** (9-30-29, Forrest) "added one more murder to the long list of such crimes now being committed on the New York stage." Kenneth Stewart (Guido Nadzo) wakes up one morning with a hangover and a wife, Vina (Glenda Farrell). He naturally is upset since he hoped to marry either Angela (Jane Kim) or Mary (Doris Freeman). Vina accepts the blame after Angela is shot dead, but she is acquitted. However, she leaves since she realizes that Mary is the best woman for Kenneth. Baldwin, a vaudevillian, vainly injected some "slam-bang" two-a-day tricks into the play to give it life, but, like Angela, it was soon dead and buried.

A foreign play fared more happily. **Candle Light** (9-30-29, Empire) was P. G. Wodehouse's redaction of a Siegfried Geyer play sometimes identified as *Kleine Komödie*. Josef (Leslie Howard), valet to Prince Rudolf (Reginald Owen), believing his master away, invites a lady he has admired over to the prince's apartment. He dresses and behaves like the prince to charm the vivacious Marie (Gertrude Lawrence). Then the prince returns unexpectedly. Understanding the situation, he goes along with the farce, even pretending to be the valet. But Marie is unmasked as a parlormaid in disguise. Critics delighted in the light-as-air comedy and in the men's performances, but both praised Miss Lawrence for her comic skills and chided her for her overacting. Her antics—such as substituting real liquor for the weak tea that served as stage liquor—may have upset Howard, who left before the sixteen-week run ended to take a totally different role in another play.

Sophie Treadwell suffered a two-week failure when she abandoned the expressionistic style she had used in *Machinal* and wrote a more commercially minded play, **Ladies Leave** (10-1-29, Charles Hopkins). She almost certainly expected the play still to be running in 1930, the year in which the action was set. Emotionally unsatisfied by her husband (Walter Connolly), a publisher preoccupied with his work, Zizi Powers (Blyth Daly) takes up with one of his editors (Henry Hull). Powers finds out, but Zizi, having been told by a visiting Viennese alienist (Charles Trowbridge) that her supposed immorality has a logical morality to it, drops both husband and lover to head for more treatment in Vienna.

Only the dwindling ranks of seventy-one-year-old Otis Skinner's admirers sustained the five-week run of **A Hundred Years Old** (10-1-29, Lyceum), which Helen and Harley Granville Barker had taken from Serafín and Joaquín Álvarez Quintero's *Papa Juan*, and in which Skinner had toured around the country the previous season. The "drowsy" play was adramatic, telling of Papa Juan's celebrating his centennial and arranging the marriage of his great-great-grandson (Hardie Albright). As usual, Skinner gave a lushly rich performance.

To many critics Martin Flavin came near fulfilling his earlier promise with **The Criminal Code** (10-2-29, National). Burns Mantle hailed it as "a thoughtful study, not only of our methods of prison conduct and corrective punishments, but also of the normal reactions, of both prisoners and keepers, to the law, to the system, and to their respective codes." A normally mild-mannered brokerage clerk, Robert Graham (Russell Hardie), is convicted by the state's attorney, Martin Brady (Arthur Byron), for a murder which the boy insists was self-defense. Brady, who is not without a certain sympathy for the boy but is politically ambitious, tells him, " 'An eye for an eye,' That's the basis and foundation of our criminal code." Six years pass. Graham, though a model prisoner, is broken in spirit. Brady's daughter, Mary (Anita Kerry), works at the prison. Having become fond of Graham, she prevails on her father to arrange a parole. But when another prisoner is killed, Graham, who has witnessed the killing, holds to the prison code that one convict will not tell on another. Just before his parole is to take effect, a cruel prison guard attempts to beat Graham, who kills him. Now there is nothing Brady can do for the boy. "It's just the way things break sometimes," a stunned Brady tells Mary. The play ran five months.

A number of failures followed. Vincent Lawrence's **Among the Married** (10-3-29, Bijou) focused on Ethel Mills (Katherine Wilson), who has repressed her feelings for Bill Minot (Edward Leiter), an attractive golf champion. Then she discovers her husband (Frank Morgan) in the embrace of her best friend (Peggy Allenby), who had been Minot's paramour. She turns at first to Minot, but then is reconciled with her husband on the understanding that they will have no double standard.

For the second time in just over a week, Pennsylvania backwaters provided the setting for a play, only this time the country was opposed to the small town. In Marie Baumer's **Town Boy** (10-4-29, Belmont), Molly Keck (Ruth Easton) brings Charlie Brownwell (Tom Douglas) home to meet her country folk. He is ill at ease, especially in the presence of Molly's husky, belligerent old flame, Ben Davis (Ralph Bellamy). Hoping to scare off Charlie, Ben provokes a fistfight and savagely bests his rival. But Molly admires the bloodied Charlie's spunk, so she sends Ben packing.

Four plays, including two importations, opened on October's first Monday night. Wall Spence's **The House of Fear** (10-7-29, Republic) was a clichéd mystery thriller, redeemed in small measure by the playing of two veteran ladies. Learning that her son has escaped from prison, where he had been sent for a murder he did not commit, Madame Zita (Effie Shannon) arranges for a seance and there unmasks the real killer. Voices and skeletons with a phosphorescent glow came from out of nowhere, hands protruded from walls, panels slid open to reveal secret passages, and bodies appeared and disappeared. Along with Miss Shannon, Cecil Spooner, who once had been a star of cheap touring melodramas when her husband, Charles A. Blaney, had run a circuit for them, and who one critic remembered as "the Bernhardt" of that bygone genre, was prominent, playing a wisecracking actress.

A. E. Thomas and Harrison Rhodes's **Her Friend the King** (10-7-29, Longacre) starred another fading oldtimer, the still slim and handsome William Faversham. Georges, the exiled king of Constantia-Felix, and his daughter, Princess Lydia (Katherine Kohler), find romance in Switzerland, he with a vivacious American widow (Ara Gerald) and she with a prince (Hugh Sinclair) who is traveling incognito.

The more interesting of the importations was the Theatre Guild's mounting of **Karl and Anna** (10-7-29, Guild), which Ruth Langner translated from Leonhard Frank's play. An atmospheric Jo Mielziner setting opened the show, depicting a Russian prisoner-of-war camp with a rude hut and, behind it, a wall topped with barbed wire. Ominous shadows of sentries moved now and then across the wall. Karl (Otto Kruger) and Richard (Frank Conroy) are German captives held in the camp. Richard has spoken lovingly of his wife, Anna (Alice Brady), so when Karl escapes he seeks Anna out and claims he is Richard, much changed by his cruel confinement. She does not believe him, but the two fall in love anyway. In time she has a child by him. Richard returns, and though Anna dissuades Karl from killing Richard, she and Karl go off together.

Claude Anet was credited with anglicizing his own play **Mademoiselle Bourrat** (10-7-29, Civic Repertory), in which a convent-trained innocent (Josephine Hutchinson) brings shame upon her horrified, intolerant family by having a child out of wedlock. She is finally married off to a local piano teacher (Harold Moulton), who, it turns out, may just have royal blood in him. The play was one of the Civic Repertory's least successful endeavors.

Margaret Ayer Barnes and Edward Sheldon were the authors of Jane Cowl's latest vehicle, **Jenny** (10-8-29, Booth). While taking a walk in Connecticut, Jenny Valentine, a famous actress, stumbles across a beautiful rose garden. The garden is the pride of John R. Weatherby (Guy Standing), and also his refuge from his mercenary, unloving family. Before long she invites him to her cabin in the Canadian woods. After their idyll, they return to Connecticut, where Jenny gives John's family a piece of her mind, then stalks out. John hesitates just long enough for a suspenseful curtain before following her. Thanks largely to the lovely, soulful-eyed Jane Cowl, the play lasted for 111 performances.

A far better play ran out the season. Robert Littel of the *World* called Ring Lardner and George S. Kaufman's **June Moon** (10-9-29, Broadhurst) "a lively show that gave *Tin Pan Alley* . . . a rich and merciless kidding." Fred Stevens (Norman Foster) gives up his job as a shipping clerk in Schenectady to try his luck as a Tin Pan Alley lyricist. His qualifications are dubious, since his speech swims in double negatives and his ignorance is evident in his reference to "a blue search [suit], with a hair-bone strip." Nonetheless he hits it big when Paul Sears (Frank Otto), who has been living off the meager royalties of his song "Paprika," puts music to Fred's lyric for "June Moon." Actually, Paul is no great shakes himself; his wife, Lucille (Jean Dixon), insists he plays the piano with ten thumbs. Success goes to Fred's head, and he drops the sweet little girl, Edna Baker (Linda Watkins), whom he met on the train from upstate, in favor of Paul's rapacious sister-in-law, Eileen (Lee Patrick). Eileen not only persuades Lucille to have a fling of her own, but she promptly

sets out to live beyond Fred's means. Just as Fred is ready to leave with Eileen for Europe—he has tickets booked optimistically as Mr. Frederick M. Stevens and wife—his eyes are opened by a caustic pianist, Maxie (Harry Rosenthal). Fred asks Maxie if the steamship line would mind his changing wives. Maxie assures him there will be no problem, "If you don't do it in midstream."

Two very short-lived duds came in the next evening. Louis Weitzenkorn's **First Mortgage** (10-10-29, Broadhurst) lasted half a week. Elmer Gray (Walter Abel) has no end of problems with his new, heavily mortgaged home in Pleasant Lawns, a place he refers to as Belly Acres. His wife (Beatrice Hendricks) goes back to mother to have her child, and he has a mildly comfortable little fling with Grace Turner (Leona Maricle), a neighbor. Learning that his newborn child has died to top everything off, Elmer burns down his house. His father (Dodson Mitchell) promptly offers to build a new one for him. The best that Elmer can hope for is to reestablish his relationship with Grace.

Ladies Don't Lie (10-10-29, Gallo), which Herman Bernstein took from an unidentified play by Paul Frank, survived only a week and a half, although it was offered at bargain prices—$2 to fifty cents—as part of a projected program of cheap attractions. It narrated the saga of three men who have found refuge from women in an isolated villa. But the woman (Spring Byington) whose plane crashes on the estate proves to be the ex-wife of two of the men and the supposed fiancée of the third. She gives them all a hard time before flying off with her new love, her pilot.

Although Chicago had embraced John C. Brownell's **The Nut Farm** (10-14-29, Biltmore), New York, as was so often its wont with Chicago hits, had little time for the comedy. The newly rich Bartons head from New Jersey to California, where they hope to start a nut farm. But Helen Bent (Natalie Schafer), the family's married daughter, comes under the influence of a baleful film producer (Edward Keane), who gets her to fork up much of the family fortune so that she can star in his latest tearjerker. The picture is a disaster until her kid brother, Willie "Boob" Barton (Wallace Ford), reworks the whole affair as a farce (shades of *Merton of the Movies*).

Jacinto Benavente's *Bonds of Interest* had failed when the fledgling Theatre Guild mounted it ten years earlier, and it failed again when Walter Hampden attempted a reconsideration the same night at the Hampden.

The New York Theatre Assembly, one of the

many groups formed during the decade in hopes of emulating the ways and success of the Theatre Guild, began its short life—seven plays in about one year's time—with Fanny Heaslip Lea's **Lolly** (10-16-29, Assembly). In a show of confidence, the company leased the famous little Princess Theatre and renamed it after itself. Lea, at the time a well-known magazine writer, recounted the adventures of a widowed southern belle (Mary Young) who had become a modern dancing mother, courted by a dashing Spanish gigolo (Albert Carillo). Her old-fashioned, girl-scoutish daughter (Elinor Bedford) tries to rectify matters, but they are not truly set aright until the reappearance of the man (Hugh Miller) whom the widow had loved and even had a fling with after the unwanted marriage she had made under parental pressure. The man is shown to be the daughter's real father.

A popular London farce, Ian Hay and Stephen King-Hall's **The Middle Watch** (10-16-29, Times Square), found few takers in New York, who had approved similar plots long ago. Two ladies go on board a navy cruiser to visit their fiancés, and the ship hurriedly leaves port with them still aboard, leading to numerous comic complications.

Alexander Woollcott and George S. Kaufman, on paper a delicious combination, received a cool response to their dramatization of Guy de Maupassant's *Boule de suif* as **The Channel Road** (10-17-29, Plymouth). During the Franco-Prussian War, a diligence arrives at a roadside inn carrying some haughty aristocrats and nuns who look down on their fellow traveler, a prostitute (Anne Forrest). Her patriotism and sense of honor compel her to rebuff the advances of the Prussian officer (Siegfried Rumann) in charge of the local army of occupation until her fear that her refusal could lead to reprisals against the other travelers softens her stance. She receives no gratitude from them for her sacrifice. Given Kaufman's sharp wit and Woollcott's delightful writing manner, the dismaying surprise of the evening was what John Mason Brown of the *Post* slammed as "reams of high-faluting dialogue" and Atkinson decried as "the fulsome literary style in which it is written, or rather overwritten."

J. W. Von Barre and Paul Krafft's **Deep Channels** (10-18-29, Waldorf), a dreadfully bad play with "a cast of misfits," was rushed in to fill a sudden booking gap but kept the house lit for only four performances. Its story depicted an affair between a sheltered, aristocratic girl and her family groom, which leads to the suicide of the groom's fiancée and her forced marriage to a neighborhood doctor.

The next Monday brought in six straight plays—three novelties and three revivals. The best of the novelties clearly was Fred Ballard's **Ladies of the Jury** (10-21-29, Erlanger). Ballard had been one of George Pierce Baker's most promising students and had been praised for early successes such as *Young America*. That play had included a superior trial scene, and his new work, which was designed as pure entertainment with no pretensions to greatness, began with another such scene. But its main interest centered on what happened in the jury room afterwards. A young and beautiful French wife (Germaine Giroux) is on trial for murdering her rich American husband. The jury is a cross-section of New Jerseyites. When they assemble to decide her fate, the first vote is eleven for conviction and one for acquittal. That lone holdout is an obstinate matron, Mrs. Livingston Baldwin Crane (Mrs. Fiske). "My instincts prove it," she tells the others. They are outraged, wanting only to convict the woman and get home. But Mrs. Crane persists; by cajoling, blackmailing, and any other means that comes to mind, she sets out to convert the panel one at a time. Thus, when a sour spinster (Clare Grenville) says all French women are bad women, Mrs. Crane comes to the defense of French ladies, thereby winning over the vote of a juror (Walter Kinsella) married to a French girl. When the spinster and the cold, narrow-minded head of the jury (George Farren) demean actresses, Mrs. Crane praises theatrical ladies and wins the vote of a former chorus girl (Hallie Manning). At sunrise two days later, only the spinster and the head of the jury are holding out for conviction. Tired and on edge, the man attacks one of the women. Mrs. Fiske cleverly covers for him, winning the last two reluctant votes. As the curtain slowly descends she embarks on a long speech congratulating her colleagues for their bravery and patience. Many of her own colleagues concurred with Alison Smith of the *World*, who lauded the play as "the most unabashed and delirious of farces," but the real paeans were reserved for the star. Charles Darnton of the *Evening World* hailed her as "Queen of our stage," Robert Garland in the *Telegram* as "The Great Lady of the Theatre," while Mantle cooed, "No one has the craft of this great planet among the stars—the richness of her comedy and the matchless pattern of her playing. . . . She is incalculable and altogether peerless." Also praised was another aging, onetime star, Wilton Lackaye, who played the judge in Act I. Unfortunately for the play, the stock market began to tumble alarmingly during the week and collapsed completely eight days after the show opened. The comedy was removed after less than three months.

The major disappointment of the night, and one of the big disappointments of the season, was George Kelly's **Maggie the Magnificent** (10-21-29, Cort), a tediously mundane drama. Critics and playgoers could not foresee that Kelly had shot his bolt and that the brilliant Pulitzer Prize–winning playwright of the twenties never again would have a major success. Maggie (Shirley Warde) is the shining light in a family of mediocrities, perhaps because she inherited the genes of her late father, who crossed her slatternly mother's path only briefly. She eventually leaves her home to live with a rich family for whom she has worked but does effect a reconciliation of sorts with her mother (Marion S. Barney). Stealing the show as Maggie's bootlegging son and his rather loose, vulgarly acquisitive wife were two figures who would find success in Hollywood, James Cagney and Joan Blondell.

If *Maggie the Magnificent* was condemned for the dreary everydayness of its writing, Jane Murfin's **Stripped** (10-21-29, Ambassador) was assailed for its wooden stiffness. Lazov (Lionel Atwill), who is thought to be a prince in exile, is embarrassed when the jewels he sells are found to be paste. It develops that the fakes were substituted by a woman (Thelma Hardwick) who is the mistress of the husband (Vernon Kelso) of Lazov's own mistress (Jessie Royce Landis). Lazov himself is exposed as a fake, a mere pretender, but that does not prevent him and his mistress from planning marriage after she obtains a divorce.

The evening's revivals, none of which ran longer than two weeks, were *Abraham Lincoln* at the Forrest, with Frank McGlynn recreating his great role; *A Tailor-Made Man* at the Gallo, with Grant Mitchell again in the title part; and the more recent *Harlem* at the Eltinge.

Two more quick failures appeared next. Austin Parker's **Week-End** (10-22-29, John Golden) was set in the home of some idle rich expatriates in Barbizon, France. Skip Penney (Grant Mills) has married Clare (Margaret Mower) for her money. Their weekend guests include Skip's wartime buddy, Brett Laney (Warren William), who writes short stories and dreams of writing a great novel, Marga (Vivienne Osborne), a girl both men once courted, and Marga's hopelessly inebriate husband (Hugh O'Connell). When Marga and Skip are caught in a tryst, Marga's husband shoots himself, and Clare thinks about leaving Skip. Marga and Brett suggest they might marry after a suitable period of mourning. O'Connell won the best notices for playing another of the drunkards he did so well.

Maurice Clark's **Button, Button** (10-23-29, Bijou)

focused on Button Woodhouse (Lynne Overman), who has been in and out of mental institutions. Brought home to live with his brother, he finds that his family and friends are as kooky as he is—"a golf fanatic, an antique furniture fanatic . . . and a scrappy female bard who sings passionately of an old horse coming out of his stable in the Spring." He makes them see they are all as eccentric as he is and elopes with an understanding young lady.

A group calling itself the Irish Theatre, Inc., took over the Greenwich Village Theatre, rechristened it, and offered Sean O'Casey's **The Silver Tassie** (10-24-29, Irish). Before the war, Harry Heegan (Sherling Oliver) had helped his football team win a silver tassie, but now, returning home a cripple, he must watch as a rival steals his girl and his old teammates ignore him. O'Casey abandoned his earlier realism for a stab at expressionism: "While the guns are thundering in the background, the soldiers in the trenches chant, sing, mock in unison and speak in series the clipped sentences peculiar to this subjective style of writing." The play survived for seven weeks.

Another importation lasted less than two weeks. **The Booster** (10-24-29, Nora Bayes) was Nat Reid's adaptation of an unidentified Viennese comedy by Louis Nertz and Armin Friedmann. It suggested that Jewish life in Vienna was not much different from Jewish life in New York. Two fathers work behind the scenes and up front to bring about the marriage of their son and daughter and to see that the son becomes a successful doctor. For nearly three acts the plans go awry, but finally pan out.

October's last arrival was another soon gone work, Hadley Waters's **The Ghost Parade** (10-28-29, Lyric). Set in a dilapidating temple in India, it told of the ruses Major Gilbert Ainslee (Oswald Marshall) employed to hide his smuggling of weapons to rebellious natives. A green spectral face appeared out of nowhere, an empty nightgown flew over the audience, and ghostly noises were common. None of this daunts Suma Singhi (Clarence Derwent), who exposes the smuggling and reveals himself as a British operative.

The first Monday after the Wall Street debacle, three hastily removed American novelties and one Anglo-American gem opened. The Anglo-American work was **Berkeley Square** (11-4-29, Lyceum). Its author was American-born John L. Balderston, who spent his playwriting years in London, where this play was first produced. Peter Standish (Leslie Howard) comes to London in 1784 to wed Kate Pettigrew (Valerie Taylor). A hundred and forty years later his descendant, another Peter Standish (Howard), having read all his ancestor's diaries and correspondence, feels he could have exchanged places with the earlier Peter. He is transported back in time, but the transition proves awkward. His special knowledge often trips him into giving away future events. More urgently, he dislikes the sharp-tongued Kate, preferring her sister, Helen (Margalo Gillmore). His discomfort wafts him back to the present, where he learns from a tombstone that Helen died just after he left the past. He tells his modern sweetheart that he has decided to remain a bachelor, and she leaves him while he reads the inscription he copied from Helen's grave. Welcomed by Heywood Broun in the *Telegram* as "easily the finest play now to be seen in New York," it ran out the season, aided immeasurably by Leslie Howard and Margalo Gillmore's "limpid acting."

The faded matinee idol Lou Tellegen was never known for limpid acting. Indeed, when he took the part of a Spanish swaggerer in Le Roy Clemens and Ralph Murphy's **Cortez** (11-4-29, Mansfield), he was ridiculed for his posturing and his absurdly un-Spanish Spanish accent. Don Hernando Cortez rescues an American movie company from Mexican bandits, only to kidnap its leading lady (Helen Baxter) and take her to his mansion. She feigns a love she does not feel for him, so he consents to return with her to Hollywood. There he suprisingly finds himself courted by film makers as a new Valentino, but having gotten the lady to genuinely love him, he heads off with her to his castle in Spain.

In Robert W. Lillard's **White Flame** (11-4-29, Vanderbilt) Don Marlowe (Kenneth Harlan), after two unsatisfactory marriages, still cannot see the love that burns like a white flame in the heart of a girl (Sydney Shields) who was raised as his sister but really was no relation. It takes his young son (Warren MacCallum) to enlighten him.

The evening's most dismissive notices were handed to D. Frank Marcus's **Make Me Know It** (11-4-29, Wallack's), in which Bulge Bannon (A. B. Comathiere), a political boss in a heavily black district, attempts to get rid of his rivals by nominating a black candidate. Marcus also took credit for the songs employed in a wild party scene.

Because first-stringers elected to attend Florenz Ziegfeld's mounting of Noel Coward's operetta *Bitter-Sweet*, Martin Flavin's second offering of the season (he would have a third a week later), **Broken Dishes** (11-5-29, Ritz), received the attention of lesser aisle-sitters. But their praises—"a clean, wholesome, charming little comedy packed with laughs," "hilarious and touching"—gave Flavin his second successive hit, its 178 performances outrun-

ning Ziegfeld's show. The harridan Mrs. Bumpstead (Eda Heinemann) has turned her two eldest daughters into mean spinsters and does everything she can to humiliate her husband (Donald Meek), who has been a mere clerk for thirty years. She refuses to keep his dinner warm when he has to remain late at the store, telling her daughters that he always has been late: "He was late to his own wedding, but— *(she sighs)*—he finally did get there, more's the pity." And she is constantly throwing up to him that she could have married rich, handsome Chet Armstrong. Only her youngest daughter, Elaine (Bette Davis), sides with her father. When the others go to the movies, she stays home with him to help clean the dishes—and to see her beau, Bill Clark (Reed Brown, Jr.). Bill comes before Mrs. Bumpstead has left, and she orders him never to see Elaine again. This so angers Elaine that she agrees to marry Bill at once. Her father, who unwittingly has managed to get tipsy on some hard cider, timidly acquiesces. Elaine brings the preacher (J. Francis-Robertson) from next door, while Mr. Bumpstead's buddy, a funeral director (Art Smith), agrees to play the organ. Never mind that the only song he knows is "Nearer My God to Thee." There is an unexpected witness at the wedding, for, of all people, Chet Armstrong (Duncan Penwarden) turns up. But so do the police, who have been hunting him for a long list of crimes. Chet flees out the window. Mrs. Bumpstead returns to find her daughter married and the dishes not yet done. But there isn't much she can say after Elaine reveals the truth about Armstrong and Mr. Bumpstead defiantly smokes a cigar as a token of his newfound mastery. Elaine tells her father that he is wonderful. His reaction is "Shucks!" The small, balding Meek, with "his nervous, frightened gestures, his apologetic geniality, his responsiveness to a pleasant word and his desire to be a doormat," walked off with acting honors.

Only a return of *Caponsacchi* at the Hampden on the same evening came between *Broken Dishes* and Flavin's next play, and his only failure of the season, **Cross Roads** (11-11-29, Morosco). Robert Edmond Jones's settings included a fraternity house, an equally spartan sorority house, and, to begin and end the play, a huge, elegantly curved stone memorial bench—which ran the length of the stage and dwarfed the players—topped by lilac bushes in bloom. Pat (Sylvia Sidney), a pretty co-ed, waiting for her beau, Mike (Eric Dressler), is approached by a campus roué, Duke (Franchot Tone), who asks her to go riding with him in the new Packard roadster his father has given him. She refuses and walks away. Mike appears with an older friend and confesses he wants to quit his pre-med studies to marry Pat. Since you cannot have your cake and eat it too, Mike prefers to eat it. But when Pat comes back she tells Mike that she insists they both finish their education. In a huff, Mike goes off with a waitress (Peggy Shannon) from a local greasy spoon. The next morning his friends learn that he and the girl were arrested in a police raid on a roadhouse. Her father (Herbert Heywood) attempts to shake down Mike. And Pat, learning of what happened, goes out for a ride with Duke. But Duke is drunk, drives too fast, and is killed when the car goes out of control. Pat is uninjured. She and Mike meet at the stone bench, and when they make up, Mike insists, "Nothing can hurt us while we have each other." Although most critics agreed with the reviewer in the *Sun* that the play had "moments of great beauty," they felt the better moments did not add up to a compelling drama.

There were few kind words for a British play, Robins Millar's **Thunder in the Air** (11-11-29, 49th St.). The specter of a dead soldier (Robert Haslam) returns to allow his family and friends to remember him. Most do not remember him kindly. But he finally confesses that his shame at his behavior prompted him to go on a suicide mission.

All of the next evening's entries flopped. Hugh Stange's **Veneer** (11-12-29, Sam H. Harris) spotlighted the caddish, self-promoting Charlie Riggs (Henry Hull), who talks a lovely, generous girl, Allie Smith (Joanna Roos), into living with him, even though she sees through him. She hopes she can change his ways. Before long she is pregnant. When he becomes bored, Charlie returns to Maysie Brady (Jeanne Greene), whom he had once promised the world, then jilted. She now strings him along, then vengefully gives him the boot. Going back to Allie, he finds her on the bed where she has killed herself. The play employed a revolving stage to move from one of its many scenes to the next—a dance hall, the public library, a Hudson River day boat, a Coney Island pavilion, a Chinese restaurant, an apartment. The entire play was performed behind a scrim which was flooded with blue light during the scene changes.

Several critics complained that they could not make heads or tails of the motivations of Walter Hackett's **Other Men's Wives** (11-12-29, Times Square). A highborn woman (Claiborne Foster) takes a job at a French inn in order to buy back her sister's jewels before her brother-in-law discovers them missing. But she voluntarily changes places with a flighty wife (Dorothy Hall) who is eloping with a young bachelor (Hugh Sinclair). By evening's end, the highborn lady and the bachelor are in love.

Louise Fox Connell and Ruth Hawthorne collaborated on **Queen Bee** (11-12-29, Belmont). Their title figure was Janice Blake (Gertrude Bryan), an imperious woman who gleefully destroys the engagement of her sister (Eleanor Phelps), then attempts to have an affair with the best friend (Brian Donlevy) of her husband (Ian Keith). All three walk out on her. Donlevy redeemed an otherwise dull evening with a superb drunk scene.

Thomas H. Dickinson's **Winter Bound** (11-12-29, Garrick) told of a woman, Tony Ambler (Aline MacMahon), who persuades Emily Fullbright (Marie Goff) to live with her on her Connecticut farm and eschew the company of men. But Emily eventually runs off with a neighboring farmer (Willard Robertson). After a young man (Richard Abbott) who adores Tony, although she refuses to offer him any encouragement, is killed in a train accident, she heads off to an uncertain future. MacMahon dressed and acted somewhat mannishly, leading some critics to suggest the play dealt with lesbianism, a point the professorial author denied.

August Strindberg's **The Pelican** (11-13-29, MacDougal St.), in a translation by Hans Alin and Raymond Jamieson, told of a selfish, heartless woman whose affair with her son-in-law drives her husband to suicide and destroys her family.

Howard Lindsay and Bertrand Robinson just missed the charmed 100-performance circle with **Your Uncle Dudley** (11-18-29, Cort). Dudley (Walter Connolly) looks to be a confirmed bachelor, so interested in civic improvement that he neglects his own business and social life. To make matters worse, he is under the thumb of his poisonously domineering sister (Beatrice Terry). To be rid of her, he helps her daughter (Eleanor Hayden) marry the boy her mother opposes, restores his business finances, then weds a Swedish beauty (Ellen Southbrook).

A single exciting scene was not enough to save Paul Osborn's **A Ledge** (11-18-29, Assembly), taken from a short story by Henry Holt. Richard Legrange (Leonard Mudie) is wrongly accused of stealing bonds from his law firm. The bonds were actually stolen by Geoffry Clarke (Gage Clarke), who hopes to use them when he elopes with the unhappy wife (Marguerite Borough) of the firm's aging head lawyer (Augustin Duncan). In a trial by terror, the partners order Legrange to walk along the ledge outside their twentieth story office. If he succeeds they will deem him innocent; if he falls they will announce his suicide. With the lights of advertising signs glowing in the distance, Legrange makes the passage. He also wins the affection of the unhappy wife, who realizes what a scoundrel her lover is.

Epilogue: 1928–1930

ng husband was the center of attrac-
'Hurlbut's farce **A Primer for Lovers**
acre). At a house party, Elkin
ert Warwick), a prosperous iron-
to have an affair with Marguerite
(Rose Hobart). But Marguerite accidentally
takes sleeping pills, so in her darkened room, Lucy
Elliott (Ann Mason), who has a crush on Elkin,
assumes her place. Learning the next morning of the
switch, Elkin exclaims, "But these things don't
happen outside of Boccaccio!"

Aurania Rouverol, who mined gold with her
Hardy family in *Skidding*, struck a much smaller lode
with **It Never Rains** (11-19-29, Republic). Just outside
Los Angeles, Henry Rogers stays one jump ahead of
the sheriff until he sells part of his property to Walter
Donovan (Phil Kelly), a friend from the East. But the
friendship sours when the deal appears to be illegal.
All is made well after the deal is shown to be proper.
Roger's son (Carl J. Julius) and Donovan's daughter
(Sidney Fox) hit it off, and the land's value skyrockets
on being rezoned for commercial use.

But there was no gold for Daniel N. Rubin's
Claire Adams (11-19-29, Biltmore). Claire (Mildred
MacLeod), having to choose between a struggling
reporter, Gene Adams (Charles Starrett), and a rich
man, Clyde Price (Buford Armitage), selects Gene.
Later, bored and unhappy with Gene's failure to rise
in the world, she runs off with Clyde, who soon
ditches her. Taking up with a distant cousin, Ted
Roper (Charles Ritchie), Claire persuades him to
kill Clyde. When the two are led off to jail, it falls to
Gene to phone the story in to his paper.

Admirers of St. John Ervine headed down to the
Village to see a play of his which was tried out last
season but, having failed, was left to an art group to
stage for New York. **The Ship** (11-20-29, Gansevoort) described the tug of war between John
Thurlow (Richard Ceough), a shipbuilder who
wants his son, Jack (John Koch), to follow in his
trade, and the young man, who hates the mecha-
nized world and longs to be a simple farmer. A
sensible grandmother (Margaret Wycherly) persuades the father to let the son select his own
occupation. But shortly before the builder's finest
vessel is ready, he falls sick. Jack agrees to sail it on
the maiden voyage. The ship is lost and Jack along
with it.

The only play to run out the season among the
next Monday's crop of openings had to thumb its
nose at a host of critical rejections to do so. David
Freedman theatricalized **Mendel, Inc.** (11-25-29,
Sam H. Harris) from his own novel *Mendel
Marantz*. Mendel (Alexander Carr) is a shiftless

Hester Street Jew, content to let his wife (Lisa
Silbert) be the breadwinner and his daughter (Helen
Dumas) help with loans from her own meager
earnings. After all, why should he move from the
East Side, "the only place in New York where you
can bargain for a price and never hit bottom"? Of
course, when he makes a million with the do-it-all
housecleaner he is inventing, matters will be different. Since this was a comedy, he finally does hit
paydirt. For many, the evening peaked with the
performance of a pair of vaudeville favorites, Joe
Smith and Charlie Dale, as Schnaps and Shtrudel,
two men always ready to buy goods from bankrupts.

Neither Cissie Loftus nor William Courtleigh,
players reared in an older school of performing,
would seem the logical casting for Boyd Smith's
modern, but apparently inane folk play, **The Patriarch** (11-25-29, 49th St.). It was the sort of piece in
which one character observes, "Wa-al, God He has
a-provided a mighty fine de-ay this yere de-ay."
Courtleigh played a revered old mountaineer, regularly called on to dispense justice in the Alleghenies
(the year's third play with the setting). When he
must sit in judgment on his own son, who has killed
another of his sons in a fight over a girl, he has no
choice but to condemn the boy to death. The
condemned youngster warns him, "Mother will fret
a lot." Mother, of course, was Loftus.

The principal players in the Theatre Guild's
mounting of Romain Rolland's **The Game of Love
and Death** (11-25-29, Guild), which Eleanor Stimson
Brooks adapted, had all been seen a few weeks
before in the company's *Karl and Anna*. The new
play told of a Girondist (Frank Conroy) who
discovers his wife (Alice Brady) is harboring a
revolutionary (Otto Kruger), a man she loves. When
a sympathetic member (Claude Rains) of the new
government gives the Girondist and his wife passports to escape, the husband self-sacrificingly surren-
ders them to his wife and her lover. This time Miss
Brady did not walk away with the best notices,
which went to Rains for his study of a man torn
between revolutionary ideals and simple human
compassion. Like its predecessor, it was not among
the Guild's better-received offerings. One critic
reported overhearing a woman say she wished she
could have fallen asleep like the man next to her
had.

Cissie Loftus and William Courtleigh were not the
only oldtimers to appear before the footlights that
evening. At seventy-four, William Gillette came out
of an eight-year retirement to give his public what it
wanted—*Sherlock Holmes*. The play began a limited engagement at the New Amsterdam on the 25th

as part of an extended cross-country tour. The production was odd in some ways. It constantly mixed canvases painted in a bygone manner with modern lighting and garbed all the players except Gillette in modern dress. Gillette's style, which once had been so daringly modern in its succinct, crisp underplaying, now seemed exactly right for a slightly musty melodrama performed only slightly tongue in cheek. Critics admitted that they could easily spot the play's creaky theatrical devices but, virtually to a man, confessed that they had a marvelous time.

Many critics also had a marvelous time at John Golden's production of Dan Jarrett's **Salt Water** (11-26-29, John Golden), yet too few playgoers lined up at the box office to turn the play into a hit. It closed after eleven weeks. The work could be perceived as a comic variation of Ervine's story for *The Ship*. John Horner (Frank Craven) of Snag Harbor, Long Island, always has wanted to follow in the footsteps of his seafaring father and grandfather. His wife (Edythe Elliott) has opposed his plans, so he secretly has dickered to use their $5000 savings to purchase a rusty freighter. Then, through the window of his cottage, he watches a local ferry hit the town pier and sink. "Before going down, the prop ferry passed back and forth in a jerky manner, as though it wanted to do a buck dance, as it may have in vaude." John then learns that his wife got to their savings first and had purchased the ferry. They are responsible for the humungous damage to the pier. But an insurance payment saves the day, and John agrees to captain the new ferry they will buy with some of the cash. The play had started life, as *Variety*'s allusion hints, as a vaudeville sketch called *Just a Pal* and still retained two-a-day gags such as "You may have been bred in Kentucky, but you're only a crumb around here."

Booth Tarkington and Harry Leon Wilson were only able to eke out an eight-week run with a play they pulled from their trunk, **How's Your Health?** (11-26-29, Vanderbilt). Dr. Pepper (Donald Brian) and his buddy, Sam Catterson (Herbert Corthell), have found amusement in the doctor's regularly prescribing sugared water for the preposterously hypochondriacal Lawrence Satterleigh (Roy Atwell). They take the wheelchair-bound patient to a party where he alarms the other guests by suggesting they show dangerous symptoms. Then Pepper tests on himself some new medicine which he discovers Satterleigh has obtained on the sly. He becomes frighteningly ill, while Catterson, finding his own blood pressure is wildly high, panics. Shortly thereafter, the men learn that the medicine was nothing but sage tea and the pressure indicator on the blink.

Meanwhile Satterleigh has come across a beautiful girl (Virginia O'Brien), whose face and figure are all the tonic he needs to abandon his wheelchair.

Broadway had no time for Charles Kenyon's **Top o' the Hill** (11-26-29, Eltinge). Nearly twenty years earlier Kenyon had written the critically admired but unsuccessful *Kindling* and since that time had largely frittered away his talent writing for silent films. His new title was something of a pun, since the action occurred in a fashionable hotel on Nob Hill and dealt with a leading Hollywood star. Sally Lawrence (Claudia Morgan) earns $7000 a week from her studio and is engaged to be married to a young socialite (Lester Vail). Then an old admirer (Charles D. Brown), who knew her when, threatens that if she won't become his mistress he will reveal that she once was Maisie Ryan and a prostitute. She refuses; he exposes her, but her fiancé could not care less.

Broadway also had no time for Max Marcin's **The Humbug** (11-27-29, Lyric), although Marcin had remained loyal to live theatre. His principal figure was Dr. Alexis Collender (John Halliday), a devious physician who employs his gift for hypnotism to seduce women. Now he hopes not only to make love to his latest victims, the wife and fiancée of two of his fellow doctors, but to use them to goad their men into furthering his petition for admission to a learned society. One of the men (King Calder), catching on to Collender's game, pretends to allow himself to be mesmerized, then, when the doctor orders him to shoot, shoots and kills Collender.

Elmer Harris's **Young Sinners** (11-28-29, Morosco), like *Mendel, Inc.*, which had opened three nights earlier, overrode a critical drubbing to play out the season. It was another look at the independence of the era's flaming youth. Seventeen-year-old Constance Sinclair (Dorothy Appleby) is a dissatisfied daughter of the ultra rich who is about to be married off to a stuffy German baron by her title-mad mother (Hilda Spong) although she loves Gene Gibson (Raymond Guion). Gibson, a ne'er-do-well society layabout, has been turned over by his disgusted father (Percy Moore) to Tom McGuire (John Harrington), who promises to make a responsible man out of him. He puts the boy through a rigorous regimen and does inculcate some morality, but he is not unwilling to obtain a girl to keep Gene company. Connie takes the girl's place and offers herself to Gene, but, with his newly learned ideals, he pushes her away, crying, "Not until you're eighteen, baby." Their parents mistakenly attempt to interfere, so the youngsters run off to get married in Iowa, where seventeen is the legal age. Whatever they thought of the play, reviewers saluted Guion's performance. *Variety* called it "corking," while Atkinson wrote, "Being a personable youth with a frank, engaging manner, Raymond Guion makes something of Gene altogether finer than the play." Hollywood talent scouts concurred, and he was soon entraining west, where film makers renamed him Gene Raymond.

John Kirkpatrick's **Charm** (11-28-29, Wallack's) proved to be merely *The Book of Charm*, which Broadway had rejected in 1925. Broadway rejected it even more firmly this time, granting it just half a week.

Another string of short-lived failures ushered in December. Ernest Pascal's **The Amorous Antic** (12-2-29, Masque) opened with Sena Balsam (Phoebe Foster), "an artist of the slanting line school," painting a portrait of Percival Redingote (Alan Mowbray) "so modernistic that it resembles a pile of soda bisquit boxes." The pair fall in love even though Percival is the best friend of Sena's husband (Frank Morgan). Being honest artists, they tell Balsam that they are going to have an affair, which they inform him will be "the quintessence of emotion sublimated by intelligence." He is baffled and at first tries to prevent the liaison, but failing in that he embarks on an affair of his own. Still, the final curtain finds the Balsams reconciled.

William Jourdan Rapp and Walter Marquiss's **Whirlpool** (12-3-29, Biltmore) folded after one of the season's shortest runs—three performances. The Reverend James Gregg (Edward Leiter) of the First Church of Kingston, Ill., is hounded out of town by the gossipy, malicious bluestockings who object to his radical pronouncements and pro-union activities. At one point they so anger him that he calls a particularly obnoxious biddy "a god damn scandal monger."

William Farnum returned to Broadway after a long absence in films but found no welcome. His vehicle was Hugh Stange's **Headquarters** (12-4-29, Forrest), with Farnum playing Inspector William Regan, who is called in to investigate the murder of a notoriously promiscuous screen star (George Baxter). A secret passage to a neighboring house leads to the discovery of a second body, Regan's wife (Lea Penman), who was having an affair with the dead man. Suspicion falls on Regan's daughter (Mildred Mitchell), but Regan proves the killer was actually a gunman hired by the actor's drug-addicted wife (Florence Johns).

The Tolstoy drama that John Barrymore had performed in 1918 as *Redemption* was offered anew to theatregoers as **The Living Corpse** (12-6-29, Civic

Repertory) with Jacob Ben Ami, who did the fresh translation and directed, in the lead. The mounting received divided notices but came to be looked back upon as one of the company's more interesting offerings.

Possibly fearing legal action, the producers of Irving Kaye Davis's **Diana** (12-9-29, Longacre) got cold feet just before the drama's premiere, dropping the original title of *Isadora*. For the play recounted episodes in the life of the late Isadora Duncan. The great dancer Diana Bolton (Mary Nash) so annoys her rich lover and backer (John Craig) by her bohemian escapades that he leaves her. She takes up with a pianist (Charles Quigley), but after her children are killed in an automobile accident she heads for Russia and there has a romance with a poet (Nicolai Oulukanof). He deserts her, and she returns to the West to appear in vaudeville. Unhappy, she begs a young man (Carleton Hildreth) to take her for a ride in his car, but her scarf catches on the wheel and she is choked to death. Oldtimer Jefferson De Angelis was applauded for his acting in the part of the dancer's loyal manager.

"Mae West's grossest production attains the grace of a psalm compared with this bawdy drama [which] reaches the bed of low drama," one critic bewailed. Never mind that **The Novice and the Duke** (12-10-29, Assembly) was technically a comedy and was better known as *Measure for Measure*. Olga Katzin "rearranged" Shakespeare's scenes but kept most of the original dialogue, which was performed by players in modern dress against an up-to-date jazz background. Leo G. Carroll was Angelo.

Bille Burke suffered the worst fiasco of her career with the one-week run of Earle Crooker and Lowell Brentano's **Family Affairs** (12-10-29, Maxine Elliott's). She took the part of a wife who is aware that her husband has a mistress, her son has an even more unsavory one, and her daughter is engaged to a ne'er-do-well. So she hires a gigolo to pose as her lover, then invites the whole caboodle to a dinner party where she opens everyone's eyes. One interesting touch, which demonstrated how quickly the theatre still could respond to recent events, was that the family was pictured as having lost much of its fortune in the stock market crash, thus justifying the wife's attempts to get rid of the expensive hangers-on.

The month's first hit, like all three of its major successes, was an importation, A. A. Milne's sugary **Michael and Mary** (12-13-29, Charles Hopkins). With Henry Hull and Edith Barrett in the title roles, it told of a couple who marry, believing the woman's first husband to be dead. They defy troublemakers and blackmailers when it is discovered the man has not died. The comedy ran into the summer at its intimate playhouse.

Most critics and playgoers passed over a revival of Chesterton's *Magic* brought out at the Gansevoort on the 16th.

To placate some of its young turks, the Theatre Guild formed a group called the Theatre Guild Studio Players. The Guild bankrolled its first mounting, Virginia and Frank Vernon's translation of V. Kirchon and A. Ouspensky's Soviet drama **Red Rust** (12-17-29, Martin Beck). It depicted a revolutionary cell leader (Herbert J. Biberman) so brutal that he even kills his own mistress (Gale Sondergaard). His superiors are finally goaded into punishing him. According to some memoirs, it was at the time of this play that Cheryl Crawford, the Guild's casting director, Harold Clurman, its play reader, and Lee Strasberg, who had a small role in the drama, began to consider breaking away from the Guild.

After years of delighting the road, and sometimes New York, in his own plays, William Hodge made what proved to be his penultimate appearance in the season's latest murder mystery, Milton Herbert Gropper and Edna Sherry's **Inspector Kennedy** (12-20-29, Bijou). A notorious, philandering drug dealer (Walter Watson), learning that he is terminally ill and has only a month to live, decides to be revenged on a girl (Margaret Mullen) who has rebuffed him. He arranges to commit suicide and make it seem the girl did it. The scheme almost succeeds. However, Inspector Kennedy, despite the further killing of a Chinese servant, numerous false leads, and false confessions, proves that the fatal shot came through a small hole in the ceiling from a gun just like the dead man's, and he fingers the person who was blackmailed by the drug dealer into firing the shot. As usual, Hodge's "easy-chair style of acting" distracted from the play's shortcomings.

Sidney Howard's **Half Gods** (12-21-29, Plymouth) received generally dismissive notices and quickly closed. Stephen and Hope Ferrier (Donn Cook and Mayo Methot) squabble incessantly. They receive particularly bad advice from a Freudian psychoanalyst (Siegfried Rumann), who tells Stephen to force his wife to have sex with him. Just as Hope is about to leave to obtain a Reno divorce, she has second thoughts. She tells Stephen that she still loves him and that they must stay together for the sake of their children. He agrees.

S. N. Behrman's often drearily discursive **Meteor** (12-23-29, Guild) lacked the wit the playwright was best known for but enjoyed a three-month run thanks to the Guild's subscription and the acting of the Lunts. Raphael Lord is convinced he can read the future and that nothing stands in the way of his success. As a result, he insists, "I don't have to be polite to people. It's more important for them to conciliate me." He leaves the college where every advantage was accorded him and, taking along his professor's ward, Ann Carr, heads for New York. Soon he is a multimillionaire. But the many enemies he has made by his rudeness, his callousness, and his achievements soon conspire to destroy him. He believes he has foreseen and thus can forestall their plans. But they act more quickly than he has imagined and bring him to the verge of ruin. He is unrepentant, unwilling to admit he has been mistaken, and tells Ann he will never change. She says that she is leaving him and that only when he finally realizes he is human and fallible will he understand he truly needs her. "When you do—you can send for me," she promises as she departs. Lord picks up the phone to resume his business dealings. The play split the critics, who were almost universally enthralled with the stars. Lunt, who was said to have consciously modeled his Lord on Jed Harris, "can plunge with all the force of his personality. He sweeps it furiously across the stage," Atkinson noted, continuing, "Miss Fontanne acts the subdued part of Ann Carr with that curiously detached animation that gives her acting individuality and lure." As a team, John Mason Brown told his readers, "the Lunts play together as no other actors in our theatre can do, with a fluency that is matchless, and an unselfish and precise sense of give and take which is a constant joy to watch."

A surprise success, since it was both a fantasy and Italian, was **Death Takes a Holiday** (12-26-29, Ethel Barrymore), translated by Walter Ferris from Alberto Casella's original. Death (Philip Merivale) throws off his frightening black robes and disguises himself as a foreign prince for an overdue vacation. He is the life of the party at the castle where he is a guest and falls in love with a beautiful woman (Ruth Hobart). She in turn falls in love with him, and when his real identity finally is disclosed, she insists on accompanying him back to his realm.

Another surprise success of sorts was Walter Hampden's revival of Edward Bulwer-Lytton's ninety-year-old drama, *Richelieu*, at the Hampden on the same night. Long a favorite of Edwin Booth and his contemporaries, the drama, dealing with the wily French religious and minister and containing memorable lines such as "The pen is mightier than the sword" and "In the bright lexicon of youth there is no such word as fail," had disappeared from twentieth-century stages. Arthur Goodrich pruned its excesses and outmoded asides but remained largely faithful to the original text. Most critics lauded Hampden's vital, passionate portrayal of the foxy manipulator, and they agreed that the play remained theatrically effective despite its Victorian mannerisms. However, some reviewers claimed that Hampden surrounded himself with an inferior supporting cast, a charge often leveled at Booth. Despite hard times and the fact that such old plays deterred many theatregoers, the drama ran for eleven weeks.

A "semi-pro group," appropriating the name employed by the Theatre Guild's predecessor, the Washington Square Players, brought out the evening's second revival, Richard Brinsley Sheridan's *The Rivals* at the Gansevoort. Two weeks later they offered George M. Cohan's *Seven Keys to Baldpate*. Both the ensemble and its mountings quickly disappeared, albeit New Yorkers would soon see a better representation of Sheridan's comedy.

Frank J. Collins's **Seven** (12-27-29, Republic) was let down easily by critics who saw it as earnest but dull. At a château converted into a hospital for wounded American airmen, a countess (Suzanne Caubaye) takes pity on one forlorn patient (Tom Douglas), who is suffering a nervous breakdown. To help restore his faith in himself she gives herself to him, but after he learns that the countess has prevailed on the officer in charge not to send him on a dangerous mission, he defiantly flies off to certain death.

Across the river at Hoboken's Rialto Theatre, Christopher Morley continued his series of nineteenth-century revivals with *The Blue and the Gray* that night. No author was credited, and while the play did use the theme of a New England officer in love with a daughter of the Confederacy that Elliott Barnes had employed in his 1884 drama with an identical title, the character names and the turns of plot were markedly different. One rumor bruited about was that Morley himself was the author, culling bits and pieces from bygone melodramas.

The month's biggest hit was St. John Ervine's **The First Mrs. Fraser** (12-28-29, Playhouse), which provided Grace George with her longest-running success. She played an understanding woman whose husband (A. E. Matthews) had divorced her to marry a pretty young chippie (Carol Goodner). Now realizing his mistake, he prevails on his ex to help rid him of his new wife. She does, but when he proposes that the first Mrs. Fraser remarry him, she demurs, prompting him to begin courting her again. The play ran ten months.

Elizabeth Miele's **City Haul** (12-30-29, Hudson) spotlighted the misbehavior of Timothy MacHugh (Herbert Rawlinson), a flagrantly corrupt big-city mayor. Besides being openly on the take, he cleverly has news leaked that he has been arrested for murder and slaps an opposing newspaper with a million-dollar libel suit after it prints the story. But when he is about to be caught for one of his peculations, his beloved daughter's fiancé (J. Anthony Hughes), whom the mayor has refused to allow his daughter (Dorothy Lebaire) to wed, quietly removes the stolen moneys from the mayor's safe and places them back where they belong. The grateful mayor consents to his daughter's marriage. Rawlinson, a fading film star, resembled New York's Mayor Walker and did everything he could to underscore the resemblance. Nonetheless, critics assured readers the action of the play occurred in Chicago.

A minor composer, Lewis Gensler, had tried his hand at producing. Now a more celebrated melodist, Vincent Youmans, who had been producing his own musicals unavailingly, turned to straight plays and met with disaster. Youmans did not stint on lavish, colorful costumes and settings depicting Batavia and New Orleans in the days when cutthroat pirates roamed the seven seas, but the gorgeous stage pictures and a bravura, swashbuckling performance by John Halliday could do nothing for Bayard Veiller and Becky Gardiner's **Damn Your Honor** (12-30-29, Cosmopolitan). The marauding pirate La Tour steals the jewels of the governor's wife (Jessie Royce Landis) but, falling in love with her, contrives to return them. His generous action almost leads to his being caught and imprisoned. Blaming the woman's treachery, he sails away in a fury, only to find that she has stolen aboard ship to remain with him. The play was taken off the boards after a single week.

So was Harry Delf's **The Unsophisticates** (12-30-29, Longacre). Delf set his play in the Plymouth colony in 1622 and filled his dialogue with annoying thees, thous, neas, and yeas. Their parents arrange for John Bradford (Vernon Rich) and Prudence Brewster (Nydia Westman) to marry. The pair are so innocent that Prudence's mother (Molly Pearson) attempts to teach her about the birds and the bees by giving her a lesson in fruit: a peach standing for admiration, a pear for companionship, and an apple for passion, with the last tasteless if not accompanied by the others. But it takes Barbara Sewell (Helen Baxter), a lusty wench just off the *Mayflower*, to indoctrinate John into the ways of the bedroom and set the two youngsters on their path.

An amateurish revival the same evening at the Macdougal Street Playhouse of W. H. Smith's 1844 temperance melodrama, *The Drunkard*, in which a vicious lawyer drives a young man to drink, found no takers in Prohibition-plagued 1929.

The Irish Theatre, Inc., a group of no particular distinction, launched the new year, 1930, with its second offering of the season at their Irish Theatre on January 2, a revival of J. M. Synge's *The Playboy of the Western World*.

Robert Sherwood offered the year's first novelty, **Waterloo Bridge** (1-6-30, Fulton), which met with a disheartening reception and struggled along for eight weeks. Roy Cronin (Glenn Hunter), a soldier from a small town near Syracuse, on sick leave from the Canadian Army, meets an attractive girl (June Walker) while walking across London's Waterloo Bridge. When he comments on her American accent, Myra tells him she had come to England to appear in *The Pink Lady* and subsequently had been stranded there. She has become a prostitute but, recognizing Roy's belief in the wholesomeness of women, refuses to tell him of her calling. Roy falls in love, although he soon discovers the truth about her. Before heading back to battle he pays her overdue rent, assigns his pay to her, and makes out an insurance policy in her name. (Sherwood later admitted that the play, aside from the ending, was autobiographical).

A much better play received much better notices, yet still failed. Unfortunately the reviews were not what Broadway called money notices. Thus, Percy Hammond wrote in the *Herald Tribune* that Edwin Justus Mayer's **Children of Darkness** (1-7-30, Biltmore) was "a literary play that acts—[and] not only has a cultivated eloquence particularly distinctive in a day given over to the cliches of naturalism in the theatre, but is a play that combines the heartiness, the cynical elegance and the cold, jesting cruelty of the early 18th Century English dramatists." It remained for an off-Broadway revival in 1958 to call proper attention to it. The action takes place on the top floor of the home of the venal Mr. Snap (Walter Kingsford), who, for an exorbitant price, houses prisoners who would otherwise be confined in Newgate Prison, next door. He professes to admire criminals: " 'Tis only the effeminate and useless young who keep out of jail completely; the young who have never been in jail are a disgrace to their youth, sir." Among his guests is the infamous Jonathan Wild (Charles Dalton). Snap conspires with another guest, the fraudulent Count La Ruse (Basil Sydney), to bilk Wild of his money and then allow him to be hanged. La Ruse had been wooing Snap's promiscuous daughter Laetitia (Mary Ellis), in hopes of finding a means of escape. He is furious when a naive poet, Mr. Cartwright (J. Kerby Hawkes), joins the household and becomes immediately enamored of Laetitia, who professes to reciprocate his feelings. At once jealous yet taken with the young man, La Ruse warns him that "there are women in whom the mother has been completely omitted, and . . . Laetitia is such a woman." Another prisoner is brought in. Lord Wainwright (Eugene Powers) has poisoned his unfaithful wife and the son she had by another man, who turns out to be La Ruse. Wainwright, a man with no time for cant, bluntly tells Laetitia that he proposes to have her favors. Both she and Wainwright so belittle La Ruse that he admits his life is worthless. He kills himself, but first gives Cartwright enough money to buy the poet's freedom—money La Ruse has stolen from both Wild and Snap. Learning of his death, Laetitia blurts out that she is pregnant with his child. The play ran for ten weeks.

Another boy from Syracuse was the pivotal figure in Jack O'Donnell and John Wray's **So Was Napoleon** (1-8-30, Sam H. Harris), which had been known in tryouts by the slightly more revealing title *The Sap from Syracuse*. The play featured Hugh O'Connell, at long last liberated from having to perform a boozer. Instead he was Littleton Looney, a dummy who inherits $18,000 from his late aunt and decides to blow much of it on a grand tour. His buddies tell him if he acts like he is important, people will believe he is. To that end his buddies send telegrams of farewell to the *Leviathan*, signing such names to them as Al Smith, Franklin Roosevelt, James Walker, and Otto Kahn. The ship's captain, duly impressed, invites Littleton to dine at the captain's table. He is pursued aboard ship by an amorous countess (Elsa Ersi), and when he stumbles on the solution to an engineering problem creating difficulties in her Bolivian mines, a wealthy marriage looms ahead.

A supposedly admired Russian actress, Maria Germanova, made her debut in the American Laboratory Theatre's revival of *The Three Sisters* the same evening but created no particular stir.

Maxim Gorky's *The Lower Depths*, which had been seen on Broadway under various titles, was brought back as **At the Bottom** (1-9-30, Waldorf), in a new version by William L. Laurence. The cast included E. J. Ballantine, Walter Abel, Barbara Bulgakov, and Anne Seymour. Leo Bulgakov's production was accorded generally laudatory notices and compiled a surprising seventy-two-performance run.

But then A. E. Snitt and L. Sand's **Phantoms** (1-13-30, Wallack's), which received one of the season's harshest critical drubbings, lingered for seven weeks, thanks to cut-rate tickets. The proprietor of a gambling house is shot. Ghosts popping in and out of sliding panels and a sleepwalking young lady complicate matters for a detective (Edwin Redding), who identifies himself as Phido Prance [read Philo Vance], and Officer Sylvester (Knox Herold), "a nance cop." However, just before the final curtain the men are shown to be escaped inmates from a lunatic asylum. The murder is never solved, but, as one critic ended his notice, "it couldn't possibly matter."

While critics did not trash Myron C. Fagan's **Nancy's Private Affair** (1-13-30, Vanderbilt), most reviews were not enthusiastic. Yet alone of the month's entries, the comedy surpassed the 100-performance mark, lasting sixteen weeks. Nancy (Minna Gombell) has become such a frump, lounging about in unbecoming woolen socks and horn-rimmed glasses, that her playwright husband (Lester Vail), who has his eyes on a pretty young gal (Marion Grant), asks for a divorce. Nancy consents, requesting only that he wait for six months before marrying her rival. In that time she changes into a ravishing clotheshorse and gets her gold-digging rival to fall for a supposedly wealthy Englishman (Gavin Muir), who is actually an out-of-work actor hired by Nancy. Hubby reconsiders.

Playgoers with fond memories of *The Old Soak* were disappointed by Don Marquis's resurrection of its principal characters in **Everything's Jake** (1-17-30, Assembly). Only this time, Clem Hawley (Charles Kennedy) and Al (Edward Donnelly) are not the center of attention. Rather their bootlegging chum, Jake Smith (Thurston Hall), takes them, along with his nouveau riche wife (Jean Adair) and daughter (Eleanore Bedford), to Paris. There, in one hilarious scene, he conspires with the British Countess of Billhorn (Ethel Morrison), who admires the openness of Jake and his friends, to smuggle back home a shipment of the famous whiskey the countess's family makes. For a time Jake also falls into the clutches of another titled English woman (Catherine Willard), who once had been an American chorus girl. Clem and Al help him escape. Marquis also had fun with Americans attempting to speak French. At a sidewalk café one of the men orders "the cat's whiskers," at the time a popular cocktail, and finds himself served four whiskeys. A short time later, mistakenly thinking *soixante* means "six," they are served sixty drinks.

In Ashley Miller and Hyman Adler's **The Challenge of Youth** (1-20-30, 49th St.) Stephen Adams (Harold De Bray) boasts that his daughter Desire (Alma Merrick) is a model youngster, unaware that she is the leader of college students insisting on a high-flying life. So he is stunned to learn she has become pregnant. Her young man, Hod Bronson (William Lovejoy), offers to do the right thing, but Desire claims that she does not love him. Adams is talked into taking Desire for a trip abroad until everything cools down. At best, Desire agrees she might marry Hod when she returns.

Ashley Dukes's theatricalization of Lion Feuchtwanger's *Power* [*Jud Süss*] had been done in London as *Jew Süss* and now was given to New York as **Josef Süss** (1-20-30, Erlanger). Josef-Süss Oppenheimer (Maurice Moscovitch), a Jew, has risen to become the power behind the throne of Karl Alexander (Malcolm Keen), Duke of Wurtemberg. He uses that power not only to line his own pockets but to secure women for the duke. The irate father (Ralph Truman) of one of the women reveals to the duke that Oppenheimer has a beautiful daughter (Janet Morrison). When the duke attempts to seduce her, she throws herself from the castle's wall. In revenge, Oppenheimer brings about the duke's downfall at the expense of his own life. Moscovitch, originally famed in Yiddish theatre, had subsequently been admired for performances in English in the West End. A decade later the Nazis made a viciously anti-Semitic film version that after the war caused its producer to be brought up for trial as a war criminal.

The Women Have Their Way (1-27-30, Civic Repertory) was the Granville Barkers' translation of another comedy by Serafín and Joaquín Álvarez Quintero, *La Puebla de las Mujeres*, and served as the chief part of a double bill. Set in a village where women outnumber men by five to one, it recounted how the town ladies cagily push a handsome Madrid lawyer (Donald Cameron) into wedding the town beauty (Eva Le Gallienne). Critics were especially pleased to be able to see one of Miss Le Gallienne's rare displays of comic technique. She showed them again in the second part of the bill, Alfred Sutro's **The Open Door**, in which a happily married woman listens to an old suitor (Cameron), and her husband's dearest friend, tell of his love for her.

One of the season's worst duds was Percival Lennon's **The Short Cut** (1-27-30, Cherry Lane). It centered on a murderous gambler who takes a short cut by jumping out of an eighth-story window just as he is about to be led off to jail.

A single smash hit during the season was all that Broadway would allow Preston Sturges in rebuffing his drama **Recapture** (1-29-30, Eltinge). A divorced couple (Melvyn Douglas and Ann Andrews) meet again after five years when they come with their current lovers (Glenda Farrell and Stuart Casey) to a hotel in Vichy. The husband still loves his ex, but she is adamant that she can never again care for him. His selfless new amour, a former chorus girl, talks her into reconsidering. However, before anything can happen the wife is killed in an elevator accident.

That same evening, the Irish Theatre brought out its latest offering, George A. Birmingham's *General John Regan*, which told how an imaginatively minded young man hoodwinks a sleepy Irish village into believing it was the birthplace of a fictitious South American hero. Despite special pleadings by a small coterie of devoted admirers, the play was rejected, much as it had been in 1913. With the play's closing, the group also closed shop.

Donald Ogden Stewart, who had appeared with Hope Williams—she of the mannish bob and mannish strides—in *Holiday*, wrote **Rebound** (2-3-30, Plymouth) for her. Together they enjoyed a smallish fourteen-week success. Sara Jaffrey realizes that Johnnie Coles (Robert Williams) is more concerned with forwarding his career than with marrying her, so when Bill Truesdale (Donn Cook), a suave ladies' man who has been spurned by Evie Lawrence (Katherine Leslie) in favor of a richer suitor, proposes to Sara, she accepts. Half a year later the Truesdales are in Paris. Bill fails to show up for a luncheon, and Sara learns that he was with Evie. At the same time, Sara encounters Johnnie, who confesses to still loving her. Back home after a few months, the situation fails to improve. Sara wonders why she married Bill. But after refusing Johnnie's suggestion to run away with him, she decides rather to tough it out. She tells Bill, "I'm alone again. But I'm not lonely. My love doesn't need you any longer." Nonetheless, she and Bill will give their marriage another try.

Edith Fitzgerald and Robert Riskin's **Many a Slip** (2-3-30, Little) failed to make the grade despite two capital performances. Jerry Brooks (Douglass Montgomery) is tricked into marrying Patsy Coster (Sylvia Sidney) by Patsy's mother (Dorothy Sands), who has hinted that Patsy is pregnant. Jerry not only weds Patsy but spends much of his savings purchasing baby clothes, cribs, and other such paraphernalia. Then he discovers that Mrs. Coster was lying. He storms out, unaware that Patsy is now truly expecting. Of course, a happy reconciliation brings down the curtain. Miss Sands, better known as a mimic in revues, was lauded for her craftily garrulous mother, while Maude Eburne all but stole the evening portraying another in her long line of loud, outspoken slaveys.

Another performance saved a show, albeit aisle-sitters scolded Katharine Cornell for selecting so trashy a vehicle as Margaret Ayer Barnes and Edward Sheldon's **Dishonored Lady** (2-4-30, Empire). In the *Herald Tribune*, Richard Watts, Jr., joined in the chiding but continued, "Miss Cornell has a dramatic power, a keen sensitivity, a sharp intelligence and an emotional vigor that are not terribly far from overwhelming. . . . You will have to accept her as our First Actress." Madeleine Cary has instigated and carried on a torrid affair with an Argentinian cabaret singer (Fortunio Bonanova) until he suddenly seems to her to stand in the way of her wedding an English lord (Francis Lister). She comes to her lover's apartment planning to put strychnine in his coffee, but her lust temporarily gains the upper hand. She tells him she is "Madeleine Cary. Your mistress and your nigger!" Adding, "I am going to hell and I can't stop myself," she seduces him into kissing her and turns out the light. The next morning she puts the poison in his coffee, pulls out the telephone cord, and starts to leave, stopping in the nick of time to reclaim her cloak, which she almost had forgotten. When she is brought to trial, the lord, her father (Fred L. Tiden), and other friends testify in her support, but after she is acquitted, they privately denounce her and leave her alone in the world. The drama ran into May, then toured the country.

There were no redeeming performances to aid Dana Burnet's **The Boundary Line** (2-5-30, 48th St.). Indeed, some reviewers lamented that the principal roles were sadly miscast. Prodded by his materialistic, greedy wife (Katharine Alexander), Allan Fenway (Otto Kruger) has abandoned his ambition to be a high-minded poet and instead writes for cheap magazines. Trouble grows after Mrs. Fenway insists that a fence surround their suburban home, even though it violates a clause stipulating a neighboring farmer (John T. Doyle) must have a right of way through the property. The farmer takes the Fenways to court but has a fatal heart attack on hearing that they have won on a technicality. Disgusted, Allan packs his bag and leaves his wife.

Out of a Blue Sky (2-8-30, Booth) was Leslie Howard's translation of Hans Chlumberg's *Das Blaue von Himmel*. It survived for just two weeks. The audience entering the theatre saw a bare stage occupied only by a few stagehands. A director (Gregory Ratoff) and his play reader (William Gargan) appear. The director announces that he lacks both a play and actors and hopes to work out a play with volunteers from the audience. The play reader selects a smug divorce attorney (Reginald Owen), who, in turn, presses his reluctant wife

(Katherine Wilson) to join him. They are to play a man with an unfaithful spouse. To the wife's dismay, the man culled from the audience to portray her imagined lover is her real lover (Warren William), and their supposed lovemaking becomes increasingly passionate, although the husband is too thick-headed to catch on.

Two more failures began their brief lives the next evening. Viva Tattersall and Sidney Toler's **Ritzy** (2-10-30, Longacre) took place in the rather seedy room at a residential hotel that the Smiths (Ernest Truex and Miriam Hopkins) call home. Their lives seem about to be changed when they are notified that they are heirs to their late Uncle Peter's $200,000 fortune, since Peter's wife and children cannot be found. Mr. Smith promptly calls his boss and quits. Mrs. Smith announces that she hereafter will have breakfast in bed and starts correcting her husband's grammar. She also gives away all her clothes, only to realize as she is standing in her undies that she has nothing to wear to go shopping in. Then a second call advises them the missing wife and children have been located. Luckily, Smith's boss, thinking Smith was bluffing, has called to offer Smith his job back, at double the salary.

Mrs. Fiske's new vehicle, Hatcher Hughes and Alan Williams's **It's a Grand Life** (2-10-30, Cort) dismayingly recalled Billie Burke's recent fiasco and gave the grand old lady one of her own. Like Burke, she played a woman whose husband (Cyril Scott) brazenly flaunts his mistresses and whose children have made unsavory alliances. However, unlike Miss Burke's character, her Mrs. Tyler agrees to accept the relationships, even to allowing one of her husband's mistresses to have her baby in the Tyler apartment. An amusing scene had Mrs. Tyler fending off most reporters but welcoming the man from the *Times*, who arrives in full dress and admires her chartreuse. The real man from the paper, Atkinson, pleaded with anyone who would listen, "Find a good play for Mrs. Fiske and do your country a service."

Biblical stories were retold in Bertram Bloch's **Joseph** (2-12-30, Liberty), but since the play starred George Jessel in the title role and was directed by George S. Kaufman, playgoers could not expect much reverence. Jessel turned Joseph into an East Side hustler, who shows Potiphar (Ferdinand Gottschalk) how to jew down a slave dealer's prices, brings sound business practices to the jail into which he has been thrown after being falsely accused by Potiphar's wife (Ara Gerald), and ultimately wins freedom by pleasing Pharaoh (Douglas Dumbrille) with his somewhat Freudian dream interpretations.

Some better satire from France by way of England fared more profitably the same night. Marcel Pagnol's **Topaze** (2-12-30, Music Box) delighted Broadway in Benn W. Levy's translation. Topaze (Frank Morgan) is a lowly, backwater schoolteacher, whose main ambition in life is to become a Doctor of Moral Philosophy. Because of his high-principled refusal to give good grades to bad students, he is fired. He pleads for help from Suzy Courtois (Phoebe Foster), whose nephew he has been coaching privately. Suzy is the mistress of Castel-Benac (Clarence Derwent), the town's biggest grafter, who consents to employ the naive Topaze as an unwitting front man for his crooked schemes. Before long Topaze catches on and comprehends the futility of his idealism, and soon he not only bests Castel-Benac in grafting but steals away Suzy. For all of this he is awarded his doctorate in Moral Philosophy.

Looking back at season's end, Burns Mantle would write that no play since *What Price Glory?* had generated such excitement as John Wexley's **The Last Mile** (2-14-30, Sam H. Harris). Mantle extolled it as "a tragedy so tense, so stripped of theatrical artificialities, and emotionally so moving" that even hardened critics were touched. Wexley based his play on a one-acter published in *American Mercury* by a man who had been executed for a killing. Wexley retained much of that play for his first act, which shows the final hours of Richard Walters (James Bell), a young man sentenced to die for killing his reluctant girl. His neighbors (the setting depicted a row of cells) point out to him how often reprieves arrive at the last minute. A giant black (Ernest Whitman), given to singing spirituals, assures him, "You'll get it, white boy," and urges him to pray. Walters tries to keep up his spirits by singing "My Blue Heaven." But the reprieve does not come. Rather, the priest (Henry O'Neill) gives him the last rites, the guards prepare him for execution by shaving him and slitting his pants, and he is led off. The whine of a motor and the momentary dimming of lights suggest the boy has been electrocuted. But the time it takes prompts the most hardboiled of the felons, "Killer" Mears (Spencer Tracy), to shout out that they are cooking the boy. Two weeks later Mears grabs a guard who has come too near his cell, strangles him, takes his keys, and releases himself and the other prisoners. They attack the guardroom and seize the guards, losing only the black man in the assault. The men then announce they will kill the guards, and the priest, one at a time, unless they are allowed to escape. Of course, the demands are refused. Mears kills the first guard, telling him, "I hope I'll miss you the first time, Drake, so you'll have to go through it a second time." There is a brief mutiny when some of the convicts protest Mears's intention of shooting a priest, but Mears stifles it by tough words and by acquiescing. When the convicts have used up all but two bullets, Mears decides to make a break for it. He dashes out, a volley of machine guns is heard, and the priest intones a prayer. Tracy was lauded for the "vibrancy" of his performance. However, the play marked his final Broadway appearance, except for one return fifteen years later.

Mei Lan-Fang, ballyhooed as China's greatest actor, began a five-week stand on the 16th at the 49th Street Theatre in a selection of one-act Chinese plays. In all of them he enacted the leading woman's role. Wearing extravagantly ornate costumes and headdresses, he pantomimed with gracefully soft, plastic gestures. In Chinese fashion only a few props and curtains served as decor. A young Chinese lady, speaking beautiful English, explained the stories.

Dorrance Davis's **Apron Strings** (2-17-30, Bijou), was one of the season's big "sleepers"—a totally unexpected hit, delighting playgoers into September. Its plot was simplicity itself. Daniel Curtis (Roger Pryor) is living an all too saintly life, following instructions left him in letters by his late mother, who had written a newspaper column on social behavior. As a result his bride (Audray Dale) is chagrined to realize she may have to remain a virgin if she does not annul the marriage. Fortunately, Daniel's sporty, rascally lawyer (Jefferson De Angelis) sits him down with a bottle of bootleg whiskey and teaches him the facts of life. The veteran comedian with his "warming, ingratiating acting is a show in itself," one pleased critic reported.

Fine performances by two younger players—Helen Menken and Leslie Banks—helped a not uninteresting British play, Norman MacOwan's **The Infinite Shoeblack** (2-17-30, Maxine Elliott's), last for ten weeks. A Scottish honor student sells his actuarial exam to a failing student and uses the money to send a stricken girl overseas for a cure. Once better, she squanders an inheritance by living in decadent luxury in Cairo, where the young man relocates her. He tries to set her on the proper path and even marries her, but she dies in childbirth.

That same night the Theatre Guild began a series of revivals, employing players it had sent around the country as the First Travelers. The performers included Earle Larimore, Sylvia Field, Sydney Greenstreet, and Henry Travers. Their repertory included *R.U.R., Marco Millions*, and *Volpone*. The first play was presented at the Martin Beck, the others, on March 3 and March 10, at the Liberty. The Capek drama ran for two weeks, the others for one.

George Abbott and S. K. Lauren's **Those We Love** (2-19-30, John Golden) failed to find much support. Abbott, along with directing the play, took the role of a writer who often lives apart from his wife (Armina Marshall), since his work requires a quiet environment while her job as a musical arranger forces her sometimes to bang away at a piano. When she wrongly believes her husband has had an affair with an unhappily married woman (Helen Flint) in her absence, she is so furious that she does, in fact, drive him into the woman's arms. But their young son (Edwin Phillips) restores matters by showing how much he needs and wants both of them. Most critics preferred Abbott's direction to his subdued acting but showered praise on Marshall.

Booth Tarkington's novel served as the basis for Arthur Goodrich's **The Plutocrat** (2-20-30, Vanderbilt). A Nebraska meat packer, Earl Tinker (Charles Coburn), his wife (Ivah Wills Coburn), and their daughter, Olivia (Emily Graham), sail for the Mediterranean to see the sights and to get Olivia away from a snooty playwright, Lawrence Ogle (Fairfax Burgher), whom Tinker detests. Tinker acts gauchely aboard ship and at their hotel on the edge of the Sahara. At the hotel he is vamped by the voluptuous Mme. Momoro (Suzanne Caubaye). He comes through with flying colors and even is reconciled to Olivia's marrying her writer. Critics thought the play was hackwork but praised the Coburns. *Variety* noted, "Without undue publicity the pair go along season after season unsupported by hits yet finding favor on a social strata all their own. 'The Plutocrat' should serve out the season locally and on the road." It did.

On the other hand, the Theatre Guild was not having a good season. It found only modest rewards with the eleven-week run of George Bernard Shaw's **The Apple Cart** (2-24-30, Martin Beck), in which King Magnus (Tom Powers) turns the tables on his rebellious prime minister (Claude Rains) and cabinet by threatening to abdicate and stand for Parliament.

Laurence Eyre's **Gala Night** (2-25-30, Erlanger) featured James Rennie as an American who has become a famous opera star in Europe under the name Paval Zala. He has become famous not only for his voice but for his giving gold keys to his apartment to beautiful women he favors. After spending much of the evening in his Pagliacci costumes, he finally finds true love, even though his wedding night is disturbed by irate former lovers and their husbands.

Epilogue: 1928–1930

Many of the same players who had performed in *At the Bottom* were seen in Bulgakov's next offering, *The Sea Gull*. Abel was lauded for his Trigorin, and Dorothy Sands for her Irina.

Just two weeks after one biblical play, with George S. Kaufman as director, began a brief life, Kaufman's erstwhile collaborator Marc Connelly garnered hosannas by theatricalizing Roark Bradford's *Ol' Man Adam an' His Chillun* as **The Green Pastures** (2-26-30, Mansfield). It recounted the Bible story in terms of simple, southern blacks. Reviewers were ecstatic. Heywood Broun in the *Telegram* called it "more stirring than anything I have seen in the theatre." The *World*'s Robert Littell hailed it as "simply and briefly one of the finest things that the theatre of our generation has seen." Atkinson pinned on the label of "the divine comedy of the modern theatre." At his simple Sunday school, the illiterate but devout Mr. Deshee (Charles H. Moore) is telling his little pupils the story of Genesis, and when one of them asks him who was in New Orleans at the time, he replies, "Dey wasn't nobody in N'Orleans on 'count dey wasn't any N'Orleans." To drive home the point, he adds there was no Canal Street, no Louisiana. He returns to his story to tell of the Creation, which, in his version, happens while the angels are enjoying a big fish fry. Gabriel (Wesley Hill), decked out in gold and purple, interrupts the festivities to shout, "Gangway! Gangway for de Lawd God Jehovah!" In the hush that follows, a large, dignified black man appears, dressed in a long but shabby Prince Albert coat and a white tie. Announcing that he will "jest r'ar back and pass a miracle," de Lawd creates the world. But in short order he is unhappy with its people. After a walk with Noah (Tutt Whitney), de Lawd and Noah return to Noah's simple cabin, with its checkered tablecloth and a chicken cooking in the pot, and they plan the ark. Bit by bit the other Old Testament stories come to life, until at another fish fry de Lawd gives special hope to the world as the Angels watch the Crucifixion down below. Robert Edmond Jones's settings combined a sense of vaulting grandeur with a humble earthly simplicity. Thus, Noah's austere cabin was framed in stylized trees rising to the top of the proscenium, with the vast blue sky behind it. De Lawd and Noah's walk was on a treadmill that gave an oddly homey touch to the scene. But, the play apart, the glory of the evening came from the performance of Richard B. Harrison as de Lawd. He was over six feet tall, with a head of leonine gray hair. His voice was richly magnificent and deep. He had never appeared in the theatre before, but he was de Lawd to the life (so much so that the rest of the cast reputedly remained in awe of him), and he toured with the play until his death five years later. The play won the Pulitzer Prize and ran for 640 performances.

What little interest Lennox Robinson's **The Round Table** (2-27-30, Gansevoort) held stemmed from Margaret Wycherly's performance as Daisy Drennan. Daisy had long held together her feckless, selfishly demanding family, so after making acceptable marriages for several of her siblings and despairing of being further help, she leaves her kin and her fiancé and sets out to see the world alone.

As if to balance the scales for Orientalists, a group of players from Japan, led by one Tsutsui, opened a two-week visit at the Booth on March 4. Although they also presented short plays, theirs were modern ones, not classics, and the cast featured numerous women.

The American Laboratory Theatre, so often neglected by critics, lured them for a second time this season when it revived Eugène Scribe's nineteenth-century favorite *A Glass of Water* on the 5th. Maria Germanova directed and took the leading role of Queen Anne of England, who makes Sarah Churchill her favorite, then dismisses her. New York had last watched it when Genevieve Ward presented it as *The Queen's Favorite* in 1886.

A second revival came in three nights later when Edwin Milton Royle's 1921 drama *Launcelot and Elaine* raised its curtain at the President, with the playwright's daughters, Selena and Josephine, as Guinevere and Elaine. Frank M. Thomas was Launcelot.

The next Monday evening was busy. Perhaps because all the other mystery yarns had departed and Bernard J. McOwen and J. P Riewerts's **The Blue Ghost** (3-10-30, Forrest) found itself the only example in town at the moment, it ran thirteen weeks despite thumbs down from the critics—the lone novelty of the month to surpass 100 performances. As happened so often in this sort of play, mysterious shrieks were heard, odd lights flashed on and off, and a frightened black servant (Nate Busby) jumped wildly on the least provocation. All this transpired in the home of a seemingly evil physician (McOwen), until it was shown to be the servant's hootch-inspired nightmare.

The evening's two other novelties had some good acting and unusual settings but very short runs. Three weeks sufficed for Marie Baumer's second play of the season, **Penny Arcade** (3-10-30, Fulton). Its action unfolded in Mrs. Delano's tawdry amusement parlor. Parts of a hot dog stand and an itinerant photographer's shop that flanked it on one side or the other could be seen in Cleon Throckmorton's set, as could the skeleton of a roller coaster behind it. Mrs. Delano's bootlegging son (James Cagney) kills a man who has sought to date his sister (Lenita Lane). The boy has used a gun belonging to an employee (Eric Dressler) of his mother (Valerie Bergere), so she takes it from him and plants it back in the employee's room. The police (in gray uniforms that made them look like postmen or Confederate soldiers) are prepared to arrest the innocent man, but Mrs. Delano's daughter had seen the shooting and, since she loved the dead man, tells all. Cagney walked off with the evening's acting honors.

Willard Robertson's **This Man's Town** (3-10-30, Ritz) was set in a cheap lunch wagon, and audiences could smell hamburgers being grilled and coffee brewing. The place is owned by Tony Fantana (Eduardo Ciannelli), a hood who railroaded innocent Eddie Anders (Walter Glass) into serving time for a crime Tony committed. Eddie is now free and bent on revenge. But before he sees Tony get his comeuppance—shot by Eddie's wife (Viola Frayne)—in the third act, Tony machine guns a cop in the first act, and stabs to death a detective who is hot on his trail in the second. A clever newspaper reporter (Pat O'Brien) arranges for Anders and his wife to depart scot-free, collects a $3000 reward for helping the police nab one of Tony's cohorts, and buys the diner with the proceeds. Robertson took the part of the wagon's likable hashslinger. But George Jessel, who had put up most of the money for his own recently failed vehicle, served as producer and lost more money when *This Man's Town* folded at the end of its first week.

A cast filled with oldtimers approaching the end of their careers and youngsters soon to move on to fame could not save Al Woods's mounting of **Love, Honor and Betray** (3-12-30, Eltinge), which Fanny and Frederic Hatton adapted from André-Paul Antoine's *L'Ennemie*. Once more the story unfolded in an unusual setting—a graveyard. There the ghosts of a Young Man (Robert Williams) who killed himself after she spurned him, her unhappy Husband (Mark Smith), and the Lover (Clark Gable) she drove to exhaustion rise to retell the stories of their relationships with the Woman (Alice Brady) in flashbacks. Unmoved, she prepares to go off with her Chauffeur (George Brent), only to find he prefers a Young Girl (Glenda Farrell). Wilton Lackaye as a Doctor completed the small cast. For the aging Lackaye and for Brent and Gable the play marked their final Broadway appearances, with the latter two heading for Hollywood—Gable by way of the lead in the West Coast company of *The Last Mile*.

Although she herself probably was unaware of it, her performances as Mrs. Malaprop in a revival of *The Rivals* at the Erlanger, beginning on the 13th, marked Mrs. Fiske's last Broadway appearances. Critics made allowances for the hurriedly thrown together nature of the enterprise and found kind words not only for Mrs. Fiske but for rubber-faced James T. Powers's Bob Acres, John Craig's Sir Anthony, Rollo Peters's Jack, and Pedro de Cordoba's Faulkland. For the first time in fifty years Mrs. Fiske's nervousness caused her to miss an important entrance. Nevertheless, Atkinson reported approvingly, "She bounces and billows around the stage, floods a huge settle with all the paraphernalia of her costume, acts with a fan and a handkerchief and storms through a variety of artifices."

Laurence Eyre's **Mayfair** (3-17-30, Belmont) was a one-week dud. Lady Clarges (Chrystal Herne) wrecks her husband's chances for advancement after she refuses to comply with his suggestion that she have an affair with the influential but venal William Danvers (Arthur Hohl). Before he is shipped back to South America, Lord Clarges (Frederick Worlock) watches bitterly as his wife has a fling with a younger, more attractive man (Derek Glynne).

Harry Wagstaff Gribble used parts of two very old English plays in combination with some new blank verse of his own to recite the tragedy of Elizabeth and Essex in **The Royal Virgin** (3-17-30, Booth). Thais Lawton was the queen; Hugh Buckler, Essex. In the fall, another blank verse drama retelling much the same story would find a welcome on Broadway, but Gribble's opus, like Eyre's, ran only a single week.

A luminous performance by Alla Nazimova and fine playing by a supporting cast that included Eliot Cabot and Dudley Digges, coupled with the loyalty of the Theatre Guild's regulars, to some extent overrode divided critical notices—which generally stressed the play's languors—to allow Ivan Turgenyev's **A Month in the Country** (3-17-30, Guild) a nine-week stand. Turgenyev's tale focused on a bored married woman's futile attempt to find romance and happiness.

The egregious miscasting of Constance Collier as a Jewish matron determined to keep her family of rich diamond merchants together and Jewish hurt what small chances Frank Vernon and G. B. Stern's **The Matriarch** (3-18-30, Longacre) had. The play was adapted from Stern's novel, which some sources said had the same name and others listed as *The Tents of Israel*. The family is ultimately bankrupted, but the matriarch passes on her ideals to her granddaughter (Jessica Tandy). Miss Tandy, making her New York debut, was perceived as performing with "fresh sincerity."

B. M. Kaye's **I Want My Wife** (3-20-30, Liberty) was waved away as amateurish. His family drug Alfred Towder (Herbert Yost), a perennial bachelor, in hopes of tricking him into marrying. He does marry, but complications arise after it is learned he was married previously to a girl he met in Philadelphia while he was suffering from amnesia.

Another oldster making his farewell Broadway appearance was William Hodge, who served as author of his final vehicle, **The Old Rascal** (3-24-30, Bijou). This time he played a retired jurist who has rushed off for a wild time in New York after his wife (Alice Fischer) has broken all the bottles in his beloved wine cellar. His wife hires some unscrupulous New York attorneys to frame him with another woman, so that she can arrange a large divorce settlement. But he outtricks them all.

Fritz Leiber brought his Chicago Civic Shakespeare Society into the Shubert for a short stand starting on the 24th. The troupe offered *Hamlet, Macbeth, King Lear, Richard III, Julius Caesar, The Merchant of Venice, Twelfth Night, The Taming of the Shrew*, and *As You Like It*. Now in his late forties, Leiber brought intelligence, vigor and freshness to both his acting and staging, yet, as always, he failed to generate much excitement.

H. F. Maltby's London comedy **Dear Old England** (3-25-30, Ritz) found impecunious aristocrats living in abandoned railroad cars. The daughter (Mary Vance) of one of the families takes work as a maid in her family's former home, now owned by a crude upstart (Edward Rigby). The upstart's son (Reginald Sheffield) falls in love with her and helps restore her family's fortune.

Mann Page's **House Afire** (3-31-30, Little) starts when the Ogdens (Florence Earle and John Hazzard) awake to find their neighbors' house on fire. Ann Elliott (May Collins) rushes in to beg them to save her cat. Frozen fire hydrants and an automobile crash prevent firefighters from doing their work swiftly, so the house burns down. Since it was known that Ann hated living in the suburbs and wanted to move to the city, she is suspected of arson. But the culprit proves to be a kindly old neighbor everyone calls Doc (William B. Mack). He understood Ann's unhappiness and wanted to give her an opportunity to enjoy herself. In fact, he admits setting a number of local fires for one reason or another. As Doc is about to be arrested he tells the group assembled in the Ogdens' home, "Don't you worry about me. I've got a lot of pleasant things to think about and no regrets." One of the pleasant

things he can dwell on is that he has just set fire to the Ogdens' house. Smoke begins to pour into the living room as the curtain falls. The comedy lasted two weeks, as did the evening's other opening.

Willard Earl Simmons's **Broadway Shadows** (3-31-30, Belmont) examined the life of a curiously mixed-up young man. Richard Alan (Howard St. John) takes a furnished apartment in the west '70s after accepting blame for a check his mother toyed with—raising the amount from $1000 to $20,000. He rejects the pleas of his socialite friends to return to them. Instead, he marries the wife (Lucille Fenton) of an ex-convict, believing the husband dead. But the man (Leo Dawn) turns up and attempts to blackmail the couple. One of the wife's lady friends shoots the blackmailer, ending Richard's problem.

Abandoning for a time her own folk plays, Lula Vollmer adapted Imre Fazekas's **Troyka** (4-1-30, Hudson) for Broadway. At a Siberian prison camp, Semion (Albert Van Dekker) and Ivan (Jack Roseleigh) share a cabin with a devout orphan girl, Natascha (Zita Johann). Both men love the girl, although Semion has a wife and children at home. When the Russian revolution leads to the prisoners being freed, Semion refuses to return to his family, preferring to remain with Natascha. He and Ivan fight over the girl, and Semion is killed. But Ivan leaves empty-handed after Natascha runs off with a captain of the guard.

The Provincetown Playhouse was briefly rechristened the Playshop Theatre and launched what it hoped would be a series of new American plays. The hopes were soon dashed, but the group did bring out Frederick Schlick and J. Barry McCarthy's **Joy of Serpents** (4-3-30, Playshop), which looked at how various wounded soldiers faced their futures as they recovered in a British hospital.

Andrew Ware (Otto Kruger), the hero of Humphrey Pearson's **They Never Grow Up** (4-7-30, Masque), has made a fortune manufacturing skillets. But his nagging wife (Kathryn March) and mother-in-law (Anne Sutherland) won't allow him to enjoy his money, so he heads off with his chauffeur (Claude Cooper) to a Mexican ranch he has bought. On the way they stop at a Mexican cantina and meet Tonia Cordoba (Mary Fowler), a Mexican who has been deported from the United States for political activities. She cajoles Andrew into trying to sneak her back across the border, but they head for the ranch first. Wife and mother-in-law arrive and raise such a to-do that Andrew runs off to South America with Tonia, who has hinted they might start a revolution there.

Broadway scuttlebutt suggested that playwright

Michael Kallesser, who produced **Live and Learn** (4-9-30, Wallack's), was also its author, albeit programs credited the writing to one Lincoln Kalworth. Displeased with the frugal domesticity of his wife, Mabel (Lois Jesson), Harold Fuller (Alden Chase) chases her from their "Love-Bird" bungalow in Leonia by paying public attention to a luscious model, Annette Roberts (Beatrice Nichols). Mabel embarks on a successful career as a singer in Europe. When she returns home, she finds Harold and Annette flinging chairs and china at each other, so she goads Annette into leaving and resumes her old place.

The Theatre Guild closed its season with Philip Barry's **Hotel Universe** (4-14-30, Martin Beck). Ann Field's guests have assembled on the terrace of her home overlooking the Mediterranean in France. They include Ann's caustic old beau, Pat Farley (Glenn Anders); Lily Malone (Ruth Gordon), an actress who longs to play Cordelia; Tom Ames (Franchot Tone), a publisher, and his wife, Hope (Phyllis Povah); Norman Rose (Earle Larimore), a rich Jew; and Alice Kendall (Ruthelma Stevens), who loves Norman. Rumor has it that the home once had been a hotel where odd things happened, where "people began to resemble other people and the place itself other places." Lily senses the strangeness: "It's fantastic, this terrace. It just hangs here. Someday it'll float off in space—and anchor there, like an island in time." All the guests early in life had enjoyed promising futures, but those promises somehow have been thwarted. They are also unnerved by the knowledge that a young man of great promise had just committed suicide by diving off the rocks and swimming out to sea. Ann's father, Stephen (Morris Carnovsky), a famous scientist who seems to have suffered a mysterious breakdown, asks probing questions and offers incisive remarks that force the guests to examine their pasts and exorcise the demons that have bedeviled them. They prepare to leave, filled with new hopes and unaware that Stephen has died quietly while sitting in his chair. The action of the play was continuous and performed, in an unusual practice for the time, without intermission. Baffled notices ("Philip Barry . . . has gone off the deep end," "boringly cryptic") and cool word of mouth meant the new play, like all the Guild's other attractions during the season, could not run much beyond its advance subscription sales.

Courtenay Savage's **Virtue's Bed** (4-15-30, Hudson) opened on the roof of a North African brothel, whose women sit about in silk nightcoats and suggestive dishabille listening to native music from the street below. The most sought-after of the girls is Eileen (Ara Gerald), an American, who learns that her husband has died and left her a fortune as well as a mansion in England. She goes there and soon is courted by several wealthy men. Then Major Harry Austin (Robert Strange), who had been one of her best customers, appears on the scene and threatens to reveal her past. She beats him to the punch. Although the snootier English shun her, the major, admiring her spunk, proposes a satisfactory relationship.

Lillian Gish won the evening's biggest round of applause when she made her first entrance as Helena, the wife of the selfish scholar (Eugene Powers), in Jed Harris's mounting of *Uncle Vanya* at the Cort the same night. However, by evening's end critics and playgoers realized that she was only part of a superbly balanced cast. Walter Connolly had the title role, Osgood Perkins was the doctor, and Joanna Roos played the pitiable Sonya. The play ran into the hot weather.

Aimee and Philip Stuart's **Lady Clara** (4-17-30, Booth) was an English drama which told of a girl (Florence Nash) who learns that she is the daughter of an earl. She successfully blackmails his family into accepting her but then, disgusted with their ways, returns to the lower-class life she has known.

In Alexander Gerry and Augusta Greely's **Penal Law 2010** (4-18-30, Biltmore) a young attorney (Frank Milan) who has won a number of cases using merely circumstantial evidence finds himself confronted with just such evidence when a maid (Janet McLeay) in his parents' home accuses him of being the father of her child. Even his family and friends believe him guilty. Not until a jury has convicted him does the vengeful wife of the family's chauffeur, the baby's real father burst into court to reveal the truth. She reveals not only that her husband is the father but that the maid is not a minor as the girl had claimed, thus making the law inapplicable.

Women with a past of one sort or another were to be popular all through April. The latest was the heroine of Adeline Leitzbach's **Dora Mobridge** (4-19-30, Little). A $400,000 inheritance creates a dilemma for Dora (Louise Carter), for it also discloses that she was raised in a brothel. Her Glendale, N.J., neighbors turn against her, and even her son calls her a harlot (for a dramatic second-act curtain). But matters turn out just swell by eleven o'clock.

If *Virtue's Bed* began with prostitutes lolling about, the curtain rose on Hadley Waters and Charles Beahan's **Little Orchid Annie** (4-21-30, Eltinge) to a parade of models displaying the latest in undies to buyers at a wholesale house. One of the models is the gold-digging Annie Westlake (Betty Lawrence), who is happy to profit from stock tips given to her by George "Georgie" Graham (Walter Davis) or to ride around in a Rolls that Myron C. "Kuppy" Kuppenheimer (Frank Wilcox) has presented her. She invites them to a Christmas party where everyone comes dressed up in kids' clothes or as Mother Goose characters. After Graham and Kuppenheimer both announce they intend to spend the night at her apartment, Danny Flynn (James Morris), a young man Annie has been helping put through Yale, announces that he, not they, will remain. A fight ensues, the police are called, and matters are not quieted until the older men learn that Danny is Annie's husband.

According to most critics, the best thing about the Civic Repertory Theatre's production of *Romeo and Juliet* on the same night was Eva Le Gallienne's "fresh, spontaneous" Juliet. Reviewers were at odds in judging the remaining cast, but the production flourished in the repertory for several seasons.

One of the season's biggest surprise hits was Howard Warren Comstock's **Stepping Sisters** (4-22-30, Waldorf), which featured yet another lady with a past. Mr. Ramsey (William Corbett) longs for the good old days when Mrs. Ramsey (Theresa Maxwell Conover) would accompany him to a baseball game, munch peanuts, and boo the ump—and when she allowed him to call her Cissie rather than Cecelia. But now that she is determined to climb in Long Island society and be president of the local woman's club, such behavior is out. She is shocked when she is advised that as part of her burden in a local charity fête she must house three stage people. One is Jack Carleton (Frederic Tozere), a leading man in musicals, with whom, Mrs. Ramsey is angered to discover, her daughter, Norma (Gertrude Moran) has fallen in love. The second is Lady Regina Chetworth-Lynde (Helen Raymond), "noted Shakespearean Reader from London, South Africa and Melbourne"—but then, as Norma's faggoty, socially approved suitor (William Lynn) consoles her, "A woman who comes from so many places would have to be good." Unfortunately, Cecelia's world starts to crumble when the lady arrives, for they recognize each other. They had been in burlesque together—but they agree to keep their secret. That secret comes out when the third guest proves to be another of their old cohorts, the outspoken Rosie O'Toole (Grace Huff). Rosie has accepted an invitation to the fête in order to unearth "Chummie," a man who lives in the town and who has shown her many favors while complaining his wife no longer understands him. Of course, Chummie turns out to be Mr.

Ramsey, whereupon his wife orders him out of the house: "Run along, Herbert! And for a wedding present I'll send you both tickets for the World Series and a *bushel* of peanuts." Only when her uppity neighbors snub her does Mrs. Ramsey recognize who her real friends are. To make matters better, Norma long has known her mother's hidden past and does not care. Neither does Norma's new husband, Jack. The season's last hit novelty, the comedy ran ten months.

April's second courtroom scene occurred in Mark Linder's **Room 349** (4-22-30, National), which confessedly was inspired by the killing of the notorious Arnold Rothstein. One of Rothstein's reputed molls, Inez Norton, was cast in the role of the fictitious hood's girl. In this case the gangster was called Harold Stromberg (Roy D'Arcy), and he was portrayed as anxious to give up his sordid trade and go straight. His killing takes place in a hotel room during a card game, and his associate, Joe "Sandy" Tully (Jack Hartley), is tried for the murder. As in some earlier courtroom dramas, a bit of the action spread into the auditorium. Supposed bailiffs were stationed in the audience and at one point noisily subdued a man threatening to leave. Tully is acquitted, leaving Stromberg's murder unsolved, much as Rothstein's was.

April closed with the quick failure of something very rare at the time, a full-length, one-character play, Irving Kaye Davis's **Courtesan** (4-29-30, President). Alice Trevor (Elsa Shelley) talks to unseen maids and servants at the hotel where she resides, speaks on the phone, reads letters aloud, and occasionally merely confers with herself as she reveals that her frustrated attempt to win the affections of a socially prominent man was followed by the offer of a musician, aware that she is a kept woman, to have an affair with her. In a fury, she has killed him and finally jumps from her balcony.

The season's shortest run—two performances—fell to Edward W. Harris's **Oh, Professor!** (5-1-30, Belmont). It featured Giuseppe Sterni, a considerable figure in New York's Italian-American theatricals. His English was not all it should have been though he played a professor of philology. He is forced out of his position on trumped up charges and shortly thereafter loses his savings in bad investments. But his nemesis, the dean (Walter Cartwright) who set all the professor's troubles in motion, is shown to be an adulterer and is made to reinstate the professor—at a substantial increase in pay.

Charles H. Brown's **The Traitor** (5-2-30, Little) brought to the stage Robert Louis Stevenson's *The*

Pavilion on the Links, in which Italian police hunt down and hound to his death an unscrupulous Englishman (Fuller Mellish) who had been entrusted with their funds. The romance of his daughter (Don Currie) and a family friend (Frank Henderson) provided a subplot.

May's lone near miss was Belford Forrest's **Lost Sheep** (5-5-30, Selwyn), expanded from a one-acter that H. L. Mencken and George Jean Nathan had published several years before in *Smart Set*. On coming to a new post, a naive minister (Ferdinand Gottschalk) is hoodwinked into renting for himself, his wife (Cecilia Loftus), and his three daughters a home that until recently had been a house—of ill repute. The good man remains totally innocent of why men of all stripes are constantly coming to the door and asking for the girls. One of the would-be clients is none other than the vicar's son (Rex O'Malley), who so falls in love with the eldest daughter (Sidney Fox) that he sets out to redeem her. Theatre folk supposedly in the know suggested that only hot weather and hard times prevented the comedy from running more than twelve weeks.

The Ada of John Kirkpatrick's **Ada Beats the Drum** (5-8-30, John Golden) was Ada Hubbard (Mary Boland). She drags her protesting family to Europe so that Mr. Hubbard (George W. Barbier) can obtain some polish and her daughter (Nydia Westman) can nab a suitably Continental husband. Regrettably, Mr. Hubbard polishes off too much French wine and winds up in jail. And young Leila does latch on to a husband in Monte Carlo—a jazz drummer from Illinois. Mr. Hubbard promises his future son-in-law a job with his firm as a reluctant Mrs. Hubbard starts packing. Boland's reluctance to remain with a failing show forced it to close.

A beautiful mounting of Henrik Ibsen's **The Vikings [of Helgeland]** (5-12-30, New Yorker) could not elicit interest in this early work of the playwright. Simple scenery and brilliantly conceived lighting, which reflected and evoked feelings of despair, high passion, and tragedy and culminated with massed shadows rushing silently across the sky toward Valhalla, enhanced the drama. Blanche Yurka had the pivotal role of Hjordis, who slaughters her deceiver (Warren William), then, being told he has become a Christian and so can never meet with her in Valhalla, leaps into the ocean and begins her journey alone to her pagan heaven. The play closed after its first Saturday night.

So did Ann Shelby's **Gold Braid** (5-13-30, Masque). On a steamy Philippine island, Major Rodney (Edward Reese), a tightfisted woman-hater, orders his long-suffering wife, Linda (Adele Ron-

son), to have an affair with Julio Cortez (Alan Devitt), a revolutionary, in order to ferret out his plans. In short order, Linda has fallen in love with Julio, especially after he rescues her from the treacherous advances of a sinister Mohammedan (Bruce Adams). She refuses to hand over his plans to her husband, and when Julio is forced to hurry into the jungle she tells him she will wait for him. Native drums throbbing ominously in the distance and a bugle playing "Taps" are heard as the curtain falls.

Martha Stanley's **Let and Sub-Let** (5-19-30, Biltmore) was a summer farce that failed to span the summer. Believing their daughter, Janet (Dorothea Chard), already has sailed for Europe, the Blairs leave their Larchmont home to catch their own ship. They are no sooner gone than Janet peeks out of a closet to make certain the house is empty. It is, but not for long, since the Blairs have rented it for a time to Edward King (George Dill), a personable bachelor who has invited a niece he has never met to spend her vacation with him. He assumes Janet is the niece. Janet takes an immediate liking to Edward, so she tricks the real niece into disappearing. The Blairs, rushing back from Europe after not finding their daughter there, discover they will soon have a son-in-law.

Three revivals closed out May and began June. At the Fulton on the 19th, George M. Cohan starred in a revival of his hit of a decade earlier, *The Tavern*. At the Empire on June 2, the Players' annual outing was a double bill. Arnold Bennett and Edward Knoblock's 1912 look at how succeeding generations move from liberal to conservative stances, *Milestones*, was coupled with Austin Strong and Lloyd Osborne's 1906 story of a meek French-Canadian priest who humbles Louis XV, *The Little Father of the Wilderness*. In the former, Edwin Milton Royle, Warburton Gamble, Tom Powers, Dorothy Stickney, and Beulah Bondi had important roles. In the latter, Francis Wilson recreated the title role he had first performed twenty-four years earlier, aided now by Walter Hampden and Margalo Gillmore. The roster clearly was not as star-studded as previous Players productions, and critics asked why such relatively unimportant pieces were selected.

The season's last novelty was Joe Byron Totten's **Spook House** (6-3-30, Vanderbilt). For the umpteenth time, a dagger-clutching hand appeared in a wall, secret panels were revealed, and guns and corpses mysteriously disappeared. The sinister Philip Haynes (John A. Lorenze) hires someone he has been told is a gunman, Spike Connelly (Leo Donnelly), to kill a man whose wife he covets. But the gunman kills Haynes instead and turns out to be the son of a man

Haynes had killed. His reward is the hand of the daughter of the man he did not shoot.

The season's last major play was also its last major hit, although it was not a new play. In fact, it was several thousand years old. Aristophanes' *Lysistrata*, translated into highly colloquial English by Gilbert Seldes and brought out on the 5th at the 44th Street, was originally mounted as a special production by Robert Edmond Jones for Philadelphia's famous old Walnut Street Theatre. Audiences entering the theatre saw no curtain. Instead, bright red steps led from the auditorium, hiding the orchestra pit, and moved up to a gaudily colored, constructivist representation of the Acropolis. Many players entered and exited from the lower boxes. Directed by Jones in a style "broader than a Second Avenue burlesque, full of rough-and-tumble, full of bawdry," a magnificent cast that included Ernest Truex, Violet Kemble Cooper, Miriam Hopkins, Sydney Greenstreet, Etienne Girardot, and Eric Dressler revitalized the old yarn about Grecian women refusing their men their beds until the men stop making war. Although most players cavorted in skimpy garments, the huge Greenstreet, as President of the Senate, was bedecked in heavy purple robes—a special ordeal on the play's sweltering opening night. Word of mouth was such that the play was able to fill the house that evening despite a steep $11.00 top and, after the reviews appeared, had little difficulty maintaining an equally stiff $5.50 top for much of its seven-month run—still a Broadway record for an ancient Greek play.

Happily, then, the season and the era it brought to a close ended on an upbeat note. That it was the greatest epoch in American theatrical history is almost beyond dispute. More than 2000 new plays—most of them by native writers—premiered between mid-June of 1914 and mid-June of 1930, a figure never before approached in so short a time, and, given modern circumstances, a figure never likely to be approached again. Yet it was not merely a quantitative achievement that made the era so exciting but the quality and diversity of the plays as well. In these few years American dramaturgy came of age and matured into a vigorous, internationally respected art form. Before 1914, Eugene O'Neill, Elmer Rice, George Kelly, Maxwell Anderson, George S. Kaufman, Marc Connelly, Sidney Howard, Robert Sherwood, and Philip Barry were unknown. By 1930, they were considerable figures, most of whom had some of their best writing ahead of them. And a score or so of lesser playwrights—to cite Martin Flaven as just one example—had also made a mark. (Of major writers, only Rachel Crothers truly spanned the period from before World War I into the later 1930s.) Moreover, it was in this era that players who were to illuminate American stages for several decades came to the fore—the Lunts, Katharine Cornell, Helen Hayes, Jane Cowl, Eva Le Gallienne, again to give only a few instances. Robert Edmond Jones, Lee Simonson, Jo Mielziner, Cleon Throckmorton, and others pioneered in developing the art of set design.

But there was little question that an epoch had ended, even though the American theatre has always been a continuum. During the 1929–30 season, Broadway bid a quiet farewell to such great or at least popular old performers as Mrs. Fiske, William Hodge, and Wilton Lackaye and a permanent or prolonged farewell to such promising youngsters as Spencer Tracy, Clark Gable, James Cagney, Claudette Colbert, and Joan Blondell. The latter all headed for Hollywood. The season also gave evidence that some of the most exciting playwrights of the twenties were written out. George Kelly, for example, would never again have a substantial hit, and Eugene O'Neill, apart from one atypical comedy, would have only a single additional dramatic success produced in his lifetime. (Though it was not immediately apparent, the next few seasons would show that the Depression destroyed the careers of virtually all of Broadway's more enlightened producers, such as Arthur Hopkins, Winthrop Ames, and Richard Herndon. And the grand old man among producers, David Belasco, would die during the next season.) But the growing Depression and breadlines had some other, particular effects. While the Depression had yet to strike bottom, and Broadway had recovered quickly from previous economic slumps, this sickeningly deep depression coincided with the rapid spread and development of radio and sound films, meaning that entertainment seekers no longer needed to disgorge pocketsful of dollars for diversions. Year by year fewer playgoers and, as a result, fewer theatres and fewer plays hereafter would testify to Broadway's ineluctable decline. More ominously, a vicious political polarization had begun and would become clearer in the next season with the emergence of the Group Theatre. The stage increasingly would become an instrument of propaganda rather than of pure pleasure-making. Much of the variety and openly theatregoer-oriented approach that had made American stages so delightful would start to disappear, never again to beckon tired businessmen for an evening's escape. Yet, decline or no, the American theatre survived, even if Broadway, as George S. Kaufman and Moss Hart were to brand it, would remain at best a fabulous invalid.

INDEX

The index is divided into two major sections. The first covers the plays discussed in the book; the second, the people.

PLAYS The Play index lists the plays treated in the book and has a subsection that lists the sources (foreign plays, foreign and domestic novels, poems, or short stories) for many of the plays. A foreign play that was a source and was also presented on Broadway in its native tongue is listed in both sections. Some plays mentioned in passing, especially in mini-biographies, and musicals mentioned as being derived from plays discussed are not indexed.

PEOPLE Playwrights and authors whose works served as sources are listed in the People index, as are producers, directors, and designers, but because listing all performers mentioned would have made the index excessively large, only those players mentioned six or more times are included. However, celebrated foreigners, performers best known in other fields (musicals, vaudeville, films), and a few deemed of special interest for other reasons have been included in spite of the six-or-more rule. Thus, exceptions have been made for some old-timers whose careers came to a halt during these years, for young actors and actresses just embarking on what became fine careers, and for a handful of players who had brief glory, but then died young. Critics per se have not been indexed; they appear solely if they wrote or worked on plays dealt with in this volume. Composers, choreographers, and similar adjunct figures mentioned in passing similarly have been ignored. Page numbers in bold print indicate mini-biographies. The People index has a subsection that lists organizations.

PLAYS

415

Index

Plays

Index

418

Plays

Index

Plays

Index

Plays

Index

Plays

Plays

Index

428

Sources

SOURCES

Index

PEOPLE

Index

People

Index

434

People

Index

Index

People

Milne, A. A., 81, 147, 166, 169, 176, 193, 194, 254, 330, 369, 379, 400
Miltern, John, 8, 43, 93, 120, 190, 377
Milton, Robert, 128
Mirande, Yves, 246, 329
Mirbeau, Octave, 228
Mitchell, Dodson, 79, 134, 142, 155, 257, 288, 331, 393
Mitchell, Grant, 8, 65, 66, 143, 144, 179, 208, 212, 248, 262, 278, 324, 377, 395
Mitchell, Helen, 375
Mitchell, Langdon, 34, 53, 384
Mitchell, Norma, 265, 298
Mitchell, Ruth C., 8
Mitchell, Thomas, 126, 148, 284, 288, 323, 333, 362
Moeller, Philip, 23, 34, 73, 98, 99, 100, 124, 241, 372, 382
Moffatt, Graham, 135
Mohr, Max, 344
Moissi, Alexander, 334, 368
Molière, 228, 229, 243
Molnár, Ferenc, 11, 149, 195, 216, 217, 241, 249, 270, 272, 302, 358, 363, 370
Montgomery, James, 50
Montgomery, Victoria, 245
Mooney, Martin, 380
Moore, Carlyle, 87, 195
Moore, Florence, 74, 122, 293
Moore, McElbert, 374
Moore, Victor, 273
Moreau, Emile, 148
Morehouse, Ward, 357
Morgan, Frank, 12, 146, 154, 191, 241, 242, 281, 296, 314, 318, 322, 392, 400, 406
Morgan, Ralph, 26, 37, 84, 106, 155, 171, 209, 230, 266, 275, 281, 310, 327, 331, 341
Morley, Christopher, 116, 370, 402
Morosco, Oliver, 226
Moroso, John A., 266
Morris, Chester, 200, 295, 314, 343
Morris, Gordon, 250
Morris, Gouverneur, 17
Morris, Grant, 90
Morris, McKay, 183, 198, 201, 208, 210, 239, 254, 258, 261, 282, 287, 313
Morrison, Anne, 222, 235, 382
Morse, N. Brewster, 290
Morton, Howard E., 167
Morton, Martha, 26
Morton, Michael, 7, 19, 62, 71, 92, 145, 204
Mouëzy-Éon, André, 329
Mowatt, Anna Cora, 226

Mowbray, Alan, 342, 386, 400
Mower, Margaret, 133, 168, 174, 192, 197, 220, 227, 252, 261, 395
Mueller, Hans, 252
Mullally, Don, 237, 245, 273, 355
Muller, Charles, 375
Mumford, Ethel Watts, 17, 78
Muni, Paul, 205, 299, 325
Munro, C. K., 289
Murfin, Jane, 58, 63, 395
Murphy, Ralph, 255, 300, 344, 396
Murphy, Rolph (*see* Murphy, Ralph)
Murray, Douglas, 89, 291
Murray, Gilbert, 217
Murray, T. C., 301
Musson, Bennet, 317
Myers, Henry, 175, 275

Nagel, Conrad, 86
Naldi, Nita, 128
Nash, Florence, 19, 70, 92, 192, 275, 411
Nash, George, 9, 26, 35, 52, 83, 94, 300, 326, 342
Nash, Mary, 34, 49, 89, 90, 140, 170, 222, 275, 288, 326, 388, 400
Natanson, Jacques, 371
Nazimova, Alla, 14, 58, 79, 80, 81, 363, 375, 379
Nelson, Jack T., 387
Népoty, Lucien, 9, 145
Nertz, Louis, 234, 395
Nesbitt, Cathleen, 52, 339
Neumann, Alfred, 340
Nevin, Hardwick, 380
Newing, DeWitt, 260
Nicander, Edwin, 54, 78, 95, 101, 117, 125, 158, 185, 195, 264, 276, 298
Niccodemi, Dario, 7, 19, 92, 270, 279
Nichols, Anne, 150, 180, 181, 242, 254, 281, 305, 309
Nichols, Robert, 370
Nicholson, Kenyon, 309, 319, 358, 382
Nicholson, Leta Vance, 125
Nivoix, Paul, 277
Noel, Joseph, 68, 111
Nordstrom, Frances, 120, 177
Norman, Christine, 35, 51, 69, 92, 239
Norman, Mrs. George, 142
North, Carrington, 234
North, Clyde, 387
Novello, Ivor, 253
Nozière, Fernand, 375
Nugent, Elliott, 179, 220, 222, 243, 259, 268, 285, 333, 348, 361

Nugent, J. C., 179, 220, 243, 259, 268, 285, 299, 319, 324, 333, 348, 361, 374
Nugent, Ruth, 179, 220, 223, 243, 263, 285
Nyitray, Emil, 9, 116, 175, 215

O'Brien, Pat, 303, 409
O'Casey, Sean, 286, 334, 336, 395
O'Connell, Hugh, 357, 395, 403
O'Connor, Una, 301
O'Donnell, Jack, 403
O'Higgins, Harvey, 16, 49, 113, 161, 228
O'Neil, Nance, 58, 120, 223, 279, 317, 327
O'Neil, Raymond, 253
O'Neill, Eugene, 54, 55, 71, 72, 81, 92, 93, 102, 114, 121, 122, 125, 139, 143, 146, 150, 174, 175, 176, 186, 224, 228, 229, 232, 243, 244, 253, 257, 277, 280, 304, 338, 341, 373, 377, 379, 414
O'Neill, James, 58
Obey, André, 167
Oenslager, Donald, 312
Oesterreicher, Rudolph, 327
Olcott, Chauncey, 82, 95
Olcott, Rita, 107
Oliver, Edna May, 159, 167, 174, 240, 251, 265
Oliver, George W., 284
Oliver, Roland, 254, 348, 366, 391
Olivier, Laurence, 388
Olivier, Stuart, 231, 288
Ongley, Byron, 9
Orbera, Rafael Marti, 223
Ord, Robert, 131
Ordynski, Richard, 60
Orkow, B. Harrison, 248, 346
Orme, Michael, 242
Osborn, Lincoln, 204
Osborn, Paul, 366, 397
Osborne, Hubert, 80, 82, 182, 233, 413
Osborne, Lloyd, 59
Osmun, Leighton Graves, 98, 183, 206, 213
Oursler, Fulton, 296, 317, 321, 331, 377
Ouspenskaya, Maria, 199, 240, 271
Ouspensky, A., 401
Owen, Bernard J., 327
Owen, Harold, 12, 56
Owen, Harrison, 349
Owen, Reginald, 283, 289, 302, 330, 391

441

Index

Index

People

Index

ORGANIZATIONS